Protecting and Promoting the
Health of NFL Players:
Legal and Ethical Analysis and Recommendations

Christopher R. Deubert

I. Glenn Cohen

Holly Fernandez Lynch

Petrie-Flom Center for Health Law Policy, Biotechnology, and Bioethics

Harvard Law School

November 2016

TABLE OF CONTENTS

ABOUT THE AUTHORS

Christopher R. Deubert is the Senior Law and Ethics Associate for the Law and Ethics Initiative of The Football Players Health Study at Harvard University. Previously, Deubert practiced commercial litigation, sports law, securities litigation, and labor/employment litigation at Peter R. Ginsberg Law, LLC f/k/a Ginsberg & Burgos, PLLC in New York City. His sports practice focused primarily on representing National Football League (NFL) players in League matters, including appeals for Commissioner Discipline, under the NFL's Policy and Program on Substances of Abuse and under the NFL's Policy on Anabolic Steroids and Related Substances (now known as the Policy on Performance-Enhancing Substances), and related litigation. Deubert also previously worked for Sportstars, Inc., one of the largest NFL-player representation firms, performing contract, statistical, and legal analysis, and he performed similar work during an internship with the New York Jets. Deubert graduated with a joint J.D./M.B.A. degree from Fordham University School of Law and Graduate School of Business in 2010, and a B.S. in Sport Management from the University of Massachusetts in 2006.

I. Glenn Cohen is a professor at Harvard Law School; Faculty Director of the Petrie-Flom Center for Health Law Policy, Biotechnology, and Bioethics; and, Co-Lead of the Law and Ethics Initiative of The Football Players Health Study. His award-winning work at the intersection of law, medicine, and ethics—in particular, medical tourism and assisted reproduction—has been published in leading journals, such as the *Harvard Law Review, Stanford Law Review, New England Journal of Medicine, Journal of the American Medical Association, American Journal of Bioethics*, and *American Journal of Public Health*. He was previously a fellow at the Radcliffe Institute for Advanced Study and a faculty scholar in bioethics with the Greenwall Foundation. He is the author, editor, and/or co-editor of several books from Oxford, Columbia, John Hopkins, and MIT University Presses. Prior to joining the Harvard faculty, Cohen served as a clerk to Chief Judge Michael Boudin, United States Court of Appeals for the First Circuit, and as an appellate lawyer in the Civil Division of the Department of Justice. He graduated from the University of Toronto with a B.A. (with distinction) in Bioethics (Philosophy) and Psychology and earned his J.D. from Harvard Law School.

Holly Fernandez Lynch is Executive Director of the Petrie-Flom Center for Health Law Policy, Biotechnology, and Bioethics; Faculty at the Harvard Medical School Center for Bioethics; and, Co-Lead of the Law and Ethics Initiative of The Football Players Health Study. Her scholarly work focuses on the regulation and ethics of human subjects research and issues at the heart of the doctor-patient relationship. Her book, *Conflicts of Conscience in Health Care: An Institutional Compromise*, was published by MIT Press in 2008; she is also co-editor with I. Glenn Cohen of *Human Subjects Research Regulation: Perspectives on the Future* (MIT Press 2014), and *FDA in the 21st Century: The Challenges of Regulating Drugs and New Technologies* (Columbia University Press 2015). Lynch practiced pharmaceuticals law at Hogan & Hartson, LLP (now Hogan Lovells), in Washington, D.C., and worked as a bioethicist in the Human Subjects Protection Branch at the National Institutes of Health's Division of AIDS. She served as senior policy and research analyst for President Obama's Commission for the Study of Bioethical Issues. Lynch is currently a member of the Secretary's Advisory Committee on Human Research Protections at the U.S. Department of Health and Human Services. She graduated Order of the Coif from the University of Pennsylvania Law School, where she was a Levy Scholar in Law and Bioethics. She earned her master's degree in bioethics from the University of Pennsylvania's School of Medicine, and her B.A. with a concentration in bioethics, also from the University of Pennsylvania.

ACKNOWLEDGMENTS

First, the authors would like to thank the staff and research assistants who assisted in the creation of this Report: Thomas Blackmon; Laura Escalona; Elizabeth Guo; Elisa Hevia; Gabrielle Hodgson; Cristine Hutchison-Jones; Jason Joffe; Jose Lamarque; Justin Leahey; Jodie Liu; Sheila Meagher; Jennifer Mindrum; Scott Sherman; Lauren Taylor; and, Valerie Wood. These individuals assisted with a variety of administrative and research tasks, including fact-checking the Report in its entirety. Particular thanks are due to Justin Leahey, Project Coordinator for the Law & Ethics Initiative of The Football Players Health Study, who provided important administrative and research assistance throughout the creation of the Report.

Second, the authors would like to thank the members of its Law & Ethics Advisory Panel for their comments and guidance during the creation of this Report: Nita Farahany; Joseph Fins; Ashley Foxworth; Walter Jones; Isaiah Kacyvenski; Bernard Lo; Chris Ogbonnaya; and, Dick Vermeil.

Third, the authors would like to thank the peer reviewers of this Report who provided valuable comments during the editing process: Andrew Brandt; Gabriel Feldman; Michelle Mello; Matt Mitten; William Sage; Paul Wolpe; and, Cindy Chang. In particular, we would like to thank Professor Feldman, who served as the "lead" peer reviewer, ensuring the thoroughness and appropriateness of our peer review process. Additional information about Professor Feldman's review is contained in Appendix O.

Fourth, the authors would like to thank the professors and academic professionals who reviewed and provided comments for parts of this Report: Peter Carfagna; John Goldberg; Michael Gusmano; John Hoberman; Howell Jackson; Vivek Krishnamurthy; Karen Maschke; Christopher Robertson; Rachel Sachs; Mildred Solomon; Holger Spamann; and, Mindy Roseman.

Fifth, the authors would like to thank the professionals who helped finalize this Report: Lori Shridhare from The Football Players Health Study at Harvard University; Kathi Hanna, who provided proofreading and editing services; and, Fassino/Design, Inc., which designed and formatted the Report.

Finally, the authors would like to thank the stakeholders, organizations, and individuals working in and around the NFL who agreed to be interviewed and/or otherwise provided relevant information for this Report. In the Introduction and in the relevant chapters we provide more detail regarding the stakeholders, organizations, and individuals who were interviewed and/or otherwise provided relevant information. Their cooperation was essential to the accuracy, fairness, and comprehensiveness of this Report. Additional information about the creation and review of this Report is contained in Appendix N.

ENSURING INDEPENDENCE AND DISCLOSURE OF CONFLICTS

The 2011 Collective Bargaining Agreement between the National Football League Players Association (NFLPA) and the National Football League (NFL) set aside funds for medical research. The NFLPA directed a portion of those funds to create The Football Players Health Study at Harvard University, of which this Report is a part. Our analysis has been independent of any control by the NFLPA, the NFL, or any other party; this independence was contractually protected in Harvard's funding agreement with the NFLPA. Per that contract, the NFLPA was only entitled to prior review of the Report to ensure that no confidential information was disclosed.[a]

This report is the principal component of the Law and Ethics Initiative of The Football Players Health Study at Harvard University. Additional background information about The Football Players Health Study is provided in the Preface. We provide more specific information about the Law and Ethics Initiative here.

The Statement of Work agreed to between the NFLPA and Harvard included as one of the Law and Ethics Initiative's projects to "Develop Ethical Framework and Accountability Structure for Player Health and Welfare." More specifically, Harvard described the work to be done as follows:

> We will conduct a research project regarding the relative primacy of players' health among potentially competing goals, and clarifying the roles of medical staff and healthcare providers, team owners, pre-professional schools and institutions (e.g., college, high school, Pop Warner, etc.), equipment manufacturers and suppliers, the media, and players themselves in protecting and advancing player health and welfare. More specifically, we will create recommendations applicable to each of these parties, supported for the first time by an overarching ethical framework and accountability structure for player health and welfare. We will also generate recommendations toward a preliminary baseline set of legally and ethically relevant protections that ought to be afforded to all players.

This project description was intended to be preliminary. The actual scope of the final Report developed over time, as expected, as the result of considerable research, internal discussion, and conversations with experts. Beyond agreeing to the Statement of Work, the NFLPA did not direct the scope or content of this Report.

As is typical with sponsored research, we provided periodic updates to the sponsor in several formats. Pursuant to the terms of Harvard-NFLPA agreement, the NFLPA receives an annual report on the progress of The Football Players Health Study as well as one Quad Chart progress report each year. Additionally, on two occasions (August 22, 2014, and January 23, 2015), we presented a summary of the expected scope and content of the Report to The Football Players Health Study Executive Committee, comprised of both Harvard and NFLPA personnel. Those meetings did not alter our approach in constructing the Report, the conclusions reached, or the recommendations made. Indeed, the only comment from the Executive Committee meetings that resulted in a change to the content of the Report was the suggestion at the beginning of the writing process to include business partners as a stakeholder, which we agreed was important.

In the Introduction, Section (D)(2): Description of Legal and Ethical Obligations, we discuss our research process for the Report. Additional information about our communications with the NFLPA and NFL is also relevant here. During the course of our research, we had multiple telephone and email communications with both NFLPA and NFL representatives to gain factual information. As will be indicated where relevant in the Report, sometimes the parties provided the requested information and sometimes they did not. These communications were not about the progress, scope, or structure of our Report.

We also concluded that it was essential to allow for substantive review of the Report by applicable stakeholders, including the NFLPA and NFL. This was necessary to ensure that we have fully accounted for the realities at hand, avoided factual errors, and fairly considered all sides. Accordingly, we provided each stakeholder group discussed in this Report and that has a clearly identified representative the opportunity to review the parts of this Report applicable to them (in draft form). A list of the stakeholders that reviewed the Report appears in Appendix N. Stakeholders had the opportunity to

---

a   The applicable contract language provides that the NFLPA is permitted to review publications 30 days in advance "for the sole purpose of identifying any unauthorized use of Confidential Information."

identify any errors, provide additional information, comment on what we planned to expect from them going forward, and raise further suggestions or objections. Sometimes these comments led to valuable changes in the Report. Other comments we found unpersuasive, and did not result in any changes. While both the NFLPA and NFL provided comments on the Report, it is critical to recognize that no external party, including the NFLPA and NFL, had the ability to direct or alter our analysis or conclusions. Finally, as part of our effort to collaboratively engage with key stakeholders, we invited both the NFLPA and NFL to write a response to the Report, which we offered to publish on The Football Players Health Study website alongside the Report. The NFL took us up on this offer while the NFLPA did not.[b]

As an additional check on our independent analysis, we engaged a Law and Ethics Advisory Panel (LEAP) with expertise in health law, bioethics, and player issues to review our work, comprised of several academics, players, a player family member, and a retired NFL coach. Additional information about the LEAP, its members, and its role in reviewing the Report is included in Appendix N. We consulted with the LEAP early in the drafting process for the Report, and members were given the opportunity to comment on its organization, selection of stakeholders, and relevant ethical principles. The LEAP also had the opportunity to review a complete draft of the Report and provide detailed feedback.

In addition, we subjected the draft Report to robust peer review by outside experts. We engaged six independent experts in fields relevant to the Report to review it for accuracy, fairness, comprehension, and its ability to positively affect the health of NFL players. Additional information about the reviewers and review process is included in Appendix N. None of these individuals had any declared conflicts of interest. To ensure that we carefully considered the comments of the reviewers and made appropriate changes, we also retained Gabriel Feldman, Associate Professor of Law and Director, Sport Law Program, Tulane University Law School, to serve as a lead peer reviewer. Professor Feldman reviewed the Report and provided comments, while also reviewing the comments of the other reviewers and any changes made by us in response to their comments. Professor Feldman's role and approval of the review process is further provided in Appendix O.

Finally, the Report's content is solely the responsibility of the authors and does not represent the official views of the NFLPA or Harvard University.

DISCLOSURES:

- The Law and Ethics Initiative's allocated budget is a total of $1,257,045 over three years, which funds not only the present Report, but also several other projects.[c]

- Deubert's salary is fully supported by The Football Players Health Study at Harvard University. From August 2010 to May 2014, Deubert was an associate at the law firm of Peter R. Ginsberg Law, LLC f/k/a Ginsberg & Burgos, PLLC. During the course of his practice at that firm, Deubert was involved in several legal matters in which the NFL was an opposing party, including several discussed in this Report. The matters discussed in this Report include the representation of: a former NFL player interested in seeking benefits pursuant to the proposed settlement in the Concussion Litigation, discussed at length in Chapter 7: The NFL and NFLPA; players disciplined pursuant to the NFL's Policy and Program on Substances of Abuse and the Policy on Anabolic Steroids and Related Substances (now known as the Policy on Performance-Enhancing Substances), discussed in Chapter 7: The NFL and NFLPA; Kevin Williams and Pat Williams in the "StarCaps" case, discussed in Chapter 7: The NFL and NFLPA; and, Jonathan Vilma in the "Bounty"-related legal proceedings, discussed at length in Chapter 9: Coaches. Deubert also was involved in the representation of former Miami Dolphins offensive line coach Jim Turner in the Jonathan Martin "bullying" situation, discussed at length in Chapter 9: Coaches, which was the result of an NFL investigation but did not involve litigation with the NFL. Additionally, Deubert was involved in the representation of both contract advisors and players in litigation and arbitrations under the NFLPA's Regulations Governing Contract Advisors, discussed at length in Chapter 12: Contract Advisors. Last, since 2007 Deubert has provided research assistance to the Sports Lawyers Association, whose Board of Directors includes many individuals with interests related to this work.

- Twenty percent of Cohen's salary is supported by The Football Players Health Study at Harvard University. Cohen has no other conflicting interests to report.

- Thirty percent of Lynch's salary is supported by The Football Players Health Study at Harvard University. Lynch has no other conflicting interests to report.

---

b   In declining the opportunity to write a response, the NFLPA stated as follows: "[O]ur primary objective in funding Harvard is to advance independent research on the many complex issues facing our members. Harvard's publications further that objective without formal comment by the PA."

c   Other Law and Ethics projects include: (1) a qualitative interview study ("listening tour") with players and their families to better understand their legal and ethical concerns related to health and well-being; (2) a comparative legal and organizational policy analysis of various professional sports leagues to identify best policies in protecting player health; (3) an analysis of the legal and ethical implications of current and potential medical tests and devices that might be used by NFL clubs and players; and, (4) an examination of how traditional workplace health and safety laws would apply to professional sports; among others.

EXECUTIVE SUMMARY

1) INTRODUCTION

Who is responsible for the health of NFL players, *why,* and *what* can be done to promote player health? These are the fundamental questions motivating this Report, authored by members of the Law and Ethics Initiative of **The Football Players Health Study at Harvard University.**[d]

To date, there has been no comprehensive analysis of the universe of stakeholders that may influence NFL player health, nor any systematic analysis of their existing or appropriate legal and/or ethical obligations. This sort of undertaking, however, is essential to uncovering areas in need of improvement and making clear that the responsibility for player health falls on many interconnected groups that must work together to protect and support these individuals who give so much of themselves—not without benefit, but sometimes with serious personal consequences—to one of America's favorite sports. It is critical to address the structural and organizational factors that shape the environment in which players live and work. Moreover, acknowledging a variety of potentiality relevant background conditions is an essential and complementary approach to clinical interventions for improving player health.

In identifying the universe of appropriate stakeholders and making recommendations regarding player health, we have taken as our threshold the moment that a player has exhausted or foregone his remaining college eligibility and has taken steps to pursue an NFL career. From that point on what needs to happen to maximize his health, even after he leaves the NFL? We have selected this timeframe not because the health of amateur players—those in college, high school, and youth leagues—is secure or unimportant. Instead, the reason is largely pragmatic: there is only

so much any one report can cover, and adding in-depth analysis of additional stakeholders such as the NCAA, youth leagues, and parents would confuse an already complicated picture.

We recognize that what happens at the professional level can have a trickle-down effect on the culture of football across the board, and also that some amateur players may be taking health risks in hopes of eventually reaching the NFL, even when that may be highly unlikely. Moreover, we acknowledge that the legal and ethical issues that arise with regard to individuals who are not competent to make their own decisions (*e.g.,* children) are substantially more difficult. Nonetheless, our goal with this Report, prompted by the limited scope of the request for proposals for this project and in part by the fact that further analysis will be possible by others, is to address the already complicated set of factors influencing the health of NFL players, current, future, and former.

This Report has four functions. First, to **identify** the various stakeholders who influence, or could influence, the health of NFL players. Second, to **describe** the existing legal and ethical obligations of these stakeholders in both protecting and promoting player health. Third, to **evaluate** the sufficiency of these existing obligations, including enforcement and current practices. And fourth, to **recommend** changes grounded in that evaluation for each of the identified stakeholders.

The issues at hand are complex and nuanced. Consequently, we urge readers to read the entire Report, or at least the Introduction and those chapters of particular interest. In this Executive Summary, we provide only a short synopsis of some of the key issues discussed in the Report.

In the remainder of this Introduction, we describe the definition of "health" used to focus the Report, discuss the ethical principles that guided our analysis, and identify the stakeholders discussed in the Report. In the second part of this Executive Summary, we summarize our discussion of the most stakeholders discussed in the Report (players, club doctors, the NFL, and the NFLPA), including highlighting major recommendations. Then, in the third part of this Executive Summary, we briefly discuss the other stakeholders analyzed in the Report and important

---

d   This Report is part of The Football Players Health Study. The 2011 Collective Bargaining Agreement (CBA) between the NFL and NFLPA allocated funds for research, and in 2014, the NFLPA and Harvard University entered into an agreement to create and support The Football Players Health Study using a portion of these funds. The contract governing this project protects our academic integrity as researchers; no external party has any editorial control over our work. A version of this Report was shared with the NFLPA, the NFL, and other stakeholders prior to publication. The NFLPA was treated the same as other stakeholders, with the exception of a contractually guaranteed 30-day review to ensure that we did not use any confidential information. We considered all feedback provided to us from all stakeholders but retained final editorial control. The content is solely the responsibility of the authors and does not necessarily represent the official views of the NFLPA or Harvard University.

recommendations concerning them. Lastly, we conclude with some final recommendations.

Before continuing with the Introduction, we provide a list of our "Top 10" recommendations; those recommendations that, if implemented, could have the most meaningful and positive impact on player health. Additional information on these recommendations, including explanations of their significance, is provided in the full Report.

Top 10 Recommendations

1. The current arrangement in which club (*i.e.,* "team") medical staff, including doctors, athletic trainers, and others, have responsibilities both to players and to the club presents an inherent conflict of interest. To address this problem and help ensure that players receive medical care that is as free from conflict as possible, division of responsibilities between two distinct groups of medical professionals is needed. Player care and treatment should be provided by one set of medical professionals (called the "Players' Medical Staff"), appointed by a joint committee with representation from both the NFL and NFLPA, and evaluation of players for business purposes should be done by separate medical personnel (the "Club Evaluation Doctor"). (Recommendation 2:1-A).

2. The NFL and NFLPA should not make player health a subject of adversarial collective bargaining. (Recommendation 7:1-A).

3. As recommended throughout the Report, various stakeholders (*e.g.,* club doctors, athletic trainers, coaches, contract advisors, and financial advisors) should adopt, improve and enforce Codes of Ethics. (Final Recommendation 3).

4. The NFL and NFLPA should continue to undertake and support efforts to scientifically and reliably establish the health risks and benefits of playing professional football. (Recommendation 7:1-B).

5. The NFL, and to the extent possible, the NFLPA, should: (a) continue to improve its robust collection of aggregate injury data; (b) continue to have the injury data analyzed by qualified professionals; and, (c) make the data publicly available for re-analysis. (Recommendation 7:1-C).

6. The NFLPA should consider investing greater resources in investigating and enforcing player health issues, including Article 39 of the 2011 CBA [covering players' rights to medical care and treatment]. (Recommendation 7:5-A).

7. Clubs and Club medical staff should support players in their right to receive a second opinion. (Recommendation 4:1-A).

8. Players diagnosed with a concussion should be placed on a short-term injured reserve list whereby the player does not count against the Active/Inactive 53-man roster until he is cleared to play by the Concussion Protocol (Recommendation 7:1-E).

9. With assistance from Contract Advisors, the NFL, the NFLPA, and others, players should familiarize themselves with their rights and obligations under the CBA, including all possible health and other benefits, and should avail themselves of applicable benefits. (Recommendation 1:1-A).

10. Players should receive a physical from their own doctor as soon as possible after each season. (Recommendation 6:1-B).

(A) Defining Health

Our definition of "health" includes and extends beyond the sort of clinical measurements that might immediately be evoked by the phrase. Indeed, the comprehensive mantra of The Football Players Health Study, "The Whole Player, The Whole Life," motivates our definition. "Health" clearly covers the conventional and uncontroversial reference to freedom from physical and mental illness and impairment. But health is much more than the mere absence of a malady. The full range of non-medical inputs that can influence health, also known as the social determinants of health, must also be considered. These social determinants extend beyond the sorts of things for which one would seek out a doctor's care, and, according to the World Health Organization, include broadly "the conditions in which people are born, grow, live, work, and age," as affected by the "distribution of money, power, and resources at global, national and local levels."

Such social determinants are fully at play in the lives of NFL players. Acknowledging these social determinants of health allows us to recognize that a set of recommendations limited exclusively to medical care, medical relationships, and medical information would not suffice to achieve our goal of maximizing player health. We cannot focus solely on avoiding brain injury, protecting joints, and promoting cardiovascular health, for example, but we must also address wellbeing more generally, which depends on other factors such as the existence of family and social support, the ability to meet economic needs, and life satisfaction.

Thus, for purposes of this Report, health is defined as "a state of overall wellbeing in fundamental aspects of a person's life, including physical, mental, emotional, social, familial, and financial components." This definition is patterned on numerous definitions of health, including that of the World Health Organization. According to our definition, we make recommendations not only about ways to influence players' medical outcomes, but also about ways to positively influence the role of social determinants of their health.

(B) Guiding Ethical Principles

We identify seven overarching ethical principles to guide our assessment of all stakeholder responsibilities and to structure the nature of our recommendations, though we also offer more tailored ethical analyses for each stakeholder. Here, we provide an abbreviated discussion of these ethical principles:

- **Respect:** The NFL is a business that relies on individuals who are exposed to health risks, but no stakeholder can treat players "merely as a means" or as a commodity solely for promotion of its own goals.

- **Health Primacy:** Avoiding serious threats to player health should be given paramount importance in every dealing with every stakeholder, subject only to the player's Empowered Autonomy.

- **Empowered Autonomy:** Players are competent adults who should be empowered to assess which health risks they are willing to undertake, provided they have been given trustworthy, understandable information and decision-making tools, and the opportunity to pursue realistic alternatives.

- **Transparency:** All parties should be transparent about their interests, goals, and potential conflicts as they relate to player health, and information relevant to player health must be shared with players immediately.

- **Managing Conflicts of Interest:** All stakeholders should take steps to minimize conflicts of interest, and when they cannot be eliminated, to appropriately manage them.

- **Collaboration and Engagement:** Protecting and promoting the health of professional football players depends on many parties who should strive to act together—and not as adversaries—whenever possible to advance that primary goal.

- **Justice:** All stakeholders have an obligation to ensure that players are not bearing an inappropriate share of risks and burdens compared to benefits reaped by other stakeholders.

(C) Stakeholders

Over several months, we conducted a comprehensive review of the sports law and ethics literature, and had in-depth conversations with a number of former players and, where they were willing to speak with us, representatives of many of the stakeholders we identified as crucial to our analysis. This allowed us to supplement our existing expertise and understanding to generate a list of 20 stakeholders on whom to focus. The stakeholders discussed in this Report are:

- Players;
- Club doctors;
- Athletic trainers;
- Second opinion doctors;
- Neutral doctors;
- Personal doctors;
- The NFL;
- The NFLPA;
- NFL clubs;
- Coaches;
- Club employees;
- Equipment managers;
- Contract advisors (aka "agents");
- Financial advisors;
- Family members;
- Officials;
- Equipment manufacturers;
- The media;
- Fans; and
- NFL business partners.

Each stakeholder is discussed in its own chapter except the NFL and NFLPA, which are discussed together in light of their interdependence.

How did we arrive at this list of stakeholders, and determine who was and was not a stakeholder within the ambit of this Report? The key criterion for inclusion was simple: who (for better or worse) does—or should—play a role in NFL player health? The answer to that question came in three parts, as there are individuals, groups, and organizations who *directly impact* player health, for example, as employers or caregivers; those who *reap substantial financial benefits* from players' work; and, those who have some *capacity to influence* player health. Stakeholders may fall under more than one of these headings, but satisfaction of at least one criterion was necessary for inclusion in this analysis. The result is an extensive mapping of a complex web of parties.

2) KEY STAKEHOLDERS

Below, we summarize some of our discussion on those stakeholders we believe to be the most important: players; club doctors; the NFL; and, the NFLPA, but the full Report contains chapters on every stakeholder.

(A) Players

The heart of this Report is about protecting and promoting player health. No one is more central to that goal than players themselves, and therefore it is important to understand who they are and what they are doing concerning their own health and the health of their NFL brethren. That said, it is also important to recognize that players are often making choices against a constrained set of background conditions, pressures, and influences—doing so often with limited expertise and information—all of which impact their capacity to optimally protect their own health. Thus, while they are competent adults with a bevy of responsibilities to protect themselves, they cannot do it alone. Players must be treated as partners in advancing their own health by offering them a variety of support systems to do so, all of which will be accompanied by recommendations geared to other stakeholders.

Significant concerns exist about players' actions regarding their own health. Historically, there is considerable evidence that NFL players underreport their medical conditions and symptoms to avoid missing playing time or jeopardizing their position within a club. This behavior is understandable, but they may be doing so at great risk. Nevertheless, we emphasize that the existing data on player health is incomplete and often unclear, leaving players without sufficient information to make truly informed decisions based on calculations of risk and benefit.

Our most important recommendation to players is **Recommendation 1:1-A: With assistance from contract advisors, the NFL, the NFLPA, and others, players should familiarize themselves with their rights and obligations under the NFL-NFLPA Collective Bargaining Agreement (CBA), including all possible health and other benefits, and should avail themselves of applicable benefits.** Our formal interviews, literature review, and other feedback from stakeholders revealed that many players are not sufficiently aware of their rights, obligations, benefits, and opportunities pursuant to the CBA, or do not take full advantage of them even if they are aware. This prevents players from truly maximizing their health.

Other recommendations concerning players are:

- Players should carefully consider the ways in which health sacrifices now may affect their future health (1:1-B).

- Players should take advantage of opportunities to prepare for life after football (1:1-C).

- Players should seek out and learn from more experienced players, including former players, concerning health-related matters (1:1-D).

- Players should take on a responsibility to one another, to support one another's health, and to change the culture for the better (1:1-E).

- Players should not return to play until they are fit to do so (1:1-F).

- Players should not sign any document presented to them by the NFL, an NFL club, or an employee of an NFL club without discussing the document with their contract advisor, the NFLPA, their financial advisor, and/or other counsel, as appropriate (1:1-G).

- Players should be aware of the ramifications of withholding medical information from the club medical staff (1:1-H).

- Players should review their medical records regularly (1:1-I).

(B) Club Doctors

The 2011 CBA between the NFL and the NFLPA requires that each club retain a board-certified orthopedic surgeon and at least one physician board-certified in internal medicine, family medicine, or emergency medicine. All physicians must also have a Certificate of Added Qualification in Sports Medicine (or be grandfathered in). In addition, clubs are required to retain consultants in the neurological, cardiovascular, nutritional, and neuropsychological fields. While each club generally has a "head" club doctor, approximately 175 doctors work with NFL clubs in total, an average of 5.5 per club. Most (if not all) of the doctors retained by NFL clubs are members of the National Football League Physicians Society (NFLPS), the professional organization for club doctors.

Club doctors are clearly important stakeholders in player health. They diagnose and treat players for a variety of ailments, physical and mental, while making recommendations to players concerning those ailments. At the same time, club doctors have obligations to the club, namely to advise clubs about the health status of players. While players and clubs share an interest in player health—both want players to be healthy so they can play at peak performance—there are several areas where their interests may diverge, such as when a player feels compelled to return to play from an injury more quickly than is recommended in order to try and help the club win or, if he does not, potentially have his contract terminated.

Given the various roles just described, it is evident that club doctors face an inherent structural conflict of interest. **This is not a moral judgment about them as competent professionals or devoted individuals, but rather a simple fact of the current organizational structure of their position in which they simultaneously perform at least two roles that are not compatible.** The intersection of club doctors' dual obligations creates significant legal and ethical quandaries that can threaten player health. Most importantly, the current structure of NFL club medical staff—how they are selected, evaluated, and terminated, and to whom they report—creates an inherent structural conflict of interest in the treatment relationship and poses concerns related to player trust, no matter how upstanding or well-intentioned any given medical professional might be.

The current structure of NFL club medical staff—how they are selected, evaluated, and terminated, and to whom they report—creates an inherent structural conflict of interest.

To see why there is an inherent structural conflict of interest, consider an analogy in clinical medicine. In the organ donation process, structural conflicts of interest are avoided as follows: both law and ethics require two separate care teams is one to care for dying patients and pronounce them dead, and one to conduct the transplant and care for the recipient. If a single medical team served both roles, the structural problem of dual loyalty to both the dying patient and the patient in need of transplant would arise, even though the interests of both parties may conflict. In particular, the donor has an interest in not being declared dead prematurely, and the recipient has an interest in the donor's death being declared quickly enough so that the organs are not rendered unusable for transplant.

Note that in the organ context, this bifurcation of roles is well-established and mandatory. For example, even if an individual doctor swears that he or she is not influenced in declaring a donor's death by the desire to get the patient an organ, and even though it would be impossible in any particular case to prove or disprove such influence, this bifurcation of roles is required. Moreover, anything short of eliminating such conflict completely would deeply undermine the public's trust and peoples' willingness to consider organ donation.

The existing ethics codes and legal requirements are insufficient to satisfy the goal of ensuring that players receive the best healthcare possible from providers who are as free from conflicts of interest as is realistically possible. Of course, achieving this goal is legally, ethically, financially, and structurally complicated. **In Recommendation 2:1-A, we propose to resolve the problem of dual loyalty by largely removing the club doctor's ties with the club and refashioning the role into one of singular loyalty to player-patients.**

The recommendation is complex and described at length in the full Report, but the main idea is to separate the roles of serving the player and serving the club and replace them with two distinct sets of medical professionals: the "Players' Medical Staff" (with exclusive loyalty to the player) and the "Club Evaluation Doctor" (with exclusive loyalty to the club). The Players' Medical Staff would be selected and reviewed by a committee of medical experts jointly selected by the NFL and NFLPA. The Players' Medical Staff would then serve as a champion for player health, while clubs are free to hire additional medical professionals for their distinct business needs. Nevertheless, the club will still be entitled to player health information through the player's medical records and regular written reports from the Players' Medical Staff, given the importance of players' physical capacity to their employment.

We believe this recommendation could substantially lessen a major concern about the current club doctor arrangement—the problem of dual loyalty and structural conflict of interest—by providing players with a medical staff that principally has the interests of the players in mind and who they can trust. The Players' Medical Staff would be almost entirely separated from the club and the pressures inherent in club employment, while being held accountable to a neutral medical committee. At the same time, this recommendation does not interfere with the clubs' legitimate interests. For these reasons, we believe that this recommendation is critical to improving player health and among the most important set forth in the Report.

Accordingly, it should be adopted as part of the Collective Bargaining Agreement.

Other recommendations concerning club doctors are:

- The NFLPS should adopt a code of ethics (2:1-B).

- Every doctor retained by a club should be a member of the NFLPS (2:1-C).

- The Concussion Protocol should be amended such that if either the club doctor or the Unaffiliated Neurotrauma Consultant diagnoses a player with a concussion, the player cannot return to the game (2:1-D).

- The NFL and NFLPA should reconsider whether waivers providing for the use and disclosure of player medical information should include mental health information (2:1-E).

- Club doctors should abide by their CBA obligation to advise players of all information the club doctors disclose to club representatives concerning the players (2:1-F).

- At any time prior to the player's employment with the club, the player should be advised in writing that the club doctor is performing a fitness-for-play evaluation on behalf of the club and is not providing any medical services to the player (2:1-G).

- The NFL's Medical Sponsorship Policy should explicitly prohibit doctors or other medical service providers from providing consideration of any kind for the right to provide medical services to the club, exclusively or non-exclusively (2:1-H).

- Club doctors' roles should be clarified in a written document provided to the players before each season (2:1-I).

- The NFL, NFLPA, and club doctors should consider requiring all claims concerning the medical care provided by a doctor who is a member of the NFLPS and is arranged for by the club to be subject to binding arbitration (2:2-A).

(C) The NFL and NFLPA

The NFL and NFLPA are clearly essential stakeholders in protecting and promoting player health. Although the parties have a long and complicated history on the issue and with each other, they have made significant progress concerning player health in recent years. Indeed, the NFL and NFLPA offer many extraordinary benefits and programs intended to help current and former players, and both deserve commendation for doing so. Nevertheless, access to the programs and benefits appears to be an issue, and questions remain whether players are sufficiently made aware or avail themselves of these programs and benefits.

Consequently, there are still many important changes that the NFL and NFLPA can make that will further advance player health.

The most straightforward way to implement many of the changes we recommend to protect and promote player health would be to include them in the next CBA between the parties. That said, whenever change is possible outside of the CBA negotiating process, such as through side letters, it should not wait—the sooner, the better. Moreover, although the CBA will often be the most appropriate mechanism for implementing our recommendations, we do not want to be understood as suggesting that player health should be treated like just another issue for collective bargaining, subject to usual labor-management dynamics. This is to say that as an ethical matter, players should not be expected to make concessions in other domains in order to achieve gains in the health domain. To the contrary, we believe firmly the opposite: player health should be a joint priority, and not be up for negotiation. **For this reason, our first recommendation, Recommendation 7:1-A, is that the NFL and NFLPA should not make player health a subject of adversarial collective bargaining.** If as part of its research or otherwise the NFL knows a policy or practice should change, it should do so without waiting for the next round of bargaining or by forcing the NFLPA to concede on some other issue. Similarly, the NFLPA should not delay on player health issues in order to advance other collective bargaining goals.

Other recommendations to the NFL and NFLPA are:

- The NFL and NFLPA should continue to undertake and support efforts to scientifically and reliably establish the health risks and benefits of playing professional football (7:1-B).

- The NFL, and to the extent possible, the NFLPA, should: (a) continue to improve its robust collection of aggregate injury data; (b) continue to have the injury data analyzed by qualified professionals; and, (c) make the data publicly available for re-analysis (7:1-C).

- The NFL and NFLPA should publicly release de-identified, aggregate data from the Accountability and Care Committee's player surveys concerning the adequacy of players' medical care (7:1-D).

- Players diagnosed with a concussion should be placed on a short-term injured reserve list whereby the player does not count against the Active/Inactive 53-man roster until he is cleared to play by the Concussion Protocol (7:1-E).

- The NFL and NFLPA should research the consequences and feasibility of guaranteeing more of players' compensation as a way to protect player health (7:1-F).

- The CBA should be amended to provide for meaningful fines for any club or person found to have violated Sections 1 through 6 of Article 39 of the CBA (7:2-A).

- The statute of limitations on filing Non-Injury Grievances, at least in so far as they are health-related, should be extended (7:2-B).

- The NFL and NFLPA should continue and improve efforts to educate players about the variety of programs and benefits available to them (7:3-A).

- The NFL and NFLPA should undertake a comprehensive actuarial and choice architecture analysis of the various benefit and retirement programs to ensure they are maximally beneficial to players (7:3-B).

- The purpose of certain health-related committees should be clarified and their powers expanded (7:3-C).

- The NFL and NFLPA should continue and intensify their efforts to ensure that players take the Concussion Protocol seriously (7:4-A).

- The NFL and NFLPA should agree to a disciplinary system, including fines and/or suspensions, for players who target another player's injury or threaten or discuss doing so (7:4-B).

- The NFLPA should consider investing greater resources in investigating and enforcing player health issues, including Article 39 of the 2011 CBA (7:5-A).

- The NFLPA should continue to assist former players to the extent such assistance is consistent with the NFLPA's obligations to current players (7:6-A).

3) OTHER STAKEHOLDERS

While above we focused on the four most important stakeholders, the remaining sixteen stakeholders are also critical to player health. In the Report, all of the stakeholders are grouped into parts as follows: Part 1: Players; Part 2: The Medical Team; Part 3: The NFL, NFLPA, and NFL Clubs; Part 4: NFL Club Employees; Part 5: Player Advisors; and, Part 6: Other Stakeholders. We briefly discuss these parts and the stakeholders included therein insofar as they were not discussed above.

(A) The Medical Team (Part 2)

A player's medical team includes not only club doctors, but also: athletic trainers; doctors whom players may consult concerning an injury or medical condition to compare or contrast that opinion to that of the club doctor (second opinion doctors); doctors who are called on when there are conflicting opinions or interests (neutral doctors); and, doctors who players see outside of the NFL environment (personal doctors). Each of these medical professionals is important in his or her own way.

Athletic trainers are generally the player's first and primary source of medical care. Nevertheless, some players distrust athletic trainers. Communications among athletic trainers, coaches, and the club's general manager place pressure on players to practice, sometimes causing them to withhold information from the athletic trainer. For this reason, **our principal recommendation concerning athletic trainers, Recommendation 3:1-A, matches Recommendation 2:1-A concerning club doctors: to separate the roles of serving "the player and serving the club and replace them with two distinct sets of medical professionals: the "Players' Medical Staff" (with exclusive loyalty to the player) and the "Club Evaluation Doctor" (with exclusive loyalty to the club).** The athletic trainers' principal day-to-day responsibilities would remain largely the same—providing medical care to the players and updating the club on player health status (just in a different way). Nevertheless, most importantly, the proposed change largely removes the structural conflict of interest in the care being provided to players by athletic trainers and other medical staff.

Under the CBA, players have the right to a second opinion doctor and the surgeon of their choice, provided the player consults with the club doctor and provides the club doctor with a report concerning treatment provided by the second opinion doctor (the full cost of which must be paid by the club). Many contract advisors arrange for their players to receive a second opinion for every injury. Given the importance of this right, **we recommend that club medical staff be more supportive of players in obtaining a second opinion (Recommendation 4:1-A).**

The 2011 CBA notes three situations where neutral doctors are required: (1) as the on-field emergency physician during games; (2) to perform examinations and provide opinions as part of the Injury Grievance process; and, (3) to investigate allegations of inadequate medical care by a club as part of the Joint Committee on Player Safety and Welfare. In addition to the CBA provisions requiring a neutral doctor, the Concussion Protocol requires an

"Unaffiliated Neurotrauma Consultant" to be assigned to each club for each game to assist in the evaluation of players suspected of having suffered a concussion. The Unaffiliated Neurotrauma Consultants are crucial to the effective operation of the Concussion Protocol, a signature component of player health. There is no indication that neutral doctors have done anything other than perform the roles assigned to them by the CBA and Concussion Protocol. Consequently, we make no recommendations concerning neutral doctors. **Indeed, the *neutrality* of these doctors is a positive benefit to players, and we should look for additional opportunities to have neutral doctor input and involvement.**

Personal doctors might be the least utilized of the doctors discussed in this Report. In talking with players, several indicated that frequent moves from city to city and their busy schedules made finding and seeing a personal doctor problematic. Consequently, many players principally rely on club doctors and second opinion doctors for their care. **Thus, we recommend that the NFLPA and clubs assist players to access and more frequently utilize the services of personal doctors (Recommendation 6:1-A).**

(B) The NFL, NFLPA, and NFL Clubs (Part 3)

Having discussed the NFL and NFLPA above, we discuss now the remaining stakeholder in Part 3: NFL Clubs. The NFL is an unincorporated association of 32 member clubs that serves as a centralized body for obligations and undertakings shared by the member clubs. Nevertheless, each member club is a separate and distinct legal entity, with its own legal obligations separate and distinct from club owners and employees. NFL clubs are the players' employers and hire many of the stakeholders discussed in this Report. In this respect, NFL clubs play an important role in dictating the culture concerning player health. They are powerful organizations that employ many people with direct day-to-day interaction concerning player health issues. Like all organizations, the specific culture on important issues varies from club to club.

NFL clubs collectively comprise the NFL. Thus, any recommendations concerning NFL clubs would ultimately be within the scope of recommendations made concerning the NFL. Moreover, NFL clubs act only through their employees or independent contractors, including coaches, other employees, and the medical staff. Thus, any recommendation we make for the improvement of clubs would be carried out through recommendations we make concerning

club employees. For these reasons, we make no separate recommendations here and instead refer to the recommendations in the chapters concerning those stakeholders for recommendations concerning NFL clubs. Nevertheless, we do stress that **it is important that club owners, as the leaders of each NFL club and its employees, personally take seriously and show leadership in player health issues, including overseeing the response to recommendations made in this Report.**

(C) NFL Club Employees (Part 4)

Part 4 discusses the non-medical stakeholders within the purview of the club: coaches; general managers; developmental staff; scouts; and, equipment managers. These stakeholders have varying degrees of influence on player health matters but are nonetheless all important.

Of all of the stakeholders considered in this Report, coaches have the most authority over players, and impose the most direct physical and psychological demands on them. Coaches can help players maximize their potential, but in some cases may also contribute to the degradation of a player's health. Head coaches are the individuals ultimately most responsible for the club's performance on the field and thus take on an immense stature and presence within the organization; indeed, some head coaches are the final decision-makers on player personnel decisions. Coaches largely determine the club's culture, dictate the pace and physicality of practice and workouts, and decide who plays—a decision often borne out by intense physical competition. Moreover, coaches must be successful in order to retain their jobs and face enormous pressure to win. That pressure no doubt affects their relationship with their players and in some cases is felt by the players. **To protect against the pressures inherent in coaches' roles, we recommend that the NFL Coaches Association adopt and enforce a code of ethics that recognizes that coaches share responsibility for player health (Recommendation 9:1-A). We also recommend specific issues that should be addressed in such a code of ethics and that the most important of these ethical principles be incorporated into the CBA (Recommendation 9:1-B).**

NFL club general managers and scouts make important decisions concerning a player's career, often based on a player's current or expected health status. Relatedly, developmental staff—often ex-players who are responsible for assisting the club's players with a blend of professional and personal issues—have the opportunity to play an important role in assisting players and making sure the actions taken are in their best interests. These club employees all have unique relationships with players that provide them an important opportunity to promote player health. Indeed, like coaches, many NFL club employees develop close relationships with players—many are former players themselves—and are thus sensitive to protecting player health. Nevertheless, the inherent pressures of winning and running a successful business can sometimes cause these employees to make decisions or create pressures that negatively affect player health. Thus, **we recommend clubs and club employees—in particular general managers and developmental staff—take steps to resolve any concerns discovered about a player's health (Recommendation 10:1-A). Relatedly, we recommend that clubs adequately support the developmental staff, something that does not appear to always be the case (Recommendation 10:1-B).**

(D) Player Advisors (Part 5)

Part 5 discusses those individuals closest to the players and who should always have the players' best interests in mind: contract advisors; financial advisors; and, family members. In reading this part, it is important to remember our broad definition of health, which includes and extends beyond clinical measurements to the social determinants of health, including financial wellbeing, education, and social support. These stakeholders are particularly critical in protecting and promoting players' long-term health in this sense.

Contract advisors, more commonly known as "agents," are often players' most trusted and important resources and allies when it comes to protecting them during their NFL career, including protecting their health. In fact, contract advisors are agents of both players and the NFLPA, pursuant to the National Labor Relations Act. The NFLPA has a program whereby it certifies contract advisors and subjects them to its Regulations Governing Contract Advisors ("Contract Advisor Regulations"). Entering the 2015 NFL season, there were 869 NFLPA-certified contract advisors

but only 420 actually had clients (48.3 percent). A contract advisor is typically involved in all aspects of a player's life, including but not limited to his personal, career, medical, legal, and financial matters. Nevertheless, there are structural and regulatory issues within the contract advisor industry that prevent players from receiving the best possible representation and the best possible protection of their health-related rights. **We therefore make multiple recommendations for amending the Contract Advisor Regulations, including prohibiting loans or advances from contract advisors to players or prospective players in excess of the costs reasonable and necessary to prepare for the NFL Draft (Recommendation 12:2-A).**

Similarly, financial advisors play a critically important role in a player's long-term health. Proper financial advice and planning can help a player determine when to retire (if he has that choice), maximize a player's career earnings, potentially provide the player with a comfortable retirement, help mitigate the consequences of the health issues suffered by many former players, and help avoid financial distress evolving into physical or mental distress. The NFLPA has a program whereby financial advisors can register with the NFLPA and are subject to its Regulations and Code of Conduct Governing Registered Player Financial Advisors ("Financial Advisor Regulations"). While there are approximately 262 NFLPA-registered financial advisors, there are many financial advisors working with NFL players who are not NFLPA-registered, many of whom likely could not meet the registration requirements. Financial advisors are governed by many robust codes of ethics that echo some of the same principles we incorporated into this Report. However, there are a variety of industry practices and realities that are preventing some players from always receiving the best possible financial guidance. Consequently, **we make multiple recommendations for amending the Financial Advisor Regulations to provide greater professionalism and transparency to the industry (Recommendation 13:1-B).**

Families can play a crucial role in protecting and promoting player health, including encouraging players to seek proper medical care and carefully consider long-term interests; they can also offer support through challenging times. Unfortunately, in some cases, family members can also put inappropriate pressure on players or otherwise negatively influence their health. Consequently, **we recommend that family members be cognizant of the gaps in their knowledge concerning the realities of an NFL career, and that the NFL and NFLPA should offer programs or materials to help them become better health advocates**

(Recommendation 14:1-A). Relatedly, players should select and rely on professionals rather than family members for managing their business, financial, and legal affairs (Recommendation 14:2-A).

(E) Other Stakeholders (Part 6)

Finally, Part 6 discusses several other stakeholders with a variety of roles in player health: officials; equipment manufacturers; the media; fans; and, NFL business partners.

Officials—as the individuals responsible for enforcing the Playing Rules—have an important role in protecting player health on the field. While the NFL consults with officials on changes to the Playing Rules, the officials' principal job is to enforce them. On that front, we found little criticism that officials are failing to enforce the Playing Rules as enacted by the NFL and thus we have no formal recommendations for them. Officials should be praised for their efforts, particularly considering the high level of scrutiny around these issues. **While officials should continue their solid work, they must always be diligent and open to change for additional ways to protect player health.**

The football equipment market is dominated by Riddell and Schutt, each of which hold at least a 45 percent share of the football equipment market, across all levels of football. An additional important party in the equipment manufacturing industry is the National Operating Committee on Standards for Athletic Equipment (NOCSAE), a non-profit organization that determines the safety standards for athletic equipment. Our review shows that equipment manufacturers are generally working to create the safest equipment possible. Equipment manufacturers for a variety of reasons (including both liability and brand image) have generally sought to make equipment safer, and the recent increased emphasis on player health and safety can only have accelerated that interest. We thus expect and recommend that equipment manufacturers continue to invest in the research and development of safer equipment. Similarly, at present, it appears that equipment manufacturers have been more careful than in years past in ensuring they accurately convey the benefits and limitations of their equipment. **In this regard, equipment manufacturers should continue this work, and we have no formal recommendations for them.**

The NFL and the media have an important and significant relationship that makes the media a key stakeholder in player health. Nevertheless, the media's coverage of player health issues has been mixed. Many reporters have done great work to expose problems in the way player health is or has been addressed and the resulting problems suffered by current and former players. At the same time, some of the coverage raises concerns. There have been many important scientific studies concerning the injuries, particularly concussions, suffered by football players. However, with the pressures of deadlines, the media may not always have adequate space or time to convey the implications and limitations of these studies. Similarly, the media has not always accurately reported on player health litigation. The scientific and legal nuances are difficult to understand, which makes accurate reporting on them critically important. Consequently, **we recommend that the media engage appropriate experts, including doctors, scientists, and lawyers, to ensure that its reporting on player health matters is accurate, balanced, and comprehensive (Recommendation 17:1-B).**

NFL football is the most popular sport in America by a variety of measures, and fans are undoubtedly a central component to the NFL's success. Fans engage with NFL football and players in a variety of ways, including by watching on television (more than 20 million people watch the primetime broadcasts), attending practices or games in-person (a mean of more than 68,000 people attend every NFL game), by gambling and playing fantasy sports, and through public events where fans might see or speak with players. Fans, ultimately, are what drive the success of the NFL, and they therefore wield incredible power. Consequently, **we recommend that fans recognize their ability to bring about change concerning player health (Recommendation 18:1-A).** At the same time, increased fan interest and engagement through social media has also resulted in inappropriate behavior, such as cheering injuries or Tweeting racist remarks. Thus, **we also recommend that fans recognize that the lives of NFL players are more than entertainment, and that NFL players are human beings who suffer injuries that may adversely affect their health (Recommendation 18:1-B).** Fans should not advocate, cheer, encourage, or incite player injuries or pressure players to play while injured.

In the 2015 season, the NFL had approximately 29 official business partners, which collectively paid the NFL more than one billion dollars annually. NFL business partners, due to the power of the purse, have a unique ability to influence the NFL to make positive changes concerning player health. Consequently, **we recommend that NFL**

business partners not remain silent on NFL player health-related policies (Recommendation 19:1-A). Moreover, NFL business partners should consider applying pressure on the NFL to improve player health (Recommendation 19:1-B), should consider supporting organizations conducting due diligence into player health issues (Recommendation 19:1-C), and should engage players concerning player health issues (Recommendation 19:1-D).

* * *

In addition to these stakeholders, there are other parties that have some role in player health and are also discussed in Part 7 of the Report: (a) the NCAA; (b) youth leagues; (c) governments; (d) workers' compensation attorneys; and, (e) health-related companies.

4) CONCLUSION

This Report explains the pressing need for research into the overall health of NFL players; the need to address player health from all angles, both clinical and structural; and, the challenges presented in conducting such research and analysis. The issues and parties involved are numerous, complex, and interconnected. To address these issues— and, ultimately, to protect and improve the health of NFL players—requires a diligent and comprehensive approach to create well-informed and meaningful recommendations for change. This is precisely the focus of this Report.

Nevertheless, our recommendations are only as useful as their implementation. For this reason, **we make the following final recommendations: the NFL, NFLPA, and other stakeholders should actively engage with and publicly respond to this Report; the stakeholders identified in this Report, media, academics, and others should actively advocate, encourage, and monitor the promotion of player health; and, as recommended throughout the Report, various stakeholders (*e.g.*, club doctors, athletic trainers, coaches, contract advisors, and financial advisors) should adopt, improve, and enforce Codes of Ethics.**

NFL football has a storied history and holds an important place in this country. The men who play it deserve to be protected and have their health needs met and it is our fervent hope that the health needs of these men will be met. We hope this Report succeeds in furthering that cause.

Preface | Introduction | Guiding Ethical Principles

THE FOOTBALL PLAYERS HEALTH STUDY AT HARVARD UNIVERSITY

There are an estimated 20,000 men alive today who at one time played professional football in the National Football League (NFL).[a] Some of these men played in "The Greatest Game Ever Played" in 1958,[b] the first Super Bowl in 1967, for the undefeated Miami Dolphins in 1973, the Chicago Bears' 46 defense in the 1980s, and so on through the course of the NFL's history. They were there when television made the game accessible to the masses, when the NFL merged with the American Football League (AFL) to create the modern NFL, and through the lawsuits of the late 1980s and early 1990s that brought us to today's NFL. And there are thousands more still playing today or about to join this elite fraternity. NFL players have always been men of seemingly supernatural physical ability, heroes to cities and sometimes the nation. Through it all, the players experience not only the benefits, but also the physical, mental, emotional, and financial tolls of their NFL careers. In the last decade or so it has become impossible to avoid accounts of how those careers affect NFL players, in particular the detrimental health effects many of them experience in the short and long term.

In response to these accounts and related concerns, the 2011 Collective Bargaining Agreement (CBA) between the NFL and the National Football League Players Association (NFLPA) added a number of new health, safety, and welfare provisions. One of these provisions sets aside $11 million per year through 2021 to be dedicated to medical research.[1] Thus, in the summer of 2012, the NFLPA issued a request for proposals to conduct original research and scientific exploration to be supported by these funds, focusing on "new and innovative ways to protect, treat, and improve the health of NFL players." The NFLPA's request for proposals specified a number of areas of particular interest, including sports medicine, repetitive brain trauma, wellness, aging, and cardiovascular disease, as well as

"Medical Ethics (e.g., examination of health care contexts to obtain a better understanding of internal morality of these practices, accountability, new interventions that avoid harms currently incurred, appropriate informed consent in the context of professional athletics, and consideration of medical care in the labor-management context of professional football)."[2]

To meet the challenge of protecting and improving player health, it is necessary to move beyond clinical issues to simultaneously address structural and organizational issues as well. This is true for healthcare more generally, where it is essential to invest not only in scientific research and development to create new clinical interventions, but also to invest in systems to efficiently administer those interventions to patients in need, as well as in public health approaches that can minimize the need for intervention in the first place. Likewise, to make headway in protecting and improving the health of NFL players, we must go beyond a single-minded focus on their clinical care and instead implement a more comprehensive strategy capable of addressing the myriad of stakeholders and contextual factors (past, present, League-wide, and individual) that play a role in their health. These include not only players' physical issues and risk factors, but also their relationships with clinicians, their professional motivations, their financial pressures, their family responsibilities, and the centrality of their health to their careers. Add to this mix the competitive nature of the business, constraints on alternative career opportunities for many players, and the like. The relevant stakeholders in player health are similarly varied and extensive.

Thus, when submitting its proposal to the NFLPA, our Harvard team included a variety of critical clinical projects alongside an equally robust set of law and ethics proposals. We agreed from the outset that a focus on diagnosing and treating player health issues—while essential—would be insufficient on its own to comprehensively resolve those issues. Instead, our approach has been to also address precisely those structural and organizational factors that are so important to player health but would be neglected by pursuing a purely clinical approach.

---

a   Included as Appendix P is a Glossary of Terms and Relevant Persons and Institutions which may help readers.

b   In 1958, the Baltimore Colts and New York Giants played in the NFL Championship Game (before the Super Bowl), in front of a national television audience and in front of 64,000 fans at Yankee Stadium. The game was a back and forth battle that wound up becoming the first ever overtime playoff game in NFL history. The Colts, led by Hall of Fame quarterback Johnny Unitas, eventually won 23–17, in what became known as "The Greatest Game Ever Played." *See Greatest Game Ever Played*, Pro Football Hall of Fame, http://www.profootballhof.com/history/release.aspx?release_id=1805 (last visited Aug. 7, 2015), *archived at* http://perma.cc/35UZ-AZRQ.

The NFLPA ultimately agreed, selecting Harvard to receive the funding after a multi-round competitive process involving several universities. In February 2014, Harvard Medical School entered into an agreement with the NFLPA to create the "Football Players Health Study at Harvard University," a transformative research initiative with the goal of improving the health of professional football players across a broad spectrum. The Football Players Health Study initially included three main components:

(1) A Population Studies component, which entails research using questionnaires and testing to better understand player health status, wellness, and quality of life, including the largest ever cohort study of living former NFL players;

(2) A Pilot Studies program aimed to develop new prevention strategies, diagnostics, and treatments by funding researchers working on innovative and promising developments that have the potential to impact the health of football players; and,

(3) A Law and Ethics component, led by the Petrie-Flom Center for Health Law Policy, Biotechnology, and Bioethics at Harvard Law School ("Law and Ethics Initiative"), which encompasses a variety of distinct projects with the primary goal of understanding the legal and ethical issues that may promote or impede player health, and developing appropriate responsive recommendations.[c]

The existence of the Law and Ethics component differentiates The Football Players Health Study from other studies concerning NFL player health. While there have been many important studies concerning the medical aspects of player health, we are not aware of any that have conducted a comprehensive analysis of the relevant legal and ethical environments.

Additionally, in the Section: Ensuring Independence and Disclosure of Conflicts, we discuss the ways in which the Law and Ethics Initiative interacted with, but was independent of, both the NFLPA and NFL in creating this Report.

In the chapters that follow, we describe the scope of the Report, its goals, and guiding ethical principles. First, however, it is essential to explain the guiding principles of The Football Players Health Study as a whole.

Most importantly, The Football Players Health Study is interested in health issues beyond concussions and neurological trauma. Although we recognize that concussions and their possible long-term sequelae are on the minds of many, and are among the most critical health issues facing players today, we simultaneously recognize that player health concerns are broader than concussions alone. Players also have concerns about cardiac health, arthritis and other joint damage, pain management, and a wide variety of other issues. Moreover, their primary concerns are likely to change over time as they transition from their playing days to retirement to old age. Thus, we have adopted the following mantra for our work: "The Whole Player, The Whole Life." Rather than a myopic approach, we are taking a wide and long view in order to make players as healthy as they possibly can be over every conceivable dimension for the entirety of their lives.

> To meet the challenge of protecting and improving player health, it is necessary to move beyond clinical issues to simultaneously address structural and organizational issues as well.

We approached this project as scholars and social scientists whose goal is to improve NFL player health. We are independent academic researchers first and foremost, regardless of the source of our funding. We have no "client" in this endeavor, other than players themselves, and we have no agenda other than to improve the lives of players, former, current, and future. Indeed, The Football Players Health Study is funded pursuant to funds set aside under the 2011 CBA for research designed to help players. Because of the way the clubs and players split revenues from NFL games and other operations, the funds used for The Football Players Health Study can reduce the amount of money available

c   Other Law and Ethics projects include: (1) a qualitative interview study ("listening tour") with players and their families to better understand their legal and ethical concerns related to health and well-being; (2) a comparative legal and organizational policy analysis of various professional sports leagues to identify best policies in protecting player health; (3) an analysis of the legal and ethical implications of current and potential medical tests and devices that might be used by NFL clubs and players; and, (4) an examination of how traditional workplace health and safety laws would apply to professional sports; among others.

current players in the form of salary.[d] Thus, the clubs and players have chosen to pay for The Football Players Health Study. In addition, although our contractual relationship is with the NFLPA, that very same contract protects our academic integrity without exception; no external party has any control whatsoever over our conclusions.

One of our primary concerns is that too little is known about player health. Specifically, too little is known from a rigorous scientific perspective about the risks and benefits of playing professional football because available data are insufficient in a variety of respects. For example, "[w]e do not know what factors exacerbate or mitigate an individual's risk, including genetics, nutrition, lifestyle, as well as length of time and position played, and injuries sustained during playing years."[3] Professional football players are an elite and unique group of men who must be studied directly and often in large numbers before we can really understand how football has affected them. Only then can we fully

address any health problems they may have. We come to this work with no pre-existing agenda—we have neither any interest in ending professional football nor any interest in looking the other way if confronted with compelling data of its downsides. Again, we are interested only in helping players lead the healthiest and most productive lives they possibly can. We are committed to going where the science takes us.

Finally, we are forward-looking. Our role is not to evaluate fault or assign blame for player health problems, and The Football Players Health Study is uninvolved in any litigation (current or past) related to these issues. Instead, we are working with a single-minded focus to develop a clear path for addressing and remediating existing player health problems, and for preventing such problems from continuing or occurring in the future, from both clinical and organizational perspectives. Although this process does include assigning shared responsibility for protecting and promoting players' health to a wide variety of parties, the past is relevant only to the extent it demonstrates ways to successfully improve going forward. We elaborate on our view of the past in the Introduction.

These are the guiding principles motivating every aspect of The Football Players Health Study at Harvard University.

---

d   The players' share of NFL revenues is referred to as the Player Cost Amount. 2011 CBA, Art. 12, § 6(c)(i). The Football Players Health Study is funded from a pool of money known as the Joint Contribution Amount. *See* 2011 CBA, Art. 12, § 5. If the NFL generates new revenue streams, the players are entitled to 50% of the net revenues from those new ventures less 47.5% of the Joint Contribution Amount. 2011 CBA, Art. 12, § 6(c)(ii). Thus, if the NFL generates new revenue streams, the amount that is passed on to the players is reduced by 47.5% of the Joint Contribution Amount, which includes The Football Players Health Study.

INTRODUCTION

This Report, the principal component of the Law and Ethics Initiative of The Football Players Health Study at Harvard University, aims to answer these fundamental questions: *Who* is responsible for the health of NFL players, why, and what can be done to promote player health? To date, there has been no comprehensive analysis of the universe of stakeholders that may influence player health, nor any systematic analysis of their existing or appropriate legal and/or ethical obligations. However, this sort of undertaking is essential to uncovering areas in need of improvement and making clear that the responsibility for player health falls on many interconnected groups that must work together to protect and support these individuals who give so much of themselves—not without personal benefit, but sometimes with serious personal consequences—to one of America's favorite sports. Without addressing and resolving these structural and organizational issues, and acknowledging a variety of potentiality relevant background conditions, any clinical approach to improving player health will necessarily fall short.

(A) The Public Debate Surrounding the Health of NFL Players

Before getting into the substance of the Report, it is important to describe our role in the public debate surrounding football. In line with the entirety of The Football Players Health Study, our goal in this Report is to be forward-looking. In seeking answers to our driving questions, we have reviewed the NFLPA, NFL, and every other stakeholder objectively and through an independent, academic lens with the exclusive goal of making the best recommendations possible to protect and promote the health of NFL players going forward. While we do sometimes provide relevant history, this is for the sole purpose of framing what is intended to be a set of prospective analyses and recommendations. In order to fully understand the current responsibilities of various stakeholders to protect and promote player health, it is essential to understand their historical relationships with players and one another, as well as their actions, omissions, controversies, and changes over time. Without this context, our recommendations would lack credibility and likely be too disconnected to influence change; they might also otherwise be simply

wrong, impracticable, or ineffective. We necessarily took history into account in making our recommendations, and felt it essential to ensure that the reader can fully grasp the rationale for our suggested approaches. Thus, in the chapters that follow, we have provided substantial factual background. Our goal, however, is not to provide a comprehensive historical account, grapple with various allegations and defenses, judge past behavior, or allocate praise and blame. Instead, our focus is on *promoting positive change* where needed moving forward, through identification of critical gaps, opportunities for improvement, recognition of power and responsibility, and the like.

With that said, we understand and acknowledge that many people believe some of the stakeholders discussed in this Report, in particular the NFL, have failed to satisfy their obligations to player health.[4] More specifically, due to a number of acknowledged and alleged shortcomings, there is an ongoing public debate about the quality of the NFL's research efforts regarding the long-term neurological effects of playing in the NFL, as well as the League's response to emerging data over time.

A series of events in spring 2016 provide a good window into the nature of public debate about professional football and neurological disease, in particular chronic traumatic encephalopathy (CTE). CTE has been defined as a "progressive neurodegenerative disease."[5] As a preliminary matter, it is essential to understand the current state of the science related to the causes, diagnosis, symptoms, and treatment of CTE. At present, diagnosis of CTE is exclusively based on a pathology diagnosis, meaning that it determined through laboratory examination of bodily tissue, in this context, from the brain. Efforts are underway to link pathological findings to a clinical phenotype, or manifestation of discrete cognitive and behavioral symptoms. However, further research is needed, as described below.

Who is responsible for the health of NFL players, why, and what can be done to promote player health?

Retrospective case reports have found CTE pathology in the brains of former athletes—including former professional football players—who manifested mood disorders, headaches, cognitive difficulties, suicidal ideation, difficulties with speech, and aggressive behavior.[6] The vast majority of cases in these studies were associated with repetitive head trauma.[7] However, a mechanistic connection between head trauma and CTE has not yet been demonstrated.[8] Similarly, whether CTE is distinct from other neurodegenerative diseases[9] or whether repetitive head traumas are necessary and sufficient to cause CTE has not been definitively established.[10]

Of note, Jeff Miller, the NFL's Executive Vice President for Health and Safety Policy, participated in a March 14, 2016 roundtable discussion before the U.S. House of Representatives Energy and Commerce Committee on concussion research and treatment. During the roundtable, Miller answered questions from Representative Anna Eshoo (D-CA) following comments from Dr. Ann McKee from Boston University, recognized as one of the foremost experts in CTE research.

> **McKee:** *I unequivocally think there's a link between playing football and CTE. We've seen it in 90 out of 94 NFL players whose brains we've examined. We've found in 45 out of 55 college players, and 6 out of 26 high school players. Now I don't think this represents how common this disease is in the living population. But the fact that over 5 years I've been able to accumulate this number of cases in football players—it cannot be rare. In fact, I think we are going to be surprised at how common it is.*

[McKee's comments about youth athletes omitted]

> **Eshoo:** *Mr. Miller, do you think there is a link between football and degenerative brain disorders like CTE?*

> **Miller:** *Well certainly Dr. McKee's research shows that a number of retired NFL players are diagnosed with CTE, so there . . . the answer to that question is certainly yes. But there are also a number of questions that come with that. What's the—*

> **Eshoo:** *So, I guess . . . Is there a link—*

> **Miller:** *Yes—*

> **Eshoo:** *'Cause we feel, or I feel, that, you know, that was not the unequivocal answer three days before the Super Bowl by Dr. Mitchell Berger.*

> **Miller:** *Well, I'm not going to speak for Dr. Berger, he's—*

> **Eshoo:** *Well you're speaking for the NFL, right?*

> **Miller:** *I . . . You asked the question about whether I thought there was a link, and I think certainly based on Dr. McKee's research there is a link because she's found CTE in a number of retired football players. My . . . I think that the broader point, and the one that your question gets to, is what that necessarily means and where do we go from here with that information. And so when we talk about a link, or you talk about the incidence or the prevalence, I think that some of the medical experts around the table—just for the record, I'm not a medical physician, so I feel limited here, or a scientist, so I feel limited in answering much more than that, other than the direct answer to your question—I would defer to number of people around the table to, you know, what the science means around the question that you're asking. And I'm happy to answer this specific question.[11]*

Miller's comments came about six weeks after Dr. Mitch Berger, a member of the NFL's Head, Neck, and Spine Committee made comments concerning a possible a link between football and CTE.[12] In fact, Berger's comments on the issue were more nuanced:

> *Well, what I would say is we know from the former players who have been evaluated, who have CTE, they've played football. So the question is, is there an association? We're concerned of course that there could be an association. Because we recognize the fact that there are long-term effects. But now we have to really understand to what degree those long-term effects occur.*

> * * *

> *There's an association between football, we think, or any traumatic brain injury, and possible long-term effects in terms of neurodegeneration. We do know, I would say unequivocally there are former players who have developed CTE. So there can be association. I would be the first one to say that.[13]*

In addition to the statistics cited by Dr. McKee in her comments, Boston University researchers have diagnosed CTE in 131 of 165 (79.4 percent) brains of individuals who, before their deaths, played football professionally, semi-professionally, in college, or in high school.[14] In one peer-reviewed study, Mayo Clinic and Boston University researchers found that the brains of 21 of 66 former contact sport athletes demonstrated CTE, while CTE pathology was not detected in any of 198 individuals without exposure to contact sports.[15]

Many claimed that Miller's comments were the first time the NFL had stated there was a connection between playing football and CTE;[16] while the NFL subsequently insisted Miller's statement was consistent with its position,[17] although the NFL had not previously expressed such a position publicly.[e] In contrast, several club owners later made comments questioning a link between CTE and NFL play.[18] The owners' comments may have been based in part on a March 17, 2016 memorandum from NFL general counsel Jeff Pash. Pash's memorandum cited the District Court's opinion in the Concussion Litigation settlement decision (discussed in Chapter 7: The NFL and NFLPA),[19] which explained that the study of CTE is in its early stages and much is still unknown, including its symptoms.[20] Pash's memorandum also cited the most recent Consensus Statement on Concussion in Sport from the world's leading concussion researchers,[21] which explained that while CTE "represents a distinct tauopathy . . . speculation that repeated concussion or sub-concussive impacts causes CTE remains unproven."[22] On the part of the NFLPA, when asked about Miller's comments, NFLPA President Eric Winston said that the NFLPA "think[s] there's a link," but, like Miller, questioned "what does that link mean?"[23] Winston further explained that the NFLPA's position will follow "[w]here the science is telling us to go."[24]

Around the same time, *The New York Times* further questioned the NFL's past research efforts[25] and ESPN questioned the NFL's current research efforts,[26] with both reports receiving immediate counter-responses from the NFL.[27] As this played out, in a March 28, 2016 *New York Times* article, Dr. McKee herself cautioned against over-interpreting her group's research findings, stating that she has "no idea" what percent of former NFL players have CTE due to the fact that her laboratory's collection of brains is not representative of the former NFL player population. She went on to note, however, that her research at the very least suggests that the condition is not rare among former NFL players.[28]

As the *New York Times* acknowledged, there "remains a quieter debate among scientists about how much risk each football player has of developing [CTE]" and unanswered questions as to why "some players seem far more vulnerable to it than others."[29] CTE can, at present, only be diagnosed after death, upon physical examination of the brain itself—again, it is exclusively a pathological diagnosis.[30] As of the date of the Court's decision (April 22, 2015), only 200 brains with CTE had ever been examined (only some of which were from former NFL players), a figure that experts testified was "well short of the sample size needed to understand CTE's symptoms with scientific certainty."[31] The Court also explained that the studies that have examined CTE have a number of important limitations, including small sample sizes, selection bias in the populations studied, lack of control groups, reliance on family members to retrospectively report subjects' behavior, and lack of controls for other risk factors such as higher body mass index (BMI), lifestyle changes, age, chronic pain, or substance abuse.[32] The National Institute of Neurological Disorders and Stroke is now funding research seeking to clarify the link between CTE pathology and specific symptoms.[33]

Clearly, this is a complicated issue. At present, there is reason to believe there is a link between CTE and professional football, which even the NFL acknowledges, but there remain significant open questions about the significance of that link.

While other components of The Football Players Health Study are working to address various clinical issues and respond to important gaps in available scientific evidence regarding player health, in part through the largest cohort study of former NFL players ever conducted, the Law and Ethics Initiative is specifically focused on the current *structural* issues influencing player health. Thus, we do not seek here to resolve debates regarding the rapidly evolving science, nor do we seek to conduct an in-depth historical analysis of the NFL or NFLPA's previous efforts, research, and reporting concerning player health. Such issues have been covered at length in news articles, books, documentaries, and movies, and we do not recapitulate that work here. This choice is guided entirely by our focus on what is needed to protect and promote player health now, rather than any desire or pressure to protect either the NFL or NFLPA; we dissect the past insofar as it is relevant to the future, and in that regard, we do not hesitate in pointing out the failures of any stakeholder to adequately address player health.

Beyond these clarifications regarding scope, it is important to note that we also have not endeavored in this Report to evaluate football as a sport or to radically change its basic nature, instead taking the current game largely as a given Critics of this approach, many of whom view the NFL as a violent gladiator spectacle, may be unsatisfied with this

---

e   In reviewing draft of this Report, the NFL stressed that "as early as 2008, the NFL acknowledged a potential link between concussions and long term problems." NFL Comments and Corrections (June 24, 2016), *citing* Alan Schwarz, *N.F.L. Acknowledges Long-Term Concussion Effects*, N.Y. Times, Dec. 20, 2009, http://www.nytimes.com/2009/12/21/sports/football/21concussions.html, *archived at* https://perma.cc/83AH-ENLP.

starting point, demanding to know why, as ethicists, we have not simply recommended that professional football cease to exist, at least in its present form. There are a number of reasons for this approach that are worth addressing explicitly here.

(B) Risks and Autonomy

As a preliminary matter, we recognize that the level of attention NFL player health is receiving at present—from Congressional hearings to daily media coverage—is such that current and future professional-level players are at least aware of the possibility of significant health risks, even if this has not always been the case in the past and even if the currently available data remain somewhat unclear. Given the range of risks we as a society allow competent adults to accept for themselves in a variety of contexts for a variety of reasons, we do not believe that it is presently appropriate or necessary to suggest that the opportunity to play professional football ought to be withheld as an ethical matter. Of course, reasonable disagreement on this score is expected, and some may prefer a precautionary approach,[34] suggesting that we ought to be convinced of the safety of professional football before allowing it to proceed. While we understand from where such a sentiment comes, our own view is that it is more appropriate to leave it to individual players to make their own decisions about whether or not to play, while empowering them with as much information and assistance to understand what is currently known and not known about the health effects of playing football and requiring all stakeholders to do their part to reduce risks of the game.

In this regard, it is helpful to consider whether there is some threshold level of risk associated with professional football that could, if eventually demonstrated through conclusive scientific evidence, alter this analysis such that simple reliance on the autonomous decisions of competent, adult professionals would no longer be ethically sufficient. In other words, when would we say that the risks of professional football are simply too high for players to be given the choice to accept them? To answer that question, it is important to contemplate when, if ever, interference with individual liberty of competent adults is acceptable, recognizing that this is a heavily contested area of political philosophy often without a clear consensus as to a "right" answer. What level of intervention is appropriate under what circumstances?

At the threshold, it is never problematic to support the exercise of individual autonomy by simply providing education and warnings based on the best available data; indeed, this ought not be considered interference with individual liberty at all, but rather is a liberty-*supporting* intervention. Thus, as discussed in more detail below, the NFL and NFLPA must, at the very least, continue to provide players with the accurate, timely, objective information likely to be material to their decisions to play and for how long.

It is also generally acceptable to interfere with individual decisions when an individual is not truly an autonomous decisionmaker, *i.e.*, if he is coerced, unduly influenced, or incapacitated in some way.[35] In some sense, this too is not true interference with individual liberty as there is some other feature inhibiting liberty itself. Below, we acknowledge the potential pressures that players may face when deciding whether to proceed in the NFL, and argue for substantial efforts to protect and support their autonomy. However, we do not maintain that these pressures ultimately render players' decisions coerced, "quasi-coerced,"[36] or impaired to such an extent that the decisions themselves ought to be ignored. Moreover, while it is certainly true that a player may become cognitively impaired, for example, after experiencing a concussion, and in that limited instance his decisions are not appropriately deemed autonomous, this is the exceptional player state—it does not justify a general disregard for player decision making, or withholding the option to play writ large.

Next, we come to the classic justification for true interference with individual liberty, which is that one individual's exercise of his liberty is interfering with the ability of others to do the same.[37] Thus, in paradigmatic public health examples, we might require vaccination to protect others from becoming sick, or even mandate the use of seatbelts or helmets to spare society from the costs associated with automobile and motorcycle accidents that extend beyond those borne by individuals directly.[38] In the context of preventing an adult from accepting the risks of playing professional football, then, we would need to ask what the externalities of accepting such risks might be—who might the cost of such risks accrue to other than the player himself? And then we must ask whether those externalities are greater than those that occur in the context of other activities that we allow competent adults to pursue.

First, society in general may have to pick up the tab for player healthcare to the extent that the benefits offered by the NFL and NFLPA are insufficient (*see* Appendix C: Summary of Collectively Bargained Health-Related Programs and Benefits). However, we do not typically require individual decisions to accept risks or incur costs to be fully self-contained; if we did, we would not allow people to smoke, drink alcohol, eat poorly, or engage in a variety of other behaviors that a free society generally permits. Beyond monetary costs, we might also consider the harm experienced by a player's family and friends if he is seriously harmed by a professional football career. In that context, however, note that we do not prevent husbands or fathers from skydiving, BASE jumping, or any number of other activities that may be seriously risky over the short or long term, the consequences of which may be borne by others beyond the individual directly taking the risks.[39] Thus, it is difficult to see here what justification there might be for treating professional football differently, especially given the substantial benefits, financial and otherwise.

Finally, there is the possibility that the existence of professional football paves the way for the existence of the game at lower levels for college and youth athletes, such that we should be wary of allowing professionals to take risks that may also then be expected or experienced by amateurs, including children. Limiting the freedom of adult professionals, however, would be an indirect and likely unnecessary approach to ensure the protection of others; instead, the risks of youth and college football could be directly regulated and restricted, if those were the externalities at issue.

In sum, it seems that costs of various kinds that may occur as a result of letting competent adults play professional football are not so much more substantial than those that may occur in other socially permissible activities to justify a prohibition on the practice. Thus, the externalities rationale appears to us to be an inadequate reason to suggest that professional football players should not be permitted to accept even substantial risks to themselves, should that be what the scientific evidence ultimately shows. Of course, we recognize that others may prefer a more paternalistic approach, one that would actually protect players from even their own autonomous decisions that may cause them harm or regret. In that case, however, it would be necessary to identify some feature of professional football that renders players in *greater* need of protection than other competent adults. We have not been able to identify any such feature, or at least no such feature that would call for an absolute bar on the opportunity to play in the NFL as it currently exists.[f]

Ultimately, we as a society have determined that it is preferable to allow people to make decisions that may cause them harm than to live in a society in which others are allowed to decide what is best for us,[40] and we believe this concept holds with regard to professional football players as well. This certainly does not mean, however, that we advocate a principle of "every man for himself." To the contrary, we noted above that efforts to educate and support player autonomy are both justified and essential. Indeed, as will be discussed in this Report, the NFL and NFLPA have made important progress in these areas, but even more is needed.

> We have not endeavored in this Report to evaluate football as a sport or to radically change its basic nature.

Accordingly, we note that it is surely not the case that the NFL can satisfy its obligations by simple acknowledgment or disclosure of risks to players, any more than a company that offers bungee jumping services can simply disclaim the risk of death — it must also take steps to provide safe bungee cords, jump training, environments, and the like. Indeed, occupational safety and health laws in the United States preclude individuals from simply consenting to any workplace risk they may be willing to accept.[41] Instead, employers are required to take various steps to protect against such workplace risks, as we discuss extensively in our forthcoming paper, *The NFL as a Workplace: The Prospect of Applying Occupational Health and Safety Laws to Protect NFL Workers*. Precisely which steps are required depends on feasibility and the nature of the industry in question, but it is clear from both legal and ethical perspectives that respect for individual autonomy in the face of even substantial risks must be paired with reasonable efforts to abate risk exposure. Again, the NFL has made changes on these issues, including providing "among other things, training on proper tackling (including youth football initiatives), helmets, and protective gear," as well as implementing "rule changes for the purpose of protecting the players."[42]

---

f   The strongest such argument would stem from the lack of relevant information regarding the risks and benefits of playing. Throughout this Report we urge the continued production of that kind of information, including through the funding of medical research on playing football. We harken back to the need for such information in our discussion of the ethical principle of Empowered Autonomy below.

Those efforts may occur through a variety of channels, but here we restrict ourselves to off-the-field interventions, rather than addressing on-the-field rules of play. As lawyers and ethicists, we believe it is beyond our legitimate expertise to recommend such specific changes. This is not to deny, of course, that the rules of play can have an important impact on player health; indeed, rule changes have historically been implemented to increase the safety of the game, and that trend continues today.[g] However, the effects of these changes are not always clear at the outset: some injury-reducing rule changes may inadvertently induce other types of risk-taking behavior, or reduce certain injuries while exacerbating others.

> The costs of letting competent adults play professional football are not so much more substantial than those that may occur in other socially permissible activities to justify a prohibition.

As in any contact sport, a certain number of injuries in football are unavoidable. To produce a truly "safe" (*i.e.*, injury-free) game would require radical reconfiguration from the current status quo, and again, we suggest that this is beyond what is ethically required for a voluntary endeavor between consenting adults (even as we recognize that those consenting adults may be faced with competing priorities between their health and other goals, and may also be constrained by a variety of background conditions addressed below). Which on-the-field changes would be desirable depends on a multifactorial analysis of the benefits and drawbacks of the current version of the game (in regards to health and otherwise), the benefits and drawbacks of moving to a radically different game, and a method of weighing those benefits and drawbacks against the consequences of injuries to players and players' own desires and goals as they define them. In this regard, we note that The Football Players Health Study is a strong example of the participatory research model: the study is funded by NFL contributions to research as well as the players themselves (through CBA funds that can otherwise be allocated to player salaries)[43] and by the NFLPA specifically, which is tasked with representing

player interests, and our study is guided by more than 30 Player Advisors. One message that we have heard loud and clear from the players is that while they hope the study will make important strides toward protecting and promoting player health, they have implored us not to make recommendations that could threaten the continued existence of the game. Thus, while we welcome recommendations for rule changes to improve player safety made by appropriate experts, evaluated in light of what players themselves want, we are not in a position to make these determinations as a definitive matter. Ultimately, we conclude that we are likely to be far more effective in protecting and promoting player health via off-the-field intervention than by suggesting that the game itself fundamentally change.

Before moving on, it is important to note that we have addressed here only the question of whether it is necessary or justifiable to eliminate the very opportunity for competent adults to play professional football, with all its attendant physical risks. As to that question, we believe the answer is "no." A distinct question exists as to whether it is ethical to watch or support professional football in various capacities as a non-player; a question we do not take on in this Report beyond addressing the roles of various stakeholders to support player health within existing parameters of the game.

* * *

With this critical background in mind, the remainder of this chapter further introduces the Report by describing its audience, articulating the process we used to develop our ultimate recommendations, and clarifying important points about scope and how the recommendations might be considered against the backdrop of the NFL's and NFLPA's historical approaches to player health. In the chapter that follows, we articulate a set of guiding ethical principles, before moving on to analysis of the wide range of stakeholders responsible for player health.

(C) **Audience**

This Report has several key audiences. First, there are the major change agents: current players; club owners; the NFL; the NFLPA; club medical staff; and, various player advisors. If change is to occur, these are the key individuals and entities that will need to effectuate it. However, we live in an era where discussions about protecting and promoting player health extend far beyond these change agents. Fans, the media, the NFL's business partners, and others all have a stake in, and more importantly, some power to shape,

g   *See* Appendix I: History of Health-Related NFL Playing Rules Changes.

how the policies and practices of the NFL might evolve to best protect and promote player health.

Writing for such divergent audiences is a significant challenge. Ultimately, we decided to err in favor of providing a more comprehensive analysis, with all the complexity and length that entails. Although the entire context of the Report is important, the chapters are intended to be read relatively independently, except where there is significant overlap between material. Knowing that some readers will only be interested in reading selected chapters, we made the editorial decision to repeat important text in more than one chapter in order to enable chapters to better stand alone. As further assistance to readers, we have created brief summaries for each of the chapters, which also include our recommendations for moving forward.

It is also important to clarify the nature of our Report, as different audiences may be more accustomed to different research designs and formats depending on their field of practice or academic discipline. Unlike other components of The Football Players Health Study, this Report is not designed or intended to be an empirical analysis, although like much legal and ethical scholarship it relies on quantitative and qualitative data where available. The Report analyzes existing literature, case law, statutes, codes of ethics, policies and practices where available, supplemented with additional information from sources with direct knowledge where possible.

(D) Goals and Process

This Report has four functions. First, to **identify** the various stakeholders who influence, or could influence, the health of NFL players. Second, to **describe** the existing legal and ethical obligations of these stakeholders in both protecting and promoting player health. Third, to **evaluate** the sufficiency of these existing obligations, including enforcement and current practices. And fourth, to **recommend** changes grounded in that evaluation and ethical principles for each of the identified stakeholders.

It is worth describing the Report's functions in greater depth.

1) IDENTIFICATION: UNDERSTANDING THE MICROENVIRONMENT AFFECTING PLAYER HEALTH

Over several months, we conducted a comprehensive review of the sports law and ethics literature, and had in-depth conversations with a number of former players and representatives of the many stakeholders we identified as crucial to our analysis. This allowed us to supplement our existing expertise and understanding to generate a list of 20 stakeholders to focus on. The stakeholders are: players; club doctors; athletic trainers; second opinion doctors; neutral doctors; personal doctors; the NFL; NFLPA; NFL clubs; coaches; club employees;

Figure Introduction-A: The Report's Goals and Process

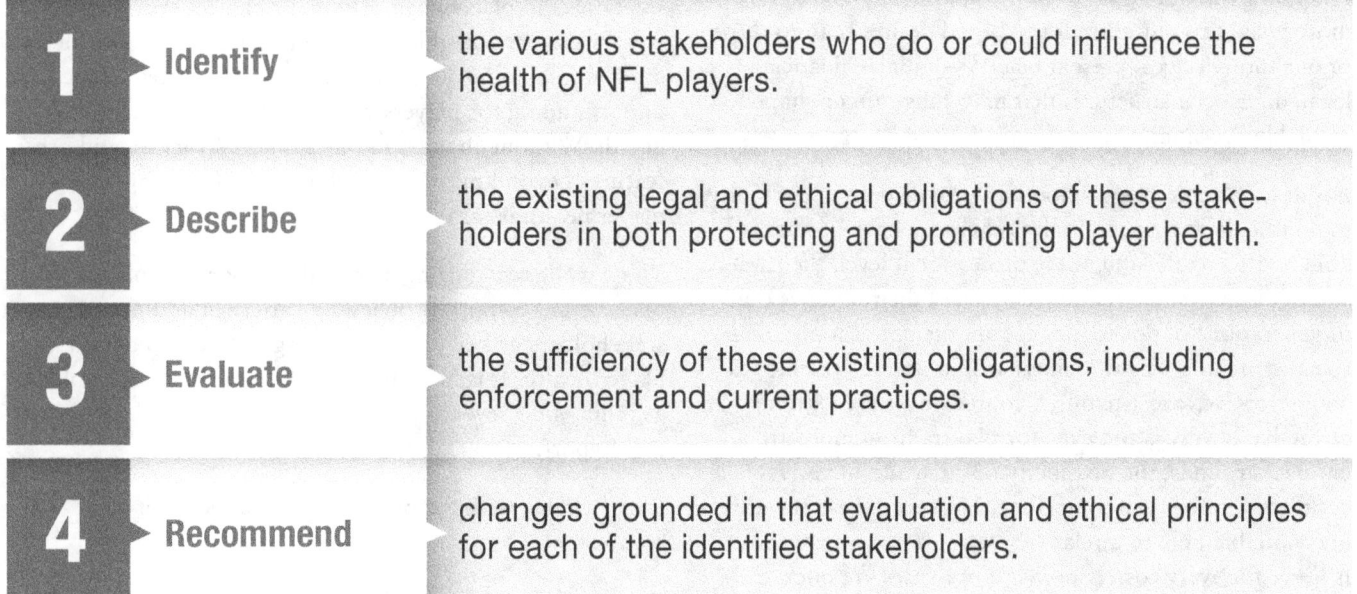

1	Identify	the various stakeholders who do or could influence the health of NFL players.
2	Describe	the existing legal and ethical obligations of these stakeholders in both protecting and promoting player health.
3	Evaluate	the sufficiency of these existing obligations, including enforcement and current practices.
4	Recommend	changes grounded in that evaluation and ethical principles for each of the identified stakeholders.

equipment managers; contract advisors; financial advisors; family members; officials; equipment manufacturers; the media; fans; and, NFL business partners. Each stakeholder is discussed in its own chapter, except the NFL and NFLPA, which are discussed together in light of their interdependence.

This comprehensive list of stakeholders is essential because one cannot understand, let alone improve, health outcomes for a population without understanding the larger context that created those health outcomes. What is instead needed is, in the words of the Institute of Medicine (now known as the National Academy of Medicine),[h] "a model of health that emphasizes the linkages and relationships among multiple factors (or determinants) affecting health."[44] When building such a model, it is essential to look at individual, interpersonal, institutional, and community domains to truly understand the terrain.

Players are, of course, the center of the universe for the purposes of this Report. After all, it is their health with which we are concerned, and it is they who make many of the key decisions that can protect and promote their health, or fail to do so. But it is essential to recognize that although they are competent adults, players make choices against a constrained set of background conditions, including limited information; it is often not as simple as saying "if you're hurt, don't play" or "if you're worried about the risks, find something else to do." These constraints include not only the kinds of limitations we all face as imperfect decision makers—for example, biases that lead us to believe that statistical predictions about scary or unpleasant outcomes will not apply to us (optimism bias), or to give more weight to our current needs and desires than to those of our future selves (present bias)[45]—but also financial, legal, and social structures that may constrain or shape available decisions.

For at least some players, football provided an opportunity to go to college that might not otherwise have been available or affordable, and at the professional level, the game can offer an avenue to pull players and their families out of generations of poverty, dangerous neighborhoods, and social strife in a way that likely would not be possible via an alternative career path. Of course, these are extremely attractive rewards, and even for players from more affluent backgrounds, the possibility of fame and lucrative contracts can be very compelling. However, these rewards are available only to a relatively select few, competition is fierce for every roster spot, and pressures are intense.

A decision not to play through injury or not to accept certain risks could make the difference between getting a contract or a contract extension and being cut. Moreover, although some players have million dollar contracts, many players make substantially less; even if their salaries are in the range of hundreds of thousands of dollars, they only have that earning potential for a relatively short period of time—they are generally not "set for life." In this context, players may feel the need to push themselves as hard as possible for as long as possible (and may also feel pressure from coaches, teammates, fans, and others), and face the consequences later. On top of all this, most players love the game. They love to play, they love the physicality, and they love the team mentality. Regardless of their physical limitations, they often *want* to play and do not want to let their teammates down.

Again, none of this is to suggest that players are not competent moral agents, making voluntary decisions to play football. They certainly are, but the background circumstances that influence their decisions, and that differ for each player, cannot be ignored. Thus, while we recognize that players bear responsibility for their own health, in many cases they simply cannot protect and promote their health entirely on their own, nor may they treat health as their unyielding primary goal. Although the competitive nature of the game and the limited available roster spots are inherent features that will not change, players need a structure that helps them make decisions that will advance their own interests, as they define those interests in the short- and long-term. This requires accurate information, unconflicted practitioners and advisors, social support and safety nets in place when they make choices that turn out poorly, easily accessible opportunities to prepare for life after football, and a culture shift toward greater respect and understanding for players who take steps to protect their health. Without changes in this support structure and other features beyond player control, meaningfully improving player health is impossible.

Thus, while recognizing a critically important role for players, this Report also views a variety of additional stakeholders as key influences, for good or for bad, on player health. It is helpful to understand these stakeholders as falling into several groupings, which mirror the Parts of this Report.

Part 1 begins with the players, the focal point of our analysis.

Part 2 is devoted to the player's medical team, those stakeholders that provide medical diagnosis and treatment, as well as athletic training, focusing directly on player health. Parts of this team (club doctors, athletic trainers) are largely

---

h The National Academy of Medicine is a nonprofit, nongovernmental organization that conducts research and provides advice concerning medical and health issues.

within the club, or at the League level (neutral doctors). Others (the player's personal doctor and second opinion doctors) are available to the player outside the ambit of the club or the League.[i]

The second grouping, contained in Part 3, includes the chief policymakers for all matters related to promoting and protecting players' health: the NFL; the NFLPA; and, the individual clubs. These stakeholders represent the club owners and the players respectively, and their policies are primarily codified in the various CBAs. Because so many of our recommendations are ones that we envision being enacted through the CBA process, we spend considerable time in this Report discussing the NFL's and NFLPA's past efforts concerning player health to ground our recommendations for the future.

While there are a number of critical League-wide policies, when it comes to player health there can also be heterogeneity among the practices of individual clubs. Our third grouping, discussed in Part 4, examines the stakeholders

that, apart from the medical team, influence player health at the club level: club employees; and, equipment managers.

Of course, players often look outside the club or the League for advice related to their health and for social support. The fourth grouping looks at who they turn to: contract advisors; financial advisors; and, family members. Part 5 examines these stakeholders.

More on the periphery is a somewhat miscellaneous set of stakeholders we discuss in Part 6: officials; equipment manufacturers; the media; fans; and, NFL business partners. In keeping with our assessment that their effects on players' health and ethical duties are more attenuated, we spend less time analyzing and making recommendations for this group. Nonetheless, they are an important part of understanding the full range of stakeholder influences on player health.

Finally, Part 7 briefly discusses several groups that are "interested parties" but do not quite rise to the level of a true stakeholder in the microenvironment that has the health of professional players at the center: the National Collegiate Athletic Association (NCAA); youth leagues; governments; worker's compensation attorneys; and, health-related companies. Understanding these parties may be helpful for understanding the broader context in which player health issues arise and are addressed, but we make no recommendations relating to these groups, for reasons discussed in Part 7.

Figure Introduction-B on the next page shows the intersections of these stakeholders in the microenvironment of player health.

---

i   At the beginning of Part 2, we acknowledge that there are other medical professionals who work with NFL players, including but not limited to physical therapists, massage therapists, chiropractors, dentists, nutritionists, and psychologists. While a health care professional from any one of these groups might play an important role in a player's health, it is our understanding that their roles are not so systematic and continuous to require in-depth personalized discussion, *i.e.,* they are typically not as enmeshed within the culture of a given NFL club to generate some of the concerns that are discussed in Part 2. Moreover, the obligations of and recommendations towards these professionals are substantially covered by other chapters in this Report. To the extent any of these healthcare professionals are employed or retained by the Club, Chapter 2: Club Doctors and Chapter 3: Athletic Trainers are of particular relevance. To the extent any of these healthcare professionals are retained and consulted with by players themselves, then Chapter 6: Personal Doctors is relevant.

It is essential to recognize that although they are competent adults, players make choices against a constrained set of background conditions.

Figure Introduction-B: Player Health Microenvironment

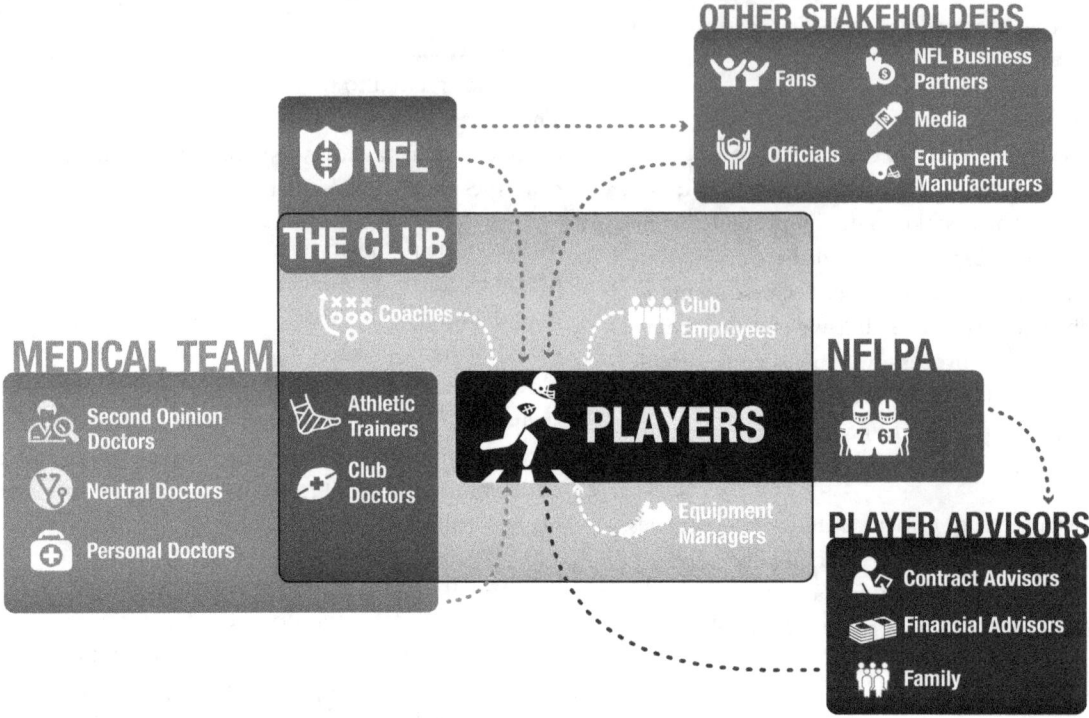

How did we arrive at this list of stakeholders? The key criterion for inclusion was simple: who (for better or worse) does—or should—play a role in NFL player health? The answer to that question came in three parts, as there are individuals, groups, and organizations who *directly impact* player health, for example, as employers or caregivers; those who *reap substantial financial benefits* from players' work; and, those who have some *capacity to influence* player health. Stakeholders may fall under more than one of these headings, but satisfaction of at least one criterion was necessary for inclusion. The result is an extensive mapping of a complex web of parties.

2) DESCRIPTION OF LEGAL AND ETHICAL OBLIGATIONS

Once our stakeholders were identified and appropriately organized in line with the microenvironment discussed above, we undertook a comprehensive analysis of their existing legal obligations and the ethical codes applicable to each (if any) through legal research, review of academic and professional literature, and interviews with key experts. We conducted formal and informal interviews with a number of current and former players, NFL and NFLPA

representatives,[j] sports medicine professionals, contract advisors, financial advisors, player family members, members of professional organizations representing coaches, athletic trainers, officials, and equipment managers, the media, and others working in and around the NFL. In the hope of encouraging full and candid disclosure, we offered these individuals the opportunity to have their comments be used confidentially and we have honored their preferences in this Report. The interviews were not intended to be representative of the different stakeholder populations or to draw scientifically valid inferences and they should not be used for that purpose. Instead, they were meant to be informative of general practices in the NFL.

Additionally, in the Section: Ensuring Independence and Disclosure of Conflicts, we discuss our methodology for obtaining relevant information from both the NFLPA and NFL. During the course of our research we had multiple telephone and email communications with both NFLPA and NFL representatives to gain factual information. As will be indicated where relevant in the Report, sometimes the parties provided the requested information and

---

j   During the course of reviewing this Report for confidential information, the NFLPA requested information obtained from the NFLPA be attributed to the NFLPA generally, rather than specific NFLPA employees. For our purposes, the specific individual that provided the information was irrelevant, so long as the NFLPA provided the information. Thus, we agreed not to identify specific NFLPA employees.

sometimes they did not. These communications were not about the progress, scope, or structure of the Report.

As is typical with sponsored research, we provided periodic updates to the sponsor in several formats: Pursuant to the terms of Harvard-NFLPA agreement, the NFLPA receives an annual report on the progress of The Football Players Health Study as well as one Quad Chart progress report each year. Additionally, on two occasions (August 22, 2014, and January 23, 2015), we presented a summary of the expected scope and content of the Report to The Football Players Health Study Executive Committee, comprised of both Harvard and NFLPA personnel. Those meetings did not alter our approach in constructing this Report, the conclusions reached, or the recommendations made. Indeed, the only comment from the Executive Committee meetings that resulted in a change to the content of the Report was the suggestion at the very beginning of the writing process to include business partners as a stakeholder, which we agreed to be important.

More specific information about our player interviews is also important. To better inform our understanding of players and all of the stakeholders and issues discussed in this Report, we conducted approximately 30-minute interviews with 10 players active during the 2015 season and 3 players who recently left the NFL (the players' last seasons were 2010, 2012, and 2012 respectively).[k] The players interviewed were part of a convenience sample identified through a variety of methods; some were interested in The Football Players Health Study more generally, some we engaged through the Law and Ethics Advisory Panel (LEAP) and Football Players Health Study Player Advisors, and some interviews were facilitated by a former player now working for the NFLPA. The players interviewed had played a mean of 7.5 seasons, with a range of 2 to 15 seasons, and for a mean of between 3 and 4 different clubs (3.4 clubs), with a range of 1 to 10 clubs. In addition, we interviewed players from multiple positions: one quarterback; two fullbacks; one tight end; three offensive linemen; two linebackers; one defensive end; two safeties; and, a special teams player (not a kicker, punter, or long snapper). We aimed for a racially diverse set of players to be interviewed: seven were white and six were African American. Finally, the players also represented a range of skill levels, with both backups and starters, including four players who had been named to at least one Pro Bowl team.

In addition to these more formal interviews, we engaged in informal discussions and interviews with many other current and former players to understand their perspectives. As stated above, these interviews were not intended to be representative of the entire NFL player population or to draw scientifically valid inferences, and should not be read as such, but were instead meant to be generally informative of the issues discussed in this Report.[l] We provide anonymous quotes from these interviews throughout the Report, and urge the reader to keep that caveat in mind throughout.

> The key criterion for inclusion was simple: who (for better or worse) does — or should — play a role in NFL player health?

We were not always able to achieve as much access to interview subjects or documents as would have been ideal. In November 2014, we notified the NFL that we intended to seek interviews with club personnel, including general managers, coaches, doctors, and athletic trainers. The NFL subsequently advised us that it was "unable to consent to the interviews" on the grounds that the "information sought could directly impact several lawsuits currently pending against the league." Without the consent of the NFL (the joint association for NFL clubs, i.e., the employers of these individuals), we did not believe that the interviews would be successful and thus did not pursue them at that time; instead, we provided those stakeholders the opportunity to review a draft of the Report. We again requested to interview club personnel in July 2016 but the NFL did not respond to that request. The NFL was otherwise cooperative; it reviewed our Report and facilitated its review by club doctors and athletic trainers. The NFL also provided information relevant to this Report, including but not limited to copies of the NFL's Medical Sponsorship Policy (discussed in Chapter 2: Club Doctors) and other information about the relationships between clubs and doctors.

---

k   The protocol for these interviews was reviewed and approved by a Harvard University Institutional Review Board.

l   We have also undertaken a "Listening Tour" of former players, current players, and their family members — a qualitative study design — to better understand their perspectives and the issues affecting them, but the results of that research are not yet available.

In April 2016, we engaged the NFL Physicians Society (NFLPS), the professional organization for club doctors, about reviewing relevant portions of a draft of the Report and related work. The NFLPS at that time questioned how many club doctors we had interviewed in developing the Report, apparently unaware of the NFL's prior response to our planned interviews. We were surprised to find that the NFL had not previously discussed the matter with the NFLPS and immediately invited the NFLPS to have individual club doctors interviewed, an offer the NFLPS ultimately declined. Instead, it chose to proceed with reviewing our work and providing feedback in that manner.

The absence of individual interview data from club personnel is an important limitation to our work. The result is that we instead rely largely on the perspectives of players concerning these individuals. Nevertheless, we believe this gap is mitigated by our extensive research and the NFL's and club doctors' review of this Report.

3) EVALUATION OF LEGAL AND ETHICAL OBLIGATIONS

Once we had a better sense of the existing obligations, or lack thereof, and how those obligations were or were not complied with or enforced, we were able to begin normative analysis, evaluating the current successes as well as gaps and opportunities for each stakeholder in protecting and promoting player health.

4) RECOMMENDATIONS

Finally, we applied a series of legal and ethical principles, discussed in the next chapter, to the current state of affairs for each stakeholder in order to arrive at recommendations for positive change where needed. For every recommendation we describe both the *reason* for the change and, where applicable, potential *mechanisms* by which it may be implemented. However, we avoided being overly specific or prescriptive when multiple options for implementation may exist, and where we lacked sufficient information to determine which mechanism might be best.

While we consider and discuss all changes that could improve player health, we purposefully chose to focus on *actionable recommendations* that could be realistically achieved between the publication of this Report and execution of the next CBA (discussed in detail below).[m] This pragmatic approach does not mean that we are giving stakeholders a pass to simply accept the many current barriers to change that may exist, but it does recognize that

change may be difficult in this complex web of relationships and in a culture that has developed over the course of many decades and is deeply entrenched. Furthermore, certain changes might require further information, research, or discussion than we were able to achieve in this Report. When we concluded that was the case, we so indicated by recommending only that a change be "considered" or that additional information be sought. Our recommendations may not be easy to achieve, but we have taken into account various realities.

Finally, it is important to recognize that we do not view our recommendations as the exclusive changes that the various stakeholders should consider. We do, however, view these as minimum next steps forward—a floor, but not a ceiling.

Each chapter largely follows the goals and process outlined above. The sections of each chapter include: (A) Background; (B) Current Legal Obligations; (C) Current Ethical Codes; (D) Current Practices; (E) Enforcement of Legal and Ethical Obligations; and, (F) Recommendations.

(E) The Collective Bargaining Agreement (CBA)

As discussed above, it is important that our recommendations be actionable. Moreover, we recognize that the most realistic way in which change will be effectuated is through the CBA. Thus, we provide a primer on the CBA.

Pursuant to the National Labor Relations Act (NLRA), the NFLPA is "the exclusive representative" of current and rookie NFL players "for the purposes of collective bargaining in respect to rates of pay, wages, hours of employment, or other conditions of employment."[46] Also pursuant to the NLRA, NFL clubs, acting collectively as the NFL, are obligated to bargain collectively with the NFLPA concerning the "wages, hours, and other terms and conditions of employment" for NFL players.[47] Since 1968, the NFL and NFLPA have negotiated 10 CBAs. The most recent CBA (executed in 2011) is 301 pages long and governs nearly every aspect of the NFL. Generally speaking, most important changes in NFL policies and practices are the result of the CBA process. Consequently, CBAs are of paramount importance to understanding how the business of the NFL functions and making recommendations for improvement. Appendix B shows the health-related changes in the CBAs over time.

---

m   The 2011 CBA expires in March 2021. 2011 CBA, Art. 69.

Figure Introduction-C: NFLPA Membership and Bargaining Unit

Throughout this Report, we refer to the CBAs by years, such as the 1968 CBA, 1993 CBA, or 2011 CBA. The years reference the dates the CBAs became effective, which is usually, but not always, the year in which the CBA was agreed to, *i.e.*, some CBAs had retroactive application.

Why discuss the past CBAs and the CBA process so heavily in this Report? The CBA represents the key covenant between players (via the NFLPA) and club owners (via the NFL), on all matters pertaining to player health (alongside many other important issues that matter to these parties). The most straightforward way to implement many of the changes we recommend to protect and promote player health will be to include them in the next CBA. That said, however, whenever change is possible outside of the CBA negotiating process, it should not wait—the sooner, the better. Moreover, although the CBA will often be the most appropriate mechanism for implementing our recommendations, we do not want to be understood as suggesting that player health should be treated like just another issue for collective bargaining, subject to usual labor-management dynamics. This is to say that as an ethical matter, players should not be expected to make concessions in other domains in order to achieve gains in the health domain. To the contrary, we believe firmly the opposite: player health should be a joint priority and not be up for negotiation.

(F) A Brief History of the NFL's and NFLPA's Approaches to Player Health

Now that we have explained the significance of the collective bargaining relationship between the NFL and NFLPA, we provide a short historical summary of the parties' approach to player health. In Chapter 7: The NFL and NFLPA, we provide a more detailed discussion (including relevant citations) of the issues summarized here.

The 1960s and 1970s were marked by the League's growth into the modern enterprise that it is today. Under the leadership of Commissioner Pete Rozelle, the NFL achieved stability by merging with its competitor league, the American Football League (AFL), and important new revenue as a result of the broadcasting of NFL games on television, aided by the passage of the federal Sports Broadcasting Act. The increased revenues coincided with an emerging NFLPA, led by its first Executive Director, Ed Garvey. Although progress was made on basic medical issues (such as medical insurance and disability benefits) during this time, the principal items of negotiation were compensation issues and free agency.

The 1980s were characterized by labor strife. The players engaged in unsuccessful strikes during the 1982 and 1987 seasons as part of their efforts to obtain a system of free agency, which by that point existed in all the other major professional sports leagues. While the players did not gain on this issue, the 1982 CBA did make progress on several health initiatives, including required certifications for club doctors and athletic trainers, the players' right to a second medical opinion paid for by their club, and the players' right to choose their own surgeon at their club's expense. In this decade, former NFL player Gene Upshaw took over for Garvey at the NFLPA, and former outside counsel Paul Tagliabue replaced Rozelle as Commissioner. The 1980s ended with a series of ongoing antitrust lawsuits concerning the NFL's compensation rules.

> As an ethical matter, players should not be expected to make concessions in other domains in order to achieve gains in the health domain.

In 1993, the NFL and NFLPA reached a settlement on the outstanding litigation and created a new, comprehensive CBA that set the framework for every CBA since. The players gained the right to unrestricted free agency for the first time in exchange for a hard Salary Cap. Nevertheless, the 1993, 1996, and 1998 CBAs made almost no substantive changes to player health provisions, other than mild increases in the benefit amounts. At the same time, concussions were starting to become an issue of concern to players and were gaining media attention. In 1994, the NFL formed the Mild Traumatic Brain Injury Committee (MTBI Committee) to study concussions, led by New York Jets club doctor Elliot Pellman.

The CBA was extended in 2002 with minimal conflict and again minimal gains on player health provisions. Of note, offseason workout programs were reduced from 16 to 14 weeks and the NFL established a Tuition Assistance Plan. Beginning in 2003, the MTBI Committee published research that became controversial, as discussed in more detail in Chapter 7: The NFL and NFLPA.

A new CBA was reached in 2006 that made some changes concerning player health, including a Health Reimbursement Account, and the "88 Benefit" to compensate retired players suffering from dementia. After completing the 2006 CBA, Roger Goodell replaced Tagliabue as NFL Commissioner.

Concerns about concussions and player health accelerated during the late 2000s. Both the NFL and NFLPA faced criticism on these issues, including at multiple Congressional hearings. At a 2009 hearing, NFLPA Executive Director DeMaurice Smith, who replaced the recently deceased Upshaw, emphasized that the NFLPA considered player health its top priority and would increase its attention to these issues. For his part, Goodell deferred to the scientific debate about the extent to which football caused brain injuries, while he also emphasized progress the NFL had made concerning its concussion protocols and research it was funding. After the hearing, the NFL effectively overhauled the MTBI Committee, renaming it the Head, Neck and Spine Committee and replacing its members with independent experts. Nevertheless, further progress on these issues was complicated by the NFL's decision, in 2008, to opt out of the 2006 CBA after the 2010 season over economic issues.

The 2011 CBA negotiations ultimately resembled a condensed version of what took place between 1987 and 1993. After extensive litigation and public politicking, the NFLPA and NFL reached a new CBA in July 2011. The 2011 CBA substantially amended and supplemented player health and safety provisions. In short, the 2011 CBA created new health-related benefits and programs, increased existing benefit amounts, reduced on-field exposure, improved the number and type of doctors clubs must retain, and set aside funds for further research. Those funds are used to fund The Football Players Health Study at Harvard University and other research initiatives.

(G) Dispute Resolution

With a brief understanding of the CBA and the NFL's and NFLPA's approaches to player health, it is important to understand how players and other stakeholders resolve disputes about the CBA or parties' policies and practices. In this Report we discuss ways in which players have enforced and can enforce stakeholder obligations, *i.e.*, ways in which players can seek to either have the stakeholder punished for failing to abide by the stakeholder's obligations, and/ or for the player to be compensated for that failure. The two principal methods by which players seek to enforce stakeholder obligations are through civil lawsuits or in arbitrations, typically through procedures outlined in the CBA. Arbitrations are a private alternative to litigation in public courthouses. As is discussed in this Report, there are often legal disputes about the forum in which a player is required bring his claim.

Nevertheless, we do not strongly advocate for one dispute resolution system over another. There are benefits and drawbacks to each, as detailed in Appendix K: Players' Options to Enforce Stakeholders' Legal and Ethical Obligations. What is important for our purposes is that players have meaningful mechanisms through which to address their claims. In places where we think players' ability to enforce stakeholder obligations is unclear or inefficient, we have made recommendations designed to improve players' rights.

Finally, it is our hope that player health will become a shared issue of concern, and less of one subject to dispute. For this reason, mediation can also be an effective form of alternative dispute resolution. Mediation involves a trained third party working with both sides to reach a mutually acceptable agreement. Through mediation, players and the various stakeholders discussed herein might be able to reach fair outcomes without resorting to more adversarial proceedings such as lawsuits and arbitrations.

(H) Scope of the Report

As already alluded to, the scope of this project is to generate legal and ethical recommendations that will improve the health of professional football players, current, future, and former. To fully grasp what is to come, it is essential to clarify these parameters.

1) DEFINING HEALTH

First, it is necessary to understand what we mean by "health" and to explain the rationale for our definition, which extends beyond the sort of clinical measurements that might immediately be evoked by the phrase. Indeed, our mantra "The Whole Player, The Whole Life" motivates definition used in this Report. "Health" clearly covers the conventional and uncontroversial reference to freedom from physical and mental illness and impairment. But health is much more than the mere absence of a malady. As a prominent medical dictionary notes, the

> . . . state of health implies much more than freedom from disease, and good health may be defined as the attainment and maintenance of the highest state of mental and bodily vigour [sic] of which any given individual is capable. Environment, including living and working conditions, plays an important part in determining a person's health, as do factors affecting access to health such as finance, ideology, and education.[n]

Other groups take the definition of "health" even further. For example, rather than recognizing environment, living and working conditions, finance, ideology, and education as factors that determine a person's health or access to health, the World Health Organization (WHO) treats them as part of health itself, which it defines as "a state of complete physical, mental and *social well-being* and not merely the absence of disease or infirmity"[48] (emphasis added). Because the WHO definition is so broad as to make nearly any question a health question, we do not directly adopt it here.

However, we do maintain the importance of considering the full range of nonmedical inputs that can influence health, also known as the social determinants of health. These social determinants extend beyond the sorts of things for which one would seek out a doctor's care, and include broadly "the conditions in which people are born, grow, live, work, and age," as affected by the "distribution of money, power, and resources at global, national and local levels."[49] Indeed, the NFL's Player Engagement Department itself includes "physical strength," "emotional strength," "personal strength," and "financial strength" within its concept of "total wellness."[50]

In Chapter 13: Financial Advisors, we discuss several reports and studies with conflicting information about the financial health of NFL players. Nevertheless, it is clear that there are serious concerns about former players' financial challenges. The relationship between physical and financial health goes in both directions. Without adequate savings and benefits during and after NFL play, players may find themselves insufficiently prepared to meet their physical and mental health needs, especially in the event of crisis.[51] On the flip side, crises in physical and mental health are closely tied to bankruptcy, home foreclosure, and other serious financial setbacks.[52] At its worst, these two outcomes can lead to a vicious cycle—poor health outcomes lead to financial losses, which worsen the ability to combat physical and mental health impairments, which in turn further deplete financial resources. Additionally, financial health is also in and of itself an important component of a person's health. Financial difficulties can cause stress that contributes to or exacerbates psychological and physical ailments.

Acknowledging these social determinants of health allows us to recognize that a set of recommendations limited exclusively to medical care, medical relationships, and medical information would not suffice to achieve our goal of maximizing player health. Acknowledging the social determinants of health recognizes that a set of recommendations limited exclusively to medical care, medical relationships,

---

n   Black's Medical Dictionary (42 ed. 2010). *See also* Black's Law Dictionary (9th ed. 2009) (defining "health" as "(1) the state of being sound or whole in body, mind, or soul. (2) Freedom from pain or sickness"); Attorney's Illustrated Medical Dictionary (American Jurisprudence Proof of Facts 3d Series 2002) (defining "health" as "[a] state of physical, mental and social well-being, characterized by optical functioning without disorders of any nature."); Stedman's Medical Dictionary (28th ed. 2006) (defining "health as "(1) The state of the organism when it functions optimally without evidence of disease or abnormality. (2) A state of dynamic balance in which an individual's or a group's capacity to cope with all the circumstances of living is at an optimal level. (3) A state characterized by anatomic, physiologic, and psychological integrity, ability to perform personally valued family, work and community roles; ability to deal with physical, biologic, psychological, and social stress; a feeling of well-being, and freedom from the risk of disease and untimely death.").

and medical information would not suffice to achieve our goal of maximizing player health. We cannot focus solely on avoiding brain injury, protecting joints, and promoting cardiovascular health, for example, but we must also address well-being more generally, which depends on other factors, such as the existence of family and social support, the ability to meet economic needs, and life satisfaction.

> Acknowledging the social determinants of health recognizes that a set of recommendations limited exclusively to medical care, medical relationships, and medical information would not suffice to achieve our goal of maximizing player health.

We define health for purposes of this Report as "a state of overall wellbeing in fundamental aspects of a person's life, including physical, mental, emotional, social, familial, and financial components." While our expansive definition of health might be more applicable to some stakeholders than others, we believe it is important to provide one definition that applies to all stakeholders.[o]

Accordingly, this Report makes recommendations not only about ways to influence players' medical outcomes, but also ways to positively influence the role of social determinants in their health. This translates to recommendations about financial management, retirement planning, the contract advisor and financial advisor industries, education and training for careers after the NFL, and others—ultimately factors that can become significant stressors if not handled appropriately, with serious consequences for physical, social, and financial health in the short and long term.[53]

Although reference to "health and well-being" is more descriptive of the breadth we have in mind, going forward, we will simply refer to "health" as shorthand to refer to both medical issues (physical and psychological) and social determinants of health.

A second clarification about our understanding of health is also worth making explicit. This is to draw a distinction, as has become common in public health, bioethics, human rights, and political philosophy, between "capabilities" and "functionings." Capabilities are central, essential entitlements needed to live a life that is a truly good life for a human being; they are what is needed to allow for human flourishing.[54] On one particularly influential list from the philosopher Martha Nussbaum these include, among other things, living a normal life span, bodily health, bodily integrity, being able to use the senses, the imagination, and thought, and experiencing normal human emotions.[55] But these capabilities are really possibilities, not mandates. They refer to the capability to do X, rather than a mandate that a person do X (a functioning). To define what makes a life good in terms of functioning instead of capability would threaten to push "citizens into functioning in a single determinate manner, [and] the liberal pluralist would rightly judge that we were precluding many choices that citizens may make in accordance with their own conceptions of the good."[56]

For this reason, whenever we discuss promoting player health in this Report we are discussing promoting players' *capabilities* related to health. As we recognize and discuss in greater depth below in our principle of "empowered autonomy," whether and how players decide to exercise those capabilities for health is something that is left up to them. We will have satisfied our duties to players if we can support their capabilities for health, whatever they decide to do with those capabilities. That said, however, we recognize, as explained above, that players face a wide variety of constraints and pressures that may influence their ability and willingness to exercise their capabilities for health. As such, we endeavor in this Report to minimize those constraints and pressures to the extent possible.

Finally, it is important to understand the temporal dimension of health we aim to improve. A driving theme for the entire Football Players Health Study is the idea that we are focused on the whole player, over his whole life. When we discuss promoting player health we have in mind the "long game," and the goal is not only to keep players healthy during their playing years or immediately afterwards, but throughout their (hopefully long) lifetimes.

---

o   For example, some might believe our definition of health is too broad to be imposed on employers such as the NFL and NFL clubs. However, as is explained in this Report, the NFL and clubs have voluntarily taken on responsibilities and facilitated many programs that address the components of our broader definition of health, including but not limited to programs concerning mental and financial health. Additionally, we note that employers are increasingly adopting initiatives, such as wellness programs, to advance employee health rather than to simply prevent injuries on the job. *See* Kristin Madison, *Employer Wellness Incentives, the ACA, and the ADA: Reconciling Policy Objectives*, 51 Willamette L. Rev. 407, 411–14 (2015).

2) A FOCUS ON PROFESSIONAL FOOTBALL PLAYERS

In identifying the universe of appropriate stakeholders and making recommendations regarding player health, we have taken as our threshold the moment that a player has exhausted or foregone his remaining college eligibility and has taken steps to pursue an NFL career. From that point on what needs to happen to maximize his health, even after he leaves the NFL? The reason we have selected this frame is not because the health of amateur players—those in college, high school, and youth leagues—is secure or unimportant. Instead, the reason is largely pragmatic: there is only so much any one report can cover, and adding analysis of additional stakeholders such as the NCAA, youth leagues, and parents would confuse an already complicated picture. We recognize that what happens at the professional level can have a trickle-down effect on the culture of football across the board, and also that some amateur players may be taking health risks in hopes of eventually reaching the NFL, even when that may be highly unlikely. Moreover, we acknowledge that the legal and ethical issues that arise regarding individuals who are not competent to make their own decisions (*e.g.,* children) are substantially more difficult. Nonetheless, our goal with this Report is to address the already complicated set of factors influencing the health of NFL players, current, future, and former.

That said, many of our recommendations will be most relevant to current and future players, simply because former players may not continue to be engaged with or affected by many of the stakeholders that we have covered, or may be past the point at which implementation of particular recommendations could help them. For example, no matter what improvements we recommend related to club doctors, these could not affect players who are no longer affiliated with any club.

We nonetheless acknowledge that concerns about the health of former NFL players have been an important contributing motivation for research on NFL player health issues, including The Football Players Health Study. Although we focus on current players, the health benefits available to players after their career are an important component of player health. We have summarized these benefits in Appendix C. In addition, in our forthcoming Report, *Comparing the Health-Related Policies and Practices of the NFL to Other Professional Sports Leagues*, we provide an in-depth analysis of these benefits and compare them to those available in other professional sports leagues. Comparing the benefits raises difficult questions of what players are entitled to and when they are entitled to it. We address these issues in our forthcoming Report.

With this Introduction to our work at hand, we next outline our governing ethical principles before moving on to discussions of the stakeholders comprising the microenvironment of player health.

Endnotes

1 CBA, Art. 12, § 5.

2 Nat'l Football League Players Ass'n, *Request for Proposals Advancing the Frontiers of Research in Professional Football* (2012), § 1(a).

3 Alvaro Pascual-Leone and Lee M. Nadler, *Let's not kill football yet*, Pitt. Post. Gazette, May 10, 2015, http://www.post-gazette.com/opinion/Op -Ed/2015/05/10/Let-s-not-kill-football-yet-Yes-players-get-injured-but -the-scope-of-the-problem-is-far-from-clear/stories/201505100034, *archived at* http://perma.cc/V3DN-Z2F3.

4 *See generally* Mark Fainaru-Wada & Steve Fainaru, League of Denial: The NFL, Concussions and the Battle for Truth (2013).

5 *See* Michelle Saulle M & Brian D. Greenwald, *Chronic Traumatic Encephalopathy: A Review*, 2012 Rehabil. Res. Pract. 1 (2012) (defining CTE as "a progressive neurodegenerative disease that is a long-term consequence of single or repetitive closed head injuries for which there is no treatment and no definitive pre-mortem diagnosis.); Bennet Omalu et al., *Emerging Histophormorphic Phenotypes of Chronic Traumatic Encephalopathy in American Athletes,* 69 Neurosurgery 173 (2011) (defining CTE as "a progressive neurodegenerative syndrome caused by single, episodic or repetitive blunt force impacts to the head and transfer of acceleration–deceleration forces to the brain."); Ann McKee et al., *Chronic Traumatic Encephalopathy in Athletes: Progressive Tauopathy After Repetitive Head Injury,* 68 J. Neuropathology & Experimental Neurology 709 (2009) (describing CTE as "shar[ing] many features of other neurodegenerative disorders").

6 *See* Joseph C. Maroon et al. *Chronic Traumatic Encephalopathy in Contact Sports: A Systematic Review of All Reported Pathological Cases*, PLOS ONE (2015) (summarizing CTE case studies to date); Ann C. McKee et al., *The spectrum of disease in chronic traumatic encepha-lopathy*, 136 Brain 43 (2013); Bennet I. Omalu, *Chronic Traumatic Encephalopathy, Suicides and Parasuicides in Professional American Athletes,* 31 Am. J. Forensic Med. Pathol. 130 (2010); *What is CTE?,* BU CTE Center, http://www.bu.edu/cte/about/what-is-cte/ (last visited Mar. 31, 2016), *archived at* https://perma.cc/W86H-886C (CTE is as-sociated with "athletes (and others) with a history of repetitive brain trauma," and "is associated with memory loss, confusion, impaired judgment, impulse control problems, aggression, depression, and, eventually, progressive dementia.")

7 *See* Maroon, *supra* note 6.

8 *See id.;* Paul McCrory et al., *Consensus statement on concussion in sport: the 4th Int'l Conference on Concussion in Sport held in Zurich, November 2012,* 47 Br. J. Sports Med. 250, 254, 257 (2013).

9 *See* Maroon, *supra* note 6.

10 *See* McCrory, *supra* note 8, at 257.

11 Concussion Research and Treatment, C-SPAN (Mar. 14, 2016), http://www.c-span.org/video/?406450-1/hearing-concussions&start =5062.

12 Mike Florio, *NFL challenged over failure to fund study for CTE test in living patients*, ProFootballTalk (Feb. 4, 2016, 8:10 PM), http://profootballtalk.nbcsports.com/2016/02/04/nfl-challenged-over -failure-to-fund-study-for-cte-test-in-live-patients/, *archived at* https:// perma.cc/R5PU-2AAH.

13 Sean Gregory, *The NFL Still Won't Tackle Brain Trauma at the Super Bowl*, TIME (Feb. 6, 2016), http://time.com/4210564/nfl-super-bowl -brain-trauma-cte/, *archived at* https://perma.cc/5RJW-FV8F.

14 Jason M. Breslow, *New: 87 Deceased NFL Players Test Positive for Brain Disease*, PBS Frontline (Sep. 18, 2015), http://www.pbs.org/wgbh /frontline/article/new-87-deceased-nfl-players-test-positive-for-brain -disease/, *archived at* https://perma.cc/GSJ5-P3DK.

15 Kevin F. Bieniek, et al., *Chronic traumatic encephalopathy pathology in a neurodegenerative disorders brain bank*, 130 Acta Neuropathologica 877 (2015).

16 *See, e.g.,* Ken Belson and Alan Schwarz, *N.F.L. Shifts on Concus-sions, and Game May Never Be the Same*, N.Y. Times, Mar. 15, 2016, http://www.nytimes.com/2016/03/16/sports/nfl-concussions-cte -football-jeff-miller.html, *archived at* https://perma.cc/JXF6-4TW7.

17 *See* Mike Florio, *More owners dispute Jeff Miller's admission of CTE-football link*, ProFootballTalk (Mar. 28, 2016, 10:58 AM), http://profootballtalk.nbcsports.com/2016/03/28/more-owners-dispute -jeff-millers-admission-of-cte-football-link/, *archived at* https://perma .cc/6QQ7-L5SZ.

18 *See id.; Jerry Jones: Need more data before linking CTE, football*, ESPN. com (Mar. 23, 2016), http://espn.go.com/nfl/story/_/id/15047068/jerry -jones-says-not-convinced-link-cte-football, *archived at* https://perma .cc/5V6Q-RS5B.

19 Letter from Jeff Pash to authors (July 15, 2016).

20 *In re Nat'l Football League Players' Concussion Injury Litigation*, 307 F.R.D. 351, 397–401 (E.D. Pa. 2015) ("Beyond identifying the existence of abnormal tau protein in a person's brain, researchers know very little about CTE.").

21 Letter from Jeff Pash to authors (July 15, 2016).

22 Paul McCrory et al., *Consensus statement on concussion in sport: the 4th Int'l Conference on Concussion in Sport held in Zurich, November 2012*, 47 Br. J. Sports Med. 250, 257 (2013).

23 Mike Florio, *NFLPA president "offended" by remarks from some owners regarding brain trauma*, ProFootballTalk (Apr. 6, 2016, 8:43 PM), http://profootballtalk.nbcsports.com/2016/04/06/nflpa-president -offended-by-remarks-from-some-owners-regarding-brain-trauma/, *archived at* https://perma.cc/25JH-VTBK.

24 *Id.*

25 *See* Alan Schwarz, Walt Bogdanich, and Jacqueline Williams, *N.F.L.'s Flawed Concussion Research and Ties to Tobacco Industry*, N.Y. Times, Mar. 26, 2016, http://www.nytimes.com/2016/03/25/sports/football/nfl -concussion-research-tobacco.html, *archived at* https://perma.cc/NM4N -SW4Q.

26 *See* Steve Fainaru and Mark Fainaru-Wada, *NFL backs away from fund-ing BU brain study; NIH to fund it instead*, ESPN.com (Dec. 22, 2015), http://espn.go.com/espn/otl/story/_/id/14417386/nfl-pulls-funding -boston-university-head-trauma-study-concerns-researcher, *archived at* https://perma.cc/2DFY-96D3.

27 *See* Steve Fainaru and Mark Fainaru-Wada, *NFL health officials confronted NIH about researcher selection*, ESPN.com (Jan. 21, 2016), http://espn.go.com/espn/otl/story/_/id/14609331/nfl-says-did-not -intervene-nih-study-selection-nih-official-says-three-league-members -tried-do-so, *archived at* https://perma.cc/84VX-RYUC. *NFL response to New York Times' concussion research story*, NFL.com (Mar. 24, 2016, 4:11 PM), http://www.nfl.com/news/story/0ap3000000647389/article/ nfl-response-to-new-york-times-concussion-research-story, *archived at* https://perma.cc/Z3XE-8FQ6.

28 Benedict Carey, *On C.T.E. and Athletes, Science Remains in Its Infancy*, N.Y. Times, Mar. 27, 2016, http://www.nytimes.com/2016/03/28/health /cte-brain-disease-nfl-football-research.html, *archived at* https://perma .cc/PU75-K9PW.

29 *Id.*

30 *Id.* at 397.

31 *Id.* at 398.

32   *Id.* at 398–99.

33   *Id.*

34   *See, e.g.,* Nicole Gelinas, *Say No to Fight Club, New York*, N.Y. Times, Apr. 6, 2016, http://www.nytimes.com/2016/04/06/opinion /say-no-to-fight-club-new-york.html?emc=edit_th_20160406&nl =todaysheadlines&nlid=58216797, *archived at* https://perma.cc/EX8B -VY4Q ("Since we are still learning about the dangers of football, for example, it is neither prudent nor moral to expose more athletes to an unknown degree of risk.").

35   Norman Daniels, *Chevron v. Echazabal: Protection, Opportunity, and Paternalism*, 93 Am. J. Pub. Health 545, 547 (2003) (acknowledging that individual workers should have less choice about which risks to undertake if they are "quasi-coerced" in the sense of having a reduced range of opportunities in terms of education, job training, and mobility than might be deemed just or fair).

36   *Id.*

37   *See* John Stuart Mill, On Liberty (1859).

38   Ronald Bayer, *The continuing tensions between individual rights and public health*, 8 EMBO Report 1099 (2007); James Colgrove and Ronald Bayer, *Manifold Restraints: Liberty, Public Health, and the Legacy of Jacobson v. Massachusetts*, 95 Am. J. Pub. Health 571 (2005).

39   Marian Moser Jones and Ronald Bayer, *Paternalism and Its Discontents: Motorcycle Helmet Laws, Libertarian Values, and Public Health*, 97 Am. J. Pub. Health 208, 213 (noting that it is possible to find a social cost for any behavior, but that approach would allow limitless interference with individual liberty).

40   *See id.*

41   *See* Daniels, *supra* n. 35; Ronald Bayer, *Workers' Liberty, Work- ers' Welfare: The Supreme Court Speaks on the Rights of Disabled Employees*, 93 Am. J. Pub. Health 541 (2003).

42   NFL Comments and Corrections (June 24, 2016).

43   The players' share of NFL revenues is referred to as the Player Cost Amount. 2011 CBA, Art. 12, § 6(c)(i). The Football Players Health Study is funded from a pool of money known as the Joint Contribution Amount. *See* 2011 CBA, Art. 12, § 5. If the NFL generates new revenue streams, the players are entitled to 50% of the net revenues from those new ventures less 47.5% of the Joint Contribution Amount. 2011 CBA, Art. 12, § 6(c)(ii). Thus, if the NFL generates new revenue streams, the amount that is passed on to the players is reduced by 47.5% of the Joint Contribution Amount, which includes The Football Players Health Study.

44   Kristine Gebbie et al., *Who Will Keep the Public Healthy? Educating Public Health Professionals for the 21st Century*, Inst. of Med. (2003), http://www.nap.edu/openbook.php?isbn=030908542X, *archived at* http://perma.cc/9U4C-5L4W.

45   For more on these issues, *see* Richard H. Thaler and Cass R. Sunstein, Nudge: Improving Decisions About Health, Wealth, and Happiness (2009); Daniel Kahneman, Thinking, Fast and Slow (2013); *see also* Ben Shipgel, *Everyone's Son*, N.Y. Times, Nov. 6, 2015, http://www .nytimes.com/2015/11/08/sports/football/lorenzo-mauldin-new-york -jets-keeps-bouncing-back.html?_r=2, *archived at* https://perma .cc/FQH6-ZQGB (discussing a young NFL player's "optimism almost beyond reason").

46   U.S.C. § 159(a).

47   U.S.C. § 158(d).

48   *Preamble to the Constitution of the World Health Organization as adopted by the International Health Conference, New York, 19 June–22 July 1946*; signed on 22 July 1946 by the representatives of 61 States (Official Records of the World Health Organization, no. 2, p. 100) and entered into force on 7 April 1948, *available at* http://www.who.int/about /definition/en/print.html, *archived at* http://perma.cc/4SQ3-AWHA.

49   *Social Determinants of Health,* World Health Org., http://www.who.int /social_determinants/sdh_definition/en/, *archived at* http://perma.cc/ USS7-8C9J; *see also* Michael Marmot & Richard G. Wilkinson, Social Determinants of Health (2d ed. 2005); For discussions of the relationship between these social determinants and ethics and political philoso- phy, *see, e.g.,* Sridhar Venkatapuram, Health Justice: An Argument from the Capabilities Approach (2011); Norman Daniels, Just Health: Meeting Health Needs Fairly (2007); Madison Powers & Ruth Faden, Social Justice: The Moral Foundations of Public Health and Health Policy (2006).

50   *See NFL Total Wellness*, NFL Player Engagement.com, https://www .nflplayerengagement.com/total-wellness/ (last visited Aug. 7, 2015), *archived at* https://perma.cc/Z368-BBV4.

51   *See* Thomas Richardson et al., *The relationship between personal unsecured debt and mental and physical health: A systematic review and meta-analysis,* Clinical Psychol. Rev. 2013;33(8):1148–62. Many experts have recognized that "financial insecurity can cause people to 'cut corners in ways that may affect their health and well-being,' like spending less on food, clothing, or prescriptions." Nadia N. Sawicki, *Modernizing Informed Consent: Expanding the Boundaries of Materiality* Univ. Ill. L. Rev. (2016), *citing* Kevin R. Riggs and Peter A. Ubel, *Overcom- ing Barriers to Discussing Out-of-Pocket Costs With Patients*, 174 Jama Int. Med. 849 (2014); Peter A. Ubel, Amy P. Abernethy, and S. Yousuf Za- far, *Full Disclosure—Out-of-Pocket Costs as Side Effects,* 369 New Eng. J. Med. 1484 (2013). Indeed, to many, "financial well-being is certainly within the boundaries of most peoples' concept of health." *Id., quoting* Michael S. Wilkes and David L. Schriger, *Caution: The Meter is Running: Informing Patients About Health Care Costs*, 165 Western J. Med. 74, 78 (1996) (noting that "discussions about the cost of care are an important part of the physician-patient relationship").

52   *See, e.g.,* Melissa B. Jacoby, Teresa A. Sullivan, & Elizabeth Warren, *Rethinking the Debates over Health Care Financing: Evidence from the Bankruptcy Courts,* 76 N.Y.U. L. Rev. 375 (2001) (empirical data demonstrating how many American families declare bankruptcy in the aftermath of illness or other healthcare crisis); Christopher Tarver Robertson, Richard Egelhof, & Michael Hoke, *Get Sick, Get Out: The Medical Causes of Home Mortgage Foreclosures*, 18 Health Matrix 65 (2008) (empirically demonstrating and discussing the role that health crises have in home foreclosures).

53   *Id.*

54   Martha C. Nussbaum, Frontiers of Justice 155–216 (2006) (setting out the Capabilities approach); *id.* at 273–315; Martha C. Nussbaum, Women and Human Development: The Capabilities Approach 4–14 (2002) (describing the Capabilities approach similarly); Amartya Sen, Inequality Reexamined 39–53 (1992) (describing the Capabilities approach similarly).

55   Nussbaum, Frontiers of Justice, *supra* note 54, at 76–78.

56   Martha C. Nussbaum, Women and Human Development 87 (2000). *See also, e.g.,* Gregory S. Alexander & Eduardo M. Peñalver, *Properties of Community*, 10 Theoretical Inquiries L. 127, 137 (2009).

GUIDING ETHICAL PRINCIPLES

As explained in the Introduction, the goal of this Report is to determine who is and should be responsible for protecting and promoting the health of NFL players, and why. In some cases, the law will at least partially answer these questions, at least from a descriptive standpoint. But in all cases it is necessary to undertake ethical analysis in order to evaluate the sufficiency of existing legal obligations, make recommendations for change, and determine the proper scope of extralegal responsibilities. It is ethics that will help us explain the conclusions and recommendations that follow.

In this chapter we outline seven foundational ethical principles that we believe ought to govern the complex web of stakeholders related to player health as described in the Introduction. These principles, generated for the unique context of professional football, served to guide the proper scope and direction of the recommendations set forth for each stakeholder in the chapters that follow, and also as a litmus test for inclusion of various recommendations in the Report. We describe these principles and their development below. Then, in each of the subsequent chapters, we consider more specific ethical obligations of each individual stakeholder as to player health, acknowledging, among other things, existing ethical codes and legal obligations.

(A) Existing General Principles

The principles that guide this Report are neither matters of natural law nor derived from pure reason, nor were they entirely driven by case study of the NFL. Instead, we recognized that "[n]either general principles nor paradigm cases adequately guide the formation of justified moral beliefs . . . ."[1] Instead, principles must be designed for specific cases and case analysis must be guided by general principles. Thus, we took both top-down and bottom-up approaches, cognizant of the sometimes fraught relationships of the relevant stakeholders, in order to develop a set of tailored principles applicable to our driving questions about the who, how, and why of protecting and promoting player health.

Stated another way, we began with widely recognized, if not necessarily universally revered, general principles from bioethics, as well as from professional and business ethics and human rights, where applicable—a top-down approach. Here, our question was "which ethical principles

have already been established or suggested that may have relevance to this context?" However, it was particularly important not to simply apply "off the shelf" general ethical principles to the setting of professional football because these principles often are meant to govern a particular kind of relationship—e.g., physician-patient, researcher-subject, business-consumer—and not all the stakeholders we examine fit those molds. Thus, we simultaneously considered unique features of the NFL context to generate more specific and novel principles for this setting—reasoning from the bottom up.

In the end, our approach was to build on ethical analyses that have come before, while recognizing that "[a]ppropriate moral judgments occur . . . through an intimate acquaintance with particular situations and the historical record of similar cases."[2]

1) GENERAL PRINCIPLES OF BIOETHICS

The literature on principles that guide bioethics is vast.[3] Not only are there numerous proposals for principles that ought to be considered, but there are also strong voices against the use of principles altogether.[4] Without providing a comprehensive review of this debate, we began our analysis with the most prominent set of principles in modern bioethics: Respect for Autonomy; Non-Maleficence; Beneficence; and, Justice. These four principles have become the foundation of an approach called "Principlism," which calls for application of these principles and balancing them against one another in order to reach moral conclusions about particular situations.[5]

What do these principles mean? In brief:

- **Respect for Autonomy** means at a minimum respecting "self-rule that is free from both controlling interference by others and limitations that prevent meaningful choice, such as inadequate understanding."[6]

- **Non-Maleficence** refers to the duty to avoid harm. It is "distinct from obligations to help others" and "requires only intentional avoidance of actions that cause harm."[7]

- **Beneficence** is the duty to positively do good, an obligation "to prevent . . . [and] remove evil or harm" and promote the welfare of the relevant party.[8]

- Finally, the principle of **Justice** refers primarily to distributive justice, the "fair, equitable, and appropriate distribution determined by justified norms that structure the terms of social cooperation."[9] This principle may be framed for our context as fairness in distribution of burdens and benefits of a given enterprise.

Other principles have also been suggested as alternatives or additions. Scholars coming from the ethics of care tradition have suggested that a principle of Compassion be added to the mix, as a supplement to Beneficence, and feminist and non-Western scholars have pressed for an approach less focused on individual autonomy, with greater recognition that individuals are situated in a much richer community and context.[10]

These values sometimes conflict, and on the Principlist view, much of the moral decisionmaker's work is to come to some appropriate balance among them. A primary criticism of Principlism, however, is that it offers no substantive guidance on how to reach such balance, leading to a great deal of subjectivity. Framed in such general terms, these principles are helpful starting points, but they cannot suffice to resolve the question driving this Report: what role should various stakeholders hold in protecting and promoting the health of NFL players? Further specification is needed.

That said, one final principle that has more recently emerged in the bioethics literature, and indeed offers some method of achieving balance among other potentially competing principles, is the principle of **Community Engagement.** Community Engagement entails collaborative inclusion in the decision-making process of those affected by particular systems and decisions, rather than relying on purely expert or hierarchical decision making.[11] This idea is related to Democratic Deliberation, or the process of actively engaging with relevant stakeholders for debate and decision making in a way that "looks for common ground wherever possible" and strives for "mutually accepted reasons to justify" policy proposals.[12]

As described in the introductory sections of this Report and in Appendix N, we endeavored to engage in a robust process for working with all available stakeholders to make sure their perspectives were appropriately accounted for in this Report and its recommendations. In addition to being ethically imperative to give weight to stakeholders' own perspectives, this approach supported the development of a set of recommendations that are well-informed, practical, and realistic. Thus, we have adopted the principle of Community Engagement, specified as "Collaboration and Engagement," in our set of guiding principles for the NFL ecosystem, as described in further detail below.

2) PROFESSIONAL ETHICS

Moving beyond broad bioethical principles, many of the stakeholders considered in this Report are members of professional groups—doctors, athletic trainers, attorneys, financial professionals, and the like—with their own systems of education, requirements for licensure or certification, special knowledge and skills, legal and ethical duties, codes of ethics, and systems of self-regulation and discipline.[13] Consequently, it was also important for us to consider the specific principles already in place to guide their behavior. Professionals have heightened ethical obligations to those they serve in part for tautological reasons: one of the things that has historically defined professions as such is the fact that they seek to help others and have goals beyond mere profit. Professionals are often granted special privileges, special access to information, and special trust, and as a result, have special duties of competence, trust, and beneficence, among others.

> Professionals are often granted special privileges, special access to information, and special trust, and as a result, have special duties of competence, trust, and beneficence, among others.

The specific principles of professional ethics applicable to each professional stakeholder are discussed in greater detail in the chapters that follow. However, several principles emerge as themes across the board (and indeed are repeatedly emphasized in sports medicine ethics): managing conflicts of interests (dual loyalty); transparency; maintaining confidentiality; and, balancing autonomy with justified paternalism.[14] In short, this means three things:

- minimizing conflicts of interest to the extent possible, and when they cannot be avoided, making sure that all those potentially affected are aware of the interests at stake;

- using confidential information only for the purpose for which it was disclosed, and being forthcoming about all of the ways in which disclosed information may be shared or protected; and,

- providing individuals with the information they need to make decisions for themselves, but in rare instances, stepping in to avoid complicity with serious and irreversible harm that would result from biased or misinformed decisions.

Each of these concepts is incorporated in our set of guiding principles below.

3) HUMAN RIGHTS NORMS

Another perspective useful as a starting point for generating governing principles comes from international human rights. In particular, the United Nations Educational, Scientific and Cultural Organization (UNESCO) has carved out a distinctive role for human rights in formulating normative principles of bioethics in its Universal Declaration on Bioethics and Human Rights, finally adopted by UNESCO in 2008.[15]

This Declaration, in its goals, goes far beyond governing the relations of states and instead aims, among other things:

> To guide the actions of individuals, groups, communities, institutions and corporations, public and private . . . to promote respect for human dignity and protect human rights, by ensuring respect for the life of human beings, and fundamental freedoms, consistent with international human rights law . . . to recognize the importance of freedom of scientific research and the benefits derived from scientific and technological developments, while stressing the need for such research and developments to occur within the framework of ethical principles set out in this Declaration and to respect human dignity, human rights and fundamental freedoms; . . . to foster multidisciplinary and pluralistic dialogue about bioethical issues between all stakeholders and within society as a whole; . . . to promote equitable access to medical, scientific and technological developments as well as the greatest possible flow and the rapid sharing of knowledge concerning those developments and the sharing of benefits, with particular attention to the needs of developing countries.[16]

The Declaration lists many principles, but particularly relevant to our context is its emphasis on respecting human dignity, empowering individuals to make their own decisions while also requiring that they bear responsibilities for those decisions, the importance of just and equitable treatment of all participants in a social institution, the recognition of conflicts of interest and the need to be transparent about them, public engagement on issues of bioethics, and the importance of using the best available scientific methods and knowledge.[17]

To be sure, some of these concepts like the notion of "human dignity" have been simultaneously criticized as too vague and championed as fundamental.[18] Moreover, we are not claiming that any of the problems we discuss in this Report or which NFL players face by playing football rise to the level of human rights violations, given the simple fact of consent to play and payment for services, the difficulties players face do not compare to the numerous and ongoing tragedies around the world that human rights law is thought to govern. Nonetheless, these UNESCO principles, like the others discussed above, form a useful foundation for generating more specific principles that can govern our analysis of protecting and promoting player health.

4) PRINCIPLES OF CORPORATE SOCIAL RESPONSIBILITY

Finally, because some of the stakeholders we examine are businesses, it is important to understand their ethical obligations through the lenses of business ethics and corporate social responsibility. The most influential articulation of corporate social responsibility principles is the United Nations Guiding Principles on Business and Human Rights, published in 2011 (Guiding Principles).[19]

We rely on these Guiding Principles in particular in Chapter 19: NFL Business Partners, but some of their spirit is more generally applicable. In particular, the emphasis on engaging in "meaningful consultation with potentially affected groups and other relevant stakeholders,"[20] and the importance of considering the "leverage" available to various stakeholders in calibrating their ethical responsibilities,[21] are two features that shape our approach in this Report more generally.

(B) Generating Specific Ethical Principles to Promote NFL Player Health

As mentioned above, we view the general principles derived from bioethics, professional ethics, human rights discourse, and corporate social responsibility as helpful starting points, but in general, insufficiently nuanced to account for the unique circumstances of the NFL. Thus, through a series of literature reviews, stakeholder interviews, and expert discussions we sought to formulate a more nuanced set of principles that address the actual issues facing NFL players through bottom-up analysis. In particular, some of the existing general principles demand modification or supplementation to go from their current role—*e.g.*, delineating the ethical roles of healthcare and other professionals—to the larger sphere of this project, analyzing the obligations and making actionable recommendations for *all* stakeholders who can or should play a role in protecting and promoting player health.

In undertaking that analysis we arrived at the following seven principles. We note that these principles are rooted in and support the foundational position described in the Introduction to this Report, in which we set forth our view that competent adults ought to be allowed the opportunity to decide to accept the risks of professional football, so long as they have adequate information and efforts are made to appropriately abate excessive risks.

Respect: The NFL is undeniably a business, but it is a business that relies on individuals who are exposed to substantial risks. These are not passive, inanimate widgets, but persons with inherent dignity and interests, social relationships, and long-term goals of their own. One principle, most prominently espoused by philosopher Immanuel Kant, is that we wrong another when we treat his person "merely as a means" rather than as an "end in himself"[22], or in other words, when we use someone only as a tool to achieve some other benefit or goal, rather than as an intrinsically valuable person. This is a paradigmatic way of treating human beings as lacking in the dignity they deserve. Thus, no matter the enjoyment gained by the half of all Americans who count themselves as professional football fans,[23] the revenue generated, or the glory to players themselves, no stakeholder may treat players "merely as a means" or as a commodity for promoting their own goals.

Health Primacy: The fact that football is a violent game and that injuries are relatively common, ranging from the transient to the severe, does not mean that player health is unimportant any more than these facts would suggest that we may permissibly ignore the health risks in other lines of potentially dangerous work. Indeed, part of what the principle of Respect dictates is valuing, protecting, and promoting players' health capability as a basic good, regardless of how many ready, willing, and able players may be queued up, eager to get their shot at professional success despite the risks.

Health is special because it is foundational to all other pursuits, from the ability to meet basic needs to higher order interests, such as pursuing education, leisure, social relationships, and the full enjoyment of life. For this reason, health capability ought to be accorded special moral weight as compared to other possible goods, and we should be particularly wary in cases where goods will accrue to those whose health is not put at risk by the activities in question.[24]

When players are expected or encouraged to sacrifice their health for the game, or even when they are simply not discouraged from doing so, they are potentially treated as mere means to an end. This is particularly problematic given the background conditions described in the Introduction in which the alternatives available to some players are

dramatically less attractive than playing professional football, potentially leading to substantial pressures to accept risks that they might otherwise prefer to avoid. Players have a moral right to have their health at the very least protected, and often promoted. To be clear, however, this does not mean that all risk must be eliminated. Bumps and bruises and even more serious harms that will be of limited duration do not raise the same kinds of red flags as the serious, long-term, irreversible health consequences that are our focus here.

Thus, as a general rule, avoiding serious threats to player health should be given paramount importance in every dealing with every stakeholder. This principle is supported by the overarching principles of Non-maleficence and Beneficence, because it calls on stakeholders to avoid harm and promote health, as well as Justice, because it prevents players from bearing unfair burdens for the benefit of others. Indeed, the NFL too acknowledges this principle. In the NFL's 2015 Health and Safety Report, Commissioner Roger Goodell declared that "[t]here must be no confusion: The health of our players will always take precedence over competitive concerns. That principle informs all of the work discussed in [the Health and Safety] report.[25]

> Roger Goodell declared that "[t]here must be no confusion: The health of our players will always take precedence over competitive concerns."

However, there may be instances when a player, acting with full information and without bias or other impairment, may rationally determine for himself that other values (such as supporting one's teammates, winning, and financial rewards) are more important than his health. As discussed in the Introduction, this is the sort of decision that we regularly allow competent adults to make without interference. Again, this determination may be colored by background conditions faced by some players that in an ideal world would not exist (*e.g.*, poverty, poor alternatives for advancement), but such a context is not unique to professional football.[a] We are extremely hesitant to suggest that

---

a   With regard to obesity, for example, we know that on the one hand, food consumption is in the realm of an individual's "choice," but on the other, it is deeply constrained by poverty, geography (*e.g.*, so-called "food deserts"), and a host of other issues.

opportunities for advancement, including those available to professional football players, be paternalistically withheld from competent adults, recognizing that we are all subject to various pressures, responsibilities, and contexts that might technically impede our unfettered autonomy. Thus, while health matters, and indeed is often at the top of any pyramid of human values, we do not maintain that players must, or even should, always choose health over all other goods. Instead, we recognize that players may be reasonably balancing along many different dimensions as to what makes a life go well, and in some instances this may mean choosing to sacrifice their health, to some extent. In these cases, we can say that Health Primacy must be balanced against the principle of Empowered Autonomy, as described below, and that in some instances Empowered Autonomy will trump.

That said, it is critically important that such tradeoffs between health and other goods ought not be accepted as conditions of entry into the game of football, signals of "toughness," or otherwise praiseworthy, per se. All stakeholders bear an obligation to try to reduce these instances of tradeoff as much as possible, and to reject an institution that demands or expects that players sacrifice their health on a regular basis.

Empowered Autonomy: Serious risks to players' health in football must be minimized as a structural matter. Beyond that, though, players are ultimately the ones most able to make decisions and take steps to protect and promote their health. In order to effectively do so, however, like all individuals they often need support and empowerment. While they need factual information (including that covered by the principle of Transparency, below), such information alone is not enough. They need information to be presented in a way they (and their families, friends, and other trusted advisors) can understand and utilize, and in a way that accounts for their own deeply held values and goals. They need decision-making tools that help them see not only short-term benefits and costs, but also longer term implications. They need to have unfettered access to competent doctors whose conflicts of interest are minimized, contract advisors, financial advisors, and others they trust to have open and frank conversations without fear of the information being shared in a way that would cause them harm. The goal is not merely to allow players to choose for themselves which capabilities and values to prioritize, but also to promote informed and authentic choice.[26]

Such choice also requires that players have access to good options and alternatives—such as unconflicted and qualified medical advisors, educational opportunities and assistance with post-play career transitions, and the like—with the freedom to select among them without undue pressure from others. Of course, this does not mean that players must be guaranteed absolute autonomy, as they will always have competing responsibilities and the compensation available in professional sports will remain more lucrative than the vast majority of alternative career paths. Thus, pressures to play are likely to remain, for some players even more than others, but their autonomous decisions about which risks to take and which to avoid nonetheless can be better supported through information and other structural changes.

In addition, players have to contend with the uncertainty of the risks they are considering. Even when the risks of injury and the health consequences of those injuries are known, well-supported statistical inferences about groups still provide no certainty about what will happen to a given individual. If there is a 50 percent risk of some injury, for example, a player will of course still not know which half of the group he will ultimately land in, injured or uninjured. In addition, some risks will be affected by the player's own circumstances. For example, while the rate of anterior cruciate ligament (ACL) injuries among NFL players may be known, an individual player's position or size might make him more or less susceptible to such an injury. As a final component of uncertainty, it is important to recognize that the contours of many risks are still unknown—many important questions about the health effects of a career in the NFL remain unclear. While the long-term effects of ACL injuries are fairly well known, the long-term effects of concussive and sub-concussive impacts are still being studied. These additional layers of uncertainty make a player's choices even more challenging.

Although perhaps not a perfect resolution of the various background pressures players may face, it is essential to take steps to at least ensure that player choice regarding matters related to their health will be free from misinformation, lack of understanding, bias, and avoidable negative influences. Other stakeholders have a responsibility to help achieve these criteria whenever possible. Where they are lacking, however, as in situations of cognitive impairment or unresolved biases, the principle of Health Primacy reigns supreme. Certain stakeholders must also be attuned to situations in which apparent restriction of autonomy might actually be autonomy enhancing, in the sense of effectuating a player's true desires. For example, given the culture of the game today, a player may prefer to be pulled "involuntarily" from play rather than being seen as not tough enough to play through injury.

Transparency: Again, to avoid treating players as mere means, and to promote Empowered Autonomy, all parties should be transparent about their interests, goals, and potential conflicts *as they relate to player health*. Failure to do so disrespects players and may also result in player health being inappropriately subrogated to other interests. Thus, information relevant to player health must be shared with players immediately and never hidden, altered, or reported in a biased or incomplete fashion. This means revealing medical information about themselves and about risks to players in general, including new information that would be sufficiently credible to be taken seriously by experts, even if not fully validated or "proven." This also means information about relationships that could influence judgment and recommendations related to player health. Promoting transparency will allow players to make better decisions for themselves, and also promote trust in all those who play a role in their health.

Managing Conflicts of Interest: Transparency alone will often be insufficient to protect and promote player health. While it is helpful to explain to players where conflicts of interest exist, as it may allow them to be on guard to better protect their own interests, mere disclosure will not help players when sufficient alternatives are lacking. Instead, all stakeholders should take steps to minimize conflicts of interest, and when they cannot be eliminated, appropriately manage them. Often conflicts of interest are painted as nefarious or the result of bad intentions by bad actors, but they need not be. Many conflicts of interest are structural; the way in which a system is set up may create challenges for even well-intentioned and ethical individuals to do the right thing. When structure is the problem, it is structure that must be changed.[b] Among other things, this will often involve removing problematic incentives, altering conflicted relationships, creating separate and independent sources of advice, and auditing the behavior of those with incentives that diverge from the primacy of player health.

Collaboration and Engagement: As will become evident in the chapters that follow, protecting and promoting the health of professional football players cannot fall to any single party given the interconnected nature of the various stakeholders. Instead, it depends on many parties who should strive to act together whenever possible to advance that primary goal. Further, part of treating players as ends in themselves and not as mere means is to refrain from

making decisions *about* them and instead to make decisions *with* them. Players should be engaged by stakeholders in all matters that influence their health.

Justice: Finally, as a simple matter of fairness, all stakeholders have an obligation to ensure that players are not bearing an inappropriate share of risks and burdens compared to benefits reaped by other stakeholders. Stakeholders should also be aware of the ways in which changing rules, laws, or programs—for example, trading benefits to former players for benefits to current players—may have differential effects on certain subcategories of players, and be attuned to ways in which those disadvantages can be blunted or recompensed. The principle of Justice also demands awareness of implications of actions beyond the NFL itself. The way in which player health is protected and promoted at the top echelons of the sport will influence policies, practices, and culture all the way down the line, influencing the health not only of future NFL players, but also the vastly larger pool of Americans who will play football and never make it to the NFL. Stakeholders should always consider the way their choices will affect this larger population and consider their policies and behaviors in this light.

* * *

In sum, the ethical principles that we advance in this Report reflect well-established principles applied to the unique context of the NFL. They may not prove exhaustive, and we anticipate several others will be generated through critical public reflection on the work herein, but they are the right starting point for further discussion. Ultimately, we can offer one simple meta-principle to guide all the relevant stakeholders, which is a combination of two prominent ethical tools: Kant's categorical imperative (which demands that we treat others the way we wish to be treated) and philosopher John Rawls' veil of ignorance (which helps identify as ethical standards those rules of behavior we would select if we did not know which role we would inhabit in a given relationship). That simple principle is this: *in every scenario, ask what system and rules you would wish to be in place to protect and promote health if you or your son were an NFL player.*

---

b   Harvard Law School professor Lawrence Lessig among others has termed this kind of structural conflict to be a problem of "institutional corruption," which he writes "is manifest when there is a systemic and strategic influence which is legal, or even currently ethical, that undermines the institution's effectiveness by diverting it from its purpose or weakening its ability to achieve its purpose, including, to the extent relevant to its purpose, weakening either the public's trust in that institution or the institution's inherent trustworthiness." Lawrence Lessig, *"Institutional Corruption" Defined*, 41 J. L. Med. & Ethics 553, 553 (2013).

> In every scenario, ask what system and rules you would wish to be in place to protect and promote health if you or your son were an NFL player.

Summary of Ethical Principles to Promote Player Health

1 ▶ **Respect**
The NFL is a business that relies on individuals who are exposed to health risks, but no stakeholder can treat players "merely as a means" or as a commodity solely for promotion of its own goals.

2 ▶ **Health Primacy**
Avoiding serious threats to player health should be given paramount importance in every dealing with every stakeholder, subject only to the player's Empowered Autonomy.

3 ▶ **Empowered Autonomy**
Players are competent adults who should be empowered to assess which health risks they are willing to undertake, provided they have been given trustworthy, understandable information and decision-making tools, and the opportunity to pursue realistic alternatives.

4 ▶ **Transparency**
All parties should be transparent about their interests, goals, and potential conflicts as they relate to player health, and information relevant to player health must be shared with players immediately.

5 ▶ **Managing Conflicts of Interest**
All stakeholders should take steps to minimize conflicts of interest, and when they cannot be eliminated, to appropriately manage them.

6 ▶ **Collaboration & Engagement**
Protecting and promoting the health of professional football players depends on many parties who should strive to act together—and not as adversaries—whenever possible to advance that primary goal.

7 ▶ **Justice**
All stakeholders have an obligation to ensure that players are not bearing an inappropriate share of risks and burdens compared to benefits reaped by other stakeholders.

Endnotes

1. Tom L. Beauchamp & James F. Childress, Principles of Biomedical Ethics 404 (7th ed. 2013).

2. *Id.* at 398 (7th ed. 2013).

3. The term "bioethics" has been defined in many different ways, but generally refers to a field of inquiry broader than medical ethics, which is specifically concerned with the relationships between patients and their healthcare providers, and focuses on the welfare of patients and medical professionalism. Bioethics, in contrast, refers to the normative analysis of ethical problems raised by advances in medicine and biology, and includes dilemmas ranging from the intimate doctor-patient relationship to those facing entire systems that influence health. For further discussion, *see* Daniel Callahan, *Bioethics and Policy—A History*, The Hastings Ctr., http://www.thehastingscenter.org/Publications/BriefingBook/Detail.aspx?id=2412 (last visited Aug. 7, 2015), *archived at* http://perma.cc/4ZPL-Q4V5. More simply, bioethics refers to the application of ethics—the philosophical discipline pertaining to notions of right and wrong—to the fields of medicine and healthcare. *What is Bioethics?*, Ctr. For Practical Bioethics, http://www.practicalbioethics.org/what-is-bioethics (last visited last visited Aug. 7, 2015), *archived at* http://perma.cc/SQ3M-9UAS.

4. For a good summary, *see* Renée C. Fox & Judith P. Swazey, Observing Bioethics 168–173 (2008).

5. For the most current version of this classic text, *see* Tom L. Beauchamp & James F. Childress, Principles of Biomedical Ethics (7th ed. 2013).

6. *Id.* at 101.

7. *Id.* at 150–153.

8. *Id.* at 152.

9. *Id.* at 250.

10. *See, e.g.*, Jan Crosthwaite, *Gender and Bioethics*, *in* A Companion to Bioethics 36 (Helga Kuhse & Peter Singer eds., 2d ed. 2009).

11. Clinical and Translational Sci. Awards Consortium and Cmty. Engagement Key Function Comm. Task Force on the Principles of Cmty. Engagement, Principles of Community Engagement at 7–8 (2d ed. 2011), available at http://www.atsdr.cdc.gov/communityengagement/, *archived at* http://perma.cc/245J-Q5FT.

12. Presidential Comm'n for the Study of Bioethical Issues, New Directions, The Ethics of Synthetic Biology and Emerging Technologies 29 (2010).

13. *See generally* Elizabeth H. Gorman & Rebecca L. Sandefur, *"Golden Age," Quiescence, and Revival: How the Sociology of Professions Became the Study of Knowledge-Based Work*, 38 Work & Occupations 275 (2011).

14. *See, e.g.*, Daniela Testoni, Christoph P. Hornik, P. Brian Smith, Daniel K. Benjamin Jr. & Ross E. McKinney Jr., *Sports Medicine and Ethics*, 13:10 Am. J. Bioethics 4–12 (2013); W.R. Dunn, M. S. George, L. Churchill & K. P. Spindler, *Ethics in Sports Medicine*, 35:5 Am. J. Sports Med. 840–844 (2007); Nancy M.P. King & Richard Robeson, *Athletes Are Guinea Pigs*, 13:10 Am. J. Bioethics (2013); Brad Patridge, *Dazed and Confused: Sports Medicine, Conflicts of Interest, and Concussion Management*, 11 J. Bioethical Inquiry, 65–74 (2014); Ron Courson et al., *Inter-Association Consensus Statement on Best Practices for Sports Medicine Management for Secondary Schools and Colleges*, 49 J. Athletic Training, 128–137 (2014).

15. Universal Declaration on Bioethics and Human Rights, United Nations Educational, Scientific and Cultural Organization, http://portal.unesco.org/en/ev.php-URL_ID=31058&URL_DO=DO_TOPIC&URL_SECTION=201.html, *archived at* http://perma.cc/T4BR-NTRG.

16. *See id.*

17. *Id.*

18. *See, e.g.*, George P. Smith II, *Human Rights and Bioethics: Formulating A Universal Right to Health, Health Care, or Health Protection?*, 38 Vand. J. Transnat'l L. 1295, 1313 (2005); Leslie A. Meltzer, *Book Review*, 359 New Eng. J. Med. 660, 660–61 (2008); Roger Brownsword, *Bioethics Today, Bioethics Tomorrow: Stem Cell Research and the "Dignitarian Alliance"*, 17 Notre Dame J.L. Ethics & Pub. Pol'y 15 (2003); Steven Pinker, *The Stupidity of Dignity: Conservative Bioethics' Latest, Most Dangerous Ploy*, New Republic (2008).

19. United Nations Office of the High Commission, Guiding Principles on Business and Human Rights, A/HRC/17/31 (Jun. 16, 2011) available at http://www.ohchr.org/Documents/Publications/GuidingPrinciplesBusinessHR_EN.pdf?v=1392752313000/_/jcr:system/jcr:versionstorage/12/52/13/125213a0-e4bc-4a15-bb96-9930bb8fb6a1/1.3/jcr:frozennode, archived at https://perma.cc/U36F-S7YR?type=pdf [hereinafter, "Guiding Principles"].

20. *Id.* at 19.

21. *Id.* at 22.

22. Immanuel Kant, Grounding for the Metaphysics of Morals 429 (James W. Ellington trans., Hackett Publ'g Co. 3d ed. 1981) (1785).

23. *Poll: 49 Percent Are Pro Football Fans*, ESPN.com, Jan. 25, 2014, http://espn.go.com/nfl/story/_/id/10350802/poll-indicates-49-percent-americans-pro-football-fans, *archived at* http://perma.cc/AJC9-8FPB.

24. *See* Norman Daniels, Just Health: Meeting Health Needs Fairly 29–78 (2008); Martha C. Nussbaum, Frontiers of Justice: Disability, Nationality, Species Membership 75–76 (2006).

25. Nat'l Football League, 2015 Player Health & Safety Report 5 (2015), http://static.nfl.com/static/content/public/photo/2015/08/05/0ap3000000506671.pdf/, *archived at* https://perma.cc/Y4BN-TUP7?type=pdf.

26. For bioethics and normative ethics literature on the requirement that choice be both informed and authentic, *see, e.g.*, Tom L. Beauchamp, *Paternalism*, in Encyclopedia of Bioethics 1914 (Warren Thomas Reich ed., 1995); Thaddeus Mason Pope, *The Maladaptation of Miranda to Advance Directives: A Critique of the Implementation of the Patient Self-Determination Act*, 9 Health Matrix 139, 189 (1999).

STAKEHOLDERS

Next, we provide an in-depth analysis of each stakeholder in NFL player health. We have organized the stakeholder discussions into parts that are indicative of their relationship to NFL players as well as other stakeholders, as follows:

- Part 1. Players.

- Part 2. The Medical Team: Club Doctors; Athletic Trainers; Second Opinion Doctors; Neutral Doctors; and, Personal Doctors.

- Part 3. The NFL; NFLPA; and, NFL Clubs.

- Part 4. Club Employees: Coaches; Club Employees; and, Equipment Managers.

- Part 5. Player Advisors: Contract Advisors; Financial Advisors; and, Family Members.

- Part 6. Other Stakeholders: Officials; Equipment Manufacturers; The Media; Fans; and, NFL Business Partners.

In addition, Part 7 examines the role of Other Interested Parties: The NCAA; Youth Leagues; Governments; Workers' Compensation Attorneys; and, Health-Related Companies.

Finally, it is important to recognize that while we have tried to make the chapters accessible for standalone reading, certain background or relevant information may be contained in other parts or chapters, specifically Part 1 discussing Players and Chapter 7 discussing the NFL and NFLPA. Thus, we encourage the reader to review other parts of this Report as needed for important context.

Stakeholders in NFL Player Health

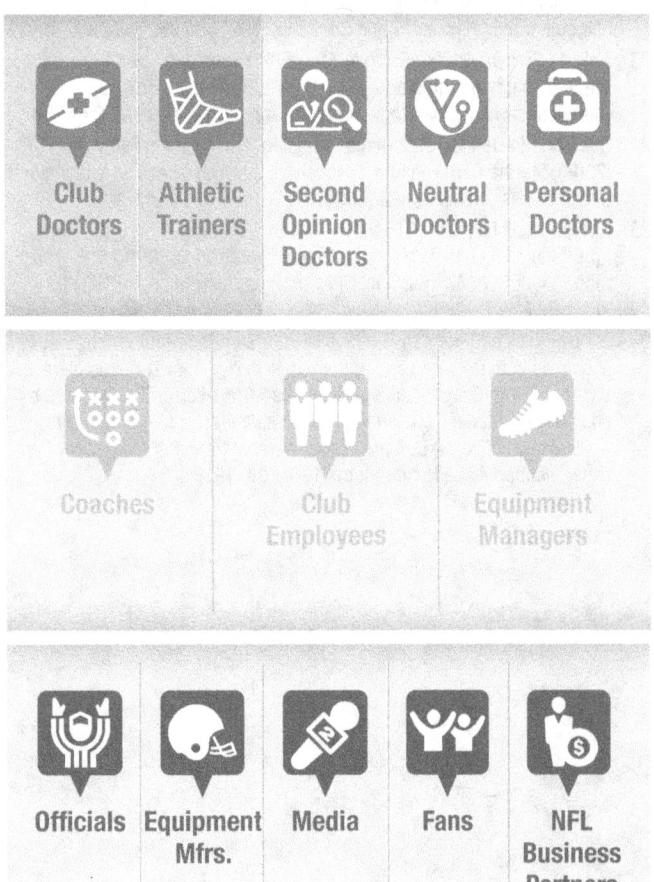

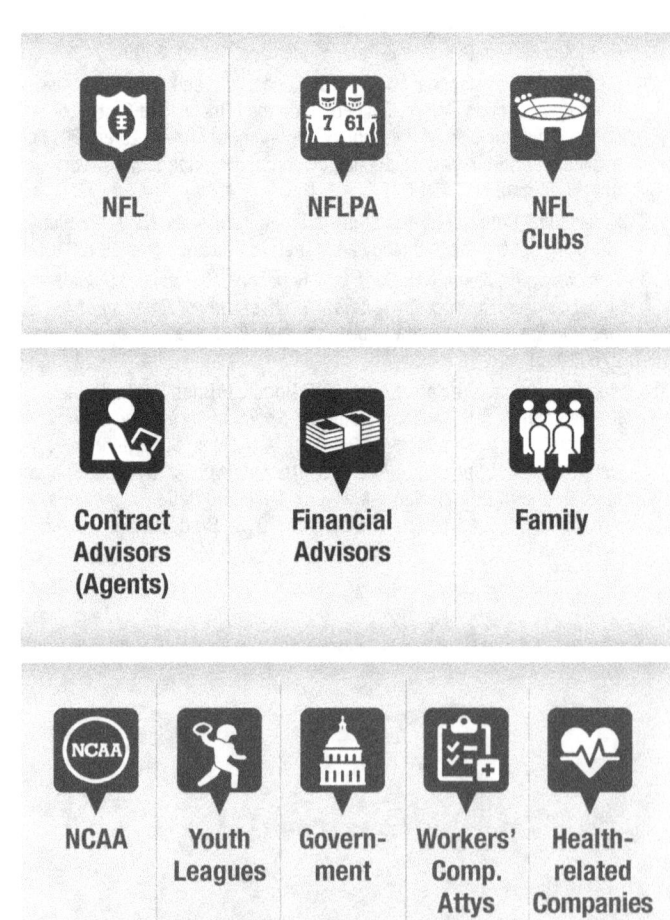

Part 1: **Players**

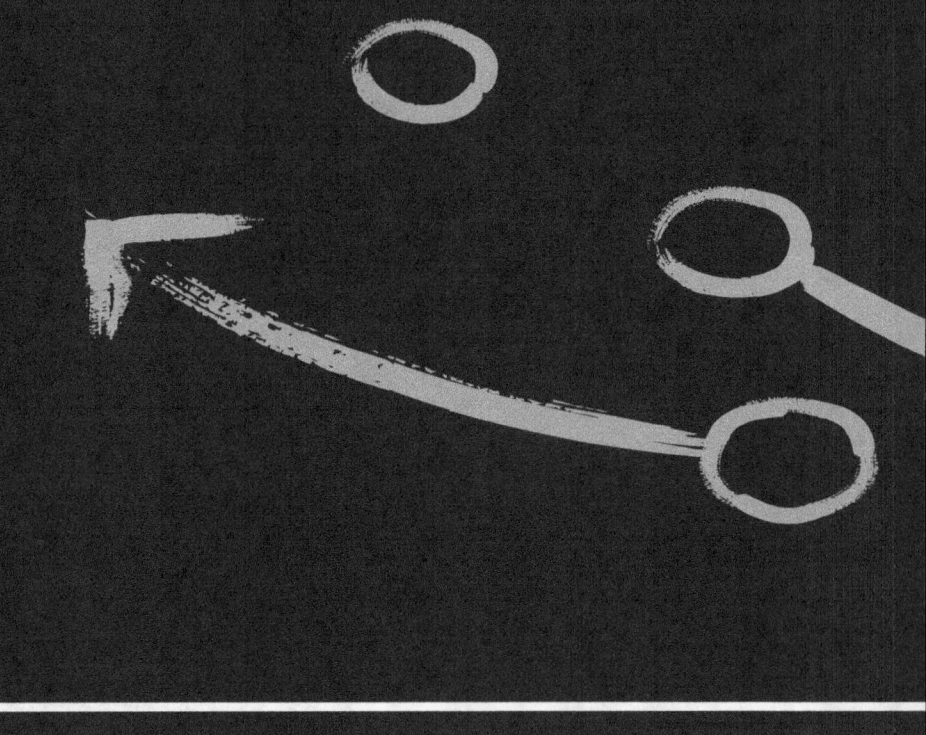

Chapter 1

Players

The heart of this Report is about protecting and promoting player health. No one is more central to that goal than players themselves. Therefore, it is important to understand who they are and what they are doing concerning their own health and the health of their NFL brethren with regard to behaviors with both positive and negative effects. That said, as we emphasized in the Introduction, players are making choices against a constrained set of background conditions, pressures, and influences, and sometimes with limited expertise and information, all of which can affect their capacity to optimally protect their own health, especially given potentially competing interests. Thus, while they are competent adults with a bevy of responsibilities to protect themselves, they cannot do it alone. Players must be treated as partners in advancing their own health by offering them a variety of support systems to do so, recommendations for which will be accompanied by others geared toward other stakeholders.

As discussed in the Description of Legal and Ethical Obligations Section of the Introduction, to better inform our understanding of players and all of the stakeholders and issues discussed in this Report, we conducted approximately 30-minute interviews with 10 players active during the 2015 season and 3 players who recently left the NFL (the players' last seasons were 2010, 2012, and 2012 respectively).[a] The players interviewed were part of a convenience sample identified through a variety of methods—some were interested in The Football Players Health Study more generally, some we engaged through the Law and Ethics Advisory Panel (LEAP) and Football Players Health Study Player Advisors, and some interviews were facilitated by a former player that now works for the National Football League Players Association (NFLPA). The players interviewed had played a mean of 7.5 seasons, with a range of 2 to 15 seasons, and for a mean of between 3 and 4 different clubs (3.4 clubs), with a range of 1 to 10 clubs. In addition, we interviewed players from multiple positions: one quarterback; two fullbacks; one tight end; three offensive linemen; two linebackers; one defensive end; two safeties; and, a special teams player (but not a kicker, punter or long snapper). We aimed for a racially diverse set of players to be interviewed: seven were white and six were African American. Finally, the players also represented a range of skill levels, with both backups and starters, including four players who had been named to at least one Pro Bowl team.

In addition to these more formal interviews, we engaged in informal discussions and interviews with many other current and former players to understand their perspectives. The interviews and discussions were not intended to be representative of the entire NFL player population or to draw scientifically valid inferences, and should not be read as such, but were instead meant to be generally informative of the issues discussed in this Report.[b] We provide anonymous quotes from these interviews throughout the Report, and urge the reader to keep that caveat in mind throughout. We also invited all 13 players that we interviewed to review a draft of this chapter prior to publication. While seven of the players agreed to review a draft, only three provided comments.

(A) Background

Each NFL club's roster has 53 players eligible to play each week, reduced to 46 active players on game days.[1] In addition, clubs are permitted to have a nine man practice squad,[2] injured players may be placed on the Injured Reserve or Physically Unable to Perform (PUP) lists, and suspended players may be placed on the Reserve/Suspended list.[3] In total, NFL clubs are permitted to have rosters of up to 80 players during the season.[4] Indeed, during an NFL season, clubs routinely approach the 80 player limit.[5] According to official NFL and NFLPA playtime figures, in 2015, 2,251 players played in at least one regular season NFL game.[6]

The age range of NFL players is narrow. On any given NFL club, the vast majority of players are in their 20s, while approximately 20 percent are in their 30s.[7] In the NFL's 94-year history, only 56 players have ever played after the age of 40.[8]

NFL players are generally either white or African American. According to the University of Central Florida's *2015 Racial and Gender Report Card*, of the 2,877 players employed by NFL clubs in 2014, 1,957 (68.0 percent) were African American, 813 were white (28.3 percent), 31 were Asian (1.1 percent), 19 were Latino (0.7 percent), 27 were other races (0.9 percent), and 30 were described as "international" (1.0 percent).[9,c] Individuals' relationships with their doctors and the medical community are always filtered through the lens of their cultural and other experiences. The strong African American demographic may be noteworthy in the context of player health, given that there is some evidence to suggest that race may be correlated with distrust of the medical profession and medical establishment, although this may be mediated by a variety of factors, including geography and socioeconomic status.[10]

NFL players come from almost every state in the country.[11] As might be expected and according to an analysis done by *Sporting News*, the states that have produced the most players are among the largest and with the highest populations: (1) California (225 players in 2013); (2) Florida (186); (3) Texas (184); (4) Georgia (95); (5) Ohio (74);

---

[a]   The protocol for these interviews was reviewed and approved by a Harvard University Institutional Review Board.

[b]   We have also undertaken a "Listening Tour" of former players, current players, and their family members to better understand their perspectives and the issues affecting them, but the results of that research are not yet available.

[c]   The approximate 600 player difference between the NFL/NFLPA playtime figure and that of the University of Central Florida can be explained by the number of players on preseason rosters, which can be as large as 90 players. *See* Marc Sessler, *NFL Increases Off Season Roster Limit to 90 players*, NFL.com (April 23, 2012, 7:19 PM), http://www.nfl.com/news/story/09000d5d82889dda/article/nfl-increases-offseason-roster-limit-to-90-players, *archived at* http://perma.cc/VM5A-SNL8. The 90-man preseason roster is reduced to 53 during the regular season, not including the Injured Reserve, Physically Unable to Perform and Reserve/Suspended lists. Thus, each preseason, there are hundreds of players who do not make the club and will not play in the regular season.

(6) New Jersey (63); (7): Louisiana (62); (8) Pennsylvania (58); (9) South Carolina (54); and, (10) Virginia (50).[12]

While all players attended college, it is unclear how many are college graduates.[d] Many (if not most) players stop attending college once their senior season is complete, spending the spring preparing for the NFL Draft rather than attending classes. However, many take online classes or return in the offseason to try and complete their degree. A 2009 NFL-funded study of *former* NFL players by the University of Michigan ("Michigan Study") provides some data.[13] The Michigan Study, conducted through telephone interviews of 1,063 former NFL players,[14] found that 56.8 percent of former players between the ages of 30 and 49 obtained their college degree before or during their NFL careers.[15] Another 12.4 percent obtained their degree after their career, for a total of 69.2 percent of former players who obtained a college degree.[16] By comparison, only 30.0 percent of American men between the ages of 30 and 49 have a college degree.[17]

The Michigan Study also found that 76.3 percent of former players between the ages of 30 and 49 were married before or during their NFL careers.[18]

There are two potential limitations to the Michigan Study. First, the Michigan Study population only included players that had vested rights under the NFL's Retirement Plan, meaning the players generally had been on an NFL roster for at least three games in at least three seasons. There is likely a significant but unknown percentage of NFL players that never become vested under the Retirement Plan. Second, responders to the survey were 36.8 percent African American and 61.4 percent white—almost a complete reversal of the NFL's population of current players. While the racial demographics of former players is likely closer to the population of the Michigan Study, *i.e.*, there were more white players than in the current NFL, the Michigan Study did not provide such data on the former player population and did not adjust or account for the racial demographics of the former player population. In a telephone call with Dr. David Weir, the lead author of the Michigan Study, he explained that: (1) due to limited resources, the population of players to be studied and contacted was restricted to the data and contact information available to and provided by the NFL; and, (2) the NFL did not provide racial demographics of former players and thus the study could not adjust for that factor. Weir also believes that the racial demographics of former players is substantially similar

to the racial demographics of the Michigan Study's participants. Finally, Weir explained that, during the internal review process with the NFL, the study was leaked to the media, preventing the study from being amended and submitted to a peer-reviewed publication.

According to official NFL and NFLPA playtime figures, in 2015, 2,251 players played in at least one regular season NFL game.

The NFL and NFLPA disagree on the mean career length of NFL players. The NFLPA has long stated that the mean career is about 3.2 years.[19] The NFL insists players' mean career length is about 6 years.[20] The difference arises from which population of players is being examined. The NFLPA seems to include in their calculation every player who ever signed a contract with an NFL club, regardless of whether they ever make it into the club or play in an NFL regular season game, while also including players who are still active (and whose careers will thus exceed their current length).[21] On the other hand, the NFL's calculation comes from players who made the opening day roster and played between 1993 and 2002, a slightly different era from today's NFL.[22] The website sharpfootballanalysis.com ultimately found that players who were drafted between 2002 and 2007 have a mean NFL career length of 5.0 years.[23,e]

The different career lengths also lead to different estimates of mean career earnings. Based on a mean career length of approximately 3 years, the NFLPA has estimated that the mean career earnings of an NFL player are $4 million after taxes.[24] Using a mean salary of $1.9 million and a mean career length of 3.5 years, others have estimated NFL players earn about $6.7 million in their careers, a figure largely on par with that of the NFLPA's.[25] However, one

---

[d]   A player is not eligible for the NFL Draft "until three NFL regular seasons have begun and ended following either his graduation from high school or graduation of the class with which he entered high school, whichever is earlier." 2011 CBA, Art. 6 § 2(b). Thus, all NFL players attend college of some kind.

[e]   A 2016 *Wall Street Journal* article estimated that the average career of an NFL player between 2008 and 2014 was 2.66 years. Rob Arthur, *The Shrinking Shelf Life of NFL Players*, Wall St. J., Feb. 29, 2016, http://www.wsj.com/articles/the-shrinking-shelf-life-of-nfl-players-1456694959, *archived at* https://perma.cc/F68T-WVAH. However, we have several questions about the methodology used to generate this statistic, including: (1) The analysis does not describe its inclusion criteria, *i.e.*, if the analysis included everyone who ever signed an NFL contract, even if they never played in a regular season game, the estimated average career length would be shorter; (2) It is unclear how players were counted who were still playing at the time of the analysis, but who also played between 2008 and 2014, *i.e.*, if a player began play in 2014 the analysis might have calculated his career length as only 1 season, when he might in fact have played 5 or 10 more seasons. This too would have caused the average estimated career to be shorter than is actually the case.

can clearly see that if one uses a longer mean career length, the mean career earnings can increase by several million dollars. Finally, it is important to point out that the mean in this case does not reflect the median career earnings of NFL players, *i.e.*, the career earnings of your typical NFL player.

Next, it is important to understand the different aspects of player health that we are looking to improve, including both physical and mental health.

1) PLAYERS AND PHYSICAL HEALTH

In 1980, the NFL created the NFL Injury Surveillance System (NFLISS) to document, track, and analyze NFL injuries and provide data for medical research.[26] When an injury occurs, the club's athletic trainer is responsible for opening an NFLISS injury form and recording the medical diagnosis (including location, severity, and mechanism of injury) and details about the circumstances (date, game or practice, field surface) in which it occurred.[27] Prior to 2015, a reportable injury was defined as only those associated with any time lost from practice or games, football-related or not, or specific conditions regardless of time lost, including but not limited to concussions, fractures, dental injuries requiring treatment, health-related illness requiring intravenous fluid administration, and injuries or illness requiring special equipment (*e.g.*, a knee brace). Beginning with the 2015 season, all injuries, regardless of whether or not they result in time lost from practice or games, are included in the NFLISS.[28] The athletic trainer is required to update the injury form with details about all medical treatments and procedures the player receives, including surgery.[29] Since 2011, the NFLISS has been managed by the international biopharmaceutical services firm Quintiles.[30] Quintiles provides injury data and reports to the NFL and NFLPA throughout the year.[31]

The NFLISS provides the best available data concerning player injuries and thus we use it here. Although the NFL's past injury reporting and data analysis have been publicly criticized as incomplete, biased, or otherwise problematic, those criticisms have been made about studies separate from the NFLISS[32] and we are not aware of any criticism of the NFLISS.[f]

The tables below compile NFLISS data on player injuries. We pulled aggregate statistics from various reports containing NFLISS data and performed simple calculations to arrive at mean figures. The NFL also provided the most recent NFLISS data. In considering these data, it is important to know that the NFL's injury reporting systems have undergone substantial change in recent years. An electronic version of the NFLISS was launched as a pilot with five clubs in 2011;[33] the electronic NFLISS expanded to all 32 clubs in 2012;[34] then, in 2013, the NFL launched an electronic medical records ("EMR") system on a pilot basis with eight NFL clubs, which was expanded to all clubs in 2014.[35] The EMR system integrates with the NFLISS and provides the most accurate injury reporting data in NFL history. Consequently, the different reporting structures over time almost certainly contributed to fluctuations in the injury rates identified below. Therefore, it is not possible to be certain whether injury *rates* have increased in recent years, or if, instead, the increases are due to improved injury *reporting*. Similarly, increased attention to player injuries in recent years, concussions in particular, might also lead to higher reported injury totals.[g]

---

f Other studies of NFL injury rates have been conducted using the clubs' publicly released injury reports. *See, e.g.,* David W. Lawrence, Paul Comper, and Michael G. Hutchison, *Influence of Extrinsic Risk Factors on National Football League Injury Rates*, Orthopaedic J. Sports Med. (2016); David W. Lawrence, Paul Comper, and Michael G. Hutchison, *Descriptive Epidemiology of Musculoskeletal Injuries and Concussions in the National Football League, 2012–2014*, Orthopaedic J. Sports Med. (2015). While these studies provide interesting analyses, NFL injury reports are not the best data source, for reasons discussed in Chapter 17: The Media.

g The costs of treating a player's injury are almost always covered by the club, as is discussed in Chapter 2: Club Doctors and Chapter 4: Second Opinion Doctors.

Table 1-A:
Number of Practice, Game and Total Injuries in NFL Preseason (2009–2015)

Year	Number of Practice Injuries	Number of Game Injuries	Total Injuries
2009	551	360	**911**
2010	560	410	**970**
2011	641	399	**1,040**
2012	675	431	**1,106**
2013	688	416	**1,104**
2014	823	503	**1,326**
2015	780	498	**1,278**
Totals	**3,138**	**2,016**	**7,735**

Table 1-B:
Mean Number of Practice, Game and Total Injuries in NFL Preseason (2009–2015)

Mean Number of Practice Injuries	Mean Number of Game Injuries	Mean Number of Total Injuries
623.0	403.2	1026.8

Table 1-C:
Number of Practice, Game and Total Injuries, and Mean Number of Injuries Per Game in NFL Regular Season (2009–2015)[h]

Year	Number of Practice Injuries	Number of Game Injuries	Total Regular Season Injuries	Injuries per Regular Season Game
2009	165	1,372	1,537	5.36
2010	176	1,346	1,522	5.25
2011	295	1,426	1,721	5.57
2012	262	1,380	1,642	5.39
2013	264	1,500	1,764	5.86
2014	401	1,823	2,224	7.12
2015	336	1,730	2,066	6.76
Totals	**1,899**	**10,577**	**12,476**	**N/A**

[h] Each year, there are 256 regular season NFL games. Thus, the injuries per regular season game statistic is derived by dividing the "number of game injuries" by 256.

Table 1-D:
Mean Number of Practice, Game and Total Injuries, and Mean Number of Injuries Per Game in NFL Regular Season (2009–2015)[i]

	Mean Number of Practice Injuries	Mean Number of Game Injuries	Mean Number of Total Regular Season Injuries	Mean Number of Injuries per Regular Season Game
	271.3	1,511.0	1,782.3	5.90

Table 1-E:
Number of Practice, Game and Total Concussions, and Mean Number of Concussions Per Game in NFL Regular Season (2009–2015)

Year	Number of Practice Concussions (Pre- And Regular Season)	Number of Preseason Game Concussions	Number of Regular Season Game Concussions	Total Concussions	Concussions per Regular Season Game
2009	25	40	159	224	.62
2010	45	50	168	263	.66
2011	37	48	167	252	.65
2012	45	43	173	261	.68
2013	43	38	148	229	.58
2014	50	41	115	206	.45
2015	38	52	182	272	.71
Totals	**283**	**312**	**1,112**	**1,707**	**N/A**

Table 1-F:
Mean Number of Practice, Game and Total Concussions, and Mean Number of Concussions Per Game in NFL Regular Season (2009–2015)

Mean Number of Practice Concussions (Pre- And Regular Season)	Mean Number of Preseason Game Concussions	Mean Number of Regular Season Game Concussions	Mean Number of Total Concussions	Mean Number of Concussions per Regular Season Game
40.4	44.6	158.9	243.9	.62

[i] Each year, there are 256 regular season NFL games. Thus, the mean number of injuries per regular season is derived by dividing the "mean number of game injuries" by 256.

Table 1-G:
Number of Regular Season Game Concussions Per Player, and Mean Number of Regular Season Game Concussions Per Player Per Season (2009–2015)[j]

Year	Number of Regular Season Game Concussions	Number of Regular Season Players	Rate of Concussions per Player-Season
2009	159	2,123	0.075
2010	168	2,187	0.077
2011	167	2,144	0.078
2012	173	2,183	0.079
2013	148	2,188	0.067
2014	115	2,202	0.052
2015	182	2,251	0.081
Totals/Rate	**1,112**	**15,278**	**0.073**

In considering the mean number of concussions per player-season, it is important to point out that the number of players who played in a regular season NFL game includes both players who played all 16 games in a season and those who played only 1 game in a season. Thus, while there is a mean of 0.073 concussions per player per regular season, the mean is likely different for different populations, i.e., depending on how many games a player played in that season.

Table 1-H:
Concussion Incidence by Player Position in the Regular Season (2013)

Position	2013
Offensive Line	19
Running Back	15
Tight End	16
Quarterback	6
Wide Receiver	17
Offense Total	**73 (49.3%)**
Defensive Secondary	25
Defensive Line	12
Linebacker	11
Defense Total	**48 (32.4%)**
Special Teams Total	**27 (18.2%)**

[j]   The number of regular season players was obtained from official NFL and NFLPA playtime figures. To be clear, these statistics only include players who played in a regular season game and thus does not include players who only played in the preseason.

Table 1-I:
Mean Number of Injuries Per Play, NFL Regular Season Games (2013)[k]

Total Number of Injuries	Total Number of Plays	Mean Number of Injuries per Play
1,500	43,090	0.035 injuries/play

While the above tables present some information concerning NFL player injuries, it is not complete. The 2015 season-end injury report from Quintiles contains data and information on other player injuries and related issues. However, we were not permitted to include that data and information in the Report. The NFLPA provided us with the 2015 season-end injury report from Quintiles but, pursuant to the terms of The Football Players Health Study—NFLPA agreement, identified the report as confidential and would not permit use of the data in this Report. The NFLPA considered the document confidential in light of alleged "player privacy concerns and regulations governing disclosure of protected health information." The NFL, in denying our request for the 2015 Quintiles report, similarly claimed that the data "is confidential and might impact individual player privacy concerns."[36] We do not agree with such concerns. The data we requested is de-identified aggregate data that does not implicate the personal medical records of any player. Additionally, the Health Insurance Portability and Accountability Act (HIPAA), which the NFLPA seems to be referencing, has no relevance here as neither we nor the NFLPA are covered entities under HIPAA.[37] Moreover, if HIPAA concerns were present in the manner the NFLPA suggests, the NFLPA would have potentially already violated HIPAA by providing us the report, regardless of whether we incorporated the data in our Report. Finally, the above tables incorporate data from the 2013 season-end Quintiles report. The 2013 season-end report was provided by the NFLPA, and it never indicated that we could not use those data in this Report for confidentiality reasons or otherwise. It is regrettable that both the NFL and NFLPA are not providing players with all data and information concerning player health that is in their possession. In Recommendation 7:1-C, we recommend that the NFL, and to the extent possible, the NFLPA, should: (a) continue to improve its robust collection of aggregate injury data; (b) continue to have qualified professionals analyze the injury data; and (c) make the data publicly available for re-analysis.

Moving on, as shown above in Table 1-I, the mean number of injuries per play in 2013 was 0.035, indicating that an injury occurred on 3.5 percent of all plays. Additionally, from the available information regarding the total number of injuries, total number of players per game, games per year, and years of data, we can calculate the overall rate of injury per player-game as 0.064 per player-game.[l] In other words, for every particular game there are 5.90 injuries (0.064 injuries per player-game x 92 players per game). That equates to one injury for every 15.6 players in that game.

We can also determine the mean rate of how often concussions occur in a game. Between 2009 and 2015 there were a total of 1,112 regular season concussions. Using the available information regarding the total number of concussions, total number of players per game, games per year, and years of data, we can calculate the overall rate of concussion per player-game as 0.0067 concussions per player-game.[m]

We can also determine the rate of injuries per player per regular season. During the 2009 to 2015 seasons, there were a total of 15,278 player-seasons played.[n] During this same time period there were a total of 10,577 game injuries. This equates to an overall rate of 0.69 injuries per player-season (10,577/15,278). Some readers, particularly players, may be surprised that this rate is not higher. It is important to remember that this statistic is the mean of *all* players who played in the NFL during these seasons, including players who might have only played in one game. Additionally, the statistic does not include injuries that occurred during preseason practices or games or regular season practices. Finally, these statistics count all injuries the same, regardless of their severity or the amount of time

[l] This statistic is calculated by dividing the total number of regular season game injuries from 2009 to 2015 (10,577) by the total number of game exposures over the same time period (164,864). The 164,864 statistic is calculated by multiplying 7 seasons by 256 regular season games per season by 92 players per game. Clubs are limited to 46 active players during a game, 2011 NFL CBA, Art. 25, § 1, thus, 92 players have the opportunity to play each week.

[m] This statistic is calculated by dividing the total number of regular season game concussions from 2009 to 2015 (1,112) by the total number of game exposures over the same time period (164,864). The 164,864 value is calculated by multiplying 7 seasons by 256 regular season games per season by 92 players per game.

[n] In other words, a mean of 2,182.6 players played in a regular season NFL game each season. The number of player-seasons was obtained from official NFL and NFLPA playtime figures.

[k] The statistic for total number of players was obtained from calculations derived from official NFL and NFLPA playtime statistics.

lost due to the injury. Thus, while helpful, this statistic is an incomplete picture of the injuries suffered by NFL players during the course of a season.

One useful question concerns ascertaining the mean number of games a player plays before suffering an injury. We calculated above that the rate of injuries per regular season game per player was 0.064. Thus, we can calculate that players play a mean of 15.6 games before suffering one injury (1/0.064). We can also calculate the mean number of games a player plays before suffering a concussion. We calculated above that the rate of concussion per regular season game per player was 0.0067. Thus, we can calculate that players play a mean of 149.25 games before suffering one concussion (1/0.0067). With 16 regular season games, players theoretically play a mean of 9.3 seasons before suffering a concussion. For context, although there is a debate about career lengths generally, the mean career length for a drafted player is about 5 years.[38] Nevertheless, it is important to remember that this is a *mean* statistic and thus includes players who play very little in the game or players who play positions less likely to suffer concussions. Players with a lot of game time and players at certain positions are likely to suffer concussions at rates higher than those provided here.

Finally, we can calculate what percentage of player injuries are concussions. Between 2009 and 2015 there were a total of 10,577 regular season injuries (Table 1-C). During this same time period, there were 1,112 regular season concussions (Table 1-E). Thus, concussions represented 10.5 percent of all regular season injuries (1,112/10,577).

Finally, below is some additional information from the NFLISS:

- The most common types of injuries during regular season practices in 2013 were hamstring strains (46), groin adductor strains (10), high ankle sprains (6), and shoulder sprains (6).

- The five most common types of injuries during regular season games in 2013 were concussions (147), hamstring strains (approximately 128[o]), medial collateral ligament (MCL) sprains (approximately 76), high ankle sprains (approximately 58), and groin adductor strains (approximately 47).

- The most common mechanisms of concussions during regular season games in 2013 were contact with other helmets (49.0 percent), contact with the playing surface (16.3 percent), contact with another player's knee (10.2 percent), and contact with another player's shoulder (7.5 percent).

Injured NFL players are placed on different lists depending on the expected duration of the injury and the timing of the injury.

If a player fails the preseason physical, *i.e.*, the club doctor determines the player is not physically ready to play football, and is unable to participate in training camp but is expected to be able to play later in the season, the player can be placed on the PUP List. A player on the PUP List cannot practice or play until after the sixth game of the regular season and does not count toward the club's 53-man Active/Inactive List during that time.[39]

Players who are injured during the preseason or regular season and are unable to return that season are placed on Injured Reserve, which typically precludes them from practicing or playing further that season. Players on Injured Reserve do not count toward the club's 53-man Active/Inactive List. In 2012, the NFL and NFLPA amended the rules to permit clubs to allow one player in any season to return from Injured Reserve after a minimum of six weeks.[40]

Finally, the less severely injured players are only given a different status on the day of the game. NFL clubs have a 53-man Active/Inactive List.[41] This is the universe of players from which clubs have to choose each week. On the day of the game, the number of players that are permitted to play, *i.e.*, the Active List, is reduced to 46 players.[42] Thus, seven players are declared Inactive and cannot play. Generally, at least some of the seven players declared Inactive have been so declared due to injury (the rest would be for skill reasons). A player is Inactive for that particular game, but can be Active for the next game. In this way, the Inactive List serves as a short-term, non-durational injured list.

Players are paid their base salaries while on any of these injury lists; however, younger players often have "split" contracts whereby if they are placed on either the PUP List or Injured Reserve, they are paid a lesser amount, typically about half of their base salary. In addition, injured players might be entitled to additional compensation pursuant to the Injury Protection benefit.[p]

Finally, despite the physical tolls of an NFL career, in a 2014–2015 survey of 763 former players by *Newsday*, 89 percent of respondents said they would still play in the NFL

---

[o] Statistics for injuries other than concussions are only available in bar graph form. Consequently, we estimate the injury statistic based on the graph available.

[p] Where a player is injured in one season, fails the preseason physical the next season because of that injury, and is terminated by the club as a result, the player is entitled to 50 percent of his salary for that season up to a maximum of $1.1 million in the 2015 season. If the player is still physically unable to play two seasons after the injury, he is entitled to 30 percent of his salary up to a maximum for $525,000 in 2015. A player is only entitled to Injury Protection once in his career. *See* 2011 CBA, Art. 45.

if they had the chance to make the decision again.[43] There are, however, limitations to the *Newsday* survey: (1) the survey was sent via email and text message by the NFLPA to more than 7,000 former NFL players, thus eliminating former players who were less technologically savvy and also possibly skewing the sample toward those former players closer to the NFLPA; (2) the response rate for the survey was low (approximately 11 percent); and, (3) the study does not discuss the demographics of those that responded, making it difficult to ascertain whether those who responded are a representative sample of all former players. Nevertheless, we provide the reader with the best existing data.

A waiver executed by players permitting disclosure of their medical information "expressly includes all records and [protected health information] relating to any mental health treatment, therapy, and/or counseling, but expressly excludes psychotherapy notes."

2) PLAYERS AND MENTAL HEALTH

As we have emphasized in the Introduction to this Report, our focus is not just players' physical health, but also their health more generally, and those factors that play a role in determining their health. This, of course, includes their mental health. According to the National Institute of Mental Health, 43.7 million American adults, or 18.6 percent, suffer from some form of mental illness.[44]

One goal of the Population Studies component of The Football Players Health Study at Harvard University is to develop better epidemiologic data specific to football players. But in the meantime, extrapolating from the above data strongly suggests that there are hundreds of current NFL players, and likely thousands of former NFL players, suffering from some form of mental illness.[45] Indeed, the Michigan Study[q] found that 25.6 percent of former

NFL players interviewed had "either been diagnosed with depression or experienced an episode of major depression in their lifetime."[46,r] However, another study (partially funded by the NFLPA) of 1,617 former players found that 14.7 percent experienced depressive symptoms.[47] Finally, a third study concerning depression among former NFL players conducted by the University of North Carolina found that of the 2,434 former players who responded to a questionnaire with complete data, 269 (11.1 percent) reported having been diagnosed previously with clinical depression.[s] Of note, the last two studies mentioned found rates of depression substantially lower than that found by the Michigan Study and also lower than the rate of depression in the general population.[t] Nevertheless, concerns about players and mental health exist. In this vein, star NFL wide receiver Brandon Marshall has been vocal in recent years about his own struggles with mental illness and has strongly advocated for acceptance and understanding in the NFL community.[48]

The issue of mental health is also important in light of the fact that "medical literature and clinical practice has *associated* [emphasis in original] psychological symptoms such as anxiety, depression, liability, irritability and aggression in patients with a history of concussions."[49] Similarly, some research has also found an association between traumatic brain injury and suicide rates.[50] Nevertheless, as the District Court in the Concussion Litigation (discussed in detail in Chapter 7: The NFL and NFLPA, Section D: Current Legal Obligations of the NFL) recognized, the question of a causal connection is contested in the medical literature, and, for at least partially this reason, the Court determined that these conditions did not need to be covered by the settlement in that case.[51] This is clearly an area of important continued research.

[q] In the background section of this chapter, we provide some limitations to the Michigan Study.

[r] Research did not reveal quality comparable data, but other studies have found that approximately 16 percent of American adults have a major depressive episode in their life. Laura Andrade, al., *The Epidemiology Of Major Depressive Episodes*, 12(1) Int'l J Methods Psychiatric Res. 3, 13–21 (2003) (16.9% rate of major depressive episodes); Ronald Kessler, et al., *The Epidemiology Of Major Depressive Disorder: Results From The National Comorbidity Survey Replication (NCS-R)*, 289 J. Am. Med. Ass'n 3095–105 (2003) (16.2% rate of major depressive disorder).

[s] Kevin Guskiewicz, et al. *Recurrent Concussion and Risk of Depression in Retired Professional Football Players*, 39 Medicine & Science in Sports & Exercise 903, 905 (2007). Also of note, the study found that retired players reporting a history of three or more previous concussions were three times more likely to be diagnosed with depression. *Id.*

[t] In addition, a 2016 study found that former NFL players who played between 1959 and 1988 died of suicide at a rate significantly less than would be expected compared with the general population. In examining the causes of death for 3,439 former NFL players, the study authors expected to find that 25.6 players had died of suicide. However, only 12 had. Everett J. Lehman, Misty J. Hein & Christine M. Gersic, *Suicide Mortality Among Retired National Football League Players Who Played 5 or More Seasons*, Am. J. Sports Med. (2016).

Players do have resources for mental healthcare. The standard training camp PowerPoint presentation includes slides about the importance of mental health and advises players to use resources available to them, including club doctors.[52] In addition, in 2012, the NFL, in partnership with other organizations, created the Life Line program, a 24/7 hotline for players and their families in need of assistance during crises.[53] Finally, players are able to receive mental healthcare through their player insurance plans.

Nevertheless, Current Player 2 indicated his belief "[t]here is not enough invested in the mental health and well-being and the emotional well-being of our players." The player also explained that he "think[s] the mental and emotional health of the players is just as important, if not more important, as the physical well-being of our players."

Aside from the resources that do exist, players are likely concerned about clubs knowing whether they have sought mental healthcare. On this issue, the NFL's insurance plan provides that the submission of claims by players or their family members for mental health, substance abuse, and other counseling services provided for under the insurance program "will not be made known to [the] Club, the NFL or the NFLPA." However, a waiver executed by players permitting the disclosure of their medical information to the NFL, the club, and others "expressly *includes* all records and [protected health information] relating to any mental health treatment, therapy, and/or counseling, but expressly excludes psychotherapy notes."[u] Thus, players are unable to receive confidential mental healthcare.

One source of assistance concerning player mental health is the club chaplain. Current Player 2 explained that he thought the club chaplain was "great" for the players. Every club generally has a chaplain who will visit practice once or twice during the week and be present before games. The chaplains often hold small studies or sermons but avoid overly religious messaging, instead focusing on themes relevant to football and the players or other themes as directed by the coaching staff. Importantly, one former player indicated that chaplains are often able to provide important words of encouragement and positive feedback in an environment that is often lacking both.

(B) Current Legal Obligations and Ethical Codes

We examine players' legal and ethical obligations from two perspectives: (1) players' obligations concerning their *own* health, as it is broadly defined for this Report; and, (2) players' obligations concerning the health of *other* players.

1) PLAYERS AND THEIR OWN HEALTH

As we will discuss, players, like all people or patients, have certain obligations concerning their own health, although they often need a range of support, education, access, and unconflicted relationships in order to fully satisfy these obligations and goals.

a) Current Legal Obligations

From a legal perspective, NFL players undoubtedly have both certain *rights* concerning their health[v] as well as *obligations*.

The Standard NFL Player Contract[w] imposes certain health-related obligations on players. Specifically, players are:

1. forbidden from engaging "in any activity other than football which may involve a significant risk of personal injury";[x]

2. obligated to maintain themselves in "excellent physical condition";[54] and,

3. obligated to "undergo a complete physical examination by the Club physician upon Club request, during which physical examination Player agrees to make full and complete disclosure of any physical or mental condition known to him which might impair his performance . . . and to respond fully and in good faith when questioned by the Club physician about such condition."[55]

---

[v] Indeed, published with this Report is a Patient Bill of Rights for NFL Players.

[w] Appendix A to the 2011 CBA is the Standard NFL Player Contract. The Standard Player Contract is 9 pages in length and contains the most basic and important provisions concerning the terms and conditions of NFL player employment. Most player contracts include multi-page addendums addressing more specific compensation or contractual issues.

[x] 2011 CBA, App. A, § 3. NFL player contracts often include addendums that prohibit "hazardous activities which involve a significant risk of personal injury and are non-football in nature, including, without limitation, water or snow skiing, surfing, hang gliding, bungee jumping, scuba diving, sky diving, rock or mountain climbing, race car driving as driver or passenger, riding a motorcycle, motor bike, all-terrain or similar vehicle as driver or passenger, travel on or flight in any test or experimental aircraft, or serving as a pilot or crew member on any flight." Copies of NFL player contracts are on file with the authors. Professional athletes have had their contracts terminated after being injured in motorcycle accidents or playing pickup basketball. *See* Herzog, Bob. *Basketball Injury Might Cost Boone Big Part of Contract*, Newsday, Jan. 28, 2004, *available at* 2004 WLNR 1117940.

---

[u] Emphasis in original. A copy of this waiver is included as Appendix L. The circumstances under which these waivers are executed is an area worthy of additional attention. For example, questions might be raised as to whether the players are providing meaningful informed consent in their execution.

Players also seemingly have an ongoing obligation to report injuries to their club, outside of the physical exam. The 2011 collective bargaining agreement (CBA) permits clubs to fine players up to $1,770 if the player does not "promptly report" an injury to the club doctor or athletic trainer.[56]

In reviewing a draft of this Report, the NFL stated that a player has an "obligation to fully and honestly disclose his physical condition to the Club," citing the above provisions,[57] while also arguing that a player who fails to be forthcoming about his medical needs is violating his contract and the CBA.[58] We think the NFL may over read the relevant provisions. It appears from the above-described provisions that NFL players have obligations to: (a) promptly report injuries; and, (b) be completely honest about their condition when undergoing a physical. However, if a player is not undergoing a physical and has not recently suffered an injury, he does not have to tell the club about his medical needs. Thus, it does not appear that the player has any obligation to keep the club medical staff apprised of his recovery from an injury previously reported to the club if the club does not request a physical. Additionally, during the offseason, it does not appear that the player has an obligation to report consultations with medical professionals outside the club or to disclose a variety of medical conditions that are not physical "injuries," such as mental health treatment, heart conditions, or general muscle soreness.

The 2011 CBA also contains numerous health benefits and programs for players. Fortunately for players, the vast majority of the programs contain no statute of limitations for filing or eligibility. The only benefit that requires filing by a certain date is the Injury Protection benefit, which requires filing by October 15 of the League Year[y] in which the benefit is being claimed.[59] The benefits available to players are discussed in more detail in Chapter 7: The NFL and NFLPA and in Appendix C: Summary of Collectively Bargained Health-Related Programs and Benefits.

Player grievances under the CBA are subject to statutes of limitations. A player must commence an Injury Grievance within 25 days if the player's contract was terminated at a time that the player was physically unable to perform the services required of him.[60] Additionally, a player could commence a Non-Injury Grievance if the player is unsatisfied with some aspect of his medical care (or a wide variety of other things) within 50 days from the date or the occurrence or non-occurrence on which the

grievance is based.[z] These grievance mechanisms will be discussed in more detail as relevant in specific chapters.

b) Current Ethical Codes

As a preliminary matter, we note that players only have obligations to promote their own health to the extent health maximization is of interest to them. In practice, we know that players often make decisions sacrificing their health in favor of some other benefit, typically career-, performance- or finance-related. In some cases, the need for those sacrifices could be avoided through structural change, and we make recommendations to that effect throughout this Report in order to advance the principle of Health Primacy. That said, our principle of Empowered Autonomy seeks to recognize a fully informed, competent player's right to voluntarily weigh his health against other interests. While we recognize that players currently lack sufficient information to be fully empowered, assuming that players are concerned with maximizing their health, they do have some obligations to help support that goal.

While not specific to NFL players, one of the most useful articulations of a player's obligations to care for his own health comes from prominent statements of patients' responsibilities. Opinion 1.1.4 of the American Medical Association's (AMA) Code of Medical Ethics, for example, recognizes a patient's right to direct his or her own healthcare but declares that "[w]ith that exercise of self-governance and choice comes a number of responsibilities."[61] The responsibilities most relevant to NFL players require them to:[aa]

(a) [Be] truthful and forthcoming with their physicians and strive to express their concerns clearly.

(b) Provide as complete a medical history as they can, including providing information about past illnesses, medications, hospitalizations, family history of illness, and other matters relating to present health.

---

z   2011 CBA, Art. 43, § 2. The term "Non-Injury Grievance" is something of a misnomer. The CBA differentiates between an "Injury Grievance" and a "Non-Injury Grievance." An "Injury Grievance" is exclusively "a claim or complaint that, at the time a player's NFL Player Contract or Practice Squad Player Contract was terminated by a club, the player was physically unable to perform the services required of him by that contract because of an injury incurred in the performance of his services under that contract." 2011 CBA, Art. 44, § 1. Generally, all other disputes (except System Arbitrations, see 2011 CBA, Art. 15) concerning the CBA or a player's terms and conditions of employment are "Non-Injury Grievances." 2011 CBA, Art. 43, § 1. Thus, there can be disputes concerning a player's injury or medical care that are considered "Non-Injury Grievances" because they do not fit within the limited confines of an "Injury Grievance." Additionally, although a Non-Injury Grievance is one method by which a player could seek changes to his medical care, there are two committees specifically designated for these issues, as discussed in more detail in Chapter 2: Club Doctors and Chapter 8: NFL Clubs.

aa   It is important to note that the AMA is an organization with a substantial interest in protecting doctors' interests and thus its description of patient obligations might not match the expectations of some patients.

---

y   An NFL League Year begins and ends in early March. 2011 CBA, Art. 1.

(c) Cooperate with agreed-on treatment plans. Since adhering to treatment is often essential to public and individual safety, patients should disclose whether they have or have not followed the agreed-on plan and indicate whether they would like to reconsider the plan.

* * *

(f) Recognize that a healthy lifestyle can often prevent or mitigate illness and take responsibility to follow preventative measures and adopt health-enhancing behaviors.

(g) Be aware of and refrain from behavior that unreasonably places the health of others at risk. They should ask about what they can do to prevent transmission of infectious disease.[62]

The principal obligations affecting NFL players are responsibilities (a) and (b) of the AMA Code, requiring open communication with doctors and full disclosure of their medical conditions and history. Although such disclosures might improve a player's treatment, as will be discussed, players are often (understandably) wary of informing the club doctor of a physical ailment because the club might use that information as a basis to terminate the player's contract or otherwise negatively affect the player's employment.

Similar codes of patient responsibility also exist from the American Hospital Association,[63] the National Health Council,[64] and individual healthcare providers.[65] These codes generally emphasize the obligation of patients to fully disclose their medical conditions and history, actively participate in medical decision making, and cooperate with and follow the recommended treatment.

Whether a patient follows these generally accepted guidelines for their own medical care can also have legal significance. Where a patient has failed to disclose important medical history, follow a doctor's recommended treatment, or otherwise engaged in behavior contrary to the patient's own medical best interests, the patient may, at least in some states, be barred or limited from recovering in a medical malpractice action.[66]

2) PLAYERS AND OTHER PLAYERS' HEALTH

a) Current Legal Obligations

NFL players also have health-related obligations toward one another that might arise from a variety of sources. However, the CBA is generally not one of them, since NFL players do not negotiate the CBA against one another. Thus, the CBA does not establish any legally enforceable obligations or rights among the players.

NFL playing rules seemingly create the principal mechanism for analyzing players' obligations to each other. The Official Playing Rules (Playing Rules) of the NFL are created and authorized pursuant to the NFL Constitution and Bylaws.[67] The NFL is empowered to enact and amend its own Constitution and Bylaws, including the Playing Rules, provided the Constitution and Bylaws does not conflict with the CBA and that any such amendment does not "significantly affect the terms and conditions of employment of NFL players."[68,ab] Paragraph 14 of the Standard NFL Player Contract, which is included as Appendix A of the 2011 CBA, also effectively obligates players to follow NFL policies.[69]

> Assuming that players are concerned with maximizing their health, they do have some obligations to help support that goal.

NFL Playing Rules come with penalties for violations, whether it be a five-yard penalty incurred by the penalized player's team or, in more extreme cases, ejection of the penalized player from the game, and possibly fines or suspension imposed after the fact by the NFL. Violations of the Playing Rules do not of themselves generate legal liability (just because a tackle amounts to the foul of unnecessary roughness does not make it a crime or a tort).[ac] However, as indicated below, intentional inflictions of injury that occur wholly outside the bounds of the game might sometimes give rise to legal liability.

[ab] For more information on NFL rules and rule changes, see Chapter 7: The NFL and NFLPA, Section A: Background on the NFL, and Appendix I: History of Health-Related NFL Playing Rule Changes.

[ac] While no court has ever cited the Playing Rules as a basis for liability, in Hackbart v. Cincinnati Bengals, Inc., 601 F.2d 516 (10th Cir. 1979), the United States Court of Appeals for the Tenth Circuit did discuss the Playing Rules as discussed in further detail below.

The Preface to the Playing Rules seeks to make clear that a violation of the Playing Rules will not necessarily, or even ordinarily, generate legal liability:

> Where the word "illegal" appears in this rule book, it is an institutional term of art pertaining strictly to actions that violate NFL playing rules. It is not meant to connote illegality under any public law or the rules or regulations of any other organization.
>
> The word "flagrant," when used here to describe an action by a player, is meant to indicate that the degree of a violation of the rules — usually a personal foul or unnecessary roughness — is extremely objectionable, conspicuous, unnecessary, avoidable, or gratuitous. "Flagrant" in these rules does not necessarily imply malice on the part of the fouling player or an intention to injure an opponent.[70]

Players also have common law[ad] obligations toward one another. In contact sports, such as football, one player can recover for injuries suffered only if the other player intentionally, recklessly, or willfully and wantonly, injured the plaintiff-player.[71] This rule has become known as the "contact sports exception."[72] The contact sports exception recognizes that "[p]articipants in team sports, where physical contact among participants is inherent and virtually inevitable, assume greater risks of injury than nonparticipants or participants in noncontact sports."[73] Thus, players can only recover from other players where the defendant player has acted exceptionally badly.[ae]

b) Current Ethical Codes

There are no known codes of ethics for players concerning the health of other players.

[ad] Common law refers to "[t]he body of law derived from judicial decisions, rather than from statutes or constitutions." Black's Law Dictionary (9th ed. 2009).

[ae] Beyond these better established theories of liability, some might argue that players could develop a fiduciary relationship with one another, thus giving rise to liability. Generally speaking, a fiduciary is "a person who is required to act for the benefit of another person on all matters within the scope of their relationship; one who owes to another the duties of good faith, trust, confidence, and candor." Black's Law Dictionary "Duty" (9th ed. 2009). Whether a fiduciary relationship exists is a fact-based inquiry into the nature of the relationship. Ritani, LLC v. Aghjayan, 880 F.Supp.2d 425, 455 (S.D.N.Y. 2012) (applying New York law); Carcano v. JBSS, LLC, 200 N.C.App. 162, 177 (N.C.App. 2009); L.C. v. R.P., 563 N.W.2d 799, 802 (N.D. 1997); Allen Realty Corp. v. Holbert, 227 Va. 441, 447 (Va. 1984); Murphy v. Country House, Inc., 307 Minn. 344, 350 (Minn. 1976). Some players, particularly younger players, might develop a relationship with a captain, veteran or other team leader whereby the younger player relies on the older player for advice and guidance. Over time, it is conceivable that a relationship of trust and confidence could develop to the point of becoming an actionable fiduciary relationship. Nevertheless, there are no known litigations in which one athlete alleged another athlete owed and/or violated a fiduciary obligation.

(C) Current Practices

Significant concerns exist about players' actions regarding their own health. Historically, there is considerable evidence that NFL players underreport their medical conditions and symptoms,[74] which is predictable, albeit undesirable. In an effort to not miss playing time, players might try to intentionally fail the Concussion Protocol's[af] baseline examination,[75] avoid going through the Concussion Protocol,[76] or avoid telling the club that he suffered a substantial blow to the head.[77,ag] Although there are no reliable statistics as to the incidence of this behavior, it does happen, and some doctors believe that players are at fault for failing to cooperate with the Concussion Protocol.[78] For these reasons, one contract advisor interviewed agreed that players can sometimes be their "own worst enemy" after sustaining a blow to the head. The players we interviewed did not believe that players were doing a good job of taking care of themselves (for a variety of reasons, ranging from youthful optimism to pressures to succeed) and all of those who were asked agreed that players often need to be protected from themselves.[ah] Nevertheless, we again emphasize that the existing data on player health are incomplete and often unclear, leaving players without sufficient information to make truly informed decisions about their own health.

The pressures to perform and remain on the field at all costs can be extraordinary. According to Hall of Fame New York Giants linebacker Harry Carson (1976–88):

> Football players are very insecure people. Players are interchangeable parts. Someone played your position before you, and when you leave, someone else is going to be in your place. You are only there for a short period of time, so you want to make as much as you can in the short time given you. You do not want to give anyone else a shot at your job. Football players understand that if they give someone the opportunity to do the job better, their days are numbered.[79]

[af] The Concussion Protocol, attached as Appendix A, dictates the way in which clubs must diagnose and manage players who have potentially suffered concussions.

[ag] A 2015 study found that 64.4 percent of clinicians (doctors or athletic trainers) in college sports reported having experienced pressure from athletes to prematurely clear them to return to participation after a concussion. Emily Kroshus, et al., *Pressure on Sports Medicine Clinicians to Prematurely Return Collegiate Athletes to Play After Concussion*, 50 J. Athletic Training 944 (2015).

[ah] Former Player 3: "You'd rather get knocked out cold than pull yourself out of the game. And there's no way they're coming out. So you do need someone that can make that decision for them at times."

There is no shortage of stories from NFL players, former and current, about the depths to which they went to continue playing—fighting through and hiding injuries to stay on the field. Players have a variety of motivations for doing so: to try and help the club win; to prove their toughness to teammates, coaches, and fans, for example; and out of for fear of losing their spot in the lineup or on the roster if they do not.[ai]

The San Francisco 49ers provided a useful recent example. In 2012, 49ers quarterback Alex Smith was having a successful season when he suffered a concussion that forced him to miss a game. Smith's backup, Colin Kaepernick played well in place of Smith.[80] Even though Smith was healthy enough to play two weeks later, the 49ers kept Kaepernick as the starter[81] and Smith never started for the 49ers again. In response, Smith stated "I feel like the only thing I did to lose my job was get a concussion."[82]

Former Player 1 gave a useful in-depth description of the pressures to keep playing:

> [T]he pressure to play when you're injured or to get back before you're healthy is just incredible . . . I saw guys play through all kinds of things . . . just knowing you had to be out there just to try to make a team and then after that trying to get your spot, trying to keep your starting spot . . . . I can't express to you the pressure you feel to play, not just games that you're a little hurt, but I mean major, major injuries. If you can walk, if you can go, if you can move your arms a little bit, you felt like you have to be out there.[aj]

Current Player 1 echoed these sentiments:

> [T]here's definitely a pressure to be out there for every practice and to never miss a game or anything like that because of injuries. Just because you know there's always a threat of another guy playing your position. And you never want somebody else to outshine you or you don't want the coaches to feel like you're unreliable and not a player that can play through injuries.[ak]

Indeed players feel pressure to play through injuries not only from their coaches[83] but also from teammates, opponents,[84] fans, media, and others.

Players and contract advisors we talked to expressed their view that club medical staff sometimes encourage players to return to the field when they are less than 100 percent healthy so that the club can obtain evidence of the player's supposed health and also his diminished performance.[85] In their perspective, the club will then terminate the player's contract, claiming it was based on the player's diminished performance and refuse to pay the player any additional compensation.[86] While the player might file an Injury Grievance seeking compensation for the duration of the injury (during the season of injury only), the player will have undermined his claim by returning to the field of play and at least appearing to be uninjured.[87]

Players we interviewed also generally did not believe that they were doing a good job of protecting their own health or that of their teammates:[al]

> **Current Player 2:** "I think as players we can do a better job of how we communicate our injuries . . . . I think that guys, and specifically as it relates to concussions, are not communicating their symptoms or not speaking up when they have taken hits to the head because they fear . . . losing playing time and . . . in the long-term the loss of potential earnings."

> **Current Player 4:** "I don't know that players genuinely care about the health of other players."

> **Current Player 5:** ""Not very good . . . . I think guys only really care about their health when they have a major health issue."

[ai] A common refrain from players, current and former, is that a player "can't make the club in the tub." Current Player 5 used this phrase as did John Yarno, Seattle Seahawks center from 1977 to 1982: "[T]here are two expressions we've always had in the NFL. One was, 'Get hurt, lose your job!' Because if you're not on the field, somebody else is, and at that level, he's probably a pretty good athlete. [. . .] The other expression is, 'You can't make the club in the tub.' If you're not on that field every day and on the practice film the coaches study at night, then you're not in their minds. I mean, it's extremely competitive. It's very difficult. When I was with the Hawks, we'd take maybe 125 guys into summer camp for 48 jobs. If somebody went down, it was like, 'Drag that carcass off the field or move the drill, and let's go!' So it was a very violent lifestyle. But I would do the whole thing again in a heartbeat. I have no remorse about that." Pierce E. Scranton, Jr., Playing Hurt: Treating and Evaluating the Warriors of the NFL 114 (2001).

[aj] Former Player 2: "I just wanted to play. The problem was that playing was the ultimate goal and most guys like myself would try to do everything they can to play . . . sometimes you have to do things that necessarily aren't right . . . I guess that's just the nature of the business we were involved in." Former Player 3: "The player is going to do anything he can to get out there."

[ak] Longtime NFL General Manager and executive Tom Donahoe explained the importance of player health in roster decisions: "Durability becomes a significant factor because there is so much money involved . . . If a guy misses five or six games a year, you'll think about whether you want to sign him. And I don't know about all coaches, but many would rather have a guy with less talent who is more dependable than a more talented guy who you don't know when he'll show up." Dave Sell, Football's Pain-Taking Process, Wash. Post, Dec. 8, 1996, available at 1996 WLNR 6482132.

[al] We reiterate that our interviews were intended to be informational but not representative of all players' views and should be read with that limitation in mind.

Current Player 6: *"Young guys have no idea how to take care of their bodies."*[am]

Players we interviewed also generally did not believe that they were doing a good job of preparing for life after football and taking advantage of the programs and benefits available to them:

Current Player 2: *"[T]he focus that's required in order to be successful at this level is off the charts. So I think it's hard for some guys to put every-thing they have into their playing career while at the same time preparing themselves for life after football . . . . [Players] are not often times tak-ing advantage of the resources that are out there for us[.]"*

Current Player 3: *"I think there are a lot of pro-grams out there that benefit guys getting ready for life after football . . . [b]ut at the end of the day, I think it's the players that have to want to prepare. The NFL can't make you go to all those programs."*

Current Player 6: *"I think there are guys that con-sider life after football and careers after football, but I wouldn't say that it's the majority."*

Current Player 10: *"I think players can do a better job of [taking advantage of programs]."*[an]

From a financial perspective, our interviews and existing reports suggest that players are often unrealistic about their likely career trajectories, believing that their careers will exceed the average length and that they will continue to make hundreds of thousands if not millions of dollars a year for the foreseeable future.[ao] Moreover, players, like many people, tend to value today over tomorrow, prefer-ring to spend now rather than save for later.

Contract advisors and financial advisors we interviewed acknowledged that young players routinely fail to grasp the likely brevity of their career[ap] and the need to handle their health and financial matters responsibly.[aq] While some players make mistakes about these matters early in their career and are able to learn from them, few players are in the NFL long enough to capitalize on that learning process. The contract advisors we interviewed maintained that this situation persists today even though players are generally more aware of the risks and realities of a football career due to increased media attention and education efforts by contract advisors, financial advisors, the NFL, and the NFLPA.[ar]

In our interviews, we found two somewhat divergent views emerged concerning players and their rights and benefits. First, some believe that players are not sufficiently made aware by either the NFL or NFLPA of their rights and benefits.[as] Second, some believe that players *are* sufficiently made aware of their rights, benefits, and opportunities, but that some players fail to take advantage of them for a variety of reasons, including lack of motivation.[at,88] Nevertheless, both views support the general belief that many players are not receiving the benefits to which they are entitled.

Players' interactions with specific stakeholders are discussed in those stakeholders' chapters.

[am] Current Player 8 had a more optimistic view: "The amount of rehab, pre-hab, strength programs, even watching diets and pills and things like that. I think players have—at least the players who stick around—have approached their health as their main concern."

[an] Current Player 10 also believes that the biggest improvement still needed concern-ing player health is "taking care of players post-career."

[ao] Contract Advisor 4: "[S]top convincing the players that they all could become super-stars and rich . . . . [B]ut no player thinks it's going to happen to them. They think they're going to be the next Richard Sherman and make $15 million and be on com-mercials. While the odds are they probably have just as good a chance of developing CTE and potentially dying as they do of becoming a $15 million player in the NFL."

[ap] Contract Advisor 5: "Every player thinks he's going to play 15 years . . . . No matter how many statistics you throw at them and tell them, they don't believe it's going to be them."

[aq] Contract Advisor 3: "[T]here's always going to be players that don't listen, don't pay attention, don't care . . . . And you know I can tell you from having been there a lot in trying to protect the player that in most circumstances no matter who you put in their life, they're not going to listen . . . . At the end of the day, it's their call." Contract Advisor 4: "It's me usually screaming at the player, you're telling me you still have a headache or if you have a headache you better let me know and you should not be on the field or anywhere near it because you need to let [the club] know."

[ar] Contract Advisors also believed that players are increasingly aware of club doctor's potential conflicts of interest and take appropriate action. Contract Advisor 5: "I think players are starting to advocate for themselves more and more these days."

[as] Current Player 5 described the NFL and NFLPA's efforts to prepare players for life after football as "below average."

[at] Jonathan Kraft, President, New England Patriots, Deans' Innovation in Sports Challenge Kickoff, Harvard Innovation Lab (Nov. 21, 2014), YouTube, https://www.youtube.com/watch?v=0_JOQb_lisw, *archived at* https://perma.cc/76JL-L7TX ("One of the things players now, at the league's expense, can go on the offseason to business schools—like Harvard, like Wharton, like Stanford—and start to get a business career. There are internship programs, there are resources that are really fantastic along many different professional levels, internship programs. But the player wants to have to do it. And I know we try to get veteran players and recently retired guys to come in and talk to them, but a guy has to want to do it. And some of them are motivated—some people like Domonique [Foxworth] are motivated—and other people just aren't. I think that's life. It's our job to make them understand what the resources are and why they are important . . . But, I think . . . like anything in life, there are people with different levels of motivation."). Contract Advisor 4: "[T]hey're clearly not hearing the information being given to them." Contract Advisor 2: "You need to want to know. This is your business. This is your career. So I think players have to take some of the responsibility."

(D) Enforcement of Legal and Ethical Obligations[au]

Almost all incidences of unnecessary player on player violence are resolved through the NFL's imposition of a fine or suspension for the player who violated the rules. The NFL's League Policies for Players contains a schedule of minimum fines for various rules violations. In 2015, on the low end of the spectrum, players who committed face masks, late hits, and chop blocks faced a minimum penalty of $8,681 for a first offense and $17,363 for a second offense.[89] On the other end of the spectrum, the largest minimum fines of $23,152 for a first offense are reserved for spearing, impermissible use of the helmet, initiating contact with the crown of the helmet, hits on defenseless players, and blindside blocks.[90]

The League Policies for Players emphasizes that the schedule of fines are minimums and that suspensions or fines are to be determined by the degree of violation.[91] Indeed, the NFL has regularly increased its discipline against repeat offenders.[au]

While the NFL's disciplinary process may partly satisfy its deterrence function, it does not provide the injured player any opportunity to recover from his injuries. Only in a

---

[au] For example, NFL safety Brandon Meriweather has been punished five times for illegal hits with increasing discipline: after his third illegal hit, Meriweather was fined $42,000; his fourth hit earned him a one-game suspension; and his fifth hit a two-game suspension. John Keim, *Brandon Meriweather Suspended*, ESPN (Aug. 26, 2014, 10:23 AM), http://espn.go.com/nfl/story/_/id/11408933/brandon-meriweather-washington-redskins-suspended-2-games-preseason-hit, *archived at* http://perma.cc/3XBY-XH2T. Meriweather indicated that he spent the 2014 offseason working on changing his tackling form to avoid further punishment. *Id.*; John Keim, *No Surprise on Brandon Meriweather*, ESPN (Aug. 25, 2014, 7:08 PM), http://espn.go.com/blog/washington-redskins/post/_/id/10225/no-surprise-on-brandon-meriweather, *archived at* http://perma.cc/V3PF-W87P.

---

handful of situations have professional athletes sought recompense for their injuries by instituting legal action against another athlete.

As discussed earlier, one player can recover for injuries suffered only if the other player intentionally, recklessly, or willfully and wantonly, injured the other player. This standard is routinely applied in youth sports.[92] Youth sports, because of their wide levels of participation, provide a forum for most tort-based sports litigation and legal rules that are then often applied in professional sports.

In *McKichan v. St. Louis Hockey Club, L.P.,*[93] a minor league hockey goalie sued an opposing player and his team after he was injured by the player's post-whistle check. A jury granted the goalie $175,000 in damages but the Missouri Court of Appeals reversed and vacated the award, finding

> *That the specific conduct at issue in this case, a severe body check, is a part of professional hockey. This body check, even several seconds after the whistle and in violation of several rules of the game, was not outside the realm of reasonable anticipation. For better or for worse, it is "part of the game" of professional hockey. As such, we hold as a matter of law that the specific conduct which occurred here is not actionable.*[94]

The *McKichan* case stands for the proposition that a violation of the playing rules generally will not be dispositive as to whether a legal duty has been violated, *i.e.,* whether a tort has been committed.

Nevertheless, a different result occurred in *Hackbart v. Cincinnati Bengals, Inc.,*[95] a lawsuit brought Denver Broncos defensive back Dale Hackbart in the 1970s. The

One player can recover for injuries suffered only if the other player intentionally, recklessly, or willfully and wantonly, injured the other player.

trial court found that a Cincinnati Bengals running back "acting out of anger and frustration, but without a specific intent to injure . . . stepped forward and struck a blow with his right forearm to the back of the kneeling plaintiff's head and neck with sufficient force to cause both players to fall forward to the ground."[96] The trial court nonetheless determined that such violent conduct was inherent to the game of football and entered judgment for the defendants.[97]

The United States Court of Appeals for the Tenth Circuit reversed, declaring that "there are no principles of law which allow a court to rule out certain tortious conduct by reason of general roughness of the game or difficulty of administering it."[98] The Tenth Circuit also discussed the Playing Rules in determining whether Hackbart consented to intentionally being injured during the course of a football game. The Court determined that the Playing Rules "are intended to establish reasonable boundaries so that one football player cannot intentionally inflict a serious injury on another."[99] The Tenth Circuit remanded the case for a new trial in which the running back's actions would be examined pursuant to a recklessness standard.[100] After remand, the case settled for an unknown sum.[101]

After the *Hackbart* case, there is only one other known case in which a player sued another player for conduct that took place during an NFL game.[102] In *Green v. Pro Football, Inc.*, former NFL player Barrett Green sued the Washington, D.C. football club, its former defensive coordinator Gregg Williams, and former Washington, D.C. player Robert Royal. Green alleged that he was injured as a result of an illegal play by Royal that was part of a scheme whereby players were financially rewarded for injuring opposing players.[103] The court denied the defendants' motion to dismiss in part and found that Green stated a viable claim for battery.[104] The case was subsequently settled on confidential terms.[105] Nevertheless, the *Green* case supports the proposition that players can be held liable for intentional acts that are beyond the reasonable bounds of the game.

It is also important to note that regardless of potential civil liability, several players have been charged criminally for dangerous actions taken on the field of play.[106]

As discussed above, players also bear responsibility and have obligations for their own health. Clubs may seek to enforce players' health disclosure obligations where the player's failure to do so negatively affects the club. In 2012, the NFL, on behalf of the New England Patriots, commenced a System Arbitration[av] against Jonathan Fanene. Prior to the 2012 season, the Patriots and Fanene agreed to a three-year contract worth close to $12 million, including a $3.85 million signing bonus.[107] As part of a pre-employment questionnaire, Fanene, according to the Patriots, stated that he took no medications regularly even though he had been taking significant amounts of painkillers to mask chronic pain in his knee.[108] The Patriots cut Fanene during training camp citing Fanene's alleged failure to disclose his medical condition,[109] and initiated a System Arbitration to recoup $2.5 million in signing bonus money already paid to Fanene.[110] Specifically, the Patriots alleged Fanene violated his obligations to negotiate the contract in good faith.[111]

The NFLPA sought to have the Patriots' claims dismissed, arguing that signing bonus forfeiture was not an available remedy for the alleged wrongful act by Fanene.[112] After the NFLPA's motion to dismiss was denied, the parties settled by allowing Fanene to keep the $2.5 million already paid, but releasing the Patriots' from their obligation to pay Fanene the remaining $1.35 million of the signing bonus.[113]

In a related proceeding, the NFLPA filed a grievance against the Patriots concerning Patriots doctor Tom Gill's care of Fanene, discussed in further detail in Chapter 8: NFL Clubs.

[av] A System Arbitration is a legal process for the resolution of disputes between the NFL and the NFLPA and/or a player concerning a subset of CBA provisions that are central to the NFL's operations and which invoke antitrust and labor law concerns, including but not limited to the NFL player contract, NFL Draft, rookie compensation, free agency, and the Salary Cap. 2011 CBA, Art. 15, § 1.

(E) Recommendations Concerning Players

This Report is intended to improve the lives and careers of players by protecting and promoting their health. While there are many stakeholders with a role to play in achieving this goal, it is important that players recognize and accept that they are on this list as well, not only with regard to their own health, but also with regard to the health of former, current and future players. Nevertheless, in many cases, players will need support from other stakeholders to fulfill the recommendations made here. In the chapters on the NFL and NFLPA, Contract Advisors, and Financial Advisors, we make recommendations to these stakeholders about how they can assist players.

While all of the recommendations in this Report concern players, certain recommendations directed toward players' conduct are made in other chapters:

- Chapter 6: Personal Doctors—Recommendation 6:1-B: Players should receive a physical from their own doctor as soon as possible after each season.

- Chapter 12: Contract Advisors—Recommendation 12:2-C: Players should be given information to ensure that they choose contract advisors based on their professional qualifications and experience and not the financial benefits the contract advisor has or is willing to provide to the player.

- Chapter 13: Financial Advisors—Recommendation 13:1-D: Players should be given information to ensure that they choose financial advisors based on their professional qualifications and experience and not the financial benefits the financial advisor has or is willing to provide to the player.

- Chapter 14: Family Members—Recommendation 14:2-A: Players should select and rely on professionals rather than family members for managing their business, financial, and legal affairs.

Additional player-specific recommendations are listed here.

Goal 1: To have players be proactive concerning their own health with appropriate support.

Principles Advanced: Health Primacy; Empowered Autonomy; and, Collaboration and Engagement.

Recommendation 1:1-A: With assistance from contract advisors, the NFL, the NFLPA, and others, players should familiarize themselves with their rights and obligations related to health and other benefits, and should avail themselves of applicable benefits.

Our formal interviews, literature review, and other feedback from stakeholders revealed that many players are not sufficiently aware of their rights, obligations, benefits, and opportunities pursuant to the CBA or other programs, or do not take full advantage of them, even if they are aware. There are numerous rights and benefits that are important to a player's health and he must be aware and take advantage of them to maximize his health. For example, a player is entitled to a second medical opinion, the surgeon of his choice, and may be entitled to tuition assistance, and a variety of injury and disability-related payments.

In Chapter 7: The NFL and NFLPA, Recommendation 7:3-A, we discuss ways in which the NFL and NFLPA have sought to advise players of certain benefits and opportunities. And while the NFL and NFLPA have an obligation to publicize

Recommendations Concerning Players – continued

these benefits and make them as easily accessible and comprehensible to the players as possible,[aw] players ultimately have to be the ones to act on the benefits.

This recommendation applies to former players as well. To the extent a former player is unaware of his rights and the benefits available to him, he should consult with his financial advisor and former contract advisor, as well as contact the NFL and the NFLPA, both of whom have staff and resources that can assist the player in understanding and obtaining benefits.

Recommendation 1:1-B: Players should carefully consider the ways in which health sacrifices now may affect their future health.

While the health of the average former player is uncertain, there is no doubt that injuries suffered during an NFL career can cause players permanent damage that could make the remainder of their life more difficult. In their desire to win, help their club and teammates, or just remain employed, players routinely play with injuries or conditions even though continuing to play might subject them to further or permanent injury. In so doing, players (like most human beings) exhibit present bias, which is the tendency to make decisions that are beneficial in the short term but are harmful in the long term.[114,ax] It is important for players (with the help of other stakeholders) to recognize the impact of this potential bias on their decision making. Some players may rationally decide that the decisions that they make now may be worth the consequences they suffer later, but it is important that those choices be as informed as possible. Players should pause—or have a support system that can help them pause—and understand the risks and benefits of playing through certain injuries or conditions, with particular emphasis on understanding the long-term implications of the decision.[115]

Relatedly, additional research must be done into ways to effectively communicate the risks and benefits of playing to NFL players. Such research can draw on effective campaigns in other areas of public health, including increased cancer awareness,[116] smoking cessation, and preventing communicable diseases.[117]

Recommendation 1:1-C: Players should take advantage of opportunities to prepare for life after football.

One reason that some players may behave in ways that jeopardize their health is because of their strong desire to remain in the NFL given the lack of attractive alternatives available to them outside the sport. The NFL and NFLPA offer a wide variety of programs and benefits to help players prepare for life after football, including educational courses and seminars. These programs are discussed in more detail in Chapter 7: The NFL and NFLPA, Appendix D: Summary of Programs Offered by NFL's Player Engagement Department and Appendix E: Summary of Programs Offered by NFLPA. As one example, the NFL's Tuition Assistance Plan reimburses players for tuition costs if they complete their college degrees within four years of leaving the NFL. Unless the player is nearly certain to have a lengthy career in coaching, broadcasting, or something else (all of which are rare), he should take advantage of this opportunity to finish his education at no or little cost.[ay] Doing so may somewhat lessen background pressures and influences to sacrifice health.

[aw] Current Player 10: "Unfortunately, advice from agents and especially the NFLPA in a long meeting with lots of information falls on deaf ears most times. Players don't care about this information until it pertains to them."

[ax] Former Player 2: "As stubborn as most of us are, I think the players truly don't understand the effects it has later in our lives."

[ay] It should also be pointed out that if the player is considering the possibility of ever coaching in college, he will likely need a college degree. *See* Brett McMurphy, *UK: Steve Masiello Didn't Graduate*, ESPN (Mar. 26, 2014, 4:30 PM), http://espn.go.com/mens-college-basketball/story/_/id/10675532/south-florida-bulls-kill-coaching-deal-steve-masiello-lying-resume, *archived at* http://perma.cc/V826-JMSZ (discussing requirement of at least an undergraduate degree to be basketball coach at the University of South Florida).

Recommendations Concerning Players – continued

Recommendation 1:1-D: Players should seek out and learn from more experienced players, including former players, concerning health-related matters.

In any line of work, younger employees are well-advised to engage with more experienced colleagues and to ask for their advice and guidance. NFL players are no different. Indeed, the uniqueness of NFL employment makes it even more important that players engage experienced players for advice.

Many of the players we interviewed told us that it took a few years in the NFL for them to learn best how to maximize their health, prepare their bodies for football, and take advantage of and protect their health-related rights, such as seeking a second medical opinion or ensuring they retain a quality financial advisor. Veteran players can provide valuable insights into these issues.[az] Moreover, while a more experienced player may not always be particularly interested in talking with the younger player, the younger player can learn a lot simply by observing.

Players have a variety of options in finding former players with whom to consult. As is discussed in detail in Chapter 10: Club Employees, each club employs a developmental employee who is charged with helping players, particularly rookies, transition to the NFL. Often this developmental employee is a former player. The club might also have former players who visit the club regularly or are involved in informal ways. Moreover, the NFLPA also employs five former players as Player Advocates, charged with serving as "the NFLPA's first line of defense in explaining and protecting player rights and benefits."[118] Each Player Advocate is assigned to a set of clubs and is responsible for helping the players on those clubs.[119] Finally, a player could ask his contract advisor about some of the contract advisor's former clients and reach out to some of them.

No matter the method, players should seek out and seize opportunities to learn from the men that came before them.

Recommendation 1:1-E: Players should take on a responsibility to one another, to support one another's health, and to change the culture for the better.

Players are in a unique and important position to help one another. There are a variety of aspects of an NFL career that only players can understand, including the incredible pressure to play and succeed and why they might sometimes make decisions that are not in the best interests of their short- or long-term health. With this understanding and the rapport that develops among teammates, players have the credibility to positively influence the decisions players make and to improve the overall culture of player health.

Given the difficult decisions players face when it comes to their careers and health, it would likely be very helpful for players to be able to rely on other players for support and advice. In addition, players can lead by example concerning their own health and the health of other players. Players are more likely able to objectively view situations and prevent players from making decisions that are not in their best interests, for example, returning to play too soon after a concussion or other major injury. At the very least, players can take it upon themselves not to pressure one another to play while injured, either explicitly or implicitly. The NFL appears to agree; as part of the standard training camp PowerPoint presentation, in discussing the importance of mental health, the NFL encourages players to "[a]dvocate for a teammate or coach if you are concerned" and declares that "[r]eaching out for assistance is not a sign of weakness but of strength!"[120]

The United States Army can serve as a useful comparison. The Army assigns each soldier a "Battle Buddy."[121] Battle Buddies help each other through training and then look out for each other physically, emotionally, and mentally when deployed.[122] Moreover, Battle Buddies remain buddies after deployment and help each other deal with the adjustment to

---

[az]   Current Player 10 explained that "there's a lot more discussions in the locker room now, especially from older guys to the younger guys just in making sure that everybody's got all the right information and making sure that everybody's healthy when they go out on the field."

Recommendations Concerning Players – continued

civilian life and with post-traumatic stress disorder.[123] A 2002 Army study of the Battle Buddy system found that soldiers overwhelmingly liked the system and found that it helped improve morale.[124]

While playing professional football should not be compared to the risks and tolls of military service, there are certain overlapping ideologies and characteristics that make the Battle Buddies analogy apt on a lesser scale. In sum, players who are well supported by their peers are likely to better handle important health issues and promote an environment in which player health is a priority.

Recommendation 1:1-F: Players should not return to play until they are fit to do so.

As discussed above, players play through all types of injuries to help the team win, protect their position on the team, prove their toughness, etc. Indeed, when a player is "fit" to return is a difficult subjective question and can involve balancing a number of factors, including but not limited to the player's short- and long-term health, the player's career goals and status with the club, and the importance of the club's upcoming games. At least some of the players and contract advisors we talked to believe that club medical staff sometimes encourage players to return to play despite being less than 100% healthy because this will allow the club to more easily terminate the player's contract or succeed in fighting a potential Injury Grievance.[ba] While clubs might not engage in such conduct with their more important players, these situations are a very real concern for many players simply seeking to retain their status on the roster.[bb] Some players indicated that they did not realize that the club would do such a thing until they saw it done or were so advised by older players.[bc] While we cannot confirm that clubs engage in such behavior, at least some players *believe* they do, which affects the trust relationship between the player and club medical staff. In sum, players need to understand the full panoply of risks when they make health-related decisions, not only to their own health, but also to their economic interests.

Recommendation 1:1-G: Players should not sign any document presented to them by the NFL, an NFL club, or an employee of an NFL club without discussing the document with their contract advisor, the NFLPA, their financial advisor, and/or other counsel, as appropriate.

As is discussed in more detail in Chapter 2: Club Doctors, players sign collectively bargained forms authorizing club doctors to disclose the players' medical records and information to club officials, coaches, and many others. A copy of this waiver is included as Appendix L. Additionally, at the NFL Combine, players similarly execute waivers and forms authorizing the disclosure of their medical records and information. The circumstances under which these waivers are executed is an area worthy of additional attention. For example, questions might be raised as to whether the players are providing meaningful and voluntary informed consent in their execution. Indeed, these forms have the potential to effectively strip players of important privacy protections and empower clubs to make adverse employment decisions about players based on the player's medical information.

As discussed in Chapter 2: Club Doctors, employers are entitled to certain parts of an employee's medical records under the Health Insurance Portability and Accountability Act, and other state laws, including worker's compensation laws.

---

ba   Peer reviewer and former NFL club executive Andrew Brandt indicated he was disappointed with some of the Injury Grievances in which he was involved, especially when players grieved about injuries for which players sought little to no treatment from club trainers or doctors. Andrew Brandt, Peer Review Response (Oct. 30, 2015).

bb   Former Player 1: "[T]his is probably the only NFL training camp they'd ever be in, but they get injured and they want to rush back and tried to get back on the field as soon as possible and the first thing that happens as soon as they get out there is the team would cut them. They get them on film running around and that's it." Current Player 10: "I think the one concern . . . [is with] young guys that are going to get released . . . . [the medical staff] hurrying to get them back on the field. Them being naïve enough to think they're getting back on the field for the right reasons and then getting released, so that the clubs don't have to pay them[.]"

bc   Former Seattle Seahawks doctor Pierce Scranton told this anecdote in his 2001 book: "One team physician complained to me that his club had cut two players after the last exhibition game, on with a ruptured disc in his neck, the other with a posterior cruciate injury to the knee. He called the club to report these injuries when the players came to his office for release physicals. 'Screw 'em,' the general manager said. 'Let 'em grieve us if they're smart enough.'

Recommendations Concerning Players – continued

Nevertheless, the waivers executed by the players are broad and potentially exceed the bounds of the aforementioned exceptions. For example, the waivers permit the player's medical records to be disclosed to and used by numerous parties *other than the player's employer*, including clubs that do not employ the player. Moreover, the waivers permit the player's medical information to be used for the NFL's publicly released injury report, discussed at length in Chapter 17: The Media, which bear no relevance to the player's ability to perform his job. Players should be careful and as knowledgeable as possible about those rights that they are waiving. Considering the stakes at hand, players would be wise to consult with the appropriate professional and expert advisors before executing any documents provided by the NFL or NFL clubs.

Recommendation 1:1-H: Players should be aware of the ramifications of withholding medical information from club medical staff.

Anecdotal evidence suggests that players routinely hide their medical conditions from the club.[125] Players principally do this to protect their status with the club and fear of being viewed as less tough by the coaches. Players know that their careers are tenuous and also know that if the club starts perceiving a player to be injury-prone, it is often not long before the club no longer employs that player. However, there are serious downsides to players not disclosing medical conditions to club medical staff. As a preliminary matter, not telling the medical staff about a condition he is suffering prevents the player from receiving necessary medical care and risks worsening the condition.[126]

Additionally, players should be aware that not advising club medical staff about their conditions might harm their financial interests. As an initial matter, as discussed above, players are obligated by the CBA and their contracts to disclose their medical conditions at certain times. Moreover, if the condition is affecting the player's performance, it increases the likelihood that the club will terminate the player's contract, generally without any further obligation to pay the player.[bd] Normally, when a player's contract is terminated because he is physically unable to perform, the club is required to continue paying the player for so long as the player is injured (during the season of injury only) via the Injury Grievance process.[127] But if the player has not advised the club that his diminished performance is the result of an injury, he has undermined his ability to bring an Injury Grievance.

Recommendation 1:1-I: Players should review their medical records regularly.

Beginning with the 2014 season, all 32 NFL clubs use electronic medical records. Players can view their records online **at any time** after registering with the website. Players should view their records regularly, including specifically at the beginning and conclusion of each season and when they are being treated for an injury or condition. Reviewing the records will ensure that the club's medical staff is properly documenting the player's condition and concerns while also helping the player to ensure he is following the proper treatment for the condition. Research has also shown that patients who have access to their medical records feel more in control of their healthcare and better understand their medical issues.[128]

Additionally, in reviewing his medical records and knowing that the club will also review them, a player might become more aware of how his medical conditions or history could adversely affect his employment. For example, the medical records might include a note from the athletic trainer that a player's knee condition prevents him from cutting and running as he had in the past, leading the club to terminate his contract. In reviewing a draft of this Report, the NFL admitted as much, stating that clubs examine a player's medical records to "evaluate whether or not a player is healthy enough to practice and play."[129] Of course, this has implications for the player's employment status.

Finally, players should also consider enlisting their family members and contract advisors to assist with regular review of medical records.

---

bd   Clubs' rights of termination are discussed as part of Recommendation 1-D in Chapter 7: NFL and NFLPA.

Endnotes

1   CBA, Art. 25.

2   *See* 2011 CBA, Art. 33, § 1 (discussing practice squad limits and also permitting the clubs to change limits from season to season).

3   *See* 2012 Constitution and Bylaws of the National Football League, § 17.1(A) (discussing the various lists on which players may be placed depending on their status).

4   *Id.*

5   During week 9 of the 2014 NFL season, the New York Giants listed 76 players on their roster: 53 players on the Active Roster; 11 players on Injured Reserve; 10 players on the Practice Squad; 1 player on the Practice Squad/Injured List; and, 1 player on Injured Reserve–Designated to Return. By contrast, the Denver Broncos only listed 67 players on their roster during week 9: 53 on the Active Roster; 3 on Injured Reserve; 10 on the Practice Squad; and, 1 on Injured Reserve–Designated to Return. There are also historical reports of clubs requesting players to fake injuries so that they can be placed on Injured Reserve and remain with the club rather than have their contract terminated. Rob Huizenga, You're Okay, It's Just a Bruise 141 (1994) (former Los Angeles Raiders Club doctor stating "I quickly learned that most teams would fake injuries, hiding talented but green prospects on the injured reserve list."); *id.* at 199 (describing a coach telling a young player "You've had neck problems before. When I tell you when, just hit the guy and lay there. You'll get your full salary this year and get a chance to make the team next year."); Pierce E. Scranton, Jr., Playing Hurt: Treating and Evaluating the Warriors of the NFL 53–55 (2001) (former Seattle Seahawks Club doctor describing how the Club used to place players on Injured Reserve with fake injuries); Samer Kalaf, *Ty Detmer Says Koy Detmer Faked An Injury So Philly Could Put Him On IR,* Deadspin (November 12, 2014, 3:07 PM), http://deadspin.com/ty-detmer-says-koy-detmer-faked-an-injury-so -philly-cou-1657968918, *archived at* http://perma.cc/8K2A-YCUD.

6   This figure was obtained from the official NFL and NFLPA playtime figures.

7   These data were derived by reviewing several NFL clubs' rosters.

8   *See History: Players Who've Played in NFL at Age 40 or Older,* Pro Football Hall of Fame, http://www.profootballhof.com/history/stats/40 _and_over_club.aspx#sthash.k0seVRUx.dpuf (last visited Aug. 7, 2015), *archived at* http://perma.cc/S87S-KKKN (listing all players to have ever played after age 40).

9   Richard Lapchick et al., *The 2015 Racial and Gender Report Card: National Football League,* The Inst. for Diversity and Ethics in Sport at the Univ. of Cent. Fl. (2015), available at http://www.tidesport.org/nfl -rgrc.html.

10 Marcella Alsan, Marianee Wanamaker, *Tuskegee and the Health of Black Men,* Nat'l Bureau of Econ. Research (2016); Katrina Armstrong et al., *Racial/Ethnic Differences in Physician Distrust in the United States,* 97 Am. J. Pub. Health (2007).

11 In 2013, the only states not to have produced NFL players were Vermont and North Dakota. *NFL 2013: Breakdown of Total Players From Each State,* SportingNews.com, September 18, 2013, http://www .sportingnews.com/nfl/story/2013-09-18/nfl-players-state-by-state -breakdown-california-florida-louisiana-texas-south-ca, *archived at* http://perma.cc/C8MC-A9MQ.

12 *Id.*

13 David R. Weir et al., *National Football League Player Care Foundation Study of Retired NFL Players,* Inst. for Social Research at Univ. of Mich. (2009), http://ns.umich.edu/Releases/2009/Sep09/FinalReport.pdf, *archived at* http://perma.cc/6G5Q-LN2M.

14 *Id.* The Michigan Study population only included players that had vested rights under the NFL's Retirement Plan, meaning the players generally had been on an NFL roster for at least three games in at least three seasons.

15 *Id.* at 14.

16 *Id.*

17 *Id.*

18 *Id.*

19 *Average NFL Career Length,* Sharp Football Analysis (Apr. 30, 2014), http://www.sharpfootballanalysis.com/blog/?p=2133, *archived at* http://perma.cc/KR58-R8DA.

20 *Id.*

21 *Id.*

22 *Id.*

23 *Id.*

24 *See* Adam Molon, *Why So Many Ex-NFL Players Struggle With Money,* CNBC (Jan. 31, 2014, 12:29 PM), www.cnbc.com/id/101377457#, *archived at* http://perma.cc/F5YN-FJE2.

25 *See* Nick Schwartz, *The Average Career Earnings Of Athletes Across America's Major Sports Will Shock You,* USA Today, Oct. 24, 2013, http://ftw.usatoday.com/2013/10/average-career-earnings-nfl-nba-mlb -nhl-mls, *archived at* http://perma.cc/9DFP-WPQ2.

26 *Injury Surveillance in the NFL: an Update from Quintiles Outcome,* Applied Clinical Trials, Aug. 30, 2012, http://www.appliedclinicaltrialsonline .com/injury-surveillance-nfl-update-quintiles-outcome (last visited Aug. 7, 2015), *archived at* http://perma.cc/5EEJ-TFA6.

27 *Id.*

28 *Transcript—2016 Injury Data Results Conference Call,* NFL Communications, Jan. 29, 2016, https://nflcommunications.com/Pages/Transcript ---2016-Injury-Data-Results-Conference-Call.aspx, *archived at* https:// perma.cc/RKC6-352G.

29 Applied Clinical Trials *supra* note 26.

30 *Id.*

31 This information was provided by the NFLPA.

32 Alan Schwarz, Walt Bogdanich, and Jacqueline Williams, *N.F.L.'s Flawed Concussion Research and Ties to Tobacco Industry,* N.Y. Times, Mar. 26, 2016, http://www.nytimes.com/2016/03/25/sports/football/ nfl-concussion-research-tobacco.html, *archived at* https://perma.cc/ NM4N-SW4Q. *See also NFL response to New York Times' concussion research story,* NFL.com (Mar. 24, 2016, 4:11 PM), http://www.nfl.com/ news/story/0ap3000000647389/article/nfl-response-to-new-york-times -concussion-research-story, *archived at* https://perma.cc/Z3XE-8FQ6.

33 Applied Clinical Trials *supra* note 26.

34 *Id.*

35 This information was provided by the NFLPA.

36 Letter from Larry Ferazani, NFL, to authors (July 18, 2016).

37 *See* 45 C.F.R. § 160.103 (defining the entities required to comply with HIPAA).

38 *See Average NFL Career Length,* Sharp Football Analysis, Apr. 30, 2014, http://www.sharpfootballanalysis.com/blog/?p=2133, *archived at* http://perma.cc/X8QV-77A3 (discussing disagreement between NFLPA and NFL and determining that the average drafted player plays about 5 years).

39 *See* 2012 NFL Constitution and Bylaws, § 12.3(E).

40 socalisteph, *NFL PUP list, Injured Reserve, NFI List rules and the 2014 San Francisco 49ers,* Superbowl Nation Blog NinersNation.com (Jul. 18, 2014, 5:30 AM), http://www.ninersnation.com/2014/7/18/5914295/nfl -pup-list-rules-injured-reserve-nfi-list-rules-49ers-2014, *archived at* http://perma.cc/6T9D-9LYM.

41 NFL CBA, Art. 25, § 4.

42 NFL CBA, Art. 25, § 1.

43 *See* Jim Baumbach, *Life After Football,* Newsday (Jan. 22, 2015),

http://data.newsday.com/projects/sports/football/life-football/, *archived at* http://perma.cc/77DP-LUUE.

44   *Any Mental Illness (AMI) Among Adults*, National Institute of Mental Health, http://www.nimh.nih.gov/health/statistics/prevalence/any-mental-illness-ami-among-adults.shtml (last visited Aug. 7, 2015), *archived at* http://perma.cc/J28R-TNXB. The National Institutes of Mental Health derived the data from the National Survey on Drug Use and Health, which defines mental illness as: "a mental, behavioral, or emotional disorder (excluding developmental and substance use disorders); diagnosable currently or within the past year; and, of sufficient duration to meet diagnostic criteria within the 4th edition of the *Diagnostic and Statistical Manual of Mental Disorders* (DSM-IV)." *Id.*

45   *See also* Jim Trotter, *Depression Prevalent in Ex-players*, ESPN (Feb. 25, 2015), http://espn.go.com/nfl/story/_/page/hotread150225/depression-suicide-raise-issue-mental-health-former-nfl-players, *archived at* http://perma.cc/K8BU-PGW6 (discussing depression among former NFL players).

46   David R. Weir et al., *National Football League Player Care Foundation Study of Retired NFL Players*, Inst. for Social Research at Univ. of Mich. (2009), *archived at* http://perma.cc/6G5Q-LN2M.

47   Thomas L. Schwenk et al., *Depression and Pain in Retired Professional Football Players*, 39 Med. & Sci. in Sports & Exercise 599 (2007).

48   *See* Marin Cogan, *The Pursuit of 'Radical Acceptance': How Brandon Marshall is Confronting the NFL's Mental Health Crisis Head-on*, ESPN (Jun. 25, 2014), http://espn.go.com/nfl/story/_/page/hotread140707/chicago-bears-brandon-marshall-spreads-awareness-nfl-mental-health-crisis-espn-magazine, *archived at* http://perma.cc/RA36-2UX7.

49   *See In re Nat'l Football League Players' Concussion Injury Litigation*, 307 F.R.D. 351, 401 (E.D. Pa. 2015) (*quoting* the Declaration of Dr. Christopher Giza) (Emphasis in the Court's opinion); *see also* Zachary Y. Kerr et al., *Nine-year risk of depression diagnosis increases with increasing self-reported concussions in retired professional football players*, 40 Am. J. Sports Med. 2206 (2012) (finding that professional football players self-reporting concussions are at greater risk for having depressive episodes later in life compared with those retired players self-reporting no concussions).

50   Thomas W. Teasdale and Aase W. Engberg, *Suicide after traumatic brain injury: a population study*, 74 J. of Neurology, Neurosurgery & Psychiatry 436 (2001).

51   *See In re Nat'l Football League Players' Concussion Injury Litigation*, 307 F.R.D. 351, 400-01 (E.D. Pa. 2015) (explaining why mood and behavioral disorders do not need to be included in settlement).

52   The NFL provided a copy of the 2016 Training Camp presentation.

53   *See Player Programs and Benefits,* NFLLifeLine.com, http://nfllifeline.org/resources/programs-and-benefits/ (last visited Aug. 7, 2015), *archived at* http://perma.cc/HJ7J-PSAW.

54   CBA, App. A, § 8. The clearest example of a potential violation of this obligation is where a player is overweight. In 2010, journalists reported that former NFL defensive lineman Albert Haynesworth showed up to training camp with the Washington Redskins overweight and out of shape and was not allowed to participate in practice. Joseph White, *Haynesworth Fails Physical Test Again*, Pitt. Post-Gazette, Jul. 31, 2010, *available at* 2010 WLNR 15233374; Michael David Smith, *Shanahan on Haynesworth: I don't get along with lazy players*, ProFootballTalk (October 31, 2013, 3:54 PM), http://profootballtalk.nbcsports.com/2013/10/31/shanahan-on-haynesworth-i-dont-get-along-with-lazy-players/, *archived at* http://perma.cc/3X2M-HJTZ.

55   CBA, App. A, § 8.

56   CBA, Art. 42, § 1(a)(iii).

57   NFL Comments and Corrections (June 24, 2016).

58   *Id.*

59   CBA, Art. 45, § 8. Relatedly, a player must file for an Extended Injury Protection benefit by January 31 following his former Club's last regular season game of the season following the season of injury. *Id.* Injury Protection and Extended Injury Protection Benefits are described in more detail in Chapter 8: NFL Clubs.

60   CBA, Art. 44, § 2. In 2014, the NFL and NFLPA litigated 31 Injury Grievances. *See Transcript from NFLPA Super Bowl XLIX Press Conference*, NFLPA, Jan. 31, 2015, http://nflpa.com/news/all-news/transcript-from-nflpa-super-bowl-xlix-press-conference, *archived at* http://perma.cc/5UJN-AGRQ.

61   *Opinion 1.1.4 – Patient Responsibilities*, Am. Med. Ass'n, *available at* http://www.ama-assn.org/ama/pub/physician-resources/medical-ethics/code-medical-ethics.page (last Aug. 1, 2016), *archived at* https://perma.cc/4QS7-F5FT.

62   *Id.*

63   *See The Patient Care Partnership*, Am. Hosp. Ass'n, http://www.aha.org/advocacy-issues/communicatingpts/pt-care-partnership.shtml (last visited Aug. 7, 2015), *archived at* http://perma.cc/HM7M-Y5PW.

64   *See Principles of Patients Rights' and Responsibilities*, Nat'l Health Council, http://www.nationalhealthcouncil.org/resources/nhc-publications/principles-patients-rights-and-responsibilities (last visited Aug. 7, 2015), *archived at* http://perma.cc/4XRF-YBKJ.

65   *See, e.g., Patients' Rights and Responsibilities*, Beth Israel Deaconess Med. Ctr., http://www.bidmc.org/Patient-and-Visitor-Information/Preparing-for-Your-Visit/Patients-Rights-and-Responsibilities.aspx (last visited Aug. 7, 2015), *archived at* http://perma.cc/P8KD-ZBJB.

66   *See* Krklus v. Stanley, 833 N.E.2d 952 (Ill. App. Ct. 2005) (patient's contributory negligence in failing to take recommended medication and continuing to smoke precluded recovery in medical malpractice case); Shinholster v. Annapolis Hosp., 685 N.W.2d 275 (Mich. 2004) (patient's failure to take prescribed medication relevant to patient's contributory negligence in medical malpractice case); Maunz v. Perales, 76 P.3d. 1027 (Kan. 2003) (patient's comparative negligence properly diminished liability of doctor in medical malpractice case); Hall v. Carter, 825 A.2d 954 (D.C. 2003) (patient's contributory negligence by smoking after surgery precluded recovery); King v. Clark, 709 N.E.2d 1043 (Ind. Ct. App. 1999) (patient's contributory negligence in delaying treatment recommended by physician precluded recovery in medical malpractice case); Carreker v. Harper, 396 S.E.2d 587 (Ga. Ct. App. 1990) (patient's failure to fully disclose all of her symptoms and medical history authorized jury charges on contributory and comparative negligence in case where jury found for defendant doctor). *See also* Matthew J. Mitten, *Emerging Legal Issues in Sports Medicine: A Synthesis, Summary, and Analysis*, 76 St. John's L. Rev. 5, 31–33 (2002).

67   *See* Constitution and Bylaws of the National Football League (2004 Rev.), Art XI. Neither the Playing Rules or the Constitution and Bylaws describe a purpose for the Playing Rules.

68   CBA, Art. 2, §§ 1, 4.

69   CBA, App. A, ¶ 14: "Player's attention is also called to the fact that the League functions with certain rules and procedures expressive of its operation as a joint venture among its member clubs and that these rules and practices may affect Player's relationship to the League and its member clubs independently of the provisions of this contract."

70   Official Playing Rules of the National Football League, Preface.

71   *See* Feld v. Borkowski, 790 N.W.2d 72 (Iowa 2010) (holding that contact sports exception applies to softball); Jaworski v. Kiernan, 696 A.2d. 332 (Conn. 1997) (applying contact sports exception to soccer); Pfister v. Shusta, 657 N.E.2d 1013 (Ill. 1995) (holding that contact sports exception applies to can kicking). *See also* Matthew G. Cole, *No Blood No Foul: The Standard of Care in Texas Owed By Participants to One Another in Athletic Contests*, 59 Baylor L. Rev. 435, 444–456 (2007) (examining the requisite degree of wrongfulness to establish liability against a sport co-participant in each of the 50 states, almost all of which require a finding beyond simple negligence).

72   *Id.*

73   *Pfister*, *supra* note 71 at 1017; *see also* Feld, *supra* note 71 at 76 (discussing same).

74   *See* Mark Fainaru-Wada & Steve Fainaru, League of Denial: The NFL, Concussions, and the Battle for Truth 26 (2013) (stating that former

Pittsburgh Steelers center Mike Webster's "rarely acknowledged his injuries, much less reported them."); Derk A. Van Kampen et al., *The "Value Added" of Neurocognitive Testing After Sports-Related Concussion*, 34 Am. J Sports Med. 1630 (2006) (concluding that "reliance on patients' self-reported symptoms after concussion is likely to result in underdiagnosis of concussion and may result in premature return to play"); *Q. and A.: Responses From an Ex-Enforcer and an Expert*, N.Y. Times, Dec. 7, 2011, http://query.nytimes.com/gst/fullpage.html?res =980DE3D71139F934A35751C1A9679D8B63, *archived at* http://perma .cc/5P5D-TRBX (discussing underreporting of concussion symptoms by football players); Tony Grossi, *Injury that Dazed McCoy Puts Focus on Concussions*, Cleveland Plain Dealer, Dec. 18, 2011, *available at* 2011 WLNR 26179502 (mentioning underreporting of concussion symptoms by NFL players).

75   Michael David Smith, *To Avoid Concussion Rules, Some Players Sandbag their Baseline Tests*, ProFootballTalk (Apr. 22, 2011, 8:25 AM), http://profootballtalk.nbcsports.com/2011/04/22/to-avoid-concussion -rules-some-players-sandbag-their-baseline-tests/, *archived at* http://perma.cc/94KW-SK7W. Experts nonetheless insist that the baseline examination cannot be cheated. *See also* Bill Pennington, *Flubbing a Baseline Test on Purpose Is Often Futile*, N.Y. Times, May 5, 2013, http://www.nytimes.com/2013/05/06/sports/sandbagging -first-concussion-test-probably-wont-help-later.html, *archived at* http://perma.cc/K8EF-G4F8.

76   Michael David Smith, *Jamaal Charles: I didn't want to go through the concussion protocol*, ProFootballTalk (Oct. 22, 2014, 9:41 AM), http://profootballtalk.nbcsports.com/2014/10/22/jamaal-charles-i-didnt -want-to-go-through-the-concussion-protocol/, *archived at* http://perma .cc/6BA2-RUPJ.

77   *See* Jason Wilde, *Aaron Rodgers says NFL's biggest concussion obstacle is players themselves*, ESPN (Jul. 14, 2016), http://espn.go.com/blog/ green-bay-packers/post/_/id/31053/aaron-rodgers-says-nfls-biggest -concussion-obstacle-is-players-themselves, *archived at* https://perma .cc/V6R7-ARXR; Joe Giglio, *NFL analyst Mark Schlereth: Why players don't report concussions*, NJ.com (Nov. 13, 2015, 9:52 AM), http://www .nj.com/sports/index.ssf/2015/11/nfl_analyst_mark_schlereth_why _players_dont_report.html, *archived at* http://perma.cc/XU5Z-TFV3; Michael David Smith, *LaAdrian Waddle: Don't blame Lions for me playing with a concussion,* ProFootballTalk (Oct. 25, 2014, 11:12 AM), http://profootballtalk.nbcsports.com/2014/10/25/laadrian-waddle -dont-blame-lions-for-me-playing-with-a-concussion/, *archived at* http://perma.cc/RMX9-VPXE.

78   *See* Kevin Seifert, *Inside Slant: The Plain Truth of NFL Sideline Concussion Tests*, ESPN (Feb.19, 2015, 12:00 PM), http://espn.go.com/blog/ nflnation/post/_/id/160927/inside-slant-the-plain-truth-of-nfl-sideline -concussion-tests, *archived at* http://perma.cc/D35A-XNF2 (quoting independent sideline neurologist Javier Cardenas as saying: "The [Concussion Protocol] is as good as we have today. We do our best. The truth of the matter is, this is a two-way street. Of course, not always are the athletes aware of their injuries. Some of them don't recognize they have a concussion, but when they do recognize, the truth is they have a responsibility to their team, to themselves, to their loved ones of declaring that they don't feel right. The tests are only as sensitive as they can be. They're imperfect.")

79   Fainaru-Wada *supra* note 74 at 63–64 (2013); *see also* Fainaru-Wada at 208 (Carson: "When someone gets hurt, you just find another part . . . [t]he reality is nobody gives a shit about those guys.")

80   Associated Press, *Alex Smith discusses demotion*, ESPN (Nov. 30, 2012), http://espn.go.com/nfl/story/_/id/8691877/alex-smith-san-francisco -49ers-wondering-how-lost-starting-job, *archived at* http://perma.cc/ GE3W-APMY.

81   *Id.*

82   *Id.*

83   *See id.* at 129 (discussing former New York Jets head coach Bill Parcells effectively ordering concussed tight end Kyle Brady to return to the field during 1999 playoff game); *id.* at 213 (discussing New England Patriots

head coach — and Parcells' protégé — Bill Belichick ordering recently concussed linebacker Ted Johnson to participate in contact drills during practice).

84   *See id.* at 79 (former NFL linebacker Gary Plummer discussing his belief, at the time, that when NFL players Al Toon and Merrill Hoge retired due to concussions that they were "pussies.")

85   "The long-established and jointly agreed-upon standard for determining when an injured player is again able to return to play in the NFL, is when 'he could play substantially up to the level of which he had been capable prior to the injury and without undue risk of further aggravation of the injury.'" Memorandum from NFLPA Legal Dep't to Contract Advisors (Jan. 18, 2012). *See also* Chris Kluwe, *How NFL teams manipulate injured players, the system for financial gain*, Sports Illustrated (Sep. 15, 2015), http://www.si.com/cauldron/2015/09/15/nfl-injuries-week -1-preseason-chris-kluwe, *archived at* http://perma.cc/2HBK-557K (describing alleged process by which Clubs force injured players back on to the field to undermine their right to future pay).

86   *Id.*

87   *Id.*

88   *See also* Kimberley A. Martin, *Life after football: How Brandon Marshall, other NFL players prepare for the next stage*, Newsday, Feb. 27, 2016, http://www.newsday.com/sports/football/life-after-football-how-brandon -marshall-other-nfl-players-prepare-for-the-next-stage-1.11517727, *archived at* https://perma.cc/P3J2-9WDB (discussing challenges of players preparing for a life after football, including taking advantage of programs available to them).

89   *Fines & Appeals*, NFL, http://operations.nfl.com/football-ops/fines -appeals/ (last visited May 17, 2016), *archived at* https://perma.cc/ M8FQ-FUJN.

90   *Id.*

91   *Id.*

92   *See* Glenn M. Wong, Essentials of Sports Law, § 4.1 (4th ed. 2010) (discussing liability of co-participants and citing relevant cases).

93   S.W.2d 209 (Miss. App. 1998).

94   *Id.* at 213.

95   F.2d 516 (10th Cir. 1979).

96   *Id.* at 519.

97   *Id.*

98   *Id.* at 520.

99   *Id.* at 521.

100 *Id.* at 524.

101 Saundra Torry, *They'd Love to Help Holyfield Get a Piece of Tyson*, Wash. Post, Jul. 7, 1997, *available at* 1997 WLNR 7365322.

102 In 2003, former Oakland Raider Marcus Williams sued his former teammate Bill Romanowski after Williams suffered a broken eye socket from a punch by Romanowski during a 2003 practice. After a jury awarded Williams $340,000, Romanowski settled the case for $415,000. *Sports Briefing*, N.Y. Times, May 28, 2005, http://www.nytimes.com/2005 /05/28/sports/sports-briefing.html, *archived at* https://perma.cc/ V4CL-49TE.

103 *See* Green v. Pro Football, Inc., 31 F.Supp.3d 714 (D.Md. 2014).

104 *Id.*

105 Email with Seth Grossman, counsel for plaintiff Barrett Green (Nov. 3, 2015).

106 *See* Wong, *supra* note 92, at § 16.1.2 (collecting cases).

107 Mike Reiss and Mike Rodak, *Source: Fanene Agrees to Terms*, ESPNBoston.com (Mar. 14, 2012, 3:45 PM), http://espn.go.com/blog/boston/new -england-patriots/post/_/id/4719093/reports-fanene-agrees-to-terms, *archived at* http://perma.cc/J777-DFFB.

108 Nat'l Football League v. Nat'l Football League Players' Ass'n In re: Jonathan Fanene, 2–3 (CBA Appeals Panel, Feb. 25, 2013).

109 Josh Alper, *Report: Pats Cut Fanene with Failure to Disclose Physical Condition Designation*, ProFootballTalk (Aug. 22, 2012, 8:47 AM),

http://profootballtalk.nbcsports.com/2012/08/22/report-pats-cut-fanene-with-failure-to-disclose-physical-condition-designation/, *archived at* http://perma.cc/G727-E7AV.

110   *See* Nat'l Football League v. Nat'l Football League Players' Ass'n In re: Jonathan Fanene (CBA Appeals Panel, Feb. 25, 2013).

111   *See* 2011 CBA, Art. 4, § 8 ("any Club, any player and any player agent or contract advisor engaged in negotiations for a Player Contract . . . is under an obligation to negotiate in good faith.")

112   Nat'l Football League v. Nat'l Football League Players' Ass'n In re: Jonathan Fanene (CBA Appeals Panel, Feb. 25, 2013).

113   Mike Reiss, *Quick-hit Thoughts Around NFL, Patriots,* ESPNBoston. com (Sept. 21, 2013, 11:15 PM), http://espn.go.com/blog/boston/new-england-patriots/post/_/id/4749358/quick-hit-thoughts-around-nfl-new-england-patriots, *archived at* http://perma.cc/FR5E-SY2B.

114   *See* Cass R. Sunstein, *The Storrs Lectures: Behavioral Economics and Paternalism,* 122 Yale L.J. 1826, 1842–43 (2013) (discussing present bias).

115   Columnist Mike Freeman has also written about the challenges in having players accept changes to the game that are for their benefit. *See, e.g.,* Mike Freeman, Two Minute Warning: How Concussions, Crime, and Controversy Could Kill the NFL (and What the League Can Do to Survive) 229 (2015) (recommending that the NFL "Keep pushing the player safety rules no matter how much the players complain.")

116   Angela Fagerlin, Brian J. Zikmund-Fisher & Peter A. Ubel, *Helping Patients Decide: Ten Steps to Better Risk Communication,* 103 J. Nat'l Cancer Inst. 19, 1436–1443 (2011).

117   Jennifer J. Infanti et al., *A literature review on effective risk communication for the prevention and control of communicable diseases in Europe—Insights into health communication,* Eur. Centre for Disease Prevention & Control (2013), http://ecdc.europa.eu/en/publications/Publications/risk-communication-literary-reviewjan-2013.pdf, *archived at* http://perma.cc/ZGN2-YZU6.

118   *See* NFLPA Player Affairs and Development, *About NFLPA—Department Contacts,* NFLPA, https://nflpa.com/about/department-contacts (last visited Aug. 7, 2015), *archived at* https://perma.cc/SYF5-6D6H?type=pdf.

119   *See id.* (listing the Clubs for which each Player Advocate is responsible).

120   The NFL provided us with a copy of the 2016 Training Camp presentation.

121   Russell Sellers, *Soldiers Helping Soldiers—Battle Buddies Assist in Military Training, Life,* U.S. Army (Aug. 26, 2010), http://www.army.mil/article/44252/Soldiers_helping_Soldiers__Battle_buddies_assist_in_military_training__life/, *archived at* http://perma.cc/ABQ9-ULR9.

122   Russel Sellers, *Soldiers Helping Soldiers: Battle Buddies Help Each Other During Tough Times,* Def. Dep't Documents, Sept. 16, 2010, *available at* 2010 WLNR 18507888.

123   *See id;* James V. Dunz, *What It Means to be a Battle Buddy,* U.S. Army, http://www.wood.army.mil/engrmag/PDFs%20for%20May-Aug%2010/Dunz.pdf (last visited Aug. 7, 2015), *archived at* http://perma.cc/HM75-YVRP.

124   *See* Peter F. Ramsberger et al., *Evaluation of the Buddy Team Assignment Program,* U.S. Army Research Inst. for the Behavioral and Soc. Sci. (2002), http://www.dtic.mil/dtic/tr/fulltext/u2/a408486.pdf, *archived at* https://perma.cc/W4V7-TWGY?type=pdf.

125   *See, e.g., Quotes from NFLPA Press Conference,* NFLPA (Feb. 4, 2016), https://www.nflpa.com/news/all-news/quotes-from-nflpa-sb50-press-conference, *archived at* https://perma.cc/2GZH-FQ37 (quarterback Matt Hasselback: "[Y]ou felt like you were a wimp if you were honest with your team doctor, trainer or a teammate or coach if something was wrong with your head"); Mike Freeman, Two Minute Warning: How Concussions, Crime, and Controversy Could Kill the NFL (and What the League Can Do to Survive) xv, 231 (2015) (mentioning players hiding injuries). *See also* Mark A. Rothstein, Jessica Roberts, Tee L. Guidotti, *Limiting Occupational Medical Evaluations Under the Americans with Disabilities Act and the Genetic Information Nondiscrimination Act,* 41 Am. J. L. & Med. 523, 531 (2015) ("In general, employees are reluctant to disclose health information that might result in a limitation on their ability to work.")

126   *See* Rothstein, *supra* n. 125 ("When employees fail to disclose symptoms or other pertinent medical information, it may impede the physician's ability to make an accurate assessment of the individual's risk or fitness for duty.")

127   *See* 2011 CBA, Art. 44 (discussing the Injury Grievance process).

128   Tom Delbanco et al., *Inviting Patients to Read Their Doctors' Notes: A Quasi-experimental Study and a Look Ahead,* Annals of Internal Med. 461 (2012).

129   NFL Comments and Corrections (June 24, 2016).

Part 2: **The Medical Team**

Club
Doctors

Athletic
Trainers

Second
Opinion
Doctors

Neutral
Doctors

Personal
Doctors

Retained by Club

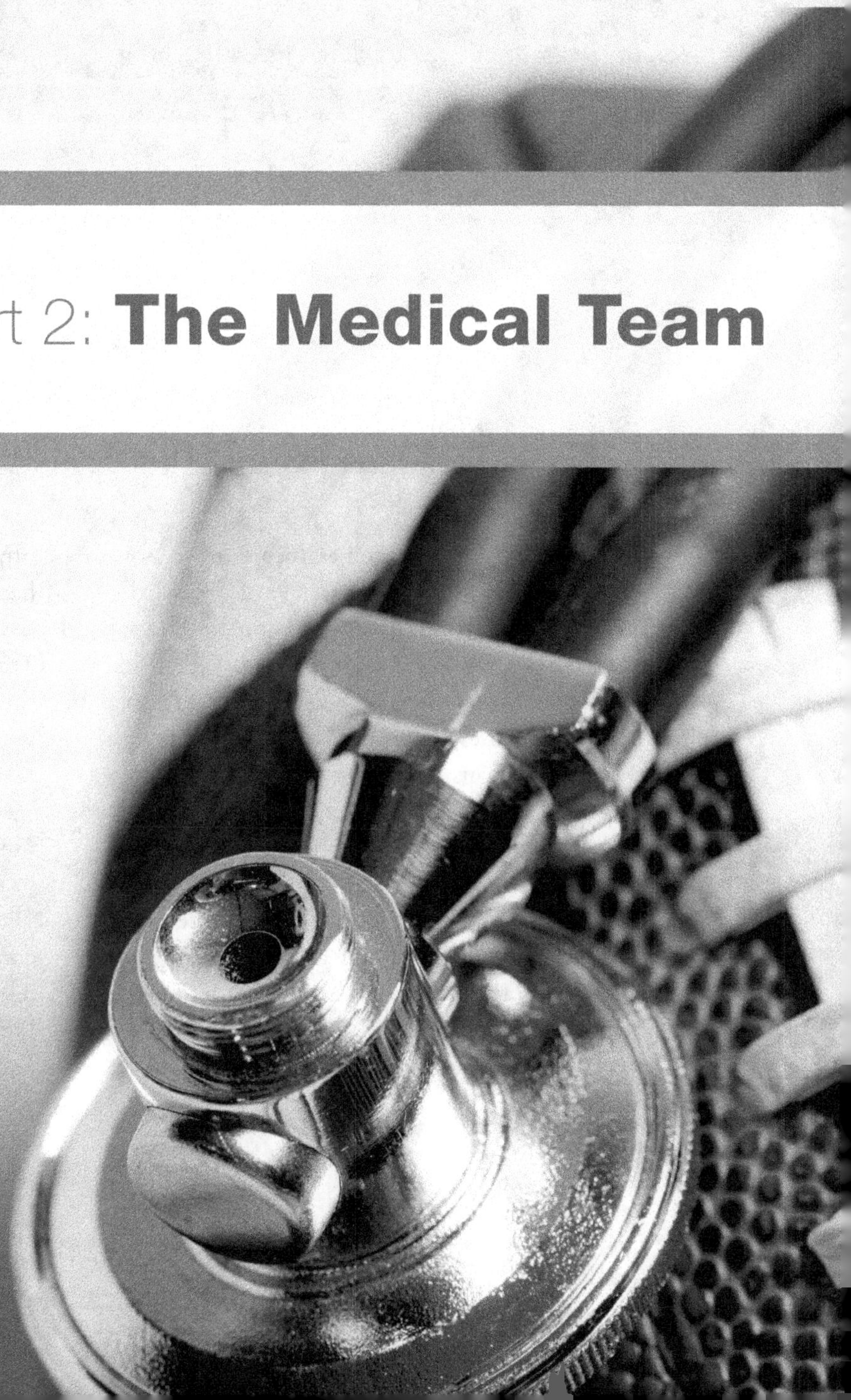

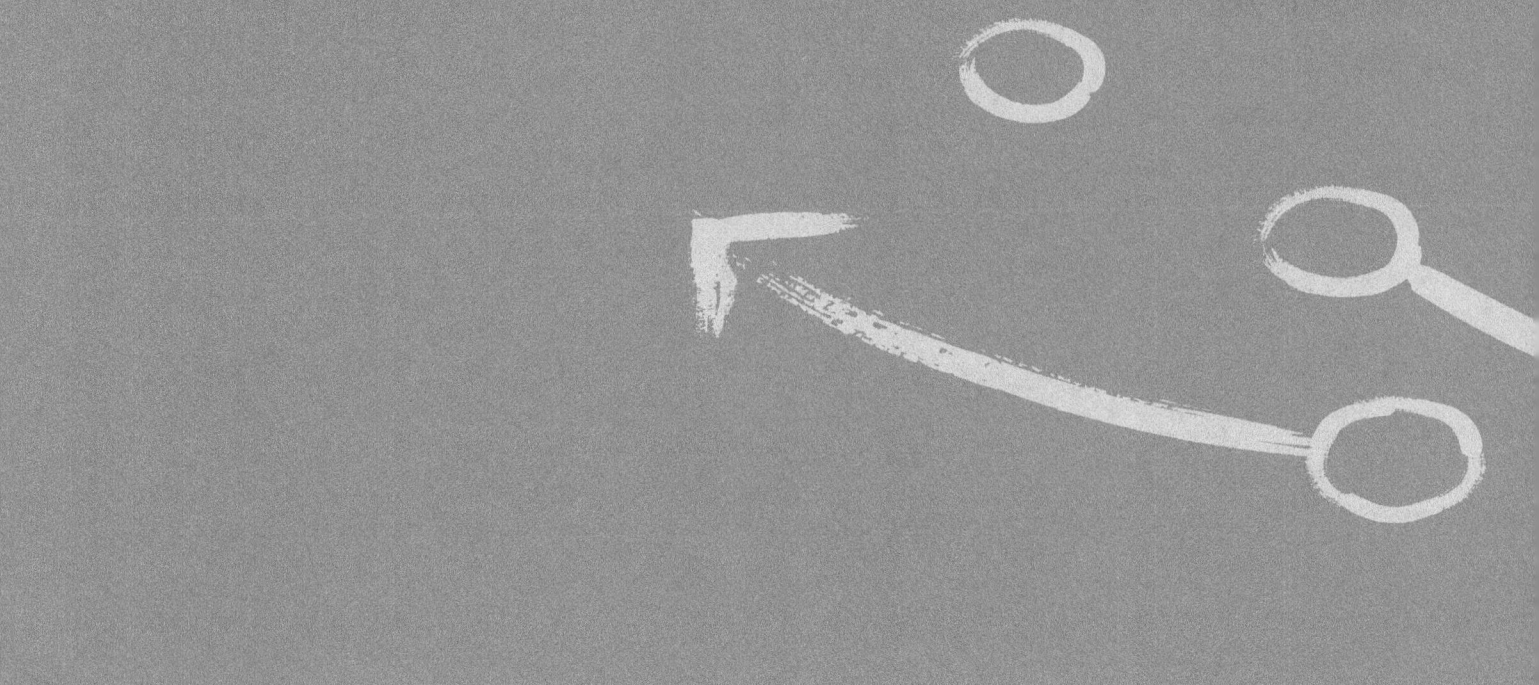

Part 2 concerns the various medical professionals who provide healthcare to the players in assorted contexts and circumstances: club doctors; athletic trainers; second opinion doctors; neutral doctors; and, personal doctors. As the players' healthcare providers, these stakeholders' actions are crucial components of player health. Some of these stakeholders reside within the club, others within the League, and still others operate outside those systems. But all must work closely with the player if player health is to be protected and promoted to the greatest extent possible.

We acknowledge that there are healthcare professionals other than those discussed in this Part who work with NFL players, including but not limited to physical therapists, massage therapists, chiropractors, dentists, nutritionists, and psychologists. Importantly, each of these groups of professionals has their own set of legal and ethical obligations governing their relationships with players. While a healthcare professional from any one of these groups might play an important role in a player's health, it is our understanding that their roles are not so systematic and continuous to require in-depth personalized discussion, *i.e.,* they are typically not as enmeshed within the culture of the NFL club to generate some of the concerns that are discussed in this Part. Moreover, the obligations of and recommendations toward these professionals are substantially covered by other Chapters of this Report. To the extent any of these healthcare professionals are employed or retained by the Club, Chapter 2: Club Doctors and Chapter 3: Athletic Trainers are of particular relevance. To the extent any of these healthcare professionals are retained and consulted with by players themselves, then Chapter 6: Personal Doctors is relevant.

Finally, we remind the reader that while we have tried to make the Chapters accessible for standalone reading, certain background or relevant information may be contained in other parts or chapters, specifically Part 1 discussing Players and Part 3 discussing the NFL and NFLPA. Thus, we encourage the reader to review other parts as needed for important context.

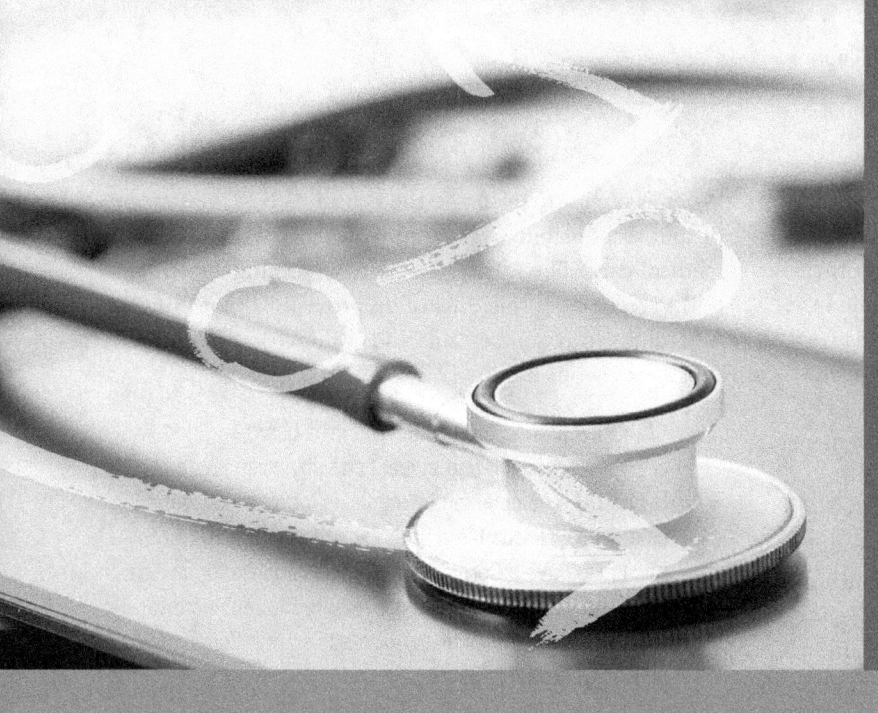

Chapter 2

Club Doctors

Club doctors are clearly an important stakeholder in player health. They diagnose and treat players for a variety of ailments, while making recommendations to players concerning those ailments. At the same time, the doctor has obligations to the club, particularly to advise it about the health status of players. While players and clubs often share an interest in player health — both want players to be healthy so they can play at peak performance — as we discuss in this chapter there are several areas where their interests are in conflict. In these areas, the intersection of the club doctors' different obligations creates significant legal and ethical quandaries that may threaten player health. Most importantly, even if club doctors are providing the best care they can to the players, the current structure of their relationship with the club creates inherent problems in the treatment relationship. It is this structural problem about which we are most concerned, as discussed below.

Before we begin our analysis, it is important to point out that throughout this chapter we emphasize that the practice of club doctors is likely heterogeneous from club to club at least to some extent. For example, some clubs may be more actively engaged with club doctors, while others may be more hands-off. Nevertheless, we were denied the opportunity to interview club doctors as part of this Report to gain a better understanding of their work. In November 2014, we notified the NFL that we intended to seek interviews with club personnel, including general managers, coaches, doctors, and athletic trainers. The NFL subsequently advised us that it was "unable to consent to the interviews" on the grounds that "the information sought could directly impact several lawsuits currently pending against the league." Without the consent of the NFL, we did not believe that the interviews would be successful and thus did not pursue the interviews at that time; instead, we have provided these stakeholders the opportunity to review draft chapters of the Report. We again requested to interview club personnel in July 2016 but the NFL did not respond to that request. The NFL was otherwise cooperative. It reviewed the Report and facilitated its review by club doctors and athletic trainers. The NFL also provided information relevant to this Report, including copies of the NFL's Medical Sponsorship Policy (discussed in Chapter 2: Club Doctors) and other information about the relationships between clubs and doctors.

In April 2016, we engaged the NFL Physicians Society (NFLPS), the professional organization for club doctors, about reviewing relevant portions of a draft of this Report and related work. The NFLPS at that time questioned how many club doctors we had interviewed in developing the Report, apparently unaware of the NFL's prior response to our planned interviews. We were surprised to find that the NFL had not previously discussed the matter with the NFLPS and immediately invited the NFLPS to have individual club doctors interviewed, an offer the NFLPS ultimately declined. Instead, it chose to proceed with reviewing our work and providing feedback in that manner.

Due to limitations on our access to club doctors we cannot generate club-by-club accounts of current practices. The result may mask a level of variation in current practice, a limitation we acknowledge.

A Background

When it comes to ensuring the health of NFL players, much of that responsibility falls on the doctors who provide them medical care. The 2011 collective bargaining agreement (CBA) recognizes this, including provisions that obligate NFL clubs to retain certain kinds of doctors. We summarize those provisions here:

- **Club Physicians:** Clubs must retain[a] a board certified orthopedic surgeon and at least one physician board certified in internal medicine, family medicine, or emergency medicine. All physicians hired after execution of the 2011 CBA must also have a Certificate of Added Qualification in Sports Medicine. In addition, clubs are required to retain consultants in the neurological, cardiovascular, nutritional, and, neuropsychological fields.[1]

- **Physicians at Games:** "All home teams shall retain at least one [Rapid Sequence Intubation] RSI physician who is board certified in emergency medicine, anesthesia, pulmonary medicine, or thoracic surgery, and who has documented competence in RSI intubations in the past twelve months. This physician shall be the neutral physician dedicated to game-day medical intervention for on-field or locker room catastrophic emergencies."[2]

As discussed in more detail in Chapter 7: The NFL and NFLPA, Section C: A History of the NFL's and NFLPA's Approaches to Player Health, the 2011 CBA added many new provisions concerning player health, including those above. However, also as detailed in that section, the changes to player health provisions in the CBA have largely been incremental, with most changes occurring as part of each CBA negotiation (others occur as part of side letter agreements between CBA negotiations). While these changes have gradually added more protections for player health, they may have also resulted in a fragmented system of care.

Of note, the above provisions added to the 2011 CBA do not require clubs to retain and have available neurological doctors at the games. The absence of this requirement is offset by the Concussion Protocol's requirement that for every game each club be assigned an Unaffiliated Neurotrauma Consultant" to assist in the diagnosis of concussions (*see* Appendix A).

Most (if not all) of the doctors retained by NFL clubs are members of the NFLPS. Founded in 1966, the NFLPS's stated mission "is to provide excellence in the medical and surgical care of the athletes in the National Football League

---

a   The CBA does not define "retain" or otherwise dictate the requisite scope of involvement by the various doctors.

and to provide direction and support for the athletic trainers in charge of the care for these athletes."[3] Approximately 175 doctors work with the 32 NFL clubs,[4] an average of 5.5 per club. The NFLPS holds annual meetings at the NFL Combine to discuss medical and scientific issues pertinent to its membership.[5]

According to NFLPS, 22 of the 32 club's head orthopedists and 14 of the 32 club's head "medicine" doctors are board certified in sports medicine.[6] In addition, although the 2011 CBA requires club doctors to have a Certificate of Added Qualification in Sports Medicine, currently only 11 of the 32 head club doctors have such a certificate. The remaining club doctors were with clubs before the 2011 CBA and were grandfathered in under the new policy.

Of the 32 clubs, only two directly employ any of their club doctors while the other 30 teams enter into independent contractor arrangements with the doctors.[7] The relevance of this distinction will be discussed in further detail below.

In most of the contracts, the club doctor reports to the club's general manager, who would have the authority to terminate the doctor.[8] The NFL does not have any policies that pertain to supervisory control of medical personnel by coaches or club personnel.[9] According to the NFL, there are no clubs in which the club doctor is supervised by the head coach.[10] Without being able to independently verify the NFL's claim, we nonetheless point out that there is no explicit prohibition against a coach having supervisory authority over a club doctor.

The quality of medical care provided by club doctors is obviously an important consideration in this work. For approximately the past 25 years, there has been a practice that has occasionally caused some to call into question the quality of healthcare being provided to players: the practice of doctors or healthcare organizations sponsoring NFL clubs or otherwise paying for the right to be the club's healthcare provider(s). Such arrangements raise concerns that clubs are retaining the doctors who provide the clubs the most money as opposed to the doctors who are most qualified and likely to provide to highest level of care.

The NFL's League Policy on Club Medical Services Agreements and Sponsorships (Medical Sponsorship Policy), discussed next, governs these types of arrangements and the relationship between NFL clubs and club doctors.

Figure 2-A: The Current Structure of Club Medical Staff

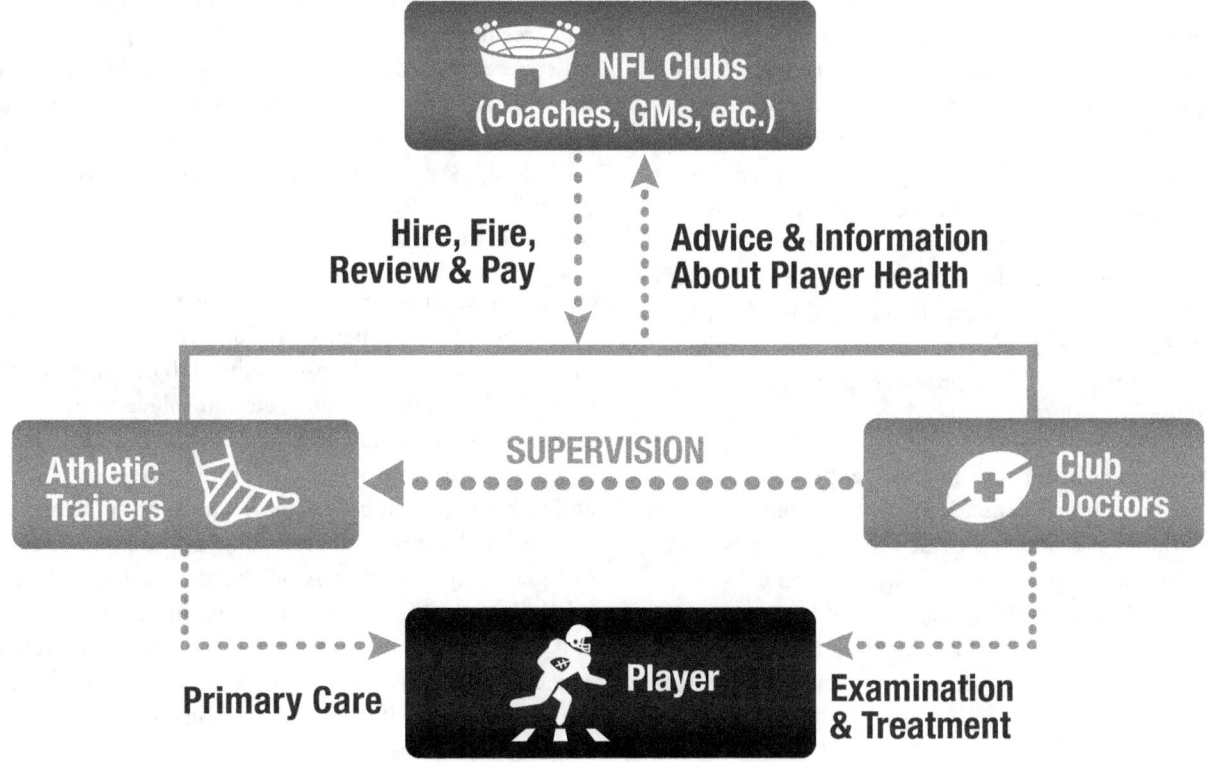

1) THE NFL'S MEDICAL SPONSORSHIP POLICY

The NFL first instituted the Medical Sponsorship Policy in 2004.[11] It prohibited clubs from entering into agreements "under which hospitals, medical facilities or physician groups were designated as club sponsors[b] and obtained the right to provide various types of medical care to the club's players and other employees."[12] Although acknowledging that such arrangements had "economic" benefits to the clubs, NFL Commissioner Paul Tagliabue determined it was best to prohibit them in light of "questions raised by players and the NFLPA," "criticism in both the lay and medical communities," and reference to them by "plaintiffs' attorneys in medical malpractice cases."[13] Additionally, Commissioner Tagliabue noted that such arrangements had resulted in an increase in players obtaining second opinions, "which, because they are paid for by the clubs, erodes the economic benefit to the sponsorship agreements."[14]

Although the Medical Sponsorship Policy was not put into place until 2004, according to former Los Angeles Raiders Club doctor Rob Huizenga, doctors began paying $1 million or more for the right to be a club's doctor in the late 1980s.[15] Huizenga noted that the doctors "could use their esteemed position as team doctor to get almost unlimited referrals[.]"[16] Furthermore, according to former Seattle Seahawks Club doctor Pierce Scranton, when the Houston Oilers moved to Tennessee and were renamed the Titans in 1997, the Titans and Baptist Memorial Hospital entered into an agreement of unknown duration whereby the hospital paid the Titans a total of $45 million for the right to be the official healthcare provider of the Titans.[17] Scranton also suggested that the agreement caused the Titans to encourage players to have all of their surgeries performed at Baptist Memorial Hospital.[c] Finally, a 2004 *New York Times* article claimed that approximately half of the teams in the Big Four sports leagues (NFL, MLB, NBA and NHL) had entered into medical sponsorship agreements, with some healthcare providers paying as much as $1.5 million annually.[18]

The 2004 Medical Sponsorship Policy explicitly permitted clubs to continue to enter into sponsorship agreements with healthcare providers, provided the agreements did not involve the healthcare provider delivering medical services to the club.[19] For example, a hospital could enter into an agreement with the club to advertise itself as the "Official Hospital of [club]" provided that very same agreement did not also call for the hospital to provide medical services to the club. The hospital could have, however, entered into a *separate* agreement to provide medical services to the club wholly apart from the sponsorship agreement. Last, under the 2004 Medical Sponsorship Policy, clubs were required to submit a copy of any proposed sponsorship agreement with a healthcare provider to the NFL for approval before execution.[20]

The Medical Sponsorship Policy was amended in 2012 in two principal ways: (1) clubs were prohibited from entering into medical services agreements whereby a particular healthcare provider became the *exclusive* provider of medical services to the club; and, (2) clubs were required to contract directly with the club's internist, orthopedist, and head physician, *i.e.*, clubs were prohibited from entering into agreements with entities (*e.g.*, hospitals) for the provision of these medical services.[21]

According to the 2012 Medical Sponsorship Policy, the NFL undertook the amendments after reviewing "relevant policies promulgated by professional associations (*e.g.*, American Orthopaedic Society for Sports Medicine) or that exist in other professional sports, or that have been recommended by experts in medical ethics and conflict of interest."[22]

The Medical Sponsorship Policy was amended again in 2014.[23] The 2014 amendments included: (1) a prohibition on agreements whereby the club doctor reports to a medical services provider (MSP) (defined below) rather than the club; (2) a prohibition on agreements whereby an MSP reserves the right to select the doctors mandated by the CBA; and, (3) a requirement that each club have a senior executive annually execute a Certification of Compliance with the Medical Sponsorship Policy.[24]

The 2014 Medical Sponsorship Policy also defined "Sponsorship Agreements" as "agreements with MSPs involving the sale or license by the club of commercial assets such as naming rights, stadium signage, advertising inventory within club-controlled media, promotional inventory (*e.g.*, day-of-game promotions), hospitality, and rights to use club trademarks for marketing and promotional purposes." According to the Policy, MSPs include "hospitals, universities, medical practice groups, rehabilitation facilities, laboratories, imaging centers and other entities that provide medical care and related services." Although doctors are not specifically included in the definition of MSPs, the NFL includes doctors as MSPs for purposes of the Policy.[25]

---

b   The 2004 Medical Sponsorship Policy did not define "sponsors."
c   Pierce E. Scranton, Jr., Playing Hurt: Treating and Evaluating the Warriors of the NFL 154 (2001) ("Does any Titans player wonder why he is so strongly encouraged to get his operation at Baptist?").

At its core, the Medical Sponsorship Policy permits clubs to enter into a Sponsorship Agreement with an MSP, but prohibits such agreements that also include the provision of medical services. Stated another way, "[n]o Club may enter into a contract for the provision of medical services to its players that is interdependent with, or in any way tied to a Sponsorship Agreement with a [MSP]." The Medical Sponsorship Policy does not define "interdependent" and instead the NFL reviews the arrangements to ensure there is no interdependence.[26]

The Policy also explicitly declares that clubs are permitted to enter into agreements with MSPs whereby the MSP obtains the right to advertise itself as an "official" or "proud" "sponsor," "partner," or "provider."[27] A review of club websites and media guides shows that at least 25 clubs currently have some type of "official" healthcare sponsor or partner.

Additionally, based on our plain text reading of the Medical Sponsorship Policy, it does not prohibit MSPs from paying for the right to provide medical services to players and also does not limit an MSP's ability to bargain for the right to provide healthcare to a club by offering discounted or free services. In reviewing a draft of this chapter, the NFLPS stated that no MSP currently pays for the right to provide medical services to players. Additionally, the NFL stated that the Medical Sponsorship Policy does prohibit MSPs from paying for the right to provide medical services and from offering discounted or free services. We disagree with the NFL's reading. While the NFL may enforce the Medical Sponsorship Policy in such a way, we disagree that the plain text of the Policy prohibits such arrangements. In any event, it appears that the NFL agrees with us that the Policy *should* prohibit any club doctor from paying for the right to pay for the right to provide healthcare to players. If the Policy is intended to prohibit club doctors from paying for the right to provide medical services to players, the text of the Policy should be clarified.

Importantly, even in situations where an MSP enters into an agreement to provide medical services to a club but has not entered into a sponsorship agreement of any kind, the MSP can benefit from the association. The MSP could still identify itself as a healthcare provider for the club on its website and in advertisements, within the bounds of relevant intellectual property, professional advertising, and consumer protection laws and regulations. In other words, the MSP likely could not use the club's logo without permission or try to make it appear that the club was actively endorsing the MSP's services. In 2004, the marketing director of Methodist Hospital explained the value of the hospital's association with the Houston Texans:

We track phone calls coming in from new patients . . . . The No. 1 driver of our calls is the association with our local teams. People say they heard that Methodist is where the players go, so it must be the best. It's not a coincidence that we are the best, but there isn't a better way to convince them. That's a win-win situation.[28]

Finally, it is worth noting that institutional MSPs can be a party to the doctor's contract with the club to the extent that such an arrangement is necessary for medical malpractice insurance or for practice privileges. In such situations, the contract must include a provision confirming the club's right to retain the doctor regardless of that doctor's relationship with the institution.

When asked for its position on medical sponsorship in the NFL, the NFLPA stated only that it "insisted upon changes that minimized conflicts of interest resulting in changes to the NFL's Medical Sponsorship Policy in 2014/15." The NFLPA declined to provide further detail on the negotiations or what specific changes it insisted upon, indicating that the discussions were confidential and that the Medical Sponsorship Policy is unilaterally promulgated by the NFL. The NFLPA indicated that its "sole objective" regarding the Medical Sponsorship Policy "is to reduce conflicts of interest and to ensure the best care possible for its members." Nevertheless, the NFLPA did not indicate that it is opposed to medical sponsorship agreements. In addition, we recognize the medical sponsorship agreements provide clubs, and thus the players, with a lucrative source of revenue.

Below are examples of relationships between MSPs, including doctors, and clubs with a discussion of whether these relationships would be prohibited or permitted by the 2014 Medical Sponsorship Policy. However, it is important to keep in mind that the 2014 Medical Sponsorship Policy is complex and, at times, unclear. Additionally, the document is not collectively bargained and there is no generally available guidance. Thus, what follows is our best interpretation of the Policy as written.

In reviewing a draft of this Report, the NFL stated that it "disagree[d] entirely with the conclusions reached in Table 2-B,"[29] without explaining why it reads the plain text of the Policy so differently than we do. The fact that two sets of trained attorneys (those who authored this Report and those at the NFL) interpret the Policy differently demonstrates that it should be clarified. Ideally, the NFL will make the Policy public to allow for further discussion and review.

Table 2-A:
Arrangements Prohibited by Medical Sponsorship Policy

Description	Explanation
Agreement with MSP to provide medical services to club on an exclusive basis.	Policy prohibits agreements with MSPs for the exclusive provision of medical services, thus enabling clubs and players to seek necessary medical care elsewhere.
Agreement allowing institutional MSP to select the doctors mandated by the CBA to provide care to the club's players.	Policy prohibits agreements that permit MSP to select CBA-mandated doctors; these doctors must be selected by the club.
Agreement with MSP to provide medical services to club on a non-exclusive basis alongside the right to post advertisements in the club's stadium using club trademarks.	Each of these agreements would be permitted on its own, but not jointly; Policy prohibits medical services agreements that are interdependent with Sponsorship Agreements with MSPs.
Agreement with MSP to provide medical services to club on a non-exclusive basis alongside naming rights to the club's practice facility.	Each of these agreements would be permitted on its own, but not jointly; Policy prohibits medical services agreements that are interdependent with Sponsorship Agreements with MSPs.
Agreement with doctor to provide medical services to club on a non-exclusive basis alongside agreement for his or her institutional MSP to post advertisements in the club's stadium using club trademarks.	Each of these agreements would be permitted on its own, but not jointly; Policy prohibits medical services agreements that are interdependent with Sponsorship Agreements with MSPs.
Agreement with doctor to provide medical services to club on a non-exclusive basis but doctor reports to institutional MSP concerning care provided to players.	Policy requires doctors to report directly to the club.

As these charts demonstrate, while the NFL has made progress in regulating the payment to and from club doctors for sponsorship, on a plain reading of the Policy, there are still a number of ethically fraught arrangements the current Policy appears to leave in place.[d]

Despite its gaps, the NFL's Medical Sponsorship Policy appears to be the most robust and protective of player health in professional sports. Major League Baseball's (MLB) medical sponsorship policy prohibits sponsorship arrangements between clubs and medical providers that included "the right of the [sponsor] to be the medical service provider for the Club's players and employees." Nevertheless, MLB has approved sponsorship arrangements with medical providers where "the Club has had a pre-existing relationship with the hospital or doctors prior to the sponsorship, and the terms of the health care agreement were unaffected by the sponsorship."[30] The National Basketball Association (NBA) only prohibits sponsorship

arrangements where the selection of healthcare providers is "based primarily on a sponsorship relationship."[31] Thus, the NBA does not prohibit agreements whereby a healthcare provider pays for the right to be the club doctor and to be a sponsor of the club, provided the sponsorship is not the primary reason for the relationship. The National Hockey League and Major League Soccer refused to provide information to us concerning a possible medical sponsorship policy.

How the leagues compare on this and other important player health issues is the subject of our forthcoming Report, *Comparing the Health-Related Policies and Practices of the NFL to Other Professional Sports Leagues.*

---

d In reviewing this Report, the National Athletic Trainers Association stated that "[p]hysician practices paying clubs to serve as team physicians may result in significant conflicts of interest (COI) in the care of the NFL athlete. Health care should be based on best practices."

Table 2-B:
Arrangements Permitted by Medical Sponsorship Policy

Description	Explanation	Potential Concerns with Practices Still Permitted
Agreement with MSP to pay the club to provide medical services to club on a non-exclusive basis.	Policy does not prohibit MSPs from paying for the right to provide medical services.	Club might choose MSP that is willing to pay the most rather than the best MSP.
Agreement with MSP to provide medical services to club on a non-exclusive basis, whereby MSP has agreed to no compensation or compensation at rates below the MSP's standard rate and market rates.	Policy does not prohibit MSPs from discounting the costs of their services for the right to provide medical services.	Club might choose MSP willing to charge lowest rates rather than the best MSP.
Agreement with MSP to provide medical services to club on a non-exclusive basis and MSP has the right to call itself the "official" doctor or healthcare provider of the club.	Policy expressly permits agreements that permit MSPs to call themselves the "official" doctor or healthcare provider.	MSP will attach monetary value to "official designation," and alter payment structure as a result, leading to clubs choosing MSPs based on reduced rates rather than skills.
Agreement with MSP to provide medical services to club on a non-exclusive basis and a separate agreement to post advertisements in the club's stadium using club trademarks.	Policy permits MSPs and clubs to enter into medical services and Sponsorship Agreements so long as they are not "interdependent."	Whether the two agreements are "interdependent" is difficult to enforce. Implied agreements and long-standing practices could result in clubs choosing MSPs based on Sponsorship Agreements rather than skills.
Agreement with MSP to pay the club for the right to call itself the "official" healthcare provider of the club and to post advertisements in the club's stadium using club trademarks but does not actually provide any medical services to the club.[e]	Policy expressly permits Sponsorship Agreements with MSPs "so long as these agreements do not involve the provision of medical service to players."	Does not directly affect player health but raises concerns about whether the general public will falsely rely on the MSP's declaration that it is the "official" healthcare provider.

B Introduction to Current Legal Obligations and Ethical Codes

At the outset it is important to restate and clarify the obvious. Club doctors provide care to players while also having some type of contractual or employment relationship with, and thus obligations to, the club. Indeed, club doctors' principal responsibilities are: (1) providing healthcare to the players; (2) helping players determine when they are ready to return to play; (3) helping clubs determine when players are ready to return to play; (4) examining players the club is considering employing, e.g., at the NFL Combine or as part of free agency; and, (5) helping clubs to determine whether a player's contract should be terminated because of the player's physical condition, e.g., whether an injury will prevent the player from playing.[32]

---

e   While some might find this practice to be misleading, raising other potential legal issues, those issues are not pertinent to player health and thus we do not address them here.

Figure 2-B: The Current Responsibilities of Club Doctors

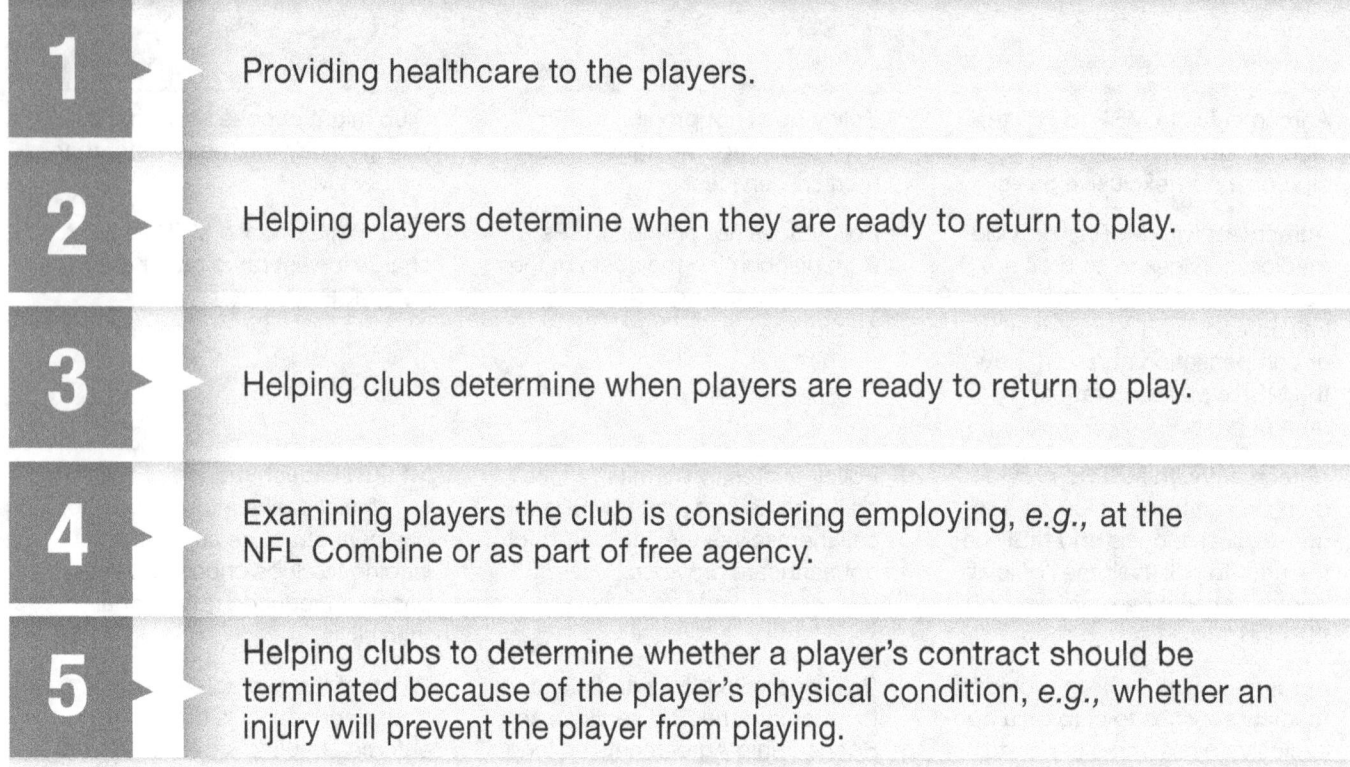

1 Providing healthcare to the players.

2 Helping players determine when they are ready to return to play.

3 Helping clubs determine when players are ready to return to play.

4 Examining players the club is considering employing, *e.g.*, at the NFL Combine or as part of free agency.

5 Helping clubs to determine whether a player's contract should be terminated because of the player's physical condition, *e.g.*, whether an injury will prevent the player from playing.

The first two responsibilities we will refer to as "Services to Player" and the last three responsibilities we will refer to as "Services to Club." The Services to Player scenario is one in which the club doctor is treating and advising the player, including taking into consideration the player's athletic goals, whereas the Services to Club scenario is one in which the doctor is exclusively advising the club. As will be discussed in detail below, in theory, club doctors' legal and ethical obligations vary depending on the two situations. Nevertheless, the club doctor's two roles are not separated in practice, potentially resulting in tension in the player healthcare system. On the one hand, club doctors engage in a doctor-patient relationship with the player, providing the player care and advice that is in the player's best interests. On the other hand, clubs engage doctors because medical information about and assessment of players is necessary to clubs' decisions related to a player's ability to perform at a sufficiently high level in the short- and long-term. These dual roles for club doctors may sometimes conflict because players and clubs often have conflicting interests, but club doctors are called to serve two parties.

Although it is common to use the word "patient" to describe the player in both of these situations, there are important differences between the Services to Player versus Services to Club setting. The essence of the doctor-patient relationship is the undertaking by a physician to diagnose and/or treat the person being diagnosed or treated with reasonable professional skill.[33] Thus, the doctor-patient relationship is established when the physician undertakes to diagnose, treat, or advise the patient as to a course of treatment.[34] Generally, this is established by mutual consent and can be based on an express or implied contract.[35] However, in the Services to Club situation, there is a limited doctor-patient relationship (or none at all), which will explain the different legal and ethical obligations.

In reviewing a draft of this Report, the NFL repeatedly analogized the NFL player healthcare model to other industries where employers provide healthcare for their employees. Indeed, doctors provide care to employees in a variety of occupational settings, such as in the military, law enforcement, and factories and other industrial settings.[36] However, the fact that these doctors, like NFL club doctors, may be placed in a position of structural conflict, whereby the doctor can be conflicted between doing what is best for the employee and what is best for the employer, is not helpful. While our review of the legal and ethical literature on occupational medicine did not reveal a one size fits all resolution to this problem,[37] our recommendations in this chapter focus on the conflict of interest embedded in the NFL healthcare structure. The fact that these structural conflicts exist elsewhere is not a defense to a problematic structure in the NFL.

Below, we discuss the sources of current legal obligations and current ethical codes and then apply those obligations and codes to both the Services to Player and Services to Club settings. Finally, we conclude this section by discussing some additional ethical considerations.

1) SOURCES OF CURRENT LEGAL OBLIGATIONS[f]

Club doctors' legal obligations derive from three sources: (1) common law; (2) statutes and regulations; and, (3) contracts.

Common law[g] and statutory obligations are generally determined by state courts (through case law) and legislatures, respectively. Each state generally has a statute setting forth the minimum requirements and qualifications to be a licensed doctor.[38] In addition, the states generally have statutes setting forth both generalized and, at times, more specific, treatment prohibitions and obligations.[39] The state statutes then empower a board or office to implement and enforce the statutes,[40] such as New York's Office of Professional Medical Conduct and The Medical Board of California. These medical boards consist largely of healthcare professionals and, for this reason, the medical field is generally considered to be self-regulated.[41] The medical boards have the authority to investigate professional misconduct by physicians and to issue appropriate discipline, which is subject to review by the courts.[42] In determining whether professional misconduct occurred, the medical boards often consult relevant statutes and regulations, as well as codes of medical ethics.

Club doctors' contractual obligations consist of two types: (1) those obligations mandated by the CBA; and, (2) those obligations mandated by the doctor's professional agreement with the club. Doctors' contractual agreements are private and not readily available; thus this chapter focuses primarily on the CBA-mandated obligations. Section D: Current Practices provides more information on the types of contractual arrangements clubs have with their doctors.

2) SOURCES OF CURRENT ETHICAL CODES

There are a wide variety of ethical codes relevant to club doctors, the most prominent of which is the American Medical Association (AMA) Code of Medical Ethics (AMA Code).[43] The AMA is a voluntary organization for doctors

with a mission "[t]o promote the art and science of medicine and the betterment of public health."[44] As a voluntary organization not all doctors are members of the AMA but the AMA Code nonetheless is still very influential.[h] The legal significance of the AMA Code is discussed in Section G: Enforcement.

In addition, NFL clubs retain in some form a wide range of doctors, including but not limited to orthopedists, internists, family medicine specialists, emergency medicine specialists, neurologists, neurosurgeons, cardiologists, and psychologists.[45] Each of these specialties generally has its own professional societies and organizations that might also have ethical codes or practice guidelines relevant to the specialty and thus also to NFL players. In particular, in 2013, the American Academy of Neurology issued guidelines for the evaluation and management of concussions in sports.[46] Similarly, there are also codes of ethics specific to doctors working in occupational settings. For example, the American College of Occupational and Environmental Medicine (ACOEM) has a Code of Ethics[47] as does the International Commission on Occupational Health.[48] These documents provide important direction on appropriate and best practices. Despite this diversity, nearly all doctors are subject to the AMA Code or a variation thereof. Thus, we only discuss those societies' ethical regulations that exceed or otherwise supplement the requirements of the AMA Code.[i]

Finally, doctors working in the sports medicine field have codified their own ethics rules. The leading international sports medicine organization is the Fédération Internationale de Médicine du Sport (FIMS), founded in 1928 in conjunction with the growth of the modern Olympic Games.[49] FIMS is an international organization comprised of national sports medicine associations across five continents that seeks to maximize athlete health and performance.[50] The American College of Sports Medicine is the American member of FIMS.[51] FIMS publishes a five-page Code of Ethics that is sports-specific and thus is relevant to this Report in its entirety.[52] Similar principles are espoused

h   The AMA Code was most recently amended in June 2016 and was still in the process of being edited as of the date of publication. Nevertheless, no substantive changes are expected and we believed it was important to use the most recent version of the AMA Code.

i   The other professional organizations whose codes of ethics we examined are the American College of Sports Medicine, American Academy of Family Physicians, American Academy of Orthopaedic Surgeons, American Association of Orthopaedic Surgeons, American Medical Society for Sports Medicine, American Orthopaedic Society for Sports Medicine, American Academy of Physical Medicine and Rehabilitation, American Osteopathic Society, American College of Physicians, American Board of Internal Medicine, American College of Physicians, American Society of Internal Medicine, American College of Emergency Physicians, American Academy of Emergency Medicine, American Association of Neurological Surgeons, American College of Cardiology, American College of Radiology, Radiological Society of North America, Academy for Sports Dentistry, American Dental Association, American Society of Anesthesiologists, National Association of Emergency Medical Technicians, and National Association of EMS Physicians.

f   The legal obligations described herein are not an exhaustive list but are those we believe are most relevant to player health.

g   Common law refers to "[t]he body of law derived from judicial decisions, rather than from statutes or constitutions." Black's Law Dictionary (9th ed. 2009).

in the *Team Physician Consensus Statement* published collectively by the American College of Sports Medicine, American Academy of Family Physicians, American Academy of Orthopaedic Surgeons, American Medical Society for Sports Medicine, American Orthopaedic Society for Sports Medicine, and the American Osteopathic Academy of Sports Medicine.[53]

The NFLPS confirmed during its review of a draft of this chapter that it does not have a Code of Ethics.[j]

It is important to point out that, at times, some of the existing ethical codes relevant to club doctors contain statements that appear internally inconsistent, in conflict with relevant laws, or incongruent with modern practices and realities. In particular, the codes are sometimes unclear about whether a player's long-term health should always be the absolute priority, as well as how player medical information should be handled. These issues will be pointed out along the way, but they do not necessarily demand criticism or revision in every instance. Indeed, legitimate and important ethical principles often come into conflict with one another as applied to particular scenarios, and the work is in determining the appropriate balance when principles must be applied to the facts at hand. The principles governing this Report are a perfect example, as the principle of Health Primacy may sometimes conflict with the principle of Empowered Autonomy, but both principles are essential to ethical analysis. Ultimately, the ethical codes applicable to club doctors should be as consistent and realistic as possible, avoid ambiguity where feasible, and be more than merely aspirational. Achieving that standard, of course, does not mean they will never contain any internal conflicts, but such conflicts should be minimized and where they persist they should be purposive.

C Current Legal Obligations and Ethical Codes When Providing Services to Player

As discussed above, club doctors' legal and ethical obligations generally differ depending on whether they are providing services to the player or to the club. Below, we discuss the Services to Player scenario, and later we discuss the realities of this distinction between possible roles. In the following sections, we will discuss a club doctor's obligations concerning (1) medical care, (2) disclosure and autonomy, (3) confidentiality, and (4) conflicts of interest when the club doctor is providing Services to Player.

---

j By contrast, the Professional Football Athletic Trainers Society (PFATS), the professional organization for NFL club athletic trainers, does have a Code of Ethics.

1) MEDICAL CARE
a) Current Legal Obligations

The topic of the legal liability and obligations of doctors is vast and would require book length treatment in its own right to be exhaustive. In what follows we highlight the main elements of this regulatory and liability structure.

Under common law, doctors have an obligation to provide medical care within an acceptable standard of care in the medical community or be subject to a medical malpractice claim.[54] Generally, the elements of a medical malpractice claim are: (1) a duty owed by the doctor to the plaintiff to abide by the prevailing standard of care; (2) a breach of that standard of care by the doctor; and, (3) the breach was the proximate cause of the plaintiff's injury.[55] The first element, the duty to provide care, is generally established by a physician-patient relationship but such a relationship is not necessarily a requirement for a medical malpractice action, as will be discussed in more detail below.[56]

Many states require a doctor with the same board certification or similar expertise as the doctor against whom the claim is brought to opine as to the appropriate standard of care.[57] Thus, in the event a club doctor were sued for medical malpractice, the claim likely could not proceed without a similarly qualified doctor—whether it be an orthopedist, neurologist or a doctor specializing in sports medicine— opining that the club doctor deviated from the applicable standard of care in the particular treatment provided (or not provided). Appendix H includes summaries of all of the medical malpractice cases against club doctors revealed by our research.

By virtue of the self-regulatory system, doctors' statutory obligations concerning medical care are effectively the same as their common law obligations: not to commit professional misconduct as judged by the state medical board.

The CBA also speaks to its conception of the club doctor's standard of care:

> [E]ach Club physician's primary duty *in providing medical care* shall be not to the Club but instead to the player-patient. This duty shall include traditional physician/patient confidentiality requirements. In addition, all Club physicians and medical personnel shall comply with all federal, state, and local requirements, including all ethical rules and standards established by any applicable government and/or other authority that regulates or governs the medical profession in the Club's city.[58] (Emphasis added.)

This CBA provision is susceptible to multiple interpretations. On a generous reading (*i.e.*, one that does not give the italicized language any special emphasis), club doctors' primary duty is to the player at all times. On a less generous reading, the CBA provision demands a primary duty to the player-patient *only* in situations where the club doctor is "providing medical care," and thus is inapplicable when the club doctor is rendering services to the club. Importantly, however, the way club doctors are currently situated within the club precludes the two roles from being truly separated, and thereby precludes club doctors from having their exclusive duty be to the players. This is because at the same time that the club doctor is providing care to the player, he is simultaneously performing duties for the club by judging the player's ability to play and help the club win.

Thus, the club doctor is required by the CBA to provide medical care that puts the player-patient's interests above the club's (in the event these interests conflict), which is as it should be. However, in most instances, and as seemingly recognized by the CBA, it is impossible under the current structure for the club doctor to *always* have a primary duty to the player-patient over the club, because sometimes the club doctor is not providing care, but rather is advising the club on business decisions, *i.e.*, fitness-for-play determinations. In other words, the club doctor cannot always hold the player's interests as paramount and at the same time abide by his or her obligations to the club. Indeed, a club doctor could provide impeccable player-driven medical care (treating the player-patient as primary in accord with the CBA), while simultaneously hurting a player's interests by advising the Club that the player's injury will negatively impact his ability to help the Club. Thus, under any reading of the CBA provision, players lack a doctor who is concerned with their best interests at all times.

Relatedly, the CBA provision also seems to require that the care relationship between players and club doctors be afforded "traditional" confidentiality protections. However, clubs request or require players to execute collectively bargained waivers, effectively waiving this requirement, and players we interviewed indicated that no player refuses to sign the waiver.[k] A copy of this waiver is included as Appendix L. The circumstances under which these waivers are executed is an area worthy of additional attention. For example, questions might be raised as to whether the players are providing meaningful and voluntary informed consent in their execution. Players are being compelled to waive certain legal rights concerning their health without meaningful options. There is no doubt that players execute the waivers because they fear that if they do not, they will lose their job. Indeed, the waivers (which are collectively bargained between the NFL and NFLPA)[59] permit the athletic trainer and club doctors to disclose the player's medical information to club employees, such as coaches and the general manager. Thus, it is unclear what work this CBA language is doing. Of course, given this communication, it is inevitable that players will be less than forthcoming about their medical needs, lest it negatively affect their career prospects.

> The club doctor cannot always hold the player's interests as paramount and at the same time abide by his or her obligations to the club.

In reviewing a draft of this Report, the NFL rejected our claim that the CBA provision "requires the traditional patient-physician confidentiality requirements of a private system,"[60] even though the provision in question specifically says club doctors have a duty to provide "traditional physician/patient confidentiality requirements." The CBA provision does not qualify the club doctor's duty in the context of the employer-employee relationship. The NFL should abide by its obligations under the CBA.

The American Psychological Association's Specialty Guidelines for Forensic Psychology provide a useful analogy. These guidelines acknowledge that a situation in which a psychologist is providing both treatment and evaluative services "may impair objectivity and/or cause exploitation or other harm." Consequently, the psychologists in such a situation "are encouraged to disclose the potential risk and make reasonable efforts to refer the request to another qualified provider."[61]

Finally, the NHL CBA contains a standard of care provision similar, but potentially superior, to the NFL's:

---

k   Current Player 5: "[O]ur first day back in camp, we sign a ton of stuff. I believe one of them is medical release form that allows our team doctors to discuss medical conditions with team officials . . . . I've seen some guys question some of the documents we have to sign but when you're given a stack of papers and it's you sign this and you play football or you don't sign it and you don't, everybody signs it. I don't know anybody who hasn't."

The primary professional duty of all individual health care professionals, such as team physicians, certified athletic trainers/therapists ("ATs"), physical therapists, chiropractors, dentists and neuropsychologists, shall be to the Player-patient *regardless of the fact* that he/she or his/her hospital, clinic, or medical group is retained by such Club to diagnose and treat Players. In addition, all team physicians who are examining and evaluating a Player pursuant to the Pre-Participation Medical Evaluation (either pre-season and/or in-season), the annual exit examination, or who are making a determination regarding a Player's fitness or unfitness to play during the season or otherwise, shall be obligated to perform complete and objective examinations and evaluations and shall do so on behalf of the Club, subject to all professional and legal obligations vis-a-vis the Player-patient.[62] (Emphasis added.)

While the NFL's standard of care fails to account for the club doctor's obligations to the club—namely to perform fitness-for-play evaluations—the NHL's provision seemingly resolves this concern in part, by requiring without limitation to the circumstances of providing medical care that the club doctor be subject to his or her obligations to the player "regardless of the fact that he/she . . . is retained by such Club[.]" Nevertheless, we have concerns about this approach, for reasons discussed in detail in Section H: Recommendations Concerning Club Doctors.

Finally, it is important to clarify how it is that the NFL CBA's standard of care provision might impose legal obligations on the club doctor. For reasons discussed in Section G: Enforcement of Legal and Ethical Obligations, players would have difficulty enforcing this provision against club doctors directly. Club doctors are not a party to the CBA and thus this provision generally cannot be enforced against them. Instead, clubs, as signatories to the CBA, are the party against whom CBA violations can be enforced. Nevertheless, club doctors are effectively bound by the CBA provision. The NFL and NFLPA, through the CBA, have legislated the required standard of care for club doctors. If a club doctor violated this standard of care, the NFLPA could challenge the club doctor's ability to remain in the position via certain CBA procedures discussed in Section G. In addition, it is possible that the club doctor's agreement with the club obligates the doctor to comply with all NFL policies and procedures, including the CBA. Thus, if a club doctor did not follow the CBA, he or she might be in violation of his or her agreement with the club.

b) Current Ethical Codes

The AMA Code's first principle is that "[a] physician shall be dedicated to providing competent medical care, with compassion and respect for human dignity and rights."[63] Similarly, the AMA Code's eighth principle declares that "physicians shall, while caring for a patient, regard responsibility to that patient as paramount."[64] Note that this mirrors the CBA language described above, but in the context of the AMA Code, it is important to recognize that many doctors do not have such stark dual obligations as club doctors. Additionally, Opinion 1.1.6–Quality, prescribes that "physicians individually and collectively share the obligation to ensure that the care patients receive is safe, effective, patient centered, timely, efficient and equitable." This obligation requires doctors, among other things, with:

(a) Keeping current with best care practices and maintaining professional competence.

(b) Holding themselves accountable to patients, families, and fellow health care professionals for communicating effectively and coordinating care appropriately.

(c) Monitoring the quality of care they deliver as individual practitioners—*e.g.,* through personal case review and critical self-reflection, peer review, and use of other quality improvement tools.

(d) Demonstrating a commitment to develop, implement, and disseminate appropriate, well-defined quality and performance improvement measures in their daily practice.

(e) Participating in educational, certification, and quality improvement activities that are well designed and consistent with the core values of the medical profession.[65]

Moreover, Opinion 1.1.1–Patient-Physician Relationship, dictates:

The relationship between patient and physician is based on trust and gives rise to physicians' ethical obligations to place patients' welfare above the physician's own self-interest and above obligations to others, to [use] sound medical judgment on patients' behalf, and to advocate for their patients' welfare.[66]

FIMS' Code of Ethics reiterates these concepts:

The same ethical principles that apply to the practice of medicine shall apply to sports medicine.[67]

Always make the health of the athlete a priority.[68]

Never do harm.[69]

* * *

The basis of the relationship between the physician and the athlete should be that of absolute confidence and mutual respect. The athlete can expect a physician to exercise professional skill at all times. Advice given and action taken should always be in the athlete's best interest.[70]

2) DISCLOSURE AND AUTONOMY

a) Current Legal Obligations

There is broad support for a patient's right to autonomy, the right to make his or her own choices concerning health and healthcare.[71] The concept is particularly important in the context of NFL player health, where treatment also includes helping players make a determination about when and whether to return to play. All patients have certain rights commensurate with their autonomy, including the rights to refuse care and to go against a doctor's recommendations. However, in this section we focus on a doctor's obligations concerning patient autonomy. With that in mind, implicit in a patient's right to make his or her own decisions is the obligation of the doctor to disclose certain relevant medical information. Our list of governing principles for this Report recognizes this by pressing for not just autonomy but also *Empowered Autonomy*.

When discussed in the legal context, these issues of disclosure and autonomy are generally framed as a patient's right to informed consent. Where a doctor fails to obtain a patient's informed consent before proceeding with a medical treatment or procedure, he is potentially subject to liability. There are two common law standards for establishing informed consent in medical cases: a professional/physician-based disclosure standard; and a patient-based standard. State courts are basically evenly split as to which standard to apply.[72]

The physician-based standard measures the physician's duty to disclose against what the reasonable medical practitioner similarly situated would disclose.[73] Jurisdictions that follow this standard ordinarily require the plaintiff to offer medical testimony to establish: (1) that a reasonable medical practitioner in the same or similar community would make the disclosure in question; and, (2) that the defendant did not comply with this community standard.[74]

The patient-based standard, in contrast, measures the physician's duty to disclose against what a reasonable patient would find material. Information is material when "a reasonable person, in what the physician knows or should know to be the patient's position, would be likely to attach significance to it."[75] The question of whether a physician disclosed risks that a reasonable person would find material

is for the trier of fact, *e.g.*, a jury, and technical expertise is not required.[76]

More than half of the states have enacted legislation dealing with informed consent, largely in response to various "malpractice crises."[77] In many states, a consent form or other written documentation of the patient's verbal consent is sufficient to establish that the patient consented to the treatment at issue.[78]

Finally, as will be addressed further in our recommendations, the CBA also imposes disclosure requirements on club doctors:

> All Club physicians are required to disclose to a player any and all information about the player's physical condition that the physician may from time to time provide to a coach or other Club representative, whether or not such information affects the player's performance or health. If a Club physician advises a coach or other Club representative of a player's serious injury or career threatening physical condition which significantly affects the player's performance or health, the physician will also advise the player in writing. The player, after being advised of such serious injury or career-threatening physical condition, may request a copy of the Club physician's record from the examination in which such physical condition was diagnosed and/or a written explanation from the Club physician of the physical condition.[79]

Additionally, club doctors are obligated to permit a player to examine his medical records once during the preseason and once after the regular season.[l] Club doctors are also obligated to provide a copy of a player's medical records to the player upon request in the offseason.[80]

b) Current Ethical Codes

The relevant provision of the AMA Code, Opinion 8.6– Promoting Patient Safety, describes a doctor's obligations to disclose medical information to patients:

> Patients have a right to know their past and present medical status, including conditions that may have resulted from medical error. Open communication is fundamental to the trust that

---

l   In 2014, the NFL instituted an electronic medical record (EMR) system, consisting of all of the athletic trainers' and doctors' diagnosis and treatment notations, including any sideline examinations performed on the player. The EMR system also includes a player portal that permits the player to access his medical records at any time, including after his career is over. This information was provided by the NFLPA. Thus, the CBA provision requiring that club doctors permit players to examine their medical records once during the preseason and then once after the regular season has become anachronistic.

underlies the patient-physician relationship, and physicians have an obligation to deal honestly with patients at all times, in addition to their obligation to promote patient welfare and safety. Concern regarding legal liability should not affect the physician's honesty with the patient.[81]

Similarly, FIMS' Code of Ethics directs that "[t]he sports medicine physician will inform the athlete about the treatment, the use of medication and the possible consequences in an understandable way and proceed to request his or her permission for the treatment."[82]

FIMS' Code of Ethics also places a great deal of emphasis on autonomy:

> A basic ethical principle in health care is that of respect for autonomy. An essential component of autonomy is knowledge. Failure to obtain informed consent is to undermine the athlete's autonomy. Similarly, failure to give them necessary information violates the right of the athlete to make autonomous choices. Truthfulness is important in health care ethics. The overriding ethical concern is to provide information to the best of one's ability that is necessary for the patient to decide and act autonomously.[83]

* * *

> Never impose your authority in a way that impinges on the individual right of the athlete to make his/her own decisions.[84]

Finally, the ACOEM Code of Ethics calls autonomy a "fundamental bioethical value," and declares that "this value respects the idea that the individual best understands his or her own best interests."[85]

3) CONFIDENTIALITY

a) Current Legal Obligations

The flip-side of disclosure by doctors is disclosure by patients, which is of course also key to the treatment relationship. Doctors have both common law and statutory obligations to keep patient information confidential.[86] "Most states provide a private common law cause of action against licensed health care providers who impermissibly disclose confidential information obtained in the course of the treatment relationship to third parties."[87] "Depending on the jurisdiction, the claim may be phrased as a breach of contract, as an act of malpractice, as a breach of fiduciary duty, [or] as an act of fraud/misrepresentation[.]"[88]

Below we discuss statutory requirements concerning the confidentiality of medical information. As will be explained in more detail below, current practices concerning the confidentiality of player medical information do not appear to violate relevant laws because of waivers executed by the players, and potentially applicable exceptions to the laws. As stated above, clubs request or require players to execute waivers permitting the player's medical information to be disclosed to and used by a wide variety of parties, including but not limited to the NFL, any NFL club, and any club's medical staff and personnel, such as coaches and the general manager. These waivers have been collectively bargained between the NFL and NFLPA.[89] Players sign these waivers without much (if any) hesitation out of fear that behaving otherwise could cost them their job.[m] Thus, one key aspect of patient confidentiality is rendered moot, at least with regard to club employees, although information must still be protected as against other third parties.

From a statutory perspective, the federal Health Insurance Portability and Accountability Act (HIPAA) likely governs club doctors' requirements concerning the confidentiality of player medical information.[90] HIPAA requires healthcare providers covered by the law to obtain a patient's authorization before disclosing health information protected by the law.[91] The waivers executed by players provide the authorization required by HIPAA.

Even without the authorizations, NFL club doctors are likely permitted by HIPAA to provide health information about players to the clubs. Covered entities under HIPAA include: "(1) A health plan[;] (2) A health care clearinghouse[; and,] (3) A health care provider who transmits any health information in electronic form."[92]

Club doctors meet the third criteria to be considered a covered entity under HIPAA.[n] A "[h]ealth care provider" is defined by HIPAA as anyone who "furnishes . . . health care in the normal course of business."[93] And "health care means care, services, or supplies related to the health of an individual" including "[p]reventive, diagnostic, therapeutic, rehabilitative, maintenance, or palliative care, and counseling, service, assessment, or procedure with respect to the physical or mental condition, or functional status, of an

---

m   A copy of this waiver is included as Appendix L. The circumstances under which these waivers are executed is an area worthy of additional attention. For example, questions might be raised as to whether the players are providing meaningful informed consent in their execution.

n   On a related point, it is not clear whether clubs would be considered covered entities under HIPAA. The application of HIPAA in this context turns on complicated questions of who is creating and receiving personal health information and the various relationships between employees and contractors of the clubs. See Memorandum Opinion and Order, In re: Nat'l Hockey League Players' Concussion Injury Litigation, 14-md-2551 (D. Minn. July 31, 2015), ECF No. 196 (discussing, but not resolving, whether NHL clubs were covered entities under HIPAA).

individual or that affects the structure or function of the body."[94] Club doctors provide healthcare within the meaning of HIPAA and thus must comply with its requirements.

However, HIPAA permits healthcare providers to provide health information about an employee to an employer without the employee's authorization when: (1) the healthcare provider provides healthcare to the individual at the request of the employer; (2) the health information that is disclosed consists of findings concerning a work-related illness or injury; (3) the employer needs the health information to keep records on employee injuries in compliance with state or federal law; and, (4) the healthcare provider provides written notice to the individual that his or her health information will be disclosed to the employer.[95]

According to the above criteria, NFL club doctors might be permitted to provide health information about players to the clubs where: (1) club doctors provide healthcare to players at the request of the employer; (2) almost every time club doctors disclose medical information to the club it is related to the player's job as an NFL player; and, (3) NFL clubs are required by law to keep records of employee injuries. For example, the Occupational Safety and Health Act requires employers with more than 10 employees to maintain records of work-related injuries and illnesses.[96] As for the fourth prong, our discussions with players make it seem unlikely that athletic trainers are providing written notice to players that their health information is being disclosed to the club at the time of injury, but it is possible that documents provided to the players before the season provide such notice.

It should also be noted that HIPAA permits an employee's health information to be disclosed to the extent necessary to comply with state workers' compensation laws.[97] Moreover, while a violation of HIPAA's Privacy Rule subjects the doctor to significant civil penalties and/or criminal liability, there is no private cause of action or remedy for the patient.[98]

In addition to the federal HIPAA, some states have passed laws restricting the disclosure of medical information by healthcare providers.[99] However, the nature and scope of these laws vary considerably in terms of restriction, disclosure exceptions, and the type of healthcare practitioners governed by the law.[100]

Furthermore, despite these common law and statutory obligations, 22 states in which NFL clubs play or practice have statutes that permit healthcare providers to provide employers with an employee's medical records and/or

information.[101,o] The reasons that disclosure is permitted are generally related to potential or actual workers' compensation claims and procuring payment. However, the state laws vary as to whether a healthcare provider is permitted to disclose medical information only where a workers' compensation claim is possible as opposed to already filed. Some states only permit disclosure after a claim has been filed.

Finally, the 2011 CBA requires the application of, but does not amend or supplement, the common law and statutory confidentiality obligations discussed above: "each Club physician's primary duty in providing player medical care shall be not to the Club but instead to the player-patient. This duty shall include traditional physician/patient confidentiality requirements."[102]

The bottom line is that by and large it seems club doctors are legally permitted to share player-patient medical information with the players' employers, the clubs, due to waivers or by statute.

> 22 states in which NFL clubs play or practice have statutes that permit healthcare providers to provide employers with an employee's medical records and/or information.

Some might question whether the waivers discussed herein should be more limited, in other words, whether club doctors should only have access to a player's medical information insofar as the medical information is related to the player's ability to play football.[p] From a clinical perspective, doctors we have spoken with indicated such an arrangement would not be acceptable, as a treating doctor needs to know the totality of a patient's conditions and medications to provide appropriate medical care. Nevertheless, whether all medical information, such as information about sexually

---

o   NFL clubs play and practice in 23 states. Wisconsin is the only state in which an NFL club plays or practices that does not have a statute permitting healthcare providers to provide employers with an employee's medical records and/information.

p   Indeed, the waiver indicates that disclosure of the player's medical information is "[f]or purposes relating only to my actual or potential employment in the National Football League[.]" *See* Appendix L. Nevertheless, the waiver permits the use and disclosure of medical information "relating to any injury, sickness, disease, mental health condition, physical condition, medical history, medical or clinical status, diagnosis, treatment or prognosis . . . ." *Id.*

transmitted diseases or mental health, is football-related and thus available to the club is still questionable.

b) Current Ethical Codes

The fourth principle of the AMA Code directs that "[a] physician shall respect the rights of patients, colleagues, and other health professionals, and shall safeguard patient confidences and privacy within the constraints of the law." Moreover, the AMA Code includes multiple Opinions concerning patient confidentiality relevant to NFL players:

> **Opinion 3.1.5 – Professionalism in Relationships with Media:** To safeguard patient interests when working with representatives of the media, all physicians should:
>
> (a) Obtain consent from the patient or the patient's authorized representative before releasing information.
>
> (b) Release only information specifically authorized by the patient or patient's representative or that is part of the public record.
>
> (c) Ensure that no statement regarding diagnosis or prognosis is made except by or on behalf of the attending physician.
>
> (d) Refer any questions regarding criminal activities or other police matters to the proper authorities.[103]

> **Opinion 3.2.1 – Confidentiality:** Patients need to be able to trust that physicians will protect information shared in confidence. They should feel free to fully disclose sensitive personal information to enable their physician to most effectively provide needed services. Physicians in turn have an ethical obligation to preserve the confidentiality of information gathered in association with the care of the patient.[104]

FIMS' Code of Ethics similarly declares that "[t]he athlete's right to privacy must be protected."[105] FIMS' Code of Ethics goes on to declare that "[n]o information about an athlete may be given to a third party without the consent of the athlete."[106] However, FIMS' Code of Ethics also declares that "[w]hen serving as a team physician, the sports medicine physician assumes the responsibility to athletes as well as team administrators and coaches . . . [and that] [i]t is essential that each athlete is informed of that responsibility and authorizes disclosure of otherwise confidential medical information, but solely to the specific responsible persons and for the expressed purpose of determining the fitness of the athlete for participation."[107]

4) CONFLICTS OF INTEREST

a) Current Legal Obligations

A doctor has a legal obligation to act in the best interests of the patient at all times that there is a doctor-patient relationship.[108] Thus, whatever other interests a doctor may have must be secondary to the interests of the patient.

The 2011 CBA appears to take a clear position about the club doctor's obligations concerning any potential conflicts of interest where the club doctor is providing care to players, as noted above:

> [E]ach Club physician's primary duty in providing player medical care shall be not to the Club but instead to the player-patient.[109]

However, also as discussed above, this CBA provision is limited to situations where the club doctor is "providing . . . medical care," and thus would be inapplicable to the Services to Club scenario (to the extent the scenarios could actually be separated).

b) Current Ethical Codes

In situations where the doctor is providing treatment to a patient, the AMA Code is clear that the doctor's principal obligation must always be to the patient:

> **AMA Code, Principle VIII:** A physician shall, while caring for a patient, regard responsibility to the patient as paramount.

> * * *

> **Opinion 11.2.2 – Conflicts of Interest in Patient Care:** The primary objective of the medical profession is to render service to humanity; reward or financial gain is a subordinate consideration. Under no circumstances may physicians place their own financial interests above the welfare of their patients . . . . Where the economic interests of the hospital, health care organization, or other entity are in conflict with patient welfare, patient welfare takes priority.[110]

> * * *

> **Opinion 1.1.1 – Patient-Physician Relationship:** The relationship between patient and physician is based on trust and gives rise to physicians' ethical obligations to place patients' welfare above the physician's own self-interest and above obligations to others, to [use] sound medical judgment on patients' behalf, and to advocate for their patients' welfare.[111]

The AMA Code also contains a sport-specific provision requiring doctors to put the athlete's interests ahead of their own or anyone else's:

Opinion 1.2.5 – Sports Medicine: Many professional and amateur athletic activities, including contact sports, can put participants at risk of injury. Physicians can provide valuable information to help sports participants, dancers, and others make informed decisions about whether to initiate or continue participating in such activities.

Physicians who serve in a medical capacity at athletic, sporting, or other physically demanding events should protect the health and safety of participants.

In this capacity, physicians should:

(a) Base their judgment about an individual's participation solely on medical considerations.

(b) Not allow the desire of spectators, promoters of the event, or even the injured individual to govern a decision about whether to remove the participant from the event.[112]

Moreover, the AMA Code contains guidance for doctors where they might be employed or supervised by nonphysicians (as may be the case in the NFL at times):

Opinion 10.2 – Physician Employment by a Nonphysician Supervisee: Accepting employment to supervise a nonphysician employer's clinical practice can create ethical dilemmas for physicians . . . . Physicians who are simultaneously employees and clinical supervisors of nonphysician practitioners must:

(a) Give precedence to their ethical obligation to act in the patient's best interest.

(b) Exercise independent professional judgment, even if that puts the physician at odds with the employer-supervisee.[113]

FIMS' Code of Ethics also contains considerable guidance for club doctors concerning conflicts of interest:

Always make the health of the athlete a priority.[114]

* * *

The physician's duty to the athlete must be his/her first concern and contractual and other responsibilities are of secondary importance. A medical decision must be taken honestly and conscientiously.[115]

* * *

The highest respect will always be maintained for human life and well-being. A mere motive of profit shall never be permitted to be an influence in conducting sports medicine practice or functions.[116]

* * *

Advice given and action taken should always be in the athlete's best interest.[117]

* * *

To enable the sports medicine physician to undertake this ethical obligation the sports medicine physician must insist on professional autonomy and responsibility for all medical decisions concerning the health, safety and legitimate interest of the athlete. No third party should influence these decisions.[118]

As mentioned earlier, most medical societies' codes of ethics track and thus do not exceed the requirements of the AMA Code. However, the American Board of Physician Specialties (ABPS)[q] Code of Ethics includes one provision that could be problematic for NFL club doctors. The ABPS Code of Ethics forbids doctors from "[a]ccept[ing] personal compensation from any party that would influence or require special consideration in the provision of care to any patient."[119] Arguably, NFL clubs can "influence or require special consideration" when a doctor is treating a player-patient. If so, doctors, according to the ABPS, would be forbidden from being compensated by the club.

The American Academy of Orthopaedic Surgeons and American Association of Orthopaedic Surgeons (AAOS), a voluntary organization, also has Standards of Professionalism that might be particularly relevant to the NFL Medical Sponsorship Policy discussed above:

An orthopaedic surgeon shall not enter into any contractual relationship whereby the orthopaedic surgeon pays for the right to care for patients with musculoskeletal conditions.

An orthopaedic surgeon shall make a reasonable effort to ensure that his or her academic institution, hospital or employer shall not enter into any contractual relationship whereby such institution

---

q   ABPS is a non-profit organization that certifies physicians in 18 different specialties, such as general surgery, orthopedic surgery, and internal medicine. *See What is the ABPS?*, Am. Bd. of Physician Specialties, http://www.abpsus.org/abps (last visited Aug. 7, 2015), *archived at* http://perma.cc/4Z2P-F8Z4. ABPS is the smaller of two organizations that certify physician specialties, the larger being the American Board of Medical Specialties. The American Board of Medical Specialties does not have a Code of Ethics.

pays for the right to care for patients with musculoskeletal conditions.

An orthopaedic surgeon or his or her professional corporation shall not couple a marketing agreement or the provision of medical services, supplies, equipment or personnel with required referrals to that orthopaedic surgeon or his or her professional corporation.[120]

An orthopedic surgeon who pays for the right to work with an NFL club would potentially be violating the AAOS Standards. Nevertheless, according to the NFL, currently no doctors pay for the right to provide care.[r] Additionally, AAOS' only enforcement mechanism is either to order the doctor's compliance or revoke the doctor's membership.[121]

D Current Legal Obligations and Ethical Codes When Providing Services to Club

Having discussed club doctors' obligations in the situation in which they are, at least in theory, only providing Services to Player, we now turn to their legal and ethical obligations where they are providing Services to Club. It is important to point out as a preliminary matter that the CBA is silent as to a club doctor's legal and ethical obligations in the Services to Club scenario.

As in the Services to Player section above, we discuss a club doctor's obligations concerning (1) medical care, (2) disclosure and autonomy, (3) confidentiality, and (4) conflicts of interest when the club doctor is providing Services to Club.

1) MEDICAL CARE

a) Current Legal Obligations

Courts have generally held that doctors performing medical examinations for non-treatment purposes have a limited patient-physician relationship.[122] However, it is also important to note that in the cases analyzing this issue, the doctors performing the medical examinations did not also have a simultaneous treatment relationship with the patient, whereas club doctors generally do have such a treatment relationship with current NFL players (though not at the NFL Combine, as discussed below). Thus, these court opinions do not address or adequately encompass the complexities of the club doctor-player relationship. Nevertheless, in the abstract these rulings are consistent with the AMA Code as is discussed below. In light of the limited relationship, doctors only performing medical examinations, such as those who evaluate fitness-for-play, have duties to exercise care consistent with their professional training and expertise so as not to cause physical harm by negligently conducting the examination.[123]

Courts have also recognized that evaluation examinations are often conducted under adversarial circumstances.[124] Consequently, some courts have held that the doctors performing such examinations have no duty to diagnose the examinee's medical conditions.[125] However, other courts have held that doctors performing evaluation exams have a duty to advise the individual of potentially serious illnesses.[126]

The CBA does not supplement club doctors' obligations when performing fitness-for-play evaluations. Instead, the CBA contains a general provision requiring club doctors to "comply with all federal, state, and local requirements, including all ethical rules and standards established by any applicable government and/or other authority that regulates or governs the medical profession in the Club's city."[127]

b) Current Ethical Codes

As an initial matter, AMA Code Opinion 1.2.6 – Work-Related & Independent Medical Examinations clearly acknowledges the issue at hand:

> Physicians who are employed by businesses or insurance companies, or who provide medical examinations within their realm of specialty as independent contractors, to assess individuals' health or disability face a conflict of duties. They have responsibilities both to the patient and to the employer or third party.[128]

Opinion 1.2.6 goes on to explain that "[s]uch industry-employed physicians or independent medical examiners establish limited patient-physician relationships. Their relationships with patients are limited to the isolated examination; they do not monitor patients' health over time, treat them, or carry out many other duties fulfilled by physicians in the traditional fiduciary role."[129] This Opinion would seem to apply to club doctors when they are performing fitness-for-play evaluations except that this Opinion is limited to situations where the medical examination is an "isolated" incident. Club doctors' examinations of current players are not isolated as there is typically an ongoing treatment

---

r   As discussed earlier in Section A(1): The NFL's Medical Sponsorship Policy, the NFL also takes the position that the Medical Sponsorship Policy prohibits club doctors from paying for the right to provide treatment to players. For the reasons discussed in that section, we disagree.

relationship as well. Thus, the application of this provision to club doctors' practices and obligations is questionable.[s]

Nevertheless, assuming Opinion 1.2.6 does apply or at least lends useful guidance, in such a situation, the doctor has the following obligations:

(a) Disclose the nature of the relationship with the employer or third party and that the physician is acting as an agent of the employer or third party before gathering health information from the patient.

(b) Explain that the physician's role in this context is to assess the patient's health or disability independently and objectively. The physician should further explain the differences between this practice and the traditional fiduciary role of a physician.

(c) Protect patients' personal health information in keeping with professional standards of confidentiality.

(d) Inform the patient about important incidental findings the physician discovers during the examination. When appropriate, the physician should suggest the patient seek care from a qualified physician and, if requested, provide reasonable assistance in securing follow-up care.[130]

The ACOEM goes one step further and seemingly does not consider there to be any patient-physician relationship where doctors are employed in occupational settings.[131] The ACOEM Code of Ethics refers to "individuals" rather than patients.[t]

In reviewing a draft of this Report, one comment from the NFL seemed to indicate that it does not believe club doctors and players are in a patient-doctor relationship. The NFL asserted that the above ACOEM position "reflects the essence of the employer-provided health care relationship."[132] The NFL's position in this regard seems to be in contradiction with the CBA, other comments from the NFL, and comments from the NFLPS. As discussed above, Article 39 of the CBA requires that "each Club physician's primary duty in providing medical care shall be not to the Club but instead to the player-patient."[133] The NFL reiterated this CBA provision in its comments, stating that "Club Physicians are required to put the player-patient's interests first."[134] In other comments, the NFL proposed that players "principally rely on Club Physicians" for their care "because of the quality of the care they receive from Club Physicians[.]"[135] Similarly, in a forthcoming commentary as part of a Special Report to The Hastings Center Report, the NFLPS maintained that "NFL physicians are accomplished medical professionals who abide by the highest ethical standards in providing treatment to all of their patients, including those who play in the NFL." Given that club doctors are clearly providing care and treatment to player, and statements acknowledging that fact in other places, we find the NFL's embrace of the ACOEM position perplexing. To be clear, we believe there is a doctor-patient relationship between club doctors and players.

2) DISCLOSURE AND AUTONOMY

a) Current Legal Obligations

As discussed above, a doctor's legal obligations when performing fitness-for-play evaluations are generally to exercise care consistent with the doctor's professional training and expertise so as not to cause physical harm by negligently conducting the examination.[136] The duties of a doctor performing a fitness-for-play evaluation are less robust than of the duties of a doctor treating a patient, but even for fitness-for-play evaluations it is indispensable that the doctor obtain the individual's informed consent for the examination, just as the doctor would when treating a patient of his or her own.[137]

b) Current Ethical Codes

As discussed above, AMA Code Opinion 1.2.6 controls a doctor's ethical responsibilities when performing "isolated" evaluation examinations. Again, assuming that Opinion 1.2.6 applies or guides club doctors when providing Services to Club, on the issues of disclosure and autonomy, Opinion 1.2.6 requires doctors to:

(a) Disclose the nature of the relationship with the employer or third party and that the physician is acting as an agent of the employer or third party before gathering health information from the patient.

(b) Explain that the physician's role in this context is to assess the patient's health or disability independently and objectively. The physician should further explain the differences between this practice and the traditional fiduciary role of a physician.

---

s   See also Tee L. Guidotti et al., Occupational Health Services: A Practical Approach 66 (2d ed. 2013) ("[W]hen there is no provider-patient relationship, the occupational health professional still has an obligation to meet professional and legal standards: inform the worker that no practitioner-patient relationship exists, obtain consent for the examination, tell the worker about significant findings, recommend medical follow-up when something abnormal is found, and manage any medical emergencies that arise during the course of an evaluation, although there is no obligation to treat the patient otherwise.").

t   See id., citing the ACOEM Code of Ethics. See also id. at 65–66 ("When the worker is being assessed and treated by the physician for an occupational injury, for example, a physician-patient relationship exists. When that same physician is conducting an evaluation for the employer for fitness to work . . . a physician-patient relationship does not exist, because the service is being performed in the interest of a third party.").

(c) Protect patients' personal health information in keeping with professional standards of confidentiality.

(d) Inform the patient about important incidental findings the physician discovers during the examination. When appropriate, the physician should suggest the patient seek care from a qualified physician and, if requested, provide reasonable assistance in securing follow-up care.[138]

3) CONFIDENTIALITY

a) Current Legal Obligations

Generally, a doctor-patient relationship is required for a doctor to be subject to common law and statutory confidentiality requirements.[139] Given the limited doctor-patient relationship in the Services to Club scenario, it is thus questionable when a state's common law or statutory obligations concerning confidentiality might apply. Nevertheless, as discussed above, the law generally makes exceptions permitting doctors to disclose medical information to employers. In light of the fact that the club doctors in the Services to Club scenario are tasked explicitly with gathering medical information for the clubs, it makes sense that they are permitted to provide medical information to the club but cannot provide it to any other party (*see* Section (C)(3)(a) above, discussing club doctors' confidentiality obligations).

The ACOEM declares that while the employer is entitled to the doctor's professional opinion as to the employee's "fitness to perform a specific job," the doctor "should not provide the employer with specific medical details or diagnoses unless the employee has given his or her permission."

b) Current Ethical Codes

AMA Code Opinion 3.2.3 – Industry-Employed Physicians & Independent Medical Examiners provides guidance on a club doctor's confidentiality obligations:

Physicians may obtain personal information about patients outside an ongoing patient-physician relationship. For example, physicians may assess an individual's health or disability on behalf of an employer, insurer, or other third party. Or they may obtain information in providing care specifically for a work-related illness or injury. In all these situations, physicians have a responsibility to protect the confidentiality of patient information.

When conducting third-party assessments or treating work-related medical conditions, physicians may disclose information to a third party:

(a) With written or documented consent of the individual (or authorized surrogate); or

(b) As required by law, including workmen's compensation law where applicable.

When disclosing information to third parties, physicians should:

(c) Restrict disclosure to the minimum necessary information for the intended purpose.

(d) Ensure that individually identifying information is removed before releasing aggregate data or statistical health information about the pertinent population.[140]

However, the application of this provision to club doctors is unclear. Opinion 3.2.3 seems to apply to those situations where there is not "an ongoing patient-physician relationship." Club doctors and players on the other hand generally are in an ongoing patient-physician relationship.

Importantly, Opinion 3.2.3 acknowledges that there may be laws, as discussed above, that permit a doctor retained by an employer to provide the employer with medical information about an employee. Similarly, also as discussed above, FIMS' Code of Ethics seems to recognize the need for medical information to be provided to clubs. While FIMS' Code of Ethics declares that "[n]o information about an athlete may be given to a third party without the consent of the athlete," [141] it also declares that it is "essential" that athletes authorize the doctor to disclose "otherwise confidential medical information" to certain club officials "for the expressed purpose of determining the fitness of the athlete for participation." [142]

Similarly, while ACOEM's Code of Ethics directs that "[o]ccupational and environmental health professionals should keep confidential all individual medical, health promotion, and health screening information," the Code of Ethics also directs that "occupational and environmental health professionals should recognize that employers may be entitled to counsel about an individual's medical work fitness."[143]

However, the ACOEM also declares that while the employer is entitled to the doctor's professional opinion as to the employee's "fitness to perform a specific job," the doctor "should not provide the employer with specific medical details or diagnoses unless the employee has given his or her permission."[u]

4) CONFLICTS OF INTEREST

a) Current Legal Obligations

As discussed above, a doctor's legal obligations when performing fitness-for-play evaluations are generally to exercise care consistent with the doctor's professional training and expertise so as not to cause physical harm by negligently conducting the examination.[144] Assuming the doctor meets that standard of care, the doctor is free to perform the fitness-for-play evaluation consistent with his or her obligations to the club.

b) Current Ethical Codes

As discussed above, AMA Code Opinion 1.2.6 potentially guides a doctor's obligations in the Services to Club scenario. In such a situation, the doctor has the following obligations:

(a) Disclose the nature of the relationship with the employer or third party and that the physician is acting as an agent of the employer or third party before gathering health information from the patient.

(b) Explain that the physician's role in this context is to assess the patient's health or disability independently and objectively. The physician should further explain the differences between this practice and the traditional fiduciary role of a physician.

(c) Protect patients' personal health information in keeping with professional standards of confidentiality.

(d) Inform the patient about important incidental findings the physician discovers during the examination. When appropriate, the physician should suggest the patient seek care from a qualified physician and, if requested, provide reasonable assistance in securing follow-up care.[145]

FIMS' Code of Ethics also contains guidance for club doctors concerning conflicts of interest:

> It is the responsibility of the sports medicine physician to determine whether the injured athletes should continue training or participate in competition. The outcome of the competition or the coaches should not influence the decision, but solely the possible risks and consequences to the health of the athlete.[146]

* * *

> At a sport venue, it is the responsibility of the sports medicine physician to determine when an injured athlete can participate in or return to an event or game. The physician should not delegate this decision. In all cases, priority must be given to the athlete's health and safety. The outcome of the competition must never influence such decisions.[147]

E Additional Ethical Obligations

FIMS' Code of Ethics declares that "[p]hysicians who care for athletes of all ages have an ethical obligation to understand the specific physical, mental and emotional demands of physical activity, exercise and sports training."[148]

Additionally, a player's right to obtain a second opinion is often an important consideration. Although the 2011 CBA provides a player the right to obtain a second medical opinion, it does not obligate the club doctor to inform or remind the player of that right.[149] In contrast, FIMS' Code of Ethics specifically obligates "[t]he team physician [to] explain to the individual athlete that he or she is free to consult another physician."[150]

AMA Code Opinion 1.2.3 – Consultation, Referral & Second Opinions also directs a doctor to cooperate with a patient's right to a second opinion:

> Physicians' fiduciary obligation to promote patients' best interests and welfare can include consulting other physicians for advice in the care of the patient or referring patients to other professionals to provide care.

u   Confidentiality of Medical Information in the Workplace, Am. Coll. of Occupational and Envtl. Med., http://www.acoem.org/Confidentiality_Medical_Information.aspx (last visited Aug. 7, 2015), archived at http://perma.cc/V7D4-3RDD. See also Tee L. Guidotti et al., Occupational Health Services: A Practical Approach 62 (2d ed. 2013) ("The occupational health professional who is working on behalf of an employer . . . has an obligation to report such information as is directly pertinent to the employee's work capacity or accommodations that are needed, but no more. The employer is entitled to a determination of "fit," "unfit," and "fit with accommodation" . . . but not to the diagnosis or medical history of the employee."); id. ("Employers have an obligation to respect the confidentiality of personal medical information of their employees. Unless informed consent is given by the worker, confidential medical information must stay within the occupational health service and cannot be shared, for example with human resources, or with management, or with coworkers."); id. at 288 ("The fitness-for-duty opinion is communicated to the employer, without disclosing any medical information, using medical terminology, or providing diagnosis. The employer only receives the final determination, which is expressed as fit, unfit, or fit subject to specific accommodations (specified).").

When physicians seek or provide consultation about a patient's care or refer a patient for health care services, including diagnostic laboratory services, they should:

(a) Base the decision or recommendation on the patient's medical needs, as they would for any treatment recommendation, and consult or refer the patient to only health care professionals who have appropriate knowledge and skills and are licensed to provide the services needed.

(b) Share patients' health information in keeping with ethical guidelines on confidentiality.

(c) Assure the patient that he or she may seek a second opinion or choose someone else to provide a recommended consultation or service . . . .

* * *

Physicians may not terminate a patient-physician relationship solely because the patient seeks recommendations or care from a health care professional whom the physician has not recommended.[151]

Similarly, the American Board of Physician Specialties obligates doctors to "[c]ooperate in every reasonable and proper way with other physicians and work with them in the advancement of quality patient care."[152]

Doctors also have ethical obligations concerning their role within the club's entire healthcare staff. As discussed in Chapter 3, athletic trainers are vital contributors to the player healthcare system. However, athletic trainers are not licensed doctors and thus it is important that they not perform any tasks which are reserved for doctors. Thus, doctors must not encourage or allow athletic trainers to undertake responsibilities that are outside the scope of their license.

On this point, AMA Code Opinion 10.2 – Physician Employment by a Nonphysician Supervisee declares:

Physicians' relationships with midlevel practitioners must be based on mutual respect and trust as well as their shared commitment to patient well-being. Health care professionals recognize that clinical tasks should be shared and delegated in keeping with each practitioner's training, expertise, and scope of practice. Given their comprehensive training and broad scope of practice, physicians have a professional responsibility for the quality of overall care that patients receive, even when aspects of that care are delivered by nonphysician clinicians.[153]

F Current Practices

As discussed above, clubs retain a wide variety of doctors. The current practices we discuss below are generally those of the head club doctor. In discussing club doctor's current practices, it is important to reiterate that some of the problems we describe are principally the result of the conflicted structure in which club doctors operate, as opposed to moral or ethical failings on the part of the doctors. Finally, it is important to recognize that there may be a good deal of variation among clubs. Without a full survey of the experience of players and doctors at each club, we cannot fully capture the nuances of local variations.

Two former NFL club doctors wrote books about their experiences which provide insight into the practices of club doctors during the doctors' tenures in the 1980s and 1990s. We fully recognize that these books cover practices from an earlier time period than present day football. Nevertheless, as is explained below, while it appears some practices have changed substantially since the time these books were written, others have not. We also recognize that these books, although they are the most complete and comprehensive coverage of the subject in existence, represent the perspectives of only two former club doctors, and that the practice and experiences of club doctors even during this time period was not uniform.

As discussed in the background of this chapter, the NFL denied our request to interview club doctors as part of this Report. Without being able to interview club doctors, where possible, we have supplemented facts discussed in the books written by former club doctors with more contemporary factual accounts, including news reports, academic and professional literature, and formal and informal interviews with NFL and NFLPA representatives, many current and former players, sports medicine professionals, contract advisors, financial advisors, and player family members. Nevertheless, the limitations discussed above are important ones and we are hopeful that we or others will be provided the necessary access and information in future work to establish a broader set of data on the experience of club doctors.

The first book, "You're Okay, It's Just a Bruise": A Doctor's Sideline Secrets About Pro Football's Most Outrageous Team, was published in 1994 by former Los Angeles Raiders club doctor Rob Huizenga. Huizenga, who was with the Raiders from 1982 to 1990, was extremely critical of the Raiders' approach to player medical issues, with particular criticism focused on Raiders' then-owner Al Davis and the Raiders' then-orthopedist and head doctor, Robert Rosenfeld. The title of the book is something Huizenga claimed Rosenfeld once told a Raiders player who had recently suffered a neck injury that had resulted in temporary paralysis, a diagnosis with which Huizenga and several other doctors disagreed.[154]

Rosenfeld, according to Huizenga, downplayed players' injuries and unabashedly placed the Raiders' interests ahead of the players'.[155] As Huizenga put it, "Rosenfeld lived for the Raider job. I suspected he would do whatever it took to keep Al Davis happy."[156] The book in many respects is an account of Huizenga's self-described efforts to balance his ethical obligations as a doctor and to the players with his obligations to the Raiders.[157] Ultimately, citing the Raiders' culture and Rosenfeld's questionable practices, Huizenga resigned his position in 1990.[158]

Then, in 2001, former Seattle Seahawks club doctor Pierce Scranton published *Playing Hurt: Treating and Evaluating the Warriors of the NFL*. Scranton was the Seahawks' club doctor from 1980 to 1998. Scranton generally believed that NFL players received outstanding care from club doctors but acknowledged the potential conflicts in the position, explaining that if a club doctor "decides to play it safe and hold [a player] out of the next game, he might feel subtle pressure from the player, his team, the player's agent, the coaches, and management."[159] "The doctor is caught in the middle, forced to distinguish between the usual aches and pains of football versus the pain of an injury that could make that player more vulnerable to serious harm."[160]

Scranton also discussed his view of the club doctor's obligations to the club and relationship with coaches. Scranton asserted that "[a] sports-medicine physician must place the interests of the team above his own. He recognizes that the team needs instant attention to injuries in order to be successful."[161] Moreover, Scranton had a close relationship with and operated on Seahawks head coach Tom Flores.[v] Nevertheless, Scranton lamented the control

coaches had over player medical issues, explaining that coaches would try to exclude doctors from team activities and make decisions about whether players were medically cleared to play.[w] Scranton further claimed that coaches would direct players not to consult the athletic trainers or doctors during the game, because "they'll take you out of the game."[162]

Below, we discuss current practices concerning club doctors from several perspectives and situations: (1) selection and payment of club doctors; (2) the NFL Combine and Draft; (3) seasonal duties; (4) game day duties; (5) relationships with coaches and club executives; and, (6) relationships with players.

1) SELECTION AND PAYMENT OF CLUB DOCTORS

Each NFL club's medical staff is chosen by the club's executives.[163] Club doctors are affiliated with a wide variety of private practice groups, hospitals, academic institutions, and other professional sports leagues. Some of these institutions have long-standing relationships with clubs, which often help lead to the doctor being retained by the club. The NFLPA plays no role in the selection of club doctors other than ensuring they have the qualifications required by the CBA and are properly licensed in the relevant state(s), via Synernet, a third-party vendor jointly selected by the NFL and NFLPA.[164] Synernet provides reports on these matters to both the NFL and NFLPA.[165] Additionally, of the NFL's 32 head club doctors, 2 are employees and 30 are independent contractors.[166]

Also, while it is our understanding that club doctors' contracts are generally reviewed and renewed on an annual basis, there is very little turnover among club doctors.

It is difficult to ascertain actual figures and practices of club doctor compensation. In the course of our research, we were informed by some familiar with the industry that club

---

v   Flores: "When I came to Seattle, I tore the cartilage in my knee, and Dr. Pierce Scranton performed the surgery in 1989. [. . .] In 1994 and 1995, I tore my right rotator cuff and then my left. Drs. Scranton and Auld, the two team physicians for the Seattle Seahawks, performed the surgery. In all of my surgeries, I was fortunate to have doctors whom I trusted and respected."
Flores: "During my years in the NFL as a head coach and general manager, I always had a close relationship with our doctors. I felt it was necessary to get to know each one, not only as a doctor, but as a person. It was important to me that our team doctors have strong feelings about our team's health and loyalty to the entire organization. When our doctors came into the training room, I didn't want the feeling that outsiders were invading us. They had to feel part of the family, and we had to treat them as such." Pierce E. Scranton, Jr., Playing Hurt: Treating and Evaluating the Warriors of the NFL viii (2001).

w   "A third reason that agents insist on outside surgery for their players is that many clubs have, in effect, neutered their team physicians. Injuries are the one thing that coaches can't control, and they drive control-freak coaches crazy. Coaches hate it when the doctor tells them that a star player will be out for four to eight weeks, maybe more. The solution to this maddening intrusion? Remove the doctor from the team. The doctors are intentionally excluded from team activities. They have to eat separately, they can't ride to the game on the team bus, and the coach will take the injury report from the trainer only. In other words, for a player who is wondering whether he can play hurt or not, the control-freak coaches want the player to ask *them* that question, not the doctor. The conventional doctor-patient relationship is nonexistent, and the trust naturally fostered by such a relationship is consciously undermined by the organization. This puts the team physicians at greater risk for malpractice." *Id.* at 174.

doctors are generally paid in relatively nominal amounts compared to what one might expect ($20,000–$30,000).[x] In reviewing a draft of this Report, the NFL stated that this estimate "grossly underestimates compensation to Head Team Physicians, Head Team Orthopedists and Head Team Internists."[167] Nevertheless, the NFL did not provide alternative compensation figures.

> The NFLPA plays no role in the selection of club doctors other than ensuring they have the qualifications required by the CBA and are properly licensed in the relevant state(s).

In addition, despite the relatively high scrutiny club doctors face, it is our understanding that their contracts with the clubs do not include any type of indemnification whereby the club would pay for the defense, settlement, or verdict of a medical malpractice claim.

Despite the various challenges, club doctors have a variety of reasons for being interested in the position. Many of them are sports fans and thus the opportunity to work up close and personal with some of the best athletes in the world is exciting. From a business perspective, a doctor's association with an NFL club could be powerful in terms of professional respect and name recognition, resulting in more patients in their practice.

We will next walk through a club doctor's typical season to provide context for the club doctor's relationships with various individuals.

2) THE NFL COMBINE AND DRAFT

Before reaching the preseason or regular season, club doctors attend the NFL Scouting Combine (Combine). The Combine is an annual event each February in which approximately 300 of the best college football players undergo medical examinations, intelligence tests, interviews and multiple football and other athletic drills and tests.[168] NFL club executives, coaches, scouts, doctors and athletic trainers attend the Combine to evaluate the players for the upcoming NFL Draft (usually in April).[169] The Combine began in the early 1980s and has been held in Indianapolis since 1987.[170]

Although called the NFL Scouting Combine, the event is actually organized by National Football Scouting, Inc., a Delaware corporation that is not owned or legally controlled by the NFL.[171] Nevertheless, the NFL exercises considerable control over the event, including involvement in decisions about the drills players perform at the Combine, selling public tickets, and broadcasting the Combine on television.[172,y] The NFL claimed that "[t]he NFLPA also exercises considerable discretion over the Combine. For example, the NFLPA prohibited the Combine medical team(s) from conducting cardiac echocardiograms on every attendee citing the potential adverse financial impact of a false positive."[173]

As an initial matter, in order to participate in the NFL Combine, players must execute waivers permitting the Combine, the NFL, and a wide variety of related parties, such as club medical staff, to obtain, use, and release the player's medical information (without any date limitation) for purposes relating to the player's potential or actual employment in the NFL. These waivers are included as Appendices in our forthcoming law review article, *Evaluating NFL Player Health and Performance: Legal and Ethical Issues*.[174]

According to Jeff Foster, the President of National Football Scouting, Inc., all 32 NFL clubs consider the medical examinations to be the most important part of the Combine.[175] Indeed, former NFL club executive Bill

---

y   It is possible that the NFL avoids direct control of the NFL Combine to avoid having to comply with the Americans with Disabilities Act (ADA). The ADA prohibits pre-employment medical examinations to determine whether a prospective employee has a disability. *See* 42 U.S.C. § 12112(d)(2)(A) (2012). The definition of "disability includes any "physical or mental impairment that substantially limits one or more major life activities," 42 U.S.C. § 12102(1). This definition of disability could arguably include any prior injury by a prospective NFL player and thus the medical examinations at the NFL Combine are potentially pre-employment medical examinations which are barred by the ADA. For more on this and related issues, see our law review article, *Evaluating NFL Player Health and Performance: Legal and Ethical Issues,* U. Penn. L. Rev. (forthcoming 2017).

---

x   In 2001, the Minnesota Vikings paid their three club doctors $4,000, $19,600 and $47,500 per year, respectively. The amounts varied based on the extent of the doctors' obligations. *See* Memorandum and Order, Stringer v. Minn. Vikings Football Club, No. 02-415, 20–23 (Minn. Dist. Ct. Apr. 25, 2003).

Polian said that "the one and only reason for the combine is the medical tests."[176] A battery of medical tests are initially performed by doctors affiliated with IU Health,[177] a healthcare system affiliated with Indiana University School of Medicine.[178] IU Health doctors have been working at the Combine since it moved to Indianapolis in 1987.[179] The IU Health doctors perform X-rays and more than 350 magnetic resonance imaging (MRI) diagnostic tests each year.[180,z]

After the tests are performed by IU Health doctors, "examinations are conducted by the physicians in the NFL Physicians Society."[181] The NFL explained that "Club medical teams each perform one element of a comprehensive evaluation and share their findings with all other clubs. In other words, a combine attendee undergoes one comprehensive examination (performed by different practitioners), not 32 comprehensive examinations."[182] According to the NFLPS, the role of the club doctor at the Combine "is to obtain a comprehensive medical and orthopaedic assessment of every player that is going to be part of the NFL Draft."[183] Also according to the NFLPS, "the team physicians along with their athletic training staff assess every player who is going to be available for the NFL Draft and provide a report back to the scouting department, the head coach, the general manager and the front office about the medical condition of each player. This information becomes very important in a team's assessment of whether or not a player will be drafted."[184] These examinations might create concerns for club doctors, as discussed below. In particular, the nature and purpose of the doctor's role might not be clear to the player being examined.[aa]

Former Seahawks club doctor Pierce Scranton discussed the Combine at length in his book. Scranton attended the Combine on behalf of the Seahawks each year to perform medical examinations on prospective NFL players. According to Scranton, "each team relies heavily on doctors in determining that its high picks are healthy and capable of contributing to the team and dominating on the field."[185] Scranton's description comports with former Los Angeles Raiders club doctor Rob Huizenga's, who described the Combine examinations as "[d]etective medicine."[186] All indications are that club doctors' responsibilities at the Combine have not changed since the period described by Scranton and Huizenga.

Scranton expressed misgivings about the Combine. He believed these examinations presented a "moral quandary" for the club doctors on whether to tell a player about medical problems he may have.[187] While Scranton felt a "responsibility to protect that athlete's health and welfare,"[188] he believed that his primary responsibility was to make sure players with relatively poor injury histories or medical conditions are not drafted by the Seahawks.[ab] It is uncertain whether Scranton's feelings are consistent with those of today's club doctors. Ultimately, Scranton said he found the "examinations . . . more dehumanizing than interesting."[189]

Nevertheless, Scranton, like all club doctors, used his medical examinations from the Combine and other pre-Draft examinations to help the club make decisions about which players to draft. According to Scranton, Mike McCormack, the Seahawks general manager from 1982 to 1989, demanded Scranton provide "an accurate assessment from the team's perspective on player health and career longevity."[190]

It is also important to note that the NFL Combine exams do include tests for conditions that could have serious health implications for players, including "sickle cell anemia, heart conditions, and other congenital conditions."[191] Although these tests can offer benefits to players, they (and other examinations conducted at the Combine) could implicate certain laws, including the Americans with Disabilities Act (ADA) and the Genetic Information Nondiscrimination Act (GINA), as discussed in our forthcoming law review article mentioned above.[192]

---

z Our research has also revealed that there have been approximately 31 published medical studies using players' medical information obtained from the examinations conducted at the NFL Combine, some involving thousands of prospective NFL players. Although some of the studies describe having received approval from an Institutional Review Board, many do not. Either way, we have concerns about whether the players voluntarily and knowingly consented to have their medical information used in these studies (to the extent consent was required).

aa In reviewing a draft of this Report, the NFL argued that the fact the "Combine attendees sign medical record release and waiver forms" indicates that players do understand the role of doctors at the Combine. NFL Comments and Corrections (June 24, 2016). We disagree. Signing a complicated legal document is far different from understanding it. Moreover, the waivers authorize the use and disclosure of the player's health information by and to a variety of parties. Nowhere does the document explain why the club doctor is performing the examination or how the results of the examination might be used.

---

ab "At the combines, a doctor can't escape the nagging sense that something's not right. As surgeons, we embody the ethical heritage of a profession that for centuries has assessed injury, made diagnoses, and provided healing treatment. Our task is to inform our patients of their condition and the relative risks of the cure. In this combine environment, however, we are only employees of a team. We may examine someone who has a life-threatening condition, but our only job is to make sure that *our* team doesn't wind up with *that* guy on its roster." Pierce E. Scranton, Jr., Playing Hurt: Treating and Evaluating the Warriors of the NFL 22 (2001).

3) SEASONAL DUTIES

Club doctors' duties are perhaps most intense during the preseason. Club rosters are much larger in the preseason (beginning with 90 active players as compared to 53 during the regular season), meaning there are many more players requiring medical care. As a result, club doctors are often at the club's training facility at least four hours a day every day. According to the NFL, for approximately the last 10 years, each club's medical staff has held a preseason meeting with players to discuss health and safety issues.[193] Beginning with the 2015 season, "[t]he content was developed by the League's medical committees, in consultation with the NFLPA's medical director."[194] The content of the presentation "include[s] information regarding heat management, concussions, infectious disease, mental health, helmet testing, controlled substances and steroids."[195]

Club doctors' daily involvement with the club actually decreases during the regular season. Club doctors generally have their own private practice where they spend most of their time.[196] In a 2008 arbitration decision, club doctors' availability and obligations to the club were described as follows:

> In general, the Club's physicians are available to address the players' injuries and problems, are present in the training room on Mondays and Wednesdays, and maintain Friday office hours for meeting with the players. They also are available on the field two hours before each game, whether at home or away, for any player who needs care. They are also in constant communication with the Club's head trainer and training staff concerning the status of players in order to implement medical plans and share notes with each other with respect to the players' progress.[197]

Club doctors' visits to the club on Monday are generally for evaluating the extent of player injuries from the previous day's game, including ordering X-rays and MRIs.[ac] The club doctor generally returns on Wednesday to reevaluate the players and assess their progress.[ad] Nevertheless, it is important to remember there is heterogeneity in club doctor's actual practices and these descriptions are offered as general practices.

Club doctors principally rely on the athletic trainers (see Chapter 3) to monitor and handle the player's care during the week. According to the NFLPS:

> The athletic trainer is often the first person to see an injured player at the game, practice, training camp, mini-camp, etc. The trainer must be accurate in the identification of injuries and must communication (sic) well with the team physician. There is a constant source of dialogue between the athletic trainers and the team physicians in all aspects of the player's care, whether it's preventative care, managing current injuries or medical problems, or the entire rehabilitation process.[198]

Club doctors then attend the club's game each week, discussed in more detail below.

At the conclusion of the season, the club doctors perform end of season physicals for every player on the roster. While the physicals can benefit the players by revealing injuries or conditions in need of care, they also provide important benefits to the club. These physicals can provide the club with a record that at the end of the season the player was healthy so that if the player's contract is terminated during the offseason, the player cannot claim that his contract was terminated because he was injured and then try to obtain additional compensation either through an Injury Grievance or the Injury Protection benefit.[ae] Additionally, the club will want an assessment of each player's health in deciding whether or not to retain that player for next season.[af]

According to the NFL, it "proposed a standard two-day post season physical examination which would include mental health evaluations and relevant player programming (career transition, substance abuse and financial education) which was rejected by the NFLPA."[199] In response, the NFLPA stated that "[t]he standard post-season physical proposal originated with the NFLPA in an effort to further player health. The NFL's counter-proposal was not acceptable to player leadership [and that] [t]hese discussions are ongoing."[200]

---

ac   See, e.g., id. at 85 ("Our injury clinic was at the Seahawk headquarters in Kirkland every Monday at 7:30 AM. This early start gave us a jump on ordering emergency MRIs for hurt players.").

ad   See id. at 87 ("Wednesday the players would put their pads back on. That afternoon, I'd come cover for the afternoon injury clinic. I'd check the progress of all our recent injuries and find out if there was anything new. Who was getting better? Who would be reclassified in that evening's injury report to coach? Who could he count on next Sunday?").

ae   See id. at 90 ("The release physical became a legal document. Our intention was to ensure that no one was released hurt. We also wanted to make sure no one demanded compensation for an injury when none had occurred.").

af   See id. at 39–40 (discussing 'Buyer-Beware' Players, including a linebacker that was "[a]n 11-year veteran who is always in the training room," a punter with "[c]hronic back spasms [and who is] [a]lways in the training room," and another linebacker who is "[a]lways on injured reserve or on an airplane for a second opinion.").

Table 2-C:
Game Day Medical Staff

For Both Clubs	For Each Club
Neurotrauma Consultants (2)	Athletic Trainers (4)
EMTs (2)	Orthopedists (2)
Athletic Trainer (1)	Primary Care Physicians (2)
Ophthalmologist (1)	Chiropractor (1)
Dentist (1)	
Radiology Technician (1)	
Airway Management Physician (1)	

4) GAME DAY DUTIES

Game days include a wide variety of medical professionals. Each club generally has four athletic trainers, two orthopedists, two primary care physicians and one chiropractor present.[201] In addition, pursuant to the Concussion Protocol (*see* Appendix A), each club is designated an Unaffiliated Neurotrauma Consultant to assess possible concussions.[ag] In addition, there are a variety of medical professionals available to both clubs, including one independent athletic trainer who views the game from the press box to spot possible injuries (the "spotter"),[ah] an ophthalmologist, a dentist, a radiology technician to handle the stadium's X-ray machine, an airway management physician, and an emergency medical technician (EMT)/paramedic crew. In total, an NFL game generally involves 27 medical personnel on site.[202]

Club doctors generally arrive at the game three to four hours before kickoff.[203] Players who are questionable for the game, will warm up on the field early, under the supervision of the club doctors.[204] The club doctor will then decide whether the player will play that day.[205] The club has until 90 minutes before kickoff to submit its Active List for the game, *i.e.*, decide which players are not eligible to play.[206]

In or about 2013, the NFL instituted a new policy requiring the club's head doctor to meet with the head referee prior to each game so that the referee knows for whom to look and with whom to talk in the event of a major injury.[207]

The club doctor's principal obligation during the games is to respond to player injuries.[208] The club doctor and athletic trainer will mutually evaluate the player and the club doctor ultimately is responsible for determining whether the player can return to play.[209]

If the player has suffered a possible concussion in a game,[ai] he must go through the Concussion Protocol (*see* Appendix A) to determine if he can return to play. Generally, the Concussion Protocol requires that the player undergo a Sideline Concussion Assessment, including the Standardized Concussion Assessment Tool (SCAT3), which consists of a series of scored symptom, cognitive, and physical assessments by the club doctor, with the potential assistance of the unaffiliated neurotrauma consultant assigned to the game.[aj] The player's score on the SCAT3 is then compared to his SCAT3 scores from a preseason baseline examination. Coupled with the doctors' other professional

---

ag The Concussion Protocol does not explain how the Unaffiliated Neurotrauma Consultant is chosen, but requires that the consultant "be a physician who is impartial and independent from any Club, is board certified or board eligible in neurology, neurological surgery, emergency medicine, physical medicine and rehabilitation physician, or any primary care CAQ sports medicine certified physician and has documented competence and experience in the treatment of acute head injuries." The Unaffiliated Neurotrauma Consultant also prepares a report after each game detailing any examinations performed.

ah "The spotter is a seasoned athletic trainer who is selected, trained and paid by the N.F.L. and who also has at his or her disposal "a video monitor and a video operator who can instantly replay a game sequence to scrutinize the mechanism of a potential head injury." "The spotter watches both teams and can communicate directly with the athletic trainers and doctors on the field via telephones that ring on the benches and walkie-talkies that are wired to earpieces." Bill Pennington, *Concussions by the New Book*, N.Y. Times, Nov. 29, 2014, http://www.nytimes.com/2014/11/30/sports/football/nfl-teams-now-operate-under-a-concussion-management-protocol.html?_r=0, *archived at* https://perma.cc/79YM-R7SN?type=pdf. In 2015, the NFL enacted a rule permitting the spotter to stop play if he or she believes a player has suffered a concussion. Darin Gantt, *Injury Timeout Proposal Unanimously Approved by NFL Owners*, ProFootballTalk (Mar. 24, 2015, 1:38 PM), http://profootballtalk.nbcsports.com/2015/03/24/injury-timeout-proposal-unanimously-approved-by-nfl-owners/, *archived at* http://perma.cc/N927-X2WL. The rule change occurred in part because, according to the NFL, during the 2014 season there were 25 incidents in which a player should have been removed from a game but was not. Mike Florio, *NFL Found 25 Failures to Remove Players from 2012 through 2014*, ProFootballTalk (Mar. 27, 2015, 8:35 PM), http://profootballtalk.nbcsports.com/2015/03/27/nfl-found-25-failures-to-remove-players-from-2012-through-2014/, archived at http://perma.cc/4BEJ-9PW9. The NFL then announced that no spotter could have worked for an NFL club within the prior 20 years. Mike Florio, *NFL Moves on from ATC Spotters with Team Affiliations*, ProFootballTalk (Apr. 25, 2015, 6:32 AM), http://profootballtalk.nbcsports.com/2015/04/25/nfl-moves-on-from-atc-spotters-with-team-affiliations, *archived at* http://perma.cc/RX9M-EXWD.

---

ai The Concussion Protocol includes a list of observable signs or player-reported symptoms that might indicate a player has suffered a concussion. *See* Appendix A.

aj The Concussion Protocol is unclear as to whether the unaffiliated neurotrauma consultant must be consulted when a Club doctor is examining a player for a potential concussion.

judgments, a determination is then made as to whether the player has in fact suffered a concussion. If the player has suffered a concussion, he cannot return to the game. The Concussion Protocol declares that "[t]he responsibility for the diagnosis of concussion and the decision to return a player to a game remains exclusively within the professional judgment of the Head Team Physician or the Team physician assigned to managing TBI." According to the NFL, there have there have never been any problems or disagreements between club doctors and the unaffiliated neurotrauma consultants.[210]

An interesting situation occurs when a visiting player is injured. Because the visiting club's doctor is often not licensed to practice in the state in which the club is playing, the home club's doctor is responsible for the visiting player's care.[ak] To address this problem, beginning in 2015, each club is assigned a Visiting Team Medical Liaison.[211] The Visiting Team Medical Liaison is a local doctor who can help provide care, medications and advice concerning local medical facilities.[212]

Additionally, legislation has been introduced to clarify the obligations of doctors and athletic trainers in these situations. In February 2015, a proposed federal law, entitled the Sports Medicine Licensure Clarity Act, was introduced that would deem medical services provided by club doctors and athletic trainers in states in which they are not licensed to have been provided in the states in which they are licensed.[213] As of the date of publication, no action has been taken since the bill's introduction.

5) RELATIONSHIPS WITH COACHES AND CLUB EXECUTIVES

Based on conversations with sports medicine professionals it is our understanding that there is much variance in the relationships between club doctors and coaches. In general, most medical information concerning a player is passed from the club doctor to the coaching staff through the athletic trainer. Athletic trainers are employees of the club and spend nearly every waking hour with the club. Thus, many club doctors might only meet with the head coach once a week to discuss the health status of players.[al] Nevertheless, there are still concerns that some club doctors have much closer relationships with, and sometimes can be pressured by, the coaching staff.

As noted above, clubs generally require players to execute waivers (which have been collectively bargained) before each season permitting the player's medical information to be disclosed to and used by a wide variety of parties, including but not limited to the NFL, any NFL club, and any club's medical staff and personnel, such as coaches and the general manager. Consequently, it is believed that club doctors provide any player medical information that might be relevant to the coaches or club executives.

Club doctors generally have minimal contact with club executives, such as general managers. The club doctors assist the club's front office during the Combine and prior to the NFL Draft by examining and evaluating the health of prospects. The club doctors might provide similar analysis

---

ak   "[I]f a visiting team's player went down, say with a severe concussion, we Seahawk physicians would assume responsibility for that player's care." Pierce E. Scranton, Jr., Playing Hurt: Treating and Evaluating the Warriors of the NFL 72 (2001).

al   *See id.* at 86 ("After we saw the game's injured players, Jimmy and I took the injury report up to the head coach. He had to know who was okay, who might need X-ray studies, who needed surgery, and who might not practice but would still be able to play on Sunday.").

Because the visiting club's doctor is often not licensed to practice in the state in which the club is playing, the home club's doctor is responsible for the visiting player's care.

during the preseason but otherwise are unlikely to communicate with club executives during the season.

St. Louis Rams club doctor and former President of the NFL Physicians Society Matthew Matava maintains that a club's on-field success bears no relation to the club doctor's obligations or status with the club:

> *Physician jobs are not dependent on wins and losses . . . . I've survived 1–15, 2–14 and 3–13 seasons with the Rams. We can go 0–16, and my job does not change one iota . . . . Obviously we know that we want to have the guys back on the field as quickly as they can be in a safe fashion—and we can be creative in the ways we do so—but there are no competitive issues involved in our decision to return to play.*[214,am]

Nevertheless, it is possible that these pressures have subtle influences that even the doctors do not themselves fully recognize. This would not be surprising as the existing literature on conflicts of interest in the medical sphere emphasizes that many doctors are influenced by incentives and other forms of judgment distortion, while strictly denying this to be the case—peoples' judgments are often compromised by conflicts they fail to recognize in themselves.[215] We discuss the problems with structural conflicts of interest in the club doctor role and our recommendations in greater depth below.

6) RELATIONSHIPS WITH PLAYERS

As discussed above, players and club doctors have regular but minimal interaction as compared to athletic trainers. Players typically only see the club doctors if they are currently being treated for an injury, in which case they might see the club doctor a few times a week. However, players typically only see the club doctor if the athletic trainer has determined the injury to be serious enough to require the club doctor's involvement. Athletic trainers are the players' first line of medical care and almost all interactions with the club doctor are facilitated through the athletic trainer.

Among the players and contract advisors we interviewed, there was a general consensus that the care provided by club doctors has gradually improved in recent years. Current Player 3 said that "team doctors for the most part . . . do a good job." Current Players 7, 8 and 10 also thought their club doctors provide good care. As one contract advisor stated, "I think that team doctors more than ever are understanding that they're an advocate for the player more

than they are an advocate for the team." Another contract advisor explained one reason why he believes the care has improved: "It seems to me that because of the high level of scrutiny involved in the concussion melodrama and drama that's occurred over the past years that there is now some sense . . . on the part of the trainers and the medical staff, there is extreme pressure on them to not mess it up." Other people we interviewed confirmed that increased scrutiny about these issues, including from the NFLPA, has likely led club doctors to be more careful about their practices.

Trust is also an important factor in the relationship between club medical staff and players. A 2016 *Associated Press* survey of 100 current NFL players addressed this issue. The survey asked players whether "NFL teams, coaches and team doctors have players' best interests in mind when it comes to injuries and player health."[216] 47 players answered yes, 39 answered no, and 14 players were either unsure or refused to respond.[217,an]

We also interviewed several former and current players to get a better understanding about NFL player health issues.[ao] It is important to note that that these interviews were intended to be illustrative but certainly not representative of all players' views and should be read with that limitation in mind. The players we spoke to generally indicated that the current structure of club medical staff often caused players to distrust club doctors, although this feeling is not universal:

- **Current Player 1:** *"I do trust our team doctors. Any time that I've dealt with them, they've been very upfront with me and gave me all the information I needed about my injuries. I never got the impression that they were hiding anything from me or putting me into a dangerous situation."*[ap]

---

an The study also found discrepancies in the responses based on the player's experience level. Of the 34 players interviewed who had between 1 and 3 years of experience, 71 percent answered "yes." Of the 66 players interviewed who had 4 or more years of experience, only 35 percent answered "yes."

ao The protocols for the interviews were reviewed and approved by a Harvard University Institutional Review Board and consisted of approximately 30-minute interviews with 10 players active during the 2015 season and 3 players who recently left the NFL (the players' last seasons were 2010, 2012, and 2012 respectively). The players interviewed were part of a convenience sample identified through a variety of methods—some were interested in The Football Players Health Study more generally, some we engaged through our Law & Ethics Advisory Panel and Football Players Health Study Player Advisors, and some interviews were facilitated by a former player now working for the NFLPA. The players interviewed had played a mean of 7.5 seasons, with a range of 2 to 15 seasons, and for a mean of between 3 and 4 different clubs, with a range of 1 to 10 clubs. In addition, we interviewed players from multiple positions: one quarterback; two fullbacks; one tight end; three offensive linemen; two linebackers; one defensive end; two safeties; and, a special teams player. We aimed for a racially diverse set of players to be interviewed: seven were white and six were African American. Finally, the players also represented a range of skill levels, with both backups and starters, including four players who had been named to at least one Pro Bowl team.

ap It is worth noting that Current Player 1 had only two years of experience in the NFL, and several other current players explained that players become wiser, and thus less trusting, as they get older. Nevertheless, Current Player 10 had played 10 seasons in the NFL and believed he received good care from the club doctors: "[G]enerally, I think I'd go with team doctors if I'm going to do certain surgeries."

---

am In reviewing this Report, a representative of the National Athletic Trainers Association stated that "I agree that some physicians possibly g[e]t caught up in the business decision rather than the best practices for proper medical care of the athletes."

- **Current Player 2:** *"I certainly think that there are a number of players that do not trust club doctors, and for various reasons. They feel as though those doctors work for the team and they do what's in the best interests of (A) the coach, and (B), ownership. And I think that a lot of times players feel as though these doctors maybe don't disclose the full extent of their injuries [and] give them a hard time about getting second opinions."*

- **Current Player 3:** *"I think that there are some instances where they don't trust the team doctors because they don't like the team, and the team doctor just wants them to get back on the field . . . . I think sometimes the doctors may . . . not tell you the full extent of what's going on . . . about a certain injury. [But] I think there is sometimes team doctors where the players trust them and the doctors are great and very trustworthy."*[aq]

- **Current Player 4:** *"I do not trust team doctors. I've had multiple occasions where I've had a team doctor tell me one thing and then I go and have a second opinion and I get a completely different answer . . . . [T]he club doctor has the same mentality as the club itself. More than anything, they want a player on the field . . . . I feel like the team doctor only has the best interest of the team in mind and not necessarily the player."*

- **Current Player 5:** *"My trust level with [my former club doctor] was very high. I know a lot of guys respected him. But I know there was a number of guys that had disagreements with him . . . . But I think generally the guys that have a problem with the doctors are guys that have had some sort of injury that affects their career and their ability to make money and support themselves and their families."*

- **Current Player 7:** *"[T]hey're doing and saying what's best to get you back on the field as soon as possible."*

- **Current Player 8:** *"I don't feel like they are diagnosing, or at least treating us like they would want to be treated or how they would treat their kids . . . . [T]hey're going to lean towards what keeps you on the field."*

- **Current Player 9:** *"I've seen times when the medical staff has lied about injuries."*

- **Current Player 10:** *"I've always had good relationships and good positive vibes from the doctors that have been out on the field . . . . I think players trust them, I think the agents don't."*

- **Former Player 2:** *"[T]hese doctors are good. I wouldn't say they are great. You know, at the end of the day . . . the organizations are paying the doctors . . . . I would say probably 65 percent of the team trusts the doctor and probably 35 percent of the team does not."*[ar]

- **Former Player 3:** *"My experience has always been very positive . . . . I know that players are told, or maybe just a little bit skeptical or suspicious of docs, thinking that they have the team's interest in mind first before the player's, but I never had an experience where I thought that was the case."*

In addition, comments from Calvin Johnson, a perennial Pro Bowl wide receiver who retired in 2016 after nine seasons, are also informative:

> *The team doctor, the team trainers, they work for the team. And I love them, you know. . . . They're some good people. They want to see you do good. But at the same time, they work for the team. They're trying to do whatever they can to get you back on the field and make your team look good.*[218]

On this point, Contract Advisor 4 even stated that when assessing a player's injury, "the club doctor has nothing to do with it . . . the club doctor's input means nothing to us."[as] Moreover, players seem to be increasingly aware of the potential conflicts of interest club doctors face in treating players.[at] For example, many question whether club doctors are telling players everything they are telling coaches or other club employees, despite an obligation to do so in the CBA.[219] In addition, players are aware of the value club doctors receive in being associated with the club; as one former player said, "I know they can go out making tremendous amounts of money . . . having that team name next to their practice."

To be sure, not all share this view of the relationship between players and club doctors, and of course, as we acknowledge, the situation varies across clubs and over time. For example, during his time as an NFL executive, peer reviewer Andrew Brandt believes that the club doctors with whom he worked "always put the player's best interests first, erring on the side of caution in treatment." At the

---

aq   Current Player 3 also stated as follows: "Sometimes they want you out there and they want to see if you can push through certain pain if the doctor feels like, okay, it's not going to get any worse if you play. You just have to deal with the pain. Can you push through that pain? I think sometimes they want to see those types of things."

ar   Former Player 2 also said he believes getting the job as club doctor "is more about who you know than what you know."

as   Contract Advisor 4: "[T]he team doctor is there to advise the team on how they should approach a player. The team doctor has nothing to do as far as I'm concerned with how the player should approach his own health . . . . The team doctor is a medical advisor to the team."

at   Contract Advisor 5: "[T]he younger generation of players absolutely, unequivocally do not trust [the club doctors]." Contract Advisor 6 similarly described the level of trust between players and club doctors as "close to zero."

same time, Brandt indicated his belief that this was not the case with at least some NFL clubs.[220]

Several players told us that players often hide injuries from club medical staff.[au] They told us that players generally believe that there is no confidentiality between them and the medical staff and that the medical staff would regularly, if not immediately, inform coaches and executives about the injury status of players, which has the potential of negatively affecting the player's status with the club. Former Player 1:

> [C]ertainly not like a modern doctor-patient relationship where confidentiality is expected. That's never going to happen . . . . [U]ltimately, they had to do their jobs and they had to disclose everything to the higher ups and to the decision makers . . . they're writing down every single little thing that you do and what happened, everything that you tell him. The first thing they're doing is sending that email or making the phone call up to the top and telling them what's going on with this guy and there's no doubt about what their motives and their intentions are, and I know a lot of it is job security and it's just part of the business, but, and you know at the end of the day, regardless of how they came across, they were all pretty much doing the same thing, just some went about it in maybe a better fashion.[av]

As discussed above, these impressions are likely correct, as players sign waivers permitting the club medical staff to share their health information with other club employees.

An additional important aspect of the player-club doctor relationship is the club doctor's cooperation with the player obtaining a second opinion, which is discussed at length in Chapter 4: Second Opinion Doctors.

Some players expressed more concerns about athletic trainers' practices as compared to club doctors.[aw] Athletic trainers spend significantly more time with players and are directly employed by the club, whereas club doctors are generally independent contractors. One current player described multiple incidents in which an athletic trainer did not disclose a player's actual diagnosis (in one case a fracture and a torn ligament in another), only to have the diagnosis revealed later by the club doctor.[ax] The same player also indicated that he believes athletic trainers are pressured by the club and coaches to have players on the field.

G Enforcement of Legal and Ethical Obligations[ay]

The 2011 CBA provides three options for players dissatisfied with the care provided by an NFL club doctor. Nevertheless, as is explained in greater depth below, these options provide remedies that do not seem adequate.

First, a player could submit a complaint to the Accountability and Care Committee (ACC). The ACC consists of the NFL Commissioner (or his designee), the NFLPA Executive Director (or his designee), and six additional members "experienced in fields relevant to health care for professional athletes," three of whom are appointed by the Commissioner and three by the NFLPA Executive Director.[221] According to the NFL, the ACC then investigates the matter and submits a report to the NFL and/or the club.[222] According to the CBA, "the complaint shall be referred to the League and the player's Club, which together shall determine an appropriate response or corrective action if found to be reasonable. The Committee shall be informed of any response or corrective action."[223]

There is thus no neutral adjudicatory process for addressing the player's claim or compensating the player for any wrong suffered. The remedial process is left entirely in the hands of the NFL and the club. It is questionable whether either has an adequate incentive to find that a club doctor acted inappropriately and to compensate the injured player in any way.

Second, a player could request the NFLPA to commence an investigation before the Joint Committee on Player Safety and Welfare (Joint Committee). The Joint Committee consists of three representatives chosen by the NFL and three

---

au Current Player 5: "[G]uys might have existing injuries . . . and they try to keep that hidden and fear that they might not be given the opportunity to show that they can still play with the injury. I think some guys are on a team and you have a history of a certain injury and it starts acting up again. You don't want to be labeled as a chronic whatever injury. So, you might want to try to treat that on your own and conceal it from the team." Current Player 7: "[W]hen you know something's worse, and you want to keep playing, you kind of look out for yourself in a sense. Okay, if I tell them all this, I can't play. So let me see if I can get through it, and I'll tell them what it is minimal." However, as discussed in Chapter 1: Players, players do have an obligation under the CBA and their contract to advise the club medical staff of their condition at certain times.

av Current Player 2: "I think the only reason that guys usually don't disclose injuries is from fear of losing their job."

aw Current Player 1: "[P]layers do trust the doctors. But I think it's more the trainers that they don't trust as much."

ax The same player complained that the athletic training staff uses outdated treatment methods, effectively using ice and electrical stimulation regardless of the injury. The player indicated that, as a result, players are less likely to report injuries so they do not have to report to practice early to undergo a minimally effective treatment they could perform at home.

ay Appendix K is a summary of players' options to enforce legal and ethical obligations against the stakeholders discussed in this Report. In addition, for rights articulated under either the CBA or other NFL policy, the NFLPA and the NFL can also seek to enforce them on players' behalves.

chosen by the NFLPA.[224] "The NFLPA shall have the right to commence an investigation before the Joint Committee if the NFLPA believes that the medical care of a team is not adequately taking care of player safety. Within 60 days of the initiation of an investigation, two or more neutral physicians will be selected to investigate and report to the Joint Committee on the situation. The neutral physicians shall issue a written report within 60 days of their selection, and their recommendations as to what steps shall be taken to address and correct any issues shall be acted upon by the Joint Committee."[225]

This remedial option faces significant limitations. While a complaint to the Joint Committee results in a neutral review process, the scope of that review process' authority is vague. The Joint Committee is obligated to act upon the recommendations of the neutral physicians, but it is unclear what it means for the Joint Committee to "act" and there is nothing obligating the NFL or any club to abide by the neutral physicians' or Joint Committee's recommendations. Moreover, there is no indication that the neutral physicians or Joint Committee could award damages to an injured player.

In 2012, the NFLPA commenced the first and only Joint Committee investigation.[226] The nature and results of that investigation are confidential per an agreement between the NFL and NFLPA,[227] and we have therefore been unable to evaluate its adequacy.

As a third remedial option, a player could commence a Non-Injury Grievance.[az] The 2011 CBA directs certain disputes to designated arbitration mechanisms[ba] and directs the remainder of any disputes involving the CBA, a player contract, NFL rules, or generally the terms and conditions of employment to the Non-Injury Grievance arbitration process.[228] Importantly, Non-Injury Grievances provide players with the benefit of a neutral arbitration and the possibility of a "money award."[229] It is worth emphasizing that in theory a player could bring a Non-Injury Grievance alleging the doctor violated ethical rules. Section 1(c) of Article 39 of the 2011 CBA requires all club medical personnel to "comply with all federal, state, and local requirements, including all ethical rules and standards established by any applicable government and/or authority that regulates or governs the medical profession in the Club's city." And Section 1 of Article 43 permits players to bring Non-Injury Grievances concerning any provision of the CBA. Thus, if a club doctor were to violate an ethical rule, he would also be violating Article 39, Section 1(c). Which ethical rules apply has never been litigated and would likely have to be determined by the arbitrator.

There are, though, several important limitations on Non-Injury Grievances.

First, in cases where the club doctor is an employee of the club—as opposed to an independent contractor as is the case for most club doctors—a player's claim against the doctor might be barred by the relevant state's workers' compensation statute. Workers' compensation statutes provide compensation for workers injured at work and thus generally preclude claims against co-workers based on the co-workers' negligence.[230,bb] This has been the result in multiple lawsuits brought by NFL players against clubs and club doctors.[231] Some states follow the "dual capacity doctrine," which allows medical malpractice lawsuits to proceed against a doctor who is also a co-employee based on the doctor having two different relationships with the allegedly injured co-employee.[232] Nevertheless, as only two current NFL club doctors are employees as opposed to independent contractors, this doctrine is less of an issue.

Second, club doctors are not parties to the CBA and thus likely cannot be the respondent in a Non-Injury Grievance for violations of the CBA.[233] Instead, the player could seek to hold the club responsible for the club doctor's violation of the CBA.[234]

Third, Non-Injury Grievances must be filed within 50 days "from the date of the occurrence or non-occurrence upon which the grievance is based,"[235] a timeframe that is difficult to meet. This is a relatively short window for players to seek relief, especially during the season. Indeed, several players have commenced arbitrations against clubs (but not doctors) concerning medical care but those claims have often been denied as outside the CBA's statute of limitations, as discussed in Chapter 8: NFL Clubs.

---

az The term "Non-Injury Grievance" is something of a misnomer. The CBA differentiates between an Injury Grievance and a Non-Injury Grievance. An Injury Grievance is exclusively "a claim or complaint that, at the time a player's NFL Player Contract or Practice Squad Player Contract was terminated by a Club, the player was physically unable to perform the services required of him by that contract because of an injury incurred in the performance of his services under that contract." 2011 CBA, Art. 44, § 1. Generally, all other disputes (except System Arbitrations, see 2011 CBA, Art. 15) concerning the CBA or a player's terms and conditions of employment are Non-Injury Grievances. 2011 CBA, Art. 43, § 1. Thus, there can be disputes concerning a player's injury or medical care that are considered Non-Injury Grievances because they do not fit within the limited confines of an Injury Grievance.

ba For example, Injury Grievances, which occur when, at the time a player's contract was terminated, the player claims he was physically unable to perform the services required of him because of a football-related injury, are heard by a specified Arbitration Panel. 2011 CBA, Art. 44. Additionally, issues concerning certain Sections of the CBA related to labor and antitrust issues, such as free agency and the salary cap, are within the exclusive scope of the System Arbitrator, 2011 CBA, Art. 15, currently University of Pennsylvania Law School Professor Stephen B. Burbank.

bb Importantly, whether the worker can recover for the injury in another way, such as by obtaining workers' compensation benefits from the employer, is a different question.

Additionally, since the execution of the 2011 CBA, there have been no grievances concerning Article 39: Players' Rights to Medical Care and Treatment decided on the merits,[236] suggesting either clubs are in compliance with Article 39 or the Article has not been sufficiently enforced.

Fourth, it is possible that under the 2011 CBA, the NFL could argue that complaints concerning medical care are designated elsewhere in the CBA and thus should not be heard by the Non-Injury Grievance arbitrator.[237,bc]

And as a fifth limitation to Non-Injury Grievances, in practice, pursuing a grievance against a club doctor would likely end the player's career with that club, and potentially his career altogether.[bd]

As a fourth remedial option, and one outside of the CBA process, players can attempt to bring civil lawsuits against NFL club doctors, principally asserting medical malpractice. However, the viability of such claims principally depends on the relationship between the club and the doctor. As discussed above, claims against doctors that are employees of the club are likely to be barred by workers' compensation statutes. By contrast, for suits against the majority of club doctors who are independent contractors, the CBA potentially presents the biggest obstacle against any medical malpractice claims. This is because the Labor Management Relations Act (LMRA)[238] bars or "preempts" state common law[be] claims, such as negligence, where the claim is "substantially dependent upon analysis of the terms" of a CBA, *i.e.*, where the claim is "inextricably intertwined with consideration of the terms of the" CBA."[239] In order to assess a club doctor's duty to an NFL player—an essential element of a negligence claim such as medical malpractice—the court may have to refer to and analyze the terms of the CBA, *e.g.*, the club doctors' obligation, resulting in the claim's preemption.[240] In these cases, player complaints must be resolved through the enforcement provisions provided by the CBA itself (*i.e.*, a Non-Injury Grievance against the club), rather than litigation. Thus, preemption may be a problem, although the matter is not crystal clear.

Lawsuits brought against clubs concerning medical care have generally been held to be preempted.[241] However, claims against doctors have found more success. To understand why, it is important to distinguish between claims brought prior to the 2011 CBA and those that might be brought under subsequent CBAs.

> There have been no grievances concerning Article 39: Players' Rights to Medical Care and Treatment decided on the merits, suggesting either clubs are in compliance with Article 39 or the Article has not been sufficiently enforced.

Prior to 2011, the CBA was not particularly robust in its description of the doctors' obligations. Thus, the chances were reduced that courts would find the medical malpractice actions preempted by the CBA, since those actions were less likely to be held inextricably intertwined with the then-existing CBA. Indeed, in the *Jeffers v. Carolina Panthers* arbitration in 2008,[242] the NFL argued that "an action in tort for malpractice against a doctor should proceed in state court, while an action against a Club, arising from a duty or obligation imposed by the CBA, must be resolved by arbitration." The arbitrator agreed, stating "that claims based on allegations of malpractice by physicians or other medical care providers deemed to be independent contractors are not arbitrable."

Research revealed 13 fully adjudicated cases brought by NFL players (or their kin) against NFL club doctors, discussed in more detail in Appendix H. All of these cases were filed prior to the 2011 CBA which at least partially explains why the claims were not preempted. Nine of the cases resulted either in settlements or jury verdicts in the player's favor, with several recoveries exceeding $1 million. In two cases, the claims were dismissed on the ground that the doctor was an employee of the club and workers' compensation laws bar claims against co-employees.[243] Both categories include the *Stringer* case, in which claims against one doctor were settled while claims against two other doctors were dismissed. Finally, in one case, the doctor was found to have been not negligent,[244] and, in another, a jury verdict was overturned by the judge.

---

bc   Nevertheless, research has not revealed any arbitration decisions in which the NFL made this argument.

bd   Current Player 8: "You don't have the gall to stand against your franchise and say 'They mistreated me.' . . . I, still today, going into my eighth year, am afraid to file a grievance, or do anything like that[.]" While it is illegal for an employer to retaliate against an employee for filing a grievance pursuant to a CBA, *N.L.R.B. v. City Disposal Systems Inc.*, 465 U.S. 822, 835–36 (1984), such litigation would involve substantial time and money for an uncertain outcome.

be   Common law refers to "[t]he body of law derived from judicial decisions, rather than from statutes or constitutions." Black's Law Dictionary (9th ed. 2009). The concept of "preemption" is "[t]he principle (derived from the Supremacy Clause [of the Constitution] that a federal law can supersede or supplant any inconsistent state law or regulation." *Id.*

The revisions to the 2011 CBA, and the new Article 39 in particular, increase the likelihood that medical malpractice actions against club doctors will now be held to be preempted. As discussed throughout this chapter, the 2011 CBA is fairly detailed in terms of club doctors' obligations to players, including an outlined standard of care. It is thus at least plausible that a court would find that analyzing a player's medical malpractice claim against a club doctor would be "inextricably intertwined with consideration of the terms of the CBA" and thus preempted. However, research has not revealed any player who has sued a club doctor for medical malpractice concerning events that took place after the execution of the 2011 CBA.

The revisions to the 2011 CBA, the new Article 39 in particular, increase the likelihood that medical malpractice actions against club doctors will now be held to be preempted.

Finally, during its review of this Report, the NFL informed us that the NFLPS "has designed and implemented a peer review process through which its membership could investigate and discipline members."[245] When we asked the NFLPS for more information on its peer review process, the NFLPS explained that it was created in 2014 pursuant to the Healthcare Quality Improvements Act (HQIA).[246] The HQIA was enacted in 1986 to improve healthcare by promoting peer review in the medical setting by immunizing such processes from antitrust scrutiny, and creating a national database of actions taken during such peer review processes called the National Practitioner Data Bank (NPDB).[247] Healthcare organizations can access the NPDB for consideration in making licensing, hiring, and credentialing decisions but the statute also declares that information reported to the NPDB is confidential.[248] However, information that does not reveal the identity of someone is not considered confidential.[249] Based on our understanding of the statute, we informed the NFLPS that our understanding was (1) that the remedial actions available as part of the NFLPS' peer review process would be limited to evaluating a club doctor's membership in the NFLPS, and (2) that the NFLPS could disclose to us de-identified aggregate data on the number of enforcement actions the NFLPS had taken under its peer review process.

The NFLPS declined to comment on our understanding of its peer review process. We then explained to NFLPS that it was our belief that the NFLPS has never taken any action under its peer review process and asked them to correct us if we were wrong. The NFLPS again declined to comment.

During its review the NFL also stated that it had "proposed enhancing the enforcement powers of [the NFLPS] by making membership in the NFLPS a prerequisite to serving on a Club's medical staff, but the NFLPA has rejected that proposal."[250] According to the NFL, such a requirement "could also serve as a dispute resolution mechanism."[251] In response, the NFLPA stated that "[t]he NFL's proposal contained a number of issues that were not in the best interest of players, including empowering a group that is not party to the CBA. With or without NFLPA agreement, the NFL and Physician Society are able to establish membership requirements and enforce the same."[252] We also note that because the NFLPS has no process by which players can make complaints or have their grievances redressed, the NFL's proposal does not provide a meaningful enforcement mechanism for players.

These options exhaust the remedies that individual players can pursue against club doctors. On the other hand, there is also the potential for actions against the doctors by accreditation bodies—an action that can be initiated by any patient against any doctor. State licensing boards have their own regulations related to violations of ethical standards that may result in disciplinary action (e.g., revoking a physician's license to practice medicine).[253] Many state licensure boards codes of ethics reference or are substantially similar to the AMA Code.[254] However, like the AMA Council on Ethical and Judicial Affairs (AMA Council), the state licensing boards have no authority to order compensation to a patient. Additionally, in the words of one of the preeminent authorities on American health law, "[m]ost boards do not have adequate staff to respond to the volume of complaints and to conduct extensive investigations of unprofessional conduct," leading consumer groups to complain about the industry's failure to self-regulate.[255]

In the event a doctor is accused of violating of the AMA Code, the AMA Council, in conjunction with the AMA President, has the power to appoint investigating juries and to institute disciplinary action against AMA members where appropriate.[256] The AMA Council has the authority to "acquit, admonish, censure, or place on probation" the accused doctor or "expel him or her from AMA membership."[257]

However, the AMA Council generally does not review complaints submitted by the general public because it believes it "is not in a position to investigation allegations of unprofessional or unethical conduct at the local level."[258] Instead, complaints referred to the AMA are usually forwarded by state medical societies and national medical societies. If the AMA Council decides the unethical conduct is "greater than local concern,"[259] it may ask the AMA President to appoint an investigating jury to determine whether there is a probable cause of action. Finally, doctors do not need to be members of the AMA to practice medicine.

The AMA Code's enforcement mechanisms are of little use as remediation to NFL players who received improper care from a team doctor. First, as discussed above, the AMA is unlikely to even review the player's complaint. Second, the AMA Code does not provide any method by which the injured patient can be compensated.

Finally, despite having a robust Code of Ethics, FIMS has no enforcement mechanism, other than the vague ability to revoke a doctor's membership by a vote of two-thirds of its Council of Delegates.[260]

In summary, although it appears that players have a variety of opportunities to enforce club doctors' legal and ethical obligations and obtain compensation, realistically, players are significantly limited by the short statute of limitations in the grievance process and by the potential preemption of claims by workers' compensation statutes and the CBA. Moreover, the remaining options seem unlikely to provide a player with a meaningful remedy.

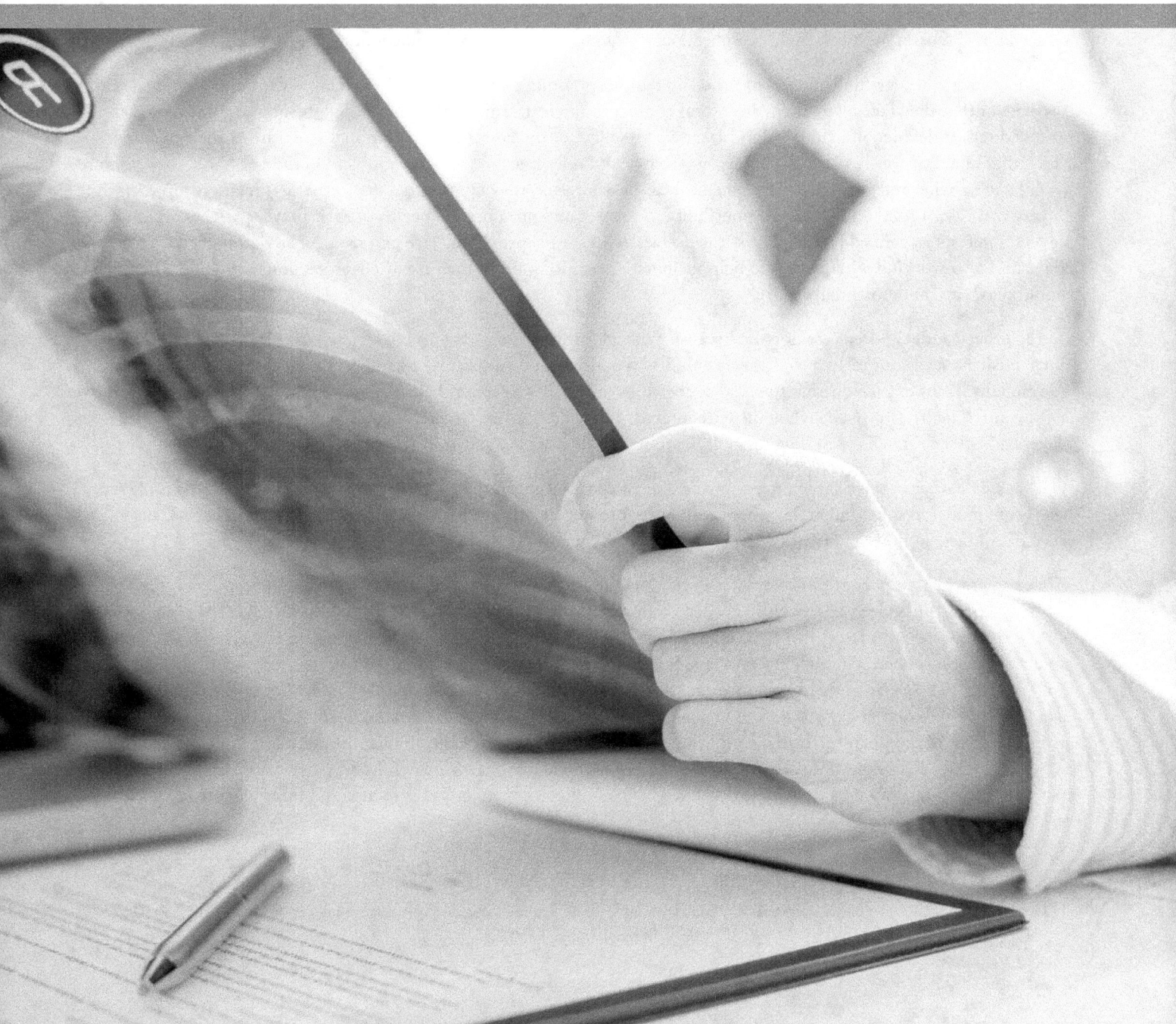

H | Recommendations Concerning Club Doctors

Club doctors are clearly one of the most important stakeholders in protecting and promoting player health. Fortunately, evidence suggests that club doctors' relationships with and treatment of players has improved in recent years. Nevertheless, there are still many important ways in which club doctors' practices and the structure in which they operate can be improved. Our recommendations below seek to address these issues.[bf]

Goal 1: To ensure that players receive the best healthcare possible from providers who are as free from conflicts of interest as possible.

Principles Advanced: Respect; Health Primacy; Empowered Autonomy; Transparency; Managing Conflicts of Interest; and, Justice.

The above-stated goal may seem obvious. Nevertheless, existing ethics codes and legal requirements are insufficient to satisfy the goal of ensuring that players receive healthcare they can trust from providers who are as free from conflicts of interest as is realistically possible. Of course, achieving this goal is legally, ethically, financially, and structurally complicated. We begin by discussing some of these complications before presenting our recommendation for how best to get there.

Club doctors are clearly fundamental to protecting and promoting player health. Yet given the various roles just described, it is evident that they face an inherent structural conflict of interest. This is not a moral judgment about them as competent professionals or devoted individuals, but rather a simple fact of the current organizational structure of their position in which they simultaneously perform at least two roles that are not necessarily compatible. On the one hand, they are hired by clubs to provide and supervise player medical care. As a result, they enter into a doctor-patient relationship with the players and have a legal and ethical responsibility to protect and promote the health of their player-patients, in line with players' interests as defined by the players themselves. This means providing care and medical advice aligned with player goals, and also working with players to help them make decisions about their own self-protection, including when they should play, rest, and potentially retire.

On the other hand, clubs engage doctors because medical information about and assessment of players is necessary to clubs' business decisions related to a player's ability to perform at a sufficiently high level in the short and long term. Additionally, clubs engage doctors to advance the clubs' interest in keeping their players healthy and helping them recover as fully and quickly as possible when they are injured. These dual roles for club doctors may sometimes conflict because players and clubs often have conflicting interests, but club doctors are called to serve both parties.

As discussed earlier in this chapter, in reviewing a draft of this Report, the NFL repeatedly analogized the NFL player healthcare model to other industries where employers provide healthcare for their employees. Again, however, the existence of conflicts in other industries does not excuse the conflict in the NFL setting.

While the practical impact of these conflicts in the NFL almost certainly varies from club to club depending on the club's approach to player health and the medical staff's autonomy, the conflict itself is unavoidable whenever the club doctor is expected to wear both hats, with simultaneous and sometimes conflicting obligations both to players and to clubs. A system that requires heroic moral and professional judgment in the face of a systemic structural conflict of interest is one that is bound to fail, even if there are individual doctors who manage to negotiate this conflict better than others. Moreover, even if a club doctor can successfully manage the conflicts, their mere existence can compromise player trust—a critical element of the doctor-patient relationship. That is why we describe the conflict of interest as inherent; the conflict is as rooted in the perceptions of others as it is in the decisions and actions of the conflicted party. Ultimately, it is the system that deserves blame, and thus, as will be discussed below, our recommendation is focused on improving that system.

---

bf   Additionally, because the roles of the various doctors with whom a player may consult are so intertwined, all recommendations made in Chapter 4: Second Opinion Doctors, Chapter 5: Neutral Doctors, and Chapter 6: Personal Doctors also can be applied to the club doctors.

Recommendations Concerning Club Doctors – continued

Additionally, there have been longstanding concerns about how club doctors are chosen, including the nature of the doctor's compensation (if any) and whether sponsorship[bg] is involved (even if the sponsorship is part of a separate agreement).

The 2011 CBA appeared to remedy some of these concerns with the addition of the below provision:

> [E]ach Club physician's primary duty in providing medical care shall be not to the Club but instead to the player-patient. This duty shall include traditional physician/patient confidentiality requirements. In addition, all Club physicians and medical personnel shall comply with all federal, state, and local requirements, including all ethical rules and standards established by any applicable government and/or other authority that regulates or governs the medical profession in the Club's city.[261]

However, this provision, while seemingly well-intentioned, is flawed or insufficient in several respects, as discussed previously in this chapter.

First, on at least one reading, the provision limits the club doctor's obligations to put the player first only to those situations in which the doctor is "providing medical care." As discussed above, club doctors have obligations to the club that extend beyond "providing medical care," specifically helping the club make determinations about the short- and long-term usefulness[bh] of a player. Thus, there are many situations in which the club doctor is not required by the above provision to put the player's interests first, because indeed he could not do so.

Second, the provision effectively acknowledges club doctors' divided loyalties when providing medical care by referencing the doctor's "primary" duty as opposed to "exclusive" duty. Clearly, the club doctor's secondary duty would be to the club, and the club's interests are therefore permissibly considered under the terms of this provision. By acknowledging that club doctors have divided loyalties, the provision cannot fully advance player health as a club doctor's primary concern.

Third, the confidentiality provision fails to account for relevant realities. As discussed above, employers are permitted to receive employee health information in many circumstances. Additionally, the club doctor could not simultaneously comply with "traditional physician/patient confidentiality requirements" and the doctor's obligations to advise the club about the health of a player. Finally, all players execute collectively bargained waivers before each season, permitting disclosure of their health information to the club. It is clear that in practice there is no confidentiality when it comes to medical information about players making its way to the club. Nevertheless, for these reasons and others that will be explained further below, the recommendations that we make also do not cloak player medical information in absolute confidentiality.

Finally, and most importantly, to the extent that the provision seeks to provide players with unconflicted healthcare, it falls short because it does not resolve the structural and institutional pressures club doctors face, whether implicitly or explicitly. So long as the club doctor is chosen, paid and reviewed by the club to both care for players and advise the club, the doctor will have, at a minimum, tacit pressures or subconscious desires to please the club by doing what is in the club's best interests.[262,bi]

In addition, like the CBA provision discussed above, many of the Codes of Ethics that would appear relevant to club doctors appear insufficient when applied to actual scenarios club doctors face. For example, AMA Code Opinion 1.2.5 declares that, in a sports medicine setting, doctors must "base their judgment about an individual's participation solely on medical considerations,"[263] when, in reality, we know players' concerns extend beyond their own health—and we are not prepared to say that this is inappropriate or unacceptable; indeed, it may be completely rational. Club doctors must take into account a player's other interests and goals and, at a certain point, our principle of Empowered Autonomy permits players to not follow a club doctor's recommendations. Similarly, the FIMS' Code of Ethics declares that "[t]he same

---

bg   As described earlier in this chapter, the 2014 Medical Sponsorship Policy defines "Sponsorship Agreements" as "agreements with M[edical Service Provider]s involving the sale or license by the club of commercial assets such as naming rights, stadium signage, advertising inventory within club-controlled media, promotional inventory (e.g., day-of-game promotions), hospitality, and rights to use club trademarks for marketing and promotional purposes."

bh   To speak of "usefulness" sounds somewhat dehumanizing. However, the term captures the cost-benefit approach to players that is at the heart of the determinations the clubs are making. To sugarcoat this reality would be to obfuscate.

bi   Current Player 3: "I think when it comes down to it, who's paying you? . . . [A]s long as the teams are paying for [the doctors], they're going to have to answer to the team; they're going to have to answer to the coach; they're going to have to answer to the boss. That's who is writing their check."

ethical principles that apply to the practice of medicine shall apply to sports medicine" but later declares that it is "essential" that athletes be informed about a doctor's responsibilities to the club and that the player authorize the doctor to disclose "otherwise confidential medical information" to certain club officials "for the expressed purpose of determining the fitness of the athlete for participation."[264] Of course, this dual loyalty is not part of the usual practice of medicine, and so the same ethical principles cannot always apply.

Given the ethics of the doctor-patient relationship, it is clear that club doctors must never sacrifice player health in order to advance *club* interests, for example by recommending treatment that will get a player back on the field quickly but result in substantial harm to the player's health in the short or long term. However, this is not to say that clubs do not have some legitimate interest in player health and player health information. Player health significantly affects the clubs' ability to win and therefore the ultimate success of their business. Thus, we acknowledge that clubs must have access to information about player health and medical treatment, including sufficient information to assess whether a player should play. Similarly, clubs have a legitimate interest in understanding a player's short- and long-term health prospects so it can make informed decisions about the player's short- and long-term prospects of assisting the club. This is the stark reality of a business driven by physical prowess and ability, but we believe there are preferable mechanisms to acknowledge that reality while accounting for player interests than are offered by the existing system.

As we said above, finding a solution to these problems is not easy. Many commentators before us have recognized the problems at hand, including discussions about conflicts of interest and pressure from the club on club medical staff, player autonomy, and decisions about when a player can return to play.[265] Some have also recommended solutions. For example, in a 1984 article, Dr. Thomas H. Murray, current President Emeritus of The Hastings Center, proposed four possible solutions for correcting conflicts of interest in sports medicine: (a) clarifying the nature of the relationship at the outset; (b) club doctors insisting on professional autonomy over the medical aspect of decisions; (c) insulating the club doctor "structurally from illegitimate pressures"; and, (d) professionalizing sports medicine.[266] We agree that the first two proposals would help,[bj] but do not believe they solve the structural conflict of interest that is at the root of the problem. The fourth proposal has seemingly largely come to fruition since the writing of Dr. Murray's article. And finally, Dr. Murray's third proposal provides support for our recommendation below.[bk] Despite the foundational work of others, the problem has not been resolved. There is a spectrum of possible approaches, each with benefits and deficiencies. Below, we discuss some of the possibilities, several of which could be further dissected or combined, before reaching our ultimate recommendation.

A. **Maintain the status quo with increased reliance on personal and second opinion doctors:** Throughout the modern history of the NFL, players have increasingly obtained second opinions to compare against those provided by the club doctor,[bl] and have also relied on their own personal doctors for care. Nevertheless, interviews we conducted with players and contract advisors indicated that seeking care from a personal doctor is a burdensome process that players are often reluctant to undertake.[bm] It is far easier for players to simply receive healthcare at the club facility where they are already spending a considerable amount of their time than to seek out a personal doctor with an office off premises, and perhaps a less robust understanding of a player's professional and physical challenges. This is especially true given how much players travel and move during, after, and between seasons. Consequently, many players, particularly the younger ones, continue to rely solely on the medical opinion of and care provided by the club doctor. It is thus uncertain how effective this approach would be. Moreover, it does not resolve the fact that club doctors would remain in a conflicted position.

B. **Maintain the status quo without the execution of confidentiality waivers:** As discussed above, players execute waivers (which have been collectively bargained between the NFL and NFLPA) permitting the club medical staff to disclose the player's health information to the club, stripping players of certain protections provided for in relevant laws and ethical codes concerning confidentiality. Players could refuse to execute these waivers and effectively preclude the clubs from knowing the specifics of a player's

---

bj   Indeed, in Recommendation 2:1-I, we recommend that "club doctors' roles should be clarified in a written document provided to the players before each season."

bk   In support of his third proposal, Dr. Murray cited a 1982 proposal from the NFLPA that club doctors be chosen jointly by the players and the clubs. *See* Bart Barnes, *Garvey: Players May Seek 65% of NFL Gross Income, NFLPA Will Seek Base Salary Scales,* Wash. Post, Nov. 25, 1981, *available at* 1981 WLNR 488341.

bl   Players have the right to a second opinion doctor and the surgeon of their choice, the full cost of which must be paid by the club, provided the player consults with the club doctor and provides the club doctor with a report concerning treatment provided by the second opinion doctor. *See* 2011 CBA, Art. 39, § 4, § 5.

bm   This issue is discussed further in Chapter 6: Personal Doctors.

medical condition. However, it is unrealistic to expect players who are constantly under threat of having their contracts terminated to risk displeasing the club's management by taking this stand on their own; it would have to be a collective approach, supported by the NFLPA. More importantly, however, as discussed herein, employers are arguably entitled to at least some information about an employee's work-related health and the club would still likely at least be entitled to know whether the player was fit to play, which may actually entail quite a wide range of medical information. Thus, the player gains little by refusing to sign the waiver and, again, the institutional and financial pressures concerning medical care provided by the club doctor would remain.

C. **Pay club doctors from a fund to which the NFL and the NFLPA jointly contribute:** The fact that the club pays the doctor (even if only small amounts) to provide services, including treating the player — whose interests may be adverse to the club's — creates an undeniable conflict of interest. A structure whereby the club doctor is paid equally by the NFL and NFLPA has the potential to remove some of the implicit structural pressures that the club doctor might feel to act in the club's best interests. However, so long as the club doctor is still chosen and reviewed by the club, and is retained to simultaneously provide services to players and clubs, the doctor is still potentially under pressure to compromise the player's best interests in favor of the club's.

D. **Choose club doctors, and subject them to review and termination, through a committee of medical experts selected equally by the NFL and the NFLPA:[bn]** The fact that club doctors are hired, paid and reviewed by the clubs presents the most foundational conflict. One way to avoid this problem is to incorporate the players into the club doctor hiring, review, and termination processes equally with the clubs themselves. A possible approach would be for the NFL and NFLPA to each select three members of a committee, and then have those six members select a seventh neutral member as chair; the committee would be responsible for selection, review, and potential replacement of the club physicians for each of the 32 clubs.[bo] Additionally, this committee could be responsible for determining the doctor's compensation, taking into account the proposed rates by the doctors interested in the position and market rates in the club's city. The doctor's compensation would still be paid by the club.

Once selected, the doctor would be subject to periodic review (perhaps once during the season and again after the season) in which the interested parties have an opportunity to weigh in on the doctor's performance. This committee could also gather data on the performance of club doctors with the potential to enable the identification of "outliers" and take corrective action. If the committee determined that the doctor's performance was unsatisfactory taking into consideration all of the parties' needs, it should then also have the ability to terminate the doctor.

Adopting this kind of solution would reduce the pressure some club doctors may feel to please the club in their treatment decisions and information disclosure, since they would no longer be linked to only one of the relevant parties. In this way, adding another party might help resolve the conflict of interest we have identified. However, even under this approach, it would remain the case that club doctors would be responsible to provide services to both players and clubs, and that can create conflicting obligations.

E. **Bifurcate doctors' responsibilities between players and clubs:** To truly address the root problem of conflicting obligations, this approach contemplates having a doctor whose sole responsibility is to provide care to the players ("Players' Doctor") and another doctor whose sole responsibility is to evaluate the player's fitness to play and advise the club accordingly ("Club Evaluation Doctor"). This solution avoids the dual loyalty problem by creating two completely separate medical roles each with a single loyalty and a distinct set of responsibilities. Such a split has the potential to ensure that the player is receiving unconflicted medical care at all times, while still allowing the club to receive the guidance it needs. In order for the Club Evaluation Doctor to still be able to perform his or her job, however, he or she would need substantial access to the player and the player's medical information.

From the players' perspective, this proposal has the potential to provide them with care from a doctor who only has their best interests in mind, and for whom they can trust that to be the case. However, if the Players' Doctor were still being selected exclusively by the club, a conflict of interest remains. Additionally, the Club Evaluation Doctor may have a diminished capacity to provide an opinion as to whether the player is fit to play if he or she is not also treating the player personally, with all of the knowledge and understanding the treatment relationship entails.

---

bn *See* Arthur L. Caplan & Lee H. Igel, *Chelsea Manager Jose Mourinho Shows Why Teams Shouldn't Hire Doctors*, Forbes (Aug. 14, 2015, 4:25 PM), http://www.forbes.com/sites/leeigel/2015/08/14/chelsea-manager-jose-mourinho-shows-why-teams-shouldnt-hire-doctors/, *archived at* http://perma.cc/CR5D-BVU8 ("In no sport should teams be allowed to hire their own physicians. Each league should hire physicians for the clubs and franchises, with the physicians reporting to a chief medical officer based in the league's headquarters.").

bo The NFL and NFLPA maintain a jointly compiled list of neutral doctors to assist in Injury Grievances, which might be a useful starting point. *See* 2011 CBA, Art. 44, § 5.

Recommendations Concerning Club Doctors – continued

Figure 2-C: Possible Approaches for Improving the NFL Player Healthcare Environment

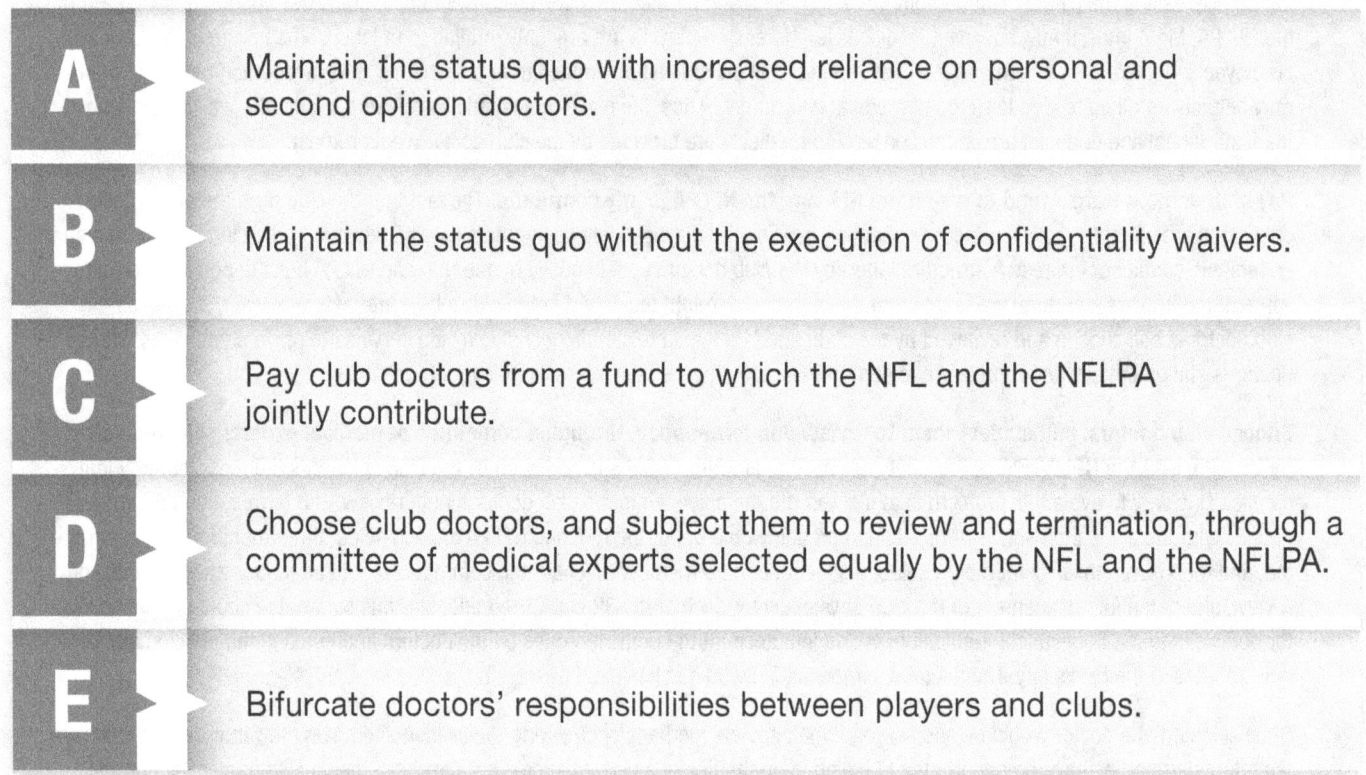

A ▸ Maintain the status quo with increased reliance on personal and second opinion doctors.

B ▸ Maintain the status quo without the execution of confidentiality waivers.

C ▸ Pay club doctors from a fund to which the NFL and the NFLPA jointly contribute.

D ▸ Choose club doctors, and subject them to review and termination, through a committee of medical experts selected equally by the NFL and the NFLPA.

E ▸ Bifurcate doctors' responsibilities between players and clubs.

While several of the above scenarios offer improvements over the current situation, each also has deficiencies. Consequently, we believe our recommendation below is the one most likely to promote and protect player health. It combines two of the possible approaches above to achieve an optimal balance. That said, if our preferred recommendation is not adopted, serious consideration should be given to the others listed above, as any would be an improvement over the status quo.[bp]

Recommendation 2:1-A: The current arrangement in which club (*i.e.,* "team") medical staff, including doctors, athletic trainers, and others, have responsibilities both to players and to the club presents an inherent conflict of interest. To address this problem and help ensure that players receive medical care that is as free from conflict as possible, division of responsibilities between two distinct groups of medical professionals is needed. Player care and treatment should be provided by one set of medical professionals (called the "Players' Medical Staff"), appointed by a joint committee with representation from both the NFL and NFLPA, and evaluation of players for business purposes should be done by separate medical personnel (the "Club Evaluation Doctor").

---

bp In theory it might be even more desirable to have different teams implement different recommendations, collect data, and then arrive at a more evidence-based recommendation for which possible approach is superior. In practice, though, we think the costs of administering those experiments, concerns about who would without conflict monitor and evaluate those experiments, and the costs of disuniformity for players in the meantime are too high to endorse that approach.

Recommendations Concerning Club Doctors – continued

This recommendation is an amalgamation of two of the possible approaches (D and E) discussed above. It is also important to remember that this recommendation encompasses athletic trainers as well, as discussed further in Chapter 3: Athletic Trainers, Section F: Recommendations. Here is how it would work.

As discussed earlier, the CBA requires clubs to retain several different types of doctors. Currently, the use of these doctors and their opinions are largely filtered through the head club doctor, who is the doctor that visits the club's practices a few times a week, directs the athletic trainers, and otherwise generally leads the medical staff. This structure and process would largely remain, but with two important distinctions. Doctors and the other medical staff[bq] for all of the clubs would: (1) be chosen, reviewed, and have their compensation determined by the joint committee of medical experts jointly selected by the NFL and NFLPA (Medical Committee) (but still paid by the club); and, (2) have as their principal obligation the treatment of players in accordance with prevailing and customary medical ethics standards and laws. For shorthand, we refer to the head doctor in this new role as the "Head Players' Doctor" and to the collection of other doctors (and medical personnel mentioned earlier) as the "Players' Medical Staff."

In this role, the Head Players' Doctor effectively replaces the individual currently known as the club doctor. In many respects, the daily responsibilities of the doctors and athletic trainers do not change under our proposed system. The key change, though, is for whom they now work—the players, as opposed to the clubs. The Head Players' Doctor would be at practices and games for the treatment of players for the same amount of time as club doctors currently are and would also still be responsible for directing the work of the athletic trainers (also part of the Players' Medical Staff). The Head Players' Doctor—and the entire Players' Medical Staff—would provide care and treatment to the players without any communications with or consideration given to the club, outside of our proposed "Player Health Report" detailed next. Moreover, the Head Players' Doctor (with input from the player) controls the player's level of participation in practices and games. Again, even though the Head Players' Doctor would still be paid by the club, he or she would be selected, reviewed, and potentially terminated by the Medical Committee, thus avoiding a key source of conflict.[br] Such a review should include a determination of whether the Head Players' Doctor has abided by all relevant legal and ethical obligations (including the administration of prescription and painkilling medications) on top of an evaluation of their medical expertise.[bs]

The value of this approach is demonstrated by the current existence of the Unaffiliated Neurotrauma Consultant as part of the Concussion Protocol. As discussed above, each club is assigned an Unaffiliated (*i.e.*, not affiliated with any club) Neurotrauma Consultant to help evaluate players for concussions during the game. In adopting this approach, the NFL and NFLPA have recognized and endorsed the importance of a player receiving healthcare free from actual or potential conflicts of interest. It is our view that player healthcare should be free of conflicts of interest at all times, not only during examination for a possible concussion. Thus, our recommendation employs a structure already in place for Unaffiliated Neurotrauma Consultants and seeks to apply it to more quotidian medical encounters.

To further understand our recommendation, we next review our proposed "Player Health Report"; the club's access to player medical records; the remaining need for doctors to provide services to the clubs; and, possible objections to our recommendation from both player-centric and club-centric perspectives.

The Player Health Report

Under our recommendation, the club would be entitled to regular written reports from the Players' Medical Staff about the status of any players currently receiving medical treatment ("Player Health Report"). Clubs—like many employers—have

---

bq At the beginning of Part 2, we explained there are many types of healthcare professionals that work with NFL clubs and players, including but not limited to physical therapists, massage therapists, chiropractors, dentists, nutritionists, and psychologists. We focus on doctors and athletic trainers because of their systematic and continuous relationship with the club and players. Nevertheless, all of these professionals would be a part of the Players' Medical Staff we recommend.

br In reviewing this Report, the National Athletic Trainers Association expressed that "[a] coach should not be able to terminate a physician."

bs One possible model for such evaluations come from The Joint Commission, a healthcare accreditation organization, which has in place processes for evaluating the care of doctors called the Ongoing Professional Practice Evaluation ("OPPE") and Focused Professional Practice Evaluation ("FPPE"). *See* Robert A. Wise, *OPPE and FPPE: Tools to help make privileging decisions*, The Joint Comm'n (Aug. 21, 2013), http://www.jointcommission.org/jc_physician_blog/oppe_fppe_tools_privileging_decisions/, *archived at* http://perma.cc/5BCR-3UBV. This is only one potential model, others are possible, and we do not purport to dictate the specific protocols for these evaluations.

Recommendations Concerning Club Doctors – continued

a legitimate business interest (and indeed in many circumstances a legal right) to know about their employees' health inso-far as it affects their ability to perform the essential functions of their jobs. The Player Health Report would serve this pur-pose by briefly describing: (1) the player's condition; (2) the player's permissible level of participation in practice and other club activities; (3) the player's current status for the next game (*e.g.,* out, doubtful, questionable, or probable);[bt] (4) any limitations on the player's potential participation in the next game; and, (5) an estimation of when the player will be able to return to full participation in practice and games. The Player Health Report would be a summary form written for the lay coaches and club officials, as opposed to a detailed medical document. Generally speaking, we propose that the Player Health Reports be provided to the club before and after each practice and game. Additionally, the club would be entitled to a Player Health Report on days where there is no practice or game if a player has received medical care or testing. The Player Health Reports should also be made available to players as they are issued, perhaps through their electronic medical records. The Players' Medical Staff shall complete the Player Health Report in a good faith effort to permit the club to be properly prepared for its next game.[bu]

Generating the Player Health Report is substantially similar to club doctors' current duties and requirements. Club doctors and athletic trainers regularly update the club on player health status and are also required to advise the player in writing of any information that the club doctor provides to the club concerning a player's condition "which significantly affects the player's performance or health."[267] That player notification requirement would stand.

The important distinction, however, is that under this recommendation, the Players' Medical Staff's determination as to a player's status would control the player's level of participation in any practice or game, excepting the player's right to obtain a second opinion, as explained below.

As an initial matter, in creating the Player Health Report, it is important that the Head Players' Doctor take into consid-eration the player's desires and not strictly clinical criteria. Players, like all patients, are entitled to autonomy-the right to make their own choices concerning healthcare. Thus, if a player who is fully informed of the risks wishes to play through an injury, the Head Players' Doctor should take that into consideration in completing the Player Health Report and decid-ing whether the player can play. Nevertheless, players who have suffered concussions or other injuries that might affect the player's cognition at the time of decision-making should be given significantly less deference.[bv]

If the Head Players' Doctor declares that a player cannot play but the player nonetheless wants to do so, the player could receive a second opinion. The logistics of when and how the player obtained the second opinion would need to be well coordinated; it would likely have to be a local doctor or practice group prepared to handle these situations for the play-ers on short notice. If the second opinion doctor says the player can play, then the player should be allowed to decide if he wants to do so. Recognizing that players may shop for doctors who will clear them to play, it is our recommendation that the Medical Committee create a list of well-qualified and approved second opinion doctors for the players to consult. This compromise also helps resolve concerns that the Head Players' Doctor for one club might be overly conservative as compared to Head Players' Doctors for other clubs.

As will be explained further below, in the event a doctor hired by the club for the purposes of advising the club (*i.e.,* not a member of the Players' Medical Staff) needs clarification from the Head Players' Doctor concerning a player's status, such communication should be permitted, as determined to be reasonably necessary by the Head Players' Doctor. While it is expected that the Players' Athletic Trainers would help create the Player Health Report, non-emergency communications

---

bt   These descriptions match the language historically used on NFL injury reports. However, prior to the 2016 season, the NFL removed the "probable" designation from the injury report and also restricted the use of the "out" designation until two days before the game. Tom Pelissero, *Major change to NFL's injury report will take some getting used to*, USA Today (Aug. 21, 2016, 4:33 PM), http://www.usatoday.com/story/sports/nfl/2016/08/21/injury-report-probable-bill-belichick-patriots/89080582/, *archived at* https://perma.cc /QT4C-MAA6. As discussed in Chapter 17: The Media, the injury report is generally meant to advise the opposing club of the status of a club's players, while also preventing the possibility of inside information to be used for gambling purposes. Those are different purposes than for which we have contemplated the Player Health Report, which is designed to advise the Club of the health status of its own players. Thus, we think the Player Health Report should be as descriptive as necessary, and does not need to track the language of the NFL's injury reports.

bu   Additional logistics of the Player Health Report are detailed in Appendix G: Model Article 39 of the Collective Bargaining Agreement–Players' Medical Care and Treatment.

bv   Our recommendation here does not change the Concussion Protocol with regard to the Unaffiliated Neurotrauma Consultant. Although the Unaffiliated Neurotrauma Consultant can help evaluate players for a concussion during the game, the club doctor's determination is controlling. In Recommendation 2:1-D, we separately recommend that the Unaffili-ated Neurotrauma Consultant also be empowered to remove a player from a game.

between the Club Evaluation Doctor (working solely on behalf of the club as explained below) and the Players' Medical Staff concerning player health should only be with the Head Players' Doctor. Beyond these minimal levels of communication, there should be no need for the Players' Medical Staff (doctors and athletic trainers) to communicate with any club employee, including a coach or general manager. By minimizing the communication in this way, and formalizing it, the goal is to minimize the club's ability to influence the medical care provided to the player, including more subtle forms of influence, *e.g.,* occasional workplace conversations. We say "minimize" because, as we discuss below, our recommendation does still allow for some communications between the Players' Medical Staff and the club. We think that this reduced level of communication is necessary and appropriate to protect player health, but nevertheless acknowledge that the existence of any such communications may cause a player to be less forthcoming to the medical staff, even if designated as the Players' Medical Staff as we recommend.

The above-described processes work well where the player's injury is pre-existing at the time of a practice or game. However, the situation is more complicated when the player suffers an injury during a practice or game. In such situations, the players' treatment clearly takes priority and it is impractical to create a Player Health Report to inform the club of the player's status. If a player suffers an injury during a practice or game, the Head Players' Doctor would retain substantial control over the player's participation, as the club doctor does under the current structure. To minimize communication between the Players' Medical Staff and club personnel, decisions about a player's practice or playing status should be communicated through the Club Evaluation Doctor, discussed below, where possible. It would be expected that the Club Evaluation Doctor would attend every game. However, given current customs, it is likely that the Club Evaluation Doctor would rarely attend practice. Consequently, if a player is injured during practice and the Players' Medical Staff is unable to relay the player's status to the club through the Club Evaluation Doctor, it is necessary and appropriate for the Players' Medical Staff to inform other club officials, including the coaches, about the player's status.

If at any time the Players' Medical Staff declares that the player cannot practice or play, through the Player Health Report or otherwise, the player cannot practice or play (except where the player has received clearance from a second opinion doctor as described above). If the club deviates from the limitations set forth by the Players' Medical Staff, the club should be subject to substantial fines or other discipline under the CBA. The club, of course, would retain the right to not play the player for any number of reasons, including injury or skill.

The Club's Access to Player Medical Records

Importantly, the Player Health Report is distinct from the player's medical records. The Player Health Report is a limited view of the player's current health and provides information on the player's immediate or near-immediate availability to the club. A player's complete medical record provides a fuller picture of the player's health and would provide additional information needed for assessing a player's long-term health, as well as a separate check on the assessment provided in the Player Health Report.

Under our recommendation, in addition to the Player Health Report, the club would also be entitled to the players' medical records, as is the case under the status quo. We reiterate the clubs' legitimate business need for a clear understanding of player health issues. Clubs would obviously and rightfully be interested in understanding a player's medical condition in both the short and long term. While some might believe that clubs should only be entitled to those medical records that are specifically relevant to football, in reality this is not a line that can easily be drawn. Clubs might believe that most of a player's medical issues, including both physical and mental health issues, are relevant to the player's status with the club. That said, as we discuss in a forthcoming article, there may be important legal restrictions on the request for and use of some of that information by an employer, including constraints imposed by the Americans with Disabilities Act and the Genetic Information Nondiscrimination Act.[268]

Providing clubs access to players' medical records raises additional issues that must be clarified. Athletic trainers are the principal providers of medical care to players under the control of club doctors and also are generally responsible for completing the players' medical records. Athletic trainers would retain these roles but our important corresponding recommendation is that athletic trainers, like the Head Players' Doctor and Players' Medical Staff, be chosen and reviewed by the Medical Committee, and that their principal obligations be to treat the players in accordance with prevailing and customary legal and ethical standards. The athletic trainers would likely assist the Head Players' Doctor in creating the Player Health Report but, like the Head Players' Doctor, should have minimal, if any, other interaction with the coaches or other club officials.

Club Evaluation Doctors

Under this new approach, clubs would be free to retain doctors and other medical professionals, as needed, who work solely for the clubs for the purposes of examining players and advising the club accordingly. These doctors, whom we call "Club Evaluation Doctors," could perform the pre-employment examinations at the Combine, during the course of free agency, and also examine players during the season. However, they would not *treat* the players in any way. The Standard Player Contract's requirement that players make themselves available for an examination by the club doctor upon request would largely remain. Additionally, the Club Evaluation Doctor would have the opportunity to review the players' medical records at any time and communicate with the Head Players' Doctor about the Player Health Report, if clarification is needed and appropriate. As is explained below, the Player Health Report should substantially minimize the need for duplicative medical examinations. This arrangement would thus permit a Club Evaluation Doctor to provide an opinion as to a player's short- and long-term usefulness to the Club, without relying on the Players' Medical Staff's opinion.[bw]

The Club Evaluation Doctor would be the only additional doctor required under our proposal. The number of other medical personnel would otherwise stay the same, but their loyalties would now be exclusively to the players.

Figure 2-D below shows the permissible forms of communication concerning player health under our proposal.

Figure 2-D: Permissible Communications Concerning Player Health

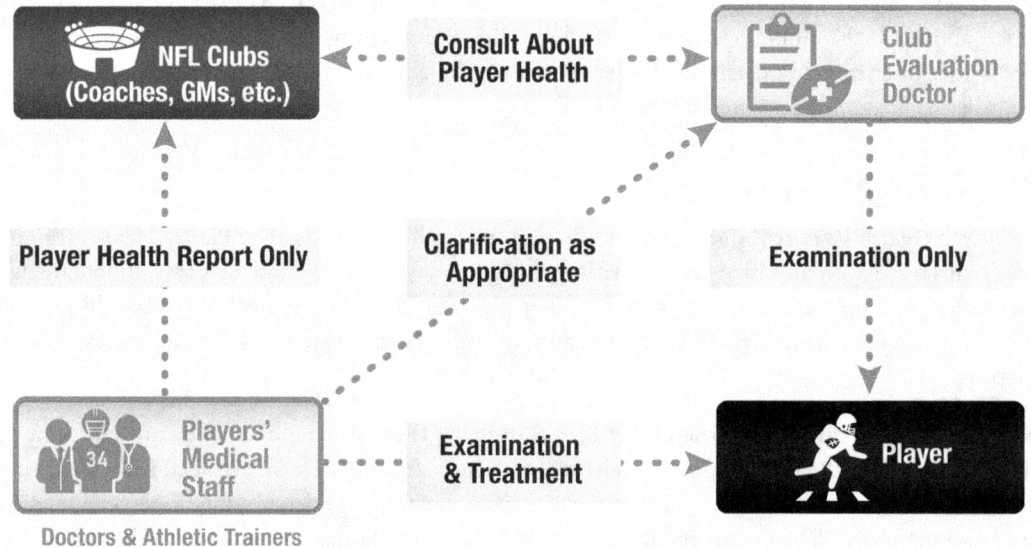

Possible Objections to our Recommendation

We understand and acknowledge potential concerns with this recommendation. As we evaluated the options, we sought the opinions of others, including several medical and sports medicine professionals. Indeed, some of the peer reviewers of the Report expressed concern about overly limiting communication between players' medical staff and the club, resulting in our

---

bw To avoid confusion between doctors providing care and performing fitness-for-duty evaluations, it may be appropriate for the doctors not providing care to have some kind of feature distinguishing them from the doctors providing care. *See, e.g.,* Rebecca Dresser, *The Ubiquity and Utility of the Therapeutic Misconception,* 19 Soc. Phil. and Pol'y 271, 293 (2002) (recommending that doctors acting as researchers rather than clinicians wear red coats).

decision to broaden the scope and frequency of permissible communications compared to our original position. On the other hand, some viewed the extent of communication that we allow as too substantial. In this regard, we note that outside of the context of professional sports, personal doctors do occasionally communicate with a patient's employer in ways sanctioned by that patient (for example, providing information to justify sick leave). Thus, we believe that this final recommendation is the best way to serve the goal of providing players healthcare they can trust from providers who are as free from conflicts of interest as possible, while acknowledging the business realities facing clubs. We recognize that it may need further adjustment as implemented, though we maintain that it is feasible to do so, although perhaps a challenging transition.

Having described our recommendation for improving the structure of player healthcare, we now consider specific possible objections to this recommendation. First, we consider possible objections from a player-centric perspective, a view that might maintain that our recommendation is not sufficiently protective of player interests. Then, we will consider possible objections from a club-centric perspective, a view that might maintain that our recommendation is unworkable or unnecessary.

Possible Objections from a Player-Centric Perspective

We consider five objections from a player-centric perspective.

First, some may question why we have not advocated for a *complete* bifurcation of roles, where there is one set of doctors that provides players with care and has no relationship or communication with the club whatsoever, and another set that provides advisory services to the club, including performing medical examinations of players. In other words, why not extend our above recommendation to prohibit all communication (including the Player Health Report) between the Head Players' Doctor and the Club Evaluation Doctor? The answer is that we believe such a proposal would not be practical for several reasons: (a) prohibiting all communication between the doctor caring for the player and the club will require the club to perform its own independent assessment of the player for every condition, likely subjecting many players to duplicative examinations, a costly and inefficient process (our Player Health Report minimizes this problem by allowing some flow of information and communication); (b) as discussed earlier, we believe clubs have a legitimate right to a player's health information and status insofar as it potentially affects his ability to play; and, (c) to the extent clubs would receive information about a player's health from the player himself, this imposes an unnecessary burden on the players and creates the risk of miscommunication and lost information. Additionally, there are also questions about whether players would adequately track and seek reimbursement for out-of-pocket healthcare expenses.

Second, some may object that our recommendation does not completely eliminate the confidentiality concerns that exist under the current model because the club would still receive medical information concerning players. This objection is true, and it may cause players to still refrain from full disclosure of their ailments to the Players' Medical Staff. However, despite this confidentiality concern, we anticipate that having a medical staff fully devoted to the players' interests will facilitate player trust that the care he is receiving has only his best interests—and not the club's—in mind. Again, with regard to the passing of at least some information to the club, we think it is a necessary business reality.

Third, some might wonder whether it is preferable to have players select the members of the Medical Committee directly, rather than via the NFLPA. Such an approach would give the players more direct input into their medical care. However, in addition to the fact that the NFLPA is the players' representative, it has experience in these types of neutral selection processes, as many are called for in the CBA (such as for the System Arbitrator, Non-Injury Grievance Arbitrator, and Benefits Arbitrator).[269] Additionally, the NFLPA has more time to devote to the selection process, as well as any subsequent issues than players would. Finally, the benefit of developing institutional knowledge over time would be challenging for a player to gather during his career.

Fourth, some might also question why the NFL would be allowed any role in selection of Players Medical Staff, even if part of a balanced Medical Committee. The reason, again, is that clubs have legitimate business-related interests in the health of their players. While these interests likely sometimes conflict with a player's interests, there is also an alignment of interests: one would generally expect that clubs have an interest in their players receiving the best possible healthcare, if for no other reason than to protect the clubs' investment in its players. Indeed, clubs invest considerable sums in players and the business of the NFL. Moreover, clubs and the NFL already have substantial knowledge about the doctors well-qualified to provide healthcare to NFL players. Consequently, it is appropriate that the NFL be involved as a voice, but not a controlling interest, in the composition of the Medical Committee.

Fifth, some might disagree with the structure of our recommendation insofar as the Head Players' Doctor, Players' Medical Staff, and athletic trainers would all still be paid by the club. Some might believe that receiving a paycheck from the club could cause the Players' Medical Staff to (at least subconsciously) favor the club's interests. In the abstract, there is some merit to this point based on what we know about subtle conflicts of interest.[270] However, the conflict here is not really the source of payment, but rather the locus of control over hiring and firing; having the Medical Committee hire and review the doctors and athletic trainers and determine their level of compensation[bx] is sufficient to manage the structural conflict of interest, and assures that the Head Players' Doctor has every reason to be concerned only about the players' interests. Consequently, it does not seem necessary to introduce the logistical complexity of having a third party pay the Players' Medical Staff.

Possible Objections from a Club-Centric Perspective

We consider four objections that clubs might raise, before also addressing comments on our recommendation provided by both the NFL and the NFLPS.

First, they might object to having to retain in some capacity their own doctors and potentially additional specialists. Clubs currently typically pay for two levels of care: the primary care by the club doctor and then also a second opinion obtained by the player. Our proposed structure does create a potential third layer of medical examination, that of the Club Evaluation Doctor. Nevertheless, we disagree with this objection for several reasons: (1) first and foremost, our proposed structure is essential for players to receive minimally conflicted healthcare; (2) by providing a Head Players' Doctor entirely devoted to the player's interests, players should have an increased level of trust in their primary level of care, which can decrease the need for and cost of second opinions (though we recognize we may not conclusively know the effect on the bottom line until after the system is implemented);[by] (3) clubs also benefit from our recommended arrangement by having a Club Evaluation Doctor who is entirely devoted to the club's interests; and, (4) at least under the current CBA, some of the costs of medical care, including physical examination costs, are at least partially paid for out of the players' share of revenue, *i.e.,* additional costs for player healthcare can decrease the amount of money available to players in salary.[bz]

Second, clubs might object by pointing out that players already have access to their own doctors, second opinion doctors, and the surgeon of their choice. While this is true, the level of access to these alternative doctors as compared to the current club doctors is dramatically different. Considering the time demands placed on them by the club, travel schedules, and movement among clubs, it is far easier (and more realistic) for a player to receive his medical care at the club facility from the club doctor now, or from the Players' Medical Staff under our proposed arrangement. Additionally, players' personal doctors and second opinion doctors are not there on the sidelines of games when important medical decisions are often made. Finally, under our recommendation, the Head Players' Doctor would have control over whether a player plays, which is not an authority that a player's personal or second opinion doctor could have.

Third, clubs might believe that coaches and club executives need to be able to speak directly to the Players' Medical Staff to be able to properly understand a player's condition and limitations. We recognize this concern and that the proposed Player Health Report is a substantial departure from existing practices whereby athletic trainers communicate regularly with the coaches and general manager. Consequently, we understand that there will be resistance to change and legitimate logistical challenges in transitioning to a new set of protocols. Nevertheless, we believe that clubs can learn to adjust to a

---

bx   The ways in which the Medical Committee determines the compensation of doctors and athletic trainers will likely need to consider antitrust laws.

by   Players might also be more likely to view the Head Players' Doctor as their personal doctor, reducing the fragmentation of care that players currently receive. Also of note, the Visiting Team Medical Liaison, discussed earlier, would still be required under our recommendation to ensure compliance with local laws.

bz   The current CBA describes what player healthcare costs are or are not considered Player Benefit Costs, *see* 2011 CBA, Art. 12, § 2, and thus count against the player's share of revenue: "Player medical costs (i.e., fees to doctors, hospitals, and other health care providers, and the drugs and other medical costs of supplies, for the treatment of player injuries) [are considered Player Benefit Costs], but . . . salaries of trainers or other Team personnel, or the cost of Team medical or training equipment" are not considered Player Benefit Costs. 2011 CBA, Art. 12, § 2(x). However, the CBA further states that "player medical costs shall include one-third of each Club's expenses for tape used on players and one-third of each Club's player physical examination costs for signed players[.]" *Id.* We thus recognize it would remain to be determined by the NFL and NFLPA whether the costs for the Club Evaluation Doctors would, like some of these other healthcare costs, be part of Player Benefit Costs, and count against the players' share of revenue.

Recommendations Concerning Club Doctors – continued

new structure—one that is necessary to ensure that players receive healthcare that is as unconflicted as realistically possible. Ultimately, the proposed Player Health Report, with the help of existing NFL club doctors and athletic trainers, can be crafted and implemented in such ways as to provide clubs with the information they need to evaluate a player's fitness to play. Additionally, to the extent clubs believe they need additional clarification, the new Club Evaluation Doctor can communicate with the Head Players' Doctor or athletic trainers, or examine a player directly, as appropriate.[ca]

Fourth, clubs and club doctors might argue that our recommendation does not resolve all trust concerns between players and club medical staff, since the club would still be receiving player medical information. We acknowledge this fact. As a result, some players will probably still withhold information about their conditions at certain times, to avoid that information being relayed to the club. We do not believe there is any realistic system that could resolve this issue given the club's business interest in player health. Yet, we believe that minimizing the structural conflict of interest by bifurcating the current club doctor role into two is a meaningful step forward in the player healthcare environment. Even if players are not always fully forthcoming, it is an improvement that they will know the care recommendations they receive from Players Medical Staff are as unconflicted as possible.

Moreover, we see no downside to our recommendation. It should impose little to no additional costs to the club and will not unreasonably delay the flow of any necessary information. Again, we welcome the involvement of the relevant stakeholders, such as the clubs and club medical staff, to resolve any logistical complexities. In the absence of a meaningful shortcoming, our recommendation offers an unquestionable improvement over the status quo.

We turn now to comments from the NFL and the NFLPS, which focus on objections to the concepts underlying the proposal. The NFL asserted that "[t]here has been no evidence of a 'conflict of interest' presented."[271] Similarly, in a commentary provided by the NFLPS as part of a forthcoming Special Report of The Hastings Center Report, the NFLPS argued that the conflict of interest discussed here is merely "theoretical." Moreover, both the NFL and NFLPS seem to take issue with what they regard as an unfair attack on highly qualified and ethical club doctors. We disagree with these viewpoints.

The existing literature on conflicts of interest in the medical sphere emphasizes that many doctors are influenced by incentives and other forms of judgment distortion while strictly denying this to be the case; judgments are often compromised by conflicts they fail to recognize in themselves.[272] Unfortunately, the NFL and the NFLPS failed to recognize that we took great care to explicitly state that the problem is structural and that we do not mean to place any fault at the feet of individual club doctors, or to denigrate the quality of care they currently provide. The NFL's and the NFLPS' refusal to recognize that there is an inherent conflict of interest contradicts an overwhelming body of literature on the issue.[273]

The NFL and the NFLPS dismiss the conflicts of interest at hand as not real, instead of acknowledging the structural nature of the problem. To see why this is erroneous, consider an analogy to the way in which structural conflicts of interest are avoided in organ donation. Both law and ethics require two separate care teams: one to care for dying patients and pronounce them dead, and one to conduct the transplant and care for the recipient.[274] If a single medical team served both roles, it would face the structural problem of dual loyalty to both the dying patient and the patient in need of transplant, even though the interests of both parties may conflict—in particular, the donor has an interest in not being declared dead prematurely and the recipient has an interest in the donor's death being declared quickly enough that the organs are not rendered unusable for transplant. Note that in the organ context, this bifurcation of roles is well-established and mandatory even if, for example, an individual doctor would swear that he or she is not influenced in declaring a donor's death by the desire to get the patient an organ, and even though it would be impossible in any particular case to prove or disprove such influence. Moreover, anything short of eliminating such conflict completely would deeply undermine the public's trust and peoples' willingness to consider organ donation. In the NFL and NFLPS' worldview, however, neither party would recognize the conflict of interest. Indeed, the NFLPS dismissed the conflict as "theoretical." It simply strains credulity

---

ca In addition to the above possible concerns, club doctors might also be concerned about how medical malpractice insurance might be affected by our recommendation. Information and data about current club doctors' medical malpractice insurance arrangements and costs is not publicly available. Consequently, it is difficult to assess how our proposed recommendation might affect those arrangements and costs. However, we acknowledge that it is essential that concerns about insurance coverage or costs (as well as salary and any other monetary issues) do not prevent players from receiving treatment from the best possible medical practitioners, *i.e.*, that the best possible Head Players' Doctors would not be scared off. Thus, while we are not in a position to conduct such an analysis, medical malpractice insurance and other financial issues must be considered alongside our recommendation.

for the NFL and the NFLPS to suggest that club doctors, who are hired, reviewed, and terminated by the club, and who communicate with and advise the club regularly about player health matters, are not placed in a position that inherently creates a conflict of interest between the interests of the club and the interests of the player. This is the equivalent of asking a single doctor to simultaneously advance the interests of both the organ donor and organ recipient.

Finally, both the NFL and the NFLPS also take issue with the methodology and sample size of players we interviewed, arguing that it was insufficient to determine that there is a problem with the current structure of NFL player healthcare. We agree that the interviews cannot serve that purpose, but that is not why we conducted them. Importantly, it is our view that even if we had not engaged in *any* interviews at all, simply examining the structure of NFL clubs' medical staff would be sufficient for our analysis, as the structure itself presents a clear conflict of interest. Nevertheless, as explained in this Report, we interviewed 10 current players and 3 players who recently left the NFL as part of a convenience sample to add the lived experience of players in their own words, explicitly noting that these interviews were intended to be illustrative but not representative of all players' views. We also engaged in informal interviews and discussions with many other current and former NFL players about NFL player healthcare, as well as other important stakeholders with insight on this issue, including contract advisors, financial advisors, and family members. Again, without making claims that these discussions were representative, they support the belief that at least some players have qualms about their ability to trust club medical staff as a result of both the perception and reality of dual loyalty.

Finally, in Recommendation 7:1-D in Chapter 7: The NFL and NFLPA, we recommend that the NFL and NFLPA publicly release the latest empirical data on this subject.

* * *

Outside of the player- and club-centric perspectives, there might also be other concerns with our recommended approach. The Head Players' Doctor may be a fan of the club, or begin to idolize the players in some way, either of which could affect the care and advice provided to the player. This is an issue the Medical Committee would have to evaluate. Additionally, players can always hide their conditions in an effort to convince the Head Players' Doctor to permit them to play. Nevertheless, we believe this recommendation could substantially resolve the major concern about the current club doctor arrangement—*i.e.*, the problem of dual loyalty and structural conflict of interest—by providing players with a medical staff dedicated solely to the interests of the players. The Head Players' Doctor would be almost entirely separated from the club and the pressures implicit in being employed by the club, while being held accountable to a neutral Medical Committee. At the same time, this recommendation does not interfere with the clubs' legitimate interests. For these reasons, we believe that this recommendation is critical to improving player health and among the most important set forth in this Report. Accordingly, it and all of its intricacies should be set forth in the CBA.

Included as Appendix G is a model CBA provision setting forth our proposal here. In addition, this recommendation is the subject of a forthcoming Special Report from The Hastings Center Report. Included with the Special Report are commentaries from a diverse group of experts, including professors, bioethicists, a former player, a former player who is now a doctor, a current player who is also a medical student in the offseason, and the NFLPS.

* * *

What follows are additional recommendations concerning club doctors. *Some of these might not be necessary or would need be altered if Recommendation 1-A above were adopted.* Nevertheless, we make all recommendations we believe can improve player health under the current structures and set of practices, even if they would become partially redundant or inconsistent if other primary recommendations are adopted.

Recommendation 2:1-B: The NFLPS should adopt a code of ethics.

Club doctors have many codes of ethics relevant to their practice. However, none of them are specific to their unique role as doctors for NFL clubs. Club doctors face a variety of complex situations that are not adequately contemplated or addressed by existing codes of ethics, most notably balancing their obligations to provide care to the player while also advising the club about players' health. A code of ethics adopted by NFLPS would supplement the club doctors' existing codes of ethics by providing guidance and tenets for the unique and competitive environment in which they must operate. Additionally, a clear code of ethics could help prevent ambiguous claims of malpractice and also foster transparency and trust in the doctor-player relationship. Importantly, the code of ethics should avoid vague aspirational language and seek to address specific situations with clear guidance and a meaningful enforcement mechanism. The code of ethics should address all of the issues discussed in this chapter, including but not limited to standards of medical care, obligations to the club, obligations in performing medical examinations on behalf of the club, handling the club doctor's dual roles, confidentiality of player medical information, player autonomy, disclosure of medical information to the player, and administration of painkillers and prescription medications. The 2013 Team Physician Consensus Statement, discussed earlier in this chapter, addresses many of these issues and would provide a useful starting point for an NFLPS code of ethics.

Finally, enforcement is essential. Violations of a professional code of ethics should include meaningful punishments, ranging from warnings and censures to fines and suspensions. In order to be effective, the enforcement and disciplinary schemes might need to be included in the CBA.

Recommendation 2:1-C: Every doctor retained by a club should be a member of the NFLPS.

While many (if not most) doctors retained by clubs are members of the NFLPS, the 2011 CBA's addition of the several different types of doctors required to be retained by clubs makes it likely that at least some doctors treating NFL players are not members of the NFLPS. In order for our recommendation that the NFLPS adopt a code of ethics to have an impact, the doctors treating players must be members of the NFLPS.

As mentioned earlier, the NFL wrote in its comments to this Report that it had "proposed that membership in the NFLPS be required for a physician to serve on a Club's medical staff to give the NFLPS enforcement authority over its membership, but that proposal was rejected by the NFLPA."[275] The NFLPA countered by explaining that "[t]he NFL's proposal contained a number of issues that were not in the best interest of players, including empowering a group that is not party to the CBA. With or without NFLPA agreement, the NFL and Physician Society are able to establish membership requirements and enforce the same."[276]

Recommendation 2:1-D: The Concussion Protocol should be amended such that if either the club doctor or the Unaffiliated Neurotrauma Consultant diagnoses a player with a concussion, the player cannot return to the game.

The Concussion Protocol requires the presence of an Unaffiliated Neurotrauma Consultant to help identify and diagnose potential concussions. However, the Concussion Protocol also declares that "[t]he responsibility for the diagnosis of concussion and the decision to return a player to a game remains exclusively within the professional judgment of the Head Team Physician or the Team physician assigned to managing TBI." Thus, the possibility exists that even if the Unaffiliated Neurotrauma Consultant diagnoses a player with a concussion, if the club doctor does not, the player can return to play.

While there is no evidence this scenario has taken place, the possibility that it could is unacceptable and unnecessary. If the Unaffiliated Neurotrauma Consultant is to have meaningful impact, he or she must have the same rights and duties concerning possible player concussions as the club doctor. If a player has been diagnosed by the Unaffiliated Neurotrauma Consultant with a concussion, he should not be able to return to play, regardless of what the club doctor believes. While we acknowledge that the club doctor is likely to have greater familiarity with the player and can thus better determine whether a player has suffered a concussion, this is a common sense protection that errs on the side of player health.

Recommendation 2:1-E: The NFL and NFLPA should reconsider whether waivers providing for the use and disclosure of player medical information should include mental health information.

In Appendices L and M we provide copies of the broad confidentiality waivers that all players execute at the request of their clubs. The first waiver authorizes the club, the NFL, and other parties to use and disclose the player's "entire health or medical record" expressly including "all records and [protected health information] relating to any mental health treatment, therapy, and/or counseling, but expressly exclude[ing] psychotherapy notes." The second waiver authorizes all of the players' "healthcare providers," including "mental health providers" to disclose player health information and records to the NFL, NFL clubs, and other parties.

These waivers are collectively bargained between the NFL and NFLPA but are nevertheless troubling. While we acknowledge, as discussed above in Recommendation 2:1-A, that clubs have a legitimate interest in player health information, mental health information is potentially different. As explained in Chapter 1: Players, players have strong reason to believe they are entitled to confidential mental healthcare because the NFL's insurance plan explicitly states that the submission of claims by players or their family members for mental health, substance abuse, and other counseling services provided for under the insurance program "will not be made known to [the] Club, the NFL or the NFLPA." This declaration suggests that the NFL and NFLPA have recognized a particular interest in enabling players to seek mental healthcare without fear that the club will terminate or otherwise alter their employment, thereby encouraging players to seek care. However, the breadth of the waivers executed by players undermines the promise of confidentiality. As a result, players may be reluctant to seek needed mental health treatment. To effectuate the goal of unencumbered access reflected in the insurance provisions, we recommend that the NFL and NFLPA re-assess whether the collectively bargained waivers executed by the players are overly broad.

Lastly, we note that while this recommendation is directed at the NFL and NFLPA, the content and issues surrounding these waivers were discussed in this chapter, and thus we thought this chapter was the best place for this recommendation.

Recommendation 2:1-F: Club doctors should abide by their CBA obligation to advise players of all information they disclose to club representatives concerning the players.

The CBA contains a requirement regarding this issue:

> All Club physicians are required to disclose to a player any and all information about the player's physical condition that the physician may from time to time provide to a coach or other Club representative, whether or not such information affects the player's performance or health. If a Club physician advises a coach or other club representative of a player's serious injury or career threatening physical condition which significantly affects the player's performance or health, the physician will also advise the player in writing.[277]

However, we have learned that in practice some players believe club doctors regularly disclose information to the club that is not disclosed to the player.[cb] In addition, many players do not believe they are ever advised about their conditions in writing, despite the CBA's requirement. As a result, players may be unaware of the full extent of their medical conditions and also how the club might take adverse employment action against the player due to his medical condition. In particular, club doctors might not be providing players with a copy of medical evaluations that he or she has provided to the club. Players are entitled by the CBA and by their status as patients to this information. It is thus imperative that club doctors comply with the CBA and that the NFLPA enforce this provision against club doctors who do not. A standard form for these types of disclosures would help to ensure compliance with this CBA provision. In addition, to the extent these disclosures are not already recorded in a player's electronic medical record (EMR), they should be.

Recommendation 2:1-G: At any time prior to the player's employment with the club, the player should be advised in writing that the club doctor is performing a fitness-for-play evaluation on behalf of the club and is not providing any medical services to the player.

Players are often confused about whether club doctors are providing care for their benefit or for the club's. This confusion sows distrust, which interferes with the effectiveness of the doctor-player relationship. This confusion and distrust begins before players are even a member of the club, including at the NFL Combine where club doctors extensively examine players. To avoid confusion and to make sure everyone's role is properly understood, players should be advised that the doctor is working only on behalf of the club in such situations. The document should clarify the role and ethical obligations of doctors in that situation.

Recommendation 2:1-H: The NFL's Medical Sponsorship Policy should prohibit doctors or other medical service providers (MSPs) from providing consideration of any kind for the right to provide medical services to the club, exclusively or non-exclusively.

The Medical Sponsorship Policy appropriately prohibits clubs from trading the right to treat a club's players in exchange for sponsorship money. This prohibition prevents clubs from choosing an MSP based on which MSP is willing to spend the most in terms of endorsement money. However, the Policy does not address, and thus permits, the open sale of the rights to provide medical services to the club (but only on a non-exclusive basis). For example, an MSP could pay $5 million for the right to treat the club's players (in addition to other MSPs). While the MSP might not obtain the right to use club trademarks or to post advertisements in the stadium, the MSP would generally be permitted to advertise the fact that it provides medical services to the club, a potentially significant reputation benefit. In reviewing a draft of this chapter, the NFLPS stated that no MSP currently pays for the right to provide medical services to players. Nevertheless, the incentive exists for MSPs to pay for the right to provide medical services, even if this not currently the practice.

If the incentive exists for MSPs to pay for the right to provide medical services, clubs would likely prefer to sell these services to the highest bidder.[cc] This scenario again raises the problematic question of whether clubs might choose MSPs based on their qualifications or instead on the amount they are willing to pay. While the NFLPS says no MSPs are currently paying for the right to provide medical services, we know that the practice existed in the past. Consequently, it is possible that the practice could return or proliferate. To ensure that clubs are choosing MSPs based solely on whether or

cb   Current Player 2: "I think that a lot of times players feel as though these doctors maybe disclose the full extent of their injuries." Current Player 3: "I think sometimes the doctors may . . . not tell you the full extent of what's going on . . . everything about a certain injury." Current Player 7: "We assume that if there's something [an injury], they [the medical staff] go and tell them [club officials]."

cc   Current Player 6 believes his club recently changed MSPs because the MSP "wrote an open check and said, 'Whatever you need, we'll give you.'" Current Player 9 expressed similar concerns: "I've come to realize that [there are] certain medical organizations, hospitals, that will pay a fee to be the official medical care of certain teams because it helps them do well. So you're not necessarily getting the best treatment for a certain injury as far as the expertise of the medical professional."

not they will do the best job in providing care to the players, it is appropriate to strictly prohibit MSPs from providing consideration of any kind—whether in the form of payment or free/discounted services—for the right to provide medical services to the club, exclusively or non-exclusively.

As discussed earlier, the NFL claims that the Medical Sponsorship Policy does prohibit MSPs from paying for the right to provide medical services and from offering discounted or free services. We disagree with the NFL's reading. While the NFL may enforce the Medical Sponsorship Policy in such a way, we disagree that the plain text of the Policy prohibits such arrangements. In any event, it appears that the NFL agrees with us that the Policy *should* prohibit any club doctor from paying for the right to pay for the right to provide healthcare to players. If the Policy is intended to prohibit club doctors from paying for the right to provide medical services to players, the text of the Policy should be clarified.

Recommendation 2:1-I: Club doctors' roles should be clarified in a written document provided to the players before each season.

As discussed throughout this chapter, club doctors play two roles: providing care to players; and, providing services to the club. When the players are under contract with the club, the club doctor is often performing both roles at the same time. Even if the club doctor is principally concerned with providing an injured player the best possible care, he cannot erase the player's injury from his mind when discussing the health status of players with the athletic trainer or coaches during the season or helping the club determine whether to retain the player at season's end. The overlap is unavoidable under the current system. Yet it causes confusion and distrust among the players that should be avoided.

Prior to the season, the club doctor should advise the players as to: (1) how often the club doctor communicates with the coaches and executives; (2) what information the club doctor communicates to the coaches and executives; (3) the doctor's relationship to the athletic trainer with an explanation of the athletic trainer's role; and, (4) the club's access to player medical records. Beyond just the preseason, this distinction should be publicized more generally to ensure the players' understanding. Finally, disclosing the club doctor's compensation might also be appropriate.

While we recommend disclosure, we recognize it is not a complete solution given the social science research on the failures of mandated disclosure of conflicts of interest.[278]

Goal 2: To provide a fair and efficient process for resolving disputes between players and club doctors.

Principles Advanced: Respect; Collaboration and Engagement; and, Justice.

Recommendation 2:2-A: The NFL, NFLPA, and club doctors should consider requiring all claims concerning the medical care provided by a doctor who is a member of the NFLPS and is arranged for by the club to be subject to binding arbitration.

As discussed in Section G: Enforcement, there are challenges to adjudicating club doctors' legal obligations to players. Arbitration is a favored dispute resolution system; it generally minimizes costs for all parties and leads to faster and more

Recommendations Concerning Club Doctors – continued

accurate resolutions of legal disputes.[cd] The CBA contains many arbitration mechanisms for almost every reasonably possible scenario involving NFL players and almost always argues in court that a player's claims must be resolved through the CBA's arbitration mechanisms. The one exception appears to be the NFL's position that club doctors can be sued in court and not through arbitration.[279] However, changes to the 2011 CBA likely increase the chances that a player's civil court claims would be preempted by the terms of the CBA and create confusion about players' rights and enforcement options. Moreover, because club doctors are not parties to the CBA, a Non-Injury Grievance against them would be unlikely to proceed. A robust arbitration process is the fairest and most efficient way of ensuring that players have the same legal rights as regular patients. It is our intention that such a system would provide players with roughly comparable remedies to those currently available to them in civil litigation, only now in a private and more efficient forum.

To the extent that the NFL is not comfortable constructing an entire medical malpractice arbitration infrastructure, including qualified arbitrators, it could use a third-party system. For example, JAMS, a worldwide leader in arbitration and mediation services, includes personal injury (including medical malpractice) as part of its services.[280]

We have recommended limiting this arbitral mechanism to NFLPS-member doctors for two reasons: (1) to create a more cohesive universe of doctors providing care to NFL players and who thus might obtain NFL-specific training or guidance and be subject to the code of ethics proposed above; and, (2) to facilitate the agreement to arbitrate. Club doctors are not signatories of the CBA and generally are not club employees, which prevents players from enforcing CBA provisions against them directly (as opposed to the club). The NFL and NFLPA would have to reach an agreement with NFLPS and its members to arbitrate medical malpractice claims. Additionally, the parties might consider requiring that all doctors who treat NFL players on behalf of a club be a member of NFLPS (which is also proposed above).

There are additional practical considerations worth mentioning. First, the arbitration mechanism should include a statute of limitations of 2 to 3 years, comparable to the statutes of many states. Second, the arbitration mechanism might require the submission of an affidavit of merit from another doctor attesting that the claim is meritorious, a common state statutory mechanism that permits doctors to obtain dismissal of medical malpractice cases at an early juncture. And third, the club doctors who are employees of the club as opposed to independent contractors might need additional consideration to agree to be a part of such an arrangement since, as employees of the club, workers' compensation laws generally bar lawsuits against them for the injuries of co-workers.

---

cd   *See* Keith N. Hylton, *Agreements to Waive or to Arbitrate Legal Claims: An Economic Analysis*, 8 Sup. Ct. Econ. Rev. 209 (2000); Steven Shavell, *Alternative Dispute Resolution: An Economic Analysis*, 24 J. Legal Stud. 1 (1995). We recognize that arbitration also raises potential concerns for claimants, including the upfront costs of the arbitration and bias in favor of repeat parties, typically the defendant. *See* David Shieh, *Unintended Side Effects: Arbitration and the Deterrence of Medical Error*, 89 N.Y.U. L. Rev. 1806 (2014). However, these concerns are not present in arbitrations involving NFL players where the NFL and NFLPA (and not the player) generally bear the costs of the arbitration equally, the NFL and NFLPA are involved in nearly all of the arbitration proceedings and both generally retain the ability to remove arbitrators with whom they are dissatisfied.

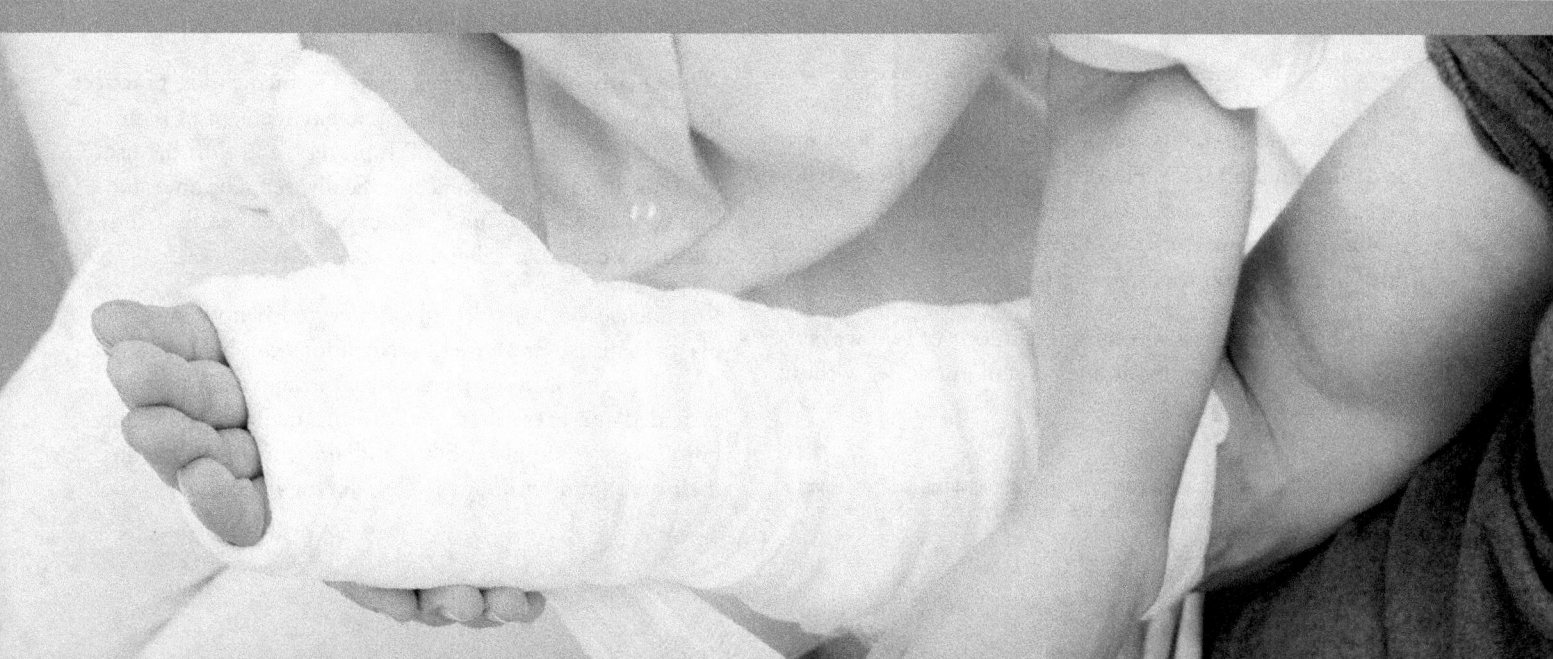

The Special Case of Medications

Like all of us, NFL players take a variety of medications to cure, mitigate, treat, or prevent a host of medical conditions. At the outset, it is important to explain what we mean by the umbrella term "medications." Medications are also generally known as pharmaceuticals or drugs. As a legal term of art, a drug is defined under the Federal Food, Drug, and Cosmetic Act (FDCA) as:

> (A) articles recognized in the official United States Pharmacopœia, official Homœopathic Pharmacopœia of the United States, or official National Formulary, or any supplement to any of them; and (B) articles intended for use in the diagnosis, cure, mitigation, treatment, or prevention of disease in man or other animals; and (C) articles (other than food) intended to affect the structure or any function of the body of man or other animals; and (D) articles intended for use as a component of any article specified in clause (A), (B), or (C).[281]

While club doctors do still prescribe medications to players (as would be expected), prescriptions are filled in a regular, commercial pharmacy and delivered to the player, with appropriate notation in the player's electronic medical record. According to the NFL, clubs no longer store or provide controlled substances to players.

Generally speaking, this section of the Report discusses drugs as defined in the FDCA. However, to avoid confusion with performance-enhancing drugs or recreational drugs (some of which are regulated by the FDCA and some of which are not), in this section we use the term "medications."[ce]

Medications are generally available in one of two ways: over-the-counter, *i.e.*, by ordinary retail purchase, without the need for a prescription; or, through a prescription from a licensed and authorized medical professional. As will be discussed further below, certain medications meet additional criteria and are classified as "controlled substances" under the Controlled Substances Act (CSA).[282] Nevertheless, many prescription medications are not controlled substances and not all controlled substances are available through a prescription (heroin, for example).

The concept of "painkillers" is also important in the context of this discussion. "Painkillers" is a generalized term for those medications that help reduce or eliminate a person's pain. Some painkillers are available as over-the-counter medications, while others are only available through a prescription. Additionally, some (but not all) painkillers are controlled substances.

Clearly there is a complex web of terminology and regulation. In this section we refer to medications generally and intend for the term to include over-the-counter medications, prescription medications, controlled substances, and painkillers. Where necessary, we will use more specific terminology.

We can now turn to the impetus for this section. In recent years, the use of medications in the NFL or by NFL players has received considerable attention. Several news reports indicate that many former NFL players have misused or abused medications. Indeed, there is ongoing litigation against the NFL concerning its medication practices, as discussed below. Moreover, there are many anecdotes of NFL clubs and club doctors having handled medications without the proper degree of care and caution. Fortunately, as will be explained, it appears the NFL's practices in this regard have substantially improved. Most importantly, while club doctors do still prescribe medications to players (as would be expected), prescriptions are filled in a regular, commercial pharmacy and delivered to the player, with appropriate notation in the player's electronic medical record.[283] According to the NFL, clubs no longer store or provide controlled substances to players.[284]

While many of the concerns related to medication practices may be a problem of the past, the management of pain is a recurring problem for NFL players, and thus the use of medications, painkillers specifically, remains an issue that can have a profound impact on player health. Consequently, we discuss it here.

It is unclear both historically and currently how much players' misuse or abuse of medications can be attributed to club doctors. In the past, clubs, through club doctors, provided and prescribed medications, including painkillers, but players could also obtain and abuse medications on their own (and without the club doctor's knowledge). For

---

ce Issues and policies concerning performance-enhancing drugs and recreational drugs are discussed in Chapter 7: The NFL and NFLPA.

this reason, this issue potentially fits into and could have been featured in several different chapters of this Report. However, because club doctors have many legal obligations concerning medications, we chose to include discussion of the special case of medications as part of this chapter.

As a final preliminary point, this section does not discuss at length the NFL-NFLPA Policy and Program on Substances of Abuse (Substance Abuse Policy), and the Policy on Performance-Enhancing Substances (PES Policy). These policies are discussed briefly in Chapter 7: The NFL and NFLPA, and analyzed at length in our forthcoming report *Comparing the Health-Related Policies and Practices of the NFL to Other Professional Sports Leagues*. While our research has not revealed any reliable data on the usage of recreational or performance-enhancing drugs by NFL players, some medications can fit into these categories. Further discussion on this point is discussed below.

1) BACKGROUND

NFL practices concerning medications appear to have substantially changed in recent years. Nevertheless, to fully understand the issue, we provide background and historical information about medication practices in the NFL.

Over the years, there have been references to a variety of medications being made readily available by NFL clubs and their medical staff to NFL players in "candy jar"-like fashion[285]—meaning without a specific prescription or individualized access. Although the "candy jar" practice reportedly ceased during the late 1980s and 1990s,[286] questions about the use of medications in the NFL persisted even recently.[287,cf]

One important study that attempted to understand the scope of the issue with one particular painkilling medication was conducted by doctors from the United States Air Force and the Denver Broncos (called the "Tokish Study" for lead author, Dr. John Tokish).[288] The Tokish Study sent questionnaires to every NFL club head doctor and head athletic trainer[289] concerning the club's use of ketorolac tromethamine, more commonly known by its brand name Toradol, during the 2000 season.

The Tokish Study described Toradol as "an effective NSAID [non-steroidal anti-inflammatory drug] for short-term relief of acute pain." The Tokish Study was motivated by concerns raised by doctors concerning Toradol's complications, "including renal failure and increased risk of bleeding."[290] The National Institutes of Health has also identified stroke, heart attack, ulcers, and holes in the stomach or intestine as potential risks of Toradol usage.[291]

The Tokish Study found that in 2000:

- 28 out of the 30 clubs that responded used Toradol;

- Clubs that used Toradol treated an average of 15 players during the season, with a range of 2 to 35;

- 26 out of 28 clubs that responded used Toradol on the day of a game;

- 24 of 27 clubs responding[cg] would allow a player as much as one injection per week throughout the season;

- 13 of 26 clubs responding found that Toradol reduced a player's pain by 51 percent or greater;

- 13 of 26 clubs responding found that Toradol reduced a player's pain by 50 percent or less; and,

- Only six clubs reported an adverse outcome related to Toradol usage during the season.

In sum, the Tokish Study concluded that "most team providers feel that ketorolac is safe when the team physician directs its use." Nevertheless, Toradol has remained a subject of study and scrutiny, as discussed below.

One category of painkillers that has received substantial attention in this context (and others) is opioids. According to the Centers for Disease Control and Prevention:

> Opioids are synthetic versions of opium. They have the ability to reduce pain but can also suppress breathing to a fatal degree when taken in excess. Examples of opioids are oxycodone

---

cf   For example, in 2016, recently retired player and perennial Pro Bowler Calvin Johnson, who played from 2007 to 2015, explained his experiences with medications: "I guess my first half of my career before they really, you know, before they started looking over the whole industry, or the whole NFL, the doctors, the team doctors and trainers, they were giving them out like candy[.]" Des Bieler, *Calvin Johnson says painkillers were handed out 'like candy' to NFL players*, Wash. Post, July 6, 2016, https://www.washingtonpost.com/news/early-lead/wp/2016/07/06/calvin-johnson-says-painkillers-were-handed-out-like-candy-to-nfl-players/, *archived at* https://perma.cc/H6HS-YVTM. Additionally, in 2010, there were allegations that both the New Orleans Saints and San Diego Chargers medical staffs were not handling medications properly. The facts of the cases are complex and do not seem to reflect modern practices, thus we do not discuss the details here. For more information, *see* Glenn Guilbeau, *Geoff Santini Speaks Out On Saints' Vicodin Case*, Shreveport Times (LA), May 12, 2010, http://archive.shreveporttimes.com/article/20100512/SPORTS/5120317/Geoff-Santini-speaks-out-Saints-Vicodin-case, *archived at* http://perma.cc/LJE9-WTGR; Sally Jenkins & Rick Maese, *Pain and Pain Management in NFL Spawn a Culture of Prescription Drug Use and Abuse*, Wash. Post, Sept. 6, 2013, *available at* 2013 WLNR 22243231; Brent Schrotenboer, *DEA: Chargers MD Wrote 108 Prescriptions to Self*, San Diego Union-Tribune, Jul. 15, 2010, *available at* 2010 WLNR 14315028; Sally Jenkins & Rick Maese, *NFL Medical Standards, Practices Are Different Than Almost Anywhere Else*, Wash. Post. Mar. 16, 2013, http://www.washingtonpost.com/sports/ redskins/nfl-medical-standards-practices-are-different-than-almost-anywhere-else/2013/03/16/b8c170bc-8be8-11e2-9f54-f3fdd70acad2_story.html, *archived at* http://perma.cc/AJ9Y-EAGY.

cg   For reasons that are unclear, not all clubs responded to all questions.

(OxyContin), hydrocodone (Vicodin) and methadone. There has been at least a 10-fold increase in the medical use of opioid painkillers during the past 20 years because of a movement toward more aggressive management of pain. Because opioids cause euphoria, they have been associated increasingly with misuse and abuse.[292]

In 2010, Washington University School of Medicine, in a study funded by ESPN, sought to examine prescription opioid use among former NFL players ("Washington/ESPN Study").[293] The Washington/ESPN Study conducted 20-minute telephone interviews with 644 former NFL players who were members of what the study referred to as the "Retired NFL Football Players Association,"[294] and retired between 1979 and 2006.

NFL practices concerning medications appear to have substantially changed in recent years.

The Washington/ESPN Study found that 52 percent of these players reported having used prescription opioids during their playing career. 71 percent of those who used prescription opioids reported having "misused" the drugs.[295] In total, 37 percent of all players studied reported having misused prescription opioids during their playing careers.

Moreover, in a 2014–2015 survey of 763 former players by *Newsday*, about 65 percent of former players responding said they used "prescription painkillers" during their career.[296] To be clear, however, not all use constitutes abuse. There are also several limitations to the *Newsday* survey: (1) the survey was sent via email and text message by the NFLPA to more than 7,000 former NFL players, thus eliminating former players that were less technologically savvy and also possibly skewing the sample toward those former players closer to the NFLPA; (2) the response rate for the survey was low (approximately 11 percent); and, (3) the study does not discuss the demographics of those that responded, making it difficult to ascertain whether those who responded are a representative sample of all former players. Importantly, the Football Players Health Study seeks to collect more data on issues such as this.

2) CURRENT LEGAL OBLIGATIONS CONCERNING MEDICATIONS

As indicated in the beginning of this section, the regulatory framework for medications depends on what type of medication is being discussed. We will discuss over-the-counter drugs, prescription drugs, and controlled substances. Again, painkillers can fit into any of these categories.

Over-the-counter drugs are those that the Food and Drug Administration has determined "to be safe and appropriate for use without the supervision of a health care professional such as a physician, and they can be purchased by consumers without a prescription."[297] Advil and Tylenol are common examples of over-the-counter painkillers. Players can obtain over-the-counter drugs on their own, without any assistance from club doctors, by purchasing them at a local pharmacy or grocery store. Club doctors can also provide players with over-the-counter medications, provided the provision of the medications and any recommend usage is within the appropriate standard of care.

Under the FDCA, a prescription drug is one that "because of its toxicity or other potentially for harmful (sic) effect, or the method of its use, or the collateral measures necessary to its use, is not safe for use except under the supervision of a practitioner licensed by law to administer such drug[.]"[298] In other words, a prescription drug is one "for which adequate directions for use cannot be written, because laypersons lack the scientific understanding needed to diagnose their disease or to use the drug in treating it."[299] Ibuprofen at certain doses and Toradol are examples of prescription painkillers (but are not controlled substances, as will be discussed below[300]). Generally speaking, club doctors can prescribe prescription medications to players provided the prescription of the medications and any recommended usage is within the appropriate standard of care.

As mentioned earlier, the CSA[301] "is the statutory framework through which the federal government regulates the lawful production, possession, and distribution of controlled substances."[302] Controlled substances are those drugs that have a "strong potential for abuse."[303] The CSA divides controlled substances into five schedules, depending on the substance's medical use, potential for abuse, and likelihood of dependence.[304] The substances considered the most dangerous are classified as Schedule I, including heroin, marijuana, LSD and ecstasy.[305] Schedule V substances, considered the least dangerous, contain limited quantities of certain narcotic and stimulant drugs and include over-the-counter cough medicines such as Robitussin.[306]

The Drug Enforcement Administration (DEA) is the federal agency primarily responsible for enforcing the CSA. "[T]he DEA is responsible for ensuring that all controlled substance transactions taken place within the 'closed system' of distribution established by [the CSA]. Under this 'closed system,' all legitimate handlers of controlled substances—manufacturers, distributors, physicians, pharmacies, and researchers—must be registered with DEA and maintain strict accounting for all distributions."[307] Generally, controlled substances that are not illegal drugs cannot be possessed or dispensed without an individual prescription.[308]

NFL club doctors, like many doctors, prescribe controlled substances—including such powerful painkillers as Vicodin, Percocet and OxyContin (all Schedule II)[309]—and thus must comply with the CSA.[310] The CSA and DEA requirements with which NFL club doctors must comply cover: registration with the DEA; the location of the doctor's registration; security of controlled substances; recordkeeping of controlled substances; and, dispensing of controlled substances, among other things.

Generally, "every person who manufactures, distributes,[311] dispenses,[312] imports, or exports any controlled substance" must register with the DEA.[313] According to the CSA, distributors of controlled substances should be granted DEA registration unless "such registration is inconsistent with the public interest."[314] One of the enumerated considerations as to whether registration would be inconsistent with the public interest is whether registration would be consistent with state law.[315] State laws generally do not allow for the prescription and distribution of controlled substances except by licensed medical professionals, such as physicians, dentists, veterinarians, and pharmacists.[316] Thus, generally, only licensed medical professionals will receive DEA registration.[317]

Doctors must obtain a separate DEA registration for each "principal place of business or professional practice" where they "dispense[]" controlled substances,[318] and must "provide effective controls and procedures to guard against theft and diversion of controlled substances."[319]

3) CURRENT ETHICAL OBLIGATIONS CONCERNING MEDICATIONS

AMA Code Opinion 9.6.6–Prescribing & Dispensing Drugs and Devices dictates that doctors should prescribe drugs . . . based solely on medical considerations, patient need, and reasonable expectations of the effectiveness for the particular patient."[320] Thus, generally doctors have an obligation to prescribe and administer prescription medications consistent with their obligation to provide medical care within an acceptable standard of care.

Of particular importance is the doctor's obligation to obtain the patient's informed consent, as discussed in Chapter 2, Section C(2)(a). Informed consent in the context of medications would importantly include advising the player about the risks of taking the medication, as well as benefits and alternatives.

4) CURRENT PRACTICES CONCERNING MEDICATIONS

As discussed earlier, medications have been misused or abused by at least some NFL clubs and NFL players in the past. Again, however, it is important to remember that players can likely obtain medications from sources other than club doctors. Moreover, the NFL's practices concerning medications have changed in recent years.

According to the NFL and NFLPS, as of February 2015, NFL clubs do not store or provide controlled substances to players.[321] Club doctors can still prescribe controlled substances to players, but the prescription is then filled at a local pharmacy.[322] Some players retrieve the prescription themselves but, according to the NFL, "[m]any players . . . request that their clubs assist them by picking up their prescriptions from a local pharmacy for them, and in many cases the clubs agree to accommodate those requests as a matter of convenience for the player."[323] The prescription is recorded in the player's electronic medical records.[324]

Clubs' practices concerning prescription medications that are not controlled substances, e.g., Toradol, are less clear. The NFL stated that it did not know whether NFL clubs or club doctors store prescription medications that are not controlled substances at stadiums and/or club facilities.[325] The NFL explained that "this practice varies from club to club and the NFL does not monitor such practices."[326]

When it comes to over-the-counter painkillers, i.e., those that do not require a prescription, club practices again vary.[327] The NFL explained that "[s]ome clubs do not provide such medications at all. Other clubs provide them at the doctors' discretion. At other clubs, ibuprofen and/or aspirin are available in the club physician's office and athletic training room and available for the players to take themselves."[328]

One useful change was made beginning with the 2015 season. As of that season, each club is assigned a Visiting Team Medical Liaison,"[329] a local doctor who can help prescribe medications as well as advice concerning local medical facilities.[330]

Some of the advances in the NFL's practices concerning painkillers and prescription medications are likely related to the increased scrutiny of the usage of Toradol (a prescription drug, but not a controlled substance). In 2012, the NFLPS commissioned a study on the use of ketorolac (brand name Toradol) in the NFL.[331] The study stated that since the Tokish Study in 2002, "it is widely believed by NFL team physicians that the use of [Toradol] has increased in prevalence not only in the NFL but also in NCAA Division I football," though there was no "objective documentation proving this hypothesis."[332]

The 2012 NFLPS study examined the pharmacological properties of Toradol, its beneficial uses (killing pain) and its possible side effects (gastrointestinal, renal, hemostasis, and cardiovascular). The study then made nine recommendations for Toradol use by NFL players, including that it only be administered under the direct supervision of a Club doctor, that it not be used prophylactically, that it be given in the lowest effective dose, and that it should be given orally except in certain situations.[333]

> "[I]f we do get painkillers, they're prescribed to us by the doctors. And they definitely go through the whole process . . . they're not just handing out a bunch of painkillers unnecessarily to guys."

The recommendations have since been adopted by NFL clubs as guidelines on the use of Toradol. Nevertheless, it has been made public that at least one club doctor began in 2012 to require players to execute a waiver for the administration of Toradol.[334,ch] The waiver included the following provisions: (1) the player's request to be treated with Toradol; (2) information about Toradol's benefits and risks; (3) the NFLPS' recommendations concerning Toradol; (4) the player's acknowledgement of having reviewed the NFLPS' study and other websites concerning Toradol; (5) the player's history of conditions related to Toradol side effects; (6) the player's acknowledgement that he had the opportunity to consult with his own doctor and an attorney about Toradol and the waiver; and, (7) a release of any possible claims the player might have against the club and the doctors related to Toradol.

As a result of the new Toradol guidelines and a grievance initiated by the NFLPA (discussed below), Toradol usage in the NFL is believed to have significantly decreased in recent years. According to St. Louis Rams club doctor and former President of the NFLPS, the practice of giving players shots of Toradol before a game has been "eliminated."[335] Current Player 1 shared his impression that painkilling medications are no longer widely dispensed:

> [I]f we do get painkillers, they're prescribed to us by the doctors. And they definitely go through the whole process . . . they're not just handing out a bunch of painkillers unnecessarily to guys—you definitely have to have a reason for it. And even when they do, they're reluctant, to give you any more than the prescribed dosage.

Current Player 5 concurred that painkillers were prescribed but also stated that "when you have a team doctor for a long time, if you build a relationship with him, then sometimes I think you have a lot of leeway in being able to get more painkillers, more drugs than he would normally prescribe." Current Player 5 also explained that painkiller misuse does still occur on some level in the NFL: "I don't think it's rampant. . . . But I think that there's probably a small percentage of guys that are actively doing whatever they can to try to get as much painkillers as they can."[ci]

On the other hand, Current Player 6 complained that his club's doctors were too conservative in providing painkillers, which is also an important concern:

> I understand not wanting to give out pain medications just freely to people who don't need it but in cases where people were in severe pain, I guess it was their call not to give out hydrocodone or pain medication that if somebody was sick in the hospital, they would be given. And instead they give them a stronger and stronger dose of Advil.[cj]

The DEA has also expressed interest in the administration of painkillers by NFL club doctors. At the 2010 NFL Combine, the DEA advised club doctors that it would be more closely monitoring the use of controlled substances by NFL clubs.[336] Then, during the 2014 season, DEA agents randomly visited several NFL clubs immediately following

---

ch   According to the NFL, only one club used such a waiver. NFL Comments and Corrections (June 24, 2016).

ci   Former Player 2 echoed that players will try to obtain painkillers without the doctor's permission: "Someone's going to have some injury where painkillers are involved. So what do you do? You go up to the guy who's hurt and say, 'Hey, let me get a couple here, maybe a couple there,' and that's how you survive[.]"

cj   Former Player 2 believes that players are "not allowed to get shots anymore."

away games.[337] The DEA agents requested to see whether the club doctors were in possession of any controlled substances and the required records.[338] The purpose of the inspections were to determine whether club doctors were prescribing and dispensing controlled substances in states in which they were not licensed to practice (and thus not registered with the DEA), and also to determine whether non-licensed staff members, such as athletic trainers, were handling controlled substances, which would violate the CSA.[339] The selected clubs were found to be in compliance and no further action was taken.[340]

To fully understand the issues raised by medications in the NFL, it is also important to understand one of the major policies addressing these issues, the NFL-NFLPA Substance Abuse Policy. The Substance Abuse Policy prohibits players "from the illegal use, possession, or distribution of drugs, including but not limited to cocaine; marijuana; opiates and opioids; methylenedioxymethamphetamine (MDMA); and phencyclidine (PCP)," as well as the "abuse of prescription drugs, over-the-counter drugs, and alcohol."[341]

According to the Substance Abuse Policy, "[t]he cornerstone of th[e] Policy is the Intervention Program."[342] "Under the NFL's Intervention Program, Players are tested, evaluated, treated, and monitored for substance abuse."[343] The Intervention Program consists of three possible stages of treatment. If the player complies with his treatment and does not fail any tests, he will be discharged from the Intervention Program. However, if the player does not comply or fails drug tests, he will be advanced into more aggressive stages of treatment and be subject to increasing discipline.

A player can enter the Intervention Program in three ways: (1) a positive test result; (2) "[b]ehavior (including but not limited to an arrest or conduct related to an alleged misuse of Substances of Abuse occurring up to two (2) football seasons prior to the Player's applicable scouting combine) which, in the judgment of the Medical Director, exhibits physical, behavioral, or psychological signs or symptoms of misuse of Substances of Abuse"; and, (3) "Self-Referral: Personal notification to the Medical Director by a Player of his desire voluntarily to enter Stage One of the Intervention Program prior to his being notified to provide a specimen leading to a Positive Test Result, and prior to behavior of the type described above becoming known to the Medical Director from a source other than the Player."[344]

Once in the Intervention Program, the players are referred to the appropriate clinical professionals to develop a treatment plan for the player.[345] The Medical Director must then approve the treatment plan.[346] Additionally, once in the Intervention Program, the player is subject to additional testing at the discretion of the Medical Director.[347]

If a player complies with his treatment plan, he can be discharged from the Intervention Program in as early as 90 days.[348] If the Medical Director believes the player needs additional treatment or if the player fails to comply with his treatment plan, such as by failing a test, the player will advance to Stage Two of the Intervention Program.[349] In Stage Two, a player can be subject to as many as 10 unannounced drug tests per month.[350]

If a player complies with his treatment plan in Stage Two, he can be discharged from the Intervention Program in as early as 12 months.[351] However, again, if the Medical Director believes the player needs additional treatment or if the player fails to comply with his treatment plan, such as by failing a test, the player will advance to Stage Three of the Intervention Program and be subject to additional treatment and evaluation.[352]

Players are not disciplined for initial positive test results under the Substance Abuse Policy. Instead, players are entered into the Intervention Program. Provided players comply with their treatment programs under the Intervention Program, they will not be disciplined. If players do not comply, there is a gradually increasing discipline scheme of fines and eventually suspension.

5) ENFORCEMENT CONCERNING MEDICATIONS

If an NFL player believes a club or club doctor has violated their obligations concerning medications, he can seek to enforce the obligations in the same manner as he might seek to enforce other obligations, including through lawsuits, investigations under the CBA, Non-Injury Grievances, and/or complaints to relevant licensing boards, as discussed above.

There has been one particularly noteworthy enforcement effort concerning the administration of medications by club doctors. In December 2012, the NFLPA commenced a Non-Injury Grievance against the NFL concerning the Toradol waiver discussed above.[353] The NFLPA contended the waiver violated three provisions of the 2011 CBA.

First, the NFLPA contended the waiver violated Paragraph 9 of the NFL Player Contract. Paragraph 9 provides that if Player is injured in the performance of his services under this contract and promptly reports such injury to the Club physician or trainer, then Player will receive such medical and hospital care during the term of this contract as the club physician may deem necessary[.]" The NFLPA argued that clubs and club doctors cannot precondition the provision of medical care they deem necessary on the acceptance of waivers.

Second, the NFLPA contended the waiver violated Article 39, Section 1 of the 2011 CBA. Section 1 provides, in relevant part, that "each Club physician's primary duty in providing player medical care shall be not to the Club but instead to the player-patient." The NFLPA argued that the waivers "are obviously not for benefit of the player-patient, but rather solely to relieve the Club and Club physician from any liability for the administration of Toradol."

Third, the NFLPA argued that the waiver violated Article 39, Section 1(c) and Article 39, Section 3(e). Section 1(c) requires "all Club physicians and medical personnel [to] comply with all federal, state and local requirements, including all ethical rules and standards established by any applicable government and/or authority that regulates or governs the medical profession in the Club's city." Section 3(e) requires a club to "use its best efforts to ensure that its players are provided with medical care consistent with professional standards for the industry." The NFLPA argued that clubs cannot precondition compliance with these provisions on the execution of a waiver.

The Non-Injury Grievance was settled,[354] and no NFL clubs currently require players to sign waivers prior to the administration of Toradol.[355]

Finally, we discuss an ongoing lawsuit against the NFL concerning medications. In May 2014, several former players, led by former Chicago Bear Richard Dent, filed a class action lawsuit alleging that the NFL and its clubs and doctors negligently and fraudulently prescribed and administered painkilling medications during their careers.[356] The lawsuit generally focused on three types of medications: opioids, which "act to block and dull pain"; nonsteroidal anti-inflammatory medications, such as Toradol, which have "analgesic and anti-inflammatory effects to mitigate pain"; and, local anesthetics, such as lidocaine.[357,ck] The former players' alleged that the doctors' inappropriate administration of the medications caused them a variety of physical and mental ailments, including heart and kidney damage and drug addiction.[358]

In December 2014, the United States District Court for the Northern District of California dismissed the case, ruling that the players' claims were preempted by the Labor Management Relations Act (LMRA).[359] Effectively, the court found that to determine the validity of the players' claims would require interpretation of the CBA, and thus the players should have pursued grievances through arbitration as opposed to lawsuits.[360] In its ruling, the Court stated:

> *In ruling against the novel claims asserted herein, this order does not minimize the underlying societal issue. In such a rough-and-tumble sport as professional football, player injuries loom as a serious and inevitable evil. Proper care of these injuries is likewise a paramount need. The main point of this order is that the league has addressed these serious concerns in a serious way—by imposing duties on the clubs via collective bargaining and placing a long line of health-and-safety duties on the team owners themselves. These benefits may not have been perfect but they have been uniform across all clubs and not left to the vagaries of state common law. They are backed up by the enforcement power of the union itself and the players' right to enforce these benefits.[361]*

The *Dent* case is currently on appeal to the United States Court of Appeals for the Ninth Circuit.[362]

Following the December 2014 ruling in the *Dent* case, the attorneys for the plaintiffs filed a separate lawsuit with new plaintiffs alleging substantially the same allegations, led by former player Chuck Evans.[363] However, the *Evans* lawsuit alleged *intentional* wrongdoing by the clubs, as opposed to merely negligent conduct.[364] In addition, in this case the defendants were the 32 individual NFL clubs, and not the NFL.[365] In July 2016, the same judge as in the *Dent* case denied the clubs' motion to dismiss the *Evans* complaint.[366] The court noted that the *Evans* plaintiffs, unlike the *Dent* plaintiffs, alleged *intentional* violations of the CSA and the FDCA.[367] The Court explained that because parties cannot agree to a CBA that permits illegal behavior (*i.e.*, behavior that violates statutes), the CBA could not preempt plaintiffs' claims.[368] As a result of the Court's decision, the *Evans* plaintiffs may have the right to investigate and discover information about medication practices in the NFL. The case is ongoing as of the time of this publication.

---

ck   The allegations in the *Dent* lawsuit mirrored revelations from Dr. Rob Huizenga, the Oakland Raiders' internist from 1983 to 1990. Huizenga, in his 1994 book "You're Okay, It's Just a Bruise," described a practice by which players received pain-killing and anti-inflammatory medications on an almost constant basis. *See* Rob Huizenga, You're Okay, It's Just a Bruise 39 (1994) ("Indocin, an Advil-like anti-inflammatory drug, was so widely used by players for aches and pains that I was tempted to put it in the water system."); *id.* at 44 ("Nearly every athlete who had seen action would request an anti-inflammatory—Indocin or maybe Naprosyn or Feldene—and sometimes a muscle-spasm medicine."); *id.* at 127 ("In order to play, he needed an injection before each game.")

6) RECOMMENDATIONS CONCERNING MEDICATIONS

The evidence available to us, though admittedly far from complete, suggests that the misuse and abuse of medications is largely a thing of the past and that, by and large, current practices involving medications comply with legal and ethical obligations. While interviews and surveys discussed above suggest that for many years NFL clubs and club doctors facilitated—or at least failed to protect against—player misuse and abuse of certain medications, this generally no longer seems to be the case. Indeed, NFL clubs no longer even store controlled substances at their facilities. For these reasons, we do not believe a formal recommendation is needed concerning medications.

Nevertheless, it is undoubtedly true that football causes pain and injuries and the use of prescription-strength painkillers and controlled substances will continue to be something many club doctors players will find necessary. Consequently, it is important that the NFL and the club doctors continue to evaluate practices concerning medications, including but not limited to how much they are being used, what types are being used and for what purposes, under what circumstances they are being used, their risks and effectiveness, prescriptions for and documentation of their use, and players' understanding of and consent to their use. Additionally, practices should be compared across the clubs, as discussions with players suggested that clubs' practices concerning medications can vary.

Endnotes

1 CBA, Art. 39, § 1.
2 CBA, Art. 39, § 1(e).
3 NFL Physicians Society Mission Statement, Nat'l Football League Physicians Soc'y, http://nflps.org/about/ (last visited Aug. 7, 2015), archived at http://perma.cc/928Z-LVZ4.
4 See Dave Siebert, What Is Medical Care Like on an NFL Sideline?, Bleacher Report (Nov. 15, 2013), http://bleacherreport.com/articles/1850732-what-is-medical-care-like-on-an-nfl-sideline, archived at http://perma.cc/7JR4-HR3G (quoting then-NFLPS President Matthew Matava describing the "about 177 NFL team physicians"); Team Physicians, Nat'l Football League Physicians Society, http://nflps.org/team-physicians/ (last visited Feb. 24, 2016), archived at https://perma.cc/HK8A-QJ9L (listing 153 club doctors as members of the NFLPS).
5 See Frequently Asked Questions—How Often Do All NFLPS Members Meet?, Nat'l Football League Physician's Soc'y, http://nflps.org/faqs/how-often-do-all-nflps-members-meet/ (last visited Aug. 7, 2015), archived at http://perma.cc/76P5-DRQX; Frequently Asked Questions—What Are Typical Topics at Members Meetings?, Nat'l Football League Physician's Soc'y, http://nflps.org/faqs/what-are-typical-topics-at-members-meetings/ (last visited Aug. 7, 2015), archived at http://perma.cc/LR79-9AN3 ("The topics at these meetings vary and address any or all of the potential injuries that a NFL player may experience. This can include orthopaedic injuries such as ACL tears, meniscus tears, cartilage injuries to the knee, multiligamentous injuries to the knee, high ankle sprains, fractures, dislocations, foot injuries, surgical techniques, rehabilitation, hip injuries, arthroscopy of the hip, sports hernia challenges, shoulder injuries such as dislocations or labral tears, rotator cuff problems, elbow dislocation, biceps or triceps injuries, wrist injuries, and hand and finger injuries or dislocations. From a medical standpoint, there has been a recent emphasis on heat-related illnesses, cardiac conditions, MRSA infections, sickle cell traits, concussions and the management of acute blunt trauma to the chest or abdomen.").
6 This information was provided by NFLPS.
7 Id. Clubs also likely do not directly hire doctors to comply with the corporate practice of medicine doctrine. The corporate practice of medicine doctrine is a state law concept that generally prohibits entities from practicing medicine or employing physicians to provide professional medical services. The prohibitions vary from state to state (with many exceptions to the general rule) and are found in common law, state statutes, regulations, and administrative opinions. See Mary H. Michal, Meg S.L. Pekarske & Matthew K. McManus, Corporate Practice of Medicine Doctrine: 50 State Survey Summary, Nat'l Hospice & Palliative Care Org. & Ctr. to Advance Palliative Care (2006), http://www.nhpco.org/sites/default/files/public/palliativecare/corporate-practice-of-medicine-50-state-summary.pdf, archived at https://perma.cc/G2QD-2EQB?type=pdf.
8 Interview with Larry Ferazani, NFL, Vice President, Labor Litigation & Policy (Oct. 6, 2014).
9 Id.
10 NFL Comments and Corrections (June 24, 2016).
11 Memorandum from NFL Commissioner Paul Tagliabue to NFL Club Chief Executives and Presidents re: Hospital and Physician Sponsorship (Sep. 7, 2004) (on file with author).
12 Id.
13 Id.
14 Id.
15 Rob Huizenga, You're Okay, It's Just a Bruise 74 (1994) ("No wonder that rumors floated, and Sports Illustrated reported that at least one NFL physician was paying the team for the privilege of being team doctor."); id. at 325 (The NFL Physicians Society is currently trying to fight off an invasion from the big business hospital chains. Turns out some health companies are actually bidding for the right to be the official team doctor/team hospital for NFL teams. The hospitals have presumably calculated that getting their hospital logo right next to one of those stadium beer commercials is worth a lot of bucks. It's rumored the bidding may have reached $1 million.")
16 Id. See also Sam Eifling, Walk It Off, Champ: Why NFL Team Doctors Are Ethically Compromised, Slate.com (Jan. 30, 2013), http://www.slate.com/articles/sports/sports_nut/2013/01/nfl_team_doctors_the_problem_with_pro_football_s_medical_sponsorship_deals.html, archived at https://perma.cc/PL2D-8JHV?type=pdf (quoting Lew Lyon, vice president of the Baltimore Ravens-affiliated MedStar Sports Medicine as saying "[t]he halo effect is huge . . . [f]riends will call me and say, 'Can you get me into see one of the Ravens docs'?").
17 Pierce E. Scranton, Jr., Playing Hurt: Treating and Evaluating the Warriors of the NFL 154 (2001).
18 Bill Pennington, Sports Turnaround: The Team Doctors Now Pay the Team, N.Y. Times, May 18, 2004, http://www.nytimes.com/2004/05/18/sports/sports-medicine-sports-turnaround-the-team-doctors-now-pay-the-team.html?pagewanted=1, archived at https://perma.cc/JW63-LZ4U?type=pdf.

19 Memorandum from NFL Commissioner Paul Tagliabue to NFL Club Chief Executives and Presidents re: Hospital and Physician Sponsorship (Sep. 7, 2004) (on file with author).

20 Id.

21 Memorandum from NFL Commissioner Roger Goodell to NFL Club Chief Executives and Presidents re: Hospital and Medical Service Provider Sponsorships (Nov. 2, 2012) (on file with author).

22 Id.

23 Memorandum from NFL Commissioner Roger Goodell to NFL Club Chief Executives and Presidents re: League Policy on Club Medical Services Agreements and Sponsorships (May 2, 2014) (on file with author).

24 Id.

25 E-mail with Larry Ferazani NFL, Vice President, Labor Litigation & Policy (Apr. 15, 2015).

26 Interview with Larry Ferazani, NFL, Vice President, Labor Litigation & Policy (Oct. 6, 2014).

27 Id.

28 Pennington, supra note 18.

29 NFL Comments and Corrections (June 24, 2016).

30 Email from Jon Coyles, MLB Labor Counsel, to Chris Deubert (Oct. 6, 2014, 15:13 EST) (on file with author).

31 NBA CBA, Art. XXII, § 5.

32 Under the 2011 CBA, this responsibility is solely the doctor's. See 2011 CBA, App. A: NFL Player Contract ¶ 8 ("If Player fails to establish or maintain his excellent physical condition to the satisfaction of the Club physician . . . then Club may terminate this contract.")

33 Lambley v. Kameny, 682 N.E.2d 907, 912 (Mass. App. Ct. 1997). See also James L. Rigelhaupt, What Constitutes Physician–Patient Relationship for Malpractice Purposes, 17 A.L.R.4th 132 (1982) (listing jurisdictions that explicitly support the view that a physician's acceptance, or undertaking treatment of a patient creates a physician–patient relationship. States listed include Cal., Ill, Mass, NJ, NY, and Wash., in addition to others.)

34 LoDico v. Caputi, 517 N.Y.S.2d 640 (N.Y. App. Div. 1987); Miller v. Sullivan, 625 N.Y.S.2d 102 (N.Y. App. Div. 1995); St. John v. Pope, 901 S.W.2d 420, 423–24 (Tex. 1995); Gallardo v. U.S., 752 F.3d 865 (10th Cir. 2014) (applying Colorado law) (recognizing that a physician's duty arises out of an express or implied contractual relationship when a physician undertakes to treat or otherwise provide medical care to another); Smith v. Pavlovich, 914 N.E.2d 1258 (Ill. App. Ct. 2009) (A physician-patient or special relationship may exist even in the absence of any meetings between the physician and patient, where the physician performs services for the patient); Harper v. Hippensteel, 994 N.E.2d 1233 (Ind. Ct. App. 2013) (where doctor does not treat, see, or in any way participate in the care or diagnosis of plaintiff-patient, doctor-patient relationship will not be found to exist such that duty owed by physician would arise); Olson v. Wrenshall, 822 N.W.2d 336 (Neb. 2012) (a physician's duty to exercise the applicable standard of care arises out of the physician-patient relationship; this relationship is said to arise when the physician undertakes treatment of the patient); Clarke v. Hoek, 219 Cal.Rptr. 845 (Cal. Ct. App. 1985) (finding no doctor-physician relationship established when doctor never entered into any contractual relationship with appellant or the proctored physician,). See also, Rigelhaupt, supra note 33.

35 Heller v. Peekskill Community Hosp., 603 N.Y.S.2d 548 (N.Y. App. Div. 1993); Lodico, 517 N.Y.S.2d 640.

36 For more on this issue, see Mark A. Rothstein, Jessica Roberts, Tee L. Guidotti, Limiting Occupational Medical Evaluations Under the Americans with Disabilities Act and the Genetic Information Nondiscrimination Act, 41 Am. J. L. & Med. 523 (2015).

37 See, e.g.,Tee L. Guidotti et al., Occupational Health Services: A Practical Approach 66 (2d ed. 2013); Jacques Tamin, Models of occupational medicine practice: an approach to understanding moral conflict in "dual obligation" doctors, 16 Med. Health Care Philos. 499 (2013); Elaine Draper, The Company Doctor: Risk, Responsibility and Corporate Professionalism (2003); and, Elaine Draper, Preventive law by corporate professional team players: liability and responsibility in the work of company doctors, 15 J. Contemp. Health Law Policy 525 (1999).

38 Barry R. Furrow et al., Health Law 61 (2d ed. 2000).

39 See, e.g., New York State Education § 6530 (defining "professional misconduct" applicable to physicians as, among other things, "practicing the profession with negligence on more than one occasion," "practicing the profession with gross negligence on a particular occasion," "[r]evealing of personally identifiable facts, data, or information obtained in a professional capacity without the prior consent of the patient, except as authorized or required by law," and "[d]elegating professional responsibilities to a person when the licensee delegating such responsibilities knows or has reason to know that such person is not qualified, by training, by experience, or by licensure, to perform them.")

40 Furrow, supra note 38, at 59. However, "[m]ost boards do not have adequate staff to respond to the volume of complaints and to conduct extensive investigations of unprofessional conduct," leading consumer groups to complain about the industry's failure to self-regulate. Mark A. Hall et al., Med. Liability and Treatment Relationships 137 (2008).

41 Id.

42 Id.

43 AMA Code of Medical Ethics, Am. Med Ass'n, http://www.ama-assn.org/ama/pub/physician-resources/medical-ethics/code-medical-ethics.page (last visited Aug. 22, 2016), archived at http://perma.cc/8JJ4-MYJX.

44 AMA Mission & Guiding Principles, Am. Med Ass'n, http://www.ama-assn.org/ama/pub/about-ama.page? (last visited Jan. 8, 2016), archived at https://perma.cc/2QCB-EADZ.

45 See 2011 CBA, Art. 39 § 1(a)-(b) (listing the various types of doctors contemplated or required to be hired by NFL Clubs).

46 See Update: Evaluation and Management of Concussion in Sports, Am. Acad. of Neurology, https://www.aan.com/uploadedFiles/Website_Library_Assets/Documents/3Practice_Management/5Patient_Resources/1For_Your_Patient/6_Sports_Concussion_Toolkit/evaluation.pdf (last visited Aug. 7, 2015), archived at https://perma.cc/4UEF-SM88?type=pdf.

47 ACOEM Code of Ethics, Am. Coll. of Occupational & Envtl. Med., http://www.acoem.org/codeofconduct.aspx (last visited Aug. 7, 2015), archived at http://perma.cc/6R8A-XN6V [hereinafter ACOEM Code of Ethics].

48 International Code of Ethics for Occupational Health Professionals, Int'l Comm'n on Occupational Health, http://www.icohweb.org/site_new/multimedia/core_documents/pdf/code_ethics_eng_2012.pdf (last visited Aug. 7, 2015), archived at https://perma.cc/2URK-LT9V?type=pdf.

49 About Us, Int'l Fed'n of Sports Med., www.fims.org/about (last visited Aug. 7, 2015), archived at http://perma.cc/458J-R3KF.

50 Our History, Int'l Fed'n of Sports Med., http://www.fims.org/about/our-history/ (last visited Aug. 7, 2015), archived at http://perma.cc/UQ33-93XZ.

51 See Member Associations, Int'l Fed'n of Sports Med., http://www.fims.org/en/associations/national/#United%20States (last visited August 6, 2015), archived at http://perma.cc/2Y7G-63Z4.

52 FIMS Code of Ethics, Int'l Fed'n of Sports Med., http://www.fims.org/files/8214/1933/5848/FIMSCodeOfEthics.pdf (last visited Aug. 7, 2015), archived at https://perma.cc/NCZ7-X3KV?type=pdf [hereinafter FIMS Code of Ethics]. FIMS also published a Team Physician Manual which is one of the preeminent manuals for sports injuries and also covers the same ethical considerations espoused in its Code of Ethics.

53 Team Physician Consensus Statement: 2013 Update, Am. Coll. of Sports Med., http://www.acsm.org/docs/other-documents/team_physician_consensus_statement___2013_update-24.pdf (last visited Aug. 7, 2015), archived at https://perma.cc/A5G5-68HJ?type=pdf.

54 See Thierfelder v. Wolfert, 52 A.3d 1251, 1264 (Pa. 2012) (discussing elements of a medical malpractice claim); Hamilton v. Wilson, 249 S.W.3d

425, 426 (Tex. 2008) (same); Sullivan v. Edward Hosp., 806 N.E.2d 645, 653 (Ill. 2004) (same).

55 Id.

56 See Greenberg v. Perkins, 845 P.2d 530, 535 (Colo. 1993) (discussing various states' positions on whether a physician-patient relationship is required for a medical malpractice action).

57 See Benjamin Grossberg, Uniformity, Federalism, and Tort Reform: The Erie Implications of Medical Malpractice Certificate of Merit Statutes, 159 U. Pa. L. Rev. 217 (2010) (identifying 25 states with statutes that require certificates of merit by another doctor for a medical malpractice claim).

58 CBA, Art. 39, § 1(c).

59 This information was provided by the NFLPA.

60 NFL Comments and Corrections (June 24, 2016).

61 Specialty Guidelines for Forensic Psychology, Am. Psychol. Ass'n, http://www.apa.org/practice/guidelines/forensic-psychology.aspx (last visited Aug. 13, 2015), archived at https://perma.cc/8H9X-3XQV?type=pdf.

62 NHL CBA, § 34.1(b).

63 AMA Code of Medical Ethics, Am. Med Ass'n, http://www.ama-assn.org/ama/pub/physician-resources/medical-ethics/code-medical-ethics/principles-medical-ethics.page? (last visited Feb. 24, 2016), archived at https://perma.cc/6YPW-G5BD.

64 Id.

65 Opinion 1.1.6 – Quality, Am. Med. Ass'n, available at http://www.ama-assn.org/ama/pub/physician-resources/medical-ethics/code-medical-ethics.page (last visited Aug.1, 2016), archived at https://perma.cc/4QS7-F5FT.

66 Opinion 1.1.1 – Patient-Physician Relationships, Am. Med. Ass'n, available at http://www.ama-assn.org/ama/pub/physician-resources/medical-ethics/code-medical-ethics.page (last Aug. 1, 2016), archived at https://perma.cc/4QS7-F5FT.

67 FIMS Code of Ethics at ¶ 1.

68 Id.

69 Id.

70 Id. at ¶ 4.

71 See, e.g., John Lantos, Ann Marie Matlock & David Wendler, Clinician Integrity and Limits to Patient Autonomy, 305 J. Am. Med. Ass'n, 495–99 (2011) ("Respect for patient autonomy plays a central role in modern clinical ethics"); Simon N. Whitney, Amy L. McGuire & Laurence B. McCullough, A Typology of Shared Decision Making, Informed Consent, and Simple Consent, 140 Ann. Intern. Med., 54–59 (2003) ("Enhancing patient choice is a central theme of medical ethics and law."); Cathy Charles, Amiram Gafni & Tim Whelan, Decision-making in the Physician-Patient Encounter: Revisiting the Shared Treatment Decision-Making Model, 49 Social Sci. & Med., 651–61 (1999) (emphasizing the need to respect differences in patient preferences). See also Stedman's Medical Stedman's Med. Dictionary (28th ed. 2006) (defining "autonomy" as "[t]he condition or state of being autonomous, able to make decisions unaided by others"); Black's Law Dictionary (9th ed. 2009) (defining "autonomy" as: "the right of self-government"; "an individual's capacity for self-determination").

72 Jamie Staples King & Benjamin Moulton, Rethinking Informed Consent: The Case for Shared Medical Decisionmaking, 32 Am. J. Law & Med. 429, 493–501 (2006). (explaining that 25 states have adopted the physician-based standard, 23 have adopted a patient-based standard and two have adopted a hybrid standard).

73 Furrow, Barry R. Furrow et al., Health Law 217 (2d ed. 2000).

74 Fuller v. Starnes, 597 S.W. 2d 88 (Ark. 1980).

75 Canterbury v. Spence, 464 F.2d 772, 787 (D.C. Cir. 1972).

76 Pedersen v. Vahidy, 552 A.2d 419 (Conn. 1989).

77 King & Moulton, supra note 72.

78 Id.

79 CBA, Art. 39, § 1(c).

80 CBA, Art. 40, § 2(a).

81 Opinion 8.6 – Promoting Patient Safety, Am. Med. Ass'n, available at http://www.ama-assn.org/ama/pub/physician-resources/medical-ethics/code-medical-ethics.page (last visited Aug. 1, 2016), archived at https://perma.cc/3APG-V3WR. See also ACOEM Code of Ethics, Ethical Principle VI: An Obligation to Advise and Report: "Occupational and environmental health professionals should communicate effectively and in a timely manner to an individual all significant observations about the health and health risk of that person and provide advice about interventions available to restore, sustain, and improve health or prevent illness."

82 FIMS Code of Ethics at ¶ 4.

83 Id. at ¶ 3.

84 Id. at ¶ 1.

85 ACOEM Code of Ethics.

86 Mark A. Hall et al., Health Care Law and Ethics 168–69 (2003) (collecting cases and statutes).

87 Id.

88 Id.

89 This information was provided by the NFLPA.

90 See Mark A. Rothstein, Jessica Roberts, Tee L. Guidotti, Limiting Occupational Medical Evaluations Under the Americans with Disabilities Act and the Genetic Information Nondiscrimination Act, 41 Am. J. L. & Med. 523, 542 (2015) ("the health care providers from whom employers obtain medical records (e.g., physicians, hospitals) are very likely to be covered entities.")

91 "Protected health information means individually identifiable health information . . . that is: (i) Transmitted by electronic media; (ii) Maintained in electronic media; or (iii) Transmitted or maintained in any other form or medium." 45 C.F.R. § 160.103. "Individually identifiable health information is information that is a subset of health information, including demographic information collected from an individual, and: (1) Is created or received by a health care provider, health plan, employer, or health care clearinghouse; and (2) Relates to the past, present, or future physical or mental health or condition of an individual; the provision of health care to an individual; or the past, present, or future payment for the provision of health care to an individual; and (i) That identifies the individual; or (ii) With respect to which there is a reasonable basis to believe the information can be used to identify the individual." Id.

92 C.F.R. § 160.103.

93 C.F.R. § 160.103.

94 Id.

95 C.F.R. § 164.512(b)(v).

96 C.F.R. § 1904.4.

97 C.F.R. § 164.512(l).

98 Hall, supra note 86, at 171.

99 See Joy Pritts et al., The State of Health Privacy: A Survey of State Health Privacy Statutes (2d ed. 2003), available at http://sharps.org/wp-content/uploads/PRITTS-REPORT1.pdf, archived at https://perma.cc/C72H-R3LK?type=pdf (describing 21 states with laws restricting doctors from disclosing healthcare information, subject to various exceptions).

100 See id.; see also Joy L. Pritts, Altered States: State Health Privacy Laws and the Impact of the Federal Health Privacy Rule, 2 Yale J. Health Pol'y, L. & Ethics 325, 335–36 (2002) (discussing variance in state laws on use and disclosure of medical information).

101 See, e.g., Arizona: A.R.S. § 12-2294(C)(9); A.R.S. § 36-509(A)(14); California: Ann. Cal. Civ. Code § 56.10(c)(2) (West 2014); Ann. Cal. Civ. Code § 56.10(c)(8)(A) (West 2014); Ann. Cal. Civ. Code § 56.10(c)(8)(B) (West 2014); Colorado: Colo. Rev. Stat. Ann. § 8-43-404(2); Colo. Rev. Stat. Ann. § 8-47-203(1)(a); 7 Colo. Code Regs. 1101-3:8; 7 Colo. Code Regs. 1101-3:8; Florida: Fla. Stat. Ann. § 440.13(4)(c); Fla. Stat. Ann. § 397.501(7)(a)(4); Georgia: Ga. Code Ann. § 34-9-207(a); Ga. Code Ann. § 34-9-207(b); Illinois: Ill. Comp. Stat. Ann 305/8(a); Indiana: Ind. Code

Ann. § 16-39-5-3; Louisiana: LSA-R.S. 23:1125; LSA-R.S. 23:1127; Maryland: MD. Code Ann. § 4-305(b)(5); Md. Code Regs. 14.09.03.07; Massachusetts: M.G.L.A. 152 § 20; Michigan: Opinion No. 6593 of the Michigan Attorney General, 1989; Minnesota: Minn. Stat. Ann. § 176.138(a); Missouri: Mo. Rev. Stat. § 287.140(7); New Jersey: N.J. Stat. Ann. § 45:14B-32; N.J. Stat. Ann. § 34:15-128(a)(2); New York: N.Y. Workers' Compensation Law § 13-(g) (McKinney); North Carolina: N.C. Gen. Stat. Ann. § 97-25.6(c)(1); N.C. Gen. Stat. Ann. § 97-25.6(c)(2); Ohio: Ohio Rev. Code Ann. § 4123.651(B); Pennsylvania: 77 Pa. Stat. Ann. § 835; 77 Pa. Stat. Ann. § 531; 50 Pa. Stat. Ann. § 711; Tennessee: Tenn. Code Ann. § 50-6-204(a)(2)(A); Texas: Tex. Labor Code Code. Ann. § 408.025(d); Virginia: Va. Code Ann. § 65.2-604(A); Va. Code Ann. § 65.2-607(A); and, Washington: Wash. Rev. Code Ann. §51.36.060; Wash. Rev. Code Ann.§ 70.02.050(1)(d).

102 CBA, Art. 39, § 1(c).

103 Opinion 3.1.5—Professionalism in Relationships with Media, Am. Med. Ass'n, available at http://www.ama-assn.org/ama/pub/physician-resources/medical-ethics/code-medical-ethics.page (last visited Aug. 1, 2016), archived at https://perma.cc/ZR8K-FC93.

104 Opinion 3.2.1—Confidentiality, Am. Med. Ass'n, available at http://www.ama-assn.org/ama/pub/physician-resources/medical-ethics/code-medical-ethics.page (last visited Aug. 1, 2016), archived at https://perma.cc/ZR8K-FC93.

105 FIMS Code of Ethics at ¶ 4.

106 Id. at ¶ 11.

107 Id. at ¶ 4.

108 Kloster v. Hormel Foods Corp., 612 N.W.2d 772, 775 (Iowa 2000) ("When a physician acts contrary to the best interests of a patient, these acts or omissions undermine the public trust, and may rise to the level of malpractice."); Pearce v. Ollie, 826 P.2d 888, 907 (Idaho 1992) ("The physician's fiduciary duty requires that he act in the best interests of his patient so as to protect the sanctity of the physician-patient relationship") (citing Petrillo v. Syntex Labs., Inc., 148 Ill. App.3d 581, 594 (Ill. App. 1986) "There is an implied promise, arising when the physician begins treating the patient, that the physician will refrain from engaging in conduct that is inconsistent with the 'good faith' required of a fiduciary. The patient should, we believe, be able to trust that the physician will act in the best interests of the patient thereby protecting the sanctity of the physician-patient relationship.").

109 CBA, Art. 39, § 1(c).

110 Opinion 11.2.2—Conflicts of Interest in Patient Care, Am. Med. Ass'n, available at http://www.ama-assn.org/ama/pub/physician-resources/medical-ethics/code-medical-ethics.page (last visited Aug. 1, 2016), archived at https://perma.cc/73DF-THU4.

111 Opinion 1.1.1—Patient-Physician Relationships, Am. Med. Ass'n, available at http://www.ama-assn.org/ama/pub/physician-resources/medical-ethics/code-medical-ethics.page (last Aug. 1, 2016), archived at https://perma.cc/4QS7-F5FT.

112 Opinion 1.2.5—Sports Medicine, Am. Med. Ass'n, available at http://www.ama-assn.org/ama/pub/physician-resources/medical-ethics/code-medical-ethics.page (last visited Aug.1, 2016), archived at https://perma.cc/4QS7-F5FT.

113 Opinion 10.2—Physician Employment by a Nonphysician Supervisee, Am. Med. Ass'n, available at http://www.ama-assn.org/ama/pub/physician-resources/medical-ethics/code-medical-ethics.page (last visited Aug.1, 2016), archived at https://perma.cc/73QV-B54W.

114 FIMS Code of Ethics at ¶ 1.

115 Id. at ¶ 3.

116 Id.

117 Id. at ¶ 4.

118 Id. at ¶ 11.

119 See Code of Ethics, Am. Bd. of Physician Specialties, http://www.abpsus.org/code-of-ethics (last visited Aug. 7, 2015), archived at http://perma.cc/S5YG-XSTR.

120 Standards of Professionalism: Providing Musculoskeletal Services to Patients ¶¶ 14–16, Am. Acad. of Orthopaedic Surgeons (2008), http://www3.aaos.org/member/profcomp/provmuscserv.pdf, archived at https://perma.cc/A4X6-V9GD?type=pdf.

121 See id.

122 See Dyer v. Trachtman, 679 N.W.2d 311, 314–15 (Mich. 2004) (collecting cases); See also Mark A. Rothstein, Jessica Roberts, Tee L. Guidotti, Limiting Occupational Medical Evaluations Under the Americans with Disabilities Act and the Genetic Information Nondiscrimination Act, 41 Am. J. L. & Med. 523, 534–35 (2015) (discussing limits of physician-patient relationship in occupational medicine).

123 Dyer, supra n. 122; Greenberg v. Perkins, 845 P.2d 530, 535 (Colo. 1993) ("physician owes a duty of care to a nonpatient examinee to conduct the examination in a manner not to cause harm to the person being examined.") (internal quotations and citations removed).

124 Bazakos v. Lewis, 911 N.E.2d 847, 849 (N.Y. 2009) ("an [independent medical examination] is essentially adversarial"); Dyer, 679 N.W. 2d at 315 (independent medical examination "physician often examines the patient under circumstances that are adversarial"); Greenberg, 845 P.2d at 539 (discussing that doctor was acting "in an adversary setting).

125 See Dyer, 679 N.W. 2d at 315 (collecting cases). See also Murphy v. Blum, 554 N.Y.S.2d 640 (App.Div. 1990) (holding that no physician-patient relationship arose out of pre-season physical exam of NBA referee conducted solely to advise league regarding referee's physical capabilities); Matthew J. Mitten, Emerging Legal Issues in Sports Medicine: A Synthesis, Summary, and Analysis, 76 St. John's L. Rev. 5, 13–14 (2002) (discussing the legal duty of care where doctor is only performing a medical examination on behalf of an employer).

126 See Reed v. Bojarski, 764 A.2d 433 (N.J. 2001) (physician retained to perform a pre-employment physical has a duty to inform the patient of a potentially serious medical condition); Green v. Walker, 910 F.2d 291 (5th Cir. 1990) (holding that, under Louisiana law, a doctor performing an examination on behalf of an employer, had "a duty to conduct the requested tests and diagnose the results thereof, exercising the level of care consistent with the doctor's professional training and expertise, and to take reasonable steps to make information available timely to the examinee of any findings that pose an imminent danger to the examinee's physical or mental well-being").

127 CBA, Art. 39 § 1(c).

128 Opinion 1.2.6—Work-Related & Independent Medical Examinations, Am. Med. Ass'n, available at http://www.ama-assn.org/ama/pub/physician-resources/medical-ethics/code-medical-ethics.page (last visited July 26, 2016), archived at https://perma.cc/4QS7-F5FT.

129 Id.

130 Id.

131 Tee L. Guidotti et al., Occupational Health Services: A Practical Approach 37 (2d ed. 2013), citing the ACOEM Code of Ethics.

132 NFL Comments and Corrections (June 25, 2016).

133 NFL CBA, Art. 39, § 1(c).

134 NFL Comments and Corrections (June 24, 2016).

135 Id.

136 Dyer, 679 N.W. 2d at 315–17 (collecting cases); Greenberg, 845 P.2d at 535 (Colo. 1993) ("physician owes a duty of care to a nonpatient examinee to conduct the examination in a manner not to cause harm to the person being examined.") (internal quotations and citations removed).

137 See, e.g., Yoder v. Cotton, 758 N.W.2d 630 (Neb. 2008); Jacobsen-Wayne v. Calvin C.M. Kam, 198 F.3d 254 (9th Cir. 1999) (both affirming granting of defendant physician who had performed independent medical examination summary judgment on informed consent claim by finding that plaintiff had consented to the examination).

138 Opinion 1.2.6—Work-Related & Independent Medical Examinations, Am. Med. Ass'n, available at http://www.ama-assn.org/ama/pub/physician

-resources/medical-ethics/code-medical-ethics.page (last visited July 26, 2016), archived at https://perma.cc/4QS7-F5FT.

139 Mark A. Hall et al., Health Care Law and Ethics 169 (2003).

140 Opinion 3.2.3–Industry-Employed Physicians and Independent Medical Examiners, Am. Med. Ass'n, available at http://www.ama-assn.org/ama/ pub/physician-resources/medical-ethics/code-medical-ethics.page (last visited Aug. 1, 2016), archived at https://perma.cc/ZR8K-FC93.

141 FIMS Code of Ethics at ¶ 10.

142 Id. at ¶ 4.

143 ACOEM Code of Ethics, Ethical Principle V.

144 Dyer, 679 N.W.2d at 315–17 (collecting cases); Greenberg, 845 P.2d at 535 ("physician owes a duty of care to a nonpatient examinee to conduct the examination in a manner not to cause harm to the person being examined.") (internal quotations and citations removed).

145 Opinion 1.2.6–Work-Related & Independent Medical Examinations, Am. Med. Ass'n, available at http://www.ama-assn.org/ama/pub/physician -resources/medical-ethics/code-medical-ethics.page (last visited July 26, 2016), archived at https://perma.cc/4QS7-F5FT.

146 FIMS Code of Ethics at ¶ 8.

147 Id. at ¶11.

148 Id. at ¶ 2.

149 See 2011 CBA, Art. 39, § 4. Second opinions are discussed in further detail below in Chapter 4: Second Opinion Doctors.

150 FIMS Code of Ethics at ¶ 4.

151 Opinion 1.2.3–Consultation, Referral & Second Opinions, Am. Med. Ass'n, available at http://www.ama-assn.org/ama/pub/physician -resources/medical-ethics/code-medical-ethics.page (last visited Aug.1, 2016), archived at https://perma.cc/4QS7-F5FT.

152 Code of Ethics, Am. Bd. of Physician Specialties, http://www.abpsus.org /code-of-ethics (last visited Aug. 7, 2015), archived at http://perma.cc/ BU3D-VAQZ.

153 Opinion 10.2–Physician Employment by a Nonphysician Supervisee, Am. Med. Ass'n, available at http://www.ama-assn.org/ama/pub/physi -cian-resources/medical-ethics/code-medical-ethics.page (last visited Aug.1, 2016), archived at https://perma.cc/73QV-B54W.

154 Rob Huizenga, You're Okay, It's Just a Bruise 259 (1994).

155 Id. at 19 (Rosenfeld telling player "It's just a stinger — you'll be fine."); id. at 21 (Rosenfeld telling player "You're okay — it's nothing serious."); id. at 58 (Rosenfeld telling Huizenga "You've got to treat [players] differently from your office patients."); id. at 147 (Rosenfeld telling player "So you really can't hurt the joint any more. We may as well just shoot it up and let you go back out there and play."). Huizenga also questioned Rosenfeld's acumen. Id. at 123 (criticizing Rosenfeld for moving the neck of a player with neck pain); id. at 149 (Rosenfeld signing a prescription for anabolic steroids); id. at 256–67 (describing disagreement with Rosenfeld about a player's condition which led to Huizenga's resignation); id. at 270–71 (alleging that Rosenfeld and his medical practice had been sued over sixty times, mostly for medical malpractice).

156 Id. at 227.

157 Id. at 57 ("There was a fuzzy boundary between good medicine and good team doctoring."); id. at 58 ("I was supposed to keep players informed of their health status, not to hide feelings from them. And every doctor knows that his legal and ethical responsibility is to the patient, regardless of who pays the bill."); id. at 103–04 (describing having player sign waiver that he understood certain risks "to protect the Raiders"); id. at 106 (describing process for having players sign a waiver stating that were healthy following pre-season physical); id. at 115 (stalling to get player off the field for competitive purposes); id. at 125 (declaring ""It's not ethical for me to stay here. I can't be associated with this kind of medicine."); id. at 240 (debating the ethics of disclosing players' medical records).

158 Id. at 266–67.

159 Pierce E. Scranton, Jr., Playing Hurt: Treating and Evaluating the Warriors of the NFL x (2001).

160 Id. at xi.

161 Id. at 32.

162 Id. at 170.

163 How does a physician become an NFL team physician? Nat'l Football League Physicians Soc'y, http://nflps.org/faqs/how-does-a-physician -become-an-nfl-team-physician/ (last visited Aug. 7, 2015), archived at http://perma.cc/AD7J-LD8A.

164 see Synernet Staff Visits NFL Headquarters, Synernet (Feb. 11, 2015), http://www.synernet.net/news/news.aspx, archived at https://perma.cc /E4UC-WNWP.

165 NFL Comments and Corrections (June 24, 2016).

166 Interview with Larry Ferazani, NFL, Vice President, Labor Litigation & Policy (Oct. 6, 2014).

167 NFL Comments and Corrections (June 24, 2016).

168 Home, NFL Scouting Combine, http://www.nflcombine.net/ (last visited Aug. 7, 2015), archived at http://perma.cc/BQW4-E66Q.

169 Id.

170 History, NFL Scouting Combine, http://www.nflcombine.net/history/ (last visited Aug. 7, 2015), archived at http://perma.cc/7V7T-HGDV.

171 See Jeff Foster Talks About Challenges of Hosting NFL Scouting Combine, NFL.com (Feb. 19, 2014), http://www.nfl.com/news/story /0ap2000000326405/article/jeff-foster-talks-about-challenges-of -hosting-nfl-scouting-combine, archived at http://perma.cc/5D2C -6G8L (discussing National Football Scouting, Inc.'s operation of the NFL Combine).

172 Albert Breer, NFL Scouting Combine's Evolution Raises Questions About Future NFL.com (Feb. 18, 2013), http://www.nfl.com/combine/story /0ap1000000139993/article/nfl-scouting-combines-evolution-raises -questions-about-future, archived at http://perma.cc/YK3Y-U6J9.

173 NFL Comments and Corrections (June 24, 2016).

174 Jessica L. Roberts et al., Evaluating NFL Player Health and Performance: Legal and Ethical Issues, Univ. Penn. L. Rev. (forthcoming 2017).

175 Breer, supra n. 172.

176 Dana Hunsinger Benbow, The real reason for the NFL Scouting Combine, Ind. Star, Feb. 25, 2016, http://www.indystar.com/story/sports/nfl/2016 /02/20/real-reason-nfl-scouting-combine/80251866/, archived at https:/ /perma.cc/7ZPW-A35X.

177 Jeff Foster Talks About Challenges of Hosting NFL Scouting Combine, supra note 171.

178 About IU Health, Ind.Univ. Health, http://iuhealth.org/about-iu-health/ (last visited Aug. 7, 2015), archived at http://perma.cc/6Z43-JKHD; see also Hunsinger Benbow, supra n. 176.

179 Breer, supra note 172.

180 See id. ("350 MRIs were conducted on 330 players in a four-day period, with IU Health").

181 This information was provided by NFLPS.

182 NFL Comments and Corrections (June 24, 2016).

183 What role do team physicians play at the NFL Combines?, Nat'l Football League Physicians Soc'y, http://nflps.org/faqs/what-role-do-team-physi -cians-play-at-the-nfl-combines/ (last visited Aug. 7, 2015), archived at http://perma.cc/57K9-W8Y5.

184 Id.

185 Id. at 26.

186 Rob Huizenga, You're Okay, It's Just a Bruise 76–77 (1994)..

187 Pierce E. Scranton, Jr., Playing Hurt: Treating and Evaluating the Warriors of the NFL 1 (2001).

188 Id. at 12.

189 Id. at 19.

190 Id. at 37.

191 NFL Comments and Corrections (June 24, 2016).

192 Jessica L. Roberts et al., Evaluating NFL Player Health and Performance: Legal and Ethical Issues, Univ. Penn. L. Rev. (forthcoming 2017).

193 NFL Comments and Corrections (June 24, 2016).

194 Id.; see also Transcript – 2016 Injury Data Results Conference Call, NFL Communications, Jan. 29, 2016, https://nflcommunications.com/Pages/Transcript---2016-Injury-Data-Results-Conference-Call.aspx, archived at https://perma.cc/RKC6-352G.

195 NFL Comments and Corrections (June 24, 2016).

196 See Do team physicians have their own practices, or do they work for the clubs full-time?, Nat'l Football Leaague Physicians Soc'y, http://nflps.org/faqs/do-team-physicians-have-their-own-practices-or-do-they-work-for-the-clubs-full-time, archived at http://perma.cc/Y535-ZMBM (last visited Aug. 7, 2015) (stating that Club doctors "have [their] own private or university practices, in addition to [their] work as team physicians.")

197 Townley, Arb. Oct. 29, 2008, available as Exhibit 16 to the Declaration of Dennis L. Curran in Support of Defendant National Football League's Motion to Dismiss Second Amended Complaint (Section 301 Preemption), Dent v. Nat'l Football League, 14-cv-2324 (N.D. Cal. Sep. 24, 2014), ECF No. 73.

198 How do NFLPS physicians collaborate with team trainers to ensure optimum health for players?, Nat'l Football League Physicians Soc'y, http://nflps.org/faqs/how-do-nflps-physicians-collaborate-with-team-trainers-to-ensure-optimum-health-for-players/ (last visited Aug. 7, 2015), archived at http://perma.cc/HVD3-BJJ5.

199 NFL Comments and Corrections (June 24, 2016).

200 This information was provided by the NFLPA.

201 Dave Siebert, What Is Medical Care Like on an NFL Sideline?, Bleacher Report (Nov. 15, 2013), http://bleacherreport.com/articles/1850732-what-is-medical-care-like-on-an-nfl-sideline, archived at http://perma.cc/7JR4-HR3G.

202 Id.

203 Id.

204 Siebert, supra note 201.

205 Id.

206 NFL Constitution and Bylaws, § 17.3.

207 Siebert, supra note 201.

208 Id.

209 Id.

210 NFL Comments and Corrections (June 24, 2016).

211 Nat'l Football League, 2015 Player Health & Safety Report 26 (2015), http://static.nfl.com/static/content/public/photo/2015/08/05/0ap3000000506671.pdf/, archived at https://perma.cc/Y4BN-TUP7?type=pdf.

212 Id.

213 H.R. 921/S. 689, 114th Cong. (2015).

214 Siebert, supra note 201.

215 See, e.g., Kirsten E. Austad, et al., Changing Interactions Between Physician Trainees and the Pharmaceutical Industry: A National Survey. 28 J. Gen. Intern. Med. 164–71 (2013) (analyzing how pharmaceutical companies' access to medical students might affect student attitudes toward the industry); Christopher T. Robertson et al., Effect of Financial Relationships on the Behaviors of Health Care Professionals: A Review of the Evidence, 40 J. L., Med., & Ethics 452 (2012) (discussing ways in which financial relationships can influence physician decisions); Kate Greenwood, Carl H. Coleman, Kathleen M. Boozang, Toward Evidence-Based Conflicts of Interest Training for Physician-Investigators, 40 J.L. Med. & Ethics 500, 505–06 (2012).

216 Howard Fendrich and Eddie Pells, AP Survey: NFL players question teams' attitudes on health, Associated Press (Jan. 30, 2016, 7:39 PM), http://pro32.ap.org/article/ap-survey-nfl-players-question-teams%E2%80%99-attitudes-health, archived at https://perma.cc/V5RR-XGY3.

217 Id.

218 Des Bieler, Calvin Johnson says painkillers were handed out 'like candy' to NFL players, Wash. Post, July 6, 2016, https://www.washingtonpost.com/news/early-lead/wp/2016/07/06/calvin-johnson-says-painkillers-were-handed-out-like-candy-to-nfl-players/, archived at https://perma.cc/H6HS-YVTM.

219 See 2011 CBA, Art. 39, § 1(c) ("All Club physicians are required to disclose to a player any and all information about the player's physical condition that the physician may from time to time provide to a coach or other Club representative, whether or not such information affects the player's performance or health. If a Club physician advises a coach or other Club representative of a player's serious injury or career threatening physical condition which significantly affects the player's performance or health, the physician will also advise the player in writing. The player, after being advised of such serious injury or career-threatening physical condition, may request a copy of the Club physician's record from the examination in which such physical condition was diagnosed and/or a written explanation from the Club physician of the physical condition.")

220 Andrew Brandt, Peer Review Response (Oct. 30, 2015).

221 CBA, Art. 39, § 3(a).

222 NFL Comments and Corrections (June 24, 2016).

223 CBA, Art. 39, § 3(d).

224 CBA, Art. 50, § 1(a).

225 CBA, Art. 50, § 1(d).

226 This information was provided by the NFLPA.

227 Id.

228 See 2011 CBA, Art. 43, § 1.

229 See 2011 CBA, Art. 43, § 6 (discussing constitution of Arbitration Panel); 2011 CBA, Art. 43 § 8 (discussing Arbitrator's authority, including to grant a "money award").

230 For articles discussing generally medical malpractice in the sports context and the preclusion of claims by workers' compensation statutes, see, e.g., Matthew J. Mitten, Team Physicians as Co-Employees: A Prescription that Deprives Professional Athletes of an Adequate Remedy for Sports Medicine Malpractice, 50 St. Louis U. L.J. 211 (2005); John Redlingshafer, Tonight's Matchup – Workers' Compensation v. Medical Malpractice: What Should Lower-Paid, Inexperienced Athletes Received When a Team Doctor Allegedly Aids in Ending Their Careers?, 2 DePaul J. Sports L. & Contemp. Probs. 100 (2004) (same).

231 See Lotysz v. Montgomery, 766 N.Y.S.2d 28 (N.Y. App. Div. 2003) (NFL player's medical malpractice claim against club doctor barred by state workers' compensation statute); Daniels v. Seattle Seahawks, 968 P.2d 883 (Wash. Ct. App. 1998) (same); Hendy v. Losse, 819 P.2d 1 (Cal. 1991) (same). See also Pam Louwagie & Kevin Seifert, Stringer Claims Against Vikings Dismissed, Newspaper of the Twin Cities (Minneapolis, MN), Apr. 26, 2003, available at 2003 WLNR 14250471 (medical malpractice claims against Club doctors barred by workers' compensation statute). See Rivers v. New York Jets, 460 F.Supp. 1233 (E.D. Mo. 1978) (player's claim that Club wrongfully concealed the true nature of player's condition barred by workers' compensation statute); Brinkman v. Buffalo Bills Football Club Division of Highwood Service, Inc., 433 F.Supp. 699 (W.D.N.Y. 1977) (player's claim that Club failed to provide adequate medical care barred by workers' compensation law). But see Bryant v. Fox, 515 N.E.2d 775 (Ill. App. Ct. 1987) (NFL player's medical malpractice claim against Club doctor not barred by workers' compensation statute where evidence established that doctor was an independent contractor). Case law from other sports leagues suggests the same outcome. See, e.g., Martin v. Casagrande, 559 N.Y.S.2d 68 (N.Y. App. Div. 1990) (NHL player's claim that Club doctor and general manager conspired to withhold information about player's medical condition barred by workers' compensation statute); Bayless v. Philadelphia National League Club, 472 F.Supp. 625 (E.D. Pa. 1979) (former MLB player's claim that Club negligently administered pain-killing drugs barred by workers' compensation statute).

232 See William J. Appel, "Dual capacity doctrine" as basis for employee's recovery for medical malpractice from company medical personnel, 73 A.L.R.4th 115 (1999); Nick DiCello, No Pain, No Gain, No Compensation: Exploiting Professional Athletes through Substandard Medical Care Administered by Team Physicians, 49 Clev. St. L. Rev. 507, 532–33 (2001).

233 See Jackson v. Kimel, 992 F.2d 1318, 1325 n.4 (4th Cir. 1993) (collecting cases holding that employees that are not signatories to the CBA cannot be sued for violations of the CBA).

234 See 2011 CBA, Art. 2, § 2 (generally discussing CBA's binding effect on NFL, NFLPA, players and Clubs but no other party).

235 CBA, Art. 43, § 2.

236 This information was provided by the NFLPA.

237 The Non-Injury Grievance arbitrator has the authority to determine whether a complaint against a doctor fit within his or her jurisdiction under Article 43. See 2011 CBA, Art. 43, § 1 (discussing scope of Non-Injury Grievance arbitrator's jurisdiction).

238 U.S.C. § 185.

239 Allis-Chambers Corp. v. Lueck, 471 U.S. 202, 213, 200 (1985).

240 See, e.g., Givens v. Tennessee Football, Inc., 684 F. Supp. 2d 985 (M.D. Tenn. 2010) (player's tort claims against Club arising out of medical treatment preempted); Williams v. Nat'l Football League, 582 F.3d 863 (8th Cir. 2009) (players' tort claims arising out of drug test preempted).

241 See, e.g., Givens, 684 F. Supp. 2d 985 (claims against Club preempted); Jeffers v. D'Alessandro, 199 N.C. App. 86 (N.C. App. 2009) (same); Sherwin v. Indianapolis Colts, Inc., 752 F.Supp. 1172 (N.D.N.Y. 1990) (claims against Club preempted; claims against doctors dismissed on jurisdictional grounds); see also Brocail v. Detroit Tigers, Inc., 268 S.W.3d 90 (Tex. App. 2008) (MLB player's claim that Club failed to provide a proper second opinion preempted).

242 (Das, Arb. Mar. 25, 2008). For a more complete discussion of Jeffers, see Chapter 8: NFL Clubs.

243 See Hendy, 819 P.2d 1; Pam Louwagie & Kevin Seifert, Stringer Claims Against Vikings Dismissed, Newspaper of the Twin Cities (Minneapolis, MN), Apr. 26, 2003, available at 2003 WLNR 14250471.

244 Felisa Cardona, Jury Finds Doctor Not Negligent in Advice to Former Bronco Al Wilson, Denver Post, Jun. 17, 2011, http://www.denverpost.com/ci_18296823, archived at http://perma.cc/QUL8-4WTU.

245 NFL Comments and Corrections (June 24, 2016).

246 U.S.C. §§ 11101–52.

247 See Michael D. Benson, Jordan B. Benson, Mark S. Stein, Hospital Quality Improvement: Are Peer Review Immunity, Privilege, and Confidentiality in the Public Interest? 11 NW J. L. & Soc. Pol'y 1 (2016).

248 U.S.C. § 11137(b)(1).

249 Id.

250 NFL Comments and Corrections (June 24, 2016).

251 Id.

252 This information was provided by the NFLPA.

253 U.S. Medical Regulatory Trends and Actions, Fed'n of State Med. Bds. 19 (2014), http://www.fsmb.org/Media/Default/PDF/FSMB/Publications/us_medical_regulatory_trends_actions.pdf.

254 See Am. Med. Ass'n, State Med. Licensure Requirements and Statistics 2014, 91–93 (2014) (discussing states which have adopted or reference the AMA Code); Ty Alper, The Role of State Medical Boards in Regulating Physician Participation in Executions, 95 Journal of Med. Licensure and Discipline 7 (2009) ("The ethical guidelines of the state-based medical associations, many of which mirror those of the AMA . . . ."); W. Noel Keyes, The Choice of Participation by Physicians in Capital Punishment, 22 Whittier L. Rev. 809 (2001) (discussing adopting of the AMA Code by many states).

255 Mark A. Hall et al., Health Care Law and Ethics 137 (2003).

256 Rules in Cases of Original Jurisdiction, Am. Med. Ass'n, http://www.ama-assn.org/ama/pub/about-ama/our-people/ama-councils/council-ethical-judicial-affairs/governing-rules/rules-cases-original-jurisdiction.page? (last visited Aug. 7, 2015), archived at http://perma.cc/P82E-TFV7.

257 Bylaw 6.50 of the Council on Ethical and Judicial Affairs, Am. Med. Ass'n, http://www.ama-assn.org/ama/pub/about-ama/our-people/ama-councils/council-ethical-judicial-affairs/ceja-bylaws.page? (last visited Aug. 7, 2015), archived at http://perma.cc/F9QQ-K57A.

258 Id.

259 Id.

260 See Art. 11 of the FIMS Statutes, Int'l Fed. of Sports Med., http://www.fims.org/en/general/statutes (last visited Aug. 7, 2015), archived at http://perma.cc/SL4Q-NHAU.

261 CBA, Art. 39, § 1(c).

262 See Christopher T. Robertson et al., Effect of Financial Relationships on the Behaviors of Health Care Professionals: A Review of the Evidence, 40 J. of L., Med. & Ethics 452 (2012) (discussing ways in which financial relationships can influence physician decisions); Aaron S. Kesselheim & David Orentlicher, Introduction: Insights from a National Conference: "Conflicts of Interest in the Practice of Medicine," 40 J. of L., Med. & Ethics 436–40 (2012) (same).

263 Opinion 1.2.5–Sports Medicine, Am. Med. Ass'n, available at http://www.ama-assn.org/ama/pub/physician-resources/medical-ethics/code-medical-ethics.page (last visited Aug.1, 2016), archived at https://perma.cc/4QS7-F5FT.

264 FIMS Code of Ethics at ¶ 1, ¶ 4.

265 See e.g., Brad Partridge, Dazed and Confused: Sports Medicine, Conflicts of Interest, and Concussion Management, 11 J. of Bioethical Inquiry 65–74 (2014); Testoni et al., Sports Medicine and Ethics, 13 Am. J. of Bioethics 10 (2013); Warren R. Dunn et al., Ethics in Sports Medicine, 35 Am. J. of Sports Med. 840–44 (2007); Ivan Waddington, Sport Health and Drugs (2000).

266 Thomas H. Murray, Divided Loyalties in Sports Medicine, 12;8 The Physician & sportsmedicine 134, 140 (1984).

267 CBA, Art. 39, § 1(c).

268 Jessica L. Roberts, et al., Evaluating NFL Player Health and Performance: Legal and Ethical Issues, U. Penn. L. Rev. (forthcoming 2016).

269 See 2011 CBA, Art. 15, § 6; Art. 16, § 7; Art. 66, § 1.

270 See, Robertson et al., supra n 263; Kesselheim and Orentlicher, supra n. 263.

271 NFL Comments and Corrections (June 24, 2016).

272 Kate Greenwood, Carl H. Coleman, Kathleen M. Boozang, Toward Evidence-Based Conflicts of Interest Training for Physician-Investigators, 40 J.L. Med. & Ethics 500, 505–06 (2012); Christopher Robertson, Susannah Rose, Aaron S. Kesselheim, Effect of Financial Relationships on the Behaviors of Health Care Professionals: A Review of the Evidence, 40 J.L. Med. & Ethics 452, 453 (2012).

273 See, e.g., Daniela Testoni, Christoph P. Hornik, P. Brian Smith, Daniel K. Benjamin Jr. & Ross E. McKinney Jr., Sports Medicine and Ethics, 13:10 Am. J. Bioethics 4–12 (2013); W.R. Dunn, M. S. George, L. Churchill & K. P. Spindler, Ethics in Sports Medicine, 35:5 Am. J. Sports Med. 840–844 (2007); Nancy M.P. King & Richard Robeson, Athletes Are Guinea Pigs, 13:10 Am. J. Bioethics (2013); Brad Patridge, Dazed and Confused: Sports Medicine, Conflicts of Interest, and Concussion Management, 11 J. Bioethical Inquiry, 65–74 (2014); Ron Courson et al., Inter-Association Consensus Statement on Best Practices for Sports Medicine Management for Secondary Schools and Colleges, 49 J. Athletic Training, 128–137 (2014).

274 See, e.g., Uniform Anatomical Gift Act (2006), § 14(i) ("Neither the physician who attends the decedent at death nor the physician who determines the time of the decedent's death may participate in the procedures for removing or transplanting a part from the decedent."); Ethical Controversies in Organ Donation After Circulatory Death, Am. Acad. of Pediatrics (2013), http://pediatrics.aappublications.org/content/131/5/1021, archived at https://perma.cc/NN9V-7RKK.

275 NFL Comments and Corrections (June 24, 2016).

276 This information was provided by the NFLPA.

277 CBA, Art. 39, § 1(c).

278 See Christopher Tarver Robertson, Biased Advice, 60 Emory L.J. 653, 666–68 (2011) (explaining study showing that disclosing parties "apparently felt that the disclosure gave them a 'moral license' to be even more biased" and that the people to the whom biases are disclosed "failed to effectively use the disclosure to adjust for the inaccuracy of the given advice[.]"); Omri Ben-Shahar & Carl E. Schneider, The Failure of Mandated Disclosure, 159 U. Penn. L. Rev. 647 (2011); I Robert Gatter, Communicating Loyalty: Advocacy and Disclosure of Conflicts in Treatment and Research Relationships, in The Oxford Handbook of U.S. Health Law (I. Glenn Cohen, Allison K. Hoffman, William M. Sage eds. 2015–2016).

279 See Defendant National Football League's Response to the Players Association's December 2, 2014 Letter Brief, Dent v. Nat'l Football League, 14-cv-2324, 2–3 (N.D. Cal. Dec. 4, 2014) (NFL explaining that the NFLPA's position "that lawsuits by players against club doctors are [not] prohibited by applicable CBAs . . . is consistent with what the NFL told [the] Court"; also explaining that "there 'very well could be' a non-preempted malpractice lawsuit against a Club doctor"; and, acknowledging that malpractice suits against Club doctors "regularly are brought to verdict against Club physicians.")

280 See Practice: Personal Injury and Tort, JAMS, http://www.jamsadr.com/personal-injury/ (last visited Aug. 7, 2015), archived at http://perma.cc/5Z2V-MHXR.

281 U.S.C. § 321(g)(1).

282 U.S.C. § 801, et seq.

283 This information was provided by the NFL and NFLPS.

284 This information was provided by the NFL.

285 See Complaint, Dent v. Nat'l Football League, 14-cv-2324 (N.D. Cal. May 20, 2014), ECF No. 1, ¶ 203 ("amphetamines in the form of yellow and purple pills were available in jars in the locker room for any and all to take as they saw fit"); Sally Jenkins & Rick Maese, Pain and Pain Management in NFL Spawn a Culture of Prescription Drug Use and Abuse, Wash. Post, April 14, 2013, available at 2013 WLNR 9074933 (William Barr, the director of New York University's Langone Medical Center, and a concussion consultant for the New York Jets from 1995 to 2004 describing a "huge candy jar of Toradol"); see Rob Huizenga, You're Okay, It's Just a Bruise 13 (1994) (former Raiders Club doctor describing the safe door where prescription medications were kept as "wide open"); id. at 40 (players complaining that Huizenga had removed the "candy jar"); Scranton, Pierce E. Scranton, Jr., Playing Hurt: Treating and Evaluating the Warriors of the NFL 27 (2001) (discussing providing the anesthetic Marcaine so that players could make it through the game; and providing Vicodin or Percocet after the game for pain management).

286 See Complaint, Dent v. Nat'l Football League, 14-cv-2324 (N.D. Cal. May 20, 2014), ECF No. 1, ¶ 204 (alleging that jars of amphetamines were removed after the death of NFL safety Don Rogers and NBA prospect Len Bias in 1986); Whatever It Takes: To Stay In The Game, Tampa Tribune (FL), Dec. 30, 2007, available at 2007 WLNR 25835392 (NFL player Brad Culpepper: "It's not like there's a giant candy jar out in the open that you just go stick your hand into and pull out the meds . . . [t]hey keep it under lock and key."); See Rob Huizenga, You're Okay, It's Just a Bruise (1994) (discussing the end to the "candy jar" practice).

287 Indeed, even if a "jar" was no longer available, Former Player 1, who retired in 2010, said Club doctors would provide "painkillers and anti-inflammatories . . . like candy." Additionally, Former Player 1 said that the Club doctors never discussed any of the risks or benefits of the painkillers with the players.

288 John Tokish, Elisha Powell, Theodore Schlegel & Richard Hawkins, Ketorolac Use in the National Football League, 30 The Physician and Sports Medicine 9 (2002).

289 of the then 31 NFL Clubs responded to the survey.

290 Id. at 21.

291 Ketorolac, Nat'l Inst. Health: U.S. Nat'l Library of Med., http://www.nlm.nih.gov/medlineplus/druginfo/meds/a693001.html (last visited Aug. 7, 2015), archived at http://perma.cc/TU2P-6FDX.

292 John Barr, Painkiller Misuse Dulls the NFL Pain, ESPN, http://sports.espn.go.com/espn/eticket/story?page=110128/painkillersnews (last visited Aug. 7, 2015), archived at http://perma.cc/FSP7-AAES, citing Centers for Disease Control and Prevention, Unintentional Drug Poisoning in the United States (July 2010).

293 Linda Cottler, Arbi Ben Abdallah, Simone Cummings, John Barr, Rayna Banks & Ronnie Forchheimer, Injury, Pain, and Prescription Opioid Use Among Former National Football League (NFL) Players, 116 Drug Alcohol Depend. 188,194 (2011).

294 It is unclear what group the Washington/ESPN study references. There are various unofficial groups of former NFL players with a variety of monikers, but research has not revealed any group using the name "Retired NFL Football Players Association."

295 The Washington/ESPN study adopted the definition of "misuse" from the U.S. National Survey on Drug Use and Health, meaning "use without a prescription or use simply for the experience or feeling the drug causes."

296 See Jim Baumbach, Life After Football, Newsday, Jan. 22, 2015, http://data.newsday.com/projects/sports/football/life-football/, archived at http://perma.cc/77DP-LUUE.

297 What are over-the-counter (OTC) drugs and how are they approved? F.D.A., http://www.fda.gov/AboutFDA/Transparency/Basics/ucm194951.htm (last visited June 17, 2016), archived at https://perma.cc/C6U2-3Q2X.

298 U.S.C. § 353(b)(1).

299 Peter Barton Hutt, Richard A. Merrill, Lewis A. Grossman, Food and Drug Law 815 (2007).

300 The list of controlled substances can be viewed from the DEA's website at http://www.deadiversion.usdoj.gov/schedules/orangebook/c_cs_alpha.pdf, archived at https://perma.cc/3WUT-FDRP?type=pdf.

301 U.S.C. § 801, et seq.

302 Brian T. Yeh, The Controlled Substances Act: Regulatory Requirements, Congressional Research Service, 1 (2012), https://www.fas.org/sgp/crs/misc/RL34635.pdf, archived at https://perma.cc/P79Q-BPXC?type=pdf.

303 Peter Barton Hutt, Richard A. Merrill, Lewis A. Grossman, Food and Drug Law 60 (2007).

304 U.S.C. §§ 811–12.

305 See 21 U.S.C. § 812(c) (listing Schedules of controlled substances); U.S. Dep't of Justice- Drug Enforcement Administration, Practitioner's Manual: An Informational Outline of the Controlled Substances Act, 5 (2006), http://www.deadiversion.usdoj.gov/pubs/manuals/pract/pract_manual012508.pdf [hereinafter DEA Practitioner's Manual] (describing Schedules of controlled substances). Schedule I substances area those that: (a) have a high potential for abuse; (b) has no currently accepted medical use in the United States; and (c) there is a lack of accepted safety for use of the drug or other substance under medical supervision. 21 U.S.C. § 812(b)(1). Cocaine is a Schedule II controlled substance. 21 U.S.C. § 812(c). Anabolic steroids are a Schedule III controlled substance. Id.

306 DEA Practitioner's Manual at 6 (describing Schedules of controlled substances).

307 Id. at 4.

308 See 21 U.S.C. § 844 (prescribing criminal penalties for possession of a controlled substance without a prescription); 21 U.S.C. § 829 (prohibiting the dispensing of Schedule II, III or IV controlled substances without a prescription).

309 Vicodin, Percocet, and OxyContin are brand names for certain types of opioid pain medications. Opioids are Schedule II controlled substances. 21 U.S.C. § 812(c).

310 See Agents Visit Cincy, Lions About Meds, ESPN (Nov. 17, 2014), http://espn.go.com/nfl/story/_/id/11895109/lions-bengals-teams-question, archived at http://perma.cc/4MHW-G7SB.

311 "The term 'distribute' means to deliver (other than by administering or dispensing) a controlled substance or a listed chemical. The term 'distributor' means a person who so delivers a controlled substance or a listed chemical." 21 U.S.C. § 802(11).

312 "The term 'dispense' means to deliver a controlled substance to an ultimate user or research subject by, or pursuant to the lawful order of, a practitioner, including the prescribing and administering of a controlled substance and the packaging, labeling or compounding necessary to prepare the substance for such delivery. The term 'dispenser' means a practitioner who so delivers a controlled substance to an ultimate user or research subject." 21 U.S.C. § 802(10).

313 C.F.R. § 1301.11.

314 U.S.C. § 823(b).

315 In considering whether someone is qualified to be registered to distribute Schedule I or II controlled substances, the DEA considers: "(1) maintenance of effective control against diversion of particular controlled substances into other than legitimate medical, scientific, and industrial channels; (2) compliance with applicable State and local law; (3) prior conviction records of application under Federal or State laws relating to the manufacture, distribution, or dispensing of such substances; (4) past experience in the distribution of controlled substances; and (5) such other factors as may be relevant to and consistent with the public health and safety." 21 U.S.C. § 823(b).

316 See Cal. Health & Safety Code § 11150 (West 2014) ("[n]o person other than a physician, dentist, podiatrist, or veterinarian, or naturopathic doctor . . . or pharmacist . . . shall write or issue a prescription"); see Cal. Health & Safety Code § 11153 (West 2014) ("[a] prescription for a controlled substance shall only be issued for a legitimate medical purpose by an individual practitioner acting in the usual course of his or her professional practice"); N.Y. Public Health Law § 3331 ("[a] practitioner [or veterinarian], in good faith, and in the course of his or her professional practice only [in the course of the practice of veterinary medicine only], may prescribe, administer and dispense [scheduled substances] or he may cause them to be administered by a designated agent under his direction and supervision"); Tex. Health & Safety Code Ann. § 481.061 ("[e]xcept as otherwise provided by this chapter, a person who is not a registrant may not manufacture, distribute, prescribe, possess, analyze, or dispense a controlled substance in this state"); Tex. Health & Safety Code Ann. § 481.002 ("'[p]ractitioner' means: (A) a physician, dentist, veterinarian, podiatrist, scientific investigator, or other person licensed, registered, or otherwise permitted to distribute, dispense, analyze, conduct research with respect to, or administer a controlled substance in the course of professional practice or research in this state. . . . 'Prescribe' means the act of a practitioner to authorize a controlled substance to be dispensed to an ultimate user").

317 See also DEA Practitioner's Manual at 47–51 (attaching DEA Form 224, Application for Registration, which requires the applicant to identify his or her "business activity" from a finite list of medical professions, and requires the applicant to provide his or her state license number).

318 C.F.R. § 1301.12; see also U.S. v. Clinical Leasing Service, Inc., 925 F.2d 120 (5th Cir. 1991) (statute requiring registration of physicians who distribute controlled substances at "each principal place of business" was not unconstitutionally vague).

319 C.F.R. § 1301.71(a).

320 Opinion 9.6.6 – Prescribing & Dispensing Drugs & Devices, Am. Med. Ass'n, available at http://www.ama-assn.org/ama/pub/physician-resources/medical-ethics/code-medical-ethics.page (last visited Aug.1, 2016), archived at https://perma.cc/D4J6-JH8K.

321 This information was provided by the NFL and NFLPS.

322 This information was provided by the NFL.

323 Letter from Larry Ferazani, NFL, to authors (July 18, 2016).

324 This information was provided by the NFL.

325 Letter from Larry Ferazani, NFL, to authors (July 18, 2016).

326 Id.

327 Id.

328 Id.

329 Nat'l Football League, 2015 Player Health & Safety Report 26 (2015), http://static.nfl.com/static/content/public/photo/2015/08/05/0ap3000000506671.pdf/, archived at https://perma.cc/Y4BN-TUP7?type=pdf.

330 Id.

331 Matthew Matava et al., Recommendations of the National Football League Physicians Society Task Force on the Use of Toradol Ketorolac in the National Football League, 4 Sports Health 377 (2012). At the time, Matava was the St. Louis Rams Club doctor, and co-authors Gritter and Heyer were Carolina Panthers Club doctors, Schlegel was a Denver Broncos Club doctor, and Yates was a Pittsburgh Steelers Club doctor.

332 Id. at 378.

333 Id. at 382.

334 Letter from Tim English, Staff Counsel, NFLPA, to Dennis Curran, Senior VP of Labor Litigation & Policy, NFL (Dec. 11, 2012), available as Exhibit 18 to the Declaration of Dennis L. Curran in Support of Defendant National Football League's Motion to Dismiss Second Amended Complaint (Section 301 Preemption), Dent v. Nat'l Football League, 14-cv-2324 (N.D. Cal. Sep. 24, 2014), ECF No. 73.

335 Dave Siebert, What Is Medical Care Like on an NFL Sideline?, Bleacher Report (Nov. 15, 2013), http://bleacherreport.com/articles/1850732-what-is-medical-care-like-on-an-nfl-sideline, archived at http://perma.cc/7JR4-HR3G.

336 Outside the Lines Discussion: Prescription Medication in the NFL, (ESPN television broadcast Nov. 17, 2014), http://espn.go.com/nfl/story/_/id/11895109/lions-bengals-teams-questioned-dea-agents, archived at http://perma.cc/4MHW-G7SB.

337 Agents Visit Cincy, Lions About Meds, ESPN (Nov. 17, 2014), http://espn.go.com/nfl/story/_/id/11895109/lions-bengals-teams-question, archived at http://perma.cc/4MHW-G7SB; Ken Belson, Federal Investigation Into Painkillers Targets N.F.L. Teams' Medical Staffs, N.Y. Times, Nov. 17, 2014, http://www.nytimes.com/2014/11/17/sports/football/dea-investigation-of-painkillers-targets-nfl-teams-medical-staffs.html?_r=0, archived at http://perma.cc/MTU2-MLC5.

338 Id.

339 Id.

340 Outside the Lines Discussion: Prescription Medication in the NFL, supra note 337.

341 NFL Substance Abuse Policy, General Policy, n. 1.

342 NFL Substance Abuse Policy at p. 1.

343 Id.

344 NFL Substance Abuse Policy, § 1.4.1.

345 NFL Substance Abuse Policy, § 1.5.1(a).

346 Id.

347 Id.

348 NFL Substance Abuse Policy, § 1.5.1(b).

349 Id.

350 NFL Substance Abuse Policy, § 1.5.2(a).

351 NFL Substance Abuse Policy, § 1.5.2(d).

352 Id.

353 Letter from Tim English, Staff Counsel, NFLPA, to Dennis Curran, Senior VP of Labor Litigation & Policy, NFL (Dec. 11, 2012), available as Exhibit 18 to the Declaration of Dennis L. Curran in Support of Defendant National Football League's Motion to Dismiss Second Amended Complaint (Section 301 Preemption), Dent v. Nat'l Football League, 14-cv-2324 (N.D. Cal. Sep. 24, 2014), ECF No. 73.

354 This information was provided by the NFLPA.

355 E-mail with Larry Ferazani NFL, Vice President, Labor Litigation & Policy (June 1, 2016). As discussed earlier, in 2012, one club doctor did require players to sign a waiver before administering Toradol.

356 See Complaint, Dent v. Nat'l Football League, 14-cv-2324 (N.D. Cal. May 20, 2014), ECF No. 1.

357 Id. at ¶ 15. In addition to state law claims sounding in fraud and negligence, the plaintiffs alleged the NFL violated several statutes. For example, the plaintiffs allege that the NFL violated: "the Controlled Substances Act's requirements governing the acquisition, storage, provision and administration of, and recordkeeping concerning, Schedule II, III and IV controlled substances"; the Food, Drug, and Cosmetic Act's "requirements for prescriptions, warnings about known and possible side effects, and proper labeling, among other violations"; and, "state laws governing the acquisition, storage and dispensation of prescription medications." Id. at ¶¶ 354–57.

358 Id.

359 Dent v. Nat'l Football League, 14-cv-2324, 2014 WL 7205048 (N.D. Cal. Dec. 17, 2014). See also Nelson v. Nat'l Hockey League, 13-cv-4846, 2014 WL 656793 (N.D.Ill. Feb. 20, 2014) (claims by estate of deceased NHL player that NHL negligently failed to monitor the player's use of addictive medications and head trauma preempted by CBA).

360 Dent v. Nat'l Football League, 14-cv-2324, 2014 WL 7205048 at *12 (N.D. Cal. Dec. 17, 2014).

361 Id.

362 Dent v. NFL, 15-15143 (9th Cir.).

363 See Complaint, Evans v. Arizona Football Clubs, LLC, 15-cv-1457 (D.Md. May 21, 2015), ECF No. 1.

364 See id.; Josh Alper, Former players file 2nd lawsuit claiming teams pushed painkillers to mask pain, ProFootballTalk (May 21, 2015, 4:21 PM), http://profootballtalk.nbcsports.com/2015/05/21/former-players-file-2nd-lawsuit-claiming-teams-pushed-painkillers-to-mask-pain/, archived at http://perma.cc/53R8-T8UK.

365 Evans v. Arizona Cardinals Football Club, 16-cv-1030, 2016 WL 3566945, *1 (N.D.Ca. July 1, 2016).

366 Id.

367 Id. at *4.

368 Id.

Chapter 3

Athletic Trainers

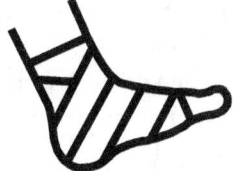

Athletic trainers are generally NFL players' first line of healthcare and are thus important stakeholders in player health. While athletic trainers may very well provide the best care possible to players, the structure in which athletic trainers — who are employees of the club and part of the club's medical staff — provide care to players has the potential to conflict with players' best interests, and raises concerns, as will be explained below. As discussed in Chapter 2: Club Doctors, on the one hand, the club's medical staff has an obligation to provide the player care and advice that is in the player's best interests. On the other hand, clubs engage athletic trainers and doctors because medical information about and assessment of players is necessary for clubs' decisions about a player's ability to perform at a sufficiently high level in the short and long-term. These dual roles for club medical staff, including athletic trainers, conflict because players and clubs often have conflicting interests, but the medical staff is called to serve both parties.

Before we begin our analysis, it is important to point out that throughout this chapter we emphasize that the practice of athletic trainers is likely heterogeneous from club to club at least to some extent. Nevertheless, we were unable to interview athletic trainers as part of this Report to gain a better understanding of their work. In November 2014, we notified the NFL that we intended to seek interviews with club personnel, including general managers, coaches, doctors, and athletic trainers. The NFL subsequently advised us that it was "unable to consent to the interviews" on the grounds that the "information sought could directly impact several lawsuits currently pending against the league." Without the consent of the NFL (the joint association for NFL clubs, *i.e.,* club athletic trainers' employers), we did not believe that the interviews would be successful and thus did not pursue the interviews at that time. Instead, we have provided these stakeholders the opportunity to review draft chapters of the Report. We again requested to interview club personnel in July 2016 but the NFL did not respond to that request. The NFL was otherwise cooperative. It reviewed our Report and facilitated its review by club doctors and athletic trainers. The NFL also provided information relevant to this Report, including copies of the NFL's Medical Sponsorship Policy (discussed in Chapter 2: Club Doctors) and other information about the relationships between clubs and doctors.

Specifically, the NFL facilitated review of Part 2: The Medical Team by four NFL club athletic trainers, all of whom were members of the Professional Football Athletic Trainers Society (PFATS), and PFATS' outside counsel, prior to publication. We did not communicate with PFATS directly. PFATS provided comments through the NFL, which were incorporated into this Report.

Also, in April 2016, we engaged the National Athletic Trainers Association (NATA), a professional organization for athletic trainers in all sports and at all levels of play, about reviewing relevant portions of a draft of this Report. Among comments provided to us, NATA asked whether we had sought to interview NFL club athletic trainers through either PFATS or NATA, apparently unaware of the NFL's prior response to our planned interviews. When we explained that we had not pursued such interviews for the reasons indicated above, NATA indicated that it would have preferred a different approach. At that time, we invited NATA to have individual club athletic trainers interviewed. Ultimately, however, NATA informed us that it discussed our invitation with PFATS and it declined.[1] Indeed, when it provided comments for this chapter, PFATS, the organization with the highest level of interest in protecting club athletic trainers, did not raise any concern that we had not interviewed athletic trainers as part of this Report.

Due to limitations on our access to club athletic trainers we cannot generate club-by-club accounts. The result may mask a level of variation in current practice, a limitation we acknowledge.

A Background

The CBA dictates the required presence, education and certification of athletic trainers:

> All athletic trainers employed or retained by Clubs to provide services to players, including any part time athletic trainers, must be certified by the National Athletic Trainers Association and must have a degree from an accredited four-year college or university. Each Club must have at least two full-time athletic trainers. All part-time athletic trainers must work under the direct supervision of a certified athletic trainer.[2]

The required education for athletic trainers has actually increased since the execution of the CBA. Athletic trainers now must have a master's degree.[3]

Each NFL club employs approximately four athletic trainers, including a head athletic trainer and three assistants. Head athletic trainers have an average of 21.9 years of experience in the NFL, while assistants average approximately 8.4 years of experience in the NFL.[4] In the 2014 season, 26 athletic trainers had at least 20 years of experience and 8 had more than 30 years of experience.[5] Athletic trainers, unlike most club doctors, are full-time employees of the club and not independent contractors.

To become a certified athletic trainer, an individual must graduate with a bachelor's or master's degree from an athletic training degree program accredited by the Commission on Accreditation of Athletic Training Education[a] and pass a test administered by the Board of Certification for the Athletic Trainer (BOC).[6] In addition, 42 states require licensure by the state, 3 states require certification (Louisiana, South Carolina, and New York) and 4 states only require registration (Oregon, Colorado, West Virginia, and Minnesota).[7] However, only three states (Illinois, Nebraska, and Vermont) require an athletic trainer to be certified by the BOC to be licensed.[8] Finally, only California has no licensure, certification, or registration requirements of any kind.[9]

States generally define athletic trainers as individuals responsible for the recognition, prevention, and treatment of athletic injuries.[10] The states that do describe athletic

---

a   According to NATA, 85 percent of PFATS' members have at least a master's degree.

trainers' duties in more detail, define such duties in broad terms. Illinois' Athletic Trainers Practice Act is instructive:[b]

Specific duties of the athletic trainer include but are not limited to:

(a) Supervision of the selection, fitting, and maintenance of protective equipment;

(b) Provision of assistance to the coaching staff in the development and implementation of conditioning programs;

(c) Counseling of athletes on nutrition and hygiene;

(d) Supervision of athletic training facility and inspection of playing facilities;

(e) Selection and maintenance of athletic training equipment and supplies;

(f) Instruction and supervision of student trainer staff;

(g) Coordination with a team physician to provide:

  i   pre-competition physical exam and health history updates,

  ii   game coverage or phone access to a physician or paramedic,

  iii follow-up injury care,

  iv   reconditioning programs, and

  v   assistance on all matters pertaining to the health and well-being of athletes.

(h) Provision of on-site injury care and evaluation as well as appropriate transportation, follow-up treatment and rehabilitation as necessary for all injuries sustained by athletes in the program;

(i) With a physician, determination of when an athlete may safely return to full participation post-injury; and

(j) Maintenance of complete and accurate records of all athletic injuries and treatments rendered.[11]

Generally, state licensing statutes and regulations require athletic trainers to work under the direction of a licensed physician.[12] Indeed, all club athletic trainers work under the supervision of a club doctor and it is important that athletic trainers act within the scope of their practice. Nevertheless, athletic trainers are often the first and most consistent source of medical care provided to players. Club doctors generally only visit practice for a few hours a few times per week (*see* Chapter 2: Club Doctors, Section F:

Current Practices), as players' conditions are unlikely to change much on a day-to-day basis. Thus, during the week, athletic trainers are responsible for treating ongoing injuries by all available methods, including, for example, ice, heat, ultrasound, massage, and stretching. The athletic trainer and club doctor remain in contact about players' conditions during the week and the club doctor directs the athletic trainer as to how treatment should proceed.[c]

Additionally, athletic trainers prepare players for each practice by taping, bracing, and padding various joints and body parts. Athletic trainers must also be prepared to respond to any new injuries that occur. Each day, athletic trainers, in consultation with the club's coaches and management, complete the daily Injury Report (discussed at length in Chapter 17: The Media), describing a player's practice participation level.[13]

Game days proceed similarly, only with the likelihood of injury significantly increased.[14] Athletic trainers assist in the evaluation of injuries, including the performance of relevant diagnostic testing. In so doing, athletic trainers work closely with the various club doctors present on game days.[15]

> ## Athletic trainers are often the first and most consistent source of medical care provided to players.

Athletic trainers are also largely responsible for maintaining the player's medical records. Beginning in 2014, all clubs utilize a customized electronic medical record (EMR) system created by eClinicalWorks.[16] A player's EMR consists of all of the athletic trainers' and doctors' diagnosis and treatment notations, including any sideline examination performed on the player.[17] Athletic trainers are generally the persons responsible for entering the notes into the EMR. Additionally, to the extent a player has obtained a second medical opinion paid for by the club, the athletic trainer will incorporate the second opinion doctor's report into the player's EMR.[18] The player's EMR also provides

---

b   Nevertheless, in reviewing a draft of this chapter, NATA indicated that "many" statutes governing athletic trainers are currently under legislative review.

c   According to the NFLPS, "[t]he athletic trainer is often the first person to see an injured player at the game, practice, training camp, mini-camp, etc. The trainer must be accurate in the identification of injuries and must communication (sic) well with the team physician. There is a constant source of dialogue between the athletic trainers and the team physicians in all aspects of the player's care, whether it's preventative care, managing current injuries or medical problems, or the entire rehabilitation process." *Frequently Asked Questions*, NFLPS, http://nflps.org/faqs/how-do-nflps-physicians-collaborate-with-team-trainers-to-ensure-optimum-health-for-players/ (last visited Aug. 7, 2015), *archived at* http://perma.cc/8FL2-F54H.

de-identified data to the NFL Injury Surveillance System (NFLISS), which tracks player injuries and is discussed in greater detail in Chapter 1: Players.[19]

The EMR system also includes a player portal that permits players to access their medical records at any time, including after their career is over.[20] The player's EMR is otherwise restricted to the club medical staff and those for whom the player has authorized access.[21] However, as explained below, players routinely execute collectively bargained waivers permitting club employees to access their medical information. Additionally, clubs interested in acquiring a player can request access to a player's medical file.[22]

Given the breadth and depth of athletic trainers' work and experience, it is not surprising that some athletic trainers are responsible for the club's entire medical operations and staff. In the 2015 season, five clubs had head athletic trainers who were also Directors of Sports Medicine or some similar title for the club (Houston Texans, Atlanta Falcons, New York Giants, San Francisco 49ers, Seattle Seahawks), even though none of the athletic trainers are doctors. In this capacity, the head athletic trainers are responsible for overseeing the entire medical staff, including doctors, and serve as an important liaison among players, coaches, and management.[23] In addition, they might be principally responsible for determining and communicating with the club's outside medical providers.[24] As a matter of law and ethics, club athletic trainers' must practice under the direction of a doctor.[25] Thus, an athletic trainer's oversight of a club doctor must be merely administrative and should not extend to medical issues. However, if the athletic trainer has the authority to terminate the club's relationship with the club doctor, there is the possibility that the club doctor will feel pressure from the athletic trainer concerning certain medical issues.

As noted above, PFATS is an organization that represents the athletic trainers of NFL clubs.[26] "[M]embership in PFATS is limited to those professionally certified in accordance with the most current NFL Collective Bargaining Agreement and who are employed full-time as head or assistant athletic trainers by any of the 32 NFL franchises."[27] PFATS' mission statement is as follows:

> The Professional Football Athletic Trainers Society (PFATS) is a Professional Association representing the athletic trainers of the National Football League. We serve the players of the NFL, the member Clubs, and other members of the community. Our purpose is to ensure the highest quality of health care is provided to the National Football League. We are dedicated to the welfare of our

members and committed to the promotion and advancement of athletic training through education and research. The Society is founded on the professional integrity and the ethical standards of our members and the fellowship that exists among us.[28]

In addition to PFATS, it is likely that many club athletic trainers are also members of NATA, mentioned above in the CBA provision. NATA is a voluntary professional membership association for certified athletic trainers across all levels of competition.[29] NATA's stated mission "is to enhance the quality of health care provided by certified athletic trainers and to advance the athletic training profession."[30] NATA informed us that 0.38 percent of its 32,651 members (equal to 124) work in the NFL.[31] At a mean of 3.875 per club, it appears almost every NFL athletic trainer is a member of NATA.

The CBA's requirement that athletic trainers be certified by NATA is actually in error and a requirement with which athletic trainers cannot comply. NATA is a voluntary professional association but does not *certify* athletic trainers. Athletic trainers are certified by the BOC.[32] The BOC used to be part of NATA, but split from the voluntary association in 1989.[33] Fortunately, the error has no impact, as all NFL athletic trainers are BOC-certified.[34] Nevertheless, to ensure players are being treated by the highest quality athletic trainers, the CBA should be amended to require the correct certification, the **Board of Certification for the Athletic Trainer.**

Lastly, the BOC promulgates Standards of Professional Practice.[35] The BOC is accredited by the National Commission for Certifying Agencies and is the only accredited certification program for athletic trainers in the United States.[36]

B | Current Legal Obligations[d]

Athletic trainers generally have a duty to conduct themselves in accordance with "the standard of care required of an ordinary careful trainer" when providing care and treatment to athletes.[37] A breach of an athletic trainer's duty could lead to a negligence or medical malpractice claim. Whether the claim is considered medical malpractice depends on each state's medical malpractice and professional negligence laws and whether the athletic trainer is considered a healthcare professional within the scope of the law.[38]

---

d   The legal obligations described herein are not an exhaustive list but are those we believe are most relevant to player health.

Athletic trainers also have legal obligations consistent with their licensure. As discussed above, the vast majority of states require athletic trainers to be licensed. Generally, each state's governing act and/or related regulations also includes standards of professional conduct with which athletic trainers must comply.[39] Many of the standards are similar to those of other licensed or certified professionals, such as prohibitions against false statements and discrimination against protected classes.[40]

State statutes and regulations governing athletic trainers are inconsistent concerning the practice of out-of-state athletic trainers. As a general rule, each state's statute or regulations require a person performing the duties of an athletic trainer to be licensed by that state. Some states (such as Pennsylvania[41]) explicitly authorize athletic trainers from out-of-state teams to work within the state. However, other states (such as Florida[42]) do not provide any exemption for out-of-state athletic trainers. Thus, theoretically, athletic trainers of clubs from outside Florida whose clubs are playing in Florida may be violating Florida's statutes governing athletic trainers by performing services in Florida. Nevertheless, we are unaware of any enforcement proceedings brought against out-of-state athletic trainers performing services with a visiting club. We do not mean to suggest athletic trainers practicing out-of-state are acting inappropriately and, in fact, believe it may be preferable if all states had statutes explicitly permitting out-of-state athletic trainers to perform their duties within the state while with a visiting club. Because this does not appear to be a problem in practice, we have not made this a formal recommendation.

Although the CBA has many provisions governing player health and safety, only two are directed at athletic trainers.

First, as discussed above, the CBA dictates the required presence, education and certification of athletic trainers.

Second, athletic trainers have an obligation to permit a player to examine his medical records once during the preseason and once after the regular season. Athletic trainers are also obligated to provide a copy of a player's medical records to the player upon request in the offseason.[43] However, these CBA provisions, agreed to in 2011, are now outdated. As discussed above, players can now obtain their medical records any time they would like via the EMR system.

Below we discuss statutory requirements concerning the confidentiality of medical information. As briefly discussed in the introduction to this chapter, an athletic trainer's conflicting interests can create complications concerning the treatment of player medical information. Indeed, in Section D: Current Practices, we provide the thoughts of some current players about these conflicts. However, before discussing the statutory requirements, it is important to first state that clubs request or require players to execute waivers permitting the player's medical information to be disclosed to and used by a wide variety of parties, including but not limited to the NFL, any NFL club, and any club's medical staff and personnel, such as coaches and the general manager. A copy of this waiver is included as Appendix L. The circumstances under which these waivers are executed is an area worthy of additional attention. For example, questions might be raised as to whether the players are providing meaningful and voluntary informed consent in their execution, even though these waivers have been collectively bargained between the NFL and NFLPA.[44]

Nevertheless, the federal Health Insurance Portability and Accountability Act (HIPAA) likely governs athletic trainer's requirements concerning the confidentiality of player medical information. HIPAA requires healthcare providers covered by the law to obtain a patient's authorization before disclosing health information protected by HIPAA.[45] Covered entities under HIPAA include: "(1) A health plan[;] (2) A health care clearinghouse[; and,] (3) A health care provider who transmits any health information in electronic form."[46]

Athletic trainers likely meet the third criteria to be considered a covered entity under HIPAA.[e] A "[h]ealth care provider" is defined by HIPAA as anyone who "furnishes . . . health care in the normal course of business."[47] And "health care means care, services, or supplies related to the health of an individual" including "[p]reventive, diagnostic, therapeutic, rehabilitative, maintenance, or palliative care, and counseling, service, assessment, or procedure with respect to the physical or mental condition, or functional status, of an individual or that affects the structure or function of the body."[48] Moreover, athletic trainers enter players' health information into EMRs that are accessed by doctors. Athletic trainers thus appear to provide healthcare within the meaning of HIPAA and thus must comply with its requirements.

In reviewing a draft of this Report, the NFL stated that "NFL Club medical teams, when providing medical care to players for football related injuries and illnesses, are not 'HIPAA-covered entities.'"[49] However, the NFL provided no explanation for this legal conclusion and did not respond specifically to our analysis in the prior paragraph.

---

e   On a related point, it is not clear whether clubs would be considered covered entities under HIPAA. See Memorandum Opinion and Order, In re: Nat'l Hockey League Players' Concussion Injury Litigation, 14-md-2551 (D. Minn. July 31, 2015), ECF No. 196 (discussing, but not resolving, whether NHL clubs were covered entities under HIPAA).

We acknowledge this is not a clear issue, but, based on our interpretation of HIPAA, it seems likely that athletic trainers are covered entities within the meaning of HIPAA and do have to comply with the law.

If athletic trainers are required to comply with HIPAA as we believe, the law nevertheless permits healthcare providers to provide health information about an employee to an employer without the employee's authorization where: (1) the healthcare provider provides healthcare to the individual at the request of the employer; (2) the health information that is disclosed consists of findings concerning a work-related illness or injury; (3) the employer needs the health information to keep records on employee injuries in compliance with state or federal law; and, (4) the healthcare provider provides written notice to the individual that his or her health information will be disclosed to the employer.[50]

NFL club athletic trainers might meet the requirements of HIPAA, permitting them to provide health information about players to the clubs under the following conditions: (1) athletic trainers provide healthcare to players at the request of the employer; (2) nearly every time athletic trainers disclose medical information to the club, it concerns a work-related illness or injury; and, (3) NFL clubs are required by law to keep records of employee injuries, for example, the Occupational Health and Safety Act requires employers with more than 10 employees to maintain records of work-related injuries and illnesses.[51] As for the fourth prong, our discussions with players make it seem unlikely that athletic trainers are providing written notice to players that their health information is being disclosed to the club at the time of injury, but it is possible that documents provided to the players before the season provide such notice.

> 22 states in which NFL clubs play or practice have statutes that permit healthcare providers to provide employers with an employee's medical records and/or information.

It should also be noted that HIPAA permits an employee's health information to be disclosed to the extent necessary to comply with state workers' compensation laws.[52]

In addition to the federal HIPAA, some states have passed laws restricting the disclosure of medical information by healthcare providers.[53] However, the nature and scope of these laws vary considerably in terms of restriction, disclosure exceptions, and the type of healthcare practitioners governed by the law.[54] Specifically, it likely varies from state to state whether athletic trainers are governed by the state confidentiality laws, e.g., whether they are considered healthcare providers within the meaning of the law.

Similar to HIPAA, 22 states in which NFL clubs play or practice have statutes that permit healthcare providers to provide employers with an employee's medical records and/or information.[55,f] The reasons that disclosure is permitted are generally related to potential or actual workers' compensation claims and procuring payment. However, the state laws vary as to whether a healthcare provider is permitted to disclose medical information only where a workers' compensation claim is possible as opposed to already filed—some states only permit disclosure after a claim has been filed.

C   Current Ethical Codes

Our initial research did not reveal any ethics code promulgated by PFATS. During its review of a draft of this chapter, PFATS did provide a non-public Code of Ethics that has existed as part of its Constitution since its formal organization in 1982. The sections of the Code most relevant to our analysis include:[56]

1. **General Principles:**

   a. The Society is unique in its scope of caring for only athletes engaged under contract to an NFL Club. The membership is charged with the responsibility of providing unique and important health care for highly visible, talented and experienced athletes that are well paid to execute their talents as professional football players.

   b. Although the primary role of the certified athletic trainer is to diligently work to make available the best possible health care for the players, the certified athletic trainer also serves as liaison between player, physician, coaching staff, management, and media and must always act in a professional manner in dealing with each of these groups.

   * * *

---

f   NFL clubs play and practice in 23 states. Wisconsin is the only state in which an NFL club plays or practices that does not have a statute permitting healthcare providers to provide employers with an employee's medical records and/information.

3. National Athletic Trainers Association Code of Ethics:

The most current version of the Code of Ethics on the National Athletic Trainers Association (NATA) shall be deemed to be incorporated by reference as part of this Code of Ethics as if fully set forth herein.

4. Responsibility of the Certified Athletic Trainer to the Player:

Player information given to the certified athletic trainer of a confidential nature with the context of the physician/patient relationship is privileged communication and must be held in trust by the certified athletic trainer.

5. Responsibility of the Certified Athletic Trainer to the Medical Staff:

a. It should be remembered that the role of the certified athletic trainer is that of a paramedical person, and that diagnosing of injuries/illnesses and prescribing remedial exercise and medication is the job of the physicians employed.

b. The certified athletic trainer shall honor the standing operating procedures established by the team physicians in the physicians' absence, and shall care for the athletes in compliance with standing orders until such time that the athletes can be seen by physicians.

6. Responsibility of the Certified Athletic Trainer to the Club:

a. The certified athletic trainer is a professional member of the NFL Club that is his employer and should be completely loyal to the Club.

b. Different Clubs and Coaches have different methods and philosophies. The certified athletic trainers are expected to provide their best professional services within the framework of the existing Club and coaching policy but should never violate professional ethics based on purported "Club Policy."

PFATS' Code of Ethics recapitulates the structural conflicts of interest in NFL player healthcare that we believe are problematic. The Code of Ethics includes multiple contradictions and troubling provisions that lay bare the inherent problem of having a medical provider provide services to both the club and players, as is discussed further in the recommendations below.

First, the Code of Ethics declares that athletic trainers must provide "the best possible health care for the players" but also declares that the athletic trainer "should be completely loyal to the Club." Providing the best possible healthcare might not always be in the club's interest. For example, recommending that a player miss games due to injury might

be best for the player, but deprives the club of the player's services. The Code of Ethics does not address how athletic trainers are supposed to resolve these competing interests.

Second, the Code of Ethics declares that communications between the player and athletic trainer are confidential and "must be held in trust." However, the Code of Ethics also declares that an athletic trainer "serves as liaison between player, physician, coaching staff, management, and media," effectively acknowledging what we know to be actual practice—that athletic trainers communicate regularly with coaches and club executives about player health. Although these communications are permitted by the collectively bargained waivers executed by players as discussed above, PFATS' Code of Ethics on this point is self-contradictory.

Third, the Code of Ethics declares that "athletic trainers are expected to provide their best professional services within the framework of the existing Club and coaching policy[.]" It is unclear why athletic trainers' purported obligations to provide "the best possible health care for the players" is subject to "Club and coaching policy."

Fourth, the Code of Ethics references that NFL players are "highly visible, talented and experienced athletes that are well paid to execute their talents as professional football players." The players' visibility and compensation should be irrelevant to the healthcare that athletic trainers provide to the players and has no place in a Code of Ethics.

Moving on, as referenced in PFATS' Code of Ethics, NATA also has a Code of Ethics.[57] The principles most relevant to our analysis include:

1: Members shall respect the rights, welfare and dignity of all.

1.3: Members shall preserve the confidentiality of privileged information and shall not release such information to a third party not involved in the patient's care without a release unless required by law.

2.1: Members shall comply with applicable local, state, and federal laws and institutional guidelines.

3.2: Members shall provide only those services for which they are qualified through education or experience and which are allowed by their practice acts and other pertinent regulation.

4: Members shall not engage in conduct that could be construed as a conflict of interest or that reflects negatively on the profession.

4.3: Members shall not place financial gain above the patient's welfare and shall not participate in any arrangement that exploits the patient.[g]

The above-stated principles leave significant room for interpretation and debate and NATA does not make any enforcement decisions public. Consequently, it is difficult to know how these principles are applied in practice.

In addition, NATA issues a variety of "Position Statements," "Official Statements," "Consensus Statements" and "Support Statements" on a variety of topics related to the health of athletes generally, including treatment of various medical conditions and issues including but not limited to concussions, psychological issues, cardiac arrest, ankle sprains, performance-enhancing drugs, nutritional supplements, and weight loss and eating disorders.[58]

NATA also has issued a Position Statement on pre-participation physical examinations (PPE) and disqualifying conditions.[59] NATA's Position Statement directs that a "licensed physician (doctor of medicine or doctor of osteopathy) is the most appropriate person to direct and conduct the PPE."[60] Additionally, the Position Statement declares that "[p]rivacy must be respected at all times when the findings of the PPE are communicated. Written authorization must be provided by the athlete . . . before any private health information is released."[61] NATA's requirement of a written authorization is generally inconsistent with the law and ethical codes of doctors in cases of fitness-for-play examinations, which generally permit doctors performing PPEs to disclose medical information about the examination and the examinee to the employer, as discussed in Chapter 2: Club Doctors.

The BOC's Standards of Professional Practice also include several relevant directives, with which all certified athletic trainers must "agree to comply,"[62] including:

- **Standard 1:** The Athletic Trainer renders service or treatment under the direction of a physician.

- **Standard 2:** Prevention: The Athletic Trainer understands and uses preventive measures to ensure the highest quality of care for every patient.

- **Standard 3:** Immediate Care: The Athletic Trainer provides standard immediate care procedures used in emergency situations, independent of setting.

- **Standard 4:** Clinical Evaluation and Diagnosis: Prior to treatment, the Athletic Trainer assesses the patient's level of function. The patient's input is considered an integral part of the initial assessment. The Athletic Trainer follows standardized clinical practice in the area of diagnostic reasoning and medical decision making.

- **Standard 5:** Treatment, Rehabilitation and Reconditioning: In development of a treatment program, the Athletic Trainer determines appropriate treatment, rehabilitation and/or reconditioning strategies. Treatment program objectives include long- and short-term goals and an appraisal of those which the patient can realistically be expected to achieve from the program. Assessment measures to determine effectiveness of the program are incorporated into the program.

- **Standard 6:** Program Discontinuation: The Athletic Trainer, with collaboration of the physician, recommends discontinuation of the athletic training service when the patient has received optimal benefit of the program. The Athletic Trainer, at the time of discontinuation, notes the final assessment of the patient's status.

- **Standard 7:** Organization and Administration: All services are documented in writing by the Athletic Trainer and are part of the patient's permanent records. The Athletic Trainer accepts responsibility for recording details of the patient's health status.

* * *

- **Code 1.2:** Protects the patient from harm, acts always in the patient's best interests and is an advocate for the patient's welfare.

- **Code 1.4:** Maintains the confidentiality of patient information in accordance with applicable law.

- **Code 1.6:** Respects and safeguards his or her relationship of trust and confidence with the patient and does not exploit his or her relationship with the patient for personal or financial gain.

Nevertheless, the above Code provisions are generalized and thus difficult to apply to NFL athletic trainers without more guidance. According to the BOC's Professional Practice and Discipline Guidelines and Procedures, it is "standard procedure" to publicly release any discipline imposed on an athletic trainer.[63] However, despite closing 304 disciplinary cases in 2015,[64] the BOC's database of disciplinary decisions only contains 63 cases from 2015,

---

g   Concerning Principles 4 and 4.3, one could imagine a situation in which an athletic trainer recommended a certain piece of equipment, apparel, or other product because he or she was being compensated or had a financial interest in the companies producing the product. For example, in the 1980s, according to former Los Angeles Raiders Club Doctor Rob Huizenga, the Professional Football Athletic Trainer's Society had an agreement with Gatorade that resulted in only Gatorade being available on NFL sidelines. Rob Huizenga, You're Okay, It's Just a Bruise 17 (1994). It is unclear whether any such conflicts exist today. Nevertheless, there remains the inherent conflict of interest between the athletic trainer treating the player but being employed and compensated by the club.

and only 99 in total, dating back to 2002.[65] Moreover, the 63 cases in 2015 that are publicly available are not helpful in interpreting the BOC's Standards of Professional Practice: 44 concern failure to receive continuing education credits; 11 concern practicing without a license; 7 concern criminal conduct; and 1 concerns voluntarily surrendering a license. The BOC stated that "[m]ost of our disciplinary cases were private censures and those are not public."[66,h]

D Current Practices[i]

Players and contract advisors we interviewed confirmed that athletic trainers are generally the player's first and primary source of medical care.[j] Club doctors are only with the club sporadically during the week of practice, while the athletic trainers are with the club at all times.[k] Players will first meet with the athletic trainer concerning a medical issue and the athletic trainer then typically determines whether the player should meet with the club doctor. Current Player 1:[l]

> [Y]ou go to your team trainers first and then the doctor comes into the facility—I think it's like two or three times during the week. If they [the trainers] think it's necessary, they'll have you meet with the actual doctors.

As discussed in the background section of this chapter, the athletic trainers and club doctors are in regular communication about players' conditions and treatment. The club doctors are responsible for directing and supervising the care of the players by the athletic trainers. Current Player 3 believes that the frequency of interaction between the players and the athletic trainers results in "better rapport" with the athletic trainers as compared to the club doctors.[m]

Nevertheless, other players expressed more concerns about athletic trainers' practices as compared to club doctors.[n] Not only do athletic trainers spend significantly more time with the players and the rest of the club's staff than the club doctor, the athletic trainers are also directly employed by the club whereas club doctors are generally independent contractors.[o] Current Player 1 described multiple incidents in which an athletic trainer did not disclose a player's actual diagnosis to the player (in one case a fracture and a torn ligament in another), which the player only discovered later from the club doctor.[p] The same player also indicated that he believes athletic trainers are pressured by the club and coaches to have players on the field. Multiple other current players we interviewed explained their distrust of athletic trainers:

- **Current Player 4:** "I don't trust [athletic trainers] at all. I feel like 90 percent of the injuries I've had have been undiagnosed or misdiagnosed before I was able to really identify what was going on. So the first analysis they always make is under-representation of the actual injury. You feel like they always downplay the situation to try to convince me you don't need to take any time off whatsoever or maybe take off as little time as possible and get back on the job immediately."[q]

- **Current Player 5:** "You know they're paid by the team and their job is to keep us healthy, keep the parts healthy so that the team as a whole works. I think sometimes there's a little bit more of a trust issue there because a player knows as soon as the trainer clears me to be healthy and I go out on the field then I'm liable to get cut if I'm not performing."

---

h   NATA suggested athletic trainers under investigation often enter into consent agreements with the BOC and that those agreements generally require that the details of the investigation and agreement not be made public. E-Mail from NATA representative to author (May 20, 2016) (on file with author).

i   As described more fully in the Introduction, Section 2(B): Description, citing ongoing litigation and arbitration, the NFL declined to consent to our request to interview current NFL club employees, including coaches, general managers, doctors, and athletic trainers. Therefore, we did not pursue interviews with these individuals.

j   Current Player 2: "[W]hen it comes to the athletic trainers, that's really where most of our medical relationships take place." Current Player 9: "[T]he training staff is the first level of contact with the players."

k   Consequently, peer reviewer and former Green Bay Packers executive Andrew Brandt refers to athletic trainers as the "bartenders" of the club. Andrew Brandt, Peer Review Response (Oct. 30, 2015).

l   To repeat information provided in the Introduction, we conducted approximately 30-minute interviews with 10 players active during the 2015 season and three players who recently left the NFL (the players' last seasons were 2010, 2012, and 2012 respectively). The players interviewed were part of a convenience sample identified through a variety of methods—some were interested in The Football Players Health Study more generally, some we engaged through the Law and Ethics Advisory Panel (LEAP) and Football Players Health Study Player Advisors, and some interviews were facilitated by a former player now working for the NFLPA. The players interviewed had played a mean of 7.5 seasons, with a range of 2 to 15 seasons, and for a mean of between 3 and 4 different clubs (3.4 clubs), with a range of 1 to 10 clubs. In addition, we interviewed players from multiple positions: one quarterback; two fullbacks; one tight end; three offensive linemen; two linebackers; one defensive end; two safeties; and a special teams player (not a kicker, punter, or long snapper). We aimed for a racially diverse set of players to be interviewed: seven were white and six were African American. Finally, the players also represented a range of skill levels, with both backups and starters, including four players who had been named to at least one Pro Bowl team. These interviews were not intended to be representative of the entire NFL player population or to draw scientifically valid inferences, and should not be read as such, but were instead meant to be generally informative of the issues discussed in this Report.

m   Current Player 8 agreed that there was more trust with athletic trainers "just because we see them more."

n   Current Player 1: "[P]layers do trust the doctors. But I think it's more the trainers that they don't trust as much." Current Player 2 described the lack of trust in athletic trainers as "even more so than the doctors." Current Player 10: "I think there's less trust in the trainers than the team doctors."

o   Current Player 2: "I don't think guys are satisfied [with the care provided by athletic trainers], that's for sure."

p   The same player complained that the athletic training staff uses outdated treatment methods, effectively using ice and electrical stimulation regardless of the injury. The player indicated that, as a result, players are less likely to report injuries so they do not have to report to practice early to undergo a minimally effective treatment they could perform at home.

q   Current Player 4 also explained "I've had trainers try to convince me not to have a second opinion."

- **Current Player 8:** *"Usually the head [athletic trainer] is more of the coaches' friend than a player's friend . . . . The training staff is meant to rehabilitate you to play on Sunday. It is not meant to rehabilitate you for . . . every-day activities later in life. The thought of 'Your playing could [cause] further damage' isn't the concern – it's 'Can you play?'"*

As mentioned above, players execute collectively bargained waivers permitting the athletic trainer and club doctors to disclose the player's medical information to club employees, such as coaches and the general manager. Athletic trainers thus keep coaches and general managers apprised of players' injury statuses during regular meetings so the general manager can make a decision about whether or not to sign another player in the event a player is unable to play.[r] Players indicated that the communications between the athletic trainers and the coaches and general manager place pressure on players to practice and also cause them to withhold information from the athletic trainer.[s] Players do not want to tell the athletic trainer that they are not healthy enough to practice, for fear that the athletic trainer will then relay that message to the general manager with the suggestion that the general manager consider signing a potential replacement player.

Our communications with players revealed a meaningful level of distrust with athletic trainers. Of course, not all players feel this way about all trainers. Indeed, some of the players we interviewed had positive comments about athletic trainers:

- **Current Player 2:** *"[W]e're fortunate enough here where we do have a trainer who's willing to stand up to our coach if he feels that guy's not ready to get back on the field."*

- **Current Player 3:** *"[T]he trainers . . . a lot of them have been very cautious about the long term goals. 'I know you might be able to come back and play this week, but you risk more potential injury. If you sit out another week, you'd be better off next week.' So, I think we have some pretty decent trainers in that regard, but I don't know."*

- **Current Player 10:** *"[T]he trainers do what's best for the players."*

- **Former Player 2:** *"I would say . . . probably 80 percent trust the trainers, 20 percent don't."*

Moreover, during its review of a draft of this chapter, both PFATS and NATA provided citations to stories in which players praised club athletic trainers.[67] In addition, while not himself a player, peer reviewer and former NFL club executive Andrew Brandt noted he "rarely" saw trust between players and athletic trainers as an issue, in part due to the longevity of the club's training and medical staff. Nevertheless, Brandt also acknowledges the dynamic is "ripe for potential conflict."[68]

Similarly, in reviewing a draft of this chapter, NATA's representative stated that some athletic trainers "were (and some still are) told to get the athlete back out at all costs. They do it or risk losing their job. Some have left the pro-ranks because of this."[69] Nevertheless, NATA's representative also indicated there are times where players ignore athletic trainers' advice not to play, and then "come back and blame the medical staff for allowing them to play!"[70]

Additionally, when players are rehabilitating their injuries, they generally do it under the supervision of the athletic trainer and strength and conditioning coach on a separate practice field away from the coaches and other players. Players we interviewed also indicated that veteran and star players are often treated differently concerning injuries than younger or less marquee name players. Current Player 1:

> *You can definitely see a very different treatment of, let's say a rookie who's injured versus a guy who's in his eighth, ninth year in the NFL. Those guys could have the same injury but the veteran, the star, he definitely gets preferential treatment, gets the benefit of the doubt that maybe he really is injured and that he needs to take a few days off. Where that rookie, he definitely doesn't get that benefit of the doubt. They expect him to have to prove himself almost every day.*

Andrew Brandt also confirmed that younger or lesser skilled players often do not receive the same treatment as star players:

> *I can recall meetings discussing injured players who had no chance of making the team, and being asked to "get them out of here." I knew that meant to contact the agent and negotiate an injury settlement for the remaining term of his injury. Thus, we would move the player out of our training room, as he was taking up resources and training staff needed for higher caliber players who were going to be key contributors on the roster.[71]*

r Current Player 1: "[O]ur head trainer has a meeting with our GM and head coach at least once a week about whatever injuries are going on in the team." Current Player 2: "Our trainer has a meeting with our head coach every day during the season. And they're constantly talking about the status of guys[.]" Current Player 6 described his communications with the club's medical staff as "not confidential." Current Player 9: "The head trainer meets with the coach every single day."

s Current Player 8: "I go into those meetings [with the athletic trainer] very conscious of the fact that anything I say or do, it's going to be relayed to the people who are there to determine my future." However, as discussed in Chapter 1: Players, players are obligated by the CBA and their contract to disclose their medical conditions at certain times.

Although we recognize that players may not be experts in treatment methods, multiple players we interviewed also complained that athletic trainers utilize outdated treatment methods:

- **Current Player 1:** *"[T]hey have the same treatment for every injury and that's just ice and [electrical] stim[ulation]."*

- **Current Player 2:** *Described his club's athletic trainers as "being dated with some of the ways that they treat us."*

- **Current Player 7:** *"A lot of us believe . . . they have the general treatment that everybody knows of . . . . It' just kind of like 'Oh, let's get an ice pack. You'll be okay.' It's for every injury."*

In reviewing a draft of this Report, the NFL stated that it believed these comments to be misplaced. Instead, the NFL believes the players' sentiments reflect that "(a) Athletic Trainers [are] not doing what doctors are supposed to do; and (b) a preference for less invasive therapies before getting to needles, drugs, MRIs, etc."[72] The NFL's point is reasonable, but to resolve the debate would require a comprehensive analysis of the type of treatments provided by athletic trainers and possible alternatives. Such an analysis is beyond our expertise and the scope of this Report.

Multiple current players explained that their concerns about athletic trainers and the club's healthcare operations caused them to self-treat or to seek care and treatment outside of the club, both during the season and in the offseason:[t]

- **Current Player 4:** *"[P]layers should seek out more outside help . . . . A lot of guys have chiropractors, massage therapists, and a number of other different people that they see that can really help to get [rehabilitation] done. The team has chiropractors and sometimes massage therapists but, again, I feel like they do the bare minimum."*

- **Current Player 5:** *"A lot of guys think the older you get the more you start working outside the system as far as not necessarily with doctors but with a different massage therapist or a different kind of trainer or a different kind of rehab . . . . The ability to go to an outside . . . physical therapy and rehab, I think that should be expanded or encouraged . . . . I go to an outside facility and hire someone to have one-on-one*

treatment for an hour instead of having to battle with being understaffed in our training room . . . . When you're going to an outside physical therapy joint, I'm paying this physical therapist money. They're giving me their time and attention. When the team is paying the trainer and I come in there, I'm demanding 100 percent of their attention but they're not giving it because they're paid to treat everybody. So they can't give you 100 percent of the treatment."

- **Current Player 6:** *"I've learned you're better off if you don't trust [athletic trainers] in dealing with the training room . . . . It seems like some people have to deal with the bureaucracy and the politics in the training room . . . . [I]f you're in pain or have an injury, just take your ass back to the hotel room and you give yourself your own massage and you treat it yourself . . . . It seems like you're constantly being evaluated in the building and it's not even separate from the training room."*

- **Current Player 8:** *"[T]he majority of guys get their therapy outside of the building, not in the training room . . . . I think the reason is trust[.]"*

Additionally, there have been reports that when conventional treatment methods have not worked, some players have reportedly turned to the developing field of stem cell therapy treatments.[73] The efficacy of stem cell therapies is unclear and the U.S. Food and Drug Administration has argued successfully that stem cell therapies require its approval before being practiced on patients.[74] As a result, many prospective patients and some players have traveled overseas to receive treatments that are not approved in the United States. These practices raise concerns that should be monitored as stem cell therapies and their use by NFL players develop, including the role of club medical personnel in potentially helping players understand the risks of seeking unapproved therapies.

E Enforcement of Legal and Ethical Obligations[u]

The 2011 CBA provides a few options for players dissatisfied with their healthcare, including athletic trainers. Nevertheless, these options, discussed below, provide questionable remedies to the players.

First, a player could submit a complaint to the Accountability and Care Committee. The Accountability and Care Committee consists of the NFL Commissioner (or his

---

t   Denver Broncos defensive lineman Antonio Smith told the Associated Press the same in 2016: "You've got to get yourself a good system. Chiropractor, massage therapist, stretch therapist. A lot of guys are doing IVs now . . . . Take care of your body. You've got to do that. If the team doesn't supply it, you spend the money." Howard Fendrich and Eddie Pells, *AP Survey: NFL players question teams' attitudes on health*, Associated Press (Jan. 30, 2016, 7:39 PM), http://pro32.ap.org/article/ ap-survey-nfl-players-question-teams%E2%80%99-attitudes-health, *archived at* https://perma.cc/V5RR-XGY3.

u   Appendix K is a summary of players' options to enforce legal and ethical obligations against the stakeholders discussed in this Report. In addition, for rights articulated under either the CBA or other NFL policy, the NFLPA and the NFL can also seek to enforce them on players' behalves.

designee), the NFLPA Executive Director (or his designee), and six additional members "experienced in fields relevant to healthcare for professional athletes," three appointed by the Commissioner and three by the NFLPA Executive Director.[75] "[T]he complaint shall be referred to the League and the player's Club, which together shall determine an appropriate response or corrective action if found to be reasonable. The Committee shall be informed of any response or corrective action."[76] There is thus no neutral adjudicatory process for addressing the player's claim or compensating the player for any wrong suffered. The remedial process is left entirely in the hands of the NFL and the club, both of which would have little incentive to find that a club medical official acted inappropriately and to compensate the injured player accordingly.

Second, a player could request the NFLPA to commence an investigation before the Joint Committee on Player Safety and Welfare (Joint Committee). The Joint Committee consists of three representatives chosen by the NFL and three chosen by the NFLPA.[77] "The NFLPA shall have the right to commence an investigation before the Joint Committee if the NFLPA believes that the medical care of a team is not adequately taking care of player safety. Within 60 days of the initiation of an investigation, two or more neutral physicians will be selected to investigate and report to the Joint Committee on the situation. The neutral physicians shall issue a written report within 60 days of their selection, and their recommendations as to what steps shall be taken to address and correct any issues shall be acted upon by the Joint Committee."[78] While a complaint to the Joint Committee results in a neutral review process, the scope of that review process' authority is vague. The Joint Committee is obligated to act on the recommendations of the neutral physicians, but it is unclear what it means for the Joint Committee to act and there is nothing obligating the NFL or any club to abide by the neutral physicians' or Joint Committee's recommendations. Moreover, there is no indication that the neutral physicians or Joint Committee could award damages to an injured player.[79]

In 2012, the NFLPA commenced the first and only Joint Committee investigation.[80] The nature and results of that investigation are confidential per an agreement between the NFL and NFLPA.[81]

Third, a player could try to commence a Non-Injury Grievance.[82] The 2011 CBA directs certain disputes to designated arbitration mechanisms[83] and directs the remainder of any disputes involving the CBA, a player contract, NFL rules or generally the terms and conditions of employment to the Non-Injury Grievance arbitration process.[84]

Importantly, Non-Injury Grievances provide players with the benefit of a neutral arbitration and the possibility of a "money award."[85]

However, there are several impediments to pursuing a Non-Injury Grievance against an athletic trainer (or any club employee). First, athletic trainers are not parties to the CBA and thus likely cannot be sued for violations of the CBA.[86] Instead, the player could seek to hold the club responsible for the athletic trainer's violation of the CBA.[87] Second, Non-Injury Grievances must be filed within 50 days "from the date of the occurrence or non-occurrence upon which the grievance is based,"[88] a timeframe that is much shorter than your typical statute of limitations. And third, players likely fear that pursuing a grievance against an athletic trainer could result in the club terminating him. Current Player 8 stated as much: "You don't have the gall to stand against your franchise and say 'They mistreated me." . . . I, still today, going into my eighth year, am afraid to file a grievance, or do anything like that[.]"

While it is illegal for an employer to retaliate against an employee for filing a grievance pursuant to a CBA,[89] such litigation would involve substantial time and money for an uncertain outcome. Moreover, given the precarious nature of players' employment and the considerable discretion the club has over the roster, any such retaliation would be challenging to prove.

Outside of the CBA, players can also attempt to bring civil lawsuits against NFL club athletic trainers for negligence or professional malpractice. However, there are serious impediments to such claims. First and foremost, the player's claim would likely be barred by workers' compensation statutes. Workers' compensation statutes provide compensation for workers injured at work and thus generally preclude lawsuits against co-workers based on the co-workers' negligence.[90] This was the result in the *Stringer* case (discussed in more detail below), in multiple cases brought by NFL players against club doctors,[91] and in a case against an NBA club athletic trainer.[92]

Our research has revealed only two cases in which an NFL club athletic trainer was sued by a player.

First, in 1989, former Seattle Seahawks safety Kenny Easley sued the Seahawks, the Seahawks doctor and athletic trainer, and Whitehall Laboratories, a maker of Advil, alleging that Easley's use of Advil had caused him kidney damage necessitating a transplant.[93] Easley alleged the Seahawks medical staff negligently provided him with large doses of the drug and did not tell him when he developed kidney problems.[94] Easley ultimately reached an undisclosed settlement with the doctor and Whitehall Laboratories in 1991.[95] The result of the case as against the athletic trainer is unclear. News reports discussed a pending workers' compensation case, which suggests that Easley's case against the athletic trainer, a co-worker, was dismissed.

In 2001, Minnesota Vikings Pro Bowl offensive tackle Korey Stringer died of complications from heat stroke after collapsing during training camp.[96] Stringer's family later sued the Vikings, Vikings coaches, athletic trainers and affiliated doctors, the NFL, and the equipment manufacturer Riddell. Of specific relevance, Stringer's family sued three Vikings athletic trainers.

A Minnesota trial court granted summary judgment[v] in favor of the Vikings, the athletic trainers, and others in an unpublished order.[97] Of relevance, the trial court determined that the athletic trainers did not owe a personal duty to Stringer and that they were not grossly negligent.[98] Stringer's representatives were required to prove both elements to avoid preemption by Minnesota's workers' compensation statute.[99]

The Minnesota Court of Appeals determined that the athletic trainers against whom appeal was sought[w] *did* owe a personal duty to Stringer but affirmed judgment in their favor by finding that they were not grossly negligent as a matter of law.[100]

The Supreme Court of Minnesota affirmed the decisions in favor of the athletic trainers and held that they *did not* owe a personal duty to Stringer.[101] Under Minnesota law, an employee owes a personal duty to an injured employee only where the employee acts "outside the course and scope of employment."[102] Because the Vikings' athletic trainers were acting within their scope of their employment when treating Stringer, they did not owe Stringer a personal duty and thus any claims against them were barred by workers' compensation laws.[103]

The fact that as a matter of Minnesota workers' compensation law the athletic trainers did not owe a personal duty to Stringer does not mean that the athletic trainers did not have obligations to Stringer or that the athletic trainers' only concern was for the club. As part of their obligations to the Vikings, the athletic trainers provided care to Stringer and other Vikings players. However, so long as the care being provided to Stringer was within the scope of the athletic trainers' employment, Minnesota's workers' compensation statutes prevented them from being held personally liable for any alleged negligence.

The CBA also presents a potential obstacle against any such claim. This is because the Labor Management Relations Act (LMRA)[104] bars or "preempts" state common law[x] claims, such as negligence, where the claim is "substantially dependent upon analysis of the terms" of a CBA, *i.e.*, where the claim is "inextricably intertwined with consideration of the terms of the" CBA."[105] In order to assess an athletic trainer's duty to an NFL player, an essential element of a negligence claim, the court may have to refer to and analyze the terms of the CBA, resulting in the claim's preemption.[106] Preemption occurs even though athletic trainers are not parties to the CBA and thus likely cannot be a party in any CBA grievance procedure. So long as the player's claim is "inextricably intertwined" with the CBA, it will be preempted. In these cases, player complaints must be resolved through the enforcement provisions provided by the CBA itself (*i.e.*, a Non-Injury Grievance against the club), rather than litigation.

PFATS' Code of Ethics also provides two purported enforcement mechanisms. First, according to PFATS, its "Constitution expressly authorizes disciplinary action against members for violations of the Constitution," of which the Code of Ethics is part.[107] However, "[d]isciplinary action for alleged violations of the PFATS Code of Ethics can only be initiated by the Executive Committee."[108] PFATS' Code of Ethics empowers the Executive Committee to "fine, suspend, or expel any member[.]"[109] When we inquired as to how often this provision had been invoked, we were informed that "[i]n the last 10 years, the Executive Committee has not initiated disciplinary action against a PFATS member for violations of the PFATS Code of Ethics."[110]

Second, PFATS' Code of Ethics also declares that any violation of the Code of Ethics may be referred to NATA.[111] According to PFATS, "[d]isciplinary actions for violations of the PFATS Code of Ethics and the NATA Code of Ethics are separate and independent. If the Executive Committee initiates disciplinary action for an alleged PFATS Code of Ethics violation, there is no requirement for such matter to be referred to the NATA. Similarly, if the Executive Committee or a PFATS member refers an alleged violation of the NATA Code of Ethics to the NATA for disciplinary

---

v   Summary judgment is "[a] judgment granted on a claim or defense about which there is no genuine issue of material fact and on which the movant is entitled to prevail as a matter of law." Black's Law Dictionary (9th ed. 2009).

w   Stringer's estate did not appeal the trial court's decision with respect to one of the athletic trainers. *See* Stringer v. Minn. Vikings Football Club, 705 N.W.2d 746, 748 n.1 (Minn. 2005).

x   Common law refers to "[t]he body of law derived from judicial decisions, rather than from statutes or constitutions." Black's Law Dictionary (9th ed. 2009). The concept of "preemption" is "[t]he principle (derived from the Supremacy Clause [of the Constitution] that a federal law can supersede or supplant any inconsistent state law or regulation." *Id.*

action, there is no requirement for the Executive Committee to initiate disciplinary action based on a violation of the PFATS Code of Ethics."[112] However, "[i]n the last 10 years, there have been no referrals by the Executive Committee or a PFATS member to the NATA for disciplinary action for violations of the NATA Code of Ethics."[113] Moreover, even if PFATS did refer a member's conduct to NATA, NATA's possible sanctions are limited to suspension or cancellation of membership, public censure or private reprimand.[114] NATA has no authority to compensate the injured player.[115]

In sum, there has been no enforcement action related to the PFATS Code of Ethics for at least the past decade. Of course, it is impossible to tell if this is a result of superb compliance or lax enforcement. Regardless of compliance, however, we believe that the Code of Ethics is insufficient for the reasons described above, and also recommend a more robust enforcement mechanism.

A player could also file a complaint with the BOC if he believes the athletic trainer has violated one of the BOC's Standards of Professional Practice.[116] While the BOC has the authority to revoke the athletic trainer's certification, the BOC has no authority to compensate the player.[117] In addition, the BOC has never disciplined an NFL club athletic trainer.[118]

F \ Recommendations Concerning Athletic Trainers

Athletic trainers are the player's principal source of healthcare. For this reason, it is important that they hold player health as their paramount responsibility and act in accordance with their legal and ethical obligations at all times. Nevertheless, as discussed above in the Current Practices Section, some players expressed concerns about athletic trainers' practice because of their close relationship to the club. To address this concern, we make the below recommendations.

Additionally, because the roles of the athletic trainer and the players' doctors are so intertwined, all recommendations made in Chapter 2: Club Doctors, Section H: Recommendations, Chapter 4: Second Opinion Doctors, Section F: Recommendations, Chapter 5: Neutral Doctors, Section F: Recommendations, and Chapter 6: Personal Doctors, Section F: Recommendations have some application to the athletic trainers. In addition to the recommendations in those chapters, and while we were unable to interview athletic trainers to gauge their viewpoints,[y] we make the recommendations below to help improve the care relationship between athletic trainers and players.

Goal 1: To ensure that players receive the best healthcare possible from providers who are as free from conflicts of interest as possible.

Principles Advanced: Respect; Health Primacy; Empowered Autonomy; Transparency; Managing Conflicts of Interest; and, Justice.

Recommendation 3:1-A: The current arrangement in which club (i.e., "team") medical staff, including doctors, athletic trainers, and others, have responsibilities both to players and to the club presents an inherent conflict of interest. To address this problem and help ensure that players receive medical care that is as free from conflict as possible, division of responsibilities between two distinct groups of medical professionals is needed. Player care and treatment should be provided by one set of medical professionals (called the "Players' Medical Staff"), appointed by a joint committee with representation from both the NFL and NFLPA, and evaluation of players for business purposes should be done by separate medical personnel (the "Club Evaluation Doctor").

This recommendation also appears in and is described at length in Chapter 2: Club Doctors. We recommend that club doctors and athletic trainers be treated the same way. This recommendation contemplates that athletic trainers (in addition to the other medical professionals treating players) be chosen, reviewed, and terminated (as necessary) by a League-wide independent Medical Committee whose members are jointly selected by the NFL and NFLPA. The athletic trainers' principal day-to-day duties would remain largely the same as they are now—providing medical care to the players and updating the club on player health status (just in a different way). However, the key distinction is that this recommendation eliminates the athletic trainer's obligations to and relationship with the club.[z] The athletic trainer would no longer report to or meet regularly with coaches and club executives concerning player health. Instead, player health status would be

---

y   As described in the background of this chapter, citing ongoing litigation and arbitration, the NFL declined to consent to our request to interview persons currently employed by or affiliated with NFL clubs, including coaches, general managers, doctors, and athletic trainers. Therefore, we did not pursue interviews with these individuals.
z   Current Player 10: "If protecting the health of players always takes precedence, as Roger Goodell has stated, then trainers need to have players', not owners', best interests in mind at all times."

transmitted to the club through a Player Health Report completed by the Players' Medical Staff.[aa] Additional logistics concerning the recommendation are discussed in Chapter 2: Club Doctors and Appendix G: Model Article 39 of the Collective Bargaining Agreement – Players' Medical Care and Treatment. Nevertheless, most importantly, the proposed structure removes any conflict of interest in the care being provided to players by athletic trainers and other medical staff. This recommendation concerns both club doctors and athletic trainers and is an important recommendation for the improvement of player health. Like club doctors, athletic trainer best practices include the avoidance and minimization of conflicts of interest.[119] Indeed, in reviewing a draft of this chapter, NATA described this recommendation as "possibly controversial," but "sound."[120] One positive sign as to the feasibility of our recommendation is that PFATS did not express any opposition to this recommendation when it reviewed a draft of this chapter.

Recommendation 3:1-B: The Professional Football Athletic Trainers Society should revise its Code of Ethics.

As discussed above, PFATS' existing Code of Ethics is contradictory and reflects the inherent conflicts of interest in the current structure of club medical staff that runs counter to the best interests of the players. The Code of Ethics should be revised to eliminate the contradictions and problematic provisions we identified above. More specifically, the PFATS Code of Ethics should emphasize the principle of health primacy and minimizing conflicts of interests by indicating (like the NATA Code of Ethics) that the athletic trainer's foremost duty is the furthering of the best interests of the player under the athletic trainer's care, regardless of the club's policies or wishes.

In addition, enforcement is essential. Violations of a professional code of ethics should include meaningful punishments, ranging from warnings and censures to fines and suspensions. However, PFATS has not initiated any enforcement proceedings in at least the last 10 years. In order to be effective, the enforcement and disciplinary schemes might need to be included in the CBA.

---

aa As explained in Chapter 2: Club Doctors, Recommendation 2:1-A, The Player Health Report would briefly describe: (1) the player's condition; (2) the player's permissible level of participation in practice and other club activities; (3) the player's current status for the next game (*e.g.*, out, doubtful, questionable, or probable); (4) any limitations on the player's potential participation in the next game; and (5) an estimation of when the player will be able to return to full participation in practice and games. The Player Health Report would be a summary form written for the lay coaches and club officials, as opposed to a detailed medical document. Generally speaking, we propose that the Player Health Reports be provided to the club before and after each practice and game. Additionally, the club would be entitled to a Player Health Report on days where there is no practice or game if a player has received medical care or testing.

Endnotes

1   E-mail from MaryBeth Horodyski, Nat'l Ath. Trainers Assoc., to Christopher R. Deubert (June 20, 2016).

2   CBA, Art. 39, § 2.

3   This information was provided by the NFLPA.

4   This information was provided by PFATS during its review of a draft of this chapter.

5   These figures were determined by compiling the data available on the Professional Football Athletic Trainers Society website. *See Member Directory,* Prof. Football Athletic Trainers Soc'y, http://www.pfats.com/directory/ (last visited Aug. 7, 2015), *archived at* http://perma.cc/PG2S-C2KH.

6   See *Athletic Training,* Nat'l Athletic Trainers Ass'n, http://www.nata.org/athletic-training (last visited Aug. 7, 2015), *archived at* http://perma.cc/8S2G-9VMJ; *Becoming an Athletic Trainer,* Professional Football Athletic Trainers Society, http://www.pfats.com/becoming-and-atc/education/ (last visited Aug. 7, 2015), *archived* at http://perma.cc/H5N8-CTQV.

7   *See Map of State Regulatory Agencies,* Board of Cert. for Athletic Trainers, http://www.bocatc.org/state-regulation (last visited Aug. 7, 2015), *archived at* http://perma.cc/5PZC-39PR.

8   *See* 68 Ill. Adm. Code 1160.20 (discussing Board of Certification for the Athletic Trainer certification as requisite to obtaining license under state law); Vt. Admin. Code 20-4-5:2; Neb. Admin. R. & Regs. Tit. 172, Ch. 17, § 002.

9   *Map of State Regulatory Agencies, supra* note 7.

10 *See e.g.,* West's F.S.A. § 468.701 ("'Athletic training' means the recognition, prevention, and treatment of athletic injuries.").

11 ILCS 5/3.

12 *See, e.g.,* Tex. Admin. Code tit. 22, § 871.13 ("An athletic trainer shall work under the direction of a licensed physician or another qualified, licensed health professional who is authorized to refer for health care services within the scope of the person's license when carrying out the practice of prevention, recognition, assessment, management, treatment, disposition, and reconditioning of athletic injuries"); Fla. Admin. Code r. 64B33-4.001 ("Each licensed Athletic Trainer is required to practice under a written protocol established between the athletic trainer and a supervising physician licensed.")

13 *See Practices,* Prof. Football Athletic Trainers Soc'y, http://www.pfats.com/nfl-workplace/practices/ (last visited Aug. 7, 2015), *archived at* http://perma.cc/HTK8-ULXB (describing an NFL athletic trainer's practice duties).

14 *See* Chapter 1: Players, Table 1-C (showing that, generally, there are about 16 percent as many injuries from regular season practices as compared to regular season games).

15 *See Game Day,* Prof. Football Athletic Trainers Soc'y, http://www.pfats.com/nfl-workplace/game-days/ (last visited Aug. 7, 2015), *archived at* http://perma.cc/BU36-CFHD (describing an NFL athletic trainer's duties on game days).

16 This information was provided by the NFLPA.

17 *Id.*

18 *Id.*

19 *Id.*

20 *Id.*

21 *Id.*

22 *Id.*

23 *See, e.g.* Greg Hanlon, *He Might Be Giants: Is Longtime Trainer Ronnie Barnes the Most Powerful Man in New York Football?,* New York Observer, Sept. 10, 2013, http://observer.com/2013/09/he-might-be-giants-is-longtime-trainer-ronnie-barnes-the-most-powerful-man-in-new-york-football/#ixzz3EAG6kCh9, *archived at* http://perma.cc/T67L-HPQ4 (discussing importance of Ronnie Barnes, the New York Giants' longtime trainer and Senior Vice President of Medical Services, within the organization).

24 *Id.* (mentioning Barnes' role in negotiating new multi-million dollar sponsorship deal with Quest Diagnostics).

25 *See, e.g.,* Fla. Stat. § 468.713 (2016) ("An athletic trainer shall practice under the direction of a physician licensed"); Tex. Occupations Code § 451.001 (2015) ("'Athletic training' means the form of health care that includes the practice of preventing, recognizing, assessing, managing, treating, disposing of, and reconditioning athletic injuries under the direction of a physician licensed"); *BOC Standards of Professional Practice,* Board of Cert. for Athletic Trainers, http://www.bocatc.org/images/stories/resources/boc_standards_of_professional_practice_1401bf.pdf ("The Athletic Trainer renders service or treatment under the direction of a physician") (last visited Aug. 7, 2015), *archived at* https://perma.cc/A36B-KM9B?type=pdf.

26 *Mission,* Prof. Football Athletic Trainers Soc'y, http://www.pfats.com/about/mission (last visited May 31, 2016), https://perma.cc/SV92-L2FC.

27 *History,* Prof. Football Athletic Trainers Soc'y, http://www.pfats.com/about/history (last visited Aug. 7, 2015), *archived at* http://perma.cc/6P8N-PZTV.

28 *Mission,* Prof. Football Athletic Trainers Soc'y, *supra* note 26.

29 *See, About the NATA,* Nat'l Athletic Trainers Ass'n, http://www.nata.org/aboutNATA (last visited Aug. 7, 2015), *archived at* http://perma.cc/5YC5-4K93.

30 *NATA Mission,* Nat'l Athletic Trainers Ass'n, http://www.nata.org/mission (last visited Aug. 7, 2015), *archived at* http://perma.cc/D96V-JL5E.

31 NATA Comments (July 14, 2016).

32 Interview with MaryBeth Horodyski, Vice President, NATA, and Jim Thornton, President, NATA (Aug. 20, 2014).

33 *See BOC Vision & Mission,* Board of Cert. for Athletic Trainers, http://bocatc.org/about-us/boc-vision-mission (last visited Aug. 7, 2015), *archived at* http://perma.cc/3J98-WU2T.

34 This information was provided by PFATS.

35 *See BOC Standards of Professional Practice,* Board of Cert. for Athletic Trainers, http://www.bocatc.org/images/stories/resources/boc_standards_of_professional_practice_1401bf.pdf.

36 *Id.* at 2.

37 Searles v. Trustees of St. Joseph's Coll., 695 A.2d 1206, 1210 (Me. 1997); *see also* Howard v. Mo. Bone and Joint Ctr., 615 F.3d 991 (8th Cir. 2010) (holding that evidence was sufficient to show that athletic trainer breached the standard of care for certified athletic trainers when the athletic trainer instructed college football player to continue to work out after the player felt back pain).

38 *See, e.g.,* Morris v. Adm'rs of Tulane Educ. Fund, 891 So.2d 57 (La. Ct. App. 2004) (holding that Louisiana's medical malpractice statute did not apply to athletic trainers); Ga. Physical Therapy v. McCullough, 466 S.E.2d 635 (Ga. Ct. App. 1996) (holding that Georgia's medical malpractice statute did apply to athletic trainer).

39 *See Map of State Regulatory Agencies,* Board of Cert. for Athletic Trainers, http://www.bocatc.org/state-regulation (last visited Aug. 7, 2015), *archived at* http://perma.cc/5PZC-39PR (collecting states' statutes and regulations governing athletic trainers).

40 *See, e.g.,* 22 Tex, Admin. Code § 871.13 (Standards of Conduct for Texas-licensed athletic trainers).

41 *See* 49 Pa. Code § 18.503 (exempting from licensure "[a]n athletic trainer from another state, province, territory or the District of Columbia, who is employed by an athletic team or organization that is competing in this Commonwealth only on a visiting basis, from providing athletic training services, provided the practice of the athletic trainer is limited to the members of the team or organization.")

42 *See* Fla. Stat. §§ 468.70-723 (governing the licensure of athletic trainers in Florida).

43 CBA, Art. 40, § 2(a).

44 This information was provided by the NFLPA.

45 "Protected health information means individually identifiable health information . . . that is: (i) Transmitted by electronic media; (ii) Maintained in electronic media; or (iii) Transmitted or maintained in any other form or medium." 45 C.F.R. § 160.103. "Individually identifiable health information is information that is a subset of health information, including demographic information collected from an individual, and: (1) Is created or received by a health care provider, health plan, employer, or health care clearinghouse; and (2) Relates to the past, present, or future physical or mental health or condition of an individual; the provision of health care to an individual; or the past, present, or future payment for the provision of health care to an individual; and (i) That identifies the individual; or (ii) With respect to which there is a reasonable basis to believe the information can be used to identify the individual." *Id.*

46 *Id.*

47 *Id.*

48 *Id.*

49 NFL Comments and Corrections (June 24, 2016).

50 C.F.R. § 164.512(b)(v).

51 C.F.R. § 1904.4.

52 C.F.R. § 164.512(l).

53 *See* Joy Pritts et al., *The State of Health Privacy: A Survey of State Health Privacy Statutes* (2d ed. 2003), http://sharps.org/wp-content/uploads/PRITTS-REPORT1.pdf, *archived at* https://perma.cc/C72H-R3LK?type=pdf (describing 21 states with statutes restricting doctors from disclosing healthcare information, subject to various exceptions).

54 *See id.*; Joy L. Pritts, *Altered States: State Health Privacy Laws and the Impact of the Federal Health Privacy Rule*, 2 Yale J. Health Pol'y, L. & Ethics 325, 335–36 (2002) (discussing variance in state laws on use and disclosure of medical information).

55 *See, e.g.,* Arizona: A.R.S. § 12-2294(C)(9); A.R.S. § 36-509(A)(14); California: Ann. Cal. Civ. Code § 56.10(c)(2) (West 2014); Ann. Cal. Civ. Code § 56.10(c)(8)(A) (West 2014); Ann. Cal. Civ. Code § 56.10(c)(8)(B) (West 2014); Colorado: Colo. Rev. Stat. Ann. § 8-43-404(2); Colo. Rev. Stat. Ann. § 8-47-203(1)(a); 7 Colo. Code Regs. 1101-3:8; 7 Colo. Code Regs. 1101-3:8; Florida: Fla. Stat. Ann. § 440.13(4)(c); Fla. Stat. Ann. § 397.501(7)(a)(4); Georgia: Ga. Code Ann. § 34-9-207(a); Ga. Code Ann. § 34-9-207(b); Illinois: Ill. Comp. Stat. Ann 305/8(a); Indiana: Ind. Code Ann. § 16-39-5-3; Louisiana: LSA-R.S. 23:1125; LSA-R.S. 23:1127; Maryland: MD. Code Ann. § 4-305(b)(5); Md. Code Regs. 14.09.03.07; Massachusetts: M.G.L.A. 152 § 20; Michigan: Opinion No. 6593 of the Michigan Attorney General, 1989; Minnesota: Minn. Stat. Ann. § 176.138(a); Missouri: Mo. Rev. Stat. § 287.140(7); New Jersey: N.J. Stat. Ann. § 45:14B-32; N.J. Stat. Ann. § 34:15-128(a)(2); New York: N.Y. Workers' Compensation Law § 13-(g) (McKinney); North Carolina: N.C. Gen. Stat. Ann. § 97-25.6(c)(1); N.C. Gen. Stat. Ann. § 97-25.6(c)(2); Ohio: Ohio Rev. Code Ann. § 4123.651(B); Pennsylvania: 77 Pa. Stat. Ann. § 835; 77 Pa. Stat. Ann. § 531; 50 Pa. Stat. Ann. § 711; Tennessee: Tenn. Code Ann. § 50-6-204(a)(2)(A); Texas: Tex. Labor Code Code. Ann. § 408.025(d); Virginia: Va. Code Ann. § 65.2-604(A); Va. Code Ann. § 65.2-607(A); and, Washington: Wash. Rev. Code Ann. §51.36.060; Wash. Rev. Code Ann.§ 70.02.050(1)(d).

56 In reviewing a draft of this Chapter, PFATS provided us with a copy of its Code of Ethics.

57 *See NATA Code of Ethics,* Nat'l Athletic Trainers Ass'n, http://www.nata.org/codeofethics (last visited Aug. 7, 2015), *archived at* http://perma.cc/A82B-2PLZ.

58 The various statements can be found on NATA's website at http://www.nata.org/press-room, *archived at* http://perma.cc/8PLT-LZUH.

59 Kevin M. Conley, Delmas J. Bolin, Peter J. Carek, Jeff G. Konin, Timothy L. Neal & Danielle Violette, *National Athletic Trainers' Association Position Statement: Preparticipation Physical Examinations and Disqualifying Conditions,* 49(1) Journal of Athletic Training 102–20 (2014).

60 *Id.* at Recommendation No. 27.

61 *Id.* at Recommendation No. 22.

62 *See BOC Standards of Professional Practice,* Board of Cert. for Athletic Trainers, http://www.bocatc.org/images/stories/resources/boc_standards_of_professional_practice_1401bf.pdf (last visited Aug. 7, 2015), *archived at* https://perma.cc/A36B-KM9B?type=pdf.

63 *BOC Professional Practice & Discipline Guidelines,* Board of Cert. for Athletic Trainers § 8.4 (2014), http://www.bocatc.org/images/stories/resources/boc_disciplinary_guidelines_1401bf.pdf (last visited Aug. 7, 2015), *archived at* https://perma.cc/Y3X5-YTSJ?type=pdf.

64 *The BOC 2015 Annual Report,* Board of Cert. for Athletic Trainers, 11 (2015), http://bocatc.org/images/stories/multiple_references/2015%20boc%20annual%20report%20vf.pdf (last visited May 18, 2016), *archived at* https://perma.cc/M4F8-GR2L.

65 *See Disciplinary Action Exchange,* Board of Cert. for Athletic Trainers, http://bocatc.org/public/disciplinary-action-exchange (last visited May 18, 2016), *archived at* https://perma.cc/GKH3-W43C.

66 Email with Shannon Leftwich, Director of Credentialing and Regulatory Affairs, Board of Certification for the Athletic Trainer (Apr. 7, 2015).

67 *See* Kyle Melnick, *Understanding risk and protocols key to concussion management*, USA Today (June 23, 2016), http://usatodayhss.com/2016/understanding-risk-and-protocols-key-to-concussion-management, *archived at* https://perma.cc/8LR7-JH73; Jayson Jenks, *Seahawks' Ricardo Lockette says he nearly died, thanks trainers, firefighters*, Seattle Times, Mar. 7, 2016, http://www.seattletimes.com/sports/seahawks/seahawks-receiver-ricardo-lockette-thanks-redmond-firefighters-and-paramedics-for-saving-his-life/, *archived at* https://perma.cc/3JJP-5CRG; *Eric Berry Health and Football Timeline Press Conference*, Kansas City Chiefs (July 29, 2015), http://www.chiefs.com/news/article-2/Eric-Berry-Health-and-Football-Timeline-Press-Conference/6c4dc83e-82a8-4c7a-883b-738126add317, *archived at* https://perma.cc/C6PS-XC37.

68 Andrew Brandt, Peer Review Response (Oct. 30, 2015).

69 E-Mail from NATA representative to author (May 23, 2016, 12:34 PM) (on file with author).

70 *Id.*

71 *Id. See also* Howard Fendrich and Eddie Pells, *AP Survey: NFL players question teams' attitudes on health*, Associated Press (Jan. 30, 2016, 7:39 PM), http://pro32.ap.org/article/ap-survey-nfl-players-question-teams%E2%80%99-attitudes-health, *archived at* https://perma.cc/V5RR-XGY3 (players discussing differences in treatment between starters and non-starters).

72 NFL Comments and Corrections (June 24, 2016).

73 Timothy Caulfield, What Does It Mean When Athletes Get 'Stem Cell Therapy'?, The Atlantic, Oct. 22, 2012, http://www.theatlantic.com/health/archive/2012/10/what-does-it-mean-when-athletes-get-stem-cell-therapy/263875/, *archived at* https://perma.cc/6PWN-3BYD; Ryan Jones, Jonathan Vilma affidavit details road to recovery from knee surgery, Times-Picayune (New Orleans, LA), July 16, 2012, http://www.nola.com/saints/index.ssf/2012/07/jonathan_vilma_affidavit_detai.html, archived at https://perma.cc/FFX4-H2U3.

74 R. Alta Charo, On the Road (to a Cure?) – Stem-Cell Tourism and Lessons for Gene Editing, 374; 10 New Engl. J. Med. 901 (2016); What are stem cells? How are they regulated?, U.S. Food and Drug Admin., http://www.fda.gov/AboutFDA/Transparency/Basics/ucm194655.htm (last visited Mar. 23, 2016), archived at https://perma.cc/EB4S-FHDL.

75   CBA, Art. 39, § 3(a).

76   CBA, Art. 39, § 3(d).

77   CBA, Art. 50, § 1(a).

78   CBA, Art. 50, § 1(d).

79   In Stringer v. Nat'l Football League, the court also expressed concerns about the effectiveness of the Joint Committee: "While the NFL is required to give 'serious and thorough consideration' to recommendations of the Joint Committee, the CBA imposes no independent duty on the NFL to consider health risks arising from adverse playing conditions, or to make recommendations for rules, regulations or guidelines for the clubs to follow." 474 F.Supp.2d 894, 896 (S.D. Ohio 2007).

80   This information was provided by the NFLPA.

81   Id.

82   The term "Non-Injury Grievance" is something of a misnomer. The CBA differentiates between an "Injury Grievance" and a "Non-Injury Grievance." An "Injury Grievance" is exclusively "a claim or complaint that, at the time a player's NFL Player Contract or Practice Squad Player Contract was terminated by a club, the player was physically unable to perform the services required of him by that contract because of an injury incurred in the performance of his services under that contract." 2011 CBA, Art. 44, § 1. Generally, all other disputes (except System Arbitrations, see 2011 CBA, Art. 15) concerning the CBA or a player's terms and conditions of employment are "Non-Injury Grievances." 2011 CBA, Art. 43, § 1. Thus, there can be disputes concerning a player's injury or medical care which are considered "Non-Injury Grievances" because they do not fit within the limited confines of an "Injury Grievance."

83   For example, Injury Grievances, which occur when, at the time a player's contract was terminated, the player claims he was physically unable to perform the services required of him because of a football-related injury, are heard by a specified Arbitration Panel. 2011 CBA, Art. 44. Additionally, issues concerning certain Sections of the CBA related to labor and antitrust issues, such as free agency and the Salary Cap, are within the exclusive scope of the System Arbitrator, 2011 CBA, Art. 15, currently University of Pennsylvania Law School Professor Stephen B. Burbank.

84   See 2011 CBA, Art. 43, § 1.

85   Id. at § 6 (discussing constitution of Arbitration Panel); Id. at § 8 (discussing Arbitrator's authority, including to grant a "money award").

86   See Jackson v. Kimel, 992 F.2d 1318, 1325 n.4 (4th Cir. 1993) (collecting cases holding that employees that are not signatories to the CBA cannot be sued for violations of the CBA).

87   See 2011 CBA, Art. 2, § 2 (generally discussing CBA's binding effect on NFL, NFLPA, players and clubs but no other party).

88   CBA, Art. 43, § 2.

89   N.L.R.B. v. City Disposal Systems Inc., 465 U.S. 822, 835–36 (1984).

90   See Alexander Cornwell, Trapped: Missouri Legislature Seeks to Close Workers' Compensation Loophole with Some Co-Employees Still Inside, 77 Mo. L. Rev. 235, 235 (2012); David J. Krco, Case Note: Torts – Narrowing the Window: Refining the Personal Duty Requirement for Coemployee Liability Under Minnesota's Workers' Compensation System – Stringer v. Minnesota Vikings Football Club, LLC, 33 Wm. Mitchell L. Rev. 739, 739 (2007); John T. Burnett, The Enigma of Workers' Compensation Immunity: A Call to the Legislature for a Statutorily Defined Intentional Tort Exception, 28 Fla. St. U. L. Rev. 491, 497 (2001).

91   See Lotysz v. Montgomery, 766 N.Y.S.2d 28 (N.Y. 2003) (NFL player's medical malpractice claim against Club doctor barred by state workers' compensation statute); Daniels v. Seattle Seahawks, 968 P.2d. 883 (Wash. Ct. App. 1998) (same); Hendy v. Losse, 819 P.2d 1 (Cal. 1991) (same). See also Bryant v. Fox, 515 N.E.2d 775 (Ill. App. Ct. 1987) (NFL player's medical malpractice claim against club doctor not barred by workers' compensation statute where evidence established that doctor was an independent contractor). For more information on the possibility of players suing coaches, see Timothy Davis, Tort Liability of Coaches for Injuries to Professional Athletes: Overcoming Policy and Doctrinal Barriers, 76 UMKC L. Rev. 571 (2008).

92   See McLeod v. Blase, 659 S.E.2d 727 (Ga. Ct. App. 2008) (former Atlanta Hawk's claim against athletic trainer for alleged negligent treated barred by workers' compensation statute).

93   See Glenn Nelson, Courting Danger Krueger's Advice to Easley: Put Up Fight, Seattle Times, May 31, 1989, available at 1989 WLNR 654489 (discussing nature of Easley's claims); Tom Farrey, Easley Settle with Doctors, Drug Maker, Seattle Times, Sept. 18, 1991, available at 1991 WLNR 984467 (identifying Whitehall Laboratories as the maker of Advil).

94   Tom Farrey, Easley Settle with Doctors, Drug Maker, Seattle Times, Sept. 18, 1991, available at 1991 WLNR 984467 (identifying Whitehall Laboratories as the maker of Advil).

95   Id.

96   Stringer v. Minnesota Vikings Football Club, 705 N.W.2d 746, 748 (Minn. 2005).

97   See Memorandum and Order, Stringer v. Minnesota Vikings Football Club, No. 02-415, (Minn. Dist. Ct. Apr. 25, 2003); Stringer v. Minnesota Vikings Football Club, No. 02-415, 2003 WL 25766738 (Minn. Dist. Ct. Dec. 8, 2003) (discussing Court's prior order). Following Stringer's death, the NFL now issues an annual memorandum to NFL Clubs warning them about the risks of players overheating during training camp. See, e.g., Memorandum from NFL Injury and Safety Panel (Elliott Hershman, M.D., Chairman), to General Managers, Head Coaches, Team Physicians, and Team Athletic Trainers re: 2014 Training Camps – Adverse Weather Conditions (July 11, 2014) (on file with author).

98   See Stringer, 705 N.W.2d at 753 (discussing trial court's order).

99   Id. at 754.

100 Stringer v. Minnesota Vikings Football Club, 686 N.W.2d 545, 551–52 (Minn. Ct. App. 2004).

101 Stringer, 705 N.W.2d 746.

102 Id. at 757–58.

103 Id. at 761–63. The result would likely have been the same under other states' workers' compensation laws. See Hendy v. Losse, 819 P.2d 1 (Cal. 1991) (NFL player's medical malpractice claim against Club doctor barred by workers' compensation statute where Club doctor was co-employee and acting within scope of employment); Macchirole v. Giamboi, 762 N.E.2d 346 (N.Y. 2001) (co-employee's negligence claims barred by worker's compensation statute where co-employee was acting within scope of employment).

104 U.S.C. § 185.

105 Allis-Chambers Corp. v. Lueck, 471 U.S. 202, 213, 200 (1985).

106 See, e.g., Givens v. Tennessee Football, Inc., 684 F.Supp.2d 985 (M.D. Tenn. 2010) (player's tort claims against Club arising out of medical treatment preempted); Williams v. Nat'l Football League, 582 F.3d 863 (8th Cir. 2009) (players' tort claims arising out of drug test preempted). However, for reasons that are not clear, LMRA preemption was not cited by any of the Minnesota state court decisions in the Stringer case.

107 This information was provided by PFATS.

108 Id.

109 PFATS Code of Ethics, Art. X.

110 E-mail from Meghan Carroll, NFL, to authors (June 20, 2016) (providing information on behalf of PFATS).

111 PFATS Code of Ethics, Art. XII, ¶ 7(b).

112 This information was provided by PFATS.

113 Id.

114 See Membership Standards and Sanctions, Nat'l Athletic Trainers Ass'n, http://www.nata.org/membership/about-membership/member-resources/membership-standards (last visited May 31, 2016), archived at https://perma.cc/A4AM-DZNU.

115 See id.

116 See Consumer Complaints, Board of Cert. for Athletic Trainers, http://www.bocatc.org/public/file-a-complaint (last visited Aug. 7, 2015), archived at http://perma.cc/L4CL-8D7T.

117 *See BOC Professional Practice & Discipline Guidelines,* Board of Cert. for Athletic Trainers § 8.4 (2014), http://www.bocatc.org/images/stories/resources/boc_disciplinary_guidelines_1401bf.pdf (last visited Aug. 7, 2015), *archived at* https://perma.cc/Y3X5-YTSJ?type=pdf.

118 Email with Shannon Leftwich, Director of Credentialing and Regulatory Affairs, Board of Certification for the Athletic Trainer (Apr. 6, 2015).

119 Ron Courson et al., *Inter-Association Consensus Statement on Best Practices for Sports Medicine Management for Secondary Schools and Colleges*, 49 J. Ath. Training 128 (2014).

120 E-Mail from NATA representative to author (May 20, 2016, 11:46 PM) (on file with author).

Chapter 4

Second Opinion Doctors

"Second opinion doctors" is a generic term for doctors whom players may consult concerning an injury or medical condition to compare or contrast that opinion to that of the club doctor. In addition, some might be the players' primary caregiver or "personal doctor," as discussed in detail in Chapter 6, and thus fall under the same recommendations we make there. Second opinion doctors are an important component of a player's healthcare protected by the CBA. That said, second opinion doctors' care of players does not include the same type of structural conflicts that potentially hinder the care provided by club doctors, so our recommended changes as to them are more sparing.

While in other chapters we provided the stakeholder an opportunity to review a draft of the relevant chapter(s) prior to publication, because there is no well-defined representative for second opinion doctors, no one reviewed this chapter on behalf of second opinion doctors prior to publication.

A Background

A player's right to a second opinion has been part of the NFL-NFLPA CBAs since 1982. The current version of this right is contained in Article 39 of the 2011 CBA:

> A player will have the opportunity to obtain a second medical opinion. As a condition of the Club's responsibility for the costs of medical services rendered by the physician furnishing the second opinion, such physician must be board-certified in his field of medical expertise; in addition, (a) the player must consult with the Club physician in advance concerning the other physician; and (b) the Club physician must be furnished promptly with a report concerning the diagnosis, examination and course of treatment recommended by the other physician.[a] A player shall have the right to follow the reasonable medical advice given to him by his second opinion physician with respect to diagnosis of injury, surgical and treatment decisions, and rehabilitation and treatment protocol, but only after consulting with the club physician and giving due consideration to his recommendations.[1]

In addition, players are entitled to have surgery performed by the surgeon of their choice:

> A player will have the right to choose the surgeon who will perform surgery provided that: (a) the player will consult unless impossible (e.g., emergency surgery) with the Club physician as to his recommendation regarding the need for, the timing of and who should perform the surgery; (b) the player will give due consideration to the Club physician's recommendations; and (c) the surgeon selected by the player shall be board-certified in his field of medical expertise. Any such surgery will be at Club expense; provided, however, that the Club, the Club physician, trainers and any other representative of the Club will not be responsible for or incur any liability (other than the cost of the surgery) for or relating to the adequacy or competency of such surgery or other related medical services rendered in connection with such surgery.[2]

Thus, to be clear, players have the right to a second opinion doctor and the surgeon of their choice, the full cost of which must be paid by the club, provided the player consults with the club doctor and provides the club doctor with a report concerning treatment provided by the second opinion doctor.

The NFLPA maintains a list of dozens of doctors around the country it recommends for second opinions. Nevertheless, players are not required to use these doctors to obtain second opinions.

B Current Legal Obligations[b]

While we discussed the controversial role of club doctors in Chapter 2, the responsibilities of a second opinion doctor are much clearer. A second opinion doctor's first and only loyalty should be to the player and they are thus bound to provide care within an acceptable standard of care, as discussed in Chapter 2: Club Doctors, Section (C)(1)(a).

Second opinion doctors are also obligated to treat player medical information confidentially in accordance with HIPAA and state laws, including the exceptions therein, as discussed in Chapter 2: Club Doctors, Section (C)(3)(a). However, as discussed above, it is important to note that pursuant to the CBA, where the player wishes to have the club pay for the second opinion, the club doctor is entitled to a report of the second opinion doctor's "diagnosis, examination and course of treatment recommended." Thus, either the player must obtain the report and provide it to the club doctor, or grant permission for the second opinion doctor to provide the report directly to the club doctor.

C Current Ethical Codes

As discussed in Chapter 2: Club Doctors, Section (C)(1)(b), doctors treating players, such as second opinion doctors, are obligated by the AMA Code and the FIMS Code of Ethics to provide care that is in the player-patient's best interests.

It is also relevant to note that while the CBA does not obligate the club doctor to take any action concerning the second opinion, ethical codes do.

---

a Presumably, if a player did not want to consult with the club doctor first or provide the club doctor with a report from the second opinion doctor, the player could pay for the second opinion doctor's services by himself. We have been told anecdotally that this does happen but there are no data on how frequently.

---

b The legal obligations described herein are not an exhaustive list but are those we believe are most relevant to player health.

FIMS' Code of Ethics obligates "[t]he team physician [to] explain to the individual athlete that he or she is free to consult another physician."[3]

AMA Code Opinion 1.2.3 – Consultation, Referral & Second also directs a doctor to cooperate with a patient's right to a second opinion:

> Physicians' fiduciary obligation to promote patients' best interests and welfare can include consulting other physicians for advice in the care of the patient or referring patients to other professionals to provide care.
>
> When physicians seek or provide consultation about a patient's care or refer a patient for health care services, including diagnostic laboratory services, they should:
>
> (a) Base the decision or recommendation on the patient's medical needs, as they would for any treatment recommendation, and consult or refer the patient to only health care professionals who have appropriate knowledge and skills and are licensed to provide the services needed.
>
> (b) Share patients' health information in keeping with ethical guidelines on confidentiality.
>
> (c) Assure the patient that he or she may seek a second opinion or choose someone else to provide a recommended consultation or service . . . .
>
> * * *
>
> Physicians may not terminate a patient-physician relationship solely because the patient seeks recommendations or care from a health care professional whom the physician has not recommended.[4]

Similarly, the American Board of Physician Specialties obligates doctors to "[c]ooperate in every reasonable and proper way with other physicians and work with them in the advancement of quality patient care."[5]

D Current Practices

Second opinion doctors play a role in player health largely as a result of contract advisors.[c] While recognizing that there may be some variation in their usage, of the six

contract advisors we interviewed, five stated that they obtain a second opinion every time or nearly every time a player is significantly injured, while the sixth stated he obtains a second opinion about 50 percent of the time.

The reasoning behind obtaining the second opinions ranges from general to specific distrust of club doctors.[d] Current Player 9 described the advantages of second opinion doctors:

> *I feel like they don't have any vested interest in keeping you on the field; their main job is that you're healthy and they check your medical condition, whatever that may be. And they don't have pressure coming from the coach or the GM [general manager] or the owner to get guys out there quickly . . . . What you have to understand is that the trainer's and the doctor's job is to get you on the field. Once you're part of the organization, it's their job to put you on the field.*[e]

Similarly, some contract advisors indicated that by almost always obtaining a second opinion, it removes any concern that the club doctor might have been making a recommendation that was in the club's interest and not the player's.[f] One contract advisor even stated that when assessing a player's injury, "the club doctor has nothing to do with it . . . the club doctor's input means nothing to us."[g] Some contract advisors also indicated that their experience with, and the reputation of, a particular club or club medical staff will color the decision of whether to obtain a second opinion or to proceed with the club doctor's recommended course of treatment.[h] Indeed, club doctors often serve as second opinion doctors for other clubs' players, often at the recommendation of contract advisors. Nevertheless, in such situations there is less concern about a structural conflict of interest since the club doctor is only serving as a second opinion doctor and not also providing advice to the club employing the player.

---

c   Current Player 2: "I think that agents do a good job of helping players with . . . seeking second opinions[.]"

d   Former Player 2: "Most of the time when I saw guys going to get second opinions . . . was because something had happened or something we heard about or the player had a multi-year contract and wanted to make sure that his diagnosis was correct."

e   Current Player 10: [P]layers have the right to get a second or third medical opinion which I think is smart to do."

f   Contract Advisor 1: "I've effectively removed any of that [concern]. I've said okay, where I feel like I need to get a second opinion almost every time, I get a second opinion. So it's become a nonissue." Contract Advisor 5: "I'm always concerned that the doctor is involved because he's, you know, an employee of the club."

g   Contract Advisor 4: "[T]he team doctor is there to advise the team on how they should approach a player. The team doctor has nothing to do as far as I'm concerned with how the player should approach his own health . . . . The team doctor is a medical advisor to the team."

h   Contract Advisor 2: "[I]t depends sometimes on the organization that we're dealing with."

The second opinion doctor typically only reviews the records, X-rays, and/or MRI films but occasionally will request to see the player in person if the doctor believes it is necessary. Contract advisors' estimates of how often a second opinion doctor's diagnosis differed from the club doctor's diagnosis were generally low ("10 to 20 percent," "as much as 20 percent," "about a third of the time," "not incredibly often"). In fact, those rates (while not necessarily representative) are slightly lower than the general population. "According to the Patient Advocate Foundation, 30 percent of patients who sought second opinions for elective surgery found the two opinions differed."[6] However, it is difficult to compare the figures because, as discussed above, players obtain second opinions almost as a matter of course while the average patient might only seek a second opinion about serious diagnoses.

> The second opinion doctor's recommended course of treatment is almost always the one taken in today's NFL.

If the second opinion doctor's diagnosis or recommended treatment plan does differ, a decision then must be made as to which course of treatment to pursue and which doctor will perform the surgery (if necessary). In some cases, the contract advisor might arrange for the second opinion doctor to talk with the club doctor to see if a consensus can be reached.[i] Sometimes a third doctor will provide an opinion. Nevertheless, the prevailing sentiment among the contract advisors interviewed is that when there is a conflict, the second opinion doctor's recommended course of treatment is almost always the one taken in today's NFL. As discussed above, some contract advisors' regard the club doctor's opinion as meaningless, and others believe that in recent years clubs and club medical staff have resigned themselves to doing what the player wants to do (as recommended by the contract advisor and second opinion doctor). Of course, just because contract advisors believe this to be the case does not necessarily mean it is true. However, in the absence of more robust evidence (and we know of no publicly available study on the subject), these perceptions are helpful even if based on incomplete data.

In talking with players and contract advisors, most believed that club doctors are generally, but not always, cooperative with players obtaining second opinions, a marked departure from historical practice and even just 5 to 10 years ago.[j] Nevertheless, former NFL club executive Andrew Brandt in his peer review comments noted his belief that clubs and club doctors maintain some level of inherent distrust of second opinion doctors chosen by contract advisors and the NFLPA; much in the same way that players and the NFLPA maintain a level of inherent distrust of club doctors.[7] For example, clubs might believe the second opinion doctors are not sufficiently qualified to treat the player.

E Enforcement of Legal and Ethical Obligations[k]

A second opinion doctor, just like any doctor, is obligated to provide care to his or her patients within an acceptable standard of care in the medical community or potentially be subject to a medical malpractice claim.[8] The extent of these obligations is discussed in much greater depth in Chapter 2: Club Doctors, Section (C)(1)(a). In brief, though, the general elements of a medical malpractice claim are: (1) a standard of care owed by the doctor to the plaintiff; (2) a breach of that standard of care by the doctor; and, (3) the breach was the proximate cause of the plaintiff's injury.[9,l]

While medical malpractice liability potentially exists, our research has not revealed any cases in which an NFL player has sued a doctor from whom he obtained a second opinion.

The CBA does not provide players with any grievance or arbitration mechanism by which players could pursue claims against second opinion doctors. Second opinions are available to players at the club's expense under the CBA, but the CBA does not in any way dictate the second opinion doctor's obligations to the player.

---

i Yet Contract Advisor 1 explained that the club doctor "will have to make a very good argument" to the second opinion doctor to convince the second opinion doctor and contract advisor to follow the club doctor's recommendation.

j Contract Advisor 1: "I will say there was a lot more pushback early in my career about second opinions and going somewhere else."

k Appendix K is a summary of players' options to enforce legal and ethical obligations against the stakeholders discussed in this Report. In addition, for rights articulated under either the CBA or other NFL policy, the NFLPA and the NFL can also seek to enforce them on players' behalves.

l Many states require a doctor with the same board certification or similar expertise as the doctor against whom the claim is brought to opine as to the appropriate standard of care. See Benjamin Grossberg, Uniformity, Federalism, and Tort Reform: The Erie Implications of Medical Malpractice Certificate of Merit Statutes, 159 U. Pa. L. Rev. 217 (2010) (identifying 25 states with statutes that require certificates of merit by another doctor for a medical malpractice claim). Thus, in the event a second opinion doctor was sued for medical malpractice, the claim likely could not proceed without a similarly qualified doctor—whether it be an orthopedist, neurologist or a doctor specializing in sports medicine—opining that the second opinion doctor deviated from the standard of care.

F   Recommendations Concerning Second Opinion Doctors

Second opinion doctors are important advocates for players' health and do not suffer from the inherent structural conflicts of interest, faced by club doctors. While we do not have recommendations directed specifically toward second opinion doctors, we do have recommendations concerning how other stakeholders can promote and support the good work of these doctors.

Goal 1: To help players obtain the best possible healthcare.

Principles Advanced: Respect; Health Primacy; Empowered Autonomy; and, Managing Conflicts of Interest.

Recommendation 4:1-A: Clubs and club medical staff should support players in their right to receive a second opinion.

The right to and value of a second medical opinion is well accepted in our society, particularly for serious conditions. This right to a second opinion is all the more important for NFL players considering that their careers depend on their health and the complexity of their conditions. Consequently, no matter the club doctor's best intentions or practices, players should regularly obtain second opinions and clubs and club medical staff should support them in exercising that right. It would be advisable that club medical staff advise players of their right to obtain a second opinion at the beginning of training camp (a right of which the NFLPA should also be advising players at the same time). Supporting a player's right to a second opinion means, among other things, advising the player of his right to a second opinion, not resisting a player's desire to obtain a second opinion, and cooperating with the second opinion doctor by providing the necessary medical records and other information in a timely fashion. Indeed, AMA Code Opinion 1.2.3 requires such cooperation. Accepting a player's right to obtain a second opinion and cooperating with that right is important for players to receive the best possible healthcare. For this reason, the parties should also consider whether this recommendation should be included in the CBA.

Recommendation 4:1-B: In the event that club medical staff diagnose or treat a player for an injury that is beyond a threshold of severity, the medical staff should remind the player of his right to obtain a second opinion at the club's expense.

As discussed above, a player's right to a second opinion is important to his health. Nevertheless, many players, particularly younger players, do not avail themselves of this right. Some players might not be aware that they have the right in the CBA to a second opinion at the club's expense or are worried about offending the club doctor and thus the club. By requiring club medical staff to advise players of their right to a second opinion in more serious situations, it is likely that players will increasingly take advantage of this right and thus also protect their own health. When a player misses a game or a week of practice it might indicate a sufficiently severe injury to trigger this obligation. Again, a player's right to receive a second opinion is important for players to receive the best possible healthcare and thus the parties should also consider whether this recommendation should be included in the CBA.

* * *

In reviewing a draft of this report, the NFL claimed that "[t]hese recommendations are already incorporated in Article 39 of the CBA."[10] While it is true that Article 39 does provide a right to a second opinion, our recommendation is not about that specific right, but about club medical staff assisting players in obtaining a second opinion. We do not read Article 39 to include these recommendations and thus believe they are important to make.

Endnotes

1 CBA, Art. 39, § 4.

2 CBA, Art. 39, § 5.

3 Féderation Internationale de Médicine du Sport, Code of Ethics, ¶ 4.

4 *Opinion 1.2.3 – Consultation, Referral & Second Opinions,* Am. Med. Ass'n, available at http://www.ama-assn.org/ama/pub/physician-resources/medical-ethics/code-medical-ethics.page (last visited Aug.1, 2016), *archived at* https://perma.cc/4QS7-F5FT.

5 *Code of Ethics,* Am. Bd. of Physician Specialties, http://www.abpsus.org/code-of-ethics (last visited Aug. 7, 2015), *archived at* http://perma.cc/BU3D-VAQZ.

6 Jerry Cianciolo, *Get a Second Opinion,* Bos. Globe, Jan. 25, 2015, *available at* 2015 WLNR 2386857.

7 Andrew Brandt, Peer Review Response (Oct. 30, 2015).

8 *See* Thierfelder v. Wolfert, 52 A.3d 1251, 1264 (Pa. 2012) (discussing elements of a medical malpractice claim); Hamilton v. Wilson, 249 S.W.3d 425, 426 (Tex. 2008) (same); Sullivan v. Edward Hosp., 806 N.E.2d 645, 653 (Ill. 2004) (same).

9 *Id.*

10 NFL Comments and Corrections (June 24, 2016).

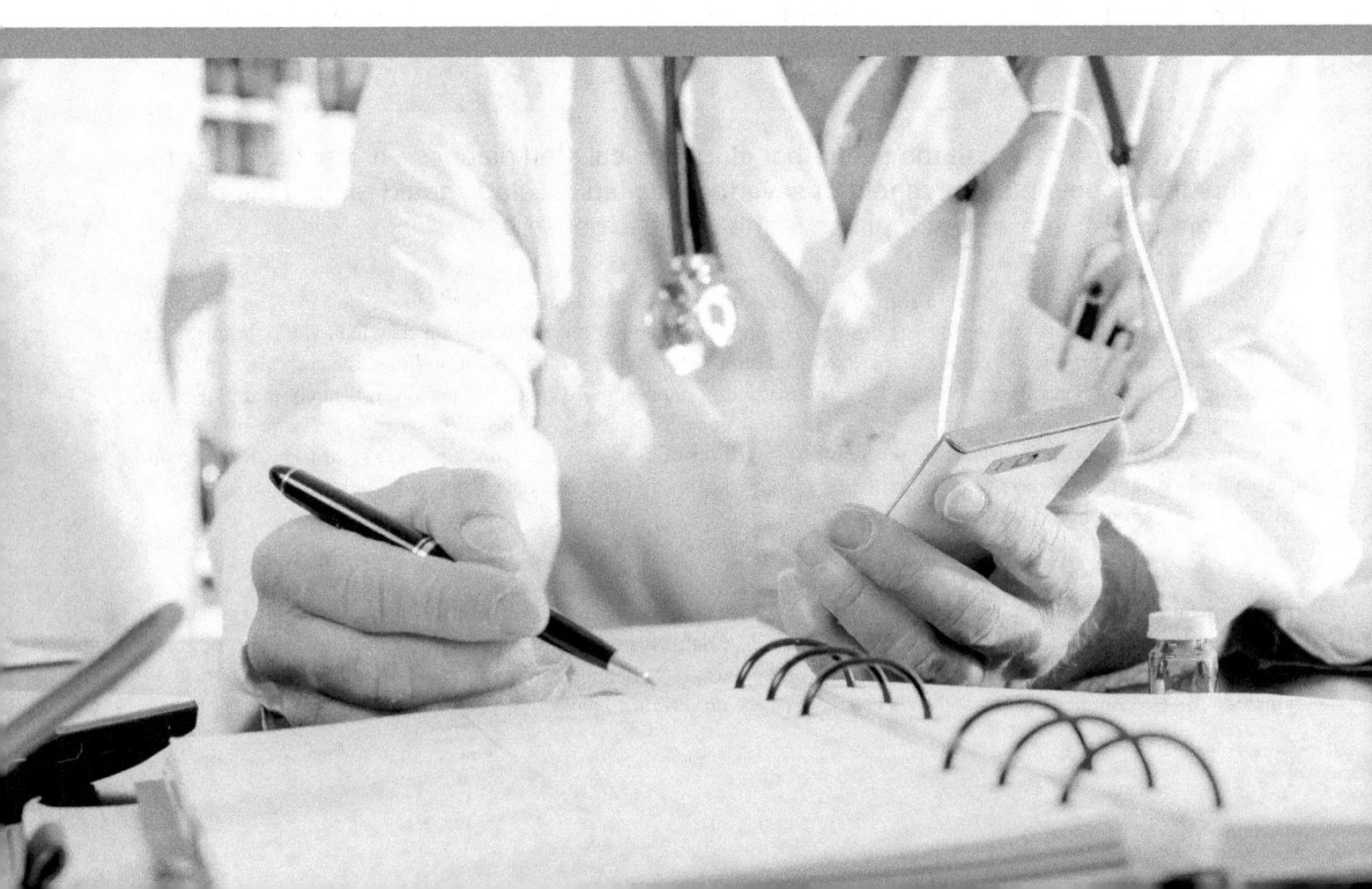

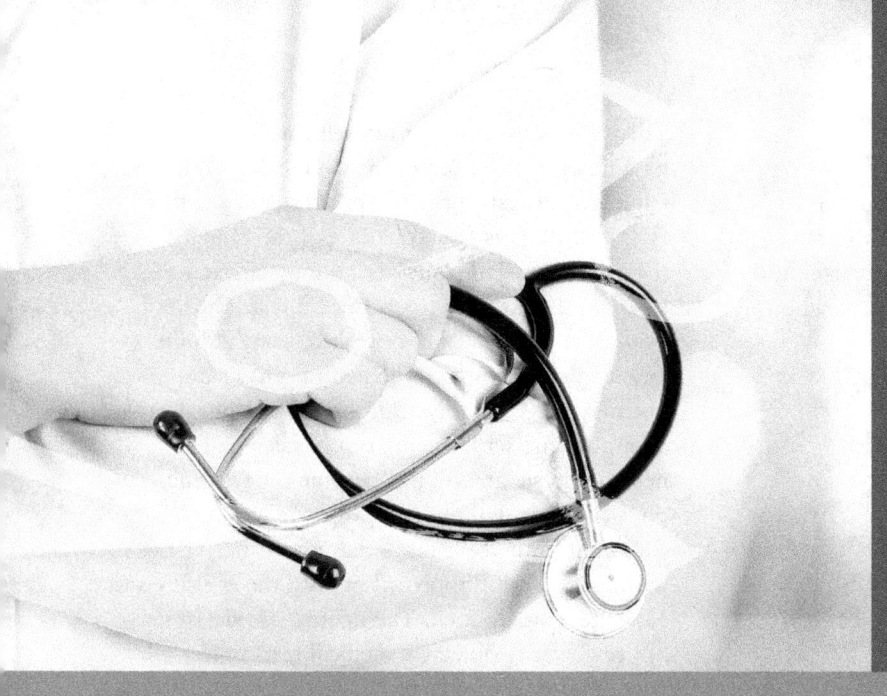

Chapter 5

Neutral Doctors

In the NFL, a third kind of doctor, what the CBA describes as a "neutral" doctor, is sometimes used when there are conflicting opinions or interests. Neutral doctors, particularly when providing care, can be an important component of a player's healthcare. As with second opinion doctors, neutral doctors' responsibilities do not include the same type of structural conflicts that potentially hinder the care provided by club doctors. Consequently, our recommendations as to them are more sparing.

While in other chapters we provided the stakeholder an opportunity to review a draft of the relevant chapter(s) prior to publication, because there is no well-defined representative for neutral doctors, no one reviewed this chapter on behalf of neutral doctors prior to publication.

A Background

The 2011 CBA demarcates three situations where neutral doctors are required. Preliminarily, it is important to note that in each of these situations, the neutral doctor is usually a different person, *i.e.*, there is not one neutral doctor who serves in each of these situations.

First, Article 39, § 1(e) concerns neutral doctors at NFL games. Section 1(e) requires that "[a]ll home teams shall retain at least one [Rapid Sequence Intubation] RSI physician who is board certified in emergency medicine, anesthesia, pulmonary medicine, or thoracic surgery, and who has documented competence in RSI intubations in the past twelve months. This physician shall be the neutral physician dedicated to game-day medical intervention for on-field or locker room catastrophic emergencies." As far as we can ascertain, there has never been a "catastrophic emergenc[y]" requiring intubation or similar emergency care.

Second, Article 44 enlists the neutral doctor in the Injury Grievance mechanism. "An 'Injury Grievance' is a claim or complaint that, at the time a player's NFL Player Contract or Practice Squad Player Contract was terminated by a Club, the player was physically unable to perform the services required of him by that contract because of an injury incurred in the performance of his services under that contract."[1] Pursuant to Article 44, the player is entitled to a neutral arbitration to determine whether the player was physically unable to perform at the time his contract was terminated. A neutral doctor plays an instrumental role in the outcome of the arbitration:

The player must present himself for examination by a neutral physician in the Club city or the Club city closest to the player's residence within twenty (20) days from the date of the filing of the grievance. This time period may be extended by mutual consent if the neutral physician is not available. Neither Club nor player may submit any medical records to the neutral physician, nor may the Club physician or player's physician communicate with the neutral physician. The neutral physician will not become the treating physician nor will the neutral physician examination involve more than one office visit without the prior approval of both the NFLPA and Management Council. The neutral physician may not review any objective medical tests unless all parties mutually agree to provide such results. The neutral physician may not perform any diagnostic tests unless all parties consent. The neutral physician is required to submit to the parties a detailed medical report of his examination.[2]

* * *

The arbitrator will consider the neutral physician's findings conclusive with regard to the physical condition of the player and the extent of an injury at the time of his examination by the neutral physician.[3]

Third, Article 50, § 1 concerns the Joint Committee on Player Safety and Welfare (Joint Committee), which also makes mention of the neutral physician. The Joint Committee consists of members from both NFL clubs and the NFLPA and is designed to discuss "the player safety and welfare aspects of playing equipment, playing surfaces, stadium facilities, playing rules, player-coach relationships,

We recommend that if the Unaffiliated Neurotrauma Consultant diagnoses a player with a concussion, the player cannot return to the game.

and any other relevant subjects."[4] The Joint Committee, at the NFLPA's behest, can also engage neutral doctors:

> The NFLPA shall have the right to commence an investigation before the Joint Committee if the NFLPA believes that the medical care of a team is not adequately taking care of player safety. Within 60 days of the initiation of an investigation, two or more neutral physicians will be selected to investigate and report to the Joint Committee on the situation. The neutral physicians shall issue a written report within 60 days of their selection, and their recommendations as to what steps shall be taken to address and correct any issues shall be acted upon by the Joint Committee.[5]

In addition to these CBA provisions requiring a neutral doctor, the NFL and NFLPA have agreed on protocols regarding the diagnosis and management of concussions ("Concussion Protocol," *see* Appendix A). The Concussion Protocol requires an "Unaffiliated Neurotrauma Consultant" to be assigned to each club for each game. The Unaffiliated Neurotrauma Consultant must "be a physician who is impartial and independent from any Club, is board certified or board eligible in neurology, neurological surgery, emergency medicine, physical medicine and rehabilitation physician, or any primary care CAQ [Certificate of Added Qualification] sports medicine certified physician and has documented competence and experience in the treatment of acute head injuries." The Unaffiliated Neurotrauma Consultant is present on the sideline during the game and "shall be (i) focused on identifying symptoms of concussion and mechanisms of injury that warrant concussion evaluation, (ii) working in consultation with the Head Team Physician or designated [Traumatic Brain Injury] TBI team physicians to implement the Club's concussion evaluation and management protocol (including the Sideline Concussion Assessment Exam) during the games, and (iii) present to observe (and collaborate when appropriate with the Team Physician) the Sideline Concussion Assessment Exams performed by Club medical staff."

Despite the important role of the Unaffiliated Neurotrauma Consultant, "[t]he responsibility for the diagnosis of concussion and the decision to return a player to a game remains exclusively within the professional judgment of the Head Team Physician or the Team physician assigned to managing TBI [traumatic brain injury]." In Chapter 2: Club Doctors, Recommendation 2:1-D, we recommend that this be changed and that if either the Unaffiliated Neurotrauma

Consultant or club doctor diagnoses a player with a concussion, the player cannot return to the game.[a]

B Current Legal Obligations[b]

The neutral doctor's role is different in each of situations described above. As a game-day doctor under Article 39 or as the Unaffiliated Neurotrauma Consultant, the neutral doctor is actually treating the player. As part of an Injury Grievance, the neutral doctor is examining, but not treating, the player. And finally, in conducting an investigation at the behest of the Joint Committee, the neutral doctor's role is less clear as the doctor might examine the player but seems unlikely to treat him.

The different contexts create different obligations on the neutral doctor.

Where the neutral doctor is treating the player, the doctor's first and only loyalty should be to the player and the doctor is thus bound to provide care within an acceptable standard of care, as discussed in Chapter 2: Club Doctors, Section (C)(1)(a).

Where the neutral doctor is evaluating the player, the doctor's obligations are the same as if the doctor were performing a fitness-for-play examination. As discussed in Chapter 2: Club Doctors, Section (D)(1)(a), doctors performing such evaluations have a limited patient-doctor relationship that obligates them to exercise care consistent with their professional training and expertise so as not to cause physical harm by negligently conducting the examination.[6]

If the neutral doctor conducting an investigation on behalf of the Joint Committee actually examines a player, then the neutral doctor will have the same obligations as if the doctor were performing a fitness-for-play evaluation as discussed above. However, if the neutral doctor does not examine (or treat) the player in any way as part of the investigation, the neutral doctor will not develop any legal responsibilities toward the player as a result of the doctor's role with the Joint Committee.

---

a   In the explanation for this recommendation, we acknowledge that because the club doctor is likely to have greater familiarity with the player, he or she might be able to better determine whether a player has suffered a concussion. Nevertheless, we believe this recommendation is a common sense protection that errs on the side of player health.

b   The legal obligations described herein are not an exhaustive list but are those we believe are most relevant to player health.

C | Current Ethical Codes

Where the neutral doctor is treating the player, a doctor-patient relationship is formed and the doctor is obligated to treat the player in accordance with applicable legal and ethical standards, as discussed at length in Chapter 2: Club Doctors, Section (C)(1)(b).

In a situation where the neutral doctor is *evaluating* but not treating the player, AMA Code Opinion 1.2.6 explains that "[s]uch industry-employed physicians or independent medical examiners establish limited patient-physician relationships. Their relationships with patients are limited to the isolated examination; they do not monitor patients' health over time, treat them, or carry out many other duties fulfilled by physicians in the traditional fiduciary role."[7] In such a situation, the doctor has the following obligations:

(a) Disclose the nature of the relationship with the employer or third party and that the physician is acting as an agent of the employer or third party before gathering health information from the patient.

(b) Explain that the physician's role in this context is to assess the patient's health or disability independently and objectively. The physician should further explain the differences between this practice and the traditional fiduciary role of a physician.

(c) Protect patients' personal health information in keeping with professional standards of confidentiality.

(d) Inform the patient about important incidental findings the physician discovers during the examination. When appropriate, the physician should suggest the patient seek care from a qualified physician and, if requested, provide reasonable assistance in securing follow-up care.[8]

D | Current Practices

Neutral doctors are a less common but nonetheless important component in the ecosystem of player health. Again, it is important to remember that neutral doctors are different professionals who are involved only in specific situations.

As discussed above, the 2011 CBA requires a neutral doctor to be present at every game. Specifically, the CBA specifies that responsibility for "catastrophic emergencies" will lie with a neutral doctor. Nevertheless, it is unclear how often, if ever, their services are required.

The reality is quite different for the Unaffiliated Neurotrauma Consultant. According to the NFL Injury Surveillance System, between 2009 and 2015, approximately 158.7 concussions occurred during games each NFL season.[9] Additionally, as discussed in greater detail in Chapter 1: Players, there is considerable evidence that NFL players underreport their medical conditions and symptoms.[10] And, in an effort not to miss playing time, players might try to intentionally fail the Concussion Protocol's baseline examination,[11] try to avoid going through the concussion diagnosis protocol,[12] or avoid telling the club that he suffered a substantial blow to the head.[13] Thus, the Unaffiliated Neurotrauma Consultant is a critical component of player health. There are no known instances in which the Unaffiliated Neurotrauma Consultant disagreed with the club doctor concerning whether a player should return to the game.[c]

In 2014, the NFL and NFLPA litigated 31 Injury Grievances that would have required examination by a neutral doctor.[14] The neutral doctors involved in Injury Grievances are selected from a list of doctors jointly approved by the NFL and NFLPA.[15] Each year, the NFL and NFLPA have the right to remove two doctors from the list.[16] In 2012, the NFLPA commenced the first and only Joint Committee investigation.[17] The nature and results of that investigation are confidential per an agreement between the NFL and NFLPA,[18] so we are unable to evaluate what role, if any, neutral doctors played there.

E | Enforcement of Legal and Ethical Obligations[d]

In a situation where the neutral doctor provides care to the player (such as the rapid sequence intubation doctor or the Unaffiliated Neurotrauma Consultant), the doctor is obligated to provide care within an acceptable standard of care in the medical community or potentially be subject to a medical malpractice claim.[19] This is discussed in much greater depth in Chapter 2: Club Doctors, Section (C)(1)(a). But briefly, in general the elements of a medical malpractice claim are: (1) a standard of care owed by the doctor to the plaintiff; (2) a breach of that standard of care by the doctor; and, (3) the breach was the proximate cause of the plaintiff's injury.[20]

---

c   The Unaffiliated Neurotrauma Consultant also prepares a report after each game detailing any examinations performed.

d   Appendix K is a summary of players' options to enforce legal and ethical obligations against the stakeholders discussed in this report. In addition, for rights articulated under either the CBA or other NFL policy, the NFLPA and the NFL can also seek to enforce them on players' behalves.

Many states require a doctor with the same board certification or similar expertise as the doctor against whom the claim is brought to opine as to the appropriate standard of care.[21] Thus, in the event a neutral doctor were sued for medical malpractice, the claim likely could not proceed without a similarly qualified doctor — whether it be an orthopedist, neurologist or a doctor specializing in sports medicine — opining that the neutral doctor deviated from the standard of care.

The CBA may limit players bringing a medical malpractice claim against a neutral doctor. This is because the Labor Management Relations Act (LMRA)[22] bars or "preempts" state common law[e] claims, such as negligence, where the claim is "substantially dependent upon analysis of the terms" of a CBA, *i.e.*, where the claim is "inextricably intertwined with consideration of the terms of the" CBA."[23] In order to assess the neutral doctor's duty to an NFL player — an essential element of a negligence claim such as medical malpractice — the court may have to refer to and analyze the terms of the CBA, *e.g.*, the neutral doctors' obligation, resulting in the claim's preemption.[24] Preemption occurs even though the neutral doctors are not parties to the CBA and thus likely cannot be a party in any CBA grievance procedure. So long as the player's claim is "inextricably intertwined" with the CBA, it will be preempted. In these cases, player complaints must be resolved through the enforcement provisions provided by the CBA itself (*i.e.*, a Non-Injury Grievance against the NFL), rather than litigation. Nevertheless, research has not revealed any litigation between a player and a neutral doctor so how a court would resolve these issues is unclear.

The player could also consider bringing a Non-Injury Grievance relating to the neutral doctor's care pursuant to the CBA.[f] The 2011 CBA directs certain disputes to designated arbitration mechanisms[g] and directs the remainder of any disputes involving the CBA, a player contract, NFL rules, or generally the terms and conditions of employment to the Non-Injury Grievance arbitration process.[25] Importantly, Non-Injury Grievances provide players with the benefit of a neutral arbitration and the possibility of a "money award."[26] However, Non-Injury Grievances must be filed within 50 days "from the date of the occurrence or non-occurrence upon which the grievance is based."[27] Additionally, it is possible that under the 2011 CBA, the NFL could argue that complaints concerning medical care are designated elsewhere in the CBA and thus should not be heard by the Non-Injury Grievance arbitrator.[28]

A player could conceivably bring a medical malpractice claim against a neutral doctor who examined the player as part of an Injury Grievance or for the Joint Committee. However, such a claim would be limited to whether the neutral doctor exercised care consistent with the doctor's professional training and expertise so as not to cause physical harm by negligently conducting the examination.[29] Additionally, the claim might be preempted by the LMRA, as discussed above.

> Research has not revealed any litigation between a player and a neutral doctor.

---

e   Common law refers to "[t]he body of law derived from judicial decisions, rather than from statutes or constitutions." Black's Law Dictionary (9th ed. 2009). The concept of "preemption" is "[t]he principle (derived from the Supremacy Clause [of the Constitution] that a federal law can supersede or supplant any inconsistent state law or regulation." *Id.*

f   The term "Non-Injury Grievance" is something of a misnomer. The CBA differentiates between an Injury Grievance and a Non-Injury Grievance. An Injury Grievance is exclusively "a claim or complaint that, at the time a player's NFL Player Contract or Practice Squad Player Contract was terminated by a club, the player was physically unable to perform the services required of him by that contract because of an injury incurred in the performance of his services under that contract." 2011 CBA, Art. 44, § 1. Generally, all other disputes (except System Arbitrations, *see* 2011 CBA, Art. 15) concerning the CBA or a player's terms and conditions of employment are Non-Injury Grievances. 2011 CBA, Art. 43, § 1. Thus, there can be disputes concerning a player's injury or medical care which are considered Non-Injury Grievances because they do not fit within the limited confines of an Injury Grievance.

g   For example, Injury Grievances, which occur when, at the time a player's contract was terminated, the player claims he was physically unable to perform the services required of him because of a football-related injury, are heard by a specified Arbitration Panel. 2011 CBA, Art. 44. Additionally, issues concerning certain Sections of the CBA related to labor and antitrust issues, such as free agency and the salary cap, are within the exclusive scope of the System Arbitrator, 2011 CBA, Art. 15, currently University of Pennsylvania Law School Professor Stephen B. Burbank.

F | Recommendations Concerning Neutral Doctors

Neutral doctors play a limited but important role in player health. Perhaps most importantly, the Unaffiliated Neurotrauma Consultants are crucial to the effective operation of the Concussion Protocol, a signature component of player health. There is no indication that neutral doctors have done anything other than perform the roles assigned to them by the CBA and Concussion Protocol. Consequently, we make no recommendations concerning neutral doctors. Indeed, as the prior chapters suggest, the *neutrality* of these doctors is a positive benefit to players, and we should look for additional opportunities to have *more* neutral doctor input and involvement.

There are additional recommendations relevant to the work conducted by neutral doctors that are made in other chapters:

- Chapter 2: Club Doctors—Recommendation 2:1-D: The Concussion Protocol should be amended such that if either the club doctor or the Unaffiliated Neurotrauma Consultant diagnoses a player with a concussion, the player cannot return to the game.

- Chapter 7: The NFL and NFLPA—Recommendation 7:4-A: The NFL and NFLPA should continue and intensify their efforts to ensure that players take the Concussion Protocol seriously.

Endnotes

1   CBA, Art. 44, § 1.

2   CBA, Art. 44, § 4(a).

3   CBA, Art. 44, § 4(d).

4   CBA, Art. 50, § 1.

5   CBA, Art. 50, § 1(d).

6   Dyer v. Trachtman, 470 Mich. 45, 51–54 (Mich. 2004) (collecting cases); Greenberg v. Perkins, 845 P.2d 530, 535 (Colo. 1993) ("physician owes a duty of care to a nonpatient examinee to conduct the examination in a manner not to cause harm to the person being examined") (internal quotations and citations removed).

7   Id.

8   Id.

9   See Chapter 1: Players, Table 1-F.

10 See Mark Fainaru-Wada & Steve Fainaru, League of Denial: The NFL, Concussions, and the Battle for Truth 26 (2013) (stating that former Pittsburgh Steelers center Mike Webster's "rarely acknowledged his injuries, much less reported them."); Derk A. Van Kampen et al., The "Value Added" of Neurocognitive Testing After Sports-Related Concussion, 34 Am. J. of Sports Med. 1630 (2006) (concluding that "reliance on patients' self-reported symptoms after concussion is likely to result in an underdiagnosis of concussions and may result in premature return to play"); Q. and A.: Responses From an Ex-Enforcer and an Expert, N.Y. Times, Dec. 7, 2011, http://query.nytimes.com/gst/fullpage.html?res=980DE3D71139F934A35751C1A9679D8B63, archived at http://perma.cc/5P5D-TRBX (discussing underreporting of concussion symptoms by football players); Tony Grossi, Injury that Dazed McCoy Puts Focus on Concussions, Cleveland Plain Dealer, Dec. 18, 2011, available at 2011 WLNR 26179502 (mentioning underreporting of concussion symptoms by NFL players).

11 Michael David Smith, To Avoid Concussion Rules, Some Players Sandbag their Baseline Tests, ProFootballTalk (Apr. 22, 2011), http://profootballtalk.nbcsports.com/2011/04/22/to-avoid-concussion-rules-some-players-sandbag-their-baseline-tests/, archived at http://perma.cc/94KW-SK7W. Experts nonetheless insist that the baseline examination cannot be cheated. See also Bill Pennington, Flubbing a Baseline Test on Purpose Is Often Futile, N.Y. Times, May 5, 2013, http://www.nytimes.com/2013/05/06/sports/sandbagging-first-concussion-test-probably-wont-help-later.html, archived at http://perma.cc/K8EF-G4F8.

12 Michael David Smith, Jamaal Charles: I Didn't Want To Go Through The Concussion Protocol, ProFootballTalk (Oct. 22, 2014), http://profootballtalk.nbcsports.com/2014/10/22/jamaal-charles-i-didnt-want-to-go-through-the-concussion-protocol/, archived at http://perma.cc/6BA2-RUPJ.

13 Michael David Smith, LaAdrian Waddle: Don't Blame Lions for Me Playing with a Concussion, ProFootballTalk (Oct. 25, 2014), http://profootballtalk.nbcsports.com/2014/10/25/laadrian-waddle-dont-blame-lions-for-me-playing-with-a-concussion/ archived at http://perma.cc/RMX9-VPXE.

14 See Transcript from NFLPA Super Bowl XLIX Press Conference, NFL Players Ass'n, https://www.nfl.com/news/all-news/transcript-from-nflpa-super-bowl-xlix-press-conference (last visited Aug. 7, 2015), archived at http://perma.cc/5UJN-AGRQ.

15 CBA, Art. 44, § 5. The list requires "at least two orthopedic physicians and two neuropsychologists in each city in which a club is located." Id.

16 Id.

17 This information was provided by the NFLPA.

18 Id.

19 See Thierfelder v. Wolfert, 52 A.3d 1251, 1264 (Pa. 2012) (discussing elements of a medical malpractice claim); Hamilton v. Wilson, 249 S.W.3d 425, 426 (Tex. 2008) (same); Sullivan v. Edward Hosp., 806 N.E.2d 645, 653 (Ill. 2004) (same).

20 Id.

21 See Benjamin Grossberg, Uniformity, Federalism, and Tort Reform: The Erie Implications of Medical Malpractice Certificate of Merit Statutes, 159 U. Pa. L. Rev. 217 (2010) (identifying 25 states with statutes that require certificates of merit by another doctor for a medical malpractice claim).

22 See 29 U.S.C. § 185.

23 Allis-Chambers Corp. v. Lueck, 471 U.S. 202, 213, 200 (1985).

24 See, e.g., Givens v. Tennessee Football, Inc., 684 F. Supp. 2d 985 (M.D. Tenn. 2010) (player's tort claims against club arising out of medical treatment preempted); Williams v. Nat'l Football League, 582 F.3d 863 (8th Cir. 2009) (players' tort claims arising out of drug test preempted).

25 See 2011 CBA, Art. 43, § 1.

26 See 2011 CBA, Art. 43, § 6 (discussing constitution of Arbitration Panel); 2011 CBA, Art. 43 § 8 (discussing Arbitrator's authority, including to grant a "money award").

27 CBA, Art. 43, § 2.

28 The Non-Injury Grievance arbitrator has the authority to determine whether a complaint against a doctor fit within his or her jurisdiction under Article 43. See 2011 CBA, Art. 43, § 1 (discussing scope of Non-Injury Grievance arbitrator's jurisdiction).

29 Dyer v. Trachtman, 470 Mich. 45, 51–54 (Mich. 2004) (collecting cases); Greenberg v. Perkins, 845 P.2d 530, 535 (Colo. 1993) ("physician owes a duty of care to a nonpatient examinee to conduct the examination in a manner not to cause harm to the person being examined") (internal quotations and citations removed).

Chapter 6

Personal Doctors

In addition to being seen by club doctors or obtaining a second opinion in response to a club doctor, players might have a personal doctor they see as a primary care physician or for other specific ailments. Personal doctors have no relationship with the NFL or NFL clubs and thus their only concern should be for the player's health. Consequently, to the extent players choose to utilize the services of their own doctor (maybe even for a second opinion), these doctors too are an important stakeholder in ensuring and promoting player health.

Additionally, in discussing personal doctors, we recognize of course that different doctors have different specialties. Thus, when discussing personal doctors in this chapter, we expect and intend players will seek out the appropriate specialist for their ailment. We intend this chapter to cover all of the various specialists (e.g., internists, orthopedists, neurologists) with whom players may consult.

Finally, while in other chapters we provided the stakeholder an opportunity to review a draft of the relevant chapter(s) prior to publication, because there is no well-defined representative for personal doctors, no one reviewed this chapter on behalf of personal doctors prior to publication.

A Background

Players' use of personal doctors is not generally discussed by the CBA. Personal doctors are not provided any rights under the 2011 CBA other than the right to, "upon presentation to the Club physician of an authorization signed by the player, inspect the player's medical and trainers' records in consultation with the Club physician or have copies of such medical and trainers' records forwarded to such player's personal physician."[1]

B Current Legal Obligations[a]

While controversy exists about the role of club doctors, the responsibilities of a player's personal doctor are clear. A player's personal doctor's first and only loyalty is to the player and the doctor is thus bound to provide care within an acceptable standard of care, as discussed in Chapter 2: Club Doctors, Section (C)(1)(a).

C Current Ethical Codes

As discussed in Chapter 2: Club Doctors, Section (C)(1)(b), doctors treating players, such as personal doctors, are obligated by the AMA Code and the FIMS Code of Ethics to provide care that is in the player-patient's best interests.

D Current Practices

Personal doctors might be the least utilized of the doctors discussed in this Report. Players principally rely on club doctors and second opinion doctors for their care. In our discussions with players, including the interviews discussed herein, several indicated that the frequent moves from city to city, the convenience of receiving healthcare at the club facility, and their busy schedules made finding and

seeing a personal doctor problematic.[b] In addition, some players also do like and prefer the care they receive from club doctors. In some circumstances, a second opinion doctor might also be or become the player's personal doctor. Current players discussed players' non-use of personal doctors:[c]

- **Current Player 4:** *"I do not have a primary care physician, no. I think most players are the same way."*

- **Current Player 5:** *"I only use doctors that are in the system . . . . I know other players will have other doctors that they used in college or whatever. But as far as routine check-ups, not much. I don't know if I've ever heard of that."*

- **Current Player 8:** *"I wouldn't think the majority of guys have a primary care physician."*

- **Current Player 10:** *"I don't think there's a whole lot of players that have their own personal doctors in whatever city they're in."*

- **Former Player 3:** *"I had never gone to the doctor. If I ever had to, I would just use our team's physician."*

In any event, there are circumstances in which players see their own personal doctors outside of the healthcare structure dictated by the CBA, particularly in the offseason.[d] If a player sees a personal doctor, the cost of that visit would likely be covered by the player's health insurance policy provided through the club, as described in Appendix C: Summary of Collectively Bargained Health-Related Programs and Benefits.

If a player's personal doctor discovers an injury, the player is required to report it to the club. The 2011 CBA permits clubs to fine players up to $1,770 if the player does not "promptly report" an injury to the club doctor or athletic trainer.[2] Nevertheless, we know that players routinely withhold injuries and medical conditions from the club medical staff for a variety of reasons, including protecting their spot on the roster and to not be viewed by the club in a negative

---

b   For comparison's sake, however, it is important to note that young men generally utilize primary care physicians less frequently than the general population. According to the United States Centers for Disease Control and Prevention, only 51.7 percent of males aged 18–44 visited a primary care physician in 2010. National Center for Health Statistics, *Health, United States, 2013: With Special Feature on Prescription Drugs*, 285 (2014), http://www.cdc.gov/nchs/data/hus/hus13.pdf, *archived at* https://perma.cc/5YX6-H7CL?type=pdf.

c   We reiterate that our interviews were intended to be informational but not representative of all players' views and should be read with that limitation in mind.

d   Current Player 3: "After the season, I think if guys have injuries, they can go [see their own doctors]. I know I've been in a situation where I've done it, and it's worked out great for me. I will say a lot of guys, when the season is over with, they get back to where they are from and they go back to the doctor they've been with a long time just to check some things out[.]"

---

a   The legal obligations described herein are not an exhaustive list but are those we believe are most relevant to player health.

light (*see* Chapter 1: Players, Recommendation 1:1-H, Chapter 3: Athletic Trainers, Section D: Current Practices).[e] Considering the perceived downsides of disclosing every injury, a $1,770 fine seems trivial and is unlikely to influence players' injury reporting behavior.

Players are also obligated to disclose their medical conditions in certain situations by their contract. The Standard NFL Player Contract obligates players to undergo a physical examination by the club doctor as a condition of the contract during which a player must "make full and complete disclosure of any physical or mental condition known to him which might impair his performance . . . and to respond fully and in good faith when questioned by the Club physician about such condition."[3] If the player does not advise the club doctor about a condition diagnosed by his personal doctor during the course of a club physical, the player might be in violation of his contract. Violating this provision carries much more serious consequences than failing to report an injury as described above. If a player fails to disclose all medical conditions during a club physical, the club may terminate the contract.[4] For an example of a club's attempts to void a player's contract under such circumstances, see Chapter 1: Players, Section D, Enforcement of Legal and Ethical Obligations.

E Enforcement of Legal and Ethical Obligations[f]

As is discussed in more depth in Chapter 2: Club Doctors, Section (C)(1)(a) and in greater depth in many other places,[5] personal doctors have the same obligations to players as any other doctor to any other patient. In brief, a doctor is obligated to provide care to his or her patients within an acceptable standard of care in the medical community or potentially be subject to a medical malpractice claim.[6] Generally, the elements of a medical malpractice claim are: (1) a standard of care owed by the doctor to the plaintiff; (2) a breach of that standard of care by the doctor; and (3) the breach was the proximate cause of the plaintiff's injury.[7]

Many states require a doctor with the same board certification or similar expertise as the doctor against whom the claim is brought to opine as to the appropriate standard of care.[8] Thus, in the event a player's personal doctor were sued for medical malpractice, the claim likely could not proceed without a similarly qualified doctor—whether it be an orthopedist, neurologist, or a doctor specializing in sports medicine—opining that the doctor deviated from the standard of care.

The CBA does not provide players with any grievance or arbitration mechanism by which players could pursue claims against their own doctors. Players may choose to see doctors on their own but the CBA does not in any way dictate that doctor's obligations to the player.

---

e   Peer reviewer and doctor for college sports teams Cindy Chang informed us that she has seen NFL players return to their college medical staff for treatment so that the care would not be known by the club. Cindy Chang, Peer Review Response (Dec. 28, 2015).

f   Appendix K is a summary of players' options to enforce legal and ethical obligations against the stakeholders discussed in this Report. In addition, for rights articulated under either the CBA or other NFL policy, the NFLPA and the NFL can also seek to enforce them on players' behalves.

F | Recommendations Concerning Personal Doctors

There is reason to believe that personal doctors are underutilized by current players. While personal doctors might not supply care as regularly as club doctors, they can be an important and trusted source of medical advice and guidance provided solely in the player's interest. While our recommendations below are principally targeted at other stakeholders, they concern the use of personal doctors and thus we include them here. Additionally, the use of personal doctors and our related recommendations would likely be less necessary if our recommendations concerning club doctors were implemented (*see* Chapter 2: Club Doctors, Section H: Recommendations).

Goal 1: To help players become proactive guardians of their own health.

Principles Advanced: Respect; Health Primacy; and, Empowered Autonomy.

Recommendation 6:1-A: The NFLPA and clubs should take steps to facilitate players' usage of personal doctors.

As discussed above, personal doctors can provide an important source of medical care and advice focused solely on the player. In particular, as is discussed below, personal doctors can provide an important perspective to players considering their long-term health and retirement.[g] However, players we interviewed indicated that logistical challenges made seeing personal doctors difficult. The NFLPA and clubs should seek to bridge that gap perhaps by generating lists of doctors for players to consider.[h] It might be even better to engage a third-party care navigation service to assist the players to avoid any appearance of conflict of interest. Another approach would be for club staff to remind players about the importance of having a personal doctor, or to confirm annually that all players who wish to have such a relationship have in fact identified a personal doctor with which they are happy. These services are particularly important for those players who have recently moved to a new city and such players should thus be given particular consideration. Players should also be given special attention when they leave the NFL to ensure smooth transition to a new medical care team.

Recommendation 6:1-B: Players should receive a physical from their own doctor as soon as possible after each season.

At the conclusion of each season, players receive a physical from the club doctor, which will list any conditions the player has at that time. While the club doctor may provide outgoing and ongoing medical advice to the player, the player should check those diagnoses and prognoses against those of an independent doctor. Additionally, given the physical and mental tolls of an NFL season, it would be wise for players to annually review their overall health with their own doctor to inform their decision-making about that offseason as well as the future of their career, including whether to retire. This physical can also be used to establish baseline measures of health for players upon retirement and to screen players for the range of medical issues for which young men should seek regular medical consultation. Moreover, having a healthcare provider familiar with their health, injury history, habits, etc., will help ensure players can make a more seamless transition into post-play health and healthcare.

A personal physical can also provide important legal and financial protections to players. In the event a club terminates a player's contract during the offseason, the club is generally under no obligation to pay the player any additional money unless

---

g   Former Player 2 thought players should have physicals done "probably three or maybe even four [times] per year."
h   Similarly, the NFLPA does generate a list of second opinion doctors.

the player was injured.[9] The club's season-end physical might describe the player as healthy. However, unless the player obtains a physical that disagrees with the club's findings around the same time as the club's season-end physical, it will be difficult for the player to dispute the club's assertion that he was healthy at the time his contract was terminated. The player's personal doctor, via a season-end physical, might provide a medical opinion that supports the player's position.

Endnotes

1   CBA, Art. 40, § 2(a).

2   CBA, Art. 42, § 1(a)(iii).

3   CBA, App. A, § 8.

4   *Id.*

5   *See, e.g.,* Barry R. Furrow et al., Health Law Ch. 6 (2d ed. 2000) (discussing doctors' obligations to patients); Mark A. Hall et al., Medical Liability and Treatment Relationships (2d ed. 2008) (same).

6   *See* Thierfelder v. Wolfert, 52 A.3d 1251, 1264 (Pa. 2012) (discussing elements of a medical malpractice claim); Hamilton v. Wilson, 249 S.W.3d 425, 426 (Tex. 2008) (same); Sullivan v. Edward Hosp., 806 N.E.2d 645, 653 (Ill. 2004) (same).

7   *Id.*

8   *See* Benjamin Grossberg, *Uniformity, Federalism, and Tort Reform: The Erie Implications of Medical Malpractice Certificate of Merit Statutes,* 159 U. Pa. L. Rev. 217 (2010) (identifying 25 states with statutes that require certificates of merit by another doctor for a medical malpractice claim).

9   *See* 2011 CBA, Art. 44 (discussing the Injury Grievance process).

Part 3: **The NFL, NFLPA, and NFL Clubs**

NFL

NFLPA

NFL
Clubs

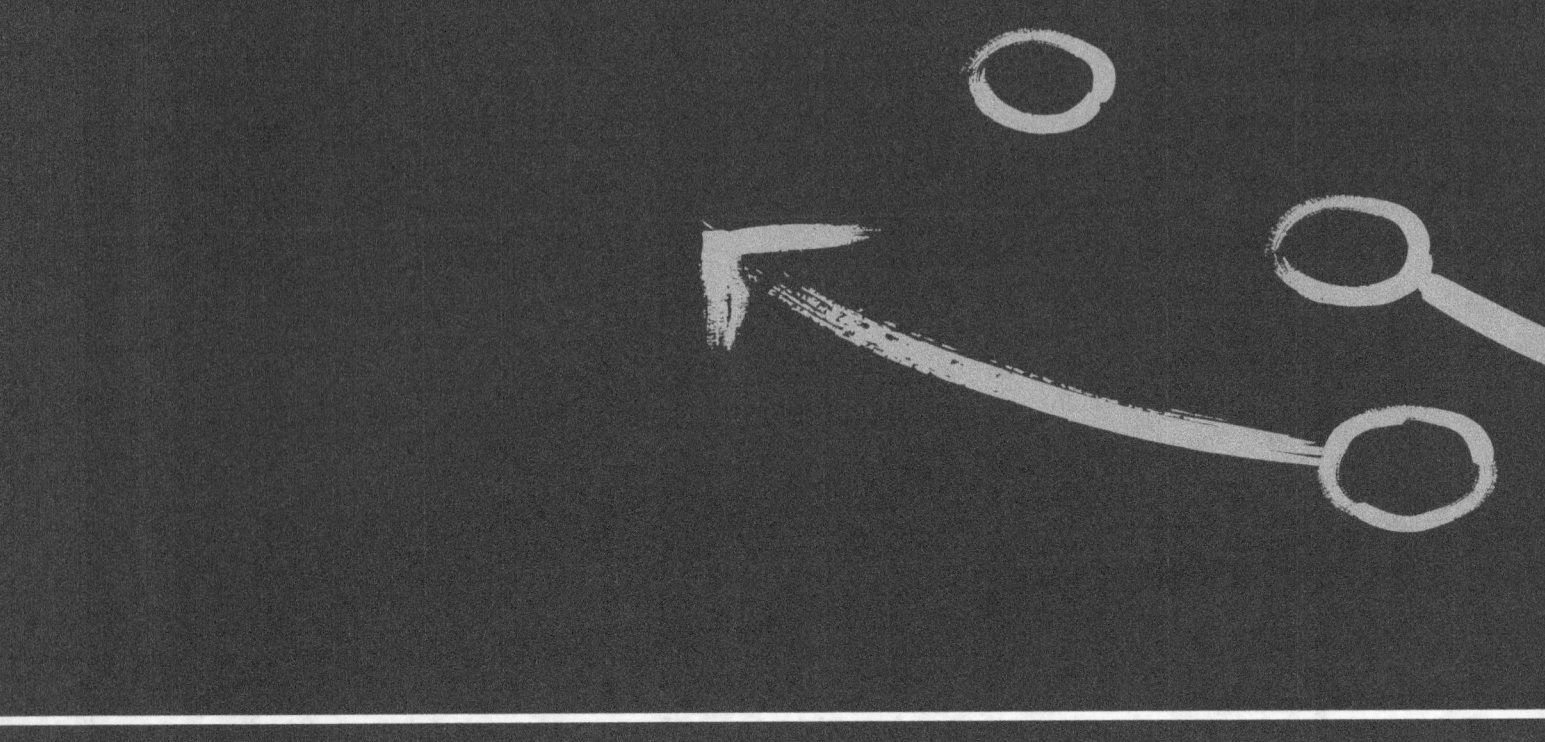

Part 3 discusses those stakeholders with the greatest ability to positively affect NFL player health: the NFL; the NFLPA; and, NFL clubs.

The NFL has been the world's premier professional football league since its inception in 1920. Through its 32 member clubs the NFL largely makes the rules of professional football, both on and off the field.

In the management/labor dyad, the counterbalance to the NFL is the NFLPA, the labor union that represents current players. The players elect the NFLPA's leadership, and, as is discussed in more detail below, the association's principal purpose is to protect and advance current player interests.

Together, the NFL and NFLPA negotiate the terms and conditions of NFL player employment in the form of the collective bargaining agreement (CBA). Thus, both organizations have a crucial role to play in protecting and promoting player health. There has been improvement on player health matters in recent years, which should

be commended. Nevertheless, there are still changes to be made, as we discuss below. Because the roles of the NFL and NFLPA are so intertwined, it is best to address them collectively.

We also include NFL clubs in this part of the Report. As will be further explained below, the NFL generally acts according to the desires and interests of the clubs (and their owners) and the clubs' actions concerning player health are generally directed by the CBA agreed to by the NFL and NFLPA. Thus, the NFL and its member clubs are best considered, and analyzed, in the same part of this Report.

Chapter 7

The NFL and NFLPA

The NFL and NFLPA are clearly lead stakeholders in protecting and promoting player health. The parties nonetheless have a long and complicated history on the issue and with each other. The most straightforward way to implement many of the changes we recommend to protect and promote player health will be to include them in the next CBA between the parties. That said, whenever change is possible outside of the CBA negotiating process, it should not wait — the sooner, the better. Moreover, although the CBA will often be the most appropriate mechanism for implementing our recommendations, we do not want to be understood as suggesting that player health should be treated like just another issue for collective bargaining, subject to usual labor-management dynamics. This is to say that as an ethical matter, players should not be expected to make concessions in other domains in order to achieve gains in the health domain. To the contrary, we believe firmly the opposite: player health should be a joint priority, and not be up for negotiation.

We begin with a brief historical overview of the activities of the NFL and NFLPA on player health since 1960. As we stressed in the Introduction to this Report, this historical information is being provided as background and context for understanding the current state of play and paths forward. Our goal is not to judge the historical record, but rather to focus on forward-looking recommendations for positive change.

(A) Background on the NFL

The NFL is an unincorporated association of 32 member clubs.[1] The NFL was historically a non-profit association,[2] but chose to give up that status in 2015.[3] Each member club is a separate and distinct legal entity,[4] with its own legal obligations as discussed in Chapter 8: NFL Clubs. However, the NFL also serves as a centralized body for obligations and undertakings shared among the member clubs.[5] This chapter focuses on the NFL as an entity, rather than on the individual clubs.

To lead the NFL, the NFL's Constitution and Bylaws dictate that club owners "select and employ a person of unquestioned integrity to serve as Commissioner[.]"[6] The Commissioner is "the principal executive officer of the League and shall have general supervision of its business and affairs."[7] The Commissioner has broad authority to conduct the business of the NFL, including but not limited to: incurring necessary expenses;[8] entering into contracts on behalf of the NFL,[9] including broadcasting agreements;[10] disciplining players, coaches, club employees, clubs, club owners or others working in the NFL for "conduct detrimental to the welfare of the League or professional football"[11]; and, resolving disputes between or among those same groups of individuals working in the NFL.[12]

Before we review the background of the NFLPA, we begin with brief discussions of the role of NFL club owners and the history of League-wide rule changes affecting player health in the NFL.

1) NFL CLUB OWNERS

It is important to understand that when we are talking about the 32 member clubs, it is the men and women who own these clubs who largely dictate their operations, and thus the NFL's operations. For all intents and purposes, when discussing the NFL, it is the 32 club owners being discussed.

The NFL's Constitution and Bylaws require individual persons, and not corporations, to own NFL clubs (holding companies created solely for the purposes of operating the club are permitted).[13] Thus, each NFL club is controlled by, and sometimes becomes synonymous with, its owner.[a]

The power of club owners cannot be understated. The owners are responsible for not only hiring the most important club employees, e.g., general managers and head coaches, but also hiring the NFL Commissioner and dictating the Commissioner's duties, obligations, and scope of authority.[14] All of the owners meet multiple times a year, when they discuss and then vote on the most important issues concerning the NFL at that time.[15] For example, during the 2015 owners' meetings, the owners discussed the possibility of a club moving to Los Angeles (which happened in 2016) and possible playoff expansion, and voted to end the NFL's "blackout" policy that required television broadcasts to be blacked out in a club's home market if attendance for that day's game was below 85-percent capacity.[16]

Owners also play a critical role in determining the culture of their club and the pressures placed on the players. The owner's attitude toward player health and safety will often be a factor in the way that the club, and ultimately the NFL, looks at the issue.[17] Unsurprisingly, there has been significant variation in how owners address and perceive player health.

On one extreme, a particularly unflattering portrait of former Oakland and Los Angeles Raiders owner Al Davis was painted in the 1994 book by former Raiders doctor Rob Huizenga, entitled *"You're Okay, It's Just a Bruise": A Doctor's Sideline Secrets About Pro Football's Most Outrageous Team*. Huizenga described Davis as placing winning above all else, including player health, and routinely pressuring players and the doctors to do anything to get a player back on the field, regardless of the risks.[18] From his perspective, Davis reportedly believed the book to be "ludicrous and untrue."[19] Huizenga's anecdotes are several decades old, but there is reason to believe that at least some owners still impose substantial pressure on injured players.

---

a   For example, George Halas founded the organization now known as the Chicago Bears in 1920, and today that Club is controlled by George McCaskey, Halas' grandson. Similarly, Tim Mara founded the New York Giants in 1925, and today that Club is controlled by his grandson, John Mara. The one notable exception is the Green Bay Packers. The Packers, as a vestige from the league's earliest days, are community-owned by individual shareholders, i.e., fans. See Birth of a Team and a Legend, Packers.com, http://www.packers.com/history/birth-of-a-team-and-a-legend.html (last visited Aug. 7, 2015), archived at http://perma.cc/DQ2F-U2GJ. Entering the 2015 season, there were 5,011,558 shares of stock owned by 360,760 stockholders. The Packers operate through Green Bay Packers, Inc., a Wisconsin corporation governed by a seven-member executive committee, elected from a board of directors. Executive Committee and Board of Directors, Packers, http://www.packers.com/team/executive-committee.html (last visited Aug. 7, 2015), archived at http://perma.cc/KW7D-MQS2.

For example, during the 2014 season, Cowboys quarterback Tony Romo suffered a back injury on Monday Night Football on October 27, after having had back surgery in the prior offseason. Two days later, Cowboys' owner Jerry Jones, who has no medical training, said on a radio station that the only thing that would prevent Romo from playing in the next week's game was "pain tolerance." Romo had already received a pain-killing injection in an effort to return to the October 27 game.[20]

Conversely, other owners have taken a different approach. For example, the San Francisco 49ers are owned by Dr. John York, a former cancer pathologist,[21] and Chairman of the NFL's Health and Safety Advisory Committee. During the 2015 offseason, several 49ers players retired due to health concerns. York generally responded with understanding and supportive statements, and has discussed the need for a culture change concerning player health.[22]

As will be shown below, the CBA serves as an important constraint on the potential variations in club owners' approaches toward player health. The CBA creates rules concerning player health, which then narrow the permissible practices by clubs.

2) PLAYING RULES CHANGES

It is frequently remarked that the NFL has significantly added or changed rules concerning and promoting player health and safety in recent years. This is certainly true, but it is important to recognize that the NFL has generally added and changed rules concerning player health and safety *throughout* its modern history (after the merger with the American Football League in 1970). Included as Appendix I of this Report is a history of NFL rule changes concerning player health and safety, and below is an illustration of the number of changes over time.

NFL rule changes are proposed by the Competition Committee, which consists of club owners, executives, and coaches.[23] In addition, the NFLPA has the right to appoint two persons to attend meetings of the Competition Committee and one of the appointees can vote on all matters related to the Playing Rules.[24] If the proposed rule change passes in the Competition Committee, the owners then vote on the proposed rule changes at their annual meeting.[25] The Competition Committee also seeks insight from outside experts, including scientists and doctors, concerning proposed rule changes.[26] "If the NFLPA believes that the adoption of a playing rule change would adversely affect player safety," then it can pursue a change through the Joint Committee on Player Safety and Welfare and arbitration.[27] The NFLPA has not brought any such challenges since 2010.[28]

Having discussed some of the key features of the NFL, we now turn to the NFLPA.

Figure 7-A: Health-Related On-The-Field Rule Changes in the NFL

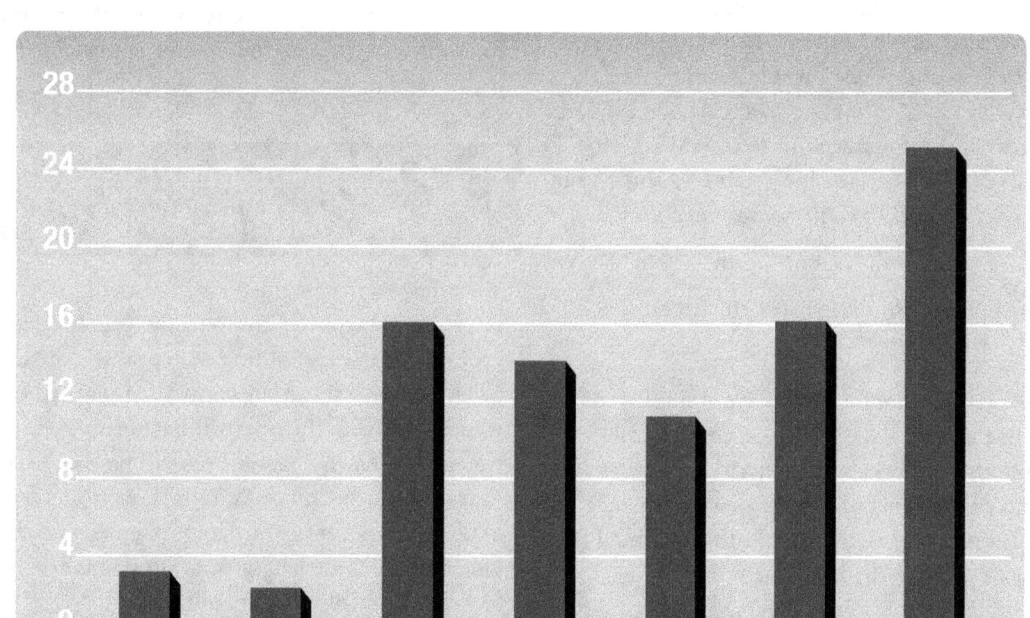

(B) Background on the NFLPA

The NFLPA in its present form is a Virginia nonprofit corporation and a tax exempt labor organization.[29] Pursuant to the National Labor Relations Act, the NFLPA is "the exclusive representative[] of all the employees in [the bargaining] unit for the purposes of collective bargaining in respect to rates of pay, wages, hours of employment, or other conditions of employment."[30]

As will be explained in more detail below, the NFLPA represents all current players, regardless of whether they are members of the union. Also, as will be explained in more detail below, the NFLPA does not represent former players, even though the NFLPA has taken actions concerning former players and might continue to do so in the future. In a lawsuit between former players and the NFLPA (discussed in more detail below), the Honorable Susan Richard Nelson of the United States District Court for the District of Minnesota was adept in describing the relationship and tension between the NFLPA and current players and former players:

> [T]he NFLPA negotiates with the League on behalf of the active players, and the interests of the active players, if not necessarily antagonistic towards the retired players, are not consistent with that of the retired players insofar as the League offers a single compensation pie to the players, such that any slice allocated to the retired players results in a smaller slice for the active players.[31]

The NFLPA, based in Washington, D.C., has a staff of approximately 100 people, led by its Executive Director.[32] The Executive Director is the "principal administrative officer of the NFLPA" and is responsible for the "day-to-day affairs of the NFLPA."[33] In many respects, the NFLPA Executive Director is the counterpoint to the NFL Commissioner. The Executive Director is elected to a three-year term by the NFLPA's Board of Representatives (discussed in more detail below),[34] which can be renewed without limit.

The NFLPA's purpose, according to its Constitution, is as follows:

> to provide professional football players employed by Clubs of the NFL with an organization dedicated to the promotion and advancement of all players and of the sport of professional football; the improvement of economic and other working conditions of players; the betterment and maintenance of relations between players, owners, coaches and staffs; the furnishing of information and the providing of membership services; the

negotiation, execution and administration of collective bargaining agreements; the resolution of player grievances, disputes and arbitrations arising under collective bargaining agreements; the representation of members in connection with common problems; the development of enterprises aimed at developing further benefits for the NFLPA and its members; assistance in providing educational advancement and training for members; encouragement of cultural, civic, legislative, charitable and other activities which further the interest of the NFLPA and its members, directly or indirectly; cooperation with and assistance to other organizations having purposes or objectives in whole or in part similar to those of the NFLPA; and the performance of all other actions consistent with this Constitution and appropriate to implement and fulfill the purposes, rights and responsibilities of the NFLPA.[35]

Each NFL club's players elect a Player Representative and an Alternate Player Representative to represent them in NFLPA matters.[36] The Executive Director, Player Representatives, and the NFLPA President collectively make up the Board of Representatives.[37] In addition, the Board of Representatives elects 10 Player Representatives as Vice Presidents.[38] The Board of Representatives is responsible for voting on matters concerning the NFLPA's business.[39]

The NFLPA President is an NFL player elected to a two-year term by the Board of Representatives,[40] and is the "principal executive officer of the NFLPA" responsible for "supervis[ing] and direct[ing] the business and affairs of the NFLPA."[41] Collectively, the President and the Vice Presidents make up the Executive Officers of the NFLPA, to whom the Executive Director is principally responsible for reporting.[42]

(C) A History of the NFL's and NFLPA's Approaches to Player Health

We briefly describe the history of the NFL's and NFLPA's efforts on player health up to the present day as background for understanding the current state of play. In order to understand the context of player health issues, we also provide the relevant background of labor relations between the parties. As will be shown, for many years, player health does not appear to have been a priority. Our treatment is far from exhaustive, but will provide a reasonable background in which to ground our forward-looking recommendations.

1) PRE-1970

Former Los Angeles Rams general manager Pete Rozelle was named NFL Commissioner in 1960.[43] For much of the 1960s, the NFL was primarily concerned with its business operations. In 1961, the NFL steered the passage of a federal antitrust exemption, the Sports Broadcasting Act, concerning NFL television broadcasts that serves as the basis for approximately two-thirds of the NFL's revenue today (see Chapter 17: The Media). Also in the 1960s, the NFL faced significant competition from the recently formed American Football League (AFL). In 1966, the AFL and NFL agreed to merge operations and play beginning with the 1970 season. Also, beginning with the 1966 season, the NFL and AFL champions played against one another in the Super Bowl.

To counter the NFL, in 1956, players formed a loosely associated NFLPA to pursue their interests.[44] The NFLPA's initial efforts to increase salaries and to require clubs to pay injured players were largely unsuccessful, but did result in the first ever professional football CBA in 1968.[45] The 1968 CBA established the players' Retirement Plan,[46] group medical insurance,[47] workers' compensation benefits,[48] a form of Injury Protection,[b] and the right to have a neutral physician assess and resolve the extent of a player's injury.[49]

2) 1970s

The year 1970 was an important turning point for the NFLPA. In that year, the NFLPA merged with the American Football League Players Association and gained formal union recognition from the National Labor Relations Board (NLRB).[50] The NFLPA and NFL also negotiated a new CBA that year, which for the first time required NFL clubs to provide disability benefits,[51] life insurance,[52] and dental benefits.[53] In 1971, the NFLPA hired labor attorney Ed Garvey, who had assisted in the CBA negotiations, to become the NFLPA's first Executive Director.[54]

The 1970 CBA expired at the end of the 1974 season. The players continued playing without a CBA, except for a 41-day strike during the 1974 preseason and a 3-day strike during the 1975 season.[55] Both strikes failed due to a lack of solidarity among the players.[56]

Finally, the parties agreed to a new CBA in 1977. The 1977 CBA made modest increases in previously agreed-upon benefit and insurance programs, such as retirement, medical, disability, life, and dental. Players had previously gained the right to grieve terminations resulting from injuries as well as Injury Protection (the right to 50 percent of his salary if a player was injured in the prior season and still unable to play). In addition, the 1977 CBA created the Joint Committee on Player Safety and Welfare, established "for the purpose of discussing the player safety and welfare aspects of playing equipment, playing surfaces, stadium facilities, playing rules, player-coach relationships, drug abuse prevention programs and other relevant subjects."[57] The Joint Committee consisted of three club representatives and three NFLPA representatives.[58] However, the CBA was very clear that the Joint Committee would "not have the power to commit or bind either the NFLPA or the [NFL] on any issue."[59] The Joint Committee continues to exist today in substantially the same form.

> Although progress was made on basic medical issues during the 1970s, the principal items of negotiation between the NFL and NFLPA at the time were compensation issues and free agency.

In the NFL context, any progress on player health issues must be viewed through, and come as a result of, the process of collective bargaining. Although progress was made on basic medical issues during the 1970s, the principal items of negotiation between the NFL and NFLPA at the time were compensation issues and free agency. Importantly, the 1977 CBA did not provide NFL players with the right to unrestricted free agency,[c] even though players in Major League Baseball (MLB), the National Basketball Association (NBA), and the National Hockey League (NHL) by then enjoyed that right due to a variety of legal proceedings.[60]

---

b   The 1968 CBA provided that "[p]layers who are removed from the active roster by reason of injury between the beginning of training camp period and the first regular season game and who have not signed new contracts, shall be guaranteed 100% of their salaries as stated on the front side of their contracts for the contract year immediately preceding the year in which they are injured." 1968 CBA, Art. XI, § 5. Under the 2011 CBA, a player who is unable to play due to an injury suffered in the prior season, is entitled to 50 percent of his salary up to a maximum of $1.1 million in the 2015 season. If the player is still unable to play in the second season following the injury, the player is entitled to 30 percent of his salary up to a maximum of $525,000 for the 2015 season. See 2011 CBA, Art. 45.

c   An Unrestricted Free Agent is a player "with four or more Accrued Seasons, who has completed performance of his Player Contract, and who is no longer subject to any exclusive negotiating rights, Right of First Refusal, or Draft Choice Compensation in favor of his Prior Club." 2011 CBA, Art. 1.

3) **1980s**

The players engaged in a 57-day strike during the 1982 preseason, following the expiration of the 1977 CBA.[61] The players began the season without a new CBA, but reached a new one in December 1982.[62] Entering negotiations for the 1982 CBA, the NFLPA sought important changes concerning players' healthcare rights:

> [T]he union wants players to have the right to be treated and examined by a physician of their choice, not the team doctor. Decisions on whether a player is healthy enough to play or when he needs an operation should not be made by a physician whose primary allegiance is to the team's management . . . . 'Team physicians (sic) . . . should be chosen jointly by the players and management and should be subject to firing by either.'[63]

The NFLPA made some progress on these issues in the 1982 CBA. The 1982 CBA required: all clubs to have a board certified orthopedic surgeon as one of its club doctors;[64] the club to pay for the cost of medical services rendered by club doctors;[65] club doctors to advise players about their condition when they have also advised the club;[66] all full-time trainers to be certified by the National Athletic Trainers Association;[67] and, for clubs to pay for education and treatment related to chemical dependence.[68] The 1982 CBA also granted players' certain rights, including: the right to a second medical opinion paid for by the club;[69] the right to choose their own surgeon at the club's expense;[70] and, the right to review their medical records twice per season.[71,d]

The 1982 CBA did not include any right of the players to choose or have input regarding club physicians, nor has any CBA since. Additionally, the NFLPA was again unable to gain free agency as part of the 1982 CBA negotiations.[72]

One of the biggest health issues in the NFL in the early 1980s was illegal drug use.[73] This was an era of escalating and worrisome drug use throughout the country,[74] and the NFL was not immune to the problem.[75] As the 1982 CBA negotiations were taking place, former star defensive end Carl Eller estimated that 20 to 25 percent of players were abusing drugs and/or alcohol.[76] Many players rejected those estimates and refused to permit drug testing.[77] The 1982 CBA ultimately included the first ever drug testing policy,[78]

permitting club physicians, "upon reasonable cause," to direct a player to a treatment facility for drug testing, but also forbidding clubs from randomly conducting drug tests on players.[79] The policy also provided for education and treatment for players.[80] Despite the new policy, drug use continued through the 1980s, as did the NFL's efforts to discipline players who had failed tests.[81]

After the 1982 CBA negotiations, Garvey chose to cede his Executive Director position to then-NFLPA President Gene Upshaw in 1983.[82] Upshaw had been an offensive lineman for the Oakland Raiders from 1967 to 1981.[e]

The expiration of the 1982 CBA in 1987 marked a dramatic and litigious turning point in NFL labor relations.[83] The players went on strike for 23 days during the 1987 season, during which time the NFL used replacement players.[84] Between 1987 and 1993, the NFLPA, NFL players and the NFL engaged in multiple courtroom battles over the NFL system, particularly the share of revenues and players' rights to free agency.[85] The NFLPA dissolved itself as the players' official bargaining representative in 1989 to improve the players' antitrust claims.[f] NFL play nevertheless continued during these years without a CBA.

With no hope of a CBA during these years, there was limited opportunity to address player health issues. The one issue that reverberated for years without much resolution was drug testing. The NFLPA successfully blocked the NFL's attempts to unilaterally impose random drug testing in 1986,[86] before ultimately agreeing to a policy in 1990.[87]

Finally, Rozelle retired as NFL Commissioner in November 1989, amid stalled CBA negotiations and extensive litigation concerning player compensation, and died in 1996 at the age of 70.[88]

---

d   During the 1982 CBA negotiations, the NFL's chief attorney, Jack Donlan, admitted that players were entitled to a doctor-patient relationship with club physicians, but refused to commit that understanding to writing and fought to prevent players from receiving their own medical records. *See* Bart Barnes and Paul Attner, *No Progress in Talks; Secret Meeting Confirmed,* Wash. Post, Oct. 1, 1982, *available at* 1982 WLNR 603101.

e   During his career, Upshaw made the Pro Bowl six times and helped the Raiders win two Super Bowls. Upshaw was elected to the Pro Football Hall of Fame in 1987. *See Hall of Famers – Gene Upshaw,* Pro Football Hall of Fame, http://www.profootballhof .com/hof/member.aspx?PLAYER_ID=220 (last visited Aug. 7, 2015), *archived at* http://perma.cc/EWF2-V3TV.

f   To simplify a complex issue for purposes of this Report, generally speaking, when NFL clubs, as separate and distinct legal entities and competitors, agree on restrictions concerning the labor market for NFL players, *e.g.,* via free agency rules, the Salary Cap, and the NFL Draft, they may be violating Section 1 of the Sherman Antitrust Act's prohibition against unreasonable restraints of trade. *See Radovich v. Nat'l Football League,* 352 U.S. 445 (1957); *Mackey v. Nat'l Football League,* 543 F.2d 606 (8th Cir. 1976); *Smith v. Pro Football, Inc.,* 593 F.2d 1173 (D.C. Cir. 1978); *Jackson v. Nat'l Football League,* 802 F. Supp. 226 (D. Minn. 1992). However, the clubs' restrictions are exempt from antitrust laws under what is known as the non-statutory labor exemption when the clubs negotiate the restrictions with a labor organization as part of the collective bargaining process. *See Brown v. Pro Football, Inc.,* 518 U.S. 231 (1996). But, if the players dissolve the union's authority, *i.e.,* remove the union's authority to negotiate on behalf of the players pursuant to the NLRA, the clubs are no longer in a bargaining relationship with a labor organization and their restrictions are no longer immune from antitrust laws. *See id.; Powell v. Nat'l Football League,* 764 F. Supp. 1351 (D. Minn. 1991). Dissolution is a powerful weapon because the Sherman Antitrust Act provides plaintiffs with treble damages. 15 U.S.C. § 15.

4) 1990s

To replace Rozelle, the NFL hired Paul Tagliabue, its chief outside counsel from the Washington, D.C. law firm of Covington & Burling LLP.[89] Compared to the NFL of 1960—with only 13 clubs, prior to the merger with the AFL, and at the beginning of the television-broadcasting era—the 1989 NFL was a different League entirely. It now included 28 clubs, worth approximately $80 million each,[90] and had television revenues of approximately $1 billion per year.[91]

In 1993, after several legal victories for the players, the NFL and the players settled the outstanding lawsuits as part of constructing a new, comprehensive CBA.[92] The NFLPA also recertified itself as the players' bargaining representative.

The 1993 CBA was groundbreaking and set the framework for every NFL-NFLPA CBA since. The players gained the right to unrestricted free agency for the first time in exchange for a hard Salary Cap. Players could become unrestricted free agents after five years of experience and clubs' payrolls were limited to a range of 62 percent to 64 percent of Defined Gross Revenue,[g] depending on the year.[93] In terms of player health provisions, the 1993 CBA increased benefit amounts (e.g., medical and life insurance, Injury Protection, and disability) but otherwise made no major changes.

A significant study concerning NFL player health was published in 1994. In the late 1980s, concern began to develop that NFL players might have shorter life spans than the general population.[94] In response, the NFLPA commissioned a study by the National Institute for Occupational Safety and Health ("NIOSH").[95] In a 1994 report, NIOSH reported somewhat reassuring results related to the health status of players. Using information from NFL pension fund databases, commercial publications, and death certificates, NIOSH examined all players who played in the NFL for at least five seasons between 1959 and 1988, 3,439 players in total.[96] NIOSH compared the death rates of the NFL players to men of similar age and race in the general population and found that 46 percent fewer NFL players had died as compared to the general population.[97] Based on the general population, NIOSH had expected that 189 NFL players would have died, but, in fact, only 103

had.[98] NIOSH acknowledged that the study contained a "relatively young group of men, only a few of which ha[d] reached the age of 50" and "[r]esearchers therefore [would] not be able to determine their average age of death for several years."[99] NIOSH updated the study's results in 2012, as will be discussed below.

The 1993 CBA was extended in 1996 and 1998, but player health provisions remained largely the same with the exception of a new Player Annuity Program in 1998,[100] discussed in further detail in Appendix C.

> The 1993 CBA was groundbreaking and set the framework for every NFL-NFLPA CBA since.

This extended era of labor peace resulted in some public criticism of the NFLPA. Critics routinely pointed out that NFL players lacked the guaranteed contracts customary to other major professional sports leagues, and surmised that Upshaw was too close with Tagliabue.[101] Upshaw's responded to his critics by highlighting the financial gains the NFLPA had made:

> "What [Commissioner Paul Tagliabue] and I try to do as stewards of the game is to try to ensure that we have stability and growth," Upshaw said. "My job is to make sure we get our fair share. I've told the players and I've told the owners the same thing. The only chance we have of not having labor peace is if either side gets greedy. For the first time the owners realize the enemy is not the union."

> "We've had ugly, nasty clashes" with owners, said Upshaw, who has led the union since 1983 and earns about $2 million a year. "We've had lockouts. We've had strikes. We've done everything everyone else does. We still do. It's just not as public as it might have been at one time. . . . To me, the test is, how much do we get of the revenues we generate? In 1987 we were getting 30 percent of the revenues and the owners were getting 70. Now we're getting two-thirds and they are getting a third. For us to do what we've been able to do has just been unbelievable."[102]

---

g   From 1993 to 2006, Defined Gross Revenue (DGR), was defined as "the aggregate revenues received or to be received on an accrual basis, for or with respect to a League Year during the term of [the CBA], by the NFL and all NFL Clubs (and their designees), from all sources, whether known or unknown, derived from, relating to or arising out of the performance of players in NFL football games," with a few specific exceptions. 1993 CBA, Art. XXIV, § 1(a)(i). In the 2006 CBA, the term was changed to Total Revenue (TR), and changed again to All Revenue ("AR") in the 2011 CBA.

While some continued to focus on the financial issues in the game, by the mid-1990s, concussions in the NFL had started to become an issue of concern to players and were gaining attention in the media.[103] The most comprehensive source for understanding the evolution of this issue in the NFL is the 2013 book *League of Denial: The NFL, Concussions and the Battle for Truth*, by ESPN writers Mark Fainaru-Wada and Steve Fainaru.[104] The NFL has never publicly disagreed with any of the factual assertions in *League of Denial*, and instead touted its past and present initiatives designed to address head injuries in sports.[105]

The media began to pay more attention to concussions around 1994.[106] Tagliabue called the concussion issue a "pack journalism issue" and insisted that concussions occurred only once every three or four games.[h] Nevertheless, by the end of year, the NFL established the Mild Traumatic Brain Injury Committee (MTBI Committee) to study concussions.[107]

> Tagliabue called the concussion issue a "pack journalism issue" and insisted that concussions occurred only once every three or four games.

The creation, constitution, and work product of the MTBI Committee would become extremely controversial. Tagliabue personally selected New York Jets Club doctor Elliot Pellman as Chairman of the Committee.[108] Although a neurologist would have seemed like the logical choice, Pellman is a rheumatologist,[109] specializing in the treatment of arthritis, and was later found to have exaggerated his resume.[110] Years later, Tagliabue insisted that he chose Pellman based on his experience in sports medicine and his recent involvement with Jets wide receiver Al Toon's concussion-related retirement.[111] Additionally, beginning in 1997, Pellman was one of Tagliabue's personal doctors, a relationship that would continue until 2006.[112]

Beyond just Pellman, the MTBI Committee seemed to many to lack appropriate expertise and independence. It consisted of several club doctors, two club athletic trainers, a consulting engineer, a club equipment manager, neurologist

Ira Casson (who had studied boxers), and Hank Feuer, an Indianapolis neurosurgeon who worked with the Indianapolis Colts.[113] The MTBI Committee did not include any NFLPA or player representation.[i] The MTBI Committee's initial composition would later be described as "comical" and "bizarre" by Kevin Guskiewicz,[114] a former athletic trainer and sports medicine academic who pioneered some of the early research into sports and concussions, and who, in 2010, joined the NFL's MTBI Committee, when it was renamed the Head, Neck and Spine Committee.[115]

5) 2000s

The CBA was extended again in 2002 and 2006. Again, player health provisions remained largely the same with the addition of a Tuition Assistance Plan in 2002,[116] the redefinition of "disability" to be in line with the American Medical Association's Guides to the Evaluation of Permanent Impairment,[j] a reduction in off-season workout programs from 16 weeks to 14 weeks;[117] and, the right of the NFLPA to commence an investigation before the Joint Committee on Player Safety and Welfare.[k] However, as is discussed in more detail below, there are important questions about the effectiveness of the Joint Committee.

In October 2003, the MTBI Committee published its first piece of work, after having gathered data with the assistance of club doctors.[118] Nevertheless, the NFL made some

---

h   Mark Fainaru-Wada & Steve Fainaru, League of Denial: The NFL, Concussions and the Battle for Truth 74 (2013). According to the NFL's Injury Surveillance System, players suffered a mean of 158.9 concussions during regular season games per season between 2009 and 2015, a rate of about .62 concussions per game. See Chapter 1: Players, Table 1-F.

i   Reports have indicated that the NFLPA played some role in the MTBI Committee, but that role is unclear. See Mike Florio, League of Denial fails to tell the whole story on concussions, ProFootballTalk (Oct. 9, 2013 9:48 PM), http://profootballtalk.nbcsports.com/2013/10/09/league-of-denial-fails-to-tell-the-whole-story-on-concussions/, archived at http://perma.cc/8LHU-PNNL; Mike Florio, NFLPA finally sued for concussions, ProFootballTalk (July 18, 2014 3:01 PM), http://profootballtalk.nbcsports.com/2014/07/18/nflpa-finally-sued-for-concussions/, archived at http://perma.cc/T35H-YDHP. Indeed, when former players sued the NFLPA concerning concussions in 2014, discussed infra, they alleged the NFLPA was involved in some way with the MTBI Committee, but provided no details of the involvement. See Class Action Complaint, Ballard v. Nat'l Football League Players Ass'n, ¶¶ 33, 56–58, 69, 82, 128, 159–60 (E.D.Mo. 2014) (No. 14-cv-01267). Attorneys for the plaintiffs in the Ballard case did not respond to an email requesting further information concerning the possible link between the NFLPA and the MTBI Committee.

j   2002 CBA, Art. XLVII, § 6. The American Medical Association's Guides to the Evaluation of Permanent Impair instructed that a permanent disability occurs where the condition: "(1) results in a 50% or greater loss of speech or sight; or (2) results in a 55% or greater loss of hearing; or (3) is the primary or contributory cause of the surgical removal or major functional impairment of a vital organ or part of the central nervous system; or (4) for orthopedic impairments . . . is (a) a 55% or greater loss of the use of the entire lower extremity; or (b) a 30% or greater loss of use of the entire upper extremity; or (c) an impairment to the spine that results in a 29% or greater whole body impairment." Id. The NFL changed the definition again in the 2011 CBA. See 2012 Bert Bell/Pete Rozelle NFL Player Retirement Plan, § 5.2 (a player "will be deemed to be totally and permanently disabled if the Retirement Board or the Disability Initial Claims Committee finds (1) that he has become totally disabled to the extent that he is substantially prevented from or substantially unable to engage in any occupation or employment for remuneration or profit, but expressly excluding any disability suffered while in the military service of any country, and (2) that such condition is permanent.")

k   2002 CBA, Art. XIII, § 1. In 2012, the NFLPA commenced the first and only Joint Committee investigation. The nature and results of that investigation are confidential per an agreement between the NFL and NFLPA. This information was provided by the NFLPA.

progress concerning concussions prior to that point. In the early 1990s, Mark Lovell—a Pittsburgh Steelers Club doctor and an original member of the MTBI Committee—had developed a neuropsychological testing program designed to diagnose players with concussion symptoms.[119] With the NFL's strong recommendation, by the end of 2001, all but three clubs (Minnesota Vikings, Carolina Panthers, and Dallas Cowboys) were using some form of Lovell's test.[120]

The MTBI Commitee's first two papers were well received by sports medicine doctors.[121] They focused on the biomechanics of NFL helmet collisions, specifically where concussive blows were actually delivered.[122] The papers were published in *Neurosurgery*,[123] the official journal of the Congress of Neurological Consultants.[124] The editor-in-chief of *Neurosurgery* was Michael Apuzzo, a professor of neurology at the University of Southern California and an NFL consultant.[125]

In total, between 2003 and 2009, the MTBI Committee published 16 articles in *Neurosurgery*.[126] By and large, the MTBI Committee's research claimed that concussion rates in the NFL were extremely low, that the number of concussions suffered by a player bears no relation to future injuries, and, that there is no link between football and brain damage.[127] The MTBI Committee's research often cited the fact that players returned to play very quickly (92 percent within seven days) after suffering a concussion as proof that concussions were not a major concern.[128] Importantly, the MTBI Committee assumed that the club doctors would not have cleared players to return to play unless they were healthy enough to do so, and thus that all of the players who returned to play after having suffered a concussion were healthy.[129]

The last 14 papers from the MTBI Committee were repeatedly and strongly criticized by the scientific community. The principal peer reviewers were Guskiewicz, Julian Bailes, a neurosurgeon who worked with the Pittsburgh Steelers, and Robert Cantu, a Boston University neurosurgeon. Cantu was also the editor of *Neurosurgery*'s sports section and responsible for the review of the MTBI Committee's publications.[130] Despite Guskiewicz', Bailes', and Cantu's criticisms and insistence that the MTBI Committee's work not be published, Apuzzo reportedly ignored standard peer-reviewed publication guidelines and published the work anyway, permitting the reviewers an opportunity to append their criticisms.[131] The criticisms generally focused on the MTBI Committee's failure to recognize that concussions were often unreported or undiagnosed and that players routinely returned to play before they were healthy.[132] Those critical of the work believed the MTBI Committee was essentially creating data designed to protect and serve the interests of the NFL.[133]

In 2005, the MTBI Committee's work came under increased scrutiny when *Neurosurgery* published an article authored by Bennet Omalu, a forensic pathologist in Pittsburgh.[134] Omalu happened to have been responsible for performing the autopsy on deceased Pittsburgh Steelers Hall of Fame center Mike Webster after Webster's death in 2002.[135] Omalu examined Webster's brain and, with the assistance of colleagues, diagnosed the brain with what Omalu labeled chronic traumatic encephalopathy ("CTE"),[I] a form of brain damage.[136] Omalu's paper claimed Webster's brain damage had been caused by "repetitive concussive brain injury" from playing football.[137]

Pellman, Casson and Dr. David C. Viano, another member of the MTBI Committee, unsuccessfully requested that Omalu's paper be retracted.[138] The doctors insisted that there was no evidence that football caused brain damage.[139]

The year after Omalu's article, the NFL and NFLPA agreed to a new CBA. The 2006 CBA made some changes concerning player health, including a Health Reimbursement Account,[140] and the "88 Benefit" to compensate retired players suffering from dementia.[141] These and other benefit programs are discussed in further detail in Appendix C. After completing negotiations of the 2006 CBA, Tagliabue announced in March 2006 that he would retire before the 2006 season.[142] The owners selected Roger Goodell, the current NFL Commissioner, to replace him.[143]

Attention to the issue of concussions continued to grow in Goodell's first year on the job, as additional deceased players were diagnosed with CTE.[144] The NFL, through Pellman and Casson, continued to deny there was any connection between brain damage and related conditions (such as depression, dementia, or Alzheimer's disease) and football.[145] Despite the denials, the board responsible for overseeing the NFL's Retirement Plan had, on several occasions, granted disability benefits to NFL players for brain damage.[146]

To assist Goodell in understanding the issues, in June 2007, the NFL held a summit of all club doctors, athletic trainers, the MTBI Committee, and those who had disagreed with the MTBI Committee's work for a variety of presentations on concussion issues.[147] The MTBI Committee members and their dissenters presented their work amid sharp disagreement.[148] Guskiewicz has said the summit was "the turning point" in the NFL's longstanding denial of the relationship between brain injuries and football,[149] and that

---

I   For a longer discussion on the issues surrounding CTE, see the Introduction.

it led Goodell and NFL General Counsel Jeff Pash to recognize the seriousness of the problem at hand.[150] Indeed, at the conclusion of the summit, Pash encouraged Guskiewicz to continue to challenge the MTBI Committee's work.[151]

The NFLPA was also facing scrutiny concerning player health issues, amid increasing stories of retired NFL players suffering from debilitating injuries and conditions.[152] Despite his own playing career, Upshaw—still NFLPA Executive Director at the time—had developed a contentious relationship with other retired players. For example, in response to criticism from retired players that the CBAs did not provide sufficient benefits to retired players, Upshaw responded: "The bottom line is I don't work for them. They don't hire me and they can't fire me. They can complain about me all day long. They can have their opinion. But the active players have the vote."[153] Additionally, according to former Seattle Seahawks club doctor Pierce Scranton and former President of the NFL Physician Society (NFLPS), the NFLPS invited Upshaw to its meetings to discuss player health but Upshaw declined to meet with or engage the NFLPS.[154]

Despite the NFL's 2007 concussion summit, the MTBI Committee continued its work and Goodell's attention shifted toward CBA negotiations. In May 2008, NFL clubs unanimously voted to opt out of the 2006 CBA, accelerating the CBA's expiration date from March 2013 to March 2011. The clubs' decision to opt out centered on their desire to receive a share of revenues beyond the approximately 50 percent to which they were entitled pursuant to the 2006 CBA.[155]

Any chance of jump starting CBA negotiations was halted when Upshaw died unexpectedly on August 21, 2008 after a brief battle with pancreatic cancer,[156] only three months after the clubs' decision to opt out of the 2006 CBA.[157] On March 16, 2009, the NFLPA elected Washington, D.C.-based litigation attorney DeMaurice Smith as its new Executive Director.[158]

As Smith began his new position, it became increasingly clear that player health issues would be a major component of the new CBA. Indeed, on October 28, 2009, the House Judiciary Committee held a hearing on football player head injuries at which both Smith and Goodell testified.[159] At that hearing, Goodell declared that in his three years as Commissioner, he had spent more time devoted to player health issues, particularly concerning retired players, than any other issue.[160] Goodell testified that the NFL had routinely increased benefit amounts, expanded benefit programs as part of collective bargaining, and had recently streamlined the benefits process for former players.[161]

Goodell, in a prepared statement, emphasized the NFL's commitment to additional research and education concerning brain injuries.[162] Moreover, he stressed that the NFL's newest guidelines concerning players suspected of having suffered a concussion returning to play:

> All return-to-play decisions are made by doctors and doctors only. The decision to return to the game is not made by coaches. Not by players. Not by teammates. If a player suffers a concussion and loses consciousness, he cannot return to the same game under any circumstances. That was not the rule as recently as 2006. Moreover, our doctors have developed guidelines that we believe are consistent with best medical practice. A player may not return to a game or practice unless he is fully asymptomatic both at rest and after exertion.[163]

Smith's prepared testimony at the same hearing emphasized his intention to focus on player health issues while also acknowledging the NFLPA's perceived past failures in this regard:

> As Executive Director, my number one priority is to protect those who play and have played this game. There is no interest greater than their health and safety. Let me say this again: Safety of the Players is Paramount.

> * * *

> I have one simple declaration on behalf of those who play and those who played this game:

> WE ARE COMMITTED TO GETTING THE RIGHT ANSWERS, TO WORK WITH EVERYONE WHO HAS THE GOAL OF PROTECTING OUR PLAYERS AND TO SERVE AS A MODEL FOR FOOTBALL AT EVERY LEVEL.

> Given that commitment, I acknowledge that the Players Union in the past has not done its best in this area. We will do better.

> * * *

> Finally we, the players, will not bargain for medical care; we will not bargain for health and safety; and we will not bargain for basic provisions of the law as patients. We will continue to work with the League but medical care is not and will never be a Collective Bargaining issue.[164]

The hearing occurred approximately six months after the NFL hosted Dr. Ann McKee, a Boston University neuropathologist, who had begun to take the lead in studying the brains of deceased NFL players and diagnosing chronic traumatic encephalopathy (CTE).[165,m] Some of the attendees indicated that the meeting was combative, including multiple interruptions.[166,n]

Also at the NFL's meeting was Peter Davies, a Long Island-based expert in Alzheimer's disease and neurological conditions.[167] At the NFL's request Davies reviewed Omalu's conclusion that brain tissue from several former NFL players demonstrated brain damage.[168] Davies substantially confirmed Omalu's findings.[169]

At the October 2009 House Judiciary Committee hearing, when pressed as to whether there was a link between football and brain injuries, Goodell deferred to the ongoing debate among the scientists.[170] Nevertheless, the October 2009 hearing marked the end of the MTBI Committee as it had previously existed. Pellman, Casson and Viano left the Committee,[171] and it was re-named the Head, Neck and Spine Committee. The NFL brought in Richard Ellenbogen and Hunt Batjer, respected neurosurgeons with no previous ties to the NFL, as co-chairmen.[172] According to Mitch Berger, a prominent San Francisco neurosurgeon who joined the Committee at that time, the Committee "essentially started from zero."[173] Guskiewicz joined the Committee in 2010, convinced that Goodell was committed to addressing the concussion issue properly.[174]

In reviewing a draft of this Report, the NFL requested that we add additional context for "the disbanding of the MTBI Committee and establishment of the Head, Neck and Spine Committee."[175] Citing a *New York Times* article, the NFL noted that Dr. Ellenbogen and Dr. Batjer "concurred that data collected by the NFL's former brain-injury leadership was 'infected' [and] that their committee should be assembled anew. The doctors said the old committee's ongoing studies on helmets and retired players' cognitive decline—whose structure and data were strongly criticized by outside experts—would not be used in any way moving forward."[176]

Eventually, several of the authors of the predecessor MTBI Committee's research later repudiated the Committee's findings and tried to distance themselves from the work.[177]

The October 2009 hearing marked the end of the MTBI Committee as it had previously existed.

The October 2009 hearing did not result in any legislation but served as a precursor for the 2011 CBA negotiations.

6) 2010–PRESENT

The 2011 CBA negotiations ultimately resembled a condensed version of what took place between 1987 and 1993, when the NFL operated without a CBA and the parties engaged in extensive litigation.[o] On March 11, 2011, after CBA negotiations centering around the split of revenues broke down, the NFLPA dissolved its status as the bargaining representative of NFL players and filed a class action antitrust lawsuit (*Brady v. NFL*).[178] After extensive litigation and public politicking, the NFLPA and NFL reached a new CBA in July 2011 (which included the NFLPA again reconstituting itself as the players' bargaining representative).[179]

The 2011 CBA substantially amended and supplemented player health and safety provisions. The most important changes include:

---

m   More information about Dr. McKee's work on CTE is provided in the Introduction.

n   Colonel Michael Jaffee, a neurologist with the Defense and Veterans Brain Injury Center who attended the meeting said "Casson interrupted the most . . . . He was the most challenging and at times mocking." Similarly, McKee said "I felt that they were in a very serious state of denial . . . . I felt like they weren't really listening. That's honestly what I thought. That's how it felt, like they had their heads in the sand. They didn't want to see it, so they didn't see it." *See* Mark Fainaru-Wada & Steve Fainaru, League of Denial: The NFL, Concussions and the Battle for Truth 268–70 (2013).

o   The 1982 CBA expired after the 1986 season. When the parties were unable to reach a new CBA, the players engaged in a failed 57-day strike followed by several lawsuits claiming that various NFL policies concerning compensation and free agency violated antitrust laws. In 1989, at the suggestion of the United States Court of Appeals for the Eighth Circuit, *see* Powell v. Nat'l Football League, 930 F.2d 1293 (8th Cir. 1989), the players voted to dissolve the NFLPA as the official bargaining representative of NFL players to eliminate the NFL's immunity from antitrust scrutiny while there was still an ongoing collective bargaining relationship. The players thereafter won two antitrust lawsuits seeking injunctive relief, *see* McNeil v. Nat'l Football League, 790 F. Supp. 871, 876 (D. Minn. 1992); Jackson v. Nat'l Football League, 802 F. Supp. 226, 228 (D. Minn. 1992), before filing a larger antitrust lawsuit seeking over $1 billion in damages, *see* White v. Nat'l Football League, 822 F. Supp. 1389, 1395 (D. Minn. 1993). The case was settled in 1993 with the creation of the modern day CBA and the recertification of the NFLPA. *See* Chris Deubert, Glenn M. Wong & John Howe, *All Four Quarters: A Retrospective and Analysis of the 2011 Collective Bargaining Process and Agreement in the National Football League*, 19 UCLA Ent. L. Rev. 1, 9–12 (2012) (discussing NFL-NFLPA labor relations between 1987 and 1993).

- The availability of "Extended Injury Protection," permitting players to earn 50 percent of their salary up to $500,000 for the second season removed from the season in which the player suffered an injury that prevented the player from continuing to play;[180]

- An overhauled disability plan providing for increased benefits depending on the cause and nature of the disability;[181]

- A reduction of offseason workouts from 14 weeks to 9 weeks in three phases of varying intensity, including new prohibitions on the use of pads during practice (contact was already prohibited);[182]

- A limit of 14 padded practices and three hours of on-field activities per day during the season with all practices filmed for possible compliance review;[183]

- A requirement that clubs have an orthopedic surgeon and an internist, family medicine, or emergency medicine physician;[184]

- A requirement that all club physicians have a Certification of Added Qualification in Sports Medicine;[185]

- A requirement that clubs have neurological, cardiovascular, nutritional, and neuropsychological consultants;[186]

- A requirement that the game-day neutral physician be experienced in rapid sequence intubation and be board certified in emergency medicine, anesthesia, pulmonary medicine, or thoracic surgery;[187]

- The NFL's agreement that "each Club physician's primary duty in providing player medical care shall be not to the Club but instead to the player-patient";[188]

- The NFLPA Medical Director's inclusion as a voting member on all NFL health and safety committees with the same access to data as the NFL Medical Advisor;[189]

- The creation of an Accountability and Care Committee to advise on player medical issues, as well as conducting a confidential survey every two years to solicit players' input regarding the adequacy of their medical care (discussed further below);[p]

- The establishment of the Legacy Benefit program for retired players with a contribution from the NFL of $620 million over the life of the CBA, to be disbursed as part of increased benefits under the Retirement Plan;[190] and,

- The creation of the Neuro-Cognitive Disability Benefit, permitting qualifying players to receive no less than $3,000 per month for a maximum of 180 months.[191,q]

In addition, the 2011 CBA allocates $22 million per year to healthcare and related benefits, funds, and programs for retired players, increasing at 5 percent annually, at the NFLPA's discretion.[192] The NFLPA used the money to create "The Trust," a program intended to be a "set of resources, programs and services designed to provide former players with the support, skills and tools to help ensure success off the field and in life after football."[193] The Trust and other programs supported by the NFLPA are discussed in further detail in the section on Current Practices of the NFLPA, below.

The 2011 CBA also allocates $11 million annually for the duration of the CBA (10 years) for medical research.[194] In 2012, the NFL announced it would be donating $30 million of these funds for brain injury research at the National Institutes of Health (NIH).[195] As discussed previously in this Report, by agreement dated February 2014, the NFLPA chose to fund The Football Players Health Study at Harvard University.

The 2011 CBA nevertheless failed to appease some former players. Former player Carl Eller filed a class action lawsuit against the NFLPA, Smith, and several players involved in the CBA negotiations alleging that they had no authority to bargain with the NFL about the terms of pension, retirement, and disability benefits.[196] Eller had previously filed a similar lawsuit against the NFL while the *Brady* case was proceeding,[197] which was settled shortly after *Brady*.[198] In his case against the NFLPA, Eller sought to have any issues relating to NFL retirees in the 2011 CBA "excised from that agreement and . . . renegotiated between Plaintiffs and the League."[199] Eller's case against the NFLPA was dismissed in May 2012.[200] The United States District Court for the District of Minnesota held that: (1) the plaintiffs could not state a claim for tortious interference; (2) that the NFLPA does not owe a fiduciary duty to former players; and, (3) the plaintiffs' claims to renegotiate the CBA were not judiciable controversies.[201]

Outside of the CBA, the NFL and NFLPA also agreed to a revised Concussion Protocol and infectious disease prevention standards. There may also be other changes to player health policy that the NFL and NFLPA have made but about which information is not publicly available. Concerning infectious disease prevention standards, the NFL and

---

p   2011 CBA, Art. 39, § 3. Despite the provisions of the CBA, the first survey was not conducted until 2015. Mike Florio, *Survey asks players how seriously they take concussions*, ProFootballTalk (Dec. 5, 2015, 6:40 AM), http://profootballtalk.nbcsports.com/2015/12/05/survey-asks-players-how-seriously-they-take-concussions/, *archived at* http://perma.cc/GE9A-RMRC.

q   For a detailed summary of the benefits available to players, including the Neuro-Cognitive Disability Benefit, *see* Appendix C.

NFLPA have partnered with the Duke Infection Control Outreach Network (DICON) Program.[202] The DICON Program has visited all of the clubs' training facilities and created a best practices manual for their use.[203]

At the same time a new CBA was being negotiated with a focus on player health issues, NIOSH was updating the results from its 1994 report that showed NFL players died at lower rates than men of similar demographics in the general population, as discussed above. By 2012, out of the 3,439 players in the study, NIOSH expected that 625 would be deceased. However, only 334 were deceased (53 percent of the expected number). NIOSH also reported that players generally died of cancer and heart disease at lower rates than the general population. Yet, NIOSH also determined that defensive linemen and players with a Body Mass Index of 30 or more were more likely to die of heart disease than the general population.[204]

As part of the 2012 update, NIOSH also examined the number of deaths caused at least in part by the neurodegenerative conditions of dementia, Alzheimer's disease, Parkinson's disease, or amyotrophic lateral sclerosis (ALS).[205] 17 of the 334 deceased former players had a neurodegenerative condition included as either the underlying or contributing cause of death listed on their death certificates, a rate three times higher than that of the general population according to the study's authors.[206] The study acknowledged that due to the low incidence of neurodegenerative conditions and deaths, it was required to adopt broad confidential intervals.[207] As an additional limitation, the study acknowledged it did not have information on environmental, genetic, or other risk factors for neurologic disorders.[208]

In July 2014, the NFLPA for the first time was sued by former NFL players for allegedly intentionally and negligently concealing the risks of traumatic brain injury from playing football.[209] Also named as defendants in the lawsuit were three former NFLPA Presidents: Trace Armstrong (1996–2003); Troy Vincent (2004–2008); and Kevin Mawae (2008–2012). The players' case was dismissed in 2015 as is discussed in more detail below.

The NFL has similarly continued to face scrutiny concerning NFL player health, including multiple lawsuits discussed in more detail below.

At the 2015 Super Bowl, the NFL announced that it had hired cardiologist Dr. Elizabeth Nabel as its first ever Chief Health and Medical Advisor. In the new role, according to the NFL, Nabel provides "strategic input to the NFL's medical, health and scientific efforts; participate[s] as an ex-officio member on each of the NFL's medical advisory committees; and identif[ies] areas for the NFL to enhance player safety, care and treatment."[210] At the time of her appointment, Nabel was president of Brigham and Women's Hospital in Boston and a professor of medicine at Harvard Medical School. Nabel continues in both positions in addition to her work with the NFL. Additionally, The Leadership Team of The Football Players Health Study at Harvard University has met with Nabel, but she is not nor has she ever been affiliated with The Football Players Health Study. According to the NFL, Nabel's appointment did not replace Pellman, who, at the time, remained an "advisor" to the NFL and provided "administrative functions" in a role that was "subordinate to Dr. Nabel."[211] Pellman retired from the NFL in July 2016.[212]

Having provided a chronological history of player health issues in the NFL, for both the NFL and NFLPA, we now explain their current legal obligations, relevant ethical codes, current practices, and possible enforcement mechanisms.

> The programs and benefits available to NFL players are extraordinary, and both the NFL and NFLPA should be commended for this fact.

(D) Current Legal Obligations of the NFL[r]

The NFL is frequently sued, and often the plaintiffs are NFL players themselves. Emerging from all these lawsuits are many different theories about the NFL's legal responsibilities to players. Ultimately, the clearest source for understanding the relationship between players and the NFL are collectively bargained documents, including the 2011 NFL-NFLPA CBA, the Policy and Program on Substances of Abuse (Substance Abuse Policy), and the Policy on Performance-Enhancing Substances (PES Policy).

---

r   The legal obligations described herein are not an exhaustive list but are those we believe are most relevant to player health.

1) COLLECTIVELY BARGAINED AGREEMENTS

The 2011 CBA contains multiple provisions governing the NFL's health obligations to its players.

The NFL is responsible for funding and administering (sometimes in conjunction with the NFLPA) various player health-related programs and benefits, including:

- Retirement Plan (created in 1968);

- Group Insurance (1968);

- Disability Plan (1970);

- Severance Pay Plan (1982);

- Second Career Savings Plan (1993);

- Player Annuity Plan (1998);

- Tuition Assistance Plan (2002);

- The 88 Plan (2006);

- Health Reimbursement Account (2006);

- Former Player Life Improvement Plan (2007);

- Legacy Benefit (2011);

- Long Term Care Insurance Plan (2011); and,

- Neuro-Cognitive Disability Benefit (2011).

These programs and benefits are discussed in detail in Appendix C. The programs and benefits available to NFL players are extraordinary, and both the NFL and NFLPA should be commended for this fact. Nevertheless, access to the programs and benefits appears to be an issue,[s] and questions remain whether players are sufficiently made aware or avail themselves of these programs and benefits, as discussed in Chapter 1: Players. The NFL stated that in 2015 that it spent $1,084,118,072 on these health-related programs and benefits.[213]

These benefits are funded by NFL and NFL club revenues and are different from health-related programs offered and funded by the NFL or the NFLPA respectively, detailed in Appendices D and E. The more than $1 billion amount mentioned above does not include the costs of these programs.[214]

In addition to the above-mentioned benefits and programs, the NFL participates in two committees with the NFLPA concerning player health (additional committees not involving the NFLPA are discussed in Section D: Current Practices).

First, as noted above, the Joint Committee on Player Safety and Welfare ("Joint Committee"), established in 1974, consists of three club representatives and three NFLPA representatives and discusses "player safety and welfare aspects of playing equipment, playing surfaces, stadium facilities, playing rules, player-coach relationships, and any other relevant subjects."[215] The Joint Committee is merely advisory and has no binding decision-making authority.[t]

Second, the NFL participates in the Accountability and Care Committee (ACC), created in 2011. The ACC consists of the NFL Commissioner (or his designee), the NFLPA Executive Director (or his designee), and six additional members "experienced in fields relevant to healthcare for professional athletes," three appointed by the Commissioner and three by the NFLPA Executive Director.[216] The ACC is obligated to: (i) encourage and support programs for outstanding professional training by club medical staffs; (ii) develop a standardized preseason and postseason physical examination and education protocol to inform players of the risks associated with playing football; (iii) conduct research into prevention and treatment of illness and injury commonly experienced by professional athletes; (iv) conduct a confidential player survey at least once every two years to solicit the players' input and opinion regarding the adequacy of medical care; (v) assist in the development and maintenance of injury surveillance and medical record systems; and, (vi) undertake such other duties as the Commissioner and Executive Director may assign.[217] Additionally, players can make complaints about

---

s   Former Player 3 explained former players' frustrations with the various benefit programs: "I think that a lot of guys get frustrated with the system . . . . I don't think guys necessarily trust when they're done playing that the PA's going to take care of them. They don't trust that the league is going to take care of them. . . . They get bombarded with paperwork. They get frustrated. They deserve better. They become bitter. Maybe they just give up on the process." As a solution, Former Player 3 explained "I would like to see a third party sort of take over the process, just somebody who really has no vested interest in anything other than serving the players and helping them. And really understands all the different things that former players go through—emotionally, mentally, physically, spiritually—experts on former players to take control."

---

t   *See* 2011 CBA, Art. 50, § 1(a). In Stringer v. Nat'l Football League, the Court also expressed concerns about the effectiveness of the Joint Committee: "While the NFL is required to give "serious and thorough consideration" to recommendations of the Joint Committee, the CBA imposes no independent duty on the NFL to consider health risks arising from adverse playing conditions, or to make recommendations for rules, regulations or guidelines for the clubs to follow." 474 F.Supp.2d 894, 896 (S.D. Ohio 2007).

their medical care to the ACC, but the ACC then refers those complaints to the NFL and Club involved.[u]

Since its creation, the ACC procured a third-party vendor, Synernet, to verify all club medical staff credentials and licensing, including with states and the Drug Enforcement Administration,[218] and also facilitated the first survey of players concerning a range of health and safety-related topics.[219] The results of that survey are not public and it is unclear whether they will ever be made public. We address this issue further in our recommendations below.

It is also important to understand the source and relative amount of funding for the various player benefits and programs mentioned above. NFL players, as a group, are entitled to different percentages of different revenue sources: (1) 55 percent of League Media, which consists of all NFL broadcasting revenues;[220] (2) 45 percent of NFL Ventures/Postseason revenue, which includes all revenues arising from the operation of postseason NFL games and all revenues arising from NFL-affiliated entities, including NFL Ventures,[221] NFL Network,[222] NFL Properties,[223] NFL Enterprises,[224] NFL Productions,[225] and NFL Digital;[226] and, (3) 40 percent of Local Revenues, which includes those revenues not included in League Media or NFL Ventures/Postseason, and specifically includes revenues from the sale of preseason television broadcasts.[227] These revenues are collectively known as All Revenue or AR.[228] AR in 2015 was approximately $12.4 billion.[229]

The players' share of AR is referred to as the Player Cost Amount.[230] The Player Cost Amount is one of two essential components for calculating the Salary Cap—the "absolute maximum amount of Salary that each Club may pay or be obligated to pay or provide to players . . . at any time during a particular League Year."[231] The other essential component of the Salary Cap calculation is Player Benefit Costs. Player Benefit Costs are the total amounts the NFL and its clubs spend on all the above-described programs and benefits, in addition to the costs of providing medical care to NFL players.[232] The Salary Cap is determined by subtracting Player Benefit Costs from the Player Cost Amount and dividing by the number of clubs in the NFL.[233] In other words, the Salary Cap equals Player Cost Amount minus Player Benefit Costs

divided by 32. *Thus, the more that is paid to NFL players, including retired players, in the form of benefits and medical care, i.e., Player Benefit Costs, the less they are able to receive in the form of salary.* Indeed, in 2015, when the Salary Cap was $143,280,000 per club, each club was charged $37,550,000 in Player Benefit Costs. Thus, out of a possible $180,830,000 that could have been spent on player salaries by each Club, 26.2 percent was allocated to player benefits.

It is important to clarify these figures. As Figure 7-B shows below, about 50 percent of a club's revenue is allocated to the players. The club keeps the other 50 percent. Of the 50 percent allocated for the players (the Player Cost Amount), in 2015, 26.2 percent of that was used on player benefits. Thus, in 2015, we can estimate that each club had approximately $361,660,000 in revenue, $180,830,000 of which would be available for players. Thus, $37,550,000 was spent on player benefits. The $37,550,000 is 26.2 percent of the Player Cost Amount and 10.4 percent of the club's revenue.

In 2015, when the Salary Cap was $143,280,000 per club, each club was charged $37,550,000 in Player Benefit Costs. Thus, out of a possible $180,830,000 that could have been spent on player salaries by each club, 26.2 percent was allocated to player benefits.

u   The three NFL-appointed members of the ACC are: Dr. Matthew Matava, Club doctor for the St. Louis Rams and former President of the NFLPS ; Rick Burkholder, athletic trainer for the Kansas City Chiefs and President of the Professional Football Athletic Trainers (PFATS); and, Dr. Elliott Hershman, Chairman of NFL Injury and Safety Panel, Department of Orthopaedic Surgery, Lenox Hill Hospital and Team Orthopedist, New York Jets. The three NFLPA-appointed members of the ACC are: Dr. Anthony Alessi, neurologist and Associate Clinical Professor of Neurology, University of Connecticut; Dr. Ross McKinney, Director, Trent Center for Bioethics, Humanities & History of Medicine, Duke University & School of Medicine; and, Dr. Johnny Benjamin, orthopedist and Director, Pro Spine Center.

In addition to the CBA, the Substance Abuse Policy contains important provisions concerning player health. The Substance Abuse Policy prohibits players from using common street drugs, such as cocaine, marijuana, amphetamines, opiates, opioids, phencyclidine (PCP), and 3,4-methylenedioxymethamphetamine (MDMA, or "ecstasy").[234] Players are subject to pre-employment tests and one test during the pre-season.[235] Players are not subject to regular season testing unless they have agreed to be or have previously failed a drug test.[236] Importantly, players who fail tests are not immediately disciplined but instead enter an intervention program where they are assessed and treated by medical personnel.[237] Players are only disciplined if they fail to comply with their treatment plans, for example, by failing additional drug tests.[238]

In contrast, players who test positive for performance enhancing drugs under the Performance-Enhancing Substance (PES) Policy are immediately disciplined and no treatment is mandated.[239] Discipline includes: a 2-game suspension for a first positive test result for diuretics or masking agents; a 4-game suspension for a first positive test for stimulants during the season or anabolic steroids; a 6-game suspension for positive test result plus a diuretic, masking agent, or attempt to substitute or dilute; a 10-game suspension for a second violation; and a 2-year ban for a third violation.[240]

Ten players per club are randomly tested for performance enhancing drugs each week of the preseason, regular season, and postseason.[241] In addition, the 2014 PES Policy initiated blood testing for human growth hormone (HGH), with a limit of six tests per player per calendar year.[242]

In our forthcoming report *Comparing the Health-Related Policies and Practices of the NFL to Other Professional Sports Leagues*, we provide an in-depth analysis of both the Substance Abuse and PES Policies. However, our research has not revealed any reliable data on the usage of recreational or performance-enhancing drugs by NFL players. Additionally, in Chapter 2: Club Doctors, Section I: The Special Case of Medications, we discuss prescription and painkilling medications as they concern NFL players at length.

2) STATUTORY OBLIGATIONS

The 2010 Patient Protection and Affordable Care Act (ACA) obligates employers who employ an average of at least 50 full-time employees on business days to provide

Figure 7-B: Division of All Revenue[w]

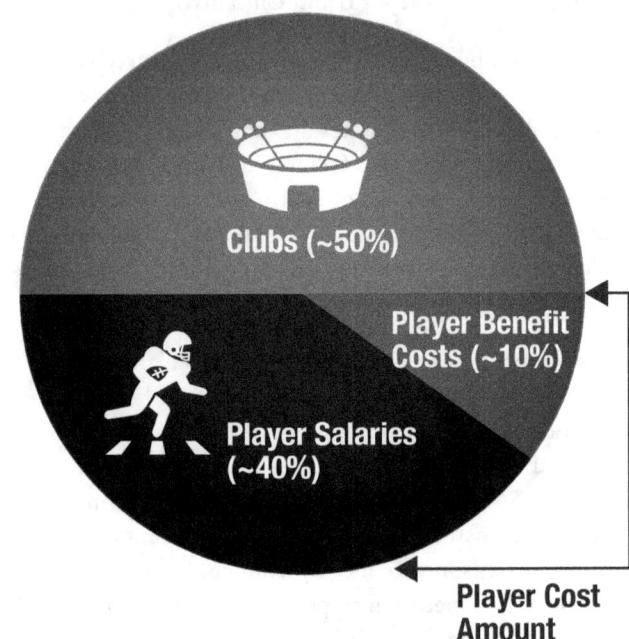

Clubs (~50%)

Player Benefit Costs (~10%)

Player Salaries (~40%)

Player Cost Amount

some basic level of health insurance to its employees or pay a financial penalty,[243] more commonly known as the employer mandate. After several delays, the employer mandate went into effect in 2015. The CBA provides health insurance to NFL players, so this is not a concern at present, but for the sake of completeness, we note that the question remains whether in the absence of the CBA, the NFL would have any obligation to provide health insurance to NFL players. While the NFL might not be considered an employer of players for purposes of the ACA,[244] the clubs certainly would be. Again, however, the issue is purely hypothetical.

The NFL also has obligations under other statutes, such as the Occupational Safety and Health Act,[245] the Americans with Disabilities Act (ADA)[246] and the Genetic Information Nondiscrimination Act (GINA). An analysis of the NFL's intersection with these statutes are the subject of future work of the Law and Ethics Initiative of The Football Players Health Study at Harvard University.[247]

3) COMMON LAW OBLIGATIONS

The existence and extent of common law[w] obligations of the NFL toward promoting and protecting the health of NFL players are debatable. *In re National Football League Players' Concussion Injury Litigation*, 12-md-2323 (E.D.Pa.) ("Concussion Litigation") concerned exactly those duties. On July 19, 2011, 75 former NFL players, led

---

v   In reviewing a draft of this Report, the NFL stated that "the roughly 50%-50% split in revenue as depicted in the chart is generally accurate, with the understanding that the revenue split does not reflect the owners' substantial costs incurred subsequent to the split of revenue." Letter from Larry Ferazani, NFL, to authors (July 18, 2016).

w   Common law refers to "[t]he body of law derived from judicial decisions, rather than from statutes or constitutions." Black's Law Dictionary (9th ed. 2009).

by former NFL linebacker Vernon Maxwell, filed a lawsuit against the NFL in California Superior Court, Los Angeles County, alleging that the NFL had negligently and fraudulently concealed the risk of brain injury associated with playing football.[248] The *Maxwell* case was the first of many concussion-related lawsuits against the NFL.

In total, former and current NFL players have filed more than 240 lawsuits against the NFL in federal and state courts all across the country.[249] On January 31, 2012, the cases existing as of that time were transferred and consolidated into the "Concussion Litigation."[250] On July 17, 2012, the plaintiffs filed an Amended Master Administrative Long-Form Complaint summarizing the various claims at issue.[251] After that date, many more lawsuits were filed, transferred, and consolidated into the Concussion Litigation.[252] In sum, more than 5,500 players filed Short-Form Complaints in the Concussion Litigation.[253]

The Concussion Litigation plaintiffs alleged the NFL owed a variety of common law and assumed duties to NFL players. These duties can generally be grouped into three categories: (1) the NFL's alleged duty to inform or disclose the risks associated with brain injuries in football;[254] (2) the NFL's alleged duty to protect NFL players;[255] and, (3) the NFL's alleged duty to competently study the risks of brain injuries in football.[256]

Whether the NFL actually owed any of these duties as a matter of law may never be resolved, *i.e.*, a court may never have to rule on whether the NFL had to actually do any of the things the Concussion Litigation plaintiffs claimed they had to do. In April 2015, the United States District Court for the Eastern District of Pennsylvania approved a settlement between the parties that provided all former NFL players the opportunity to undergo baseline neurological and neuropsychological examination and the opportunity for monetary awards (subject to various adjustments) for the following conditions:

- Amyotrophic lateral sclerosis (ALS): $5 million;

- Death with CTE prior to the date of the settlement (diagnosed after death): $4 million;

- Parkinson's disease: $3.5 million;

- Alzheimer's disease: $3.5 million;

- Level 2 Neurocognitive Impairment (*i.e.*, moderate Dementia): $3 million; and,

- Level 1.5 Neurocognitive Impairment (*i.e.*, early Dementia): $1.5 million.[257]

The players are not required to prove that their conditions are related to having played in the NFL to obtain an award. Additionally, the NFL did not admit any wrongdoing or liability as part of the settlement. In approving the settlement, the Court cited numerous expert opinions in noting that "[a] consensus is emerging that repetitive mild brain injury is associated with [the conditions covered by the settlement]."[258,x] The NFL's financial obligations under the settlement are not capped, except that the settlement expires after 65 years.

In April 2016, the United States Court of Appeals for the Third Circuit affirmed the District Court's approval of the settlement.[259] In August 2016, some of the plaintiffs petitioned the Supreme Court of the United States to review the case.[260] At that time, approximately 169 former players and 20 former player family members had chosen to opt out of the settlement, providing them the opportunity to press their claims and the NFL's alleged duties in new lawsuits.

(E) Current Ethical Codes Relevant to the NFL

There are no known codes of ethics currently applicable to the NFL and player health.

(F) Current Practices of the NFL

As discussed in the background to this chapter, the NFL's practices and policies concerning player health have improved dramatically over the decades. Moreover, those improvements have accelerated in recent years following leadership changes at both the NFL and NFLPA and with the execution of the 2011 CBA. Table 7-A below lists NFL committees that perform player health-related work, as of the 2016 season.[261] It is important to note that these committees are created and facilitated by, and principally serve in an advisory capacity to, the NFL. As a result, it is difficult to fully evaluate their work.

---

x   The Court, however, denied the argument that CTE after the date of the settlement should be covered, noting that the study of CTE is in its early stages and much is still unknown, including its symptoms. *In re Nat'l Football League Players' Concussion Injury Litigation*, 307 F.R.D. 351, 397–401 (E.D. Pa. 2015) ("Beyond identifying the existence of abnormal tau protein in a person's brain, researchers know very little about CTE."). The Court also denied arguments that mood and behavioral disorders should be covered by the settlement. *See id.* at 401 (*quoting* the Declaration of Dr. Christopher Giza: "While medical literature and clinical practice has *associated* psychological symptoms such as anxiety, depression, liability, irritability and aggression in patients with a history of concussions, this association has not led to *conclusive causation*.") (Emphasis in the Court's opinion).

Table 7-A: NFL Health and Safety Committees[z]

Committee	Areas of Focus	Membership
General Medical Committee	• Behavioral health • Cardiovascular • Environmental • Infectious disease • Pain management • Miscellaneous	• Dr. Andrew Tucker • Dr. Deverick Anderson • Rick Burkholder • Dr. Doug Casa • Dr. Rob Heyer • Dwight Hollier • Dr. Patrick Strollo • Dr. Robert Vogel • Dr. Elizabeth Nabel • Dr. Thom Mayer
Musculoskeletal Committee	• Foot and ankle • Lower extremity trauma • Upper extremity trauma • Studies	• Dr. Robert Anderson • Dr. Ed Wojtys • Dr. Asheesh Bedi • Dr. Robert Brophy • Rick Burkholder • Dr. Mike Coughlin • Dr. Rob Heyer • Dr. Thomas Hunt • Dr. William Levine • Joe Skiba • Dr. Kurt Spindler • Dr. Elizabeth Nabel • Dr. Thom Mayer
Head, Neck and Spine Committee	• Concussion • Moderate and severe brain injury • Neck and spine	• Dr. Hunt Batjer • Dr. Rich Ellenbogen • Dr. Mitch Berger • Dr. Javier Cardenas • Dr. Russell Lonser • Dr. Margot Putukanian • Dr. Robert Cantu • Dr. Joseph Maroon • Dr. Elizabeth Nabel • Dr. Thom Mayer

z   Also of note, according to former Seattle Seahawks club doctor Pierce Scranton, at some point in the 1990s, the NFL did establish a Safety Committee that included the NFLPS President as a member and began to study issues affecting player health and safety, including playing surfaces and concussions. Pierce E. Scranton, Jr., Playing Hurt: Treating and Evaluating the Warriors of the NFL 145–46 (2001).

Thom Mayer, the NFLPA's Medical Director, is a voting member on all NFL health and safety committees.[262] In addition, the NFLPA has "the right to appoint two persons to attend those portions of the annual meeting of the NFL Competition Committee dealing with playing rules to represent the players' viewpoint on rules. One of the appointees shall have a vote on all matters considered at the meeting which relate to playing rules."[263] A history of health-related rule changes in the NFL is included as Appendix I.

We were unable to extensively document all of the information the NFL, through these committees or otherwise, provides to NFL players concerning health and safety issues. Nevertheless, it is clear that the NFL does provide at least some information. Prior to the 2015 season, for the first time ever, each club's medical staff held a one-hour pre-season meeting with the club's players to discuss health and safety issues.[264] In addition, NFL clubs post a large poster in their locker room detailing facts about concussions, including symptoms and recommended steps in the event a player suspects he has a concussion.[265] The poster was developed in conjunction with the NFLPA, NFL Physicians Society, Professional Football Athletic Trainers Society, and the Centers for Disease Control and Prevention.

In addition to the above committees and the collectively bargained benefits and programs mentioned earlier, the NFL has a Player Engagement Department[266] that provides a number of programs designed to help players as well as others involved in the world of football, including:

- NFL Prep 100;

- Prep Leadership Program;

- NFL Prep Sports Career Expo;

- NFL-NCAA Summit;

- NFL-NCAA Life Skills Roundtable;

- 1st & Goal Program;

- Broadcast Boot Camp;

- Business Management and Entrepreneurial Program;

- Business of Music Boot Camp;

- Financial Education;

- Franchising Boot Camp;

- Hospitality & Culinary Management Workshop;

- NFL-NCAA Champion Forum;

- NFL-NCAA Coaches Academy;

- NFL-NCAA Future Football Coaches Academy;

- Rookie Transition Program;

- Pro Hollywood Boot Camp;

- Sports Journalism & Communications Boot Camp;

- Consumer Products Boot Camp;

- Bill Walsh NFL Minority Coaching Fellowship;

- Transition Assistance Program; and,

- Legends Community.

Each of these programs offesred by the NFL's Player Engagement Department is discussed in detail in Appendix D. In addition, the NFL's Player Engagement Department works with players to place them in off-season or post-career internships in a wide variety of industries.[z]

Moreover, in 2007, the NFL and NFLPA jointly created the NFL Player Care Foundation, which funds research into issues affecting NFL players, provides grants to former players in need, and otherwise assists former players in obtaining support for a healthy life.[267] Entering the 2015 season, the NFL Player Care Foundation had arranged for 3,599 former players to undergo a series of private and comprehensive medical examinations.[268]

Despite these extensive programs, committees, and other attention from the NFL, in discussing the NFL's approach to player health, players, contract advisors and financial advisors generally (but not universally) had a negative reaction:[aa]

- **Current Player 1:** *"[I]t would seem that they're more concerned about making money than protecting their players."*

- **Current Player 2:** *"I think that the changes are more for public image . . . . I don't really think that player safety and health is as big a concern for them and has as much importance to them as they portray. I think at the end of the day, it's still big business and they're still trying to put a product out there that's going to be profitable."*

---

z   The industries include: advertising/media; consulting; consumer products; corporate finance; financial services; gaming/digital media; hospitality management; mortgage banking; the National Football League; non-profit/advocacy; public relations; real estate; scouting; sports marketing; television production and development; and, youth football.

aa   We reiterate that our interviews were intended to be informational but not representative of all players', contract advisors', or financial advisors' views, and should be read with that limitation in mind.

- **Current Player 3:** *"[The NFL is] trying to do a good job to make the game safer at the end of the day."*

- **Current Player 4:** *"I think they're trying to avoid the hundred million dollar settlements like they recently had more than they are generally concerned with player safety. I think it's more about public image more than it is really caring about players' health and safety."*[ab]

- **Current Player 5:** *"As far as the Concussion Protocol, I think that they're doing a great job . . . . I don't think there has been an interest in player safety from the league besides the Concussion Protocol."*

- **Current Player 6:** *"I think the NFL is more concerned about the appearance of taking care of players more than actually taking care of players."*

- **Current Player 8:** The NFL takes player health *"as serious as the [Concussion] lawsuit indicates . . . . I think the NFL is concerned with player health as far as they can afford it."*

- **Current Player 9:** *"I would say the NFL's approach is, to me, reactionary . . . . [T]he bottom line for the NFL is to increase revenues. So when it comes to player safety, sometimes that's an afterthought[.]"*

- **Current Player 10:** *"I think [the NFL] has been great . . . . [T]he changes that I've seen in the last 10 years, I think they've really made it a priority. And I think that has changed."*

- **Former Player 1:** *"[F]or sure they want to have this great product just for the fans, all the revenue that they can, also just like any business . . . I mean they want to have the best product and what does that mean? Keeping their top superstar athletes in the best health."*

- **Former Player 2:** *"I think they've done an okay job. I wouldn't say great."*

- **Former Player 3:** *"I don't think anybody is out there saying 'hey, screw the players.' I think they have honestly invested significant resources into it."*

- **Contract Advisor 1:** *"I think it's mixed . . . . You can say I don't want to blow up the NFL with how much we're going to have to pay in litigation and on the other side of it . . . Roger Goodell is not going to want to watch every player he's come to know have issues ten years after they're playing."*

- **Contract Advisor 3:** *"[The NFL's approach] has definitely gotten a lot better as the NFL teams made it a bigger issue, but to say that they do it just because they want to be good guys, I wouldn't put it in that category."*

- **Contract Advisor 4:** *"[T]he NFL is strictly a business. People always say that there's a business side. There is no business side. It is a business."*

- **Contract Advisor 5:** *"They don't care . . . . They're going to keep it under the rug as long as they can until something really comes into play."*

- **Contract Advisor 6:** *"Litigation avoidance."*

Multiple contract advisors specifically identified the NFL's interest in expanding the regular season from 16 to 18 games[ac] as evidence that the NFL's financial interests are more important than player health.[ad]

A 2014–2015 survey of former players by *Newsday* garnered responses from 763 individuals, 85 percent of whom did not feel that the NFL adequately prepared them for the transition to post-football life.[269] However, 48 percent of respondents believed the NFL is doing enough to make the game safer, as compared to only 31 percent who do not.[270] The survey did not ask the former players whether they felt the NFLPA had adequately prepared them for the transition to post-football life. There are also several other limitations to the survey: (1) the survey was sent via email and text message by the NFLPA to more than 7,000 former NFL players, thus eliminating former players that were less technologically savvy and also possibly skewing the sample towards those former players closer to the NFLPA; (2) the response rate for the survey was low (approximately 11 percent); and, (3) the study does not discuss the demographics of those that responded, making it difficult to ascertain whether those who responded are a representative sample of all former players. Nevertheless, we provide the reader with the best existing data.

For more specific guidance, the NFL's current practices concerning health are best understood by examining the practices of the NFL-affiliated stakeholders discussed in this Report: Chapter 2: Club Doctors; Chapter 3: Athletic Trainers; Chapter 8: NFL Clubs; Chapter 9: Coaches; Chapter 10: Other NFL Club Employees; and, Chapter 11: Equipment Managers.

---

ab Current Player 4 also praised the NFL for its rules protecting "defenseless players" but also thought more needed to be done to protect defensive linemen from cut blocking and blocks on interceptions.

ac The NFL cannot increase the length of the regular season without the NFLPA's approval. 2011 CBA, Art. 31.

ad In reviewing a draft of this Report, the NFL clarified that any proposal to increase the regular season from 16 to 18 games would also reduce the preseason from 4 to 2 games. NFL Comments and Corrections (June 24, 2016).

(G) Enforcement of the NFL's Legal and Ethical Obligations[ae]

As discussed above, the NFL's principal legal obligations concerning player health, as opposed to those of the clubs, are to fund and administer various benefit programs. In the event any player is dissatisfied with his benefits, *i.e.,* believes he is entitled to more than he is receiving, he can commence an arbitration before the neutral Benefits Arbitrator.

Aside from the NFL's benefit-related obligations, if a player believes the NFL has violated some other obligation he could commence a Non-Injury Grievance.[af] The 2011 CBA directs certain disputes to designated arbitration mechanisms[271] and directs the remainder of any disputes involving the CBA, a player contract, NFL rules, or generally the terms and conditions of employment to the Non-Injury Grievance arbitration process.[272] Importantly, Non-Injury Grievances provide players with the benefit of a neutral arbitration and the possibility of a "money award."[273] Many of the NFL's above-described legal obligations could be the subject of a Non-Injury Grievance. However, Non-Injury Grievances must be filed within 50 days "from the date of the occurrence or non-occurrence upon which the grievance is based."[274] Additionally, it is possible that under the 2011 CBA, the NFL could argue that complaints concerning medical care are designated elsewhere in the CBA and thus should not be heard by the Non-Injury Grievance arbitrator.[275]

Lawsuits against the NFL are another possible enforcement method, but face significant barriers. This is because the Labor Management Relations Act (LMRA)[276] bars or "preempts" state common law[ag] claims, such as negligence, where the claim is "substantially dependent upon analysis of the terms" of a CBA, *i.e.,* where the claim is "inextricably intertwined with consideration of the terms of the"

CBA."[277] In these cases, player complaints must be resolved through the enforcement provisions provided by the CBA itself (*i.e.,* a Non-Injury Grievance), rather than through litigation. Next, we provide a summary of some important lawsuits involving the NFL that also exemplify the preemption defense.

In *Williams v. NFL*, the United States Court of Appeals for the Eighth Circuit held that common law claims by Minnesota Vikings players Kevin Williams and Pat Williams against the NFL concerning a failed test under the NFL's Policy and Program on Anabolic Steroids and Related Substances ("Steroid Policy")[ah] were preempted by the LMRA. However, non-common law claims brought pursuant to Minnesota state *statutes* were not.[278,ai] The most important outcome of the "StarCaps" case, as it has become known, is the clear message that the CBA, Steroid Policy, and any other collectively bargained agreement, such as the NFL's Policy and Program for Substances of Abuse, must comply with each individual state's laws. The NFL argued that "subjecting the [Steroid] Policy to divergent state regulations would render the uniform enforcement of its drug testing policy, on which it relies as a national organization for the integrity of its business, nearly impossible."[279] The Eighth Circuit rejected this argument, explaining that deference to collective bargaining does not "grant the parties to a CBA the ability to contract for what is illegal under state law."[280] Indeed, throughout the StarCaps case, "the NFL concede[d] that its steroid testing procedures do not comply with the letter of Minnesota state law."[281]

Another prominent case concerning the NFL and the defense of preemption is *Stringer v. Nat'l Football League*.[282] In 2001, Minnesota Vikings Pro Bowl offensive tackle Korey Stringer died of complications from heat stroke after collapsing during training camp.[283] Stringer's family filed two lawsuits: one against the Vikings, Vikings coaches, trainers, and affiliated doctors;[284] and a second against the NFL and Riddell, the equipment manufacturer. In the second suit, Stringer's family alleged that the NFL was negligent in its regulation and control of training camps, equipment, and working conditions, and that Riddell sold defectively designed equipment.[285] In a February 2007 decision, the United States District Court for the Southern District of Ohio held that Stringer's common

---

ae Appendix K is a summary of players' options to enforce legal and ethical obligations against the stakeholders discussed in this Report. In addition, for rights articulated under either the CBA or other NFL policy, the NFLPA can seek to enforce them on players' behalves.

af The term "Non-Injury Grievance" is something of a misnomer. The CBA differentiates between an "Injury Grievance" and a "Non-Injury Grievance." An Injury Grievance is exclusively "a claim or complaint that, at the time a player's NFL Player Contract or Practice Squad Player Contract was terminated by a club, the player was physically unable to perform the services required of him by that contract because of an injury incurred in the performance of his services under that contract." 2011 CBA, Art. 44, § 1. Generally, all other disputes (except System Arbitrations, *see* 2011 CBA, Art. 15) concerning the CBA or a player's terms and conditions of employment are Non-Injury Grievances. 2011 CBA, Art. 43, § 1. Thus, there can be disputes concerning a player's injury or medical care that are considered Non-Injury Grievances because they do not fit within the limited confines of an Injury Grievance.

ag Common law refers to "[t]he body of law derived from judicial decisions, rather than from statutes or constitutions." Black's Law Dictionary (9th ed. 2009). The concept of "preemption" is "[t]he principle (derived from the Supremacy Clause [of the Constitution]) that a federal law can supersede or supplant any inconsistent state law or regulation." *Id.*

ah In 2014, the Steroid Policy was renamed the "Policy on Performance-Enhancing Substances."

ai Christopher R. Deubert, an author of this Report, formerly practiced at the law firm of Peter R. Ginsberg Law, LLC, which represented the Williamses in the StarCaps case. However, the case decisions discussed here occurred prior to Deubert joining the firm. Also of note, the StarCaps case involves multiple decisions in both state and federal courts, with varying degrees of success for the parties.

law wrongful death claim was "inextricably intertwined and substantially dependent upon an analysis of certain CBA provisions" and thus preempted.[286] However, the Court held that Stringer's negligence claims against the NFL concerning equipment safety were not preempted, since the CBA imposes no obligations concerning equipment.[287] Stringer's family and the NFL settled the lawsuit in January 2009.[288]

Prior to settlement of the Concussion Litigation, courts in a handful of cases had decided whether players' concussion-related claims were preempted. In December 2011, in three related cases, the United States District Court for the Central District of California determined that at least some of the plaintiffs' claims were preempted and thus denied the plaintiffs' motion to remand the action back to state court (the Court, at that stage of the legal proceedings, did not have to consider whether all the claims were preempted).[289] Similarly, in a lawsuit brought by the estate of former Chicago Bear and suicide victim David Duerson, the United States District Court for the Northern District of Illinois held that Duerson's estate's concussion-related claims were "substantially dependent on the interpretation of CBA provisions" and thus preempted.[290] All of these cases were later transferred and consolidated into the Concussion Litigation. The NFL's principal defense in the Concussion Litigation—as it has been in almost any case brought by players alleging common law violations—was preemption.

In contrast, in *Green v. Arizona Cardinals Football Club LLC*, the United States District Court for the Eastern District of Missouri held that a former player's concussion-related claims against the Arizona Cardinals (but not the NFL) merely required reference to, and not interpretation of, the CBA and thus were not preempted.[291] As a result, the plaintiffs in the *Green* case potentially had the unique opportunity to pursue discovery against an NFL club on his claims.[292] However, in December 2015, after some of the plaintiffs left the case and the remaining plaintiffs filed an amended complaint, the Cardinals removed the case from Missouri state court to federal court and successfully had it consolidated with the Concussion Litigation.[293] Thus, the unique opportunity presented by the initial decision of the Eastern District of Missouri court seems to have dissolved.

In addition to the concussion-related litigation, in May 2014, several former players, led by former Chicago Bear Richard Dent, filed a class action lawsuit alleging that the NFL and its clubs negligently and fraudulently prescribed and administered painkilling medications during their careers.[294] The lawsuit generally focused on three types of medications: opioids, which "act to block and dull pain"; non-steroidal anti-inflammatory medications, such as Toradol, which have "analgesic and anti-inflammatory effects to mitigate pain"; and, local anesthetics, such as lidocaine.[295] In December 2014, the United States District Court for the Northern District of California ruled that the players' claims were preempted by the LMRA.[296] Effectively, the court found that to determine the validity of the players' claims would require interpretation of the CBA, and thus the players should have pursued grievances as opposed to lawsuits.[297] In Chapter 2: Club Doctors, Section I: The Special Case of Medications, we discuss issues concerning painkilling and prescription medication in the NFL.[aj]

The above cases demonstrate the difficulty players are likely to have in pursuing health-related lawsuits against the NFL. Generally speaking, if a player's common law claim requires the Court to analyze the terms of the CBA, the player will be unable to pursue that claim in a lawsuit.[ak] The concept of preemption effectively forces parties to settle their disputes via collectively bargained arbitration procedures rather than in lawsuits.[al]

While arbitration can provide meaningful recourse for the players, the short statute of limitations makes it difficult to pursue claims.

---

aj   In that section, we discuss a case related to the *Dent* lawsuit, led by former player Chuck Evans. The *Evans* plaintiffs alleged substantially the same allegations as in the *Dent* case, but alleged *intentional* wrongdoing by the clubs, as opposed to merely negligent conduct. For reasons discussed in that section, the court denied a motion to dismiss by NFL clubs and the case is ongoing as of the time of this publication. *See* Evans v. Arizona Cardinals Football Club, 16-cv-1030, 2016 WL 3566945, *1 (N.D.Ca. July 1, 2016).

ak   Nevertheless, it is important to note that, in May 2016, in a lawsuit substantially similar to the NFL's Concussion Litigation, the United States District Court for the District of Minnesota denied the National Hockey League's motion to dismiss concussion-related claims on preemption grounds. In many respects, the Court held that the issue would have to be decided on summary judgment after additional discovery in the case. *See* In re Nat'l Hockey League Players' Concussion Injury Litigation, 14-md-2551, 2016 WL 2901736 (D. Minn. May 18, 2016).

al   Arbitration generally minimizes costs for all parties and leads to faster and more accurate resolutions of legal disputes. *See* Keith N. Hylton, *Agreements to Waive or to Arbitrate Legal Claims: An Economic Analysis*, 8 Sup. Ct. Econ. Rev. 209 (2000); Steven Shavell, *Alternative Dispute Resolution: An Economic Analysis*, 24 J. Legal Stud. 1 (1995). We recognize that arbitration also raises potential concerns for claimants, including the upfront costs of the arbitration and bias in favor of repeat parties, typically the defendant. *See* David Shieh, *Unintended Side Effects: Arbitration and the Deterrence of Medical Error*, 89 N.Y.U. L. Rev. 1806 (2014). However, these concerns are not present in arbitrations involving NFL players where the NFL and NFLPA (and not the player) generally bear the costs of the arbitration equally, the NFL and NFLPA are involved in nearly all of the arbitration proceedings, and both generally retain the ability to remove arbitrators with whom they are dissatisfied.

(H) Current Legal Obligations of the NFLPA[am]

It is important to situate the NFLPA's legal obligations within its role as a labor union, which requires clarifying the difference between the NFLPA's membership and the bargaining unit it is bound to represent. First, in terms of membership, the NFLPA Constitution declares that "[t]here shall be three types of membership in the NFLPA: active, retired and associate membership."[an] However, "[o]nly active members in good standing shall be eligible to vote in elections of Player Representatives and Alternates, contract ratification or any other matter which affects active players."[298] In 2013, there were 5,430 total members: 2,006 active (nearly all active players in the NFL); 3,230 former (out of an estimated 20,000); and 194 associate.[299]

Membership in the NFLPA must be differentiated from the bargaining unit, i.e., the persons the NFLPA represents in collective bargaining negotiations and other NFL-employment matters. The bargaining unit consists of:

"(1) All professional football players employed by a member club of the National Football League; (2) All professional football players who have been previously employed by a member club of the National Football League who are seeking employment with an NFL Club; (3) All rookie players once they are selected in the current year's NFL College Draft; and (4) All undrafted rookie players once they commence negotiation with an NFL Club concerning employment as a player."[300] In contrast, the union only consists of those players within the bargaining unit that choose to be members of the union, which almost all do. It is important to note that the bargaining unit does not include players until the NFL Draft takes place, i.e., players at the NFL Combine are not within the bargaining unit and thus are not protected or represented by the NFLPA.

Importantly, players who previously played in the NFL but are no longer seeking employment with an NFL club, i.e., retired or former players, are not part of the bargaining unit. Former players remain NFLPA members, in their limited capacity, only so long as they pay NFLPA dues.[301]

Active NFL players, i.e., those within the bargaining unit, similarly remain an NFLPA member only so long as they pay their dues.[302] As part of the CBA, NFL clubs agree to provide "check-off" authorization forms to the players,

---

am The legal obligations described herein are not an exhaustive list but are those we believe are most relevant to player health.

an When asked, the NFLPA was uncertain as to what an "associate" member was and such membership is not described in the NFLPA Constitution.

Figure 7-C: NFLPA Membership and Bargaining Unit

permitting the clubs to directly withhold a portion of the players' paychecks to be sent to the NFLPA for dues.[303] In the event a player chooses not to join the NFLPA, he still must pay "an annual service fee in the same amount as any initiation fee and annual dues required of members of the NFLPA."[304] This is essentially a protection against non-member players receiving the benefits the NFLPA negotiates on behalf of the entire bargaining unit, which cannot be segregated from benefits available only to members. If the player refuses to pay the initiation fee, the NFLPA has the right to request that the player be suspended without pay until the fee is paid.[305] Nevertheless, even if an active player is not an NFLPA member, he is still within the bargaining unit and thus entitled to the rights, benefits, and obligations provided for in the CBA.[306]

All of this is to say that, even though retired players can be "members" of the NFLPA, they are not in the same legal relationship with the NFLPA as those players in the bargaining unit ("Active Members" for purposes of this chapter). The differences in these legal relationships are discussed below.

The NFLPA has legal obligations towards those players in the bargaining unit (generally, current players and those actively seeking employment in the NFL). Specifically, the NFLPA owes a duty of fair representation to those in the bargaining unit.[307] A union breaches its duty of fair representation when its "conduct toward a member of the collective bargaining unit is arbitrary, discriminatory, or in bad faith."[308] Although a union has wide discretion in representation of its the bargaining unit, it must exercise that discretion in good faith.[309] If players believe the NFLPA had failed to make a good faith effort to protect their health or otherwise abide by its obligations under its Constitution,

they could seek legal recourse against the NFLPA.[310] Situations in which players have sued the NFLPA are discussed later in this chapter.

Unions in any industry do not owe a duty of fair representation to former members, *i.e.,* anyone outside of the bargaining unit.[311] Thus, the NFLPA does not owe a duty of fair representation to former NFL players.

The NFLPA might also have fiduciary obligations towards those in the bargaining unit. A fiduciary duty obligates the fiduciary "to act with the highest degree of honesty and loyalty toward another person and in the best interests of the other person."[312] Determining whether a fiduciary relationship exists between two parties requires a fact-based inquiry into the relationship.[313] The duty of fair representation is considered a fiduciary duty[314] and thus there exists a strong argument that the NFLPA owes a fiduciary duty to players in the bargaining unit, which would include looking out for their best interests.

On multiple occasions, courts have found that the NFLPA did not owe a fiduciary duty to retired players,[315] but the courts have not addressed that question as it concerns current players.

(l) Current Ethical Codes Relevant to the NFLPA

The NFLPA does not have a governing code of ethics. This is not unusual for a labor organization. Nevertheless, the NFLPA Constitution does contain some statements of ethical responsibility, as discussed in the background to this chapter.

Generally speaking, if a player's common law claim requires the court to analyze the terms of the CBA, the player will be unable to pursue that claim in a lawsuit.

(J) Current Practices of the NFLPA

Despite the NFLPA's structural challenges, discussed in more detail below, substantial progress on player health issues has been made during NFLPA Executive Director Smith's tenure, particularly as part of Article 39 of the 2011 CBA, as previously discussed. Appendix C summarizes the various health-related programs and benefits available to players, Appendix D summarizes the various programs available to players through the NFL's Player Engagement Department, and Appendix E summarizes programs available to players through the NFLPA.

In addition to the above-mentioned programs, the NFLPA offers several programs to help current and former players, including: (1) an externship program with a variety of companies; (2) business classes through Indiana University's Kelley School of Business; (3) a college coaching internship; (4) The Trust—a "set of resources, programs and services designed to provide former players with the support, skills and tools to help ensure success off the field and in life after football";[316] and, (5) the Gene Upshaw Player Assistance Trust Fund, which provides former players facing financial hardship or who wish to finish their undergraduate degrees with financial grants.[317]

The NFLPA also employs five former players as Player Advocates to assist players.[318] The Player Advocates are assigned to specific regions and are responsible for the players of the clubs in their region. The Player Advocates are generally available to the players to help them with club-related matters, to steer them to the appropriate resources such as the NFLPA, and to provide general support.

The NFLPA meets with players during training camp and during the season to discuss relevant issues, including injury trends, existing science, the Concussion Protocol and health-related rights under the CBA.[319] The NFLPA also sends players quarterly emails on these issues and a pamphlet concerning concussions created in collaboration with the American Academy of Neurology.[320] Finally, the NFLPA is currently in the process of creating a video concerning concussions for presentation to the players.[321]

In addition to the NFLPA's programs, beginning in 2014, the NFLPA has sponsored The Football Players Health Study at Harvard University, of which this Report is a part. The Study is a long-term research project with the goal of improving the health of NFL players, including

by understanding the health consequences of an NFL career; identifying and supporting groundbreaking medical research that can benefit players; and, analyzing the legal and ethical issues affecting player health.

Finally, in 2009, the NFLPA created the Mackey-White Committee,[ao] consisting of current players, former players, doctors, and others for the purpose of "assist[ing] the NFLPA in its development of policies concerning workplace safety and the health of NFLPA members."[322] The Mackey-White Committee has four objectives:

(1) identify and analyze the health and safety hazards in the NFL and recommend control measures to eliminate or reduce the risks to players from such hazards;

(2) interpret the science related to work place injuries and conditions arising from employment in the NFL, including, without limitation, repetitive brain trauma, and to disclose the short and long term risks associated therewith, in an effort to better inform and protect NFLPA members, past, present and future;

(3) change the culture of professional football by (i) educating players, coaches and members of the medical community about the short and long-term effects of concussions and other injuries and (ii) advocating for progressive changes, based on science, to the ways in which injuries are managed by the NFL and its Clubs whenever necessary; and

(4) protect youth athletes by raising awareness of the risks associated with repeat concussions, and help educate our elected officials and the general public about health issues related to the professional football occupation.[323]

According to the NFLPA, the Mackey-White Committee has played an advisory role in essentially all of the NFLPA's accomplishments concerning player health and safety, including but not limited to the credentialing of medical staff, revisions to the Concussion Protocol, and the decision to fund The Football Players Health Study at Harvard University.[324]

Notwithstanding the programs and efforts described above, discussions and interviews with current and former players revealed a wide variety of reactions to the NFLPA. Some place the blame for any issues players face at the feet of the NFL and believe the NFLPA has fought hard to protect players. Some—former players in particular—think the

---

ao The Mackey-White Committee is named for Hall of Fame tight end John Mackey who was the first President of the NFLPA (1970–73), and Hall of Fame defensive end Reggie White. Both Mackey and White were lead plaintiffs in lawsuits challenging the NFL's player movement and salary restrictions.

NFLPA has failed and continues to fail to protect players.[ap] Players sometimes express concern that the NFLPA works much harder on behalf of star players than the rank and file.[aq] Of course, there are also many with a viewpoint somewhere in between. Below we offer a sampling of the perspectives of current players that we interviewed concerning the NFLPA,[ar]

- **Current Player 1:** *"I feel like they have our best interests at heart [but] I don't know if I would say they're that effective but I think . . . they're kind of limited as to what they can do for us."*

- **Current Player 2:** *"I think that they've certainly made strides in the right direction . . . but I still think that there's a long way for us to go in order to get where we'd all like to see it go."*

- **Current Player 3:** *"I think the NFLPA has done a good job because we've been in situations where we've been able to negotiate and get some things done with practice scheduling . . . . [W]hen you talk about the NFLPA, you're going to have some guys that love the PA and other guys who hate it . . . . There's no way you can make everything perfect for each individual. You just have to make it good for the whole . . . . That's just part of dealing with that many different people because if you've got 2,000 players, you've got 2,000 different situations and there's just no way that you can instantly cover each situation."*

- **Current Player 4:** *"I'm definitely not [happy with the NFLPA] . . . . It seems very disorganized . . . . I think it does not do enough to help players avoid problematic situations with financial advisors and agents . . . . I don't think they're very good as it relates to player health."[as]*

- **Current Player 5:** *"I believe in the union and everything like that but I think in general they're not seen as doing very much for the players."*

- **Current Player 6:** *"I think the PA is doing a really good job. Whether that's helping guys find out their rights, whether*

that's offering resources like through the PA office, I'm really happy with the PA's work."*

- **Current Player 8:** *"I think there are a lot of great ideas being thrown around. I think there's a lot of movement and momentum starting."* However, Current Player 8 also stated: *"I am frustrated with the lack of consensus [in medical information], but I wish the PA could provide a direct source to the information."*

- **Current Player 9:** *"I think the PA has done a good job protecting players . . . . I'm not going to sit here and say that the PA in the past has acted always as quickly as we needed them to."*

- **Current Player 10:** *"They've done well in that they can bring the issue up, they can talk to us in our meetings about it, but I don't think they are a very big player in it to be honest . . . . The NFLPA's whole tune is always anti-establishment, basically us against them . . . but I think the NFL, in general, has done a good job by themselves with player issues in the forefront . . . . [The NFLPA] is a lot about politics and I don't know if it's always necessarily about the players first more so than some of the people in the organization."*

The NFLPA's membership composition poses considerable challenges. As discussed above, the NFLPA has approximately 2,000 active members, only slightly less than the estimated 2,340 active members of the Major League Baseball Players Association, National Basketball Players Association and National Hockey League Players Association combined.[325] When coupled with the fact that the average NFL player's career is generally shorter than that of players in the other leagues,[326] it is clear that the NFLPA membership is a massive and constantly changing group. Members of this group are likely to have heterogeneous or in some cases conflicting interests.

There are also potential concerns about the enforcement of player health rights. Since the execution of the 2011 CBA, there have been no grievances concerning Article 39: Players' Rights to Medical Care and Treatment decided on the merits.[327] Additionally, the Joint Committee on Player Safety and Welfare has only conducted one investigation concerning the medical care of a club.[328] These facts suggest that either there are no problems, which seems unlikely considering the issues discussed in this Report and the contentious relationship between the NFL and NFLPA, or that there are opportunities for additional enforcement of player health provisions.

---

ap Former Player 1: "The NFLPA is the most inept organization in professional sports. That's my personal opinion. I've had multiple dealings with the NFLPA and I have never felt so underserved . . . . I think it is an incompetent body that's basically beholden to the ownership and the NFL and they do not have the players' best interests in mind regardless of what they say." Former Player 2: "I think it's a weak union, a very weak union. I think the NFL and the owners they dominate everything." Also, in a 2014–2015 survey of 763 former players by *Newsday*, *Newsday* reported "many" former players "blamed the union for not looking out for them during previous collective bargaining." *See* Jim Baumbach, *Life After Football*, Newsday (Jan. 22, 2015), http://data.newsday.com/projects/sports/football/life-football/, *archived at* http://perma.cc/77DP-LUUE.

aq Former Player 1: "They might have some of the top players, but they don't have every NFL player in mind and it's very obvious."

ar We reiterate that our interviews were intended to be informational but not representative of all players' views, and should be read with that limitation in mind.

as Current Player 4 did praise the NFL for offering "a number of different programs in the offseason for players."

Multiple contract advisors attributed the lack of enforcement to the NFLPA's relatively small legal staff. One contract advisor that we spoke with expressed the belief that "the NFLPA is severely understaffed," while another explained that in his opinion the NFLPA does a "terrible job" of policing club medical staff and enforcing player health and safety provisions of the CBA because, in part, it is "absolutely not" adequately staffed. He recommended the NFLPA have an attorney in every city where there is an NFL club to constantly monitor the club and its medical staff. Similarly, another contract advisor said it would help "100 percent" if the NFLPA hired more attorneys focused on health issues.[at]

In addition to enforcement, questions have been raised concerning potential conflicts of interest between the NFLPA and the players. By way of background, the NFLPA routinely negotiates (or attempts to negotiate) settlements of multiple players' grievances, for appeals for Commissioner discipline, and for appeals under the Policy and Program of Substances of Abuse ("Substance Abuse Policy") and the Policy on Performance-Enhancing Substances ("PES Policy"). For example, when the parties agreed to a revised Substance Abuse Policy and PES Policy in September 2014, they also agreed to amended discipline for six players.[329] Additionally, as part of the 2011 CBA, the NFL and NFLPA agreed to reduced discipline for four players involved in the "StarCaps" case, discussed above.[330] Moreover, the 2014 PES Policy specifically created an "Appeals Settlement Committee" consisting of the NFL Commissioner and NFLPA Executive Director (or their designees) that has "the authority to resolve any appeal under th[e] [Steroid] Policy, which resolution shall be final and binding." Importantly, the Appeals Settlement Committee does not mention requiring the potentially suspended player's input or preference concerning a possible settlement.

Some have suggested that these settlements raise concerns that the NFLPA might favorably settle one player's case at the expense of another player's, or that the NFLPA advances other bargaining agendas at the expense of potential settlements for players. For example, the conflict of interest issue was raised in 1996 by former Pro Bowl wide receiver Sterling Sharpe in an unsuccessful lawsuit against the NFLPA,[au] and again by Honorable Helen G. Berrigan of the United States District Court for the Eastern District of Louisiana in 2012. In response to the "bounty" allegations from the NFL, discussed at length in Chapter 9: Coaches, the NFLPA and three of the players alleged to have been involved filed a lawsuit against the NFL in the Eastern District of Louisiana.[av] The NFLPA and all three players were represented by the NFLPA's longtime outside counsel Jeffrey Kessler of Winston Strawn LLP (formerly of Dewey & LeBoeuf and Weil, Gotshal & Manges LLP). Judge Berrigan expressed concern that Kessler had a conflict of interest by representing both the NFLPA and the players and ordered Kessler to show cause why he and his firm should not be disqualified.[331] It would seem that Berrigan was concerned that Kessler's firm would be advocating for the interests of the NFLPA, including a potential settlement, which might not have corresponded with the interests of the players.

Kessler and the NFLPA responded by explaining that Kessler "has represented the NFLPA along with thousands of NFL players for more than 20 years in various disputes against the NFL," including "[m]ore than a hundred arbitrations . . . filed each year, plus occasional court cases."[332] Additionally, the NFLPA argued that, "[a]s a union, [it] is the exclusive collective bargaining representative of NFL players, and as such has the authority under federal labor laws to negotiate and resolve disputes on behalf of its members, both in negotiations with management and in the arbitral process."[333]

Ultimately, Judge Berrigan did not issue any reaction to the NFLPA's response and did not disqualify Kessler and his firm.

---

at A 2008 report prepared by the Congressional Research Service also questioned the NFLPA's ability to address player health matters at that time: "The subject of MTBI research and guidelines, in particular, raises several questions regarding whether the players association has sufficient capacity and authority to participate effectively in matters involving safety and health issues. For example, while members of the MTBI Committee have been involved in an ongoing dialogue with other professionals in the field of neurology (as documented above), it appears that the NFLPA has not commented publicly on any of the issues, such as the possible long-term effects of concussions and the possibility that multiple mild traumatic brain injuries could result in CTE." L. Elaine Halchin, Cong. Research Serv., RL34439, NFL Players: Disabilities, Benefits, and Related Issues (2008) *available at* http://digitalcommons.ilr .cornell.edu/key_workplace/525, *archived at* http://perma.cc/FT92-ECEL.

au In 1994, Sharpe suffered a career-ending injury and filed a grievance against his Club, the Green Bay Packers, seeking payment for portions of his contract. Sharpe sued the NFLPA alleging it had breached its duty of fair representation by agreeing with the NFL that Sharpe's grievance would not be expedited and would not be treated as an Injury Grievance, creating the impression with the arbitrator that the NFLPA did not believe in the legitimacy of Sharpe's case. The United States District Court for the District of Columbia dismissed Sharpe's claim as premature, since no arbitration decision had yet been rendered. Sharpe v. Nat'l Football League Players Ass'n, 941 F. Supp. 8 (D.D.C. 1996). Sharpe later voluntarily dismissed the case. Oscar Dixon, *Sharpe, Dent Suits Dismissed By Court*, USA Today, Jun. 30, 1995, *available at* 1995 WLNR 2566365.

av Christopher R. Deubert, an author of this Report, and the firm at which he formerly practiced, Peter R. Ginsberg Law, LLC, represented former New Orleans Saints player Jonathan Vilma in the "Bounty"-related legal proceedings, but was uninvolved in the issue discussed here.

(K) Enforcement of the NFLPA's Legal and Ethical Obligations[aw]

A player's only recourse against the NFLPA is a civil lawsuit. While other claims might exist depending on the particular circumstances, lawsuits by union members against the union are generally framed as alleged breaches of the duty of fair representation. However, such claims are generally difficult to prove and have been rarely brought against the NFLPA. In addition to the *Sharpe* case mentioned above, research has only revealed two other lawsuits in which players alleged the NFLPA violated its duty of fair representation.

In *Chuy v. Nat'l Football League Players Ass'n*,[334] former player Donald Chuy alleged the NFLPA breached its duty of fair representation when it refused to process Chuy's Injury Grievance against his former club (the club refused to pay Chuy after he was injured during the 1969 season). The United States District Court for the Eastern District of Pennsylvania denied the NFLPA's motion to dismiss, holding that Chuy stated a viable claim.[ax]

The NFLPA made no public statement regarding the merits of the Concussion Litigation, provided no legal advice or guidance to players, and made no statement regarding the proposed or eventual settlement in the Concussion Litigation.

Former player James Peterson was less successful in his breach of the duty of fair representation claim against the NFLPA. In his case,[335] the United States Court of Appeals for the Ninth Circuit affirmed the vacatur[ay] of a jury verdict in Peterson's favor. Peterson alleged that, in 1977, the NFLPA and two of its lawyers failed to timely file an Injury Grievance on Peterson's behalf despite handling

the matter for Peterson. The Ninth Circuit held that the NFLPA's conduct was not arbitrary, discriminatory, or in bad faith sufficient to state a claim. The court explained that, generally, acts of negligence by union officials will not state a claim for breach of the duty of fair representation.

The most significant lawsuit concerning the NFLPA's health obligations was brought in 2014. In *Smith v. Nat'l Football League Players Ass'n*,[336] former NFL players sued the NFLPA alleging that it had intentionally and fraudulently failed to protect them from the risk of concussions during their careers. The lawsuit was brought by some of the same attorneys involved in the Concussion Litigation against the NFL and substantially duplicated the allegations in that lawsuit. The NFLPA responded by having the case removed from Missouri state court to the United States District Court for the Eastern District of Missouri and asserting the same defense as the NFL in the Concussion Litigation – that the players' claims were preempted by the LMRA. Additionally, the NFLPA argued that the players' claims were preempted by the NLRA, *i.e.*, that the plaintiffs' claims had to be brought as breach of the duty of fair representation claims.

The NFLPA's defense in the *Smith* case was the first time the NFLPA had expressed publicly any opinion about concussion-related claims by former players. Ultimately, the court sided with the NFLPA on all counts, *i.e.*, agreed that the players' claims were preempted by the LMRA and the NLRA, and denied the plaintiffs' motion to remand the case to state court.[337] After denying the motion to remand, the court granted the NFLPA's motion to dismiss the case, again finding that the players' claims were preempted.[338]

This case is particularly important not only because it highlights the sometimes fractious relationship between the NFLPA and former players, but also because it reveals a potential structural tension the NFLPA's self-interest and its responsibility to players. The NFLPA made no public statement regarding the merits of the Concussion Litigation against the NFL, provided no legal advice or guidance to players deciding whether to join the class action or not, offered no guidance on legal strategies most likely to be successful against the NFL, and made no statement regarding the proposed or eventual settlement in the Concussion Litigation and its adequacy.[339] Some commentators opined that the NFLPA abstained from expressing any opinion about the Concussion Litigation for fear that it would highlight the NFLPA's own actions or inactions concerning concussions:

---

aw Appendix K is a summary of players' options to enforce legal and ethical obligations against the stakeholders discussed in this Report.
ax The result of the lawsuit is unclear.
ay "Vacatur" refers to the judicial "act of annulling or setting aside." Black's Law Dictionary (9th ed. 2009). In this case, the United States District Court for the Southern District of California set aside a jury verdict in Peterson's favor, a decision affirmed by the Ninth Circuit.

The NFLPA has kept its head low throughout the concussion litigation, in large part because none of the plaintiffs had sued the players' union—but any, some, or all of them could have sued.[340]

* * *

At a time when some are lamenting the fact that the settlement of the concussion lawsuits will prevent the public from knowing what the NFL knew and when the NFL knew it, those same questions will never be answered regarding the NFLPA. What did the NFLPA know, when did the NFLPA know it, and why didn't the NFLPA do a better job of protecting its men? [. . .] The simple fact is that, under the late Gene Upshaw, the NFLPA was a major part of the problem.[341]

A final case worth mentioning concerns the NFLPA's Financial Advisor program (discussed at length in Chapter 13: Financial Advisors). In *Atwater v. Nat'l Football League Players Ass'n,*[342] six former players sued the NFLPA for losses they suffered by investing with NFLPA-registered financial advisors. The Court granted the NFLPA summary judgment,[az] holding that the players' claims were preempted by the LMRA.[ba]

---

az Summary judgment is "[a] judgment granted on a claim or defense about which there is no genuine issue of material fact and on which the movant is entitled to prevail as a matter of law." Black's Law Dictionary (9th ed. 2009).

ba Similarly, in June 2015, former NFL player Richard Goodman sued the NFLPA alleging that it was negligent and breached its fiduciary duties in regulating Goodman's former contract advisor, causing Goodman financial damages. *See* Complaint, Goodman v. Nat'l Football League Players Ass'n, No. 15011396 (Fla. Cir. Ct. June 30, 2015). Less than two weeks after it was filed, Goodman and the NFLPA settled the lawsuit on confidential terms. E-mail with Darren Heitner, Heitner Legal, P.L.L.C., Counsel for Goodman (Aug. 25, 2015).

(L) Recommendations Concerning The NFL and NFLPA

The NFL and NFLPA are clearly in a position to protect and promote player health. There is also no doubt that both parties have made significant progress on this front in recent years, and that the NFL and NFLPA offer many benefits and programs intended to help current and former players. Nevertheless, there are still many important changes the NFL and NFLPA can make that will further advance player health and likely the game of football in the process.

Before explaining our recommendations for the NFL and NFLPA, it is important to review a key principle of labor law. The NLRA obligates employers and unions to collectively bargain "in good faith with respect to wages, hours, and other terms and conditions of employment."[343] Within this obligation, there is ongoing legal debate as to which issues are mandatory subjects of bargaining and which are merely permissible subjects of bargaining, *i.e.*, which subjects the NLRA requires the parties to negotiate, and which the parties are not required to negotiate but may.[344] Some of our recommendations concern mandatory subjects of bargaining while others likely do not. We recognize the NFL and NFLPA might reasonably disagree about which issues are mandatory subjects of bargaining and thus do not intend to suggest that each of the below recommendations must be collectively bargained. We encourage collaboration between the parties but nonetheless urge progress first and foremost, including where that progress can be made unilaterally.

Additionally, it is again important to remember that the NFLPA's legal duties are to current players, not former players. This is true even though the NFLPA has negotiated increased benefits and additional programs for former players many times. Indeed, beyond the NFLPA's legal duties, we recognize that many former players rely on the NFLPA for information and assistance. Nevertheless, for reasons discussed in the Introduction, Section H: Scope of the Report, our recommendations focus on current players.

Finally, there are also recommendations directly concerning the NFL and NFLPA that are made in other chapters:

- Chapter 1: Players — Recommendation 1:1-G: Players should not sign any document presented to them by the NFL, an NFL club, or employee of an NFL club without discussing the document with their contract advisor, the NFLPA, their financial advisor, and/or other counsel, as appropriate.

- Chapter 2: Club Doctors — Recommendation 2:1-A: The current arrangement in which club (*i.e.*, "team") medical staff, including doctors, athletic trainers, and others, have responsibilitiefos both to players and to the club presents an inherent conflict of interest. To address this problem and help ensure that players receive medical care that is as free from conflict as possible, division of responsibilities between two distinct groups of medical professionals is needed. Player care and treatment should be provided by one set of medical professionals (called the "Players' Medical Staff"), appointed by a joint committee with representation from both the NFL and NFLPA, and evaluation of players for business purposes should be done by separate medical personnel (the "Club Evaluation Doctor").

- Chapter 2: Club Doctors — Recommendation 2:1-H: The NFL's Medical Sponsorship Policy should prohibit doctors or other medical service providers (MSPs) from providing consideration of any kind for the right to provide medical services to the club, exclusively or non-exclusively.

- Chapter 9: Coaches — Recommendation 9:1-B: The most important ethical principles concerning coaches' practices concerning player health should be incorporated into the CBA.

- Chapter 13: Financial Advisors — Recommendation 13:1-A: Players should be encouraged by the NFL, NFLPA, and contract advisors to work exclusively with NFLPA-registered financial advisors.

- Chapter 13: Financial Advisors — Recommendation 13:2-A: The NFLPA and NFL should consider holding regular courses on financial issues for players.

- Chapter 13: Financial Advisors — Recommendation 13:2-B: The NFL and NFLPA should consider amending the player payment schedule so that players, by default, are paid over a 12-month period.

Recommendations Concerning The NFL and NFLPA – continued

- Chapter 14: Family Members—Recommendation 14:1-A: Family members should be cognizant of the gaps in their knowledge concerning the realities of an NFL career, and the NFL and NFLPA should offer programs or materials to help them become better health advocates.

Goal 1: To make player health a priority.

Principles Advanced: Respect; Health Primacy; Empowered Autonomy; Transparency; Managing Conflicts of Interest; Collaboration and Engagement; and, Justice.

Recommendation 7:1-A: The NFL and NFLPA should not make player health a subject of adversarial collective bargaining.

As discussed throughout this Report, collective bargaining is the principal method by which changes are made to NFL player health policies. Pursuant to federal labor law, this will and should continue to be the case. However, we do not believe that collective bargaining over player health issues should be an *adversarial* process.

We acknowledge the realities of labor negotiations and do not mean to naively suggest that the one party accept at face value every player health proposal the other might make. Nevertheless, if as part of its research or otherwise the NFL knows a policy or practice should change, it should do so without waiting for the next round of bargaining or by forcing the NFLPA to concede on some other issue. Indeed, for the NFL to demand a quid pro quo in exchange for improving player health policies or practices would be ethically problematic. For player health to be maximized, it is important that the NFL view the issue as an independent obligation of its own, rather than an issue to be forced upon it. Similarly, the NFLPA should not delay on addressing player health issues in order to advance other collective bargaining issues. We hope the NFL and NFLPA have adopted and will in the future adopt this attitude toward collective bargaining.

Relatedly, the NFL should also more substantially engage with current players about player health issues, including incorporating their input on some of the NFL's committees.

Recommendation 7:1-B: The NFL and NFLPA should continue to undertake and support efforts to scientifically and reliably establish the health risks and benefits of playing professional football.[bb]

The MTBI Committee's work is widely considered to have been flawed and incorrect in many ways. Since overhauling that Committee in 2009, the NFL has committed funds to several external organizations primarily to study traumatic brain injury, including but not limited to providing $1 million to Boston University in 2010[345] and $30 million to the National Institutes of Health (NIH) in 2012, $6 million of which, according to the NFL, was eventually awarded to Boston University.[346,bc] In total, the NFL stated that "over the past six years the NFL has dedicated more than $93 million in funds for scientific and medical research."[347] Research concerning brain injuries is very important. In addition, as we have

---

bb   Dr. Elizabeth Nabel, the NFL's Chief Health and Medical Adviser, has also recommended that the NFL continue to fund medical research concerning player health. *See* Ben Tinker, *CNN exclusive: NFL's first medical adviser sits down with Dr. Sanjay Gupta*, CNN (Aug. 4, 2015), http://www.cnn.com/2015/08/04/health/nfl-health-chief-interview/, *archived at* http://perma.cc/CR8S-898C.

bc   The funds to NIH might also be used for studying health conditions other than brain injuries, but the focus of the study is clearly on brain injuries. *See The National Football League Commits $30 Million Donation to the Foundation for the National Institutes of Health to Support Medical Research*, Nat'l Insts. of Health (Sept. 5, 2012), http://www.nih .gov/news/health/sep2012/od-05.htm, *archived at* http://perma.cc/LR65-9CYR.

Recommendations Concerning The NFL and NFLPA – continued

emphasized in this Report, it is important to focus on the health of the whole player for the whole lifetime, which means also supporting research in other health domains. Without knowing the actual results of a football career, it is difficult to craft policies and practices that can maximize player health. On this point, the NFL has funded studies derived from data collected from medical screenings of 3,599 former players through the Player Care Foundation[348] and the NFLPA has awarded funding to Harvard University for The Football Players Health Study at Harvard University. Research on these issues should continue.

We also emphasize the importance of studying and better articulating the benefits of playing professional football. On this point, we agree with the NFL:

> Football is a sport that truly unites people. Our players feel connected to their team, their community and their fans. They are taking part in a cultural institution in this country that provides inspiration and joy to millions of people. While those are not financial benefits, those are benefits that provide our players with tremendous personal satisfaction and value, and should not be overlooked[.][349]

Better understanding of both the risks and benefits of playing professional football will help to empower players in making choices about football and their health.

Recommendation 7:1-C: The NFL, and to the extent possible, the NFLPA, should: (a) continue to improve its robust collection of aggregate injury data; (b) continue to have qualified professionals analyze the injury data; and, (c) make the data publicly available for re-analysis.

As explained in Chapter 1: Players, the NFL Injury Surveillance System (NFLISS) allows for the accumulation of current information about the nature, duration, and cause of player injuries. Also as stated in Chapter 1, we rely on NFLISS data in this Report because it provides the best available data concerning player injuries, although we cannot independently verify the data's accuracy. We acknowledge that the NFL's past injury reporting and data analysis have been publicly criticized as incomplete, biased, or otherwise problematic, although we are not aware of any criticism of the NFLISS specifically.[350] Without resolving the debate concerning the NFL's collection and use of injury data, we nonetheless stress the importance of accurate, comprehensive, and mandatory injury data collection—and meaningful disciplinary action for responsible parties (e.g., club medical staff) who fail to accurately record injury data.

If accurately collected, these datasets have the potential to improve player health through analysis by qualified experts, so long as they are made available to them. In particular, analysis can be performed to determine, among other things, the effects of rule changes, practice habits, scheduling, new equipment, and certain treatments, while also identifying promising or discouraging trends and injury types in need of additional focus.[351] Notably, the NFL already conducts this type of analysis through Quintiles, as explained in Chapter 1: Players.[bd] However, the NFL does not publicly release its injury data (nor does any other major professional league as far as we are aware). The NFL does release some data at its annual Health & Safety Press Conference at the Super Bowl. However, the data released at the Press Conference are minimal compared to the data available and the analyses performed by Quintiles. Also as explained in Chapter 1: Players, the NFL and NFLPA denied our request to incorporate additional data from the 2015 Quintiles report into this Report, for reasons with which we disagree. It is regrettable that both the NFL and NFLPA are not providing players with all data and information concerning player health that is in their possession.

---

bd The Football Players Health Study is also collecting data about former NFL players, their injury histories, and other factors that can help better elucidate the risks faced by players.

Recommendations Concerning The NFL and NFLPA – continued

For the data collected to have the potential meaningful applications mentioned above, it must be made available in a form as close to its entirety as possible. Such disclosure would permit academics, journalists, fans, and others to scrutinize and analyze the data in any number of ways, likely elucidating statistical events, trends and figures that have the opportunity to improve player health, as well as simply providing independent verification of any analysis done by Quintiles for added public trust. To be clear we are recommending the release of more *aggregate* data, not data that could lead to identification of the injuries of any particular player or cause problems concerning gambling (*see* Chapter 18: Fans).

Publicly releasing injury data, nevertheless, comes with complications that we must acknowledge. While more transparency in injury reporting is necessary, the nuances of such data can easily be lost on those without proper training. Sports injury prevention priorities in public health can be swayed by public opinion and heavily influenced by those with the most media coverage. Making injury data publically available may allow those with the media access to dictate the agenda regardless of the actual implications of the data. As a result, it may be harder for injury trends that may be more hazardous, but less visible in the media, to get the attention they need, even when the data clearly state their importance. Thoughtful, balanced, peer-review results may have difficulty competing against those statistics which garner the most media attention. For this and other reasons, in Chapter 17: The Media, we recommended that "[t]he media should be accurate, balanced, and comprehensive in its reporting on player health issues." The medical, scientific and legal issues concerning player health are extremely complicated, which demands that the media take care to avoid making assertions that are not supported or that do not account for the intricacies and nuance of medicine, science and the law.

In light of these concerns, one possible intermediate solution is to create a committee of experts that can review requests for data and determine whether or not the usage of the data is appropriate and will advance player health. Indeed, the Datalys Center for Sports Injury Research and Prevention performs this role concerning access to NCAA student-athlete injury data.[352] Moreover, such committees have also been formed in the clinical research setting.[353]

Recommendation 7:1-D: The NFL and NFLPA should publicly release de-identified, aggregate data from the Accountability and Care Committee's player surveys concerning the adequacy of players' medical care.

As discussed earlier, as part of the 2011 CBA, the NFL and NFLPA created a joint Accountability and Care Committee (ACC), which is to "provide advice and guidance regarding the provision of preventive, medical, surgical, and rehabilitative care for players[.]"[354] Among the ACC's responsibilities is to "conduct a confidential player survey at least once every two years to solicit the players' input and opinion regarding the adequacy of medical care provided by their respective medical and training staffs and commission independent analysis of the results of such surveys." Despite the provisions of the CBA, the first survey was not conducted until 2015.[355] Moreover, no results of the survey have been made public.

We believe de-identified aggregate data from the results from the 2015 survey and all subsequent surveys should be made public, or at least made available to appropriate outside researchers. As discussed at length in Chapter 2: Club Doctors and Chapter 3: Athletic Trainers, there are serious questions concerning the relationship between club medical staff and players, including the possibility that at least some players do not trust the club medical staff—a serious concern for the efficacy of the patient-doctor relationship. Independent research on these issues is important, as it can allow qualified experts to analyze the data and identify potential areas of improvement. Nevertheless, as evidenced by the challenges in our own work, engaging players and club medical staff (including NFL permission) to participate in a research study is extremely difficult. The NFL and NFLPA have these data sets and thus can make them public to facilitate additional research.

Recommendations Concerning The NFL and NFLPA – continued

This recommendation is reiterated in a forthcoming Special Report from The Hastings Center Report, to be published in December 2016.

The NFL denied our request for this data, citing a confidentiality agreement between the NFL and NFLPA. The NFL explained

> [u]nder the terms of the confidentiality agreement, the results of the survey were provided to only certain, specifically-named individuals at the League and the Players Association and to certain individuals at each club, who are bound by the terms of the agreement. The results were collected, tabulated and analyzed by the survey company which then met with the NFL and NFLPA to discuss the results. Representatives of many of the clubs, the NFL and the NFLPA have also met to discuss the results of the survey and to share best practices regarding player medical care as part of their ongoing efforts in this realm. These best practices will be further discussed when the representatives of the NFL and NFLPA (including the NFLPA's Medical Director) visit training camps to meet with club medical staffs this summer, as they do every year.

For the reasons stated above, we believe it is important that this data be analyzed beyond a small group of people at the NFL, NFLPA and NFL clubs.

Recommendation 7:1-E: Players diagnosed with a concussion should be placed on a short-term injured reserve list whereby the player does not count against the Active/Inactive 53-man roster until he is cleared to play by the Concussion Protocol (see Appendix A).

For each game, NFL clubs must divide their 53-man rosters into 46 active players, those eligible to play in the game, and 7 inactive players, those who cannot play in the game.[356] There is no limitation on how often a player can be declared inactive. While concussed players can be declared inactive for one or more games, we believe concussions present a unique situation that requires a unique approach.

According to the leading experts, 80 to 90 percent of concussions are resolved within 7 to 10 days.[357] Thus, concussion symptoms persist for longer than 10 days for approximately 10 to 20 percent of athletes. In addition, a variety of factors can modify the concussion recovery period, such as the loss of consciousness, past concussion history, medications, and the player's style of play.[358] Consequently, a player's recovery time from a concussion can easily range from no games to several. The uncertain recovery times create pressure on the player, club, and club doctor. Each roster spot is valuable and clubs constantly add and drop players to ensure they have the roster that gives them the greatest chance to win each game day. As a result of the uncertain recovery times, clubs might debate whether they need to replace the player for that week or longer. The club doctor and player might also then feel pressure for the player to return to play as soon as possible. By exempting a concussed player from the 53-man roster, the club has the opportunity to sign a short-term replacement player in the event the concussed player is unable to play. At the same time, the player and club doctor would have some of the return-to-play pressure removed.[359]

In fact, MLB already has such a policy. MLB has a 7-day Disabled List (as compared to its normal 15 and 60 day Disabled Lists) "solely for the placement of players who suffer a concussion."[360]

Why treat concussions differently than other injuries in this respect? This is a fair question to which there are a few plausible responses. First, in terms of the perception of the game by fans, concussions have clearly received more attention than any of the other injuries NFL players might experience and thus the future of the game depends more critically on adequately protecting players who suffer from them. Second, concussions are harder to diagnose than other injuries, such that there may be a period of uncertainty in which it would be appropriate to err on the side of caution.[361] Third, both players and medical professionals have more difficulty anticipating the long-term effects of concussions as compared

Recommendations Concerning The NFL and NFLPA – continued

to other injuries, given current scientific uncertainties concerning brain injury.[362] Fourth, and perhaps most importantly, it is harder to determine the appropriate recovery times for concussions as compared to other injuries.[363] These reasons all support a recommendation to exclude concussed players from a club's Active/Inactive roster, but we recognize that the key feature of players potentially feeling or facing pressure to return before full recovery may be shared across any injury a player may experience. Thus, it may also be reasonable to consider extending this recommendation beyond concussions.[be]

In reviewing a draft of this Report, the NFL argued that "[t]he current NFL roster rules actually provide greater flexibility" than is recommended here.[364] The NFL explained that because "[t]here is no limitation on how long a player may be carried on the 53-man roster throughout the season without being 'activated,' . . . a player who is concussed routinely is carried on his club's 53-man roster without being activated until he is cleared."[365] However, for the reasons explained above, we believe concussions should be treated differently. All 53 spots on the roster are precious to both the club and the players. The uncertainty surrounding recovery from a concussion presents unique pressures that can be lessened with the approach recommended here.

Recommendation 7:1-F: The NFL and NFLPA should research the consequences and feasibility of guaranteeing more of players' compensation as a way to protect player health.

Guaranteed compensation in the NFL is a complicated issue, and we are not making a recommendation that NFL player contracts be fully guaranteed, as is generally the case in MLB, the NBA and, to a lesser extent, the NHL. Many people, particularly some players, feel that fully guaranteeing a player's contract is a fair trade for the health risks players undertake, a notion consistent with our ethical principle of Respect. More important for our purposes here, focused on protecting and promoting player health, is that, if a player's contract were fully guaranteed, he would likely feel less pressure to play through injuries in an effort to continually prove himself to the club,[366] a notion consistent with our ethical principle of Health Primacy.[bf] Relatedly, job and income insecurity likely cause stress and psychological harm for some players. However, we have concerns about the possibility of unintended consequences, as well as the feasibility, of such a recommendation to fully guarantee player compensation.

To understand these concerns, a brief explanation of guaranteed compensation in the NFL is important. Generally, NFL clubs are permitted to terminate a player's contract without any further financial obligation to the player for five reasons:

(1) the player "has failed to establish or maintain [his] excellent physical condition to the satisfaction of the Club physician";

(2) the player has "failed to make a full and complete disclosure of [his] physical or mental condition during a physical examination";

(3) "[i]n the judgment of the Club, [the player's] skill or performance has been unsatisfactory as compared with that of other players competing for positions on the Club's roster";

(4) the player has "engaged in personal conduct which, in the reasonable judgment of the Club, adversely reflects on the Club"; and,

(5) "[i]n the Club's opinion, [the player is] reasonably anticipated to make less of a contribution to the Club's ability to compete on the playing field than another player or players whom the Club intends to sign or attempts to sign, or already on the roster of the Club, and for whom the Club needs Room."[367]

---

be We recognize that this new injured reserve list is subject to gaming by clubs, whereby a club might designate a player as concussed in order to add another player and effectively expand the roster. We do not view this this concern to be sufficient to outweigh the health benefits of the proposal. Moreover, all injury lists are subject to some risk of being gamed in this manner, and thus the issue is not unique to what we propose.

bf In reviewing a draft of the Chapter 14: Family Members, the wife of a former NFL player stated: "if you don't have any guarantees in your contract and you are a game or practice away from being released/fired, you are less likely to take on the role of a change agent[.]"

Recommendations Concerning The NFL and NFLPA – continued

Players and their contract advisors seek to curtail the clubs' termination rights as to individual players by negotiating for some of the player's compensation to be guaranteed. Guaranteed compensation takes a wide variety of forms (most notably in signing bonuses),[368] but generally players and their contract advisors seek to guarantee the player's contract even where he is terminated for "injury," "skill" or "Salary Cap." An "injury" guarantee will protect against the first reason listed above for which clubs can generally terminate a player's contract; a "skill" guarantee will protect against the third reason, and a "Salary Cap" guarantee will protect against the fifth reason. A player might have all or just some seasons of his contract guaranteed for skill, injury and/or Salary Cap. In addition, there are other mechanisms in the CBA that can effectively guarantee some or all of a player's salary, including Injury Protection[bg] and Termination Pay.[bh]

Generally, players and their contract advisors seek to obtain as much guaranteed money as possible in contract negotiations. Guaranteed compensation provides the player with a secure income that is otherwise typically threatened by injury. However, there are times when a player might not want to sign the contract that offers him the most money, guaranteed or unguaranteed. Younger players might eschew the last year or two of a contract and the money that comes with it in favor of a shorter contract. In doing so, the player is hoping or expecting that he will be able to complete the shorter contract, re-enter the free agency market and sign another contract. Such decisions are obviously risky—the player's career might end for skill or health reasons under the shorter contract and the player will never have another chance at another contract. However, if the player is healthy, securing a second free agent contract can be lucrative.

From a club's perspective, guaranteed compensation is something to be avoided. Guaranteeing all or a portion of a player's contract commits the club to a player financially, regardless of whether the player performs poorly under the contract or suffers a career threatening injury. Nevertheless, clubs often agree to guarantee compensation to players to persuade them to join or stay with the club.

Changes to the Salary Cap rules as part of the 2011 CBA potentially increased the use of guaranteed money. Technically, whether a player's compensation is guaranteed has no effect on the Salary Cap—a club is limited to a certain amount of player compensation costs regardless of whether that amount is guaranteed or unguaranteed. Importantly, the amount of player salary that is counted against a club's Salary Cap does not necessarily reflect the amount actually being paid to players. As a result of the Salary Cap's accounting rules, in any given year a significant portion of a club's Salary Cap allocation might be consumed by charges that do not actually reflect a payment being made from the club to players. However, the 2011 CBA addressed this discrepancy by adding a requirement that clubs spend a certain amount of the Salary Cap in cash, that is, actual payments to the players, regardless of the accounting rules. Probably the easiest way for a club to ensure that it spends a sufficient amount in cash is to pay lump sum signing bonuses. Signing bonuses are the most traditional form of guaranteed compensation.

The website spotrac.com provides the most reliable publicly available data on player contracts. Using data from spotrac.com during week 2 of the 2015 regular season, approximately 44 percent of all contracted compensation was guaranteed. Importantly, this statistic represented the aggregate of player contracts, but does not necessarily reflect any single player's contract. On that front, approximately 70 percent of players had at least some guaranteed compensation in their contract and the average amount of guaranteed compensation in an NFL player contract was $3.4 million. Additionally, 251 players had a contract that included at least $10 million in guaranteed compensation and 740 players had a contract that included at least $1 million in guaranteed compensation.

In recent years, the percentage of an NFL player's contract that is guaranteed appears to have risen. Although the scope of the guarantees is sometimes debated,[369] it is not uncommon for marquee players to sign contracts that guarantee 50

---

bg Where a player is injured in one season, fails the preseason physical the next season because of that injury, and is terminated by the club as a result, the player is entitled to 50 percent of his salary for that season up to a maximum of $1.1 million in the 2015 season. If the player is still physically unable to play two seasons after the injury, he is entitled to 30 percent of his salary up to a maximum for $525,000 in 2015. A player is only entitled to Injury Protection once in his career. *See* 2011 CBA, Art. 45.

bh A player with at least four years of experience who has his contract terminated after the first game of the season is entitled to the remainder of his salary for that season once in his career. 2011 CBA, Art. 30.

Recommendations Concerning The NFL and NFLPA – continued

percent or more of their compensation.[370] Moreover, the 2011 CBA significantly curtailed rookie compensation, cutting the amount top draft picks earned by more than 50 percent.[371] In exchange, however, many first round draft picks' contracts are now fully guaranteed.[372]

The NFLPA has also expressed mixed views about the existence of guaranteed contracts. In a 2002 editorial in *The Washington Post*, then-NFLPA Executive Director Gene Upshaw acknowledged that the possibility of guaranteed contracts "is severely undermined by the risk of a career-ending injury" and touted the benefits available to players as an alternative.[373] Then, in two reports issued by the NFLPA in or about 2002 and 2007 respectively, the NFLPA asserted that NFL player compensation is, in fact, largely guaranteed by explaining that more than half of all compensation paid to players is guaranteed.[374] However, importantly, this statistic does not mean that half of all compensation contracted was guaranteed—indeed, as discussed above, approximately 44 percent of all contracted compensation is guaranteed. Players are often paid guaranteed money (*e.g.*, a signing bonus or roster bonus) in the first or second year of the contract only to have the base salaries (the unguaranteed portions) in the later years of the contract go unpaid because the player's contract was terminated.

With this background in mind, there are several reasons why fully guaranteed compensation might not be beneficial to players collectively. First, while fully guaranteed contracts might be good for the players that receive them, it could result in many players not receiving any contract at all. If clubs were forced to retain a player of diminishing skill because his contract was guaranteed, a younger or less proven player might never get the opportunity to sign with the club.[375] Relatedly, clubs might continue to provide playing opportunities to the players with larger contracts in order to justify those contracts, preventing younger players from establishing themselves as starting or star players and earning higher salaries. It is also likely that under a system of guaranteed compensation, player salaries would decrease (at least in the short-term), particularly the salaries of the highest paid players and players who are less certain to add value to a roster, as clubs would be more cautious about taking on the financial liabilities, especially given the Salary Cap in place in the NFL. Similarly, clubs also may seek to minimize their financial liabilities by reducing roster sizes, which might cost marginal players their jobs, while again reducing opportunities for young or unproven players to join a club.

Clearly this is a complex issue, with the potential for substantial unintended consequences. Thus, we recognize the likely health value of guaranteed contracts, while simultaneously recognizing that it may not be the right solution for all players. Importantly, as discussed above, players who value a contractual guarantee over potentially higher but uncertain compensation may negotiate for that protection individually, as many currently do. Moreover, we expect that other recommendations made throughout this Report, including key recommendations related to the medical professionals who care for players, will make great strides toward protecting and promoting player health such that guaranteed compensation will be less critical for that purpose.

There are also logistical challenges to implementing fully guaranteed contracts. The finances and operations of the NFL and its clubs are greatly intertwined with the fact that NFL contracts have never been fully guaranteed. Since 1993, NFL clubs have had to comply with a strict Salary Cap that necessarily influences the types of contracts clubs are willing to offer, including the possibility of guaranteed compensation. Fully guaranteed contracts would be a fundamental and monumental alteration to the current business of the NFL that, at a minimum, would require a gradual phasing in process.[bi]

It is possible that a rate of guaranteed contracts less than 100 percent but more than the current 44 percent is also optimal. Given the varying factors to be weighed and considered, it is not clear percentage of guaranteed compensation would maximize player health for the most NFL players.

---

bi   For example, one rule that would likely have to be removed is the NFL's requirement that clubs deposit into a separate account the present value, less $2 million, of guaranteed compensation to be paid in future years. 2011 CBA, Art. 26 § 9. Peer reviewer and former NFL club executive Andrew Brandt believes clubs "hide behind" the funding rule to avoid guaranteeing player compensation, and have been largely successful in doing so. Andrew Brandt, Supplemental Peer Review Response (Nov. 6, 2015).

Recommendations Concerning The NFL and NFLPA – continued

Ultimately, we recommend further research into this question, including player and club perspectives, economic and actuarial analysis, and comprehensive consideration of the relevant trade-offs, ramifications, and potential externalities. In the meantime, we note that the trend toward greater use of contractual guarantees can help promote player health and allow individual negotiation by players based on their own goals and priorities.

Goal 2: To ensure that there are effective enforcement mechanisms when players' rights related to health are violated.

Principles Advanced: Respect; Health Primacy; and, Justice.

Recommendation 7:2-A: The CBA should be amended to provide for meaningful fines for any club or person found to have violated Sections 1 through 6 of Article 39 of the CBA.

Sections 1 through 6 of Article 39 contain a multitude of rules for clubs and club medical providers concerning player healthcare (*see* Appendix F). However, Article 39 does not contain any enforcement mechanisms. While the NFLPA or players could bring a Non-Injury Grievance or request an investigation before the Joint Committee (discussed in greater detail in Chapter 2: Club Doctors and Chapter 8: NFL Clubs), these processes are more likely to result in remedial and not financial action, particularly if no player has suffered distinct damage from the violation.[376] Additionally, Recommendation 2:2-A in the Club Doctors Chapter proposed a system of arbitration for resolving disputes between players and club doctors, *e.g.,* claims of medical malpractice. While this recommendation offers possible remedial benefit to players, it should not be viewed as the exclusive enforcement mechanism against club doctors and other employees. Clubs and club medical providers should be penalized for violating the player healthcare provisions regardless of whether their bad acts result in clear and compensable harm to a player.[bj] Indeed, the CBA contains many provisions that permit fines without evidence of actual harm.[377] If Article 39 is to be maximally effective, it should contain a fine system sufficient to deter violations and punish violators.[378]

There is precedent for our recommendation. Prior to the 2016 season, the NFL and NFLPA agreed to a disciplinary scheme and process for violations of the Concussion Protocol.[379] Under the agreement, both the NFL and NFLPA have the power to submit potential violations of the Concussion Protocol to a third-party arbitrator for evaluation.[380] The arbitrator then will issue a report to the Commissioner who can issue fines or strip the club of draft picks depending on the severity of the violation.[381] The Commissioner nevertheless retains "absolute discretion" to determine the penalties.[382] Article 39, like the Concussion Protocol, is deserving of meaningful discipline in the event of noncompliance.

Recommendation 7:2-B: The statute of limitations on filing Non-Injury Grievances, at least insofar as they are health-related, should be extended.[bk]

---

bj   An instructive example occurred during the 2015 NFL season. During week 11, St. Louis Rams quarterback Case Keenum sustained a head injury and noticeably had trouble walking after a play. A Rams trainer went on to the field to check on Keenum but did not remove Keenum from the game to undergo a concussion evaluation. Keenum was later diagnosed with a concussion. The NFL investigated the incident and the Rams' apparent mishandling of the Concussion Protocol but did not impose any discipline against the Rams or their medical staff. *See* Mike Florio, *Report: Rams won't be penalized for concussion debacle*, ProFootballTalk (Nov. 29, 2015, 8:12 AM), http://profootballtalk.nbcsports .com/2015/11/29/report-rams-wont-be-penalized-for-keenum-concussion-debacle/, *archived at* http://perma.cc/WR62-VQT2; Darin Gantt, *NFL has conference call to remind all teams of concussion protocol*, ProFootballTalk (Nov. 25, 2015, 12:09 PM), http://profootballtalk.nbcsports.com/2015/11/25/nfl-has-conference-call-to-remind-all-teams-of -concussion-protocol/, *archived at* http://perma.cc/TS3D-M4S3. Weeks later, it was announced that clubs would be disciplined (including fines or suspensions) for future violations of injury protocols. Darin Gantt, *NFL to fine, suspend teams who don't follow injury protocols*, ProFootballTalk (Dec. 17, 2015, 6:00 AM), http://profootballtalk.nbcsports.com /2015/12/17/nfl-to-fine-suspend-teams-who-dont-follow-injury-protocols/, *archived at* https://perma.cc/8CH3-77F9.
bk   The focus of this Report is on player health issues and thus we do not specifically address Non-Injury Grievances outside of the health context.

Recommendations Concerning The NFL and NFLPA – continued

The rights afforded to players under the CBA are only meaningful if there is meaningful enforcement. Nevertheless, there are at most a few health-related Non-Injury Grievances each year. This may be a result of few problems actually occurring, but it may alternatively reflect player concern about losing their job or status with the club. In particular, a player may fear that filing a Non-Injury Grievance would jeopardize the player's career, therefore causing him to forego the opportunity to pursue viable claims.[bl] Discussions with contract advisors confirmed that filing a Non-Injury Grievance is generally not considered a viable option because of the likely effect on the player.

Currently, players have 50 days "from the date of the occurrence or non-occurrence upon which the grievance is based . . . or from the date on which the facts of the matter became known or reasonably should have been known" to file a Non-Injury Grievance.[bm] Setting a statute of limitations always requires trading-off protecting the injured party against the other side's interests in preserving evidence. There are tough judgment calls to be made in some cases, but the statute of limitations in this case is clearly too short to be fair. This statute of limitations is far shorter than the two- or three-year statute of limitations typical to negligence or medical malpractice actions under most states laws.[383] Moreover, unless the player has left the club very close to the date of the action or omission that gave rise to the grievance, the player is unlikely to pursue a timely grievance.

We propose that the statute of limitations for Non-Injury Grievances be the latest of: (1) one year from the date of the occurrence or non-occurrence upon which the grievance is based; (2) one year from the date on which the facts of the matter became known or reasonably should have been known; or, (3) 90 days from the date of the player's separation[bn] from the club, provided the Non-Injury Grievance is filed within three years from the date of the occurrence or non-occurrence upon which the grievance is based.

The problem with the current short statutes of limitations on grievances is evident in the Concussion Litigation. The NFL's principal defense in the Concussion Litigation was that the players' claims were preempted by the LMRA—in other words, that the players' claims were required to be brought as grievances under the CBA and not in court. Had the NFL succeeded (the case was ultimately settled) and the players faced arbitration, they would have had great difficulty due to the short statute of limitations on Non-Injury Grievances, which would likely have barred their claims.[384] If the NFL's position is that these kinds of claims are preempted and should instead be arbitrated, it must allow for a fair Non-Injury Grievance process, including a fairer statute of limitations. The proposed statute of limitations would provide players a meaningful opportunity to consider their options and pursue claims for wrongs committed in arbitration without jeopardizing their often tenuous careers.

Goal 3: To improve player access to and understanding of their health rights and benefits.

Principles Advanced: Respect; Empowered Autonomy; Transparency; Collaboration and Engagement; and, Justice.

Recommendation 7:3-A: The NFL and NFLPA should continue and improve efforts to educate players about the variety of programs and benefits available to them.

---

bl Current Player 8: "You don't have the gall to stand against your franchise and say 'They mistreated me.'" . . . I, still today, going into my eighth year, am afraid to file a grievance, or do anything like that[.]" While it is illegal for an employer to retaliate against an employee for filing a grievance pursuant to a CBA, *N.L.R.B. v. City Disposal Systems Inc.*, 465 U.S. 822, 835–36 (1984), such litigation would involve substantial time and money for an uncertain outcome.

bm 2011 CBA, Art. 43 § 3. Other American professional sports leagues have similar statutes of limitations: the NBA provides 30 days, 2011 NBA CBA, Art. XXXI; MLB provides 45 days, 2012 MLB CBA, Art. XI; and, the NHL provides 60 days, 2013 NHL CBA, Art. 17. However, the CFL permits players one year to initiate grievance. 2014 CFL CBA, § 4.02.

bn Separation would include the club terminating the player's contract, the expiration of the player's contract or the player's filing of retirement papers with the NFL.

Recommendations Concerning The NFL and NFLPA – continued

As discussed above and detailed in Appendices C and D, the NFL and NFLPA offer many benefits and programs to current and former players to help them on a wide spectrum of issues, including most importantly healthcare and career-related guidance. However, it appears that many players are not taking full advantage of these programs.[bo]

The NFL and NFLPA both make some efforts to address this problem.

In comments provided to us, the NFL explained that "[t]he NFL Retirement Plan now sends out one mailing that summarizes all potential benefits. There is also one telephone number that will direct a player to the appropriate resource. Finally, retired players may access all of the relevant information at www.MyGoalLine.com."[385]

As for the NFLPA, at the conclusion of each season, the NFLPA provides the contract advisors an "End of Season Player Checklist." The Checklist is a multi-page document summarizing many of the players' important rights, benefits, and opportunities, such as obtaining medical records, obtaining second medical opinions, filing for workers' compensation, Injury Protection or disability benefits, understanding their insurance options, understanding off-season compliance with the Policies on Performance-Enhancing Substances and Substances of Abuse, and preparing for life after football by engaging the benefits and programs offered by the NFL and NFLPA. Contract advisors are required to provide the Checklist to all of their clients and certify in writing to the NFLPA that they have discussed the contents with their clients. In short, the Checklist is an excellent document and the NFLPA should be commended for its creation and use. Similarly, the NFLPA has on its website a Benefits Book, summarizing the various benefit plans. Nevertheless, it is unclear if these documents are ever provided directly to the player.

Each preseason every player should be given a manual that lists and explains all of the different programs and benefits for which they are eligible, either through the NFL, NFLPA, or otherwise. Players should receive the manual again whenever their contract is terminated and again at or near the conclusion of the season. Providing the manual near the conclusion of the season is important because many useful programs and seminars are conducted during the offseason. We further recommend that this manual be a joint creation of the NFL and NFLPA, and that an electronic copy be provided to every contract advisor and financial advisor so they can advise their clients accordingly.

The NFL already does create a document along these lines, entitled the Player Engagement Resource Guide, which lists and describes current and former player programs and resources.[386]

The above-mentioned efforts to inform players about these programs and benefits are steps in the right direction. However, they do not appear to have been fully successful, a problem with which many employers struggle. In interviews we conducted, current and former players were generally unclear and unsure about what information they had received. Although this is also a responsibility of the players, there is room for additional ideas and efforts in this area by the NFL and NFLPA.

We believe the NFL and NFLPA should make all benefit and retirement plans publicly available on their websites. Information about NFL player benefits is made available to players by the NFL and NFLPA through the website mygoalline.com, and to contract advisors and financial advisors through the NFLPA's website. However, players can only access mygoalline.com with a username and password, the full plan documents are not readily available to contract advisors and financial advisors, and neither the NFL nor the NFLPA websites otherwise make publicly available information about any of the various benefit and retirement programs that are available to NFL players. These plans should be readily available so that current, former, and future players, player family members, and other trusted advisors can review them to assist players. Public access will also allow academics, government officials, and others with an interest in the topic to review the plans and potentially make recommendations that would improve the plans and players' health.

---

bo Indeed, in a 2014 interview, Troy Vincent, a former Pro Bowl cornerback and former President of the NFLPA who is now the NFL's Executive Vice President of Football Operations, explained that the NFL's Player Care Foundation offers former players comprehensive medical examinations free of charge but that "the lines are empty." Jim Baumbach, *Life After Football*, Newsday, Jan. 25, 2015, *available at* 2015 WLNR 2381142.

Recommendations Concerning The NFL and NFLPA – continued

Finally, bare provision of information and documents to the players is not sufficient. Although players are ultimately responsible for taking advantage of benefits available to them, we know from behavioral science that too much information can be overwhelming[bp] and that certain approaches are more likely to result in comprehension and action. The NFL and NFLPA must work together (including potentially with experts in behavioral science) to ensure that the information being provided to the players is understandable, digestible, and actionable and that the players are actually processing the information. This will likely require substantial investments in education along with attempts to monitor whether players understand what they are being told. For example, quizzes after providing information, as are sometimes used in clinical trial informed consent, are one method of ensuring players are taking the information provided to them seriously.

Recommendation 7:3-B: The NFL and NFLPA should undertake a comprehensive actuarial and choice architecture analysis of the various benefit and retirement programs to ensure they are maximally beneficial to players.

Choice architecture refers to the ways in which choices are presented to consumers.[387] A common and relevant choice architecture example is constructing retirement plans such that employees are automatically enrolled in them but allowed to opt out if they so choose, which has the effect of "nudging" individuals into more sensible amounts of retirement savings.[388] According to Aon Hewitt, one of the world's leading human resources consulting firms, 61.7 percent of firms automatically enroll employees in retirement plans.[389] In addition to auto-enrollment, there are several other relevant choice architecture constructs, including claims processes, required documentation, payment schedules, notifications and assumptions about age, marital and dependent status, income, and other information. A comprehensive analysis of how the NFL and NFLPA benefit and retirement programs are configured from a choice architecture perspective will help ensure that the maximum number of players are receiving the benefits to which they are entitled and in a manner that is most helpful to them.

Recommendation 7:3-C: The purpose of certain health-related committees should be clarified and their powers expanded.

As is discussed in the Enforcement section of various stakeholder chapters, players generally have three options within the confines of the CBA concerning healthcare-related problems they can file: (1) a Non-Injury Grievance; (2) a complaint with the ACC; or (3) a complaint with the Joint Committee. While a Non-Injury Grievance can provide a player the opportunity to be compensated for a wide variety of wrongs, the Joint Committee and ACC are both supposed to be responsible for player health matters, including the possibility of conducting investigations. However, the authority of these Committees is unclear.

The Joint Committee has the authority to initiate an investigation run by neutral doctors, but the Joint Committee is only obligated to "act[] upon" the doctors' recommendations, which is somewhat vague. It is unclear what it means for the Joint Committee to "act[] upon" the recommendations and there is nothing binding the NFL or the clubs to "act[] upon" the doctors' recommendations.

The ACC is even weaker than the Joint Committee. The ACC merely refers complaints to the NFL and the club involved and the NFL and the club are then free to "determine an appropriate response."

---

bp   Current Player 10: "Unfortunately, advice from agents and especially the NFLPA in a long meeting with lots of information falls on deaf ears most times. Players don't care about this information until it pertains to them."

Recommendations Concerning The NFL and NFLPA – continued

At least one of the committees should have the ability to conduct a thorough investigation and/or hold a hearing and make binding their findings and recommendations. If the responsible parties fail to comply with the recommendations, they should be meaningfully fined until there is compliance.

The purpose of the committees should also be clarified to differentiate them from a Non-Injury Grievance. The current advantage of the committees from the players' perspective is that complaints to the committees are not subject to the strict 50-day statute of limitations for Non-Injury Grievances. Additionally, the committees consist generally of persons working in the medical field as opposed to the lawyer presiding over a Non-Injury Grievance. Although the arbitrator might consider expert medical testimony in deciding a Non-Injury Grievance, the committees might offer expertise or recommendations befitting their qualifications before matters reach the point of a Non-Injury Grievance.

Any change to the committees should also take into consideration other recommendations made herein, including the creation of a Medical Committee jointly selected by the NFL and NFLPA to hire, review, and terminate club doctors, as outlined in Chapter 2: Club Doctors, Recommendation 2:1-A. Our proposed Medical Committee may have overlapping areas of expertise and responsibilities as the committees discussed in this recommendation.

By reorganizing and clarifying the roles and authority of the committees, they will be more effective for all parties involved.

Goal 4: To hold players accountable for their own acts affecting their health and the health of other players.

Principles Advanced: Respect; Health Primacy; and, Justice.

Recommendation 7:4-A: The NFL and NFLPA should continue and intensify their efforts to ensure that players take the Concussion Protocol seriously.

As discussed in Chapter 1: Players, Section C: Current Practices, at least some players have sought to avoid undergoing the Concussion Protocol after suffering a suspected concussion. It is possible that players' non-cooperation is sometimes a result of the concussion suffered and diminished capacity. However, other players who do so either do not fully understand the risks of playing with a concussion or are so committed to playing and winning that they will continue to play no matter the possible health consequences. It is our understanding that both the NFL and NFLPA are providing players with information about the risks of concussions. Nevertheless, steps should be taken by the NFL and NFLPA, among others, to resolve issues concerning players' cooperation with the Concussion Protocol.

While the Concussion Protocol is generally helpful for ensuring players do not play with suspected or actual head injuries, it only works if players cooperate.[bq] Consequently, it is important that the NFL and NFLPA continue to educate players on the risks of concussions and the importance of the Concussion Protocol for both their short- and long-term health.

---

bq   A positive example occurred during the 2015 season when Pittsburgh Steelers quarterback Ben Roethlisberger self-reported concussion symptoms during the fourth quarter of a close game. Mike Florio, *Roethlisberger self-reported concussion symptoms*, ProFootballTalk (Nov. 29, 2015, 10:15 PM), http://profootballtalk.nbcsports.com/2015/11/29/roethlisberger-self-reported-concussion-symptoms/, *archived at* http://perma.cc/52EZ-D2W9.

Recommendations Concerning The NFL and NFLPA – continued

If players do not cooperate with the Concussion Protocol even after substantial effort has been made to educate them on its importance, it may be in the interests of player health to adopt stronger deterrent mechanisms, including fines and/or suspensions.

Recommendation 7:4-B: The NFL and NFLPA should agree to a disciplinary system, including fines and/or suspensions, for players who target another player's injury or threaten or discuss doing so.

Prior to the 2015 Super Bowl, New England Patriots cornerback Brandon Browner said he would encourage his team-mates to target and try to hit the injured shoulder of Seattle Seahawks safety Earl Thomas and the injured elbow of Seahawks cornerback Richard Sherman.[390] Similarly, in the 2012 NFC Championship game, New York Giants special teams players Jacquian Williams and Devin Thomas discussed targeting San Francisco 49ers kick returner Kyle Williams due to his history of concussions.[391] Generally, the NFL does not fine and/or suspend players unless they have violated the Playing Rules in an egregious way. However, when such threats are made, the NFL should not need to wait until the Playing Rules have been broken or a player is actually injured before taking action. The discussion or encouragement of targeting players' injuries increases the likelihood of players taking actions that unnecessarily harm other players and thus should not be tolerated. On this point, the threat to player health is too real not to act proactively.

i) NFLPA-Specific Recommendations

The below recommendations are NFLPA-specific. In other words, they are either within the NFLPA's unique control or potentially adverse to the NFL's interests.

Before getting to these recommendations, there are additional recommendations concerning the NFLPA that are made in other chapters:

- Chapter 1: Players—Recommendation 1:1-A: With assistance from contract advisors, the NFL, the NFLPA, and others, players should familiarize themselves with their rights and obligations related to health and other benefits, and should avail themselves of applicable benefits.

- Chapter 6: Personal Doctors—Recommendation 6:1-A: The NFLPA and clubs should take steps to facilitate players' usage of personal doctors.

Additionally, because the NFLPA regulates contract advisors and financial advisors, all recommendations made in those chapters also concern the NFLPA. NFLPA-specific recommendations are listed here.

Goal 5: For the NFLPA to take additional affirmative steps to hold accountable those stakeholders who do not meet their legal and ethical obligations concerning player health.

Principles Advanced: Respect; Health Primacy; Transparency; Managing Conflicts of Interest; and, Justice.

Recommendation 7:5-A: The NFLPA should consider investing greater resources in investigating and enforcing player health issues, including Article 39 of the 2011 CBA.

Recommendations Concerning The NFL and NFLPA – continued

The 2011 CBA contains many provisions and rules concerning player health and club and club doctors' obligations related thereto. Article 39 of the CBA houses many of these obligations. However, as discussed above, questions have been raised by some stakeholders we interviewed about the NFLPA's ability to investigate and enforce player health provisions through grievances. One possibility is for the NFLPA to hire additional attorneys with a focus on investigating and litigating player health, safety and welfare matters.

Goal 6: To provide current and former players with the resources necessary to maximize their health.

Principles Advanced: Health Primacy; Empowered Autonomy; and, Collaboration and Engagement.

Recommendation 7:6-A: The NFLPA should continue to assist former players to the extent such assistance is consistent with the NFLPA's obligations to current players.

As discussed above, the NFLPA's principal obligations are to current players, not former players. This legal reality creates tension between the NFLPA and former players. In recent years, the NFLPA has made efforts to smooth this tension by negotiating benefits and creating programs that help former players. It is admirable of the current players that they effectively agreed to give up a portion of their potential income to help the players that came before them. The NFLPA should continue to try and balance these, at times, incongruent interests. To do so, the NFLPA can remind current players of the sacrifices made by former players and the different circumstances under which they played. The NFLPA works to advance the interests of current players, many of whom quickly become former players. Thus, the NFLPA should try to continue and help those men as much as it can.

Endnotes

1   American Needle, Inc. v. Nat'l Football League, 560 U.S. 183, 187 (2010).

2   *See* 26 U.S.C. § 501(c)(6) (2012) (specifying "professional football leagues" as tax exempt).

3   Drew Harwell and Will Hobson, *The NFL is dropping its tax-exempt status. Why that ends up helping them out ends up helping them out.* Wash. Post, Apr. 28, 2015, http://www.washingtonpost.com/news/business/wp/2015/04/28/the-nfl-is-dropping-its-tax-exempt-status-why-that-ends-up-helping-them-out/, *archived at* http://perma.cc/XH58-QCKG.

4   *See* Brady v. Nat'l Football League, 640 F.3d 785 (8th Cir. 2011) (listing each of the 32 different entities as defendants in lawsuit).

5   *See* 2012 NFL Constitution and Bylaws, Art. II, § 2.1 (the purpose of the NFL is "[t]o promote and foster the primary business of League members, each member being an owner of a professional football club located in the United States.").

6   *See* 2012 NFL Constitution and Bylaws, Art. VIII, § 8.1.

7   *See id.* at § 8.4(b).

8   *See id.* at § 8.4(a).

9   *See id.* at § 8.10.

10 *See id.* at § 8.9.

11 *See id.* at § 8.13(A).

12 *See id.* at § 8.3.

13 *See* 2012 NFL Constitution and Bylaws, Art. III (discussing eligibility of members). The NFL's rule has withstood legal challenges. *See* Sullivan v. Nat'l Football League, 34 F.3d 1091 (1st Cir. 1994) (reversing judgment of $51 million for former New England Patriots owner Billy Sullivan and remanding for a new trial). In 1998, Sullivan settled the case for $11.5 million, leaving the NFL's policy in effect. *See* Frank Litsky, *Billy Sullivan, 86, Founder Of Football Patriots, Dies*, N.Y. Times, Feb. 24, 1998, http://www.nytimes.com/1998/02/24/sports/billy-sullivan-86-founder-of-football-patriots-dies.html, *archived at* http://perma.cc/8V2F-Y8NU. *See also* Drew D. Kause, *The National Football League's Ban on Corporate Ownership: Violating Antitrust Law to Preserve Traditional Ownership – Implications Arising from William H. Sullivan's Antitrust Suit*, 2 Seton Hall J. Sports L. 175 (1992).

14 *See* 2012 NFL Constitution and Bylaws, Art. VIII (describing the process for hiring the Commissioner and the Commissioner's responsibilities and authority).

15 *See* Lindsay H. Jones, *NFL Owners Have Lots to Tackle at Annual Meeting*, USA Today, Mar. 23, 2014, http://www.usatoday.com/story/sports/nfl/2014/03/23/nfl-owners-meetings/6804693/, *archived at* http://perma.cc/FY7A-BGZK (discussing agenda for March 2014 meeting including potential rules changes, selection of Super Bowl hosts, disciplining Colts' owner Jim Irsay for a DUI, and, determining the schedule); Monique N Jones, *Recap: NFL Commissioner Roger Goodell Recaps Owners Meetings*, USA Today, Oct. 9, 2014, http://www.usatoday.com/story/sports/nfl/teams/2014/10/08/roger-goodell-news-conference-owners-meetings/16938197, *archived at* http://perma.cc/MLQ9-C86M (discussing agenda for October 2014 meeting including the sale of the Buffalo Bills, a new drug program, Commissioner discipline and the NFL's personal conduct policy, domestic violence issues, and, the possibility of a club moving to Los Angeles).

16 Ben Volin, *Still No Timetable on 'Deflategate' Report*, Bos. Globe, Mar. 25, 2015, *available at* 2015 WLNR 8888394.

17 *See* Mike Freeman, Two Minute Warning: How Concussions, Crime, and Controversy Could Kill the NFL (and What the League Can Do to Survive) 98 (2015) ("Some . . . owners see their teams simply as ATM machines, and players as interchangeable parts.")

18 *See* Rob Huizenga, You're Okay, It's Just a Bruise 124 (1994) (The Raiders orthopedist, Dr. Robert Rosenfeld, explaining to Huizenga "Al doesn't like us to use stretchers . . . [t]he team gets demoralized and plays less aggressively when they see a teammate getting carted off the field on a stretcher."); *id.* at 150, 166 (Davis pressuring players to take pain-killing injections); *id.* at 239 (Davis pressuring Club doctors not to tell players about the risks of playing football or the full extent of their injuries); *id.* at 76 (A Raiders' questionnaire to college athletic trainers asking: "Is the athlete injury prone?" "Does he recover quickly?" "Will he play when he's ailing?").

19 Carlton Thompson, *Raiders, Davis Takes a Hit from Former Internist: Huizenga's Book Details Some Questionable Medical Practices*, Hous. Chronicle, Oct. 15, 1995, *available at* 1995 WLNR 5230160.

20 Todd Archer, *Jerry: Romo Injury Not Season-ending*, ESPN (Oct. 29, 2014, 1:29 PM), http://espn.go.com/dallas/nfl/story/_/id/11784154/dallas-cowboys-owner-jerry-jones-says-qb-tony-romo-play-sunday-arizona-cardinals, *archived at* http://perma.cc/RQ2F-HUDM.

21 Mark Purdy, *Purdy: John York enjoys San Francisco 49ers' return to the Super Bowl from the background,* San Jose Mercury-News, Jan. 22, 2013, http://www.mercurynews.com/ci_22429014/purdy-john-york-enjoys-san-francisco-49ers-return, *archived at* http://perma.cc/7LGM-4YKV.

22 *See* Paul Gutierrez, *NFL health chair says game 'safer,'* ESPN, (Mar. 23, 2015), http://espn.go.com/nfl/story/_/id/12548062/john-york-nfl-health-safety-advisory-committee-cites-culture-change, *archived at* http://perma.cc/WTE9-QQUM; David Fucillo, *John York discusses concussions, recent 49ers retirement,* SB Nation (Jun. 17, 2015), http://www.ninersnation.com/2015/6/17/8797057/john-york-discusses-concussions-recent-49ers-retirements, *archived at* http://perma.cc/NM2A-YW3Q.

23 *See* Samer Kalaf, *The Colts' New Rule Proposal: Touchdown Drives Worth Up To Nine Points*, Deadspin (Mar. 18, 2015, 3:33 PM), http://deadspin.com/the-colts-new-rule-proposal-touchdown-drives-worth-up-1692203684, *archived at* http://perma.cc/UHV8-EFVY (providing NFL's internal summary document of proposed rule changes and describing 2015 Competition Committee as Atlanta Falcons President Rich McKay, St. Louis Rams Head Coach Jeff Fisher, Dallas Cowboys Chief Operating Officer Stephen Jones, Cincinnati Bengals Head Coach Marvin Lewis, New York Giants Owner John Mara, Green Bay Packers President Mark Murphy, Baltimore Ravens General Manager Ozzie Newsome, Houston Texans General Manager Rick Smith and Pittsburgh Steelers Head Coach Mike Tomlin).

24 CBA, Art. 50, § 2.

25 Michael David Smith, *Five Rules Changes Get NFL Owners' Approval at League Meeting,* ProFootballTalk (Mar. 26, 2014, 10:11 AM), http://profootballtalk.nbcsports.com/2014/03/26/five-rules-changes-pass-as-nfl-owners-vote-at-league-meeting/, *archived at* http://perma.cc/6Z49-4J3J.

26 *See* Mark Fainaru-Wada & Steve Fainaru, League of Denial: The NFL, Concussions and the Battle for Truth 344 (2013) [hereinafter, "*League of Denial*"] (describing how the NFL agreed to move the yard line from where kickoffs take place from the 30 yard line to the 35 yard line at the insistence of Kevin Guskiewicz, a University of North Carolina scientist and concussion expert).

27 CBA, Art. 50, § 1(c).

28 NFL Comments and Corrections (June 24, 2016).

29 *See* 26 U.S.C. § 501(c)(5) (listing labor organizations as those exempted from taxation). An additional aspect of the NFLPA's operations also bears mentioning. In 1994, the NFLPA formed a Virginia for-profit entity known as the National Football League Players Association, Incorporated, or "Players, Inc." Players, Inc. is responsible for group licensing of NFL player rights. In 2013, each NFL player received $8,800 in royalties from Players, Inc. *See* NFLPA Department of Labor Form LM-2 Labor Organization Annual Report (2013). *See also* Adderley v. Nat'l Football

League Players Ass'n, 07-cv-943, 2008 WL 3287030 (N.D. Cal. Aug. 6, 2008) (denying NFLPA's motion to dismiss lawsuit by former players concerning Players, Inc. royalties); David Elfin, NFLPA settles lawsuit with Adderly for $26.5M, Wash. Times, Jun. 6, 2009, available at 2009 WLNR 10883474; Grant v. Nat'l Football League Players Ass'n, 11-cv-3118, 2012 WL 1870974 (C.D.Cal. May 22, 2012) (rejecting former players' claims that NFLPA breached its fiduciary duty to them by having failed to seek licensing opportunities for them and by alleging having failed to distribute royalty income accurately), aff'd 566 Fed.Appx. 569 (9th Cir. 2014).

30 U.S.C. § 159(a).

31 Eller v. Nat'l Football League Players Ass'n, 872 F. Supp. 2d 823, 834 (D.Minn. 2012).

32 See Department Contacts, Nat'l Football League Players Ass'n, https ://www.nflplayers.com/about-us/Department--Contacts/ (last visited Aug. 7, 2015) (listing NFLPA employees in the following departments: Executive; Benefits; Communications; Finance and Asset Management; Former Player Services; Human Resources; Information Systems; Legal; Player Affairs and Development; Salary Cap and Agent Administration; Security and Operations; and Players, Inc.).

33 NFL Players Association Constitution, Art. 3 (2007), available at http://www.ipmall.info/hosted_resources/SportsEntLaw_Institute/ League%20Constitutions%20&%20Bylaws/NFLPA%20Constitution%20 -%20March%202007.pdf, archived at https://perma.cc/HAF5-24E8 ?type=pdf ("NFLPA Constitution").

34 NFLPA Constitution, § 4.01(b).

35 NFLPA Constitution, § 1.03.

36 NFLPA Constitution, Art. 3.

37 NFLPA Constitution, § 5.01.

38 NFLPA Constitution, §§ 4.01–02.

39 NFLPA Constitution, § 5.02.

40 NFLPA Constitution, § 4.01(a). "A person is not eligible for election or re-election as an Executive Officer [, including President,] unless he has been on the roster of an NFL Club during the previous twelve (12) months." NFLPA Constitution, § 4.03. There has been speculation that NFL Clubs intentionally refuse to sign NFLPA Presidents. See, e.g., Mike Florio, NFLPA president gets another NFL gig, ProFootballTalk (Jul. 29, 2014, 10:31 AM), http://profootballtalk.nbcsports.com/2014/07/29/ nflpa-president-gets-another-nfl-gig/, archived at http://perma.cc/RF2Q -D3C6.

41 NFLPA Constitution, § 4.06.

42 NFLPA Constitution, §4.01.

43 Bob Carter, Rozelle Made NFL What It Is Today, ESPN, http://espn.go .com/classic/biography/s/rozelle_pete.html (last visited Aug. 7, 2015), archived at http://perma.cc/9NS6-D4R2.

44 History, Nat'l Football League Players Ass'n, https://www.nflpa.com/ about/history (last visited Aug. 7, 2015), archived at https://perma.cc /3D2R-8EQG?type=pdf [hereinafter "NFLPA History"].

45 Id.

46 CBA, Art. VII.

47 CBA, Art. VII, § 2(f). By the conclusion of Rozelle's tenure, medical insurance coverage increased to a maximum of $1 million. 1982 CBA, Art. XXXIV.

48 CBA, Art. XI, § 4.

49 CBA, Art. XI, § 5.

50 NFLPA History supra n. 44.

51 Players deemed to have suffered "substantial partial or total disablement as determined by the Retirement Board which is deemed to be permanent" eligible for $200/month in benefits for the duration of the disability. 1970 CBA, Art. VI § 2(c)(2). When Rozelle retired as Commissioner in 1989, the benefits were $4,000/month for football-related injuries and $750/month for non-football related injuries. 1982 CBA, Art. XXXIV, § 8.

52 CBA, Art. VI, § 4. The amounts of coverage were not identified. When Rozelle retired, a player could obtain a $50,000 life insurance policy plus $10,000 of coverage for each Credited Season up to $100,000. 1982 CBA, Art. XXXIII, § 1.

53 CBA, Art. VI, § 4.

54 NFLPA History supra n. 44.

55 See Glenn M. Wong, Essentials of Sports Law, § 11.3 (4th ed. 2010) (providing summary of NFL-NFLPA labor history).

56 Id.

57 CBA, Art. XI.

58 Id. at § 1.

59 Id. at § 3.

60 See Chris Deubert & Glenn M. Wong, Understanding the Evolution of Signing Bonuses and Guaranteed Money in the National Football League: Preparing for the 2011 Collective Bargaining Negotiations, 16 UCLA Ent. L. Rev. 179, 187 (2009) (describing the various legal proceedings leading to free agency in those sports).

61 See Wong, supra n. 55.

62 Id.

63 Bart Barnes, Garvey: Players May Seek 65% of NFL Gross Income, NFLPA Will Seek Base Salary Scales, Wash. Post, Nov. 25, 1981, available at 1981 WLNR 488341.

64 CBA, Art. XXI, § 1.

65 Id.

66 Id.

67 CBA, Art. XXXI, § 2.

68 CBA, Art. XXXI, § 6.

69 CBA, Art. XXXI, § 3.

70 CBA, Art. XXXI, § 4.

71 CBA, Art. XXXII, § 2.

72 NFLPA History, supra n. 44.

73 See Bart Barnes, Players Adamant About Drug Test, Wash. Post, July 15, 1982, available at 1982 WLNR 594666; Ken Denlinger, Teamwork is the Solution, Wash. Post, July 2, 1982, available at 1982 WLNR 587496; Bart Barnes, Rozelle, Garvey: Different Views on Drug Abuse, Wash. Post, June 19, 1982, available at 1982 WLNR 569668.

74 See A Brief History of the Drug War, DrugPolicy.org, http://www .drugpolicy.org/new-solutions-drug-policy/brief-history-drug-war (last visited Aug. 7, 2015), archived at http://perma.cc/39W2-7PM5; II. America's Drug Use Profile — Cocaine Abuse: We Are Still Paying The Price For The 1980s, Office of National Drug Control Policy, https://www .ncjrs.gov/ondcppubs/publications/policy/99ndcs/ii-e.html (last visited Aug. 7, 2015), archived at https://perma.cc/4X77-45E5 (discussing significant increases in cocaine usage during the 1980s).

75 See Cocaine And A Super Bowl Team: The Last Straw: Drugs In The NFL: A Chronology, L.A. Times, Jan. 29, 1986, http://articles.latimes.com /1986-01-29/sports/sp-1319_1_cocaine, archived at http://perma.cc/ FGW9-QF9U (discussing drug-related incidents and policies in the NFL from 1972–86); Frank Litsky, Player Tells of Wide Drug Use in the N.F.L., N.Y. Times, Jun. 10, 1982, http://www.nytimes.com/1982/06/10/sports /player-tells-of-wide-drug-use-in-nfl.html, archived at http://perma.cc/ E9GA-V6JK (discussing allegations by former player that cocaine usage was rampant throughout the NFL); David J. Sisson & Brian D. Trexell, The National Football League's Substance Abuse Policy: Is Further Conflict Between Players and Management Inevitable? 2 Marq. Sports. L.J. 1 (1991).

76 Barnes, supra note 73, at 1982 WLNR 569668.

77 Id. at 1982 WLNR 594666.

78 See Sisson, supra note 75, at 3–10 (discussing evolution of drug testing in the NFL during the 1980s).

79 CBA, Art. XXXI, § 7.

80 See Sisson, supra note 75, at 3–10 (discussing evolution of drug testing in the NFL during the 1980s).

81   *Id.*

82   NFLPA History, *supra* n. 44.

83   *See* Chris Deubert, Glenn M. Wong & John Howe, *All Four Quarters: A Retrospective and Analysis of the 2011 Collective Bargaining Process and Agreement in the National Football League*, 19 UCLA Ent. L. Rev. 1, 9–12 (2012) (discussing NFL-NFLPA labor relations between 1987 and 1993).

84   *Id.*

85   *See id.* at 6–13; NFLPA History.

86   Gary Pomerantz, *Arbitrator Rejects NFL Drug Testing*, Wash. Post, Oct. 28, 1986, *available at* 1986 WLNR 1907666

87   Christine Brennan, *NFL to Institute Year-Round, Random Testing for Steroids*, Wash. Post, Mar. 15, 1990, *available at* 1990 WLNR 4588145

88   Bob Carter, *Rozelle Made NFL What It Is Today*, ESPN.com, http://espn.go.com/classic/biography/s/rozelle_pete.html (last visited Aug. 7, 2015), *archived at* http://perma.cc/9NS6-D4R2.

89   *Paul Tagliabue*, Covington & Burling, LLP, http://www.cov.com/ptagliabue/ (last visited Aug. 7, 2015), *archived at* http://perma.cc/P8QR-CCHA.

90   *See* Marty York, *Price Tag of $80 Million NFL Version of Hard Times*, Globe & Mail (Toronto, ON), Mar. 22, 1984, *available at* 1984 WLNR 830899.

91   *See* Prentis Rogers, *CBS Drops Another $1 Billion into the NFL's Coffers*, Atlanta J-Const. (GA), Mar. 8, 1990, *available at* 1990 WLNR 2057314 (discussing CBS' agreement to pay more than $1 billion for a four year deal; NBC paying between $700 and $900 million for a multi-year deal and club television revenues equaling $32 million per year); Michael Janofsky, *$1.4 Billion Deal Adds Cable to N.F.L. Picture*, N.Y. Times, Mar. 16, 1987, *available at* 1987 WLNR 995997 (on file with author) (discussing ESPN's agreement to pay $1.42 billion to television NFL games over a three-year period).

92   *See* NFLPA History *supra* note 44; Deubert, *supra* note 83.

93   Deubert, *supra* note 83.

94   Leonard Shapiro, *NFL Players Making More Money, Living Longer, Report Says*, Wash. Post, Jan. 28, 1994, *available at* 1994 WLNR 5690724; Paul Needell, *There Is Life After Football Study: NFL Players Don't Die Young*, N.J. Star-Ledger, Sept. 29, 2002, *available at* 2002 WLNR 12895808; Alan Greenberg, *Case of Ticker Shock: Down the Road, that Hulking Lineman is Likely to Have a Heart in Sad Shape*, Hartford Courant, June 17, 2001, *available at* 2001 WLNR 10659744.

95   *Id.*

96   *See Heart Health Concerns for NFL Players*, Nat'l Inst. Occupational Health-Safety, Mar. 2012 (discussing methodology and results of 1994 study), *available at* http://www.cdc.gov/niosh/pgms/worknotify/pdfs/NFL_Notification_01.pdf, *archived at* https://perma.cc/LCT5-K9UD?type=pdf; *NFL Mortality Study*, Nat'l Inst. Occupational Health-Safety, Jan. 1994 (same), *available at* http://www.cdc.gov/niosh/pdfs/nflfactsheet.pdf, *archived at* https://perma.cc/PW3S-HXT2?type=pdf.

97   *NFL Mortality Study*, Nat'l Inst. Occupational Health-Safety, *supra* note 96.

98   *Id.*

99   *Id.*

100 CBA, Art. XLVIII-A.

101 Thomas Heath and Leonard Shapiro, *For NFL Players, There Are No Guarantees; Contracts Illustrate Issues With Union*, Wash. Post, Dec 15, 2002, *available at* 2002 WLNR 15313660.

102 *Id.*

103 *See* Jarrett Bell, *Grading Scale One Hurdle to Spotting Trend*, USA Today, Feb. 17, 1995, *available at* 1995 WLNR 2568233; Steve Jacobson, *Concussion Issue Must Be Tackled*, Newsday, Nov. 30, 1994, *available at* 1994 WLNR 475550.

104 *League of Denial*, Mark Fainaru-Wada & Steve Fainaru, League of Denial: The NFL, Concussions, and the Battle for Truth 24 (2013).

105 Gary Mihoces, *Documentary: For Years, NFL Ignored Concussion Evidence*, USA Today, Oct. 7, 2013, http://www.usatoday.com/story/sports/nfl/2013/10/07/frontline-documentary-nfl-concussions/2939747/, *archived at* http://perma.cc/N8H2-WMWV.

106 *League of Denial, supra* note 104, at 71–73.

107 *Id.* at 75.

108 *See id.* at 131 (discussing Pellman's appointment as Chairman of the MTBI Committee).

109 *Id.*

110 *Id.* at 127–28.

111 *Id.* at 131.

112 *Id.*

113 *Id.* at 126.

114 *Id.* at 131.

115 *Kevin Guskiewicz, Senior Associate Dean for Natural Sciences*, Univ. of N.C., http://college.unc.edu/administrationcontacts/guskiewicznaturalsciences/ (last visited Aug. 7, 2015), *archived at* http://perma.cc/JN4T-KP4M.

116 CBA, Art. XLVIII-B.

117 CBA, Art. XXXV.

118 *League of Denial, supra* note 104, at 131.

119 *Id.* at 132.

120 *Id.* at 138–39. The test, known as ImPACT, became widely used in all levels of sports and thus very profitable for Lovell. *Id.* at 183. The MTBI Committee even promoted its usage. *Id.*

121 *Id.* at 142–44.

122 *Id.*

123 *See id.* at 180 (mentioning that the MTBI Committee published a total of 16 articles in *Neurosurgery*); *id.* at 276 (discussing the MTBI Committee's sixteenth paper in June 2009).

124 *Id.* at 139.

125 *Id.*

126 *See id.* at 180 (mentioning that the MTBI Committee published a total of 16 articles in *Neurosurgery*); *id.* at 276 (discussing the MTBI Committee's sixteenth paper in June 2009).

127 *Id.* at 144; 166; 174; 276.

128 *Id.* at 167.

129 *Id.* at 144; 167.

130 *Id.* at 146 (discussing Cantu's role as the sports section editor of *Neurosurgery*).

131 *Id.*; *id.* at 172.

132 *Id.* at 171–72.

133 *Id.*

134 *See id.* at 188–89 (discussing Omalu's article).

135 *Id.* at 9–10; 151–61.

136 *Id.*; *id.* at 163.

137 *Id.* at 164.

138 *Id.* at 189.

139 *Id.* at 189–91.

140 CBA, Art. XLVIII-C.

141 CBA, Art. XLVIII-D.

142 Ken Murray, *Tagliabue to Retire as NFL's Chief in July; He Made Baltimore Wait for a New Team*, Balt. Sun, Mar. 21, 2006, *available at* 2006 WLNR 4664231.

143 *Id.*; Rick Gosselin, *Goodell's No Rookie When It Comes To The NFL*, Dallas Morning News, Aug. 8, 2006, *available at* 2006 WLNR 13712449.

144 The players included former Pittsburgh Steelers lineman Terry Long who committed suicide in July 2005, Mark Fainaru-Wada & Steve Fainaru, League of Denial: The NFL, Concussions, and the Battle for Truth 193–96 (2013), and Andre Waters, a former Philadelphia Eagles and Arizona Cardinals safety who committed suicide in November 2006, *id.* at 201–04.

145 *League of Denial, supra* note 104, at 217–18.

146 *Id.* at 168.

147 Gary Mihoces, *Issues Debated on Concussions, Doctors Disagree at NFL Meeting,* USA Today, Jun. 20, 2007, *available at* 2007 WLNR 11537008; *League of Denial, supra* note 104, at 219 (describing concussion summit as "designed to get the new commissioner up to speed").

148 *League of Denial, supra* note 104, at 219–28 (describing meeting).

149 *Id.* at 228.

150 *Id.*

151 *Id.* ("'Keep doing what you're doing,' he told Guskiewicz.")

152 *See* Harvey Araton, *Stealth Killer Puts Doctor On Mission With N.F.L.,* N.Y. Times, May 8, 2007, http://www.nytimes.com/2007/05/08/sports/football/08araton.html, *archived at* http://perma.cc/Y4EU-FRYW; Jodie Valade, *NFL Glories Come With A Price: A Career In Football Rewards Almost All Former Players With A Lifetime of Pain And Few Options To Deal With It,* Cleveland Plain Dealer, Aug. 17, 2003, *available at* 2003 WLNR 517073; Jeannine Stein, *This Sport Stays In Contact, Ailments Haunt NFL Retirees,* Chicago Trib., Jun. 15, 2003, *available at* 2003 WLNR 15259601.

153 Bob Raissman, *NFL's Secret Shame: Players Association Turn Backs On Down-and-Outsiders,* N.Y. Daily News, Jan. 21, 2007, *available at* 2007 WLNR 1263471. Upshaw's comments run counter to the NFLPA Constitution which includes Retired Members among its membership and also "recogniz[es] that retired players still have a stake in the actions of the NFLPA." NFLPA Constitution.

154 Pierce E. Scranton, Jr., Playing Hurt: Treating and Evaluating the Warriors of the NFL 145 (2001).

155 John Clayton, *NFL Owners Vote Unanimously to Opt Out of Labor Deal,* ESPN (May 20, 2008, 10:10 PM), http://sports.espn.go.com/nfl/news/story?id=3404596, *archived at* http://perma.cc/MZ2C-9AYZ.

156 William C. Rhoden, *Remembering Player, Friend And Enemy,* N.Y. Times, Aug. 22, 2008, http://www.nytimes.com/2008/08/22/sports/football/22rhoden.html, *archived at* http://perma.cc/FJ9N-EVSL.

157 Mike Florio, *De Smith Declares "War" Against the Owners,* ProFootball-Talk (Jan. 23, 2011, 12:21 PM), http://profootballtalk.nbcsports.com/2011/01/23/de-smith-declares-war-against-the-owners/, *archived at* http://perma.cc/3QVF-6NJB.

158 Mike Florio, *De Smith's Contract Expires in March 2012,* ProFootball-Talk (Jun. 13, 2011, 11:41 AM), http://profootballtalk.nbcsports.com/2011/06/13/de-smiths-contract-expires-in-march-2012/, *archived at* http://perma.cc/KH5W-Z472.

159 *Hearing On: Legal Issues Relating to Football Head Injuries,* Hearing Before the H. Comm. on the Judiciary, 111th Cong. (Oct. 28, 2009 and Jan. 4, 2010), *available at* http://judiciary.house.gov/index.cfm/hearings?ID=38827733-BF15-230A-9520-EA74C061B19D, *archived at* http://perma.cc/3H3U-6A4B?type=live.

160 *Id.* at 29.

161 *Id.* at 29–36.

162 *Id.*

163 *Id.* at 34.

164 *Football Players Head Injuries Before the H. Comm. on the Judiciary,* 111th Cong. (2009) (statement of DeMaurice Smith Executive Director, National Football Players Ass'n) *available at* http://judiciary.house.gov/_files/hearings/pdf/Smith091028.pdf, *archived at* https://perma.cc/3F3T-T6PZ?type=pdf; *see also* Alan Schwarz, *N.F.L. Union Says It Shares Blame On Head Injuries,* N.Y. Times, Nov. 1, 2009, http://www.nytimes.com/2009/11/01/sports/football/01union.html, *archived at* 2009 WLNR 21793818.

165 Mark Fainaru-Wada & Steve Fainaru, League of Denial: The NFL, Concussions, and the Battle for Truth 266–71 (2013) (discussing meeting).

166 *Id.*

167 *Id.* at 267 (mentioning Davis' presence); *id.* at 235 (discussing Davies' background).

168 *Id.* at 235.

169 *See id.* at 235–39 (discussing Davies' review and findings).

170 *Id.* at 279.

171 *Id.* at 283–88.

172 *Id.* at 286–88.

173 *Id.* at 286.

174 *Id.* at 344.

175 NFL Comments and Corrections (June 24, 2016), *citing* Alan Schwarz, *Concussion Committee Breaks with Predecessor,* N.Y. Times, June 1, 2010, http://www.nytimes.com/2010/06/02/sports/football/02concussion.html?_r=1, *archived at* https://perma.cc/E43W-V46E.

176 *Id.*

177 *See id.* at 210 (2013) (discussing Colt neurological consultant Hank Feuer and Cynthia Arfken, an associate professor at Wayne State University, stating there was no basis for the MTBI Committee's finding, in its seventh paper, that "it might be safe for college/high school football players to be cleared to return to play on the same day as [a concussion]."); *id.* at 178–79 (discussing Mark Lovell's disavowing responsibility for certain of the MTBI Committee's research).

178 *See* Chris Deubert, Glenn M. Wong & John Howe, *All Four Quarters: A Retrospective and Analysis of the 2011 Collective Bargaining Process and Agreement in the National Football League,* 19 UCLA Ent. L. Rev. 1 (2012).

179 *Id.*

180 CBA, Art. 45.

181 CBA, Art. 61.

182 CBA, Art. 21.

183 CBA, Art. 24.

184 CBA, Art. 39, § 1(a).

185 CBA, Art. 39, § 1(a).

186 CBA, Art. 39, § 1(b).

187 CBA, Art. 39, § 1(e).

188 CBA, Art. 39, § 1(c).

189 CBA, Art. 39, § 1(d).

190 CBA, Art. 57.

191 CBA, Art. 65.

192 CBA, Art. 12, § 5.

193 *See* Emily Kaplan, *The Games Go On, And So Does Life,* MMQB (Dec. 26, 2013), http://mmqb.si.com/2013/12/26/nfl-nflpa-the-trust-player-retirement-benefits/, *archived at* http://perma.cc/Z2LH-V8PM (discussing creation of the Trust); *Frequently Asked Questions,* Trust, http://playerstrust.com/frequently-asked-questions (last visited Aug. 7, 2015), *archived at* http://perma.cc/7NLC-HDTB (describing The Trust and its purpose).

194 CBA, Art. 12, § 5.

195 Mark Maske, *NFL Donating $30 Million to NIH for Brain Injury Research,* Wash. Post, Sept. 5, 2012, http://www.washingtonpost.com/blogs/football-insider/wp/2012/09/05/nfl-donating-30-million-to-nih-for-brain-injury-research/, *archived at* http://perma.cc/EKJ9-KR5Y.

196 Class Action Complaint, Eller v. Nat'l Football League Players Ass'n, (D. Minn. 2011) (No. 11-cv-2623), ECF No. 1.

197 Class Action Complaint, Brady v. Nat'l Football League, 779 F. Supp. 2d 992 (D. Minn. 2011) (No. 11-cv-639), ECF No. 57.

198 Stipulation of Dismissal, Brady v. Nat'l Football League, 779 F. Supp. 2d 992 (D. Minn. 2011) (No. 11-cv-639), ECF No. 199; *see also* Mike Florio, *Carl Eller Case is Dismissed,* ProFootballTalk, Aug. 24, 2011, http://profootballtalk.nbcsports.com/2011/08/24/carl-eller-case-is-dismissed/, *archived at* http://perma.cc/G2DT-XSVL.

199 Class Action Complaint, Eller v. Nat'l Football League Players Ass'n, *supra* note 196 at ¶ 136.

200 Eller v. Nat'l Football League Players Ass'n, 872 F. Supp. 2d 823 (D. Minn. 2012), *aff'd* 731 F.3d 752 (8th Cir. 2013).

201 *See id.*

202 *Duke Provides Infection Control Steps to Keep Pro Football Players Healthy,* Duke Med. News & Comm., https://pdc.dukemedicine.org/news/duke-provides-infection-control-steps-keep-pro-football-players-healthy, (last visited Mar. 15, 2016), *archived at* https://perma.cc/FSY4-KKSC.

203 *Id.*

204 *See Heart Health Concerns for NFL Players,* Nat'l Inst. Occupational Health-Safety, Mar. 2012 (discussing methodology and results of 1994 study), *available at* http://www.cdc.gov/niosh/pgms/worknotify/pdfs/NFL_Notification_01.pdf, *archived at* https://perma.cc/LCT5-K9UD?type=pdf.

205 Everett J. Lehman et al., *Neurodegenerative causes of death among retired National Football League players,* Neurology 2012;79:1970–74.

206 *See id.*

207 *Id.*

208 *Id.*

209 Class Action Complaint, Ballard v. Nat'l Football League Players Ass'n, (E.D.Mo. 2014) (No. 14-cv-01267).

210 *NFL Names Dr. Elizabeth Nabel First Chief Health And Medical Advisor,* NFL Communications (Feb. 9, 2015), http://nflcommunications.com/2015/02/09/nfl-names-dr-elizabeth-nabel-first-chief-health-and-medical-advisor/, *archived at* http://perma.cc/V9RV-DSKV.

211 NFL Comments and Corrections (June 24, 2016).

212 Nathaniel Vinton, *NFL hiring chief medical officer as controversial Dr. Elliot Pellman, who downplayed concussions, retires,* N.Y. Daily News, July 20, 2016, http://www.nydailynews.com/sports/football/controversial-doc-behind-nfl-concussion-policies-retires-article-1.2718836, *archived at* https://perma.cc/FGR6-HW8Z.

213 NFL Comments and Corrections (June 24, 2016).

214 NFL Comments and Corrections (June 24, 2016).

215 CBA, Art. 50, § 1(a).

216 CBA, Art. 39, § 3(a).

217 *Id.*

218 This information was provided by the NFLPA; *see also Synernet Staff Visits NFL Headquarters,* Synernet (Feb. 11, 2015), http://www.synernet.net/news/news.aspx, *archived at* https://perma.cc/E4UC-WNWP.

219 Mike Florio, *Survey asks players how seriously they take concussions,* ProFootballTalk (Dec. 5, 2015, 6:40 PM), http://profootballtalk.nbcsports.com/2015/12/05/survey-asks-players-how-seriously-they-take-concussions/, *archived at* https://perma.cc/P5NZ-XVS4.

220 The NFL currently has television broadcasting agreements with ESPN, NBC, CBS, FOX, NFL Network and DirecTV. In addition, the NFL has a radio broadcasting agreement with Westwood One. In total, the broadcasting agreements bring in approximately $7 billion in annual revenue to the NFL. Kurt Badenhausen, *The NFL Signs TV Deals Worth $27 Billion,* Forbes (Feb. 14, 2011, 6:13PM), http://www.forbes.com/sites/kurtbadenhausen/2011/12/14/the-nfl-signs-tv-deals-worth-26-billion/, *archived at* https://perma.cc/B64R-2GHV?type=pdf.

221 NFL Ventures is responsible for negotiating all of the league's major sponsorship, marketing, and media rights deals. NFL Ventures, which Commissioner Goodell ran before becoming Commissioner, includes four wholly-owned subsidiaries: NFL Enterprises, NFL Properties, NFL Productions, and NFL International. *See* Tommy Craggs, *Exclusive: Leaked Documents Show Operating Profits for NFL Ventures Rose 29 Percent Last Year,* Deadspin (July 15, 2011, 1:10 PM), http://deadspin.com/5821386/audited-financials-operating-profit-for-nfl-ventures-lp-rose-from-999-million-to-13-billion-last-year, *archived at* https://perma.cc/N9KB-7KGP?type=source.

222 NFL Network is the league-owned and operated television network devoted full-time to the NFL, including broadcasting select Thursday night games. For more information, see www.nfl.com/nflnetwork.

223 NFL Properties is responsible for licensing, sponsorship, and marketing. NFL Properties was the subject of Am. Needle, Inc. v. Nat'l Football League, 560 U.S. 183 (2010). NFL Properties was created by the 32 individual clubs to collectively market and license the clubs' individual intellectual property, such as names, colors, logos, and trademarks. In 2000, the clubs—through NFL Properties—granted Reebok an exclusive license to produce and sell trademarked headwear for the 32 clubs. American Needle, a former licensee and creator of NFL appareled headwear, could no longer create headwear with NFL logos and trademarks. American Needle challenged the exclusive license as an illegal restraint of trade by the 32 NFL clubs. The Northern District of Illinois granted the NFL summary judgment after finding that NFL Properties constituted a single entity for antitrust purposes, and therefore there was no contract, combination, or conspiracy to restrain trade. *See* Am. Needle, Inc. v. New Orleans La. Saints, 496 F. Supp. 2d 941, 943 (N.D. Ill. 2007). The Seventh Circuit affirmed. Am. Needle, Inc. v. Nat'l Football League, 538 F.3d 736 (7th Cir. 2008). The Supreme Court reversed. *Am. Needle,* 560 U.S. 183. While the Court noted that NFL clubs "depend upon a degree of cooperation for economic survival," the necessity of cooperation does not transform concerted action into the independent action of a single-entity. *Id.* at 198. Furthermore, that "even if league-wide agreements are necessary to produce football, it does not follow that concerted activity in marketing intellectual property is necessary to produce football." *Id.* at n.7.

224 NFL Enterprises is responsible for advertising, publicizing, promoting, marketing, and selling broadcasts of NFL games.

225 NFL Productions, also known as NFL Films, is the league-owned film company that for more than 50 years has produced award-winning films about the NFL. For more information *see* www.nflfilms.com.

226 NFL Digital is responsible for the league's technology and new media ventures, including www.nfl.com and NFL Mobile.

227 CBA, Art. 12, § 6.

228 CBA, Art. 12, §1, § 6.

229 Mark Leibovich, *Roger Goodell's Unstoppable Football Machine,* N.Y. Times, Feb. 3, 2016, http://www.nytimes.com/2016/02/07/magazine/roger-goodells-unstoppable-football-machine.html?_r=0, *archived at* https://perma.cc/Y7L5-A99L.

230 CBA, Art. 12, § 6(c)(i).

231 CBA, Art. 1.

232 CBA, Art. 12, § 2.

233 CBA, Art. 12, § 6(c)(v).

234 Substance Abuse Policy, § 1.3.

235 Substance Abuse Policy, § 1.3.1.

236 *Id.*

237 *See generally* 2014 Substance Abuse Policy, § 1.

238 *See* 2014 Substance Abuse Policy, § 1.4 – 1.5.

239 *See generally* 2014 Steroid Policy.

240 Steroid Policy, § 6.

241 *Id.* at § 3.1

242 *Id.* at § 7.

243 *See* 26 U.S.C. § 4980H.

244 Courts have considered whether the NFL is an employer of NFL players with mixed results.

In *Williams v. Nat'l Football League,* a Minnesota trial court determined that the NFL was a joint employer of two members of the Minnesota Vikings for purposes of Minnesota's Drug and Alcohol Testing in the Workplace Act (DATWA). Articulating the Minnesota Supreme Court's five-part test to determine whether an employment relationship exists, the court found that the NFL controlled the drug testing process, controlled the means and manner of performance and the location of team play, controlled the mode of payment to players, controlled the materials and tools used by players, and controlled the right to discipline and discharge players. Taken together, these factors supported the conclusion that the NFL is an employer for the purposes of DATWA and that DATWA applied in that case. 27-cv-08-29778, 2010 WL 1793130 (Minn.Dist.Ct. May 6, 2010).

Conversely, in *Brown v. Nat'l Football League,* the United States District Court for the Southern District of New York found that the NFL was not a former player's employer. In *Brown*, a former NFL player brought a personal injury action in state court against the NFL, seeking damages for a career-ending eye injury he sustained during a game when a referee threw a penalty flag that struck the player in the eye. The Court observed, "[a]t the time of his injury, Brown worked not for the NFL, but for the Cleveland Browns Football Company, a Delaware limited partnership and an entirely separate entity which happens to be a member of the NFL." 219 F. Supp. 2d 372, 383 (S.D.N.Y. 2002).

245 *See* 29 U.S.C. § 651, et seq.

246 *See* 42 U.S.C. § 12101, et seq.

247 Jessica L. Roberts et al., *Evaluating NFL Player Health and Performance: Legal and Ethical Issues*, Univ. Penn. L. Rev. (forthcoming 2017).

248 *See* Complaint, Maxwell v. Nat'l Football League, BC465842 (Cal.Sup.Ct. July 19, 2011), Dkt. No. 1.

249 *See Plaintiffs/Former Players*, NFL Concussion Litig., http://nflconcussionlitigation.com/?page_id=274 (last visited Aug. 7, 2015) (stating that as of June 1, 2013, there were more than 4,800 named player-plaintiffs in 242 concussion-related lawsuits).

250 *See* 28 U.S.C. § 1407 (describing grounds and process for transferring and consolidating multidistrict litigation).

251 Plaintiffs' Amended Master Administrative Long-Form Complaint, In re Nat'l Football League Players' Concussion Injury Litig., 2:12-md-2323 (E.D.Pa. July 17, 2012), ECF No. 2642.

252 *See generally* Docket, In re Nat'l Football League Players' Concussion Injury Litig., 2:12-md-2323 (E.D.Pa. July 17, 2012) (including many case transfer orders).

253 *See id.*

254 *See* Plaintiffs' Amended Master Administrative Long-Form Complaint at ¶ 6, In re Nat'l Football League Players' Concussion Injury Litig., 2:12-md-2323 (E.D.Pa. July 17, 2012), ECF No. 2642 ("to provide players with . . . information that protect them as much as possible from short-term and long-term health risks"); ¶ 90 ("to provide truthful information to NFL players regarding risks to their health"); ¶ 91 ("to keep the players informed of safety information they needed to know"); ¶ 99 ("to keep NFL players informed of neurological risks, to inform NFL players truthfully, and not to mislead NFL players about the risks of permanent neurological damage that can occur from MTBI incurred while playing football"); ¶ 222 ("to educate [the public] as to the risks of concussions due to the League's unique position of influence"); ¶ 248 ("to advise Plaintiffs of th[e] heightened risk" "that the repeated traumatic head impacts the Plaintiffs endured while playing NFL football were likely to expose them to excess risk to neurodegenerative disorders and diseases, including but not limited to CTE, Alzheimer's disease or similar cognitive-impairing conditions"); ¶ 304 ("to disclose accurate information to the Plaintiffs"); ¶ 324 ("to inform and advise players and teams of the foreseeable harm that can arise from such things as the use of leather helmets, the need to wear hard plastic helmets to reduce head wounds and internal injury (1943) and the grabbing of an opponent's facemask—to minimize or avoid head and neck injuries (1956/1962)").

255 *See id.* at ¶ 6 ("to provide players with rules . . . that protect them as much as possible from short-term and long-term health risks"); ¶ 90 ("to act in the best interests of the health and safety of NFL players"); ¶ 90 ("to take all reasonable steps necessary to ensure the safety of players"); ¶ 91 ("to make the game of professional football safer for the players"); ¶ 103 ("to govern player conduct on and off the field"); ¶ 323 ("to supervise how the game of football was played in the United States"); and, ¶ 324 ("to provide a safe environment for players and because of its superior knowledge of the risks of injury to players").

256 *See id.* at ¶ 17 ("to investigate, study, and truthfully report the medical risks associated with MTBI [(mild traumatic brain injuries)] in football"); ¶ 106 ("to provide truthful scientific research and information about the risks of concussive and sub-concussive injuries to NFL players"); ¶ 150 ("to use reasonable care in the study of concussions and post-concussion syndrome in NFL players; the study of any kind of brain trauma relevant to the sport of football; the use of information developed; and the publication of data and/or pronouncements from the MTBI

Committee"); ¶¶ 340, 358 ("to exercise reasonable care in the MTBI Committee's work and the NFL and its agents' public statements about the substance of the Committee's work"); ¶ 372 ("to retain and employ persons within the MTBI Committee who were professionally competent to study and render opinions on the relationship between repetitive head impacts in football and brain injury and to ensure that those whom it hired had no conflict of interest and that each had the professional and personal qualifications to conduct those studies and render opinions that were scientifically rigorous, valid, defensible, and honest"); ¶ 378 ("not to allow those incompetent persons it had hired within the MTBI Committee to continue to conduct incompetent and falsified studies and render incompetent opinions on the relationship between repetitive head impacts in football and brain injury.")

257 *See* Class Action Settlement Agreement (As Amended), In re Nat'l Football League Players' Concussion Injury Litigation, 12-md-2323 (Feb. 13, 2015), ECF No. 6481-1.

258 *In re Nat'l Football League Players' Concussion Injury Litigation*, 307 F.R.D. 351, 393 (E.D. Pa. 2015).

259 *In re Nat'l Football League Players' Concussion Injury Litigation,* 2016 WL 1552205 (3d Cir. Apr. 18, 2016).

260 Mike Florio, *Apparently, not all former players dropped their objection to the concussion settlement*, ProFootballTalk (Aug. 31, 2016, 12:05 PM), http://profootballtalk.nbcsports.com/2016/08/31/apparently-not-all-former-players-dropped-their-objection-to-the-concussion-settlement/, *archived at* https://perma.cc/R34V-3C8H.

261 This information was provided by the NFL prior to the 2016 season.

262 CBA, Art. 39, § 1(d); this information was also provided by the NFLPA.

263 CBA, Art. 50, § 2.

264 *Transcript – 2016 Injury Data Results Conference Call*, NFL Communications, Jan. 29, 2016, https://nflcommunications.com/Pages/Transcript---2016-Injury-Data-Results-Conference-Call.aspx, *archived at* https://perma.cc/RKC6-352G.

265 The NFL provided us with a copy of the poster.

266 Former New York Giants running back Charles Way is the Director of the NFL's Player Engagement Department. Michael Eisen, *Charles Way Named Head of NFL's Player Engagement Department*, Giants.com (Jul, 2, 2014), http://www.giants.com/news-and-blogs/article-1/Charles-Way-named-head-of-NFLs-Player-Engagement-Department/d98165b5-1b82-4243-a3d0-5746aae812e1, *archived at* http://perma.cc/QBN8-7Z2M.

267 *See Player Care Foundation*, NFL Player Care Found., http://www.nflplayercare.com/ (last visited Aug. 7, 2015), *archived at* http://perma.cc/93M6-XCN2.

268 Nat'l Football League, 2015 Player Health & Safety Report 30 (2015), http://static.nfl.com/static/content/public/photo/2015/08/05/0ap3000000506671.pdf/, *archived at* https://perma.cc/Y4BN-TUP7?type=pdf.

269 *See* Jim Baumbach, *Life After Football,* Newsday (Jan. 22, 2015), http://data.newsday.com/projects/sports/football/life-football/, *archived at* http://perma.cc/77DP-LUUE.

270 *See* Jim Baumbach, *Life After Football,* Newsday (Jan. 22, 2015), http://data.newsday.com/projects/sports/football/life-football/, *archived at* http://perma.cc/77DP-LUUE.

271 For example, Injury Grievances, which occur when, at the time a player's contract was terminated, the player claims he was physically unable to perform the services required of him because of a football-related injury, are heard by a specified Arbitration Panel. 2011 CBA, Art. 44. Additionally, issues concerning certain Sections of the CBA related to labor and antitrust issues, such as free agency and the Salary Cap, are within the exclusive scope of the System Arbitrator, 2011 CBA, Art. 15, currently University of Pennsylvania Law School Professor Stephen B. Burbank.

272 *See* 2011 CBA, Art. 43, § 1.

273 *See* 2011 CBA, Art. 43, § 6 (discussing constitution of Arbitration Panel); 2011 CBA, Art. 43 § 8 (discussing Arbitrator's authority, including to grant a "money award").

274 CBA, Art. 43, § 2.

275 The Non-Injury Grievance arbitrator has the authority to determine whether a complaint against a doctor fit within his or her jurisdiction under Article 43. *See* 2011 CBA, Art. 43, § 1 (discussing scope of Non-Injury Grievance arbitrator's jurisdiction).

276 U.S.C. § 185.

277 Allis-Chambers Corp. v. Lueck, 471 U.S. 202, 213, 200 (1985).

278 Williams v. Nat'l Football League, 582 F.3d 863, 870–72 (8th Cir. 2009). The case was subsequently remanded to Minnesota state court for resolution of the Williamses' state law claims on the merits. Williams v. Nat'l Football League, 10-cv-613, 2010 WL 760701 (D. Minn. Mar. 4, 2010). The case proceeded to trial after certain parts of the Williamses' statutory claims were dismissed on summary judgment. Williams v. Nat'l Football League, 27-cv-08-29778, 2010 WL 547537 (Minn. Dist. Ct. Feb. 18, 2010). At trial the court determined that the Williamses were not harmed by the NFL's state law violations and thus denied their request for a permanent injunction and dissolved a prior temporary restraining order. Williams v. Nat'l Football League, 27-cv-08-29778, 2010 WL 1793130 (Minn. Dist. Ct. May 6, 2010); *aff'd on different grounds*, Williams v. Nat'l Football League, 794 N.W.2d 391 (2011). As part of 2011 CBA, the NFL agreed to reduce the players' suspensions from four games to two. *See* Mike Florio, *StarCaps Suspensions Finally Are Finalized*, ProFootballTalk (Sept. 2, 2011, 5:07 PM), http://profootballtalk .nbcsports.com/2011/09/02/starcaps-suspensions-finally-are-finalized/, *archived at* http://perma.cc/BRR8-RPPL.

279 *Williams*, 582 F.3d 863.

280 *Id.* at 878, *quoting* Lueck, 471 U.S. at 211–12.

281 Nat'l Football League Players Ass'n v. Nat'l Football League, 654 F. Supp. 2d 960,972 (D. Minn. 2009).

282 F. Supp. 2d 894 (S.D. Ohio 2007).

283 *Id.* at 898.

284 *See* Stringer v. Minnesota Vikings Football Club, LLC, 705 N.W.2d 746 (Minn. 2005).

285 *See* Stringer v. Minnesota Vikings Football Club, LLC, 474 F. Supp. 2d 894, 898 (S.D. Ohio 2007).

286 *Id.* at 909.

287 *Id.* at 912.

288 *NFL, Stringer's Widow Settle Lawsuit*, ESPN (Jan. 26, 2009, 4:25 PM ET), http://sports.espn.go.com/nfl/news/story?id=3861331, *archived at* http://perma.cc/UM7H-HD45. Following Stringer's death, the NFL now issues an annual memorandum to NFL Clubs warning them about the risks of players overheating during training camp. *See, e.g.*, Memorandum from NFL Injury and Safety Panel (Elliott Hershman, M.D., Chairman), to General Managers, Head Coaches, Team Physicians, and Team Athletic Trainers re: 2014 Training Camps – Adverse Weather Conditions (July 11, 2014) (on file with author). In addition, a preseason training camp presentation to players includes materials from the Korey Stringer Institute on the risks of overheating. The NFL provided us with a copy of the preseason training camp presentation.

289 *See* Order Denying Plaintiffs' Motion to Remand, Maxwell v. Nat'l Football League, 11-CV-08394 (C.D.Cal. Dec. 8, 2011); Order Denying Plaintiffs' Motion to Remand, Pear v. Nat'l Football League, 11-CV-08395, Dec. 8, 2011 (C.D.Cal Dec. 8, 2011.), ECF No. 61; Order Denying Plaintiffs' Motion to Remand, Barnes v. Nat'l Football League, 11-CV-08396, Dec. 8, 2011 (C.D. Cal. Dec. 8, 2011), ECF No. 58.

290 Duerson v. Nat'l Football League, 12-cv-2513, 2012 WL 1658353, *6 (N.D.Ill. May 11, 2012).

291 Green v. Arizona Cardinals Football Club LLC, 21 F.Supp.3d 1020 (E.D.Mo. May 14, 2014).

292 Mike Florio, *NFL Suffers Major Setback in Concussion Cases*, ProFootballTalk (May 14, 2014, 9:28 PM), http://profootballtalk.nbcsports.com /2014/05/14/nfl-suffers-major-setback-in-concussion-case/, *archived at* http://perma.cc/3VQD-DCH9.

293 *See* Transfer Order, *In re: Nat'l Football League Players' Concussion Injury Litigation*, 15-cv-1903 (E.D. Mo. Apr. 11, 2016), ECF No. 38.

294 *See* Complaint, Dent v. Nat'l Football League, 14-cv-2324 (N.D. Cal. May 20, 2014), ECF No. 1.

295 *Id.* at ¶ 15. In addition to state law claims sounding in fraud and negligence, the plaintiffs alleged the NFL violated several statutes. For example, the plaintiffs allege that the NFL violated: "the Controlled Substances Act's requirements governing the acquisition, storage, provision and administration of, and recordkeeping concerning, Schedule II, III and IV controlled substances"; the Food, Drug, and Cosmetic Act's "requirements for prescriptions, warnings about known and possible side effects, and proper labeling, among other violations"; and, "state laws governing the acquisition, storage and dispensation of prescription medications." *Id.* at ¶¶ 354–57.

296 Dent v. Nat'l Football League, 14-cv-2324, 2014 WL 7205048 (N.D. Cal. Dec. 17, 2014). *See also* Nelson v. Nat'l Hockey League, 20 F.Supp.3d 650 (N.D.Ill. Feb. 20, 2014) (claims by estate of deceased NHL player that NHL negligently failed to monitor the player's use of addictive medications and head trauma preempted by CBA).

297 Dent v. Nat'l Football League, 14-cv-2324, 2014 WL 7205048, *12 (N.D. Cal. Dec. 17, 2014) ("In ruling against the novel claims asserted herein, this order does not minimize the underlying societal issue. In such a rough-and-tumble sport as professional football, player injuries loom as a serious and inevitable evil. Proper care of these injuries is likewise a paramount need. The main point of this order is that the league has addressed these serious concerns in a serious way – by imposing duties on the clubs via collective bargaining and placing a long line of health-and-safety duties on the team owners themselves. These benefits may not have been perfect but they have been uniform across all clubs and not left to the vagaries of state common law. They are backed up by the enforcement power of the union itself and the players' right to enforce these benefits. Given the regime in place after decades of collective bargaining over the scope of these duties, it would be impossible to fashion and to apply new and supplemental state common law duties on the league without taking into account the adequacy and scope of the CBA duties already set in place. That being so, plaintiffs' common law claims are preempted by Section 301 of the Labor Management Relations Act of 1947. The motion to dismiss all of plaintiffs' claims based on preemption grounds under Section 301 is Granted.")

298 NFLPA Constitution, § 2.00.

299 *See* NFLPA Department of Labor Form LM-2 Labor Organization Annual Report (2013), p. 27.

300 CBA, Preamble.

301 *See* NFLPA Constitution, § 2.06 (discussing suspension of a member's membership for failure to pay dues regardless of type of membership); *see also* NFLPA Constitution, § 2.11 (providing all retired players with two years of membership in the NFLPA at no cost). The NFLPA Constitution never discusses what it means to an "associate" member.

302 *See* NFLPA Constitution, § 2.06 (discussing suspension of a member's membership for failure to pay dues regardless of type of membership).

303 CBA, Art. 47, § 2.

304 CBA, Art. 47, § 1.

305 CBA, Art. 47, § 6.

306 *Schneider Moving & Storage Co. v. Robbins*, 466 U.S. 364, 376 n. 22 (1984) ("Because a union so selected is the exclusive representative of all employees in a bargaining unit, the union bears a concomitant duty to represent the interests of each and every employee in that unit fairly"); *see also* Gilpin v. Am. Fed'n of State, Cnty, and Mun. Emps, AFL-CIO, 875 F.2d 1310, 1311 (7th Cir. 1989) ("A union that has been certified as the exclusive bargaining representative for a group of employees must represent every employee in the bargaining unit, even those who don't belong to the union.")

307 *See, e.g.*, Peterson v. Kennedy, 771 F.2d 1244, 1253 (9th Cir. 1985) (reviewing player's claim for a breach of the NFLPA's duty of fair representation); Sharpe v. Nat'l Football League Players Ass'n, 941 F.Supp. 8 (D.D.C. 1996) (same); Chuy v. Nat'l Football League Players Ass'n, 495 F.Supp. 137 (E.D.Pa. 1980) (same).

308 Vaca v. Sipes, 386 U.S. 171, 207 (1967).

309 Ford Motor Co. v. Huffman, 345 U.S. 330, 338 (1953); *see also* Clarett v. Nat'l Football League, 369 F.3d 124, 138 (2d Cir. 2004) (discussing NFLPA's discretion in setting policy concerning NFL players).

310 *See, e.g.,* Wooddell v. Int'l Broth. of Elec. Workers, Local 71, 502 U.S. 93 (1991) (reinstating plaintiff union-members breach of union constitution claim).

311 Merk v. Jewel Co., 848 F.2d 761, 766 (7th Cir. 1988) ("because the 2,000 former workers are not statutory 'employees', the Union does not represent them. The Union owes no duty to those it does not represent. If it does not have a duty to represent them at all, it does not have a duty to represent them 'fairly'."); Anderson v. Alpha Portland Indus., 727 F.2d 177, 181 (8th Cir. 1984) (union did not have a duty to fairly represent former members who had retired even though the union had negotiated a collective bargaining agreement providing for retirement benefits); *Cooper v. Gen. Motors Corp.*, 651 F.2d 249 (5th Cir.1981) (union did not owe supervisors who were former members of the union a duty of fair representation with regard to their seniority rights); McCormick v. Aircraft Mechanics Fraternal Ass'n, 225 F. Supp. 2d 1131, 1135 (D.Minn. 2002) (denying former union members' claim for breach of the duty and fair representation and explaining that "courts have repeatedly rejected the notion that a union has a duty to fairly represent its former members").

312 Black's Law Dictionary, "Duty" (9th ed. 2009).

313 *See, e.g.,* Grant v. Nat'l Football League Players Ass'n, 11-cv-3118, 2012 WL 1870974, *2-6 (C.D.Cal. May 22, 2012) (examining relationship between retired player and NFLPA to see if fiduciary relationship existed); Parrish v. Nat'l Football League Players Ass'n, 07-cv-943, 2007 WL 3456988, *6-7 (N.D. Cal. Nov. 14, 2007) (same).

314 *See* Bell v. DaimlerChrysler Corp., 547 F.3d 796, 804 (7th Cir. 2008) (discussing history of cases recognizing "that a union owes a fiduciary duty to represent its members fairly").

315 *See* Grant *supra* 313 at 110; Eller v. Nat'l Football League Players Ass'n, 872 F. Supp. 2d 823 (D.Minn. 2012), *aff'd* 731 F.2d 752 (8th Cir. 2013) (NFLPA Executive Director DeMaurice Smith's public statement "that the NFLPA owes a fiduciary duty to retired NFL players" did not create any legal obligations for the NFLPA); *see also* Soar v. Nat'l Football League Players Ass'n, 438 F.Supp. 337, 345 (D.R.I. 1975) (NFLPA did not violate purported fiduciary duty to seek pension benefits on behalf of retired players).

316 *See* Emily Kaplan, *The Games Go On, And So Does Life,* MMQB (Dec. 26, 2013), http://mmqb.si.com/2013/12/26/nfl-nflpa-the-trust -player-retirement-benefits/, *archived at* http://perma.cc/Z2LH-V8PM (discussing creation of the Trust); *Frequently Asked Questions,* Trust, http://playerstrust.com/frequently-asked-questions (last visited Aug. 7, 2015), *archived at* http://perma.cc/7NLC-HDTB (describing The Trust and its purpose).

317 Gene Upshaw Player Assistance Trust Fund, https://www.yourpaf.com /gupat/#.VuhhvnOrLIU (last visited Mar. 15, 2016), *archived at* https:// perma.cc/S9T8-RYHF.

318 *About NFLPA—Department Contacts,* NFLPA, https://www.nflpa.com/ about/department-contacts (last visited May 18, 2016), *archived at* https ://perma.cc/HK96-DQKA.

319 This information was provided by the NFLPA.

320 *Id.*

321 *Id.*

322 NFLPA Mackey-White Committee Charter, ¶ 2.

323 *Id.*

324 This information was provided by the NFLPA.

325 The 30 Major League Baseball Clubs each have a 40-man roster, *see* 2012–16 Basic Agreement between MLB and MLBPA, Art. XX, § A, resulting in 1,200 MLB players. Generally, each of the 30 NBA Clubs has a 15-man roster, *see* Constitution and Bylaws of the National Basketball Association, Bylaws § 6, resulting in 450 NBA players. Each of the 30 NHL clubs has a 23-man roster, *see* Collective Bargaining Agreement between National Hockey League and National Hockey League Players' Association (Feb. 15, 2013), § 16.4, resulting in 690 NHL players.

326 *See What is Average NFL Player's Career Length? Longer Than You Might Think, Commissioner Goodell Says,* NFL.com (Apr. 18, 2011), http://nflcommunications.com/2011/04/18/what-is-average-nfl -player%E2%80%99s-career-length-longer-than-you-might-think -commissioner-goodell-says/, *archived at* http://perma.cc/PX5U-9SFK (discussing dispute between NFLPA's assertion that the average career is 3.5 years and the NFL's assertion that the average career is 6 years); *Average NFL Career Length,* Sharp Football Analysis (Apr. 30, 2014), http://www.sharpfootballanalysis.com/blog/?p=2133, *archived at* http://perma.cc/KR58-R8DA (discussing disagreement between NFLPA and NFL and determining that the average drafted player plays about 5 years). The average career in the NBA is about 4.8 years according to the National Basketball Players Association, *see* Susan Koenig, *Financial Planning for the Pros,* Registered Rep. 34, Apr. 1, 2010, *available at* 2010 WLNR 26366417; the average career in MLB is about 5.6 years, *see* William D. Witnauer, Richard G. Rogers & Jarron M. Saint Onge, *Major League Baseball Career Length in the 20th Century,* 26 Popul. Res. Policy Rev., 371–386 (2007), *available at* http://link.springer.com/article /10.1007/s11113-007-9038-5/fulltext.html, *archived at* http://perma.cc /UY9E-HCHL; and the average career in the NHL is about 5.6 years, *see Average Length of an NHL Player Career,* QuantHockey.com, http://www .quanthockey.com/Distributions/CareerLengthGP.php (last visited Aug. 7, 2015), *archived at* http://perma.cc/9Q22-BNLF.

327 This information was provided by the NFLPA.

328 *Id.*

329 *See Joint NFL NFLPA Statement on Wide-Ranging Changes to Drug Programs* Nat'l Football League Communications, http://nflcommunications .com/2014/09/19/joint-nfl-nflpa-statement-on-wide-ranging-changes -to-drug-programs/ (last visited Aug. 7, 2015), *archived at* http://perma .cc/7JNE-GY4R. Wes Welker of the Denver Broncos, Eric Herman of the New York Giants, Orlando Scandrick of the Dallas Cowboys and Stedman Bailey of the St. Louis Rams, each formerly serving four game suspensions, were permitted to return to their teams immediately. Josh Gordon of the Cleveland Browns and free agent LaVon Brazill were eligible to return after 10 games. Mark Daniels, *Drug-Policy Tweaks Could Affect Pats,* Providence Journal (RI), Sept. 17, 2014, *available at* 2014 WLNR 25824590.

330 *See* Mike Florio, *StarCaps Suspensions Finally are Finalized,* ProFootballTalk (Sept. 2, 2011, 5:07 PM), http://profootballtalk.nbcsports.com /2011/09/02/starcaps-suspensions-finally-are-finalized/, *archived at* http://perma.cc/BRR8-RPPL.

331 Order, Vilma v. Goodell, 12-cv-1283 (E.D.La. Sep. 5, 2012), ECF No. 121.

332 Submission of the NFLPA and the Players in Response to the Court's Order Concerning Joint Representation, Vilma v. Goodell, 12-cv-1283 (E.D.La. Sep. 5, 2012), ECF No. 122.

333 *Id.* at 4, *citing* Wood v. NBA, 809 F.2d 954, 959 (2d Cir. 1987).

334 F.Supp. 137 (E.D.Pa. 1980). Research did not reveal the outcome of the lawsuit after the court denied the NFLPA's motion to dismiss.

335 F.2d 1244 (9th Cir. 1985). *See also* Boogaard v. Nat'l Hockey League Players' Ass'n, 12-cv-9128, 2013 WL 1164301 (C.D.Cal. Mar. 20, 2013) (Dismissing duty of fair representation claim against NHLPA and finding NHLPA had no duty to advise estate of deceased player as to the statute of limitations on a duty of fair representation claim).

336 -cv-1559, 2014 WL 6776306 (E.D.Mo. Dec. 2, 2014).

337 *Id.*

338 Ballard v. Nat'l Football League Players Ass'n, 123 F. Supp.3d 1161 (E.D. Mo. 2015).

339 *See Quotes from NFLPA Press Conference,* NFLPA (Feb. 4, 2016), https ://www.nflpa.com/news/all-news/quotes-from-nflpa-sb50-press -conference, *archived at* https://perma.cc/2GZH-FQ37 (NFLPA Executive Director DeMaurice Smith commenting on the Concussion Litigation: "we don't represent the people in the concussion settlement . . . we're not a part of it. [I am] not in a position to advise or give legal advice to people about whether they opted into the settlement or not.")

340   Mike Florio, *NFLPA Issues Brief Statement On Settlement of Concussion Lawsuits*, ProFootballTalk (Aug. 29, 2013, 3:41 PM), http://profootballtalk .nbcsports.com/2013/08/29/nflpa-issues-brief-statement-on-settlement -of-concussion-lawsuits/, *archived at* http://perma.cc/2NKD-MKKY; Mike Florio, *NFLPA Addresses Its Failure to be Mentioned in League of Denial*, ProFootballTalk (Oct. 13, 2013, 8:59 AM), http://profootballtalk.nbcsports .com/2013/10/13/nflpa-addresses-its-failure-to-be-mentioned-in -league-of-denial/, *archived at* http://perma.cc/3JWG-SZCF; *see also* Mike Freeman, Two Minute Warning: How Concussions, Crime, and Controversy Could Kill the NFL (and What the League Can Do to Survive) xxii (2015) (quoting former player Sean Morey as stating "Every player that ever played the game, every player that plays the game today, is being betrayed by their union. Because they're dismissing this issue [football causing serious brain trauma] because they don't want to incur additional liability, and they're trying to protect themselves.").

341   Mike Florio, *NFLPA Addresses Its Failure to be Mentioned in League of Denial*, ProFootballTalk (Oct. 13, 2013, 8:59 AM), http://profootballtalk .nbcsports.com/2013/10/13/nflpa-addresses-its-failure-to-be -mentioned-in-league-of-denial/, *archived at* http://perma.cc/3JWG -SZCF.

342   F.3d 1170 (11th Cir. 2010).

343   U.S.C. § 158(d).

344   *See* Ford Motor Co. v. N.L.R.B., 441 U.S. 488 (1979) (discussing what issues are mandatory subjects of collective bargaining); Allied Chemical and Alkali Workers of America, Local Union No. 1 v. Pittsburgh Plate Glass Co., Chemical Division, 404 U.S. 157 (1971).

345   *NFL Gives $1 Million to Boston University for Study of Brain Injuries*, Nat'l Football League (Updated Jul. 26, 2012, 8:42 PM), http://www .nfl.com/news/story/09000d5d817a2623/article/nfl-gives-1-million-to -boston-university-for-study-of-brain-injuries, *archived at* http://perma .cc/D5LZ-NYMM.

346   NFL Comments and Corrections (June 24, 2016).

347   *Id.*

348   *See* Nat'l Football League, 2015 Player Health & Safety Report 30 (2015), http://static.nfl.com/static/content/public/photo/2015/08/05 /0ap3000000506671.pdf/, *archived at* https://perma.cc/Y4BN-TUP7 ?type=pdf.

349   NFL Comments and Corrections (June 24, 2016).

350   Alan Schwarz, Walt Bogdanich, and Jacqueline Williams, *N.F.L.'s Flawed Concussion Research and Ties to Tobacco Industry*, N.Y. Times, Mar. 26, 2016, http://www.nytimes.com/2016/03/25/sports/football/ nfl-concussion-research-tobacco.html, *archived at* https://perma.cc/ NM4N-SW4Q. *See also NFL response to New York Times' concussion research story*, NFL.com (Mar. 24, 2016, 4:11 PM), http://www.nfl.com/ news/story/0ap3000000647389/article/nfl-response-to-new-york-times -concussion-research-story, *archived at* https://perma.cc/Z3XE-8FQ6.

351   For examples of such studies in high school and college sports, *see* Barry P. Boden et al., *Catastrophic Injuries in Pole Vaulters, A Prospective 9-Year Follow-up Study*, 40 Am. J. Sports Med. 1488 (2012); Frederick O. Mueller and Robert C. Cantu, *Catastrophic injuries and fatalities in high school and college sports, fall 1982-spring 1988*, 22 Med. & Sci. in Sports & Exercise 737 (1990).

352   *See The Datalys Center for Sports Injury Research and Prevention*, NCAA, http://www.ncaa.org/health-and-safety/medical-conditions /datalys-center-sports-injury-research-and-prevention (last visited Aug. 3, 2016), *archived at* https://perma.cc/2M75-B24L.

353   *See, e.g., Data transparency*, GlaxoSmithKline, http://www.gsk.com/en -gb/behind-the-science/innovation/data-transparency (last visited June 20, 2016), *archived at* https://perma.cc/M5HN-NLHN; *Frequently Asked Questions*, the YODA Project, http://yoda.yale.edu/frequently-asked -questions-faqs#Data (last visited June 20, 2016), *archived at* https:// perma.cc/2Z98-R7HC.

354   CBA, Art. 39, § 3(a).

355   Mike Florio, *Survey asks players how seriously they take concussions*, ProFootballTalk (Dec. 5, 2015, 6:40 AM), http://profootballtalk.nbcsports .com/2015/12/05/survey-asks-players-how-seriously-they-take -concussions/, *archived at* http://perma.cc/GE9A-RMRC.

356   NFL CBA, Art. 25, § 4.

357   *See* Paul McCrory et al., *Consensus statement on concussion in sport: the 4th Int'l Conference on Concussion in Sport held in Zurich, November 2012*, 47 Br. J. Sports Med. 250, 251 (2013).

358   *Id.* at 253.

359   Columnist Mike Freeman has made a similar recommendation. *See* Mike Freeman, Two Minute Warning: How Concussions, Crime, and Controversy Could Kill the NFL (and What the League Can Do to Survive) 230–31 (2015) ("Make players sit for at least one game after a concussion, no matter if they pass concussion protocol tests or not. These tests are not infallible, and while sitting one game isn't a perfect solution, it helps prevent players from circumnavigating the system post-concussion.")

360   MLB CBA, Att. 36, ¶ 2.

361   *See* Paul McCrory et al., *Consensus statement on concussion in sport: the 4th Int'l Conference on Concussion in Sport held in Zurich, November 2012*, 47 Br. J. Sports Med. 250, 250–58 (2013) (discussing the challenges of and best practices for diagnosing concussions).

362   *See id.* at 254 (discussing the possibility of long-term problems for athletes that have suffered concussions).

363   *See id.* at 252–58 (discussing generally the challenges of determining when an athlete has recovered from a concussion).

364   Letter from Larry Ferazani, NFL, to authors (July 18, 2016).

365   *Id.*

366   *See* Sally Jenkins, *NFL's concussion priorities: Dodging blame, making players responsible*, Wash. Post, Dec. 3, 2015, https://www .washingtonpost.com/sports/redskins/nfls-concussion-priorities -dodging-blame-making-players-responsible/2015/12/03/1b8752f8 -99d2-11e5-94f0-9eeaff906ef3_story.html, *archived at* https://perma .cc/JT6P-JX44 ("The heart of the NFL's concussion problem is not that players hide symptoms; it's a compensation structure that forces them to play hurt, or get cut.")

367   CBA, App. H: Notice of Termination; *see also* 2011 CBA, Art. 4, § 5(d); 2011 CBA, App. A: NFL Player Contract, ¶¶ 8, 11. "'Room' means the extent to which a Team's then-current Team Salary is less than the Salary Cap." 2011 CBA, Art. 1.

368   *See* Chris Deubert & Glenn M. Wong, *Understanding the Evolution of Signing Bonuses and Guaranteed Money in the National Football League: Preparing for the 2011 Collective Bargaining Negotiations*, 16 UCLA Ent. L. Rev. 179, 193–95 (2009) (describing the various forms of guaranteed compensation in the NFL).

369   *See* Mike Florio, *The Full Kaepernick Contract Details*, ProFootballTalk (Jun. 5, 2014, 12:46 AM), http://profootballtalk.nbcsports.com/2014/06 /05/the-full-kaepernick-contract-details/, *archived at* http://perma.cc/ BM65-VHRR (discussing details of Colin Kaepernick's 2014 contract with the San Francisco 49ers. Despite reports that Kaepernick had received $61 million guaranteed, only about $13 million was guaranteed against skill, injury and Salary Cap).

370   *See* Chris Deubert, Glenn M. Wong & John Howe, *All Four Quarters: A Retrospective and Analysis of the 2011 Collective Bargaining Process and Agreement in the National Football League*, 19 UCLA Ent. L. Rev. 1 (2012) (discussing the movement towards more guaranteed compensation). In 2012, Peyton Manning signed a five-year deal with the Denver Broncos for $96 million, $58 million of which was guaranteed. Mike Klis and Jeff Legwold, *Peyton Manning's $96 Million Deal With Broncos Includes Neck Injury Clause*, Denver Post, (Mar. 20, 2012), http://www .denverpost.com/ci_20213659/peyton-mannings-deal-broncos-5-years -96-million, *archived at* http://perma.cc/3NPD-MJDW. In 2014, J.J. Watt signed a six-year deal with the Houston Texans for $100 million, $51.8 million of which was guaranteed. *Texans Give J.J. Watt $100M Deal*, ESPN.com (Sept. 2, 2014), http://espn.go.com/nfl/story/_/id/11451373 /jj-watt-houston-texans-reach-agreement-6-year-100-million-deal, *archived at* http://perma.cc/HRE6-TNKX. And, in 2015, Ndamukong Suh signed a six-year deal with the Miami Dolphins for $114 million, $60 million of which was guaranteed. Josh Alper, *Dolphins Make It*

Official With Ndamukong Suh, ProFootballTalk (Mar. 11, 2015, 4:14 PM), http://profootballtalk.nbcsports.com/2015/03/11/dolphins-make-it -official-with-ndamukong-suh/, *archived at* http://perma.cc/8BPH-R5T5.

371   *See* Deubert *supra* note 370 at 52–61 (discussing changes to rookie compensation scheme).

372   *Id.*

373   Gene Upshaw, *NFLPA's Upshaw Responds,* Wash. Post, Dec. 22, 2002, *available at* 2002 WLNR 15865309.

374   NFLPA, *A New Look at Guaranteed Contracts in the NFL* (circa 2002) (on file with authors) ("Over half of all salary earned by NFL players now is guaranteed"); NFLPA, *Guaranteed Contracts in Professional Team Sports: How Does the NFL Compare?* (circa 2007) (on file with authors) ("at least 52% of all compensation in the NFL is, in fact, 'guaranteed' to players.'")

375   Mike Florio, *Fully-guaranteed contracts could cause problems for teams, players,* ProFootballTalk (May 29, 2015, 9:55 AM), http://profootballtalk .nbcsports.com/2015/05/29/fully-guaranteed-contracts-could-cause -problems-for-teams-players/, *archived at* http://perma.cc/GE9E-YSME (discussing potential problems with guaranteed contracts in the NFL).

376   *See* 2011 CBA Art. 43, § 8 (empowering Non-Injury Grievance arbitrator to issue an "a money award, order of reinstatement, suspension without pay, a stay of suspension pending decision, a cease and desist order, a credit or benefit award under the Bert Bell/Pete Rozelle NFL Player Retirement Plan, or an order of compliance with a specific term of [the CBA] or any other applicable document, or an advisory opinion pursuant to Article 50, Section 1(c)."); 2011 CBA Art. 50, § 1(d) (Joint Committee obligated to "address and correct" issues identified by investigating neutral physicians).

377   *See, e.g.,* 2011 CBA, Art. 14, § 6 (permitting fines of $500,000 on play-ers, Contract Advisors and Club officials and $6,500,000 on Clubs found to have violated the Rookie Compensation Pool); 2011 CBA, Art. 18, § 3 (permitting fines of $375,000 on any person or Club that falsely certi-fies certain information); 2011 CBA, Art. 21, § 8(d)(i) (requiring fines of $100,000 for head coaches that have violated offseason workout rules the first time); 2011 CBA, Art. 42, § 1(a) (permitting Clubs to fine players for a variety of items, including being overweight, missing practice and violating curfew); 2011 CBA, Art. 48, § 3 (imposing fine of $30,000 on any Club that negotiates a player contract with a Contract Advisor not certified by the NFLPA).

378   The various fines discussed above are generally the result of findings by either the Commissioner or an arbitrator. Similarly, fines for Article 39 violations could be subject to a finding of violation by the Non-Injury Grievance arbitrator pursuant to Article 43.

379   Mike Florio, *NFL, NFLPA unveil new concussion protocol enforcement policy,* ProFootballTalk (July 25, 2016, 5:01 PM), http://profootballtalk .nbcsports.com/2016/07/25/nfl-nflpa-unveil-new-concussion-protocol -enforcement-policy/, *archived at* https://perma.cc/2U94-JU92.

380   *Id.*

381   *Id.*

382   *Id.*

383   *See Medical Malpractice Statute of Limitations by State,* Rocket Lawyer, https://www.rocketlawyer.com/article/medical-malpractice-statute-of -limitations-by-state.rl (last visited Aug. 7, 2015), *archived at* https:// perma.cc/9VFH-METW (providing medical malpractice statute of limita-tions in each state); *Chart: Statutes of Limitations in All 50 States,* NOLO. com, http://www.nolo.com/legal-encyclopedia/statute-of-limitations -state-laws-chart-29941.html (last visited Aug. 7, 2015), *archived at* http://perma.cc/MZ62-H475 (providing negligence statute of limitations in each state).

384   Throughout the litigation, news articles routinely and erroneously—either explicitly or implicitly—claimed that if the players' concussion-related claims were dismissed in court, they'd have the ability to pursue their claims in arbitration. *See, e.g.,* Michael Sokolove, *How One Lawyer's Crusade Could Change Football Forever,* N.Y. Times (Mag.), Nov. 6, 2014, http://www.nytimes.com/2014/11/09/magazine/how-one -lawyers-crusade-could-change-football-forever.html?_r=0, *archived at* https://perma.cc/4DJ6-XMQV?type=pdf ("a ruling for the league would have forced the players into mediation or arbitration and most likely only modest payouts"); Peter Keating, *An Unsettling Deal On Concussions,* ESPN Magazine, Nov. 18, 2014, *available at* http://espn.go.com/nfl/story /_/id/11899196/pnfl-concussion-settlement-bob-stern-objection-p, *ar-chived at* http://perma.cc/VL28-MQW6 ("in August 2012, the NFL moved to dismiss their cases entirely, arguing that the league's labor deal, not the courts, should resolve injury disputes").

385   NFL Comments and Corrections (June 24, 2016).

386   The NFL provided us with a copy of the Player Engagement Resource Guide.

387   *See* Cass R. Sunstein, *The Storrs Lectures: Behavioral Economics and Paternalism,* 122 Yale L.J. 1826, 1834 (2013).

388   *See* Cass R. Sunstein, *Deciding by Default,* 162 U. Pa. L. Rev. 1, 3 (2013).

389   Marlene Satter, *Employers Auto Enrolling at Company Match,* Ben-efitsPro.com (Jan. 21, 2015), http://www.benefitspro.com/2015/01/21/ employers-auto-enrolling-at-company-match, *archived at* http://perma .cc/33VA-X6F6.

390   Josh Alper, *Brandon Browner on Earl Thomas, Richard Sherman: Hit That Shoulder, Hit That Elbow,* ProFootballTalk (Jan. 26, 2015, 3:15 PM), http://profootballtalk.nbcsports.com/2015/01/26/brandon-browner -on-earl-thomas-richard-sherman-hit-that-shoulder-hit-that-elbow/, *archived at* http://perma.cc/DBL9-65CD.

391   Mike Florio, *Concussions Take on a Strategic Component,* ProFootball-Talk (Jan. 23, 2012, 10:09 PM), http://profootballtalk.nbcsports.com /2012/01/23/concussions-take-on-a-strategic-component/, *archived at* http://perma.cc/9FD8-Q98C.

Chapter 8

NFL Clubs

The NFL is an unincorporated association of 32 member clubs.[97] It serves as a centralized body for obligations and undertakings shared by the member clubs. Nevertheless, each member club is a separate and distinct legal entity,[98] with its own legal obligations separate and distinct from club owners and employees. This chapter focuses on NFL clubs as individual entities, rather than the clubs' employees, many of whom are discussed in other chapters. Additionally, the role of NFL club owners is discussed in Chapter 7: The NFL and NFLPA.

NFL clubs are the players' employers and hire many of the stakeholders discussed in this report. In this respect, NFL clubs play a powerful role in dictating the culture concerning player health.

(A) Background

NFL clubs are important stakeholders in player health. They are powerful organizations that employ many people with direct day-to-day interaction concerning player health issues. Club owners typically hire a general manager who then hires the coaching and football operations staff. The general manager and other executives are also likely involved with the hiring of the medical staff. Like all organizations, there is thus likely to develop a specific culture surrounding important issues, which will vary from club to club. In football, the club's attitude towards player health can have a significant impact.

NFL clubs are the players' employers and hire many of the stakeholders discussed in this report. In this respect, NFL clubs play a powerful role in dictating the culture concerning player health.

(B) Current Legal Obligations[a]

The 2011 CBA contains multiple provisions governing clubs' health obligations to its players:[b]

1. **Medical Care Generally:** "Each Club shall use its best efforts to ensure that its players are provided with medical care consistent with professional standards for the industry."[1]

2. **Physically Unable to Perform (PUP) List:** Any player who is placed on the PUP List as a result of a football-related injury "will be paid his full Paragraph 5 Salary while on such list."[2] In practice, this provision differentiates the PUP List from the Non-Football Injury ("NFI") List. A player is placed on the NFI List when he suffers an injury outside of football and clubs are not required to pay players their Paragraph 5 Salary while they are on the NFI List.

3. **Club Physicians:** Clubs must retain a board-certified orthopedic surgeon and at least one physician board-certified in internal medicine, family medicine, or emergency medicine. All physicians also must have a Certificate of Added Qualification in Sports Medicine.[3] In addition, clubs are required to retain consultants in the neurological, cardiovascular, nutritional, and, neuropsychological fields.[4]

4. **Physicians at Games:** "All home teams shall retain at least one [Rapid Sequence Intubation] RSI physician who is board certified in emergency medicine, anesthesia, pulmonary medicine, or thoracic surgery, and who has documented competence in RSI intubations in the past twelve months. This physician shall be the neutral physician dedicated to game-day medical intervention for on-field or locker room catastrophic emergencies."[5]

5. **Club Athletic Trainers:** "All athletic trainers employed or retained by Clubs to provide services to players, including any part time athletic trainers, must be certified by the National Athletic Trainers Association and must have a degree from an accredited four-year college or university. Each Club must have at least two full-time athletic trainers. All part-time athletic trainers must work under the direct supervision of a certified athletic trainer."[6]

6. **Second Medical Opinion:** Clubs are obligated to pay for a player's consultation with a physician for a second medical opinion provided the player first consults with the club physician and the club physician is provided a report of the second physician's examination and diagnosis.[7]

7. **Player's Right to a Surgeon of His Choice:** Players have the right to choose the surgeon who will perform a surgery and the club must pay for the surgery provided the player first consulted with the club physician.[8]

8. **Workers' Compensation:** Clubs are required to provide workers' compensation coverage or comparable benefits to its players.[9]

9. **Injury Protection:** If a player is physically unable to play in the season following a season in which he was injured but remains under contract with the club, clubs are required to pay an amount equal to 50 percent of the player's Paragraph 5 salary in the subsequent season, up to a range of $1–1.2 million.[10]

    a) Players can also earn "Extended Injury Protection" benefits up to a range of $500–575,000 for the second season after the season in which the player was injured.[11]

In addition to their obligations under the CBA, NFL clubs also have statutory obligations to provide health insurance to NFL players. Starting in 2015, the 2010 Patient Protection and Affordable Care Act (ACA) obligates employers who employ an average of at least 50 full-time employees

---

a   The legal obligations described herein are not an exhaustive list but are those we believe are most relevant to player health.

b   The club obligations discussed herein are separate and apart from those of the NFL as a centralized entity.

on business days to provide some basic level of health insurance to its employees or pay a financial penalty.[12] NFL clubs certainly employ more than 50 people (NFL clubs have 53 players, not including players placed on Injured Reserve, and a host of other employees)[13] and thus are obligated by the ACA to provide basic health insurance to their players.

Additionally, it is possible that NFL clubs are obligated to take certain measures concerning employee health and safety as a result of the Occupational Safety and Health Act[14] or a similar state or federal regulatory scheme. However, research has not revealed the application of any such scheme to the NFL in practice, and we thus avoid a theoretical analysis here. The application of the Occupational Safety and Health Act is the subject of future work by the Law & Ethics Initiative of The Football Players Health Study.

However, one statutory employee-benefit mechanism with which NFL clubs do have regular interactions is workers' compensation laws. Before we discuss the current ethical codes and current practices of the clubs, we discuss in detail the application of workers' compensation laws to NFL clubs.

1) WORKERS' COMPENSATION

Workers' compensation benefits and statutes have been contentious issues in the NFL.

"Workers' compensation laws provide protections and benefits for employees who are injured in the course of their employment. In the typical case, the workers' compensation regime grants tort immunity to employers in exchange for the regime's protections and benefits to the employee."[15] Since the first CBA in 1968, NFL clubs have been obligated to make the necessary arrangements to provide workers' compensation benefits to their players. If the state in which the club operates does not have workers' compensation or specifically excludes professional athletes from workers' compensation coverage, the CBAs have required those clubs to "guarantee equivalent benefits to its players."[16]

As a preliminary matter, it is important to point out that workers' compensation laws, systems and benefits vary widely among the states. Below, we try to provide a general description of workers' compensation rights and their relevance to NFL players.

Workers' compensation provides two important benefits to workers: monetary compensation; and, coverage for medical care. We discuss each of these benefits in turn.

Workers' compensation payments typically depend on the employee's level of injury or disability and the extent to which the injury or disability affects the employee's ability to continue working. Generally, workers receive "around one-half to two-thirds of the employee's average weekly wage."[17] In addition, the amount of benefits is subject to maximums which are usually tied to the state's average weekly wage,[18] and are generally between $500 and $1,000.[19] The benefits continue so long as the employee is disabled or unable to work. Additionally, the amount a player receives in workers' compensation reduces the amount the club is obligated to pay the player for certain other CBA-provided benefits.[20]

Medical care coverage is an important benefit available to players through workers' compensation. If a player is injured during the season, he is entitled to medical care from the club "during the season of injury only[.]"[21] Consequently, if a player suffers an injury that causes him to have ongoing or recurring healthcare needs (such as surgeries) well beyond the season of injury (and for perhaps the rest of his life), the club will have no obligation to pay for such care. Workers' compensation fills that gap. Workers' compensation statutes generally require the employer (really the employer's insurance carrier) to pay for reasonable and necessary medical expenses that are the result of an injury suffered at the workplace in perpetuity. More importantly, the worker does not have to pay for any part of the care.

Players must be diligent in protecting their rights. Even if a player suffers an injury and believes it has healed well, the player cannot know if the injury will resurface or cause problems later in life. Thus, the player must protect his rights by filing for workers' compensation benefits within the applicable statute of limitations, generally between one and three years. The workers' compensation claim is then adjudicated by a panel or board commissioned by the state. If the player is successful in his claim, he will be entitled to future medical care concerning the injury, even if no further care is needed at the time.

The trade-off for workers' compensation benefits from an employee's perspective is that the laws generally bar any civil lawsuit against the employer or other employees. Workers' compensation statutes provide compensation for workers injured at work (without having to prove the employer was at fault) and thus generally preclude lawsuits based on the co-workers' negligence.[22] This preemption applies with regard to the negligence of any co-worker, regardless of hierarchy or reporting structure. So, for example, as is discussed in detail in Chapter 9: Coaches, players generally cannot sue coaches for negligence due to workers' compensation statutes.

The clubs contract with insurance companies to pay for workers' compensation benefits. It is believed that clubs pay approximately $1.2 to $1.5 million in workers' compensation insurance premiums each year. Once a player files for workers' compensation benefits, the insurance carrier will be responsible for handling the litigation as well as paying any benefits.

In recent years, California received a flood of NFL player workers' compensation claims because of some unique (but now amended) statutory provisions.

First, California's workers' compensation law extended broadly to cover employees of non-California employers who were injured while in California temporarily on behalf of their employers.[23] Section 3600.5 of California's Labor Code previously dictated that if an employee "who has been hired or is regularly employed in the state receives personal injury by accident arising out of and in the course of such employment outside of this state, he . . . shall be entitled to [workers'] compensation" benefits under California law.[24] "The California Workers' Compensation Board has taken a wide view of the phrase 'regularly employed' that has allowed NFL players to be covered under the broad umbrella of workers' compensation rights in the state."[25]

Second, California permitted employees to recover for "cumulative" injuries. A cumulative injury is an injury that is "occurring as repetitive mentally or physically traumatic activities extending over a period of time, the combined effect of which causes any disability or need for medical treatment."[26] Recent controversy concerning NFL player injuries has centered on head, neck, and neurological conditions. These types of injuries generally have been diagnosed and recognized as injuries that did not occur as the result of any specific play or incident but instead are the cumulative result of decades of playing football.[27] Thus, California's cumulative injury designation appeared to perfectly suit the recent claims by current and former NFL players.

Third, the statute of limitations on an employee's workers' compensation claim in California did not begin to run until the employer formally notified the employee of his or her rights under California's workers' compensation laws.[28] "NFL teams, either believing that they had adequately taken care of their players' medical conditions at the time, or hoping to avoid workers' compensation claims, or simply being unaware of the possibility of such claims, historically had not informed their players of their rights under California's regime."[29]

Likely as a result of California's liberal workers' compensation laws, between 2006 and 2013, 3,400 former NFL players filed for workers' compensation in California alleging head or brain injuries.[30] The NFL estimated that the average California workers' compensation claim cost the club $215,000 to resolve, though it is unclear whether this figure refers to payments to players, or also includes legal fees.[31] Additionally, more than two-thirds of all California workers' compensation claims made by professional athletes and which cited cumulative trauma were made by players who never played for a California club.[32]

The NFL, not surprisingly, pushed for changes to California's workers' compensation scheme. In 1997, the NFL unsuccessfully sponsored legislation that would have limited California's workers' compensation benefits to athletes who lived in the state and would have prevented athletes from collecting benefits for cumulative injuries.[33] The NFL seemingly pursued this legislation despite the fact that the 1993 CBA imposed a moratorium on lobbying related to workers' compensation that was not lifted until June 1, 1999.[34]

Having failed to change the law, NFL clubs then began to contract around the law by inserting a provision into player contracts that require players to file their workers' compensation claims in the club's home state and under the law of the club's home state.[35] The NFL has prevailed in its efforts to enforce these provisions.[36]

These successes did not stop the NFL from pursuing amendments to California's workers' compensation laws.

In early 2012, only months after the execution of the most recent CBA, the NFL renewed its efforts to have California's workers' compensation statutes amended.[37] After extensive lobbying from the NFL and to a lesser extent the NFLPA on the opposite side of the issue,[38] on October 8, 2013, California Governor Jerry Brown signed into law amendments to California's workers' compensation statutes that affected all claims filed on or after January 1, 2014.

This legislation amended California's workers' compensation statute in two significant ways.

First, athletes who did not play for California teams can no longer file claims under California's workers' compensation laws if the athlete's employer "has furnished workers' compensation insurance coverage or its equivalent under the laws of a state other than California."[39] Since the CBA requires clubs to obtain workers' compensation insurance coverage or its equivalent, the amended legislation effectively precludes out-of-state players from filing for benefits in California.

Second, even players who played for California-based teams must meet certain criteria to file for workers' compensation in California. The player must have: (a) played for a California-based team for at least two seasons or 20% of his or her career; and (b) "worked for fewer than seven seasons for any team or teams other than a California-based team."[40] This second provision, had it been in place when they played, would have effectively precluded some of California's most high-profile athletes from filing for workers' compensation.[c]

The legislation easily passed despite questions as to whether the bill provided any clear benefit to the state. By curtailing potentially thousands of annual workers' compensation claims, the state saves the administrative costs related to adjudicating workers' compensation claims. Nevertheless, some critics argued that the NFL was able to get the bill passed by erroneously suggesting the state in some way was responsible for paying the players' workers' compensation benefits.[41] As the bill's author Assemblyman Henry Perea admitted, clubs – and not the state – pay for the benefits.[42,d]

Moreover, the NFLPA has argued that in fact the players pay for the benefits.[43] The NFL-NFLPA CBA sets a "Player Cost Amount," effectively an upper limit on the total salary and benefits NFL clubs can expend on players. The CBA also permits a Salary Cap, limiting the total amount clubs can spend on players and effectively curtailing player salaries. The Salary Cap is determined by deducting player benefits from the Player Cost Amount.[44] Thus, the more clubs pay in benefits, the less they pay in salary. Workers' compensation payments (including to former players) and premiums are among the benefits deducted from the Player Cost Amount to set the Salary Cap.[45] Players, through the CBA, have thus accepted less salary in exchange for increased benefits, including workers' compensation benefits.

> Workers' compensation statutes generally require the employer (really the employer's insurance carrier) to pay for reasonable and necessary medical expenses that are the result of an injury suffered at the workplace in perpetuity.

The NFL's workers' compensation issues did not end with California. In May 2014, Louisiana legislators introduced a bill, with the support of the New Orleans Saints, to address the method for calculating a player's workers' compensation benefits.[46] Workers' compensation benefits are determined based on the workers' salary. Louisiana Administrative Law Judges adjudicating workers' compensation claims had generally determined that an athlete's benefits should be determined by the athlete's salary at the time the athlete was injured.[47] The athletes argued that their benefits should instead be determined by considering their entire compensation for the year in which they are injured.[48]

The difference in calculation methods used by the state of Louisiana is quite large. NFL player salaries are paid out during the 17-week regular season; they earn considerably less during minicamps and training camps. In 2015, all veterans—regardless of skill and regular season salary—received only $1,800 per week during training camp,[49] whereas the minimum weekly salary for a four-year veteran during the regular season was $43,823.53.[50] Thus, it is clear a player injured during training camp rather than the regular season will receive significantly less workers' compensation benefits.[e]

The NFLPA and its players mobilized against the 2014 bill, led by Saints' star quarterback Drew Brees.[51] After a few weeks of debate, the Louisiana proposed bill was tabled for further discussion among the parties on the best way to calculate the benefits.[52]

---

c   For instance, Wayne Gretzky, widely considered the greatest hockey player of all-time, could not file for worker's compensation under this rule even though he spent 7.5 of years of his 21 year career with the Los Angeles Kings. Terrell Owens, one of the most-accomplished 49ers wide receiver of all-time would also be precluded, having followed his first six years in San Francisco with seven years with other NFL clubs. Lastly, Barry Bonds, arguably one of the greatest baseball players ever (and certainly one of the most controversial), is ineligible for workers' compensation benefits despite having hit 586 home runs for the San Francisco Giants because he also played seven years with the Pittsburgh Pirates.

d   Ironically, some have also argued that the changes to California's workers' compensation statutes will increase costs to the state. Modesto Diaz, a California workers' compensation attorney specializing in representing athletes, contended that injured former athletes who are no longer eligible to receive workers' compensation payments from their teams will now have to resort to Social Security disability benefits, Medicaid, and other forms of government aid, Ken Bensinger & Marc Lifsher, *California Limits Workers' Comp Sports Injury Claims*, L.A. Times, Oct. 3, 2013, http://articles.latimes.com/2013/oct/08/business/la-fi-workers-comp-nfl-20131009, *archived at* http://perma.cc/2JTS-83KK, effectively shifting player health costs from the clubs to the state.

e   In reviewing this Report, the NFL explained that "[a]t least some states pay workers' comp benefits based on the contract salary, regardless of when the player gets hurt." NFL Comments and Corrections (June 24, 2016).

Other states' workers' compensation laws have athlete-specific language. For example, Pennsylvania's workers' compensation statute reduces the athlete's workers' compensation benefits by any amounts received by the athlete from the club during the time the athlete was injured, including salary, club-funded insurance, and any other benefit paid as a result of the CBA.[53] These types of statutes coupled with benefit maximums effectively prevent many athletes from receiving any workers' compensation benefits. Moreover, according to the NFLPA, every year NFL clubs sponsor state level legislation that seeks to curtail players' workers' compensation benefits in some way.

To assist NFL players with workers' compensation claims, the NFLPA makes available to players and their contract advisors a document describing the benefits claim process, benefits amount and statutes of limitations. Additionally, the NFLPA has recommended workers' compensation attorneys in each city in which an NFL club plays (collectively, the "Panel"). The Panel consists of approximately 60 attorneys. Because players play in many states, they are often eligible for workers' compensation benefits in many states. The advantage of the Panel is coordination and communication (with the NFLPA' assistance) that permits a player to determine which state will provide the player with the best benefits. Finally, contract advisors are prohibited from referring a player to a workers' compensation attorney who is not a member of the Panel.[54]

(C) Current Ethical Codes

Research has not revealed any ethical code that governs NFL clubs as such.

(D) Current Practices

The best way to understand NFL clubs' current practices concerning player health is to examine the current practices of the relevant NFL club employees or contractors: see Chapter 2: Club Doctors; Chapter 3: Athletic Trainers; Chapter 9: Coaches; Chapter 10: Club Employees; and Chapter 11: Equipment Managers. These employees carry out the day to day tasks of the club, interact with the players, and dictate the club's culture accordingly.

(E) Enforcement of Legal and Ethical Obligations[f]

The 2011 CBA provides a few options for players dissatisfied with the medical care provided by an NFL club. Nevertheless, these options, discussed below, provide questionable remedies to the players for a club's health-related obligations.

First, a player could submit a complaint to the Accountability and Care Committee (ACC), which consists of the NFL Commissioner (or his designee), the NFLPA Executive Director (or his designee), and six additional members "experienced in fields relevant to health care for professional athletes," three appointed by the Commissioner and three by the NFLPA Executive Director.[55] "[T]he complaint shall be referred to the League and the player's Club, which together shall determine an appropriate response or corrective action if found to be reasonable. The Committee shall be informed of any response or corrective action."[56] There is thus no neutral third-party adjudicatory process for addressing the player's claim or compensating the player for any wrong suffered. The remedial process is left entirely in the hands of the NFL and the club, both of which may face a significant conflict of interest and have reasons not to find that a club's medical staff acted inappropriately and to compensate the injured player accordingly.

Second, a player could commence a Non-Injury Grievance.[g] The 2011 CBA directs certain disputes to designated arbitration mechanisms[57] and directs the remainder of any disputes involving the CBA, a player contract, NFL rules or generally the terms and conditions of employment to the Non-Injury Grievance arbitration process.[58] Importantly, Non-Injury Grievances provide players with the benefit of a neutral arbitration and the possibility of a "money award."[59] Many of the clubs' above-described legal obligations could be the subject of a Non-Injury Grievance. However, Non-Injury Grievances must be filed within 50 days "from the date of the occurrence or non-occurrence upon which the grievance is based."[60] Additionally, it is possible

---

f   Appendix K is a summary of players' options to enforce legal and ethical obligations against the stakeholders discussed in this Report. In addition, for rights articulated under either the CBA or other NFL policy, the NFLPA and the NFL can also seek to enforce them on players' behalves.

g   The term "Non-Injury Grievance" is something of a misnomer. The CBA differentiates between an "Injury Grievance" and a "Non-Injury Grievance." An Injury Grievance is exclusively "a claim or complaint that, at the time a player's NFL Player Contract or Practice Squad Player Contract was terminated by a Club, the player was physically unable to perform the services required of him by that contract because of an injury incurred in the performance of his services under that contract." 2011 CBA, Art. 44, § 1. Generally, all other disputes (except System Arbitrations, see 2011 CBA, Art. 15) concerning the CBA or a player's terms and conditions of employment are Non-Injury Grievances. 2011 CBA, Art. 43, § 1. Thus, there can be disputes concerning a player's injury or medical care which are considered Non-Injury Grievances because they do not fit within the limited confines of an Injury Grievance.

that under the 2011 CBA, the NFL could argue that complaints concerning medical care are designated elsewhere in the CBA and thus should not be heard by the Non-Injury Grievance arbitrator.[61]

In the 2011 CBA, the parties added Article 39: Players' Rights to Medical Care and Treatment (Appendix F), supplementing and amending some provisions from prior CBAs. Article 39 reaffirms some of the clubs' obligations concerning player health and the rights of players concerning their health that were expressed in past CBAs. Article 39 also added and clarified several substantive provisions.[h] Nevertheless, since the execution of the 2011 CBA, there have been no Non-Injury Grievances concerning Article 39 decided on the merits,[62] suggesting either clubs are in compliance with Article 39 or the Article has not been sufficiently enforced.

Although no Article 39 Non-Injury Grievances have been adjudicated on the merits, there was a significant grievance concerning Article 39 between the New England Patriots and former Patriots' defensive lineman Jonathan Fanene. In that matter, the NFLPA alleged that Patriots club doctor Tom Gill violated Article 39, § 1(c)'s requirement that Gill's primary duty in providing player medical care shall be to the player and that he comply with all medical ethics rules concerning his treatment of Fanene.[63] Prior to the 2012 season, the Patriots and Fanene agreed to a three-year

contract worth close to $12 million, including a $3.85 million signing bonus.[64] As part of a pre-employment questionnaire, Fanene, according to the Patriots, stated that he took no medications regularly even though he had been taking significant amounts of painkillers to mask chronic pain in his knee.[65] The Patriots terminated Fanene's contract during training camp, citing Fanene's alleged failure to disclose his medical condition,[66] and initiated a System Arbitration[i] to recoup $2.5 million in signing bonus money already paid to Fanene (discussed further in Chapter 1: Players).[67] Specifically, the Patriots alleged Fanene violated his obligations to negotiate the contract in good faith.[68]

The NFLPA alleged that during the 2012 training camp, Gill told Patriots owner Robert Kraft and club President Jonathan Kraft that he was "trying to put together a case" against Fanene so that the club could seek the return of the signing bonus paid. The NFLPA further alleged that, at the direction of Patriots head coach Bill Belichick, Gill intentionally delayed and ultimately refused performing surgery on Fanene so the Patriots could convince him to retire. Moreover, the NFLPA alleged that Gill fabricated and/or back-dated notes to help the Patriots' grievance against Fanene. All of these actions, according to the NFLPA, violated Article 39, § 1(c).

---

i   A System Arbitration is a legal process for the resolution of disputes between the NFL and the NFLPA and/or a player concerning a subset of CBA provisions that are central to the NFL's operations and which invoke antitrust and labor law concerns, including but not limited to the NFL player contract, NFL Draft, rookie compensation, free agency, and the Salary Cap. 2011 CBA, Art. 15, § 1.

---

h   For a description of these health-related changes, see Appendix B.

There have been no Non-Injury Grievances concerning Article 39 decided on the merits, suggesting either clubs are in compliance with Article 39 or the Article has not been sufficiently enforced.

Gill generally denied the allegations and insisted that his comments were taken out of context.[69] The dueling grievances were settled in September 2013 when the Patriots let Fanene keep $2.5 million in signing bonus money already paid but did not have to pay the $1.35 million still owed.[70] The settlement thus prevented any precedential legal authority.[j]

Prior to the 2011 CBA, there were some arbitrations against clubs concerning medical care but all of the cases revealed by our research were denied as untimely.[71] In addition, each of these cases discuss that the CBA's statutes of limitations have been and are to be construed strictly by the arbitrators.

The third option for a player seeking to enforce a club's health-related obligations is to request the NFLPA to commence an investigation before the Joint Committee on Player Safety and Welfare ("Joint Committee"). The Joint Committee consists of three representatives chosen by the NFL and three chosen by the NFLPA.[72] "The NFLPA shall have the right to commence an investigation before the Joint Committee if the NFLPA believes that the medical care of a team is not adequately taking care of player safety. Within 60 days of the initiation of an investigation, two or more neutral physicians will be selected to investigate and report to the Joint Committee on the situation. The neutral physicians shall issue a written report within 60 days of their selection, and their recommendations as to what steps shall be taken to address and correct any issues shall be acted upon by the Joint Committee."[73] While a complaint to the Joint Committee results in a neutral review process, the scope of that review process' authority is vague. The Joint Committee is obligated to act upon the recommendations of the neutral physicians, but it is unclear what it means for the Joint Committee to act and there is nothing obligating the NFL or any club to abide by the neutral physicians' or Joint Committee's recommendations. Moreover, there is no indication that the neutral physicians or Joint Committee could award damages to an injured player.[74]

In 2012, the NFLPA commenced the first and only Joint Committee investigation.[75] The nature and results of that investigation are confidential per an agreement between the NFL and NFLPA.[76]

Lawsuits against clubs are another possible avenue of relief, but prove difficult to pursue. The CBA presents the biggest obstacle against any such claim. This is because the Labor Management Relations Act (LMRA)[77] bars or "preempts" state common law[k] claims, such as negligence, where the claim is "substantially dependent upon analysis of the terms" of a CBA, *i.e.,* where the claim is "inextricably intertwined with consideration of the terms of the" CBA."[78] In order to assess a club's duty to an NFL player—an essential element of a negligence claim—the court would likely have to refer to and analyze the terms of the CBA, resulting in the claim's preemption.[79] In these cases, player complaints must be resolved through the enforcement provisions provided by the CBA itself (*i.e.,* a Non-Injury Grievance against the club), rather than through litigation.

In cases where the club doctor is an employee of the club—as opposed to an independent contractor—a player's lawsuit against the club is likely to be barred by the relevant state's workers' compensation statute. As discussed earlier, workers' compensation statutes provide compensation for workers injured at work and thus generally preclude lawsuits based on the co-workers' negligence.[80] This has been the result in multiple cases brought by NFL players against clubs and club doctors.[81]

Several players have sued their clubs concerning medical issues, with mixed results. In recent years, courts generally have determined that players' claims for negligent or otherwise improper medical care are preempted.[82] However, some cases concerning medical issues survive preemption. For example, between 2005 and 2008, six Cleveland Browns players became infected with staphylococcus ("staph"), raising concerns about the cleanliness of the Browns' facilities.[83] Among the infected, wide receiver Joe Jurevicius and center LeCharles Bentley filed lawsuits against the Browns.

---

j Gill was removed as the Patriots' Club doctor in April 2014. Liz Kowalczyk, *Troubles In Their Field*, Bos. Globe, Apr. 12, 2014, *available at* 2014 WLNR 9885884. The Patriots stated the change was because Gill was no longer chief of sports medicine at Massachusetts General Hospital and that the Club's doctor had "always" been the chief of sports medicine at the Hospital. *Id.* The Patriots made the change even though some reports indicated he was well-liked and trusted by the players. Bob Hohler, *Gill Denies He Sided With Team Over Player*, Bos. Globe, Dec. 13, 2014, *available at* 2014 WLNR 35249641.

---

k Common law refers to "[t]he body of law derived from judicial decisions, rather than from statutes or constitutions." Black's Law Dictionary (9th ed. 2009). The concept of "preemption" is "[t]he principle (derived from the Supremacy Clause [of the Constitution] that a federal law can supersede or supplant any inconsistent state law or regulation." *Id.*

In 2009, Jurevicius sued the Browns and Browns' doctors in Ohio state court, alleging causes of action for negligence, negligent misrepresentation, fraud, constructive fraud, breach of fiduciary duty, common law intentional tort, and statutory intentional tort against the Browns.[84] Jurevicius generally alleged that the Browns failed to take proper precautions to prevent staph infections and lied to players about what steps the Club had taken to prevent infections.[85] The Browns attempted to remove the case to federal court (and then argued that it was preempted), arguing that Jurevicius' claims were barred by the CBA.[86] In a March 31, 2010 decision, the United States District Court for the Northern District of Ohio determined that Jurevicius' negligence, negligent misrepresentation, fraud, common law intentional tort and statutory intentional tort claims were not preempted, while the constructive fraud and breach of fiduciary duty claims were. The Court generally found that the CBA did not address a club's obligations concerning facilities and thus did not need to be interpreted to resolve Jurevicius' claims.[87] The lawsuit was settled a few months after the Court's decision.[88]

In 2010, Bentley sued the Browns, alleging facts and claims similar to Jurevicius'.[89] Likely because the Browns had already lost the argument that claims arising out of these facts were preempted, the Browns did not attempt to remove the case to federal court and have it dismissed on the preemption ground. Instead, the Browns filed a motion to compel Bentley's claims to the arbitration procedures outlined in the CBA.[90] In July 2011, relying on the *Jurevicius* decision, the Court of Appeals of Ohio affirmed the denial of the Browns' motion.[91] Bentley and the Browns settled the case a month later.[92]

In a very similar case, in 2015 kicker Lawrence Tynes sued the Tampa Bay Buccaneers after he contracted methicillin-resistant Staphylococcus aureus (MRSA) from the club's training facility. Relying in part on *Jurevicius*, the United States District Court for the Middle District of Florida ruled that Tynes' claims were not preempted.[93] The court found that Tynes' claims had "nothing to do with medical treatment" and that "there is nothing in the CBA regarding the condition of facilities."[94] The case was remanded to Florida state court and is ongoing as of the date of publication.

One additional case bears mentioning. In *Chuy v. Philadelphia Eagles Football Club*,[95] former Eagles lineman Don Chuy successfully recovered against the Eagles for intentional infliction of emotional distress after the Eagles' Club doctor told a reporter that Chuy suffered from a fatal disease after the 1969 season. In a 1979 opinion, the United States Court of Appeals for the Ninth Circuit affirmed the jury verdict in Chuy's favor, finding that the allegations, if true as the jury found, "constituted intolerable professional conduct."[96] Considering the age of the case, its relevance today is unclear, particularly because it is questionable whether such a claim would survive preemption.

While players do have options for seeking redress against clubs concerning player health (probably arbitration more so than litigation), practical considerations often prevent players from pursuing these options. Players are constantly concerned about losing their job or status with the club. Filing a Non-Injury Grievance against a club is a surefire way to anger the club and jeopardize the player's career.[l] Thus, players often forego pursuing viable claims.

---

l   Current Player 8: "You don't have the gall to stand against your franchise and say 'They mistreated me.' . . . I, still today, going into my eighth year, am afraid to file a grievance, or do anything like that[.]"

(F) Recommendations Concerning NFL Clubs

NFL clubs collectively comprise the NFL. Thus, any recommendations concerning NFL clubs would ultimately be within the scope of recommendations made concerning the NFL. Moreover, NFL clubs act only through their employees or independent contractors, including coaches, other employees, and the medical staff. Thus, any recommendation we make for the improvement of clubs would be carried out through recommendations we make concerning club employees. For these reasons, we make no separate recommendations here and instead refer to the recommendations in the chapters concerning those stakeholders for recommendations concerning NFL clubs. Nevertheless, we do stress that it is important that club owners, as the leaders of each NFL club and its employees, take seriously and personally participate in player health issues, including overseeing the response to recommendations made in this Report.

Additionally, there is one recommendation contained in another chapter that is also directly relevant to NFL clubs:

- Chapter 1: Players—Recommendation 1:1-G: Players should not sign any document presented to them by the NFL, an NFL club, or employee of an NFL club without discussing the document with their contract advisor, the NFLPA, their financial advisor, and/or other counsel, as appropriate.

Endnotes

1   American Needle, Inc. v. Nat'l Football League, 560 U.S. 183, 187 (2010).

2   See Brady v. Nat'l Football League, 640 F.3d 785 (8th Cir. 2011) (listing each of the 32 different entities as defendants in lawsuit).

3   CBA, Art. 39, § 3(e).

4   CBA, Art. 20, § 2. It is most likely the General Manager or person with control over personnel decisions who makes the decision whether to place a player on the PUP List.

5   The American Board of Family Medicine issues Certificates of Added Qualifications in several areas, including Sports Medicine. See Certificates of Added Qualifications (CAQs), Am. Bd. Family Med., https://www.theabfm.org/caq/index.aspx (last visited Aug. 7, 2015), archived at https://perma.cc/R6JS-D2Z5.

6   CBA, Art. 39, § 1. It is the American Board of Family Medicine which issues Certificates of Added Qualification in Sports Medicine. See Sports Medicine, Am. Bd. Family Med., https://www.theabfm.org/caq/sports.aspx (last visited Aug. 7, 2015), archived at https://perma.cc/R6JS-D2Z5.

7   CBA, Art. 39, § 1(e).

8   CBA, Art. 39, § 2.

9   CBA, Art. 39, § 4.

10 CBA, Art. 39, § 5.

11 CBA, Art. 41, § 1.

12 CBA, Art. 45.

13 CBA, Art. 45, § 4.

14 See 26 U.S.C. § 4980H.

15 CBA, Art. 25, § 4.

16 See 29 U.S.C. § 651, et seq.

17 Gabriel Feldman, Closing the Floodgates: The Battle Over Workers' Compensation Rights in California, 8 Fla. Int'l Univ. L. Rev. 107, 109 (2012).

18 See, e.g., 2011 CBA, Art. 41, § 1.

19 Lex Larson, Workers' Compensation Law, § 1.01 (Matthew Bender 2014).

20 Lex Larson, Workers' Compensation Law, § 1.03 (Matthew Bender 2014).

21 Howard Berkes, Injured Workers Suffer As 'Reforms' Limit Workers' Compensation Benefits, Nat'l Pub. Radio (Mar. 4, 2015), http://www.npr.org/2015/03/04/390441655/injured-workers-suffer-as-reforms-limit-workers-compensation-benefits, archived at http://perma.cc/X5WN-5TRG (discussing states' reductions in maximum workers' compensation benefits).

22 See 2011 CBA, Art. 41, § 4.

23 CBA, App. A, ¶ 9.

24 See Matthew J. Mitten, Team Physicians as Co-Employees: A Prescription that Deprives Professional Athletes of an Adequate Remedy for Sports Medicine Malpractice, 50 St. Louis U. L.J. 211 (2005) (discussing generally medical malpractice in the sports context and the preclusion of claims by workers' compensation statutes); John Redlingshafer, Tonight's Matchup – Workers' Compensation v. Medical Malpractice: What Should Lower-Paid, Inexperienced Athletes Received When a Team Doctor Allegedly Aids in Ending Their Careers?, 2 DePaul J. Sports L. & Contemp. Probs. 100 (2004) (same).

25 Gabriel Feldman, Closing the Floodgates: The Battle Over Workers' Compensation Rights in California, 8 Fla. Int'l Univ. L. Rev. 107, 111 (2012).

26 Id.

27 Id., citing Injured Workers' Ins. Fund of Md. v. Workers' Comp. Appeals Bd., 29 Cal. Workers' Comp. Rep. 182 (2001); Carroll v. New Orleans Saints, No. ADJ2295331 (ANA0397551) (Workers' Comp. Appeals Bd. Jan. 24, 2011).

28 Cal. Labor Code § 3208.1.

29 Gabriel Feldman, Closing the Floodgates: The Battle Over Workers' Compensation Rights in California, 8 Fla. Int'l Univ. L. Rev. 107, 110 (2012).

30 Id. at *110, n. 18, citing Cal. Labor Code § 3550 (2012) (requiring employers to post in a conspicuous place the name of their insurance carrier and the entity responsible for workers compensation claims); see, e.g., Kaiser Found. Hosp. v. Workers' Comp. Appeals Bd., 702 P.2d 197, 201 (1985) ("[W]hen an employer fails to perform its statutory duty to notify an injured employee of his workers' compensation rights, the injured employee is unaware of those rights from the date of injury through the date of the employer's breach, then the statute of limitations will be tolled until the employee receives actual knowledge that he may be entitled to benefits under the workers' compensation system.").

31 Gabriel Feldman, Closing the Floodgates: The Battle Over Workers' Compensation Rights in California, 8 Fla. Int'l Univ. L. Rev. 107, 110–111 (2012).

32 Ken Bensinger & Marc Lifsher, California Limits Workers' Comp Sports Injury Claims, L.A. Times, Oct. 3, 2013, http://articles.latimes.com/2013/oct/08/business/la-fi-workers-comp-nfl-20131009, archived at http://perma.cc/2JTS-83KK.

33 Armand Emamdjomeh & Ken Bensinger, NFL Workers' Comp Victory Comes at a Price, L.A. Times, Feb. 1, 2014, http://www.latimes.com/business/la-fi-nfl-claims-20140201-dto-htmlstory.html, archived at http://perma.cc/JNF5-42RR.

34 Bensinger, supra note 32.

35 Id., citing NFL Tackles Benefits, L.A. Times, Apr. 11, 1997, http://articles.latimes.com/1997-04-11/business/fi-47559_1_compensation-benefits, archived at http://perma.cc/EB2S-B54W.

36 CBA, Art. LIV.

37 Bensinger, supra note 32.

38 See Matthews v. Nat'l Football League Mgmt. Council, 688 F.3d 1107 (9th Cir. 2012); Chicago Bears Football Club, Inc. v. Haynes, 816 F. Supp. 2d 534 (N.D. Ill. 2011); New Orleans Saints, LLC v. Cleveland, No. 2:11-cv-02093 (E.D. La. Aug. 24, 2011) (Beck, Arb.); Kansas City Chiefs Football Club, Inc. v. Allen, No. 4:12-cv-00238 (W.D. Mo. Feb. 24, 2012) (Beck, Arb.), and Atlanta Falcons Football Club LLC v. Nat'l Football League Players Ass'n, No. 1:12-cv-00753 (N.D. Ga. Feb. 23, 2012) (Beck, Arb.).

39 See Michael Hiltzik, California Gives a Huge Payoff to the NFL, L.A. Times, Oct. 8, 2013, http://articles.latimes.com/2013/oct/08/business/la-fi-mh-nfl-20131008, archived at http://perma.cc/6V33-FCPB (discussing, among other things, timeline of amendments to California's workers' compensation laws).

40 The NFLPA issued a memorandum to agents and players about the issue. See Mike Florio, California Overreacts to NFL Workers' Compensation Loophole, ProFootballTalk (May 3, 2013, 10:11 AM), http://profootballtalk.nbcsports.com/2013/05/03/california-overreacts-to-nfl-workers-compensation-loophole, archived at http://perma.cc/TJZ3-X2LC. Also, star quarterbacks Tom Brady of the New England Patriots and Drew Brees of the New Orleans Saints wrote an editorial in the San Francisco Chronicle decrying the proposed legislation. Tom Brady & Drew Brees, Injured Pro Athletes Deserve Workers' Comp, S.F. Chronicle, June 23, 2013, http://www.sfchronicle.com/opinion/openforum/article/Injured-pro-athletes-deserve-workers-comp-4617644.php?t=7ce9302705cefdcb88, archived at http://perma.cc/R97F-J2TC.

41 Cal. Labor Code § 3600.5(c).

42 Cal. Labor Code § 3600.5(d).

43 See Hiltzik *supra* note 39; Florio *supra* note 40.

44 Brady *supra* note 40.

45 Florio *supra* note 40.

46 CBA, Art. 12, § 6(c)(v).

47 *See* 2011 CBA, Art. 12, § 2(a)(iv) (listing workers' compensation benefits among "Benefits" to be deducted).

48 Michael David Smith, *Brees, NFLPA Speak Against Saints-supported Workers' Comp Bill,* ProFootballTalk (May 16, 2014, 7:17 PM), http://profootballtalk.nbcsports.com/2014/05/16/drew-brees-nflpa -speak-against-saints-supported-workers-comp-bill/, *archived at* http://perma.cc/G57L-Z784; Mike Florio, *Louisiana Workers' Compensation Fight Could Be Easily Solved,* ProFootballTalk (May 17, 2014, 12:44 PM), http://profootballtalk.nbcsports.com/2014/05/17/louisiana-workers -compensation-fight-could-be-easily-solved/, *archived at* http://perma .cc/2BGU-Z9PP.

49 Florio *supra* note 48.

50 *Id.*

51 CBA, Art. 23, § 4.

52 See 2011 CBA, Art. 26, § 1 (listing a four-year veteran's minimum salary for the 2015 season as $745,000). $745,000 divided by 17 weeks equals $43,823.53.

53 *House Bill 1069 is Wrong for Louisiana,* NFL Players Ass'n (May 13, 2014), https://www.nflpa.com/news/all-news/house-bill-1069-is-wrong -for-louisiana, *archived at* https://perma.cc/5JM3-EB8Q.

54 Mike Florio, *Sponsor Pulls Controversial Louisiana Workers' Compensation Bill,* ProFootballTalk (May 27, 2014, 4:36 PM), http://profootballtalk .nbcsports.com/2014/05/27/sponsor-pulls-controversial-louisiana -workers-compensation-bill/, *archived at* http://perma.cc/E7DT-BGE9.

55 P.S. § 565.

56 NFLPA Regulations, § 3(B)(28).

57 CBA, Art. 39, § 3(a).

58 CBA, Art. 39, § 3(d).

59 For example, Injury Grievances, which occur when, at the time a player's contract was terminated, the player claims he was physically unable to perform the services required of him because of a football-related injury, are heard by a specified Arbitration Panel. 2011 CBA, Art. 44. Additionally, issues concerning certain Sections of the CBA related to labor and antitrust issues, such as free agency and the Salary Cap, are within the exclusive scope of the System Arbitrator, 2011 CBA, Art. 15, currently University of Pennsylvania Law School Professor Stephen B. Burbank.

60 *See* 2011 CBA, Art. 43, § 1.

61 *See* 2011 CBA, Art. 43, § 6 (discussing constitution of Arbitration Panel); 2011 CBA, Art. 43 § 8 (discussing Arbitrator's authority, including to grant a "money award").

62 CBA, Art. 43, § 2.

63 The Non-Injury Grievance arbitrator has the authority to determine whether a complaint against a doctor fit within his or her jurisdiction under Article 43. *See* 2011 CBA, Art. 43, § 1 (discussing scope of Non-Injury Grievance arbitrator's jurisdiction).

64 This information was provided by the NFLPA.

65 Letter from Thomas J. DePaso, NFLPA General Counsel, to W. Buckley Briggs, Vice President of Labor Arbitration and Litigation, NFL Management Council re: NFLPA v. New England Patriots (June 19, 2013).

66 Mike Reiss and Mike Rodak, *Source: Fanene agrees to terms,* ESPNBoston.com (Mar. 14, 2012, 3:45 PM), http://espn.go.com/blog/boston/new -england-patriots/post/_/id/4719093/reports-fanene-agrees-to-terms, *archived at* http://perma.cc/J777-DFFB.

67 Opinion, Nat'l Football League v. Nat'l Football League Players' Ass'n In re: Jonathan Fanene, 2–3 (CBA Appeals Panel, Feb. 25, 2013).

68 Josh Alper, Report: Pats Cut Fanene with Failure to Disclose Physical Condition Designation, ProFootballTalk (Aug. 22, 2012, 8:47 AM), http:// profootballtalk.nbcsports.com/2012/08/22/report-pats-cut-fanene-with

-failure-to-disclose-physical-condition-designation/, archived at http:// perma.cc/G727-E7AV.

69 Opinion, Nat'l Football League v. Nat'l Football League Players' Ass'n In re: Jonathan Fanene, *supra* note 67.

70 *See* 2011 CBA, Art. 4, § 8 ("any Club, any player and any player agent or contract advisor engaged in negotiations for a Player Contract . . . is under an obligation to negotiate in good faith.")

71 Bob Hohler, *Gill Denies He Sided With Team Over Player,* Bos. Globe, Dec. 13, 2014, *available at* 2014 WLNR 35249641.

72 Mike Reiss, *Quick-hit Thoughts Around NFL, Patriots,* ESPNBoston. com (Sept. 21, 2013, 11:15 PM), http://espn.go.com/blog/boston/new -england-patriots/post/_/id/4749358/quick-hit-thoughts-around-nfl -new-england-patriots, *archived at* http://perma.cc/FR5E-SY2B.

73 In *Bunch v. New York Giants,* former New York Giants fullback Jarrod Bunch commenced a Non-Injury Grievance against his former Club alleging that the Giants violated the CBA by failing to advise Bunch that he had sustained a torn MCL during a 1993 training camp scrimmage. The arbitrator dismissed Bunch's claim as outside the 45-day statute of limitations. (Creo, Arb. Dec. 10, 1997), available as Exhibit 19 to the Declaration of Dennis L. Curran in Support of Defendant National Football League's Motion to Dismiss Second Amended Complaint (Section 301 Preemption), Dent v. Nat'l Football League, 14-cv-2324 (N.D. Cal. Sep. 24, 2014), ECF No. 73.

In *Jeffers v. Carolina Panthers,* former Carolina Panthers wide receiver Patrick Jeffers brought suit against the Panthers and Panthers' doctor Donald D'Alessandro in North Carolina state court for medical malpractice alleging that D'Alessandro performed "high-risk surgical procedures upon Jeffers' knees without Jeffers' knowledge or consent." The North Carolina Superior Court denied the Panthers' motion to dismiss but granted the Club's motion to compel the action to arbitration. Jeffers thereafter filed a Non-Injury Grievance pursuant to the CBA. Before a hearing on the merits, the parties submitted two issues to the arbitrator: (1) whether Jeffers' claims against the Panthers were subject to arbitration; and, (2) whether Jeffers' claims were barred by the CBA's statute of limitations. The arbitrator found that Jeffers' claims against the Club were required to be brought under the CBA because the claims would require "consideration of the express and implied terms of the CBA." The arbitrator then dismissed Jeffers' claims as time-barred by the CBA's 45-day statute of limitations. (Das, Arb. Mar. 25, 2008), available as Exhibit 15 to the Declaration of Dennis L. Curran in Support of Defendant National Football League's Motion to Dismiss Second Amended Complaint (Section 301 Preemption), Dent v. Nat'l Football League, 14-cv-2324 (N.D. Cal. Sep. 24, 2014), ECF No. 73.

In *Wilson v. Denver Broncos,* former Denver Broncos linebacker Al Wilson commenced a Non-Injury Grievance against his former Club alleging that the Broncos violated Art. XLIV, § 1 of the 2006 CBA (discussed above in *Bunch*) by failing to advise Wilson of the adverse effects of a neck injury sustained during the 2006 season. Wilson sought his 2007 salary after having been terminated prior to the 2007 season. The arbitrator dismissed Wilson's claim as outside the 45-day statute of limitations. (Townley, Arb. Oct. 29, 2008), available as Exhibit 16 to the Declaration of Dennis L. Curran in Support of Defendant National Football League's Motion to Dismiss Second Amended Complaint (Section 301 Preemption), Dent v. Nat'l Football League, 14-cv-2324 (N.D. Cal. Sep. 24, 2014), ECF No. 73.

See also Stevenson v. Houston Texans (Das, Arb. Feb. 4, 2013) (player's Non-Injury Grievance that Club violated CBA by conducting contact drills in minicamp resulting in player's injury barred by CBA's 45-day statute of limitations), available as Exhibit 18 to the Declaration of Dennis L. Curran in Support of Defendant National Football League's Motion to Dismiss Second Amended Complaint (Section 301 Preemption), Dent v. Nat'l Football League, 14-cv-2324 (N.D. Cal. Sep. 24, 2014), ECF No. 73.

74 CBA, Art. 50, § 1(a).

75 CBA, Art. 50, § 1(d).

76   In Stringer v. Nat'l Football League, the Court also expressed concerns about the effectiveness of the Joint Committee: "While the NFL is required to give "serious and thorough consideration" to recommendations of the Joint Committee, the CBA imposes no independent duty on the NFL to consider health risks arising from adverse playing conditions, or to make recommendations for rules, regulations or guidelines for the clubs to follow." 474 F. Supp. 2d 894, 896 (S.D.Ohio 2007).

77   This information was provided by the NFLPA.

78   *Id.*

79   U.S.C. § 185.

80   Allis-Chambers Corp. v. Lueck, 471 U.S. 202, 213, 200 (1985).

81   *See, e.g.,* Givens v. Tennessee Football, Inc., 684 F. Supp. 2d 985 (M.D.Tenn. 2010) (player's tort claims against Club arising out of medical treatment preempted); Williams v. Nat'l Football League, 582 F.3d 863 (8th Cir. 2009) (players' tort claims arising out of drug test preempted).

82   *See* Matthew J. Mitten, *Team Physicians as Co-Employees: A Prescription that Deprives Professional Athletes of an Adequate Remedy for Sports Medicine Malpractice,* 50 St. Louis U. L.J. 211 (2005) (discussing generally medical malpractice in the sports context and the preclusion of claims by workers' compensation statutes); John Redlingshafer, *Tonight's Matchup – Workers' Compensation v. Medical Malpractice: What Should Lower-Paid, Inexperienced Athletes Received When a Team Doctor Allegedly Aids in Ending Their Careers?,* 2 DePaul J. Sports L. & Contemp. Probs. 100 (2004) (same).

83   *See* Lotysz v. Montgomery, 309 A.D.2d 628 (N.Y. App. Div. 2003) (NFL player's medical malpractice claim against club doctor barred by state workers' compensation statute); Daniels v. Seattle Seahawks, 968 P.2d 883 (Wash. Ct. App. 1998) (same); Hendy v. Losse, 819 P.2d 1 (Cal. 1991) (same); Rivers v. New York Jets, 460 F.Supp. 1233 (E.D.Mo. 1978) (player's claim that club wrongfully concealed the true nature of player's condition barred by workers' compensation statute); Brinkman v. Buffalo Bills Football Club Division of Highwood Service, Inc., 433 F.Supp. 699 (W.D.N.Y. 1977) (player's claim that Club failed to provide adequate medical care barred by workers' compensation law). *See also* Bryant v. Fox, 515 N.E.2d 775 (Ill. App. Ct. 1987) (NFL player's medical malpractice claim against Club doctor not barred by workers' compensation statute where evidence established that doctor was an independent contractor); Martin v. Casagrande, 559 N.Y.S.2d 68 (N.Y. App. Div. 1990) (NHL player's claim that Club doctor and general manager conspired to withhold information about player's medical condition barred by workers' compensation statute); Bayless v. Philadelphia National League

Club, 472 F.Supp. 625 (E.D.Pa. 1979) (former MLB player's claim that Club negligently administered pain-killing drugs barred by workers' compensation statute).

84   *See, e.g.,* Givens v. Tennessee Football, Inc., 684 F. Supp. 2d 985 (M.D.Tenn. 2010); Jeffers v. D'Alessandro, 681 S.E.2d 405 (N.C. Ct. App. 2009); Sherwin v. Indianapolis Colts, Inc., 752 F.Supp. 1172 (N.D.N.Y. 1990); *see also* Brocail v. Detroit Tigers, Inc., 268 S.W.3d 90 (Tex. App. 2008) (MLB player's claim that Club failed to provide a proper second opinion preempted). Older cases do not even incorporate a preemption analysis, as the CBA then-controlling was likely less substantive in player health and welfare provisions. *See, e.g.,* Krueger v. S.F. Forty Niners, 234 Cal.Rptr. 579 (Cal.App. 1987) (ordering judgment in favor of player who played from 1958–73 and who alleged 49ers fraudulently concealed medical information).

85   *Jurevicius Becomes Sixth Browns Player in 4 Years to Contract Staph Infection,* ESPN (Apr. 11, 2008, 6:06 PM), http://sports.espn.go.com/nfl/news/story?id=3341171, *archived at* http://perma.cc/5Q7K-6ZWK.

86   *See* Jurevicius v. Cleveland Browns Football Co. LLC, 09-cv-1803, 2010 WL 8461220 (N.D.Ohio Mar. 31, 2010).

87   *Id.*

88   *Id.*

89   *Id.*

90   *Jurevicius Settles Lawsuit with the Browns,* ESPN (June 15, 2010, 6:37 PM), http://sports.espn.go.com/nfl/news/story?id=5289486, *archived at* http://perma.cc/5FYK-KB94.

91   *See* Bentley v. Cleveland Browns Football Co., 958 N.E.2d 585 (Ohio Ct. App. 2011).

92   *Id.*

93   *Id.*

94   *Browns, LeCharles Bentley Settle,* ESPN (Aug 15, 2012, 8:50 PM), http://espn.go.com/nfl/story/_/id/8272933/cleveland-browns-settle-former-lineman-lecharles-bentley-2010-staff-infection-lawsuit, *archived at* http://perma.cc/D87L-LZGY.

95   Tynes v. Buccaneers Limited Partnership, 15-cv-1594, 2015 WL 5680135 (M.D. Fl. Sep. 24, 2015).

96   *Id.* at *5–6.

97   F.2d 1265 (3d Cir. 1979).

98   *Id.* at 1274.

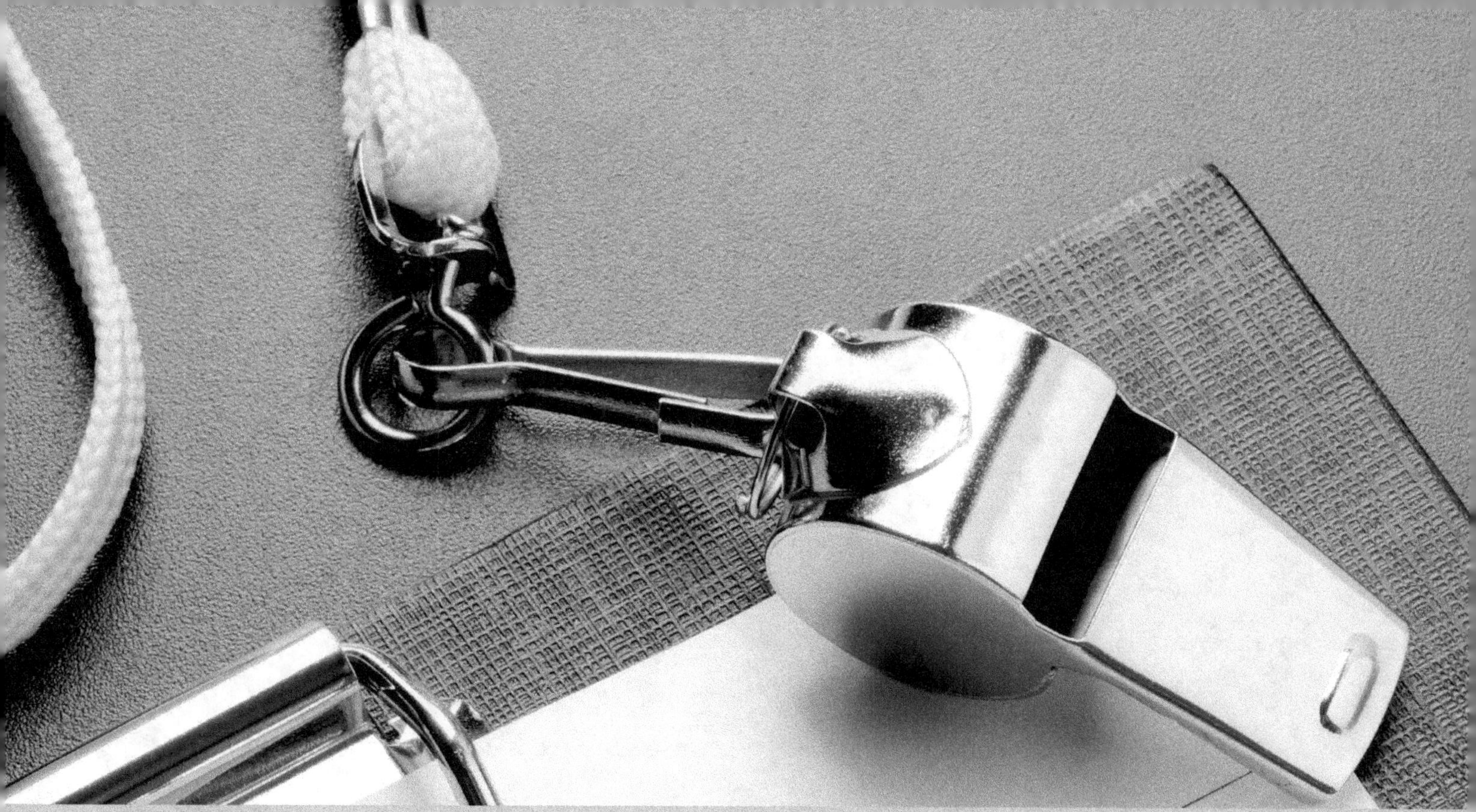

Part 4: **NFL Club Employees**

Coaches

Club
Employees

Equipment
Managers

Part 4 discusses those stakeholders who are not a part of the medical staff but otherwise fall under the control of the club, including: coaches; club employees; and, equipment managers. Additionally, we remind the reader that while we have tried to make the chapters accessible for standalone reading, certain background or relevant information may be contained in other parts or chapters, specifically Part 1 discussing Players and Part 3 discussing the NFL and NFLPA. Thus, we encourage the reader to review other parts of this Report as needed for important context.

Chapter 9

Coaches

Of all of the stakeholders considered in this Report, coaches have the most authority over players, and impose the most direct physical and psychological demands on them. Coaches can help players maximize their potential, but in some cases, may also contribute to the degradation of players' health. For these reasons and those discussed below, coaches are important stakeholders in player health.

Before we begin our analysis, it is important to point out that throughout this chapter we emphasize that the practice of coaches is likely heterogeneous from club to club at least to some extent. Nevertheless, we were unable to interview coaches as part of this Report to gain a better understanding of their work. In November 2014, we notified the NFL that we intended to seek interviews with club personnel, including general managers, coaches, doctors, and athletic trainers. The NFL subsequently advised us that it was "unable to consent to the interviews" on the grounds that the "information sought could directly impact several lawsuits currently pending against the league." Without the consent of the NFL, we did not believe that the interviews would be successful and thus did not pursue the interviews at that time. Instead, we have provided these stakeholders the opportunity to review draft chapters of the Report. We again requested to interview club personnel in July 2016 but the NFL did not respond to that request. The NFL was otherwise cooperative—it reviewed our Report and facilitated its review by club doctors and athletic trainers. The NFL also provided information relevant to this Report, including but not limited to copies of the NFL's Medical Sponsorship Policy (discussed in Chapter 2: Club Doctors) and other information about the relationships between clubs and doctors.

In addition, in order to ensure that this chapter was as accurate and valuable as possible, we invited the American Football Coaches Association (AFCA) and the National Football League Coaches Association (NFLCA), both described below, to review a draft version of this chapter prior to publication. The AFCA reviewed the chapter but had no comments or suggested edits.[1] David Cornwell, the Executive Director of the NFLCA, reviewed the chapter and provided comments.

(A) Background

The importance of NFL coaches to a player's career is obvious but cannot be understated. NFL coaches work incredible hours and face unrelenting criticism and pressure to succeed.[2] Coaches must be successful in order to retain their jobs and face pressure to provide good outcomes for the team. That pressure no doubt infects their relationship with their players and in some cases is transferred to the players. Head coaches are the individuals ultimately most responsible for the club's performance on the field and thus take on an immense stature and presence within the organization.[a] Coaches largely determine the club's culture,[3] dictate the pace and physicality of practice and workouts, and decide who plays—a decision often borne out by intense physical competition.[b] Moreover, some head coaches are the final decision-makers on player personnel decisions.[4]

In a 2012 arbitration decision concerning allegations that New Orleans Saints coaches had instituted a "bounty"

scheme to injure opposing players, discussed in detail below, former NFL Commissioner Paul Tagliabue, acting as arbitrator, described the control coaches have over players:[c]

> NFL players on average have short careers; their careers can end suddenly through injury or declining skills; players want to be good, cohesive members of the team, or unit, not complainers or dissenters; and players accept that they work for coaches, in "programs" conceived by coaches. These are programs for which coordinators and assistant coaches are often specially selected and hired to execute. Here we have a classic example: Head Coach Payton hired Defensive Coordinator Williams with directions to make the Saints' defense "nasty."

> In such circumstances, players may not have much choice but to "go along," to comply with coaching demands or directions that they may question or resent. They may know—or believe—that from the coaches' perspective, "it's my way or the highway." Coaching legends such as George Halas and Vince Lombardi are not glorified or remembered because they offered players "freedom of choice."

> While more recent and current coaches may debate whether and how much coaching approaches to "do it my way" have changed over time, it is clear that directions such as those given by the Saints' coaches in creating the Program are usually followed by most players. NFL head coaches told me in my seventeen years as Commissioner, "If players don't do it our way, they can find another team to pay them."[5]

NFL club coaching staffs are large. A typical NFL coaching staff consists of 15 to 20 people: the head coach; an offensive coordinator responsible for the offensive plays and players; a defensive coordinator responsible for the defensive plays and players; a special teams coordinator responsible for the special teams plays and players; and, position coaches and assistant position coaches at every nearly every position in the game of football.

Considering the size of NFL rosters and the scope of a head coach's duties, most players communicate principally with their position coaches.[d] For example, position coaches are the ones instructing and working with the players during practice. Yet given the rigid limits on on-field practice time

---

a   *See, e.g.,* Mark Fainaru-Wada & Steve Fainaru, League of Denial: The NFL, Concussions, and the Battle for Truth 213 (2013) (discussing New England Patriots head coach Bill Belichick ordering recently concussed linebacker Ted Johnson to participate in contact drills during practice and Johnson describing such pressure as common among NFL coaches).

b   *See, e.g., id.* at 14 (discussing a particularly violent drill known as the "Nutcracker" and New England Patriots coach Bill Belichick's affinity for it: "Belichick believed the Nutcracker answered some of football's most fundamental questions: 'Who is a man? Who's tough? Who's going to hit somebody?'").

c   Christopher R. Deubert, an author of this Report, and the firm at which he formerly practiced, Peter R. Ginsberg Law, LLC, represented former New Orleans Saints player Jonathan Vilma in the "Bounty"-related legal proceedings.

d   Former Player 1 described his interactions with the head coach as "minimal interaction," while Current Player 1 stated "we spend every day with our position coach."

(three hours per day),[6] it is the off-field work that is increasingly important. It is perhaps in meetings and video sessions where position coaches provide their best instruction and get to know the players best.

Strength and conditioning coaches also play an important role in a player's career. As their title implies, strength and conditioning coaches are responsible for overseeing a player's general fitness and physical preparedness for NFL games.[7] Strength and conditioning coaches create weight-lifting and stretching programs for players and otherwise monitor and assist players to ensure that they are in the best possible condition to play each week.[8] Given the importance of NFL players' health to the success of the team, NFL clubs and players consider strength and conditioning coaches to be among their most important coaches and staff.[9,e]

The collective bargaining agreement (CBA) contains no references to or requirements for strength and conditioning coaches. Nevertheless, NFL strength and conditioning coaches typically have a college degree in exercise science or a similar discipline and certification from the National Strength and Conditioning Association.[10]

NFL coaches might be members of one, both, or neither of two relevant professional associations: the AFCA; and, the NFLCA.

The AFCA is a voluntary organization of more than 11,000 high school, college or professional football coaches.[11] The AFCA is largely directed towards college coaches. AFCA members vote for the weekly Coaches Poll, which is one of the long-standing principal methods for ranking and evaluating college football teams.[12] Nevertheless, the AFCA occasionally consults with the NFL[13] and it is a well-respected organization with a Boards of Trustees past and present that includes many of the most successful college football coaches in history.[14]

The NFLCA is more loosely organized than the AFCA. The NFLCA, in its own language, "is a voluntary non-union association that represents the over six hundred coaches and assistant coaches currently employed by the thirty-two individual National Football League Clubs, as well as many retired coaches formerly employed by the NFL teams."[15,f] In February 2012, the NFLCA hired longtime

sports attorney David Cornwell as its Executive Director in a part-time capacity.[16]

Nevertheless, the NFLCA has a more subdued public status compared to the AFCA. The NFLCA has no website, does not negotiate the terms and conditions of coaches' employment, and rarely makes any positions known (to the extent it has any).

(B) Current Legal Obligations[g]

The principal source for regulating the behavior of coaches is the CBA. The 2011 CBA contains multiple provisions governing coaches' health obligations to players. We summarize those provisions here:

1. **Offseason Workouts:** Offseason workout programs are limited to nine weeks total, separated into three phases of varying intensity and strict prohibitions against live contact.[17] The 9-week limitation is reduced from the 14 weeks permitted under the prior CBA.[18] "The head coach and the Club[] are jointly responsible" for ensuring compliance with the offseason workout rules and are subject to fines beginning at $100,000 for any violations.[19]

2. **Minicamps:** Each club is limited to one maximum mandatory minicamp for veterans, unless the club hired a new coach, in which case it can hold two mandatory minicamps.[20] Minicamps are limited to three days in length,[21] and there is a strict prohibition against contact during minicamps.[22] In addition, all on-field activities from minicamps must be filmed to ensure compliance.[23] The head coach and club are jointly responsible for ensuring compliance with the preseason training camp rules and are subject to the same discipline scheme outlined in Article 21 governing Offseason Workouts.[24]

---

e   Current Player 6: "I think an important part in player health is the strength coach."

f   The NFLCA's status as a "non-union association" is important. If the NFLCA were to seek recognition as a union from the National Labor Relations Board, it might not be able to include all coaches in its membership. The National Labor Relations Act, the federal statute governing labor relations, exempts "supervisors" from its protections, which may include some coaches, particularly head coaches. Supervisors are defined as "any individual having authority, in the interest of the employer, to hire, transfer, suspend, lay off, recall, promote, discharge, assign, reward, or discipline other employees, or responsibly to direct them, or to adjust their grievances, or effectively to recommend such action[.]" 29 U.S.C. § 152(11); 29 U.S.C. § 164.

g   The legal obligations described herein are not an exhaustive list but are those we believe are most relevant to player health.

3. **Preseason Training Camps:** Preseason training camps begin on July 15 at the earliest.[25] Two-a-day practices can occur only if certain criteria are met: "(i) players may be on the field for a total of no more than four hours per day; (ii) players may participate in no more than one padded practice per day, which shall be no longer than three hours of on-field activities; (iii) there must be at least a three hour break after the practice; and (iv) the second practice on the same day may only be for a maximum of the remaining available on-field time, and shall be limited to only 'walk-through' instruction (i.e., no helmets, full-speed pre-snap, and walking pace after the snap)."[26] In addition, all on-field activities from preseason training camp must be filmed to ensure compliance.[27] The head coach and club are jointly responsible for ensuring compliance with the preseason training camp rules and are subject to the same discipline scheme outlined in Article 21 governing Offseason Workouts.[28]

4. **Regular Season and Postseason Practices:** Clubs are limited to 14 padded practices during the season and one per week during the postseason.[29] During such practices, on-field activities are limited to three hours per day.[30] Players must have at least four consecutive off days during bye weeks.[31] All regular and postseason practices must be filmed to ensure compliance.[32] The head coach and club are jointly responsible for ensuring compliance with the preseason training camp rules and are subject to the same discipline scheme outlined in Article 21 governing Offseason Workouts.[33]

5. **Days Off:** Clubs are required to provide players with five off days during preseason and four off days per month during the regular season (not including days off during bye weeks).[34]

(C) Current Ethical Codes

The AFCA maintains a Code of Ethics.[35] The Code of Ethics, last updated in 1997, is 20 pages long and covers nine coaching contexts: responsibilities to players; responsibilities to the institution; rules of the game; officials; public relations; scouting; recruiting; game day; and, all-star games.[36] The AFCA's Code of Ethics is principally geared toward college football coaches with its references to recruiting and academic endeavors. Consequently, our analysis focuses on those provisions relevant to players, and, player health in particular.

The Code of Ethics is premised on a 1927 report from Fielding Yost,[37] a college football coach from 1897 to 1926, including 25 seasons at the University of Michigan. Yost's report included ten ethical standards by which he believed all coaches ought to abide, including "to consider the welfare of the players of paramount importance at all times and not to countenance their exploitation for personal or private gain."[38] Article One of the current Code of Ethics, entitled Responsibilities to Players, expounds on Yost's proclamation:

1. In his relationships with players under his care, the coach should always be aware of the tremendous influence he wields, for good or bad. Parents entrust their dearest possession to the coach's charge; and, the coach, through his own example, must always be sure that the young men who have played under him are finer and more decent men for having done so. The coach should never place the value of a win above that of instilling the highest desirable ideals and character traits in his players. The safety and welfare of his players should always be uppermost in his mind, and they must never be sacrificed for any personal prestige or selfish glory.

2. In teaching the game of football, the coach must realize that there are certain rules designed to protect the player and provide common standards for determining a winner and loser. Any attempts to circumvent these rules, to take unfair advantage of an opponent, or to teach deliberate unsportsmanlike conduct, have no place in the game of football, nor has any coach guilty of such teaching any right to call himself a coach. The coach should set the example for winning without boasting and losing without bitterness. A coach who conducts himself according to these principles need have no fear of failure, for in the final analysis, the success of a coach can be measured in terms of the respect he has earned from his own players and from his opponents.

3. Prompt and professional medical attention is a responsibility of the coach. The diagnosis and treatment of injuries is a medical problem; a coach should not involve himself with the diagnosis of any injury. It is important that a solid, independent, and competent medical program of diagnosis and treatment be established and that a coach support such a program in the best interest and well-being of his players.

4. Under no circumstances should a coach authorize or tolerate the use of illegal or performance enhancing drugs. All medicines used by student-athletes should be under the direction of a physician or other appropriate medical personnel.

5. A coach should know and understand rules of eligibility and not violate any rules that would jeopardize his institution or players under his direction.

6. Academics and athletics are a joint effort, each providing benefits to the participants. A coach should encourage the proper time-management skills to his men that will allow them to achieve success both on the playing field and in the classroom. A coach should support the academic endeavors of his players.

The NFLCA does not have a Code of Ethics.

D Current Practices

As described in the Background, coaches remain predominant figures in an NFL player's career. Players indicated that their relationships with coaches varied (Current Player 5: "it's very individual"; Current Player 6: "it depends on the coach.")[h] Nevertheless, players also discussed that there is often a very different relationship between players and coaches when the coaches were themselves NFL players. Players generally view these coaches as more credible and sympathetic.[i] Current Player 6 said "I think coaches that have played kind of understand things a little bit better." Similarly, players also often develop close relationships with their position coaches, with whom they spend most of their time.[j] Despite these bonds, players are still reluctant to discuss health-related issues with the coaches for fear that the information will be relayed through the organizational hierarchy.

Interviews and discussions with players and contract advisors revealed continuing concern that coaches place strong implicit (and sometimes explicit) pressure on the players and medical staff concerning a player's treatment and return to play:[k]

- **Current Player 4:** *"I think that [player health] is much less of a priority to them than winning and/or producing the best players on the field and getting the best production out of them . . . . [T]here is a certain level of distrust with the coaches."*

- **Current Player 5:** *"I've heard a coach tell a player, 'You need to get better, you need to get healthy or else you're going to get cut because you're missing out on [practice]." "I heard a coach . . . say 'If you pull this muscle again, I'm cutting you or I'm fining you[.]"*

- **Current Player 7:** *"[I have heard coaches say] so what's the verdict on him? Are they going to be back in time? We need him."*

- **Current Player 8:** *"The head coach meets with the head trainer and says, 'You know, this guy's on the bubble . . . we need him this Sunday.' And he gets bumped off of the bubble."*

- **Current Player 10:** *"[I]t can get a little testy because, in general, the coaches want the players on the field and the trainers do what's best for the players . . . . But [the] coaches, their job is to win games, and it's such a bottom line business for them and so they want their best players out there."*

- **Former Player 2:** *"The NFL is a performance business . . . . So if you're not winning football games and the head coach is on the hot seat and his star player is nursing their hamstring issue, there's going to be pressure on the trainer to get the guy out there."[l]*

Moreover, one contract advisor interviewed relayed that he has had players tell him that assistant coaches have told players that "the concussion protocol that the NFL has in place is nonsensical and that if they feel good enough to go, they should." Nevertheless, Current Player 2 did also "think that the coaches are genuinely concerned about player health."[m] Former Player 2 agreed that coaches are generally "concerned" about player health but noted that the high turnover of players in the NFL often prevents coaches and players from having any relationship that would cause the coach to care.[n] Finally, Current Player 10 believes that, while "there's been a [positive] shift in the last five to ten years" concerning coaches' attitudes towards player health, he did not "think player health is the number one concern for coaches. It's wins and losses."

The implicit pressure to play often comes from comments made by coaches.[39] A common phrase attributed to NFL coaches is that "sometimes the best ability is availability."[40,o] Former San Francisco 49ers linebacker

---

h   Current Player 8 said: "For guys like me who bounce around, and spend a season or a few weeks in a place, I don't think coaches care that much about my health."

i   *See also* Rob Huizenga, You're Okay, It's Just a Bruise 231–32 (1994) (in discussing former Raiders coach Art Shell, "Shell looked me straight in the eye and said, 'Tell [the player] not to worry, I understand perfectly. I was a player. I'm not going to let him put one foot on the practice field until he's one hundred percent.'").

j   Current Player 9: "I think position coaches have a little more invested in the individual players and so they care a little bit more about your situation." We reiterate that our interviews were intended to be informational but not representative of all players' views and should be read with that limitation in mind.

k   Former Player 3 disagreed: "Coaches would obviously want to know from the medical staff, 'hey, will the guy be able to play?' But I would say they never put any pressure." Also of note, A 2015 study found that 53.7 percent of clinicians (doctors or athletic trainers) in college sports reported having experienced pressure from coaches to prematurely clear athletes to return to participation after a concussion. Emily Kroshus et al., *Pressure on Sports Medicine Clinicians to Prematurely Return Collegiate Athletes to Play After Concussion*, 50 J. Athletic Training 944 (2015).

l   For examples of situations in which coaches allegedly pressured players to return to play, Mark Fainaru-Wada & Steve Fainaru, League of Denial: The NFL, Concussions and the Battle for Truth 129 (2013) (discussing former New York Jets head coach Bill Parcells effectively ordering concussed tight end Kyle Brady to return to the field during 1999 playoff game); *id.* at 213 (discussing New England Patriots head coach Bill Belichick ordering recently concussed linebacker Ted Johnson to participate in contact drills during practice). In addition, strength and conditioning coaches should be differentiated from the football-specific coaches. When players are rehabilitating their injuries, they generally do it under the supervision of the athletic trainer and strength and conditioning coach on a separate practice field away from the coaches and other players.

m   "I've noticed our coaching staff say, 'Hey, get him out of there, he doesn't look right.'"

n   Former Player 3 also believes that coaches care about player health: "It doesn't do the coach any good if the guy is out there and he's not right."

o   Similarly, according to former Seattle Seahawks club doctor Pierce Scranton, one former Seahawks head coach instituted a "no practice, no play" rule, whereby if players were too injured to practice, they could not play in the next game. According to Scranton, the rule was intended to pressure players to practice even while hurt or injured. Pierce E. Scranton, Jr., Playing Hurt: Treating and Evaluating the Warriors of the NFL 169 (2001).

Gary Plummer described the pressure from coaches as follows:

> The coaches had euphemisms. They'll say: 'You know, that guy has to learn the difference between pain and injury.' Or: 'He has got to learn the difference between college and professional football.' What he's saying is the guy's a pussy and he needs to get tough or he's not going to be on the team. It's a very, very clear message.[41]

Interviews and discussions with players and contract advisors revealed continuing concern that coaches place strong implicit (and sometimes explicit) pressure on the players and medical staff concerning a player's treatment and return to play.

Plummer's comments are buttressed by a 2016 comment from Miami Dolphins head coach Adam Gase concerning star wide receiver DeVante Parker's injury problems:

> Sometimes it takes some guys more time to learn more than others. Eventually you get tired of being the guy standing on the sideline. I do think he's a little frustrated. He's been the odd man out all the time. Eventually . . . he will know how to push through certain kinds of pain.[42]

Nevertheless, several players also seemed to excuse the coaches' actions as inherent to the NFL:

- **Current Player 2:** *"It's the culture of football, coaches want their players on the field and they're going to apply that pressure to their trainers."*[p]

- **Current Player 6:** *"[M]ost coaches and pretty much anyone in this business has to look out for themselves."*

- **Current Player 8:** *"I don't want to condemn them for [placing pressure on the medical staff], but that's the job. The coach absolutely needs the parts to the machine to be out there for it to function."*

- **Former Player 2:** *"[Putting pressure on the medical staff] is just the nature of the beast."*

Additionally, there is some evidence that in recent years coaches have largely removed themselves from player health decisions, perhaps a change from years past. Moreover, coaches that do not have good reputations among players might find it challenging to recruit players to join the club during free agency.

One incident in which a coach positively involved himself in a player health matter is worth mentioning. In a 2015 game, the Pittsburgh Steelers' medical staff suspected a player of having sustained a concussion and thus attempted to evaluate the player. When the player resisted the evaluation in hopes of staying in the game, Steelers head coach Mike Tomlin intervened and told the player "You will listen to these doctors, and you'll do it now." The player was then evaluated and removed from the game.[43]

Two additional incidents bear mentioning to shed light on the role of coaches in today's NFL.

First, in March 2012, the NFL issued a press release alleging that New Orleans Saints coaches and players had participated in a "bounty" scheme whereby coaches and players provided financial rewards for good plays as well as for injuring opposing players in violation of NFL rules.[44] On March 21, 2012, about three weeks after the initial press release, the NFL suspended and fined Saints coaches and officials.[45] The Saints were also fined $500,000 and required to forfeit second round draft picks in the 2012 and 2013 NFL Drafts.[46]

The Saints and the coaches accepted the punishments, *i.e.*, did not pursue legal action, while denying the facts upon which the punishments were based.[47]

On May 2, 2012, the NFL suspended four players for their alleged involvement in the "bounty" program.[48] The players challenged their discipline through various legal options including through CBA arbitration mechanisms and in federal court.[49] Ultimately, former NFL Commissioner Paul Tagliabue presided over a four-day arbitration designed to ascertain the truth of the NFL's allegations and the fairness of the NFL's punishment.[50]

On December 11, 2012, former Commissioner Tagliabue issued his decision, vacating all discipline against the players but "affirm[ed]" Commissioner Goodell's finding that the players engaged in conduct detrimental to the game of football, except as to one of the four players. Commissioner Tagliabue principally placed the blame for any wrongdoing on the Saints' coaches and organization and faulted

---

p   Contract Advisor 6 expressed a similar sentiment: "[S]o many coaches believe you play hurt."

Commissioner Goodell's efforts to change a long-standing practice in the NFL too quickly and with insufficient notice to the clubs and players.[51] Tagliabue's decision made clear that the players were under tremendous pressure to follow the coaches' lead.

Commissioner Tagliabue had particularly strong words for the coaches. Tagliabue "condemn[ed]" the Saints' coaches for having created the pay-for-performance program, for pressuring a player to lie, and for their "irresponsible," "persistent and flagrant contempt for clear League rules and policies regarding player safety."[52] By vacating the player discipline, Commissioner Tagliabue principally laid the blame for any wrongdoing on the Saints' coaches.

Second, on October 28, 2013, Miami Dolphins offensive lineman Jonathan Martin left the Dolphins and checked himself into a nearby hospital, requesting psychological treatment. In the weeks and months that followed, it was reported that Martin had left the club as a result of bullying and harassment from his teammates, in particular fellow offensive lineman Richie Incognito.

On February 14, 2014, attorney Ted Wells and his law firm Paul, Weiss, Rifkind, Wharton & Garrison LLP released a report, commissioned by the NFL, entitled "Report to the National Football League Concerning Issues of Workplace Conduct at the Miami Dolphins." ("Wells Report.")[53] To summarize, the Wells Report found the Dolphins locker room to be a place of inappropriate and abusive conduct by the players as well as, at times, some coaches. Of relevance, the Wells Report gave a generally negative view of offensive line coach Jim Turner's involvement in the situation, suggesting that Turner had failed to take action to correct some of the inappropriate behavior and improperly defended Incognito.

The Dolphins fired Turner five days after the Wells Report.

In September 2014, Turner, through the law firm Peter R. Ginsberg Law, LLC, issued a Response to the Wells Report which explained his exemplary career and his involvement in the Martin-Incognito situation.[54] Turner's response also included interviews with several Dolphins offensive linemen who disagreed with all or parts of the Wells Report.[q]

Although neither situation resulted in litigation in which a coach was a party, both situations raised interesting questions concerning a coach's perceived and actual duties to his players.

(E) Enforcement of Legal and Ethical Obligations[r]

In the event a player or the NFLPA believes a coach has violated his obligations to the players, the player could try to commence a Non-Injury Grievance in accordance with the CBA.[s] The 2011 CBA directs certain disputes to designated arbitration mechanisms[t] and directs the remainder of any disputes involving the CBA, a player contract, NFL rules or generally the terms and conditions of employment to the Non-Injury Grievance arbitration process.[55] Importantly, Non-Injury Grievances provide players with the benefit of a neutral arbitration and the possibility of a "money award."[56]

However, there are several impediments to pursuing a Non-Injury Grievance against a coach (or any club employee). First and foremost, coaches are not parties to the CBA and thus likely cannot be sued for violations of the CBA.[57] Instead, the player could seek to hold the club responsible for the coach's violation of the CBA.[58] Second, the player's claim might be barred by workers' compensation statutes. Workers' compensation statutes provide compensation for workers injured at work and thus generally preclude lawsuits against co-workers based on the co-workers' negligence.[59] This was the result in the *Stringer* case (discussed in more detail below), and in multiple cases brought by NFL players against club doctors.[60] It is unclear how this bar would apply in an arbitration. Third, Non-Injury Grievances must be filed within 50 days "from the date of the occurrence or non-occurrence upon which the grievance is based,"[61] a timeframe that is much shorter than your typical statute of limitations. And fourth, players

---

q   Christopher R. Deubert, an author of this Report, previously practiced at Peter R. Ginsberg Law, LLC, and participated in the creation of Turner's response to the Wells Report prior to joining The Football Players Health Study at Harvard University.

r   Appendix K is a summary of players' options to enforce legal and ethical obligations against the stakeholders discussed in this Report. In addition, for rights articulated under either the CBA or other NFL policy, the NFLPA and the NFL can also seek to enforce them on players' behalves.

s   *See* 2011 CBA, Art. 43 (discussing Non-Injury Grievance procedures). The term "Non-Injury Grievance" is something of a misnomer. The CBA differentiates between an "Injury Grievance" and a "Non-Injury Grievance." An Injury Grievance is exclusively "a claim or complaint that, at the time a player's NFL Player Contract or Practice Squad Player Contract was terminated by a Club, the player was physically unable to perform the services required of him by that contract because of an injury incurred in the performance of his services under that contract." 2011 CBA, Art. 44, § 1. Generally, all other disputes (except System Arbitrations, *see* 2011 CBA, Art. 15) concerning the CBA or a player's terms and conditions of employment are Non-Injury Grievances. 2011 CBA, Art. 43, § 1. Thus, there can be disputes concerning a player's injury or medical care which are considered Non-Injury Grievances because they do not fit within the limited confines of an Injury Grievance.

t   For example, Injury Grievances, which occur when, at the time a player's contract was terminated, the player claims he was physically unable to perform the services required of him because of a football-related injury, are heard by a specified Arbitration Panel. 2011 CBA, Art. 44. Additionally, issues concerning certain Sections of the CBA related to labor and antitrust issues, such as free agency and the Salary Cap, are within the exclusive scope of the System Arbitrator, 2011 CBA, Art. 15., currently University of Pennsylvania Law School Professor Stephen B. Burbank.

likely fear that pursuing a grievance against a coach could result in the club terminating him.[u]

As an alternative to pursuing a Non-Injury Grievance, the NFLPA (at the player's request) might request the NFL to enforce the terms of the CBA and issue the required punishment. For example, after reports of a fight between players during a June 18, 2014 minicamp for the defending Super Bowl champion Seattle Seahawks, the NFLPA filed a complaint and requested the videotape from the practice as was its right.[62] The videotapes revealed extensive violations of the prohibitions against live contact during minicamps, resulting in a $100,000 fine for Seahawks head coach Pete Carroll, a $200,000 fine for the Seahawks, and the loss of two minicamp practices for the Seahawks in 2015.[63] Moreover, the Seahawks were repeat offenders, having also violated the no-contact rules in 2012.[64]

A player might also sue in court, but such lawsuits are unlikely to succeed for reasons discussed below. As a preliminary matter, while it is not uncommon for high school and youth sport coaches to be sued for their alleged involvement in a player injury,[65] research has only revealed two cases in which an NFL player (or someone on his behalf) sued an NFL coach.

In 2001, Minnesota Vikings Pro Bowl offensive tackle Korey Stringer died of complications from heat stroke after collapsing during training camp.[66] Stringer's family later sued the Vikings, Vikings coaches, trainers and affiliated doctors, the NFL, and equipment manufacturer Riddell. Of specific relevance, Stringer's family sued the Vikings' head coach and offensive line coach. In 2003, a Minnesota trial court granted summary judgment[v] in favor of the Vikings, the head coach and the offensive line coach.[67] The court determined that the head coach and the offensive line coach were acting within the scope of their employment concerning Stringer's medical situation, were not grossly negligent, and thus were immune from liability pursuant to Minnesota's workers' compensation laws.[68]

In addition to workers' compensation statutes, the CBA also presents a major obstacle for a player suing a coach. Lawsuits are another possible enforcement method, but face significant barriers. This is because the Labor Management Relations Act ("LMRA")[69] bars or "preempts" state common law[w] claims, such as negligence, where the claim is "substantially dependent upon analysis of the terms" of a CBA, i.e., where the claim is "inextricably intertwined with consideration of the terms of the" CBA."[70] In order to assess a coach's duty to an NFL player and whether it was satisfied—an essential element of a negligence claim—the court would likely have to refer to and analyze the terms of the CBA, resulting in the claim's preemption.[71] Preemption occurs even though coaches are not parties to the CBA and thus likely cannot be a party in any CBA grievance procedure. So long as the player's claim is "inextricably intertwined" with the CBA, it will be preempted. In these cases, player complaints must be resolved through the enforcement provisions provided by the CBA itself (i.e., a Non-Injury Grievance against the club), rather than litigation.

In a 1995 lawsuit, two Houston Oilers players alleged that the Houston Oilers general manager and strength and conditioning coach subjected the players to a phony and brutal rehabilitation program designed to coerce the players into quitting the club.[72] The players alleged state law claims of coercion, duress, extortion, assault and battery, and intentional infliction of emotional distress. The United States District Court for the Southern District of Texas held that the players' claims were preempted by the CBA, because the CBA and the players' contracts governed rehabilitation programs.[73] The United States Court of Appeals for the Fifth Circuit affirmed.[74]

While these avenues for actions against coaches seem unfruitful, the AFCA Code of Ethics does provide a potential enforcement mechanism. Pursuant to the Code of Ethics, the AFCA Committee on Ethics "is empowered to investigate any and all alleged violations of the Code . . . from any source[.]"[75] The Code of Ethics includes a robust hearing mechanism, including the presentation of evidence and calling of witnesses.[76] Nevertheless, the Committee's disciplinary authority is limited to a letter of reprimand or

---

u   Current Player 8: "You don't have the gall to stand against your franchise and say 'They mistreated me.' . . . I, still today, going into my eighth year, am afraid to file a grievance, or do anything like that[.]" While it is illegal for an employer to retaliate against an employee for filing a grievance pursuant to a CBA, *N.L.R.B. v. City Disposal Systems Inc.*, 465 U.S. 822, 835–36 (1984), such litigation would involve substantial time and money for an uncertain outcome.

v   Summary judgment is "[a] judgment granted on a claim or defense about which there is no genuine issue of material fact and on which the movant is entitled to prevail as a matter of law." Black's Law Dictionary (9th ed. 2009).

w   Common law refers to "[t]he body of law derived from judicial decisions, rather than from statutes or constitutions." Black's Law Dictionary (9th ed. 2009). The concept of "preemption" is "[t]he principle (derived from the Supremacy Clause [of the Constitution] that a federal law can supersede or supplant any inconsistent state law or regulation." *Id.*

the suspension of membership.[77] Moreover, the AFCA typically does not go that far.[x] Each year, the AFCA's Committee on Ethics meets at the AFCA's annual convention and reviews recent charges brought by the National Collegiate Athletic Association (NCAA) for violations of NCAA Bylaws and which involve college football coaches. The AFCA generally does not discipline the coaches involved in any way, and instead issues generic aspirational statements recommending and reminding coaches to be ethical and to follow NCAA Bylaws. Additionally, the AFCA's Committee on Ethics seemingly does not conduct any investigation of its own and only considers cases already adjudicated by the NCAA.

Finally, of the most relevance, the AFCA does not undertake to investigate or discipline NFL coaches for any violations of the AFCA's Code of Ethics, instead deferring to the NFL to handle such matters.[78] For these reasons the AFCA route for enforcing the legal and ethical obligations of the coach seems anemic.

Currently, the only enforcement of coaches' obligations concerning player health tends to be discipline by the NFL. It is thus suspect whether current practices and the current enforcement scheme are sufficiently protective of player health.

---

x   The AFCA provided us copies of its Ethics Committee Reports from 2006 to 2015.

Currently, the only enforcement of coaches' obligations concerning player health tends to be discipline by the NFL. It is thus suspect whether current practices and the current enforcement scheme are sufficiently protective of player health.

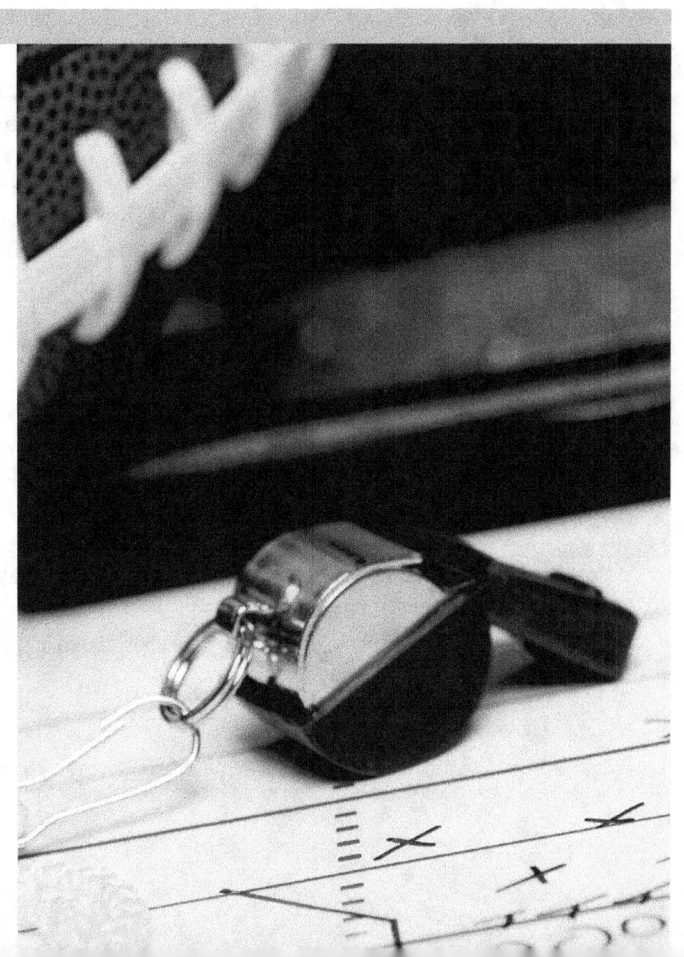

(F) Recommendations Concerning Coaches

Coaches have tremendous influence over a player's career and can make decisions or dictate policies or culture that have a substantial impact on a player's health. Many coaches develop close relationships with players, or are former players themselves, and are thus sensitive to protecting player health. Nevertheless, the inherent pressures of coaching sometimes cause coaches to make decisions or create pressures that are not in the best interests of player health. Unfortunately, when things go wrong, there are currently few, if any, fruitful avenues for players to pursue complaints against coaches related to their health. While we were unable to interview current coaches to gauge their viewpoints,[y] we make the below recommendations to help improve the role of coaches in player health.

Goal 1: To hold coaches accountable for their role in player health.

Principles Advanced: Respect; Health Primacy; and, Justice.

Recommendation 9:1-A: The NFLCA should adopt and enforce a Code of Ethics that recognizes that coaches share responsibility for player health.

Codes of ethics provide important guidelines and instructions for a wide variety of professionals to ensure that they are conducting themselves in an appropriate and ethical manner. Currently, there is no code of ethics actively governing NFL coaches, which can and does allow for serious lapses concerning player health. To resolve the ethical void for NFL coaches, there are seemingly three options.

First, the AFCA could take a more active role in NFL coaching matters, including enforcing its code of ethics against NFL coaches who are members of the AFCA. However, the AFCA's focus on college coaches and issues seems appropriate and it would likely be better if there were an organization solely focused on NFL coaches.

Second, if the AFCA is not well-suited to regulate NFL coaches, the NFLCA should be. The NFLCA seemingly has minimal resources and employees and engages in limited work. This seems to be a missed opportunity not only to advance the interests of NFL coaches but, also for our concerns here, to ensure the proper involvement of coaches in the lives and health of their players. Thus our preferred solution and the one we recommend here is that the NFLCA evolve into a more robust and active organization, including the self-regulation of its coaches.

Third, in addition to self-regulation, if the NFLCA is unable or unwilling to take on the role of enforcing the ethical obligations of its coaches, the next best option is likely for such obligations to be included in the CBA. It would be preferable if coaches and the NFLCA voluntarily undertook to recognize and clarify their responsibilities, but if they do not, the NFLPA should seek to have such responsibilities outlined in the CBA—a change the NFL should appreciate and willingly accept.

A code of ethics for NFL coaches should cover at least the following topics: coaches' obligations to players, including to help support players in preparation for post-football life; coaches' obligations to other players; communications with medical staff; use of player medical information; and, handling conflicts of interest, including winning and player health. Below, we elaborate on some of these issues.

- **Coaches should establish a locker room culture in which players and their health and safety are respected.** Coaches' influence in the locker room cannot be understated—they set the tone and culture for the organization and players respond and comport themselves according to the culture preferred by the coaches. To that end, if the coaches create a locker room centered around toughness

---

and where playing through injuries is required, players are likely to make decisions that negatively affect their health. Moreover, such decisions could negatively affect the club if the player returns to play too soon and worsens his injury, requiring him to miss even more playing time. Ideally, coaches will respect a player's medical condition and his right to be treated in a way that is in the player's best interests.

- **Coaches should orient communications with players about their health so as not to create undue pressure on the player where it may be detrimental to player health.**[z] Players are under incredible pressure to play and to play well. They know that coaches control their careers in many respects and thus feel intense pressure to impress the coaches, including their ability to play through injuries. Questions and comments from coaches such as, "How are you feeling?" "Are you good to go today?" or "You know we really need you out there" carry the implications that the player must be ready to play and perform, regardless of the player's actual health status.[aa] We recognize that such questions from coaches might come from genuine concern and that we want players and coaches to establish a meaningful relationship in this regard. Nevertheless, coaches should also recognize the implicit pressures created by these types of comments. Additionally, coaches cannot be faulted for later using the information conveyed by the player in considering the player's roster status, whether in the short or long term. Consequently, coaches should approach conversations with players concerning their health with sensitivity and the players' potential concerns in mind.

- **Coaches should consider, respect and care about players' post-career lives while the player is playing for that coach.** Although the NFL and NFLPA disagree as to the average length of an NFL player's career, it is undeniably short—somewhere in the three to six year range.[79] Thus the average NFL player will be out of the NFL well before his 30th birthday. And although NFL player salaries are relatively substantial, few, if any, NFL players could reasonably be expected to live another 50 to 60 years on the income earned in their 20s. Almost all players will need to find a career after football. Coaches and club executives should actively encourage their players to consider their post-career options and provide them the flexibility to further their post-career options where it does not undermine the player's and coach's commitment to winning.[ab]

- **Coaches should not encourage in any way the injury of opposing players.** While the exact details of the New Orleans Saints' "pay-for-performance"/"bounty" system are unclear and debated, the situation did bring into focus the possibility that NFL coaches, in their attempts to motivate their players, might occasionally use language that promotes or suggests that players should attempt to injure their opponents, or go even further to encourage such behavior. Even if such language is hyperbole or overheated rhetoric, players may take such words literally as part of their enthusiasm for the game and in an effort to please their coaches. Moreover, it is the coaches' obligation to ensure that their players play and conduct themselves within the rules. Language tending to promote the injury of opposing players does not serve this obligation and threatens the safety of players.

- **Coaches should ensure that the medical staff acts independently and does not feel pressured to act in any way other than in the player's best interests.** Coaches are not medical professionals and thus are not qualified to opine on a player's medical condition or treatment course. Historically, at least some coaches have unduly influenced club doctors, clubs, and players to take actions that might jeopardize the player's health for the sake of winning. Such actions violate the player's right to a doctor concerned with his best interests and unfairly take advantage of players' (and perhaps also the club doctor's) eagerness to win the approval of their coaches. In order to prevent these situations, clubs and coaches should provide the medical staff the latitude to provide medical care to the players without influence from non-medical staff. Fortunately, there is reason to believe coaches are largely uninvolved in player health decisions today, but a clear ethical rule prohibiting any such involvement is still necessary to avoid these dangerous situations.

---

z   As is explained in Chapter 2: Club Doctors, we recommend that information about player health be relayed to coaches through a summary form known as the Player Health Report. This approach minimizes some of the concerns explained in this Section.

aa Current Player 9: "A lot of time the coaches can't help themselves but to throw little comments about, 'When can we have you back,' 'how do you feel.' And sometimes they're honest questions, but a lot of times they are probing questions because they want to know when they're going to get that player back . . . . I hate it when I hear a coach ever making light of an injury 'this is not something serious enough to keep somebody out,' or whenever they try to challenge someone's manhood so to speak and their toughness. Those just are things that don't need to be said."

ab For example, during the 2014 season, Chicago Bears head coach Marc Trestman approved of star wide receiver Brandon Marshall flying back to New Jersey each Tuesday to tape the television program "Inside the NFL." Trestman stated: "I trust Brandon . . . . He asked me about it. I trust him to make decisions that are in the best interests of the team first. I know Brandon. I know he'll do that. So I have complete faith that the team always comes first, football has always come first to him, and I believe he'll work it out to where it won't distract him from doing his job." Bob Wolfley, *Bears' Coach Marc Trestman Approves of Brandon Marshall's 'Inside the NFL' Gig,* SportsDay with Bob Wolfley Blog (Aug. 18, 2014), http://www.jsonline.com/blogs/sports/271721501.html, *archived at* http://perma.cc/4N68-3ENY.

- **Coaches' interests in winning should not supersede player health.** While coaches have legitimate interests in winning, and face tremendous pressure to do so, those interests cannot cause coaches to act in such a way that jeopardizes player health. We recognize it is difficult to determine at what point a player's health, whether short- or long-term, becomes jeopardized and that coaches are not medical professionals. Consequently, if the above-bulleted recommendations concerning the independence of the medical staff are followed, coaches should be free from concerns about player health and can focus solely on winning. To the extent coaches are still in a position to affect player health, they should immediately involve the proper medical staff to ensure that the situation is handled with the appropriate expertise and care.

In order for the recommended NFLCA Code of Ethics to be effective, all NFL coaches must be members of the NFLCA. While it is unclear whether or not all coaches currently are members, it might be necessary for the CBA to require that all coaches be members or otherwise be bound by the proposed Code of Ethics.

Finally, enforcement is essential. Violations of a professional code of ethics should include meaningful punishments, ranging from warnings and censures to fines and suspensions. Again, in order to be effective, the enforcement and disciplinary schemes might need to be included in the CBA.

Recommendation 9:1-B: The most important ethical principles concerning coaches' practices concerning player health should be incorporated into the CBA.

As discussed above, professional self-regulation is important and useful. However, professional codes often fail to be sufficiently enforced. Additionally, player health and coaches' obligations towards player health are too important to leave in the hands of coaches alone. In particular, it currently seems unlikely that the NFLCA has the resources to adopt and enforce a meaningful code of ethics. Consequently, incorporating at least some of the above-mentioned ethical concepts, particularly those concerning player health primacy, into the CBA is likely necessary, along with appropriate enforcement mechanisms.

Recommendation 9:1-C: Coaches should consider innovative ideas and methods that might improve player health.

Helmet-to-helmet hits are a leading cause of concussions.[80] As a result, the NFL has increasingly penalized such hits while also emphasizing safer tackling methods, which reduce helmet-to-helmet contact. To reinforce those safer tackling methods, the University of New Hampshire football team occasionally practices tackling without helmets.[81] Players believed that the drills helped them to learn how to tackle by using their chest and legs as opposed to their heads.[82] Similarly, NFL coaches and players should consider whether new practice drills can be implemented that might improve player health.

For example, in 2015, Dartmouth College's football team also introduced a new practice component designed to improve player health. Engineering students at the college created motorized tackling dummies that players can tackle during practice, as opposed to other players.[83] Indeed, in 2016, the Pittsburgh Steelers began using a motorized tackling dummy.[84] Moreover, based in part on Dartmouth College's new tackling dummy, in 2016, the Ivy League banned full-contact hitting and tackling during regular season practices.[85] Such innovations should continue to be studied and, if successful, might also prove useful to NFL coaches and players and thus should be considered.

Additionally, it would likely be helpful if coaches had a forum in which to share innovative ideas and methods that might improve player health. Nevertheless, we acknowledge that coaches are likely to have concerns about sharing information they might regard as a competitive advantage with other clubs.

Endnotes

1   E-mail from Vince Thompson, AFCA, Director of Media Relations, to author (Apr. 5, 2016, 2:31 PM) (on file with authors).

2   See Paul Woody, NFL Coaching Not a Healthy Occupation, Richmond Times Dispatch, Dec. 18, 1998, available at 1998 WLNR 1242844.

3   See Nate Ulrich, Pettine's New Boys, Akron Beacon Journal, Mar. 27, 2014, available at 2014 WLNR 8435196; Rainer Sabin, Cowboys Blog: Garrett's Message of Toughness Being Heeded by Cowboys, Dall. Morning News, Sept. 24, 2011, available at 2011 WLNR 19451135; Lions Hire Marinelli Tampa Bay Assistant Brings Toughness to Wayward Team, Detroit News, Jan. 19, 2006, available at 2006 WLNR 25099694; Larry Weisman, Athletes Victims of Culture That Likes Its Heroes Tough, USA Today, May 16, 1996, available at 1996 WLNR 2832770; Larry Weisman, In NFL, Pain is Part of the Game, Seattle Times, May 26, 1996, available at 1996 WLNR 1342239.

4   Christopher R. Deubert, Glenn M. Wong & Daniel Hatman, National Football League General Managers: An Analysis of the Responsibilities, Qualifications, and Characteristics, 20 Jeffrey S. Moorad Sports L.J. 427, 477 (2013) (identifying head coaches who also held general manager/personnel decision responsibilities).

5   Final Decision on Appeal, In the Matter of New Orleans Saints Pay-for-Performance/"Bounty," at 16–17 (Tagliabue, Arb. Dec. 11, 2012).

6   CBA, Art. 24, § 1(d).

7   See How to Become an NFL Strength and Conditioning Coach, Sports Rehab and Performance Group, Feb. 28, 2014, http://sportsrehabandperformancegroup.org/?p=494, archived at http://perma.cc/U6E4-C7V5 (interview with Cincinnati Bengals strength and conditioning coach Ron McKeefery about the role of a strength and conditioning coach); Mike Vandermause, Green Bay Packers Assistant Strength and Conditioning Coach Dave Redding Played 'Big Role' in Success, Green Bay Press-Gazette, Feb. 23, 2011, available at 2011 WLNR 3564295 (discussing role of NFL strength and conditioning coach); Allen Wilson, By the Power Vested in Him . . . Strength and Conditioning Coach Allaire Helps Bills Meet Fitness Goals for the Long Season, Buffalo News, Oct. 15, 2006, available at 2006 WLNR 17952756 (same); Mike Preston, Bigger, Faster, Stronger; Fitness: Looking to Protect Their Investment in Players, NFL Teams Put Their Stock and Faith In Year-Round Strength and Conditioning Programs, Balt. Sun, Sept. 20, 1996, available at 1996 WLNR 923238 (same); Thomas George, Strength and Conditioning Coaches: The Force Is With Them, N.Y. Times, Jun. 27, 1993, http://www.nytimes.com/1993/06/27/sports/pro-football-strength-and-conditioning-coaches-the-force-is-with-them.html archived at http://perma.cc/QH9X-FH25 (same).

8   See id.

9   See id.

10 See How to Become an NFL Strength and Conditioning Coach, supra note 7.

11 American Football Coaches Association – Who We Are, Am. Football Coaches Ass'n (Sept. 22, 2014), http://www.afca.com/article/article.php?id=1135, archived at http://perma.cc/EKL5-KNUL. The AFCA's Executive Director is former Baylor head coach and College Football Hall of Famer Grant Teaff.

12 See Amway Coaches Poll, USA Today, http://www.usatoday.com/sports/ncaaf/polls/ (last visited May 18, 2016), archived at https://perma.cc/GZ9A-JCU6 (explaining the AFCA's involvement in the polls).

13 See Pitt State Football: Gorillas Hire NFL All-Pro Gordon, Morning Sun (Pittsburg, KS), July 25, 2013, available at 2013 WLNR 18347003 (NFL, NCAA and AFCA collaborated to create coaching intern program); William C. Rhoden, N.F.L. Crosses A Boundary In the Pryor Case, N.Y. Times, Aug. 21, 2011, http://www.nytimes.com/2011/08/22/sports/football/pryor-case-highlights-nfls-uncomfortably-cozy-ties-with-ncaa.html, archived at http://perma.cc/5X78-DJWC (NFL, NCAA and AFCA collaborated on efforts to prevent student-athletes from losing their eligibility); Slive: SEC Will Talk On Agents, Rosters, Rules, Birmingham News (AL), April 19, 2011, available at 2011 WLNR 7702131 (NFL, NCAA and AFCA collaborated on efforts to curtail unethical agents).

14 See AFCA Board of Trustees, Am. Football Coaches Ass'n (Sept. 22, 2014), http://www.afca.com/article/article.php?id=5, archived at http://perma.cc/S9UA-E8VT. The Trustees entering the 2015 season were Todd Berry, University of Louisiana-Monroe, First Vice President; Lee Owens, Ashland University, Second Vice President; Rich Rodriguez, University of Arizona, Third Vice President; Bill Cronin, Georgetown College; Frank Solich, Ohio University; Mike Riley, Oregon State University; Gary Patterson, TCU; David Bailiff, Rice University; Mark Richt, University of Georgia; Pete Fredenburg, University of Mary Hardin-Baylor; Turner Gill, Liberty University; Pat Fitzgerald, Northwestern University; Craig Bohl, University of Wyoming; Bronco Mendenhall, Brigham Young University; Todd Knight, Ouachita Baptist University; David Cutcliffe, Duke University; Dale Lennon, Southern Illinois University; Bobby Kennedy, University of Iowa; Dino Babers, Bowling Green State University; and,w Sam Knopik, The Pembroke Hill School (Mo.).

15 Amicus Brief of the National Football League Coaches Association in Support of Petitioner, American Needle, Inc. v. Nat'l Football League, 560 U.S. 183 (2010) (No. 08-661), 2009 WL 3143713, at *1.

16 Mike Florio, Cornwell Named NFLCA Executive Director, ProFootballTalk (Feb. 21, 2012, 5:03 PM), http://profootballtalk.nbcsports.com/2012/02/21/cornwell-named-nflca-executive-director/, archived at http://perma.cc/3SGB-ZTQT; see also Barnes &Thornburg, LLP Directory: David Cornwell Sr., http://www.btlaw.com/david-cornwell/ (last visited Aug. 7, 2015), archived at http://perma.cc/7GF8-V7MV, (discussing Cornwell's ongoing legal practice outside of his duties at the NFLCA).

17 CBA, Art. 21.

18 CBA, Art. XXXV.

19 CBA, Art. 21, § 8.

20 CBA, Art. 22, § 1.

21 CBA, Art. 22, § 2.

22 CBA, Art. 22, § 5.

23 CBA, Art. 22, § 8.

24 CBA, Art. 22, § 9.

25 CBA, Art. 23, § 5.

26 CBA, Art. 23, § 6.

27 CBA, Art. 23, § 10.

28 CBA, Art. 23, § 11.

29 CBA, Art. 24, § 1(a), (b).

30 CBA, Art. 24, § 1(d).

31 CBA, Art. 24, § 2.

32 CBA, Art. 24, § 4.

33 CBA, Art. 24, § 3.

34 CBA, Art. 35.

35 AFCA Code of Ethics Summary, Am. Football Coaches Ass'n (Sept. 22, 2014), http://www.afca.com/article/article.php?id=8, archived at http://perma.cc/KJ49-N68E. The complete Code of Ethics can be obtained by contacting the AFCA.

36 Id.

37 Id.

38 Id.

39 See, e.g., Michael David Smith, Chip Kelly, Earl Wolff not seeing eye to eye on recovery from injury, ProFootballTalk (Jun. 10, 2015, 12:06 PM), http://profootballtalk.nbcsports.com/2015/06/10/chip-kelly-earl-wolff-not-seeing-eye-to-eye-on-recovery-from-injury/, archived at http://perma.cc/Z7P6-JCKQ (Philadelphia Eagles head coach Chip Kelly publicly stating that the only thing holding a player back from participating in practice was pain tolerance); Josh Alper, Marvin Lewis: Marvin Jones has to "find a way to get out there," ProFootballTalk (Aug. 7, 2015, 9:41 AM), http://profootballtalk.nbcsports.com/2015/08/07/marvin-lewis-marvin-jones-has-to-find-a-way-to-get-out-there/, archived at http://perma.cc/8YBW-4GRP.

40 Rick Stroud, *Thomas Catches On Again,* St. Petersburg Times (FL), Sept.18, 1998, *available at* 1998 WLNR 2608915.

41 Mark Fainaru-Wada & Steve Fainaru, League of Denial: The NFL, Concussions, and the Battle for Truth 80 (2013).

42 Adam H. Beasley, *Dolphins' Gase challenges Parker to do what it takes to stay on the field,* Miami Her., Aug. 30, 2016, http://www.miamiherald .com/sports/nfl/miami-dolphins/article98878327.html, *archived at* https ://perma.cc/6E6P-9RBT.

43 Mike Florio, *NFL really is doing a better job of spotting concussions,* ProFootballTalk (Dec. 1, 2015, 9:19 AM), http://profootballtalk .nbcsports.com/2015/12/01/nfl-really-is-doing-a-better-job-of-spotting -concussions/, *archived at* http://perma.cc/BPN9-E64P.

44 *See* Christopher R. Deubert, *A Summary of the NFL's Investigation Into the New Orleans Saints Alleged Bounty Program and Related Proceedings,* 9 DePaul J. Sports L. & Contemp. Probs. 123 (2013).

45 *Id.*

46 *Id.*

47 *Sean Payton Proud of Saints,* ESPN (Sept. 5, 2012), http://espn.go.com /nfl/story/_/id/8339699/sean-payton-expects-new-orleans-saints-do -well-him, *archived at* http://perma.cc/3QEB-A4R4.

48 *See* Deubert, *supra* note 44.

49 *Id.*

50 *Id.*

51 *Id. See* Final Decision on Appeal, *In the Matter of New Orleans Saints Pay-for-Performance/"Bounty"* (Tagliabue, Arb. Dec. 11, 2012).

52 *Id.*

53 The Wells Report is available from a variety of online sources, most reliably the Sports Lawyers Association, www.sportslaw.org (membership required).

54 Turner's response can be found at http://espn.go.com/pdf/2014/0911/ turner-response_r.pdf, *archived at* https://perma.cc/74B3-78AT?type=pdf.

55 *See* 2011 CBA, Art. 43, § 1.

56 *See* 2011 CBA, Art. 43, § 6 (discussing constitution of Arbitration Panel); 2011 CBA, Art. 43 § 8 (discussing Arbitrator's authority, including to grant a "money award").

57 *See* Jackson v. Kimel, 992 F.2d 1318, 1325 n.4 (4th Cir. 1993) (collecting cases holding that employees that are not signatories to the CBA cannot be sued for violations of the CBA).

58 *See* 2011 CBA, Art. 2, § 2 (generally discussing CBA's binding effect on NFL, NFLPA, players and Clubs but no other party).

59 *See* Alexander Cornwell, *Trapped: Missouri Legislature Seeks to Close Workers' Compensation Loophole with Some Co-Employees Still Inside,* 77 Mo. L. Rev. 235, 235 (2012); David J. Krco, *Case Note: Torts – Narrowing the Window: Refining the Personal Duty Requirement for Coemployee Liability Under Minnesota's Workers' Compensation System – Stringer v. Minnesota Vikings Football Club, LLC,* 33 Wm. Mitchell L. Rev. 739, 739 (2007); John T. Burnett, *The Enigma of Workers' Compensation Immunity: A Call to the Legislature for a Statutorily Defined Intentional Tort Exception,* 28 Fla. St. U. L. Rev. 491, 497 (2001).

60 *See* Lotysz v. Montgomery, 309 A.D.2d 628 (N.Y. App. Div. 2003) (NFL player's medical malpractice claim against club doctor barred by state workers' compensation statute); Daniels v. Seattle Seahawks, 968 P.2d 883 (Wash. Ct. App. 1998); Hendy *v.* Losse, 819 P.2d 1 (Cal. 1991). *See also* Bryant v. Fox, 515 N.E.2d 775 (Ill. App. Ct. 1987) (NFL player's medical malpractice claim against Club doctor not barred by workers' compensation statute where evidence established that doctor was an independent contractor). For more information on the possibility of players suing coaches, see Timothy Davis, *Tort Liability of Coaches for Injuries to Professional Athletes: Overcoming Policy and Doctrinal Barriers,* 76 UMKC L. Rev. 571 (2008).

61 CBA, Art. 43, § 2.

62 Mike Florio, *Report of Richard Sherman Minicamp Fight Sparked NFLPA Investigation,* ProFootballTalk (Aug. 27, 2014), http://profootballtalk.nbcsports .com/2014/08/27/report-of-richard-sherman-minicamp-fight   -sparked -nflpa-investigation/, *archived at* http://perma.cc/Y4RT-D8XW. *See also* 2011 CBA, Art. 22, § 8 (discussing NFLPA's rights to films from minicamps).

63 Chris Mortensen, *NFL Fines Pete Carroll, Seahawks,* ESPN (Aug. 26, 2014 8:00 PM), http://espn.go.com/nfl/story/_/id/11414018/seattle -seahawks-pete-carroll- . . . 1, *archived at* http://perma.cc/46ZR-HWX7.

64 *Id.*

65 *See* Glenn M. Wong, Essentials of Sports Law, § 4.2 (4th ed. 2010) (discussing liability of coaches and gathering cases).

66 Stringer v. Minnesota Vikings Football Club, LLC, 705 N.W.2d 746, 748 (Minn. 2005).

67 *See* Memorandum and Order, Stringer v. Minnesota Vikings Football Club, LLC, No. 02-415 (Minn. Dist. Ct. Apr. 25, 2003); Stringer v. Minnesota Vikings Football Club, LLC, No. 02-415, 2003 WL 25766738 (Minn. Dist. Ct. Dec. 8, 2003) (discussing Court's prior order). Following Stringer's death, the NFL now issues an annual memorandum to NFL Clubs warning them about the risks of players overheating during training camp. *See, e.g.,* Memorandum from NFL Injury and Safety Panel (Elliott Hershman, M.D., Chairman), to General Managers, Head Coaches, Team Physicians, and Team Athletic Trainers re: 2014 Training Camps – Adverse Weather Conditions (July 11, 2014) (on file with author).

68 *See* Memorandum and Order, Stringer v. Minnesota Vikings Football Club, LLC, No. 02-415, 71–76 (Minn. Dist. Ct. Apr. 25, 2003).

69 U.S.C. § 185.

70 Allis-Chambers Corp. v. Lueck, 471 U.S. 202, 213, 200 (1985).

71 *See, e.g.,* Givens v. Tennessee Football, Inc., 684 F. Supp. 2d 985 (M.D.Tenn. 2010) (player's tort claims against Club arising out of medical treatment preempted); Williams v. Nat'l Football League, 582 F.3d 863 (8th Cir. 2009) (players' tort claims arising out of drug test preempted).

72 Smith v. Houston Oilers, Inc., 87 F.3d 717 (5th Cir. 1996).

73 *Id.*

74 *Id.*

75 AFCA Code of Ethics at p. 9.

76 *Id.* at 9–10.

77 *Id.* at 10.

78 E-mail from Vince Thompson, Director of Media Relations, AFCA, to Christopher R. Deubert (Feb. 26, 2015).

79 *See Average NFL Career Length,* Sharp Football Analysis, Apr. 30, 2014, http://www.sharpfootballanalysis.com/blog/?p=2133, *archived at* http://perma.cc/X8QV-77A3 (discussing disagreement between NFLPA and NFL about average career length and determining that the average drafted player plays about 5 years).

80 At Super Bowl XLIX, the NFL presented data showing that between 2012 and 2014 that helmet-to-helmet hits were responsible for 49.7% of concussions. The next most likely cause was the playing surface, which accounted for only 12.9% of concussions. *See Super Bowl XLIX Health & Safety Press Conference,* NFL (May 1, 2015), http://static.nfl.com/static /content/public/photo/2015/01/29/0ap3000000465343.pdf, *archived at* https://perma.cc/8GV6-JJ7W?type=pdf.

81 Jenny Ventras, *Helmetless Football? It's the New Practice at New Hampshire,* Sports Illustrated, Dec. 4, 2014, http://mmqb.si.com/2014/12/04/ helmetless-football-practice-university-of-new-hampshire/, *archived at* http://perma.cc/6CBB-8Y5J.

82 *Id.*

83 Holly Ramer, *In bid to reduce concussions, Dartmouth debuts remote-controlled tackling dummy,* U.S. News & World Report (Aug. 26, 2015 1:16 PM), http://www.usnews.com/news/sports/articles/2015/08/26 /tackling-goes-high-tech-at-dartmouth, *archived at* http://perma.cc /2UXD-LB4K.

84 Josh Alper, *Steelers experimenting with robots in practice,* ProFootballTalk (May 20, 2016, 7:28 AM), http://profootballtalk.nbcsports.com/2016 /05/20/steelers-experimenting-with-robots-in-practice/, *archived at* https://perma.cc/TBD2-NLEX.

85 Ken Belson, *Ivy League Moves to Eliminate Tackling at Football Practices,* N.Y. Times, Mar. 1, 2016, http://www.nytimes.com/2016/03/02/ sports/ncaafootball/ivy-league-moves-to-eliminate-tackling-at-practices .html, *archived at* https://perma.cc/24W6-VKG2.

Chapter 10

Club Employees

This chapter discusses the roles of NFL club general managers (often referred to as "GMs"), developmental staff, and scouts. Each of these employees has involvement with players at key moments in players' careers. For example, as will be explained further below, general managers draft, sign, and release players; developmental staff help players after they have been drafted; and scouts gather as much information as possible on players. Consequently, these club employees have the potential to influence player health in important ways.

Before we begin our analysis, it is important to point out that throughout this chapter we emphasize that the practice of club employees is likely heterogeneous from club to club at least to some extent. Nevertheless, we were unable to interview club employees as part of this report to gain a better understanding of their work. In November 2014, we notified the NFL that we intended to seek interviews with club personnel, including general managers, coaches, doctors, and athletic trainers. The NFL subsequently advised us that it was "unable to consent to the interviews" on the grounds that the "information sought could directly impact several lawsuits currently pending against the league." Without the consent of the NFL, we did not believe that the interviews would be successful and thus did not pursue the interviews at that time; instead, we have provided these stakeholders the opportunity to review draft chapters of the Report. We again requested to interview club personnel in July 2016 but the NFL did not respond to that request. The NFL was otherwise cooperative—it reviewed our Report and facilitated its review by club doctors and athletic trainers. The NFL also provided information relevant to this Report, including but not limited to copies of the NFL's Medical Sponsorship Policy (discussed in Chapter 2: Club Doctors) and other information about the relationships between clubs and doctors. Nevertheless, the NFL did not facilitate review of this chapter by any of the types of club employees discussed: general managers; developmental staff; and, scouts.

(A) Background

1) GENERAL MANAGERS

NFL general managers by and large are the persons responsible for every aspect of the club. General managers report directly to the club's owner and are responsible for putting together a cohesive and well-functioning organization that wins on the field and is maximally profitable off of it. To that end, general managers handle some of the most important football-related tasks, such as hiring the coach and making player personnel decisions, but also a variety of non-football specific tasks, including overseeing and directing the financials, human resources, marketing, stadium development, and media and community relations.[1] Additionally, general managers come from a variety of career paths, including many who played in either college and/or the NFL. Generally, about two-thirds of general managers played college football and about a fifth played in the NFL.[2]

General managers are an integral part of the entire NFL club and thus are an integral part of the process for identifying and addressing player health and welfare matters. General managers are responsible for, or at least intimately involved in, hiring coaches, doctors, athletic trainers and other club staff involved in player health matters.

Perhaps most importantly to the players, general managers make roster decisions affecting the player's employment and contract decisions affecting the player's compensation.[a] During the season, clubs are limited to a 53-man roster and general managers are constantly looking to replace injured players with healthy players and underperforming players with better players. It is thus vital that players be seen positively in the eyes of the general manager.

2) DEVELOPMENTAL STAFF

Each NFL club employs someone with the title of Director of Player Development or Director of Player Engagement. These employees are often ex-players who are responsible for assisting the club's players with a blend of professional and personal issues, including transitioning from college to the NFL, getting the player and his family settled in a new environment, dealing with the media, continuing their education, planning for retirement, and providing general life coaching and guidance.[3] As respected elder statesmen of the game, these individuals have the opportunity to play an important role in assisting players and making sure the actions taken are in their best interests.

Nevertheless, the ability of these staff members to have a meaningful impact on the club and players depends on the resources provided and the club's commitment to player development. For example, in February 2012, the Washington football club hired 15-year veteran defensive end Phillip Daniels as their Director of Player Development.[4] Daniels left the organization after one season because he felt the club did not take his position or player development seriously.[5] Daniels never met with head coach Mike Shanahan or General Manager Bruce Allen and said he was not given any financial resources to implement the types of programs he thought would be beneficial to the club's players and their families.[6]

3) SCOUTS

Quality scouts can also be the core of a successful football team. Each NFL club employs approximately 10 to 15 people in their player personnel/scouting departments. Scouts are separated into two categories: professional and college. Professional scouts are responsible for scouting players on other NFL clubs, while the college scouts fan out across the country and provide scouting reports on thousands of college football players.[7]

Scouts seek out every personal and professional detail on players and thus provide valuable insight to a club when it comes time for personnel decisions. For example, in

---

a   In any given season, there are, however, a handful of head coaches who possess final control over the club's roster as opposed to the general manager.

addition to how well they play football, scouting reports often include details of family and romantic relationships, academic performance, troubles with the law or coaches, personality profiles, injury history, and perceived toughness and intelligence.[b] Scouts often interview the players, their high school and college coaches, college medical staff, and others who know the players to obtain these details.[8] Scouts then have the power to decide whether to label a prospect as "injury prone" or someone with "bad character."

Moreover, it is important to note that many NFL clubs share scouting reports through one of two scouting services: National and BLESTO.[9] Both services employ scouts who provide comprehensive reports to multiple clubs.[10] Consequently, one scout can have a very big impact on a player's future. It is thus essential that the scout's information be accurate.

Scouting information can also play an important role once a player joins a club. If a club knows from a scouting report that a player has any particular social issues, such as family, friends or drugs, the club is potentially in a position to effectuate positive change.[c] Additionally, if a scouting report reveals that a player suffers or has suffered from a physical ailment of some kind, the club can ensure that the player is treated appropriately. Indeed, out of their own self-interest, clubs are likely to try and provide a player with the support (physical, social, and otherwise) he needs to be a successful football player.

B Current Legal Obligations[d]

The 2011 CBA contains no provisions specifically addressing the obligations of general managers, developmental staff, or scouts.

The CBA does contain many provisions concerning the responsibilities of clubs. General managers, as the persons at the top of the club's football hierarchy, are generally responsible for ensuring the clubs' compliance with its various CBA-identified obligations. Indeed, it is not uncommon for general managers to be fined when a club fails to comply with NFL policies.[11]

Although scouts and development staff could potentially be complicit in the violation of the CBA or NFL policy, they are under no general obligation to ensure compliance with the CBA or NFL policies.

C Current Ethical Codes

There are no ethical codes specific to general managers, developmental staff, or scouts.[e]

D Current Practices

It is generally believed that general managers have little involvement with player health decisions or treatment, other than in an administrative capacity such as relaying information from the club doctor to the contract advisor or letting the contract advisor know if the player is being placed on Injured Reserve. Moreover, the players we interviewed generally said they have had no relationship with their general managers.[f] Some contract advisors believe general managers' involvement in player health decisions has decreased in the last five years or so, as clubs have looked to avoid conflict and/or liability concerning these issues.[g]

General managers are involved with the player's health to the extent that it affects the club's roster.[h] Athletic trainers and, to a lesser extent, club doctors keep coaches and general managers apprised of players' injury status during weekly meetings so the general manager can make a decision about whether or not to sign another player in the

b   One scout described his efforts to obtain information about a college player as follows: "When you arrive at a school, you get there early in the morning and you meet with the football operations director. He gives you background information on the kid: the hometown, their family and those types of things. After that, you'll go to a film room and watch tape for the biggest part of the day. You meet with the strength coach. You meet with an academic advisor that gives you some background on the player's performance in those areas. You meet with the trainer to see if they have ever been injured, how their rehab habits are. Then you go to practice. You get a feel for their effort in practice, how hard they work and that type of thing." *See* John Zernhelt, *Scout's Tales: Aaron Donald*, St. Louis Rams (Mar. 27, 2015), http://www.stlouisrams.com/news-and-events/article-1/Scouts-Tales-Aaron-Donald/910aff46-e2cd-49d5-8a7a-45814fa773de, *archived at* http://perma.cc/VSJ6-4Q7L.

c   For example, when the Dallas Cowboys drafted wide receiver Dez Bryant in the first round of the 2010 NFL Draft, after Bryant's college career had ended in suspension, the Cowboys and Bryant negotiated a set of regulations concerning Bryant's off-field activities and provided Bryant with a three-man security team. Josh Alper, *Cowboys Enact Set of Behavioral Rules for Dez Bryant*, ProFootballTalk (Aug. 26, 2012, 12:07 PM), http://profootballtalk.nbcsports.com/2012/08/26/cowboys-enact-set-of-behavioral-rules-for-dez-bryant/, *archived at* http://perma.cc/6LFT-XYFL.

d   The legal obligations described herein are not an exhaustive list but are those we believe are most relevant to player health.

e   If any of these club employees were licensed in some other way, they might have additional obligations.

f   Current Player 7: "For the most part, the General Managers are up in the office. We don't really see them, or the owners." Current Player 8: "[T]he top 10 to 20 percent on each team, I think, have a passing relationship with [the General Manager], or some may have more but, again, this is going into my eighth year and I've never had a relationship with any General Manager."

g   Contract Advisor 1: "I think in the last five to seven years, the coaches and general managers have taken a step back from the medical component. There's too much risk and owners have probably told them . . . why would you do this, not to mention for the most part, general managers are not interested in having players get hurt on their watch more severely than they needed to be." Contract Advisor 6: "[V]ery few general managers have a clue. They rely strictly on their medical staff. So they don't really spend a lot of time [dealing with player health issues]."

h   Former Player 3: "I think general managers are probably better than coaches at looking at the long view [on player health] because they have a little bit longer shelf life."

event a player is unable to play.[i] Club medical staff keep coaches and general managers apprised of players' injury status during weekly meetings so the general manager can make a decision about whether or not to sign another player in the event a player is unable to play. Players indicated that these meetings place pressures on players to practice to avoid having the athletic trainer tell the general manager that he should consider signing a potential replacement.

Current players often recognize the tenuous nature of their career and that it lays in the hands of the general manager and coaches, as Current Player 1 stated:

> [Y]ou like to think that they care about you but I think you kind of realize that it's a business. They're just trying to get the most out of you for as many years as they can [while] they feel that you're still serviceable and productive.

Players indicated that developmental staff is a "great resource" for a player, particularly when he is new to the club or city. The staff is able to get them situated with housing, transportation, and other living necessities. In addition, some players explained that the developmental staff would meet with rookies before the season to try to help them adjust to the NFL and also to understand the realities of the NFL.[j] For example, the developmental staff might try to make the player aware of the possible brevity of his career and encourage him to spend his money wisely and to begin to consider life after football. Nevertheless, players also indicated that the development staff is generally far removed from matters concerning player health or the player's status on the club.

Despite the incredible amount of information and data that scouts collect about players, scouts generally do not play any role in player health once the player joins the club.

---

i   Current Player 1: "[O]ur head trainer has a meeting with our GM and head coach at least once a week about whatever injuries are going on in the team." Current Player 9: "[General Managers] are in meetings with the head coaches and with the head trainers."

j   Current Player 1: "[W]hen you're a rookie you spend a ton of time with the director of player of development. We have numerous meetings talking about how to spend your money, how to deal with family relationships now that you're in the NFL, [and] how to deal with outside influences. He really helps you to develop[.]" Current Player 8: "I think that the player development guy on each team assists the young guys in kind of the mental and social changes that they have to go through."

Club medical staff keep coaches and general managers apprised of players' injury status during weekly meetings so the general manager can make a decision about whether or not to sign another player in the event a player is unable to play.

(E) Enforcement of Legal and Ethical Obligations[k]

In the event a player or the NFLPA believes a club employee has violated his obligations to the players, the player could try to commence a Non-Injury Grievance in accordance with the CBA.[l] The 2011 CBA directs certain disputes to designated arbitration mechanisms[m] and directs the remainder of any disputes involving the CBA, a player contract, NFL rules, or generally the terms and conditions of employment to the Non-Injury Grievance arbitration process.[12] Importantly, Non-Injury Grievances provide players with the benefit of a neutral arbitration and the possibility of a "money award."[13]

However, there are several impediments to pursuing a Non-Injury Grievance against a club employee. First and foremost, club employees are not parties to the CBA and thus likely cannot be sued for violations of the CBA.[14] Instead, the player could seek to hold the club responsible for the club employee's violation of the CBA.[15] Second, the player's claim might be barred by workers' compensation statutes. Workers' compensation statutes provide compensation for workers injured at work and thus generally preclude lawsuits against co-workers based on the co-workers' negligence.[16] This was the result in the *Stringer* case (discussed in detail in Chapter 9: Coaches), and in multiple cases brought by NFL players against club doctors.[17] It is unclear if or how this bar would apply in an arbitration. Third, Non-Injury Grievances must be filed within 50 days "from the date of the occurrence or non-occurrence upon which the grievance is based,"[18] a timeframe that is much shorter than your typical statute of limitations. And fourth,

players likely fear that pursuing a grievance against a club employee could result in the club terminating him.[n]

In addition to workers' compensation statutes, the CBA also presents a major obstacle for a player suing a club employee. This is because the Labor Management Relations Act (LMRA)[19] bars or "preempts" state common law[o] claims, such as negligence, where the claim is "substantially dependent upon analysis of the terms" of a CBA, *i.e.*, where the claim is "inextricably intertwined with consideration of the terms of the" CBA."[20] In order to determine whether a club employee was appropriately attentive to a player's health or welfare needs, the court might have to refer to and analyze the terms of the CBA governing player health, resulting in the claim's preemption.[21] Preemption occurs even though club employees are not parties to the CBA and thus likely cannot be a party in any CBA grievance procedure. So long as the player's claim is "inextricably intertwined" with the CBA, it will be preempted. In these cases, player complaints must be resolved through the enforcement provisions provided by the CBA itself (*i.e.*, a Non-Injury Grievance against the club), rather than through litigation.

In a 1995 lawsuit, two Houston Oilers players alleged that a Houston Oilers general manager and strength and conditioning coach subjected the players to a phony and brutal rehabilitation program designed to coerce the players into quitting the club.[22] The players alleged state law claims of coercion, duress, extortion, assault and battery, and intentional infliction of emotional distress. The United States District Court for the Southern District of Texas held that the players' claims were preempted by the CBA, because the CBA and the players' contracts governed rehabilitation programs.[23] The United States Court of Appeals for the Fifth Circuit affirmed.[24]

Currently, the only enforcement of club employees' obligations concerning player health tends to be discipline by the NFL. It is thus suspect whether current practices and the current enforcement scheme are sufficiently protective of player health.

---

k   Appendix K is a summary of players' options to enforce legal and ethical obligations against the stakeholders discussed in this Report. In addition, for rights articulated under either the CBA or other NFL policy, the NFLPA and the NFL can also seek to enforce them on players' behalves.

l   *See* 2011 CBA, Art. 43 (discussing Non-Injury Grievance procedures). The term "Non-Injury Grievance" is something of a misnomer. The CBA differentiates between an "Injury Grievance" and a "Non-Injury Grievance." An Injury Grievance is exclusively "a claim or complaint that, at the time a player's NFL Player Contract or Practice Squad Player Contract was terminated by a Club, the player was physically unable to perform the services required of him by that contract because of an injury incurred in the performance of his services under that contract." 2011 CBA, Art. 44, § 1. Generally, all other disputes (except System Arbitrations, *see* 2011 CBA, Art. 15) concerning the CBA or a player's terms and conditions of employment are Non-Injury Grievances. 2011 CBA, Art. 43, § 1. Thus, there can be disputes concerning a player's injury or medical care which are considered Non-Injury Grievances because they do not fit within the limited confines of an Injury Grievance.

m   For example, Injury Grievances, which occur when, at the time a player's contract was terminated, the player claims he was physically unable to perform the services required of him because of a football-related injury, are heard by a specified Arbitration Panel. 2011 CBA, Art. 44. Additionally, issues concerning certain Sections of the CBA related to labor and antitrust issues, such as free agency and the Salary Cap, are within the exclusive scope of the System Arbitrator, 2011 CBA, Art. 15, currently University of Pennsylvania Law School Professor Stephen B. Burbank.

n   Current Player 8: "You don't have the gall to stand against your franchise and say 'They mistreated me.' . . . I, still today, going into my eighth year, am afraid to file a grievance, or do anything like that[.]" While it is illegal for an employer to retaliate against an employee for filing a grievance pursuant to a CBA, *N.L.R.B. v. City Disposal Systems Inc.*, 465 U.S. 822, 835–36 (1984), such litigation would involve substantial time and money for an uncertain outcome.

o   Common law refers to "[t]he body of law derived from judicial decisions, rather than from statutes or constitutions." Black's Law Dictionary (9th ed. 2009). The concept of "preemption" is "[t]he principle (derived from the Supremacy Clause [of the Constitution] that a federal law can supersede or supplant any inconsistent state law or regulation." *Id.*

(F) Recommendations Concerning Club Employees

NFL club general managers and scouts make important decisions concerning a player's career, often based on a player's current or expected health status. In addition, general managers, scouts, and developmental staff all have unique relationships with players that provide them a unique opportunity to promote player health. Indeed, like coaches, many NFL club employees develop close relationships with players, or are former players themselves, and are thus sensitive to protecting player health. Nevertheless, the inherent pressures of winning and running a successful business can sometimes cause these employees to make decisions or create pressures that negatively affect player health. While we were unable to interview these employees to gauge their viewpoints,[p] we make the below recommendations to help improve the role of club employees in player health.

In Chapter 9: Coaches, we recommended that the NFLCA adopt and enforce a Code of Ethics that demands that coaches be responsible for player health. We then highlighted several important ethical concepts or practices for coaches, including that:

- Coaches should establish a locker room culture in which players and their health and safety are respected.

- Coaches should keep communications with players about their health to a minimum.

- Coaches should consider, respect, and care about players' post-career lives.

- Coaches should not encourage in any way the injury of opposing players.

- Coaches should ensure that the medical staff acts independently and does not feel pressured to act in any way other than in the player's best interests.

- Coaches' interests in winning cannot supersede player health.

Each of the above-listed ethical concepts or practices can also be applied to the club employees discussed in this chapter.

Additionally, while we recommended that the NFLCA enact and enforce such a Code of Ethics, we recognized that it might not have the resources or will to do so. Consequently, we recommended that the most important principles concerning coaches' conduct be incorporated into the CBA. Similarly, since there are generally no professional societies governing general managers, developmental staff, or scouts, these principles as applied to those club employees should be incorporated into the CBA.

Below are recommendations more specific to the club employees discussed in this chapter.

Goal 1: To encourage clubs and their employees to advance a culture of health.

Principles Advanced: Respect; Health Primacy; Managing Conflicts of Interest; and, Collaboration and Engagement.

Recommendation 10:1-A: Clubs and club employees, in particular general managers and developmental staff, should take steps to resolve any concerns discovered about a player's health.[25]

---

p   As described more fully in the Introduction, Section D(2): Description of Legal and Ethical Obligations, citing ongoing litigation and arbitration, the NFL declined to consent to our request to interview persons currently employed by or affiliated with NFL clubs, including coaches, general managers, doctors, and athletic trainers. Therefore, we did not pursue interviews with these individuals.

Clubs expend considerable effort to learn a great deal of information about players, including their medical, family, intellectual, personality, financial and social issues. These issues can threaten a promising career. Clubs learn about these issues during the pre-Draft process, when considering signing the player as a free agent, and when the player is a member of their club. While clubs are interested in helping players address these issues to protect their investment in the player, clubs should look beyond what might only be short-term solutions that help the player while he is with the club to include longer-term solutions, such as a variety of programs offered by the NFL and NFLPA, that will improve player health over a more extended period of time.

Recommendation 10:1-B: Clubs should adequately support the developmental staff.

Players we interviewed generally spoke well of the effort by developmental staff to assist players, particularly young players. Nevertheless, through these interviews and news articles, it also seems likely that the developmental staff can sometimes be under-resourced and limited in its role. The developmental staff has the potential to be a powerful resource for players, particularly in pointing them to the various programs and benefits offered by the NFL and NFLPA, and helping them through the process of taking advantage of those programs and benefits. By better supporting these staffs and professionalizing their role, clubs can make gains in player health.

Endnotes

1   For a discussion of the role of NFL General Managers, see Christopher R. Deubert, Glenn M. Wong & Daniel Hatman, *National Football League General Managers: An Analysis of the Responsibilities, Qualifications, and Characteristics*, 20 Jeffrey S. Moorad Sports L.J. 427 (2013).

2   *See id.* at 475 (chart showing playing experience of NFL General Managers in 1992, 2002 and 2012).

3   *See* Mike Chappel, *Ex-Colt Pollard Feeling Blessed*, Indianapolis Star, Jun. 9, 2014, *available at* 2014 WLNR 15630530 (discussing fourteen-year veteran Marcus Pollard's hiring as the Jacksonville Jaguars Director of Player Development); Conor Orr, *Tyree's Hiring Comes With Controversy, Former WR Blasted For His Personal Views*, Star-Ledger (Newark, NJ), Jul. 23, 2014, *available at* 2014 WLNR 20130392 (discussing former wide receiver David Tyree's hiring as the New York Giants Director of Player Development).

4   Dan Steinberg, *Phillip Daniels Said He Was 'On an Island' When He Worked for the Redskins*, Wash. Post DC Sports Blog (Jun. 30, 2014), http://www.washingtonpost.com/blogs/dc-sports-bog/wp/2014/06/30/phillip-daniels-said-he-was-on-an-island-when-he-worked-for-the-redskins/, *archived at* http://perma.cc/NZ5K-DW5K.

5   *Id.*

6   *Id.*

7   *See* Deubert, *supra* note 1, at 466–72 (discussing composition, purpose and duties of scouting departments).

8   Ben Volin, *NFL Teams Go Extra Yard to Vet Prospects Before Draft*, Bos. Globe, Apr. 26, 2015, http://www.bostonglobe.com/sports/2015/04/25/nfl-teams-homework-including-spying-draft-prospects/I5ElHKwSQBvI6fvwQNVkyL/story.html, *archived at* http://perma.cc/8NNY-GPR3.

9   *Id.* BLESTO stands for Bears, Lions, Eagles and Steelers Talent Organization, although now approximately twelve Clubs use BLESTO.

10 Volin, *supra* note 8.

11 *See Fall From Grace, Saints Suffer Unprecedented Penalties from NFL for Running Bounty Program*, New Orleans Times Picayune, Mar. 22, 2012, *available at* 2012 WLNR 6061758 ($500,000 fine for New Orleans Saints General Manager Mickey Loomis for alleged involvement in bounty program); J.P. Pelzman, *NFL Hits Jets with $100K Fine*, N.J. Record, Sept. 17, 2009, *available at* 2009 WLNR 20070367 ($25,000 fine for New York Jets General Manager Mike Tannenbaum for Club's failure to include injured quarterback Brett Favre on injury report); Mike Freeman, *Pro Football Notebook: Mara Not Blaming Tagliabue*, N.Y. Times, Dec. 17, 2000, http://www.nytimes.com/2000/12/17/sports/pro-football-notebook-mara-not-blaming-tagliabue.html, *archived at* http://perma.cc/ZP64-WVUP ($400,000 fine for San Francisco 49ers General Manager Carmen Policy for Salary Cap violations).

12 *See* 2011 CBA, Art. 43, § 1.

13 *See* 2011 CBA, Art. 43, § 6 (discussing constitution of Arbitration Panel); 2011 CBA, Art. 43 § 8 (discussing Arbitrator's authority, including to grant a "money award").

14 *See* Jackson v. Kimel, 992 F.2d 1318, 1325n.4 (4th Cir. 1993) (collecting cases holding that employees that are not signatories to the CBA cannot be sued for violations of the CBA).

15 *See* 2011 CBA, Art. 2, § 2 (generally discussing CBA's binding effect on NFL, NFLPA, players and Clubs but no other party).

16 *See* Alexander Cornwell, *Trapped: Missouri Legislature Seeks to Close Workers' Compensation Loophole with Some Co-Employees Still Inside*, 77 Mo. L. Rev. 235, 235 (2012); David J. Krco, *Case Note: Torts – Narrowing the Window: Refining the Personal Duty Requirement for Coemployee Liability Under Minnesota's Workers' Compensation System – Stringer v. Minnesota Vikings Football Club, LLC*, 33 Wm. Mitchell L. Rev. 739, 739 (2007); John T. Burnett, *The Enigma of Workers' Compensation Immunity: A Call to the Legislature for a Statutorily Defined Intentional Tort Exception*, 28 Fla. St. U. L. Rev. 491, 497 (2001).

17 *See* Lotysz v. Montgomery, 766 N.Y.S.2d 28 (N.Y. 2003) (NFL player's medical malpractice claim against Club doctor barred by state workers' compensation statute); Daniels v. Seattle Seahawks, 968 P.2d. 883 (Wash. Ct. App. 1998) (same); Hendy v. Losse, 819 P.2d 1 (Cal. 1991) (same). *See also* Bryant v. Fox, 515 N.E.2d 775 (Ill. App. Ct. 1987) (NFL player's medical malpractice claim against Club doctor not barred by workers' compensation statute where evidence established that doctor was an independent contractor). For more information on the possibility of players suing coaches, see Timothy Davis, *Tort Liability of Coaches for Injuries to Professional Athletes: Overcoming Policy and Doctrinal Barriers*, 76 UMKC L. Rev. 571 (2008).

18 CBA, Art. 43, § 2.

19 U.S.C. § 185.

20 Allis-Chambers Corp. v. Lueck, 471 U.S. 202, 213, 200 (1985).

21 *See, e.g.*, Givens v. Tennessee Football, Inc., 684 F. Supp. 2d 985 (M.D. Tenn. 2010) (player's tort claims against Club arising out of medical treatment preempted); Williams v. Nat'l Football League, 582 F.3d 863 (8th Cir. 2009) (players' tort claims arising out of drug test preempted).

22 Smith v. Houston Oilers, Inc., 87 F.3d 717 (5th Cir. 1996).

23 *Id.*

24 *Id.*

25 Mark Cuban, owner of the NBA's Dallas Mavericks, has advocated such an approach: ""You don't go from the minors or college to the pros and all of a sudden become a spouse abuser, or any of a number of other serious personal issues. Those traits don't suddenly appear when you make a pro roster. They were there in college. They were probably there prior to college. Yet we as leagues ignore those issues when we sign and draft players. That has to change. We need to participate in programs that publicly identify those athletes that have issues, and not allow them to play unless they go through rigorous counseling. We need to demand that colleges and minor leagues and high schools and summer travel programs identify and report issues. By not reporting abuse or other issues with their players, they could be costing them a shot at the pros. It's our fault for not being more proactive. It's college's fault for not red-flagging these kids and getting them help." Tim MacMahon, *Cuban: Be Proactive About Red Flags*, ESPN (Nov. 8, 2014, 1:46 PM), http://espn.go.com/dallas/nba/story/_/id/11836940/mark-cuban-need-more-proactive-athlete-red-flags, *archived at* http://perma.cc/5U2J-7KNS.

Chapter 11

Equipment Managers

Each NFL club employs three to four equipment managers. While equipment managers assist players in a variety of ways, their principal job is to help outfit players in equipment that will maximize their safety on the field, a crucial component of player health.

Before we begin our analysis, it is important to point out that throughout this chapter we emphasize that the practice of equipment managers is likely heterogeneous from club to club at least to some extent. Nevertheless, we were unable to interview equipment managers as part of this Report to gain a better understanding of their work. In November 2014, we notified the NFL that we intended to seek interviews with club personnel, including general managers, coaches, doctors, and athletic trainers. The NFL subsequently advised us that it was "unable to consent" to the interviews on the grounds that the "information sought could directly impact several lawsuits currently pending against the league." Without the consent of the NFL, we did not believe that the interviews would be successful and thus did not pursue the interviews at that time; instead, we have provided these stakeholders the opportunity to review draft chapters of the Report. We again requested to interview club personnel in July 2016 but the NFL did not respond to that request. The NFL was otherwise cooperative—it reviewed our Report and facilitated its review by club doctors and athletic trainers. The NFL also provided information relevant to this Report, including but not limited to copies of the NFL's Medical Sponsorship Policy (discussed in Chapter 2: Club Doctors) and other information about the relationships between clubs and doctors.

Nevertheless, the NFL did not facilitate review of this chapter by any equipment managers. On the other hand, the American Equipment Managers Association (AEMA) did review the Report and provide comments.

(A) Background

Equipment managers are responsible for million dollar or more budgets and for ordering and constantly stocking hundreds of items players want and need in every conceivable variety, from their helmets and cleats to gum, washcloths, and toothpaste.[1] Equipment managers take pride in being responsive to the players' every need to make sure they are maximally comfortable and prepared to play.[2] Perhaps most importantly, equipment managers help players select equipment and make sure the equipment fits according to the manufacturer's guidelines.[3]

Equipment managers are also a critical link between equipment manufacturers (discussed in Chapter 16) and players. Equipment managers deal directly with equipment manufacturers and attend two NFL-organized seminars a year to keep up to date on the latest equipment so that they can provide the players the best available options.[4]

In summary, players rely on the equipment managers to help prepare and protect them. Not surprisingly, players and equipment managers sometimes develop close, personal relationships during their tenures with a club.[5]

The AEMA, a voluntary organization, provides certification to equipment managers working in sports across the country.[6] The certification process requires: (1) a four-year college degree; (2) at least two years of experience working in athletics; and, (3) passing a written examination.[7] The written examination covers management, administration, professional development, procurement, accountability, maintenance, and fitting and safety.[8]

The AEMA has a limited role in the NFL, in part because the AEMA's limited resources prevent the AEMA from engaging with the NFL and other leagues as robustly as it would like.[9] Approximately 60 to 70 percent of NFL equipment managers are AEMA-certified but neither the CBA nor the NFL independently requires any certification for equipment managers.[10] Nevertheless, in recent years, the NFL has increasingly shown an interest in the AEMA's work and the importance of qualified, well-trained equipment managers.[11]

(B) Current Legal Obligations[a]

The CBA contains no provisions specifically relevant to equipment managers or equipment. The NFL does have detailed policies on what equipment is mandatory for players, but these rules are directed at players, not equipment managers.

Employers have a common law non-delegable obligation to provide safe equipment to their employees.[12] A non-delegable duty is one whereby the employer cannot escape liability by having passed along the task to an employee; the employer will generally be held vicariously liable for the employee's conduct concerning the provision of equipment regardless.[13] In the context of NFL equipment managers, the law thus imposes the obligation to provide safe equipment to the players on the club, rather than the equipment managers.

Lastly, it is plausible that NFL players and equipment managers have a fiduciary relationship. Nevertheless, there are no known cases in which a player has alleged an equipment manager owed or breached a fiduciary duty and enforcing an alleged fiduciary relationship poses legal problems discussed below.[b]

(C) Current Ethical Codes

The AEMA has a Code of Ethics for equipment managers.[14] Of relevance, the fifth objective of the AEMA Code of Ethics is: "[t]o work as a group to bring about equipment improvements for greater safety of participants in all

---

a   The legal obligations described herein are not an exhaustive list but are those we believe are most relevant to player health.

b   Generally speaking, a fiduciary is "a person who is required to act for the benefit of another person on all matters within the scope of their relationship; one who owes to another the duties of good faith, trust, confidence, and candor." "Duty," Black's Law Dictionary (9th ed. 2009). Whether a fiduciary relationship exists is a fact-based inquiry into the nature of the relationship. Ritani, LLC v. Aghjayan, 880 F. Supp. 2d 425, 455 (S.D.N.Y. 2012) (applying New York law); Carcano v. JBSS, LLC, 684 S.E.2d 41, 53 (N.C. Ct. App. 2009); L.C. v. R.P., 563 N.W.2d 799, 802 (N.D. 1997); Allen Realty Corp. v. Holbert, 318 S.E.2d 592, 595 (Va. 1984); Murphy v. Country House, Inc., 240 N.W.2d 507, 511 (Minn. 1976). An argument could exist that the relationship of trust and confidence between a player and the equipment managers rises to that of a fiduciary relationship.

sports." The AEMA Code of Ethics describes equipment manager's obligations to players as follows:

> Each and every member of an athletic squad should be treated conscientiously without discrimination or partiality. An athletic equipment manager can wield a great amount of influence on members of athletic squads by proper conduct and the use of good judgment in dealing with various personalities and temperaments.
>
> In the care of equipment, the athletic equipment manager must be thorough in carrying out the accepted procedures and instructions. Any carelessness or laxity on the part of the athletic equipment manager in following through his responsibilities to players is a breach of ethical conduct (sic).[15]

(D) Current Practices

Equipment managers' responsibilities have not changed much over time. As discussed above, they are focused on providing players not only their equipment, but also all the little things that make it easier for players to succeed. They are important but not particularly powerful employees in the NFL club hierarchy. Current players we interviewed had only good things to say about equipment managers:

- **Current Player 1:** *"I would say [they] are really good. Any time I need something, they've always taken care of it for me. And even for certain injury specific equipment, maybe it's like an extra pad, shoulder pads or shin guards, something like that, or something you need done to your helmet, they've always been good about that – done whatever I've asked of them."*

- **Current Player 2:** *"They do play a big role. Especially when it comes to helmets . . . , making sure that our helmets fit properly, that we're in technology that's up to date . . . I know that our guy here does a great job of that. He goes above and beyond to make sure everything that we wear . . . are up-to-date and fitting us properly."*

- **Current Player 4:** *"I think they do a great job of getting players the equipment they want/or need."*

Today, equipment managers seem to take serious their responsibility to help players understand the different helmet options and to choose one that fits best for that player. The New York Giants maintain two racks of possible helmet options for players to try on and consider.[16] There, Joe Skiba, the Giants' equipment director and a member of the NFL's Subcommittee on Safety Equipment and Playing Rules, can explain to the players "the intricacies of helmet technology."[17]

The equipment manager's assistance in helping a player finding the right helmet is crucial. According to the American Academy of Neurology, "[t]here is moderate evidence indicating that use of a helmet (when well fitted, with approved design) effectively reduces, but does not eliminate, risk of concussion and more-serious head trauma in hockey and rugby; [and] similar effectiveness is inferred for football."[18]

> According to the American Academy of Neurology, "[t]here is moderate evidence indicating that use of a helmet (when well fitted, with approved design) effectively reduces, but does not eliminate, risk of concussion and more-serious head trauma in hockey and rugby; [and] similar effectiveness is inferred for football."

To assist equipment managers help players with their helmet decisions, in 2015, the Engineering Subcommittee of the NFL's Head, Neck and Spine Committee completed a study evaluating the ability of 17 different helmets to absorb impacts, including accounting for rotational velocity and rotational acceleration.[19] Based on the test results, the NFL created a poster listing the helmets in order of performance for equipment managers to display for the players' review.[20] The study was repeated in 2016, and again presented to the players in both a memorandum and as a poster.[21] Similarly, according to the NFL, the NFL and NFLPA have also commissioned studies concerning cleats and shoes, and have created posters warning players about certain shoes and cleats that are not recommended for use.[22] More information on player equipment can be found in Chapter 16: Equipment Manufacturers.

The difficulty equipment managers sometimes face is player cooperation. Linebacker Keith Rivers admitted that appearance generally mattered more than safety: "a lot of guys go looks first."[23] Additionally, many players are reluctant to change helmets from the ones they have been playing with for their entire NFL career, if not since college.[24] This practice may stand in the way of adopting safer helmets or other equipment by players. Nevertheless, while some players might choose their helmet based on looks, what is important is that they are choosing among helmets that have met threshold requirements for safety. What is essential is that equipment managers help players find the best helmet for them.

(E) Enforcement of Legal and Ethical Obligations[c]

Any claim brought by a player against an equipment manager would likely be barred by workers' compensation laws. Workers' compensation statutes provide compensation for workers injured at work and thus generally preclude lawsuits against co-workers (such as NFL players and equipment mangers) based on the co-workers' negligence.[25]

The CBA also presents a potential obstacle for claims against an equipment manager. This is because the Labor Management Relations Act (LMRA)[26] bars or "preempts" state common law[d] claims, such as negligence, where the claim is "substantially dependent upon analysis of the terms" of a CBA, i.e., where the claim is "inextricably intertwined with consideration of the terms of the" CBA."[27] In these cases, player complaints must be resolved through the enforcement provisions provided by the CBA itself (i.e., a Non-Injury Grievance against the Club), rather than litigation. In the case of equipment managers, the CBA is generally silent as to the provision of equipment and thus it is not certain that claims concerning equipment against either the club or equipment manager would be preempted by the LMRA. Nevertheless, as discussed in several chapters of this Report, the NFL has successfully asserted the preemption defense in many lawsuits concerning the health of NFL players.

Instead of attempting a lawsuit, players who believe they have been harmed by the actions of their equipment managers could likely commence a Non-Injury Grievance.[e] The 2011 CBA directs certain disputes to designated arbitration mechanisms[f] and directs the remainder of any disputes involving the CBA, a player contract, NFL rules, or generally the terms and conditions of employment to the Non-Injury Grievance arbitration process.[28]

However, there are several impediments to pursuing a Non-Injury Grievance against an equipment manager. First and foremost, club employees are not parties to the CBA and thus likely cannot be sued for violations of the CBA.[29] Instead, the player could seek to hold the club responsible for the equipment manager's violation of the CBA.[30] Second, as discussed above, the player's claim might be barred by workers' compensation statutes. Third, Non-Injury Grievances must be filed within 50 days "from the date of the occurrence or non-occurrence upon which the grievance is based,"[31] a timeframe that is much shorter than your typical statute of limitations. And fourth, players likely fear that pursuing a grievance against an equipment manager could result in the club terminating him.[g]

The AEMA is empowered to investigate possible breaches of its Code of Ethics but its remedial authority is limited to a "letter or censorship, letter of censorship with a period of probation, or cancellation of membership."

---

c   Appendix K is a summary of players' options to enforce legal and ethical obligations against the stakeholders discussed in this Report. In addition, for rights articulated under either the CBA or other NFL policy, the NFLPA and the NFL can also seek to enforce them on players' behalves.

d   Common law refers to "[t]he body of law derived from judicial decisions, rather than from statutes or constitutions." Black's Law Dictionary (9th ed. 2009). The concept of "preemption" is "[t]he principle (derived from the Supremacy Clause [of the Constitution] that a federal law can supersede or supplant any inconsistent state law or regulation." Id.

e   The term "Non-Injury Grievance" is something of a misnomer. The CBA differentiates between an "Injury Grievance" and a "Non-Injury Grievance." An Injury Grievance is exclusively "a claim or complaint that, at the time a player's NFL Player Contract or Practice Squad Player Contract was terminated by a Club, the player was physically unable to perform the services required of him by that contract because of an injury incurred in the performance of his services under that contract." 2011 CBA, Art. 44, § 1. Generally, all other disputes (except System Arbitrations, see 2011 CBA, Art. 15) concerning the CBA or a player's terms and conditions of employment are Non-Injury Grievances. 2011 CBA, Art. 43, § 1. Thus, there can be disputes concerning a player's injury or medical care which are considered Non-Injury Grievances because they do not fit within the limited confines of an Injury Grievance.

f   For example, Injury Grievances—which occur when at the time a player's contract was terminated the player claims he was physically unable to perform the services required of him because of a football-related injury—are heard by a specified Arbitration Panel. 2011 CBA, Art. 44. Additionally, issues concerning certain Sections of the CBA related to labor and antitrust issues, such as free agency and the Salary Cap, are within the exclusive scope of the System Arbitrator, 2011 CBA, Art. 15, currently University of Pennsylvania Law School Professor Stephen B. Burbank.

g   Current Player 8: "You don't have the gall to stand against your franchise and say 'They mistreated me.' . . . I, still today, going into my eighth year, am afraid to file a grievance, or do anything like that[.]" While it is illegal for an employer to retaliate against an employee for filing a grievance pursuant to a CBA, N.L.R.B. v. City Disposal Systems Inc., 465 U.S. 822, 835–36 (1984), such litigation would involve substantial time and money for an uncertain outcome.

(F) Recommendations Concerning Equipment Managers

As a preliminary matter, we recommend equipment managers continue to act as they have. Reports indicate that equipment managers work diligently and take seriously their role in providing players with equipment that will minimize the health and safety risks of playing football. Equipment managers do not appear to have any incentive to make decisions which might jeopardize player health, *e.g.,* such as pressuring a player to play with an injury, like other club employees, such as coaches or medical staff. Additionally, the twice-annual meetings for equipment managers and manufacturers seem like an appropriate way for the equipment managers to remain current and educated on the latest equipment. Minimal other recommendations are needed concerning equipment managers.

Goal 1: To ensure that players are served by the best possible equipment managers.

Principles Advanced: Respect; Health Primacy; and, Collaboration and Engagement.

Recommendation 11:1-A: The CBA should require that all equipment managers be certified by the AEMA.

As discussed above, the AEMA's certification program sets reasonable minimum education and experience requirements and requires equipment managers to pass a test certifying their competence in a variety of issues pertinent to the equipment industry, including fitting and safety. In addition, the AEMA requires its members to attend continuing education courses. Requiring NFL equipment managers to be AEMA-certified is a meaningful way of ensuring that the equipment managers working with NFL players are among the most qualified and educated in the industry. The requirement is meaningful enough that it should be codified in the CBA. Ensuring highly-qualified equipment managers will help ensure that players are using the best, well-fitting, and safest equipment possible.

Endnotes

1   *See* Bill Pennington, *A Full-Gear Operation,* N.Y. Times, Aug. 17, 2013, http://www.nytimes.com/2013/08/17/sports/football/for-the-giants-a -full-gear-operation.html *archived at* http://perma.cc/2SQB-LUSR; Kevin Baxter, *NFL: Gearing Up for the Game, a Whole Laundry List,* L.A. Times, Nov. 6, 2012, *available at* 2012 WLNR 23540542; Craig K. Paskoski, *Littlestown Resident Helps the Ravens Look Good, Play Well,* Evening Sun (Hanover, PA), Oct. 16, 2011, *available at* 2011 WLNR 21180003; Danny Woodward, *All the Right Equipment: Cowboys Staff Makes Sure Team Has Everything It Needs,* Dall. Morning News, Nov. 21, 2001, *available at* 2001 WLNR 11689243; Rob Huizenga, M.D., You're Okay, It's Just a Bruise 13 (1994) (discussing Los Angeles Raiders players "stealing various toiletries").

2   *See id.*

3   Interview with Kelly Jones, Certification Steering Committee Chair, AEMA, and Equipment Manager, Gettysburg College, and Mike Royster, Executive Director, AEMA, and Equipment Manager, University of Tennessee Chattanooga (Oct. 27, 2014).

4   *See* Sam Borden, *Despite Risks, N.F.L. Leaves Helmet Choices in Players' Hands,* N.Y. Times, Sept. 20, 2012, http://www.nytimes.com /2012/09/21/sports/football/despite-risks-nfl-leaves-helmet-choices -in-players-hands.html, *archived at* https://perma.cc/K4YB-PBT7?type =pdf. Research did not reveal the details about the nature of these seminars, *e.g.,* whether they are more like trade shows than informational seminars.

5   *See, e.g.,* Paskoski *supra* note 1 (discussing Baltimore Ravens Pro Bowl defensive end Terrell Suggs referring to Ravens' equipment manager Ed Carroll as "dad").

6   For more information on the AEMA, see its website at http://equipmentmanagers.org.

7   Interview with Jones and Royster, *supra* note 3.

8   *Certification,* Athletic Equipment Managers Ass'n, http://equipmentmanagers.org/certification (last visited Aug. 7, 2015), *archived at* http://perma.cc/2SSQ-9JGS.

9   Interview with Jones and Royster, *supra* note 3.

10 *Id.* By comparison, approximately 90 percent of NCAA Division I equipment managers are AEMA members.

11 *Id.*

12 Suburban Hospital, Inc. v. Kirson, 763 A.2d 185, 205 (Md. 2000); Gerrish v. Savard, 739 A.2d 1195, 1199 (Vt. 1999); Johansen v. Anderson, 555 N.W.2d 588, 593 (N.D. 1996); Smith v. Massey-Ferguson, Inc., 883 P.2d 1120, 1131 (Kan. 1994); Kennemer v. McFann, 470 So.2d 1113, 1116 (Ala. 1985); Gerger v. Campbell, 297 N.W.2d 183, 186 (Wis. 1980).

13 *See id.*

14 The AMEA Code of Ethics is on file with the authors.

15 *Id.*

16 Borden, *supra* note 4.

17 *Id.*

18 *Update: Evaluation and Management of Concussion in Sports — 2013,* Am. Acad. Neurology, https://www.aan.com/uploadedFiles/Website_ Library_Assets/Documents/3Practice_Management/5Patient_Resources /1For_Your_Patient/6_Sports_Concussion_Toolkit/evaluation.pdf (last visited Aug. 7, 2015), *archived at* https://perma.cc/7943-3EXG?type =pdf.

19 Nat'l Football League, 2015 Player Health & Safety Report 12 (2015), http://static.nfl.com/static/content/public/photo/2015/08/05 /0ap3000000506671.pdf/, *archived at* https://perma.cc/Y4BN-TUP7 ?type=pdf.

20 *Id.*

21 NFL Comments and Corrections (June 24, 2016).

22 *Id.*

23 Borden, *supra* note 4.

24 *Id.* (Giants center David Baas, who is in his eighth NFL season, said veterans can be hesitant to change anything related to their equipment. "Some guys don't want to switch because they're comfortable in the same one they've had since college or whatever," he said.)

25 *See* Alexander Cornwell, *Trapped; Missouri Legislature Seeks to Close Workers' Compensation Loophole with Some Co-Employees Still Inside,* 77 Mo. L. Rev. 235, 235 (2012); David J. Krco, *Case Note: Torts – Narrowing the Window: Refining the Personal Duty Requirement for Coemployee Liability Under Minnesota's Workers' Compensation System – Stringer v. Minnesota Vikings Football Club, LLC,* 33 Wm. Mitchell L. Rev. 739, 739 (2007); John T. Burnett, *The Enigma of Workers' Compensation Immunity: A Call to the Legislature for a Statutorily Defined Intentional Tort Exception,* 28 Fla. St. U. L. Rev. 491, 497 (2001).

26 U.S.C. § 185.

27 Allis-Chambers Corp. v. Lueck, 471 U.S. 202, 213, 200 (1985).

28 *See* 2011 CBA, Art. 43, § 1.

29 *See* Jackson v. Kimel, 992 F.2d 1318, 1325 n.4 (4th Cir. 1993) (collecting cases holding that employees that are not signatories to the CBA cannot be sued for violations of the CBA).

30 *See* 2011 CBA, Art. 2, § 2 (generally discussing CBA's binding effect on NFL, NFLPA, players and clubs but no other party).

31 CBA, Art. 43, § 2.

Part 5: **Player Advisors**

Contract Advisors (Agents)

Financial Advisors

Family

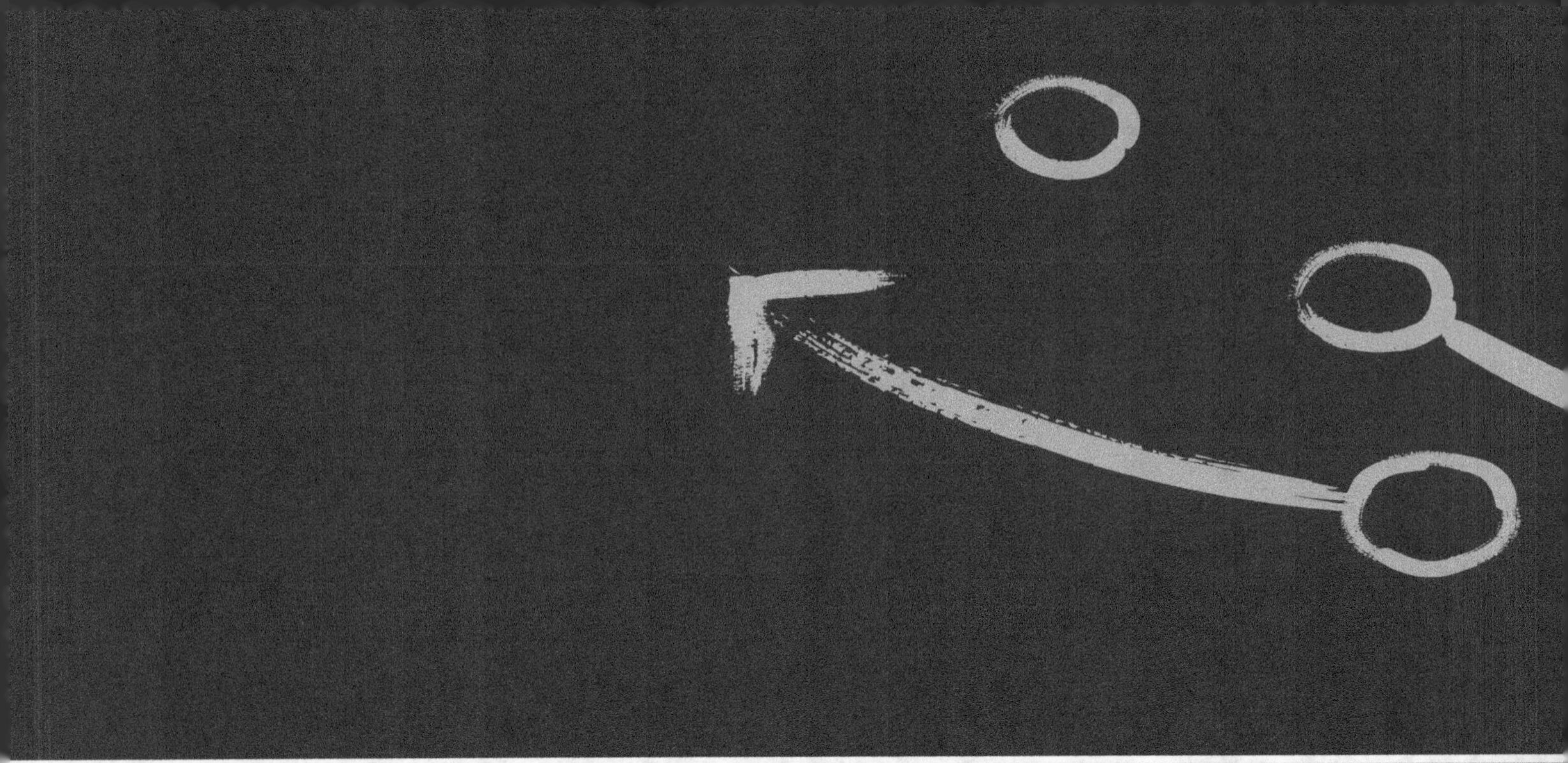

Part 5 discusses those individuals closest to the players and who should always be looking out for the players' best interests: contract advisors, financial advisors, and family members.

In reading this part, it is important to remember our broad definition of health, which includes and extends beyond clinical measurements to the social determinants of health, including financial wellbeing, education, and social support. The stakeholders discussed in this part are particularly important in these broader aspects of health. As a result, these stakeholders are also critical stakeholders in protecting and promoting players' long-term health.

Additionally, we remind the reader that while we have tried to make the chapters accessible for standalone reading, certain background or relevant information may be contained in other parts or chapters, specifically Part 1 discussing Players and Part 3 discussing the NFL and NFLPA. Thus, we encourage the reader to review other parts as needed for important context.

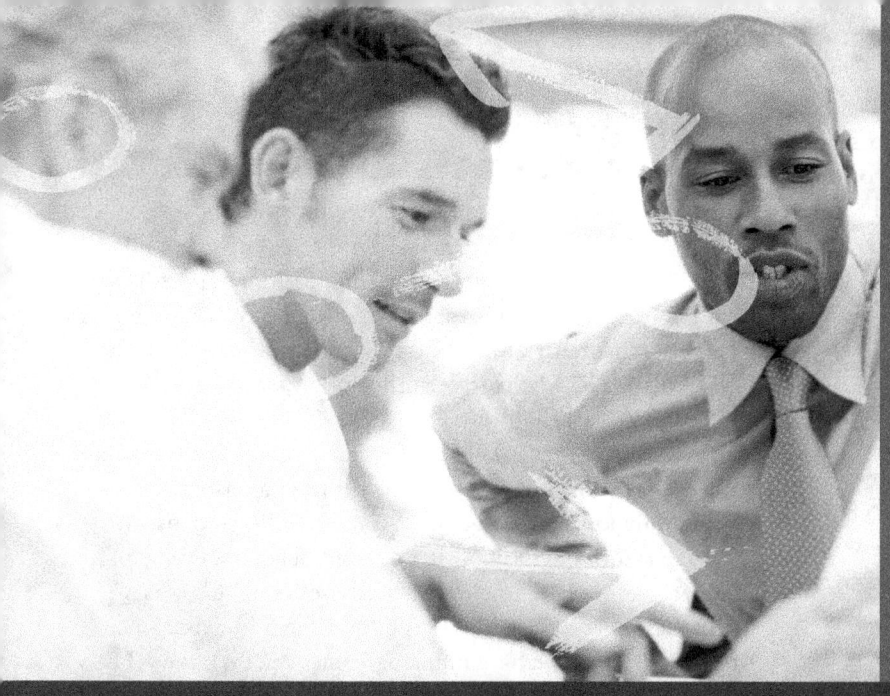

Chapter 12

Contract Advisors
(aka "Agents")

Contract advisors, more commonly known as "agents," are often players' most trusted and important resources and allies when it comes to protecting them during their NFL career, including their health. In fact, as will be explained below, contract advisors are "agents" of both players and the NFLPA. They often communicate with players on a nearly daily basis during the season and are obligated to represent the players' interests, particularly when those interests conflict with those of the club. Consequently, contract advisors are typically the first and most important line in ensuring that player's health-related rights (and other rights) are followed and enforced. As we emphasized in the Introduction to the Report, we employ a broad definition of "health," which includes and extends beyond clinical measurements to the social determinants of health, including financial wellbeing, education, and social support. Contract advisors play a key role concerning these issues, as well as those related to the player's medical health. Below, we describe the legal and regulatory background of contract advisors, how they come to represent NFL players, and the types of services they generally provide to players, current and former. Additionally, it is useful to keep in mind that approximately 62 percent of contract advisors are attorneys, creating unique obligations and relationships, as will be discussed in more detail below.

To better inform our understanding of contract advisors' obligations and practices, we conducted approximately hour-long interviews with six currently active contract advisors. On average, those interviewed had been NFLPA-certified contract advisors for 17 years, had each represented an estimated 275 players in their careers, and currently represent 23 players. The interviews were not intended to be representative of the entire contract advisor population or to draw scientifically valid inferences, but were instead meant to be informative of general practices among these advisors. We provide anonymous quotes from these interviews throughout this Report, and urge the reader to keep that caveat in mind throughout. We then invited all six contract advisors to review a draft of this chapter prior to publication. Although five agreed to review a draft, only three provided comments. In addition, we interviewed an NFLPA representative to understand the NFLPA's perspective of the contract advisor industry.[a]

Finally, this chapter contains significant discussion about the contract advisor industry and practices. On their face, these items may not seem directly related to player health. However, as mentioned above and as will be explained below, contract advisors are a crucial advocate and defender of players concerning all matters, and their health in particular. For example, it would be a very rare occurrence for a player to commence a Non-Injury Grievance, Injury Grievance, or lawsuit without the support and advice of his contract advisor. Nevertheless, as will also be explained below, there are serious problems in the contract advisor industry. Until and unless these problems are addressed, there will continue to be problems promoting and protecting player health. Hence, resolving issues in the contract advisor industry is an important step in promoting and protecting player health.

(A) Background

Pursuant to the National Labor Relations Act (NLRA), the NFLPA is currently "the exclusive representative[] of all the employees in [the bargaining] unit for the purposes of collective bargaining in respect to rates of pay, wages, hours of employment, or other conditions of employment."[1] The NFLPA thus has "exclusive authority to negotiate with NFL Clubs on behalf of NFL players."[2] The NFLPA, as is its prerogative, nevertheless delegates a portion of its exclusive representational authority to contract advisors,[3] more commonly known as "agents." If the NFLPA so chose, it has the right under the NLRA to itself negotiate every NFL player's contract. Thus, contract advisors only exist as a profession because the NFLPA allows them to exist. Since the 1993 collective bargaining agreement (CBA), the NFL has explicitly recognized the NFLPA's authority to govern contract advisors and has agreed to fine clubs that negotiate with contract advisors not certified by the NFLPA.[4]

Contract advisors were not historically well received by clubs. Vince Lombardi, the Hall of Fame coach of the Green Bay Packers from 1959 to 1967 who also negotiated the Club's contracts, famously refused to deal with agents, including trading a player who had shown up to a contract negotiation with a lawyer.[5]

Nevertheless, as the business of football grew, so did the concept of players using advisors to assist with contract negotiations, marketing, and other business items. Today, all but a handful of NFL players retain contract advisors. The NFLPA has been certifying contract advisors in at least some fashion since 1983.[6] However, the NFLPA's certification and enforcement procedures in the 1980s were largely considered ineffective.[7]

When the NFLPA de-certified itself as the official and exclusive bargaining representative of NFL players in 1989,[8] it also lost the legal authority to regulate contract advisors pursuant to the NLRA.[9] Thus, no progress was made on tightening contract advisor regulation until the NFLPA re-certified itself in 1993.[10]

In 1994 and the years shortly thereafter, the NFLPA released new and more comprehensive Regulations Governing Contract Advisors ("Contract Advisor Regulations"), including new certification requirements, a standard code of conduct for contract advisors, an arbitration mechanism for disputes between or among players and/or contract advisors, and a cap on contract advisor's fees equal to 3 percent of a player's negotiated compensation. Of note, the new Contract Advisor Regulations explicitly obligated contract advisors to "[a]ct at all times in a fiduciary capacity on behalf of players,"[11] an obligation that continues to this day.

---

a   During the course of reviewing this Report for confidential information, the NFLPA requested information obtained from the NFLPA be attributed to the NFLPA generally, rather than specific NFLPA employees. For our purposes, the specific individual that provided the information was irrelevant, so long as the NFLPA provided the information. Thus, we agreed not to identify specific NFLPA employees.

The Contract Advisor Regulations have been amended from time to time since 1994, most recently in 2012,[12] but still largely follow the structure and rules set forth in the 1990s. The 2012 Contract Advisor Regulations, discussed in more detail below, require individuals seeking certification as contract advisors to have a college degree and postgraduate degree or, as an alternative, at least seven years of sufficient negotiating experience at the NFLPA's discretion.[13] In addition, they must pass a written examination covering the provisions of the Contract Advisor Regulations and CBA.[14]

Contract advisors who represent fewer than 10 active players pay an annual fee to the NFLPA of $1,500.[15] Contract advisors who represent 10 or more active players pay an annual fee of $2,000.[16]

1) FORMATION OF THE PLAYER-CONTRACT ADVISOR RELATIONSHIP

Contract advisors typically begin recruiting players as soon as the player demonstrates that he might become an NFL player. For some players, this might mean they will begin receiving phone calls, text messages and recruitment materials from contract advisors their freshman year of college—even though they cannot enter the NFL Draft until after their junior year.[17] For most players, the recruiting efforts become most intense in the summer preceding their senior season. Beginning with that summer and continuing through the season, players will hear from contract advisors according to their perceived Draft status: top prospects will hear from dozens of contract advisors, while players who are questionable to be drafted might only hear from a few.

Ultimately, the college players, with the help of their family, friends, and college, will sort through the multitude of contract advisors, meet with a few, and choose one. The player and contract advisor formalize the relationship by executing the NFLPA's Standard Representation Agreement (SRA), which dictates the parties' obligations to one another with minimal permitted variation.[b] The SRA is typically executed within days of the player's collegiate season being completed.

Within weeks (if not days) of the SRA's execution, the contract advisor will typically arrange (*i.e.,* pay) for the player to be flown to a training facility. Over the next few months, the player, under the tutelage of professional athletic trainers and football coaches (often former NFL players or

coaches), will prepare for the NFL Combine in February as well as additional workouts that may be held at the player's college or at an NFL club's facility around the same time to help advance the player's stock before the NFL Draft in April or May. The costs of training are typically between $15,000 and $35,000 per player.

> If the NFLPA so chose, it has the right under the NLRA to itself negotiate every NFL player's contract. Thus, contract advisors only exist as a profession because the NFLPA allows them to exist.

The contract advisors almost always pay the full cost of the player's training and housing during this crucial time period. However, most contract advisors require players to execute an agreement obligating the player to repay the costs of training in the event the player terminates the contract advisor prior to the contract advisor negotiating a contract on behalf of the player (at which point the player will be obligated to pay the contract advisor commissions on that contract).

Contract advisors will also look to make sure their client is in optimal physical health for the NFL Combine and NFL Draft. The contract advisor will often receive the player's college medical records and have any condition that might cause concern to an NFL club (such as a prior injury) be examined and treated by a doctor trusted by the contract advisor. The contract advisor will also often enlist the services of nutritionists, massage therapists, tutors, and others to ensure the players are maximally prepared for the Combine and other workouts.

In addition to paying for training, many (but not all) contract advisors routinely provide new clients with tens or hundreds of thousands of dollars in loans or advances which generally do not have to be repaid if the player continues to retain the contract advisor. The legality of these advances will be discussed in further detail below.

In sum, the contract advisor and his staff will be involved in the player's life on a near constant basis from the moment the player signs the SRA until he is drafted. What happens after the player is officially a member of an NFL club is discussed below.

---

b   The SRA requires the parties to set forth the contract advisor's compensation, up to the maximum of 3 percent. Additionally, the SRA permits the parties to execute other agreements concerning the representation, including loans or advances paid to the player by the contract advisor.

2) SERVICES PROVIDED TO CURRENT PLAYERS

A contract advisor's duties run the gamut of almost every service a professional could offer a client. Services range from the more intellectual tasks of negotiating contracts, securing endorsements, handling relations with the club, providing career and post-career counseling (including taking advantage of programs and benefits offered by the NFL and NFLPA), and providing legal services and financial advice, to the most mundane and personal tasks, such as making travel and dinner reservations, resolving housing and parking issues, purchasing the latest cellular phones and technological gadgets, arranging for free clothing, and helping handle domestic issues.[18] More established contract advisors generally enlist client service representatives, recently certified contract advisors, and interns to handle these pettier matters. Nevertheless, in general, contract advisors provide advice for every aspect of an NFL player's life. Contract Advisor 4:

> *I end up, in the role of agent as being the quarterback for everything that happens in their life or in their career. And so it ends up being a wide range of things from 'I want to go on vacation,' 'I want to rent a car,' to 'I just blew out my knee, what do I do.'*

For their efforts, contract advisors can be compensated a maximum of 3 percent of the compensation[19] a player receives in each playing season covered by the contract negotiated by the contract advisor.[20] Contracts executed pursuant to the Franchise or Transition tag provisions of the CBA,[21] are further limited to between 1 percent and 2 percent depending on how many times the player has previously been so designated.[22] Nevertheless, competition among contract advisors routinely drives them to offer their services for less than 3 percent. Importantly, a "Contract Advisor is prohibited from receiving any fee for his/her services until and unless the player receives the compensation upon which the fee is based."[23,c]

Players can and do switch contract advisors very easily. Players can terminate the Standard Representation Agreement at any time, effective five days after written notice of termination to the contract advisor.[24]

3) RELATIONSHIP WITH FORMER PLAYER-CLIENTS

Once a player's NFL career has ended, his relationship with the contract advisor is generally no longer governed by the Contract Advisor Regulations[d] and the contract advisor and player have no more contractual obligations to one another. Thus, contract advisors generally do not receive any compensation from a player after his playing career ends (unless they represent them in marketing, coaching or broadcasting deals). Nevertheless, the contract advisors interviewed generally expressed that they believe their role is unchanged— to provide the player with whatever guidance and support he needs. The contract advisors we interviewed admitted that the degree of assistance provided to a player after his career is over depends on the strength of the relationship between the contract advisor and player; some former players will communicate with their contract advisor almost every day, just as they did when they were playing; while those who communicated less with their contract advisor during their career could easily break off all communication with their former contract advisor.[e]

Contract advisors have multiple reasons for continuing to help players after their career. First, many develop very close, almost sibling-like relationships with their clients. Second, they can often continue to benefit from their association with their former clients. In particular, if a former NFL player happens to stay involved with his former college football team, the contract advisor might use his former client to facilitate meetings with players from that team. Generally speaking, success in the contract advisor industry is very reputation-driven; thus, contract advisors will generally try to avoid doing things that could make them look bad in the eye of players—current, former, and future.

Not surprisingly, multiple contract advisors discussed the difficulty players have in transitioning from a highly competitive and structured life in the NFL to being unsure of what to do next. Contract advisors explained that those who prepare themselves for the transition understandably handle it much better. Thus, all of the interviewed contract advisors expressed the importance of preparing for a

---

c   Current Player 9: "One thing that guys aren't as happy about, I think across the board, is agent fees and paying agents 3 percent."

d   The contract advisor will still be subject to the contract advisor's broad prohibition against "[e]ngaging in unlawful conduct and/or conduct involving dishonesty, fraud, deceit, misrepresentation, or other activity which reflects adversely on his/her fitness as a Contract Advisor or jeopardizes his/her effective representation of NFL players." 2012 NFLPA Contract Advisor Regulations, § 3(B)(14).

e   Contract Advisor 3: "[I]t all depends on the player. Some I'm still pretty involved with, others just kind of disappear and fade away. It really depends on what your relationship was with the guy during their career and kind of what their motivations are post career. So you know there's a few that I still send Christmas cards to. There's others that I don't even know if they have my e-mail."

player's exit from the NFL as soon as possible. To prepare players for their life after football, the contract advisors often encourage players to finish their degree if necessary in the offseason, consult with a financial advisor (assuming it is one the contract advisor trusts), get media training, take advantage of workshops offered by the NFL and NFLPA, and participate in internships in the offseason.

(B) Current Legal Obligations[f]

Contract advisors are regulated by several bodies of law: 1) common law; 2) Contract Advisor Regulations; 3) state statutes; and, 4) federal statutes.

1) COMMON LAW

First and foremost, pursuant to the NLRA, contract advisors exist to represent and protect the player's best interests in dealings with the club. More broadly, contract advisors are "agents," which, by law, are authorized to act on the behalf of another individual (the "principal") and must act in the best interests of the principal at all times.[25] The agent has many duties to the principal, including loyalty, care, good faith, competence and diligence.[26] These duties are more generally known as fiduciary duties. Generally speaking, a fiduciary is "a person who is required to act for the benefit of another person on all matters within the scope of their relationship; one who owes to another the duties of good faith, trust, confidence, and candor."[27] While the existence of a fiduciary relationship generally requires a fact-based inquiry,[28] there is little doubt that contract advisors and their player-clients are in a fiduciary relationship.

2) CONTRACT ADVISOR REGULATIONS

The Contract Advisor Regulations are a set of obligations established by the NFLPA by which contract advisors have agreed to abide.

The Contract Advisor Regulations include a comprehensive list of 19 actions a contract advisor is "required" to take.[29] Of the most relevance, they must:

(7) Advise the affected player and report to the NFLPA any known violations by an NFL Club of a player's individual contract or of his rights under any applicable Collective Bargaining Agreement;

* * *

(14) Fully comply with applicable state and federal laws;

(15) Become and remain sufficiently educated with regard to NFL structure and economics, applicable Collective Bargaining Agreements and other governing documents, basic negotiating techniques, and developments in sports law and related subjects[.];

(16) Disclose in an addendum (in the form attached as Appendix G) attached to the Standard Representation Agreement between the Contract Advisor and player, the names and current positions of any NFL management personnel or coaches whom Contract Advisor represents or has represented in matters pertaining to their employment by or association with any NFL club;

(17) Act at all times in a fiduciary capacity on behalf of players;

* * *

(20) Educate player-clients as to their benefits, rights and obligations pursuant to the Collective Bargaining Agreement; and to advise and assist those player-clients in taking maximum advantage of those benefits and rights, including, without limitation, Termination Pay, Severance Pay, Bert Bell/Pete Rozelle disability benefits, workers compensation benefits, second medical opinions, and right to chose (sic) their own surgeon.[g]

Just as importantly, the Contract Advisor Regulations list 31 specific actions in which contract advisors are **prohibited** from engaging. Of particular relevance, they are prohibited from:

(2) Providing or offering money or any other thing of value to any player or prospective player to induce or encourage that player to utilize his/her services;

(3) Providing or offering money or any other thing of value to a member of the player's or prospective player's family or any other person for the purpose of inducing or encouraging that person to recommend the services of the Contract Advisor;

(4) Providing materially false or misleading information to any player or prospective player in the context of recruiting the player as a client or in the course of representing that player as his Contract Advisor;

* * *

---

f   The legal obligations described herein are not an exhaustive list but are those we believe are most relevant to player health.

g   The contract advisor's obligation to help players obtain second medical opinions and to receive treatment from the surgeon of their choice demonstrates the unique and significant role contract advisors play in player health.

(8) Engaging in any other activity which creates an actual or potential conflict of interest with the effective representation of NFL players;

* * *

(12) Concealing material facts from any player whom the Contract Advisor is representing which relate to the subject of the player's individual contract negotiation;

(13) Failing to advise the player and to report to the NFLPA any known violations by an NFL Club of a player's individual contract;

(14) Engaging in unlawful conduct and/or conduct involving dishonesty, fraud, deceit, misrepresentation, or other activity which reflects adversely on his/her fitness as a Contract Advisor or jeopardizes his/her effective representation of NFL players;

* * *

(19) Violating the confidentiality provisions of the National Football League Policy and Program for Substances of Abuse. The NFLPA Executive Director in consultation with the Disciplinary Committee may fine a Contract Advisor in accordance with the terms of the National Football League Policy and Program for Substances of Abuse. Such fine, if imposed, shall be in addition to, and not a substitute for, discipline which may be imposed pursuant to Section 6 of these Regulations;

* * *

(21) (a) Initiating any communication, directly or indirectly, with a player who has entered into a Standard Representation Agreement with another Contract Advisor and such Standard Representation Agreement is on file with the NFLPA if the communication concerns a matter relating to the: (i) Player's current Contract Advisor; (ii) Player's current Standard Representation Agreement; (iii) Player's contract status with any NFL Club(s); or (iv) Services to be provided by prospective Contract Advisor either through a Standard Representation Agreement or otherwise.

(b) If a player, already a party to a Standard Representation Agreement, initiates communication with a Contract Advisor relating to any of the subject matters listed in Section 3(B)(21)(a) the Contract Advisor may continue communications with the Player regarding any of those matters.

(c) Section 3(B)(21) shall not apply to any player who has less than sixty (60) days remaining before his NFL Player Contract expires, and he has not yet signed a new Standard Representation Agreement with a Contract Advisor within the sixty (60) day period.

(d) Section 3(B)(21) shall not prohibit a Contract Advisor from sending a player written materials which may be reasonably interpreted as advertising directed at players in general and not targeted at a specific player.

* * *

(24) Affiliating with or advising players to use the services of a person who is not an NFLPA Registered Player Financial Advisor for purposes of providing financial advice to the player; or acting as a "Financial Advisor" and/or providing "Financial Advice" to an NFL player as those terms are defined in the NFLPA Regulations and Code of Conduct Governing Registered Player Financial Advisors, without first becoming a Registered Player Financial Advisor pursuant to the NFLPA Regulations and Code of Conduct Governing Registered Player Financial Advisors;

* * *

(28) Referring a player to a workers compensation attorney who is not a member of the NFLPA Panel of Workers Compensation Attorneys;

* * *

(32) Using, associating with, employing or entering into any business relationship with any individual in the recruitment of prospective player-clients who is not Certified and in good standing as a Contract Advisor pursuant to these Regulations[.]

3) STATE STATUTES

Forty-three states have enacted some version of the Uniform Athlete Agents Act (UAAA).[h] The UAAA is principally concerned with the transition from college student-athlete to professional athlete but also governs contract advisors' conduct more generally as well. The UAAA requires persons representing athletes,[30] *i.e.,* "agents," to register with the relevant state's Secretary of State and to notify the college when an agent signs an agreement with a college player in the process of turning professional.[31] The UAAA also prohibits many of the actions discussed in the Contract Advisor Regulations, including "giv[ing] any materially false or misleading information or mak[ing] a materially false promise or representation," and, "furnish[ing] anything of value to a student-athlete before the student-athlete enters into the agency contract."[32] Finally, the UAAA gives colleges the right to sue agents for failing to comply with

---

h   In 2015, the Uniform Law Commission of the National Conference of Commissioners on Uniform State Laws approved a revised version of the UAAA, first approved in 2000. Nevertheless, the revised law does not substantially implicate player health in any new ways and, as of October 2016, had only been adopted by three states.

the law,[33] since colleges could be forced to declare players ineligible under National Collegiate Athletic Association (NCAA) Bylaws for having accepted gifts or money from an agent.

While the UAAA was designed to protect colleges and players from unscrupulous agents, unfortunately, it has done little but increase agents' costs of doing business through increased registration fees since few states take any measures to enforce the law.[34] In addition, California, Michigan, and Ohio have passed their own agent laws that also require registration and forbid certain acts.[35]

Research has not revealed any litigation involving any state's version of the UAAA. However, in 2006, former NFL player Chad Morton sued former contract advisor Leigh Steinberg alleging Steinberg had violated California's Miller-Ayala Athlete Agents Act.[36] Morton alleged Steinberg and his firm failed to repay $500,000 in loans.[37] The case was settled when Steinberg agreed to repay the loan.[38]

The UAAA does not contain any language directly concerning player health, safety, or welfare.

4) FEDERAL STATUTES

Contract advisors must comply with the federal Sports Agent Responsibility and Trust Act (SPARTA),[39] passed in 2004. SPARTA, like the UAAA, is principally concerned with student-athlete recruitment but also governs contract advisors more generally. SPARTA prohibits sports agents from soliciting clients with misleading information, making false promises, providing anything of value as an inducement, or neglecting to provide a required disclosure statement warning the student-athlete that he or she may lose his or her eligibility.[40] The Federal Trade Commission is responsible for enforcing SPARTA but has never brought any legal action against an agent.[41]

SPARTA does not contain any language directly concerning player health, safety, or welfare.

5) OTHER CONSIDERATIONS – NCAA BYLAWS

The NCAA bears mentioning in this context, as many might believe (incorrectly) that it has some authority over agents. The NCAA is a private organization through which the nation's colleges and universities govern their athletic programs. The NCAA consists of more than 1,200 member institutions, all of which participate in the creation of

NCAA rules and voluntarily submit to its authority.[42] As a voluntary organization, the NCAA can only exercise plenary power over its member institutions, their employees, and their student-athletes.[43] Consequently, while the NCAA prohibits student-athletes from entering into agreements with agents,[44] the NCAA has no authority to discipline contract advisors.

Although the NCAA has no direct jurisdiction over agents, as described earlier, the UAAA does empower educational institutions with certain regulatory powers and the ability to file civil suits against agents.[45] Many NCAA member institutions require each agent wishing to recruit a player at that school to also register with the school's athletic department or compliance office.[46] Contract advisors wishing to remain in the good graces of the school will comply with the school's regulations.

(C) Current Ethical Codes

Attorney's Rules of Professional Conduct, like the Contract Advisor Regulations, are quasi-legal/quasi-ethical in nature, in that they are ethical rules that can be legally enforced.

Contract advisors who are also attorneys must comply with their respective state bar's attorney ethics rules. In 2015, 545 of the 875 certified contract advisors (62 percent) had a law degree.[47] While we do not know the number of contract advisors who subsequently were admitted to practice law by a state bar, it seems likely that many did. The Model Rules of Professional Conduct (which serve as guidance for every state's Attorney's Rules of Professional Conduct) include several rules that could be implicated by some of the alleged wrongful behavior of contract advisors. For example, Rule 1.1 requires "competent" representation, Rule 1.7 governs conflicts of interest, Rule 1.15 strictly directs how a lawyer is to handle client money, and Rule 5.3 holds attorneys liable for the conduct of non-lawyer employees, such as the "runners" often employed by contract advisors.[48] In addition, Rule 7.1 prohibits false or misleading communications about a lawyer's services, Rule 7.2 prohibits a lawyer from giving anything of value to a person for recommending the lawyer's services, and Rule 7.3 limits a lawyer's ability to solicit clients.[49]

(D) Current Practices

Players generally have mixed feelings about the contract advisor industry.[i] While many like their advisors, they have also heard horror stories about others. In particular, players believe many contract advisors look to take advantage of players in whatever way they can.[j] Below, we discuss some most important areas where contract advisors have an opportunity to influence player health, including Recruiting, Negotiating Contracts, Assisting with Medical Care, Engaging with the NFLPA, and Potential Conflicts of Interest.

1) RECRUITING

The extreme competitiveness of the industry prevents contract advisors from promoting and protecting player health as one might hope they could. Entering the 2015 NFL season, there were 869 NFLPA-certified contract advisors but only 420 actually had clients (48.3 percent).[50] Importantly, "[t]he Certification of any Contract Advisor who has failed to negotiate and sign a player to an NFL Player Contract (excluding Practice Squad Contracts) for at least one NFL player during any three-year period shall automatically expire at the end of such three-year period."[51] Thus, in the rare case that a contract advisor has one or multiple clients and none of their contracts expire during a three-year period, those advisors will need to go through the contract advisor certification process again, including retaking the contract advisor examination.[52] The NFLPA representative we interviewed explained that the purpose of the rule is to ensure that contract advisors remain "active in the business."

Entering the 2015 NFL season, there were 869 NFLPA-certified contract advisors but only 420 actually had clients (48.3 percent).

Contract advisors interviewed, on average, spent 30 percent of their time recruiting players, a proportion that has only increased over time. Recruiting thus diminishes the amount of time and resources available for contract advisors to devote to their current clients.

Some scholars have commented that the competition and allure of the industry have resulted in a ruthless professional environment and nearly continuous allegations of wrongdoing.[53] Contract advisors engage in protracted recruiting battles for the right to represent college football players entering the NFL.[54] Even though the Contract Advisor Regulations have long forbid "[p]roviding or offering money or any other thing of value to any player or prospective player to induce or encourage that player to utilize his/her services,"[55] as discussed above, many (but not all) contract advisors routinely provide new clients with tens or hundreds of thousands of dollars in loans or advances which generally do not have to be repaid if the player continues to retain the contract advisor.[56] Perhaps counterintuitively, such arrangements have repeatedly been approved by NFLPA arbitrator Roger Kaplan[k] in disputes between players and contract advisors.[57] Recently, in *Rosenhaus v. Jackson*, NFLPA Case No. 13-31 (Kaplan, Arb. Apr. 10, 2014), Kaplan held that since the loan agreements between contract advisor Drew Rosenhaus and player DeSean Jackson explicitly stated that the loans were not conditioned on the signing of an SRA, "[t]he mere existence of the loan and/or the possibility that some or all of it might be interest free or forgiven entirely does not render it an improper inducement."[58]

Also as discussed above, contract advisors typically pay $15,000 to $35,000 to prepare their clients for the NFL Combine and Draft. Players are typically only obligated to repay the training costs in the event they terminate the contract advisor prior to signing an NFL contract. Arbitrator Kaplan has held that such expenses are reasonable and necessary to the negotiation of the player's first contract and thus the player is obligated to repay them if he has agreed to do so as part of the SRA.[59]

Former Player 1 explained that the loans and advances are "one of the biggest selling points for most kids out of college":

> [T]hose kids for the most part come from modest means and haven't seen the type of money thrown around and thrown at them and all of a sudden

---

i   Current Player 5: "Some guys love their agents, have a great relationship and some guys don't. I think it would be split pretty close down the middle." Current Player 6: "Most agents don't really do anything apart from negotiating the contract." Current Player 10: "Agents do a good job of looking after players." Former Player 3: "For the most part, agents do a pretty good job."

j   Current Player 4: "I think there are a lot of those guys that are preying on players."

k   Arbitrator Roger Kaplan has presided over almost every NFLPA arbitration since 1994. *See* Weinberg v. Nat'l Football League Players Ass'n, 06-cv-2332, 2008 WL 4808920, at *2 (N.D. Tex. Nov. 5, 2008) (citing affidavit from Kaplan in which he explained he has been the NFLPA arbitrator since 1994).

you have this guy that's willing to put up the cash for cars and jewelry and clothes and everything else and you know it's quite alluring for a lot of kids that have never seen that.[1]

Several current players also expressed concern with the loans and advances from contract advisors to players:

- **Current Player 4:** *"It definitely creates a problem where guys are in the hole that amount of money before they've ever made a dollar."*

- **Current Player 5:** *"I think it's one of the worst things that you can possibly do. I'm 100 percent against it. I think that it's basically agents buying players . . . . I can understand why a player may need money . . . before the draft to help him train and all that. But I think it's gotten way out of control."*

- **Current Player 8:** *"I think that it's highway robbery because I've seen some of the interest rates that they've charged these guys. I think that's a person of power taking advantage of an uneducated kid . . . . I think it's become kind of a competitive market that definitely has its downfalls."*

- **Current Player 9:** *"I view it as a major problem because it's just the player already in debt before he even has money."*

The NFLPA representative we interviewed also explained the players' and NFLPA's concern with these arrangements:

From the agent's perspective, the financial output they have to put into a player prior to the draft has certainly grown exponentially over the last five, ten years.

* * *

[W]ith the increased competition in the agent business—for clients coming out of college especially—it has led to agents having to put out more dollars financially in pre-Combine training and stipends and whatever you want to call it, pre-draft loans, whatever you want to call it.

And it may be that some players make their choice of agent solely based on the amount of money that the agent's willing to pay out, rather than necessarily signing with the one that's the best fit for them. Has that harmed players? That's hard to quantify—whether or not that's harmed anybody. But I think certainly that does put a player in a position where maybe he's making the choice of

an agent not using the right criteria, or at least not prioritizing it the right way.

The NFLPA representative also explained that the possibility of amending the Contract Advisor Regulations to restrict pre-Draft loans and advances in some way has "been discussed," but that "the player rep[resentative]s haven't taken any action to change our rules as of yet."

2) NEGOTIATING CONTRACTS

The principle responsibility of contract advisors, in accord with the delegation of that responsibility to them by the NFLPA as discussed above, is to represent players in contract negotiations with clubs. However, contract advisors generally only negotiate contracts in two windows: (1) around the beginning of a new League Year in March when veteran players become free agents; and, (2) in the summer after rookies have been drafted. However, the 2011 CBA significantly reduced and restricted rookie compensation and thus also the rookie contract negotiations. While veteran players might sign contract extensions or renegotiations at a variety of times during the year, the truth is that negotiating contracts does not consume a majority of a contract advisor's time.

This is not to say, however, that contract advisor's negotiating services are not important. They are extremely important. A skilled contract advisor will perform comprehensive statistical and economic analysis of a player's worth in preparation for a contract negotiation. Moreover, quality contract advisors will be able to negotiate with multiple clubs, judge the market, and sell the player's skill to obtain a contract acceptable to the player. Contract advisors and their negotiations are a critical component to maximizing career earnings, an important consideration when discussing player health.

3) ASSISTING WITH MEDICAL CARE

As the player's principal advocate and advisor, contract advisors play an important role in player health matters. Indeed, they have an important obligation to ensure players understand and take advantage of the myriad of programs and benefits offered by the NFL and NFLPA. Many of the contract advisors interviewed explained that very early on in the contract advisor-player relationship, they have a meeting or telephone call with the player to explain the realities of the business, *i.e.*, that they are likely to get injured and have short careers and thus must be responsible and plan accordingly. Whether players are receptive to and understand this advice is another question.

---

[1] We reiterate that our interviews were intended to be informational but not representative of all players' views and should be read with that limitation in mind.

Contract advisors also guide players after they have been injured. In a typical scenario where a player suffers an in-season or in-game injury, the contract advisor will often be in touch with the player and someone from the club's front office as soon as possible to learn the extent of the injury. Within 24 hours, the player will undergo a variety of possible examinations by club doctors, including but not limited to X-rays, MRIs,[60] or CT scans.[61] The contract advisor will then obtain the films from the examinations, by requesting them from the player, the club's medical staff, or the club's front office. The contract advisor will then have the films sent to another doctor chosen by them for a second opinion.

Of the six contract advisors interviewed, five stated that they obtain a second opinion every time or nearly every time a player is injured while another stated he obtains a second opinion about 50 percent of the time.[62] The motivation behind obtaining the second opinions stems from both general and specific distrust of club doctors by the contract advisors. Some contract advisors indicated that by almost always obtaining a second opinion, it removes any concern that the club doctor might have been making a recommendation that was in the club's interest and not the player's.[m] One contract advisor even stated that when assessing a player's injury, "the club doctor has nothing to do with it . . . the club doctor's input means nothing to us."[n] Some contract advisors also indicated that their experience with, and the reputation of, a particular club or club medical staff will color the decision of whether to obtain a second opinion or to proceed with the club

doctor's recommended course of treatment.[o] It is important to emphasize that we are merely reporting the perception of the contract advisors. We lack the relevant data to evaluate whether second opinion doctors are superior to club doctors in any way.

The second opinion doctor typically only reviews the film but occasionally will request to see the player in person if the doctor believes it is necessary. Contract advisors' estimates of how often a second opinion doctor's diagnosis differed from the club doctor's were generally low ("10 to 20 percent," "as much as 20 percent," "about a third of the time," "not incredibly often"). "According to the Patient Advocate Foundation, 30 percent of patients who sought second opinions for elective surgery found the two opinions differed."[63] However, it is difficult to compare the figures because, as discussed above, players obtain second opinions almost as a matter of course while the average patient might only seek a second opinion about serious diagnoses.

If the second opinion doctor's diagnosis does differ, a decision then must be made as to which course of treatment to pursue and which doctor will perform the surgery (if necessary). In some cases, the contract advisor might arrange for the second opinion doctor to talk with the club doctor to see if a consensus can be reached.[p] Sometimes a third doctor will provide an opinion. Nevertheless, the prevailing sentiment among the advisors interviewed is that the second opinion doctor's recommended course of treatment almost always is the one taken in today's NFL.

There are two main reasons why the second opinion doctor's recommended course is followed. First, as discussed above, some contract advisors regard the club doctor's opinion as meaningless and will not follow it (unless, of course, it concurs with that of the second opinion doctor). Second, some contract advisors believe that in recent years clubs and club medical staff have resigned themselves to doing what the player wants to do (as recommended by the contract advisor and second opinion doctor).

In the course of this process, contract advisors are also likely to review the player's contract to refresh their understanding as to any provisions which might be relevant to the player's health and gauge how the injury might

> Of the six contract advisors interviewed, five stated that they obtain a second opinion every time or nearly every time a player is injured while another stated he obtains a second opinion about 50 percent of the time.

---

m   Contract Advisor 1: "I've effectively removed any of that [concern]. I've said okay, where I feel like I need to get a second opinion almost every time, I get a second opinion. So it's become a nonissue." Contract Advisor 5: "I'm always concerned that the doctor is involved because he's, you know, an employee of the club."

n   Contract Advisor 4: "[T]he team doctor is there to advise the team on how they should approach a player. The team doctor has nothing to do as far as I'm concerned with how the player should approach his own health . . . . The team doctor is a medical advisor to the team."

o   Contract Advisor 2: "[I]t depends sometimes on the organization that we're dealing with." Nevertheless, Clubs seem to have become less adversarial about a player choosing to obtain a second opinion. Contract Advisor 1: "I will say there was a lot more pushback early in my career about second opinions and going somewhere else."

p   Yet, Contract Advisor 1 explained that the club doctor "will have to make a very good argument" to the second opinion doctor to convince the second opinion doctor and contract advisor to follow the club doctor's recommendation.

affect the player's contract status. In addition, the contract advisor will likely review relevant CBA provisions and advise the player of his rights, such as the right to a second opinion, the surgeon of his choice, workers' compensation benefits, and the Injury Protection benefit. Contract advisors generally stressed the importance of taking advantage of these safeguards to protect a player's health.

There was also a general consensus among the contract advisors that they themselves have become, and are, increasingly sensitive to player health issues, and to concussions in particular.[64] Of course, such self-evaluations have to be viewed with that perspective in mind. One contract advisor explained an effort he made to prevent a player from suffering a future injury. Understanding that his client had played defensive end on only one side of the line his entire career, the contract advisor was concerned that the player's hips and legs would become unbalanced, increasing the risk of injury. The contract advisor worked with the player and the player's athletic trainer to make sure the player's hips were equally strong and flexible.

Another contract advisor had a creative idea for helping his players. Throughout his career, he has recommended his clients to maintain an "injury diary," contemporaneously listing each condition the player has and the treatment recommended and received. The contract advisor believes the diary could serve multiple purposes: (1) ensure the player's medical condition is accurately described and understood to assist with treatment; (2) help the player improve treatment in the future in the event the condition recurs; and, (3) for possible use during an Injury Grievance against the club.

4) ENGAGING WITH THE NFLPA

Contract advisors and the NFLPA are two stakeholders intimately involved in protecting players' health. However, some of the contract advisors we interviewed suggested that a poor relationship between the two groups reduces the effectiveness of both groups in assisting players.

The sentiment among the contract advisors interviewed was near universal that the relationship between contract advisors and the NFLPA is mediocre at best, "horrible" at worst. Contract Advisor 1 explained that, in his opinion:

> [I]f you can't win the war with 32 owners, you show the players that you're saving money, say cutting agent fees or having the ability to do certain things with the agents and showing that power[.]

The contract advisors we spoke to indicated their view that the principle issue preventing the NFLPA and contract advisors from working well together centers around a lack of communication and trust. In general, contract advisors seem to believe that the NFLPA is missing out on a valuable opportunity to help players by not engaging contract advisors more fully. As explained by Contract Advisor 1:

> [N]obody knows the players as well as we do and nobody has more day-to-day interaction with them. So the issues they face—while we're told we have a platform and an avenue to articulate [the issues to the NFLPA]—never really comes to bear.

Similarly, Contract Advisor 4, explained "they [the NFLPA] don't quite understand the influence that we could have and that we may have in a player's life." Contract Advisor 6 expressed his opinion that the NFLPA thinks contract advisors are "idiots . . . , a nuisance." Of course, this may just be their own biases as to their importance and relevance, and the opinions need to be evaluated in that light.

Multiple contract advisors did, however, recognize the difficulty the NFLPA faces with such a large and constantly changing membership. Additionally, several contract advisors believed the NFLPA's work on player health matters has improved in recent years and that the NFLPA is taking those issues seriously.[q]

In reviewing a draft of this Report, peer reviewer and former contract advisor and club executive Andrew Brandt had this to say about the relationship between contract advisors and the NFLPA:

> The Chapter does a good job of explaining the tense relationship—or lack of relationship between agents and the NFLPA. Even though they are both on the same side of looking out for the best interests of players, there is an apprehension from each side in dealing with the other. The reasons are several, often due to personalities, but emanate from the collective versus individual nature of their representation. The union is looking out for the overall constituency and providing collective benefit; agents are concerned about maximizing income and benefits for their clients rather than the general population of players. I know that, as the Chapter says, there are annual meetings at the Combine for all agents and for a select group of agents with union representatives, but I often hear negative viewpoints about

---

q   Contract Advisor 1: "[O]ne of the good things that the NFL has done and the PA has done is ensuring that these guys can have an easy way to get their degree[.]"

these meetings, especially from agents that are excluded.[65]

For the NFLPA's part, the NFLPA representative we interviewed was more optimistic and generally praised contract advisors:

> *To the best of my knowledge, they're doing fine . . . . 99 times out of 100 they are aware of filing deadlines for grievance purposes and stuff like that. I think most agents genuinely care about the welfare of their players. It's in their best interest. The longer the player plays, the more money the agent's going to make.*[r]

The NFLPA representative also believed that the NFLPA's relationship with agents was "generally . . . good." Nevertheless, the NFLPA representative acknowledged that "a lot of [contract advisors] would probably say we need to do more in the discipline area."

At the conclusion of each season, the NFLPA provides the contract advisors an "End of Season Player Checklist." The Checklist is a multi-page document summarizing many of the players' important rights, benefits, and opportunities, such as obtaining medical records, obtaining second medical opinions, filing for workers' compensation, Injury Protection or disability benefits, understanding their insurance options, understanding off-season compliance with the Policies on Performance-Enhancing Substances and Substances of Abuse, and preparing for life after football by engaging the benefits and programs offered by the NFL and NFLPA. Contract advisors are required to provide the Checklist to all of their clients and certify in writing to the NFLPA that they have discussed the Checklist with their clients. In short, the Checklist is an excellent document and the NFLPA should be commended for its creation and use.

Nevertheless, contract advisors we interviewed expressed that there is an insufficient opportunity for contract advisors and the NFLPA to discuss issues affecting players. Several contract advisors indicated that the NFLPA only ever solicits advice from, or listens to, the most successful and powerful contract advisors. The NFLPA representative we interviewed explained that every year at the NFL Combine, the NFLPA holds an invitation-only meeting with approximately 20 contract advisors to discuss issues affecting contract advisors and players. The invited contract advisors are selected by the NFLPA.

5) POTENTIAL CONFLICTS OF INTEREST

While contract advisors' and players' interests are generally well-aligned, an NFL player should be aware of a variety of situations in which his contract advisor's interests might conflict with his own. It is quite clear that there are many situations which on their face present the perception of a conflict.[s] What is not clear is the extent to which these conflicts are real or hurt players. It is, however, paramount that players be aware of the potential conflicts. As discussed above, contract advisors are typically the player's most trusted and involved advocate. They play a critical role in protecting and advancing player health. A situation in which a contract advisor is not wholly committed to the player's interests undermines the contract advisor's representation and zealous advocacy on behalf of the player, potentially damaging to the player's short-term and/or long-term health.

Before turning to the explanation of each potential conflict, it is important to recognize that conflicts and potential conflicts—including those of the type faced by contract advisors—are common in many professional industries. Thus, that contract advisors face potential conflicts is not necessarily problematic. Instead, what is important is that players (like all professional clients) be aware of the potential conflict and that the contract advisor (like all professionals) attempt to minimize those conflicts, and where not possible to do so, be transparent about the conflict and attempt to manage it appropriately.

The potential conflicts include:

- **The contract advisor's relationship with club officials.** Generally speaking, contract advisors rely on their professional network and contacts as much as any other industry. Club officials—particularly general managers and other front office executives such as the Directors of Football Administration—are important and powerful contacts for contract advisors. Contract advisors can obtain important information from club officials about any number of football-related items (perhaps most importantly, information, *e.g.,* telephone numbers, of college players the contract advisor might want to recruit). Contract advisors might even be able to secure favorable contract terms for a player when he has a good relationship with a particular club. As a result, contract advisors occasionally walk a fine line between zealous advocacy on behalf of their client and refraining from angering club

---

r   The NFLPA representative also explained that contract advisors might pressure players to continue their careers: "I'm not saying there's agents that are encouraging players to continue their careers when maybe the player shouldn't. But I wouldn't be surprised if that's happened a few times."

s   Current Player 2: "There's always going to be agents out there that are just doing what they do to benefit themselves personally."

officials. To this end, the possibility exists that a contract advisor might avoid a confrontation with a club for one player to benefit another player that is a member, or potential member, of the same club. Contract Advisor 4 confirmed this rare but troublesome practice:

I've heard of some larger scale agents kind of wheeling and dealing in order to make one thing better for someone [saying] "I let you have a point last time on the last player, so you owe me on this player."[t]

Moreover, the contract advisor business is highly competitive and fraught with challenges, as described above. Some contract advisors might decide they are more interested in working for an NFL club than representing NFL players.[u] Thus, the possibility exists that some contract advisors might have an interest in maintaining a good relationship with a club at the expense of his client (even if unconsciously).

- **The contract advisor's compensation structure.** As discussed above, contract advisors are paid a percentage of the player's contract. Thus, until a contract is finally signed, a contract advisor is entitled to nothing. The contract advisor business model revolves around players reaching a "second contract." In other words, contract advisors generally do not generate a profit from representing players during the term of their rookie contracts, particularly after the 2011 CBA, which significantly reduced rookie compensation.[v] A player's

financial value is generally at its maximum when his rookie contract expires (or is near expiration) and he reaches (or nears) free agency for the first time (usually after four seasons in the NFL). It is at this point that players are able to offer their services to any and all clubs for whatever price the free agency market will bear. This "second contract" is a significant financial moment for the player, the club, and the contract advisor.

As a result of the significance of the second contract, contract advisors are under pressure to successfully negotiate the second contract. Not surprisingly, these more important and costly contract negotiations tend to be more difficult and subject to media attention. Players therefore may begin questioning whether another contract advisor might be more successful at "closing the deal" on the second contract (often at the prompting of a competing contract advisor). In this environment, a contract advisor likely feels pressure to have a contract executed before he or she can be terminated by the player or else the contract advisor risks losing out on a significant income stream. Contract advisors with a questionably committed client might therefore refrain from continued difficult negotiations with a club and instead recommend a player sign a contract of perhaps less than maximum value to ensure that the contract advisor will be paid. Contract Advisor 4 also confirmed this practice:

[I]f players are incentivized to leave their agent by other agents, at some point in time, an agent is going to recognize that "Hey, it's in my best interest personally to get a deal done." I am sure that has occurred multiple times, many times.

* * *

t   Interviewer: Do you think sometimes agents are reluctant to push hard on teams because they don't want to ruin the relationship with the club?
     Contract Advisor 4: Yes, I do.

u   For example, Andrew Brandt was a contract advisor before becoming Vice President of the Green Bay Packers in 1999. *WSBI Bios,* Wharton Sports Bus. Inst., http://wsb.wharton.upenn.edu/wsbibios-brandt.html (last visited Aug. 7, 2015), *archived at* http://perma.cc/RWN7-2E7T. Brandt's switch came soon after he was representing top draft pick Ricky Williams; he was approached by the Packers within a week after Williams informed Brandt he wanted him to work with the rapper Master P, who was starting a sports management firm. Andrew Brandt, Peer Review Response (Oct. 30, 2015). Similarly, Cliff Stein, current Vice President of Football Administration and General Counsel for the Chicago Bears, was a contract advisor for nine years before joining the Bears in 2002. *Front Office – Cliff Stein,* Chi. Bears, http://www.chicagobears.com/team/staff/Cliff-Stein/8dbdd7b5-9ffa-4612-8ddd-902086ec91a3, *archived at* http://perma.cc/ZKL9-JX7H (last visited Aug. 7, 2015). Both Stein and Brandt are very well-regarded in the sports industry and thus we do not mean to suggest that either engaged in a conflicted manner while contract advisors.

v   For example, the Houston Texans selected C.J. Fiedorowicz with the first pick of the third round in the 2014 NFL Draft. *C.J. Fiedorowicz,* Spotrac, http://www.spotrac.com/nfl/houston-texans/c.j.-fiedorowicz (last visited Aug. 7, 2015), *archived at* http://perma.cc/DBU2-MBRV. Fiedorowicz signed a four-year contract with a maximum value of $3,195,114. *Id.* If a contract advisor were to recoup 3% of Fiedorowicz' contract, and Fiedorowicz is able to play all four years of the contract (far from a guarantee) the contract advisor would make $95,853. A contract advisor could easily spend $35,000 recruiting a player and preparing him for the NFL Draft, not to mention the contract advisor's other professional and administrative costs. If the contract advisor were only receiving a 2% commission, which is often the case, he or she would only earn $63,902. Thus, the contract advisor stands to make very little, if any, profit from a player's rookie contract.

> Contract advisors with a questionably committed client might therefore refrain from continued difficult negotiations with a club and instead recommend a player sign a contract of perhaps less than maximum value to ensure that the contract advisor will be paid.

You have to choose. You have to decide what side of the line do you want to come down on. Do you want to come down on the side of the line where you want to do the best job? Or do you want to come down on the side of the line where you got a deal done and locked in a commission when it could be a fine deal, but not the best deal. That's the choice agents have to make, and . . . I'd be pretty sure on a regular basis, agents come down on the side of the line where it's, "Okay, let me get this done."

* * *

I think some agents are just looking to get deals done . . . . I've seen the agents that just want to sign off and move on to the next one.[w]

The contract advisor-player Standard Representation Agreement (SRA) attempts to alleviate these concerns by providing terminated contract advisors "the reasonable value of the services performed in the attempted negotiation of such contract(s) provided such services and time spent thereon are adequately documented by Contract Advisor."[66] Indeed, this *quantum meruit* provision of the SRA is a frequent subject of arbitrations between players and their former contract advisors.[67] However, NFLPA Arbitrator Kaplan strictly applies the documentation requirements and limits the hourly rate a contract advisor can obtain to $250/hour,[68] and the amounts awarded are generally far less than the commission would have been had the contract advisor completed negotiations.[x]

Relatedly, there is a potential conflict concerning short- and long-term interests. The contract advisor only gets paid while the player is playing, and thus may have an interest in having the player continue playing, even when it might not be in the best interests of the player's long-term health.

- **The contract advisor's representation of multiple players on the same club.** Each NFL club is only permitted to pay players in aggregate up to the limit of the Salary Cap. Thus, there is a finite amount of money to be divided among the club's players. If a contract advisor represents two players on the same club, every dollar a contract advisor is able to secure for one player is one less dollar that is available to the other player.

- **The contract advisor's representation of multiple players at the same position.** If the players are comparably skilled, contract advisors might market one player's services at the expense of the other. Creative Artists Agency (CAA) Contract Advisor Tom Condon and former CAA Contract Advisor Ben Dogra,[69] among the most powerful in the business, have faced some scrutiny for being in such a situation. For example, in the 2012 NFL Draft, CAA was recruiting top quarterback prospect Andrew Luck who was expected to be and ultimately was chosen with the first overall pick by the Indianapolis Colts.[70] However, at the same time, CAA represented then Colts quarterback Peyton Manning, recovering from an injury.[71] Some commentators thus questioned whether CAA could encourage the Colts to draft Luck while also looking out for the best interests of Manning.[72] In addition, CAA represented several of the other top quarterbacks in the NFL at the time, including Drew Brees, Eli Manning, Matt Ryan, Matthew Stafford, and Sam Bradford.[73] In the end, Luck decided not to sign with CAA.[74]

Moreover, in that same offseason, San Francisco 49ers quarterback Alex Smith, also represented by CAA, reportedly contemplated terminating CAA as his representatives because there was speculation that the 49ers wanted Manning as their quarterback.[75] Smith was ultimately traded to the Kansas City Chiefs, did not terminate CAA,[76] and Manning signed with the Denver Broncos. In CAA's defense, CAA's experience in negotiating quarterback contracts, generally the richest in the NFL, certainly serves Smith and the other quarterbacks represented by CAA well.

- **The contract advisor's representation of multiple players contemplated to be the top pick in the NFL Draft.** For example, speculation has been raised in multiple NFL Drafts that contract advisors, by representing several of the top prospects, could not properly advocate for each player to be considered the top pick and thus receive a larger contract.[77] Although the issue has been raised,[78] no known action has been taken against any contract advisor (which is not to necessarily suggest that any conflicts of interest rules have been violated).

---

w   Contract Advisor 4 also believes that the NFLPA's failure to enforce the Contract Advisor Regulations prohibitions against soliciting and offering inducements to players that are other contract advisors' clients contributes to this conflicted scenario: "[T]he NFLPA doesn't really care about [these situations; they have] turned a blind eye." Relatedly, Contract Advisor 4 explained: "I think we agents probably feel the most pressure, and that's where the conflicts come from, is the idea of losing players for no good reason when you're trying to do your best job. There are a lot of agents who do try to do their best job but have to worry about the idea of a player being scooped up because someone else stole them."

x   In rare instances, Arbitrator Kaplan has awarded the terminated contract advisor a percentage of the contract ultimately negotiated by the player or another contract advisor if the terms were significantly similar to those negotiated by the terminated contract advisor. *See* Harrison v. Peek, NFLPA Case No. 07-38 (Kaplan, Arb. 2007) (awarding terminated contract advisor the agreed-upon 2 percent commission where player terminated contract advisor but signed contract negotiated by contract advisor); Lock/Metz v. Galloway, NFLPA Case No. 00-26 (Kaplan, Arb. 2001) (awarding terminated contract Advisors 1.25% of $12 million signing bonus where contract's elements "had been primarily and substantially negotiated" by prior Contract Advisors); Professional Stars, Inc. v. Townsend, NFLPA Case No. 95-11 (Kaplan, Arb. 1996) (awarding terminated Contract Advisor the agreed-upon 2% commission where player terminated Contract Advisor but signed contract negotiated by Contract Advisor).

In each of the above-described situations where a contract advisor's loyalties to two clients might seem at odds, the contract advisor's defense is likely to be that his or her role or ability to influence NFL clubs is being overstated, that clubs carefully make personnel and contract decisions and are not likely to be influenced in any way by a contract advisor's sales pitches. As Contract Advisor 4 explained: "The team is deciding who they want. I would describe the agent's role more in terms of helping the player get as much money as possible."

- **The contract advisor's representation of club executives and coaches.** Contract advisors are permitted to represent club executives and coaches provided they disclose those representations to the player-clients.[79] These relationships (which are not uncommon)[y] are not surprising considering many players go on to become coaches or executives and wish to retain the services of the contract advisor from their playing days. The potential conflicts in these situations are obvious—a contract advisor's advocacy and negotiation efforts on behalf of a player could be in direct conflict with the interests (financial or otherwise) of the club executive or coach the contract advisor also represents.

Figure 12-A: Potential Conflicts of Interest for Contract Advisors

1	The contract advisor's relationship with club officials.
2	The contract advisor's compensation structure.
3	The contract advisor's representation of multiple players on the same club.
4	The contract advisor's representation of multiple players at the same position.
5	The contract advisor's representation of multiple players contemplated to be the top pick in the NFL Draft.
6	The contract advisor's representation of club executives and coaches.

---

y   There are and have been several successful contract advisors who represent both NFL players and club personnel. *See* Pete Thamel, *How Jimmy Sexton became college football's most powerful agent,* Sports Illustrated, Jan. 3, 2014, http://www.si.com/college-football/2014/01/03/jimmy-sexton-college-football, *archived at* http://perma.cc/N5UT-HXMF; Anthony L. Salvador, *The Regulation of Dual Representation in the NFL,* 13 Tex. Rev. Ent. & Sports L. 63, 65–66 (2011).

(E) Enforcement of Legal and Ethical Obligations[z]

The Contract Advisor Regulations provide an arbitration mechanism that is generally the exclusive mechanism by which NFL players can bring a claim against a contract advisor for a violation of the contract advisor's obligations. Specifically, the Contract Advisor Regulations arbitration procedures govern, in relevant part, "[a]ny dispute between an NFL player and a Contract Advisor with respect to the conduct of individual negotiations by a Contract Advisor," "[t]he meaning, interpretation or enforcement of a fee agreement," and "[a]ny other activities of a Contract Advisor within the scope of the[] [NFLPA] Regulations."[80]

The arbitrations are commenced with the filing of a grievance, generally followed by a hearing where each side has the opportunity to present evidence and witnesses.[81] Arbitrator Roger Kaplan has presided over almost every NFLPA arbitration since 1994.[82] Kaplan is empowered to and regularly awards monetary damages to both contract advisors and players.

The NFLPA's arbitration provisions preempt civil lawsuits and thus have effectively eliminated player-contract advisor litigation. Consequently, a player's best recourse against a contract advisor is to pursue damages through the NFLPA arbitration process.[83] Each year there are dozens of grievances filed between contract advisors and players. However, a review of the NFLPA's arbitration cases reveals only one case concerning player health, safety or welfare: *Mayes v. Zucker.*

In *Mayes v. Zucker*,[84] the arbitrator awarded former Miami Dolphin Alonzo Mayes $100,000 in damages against his former contract advisor. The Dolphins had cut Mayes after he suffered a knee injury and his contract advisor failed to file an Injury Grievance on Mayes' behalf, which would have entitled Mayes to his salary for the amount of games for which the injury would have prevented him from playing. The contract advisor's NFLPA-certification was also revoked in a separate decision arising out of the same facts.

Importantly, while the arbitration process settles disputes between contract advisors and players (or other contract advisors), it is not the process by which contract advisors are disciplined for violations of the Contract Advisor Regulations. The NFLPA has a three- to five-player Committee on Agent Regulation and Discipline (CARD), which is responsible for investigating and taking disciplinary action against contract advisors.[85] CARD issues a complaint to the contract advisor and, after the contract advisor files an answer, CARD issues its discipline.[86] CARD's disciplinary authority includes letters of reprimand, suspensions, fines, prohibitions on recruiting, and revocation of the contract advisor's NFLPA-certification.[87] The contract advisor can appeal any discipline to Kaplan, who will hold a hearing as he would pursuant to a dispute between or among contract advisors and players.[88]

At the 2015 Harvard Symposium on Sports & Entertainment Law, NFLPA Assistant General Counsel Heather McPhee explained that the quality of contract advisors "run[s] the gamut" and that enforcement of the Contract Advisor Regulations is difficult because the NFLPA only has five attorneys who work on those types of issues in addition to their other legal work.[aa] McPhee further explained that "evidentiary" issues create enforcement issues, *e.g.*, allegations are hard to prove, particularly if players are unwilling to testify. Consequently, McPhee expressed that the NFLPA is often only able to enforce "really egregious" violations of the Contract Advisor Regulations.

The NFLPA representative we interviewed echoed McPhee's comments in many respects, explaining that when it comes to proving a violation of the Contract Advisor Regulations, "filing a sworn statement or turning over proof, all of a sudden [the Contract Advisors] start clamming up." The NFLPA representative believes that the NFLPA has done "a pretty good job" of enforcing the Contract Advisor Regulations, but that "[i]t could always be improved." Finally, the NFLPA representative affirmed that "where a player's being harmed financially, that's something that we go after hard and heavy."

---

z   Appendix K is a summary of players' options to enforce legal and ethical obligations against the stakeholders discussed in this Report.

aa   As discussed in Chapter 7: The NFL and NFLPA, Section J: Current Practices of the NFLPA, many contract advisors also believe the NFLPA is understaffed. One contract advisor that we spoke with expressed the belief that "the NFLPA is severely understaffed," while another explained that in his opinion the NFLPA does a "terrible job" of policing club medical staff and enforcing player health and safety provisions of the CBA because, in part, it is "absolutely not" adequately staffed. Similarly, another contract advisor said it would help "100 percent" if the NFLPA hired more attorneys focused on health issues.

(F) Recommendations Concerning Contract Advisors

Contract advisors are a critical stakeholder in protecting and advancing player health.[ab] Indeed, peer reviewer and former contract advisor and NFL club executive Andrew Brandt noted in his comments that contract advisors "are the gateway to the player" and thus are "key stakeholders in player health issues."[89] A contract advisor is typically involved in all aspects of a player's life, including but not limited to his personal, career, medical, legal, and financial matters. They have the ability to ensure that the player receives proper medical care during his career, that the player's health-related rights are respected and that the player considers the risks of an NFL career while at the same time helping to prepare the player for a life after football.

While some may think that the role of contract advisors is further afield from health than other stakeholders in this Report, it is important to bear in mind our broad definition of health, as explained in the Introduction. We define health for purposes of this Report as "a state of overall wellbeing in fundamental aspects of a person's life, including physical, mental, emotional, social, familial, and financial components." To truly improve player health we cannot focus solely on avoiding brain injury, protecting joints, and promoting cardiovascular health, for example, but we must also address well-being more generally, which depends on other factors, such as the existence of family and social support, the ability to meet economic needs, and life satisfaction. Contract advisors play a critical role in all of these aspects of player health.

Nevertheless, as explained above, there are structural and regulatory issues with the contract advisor industry that prevent players from receiving the best possible representation and the best possible protection of their health-related rights. Improvements to the contract advisor industry should increase the level of professionalism in the industry, reduce unethical behavior, increase stability in contract advisor operations, and most importantly, help players receive the guidance and representation they deserve, particularly on health-related matters. Simply put, improvements in player health require sufficient representation and enforcement concerning player rights. Sufficient representation and enforcement will not come unless the contract advisor industry is improved.

Before getting to contract advisor-specific recommendations, there are additional recommendations concerning contract advisors that are made in other chapters:

- Chapter 1: Players—Recommendation 1:1-A: With assistance from contract advisors, the NFL, the NFLPA, and others, players should familiarize themselves with their rights and obligations related to health and other benefits, and should avail themselves of applicable benefits.

- Chapter 13: Financial Advisors—Recommendation 13:1-A: Players should be encouraged by the NFL, NFLPA, and contract advisors to work exclusively with NFLPA-registered financial advisors.

In addition to these recommendations, and in light of the above background and the important role that contract advisors are capable of playing in protecting and promoting player health, we recommend the following:

> **Goal 1: To recognize contract advisors as an important resource alongside the NFLPA in their shared endeavor to advance player interests, and to seek opportunities to strengthen their connections whenever possible.**

Principles Advanced: Respect; Health Primacy; and, Collaboration and Engagement.

---

ab   Current Player 8 explained that "there are many, many guys that . . . need an agent to help them transition, and help them in their everyday lives of the NFL."

Recommendations Concerning Contract Advisors – continued

Recommendation 12:1-A: The NFLPA should create a Contract Advisor Committee that meets with NFLPA representatives at least twice a year to discuss issues affecting NFL player health, as defined broadly in this Report to include health, finances, education, and the like.

It seems clear that the relationship between the NFLPA and contract advisors could be considerably stronger. By law, contract advisors are agents of the NFLPA—acting in largely the same capacity as the NFLPA, *i.e.*, protecting players' best interests. Contract advisors are typically players' most trusted guides and the ones who take on almost all dealings with NFL clubs. For these reasons, the NFLPA should view contract advisors as partners in protecting players' rights, particularly when it comes to their health, and should develop formal mechanisms for contract advisors to pass along their knowledge, experience, concerns, and suggestions. A committee comprised of contract advisors would provide such a mechanism. Without getting into the specifics of the precise structure and terms of this proposed committee, we simply emphasize that the committee members should reflect a wide range of clientele, and systems should be put in place to allow all contract advisors to be heard.

Recommendation 12:1-B: The NFLPA should provide contract advisors with a copy of all materials and advice that it provides to players concerning player health.

Contract advisors typically serve as the main conduits and filters for information and documents to players. Given their trust in their contract advisors and competing demands for their time, many players might only pay serious attention to information or a document if their contract advisor tells them to read it. The NFLPA provides players with documents during training camp and at other times during the season and offseason concerning various topics, including their rights, current issues, and their health. While the NFLPA does make summaries of the benefit plans available to contract advisors via a password-protected website, contract advisors that we interviewed expressed that the NFLPA does not otherwise provide contract advisors with copies of the documents it is providing to players.[ac] During its review of this Report, the NFLPA stated that it believes it does provide contract advisors with all such documents. Without resolving this dispute, in order to ensure that the players take the notices seriously, the NFLPA should provide a copy of these documents related to health, as defined broadly by this Report, to contract advisors so that they can confirm that the player received and properly considered the information. Again, the NFLPA should consider contract advisors as its partners in representing and protecting players.

Goal 2: To improve professionalism and ethical conduct within the contract advisor industry.

Principles Advanced: Respect; Health Primacy; Empowered Autonomy; Transparency; Managing Conflicts of Interest; and, Justice.

Recommendation 12:2-A: The NFLPA should amend the Contract Advisor Regulations to prohibit loans or advances from contract advisors to players or prospective players in excess of the costs reasonable and necessary to prepare for the NFL Draft.

ac   Contract Advisor 4: "I don't know what they [the NFLPA] share with the players."

Recommendations Concerning Contract Advisors – continued

The NFLPA Contract Advisor Regulations forbid "[p]roviding or offering money or any other thing of value to any player or prospective player to induce or encourage that player to utilize his/her services."[90] However, many (but not all) contract advisors routinely provide new clients with tens or hundreds of thousands of dollars in loans or advances that generally do not have to be repaid if the player continues to retain the contract advisor. The NFLPA arbitrator has routinely found such arrangements not to be in violation of the NFLPA Contract Advisor Regulations based on a questionable legal analysis.

Although such arrangements would seem to benefit players by providing them with significant amounts of money up front, permitting these loans and advances may actually work to the detriment of players to the extent they cause players to choose their contract advisors for the wrong reasons—cash over competence, integrity, and experience. As a result, what appears to be a windfall in the short-term can result in long-term deficits to the player.

For example, an inadequate contract advisor might fail to tell the player he has the right to a second medical opinion or might arrange for a second medical opinion by an unqualified doctor. The contract advisor might not know how to appropriately work with the NFLPA in protecting a player's rights, such as filing a grievance. The contract advisor might also avoid filing a grievance to avoid spoiling his or her relationship with the club. Moreover, the contract advisor might not adequately assist the player in taking advantage of the benefits and programs available to him to prepare for life after football.

Accordingly, we recommend limiting loans and advances from contract advisors to the costs reasonable and necessary to prepare players for the NFL Draft. The NFLPA should consider developing a maximum amount (to grow annually at some nominal rate) that contract advisors may loan or advance to players for training purposes and treat any amount above that as presumptively violative. This will help players focus on competence over short-term benefits when selecting contract advisors and allow them more freedom to end relationships with contract advisors who are not working out, as they will avoid having large debts that come due only if and when they select a new contract advisor.

In terms of enforcement, NFLPA Contract Advisor Regulations already require contract advisors to provide the NFLPA with a copy of any agreement between the contract advisor and player.[91] Thus, the NFLPA should review those agreements to determine whether the amounts being advanced or loaned appear to be acceptable and investigate as appropriate. To further assist in enforcement, the NFLPA should also require that all agreements between a contract advisor and a player be in writing.

Recommendation 12:2-B: The NFLPA should consider investing greater resources in investigating and enforcing the Contract Advisor Regulations.

As discussed above, there are serious problems with the contract advisor industry that sometimes result in substandard representation for and advice to the players, including poor handling of player health matters. Additionally, the NFLPA admittedly has difficulty enforcing the Contract Advisor Regulations. Without meaningful enforcement, the Regulations lose their effectiveness to the detriment of players. One possibility is hiring more attorneys to focus on these matters.

Recommendation 12:2-C: Players should be given information to ensure that they choose contract advisors based on their professional qualifications and experience and not the financial benefits the contract advisor has or is willing to provide to the player.

Recommendations Concerning Contract Advisors – continued

As discussed above, prospective NFL players often choose their contract advisors not based on their professional qualifications but instead on how much the contract advisor is willing to "loan" or "advance" to the player. Players understandably are excited about the opportunity to receive large sums from the contract advisors simply for letting the contract advisor represent them. However, players do so at their own peril. As Contract Advisor 4 stated:

> "[I]f a player wants to make a business decision based on how much money they're being given or advanced, well, then that's their right . . . . The sad thing, of course, is when they're young, they're from more difficult socioeconomic backgrounds, so they don't understand that when you take money or you take some sort of favor for the right to represent them, that . . . you're only going to get what you paid for . . . . [J]ust as you wouldn't go to the heart doctor for your heart surgery that's going to give you the most money . . . [y]ou want to go to the best doctor. And we see every day players wondering why am I getting improper guidance, why am I getting poor advice, why am I being left to hang out to dry. And sometimes I'll tell them to look in the mirror and ask why did I choose the people around me that I did. And often times it's because of the financial advances, financial favors that they were given."

If the Contract Advisor Regulations are not amended to prohibit such arrangements as recommended above, it is important that the players at least understand the downsides of choosing their contract advisor based on loans or advances.[ad]

However, presently, there are minimal resources for players about how to choose a contract advisor. While colleges might be able to help players, they are not experts in the contract advisor industry and often have their own interests which might conflict with the player's—such as when the player is considering leaving college even though he has college eligibility remaining.[92]

The NFLPA has the potential to be the best resource for helping players choose contract advisors appropriately and does make some effort on this topic. The NFLPA conducts "Pipeline to the Pros" with current college football players to try to inform them about the process of becoming an NFL player, including hiring a contract advisor.[93] In addition, the NFLPA's website includes a page advising "Active Players" on "How to Pick Your Agent,"[94] but the page is sparse on information. The NFLPA only lists five recommendations for consideration in picking a contract advisor:

(1) The primary reason you hire an agent is to negotiate your NFL Player Contract. Your agent should be skilled at negotiating the following: Signing Bonus; Paragraph 5 Salary; Roster, Report and Workout Bonuses; and, Incentives.

(2) Interview several there are more than 850 certified agents (sic).

(3) Verify clients represented.[ae]

(4) Contact the NFLPA and/or utilize the agent search feature on this website to ensure the agent is active and in good standing.

(5) Familiarize yourself with the NFLPA Regulations Governing Contract Advisors and understand required and prohibited conduct for the agents.

---

ad Contract Advisor 5: "[P]layers have a tendency to focus in on the fee, focus in on the flavor of the month, so to speak, and just worry about what kind of contract they think they're gonna get or what the agent promises them. And I think what happens is that the player doesn't understand that really this is from A, which is the start of their career, to B, the end of their career, to C, which is after their career."

ae During the recruiting process, the contract advisor will generally make the player aware of other players the contract advisor purportedly represents, to try and demonstrate the contract advisor's skill. A list of contract advisor's clients is available to players after they are in the NFL—but not before. Thus, before the player enters the NFL, the best resource for confirming a contract advisor's clients is the NFLPA. Players should also seek to discuss the quality of a contract advisor's services with current and/or former clients.

Recommendations Concerning Contract Advisors – continued

Notably, each of these steps is fairly burdensome for the players. Additionally, the NFLPA's site does not include any information on the contract advisor hiring process, the types of services contract advisors must or can provide, potential conflicts of interest, or the types of fee and contractual arrangements between contract advisors and players (such as loans and advances) and the benefits and drawbacks of such arrangements.

The NFLPA is in a powerful position to help prospective NFL players pick contract advisors. While such players are not yet in the NFLPA's bargaining unit (and thus the NFLPA has no legal obligations towards them, see Chapter 7: The NFL and NFLPA), hundreds of college players will soon be NFLPA members and their decisions concerning a contract advisor while still in college can have a significant impact on their NFL career. Although the NFLPA provides some guidance to players about the process, problems clearly remain. The NFLPA could expand and intensify the information made available to prospective NFL players and could work with both the NCAA and the NFL (both of which more closely track potential NFL players) to ensure that the right players are receiving the necessary information. The NFLPA should also consider creating a system whereby players are able to rate their contract advisors' performance and that data could be made available, including but not limited to a regular survey, a Yelp-like service, or some other form of information-sharing.

Recommendation 12:2-D: The Contract Advisor Regulations should be amended to require contract advisors to consider a player's long-term health interests in providing representation and advice.

It is clear that a player's career can be short and that the physical and mental tolls of a career can be permanent. Players will often take physical risks to maximize their earnings, even if those earnings come at the cost of future health. Balancing these risks and rewards is difficult. Nevertheless, the long-term effects of a player's decision—including whether to play through an injury and how to structure a contract—must be taken into consideration. Contract advisors must be aware, and make sure the players are aware, of these short-term versus long-term trade-offs.

Contract advisors should continue to be a resource for players after their careers are over. Even though contract advisors are no longer compensated once a player's career ends, players are still likely to view them as their most trusted and best resource for many matters in life, including, specifically, items related to the CBA, such as various benefits and programs. While contract advisors are likely to help former players because it is in their own business interests, they should also recognize that a player will view ongoing assistance as a logical and natural extension of their relationship during the player's playing days.

Recommendation 12:2-E: The NFLPA should amend the Contract Advisor Regulations to prohibit contract advisors from revealing a player's medical information or condition to anyone without the player's consent.

Players are obligated by the CBA to advise the club of any injury or medical condition. Contract advisors might often be a conduit for this information, particularly where the player has been seen by a second opinion doctor. Thus, it is unclear that there is a problem with contract advisors disclosing player medical information to clubs without the player's consent. Nevertheless, considering the importance of the information, we believe it is a practice that should be more closely examined.

Recommendations Concerning Contract Advisors – continued

There are numerous laws and ethical rules that make clear that an individual's medical history, conditions, and records are entitled to the utmost confidentiality. These laws and rules emanate from respect for people's privacy and recognition that people generally should not be discriminated against based on medical conditions. As explained in Chapter 2: Club Doctors, these confidentiality protections can only be bypassed with the individual's consent or in certain rare situations. Contract advisors should similarly be required to hold in confidence a player's medical condition where the condition is not otherwise public knowledge. While there may be many legitimate reasons for a contract advisor to disclose a player's medical history or condition to a third party, such as a club interested in drafting or signing the player, considering the sensitivity of the information, the contract advisor should involve the player in important processes related to their health and obtain consent to disclose such information.

Recommendation 12:2-F: The NFLPA should consider including at least one non-player member on the Committee on Agent Regulation and Discipline (CARD).

CARD is responsible for investigating and disciplining contract advisors for violations of the NFLPA Contract Advisor Regulations. However, the most egregious and regular violations of the NFLPA Contract Advisor Regulations are those that, on their face, seem to benefit players—large payouts and other improper inducements. As discussed above, these practices undermine the industry's professionalism at the expense of the players and their health. Yet players serving on CARD might not consider these practices to be as detrimental as they are, perhaps because they themselves took benefits or inducements at one time, or know teammates or friends who have, or know and like contract advisors who have provided such inducements.

Adding a law professor or attorney familiar with the sports industry to CARD would provide a different and independent perspective on the relevant issues and practices. Although the NFLPA assists CARD members in their investigations, adding a neutral member to the Committee would strengthen the process.

Recommendation 12:2-G: The NFLPA should consider whether there are structural or regulatory changes that can be made to the contract advisor industry to remove or reduce possible conflicts of interests, including situations where the contract advisor represents players on the same club, players at the same position, and/or players in the same NFL Draft.

As discussed above, there are a variety of situations and practices that could pose conflicts for contract advisors or, at a minimum, present the appearance of a conflict. It is not clear whether these potential conflicts are in fact harming players or how these conflicts can be removed or reduced without also harming players. For example, if a player were to be represented by a contract advisor devoid of any possible conflicts, *i.e.*, one who does not represent any other players at the same position, on the same team, in free agency, or have relationships with club personnel, the player might easily end up being represented by an inexperienced and marginally skilled advisor.

Recommendations Concerning Contract Advisors – continued

One possibility is for contract advisors to disclose these potential conflicts to their clients. Indeed, those contract advisors who are also attorneys are required to obtain their client's informed consent before proceeding with a conflicted representation.[95] However, research has shown that sometimes disclosing conflicts can actually increase the level of trust between the biased advisor and the person to whom the conflict is disclosed.[96] Moreover, disclosure does not remove the potential conflict.

There are no clear answers, but the NFLPA should more closely examine the issue via analyzing past and future situations that might present conflicts, and by discussing the issue with players and contract advisors.

Endnotes

1 U.S.C. § 159(a).

2 White v. Nat'l Football League, 92 F. Supp. 2d 918, 924 (D. Minn. 2000).

3 *See* Black v. Nat'l Football League Players Ass'n, 87 F. Supp. 2d 1, 2 (D.D.C. 2000) ("NFLPA nevertheless permits individual agents, or 'contract advisors,' to represent individual players in negotiations with NFL Clubs."); White v. Nat'l Football League, 92 F. Supp. 2d 918, 924 (D.Minn. 2000) ("Player agents are permitted to negotiate player contracts in the NFL only because the NFLPA has delegated a portion of its exclusive representational authority to them."). *See also* Magic Pan, Inc. v. NLRB, 627 F.2d 105, 109–10 (7th Cir. 1980), *citing* General Electric Co. v. NLRB, 412 F.2d 512, 520 n.6 (2d Cir. 1969) (explaining relationship between unions and agents); Richard T. Karcher, *Fundamental Fairness in Union Regulation of Sports Agents*, 40 Conn. L. Rev. 355, 359 (2007) (describing union's authority to delegate responsibility for player contract negotiations to agents).

4 *See* 1993 CBA, Art. VI; see also 2011 CBA, Art. 48 (discussing NFLPA's authority to govern agents and discipline for Clubs which negotiate with non-certified agents).

5 *See* Dan Cook. *Sports agents busy chasing sweetest deals,* San Antonio Express-News, July 4, 1999, available at 1999 WLNR 7890207.

6 Anndee Hochman, *Manley Case to Players Union,* Wash. Post, Jan. 26, 1985, available at 1985 WLNR 1507095.

7 *See* Brian Schmitz, *Agents Agree that Unscrupulous Practitioners Give Field Bad Name*, Orlando Sentinel, Jun. 12, 1988, *available at* 1988 WLNR 2014977 (discussing problems in the sports agency business with focus on football and basketball industries); Doug Bedell, *The Crackdown on Agents,* Dallas Morning News, July 19, 1987, *available at* 1987 WLNR 1923190 (same); Mitch Lawrence, *A Bad Deal: Player Agents and College Athletes,* Dallas Morning News, Nov. 10, 1985, *available at* 1985 WLNR 1326922 (same).

8 *See NFLPA is no longer labor group,* Dallas Morning News, Dec. 6, 1989 available at 1989 WLNR 3102115.

9 See Larry Weisman, *Redskins Get a Good Four-Year Deal in Harvey,* USA Today, Mar. 9, 1994, available at 1994 WLNR 2322485 (referencing NFLPA's inability to regulate Contract Advisors during legal dispute with NFL).

10 See Bob Oates, *With Free Agency Won, NFLPA Ready to Recertify as a Union,* L.A. Times, Mar. 14, 1993, *available at* 1993 WLNR 3986006.

11 Contract Advisor Regulations, § 3(A)(17).

12 The 2012 Contract Advisor Regulations are available from the NFLPA's website at http://nflparesources.blob.core.windows.net/mediaresources/files/PDFs/SCAA/2012_NFLPA_Regulations_Contract_Advisors.pdf.

13 Contract Advisor Regulations, § 2(A).

14 *Id.* The NFLPA's enforcement of its rules was tested when the rap and entertainment mogul Jay-Z announced the creation of Roc Nation Sports, a prospective athlete representation firm, in 2013. Jay-Z did not graduate high school and was presumably not interested in taking the NFLPA's exam. Jay-Z evaded the Contract Advisor Regulations by hiring Kim Miale, a certified contract advisor, to work for Roc Nation Sports. Nevertheless, because he was not certified, Jay-Z was thought not to be permitted to engage in recruiting on behalf of Roc Nation Sports. The NFLPA provided Jay-Z a reprieve when it issued a memorandum stating non-Contract Advisor employees could sit in on recruiting meetings held at the contract advisor's office. *See* Darren A. Heitner and Bryan Saul, *Jay Z Has 99 Problems, And Being a Sports Agent May Be One*, 24 Marq. Sports L. Rev. 59 (2013); Jason Cole, *NFLPA Adopts Jay-Z Rule*, Nat'l Football Post (Dec. 6, 2013, 5:53 PM), http://www.nationalfootballpost.com/NFLPA-adopts-JayZ-Rule.html, *archived at* http://perma.cc/7YD9-JYLP (discussing NFLPA's memorandum on the issue).

15 Agent Certification FAQs, NFLPA, https://nflpa.com/agents/faq (last visited Aug. 7, 2015).

16 *Id.*

17 A player is not eligible for the NFL Draft "until three NFL regular seasons have begun and ended following either his graduation from high school or graduation of the class with which he entered high school, whichever is earlier." 2011 CBA, Art. 6, § 2. From 2007 to 2012, contract advisors were prohibited from recruiting players until they were eligible for the NFL Draft. The "Junior Rule," as it was known, only empowered those contract advisors who disregarded the Junior Rule as well as "runners," who are not regulated by the NFLPA. As a result, in 2012, the Contract Advisor Regulations were amended to remove the Junior Rule. Mike Florio, *NFLPA dumps "junior rule"* ProFootballTalk (Mar. 27, 2012, 6:00 PM), http://profootballtalk.nbcsports.com/2012/03/27/nflpa-dumps-junior-rule/, *archived at* http://perma.cc/W53W-KT7H.

18 *See* Mike Florio, *Good agents do a lot more than negotiate contracts,* ProFootballTalk (July 23, 2015, 11:01 AM), http://profootballtalk.nbcsports.com/2015/07/23/good-agents-do-a-lot-more-than-negotiate-contracts/, *archived at* http://perma.cc/UWB8-DXC3.

19 "The term "compensation" shall be deemed to include only salaries, signing bonuses, reporting bonuses, roster bonuses, Practice Squad salary in excess of the minimum Practice Squad salary specified in Article 33 of the Collective Bargaining Agreement, and any performance incentives earned by the player during the term of the contract (including any option year) negotiated by the Contract Advisor. For example, and without limitation, the term compensation shall not include any "honor" incentive bonuses (e.g. ALL PRO, PRO BOWL, Rookie of the Year), or any collectively bargained benefits or other payments provided for in the player's individual contract." 2012 NFLPA Contract Advisor Regulations, § 4(B)(3).

20 NFLPA Contract Advisor Regulations, § 4(B)(1).

21 Each year, clubs can designate one unrestricted free agent as a "Franchise Player" and one unrestricted free agent as a "Transition Player." These designations provide the clubs the opportunity to match any offers made to the players and to receive draft picks as compensation in the event the players sign with another club. In exchange, the players are guaranteed a one-year contract that makes them among the highest paid at their position. *See* 2011 CBA, Art. 10.

22 NFLPA Contract Advisor Regulations, § 4(B)(1)(a).

23 NFLPA Contract Advisor Regulations, § 4(B)(4).

24 ¶ 12 of the NFLPA Standard Representation Agreement, which can be found as Appendix D-4 to the 2012 NFLPA Contract Advisor Regulations.

25 *See* Restatement (Third) of Agency § 1.01 (2006) ("Agency is the fiduciary relationship that arises when one person (a 'principal') manifests assent to another person (an 'agent') that the agent shall act on the principal's behalf and subject to the principal's control, and the agent manifests assent or otherwise consents so to act.")

26 *See id.* § 8.03, cmt. d (describing agent's duty of undivided loyalty); *id.* § 8.08 (2006) (explaining agent's duty to act with care, competence and diligence of agents in similar circumstances); *id.* § 8.10 (stating that agent has duty "to refrain from conduct that is likely to damage the principal's enterprise").

27 "Duty," Black's Law Dictionary (9th ed. 2009).

28 Ritani, LLC v. Aghjayan, 880 F. Supp. 2d 425, 455 (S.D.N.Y. 2012) (applying New York law); Carcano v. JBSS, LLC, 200 N.C.App. 162, 177 (N.C.App. 2009); L.C. v. R.P., 563 N.W.2d 799, 802 (N.D. 1997); Allen Realty Corp. v. Holbert, 227 Va. 441, 447 (Va. 1984); Murphy v. Country House, Inc., 307 Minn. 344, 350 (Minn. 1976).

29 NFLPA Contract Advisor Regulations, § 3(A).

30 The UAAA defines an "athlete agent" as: an individual who enters into an agency contract with a student-athlete or, directly or indirectly, recruits or solicits a student-athlete to enter into an agency contract. The term includes an individual who represents to the public that the individual

is an athlete agent. The term does not include a spouse, parent, sibling, [or] grandparent[, or guardian] of the student-athlete or an individual acting solely on behalf of a professional sports team or professional sports organization. UAAA, § 2(2).

31 *Uniform Athletes Agents Act*, National Conference of Commissioners on Uniform State Laws, Aug. 4, 2000, http://www.uniformlaws.org/shared/docs/athlete_agents/uaaa_finalact_2000.pdf, *archived at* https://perma.cc/798J-QENC?type=pdf.

32 *Id.*

33 Marc Edelman, *Will The New Uniform Athlete Agents Act Continue To Pander To The NCAA?*, Forbes (June 4, 2013 9:00 AM), http://www.forbes.com/sites/marcedelman/2013/06/04/will-the-new-uniform-athlete-agents-act-continue-to-pander-to-the-ncaa/, *archived at* https://perma.cc/ALC6-79CS?type=pdf; *see also Athlete Agents Acts*, Uniform Laws Comm'n, http://www.uniformlaws.org/Act.aspx?title=Athlete%20Agents%20Act (last visited Aug. 7, 2015), *archived at* http://perma.cc/V223-PE7Q (showing the status of the UAAA across the country).

34 *See* Chris Deubert, *What's A Clean Agent to Do? The Case for a Cause of Action Against a Players Association*, 18 Vill. Sports & Ent. L.J. 1, 6–10 (2011) (discussing problems with the UAAA).

35 *See id.* at 10–11 (discussing other states' agent laws).

36 *See* Morton v. Steinberg, No. G037793, 2007 WL 3076934 (Cal.Ct.App. Oct. 22, 2007).

37 *Id.*

38 *See* Bernie Wilson, *Steinberg is Dealing with the Fallout from Drinking*, The Augusta Chronicle Jan. 15, 2012, available at 2012 WLNR 1050482 (discussing Steinberg's outstanding debt to Morton of $450,000 as of January 2012).

39 Sports Agent Responsibility and Trust Act, 15 U.S.C. §§ 7801–7807.

40 *See* Deubert, *supra* note 34 at 11–12 (discussing problems with SPARTA).

41 *Id.*

42 *See Who We Are*, Nat'l Collegiate Athletic Ass'n, http://www.ncaa.org/about/who-we-are (last visited Aug. 7, 2015), *archived at* http://perma.cc/2S7M-GL89; *Membership*, Nat'l Collegiate Athletic Ass'n, http://www.ncaa.org/about/who-we-are/membership (last visited Aug. 7, 2015), *archived at* http://perma.cc/5J5P-RQ2V (describing membership as more than 1,200 schools).

43 *See* NCAA v. Tarkanian, 488 U.S. 179 (1988) (discussing scope of NCAA's power).

44 −14 NCAA Division I Manual, § 12.1.2.

45 *See* UAAA §§ 15, 17 (2000) (explaining that violations of parts of act prohibiting certain conduct may result in criminal and administrative punishments).

46 Deubert, *supra* note 34 at 14.

47 This information was provided by the NFLPA.

48 "The term 'runner' generally describes someone employed by an agent, typically a young person, whose job is to become friendly with the student-athlete, providing the student-athlete with cash, meals, clothes or other gifts and ultimately steering the student-athlete towards the employing agent." Deubert, *supra* note 34 at 6.

49 *Model Rules of Prof'l Conduct*, Am. Bar Ass'n (2013), available at www.americanbar.org/groups/professional_responsibility/publications/model_rules_of_professional_conduct.html.

50 Information about the number of Contract Advisors and their clientele is on file with the NFLPA.

51 Contract Advisor Regulations, § 2(G). *See also* Kivisto v. Nat'l Football League Players Ass'n, 10-cv-24226, 2011 WL 335420 (S.D.Fla. 2011) (dismissing Contract Advisor's challenge to his decertification for having not negotiated an NFL contract in a three-year period), *aff'd* 435 Fed. Appx. 811 (11th Cir. 2011).

52 This information was provided by the NFLPA.

53 *See* Scott Kestenbaum, *Uniform Alternative Dispute Resolution: The Answer to Preventing Unscrupulous Agent Activity*, 14 Pepp. Disp. Resol.

L.J. 55, 56–58 (2014) (discussing recent scandals involving sports agents); James Masteralexis, Lisa Masteralexis and Kevin Snyder, *Enough is Enough: The Case for Federal Regulation of Sport Agents*, 20 Jeffrey S. Moorad Sports L.J. 69, 71 (2013) (same); Deubert, *supra* note 34 (discussing problems with the current agent regulatory scheme).

54 *See* Andrew Brandt, *An agent's life isn't all glamour*, ESPN, Nov. 27, 2012, http://espn.go.com/nfl/story/_/id/8681968/nfl-agent-life-all-glamour, *archived at* http://perma.cc/7VVL-CYBG (discussing realities of Contract Advisor industry).

55 See 2012 Contract Advisor Regulations, § 3(B)(2).

56 *See* Champion Pro Consulting Group, LLC v. Impact SportsFootball, LLC, 12-cv-27, 2015 WL 4392994, *2 (M.D.N.C. July 15, 2015) (discussing $100,000 advanced to NFL player Robert Quinn); Mike Florio, *As rookie money dries up, agents continue to cut great deals for players*, ProFootballTalk (Jan. 11, 2012, 1:17 PM), http://profootball-talk.nbcsports.com/2012/01/11/as-rookie-money-dries-up-agents-continue-to-cut-great-deals-for-players/, *archived at* http://perma.cc/KUM5-WFPB (discussing large advances and loans being provided to prospective clients).

57 *See, e.g.,* Rosenhaus v. Jackson, NFLPA Case No. 13-31 (Kaplan, Arb. Apr. 10, 2014) (player required to repay Contract Advisor $361,415 in loans made at the time the player became a client or shortly thereafter); Fleming v. Brown, NFLPA Case No. 13-29 (Kaplan, Arb. Mar. 18, 2014) (player required to repay Contract Advisor $60,875.45 in pre-draft loans and advances); Kiernan v. Rachal, NFLPA Case No. 13-2 (Kaplan, Arb. Jul. 18, 2013) (player required to repay Contract Advisor $43,573.76 in loans and advances); Martin v. Galette, NFLPA Case No. 10-40 (Kaplan, Arb. Mar. 1, 2011) (player required to repay Contract Advisor $21,978.10 in pre-draft loans); Canter v. Lee, NFLPA Case No. 08-40 (Kaplan, Arb. Apr. 9, 2009) (player required to repay Contract Advisor $9,228.42 in pre-draft loans).

58 Rosenhaus v. Jackson, NFLPA Case No. 13-31 (Kaplan, Arb. Apr. 10, 2014), at 34–35.

59 See, e.g., Mackler & Archambeau v. Nicks, NFLPA Case No. 08-38 (Kaplan, Arb. May 7, 2009) (player required to repay Contract Advisors $25,493.96 in training expenses).

60 "Magnetic resonance imaging (MRI) is a test that uses a magnetic field and pulses of radio wave energy to make pictures of organs and structures inside the body. In many cases, MRI gives different information about structures in the body than can be seen with an X-ray, ultrasound, or computed tomography (CT) scan." *Magnetic Resonance Imaging (MRI)*, WebMD, May 24, 2013, http://www.webmd.com/a-to-z-guides/magnetic-resonance-imaging-mri, *archived at* http://perma.cc/QC93-HA5B.

61 "A computed tomography (CT) scan uses X-rays to make detailed pictures of structures inside of the body." CT or CAT Scan, WebMD, Jun. 5, 2013, http://www.webmd.com/hw-popup/ct-or-cat-scan, *archived at* http://perma.cc/FB76-AP2P.

62 *See also* David Canter, *From Doctor to Watchdog to Friend*, ESPN (2000), http://espn.go.com/page2/s/confessions/001115agent.html, *archived at* http://perma.cc/8KTJ-S2CB (NFL Contract Advisor David Canter: "For some clients, I play doctor. I have to know detailed physical information about the injuries the players have suffered in the past. I have to know whether or not those injuries could be career-threatening or career-ending, and whether or not my client should see a doctor for a second opinion or if he should see a certain specialist."); Sally Jenkins & Rick Maese, *NFL Medical Standards, Practices Are Different Than Almost Anywhere Else*, Wash. Post. Mar. 16, 2013, http://www.washingtonpost.com/sports/redskins/nfl-medical-standards-practices-are-different-than-almost-anywhere-else/2013/03/16/b8c170bc-8be8-11e2-9f54-f3fdd70acad2_story.html, *archived at* http://perma.cc/AJ9Y-EAGY ("[NFL Contract Advisor] Smith demands his clients receive an MRI and second opinion for every injury. He estimates they diverge from the club physician's opinion 'four to five times out of every 25.'");

63 Jerry Cianciolo, *Get a second opinion*, Bos. Globe, Jan. 25, 2015, available at 2015 WLNR 2386857; *see also* Robert Klitzmann, *Second*

Opinions, Through a Patient's Eyes, N.Y. Times, Feb. 12, 2008, http://www.nytimes.com/2008/02/12/health/views/12essa.html?_r=0, *archived at* https://perma.cc/Z4AA-S386?type=pdf ("For 30 percent of patients who voluntarily seek second opinions for elective surgery and 18 percent of those whose insurance companies require it, the second doctors disagree with the first.")

64 *See also* Mark Fainaru-Wada and Steve Fainaru, League of Denial: The NFL, Concussions, and the Battle for Truth 76–82 (2013) (discussing the efforts of Leigh Steinberg, at one time one of the most powerful sports agents in the world, to educate his clients on the risks of concussions in the mid-1990s).

65 Andrew Brandt, Peer Review Response (Oct. 30, 2015).

66 NFLPA Contract Advisor Regulations, App. D, ¶ 12.

67 *See, e.g.*, Elnitski/Redden v. Wake, NFLPA Case No. 09-28 (Kaplan, Arb. 2010) (awarding terminated Contract Advisors $6,000 in *quantum meruit* for their efforts in negotiating contract before termination); Sarnoff v. Boldin, NFLPA Case No. 06-6 (Kaplan, Arb. 2006) (awarding terminated Contract Advisor $18,000 in *quantum meruit* for his efforts in negotiating contract before termination); Segal/Levy v. Lincoln, NFLPA Case No. 96-3 (Kaplan, Arb. 1997) (awarding terminated Contract Advisors $11,250 in *quantum meruit* for their efforts in negotiating contract before termination).

68 *See, e.g.*, Carey v. Quinn, NFLPA Case No. 12-13 (Kaplan, Arb. 2013) (awarding Contract Advisor Carl Carey only 70 hours of the 650 hours he requested for *quantum meruit* based on Carey's failure to provide sufficient documentary evidence of his alleged work).

69 CAA terminated Dogra in November 2014. Michael David Smith, *High-profile agent Ben Dogra out at CAA*, ProFootballTalk (Nov. 13, 2014, 5:41 PM), http://profootballtalk.nbcsports.com/2014/11/13/high-profile-agent-ben-dogra-out-at-caa/, *archived at* http://perma.cc/NC6P-LFHB.

70 Mike Florio, *Report: Luck could be signing with CAA*, ProFootballTalk (Dec. 20, 2011, 6:21 PM), http://profootballtalk.nbcsports.com/2011/12/20/report-luck-could-be-signing-with-caa/, *archived at* http://perma.cc/7FNU-JX9K.

71 *Id.*

72 *Id.*; Jarrett Bell, *Condon has big clients, a lot of clout, Elite agent's negotiating plate full*, USA Today, Jan. 27, 2012, *available at* 2012 WLNR 1855278.

73 Doug Tatum, *The Power Brokers*, New Orleans Times Picayune, Mar. 2, 2012, available at 2012 WLNR 4602944.

74 *See* Florio, *supra* note 70 (mentioning that Luck's father, Oliver Luck, also West Virginia University's Athletic Director, is an attorney); Mike Florio, *Trent Richardson lands with CAA*, ProFootballTalk (Jan. 25, 2012, 1:32 PM), http://profootballtalk.nbcsports.com/2012/01/25/trent-richardson-lands-with-caa/, *archived at* http://perma.cc/MW7P-2H62 (mentioning that Luck chose not to be represented by CAA).

75 Mike Florio, *Report: Alex Smith may part ways with CAA*, ProFootballTalk (Mar. 17, 2012, 6:33 PM), http://profootballtalk.nbcsports.com/2012/03/17/report-alex-smith-may-part-ways-with-caa/, *archived at* http://perma.cc/SPQ3-FQPR.

76 *See* Mike Florio, *Impasse lingers between Alex Smith, Chiefs*, ProFootballTalk (Aug. 9, 2014, 8:18 PM) http://profootballtalk.nbcsports.com/2014/08/09/impasse-lingers-between-alex-smith-chiefs/, *archived at* http://perma.cc/4LA4-UJR2 (discussing contract negotiations between CAA, on Smith's behalf, with the Chiefs prior to the 2014 season).

77 Mike Florio, *Conflict Of Interest Issue Comes Back Into Focus*, ProFootballTalk (Apr. 14, 2009, 12:36 PM), http://profootballtalk.nbcsports.com/2009/04/14/conflict-of-interest-issue-comes-back-into-focus/, *archived at* http://perma.cc/598K-XM2U; Mike Florio, *Goff, Wentz have same agents*, ProFootballTalk (Apr. 14, 2016, 7:30 PM), http://profootballtalk.nbcsports.com/2016/04/14/goff-wentz-have-same-agents/, *archived at* https://perma.cc/MH46-B44V.

78 For more on potential conflicts of interests among sports agents, *see* Jeffrey C. Meehan, *Harvard or Hardball? An Examination of the Ethical Issues Faced by Lawyer-Agents*, 21 Sports L.J. 45 (2014); Scott R. Rosner, *Conflicts of Interest and the Shifting Paradigm of Athlete Representation*, 11 UCLA Ent. L. Rev. 193 (2004); Mark Doman, *Attorneys as Athlete-Agents: Reconciling the ABA Rules of Professional Conduct with the Practice of Athlete Representation*, 5 Tex. Rev. Ent. & Sports L. 37 (2003).

79 *See* 2012 NFLPA Contract Advisor Regulations, § 3(A)(16).

80 Contract Advisor Regulations, § 5(A). The Contract Advisor Regulations also govern disputes between Contract Advisors. *See id.*

81 *See* 2012 Contract Advisor Regulations, § 5 (discussing the arbitration procedures).

82 *See* Weinberg v. Nat'l Football League Players Ass'n, 06-cv-2332, 2008 WL 4808920, at *2 (N.D.Tex. Nov. 5, 2008) (citing affidavit from Kaplan in which he explained he has been the NFLPA arbitrator since 1994).

83 Contract Advisor-player lawsuits occurred occasionally prior to the NFLPA arbitration mechanism. *See, e.g.*, Detroit Lions, Inc. v. Argovitz, 580 F.Supp. 542 (E.D.Mi. 1984) (Court rescinded contract between player and USFL club because of agent's interest in USFL club); Zinn v. Parrish, 644 F.2d 360 (7th Cir. 1981) (Contract Advisor entitled to damages for breach of contract on contract commissions). *But see also* Hilliard v. Black, 125 F. Supp. 2d 1071 (2000) (denying contract advisor's motion to dismiss breach of fiduciary duty, conversion, conspiracy and securities law claims); Total Economic Athletic Management of America, Inc. v. Pickens, 898 S.W.2d 98 (Mo.App. 1995) (Contract advisor entitled to damages for anticipatory breach of contract). The *Black* case may not have been subject to the NFLPA's arbitration mechanism because it concerned statutory claims. Additionally, the *Pickens* case may not have been subject to the NFLPA's arbitration mechanism because the alleged wrongdoing occurred at the time the NFLPA was dissolved as a union, which would have made the contract advisor Regulations unenforceable.

84 NFLPA Case No. 03-64 (Kaplan, Arb. Nov. 1, 2004).

85 Contract Advisor Regulations, § 6(A).

86 *See* 2012 Contract Advisor Regulations, § 6 (describing disciplinary process).

87 Contract Advisor Regulations, § 6(D).

88 *See* 2012 Contract Advisor Regulations, § 6 (describing disciplinary process).

89 Andrew Brandt, Peer Review Response (Oct. 30, 2015).

90 *See* 2012 Contract Advisor Regulations, § 3(B)(2).

91 NFLPA Contract Advisor Regulations, § 3(A)(6).

92 For more on the complicated process of athletes transferring from the amateur to professional ranks, *see* Glenn M. Wong, Warren Zola and Chris Deubert, *Going Pro in Sports: Providing Guidance to Student-Athletes in a Complicated Legal & Regulatory Environment*, 28 Cardozo Arts & Ent. L.J. 553 (2011).

93 *Pipeline to the Pros*, NFLPA, https://www.nfl.com/pipeline (last visited Aug. 7, 2015), *archived at* https://perma.cc/M8VS-4BM4; *Getting To Know Mark Levin*, NFLPA, Jun. 19, 2014, http://www.nflpa.com/news/all-news/getting-to-know-mark-levin, *archived at* http://perma.cc/27VK-G784.

94 *How to Pick Your Agent*, NFLPA, https://nflpa.com/active-players/how-to-pick-your-agent (last visited Aug. 7, 2015), *archived at* https://perma.cc/TA4L-8VM9.

95 *See Rule 1.7: Conflict of Interest: Current Clients*, Am. Bar Ass'n, http://www.americanbar.org/groups/professional_responsibility/publications/model_rules_of_professional_conduct/rule_1_7_conflict_of_interest_current_clients.html (last visited Aug. 7, 2015), *archived at* http://perma.cc/7UVR-44A6.

96 *See* Christopher Tarver Robertson, *Biased Advice*, 60 Emory L.J. 653, 666–68 (2011) (explaining study showing that disclosing parties "apparently felt that the disclosure gave them a 'moral license' to be even more biased" and that the people to the whom biases are disclosed "failed to effectively use the disclosure to adjust for the inaccuracy of the given advice[.]")

Financial Advisors

As we discussed in the Introduction to this Report, our goal is to examine all the inputs that may influence players' health, including the so-called "social determinants of health." Financial health is a major contributor to physical and mental health, and also, in turn, affected by physical and mental health.[a] Indeed, many studies have shown a correlation between financial debt and poor physical health.[1] For these reasons, financial advisors are a critical stakeholder in players' long-term health. Despite multiple layers and the availability of well-qualified financial professional regulation (discussed below), there are many stories of NFL players suffering from financial difficulties. While the

---

a   Many experts have recognized that "financial insecurity can cause people to 'cut corners in ways that may affect their health and well-being,' like spending less on food, clothing, or prescriptions." Nadia N. Sawicki, *Modernizing Informed Consent: Expanding the Boundaries of Materiality*, Univ. Ill. L. Rev. (2016), *citing* Kevin R. Riggs and Peter A. Ubel, *Overcoming Barriers to Discussing Out-of-Pocket Costs With Patients*, 174 Jama Int. Med. 849 (2014); Peter A. Ubel, Amy P. Abernethy, and S. Yousuf Zafar, *Full Disclosure— Out-of-Pocket Costs as Side Effects,* 369 New Eng. J. Med. 1484 (2013). Indeed, to many, "financial well-being is certainly within the boundaries of most peoples' concept of health." *Id., quoting* Michael S. Wilkes and David L. Schriger, *Caution: The Meter is Running: Informing Patients About Health Care Costs*, 165 Western J. Med 74, 78 (1996) (noting that "discussions about the cost of care are an important part of the physician-patient relationship").

actual career earnings of NFL players are difficult to ascertain,[b] there have been multiple studies about NFL player financial health with a variety of results.

According to a 2009 *Sports Illustrated* article, by the time NFL players have been retired for two years, 78 percent of them are bankrupt or in financial distress.[2] However, according to a 2009 NFL-funded study of former NFL players by the University of Michigan, the median income of a former player between the ages of 30 and 49 is $85,000, compared to $55,000 for the general population. The study also found that 8.4 percent of former players between ages 30 and 49 were below the poverty level, as compared to 9.5 percent of the general population. A 2015 academic study also refuted the figures in the *Sports Illustrated* article, finding that within two years of the end of their career, only 1.9 percent of players were bankrupt, while also finding that one in six players was bankrupt within 12 years of leaving the NFL.[c] Moreover, in 2012, ESPN released the documentary "Broke" detailing the financial problems of professional athletes, and exploring how they had gotten there.[3] And in a 2014–2015 survey of 763 former players by *Newsday*, 50.59 percent of former players interviewed said they had struggled financially since their playing career ended.[4]

There are, however, important limitations to the above-mentioned studies.

To support its findings *Sports Illustrated* cited "reports from . . . athletes, players' associations, agents and financial advisers" but no additional details and no information that can be independently verified.

There are two potential limitations to the Michigan Study. First, the Michigan Study population only included players who had vested rights under the NFL's Retirement Plan, meaning that the players generally had been on an NFL roster for at least three games in at least three seasons. There is likely a significant but unknown percentage of NFL players who never become vested under the Retirement Plan. Second, responders to the survey were 36.8 percent African American and 61.4 percent white—almost a complete reversal of the NFL's population of current players. While the racial demographics of former players is likely closer to the population of the Michigan Study, *i.e.*, there were more white players than in the current NFL, the Michigan Study did not provide such data on the former player population and did not adjust or account for the racial demographics of the former player population.

In a telephone call with Dr. David Weir, the lead author of the Michigan Study, he explained that: (1) due to limited resources, the population of players to be studied and contacted was limited to the data and contact information available to and provided by the NFL; and, (2) the NFL did not provide racial demographics of former players and thus the study could not adjust for that factor. Weir also believes that the racial demographics of former players is substantially similar to the racial demographics of the Michigan Study's participants. Finally, Weir explained that, during the internal review process with the NFL, the study was leaked to the media, preventing the study from being amended and submitted to a peer-reviewed publication.

Finally, there are also limitations to the *Newsday* survey: (1) the survey was sent via email and text message by the NFLPA to more than 7,000 former NFL players, thus eliminating former players who were less technologically savvy and also possibly skewing the sample towards those former players closer to the NFLPA; (2) the response rate for the survey was low (approximately 11 percent); and, (3) the study does not discuss the demographics of those that responded, making it difficult to ascertain whether those who responded are a representative sample of all former players.

Despite these limitations, we provide the reader with the best existing data. Moreover, while there are limitations to the data collected to date as well as differences in the figures presented, it is clear that there are serious concerns about former players' financial difficulties.[5]

---

b   Based on an average career length of approximately three years, the NFLPA has estimated that the average career earnings of an NFL player are $4 million after taxes. *See* Adam Molon, *Why So Many Ex-NFL Players Struggle With Money*, CNBC (Jan. 31, 2014, 12:29 PM), www.cnbc.com/id/101377457#, *archived at* http://perma.cc/F5YN-FJE2. Using an average salary of $1.9 million and an average career length of 3.5 years, others have estimated NFL players earn about $6.7 million in their careers, a figure largely on par with that of the NFLPA's. *See* Nick Schwartz, *The Average Career Earnings Of Athletes Across America's Major Sports Will Shock You*, USA Today, Oct. 24, 2013, http://ftw.usatoday.com/2013/10/average-career-earnings-nfl-nba-mlb-nhl-mls, *archived at* http://perma.cc/9DFP-WPQ2. However, the NFL has disputed the 3.5 years figure generally provided by the NFLPA, stating instead that players who actually make an NFL Club have, on average, careers of about 6 years. *See What is average NFL player's career length? Longer than you might think, Commissioner Goodell says*, NFL (Apr. 18, 2011), http://nflcommunications.com/2011/04/18/what-is-average-nfl-player%E2%80%99s-career-length-longer-than-you-might-think-commissioner-goodell-says/, *archived at* http://perma.cc/PX5U-9SFK. Finally, it is important to point out that the average in this case does not reflect the median career earnings of NFL players, *i.e.*, the career earnings of a typical NFL player.

c   Kyle Carlson, et al., *Bankruptcy Rates Among NFL Players with Short-Lived Income Spikes*, Nat'l Bureau of Econ. Research (April 2015). The study found that the rate of bankruptcy among the general population in the 25–34 year age group was very similar to the bankruptcy rate of NFL players. However, the general population's average income is almost certainly substantially less than that of the average NFL player's.

The relationship between physical and financial health goes in both directions. Without adequate savings and benefits during and after NFL play, players may find themselves insufficiently prepared to meet their physical and mental health needs, especially in the event of crisis. On the flip side, crises in physical and mental health are closely tied to bankruptcy, home foreclosure, and other serious financial setbacks.[6] At its worst, these two outcomes can lead to a vicious cycle—poor health outcomes lead to financial losses, which worsen the ability to combat physical and mental health impairments, which in turn further deplete financial resources.

Financial health is also in and of itself an important component of a person's health. Financial difficulties can cause stress that contributes to or exacerbates psychological and physical ailments.

For all of the above reasons, it is thus critical to consider a stakeholder with a key role in helping players cope and plan financially—financial advisors. It is also critical to recognize that even though NFL players may make a sizeable income during their playing years, they do not all have million dollar contracts, and depending on their career options outside of football, the money they earn may need to see them and their families through decades.

To better inform our understanding of financial advisors' obligations and practices, we conducted 30–60 minute interviews with three active financial advisors. On average, the financial advisors interviewed had been NFLPA-registered financial advisors for 15 years and had 34 active or former NFL players as clients. The interviews were not intended to be representative of the entire financial advisor population or to draw scientifically valid inferences, but were instead meant to be informative of general practices among financial advisors. We provide quotes from these interviews and urge the reader to keep that caveat in mind throughout. We then invited all three financial advisors to review a draft of this chapter prior to publication. Although two agreed to review a draft of the chapter, only one, Mark Doman of The Doman Group, provided comments. Finally, while two of the financial advisors we interviewed preferred to remain anonymous, Doman preferred to be identified by name in the Report.

(A) Background

Financial advisors are a variety of professionals whose services depend on their area of expertise but can include services such as tax planning, investment advice and services, budgeting, financial planning, insurance, estate planning, and retirement planning.[d] While many financial advisors working on behalf of NFL players try to focus their efforts in the world of professional sports, the majority of them have a wide range of clients.

As described in Chapter 12: Contract Advisors, under the National Labor Relations Act (NLRA), the NFLPA is the exclusive representation of players in negotiations with NFL clubs. By choosing to delegate this authority to contract advisors, the NFLPA has the legal authority to certify, regulate and discipline contract advisors. The NFLPA is able to further strengthen its control over contract advisors by requiring NFL clubs to only deal with contract advisors who have been certified by the NFLPA, or be subject to a $30,000 fine.[7]

> Without adequate savings and benefits during and after NFL play, players may find themselves insufficiently prepared to meet their physical and mental health needs.

The NFLPA has no such authority over financial advisors. Neither the NLRA nor any other law confers any status on the NFLPA that gives it the right to regulate financial advisors. More specifically, financial advisors are not involved in the labor dynamics that create the NFLPA's legal authority over contract advisors, *i.e.,* financial advisors do not negotiate contracts and generally have no contact with the NFL or NFL clubs.

---

d   The NFLPA Financial Advisor Regulations define "Financial Advice" as "any form of advice, guidance, recommendation, direction, or control, directly or indirectly, over a Player's funds, property and/or investments, and shall include, but not be limited to, investment advice (including securities, commodities, banking, insurance, or real estate), financial planning, budgeting, money management, retirement planning, the purchase of insurance, tax and estate planning, and any other form of financial consultation that permits the advisor to exercise discretion or control over a Player's funds, property, and/or investments. As such, 'Financial Advisors' includes 'Brokers,' 'Dealers,' 'Investment Advisers,' and 'Financial Planners,' each as defined herein. 'Financial Advisors' also expressly includes insurance agents, accountants, and attorneys." 2012 NFLPA Financial Advisor Regulations, § 1.

Nevertheless, after an estimated 78 players were defrauded of $42 million in a three-year period, the NFLPA began a system of regulating financial advisors in 2002.[8] That year, the NFLPA launched a program whereby financial advisors could register with the NFLPA and released its Regulations and Code of Conduct Governing Registered Player Financial Advisors ("Financial Advisor Regulations").[e] The NFLPA's financial advisor program was, and remains, the only one of its kind among the major American sports unions, and deserves praise in this regard.

It is important to note that the NFLPA only "registers" financial advisors while it "certifies" contract advisors. This distinction likely exists for several reasons: the NFL lacks legal authority over financial advisors as described above; and, the NFLPA does not want to be seen as endorsing any financial advisor and becoming liable for the wrongdoing of any financial advisor.[9] Indeed, the NFLPA requested and received a No-Action Letter from the Securities and Exchange Commission (SEC) agreeing with the NFLPA's position that by operating the financial advisor program, the NFLPA would not be considered an investment adviser or solicitor within the meaning of federal securities laws.[10]

Significantly, this distinction means that while contract advisors are *required* to be certified by the NFLPA to perform their duties, financial advisors are under no obligation to register with the NFLPA.

There are many financial advisors who refuse to engage in recruiting as a matter of professional ethics.

The Financial Advisor Regulations have been amended from time to time, most recently in 2012.[11] Like the NFLPA's Contract Advisor Regulations, the Financial Advisor Regulations contain extensive eligibility requirements, including: a bachelor's degree; a minimum of eight years of experience with appropriate financial industry licensure; minimum of $4 million in insurance coverage; and, no civil, criminal or regulatory history relevant to financial services or fiduciary duties.[12]

While there are currently 262 NFLPA-registered financial advisors, there are many financial advisors working with NFL players who are not NFLPA-registered, many of whom likely could not meet the registration requirements.

I) FORMATION OF THE PLAYER-FINANCIAL ADVISOR RELATIONSHIP

The financial advisor industry has become as competitive as the contract advisor industry, if not more so.[13] Many financial advisors recruit clients in the same manner as contract advisors, by calling them, texting them, and sending recruitment materials as soon as the player demonstrates that he might become an NFL player.[f] In addition, some financial advisors offer financial incentives as inducements to hire them, including payments in the tens or hundreds of thousands of dollars to players. Indeed, it was reported that one firm offered 2015 draft picks six-month loans of $55,000–75,000.[14] Such payments are not expressly prohibited by the Financial Advisor Regulations, as discussed in more detail below in Section E: Recommendations. Financial Advisor Mark Doman explained that, in addition to receiving interest on the loans provided to the players, some financial advisors (but not he) will advise the players to use some of the loaned money to purchase financial products, such as an annuity or insurance, from or through the financial advisor, off which the financial advisor can make additional income.

Nevertheless, as will be discussed more below, there are many financial advisors who refuse to engage in recruiting as a matter of professional ethics. These financial advisors generally receive their clients through referrals from other players or contract advisors. Because contract advisors are often recruiting the player at the same time as the financial advisor, contract advisors often do not have the ability to recommend a financial advisor to a player. Additionally, since college players are generally permitted by NCAA Bylaws to have financial advisors while they cannot have contract advisors, players often retain a financial advisor before a contract advisor.

Ultimately, the college players, with the help of their family, friends and college, will sort through the multitude of financial advisors, meet with a few, and choose one. The player and financial advisor formalize the relationship by executing the financial advisor's individualized services agreement,

---

e   The Financial Advisor Regulations define a "Financial Advisor" as "any person who, for compensation in any form, gives any financial advice with respect to a Player's funds, property, and/or investments of any kind, including, but not limited to, any 'Alternative Investment' as defined herein, as well as any other security, commodity, or financial product, whether or not traded on an organized public market in the United States (*e.g.,* The New York Stock Exchange or the NASDAQ) or abroad." 2012 NFLPA Financial Advisor Regulations, § 1.

f   During the recruiting process, the financial advisor will generally make the player aware of other players with whom the financial advisor purportedly work, to try and demonstrate the financial advisor's skill. For those financial advisors registered with the NFLPA, the NFLPA is the best resource for confirming a financial advisor's bona fides, as is discussed in the Recommendations section. Players should also seek to discuss the quality of a financial advisor's services with current and/or former clients.

as the NFLPA does not have a standard services agreement like with contract advisors.

II) SERVICES PROVIDED TO PLAYERS (CURRENT AND FORMER)

Financial advisors generally provide advice and assistance concerning any of the player's financial matters, including investment management, income tax preparation, budgeting, estate planning, post-career planning, and insurance (including, *e.g.*, homeowner's, renter's, car, life, disability). In addition, some financial advisors will provide a bill paying service or recommend a firm that can handle these tasks for the players.[g] Perhaps one of the financial advisor's most important responsibilities is making sure players are aware of and take advantage of the various financial benefits under the CBA, including but not limited to the Retirement Plan, Player Annuity Program, Tuition Assistance Plan, Severance Pay, Second Career Savings Plan, and Health Reimbursement Account.[h]

Financial advisors generally work with players and their family for the player's entire life. In this respect, financial advisors are more important than contract advisors and are crucial stakeholders when it comes to the player's post-career health. A 2014–2015 survey of 763 former players by *Newsday* shows the importance of post-career planning: 34.5 percent of former players interviewed said they had difficulty finding employment after their NFL career ended, and 37.1 percent said they did not prepare for life after football during their playing career.[i] The financial advisors interviewed explained that retirement is the opportunity to show the player that the post-career plan they had put together works and to begin to take the next steps, including for the player to potentially finish his education and obtain another job.[j]

The level of communication between the financial advisor's firm and the player varies depending on the needs of the player. Younger players may speak with their financial advisor once a week while more experienced players might only communicate with their financial advisors once a month. The financial advisors generally send monthly statements concerning the player's finances, even though the NFLPA only requires them to be sent quarterly.[15]

More specifics on some of these services will be discussed below, in Section C: Current Practices.

(B) Current Legal Obligations[k]

The financial advisor industry is heavily regulated by both governmental and private organizations that perform quasi-governmental functions. Financial advisors are subject to federal and state statutes and regulations concerning the various financial industries in which they may practice. Most importantly, all financial advisors must comply with the Securities Exchange Act and its regulations, as enforced by the SEC.

In addition, many financial advisors are subject to oversight by the Financial Industry Regulatory Authority (FINRA). FINRA is a private, non-profit "self-regulatory organization" within the meaning of the Securities and Exchange Act, registered with the SEC, and responsible for enforcing FINRA rules, SEC regulations, and federal securities statutes against FINRA members.[16] FINRA promulgates and enforces rules governing more than 4,000 securities firms and approximately 630,000 financial professionals.[17] FINRA brings disciplinary actions against its members and also provides an arbitration mechanism that is the chief forum for resolving disputes between financial advisors and their clients.[18]

A financial advisor's precise legal obligations might depend on his or her qualifications, licensure, and the services he or she provides to a player. While we briefly describe these possible distinctions below, none of our recommendations turns on the exact nature of the financial advisor's legal duty to his or her player-client. Moreover, there is an ongoing debate in the financial services industry about the duties owed by certain types of financial professionals to their clients, and much will depend on specific facts.

Some financial advisors might only be registered as "brokers" or "dealers" under the Securities Exchange Act of 1934. Broker-dealers are individuals engaged in the business of buying and selling stocks,[19] who traditionally earn the majority of their income from commissions on the stock sales or purchases.[20] Broker-dealers are historically held to a "suitability," as opposed to a fiduciary standard.[21]

---

g   Bill paying services generally are responsible for ensuring the timely and proper payment of a player's various expenditures, including housing payments, utilities, car payments, cellular telephone payments, contract advisor, financial advisor and attorneys' fees, child support, etc. Nevertheless, Financial Advisor 1 explained that he prefers players pay their own bills so that players are aware of their expenses and "feel[] the same pain that anybody else feels."

h   Financial Advisor 1 estimated that the annual value of benefits players are entitled to is "almost $200,000."

i   *See* Jim Baumbach, *Life After Football*, Newsday, Jan. 22, 2015, http://data. newsday.com/projects/sports/football/life-football/, *archived at* http://perma. cc/77DP-LUUE. In the introduction to this chapter, we described some limitations to *Newsday's* analysis.

j   To assist players in preparing for careers after football, Financial Advisor Mark Doman offers his players the opportunity to intern at his office during the offseason. During the internship, the players study their own financial portfolios and the related concepts.

---

k   The legal obligations described herein are not an exhaustive list but are those we believe are most relevant to player health.

The suitability standard only requires broker-dealers to recommend investments that are suitable based on the client's needs and goals.[22] The broker-dealer "must have an adequate and reasonable basis for any recommendation that [he or she] makes,"[23] but are not necessarily required to provide investment advice that puts the client's interest first, as a fiduciary would.[24] This looser standard permits broker-dealers to recommend its clients to buy stocks currently owned by the broker-dealer's firm, thus benefiting the firm. Nevertheless, broker-dealers can develop fiduciary relationships with their clients if the broker-dealer takes on greater responsibilities towards the client, such as having discretionary authority over the client's account.[25]

The potentially limited obligations of broker-dealers are complicated by the Investment Advisers Act of 1940.[26] An investment adviser is "any person, who, for compensation is engaged in a business of providing advice to others or issuing reports or analyses regarding securities."[27] Traditionally, investment advisers, charge a fee based on the amount of assets managed by the investment adviser.[28] Investment advisers *do* have a fiduciary relationship with their clients, requiring them to put the interests of their clients first and to avoid conflicts of interest.[29] Under common law,[l] from which the securities statutes and regulations are generally derived, a fiduciary is "a person who is required to act for the benefit of another person on all matters within the scope of their relationship; one who owes to another the duties of good faith, trust, confidence, and candor; . . . [o]ne who must exercise a high standard of care in managing another's money or property."[30]

Depending on the broker-dealer's compensation structure, he or she too may also be subject to the higher standards of the 1940 Act. A broker-dealer who provides investment advice to clients is not considered an investment adviser only so long as the broker-dealer's advice is "solely incidental" to the broker-dealer's services and the broker-dealer charges only commissions and not asset-based fees.[31] Nevertheless, the interpretation of this exception remains open to debate and is often a fact-specific inquiry.[32]

In 2016, the Department of Labor potentially further complicated matters with a new regulation set to take effect in April 2017. The new regulation requires that individuals that invest a client's money as part of a tax-deferred retirement account, such as a 401(k) or IRA, act in a fiduciary capacity toward the client, regardless of whether they are a broker-dealer or investment adviser.[33]

While the above uncertainty demonstrates that some NFL player financial advisors might be able to avoid having a fiduciary relationship with their clients, they almost certainly cannot if they choose to register with the NFLPA. The Financial Advisor Regulations, which are a quasi-legal/ethical code, dictate that financial advisors "have the duty to act in the best interest of his/her Player-clients."[34] Moreover, by agreeing to be registered with the NFLPA, each financial advisor

> acknowledges[m] that it is a fiduciary with respect to each of its Player-clients and agrees to perform its duties as a Financial Advisor to such Player-client in good faith and with the care, skill, prudence, and diligence under the circumstances then prevailing that a prudent person acting in a like capacity and familiar with such matters would use in the conduct of an enterprise of a like character and with like aims and consistent with the Registered Player Financial Advisor's obligations and duties under applicable law, and consistent with the Registered Player Financial Advisor's existing practices and procedures, obligations, powers and duties under its written contract with the Player-client required under Section Three (H) of the Regulations.[35]

Despite the fiduciary standard imposed by the Financial Advisor Regulations, as will be discussed below in Section E: Enforcement, the Financial Advisor Regulations provide players with minimal recourse in the event of a violation.

Generally, the Financial Advisor Regulations require financial advisors to "[f]ully comply with all federal and state laws governing the . . . Financial Advisor's professional activities."[36] The Financial Advisor Regulations prohibit a wide variety of conduct subject to abuse in the financial advisor industry, including:

1. Employing any device, scheme, or artifice to defraud a Player;

2. Inducing any activity in a Player's account that is excessive in size or frequency in view of the Player's financial resources and/or sophistication, and the character of the account;

3. Soliciting or obtaining any general power of attorney from a Player over his assets or investment;

---

l   Common law refers to "[t]he body of law derived from judicial decisions, rather than from statutes or constitutions." Black's Law Dictionary (9th ed. 2009).

m   A broker-dealer might theoretically argue that since he or she never had a fiduciary relationship with a player-client, he or she cannot "acknowledge" such an obligation. It nonetheless seems more likely that a financial advisor who registers with the NFLPA who otherwise would not be in a fiduciary relationship with his or her clients voluntarily assumes fiduciary obligations as part of the NFLPA registration.

4. Soliciting or obtaining any limited power of attorney or discretionary authority which is not specifically and reasonably necessary for the Registered Player Financial Advisor to perform his/her services;

5. Commingling any Player's funds or other property with the Registered Player Financial Advisor's personal funds. Commingling one or more client funds together is permitted, subject to applicable legal requirements and proper accounting;

6. Having custody of a Player's funds or other property unless the Registered Player Financial Advisor is a Qualified Custodian;

7. Placing an order for the purchase or sale of a security if that security is not either registered or exempt from registration under applicable law;

8. Providing false or misleading information to any Player, or concealing material facts from any Player, in the course of recruiting the Player as a client, or in the course of representing or consulting with that Player as a Registered Player Financial Advisor;

9. Making any false or misleading statement about his or her ability, degree, or area of competence;

10. Engaging in any unlawful conduct and/or conduct involving dishonesty, fraud, deceit, misrepresentation, or any other activity which reflects adversely on his/her honesty, trustworthiness, professional competence, and fitness as a Registered Player Financial Advisor, or which otherwise jeopardizes his/her effective representation of Players;

11. Representing or suggesting to anyone that his/her status as a Registered Player Financial Advisor constitutes an endorsement or recommendation by the NFLPA of the Registered Player Financial Advisor, or his/her qualifications, or services;

12. Providing or offering money or any other thing of value, or extending credit or loaning money, to any Player, or member of a Player's family, or anyone in a position to influence the Player, where such payment or loan would violate any applicable law, regulations, rule, or ethical standard;

13. Engaging in any activity which creates an actual or potential conflict of interest with the effective representation of a Player, including, but not limited to, the following:

a) Convincing a Player to purchase stock or property, or to invest in any manner, or loan money or extend credit from, any enterprise or entity in which the Registered Player Financial Advisor fails to disclose, in advance and in writing, his/her own financial or ownership interest, or that of an affiliate or a family member, to the Player;

b) Failing to disclose, in advance and in writing, any commission, finder's fee, or other thing of value that the Registered Player Financial Advisor receives, or is to receive, from any third party or entity, in return for convincing a Player to make or not make an investment, or to retain or not to retain a Certified Contract Advisor, or any other person;

c) Failing to disclose, in advance and in writing, any commission, finder's fee, or referral fee, promised and/or paid to, any third party, in return for that party's agreement to refer a Player to him or her[.][37]

(C) Current Ethical Codes

In addition to legal obligations, depending on the financial advisor's expertise or experience, he or she is likely subject to additional ethics rules. For example, the Chartered Financial Analyst Institute (CFA Institute),[38] Certified Financial Planner Board of Standards (CFP Board),[39] National Association of Personal Financial Advisors (NAPFA),[40] National Association of Insurance and Financial Advisors (NAIFA),[41] and American Institute of Certified Public Accountants (AICPA)[42] all have an ethics code of some kind regulating the professional responsibilities of their members.

The codes of ethics for the CFP Board, NAPFA, and NAIFA are not particularly lengthy and instead generally identify principles by which members are required to act. For example, the totality of the CFP Board's Code of Ethics and Professional Responsibility reads as follows:

Principle 1 – Integrity: Provide professional services with integrity.

Integrity demands honesty and candor which must not be subordinated to personal gain and advantage. Certificants are placed in positions of trust by clients, and the ultimate source of that trust is the certificant's personal integrity. Allowance can be made for innocent error and legitimate differences of opinion, but integrity cannot co-exist with deceit or subordination of one's principles.

Principle 2 – Objectivity: Provide professional services objectively.

Objectivity requires intellectual honesty and impartiality. Regardless of the particular service rendered or the capacity in which a certificant functions, certificants should protect the integrity of their work, maintain objectivity and avoid subordination of their judgment.

Principle 3 – Competence: Maintain the knowledge and skill necessary to provide professional services competently.

Competence means attaining and maintaining an adequate level of knowledge and skill, and application of that knowledge and skill in providing services to clients. Competence also includes the wisdom to recognize the limitations of that knowledge and when consultation with other professionals is appropriate or referral to other professionals necessary. Certificants make a continuing commitment to learning and professional improvement.

Principle 4 – Fairness: Be fair and reasonable in all professional relationships. Disclose conflicts of interest.

Fairness requires impartiality, intellectual honesty and disclosure of material conflicts of interest. It involves a subordination of one's own feelings, prejudices and desires so as to achieve a proper balance of conflicting interests. Fairness is treating others in the same fashion that you would want to be treated.

Principle 5 – Confidentiality: Protect the confidentiality of all client information.

Confidentiality means ensuring that information is accessible only to those authorized to have access. A relationship of trust and confidence with the client can only be built upon the understanding that the client's information will remain confidential.

Principle 6 – Professionalism: Act in a manner that demonstrates exemplary professional conduct.

Professionalism requires behaving with dignity and courtesy to clients, fellow professionals, and others in business-related activities. Certificants cooperate with fellow certificants to enhance and maintain the profession's public image and improve the quality of services.

Principle 7 – Diligence: Provide professional services diligently.

Diligence is the provision of services in a reasonably prompt and thorough manner, including the proper planning for, and supervision of, the rendering of professional services.

The CFA Institute's Code of Ethics and Standards of Professional Conduct is similar, but provides more specific guidance in the following areas: professionalism; integrity of capital markets; duties to clients; duties to employers; investment analysis, recommendations, and actions; conflicts of interest; and, responsibilities as a CFA Institute member or CFA candidate.

In contrast, the AICPA's Code of Professional Conduct is far more complicated and includes interpretations of the relevant rules. Moreover, the AICPA's Code is divided into the following sections: Principles of Professional Conduct; Independence, Integrity and Objectivity; General Standards Accounting Principles; Responsibilities to Clients; Responsibilities to Colleagues; and, Other Responsibilities and Practices. The AICPA's Code is likely longer to ensure its' members compliance with generally accepted accounting principles.

(D) Current Practices

Players were near unanimous in explaining the importance of financial advisors and financial health, while having mixed feelings about financial advisors themselves:[n]

- **Current Player 2:** *"Those financial advisors are huge."* *"[F]inancial health is important and that is a great opportunity for a young man to jumpstart their lives financially, and put themselves at an advantage moving forward to their next career."*

- **Current Player 4:** *"I personally was able to find a financial advisor who I trust and I think he's doing an excellent job. But I would say probably about one in three guys have a problem with their Financial Advisor."*

- **Current Player 5:** *"Financial education is hugely important. And we get some but not nearly enough." "I think there are some good financial advisors, some bad financial advisors . . . . They have a vested interest in helping to make sure the player keeps his money but they have a bigger vested interest in keeping the player as a client. So, whether the player is burning through his money or not, the financial advisor he keeps getting paid a percentage until the player runs out of money . . . [but] in general, financial advisors do a pretty good job of advising their clients and preparing them for life outside the NFL."*

- **Current Player 6:** *"That's the biggest question I'd like to try to figure out. What can be done to help players be better with their finances?"*

- **Current Player 9:** *"Financial health is important to NFL players and everybody . . . . So I think planning and education is very important."*

---

n   We reiterate that our interviews were intended to be informational but not representative of all players' views.

- **Former Player 3:** *"You have the full gamut . . . . Good financial advisors are the ones that can tell their clients 'no,' [but] you'll probably get fired but players need to hear 'no' a lot more than they tell them 'yes.'"*

The financial advisors interviewed were similarly unanimous in their assessment that players are generally not well served by the current crop of financial advisors.[o] The financial advisors' sentiment matched that of contract advisors interviewed. The contract advisors noted that while there are some well-qualified and ethical financial advisors, there are many who are not. However, some contract advisors recognized that financial advisors often have difficulty convincing the players to take certain financially responsible actions.[p] Below, we discuss the most important areas where financial advisors have an opportunity to influence player health, including Recruiting, Educating and Budgeting, Insurance, and Fees.

1) RECRUITING

As discussed in the background to this chapter, the recruiting of prospective clients is intensely competitive in the financial advisor industry. As a result, some financial advisors offer players payments and other inducements in order to obtain the client. All of the financial advisors we interviewed worried about this practice. Mark Doman, one of the financial advisors we interviewed, explained:

> *I think [financial advisor recruiting] is without any exaggeration or hyperbole, the most dangerous of the issues that face professional athletes off the field. Aside from their own personal health, the financial health of these young men and these horrible statistics of them going bankrupt due to . . . being exposed to people that are not sophisticated enough to actively manage the financial needs of these athletes. And even more specifically providing the financial literacy that they so desperately need.[q]*

While competition in industry is often good,[r] the intensity and form of competition in the financial advisor industry may raise concerns. Indeed, Former Player 1 described being recruited by financial advisors as "a crazy experience . . . a meat market."

The financial advisors interviewed further explained that their firms refused to recruit out of principle. Instead, these financial advisors generally obtain clients via referrals from players and contract advisors.

2) EDUCATING AND BUDGETING

The financial advisors and players we interviewed expressed that financial literacy among the players remains a major issue.[s] Most NFL players and their families are unlikely to have ever had the type of money that is available through an NFL career. In addition, most NFL players are young men in their 20s with limited time spent having lived on their own. Thus, most NFL players are unfamiliar with the different types of financial products and services that might be available to them and are unlikely to have a good understanding of how to spend and save their money.

All of the financial advisors we interviewed stressed the importance of an initial meeting with their clients where they can try to explain to the player the various financial issues he will likely have to address, how to develop responsible financial habits, and to plan properly for the future.[t] Financial Advisor 1 also explained a method his firm uses to help reign in client spending. The player's paycheck is directly deposited into an account to which the financial advisor has access. On the first of each month, a budgeted amount is transferred from the initial account to a checking account that the player is able to access for his personal spending. The arrangement prevents the player from

---

o   Financial Advisor 2: "I think there are a lot of people that don't know what they're doing . . . . And you see some of the people in the room [at the NFLPA Financial Advisor conferences] and . . . it's scary that they're thinking about trying to work with players. They don't know anything." Also Financial Advisor 2: There are "a lot of people out there running around trying to work with players for all the wrong reasons . . . but I don't know how you regulate incompetency." We reiterate that our interviews were intended to be informational but not representative of all financial advisors' views. Additionally, we acknowledge the possibility of bias among the financial advisors we interviewed — they believe they are conducting themselves competently and professionally while their competitors are not.

p   Contract Advisor 1: "[Y]ou can only take a horse to water, you can't make them drink."

q   Doman also explained that he thinks the problem "has gotten infinitely worse" since he started working with NFL players.

r   Indeed, in Speakers of Sport, Inc. v. ProServ, Inc., 178 F.3d 862 (7th Cir. 1999), Judge Richard Posner dismissed tortious interference and unfair competition claims brought by one sports agent against another, stating "[t]here is in general nothing wrong with one sports agent trying to take a client from another if this can be done without precipitating a breach of contract. That is the process known as competition, which though painful, fierce, frequently ruthless, sometimes Darwinian in its pitilessness, is the cornerstone of our highly successful economic system."

s   Financial Advisor 1: "[I]t's really just about capitalizing on [the benefits offered], understanding them and capitalizing on them. Most guys just don't understand them." Financial advisor Mark Doman: "I emphasize to them that trust is great but knowledge is better. I don't need them to trust me. I need them to understand what we're doing. And if they understand what we're doing then they don't need to trust. Trust is a luxury." Current Player 9: "The PA and the NFL, there are some programs in place that players can learn [about financial matters]. But you know a lot of it is about motivating guys to actually take hold of it and actually become involved and engaged."

t   Financial Advisor 1: "If I have a guy who's in his first year in the league, we're already talking about post-career. . . . I think it goes without saying that the NFL career has a very short life expectancy. So we usually talk to the guys right from the beginning about worst case scenario and this might be your only year in the league, so you need to plan as such."

spending beyond his means while still having control over his spending choices.

In addition to their financial advisors, players also are exposed to some financial education through the Rookie Transition Program. The Rookie Transition Program is a three-day program offered by each club in which rookies are presented with seminars, discussions, and information on a variety of topics intended to help the rookie make a successful transition to the NFL and to avoid some of the problems past NFL players have suffered.[43] The Rookie Transition Program replaced the Rookie Symposium in 2016, an event which previously hosted all incoming NFL rookies in one central location and provided the same types of services.[44] Nevertheless, there are questions as to whether players are sufficiently understanding the information presented to them.

Despite the Rookie Symposium and Transition Program, the financial advisors interviewed were mixed in their feelings towards existing programs and support for players in their financial matters. Appendix D includes a list of programs offered by the NFL's Player Engagement Department on financial and other matters. Financial Advisor 1 believes the NFLPA has not done a good job of educating players about financial issues but does provide useful resources to the financial advisors. Doman believes that both the NFL and NFLPA "could do a lot better" when it comes to educating players about financial matters.[u] Meanwhile, Financial Advisor 2 expressed uncertainty as to whether the NFLPA could do anything more to educate players. Additionally, the financial advisors were generally pleased with the type and availability of benefits (Financial Advisor 2: "I think they've done a tremendous job of improving the benefits.")

3) INSURANCE

One potentially important aspect of a financial advisor's duties is obtaining a disability or career ending insurance policy for the player. The financial advisors are generally responsible for soliciting, reviewing, and negotiating the insurance policies on behalf of the player. The financial

advisors interviewed explained that whether players require the insurance is judged on a case-by-case basis, including an analysis of the player's age, contract structure, and status and financial security. For $1 million in coverage, a rookie will pay approximately $10,000 (1 percent) in premiums while a player in his mid-thirties can easily pay over $100,000 (10 percent) in premiums.[v]

There are other insurance options players might consider. For example, players might obtain an insurance policy on the unguaranteed portions of their contract in the event their contracts are terminated. Players might also obtain "loss of value" insurance policies when they are approaching free agency. The loss of value insurance policy will let a player recover in the event his next contract is not as expected due to injury or diminished skill.[45]

4) FEES

For their services, financial advisors are generally paid an amount equal to 1 percent (annualized) of assets under management. Thus, if a financial advisor is overseeing $1 million of a player's money, he or she will be paid $10,000 per year. Financial advisors with more total assets under management may charge lower fees.

There are concerns that financial advisors find a number of ways to inflate their fees. For example, some financial advisors include as assets under management the amount in the player's retail checking account, even though the financial advisor is not investing those assets. Additionally, some financial advisors invest players' money in investment vehicles which provide the financial advisor a referral fee or commission, even though such fees are in violation of the Financial Advisor Regulations. Doman explained:

> [T]he other things that these advisors are doing these days is they will tell the client that they'll do investment services and they won't charge them . . . . And the reality is what they are, are conduits to mutual funds and other very basic types of structured bank investment vehicles where there are built-in expense ratios and people who refer those funds money are able to get some sort of fee. Now, separately what they do is instead of charging them for business management . . . they'll sell a young person who has no dependents a multimillion dollar annuity or whole life product which has an enormous commission for [the financial advisor].

---

u   The St. Louis Rams provide an interesting example of a Club that perhaps takes educating its rookies on financial matters seriously. In 2012, Rams head coach Jeff Fisher had a Brinks truck deliver $1 million in cash to the Club's facility. Fisher put the money on the table in front of his rookies and took away portions for taxes, parents, cars, and living and other expenses to show how much money the rookies would actually have left. Jason La Canfora, *Rams' Calculated Risk-Taking On Prospects Working Wonders So Far*, CBS Sports (Aug. 9, 2013, 10:52 AM), http://www.cbssports.com/nfl/writer/jason-la-canfora/23082070/rams-calculated-risktaking-on-prospects-working-wonders-so-far, *archived at* http://perma.cc/X3HV-FYCZ. In addition, the Rams hold educational classes on financial planning, home ownership, investing and other everyday items. Nick Wagoner, *Rams Will Have Rookies Signed Soon*, ESPN (Jun. 10, 2014), http://espn.go.com/blog/st-louis-rams/post/_/id/9148/rams-will-have-rookies-signed-soon, *archived at* http://perma.cc/G6UZ-FXL4.

v   Financial Advisor 1 explained that each week his firm reviews which of its clients were injured and provides notice to disability insurers to protect the player's right to a possible future claim.

(E) Enforcement of Legal and Ethical Obligations[w]

Despite the Financial Advisor Regulations' rigorous standards, the NFLPA currently lacks meaningful enforcement authority over financial advisors. The NFLPA requires registered financial advisors to consent to arbitration, but the arbitration mechanism only governs disputes concerning denial, suspension or revocation of the financial advisor's registration.[46] The totality of the NFLPA's disciplinary authority where the Financial Advisor Regulations have been violated is the issuance of a letter of reprimand or to suspend or revoke the financial advisor's registration.[47] Moreover, the NFLPA and its arbitration mechanism, unlike the contract advisor arbitration mechanism, have no authority to provide damages to a player adversely affected by a financial advisor as a result of a breach of the Financial Advisor Regulations.[48]

The relatively meek regulatory enforcement scheme begs the question why financial advisors register with the NFLPA at all. Indeed, while there are currently about 262 NFLPA-registered financial advisors, there are many players involved with financial advisors who are not NFLPA-registered and the NFLPA has no recourse other than to advise its players to only use registered financial advisors.[x]

As discussed above, financial advisor recruiting is extremely intense and thus players are inundated with recruitment pitches and might choose to hire a non-registered financial advisor. Nevertheless, it benefits financial advisors to register with the NFLPA for a variety of reasons: the financial advisor can explain the importance of meeting the NFLPA's registration requirements and having been vetted by the NFLPA; the NFLPA gives financial advisors financial, salary and benefit information relevant to NFL players, which can assist in their work;[49] and, a quality contract advisor will likely encourage the player to use only an NFLPA-registered financial advisor for the same reasons.

NFL players seeking recompense for damages caused by a financial advisor cannot rely on the Financial Advisor Regulations. Players can and have brought lawsuits or arbitrations (typically via FINRA) against financial advisors alleging breach of fiduciary duty, negligence, breach of contract, fraud, and other relevant causes of action.[50] Some courts have recognized a cause of action for financial advisor or stockbroker malpractice,[51] and most recognize a cause of action for accountant malpractice, if appropriate.[52] Lastly, causes of action and restitution claims likely exist under various federal and state securities laws.[53]

Enforcement of the ethics codes of the CFA Institute, CFP Board, NAPFA, NAIFA, and AICPA are of minimal importance to NFL players. While the organizations are empowered to expel their members and retract their certifications, these punishments provide no benefit to NFL player-clients.

---

w   Appendix K is a summary of players' options to enforce legal and ethical obligations against the stakeholders discussed in this Report.

x   There are no data on how many players use financial advisors not registered with the NFLPA. Current Player 10 commended the NFLPA for its financial advisor program: "I think the NFLPA has done a good job in terms of making financial advisors register and doing background checks and the criminal checks on all the financial advisors that are trying to come in. So there's a long list of guys that have been okayed by the PA."

While there are currently about 262 NFLPA-registered financial advisors, there are many players involved with financial advisors who are not NFLPA-registered.

(F) Recommendations Concerning Financial Advisors

Financial advisors play perhaps the most important role in a player's long-term health. Proper financial advice and planning can help a player determine when to retire (if he has that choice), maximize a player's career earnings, potentially provide the player with a comfortable retirement, help mitigate the consequences of the health issues suffered by many former players, and help avoid financial distress evolving into physical or mental distress. Additionally, financial advisors are governed by many robust codes of ethics that echo some of the same principles we incorporated into this Report, including Respect, Health Primacy, Empowered Autonomy, Transparency, Managing Conflicts of Interest, and Collaboration and Engagement. However, there are a variety of industry practices and realities that are preventing players from receiving the best possible financial guidance. Below are recommendations designed to improve the financial support provided to players.

Goal 1: To make sure players get the best financial advice possible.

Principles Advanced: Respect; Empowered Autonomy; Transparency; and, Collaborative Engagement.

Recommendation 13:1-A: Players should be encouraged by the NFL, NFLPA, and contract advisors to work exclusively with NFLPA-registered financial advisors.

There is significant concern and evidence that players are not well-served by the financial advisor industry and otherwise are prone to mishandling their finances. The NFLPA's financial advisor program is a well-intentioned program that at least sets basic requirements for financial advisors and attempts to weed out those with criminal and otherwise concerning pasts. In addition, the financial advisor registration scheme provides the NFLPA with at least some oversight over the financial advisor industry as it concerns NFL players. Nevertheless, a significant (but unknown) portion of players are persuaded to retain financial advisors who do not register with the NFLPA and whose experience and intentions may be questionable. The NFLPA should encourage players to use those financial advisors which it has determined have at least the minimal qualifications it is able to impose through its registration program. In so doing, the NFLPA should remind players of the advantages of using NFLPA-registered financial advisors, including access to NFL-specific benefit and financial information through the NFLPA.

One possible mechanism by which the NFLPA could encourage players to use NFLPA-registered financial advisors is to collect the names of players' financial advisors each preseason. If a player is using a financial advisor who is not registered with the NFLPA, the NFLPA should advise the player of the purposes and benefits of the NFLPA's registration system. If the player does not have a financial advisor, the NFLPA could advise the player to retain one and follow-up with the player to ensure that he does.[54]

Although the NFLPA financial advisor registration system does not guarantee a player will receive sound financial advice and assistance, it increases the odds as compared to non-registered financial advisors.

Recommendation 13:1-B: The NFLPA should strengthen its Financial Advisor Regulations.

The current Financial Advisor Regulations are robust and align well with other regulations and codes of ethics in the financial industry. Nevertheless, there are potential areas of improvement, including:

- **Requiring financial advisors to pass an examination concerning NFL economic and benefit provisions in order to be registered.** The NFLPA has long required contract advisors to pass an examination concerning the NFL CBA to be certified. There is no reason why financial advisors should be treated differently. It is clear that financial advisors are as much a part of players' lives as contract advisors

Recommendations Concerning Financial Advisors – continued

and perhaps even more important considering that they handle players' money. Nevertheless, financial advisors are not regulated as closely as contract advisors and thus have the potential to be more destructive to the health of players. An examination would provide an additional and meritorious barrier to entry into the NFL player-financial advisor industry. Financial advisors should understand the unique circumstances of NFL player employment while also understanding the variety of benefits available to players. An examination will force financial advisors to educate themselves on these issues while also eliminating the financial advisors unable or unwilling to do so.

- **Prohibiting registered financial advisors from providing or offering money or any other thing of value to any player or any other person (e.g., the player's family member) to induce or encourage the player to utilize the financial advisor's services.** The Financial Advisor Regulations currently prohibit "[p]roviding or offering money or any other thing of value, or extending credit or loaning money, to any Player, or member of a Player's family, or anyone in a position to influence the Player, where such payment or loan would violate any applicable law, regulations, rule, or ethical standard."[55] This rule, however, is unnecessarily vague. There is no reason for the NFLPA to defer to other laws, regulations, rules or ethical standards. There is clearly a problem whereby financial advisors are inducing players to retain them with large payments and players are thereafter receiving poor financial advice and assistance. The NFLPA should prohibit such payments to ensure players are choosing financial advisors based exclusively on their merit and qualifications.

- **Providing the NFLPA with greater authority to conduct audits of financial advisors' activities.** Section 3(I)(D) requires financial advisors to consent to audits by a Certified Public Accountant (CPA) at the player's request. Players are unlikely to know when an audit might be necessary and are also unlikely to take advantage of this right. The NFLPA in coordination with the right financial professionals could undertake this action on behalf of players randomly. Even though the NFLPA would be unable to catch every bad actor, making it known that it conducts such audits should have at least some deterrent effect.

The NFLPA could also require financial advisors to provide the NFLPA with copies of the itemized statements they provide to players. Section 3(I)(A) of the Financial Advisor Regulations requires financial advisors to provide players "at regular intervals, but in no event less than quarterly, itemized statements setting forth the amount charged to the Player-client for Financial Advice, the identity of any investments made in conjunction with that advice, and an accurate account of the increase or decrease in the economic value of any such investments." However, the majority of players are unlikely to review or understand the statements provided to them, and thus identify possible inconsistencies or troubling activities. While the NFLPA likely does not have the resources (and would probably have to hire financial experts) to check quarterly statements for all of its members, it could at a minimum conduct a random review of selected statements. Collection of the statements would identify those financial advisors who failed to follow a simple record production requirement while also having at least some deterrent effect. An alternative approach would be to rely on contract advisors to police financial advisors through inspection of these statements. More broadly, this recommendation could be extended from audits of itemized statements to audits of any financial advisor's activity concerning NFL players.

- **Requiring financial advisors to send the itemized statements required by Section 3(I)(A) of the Financial Advisor Regulations to the player's contract advisor, unless the player objects.** As discussed above, there is currently a lack of oversight concerning financial advisor fees and services. Contract advisors, like financial advisors, are professionals with a fiduciary obligation to look out for the player's best interests. Almost every player has a contract advisor and almost every player has a financial advisor. Thus, in the absence of NFLPA resources to do the same, contract advisors can provide a valuable check on financial advisor fees and activities.[y]

- **Requiring that financial advisors provide the NFLPA with a copy of any agreement with a player.** Section 3(I)(H) of the Financial Advisor Regulations requires all agreements between a financial advisor and player comply with applicable laws and regulations and be in writing. However, financial advisors are only required to provide a copy of the agreement to the NFLPA "upon request." In contrast, contract advisors are required to provide the NFLPA with a copy of any agreement between the contract advisor and player.[56] The NFLPA also generally reviews the contract advisor-player agreements to ensure they are in compliance with Contract Advisor Regulations. Similarly, the NFLPA should review financial advisor-player agreements to ensure they are in compliance with the Financial Advisor Regulations and not otherwise concerning.

---

y   Conversely, there is no need for contract advisors to provide statements of their fees to financial advisors. First, the financial advisors likely have access to the accounts and can see the fees anyway. Second, contract advisor fees are capped at 3 percent of a player's compensation by the Contract Advisor Regulations, eliminating much of the worry that contract advisors can financially take advantage of players.

Recommendations Concerning Financial Advisors – continued

- **Requiring financial advisors to stay abreast of current issues affecting NFL players (with the NFLPA providing the necessary courses and information).** The economics of the NFL are unique, complicated and often changing. Moreover, the application of mainstream financial issues might incur unexpected complications due to the dynamics of the NFL. It is thus important that financial advisors remain current on issues affecting NFL players. The NFLPA could provide relevant information, materials, and updates to financial advisors on a more regular basis or also require financial advisors to attend conferences more regularly. Section 3(I)(J) of the Financial Advisor Regulations only requires financial advisors to attend a conference every two years. In contrast, contract advisors are required to attend a conference every year. Requiring financial advisors to attend conferences more regularly not only ensures that they stay abreast of current financial issues affecting NFL players but also serves as another opportunity to weed out those who are less professional and do not attend.

* * *

We recognize that the above recommendations would increase the NFLPA's involvement in the financial advisor industry and would potentially require delicate maneuvering through complicated financial laws and regulations. Nevertheless, the NFLPA is in the most powerful position, and has as its mission to help players. Thus, it should take every step that it reasonably can to help players by overseeing the actions of financial advisors.

Recommendation 13:1-C: The NFLPA should consider investing greater resources in investigating and enforcing the Financial Advisor Regulations.

As discussed above, there are serious problems with the financial advisor industry that frequently result in substandard representation for and advice to the players, including poor handling of player health matters. Without meaningful enforcement, the Regulations lose their effectiveness to the detriment of players. One possibility is hiring more attorneys to focus on these matters.

Recommendation 13:1-D: Players should be given information to ensure that they choose financial advisors based on their professional qualifications and experience and not the financial benefits the financial advisor has or is willing to provide to the player.

As discussed in more detail above, prospective NFL players are routinely choosing their financial advisors not based on the financial advisor's professional qualifications but instead on how much the financial advisor provides the player at the outset. The players are excited about the opportunity to receive tens if not hundreds of thousands of dollars from the financial advisors for letting the financial advisor provide services to them. However, players do so at their own peril, sometimes agreeing to retain substandard financial advisors.

If the Financial Advisor Regulations are not amended to explicitly prohibit such arrangements as recommended above, it is important that the players understand the downsides of choosing their financial advisor based on loans or advances.

However, presently, there are minimal to no resources for players about how to choose a financial advisor. The NFLPA has the potential to be the best resource for helping players choose financial advisors appropriately but it is unclear what efforts it makes on this topic. The NFLPA conducts "Pipeline to the Pros" with current college football players to try to inform them about the process of becoming an NFL player, including hiring a contract advisor,[57] but it is unknown whether that advice also extends to financial advisors. Similarly, while the NFLPA's website includes a page advising "Active Players" on "How to Pick Your Agent,"[58] there is no similar advice concerning financial advisors.

Recommendations Concerning Financial Advisors – continued

The NFLPA is in a powerful position to help prospective NFL players pick financial advisors. While such players are not yet in the NFLPA's bargaining unit (and thus the NFLPA has no legal obligations toward them, see Chapter 7: The NFL and NFLPA), hundreds of college players will soon be NFLPA members and their decisions concerning a financial advisor while still in college can have a significant impact on their NFL career. Yet it does not appear that the NFLPA currently provides players with any assistance concerning the selection of financial advisors. The NFLPA could expand and intensify the information made available to prospective NFL players and could work with both the NCAA and the NFL (both of which more closely track potential NFL players) to ensure that the right players are receiving the necessary information. The NFLPA should also consider creating a system whereby players able to rate their financial advisors' performance and that data could be made available, including but not limited to a regular survey, a Yelp-like service, or some other means of information-sharing.

Goal 2: To help players better manage their finances.

Principles: Health Primacy; and, Empowered Autonomy.

Recommendation 13:2-A: The NFLPA and NFL should consider holding regular courses on financial issues for players.

As is true of the population more generally, players often lack the financial sophistication to make sound financial decisions, such as budgeting expenditures, saving for retirement, and planning for a post-career life. Additionally, players' lack of financial sophistication prevents them from monitoring the actions of their financial advisors and leaves them vulnerable to others who might seek to take advantage of them.

To assist players in learning important financial skills, the NFL has partnered with Money Management International, the country's largest non-profit credit and counseling service, to provide players with an educational website and a 24 hours a day, seven days a week advice hotline.[59] The NFLPA has established a near identical partnership with Financial Finesse, a company that provides financial education services.[60] Both the NFL and NFLPA should be commended for these partnerships.

However, players might not take advantage of these services. Consequently, an in-person introductory financial course would help to bridge the knowledge gap. Although the NFL's annual Rookie Transition Program likely includes discussions of financial issues (as its predecessor the Rookie Symposium did[61]), those are just some of the many issues players are presented with in a three-day event. Moreover, the Rookie Transition Program occurs before the player's first season and thus before players begin to receive their weekly pay, which is almost certainly the largest check the player has ever received. It would be beneficial to hold additional financial-focused courses or seminars after players begin to receive (and thus have the ability to spend) money. Two of the financial advisors interviewed recommended players take such a course. These would be useful supplements to the kinds of courses already offered by the NFL and NFLPA.

Relatedly, such courses could advise players of their rights concerning financial advisors, including the right to have their financial advisors' work audited.

Recommendations Concerning Financial Advisors – continued

Recommendation 13:2-B: The NFL and NFLPA should consider amending the player payment schedule so that players, by default, are paid over a 12-month period.

Players receive a check for each game they play. Thus, players generally only receive pay during the season.[z] As discussed above, some players might spend recklessly during the season, causing financial problems in the off-season or when their career is over. By paying a player over an entire year or deferring a player's salary payments for some period of time, the player will have additional income at a later point when he may not have otherwise saved for it. Indeed, in June 2014, the NFLPA was reportedly considering approaching the NFL about players being paid in 26 installments over a year,[62] and the issue is regularly considered at NFLPA Executive Committee meetings.[63]

In reviewing a draft of this Report, the NFL stated that "[t]here is no evidence cited in the Report that players face short-term stress during the year (or that they do so any more than other people), or that any longer- term financial problems would be alleviated by moving to a 12-month payment schedule."[64] Nevertheless, at least one club, the Tennessee Titans, does pay their players over a longer period of time, through March (when the League Year ends).[65] While it is uncertain if there is a problem with players spending too much money during the season, many players and contract advisors believe there is.[66] At a minimum, it is an issue in need of further consideration.

Andrew Brandt, a peer reviewer of this Report and a former Green Bay Packers executive, noted in his review that he used to provide players with the option of receiving their salary year-round in light of concerns he had about players' spending. While some players took the Packers up on the offer, the majority of players did not, as contract advisors often wanted interest to be paid on the deferred compensation.[67] While contract advisors are correct that players paid year round would be receiving slightly less based on the time value of money, a revised payment schedule would likely benefit players more than hurt them.

Making a 12-month payment schedule the default option could help ensure that all players have the opportunity to benefit from this possible change in payment schedule. Players should be free to opt out of a 12-month payment schedule if they like, but research suggests that most players will stay with the default option.[68]

Our recommendation supplements deferred compensation plans that the NFL offers, including the Player Annuity Plan and a 401(k) plan (the Second Career Savings Plan), discussed in detail in Appendix C. While these deferred compensation plans are retirement-focused, our recommendation is meant to help players better handle their income in the short term.[aa]

---

z   Players might receive bonuses during the offseason.

aa In Chapter 7: The NFL and NFLPA, Recommendation 7:3-B recommends that the NFL and NFLPA undertake a comprehensive actuarial and choice architecture analysis of the various benefit and retirement programs to ensure they are maximally beneficial to players.

Endnotes

1   *See* Thomas Richardson et al., *The relationship between personal un-secured debt and mental and physical health: A systematic review and meta-analysis,* Clinical Psychol. Rev. 2013;33(8):1148–62.

2   Pablo S. Torre, *How (and Why) Athletes Go Broke,* Sports Illustrated, Mar. 23, 2009, http://www.si.com/vault/2009/03/23/105789480/how-and-why-athletes-go-broke, *archived at* http://perma.cc/4E3Z-NHL6.

3   Linda Holmes, *ESPN's 'Broke' Looks At The Many Ways Athletes Lose Their Money,* NPR (Oct. 2, 2012 1:35 PM), http://www.npr.org/blogs/monkeysee/2012/10/02/162162226/espns-broke-looks-at-the-many-ways-athletes-lose-their-money, *archived at* http://perma.cc/4HDY-6AZ2.

4   *See* Jim Baumbach, *Life After Football,* Newsday, Jan. 22, 2015, http://data.newsday.com/projects/sports/football/life-football/, *archived at* http://perma.cc/77DP-LUUE.

5   *See* Ken Belson, *When Settlement Buys Time,* N.Y. Times, Jul. 19, 2014, http://www.nytimes.com/2014/07/19/sports/football/former-nfl-players-make-difficult-choice-in-opposing-concussion-settlement.html, *archived at* http://perma.cc/5P3D-94A8; Sally Jenkins and Rick Maese, *Do No Harm: Who Should Bear The Costs Of Retired NFL Players' Medical Bills?* Wash. Post, May 9, 2013, http://www.washingtonpost.com/sports/redskins/do-no-harm-who-should-bear-the-costs-of-retired-nfl-players-medical-bills/2013/05/09/2dae88ba-b70e-11e2-b568-6917f6ac6d9d_story.html, *archived at* http://perma.cc/VER2-EM24.

6   *See, e.g.,* Melissa B. Jacoby, Teresa A. Sullivan, & Elizabeth Warren, *Rethinking the Debates over Health Care Financing: Evidence from the Bankruptcy Courts,* 76 N.Y.U. L. Rev. 375 (2001) (empirical data demonstrating how many American families declare bankruptcy in the aftermath of illness or other healthcare crisis); Christopher Tarver Robertson, Richard Egelhof, & Michael Hoke, *Get Sick, Get Out: The Medical Causes of Home Mortgage Foreclosures,* 18 Health Matrix 65 (2008) (empirically demonstrating and discussing the role that health crises have in home foreclosures).

7   CBA, Art. 48, § 3.

8   *Report: Players Getting Bilked,* N.Y. Daily News, Feb. 4, 2002, *available at* 2002 WLNR 13839496. The figures in this report were aggregated by the NFLPA and include a variety of incidents, the details of which were not disclosed by the NFLPA in this publication.

9   Indeed, in *Atwater v. Nat'l Football League Players Ass'n,* 06-cv-1510, 2009 WL 3254925 (N.D.Ga. Mar. 27, 2009) *aff'd* 626 F.3d 1170 (11th Cir. 2010), six former players sued the NFLPA for losses they suffered by investing with NFLPA-registered Financial Advisors. The Court granted the NFLPA summary judgment, holding that the players' claims were preempted by the Labor Management Relations Act.

10 SEC No-Action Letter, Nat'l Football League Players Ass'n (Jan. 25, 2002), *available at* 2002 WL 100675.

11 The Financial Advisor Regulations are available from the NFLPA's website at http://nflparesources.blob.core.windows.net/mediaresources/files/PDFs/SCAA/2012_NFLPA_Regulations_Contract_Advisors.pdf, *archived at* https://perma.cc/D6E4-7USM?type=pdf.

12 *See* 2012 Financial Advisor Regulations, § 2(II).

13 *See* Julie Steinberg, *Colleges Push to Keep Financial Advisers Away From Athletes,* Wall St. J., Nov. 6, 2014, http://www.wsj.com/articles/colleges-push-to-keep-financial-advisers-away-from-athletes-1415331002?mod=WSJ_hp_RightTopStories, *archived at* http://perma.cc/HP9N-CKKF (discussing the increased recruiting efforts and unscrupulous practices of Financial Advisors).

14 Daniel Kaplan, *Show Me The Money: Morgan Stanley Offering Loans To Top NFL Draft Picks,* Sports Bus. Daily (May 11, 2015), http://www.sportsbusinessdaily.com/Daily/Issues/2015/05/11/Finance/Morgan-Stanley.aspx, *archived at* http://perma.cc/R3QV-MVA7.

15 *See* 2012 Financial Advisor Regulations, § 3(I)(A).

16 *See* Fiero v. Financial Industry Regulatory Authority, Inc., 660 F.3d 569 (2d Cir. 2011); *About FINRA,* Fin. Indus. Regulatory Auth., http://www.finra.org/AboutFINRA/ (last visited Aug. 7, 2015).

17 *Id.*

18 *About FINRA – What We Do,* Fin. Indus. Regulatory Auth., http://www.finra.org/AboutFINRA/WhatWeDo/ (last visited Aug. 7, 2015), *archived at* http://perma.cc/HWJ3-FCX7. In 2013, former NFLPA-registered Financial Advisor Jinesh "Hodge" Brahmbatt was banned by FINRA for his participation in an alleged fraud that cost NFL and NBA players an estimated $18 million. Rand Getlin, *Former Financial Adviser For NFL Players Banned From Industry By FINRA,* Yahoo! Sports (Nov. 18, 2013 1:33 PM), http://sports.yahoo.com/blogs/not-for-attribution/former-financial-adviser-nfl-players-banned-industry-finra-183315178.html, *archived at* http://perma.cc/7ZCW-EJHC.

19 *Guide to Broker-Dealer Registration,* U.S. Securities and Exchange Comm'n, https://www.sec.gov/divisions/marketreg/bdguide.htm (last visited Apr. 25, 2016), *archived at* https://perma.cc/W3G3-2K3Y.

20 Arthur B. Laby, *Fiduciary Obligations of Broker-Dealers and Investment Advisers,* 55 Vill. L. Rev. 701, 701 (2010).

21 *Guide to Broker-Dealer Registration,* U.S. Securities and Exchange Comm'n, https://www.sec.gov/divisions/marketreg/bdguide.htm (last visited Apr. 25, 2016), *archived at* https://perma.cc/W3G3-2K3Y; Michael S. Barr, Howell E. Jackson, Margaret E. Tahyar, Financial Regulation: Law and Policy 470 (2016).

22 *Id.*

23 *Id.*

24 Laby, *supra* note 20 at 702.

25 *Id.* at 714.

26 U.S.C. § 80b-3.

27 Michael S. Barr, Howell E. Jackson, Margaret E. Tahyar, Financial Regulation: Law and Policy 481 (2016).

28 Laby, *supra* note 20 at 702.

29 *Id.* at 716.

30 "Duty," Black's Law Dictionary (9th ed. 2009).

31 *Id.* at 702.

32 *See* Barr et al., *supra* note 27 at 480, *citing* RAND Institute for Civil Justice, *Investor and Industry Perspectives on Investment Advisors and Broker-Dealers* (2008).

33 C.F.R. § 2509–§ 2510; Tara Siegel Bernard, *'Customers First' to Become the Law in Retirement Investing,* N.Y. Times, Apr. 6, 2016, http://www.nytimes.com/2016/04/07/your-money/new-rules-for-retirement-accounts-financial-advisers.html, *archived at* https://perma.cc/5V38-4S2Q.

34 NFLPA Financial Advisor Regulations, § 4.

35 *Id.* at § 4(III).

36 *Id.* at § 3(I)(C).

37 *Id.* at § 4(II)(A).

38 *See Code of Ethics & Standards of Professional Conduct,* Cfa Inst., http://www.cfainstitute.org/ethics/codes/ethics/pages/index.aspx (last visited Aug. 7, 2015), *archived at* http://perma.cc/6T2Q-BF7V.

39 *See Code of Ethics & Professional Responsibility,* CFP Board, http://www.cfp.net/for-cfp-professionals/professional-standards-enforcement/standards-of-professional-conduct/code-of-ethics-professional-responsibility (last visited Aug. 7, 2015), *archived at* http://perma.cc/JQ4J-S4W4.

40 *See NAPFA Code of Ethics,* Nat'l Ass'n of Personal Fin. Advisors, http://napfa.org/about/CodeofEthics.asp (last visited Aug. 7, 2015), *archived at* http://perma.cc/Q96W-AXTK.

41 *See Id.*

42 *See Professional Ethics, Am. Ass'n of CPAs,* http://www.aicpa.org/interestareas/professionalethics/Pages/professionalethics.aspx (last visited Aug. 7, 2015), *archived at* http://perma.cc/NF7D-DAJS.

43 Michael David Smith, *NFL replaces rookie symposium with new rookie transition program,* ProFootballTalk (Apr. 5, 2016, 1:51 PM), http://profootballtalk.nbcsports.com/2016/04/05/nfl-replaces-rookie-symposium-with-new-rookie-transition-program/, *archived at* https://perma.cc/ML6Z-LVR5.

44 *See* Robert Klemko, *So This is the NFL, Part I,* The MMQB (July 8, 2014), http://mmqb.si.com/2014/07/08/nfl-rookie-symposium-part-1/, *archived at* http://perma.cc/2E8R-3S38; Robert Klemko, *So This is the NFL, Part II,* The MMQB (July 9, 2014), http://mmqb.si.com/2014/07/09/nfl-rookie-symposium-part-2/, *archived at* http://perma.cc/A9ZM-3WDD.

45 For more on the insurance options in professional sports, see Glenn M. Wong, Chris Deubert, *The Legal & Business Aspects of Career-Ending Disability Insurance Policies in Professional and College Sports,* 17 Vill. Sports & Ent. L.J. 473, 495 (2010).

46 Financial Advisor Regulations at § 3(E).

47 *Id.* at App. C, ¶ D.

48 *Id.* at § 6.

49 *See* 2012 Financial Advisor Regulations, Introduction.

50 *See, e.g.,* McFadden v. Vick, 16-cv-319 (E.D. Ark.); Vick v. Wong, 263 F.R.D. 325 (E.D. Va. 2009); Anderson v. Branch Banking and Trust Company, 2013-cv-62381 (S.D.Fla.); Johnson v. Amerus Life Ins. Co., 05-cv-61363, 2006 WL 3826774 (S.D.Fla. Dec. 27, 2006); *Clark v. Weisberg,* 98-cv-6214, 1999 WL 543191 (N.D. Ill. Jul. 23, 1999); Josh Alper, *Jared Odrick Sues Investment Adviser In Alleged Fraud,* ProFootballTalk (Apr. 21, 2013, 11:23 AM), http://profootballtalk.nbcsports.com/2013/04/21/jared-odrick-sues-investment-adviser-in-alleged-fraud/, *archived at* http://perma.cc/4U6D-R7KB.

51 *See, e.g.,* Devonshire v. Johnston Group First Advisors, 338 F. Supp. 2d 823 (N.D.Ohio 2004); Dymm v. Cahill, 730 F.Supp. 1245 (S.D.N.Y. 1990).

52 *See, e.g.,* Jordache Enterprises, Inc. v. Brobeck, Phleger & Harrison, 958 P.2d 1062 (Cal. 1998); Murphy v. Campbell, 964 S.W.2d 265 (Tex. 1997); Congregation of the Passion, Holy Cross Province v. Touche Ross & Co., 636 N.E.2d 503 (Ill. 1994); Peat, Marwick, Mitchell & Co. v. Lane, 565 So.2d 1323 (Fla. 1990).

53 *See, e.g.,* Thomas Lee Hazen, Treatise on the law of securities Regulation (2009).

54 Columnist Mike Freeman has made a similar recommendation. *See* Mike Freeman, Two Minute Warning: How Concussions, Crime, and Controversy Could Kill the NFL (and What the League Can Do to Survive) 225 (2015) ("as part of the CBA, every player in the league must show proof to the union that he meets with a union-approved financial advisor once every six months.").

55 Financial Advisor Regulations, § 4(II)(A)(12).

56 Contract Advisor Regulations, § 3(A)(6).

57 *Pipeline to the Pros,* NFLPA, https://www.nflpa.com/pipeline (last visited Aug. 7, 2015), *archived at* https://perma.cc/M8VS-4BM4; *Getting To Know Mark Levin,* NFLPA, Jun. 19, 2014, http://www.nflpa.com/news/all-news/getting-to-know-mark-levin, *archived at* http://perma.cc/27VK-G784.

58 *How to Pick Your Agent,* NFLPA, https://nflpa.com/active-players/how-to-pick-your-agent (last visited Aug. 7, 2015), *archived at* https://perma.cc/TA4L-8VM9.

59 *Financial Education,* NFL Player Engagement, https://www.nflplayerengagement.com/financial-education/ (last visited Aug. 7, 2015), *archived at* https://perma.cc/8FFU-ANMA?type=image.

60 *Financial Finesse,* Trust, http://playerstrust.com/your-trust/financial/financial-finesse (last visited Aug. 7, 2015), *archived at* http://perma.cc/Z7TM-FCNG.

61 *See* Robert Klemko, *So This is the NFL, Part I,* The MMQB (July 8, 2014), http://mmqb.si.com/2014/07/08/nfl-rookie-symposium-part-1/, *archived at* http://perma.cc/2E8R-3S38; Robert Klemko, *So This is the NFL, Part II,* The MMQB (July 9, 2014), http://mmqb.si.com/2014/07/09/nfl-rookie-symposium-part-2/, *archived at* http://perma.cc/A9ZM-3WDD.

62 Tom Pelissero, *Debates Simmer Over NFLPA Deferred Pay Proposal,* USA Today, Jun. 3, 2014, http://www.usatoday.com/story/sports/nfl/2014/06/03/kevin-williams-nflpa-payment-plan/9930969/, *archived at* http://perma.cc/3KPN-QX6B.

63 This information was provided by the NFLPA.

64 NFL Comments and Corrections (June 24, 2016).

65 Praesh Dave, *By Deferring Some Earnings, Athletes Can Help Themselves And Their Teams,* L.A. Times (Nov. 17, 2013, 5:00 AM), http://www.latimes.com/sports/la-sp-worst-sports-contracts-20131117-story.html#page=1.

66 Pelissero, *supra* n. 62.

67 Andrew Brandt, *Peer Review Response* (Oct. 30, 2015).

68 *See* Cass R. Sunstein, *Deciding by Default,* 162 U. Pa. L. Rev. 1, 3 (2013).

Chapter 14

Family Members

Families can play a crucial role in protecting and promoting player health, including by encouraging players to seek proper medical care and appropriately consider long-term interests, and they can offer support through challenging times. Unfortunately, in some cases, family members can also put inappropriate pressure on players or otherwise negatively influence their health. Thus, players' families, which include spouses, siblings, parents, adult children, and extended relatives, are an important set of stakeholders whose roles we must address.[a]

Additionally, friends often play a similar role to that of family members and thus much of what we say in this chapter can also apply to them.

---

a   We acknowledge that the issue of NFL players and domestic violence is an important one. However, these issues are outside the scope of this Report. Our focus here is on the effect of a family on the player and his health, not the effect of a player on family health.

In order to ensure that this chapter was as accurate and valuable as possible, the President of the Off the Field Players' Wives Association (a group of NFL player wives), Ericka Lassiter, who is also a Family Advisor to The Football Players Health Study at Harvard University, arranged for three wives of former NFL players to review a draft of this chapter prior to publication. Two of the wives provided comments.

(A) Background

When it comes to a person's health, family is extremely important.[1] NFL players are no different. Family members can provide guidance, comfort, love and support. NFL players—given the multitude of issues with which they must deal—certainly benefit from having a caring and supportive family.

However, NFL family members sometimes may be the source of problems for players. In 2016, the minimum salary for an NFL player is $450,000 for a rookie and $675,000 for a player with at least three years' experience.[2] Clearly, NFL players are paid well while playing as compared to the general population. Thus, it should not be surprising that NFL players frequently feel pressure from family members for financial support.[3] Coupled with the short careers of NFL players, it is also not surprising that family pressure can financially ruin current or former professional athletes.[4]

As with the general population, NFL players marry and divorce. A 2009 NFL-funded study of former NFL players by the University of Michigan (Michigan Study) provides some data.[5] The Michigan Study found that, of 1,063 former players interviewed, 76.3 percent between the ages of 30 and 49 at the time of the study were married before or during their NFL careers.[6] In addition, of the former players interviewed and between 30 and 49, 75.5 percent were currently married (a statistic that would include second marriages).[7] By comparison, only 64.4 percent of American men between 30 and 49 are married.[8]

The divorce rate for professional athletes has been estimated at 60 to 80 percent,[9] though the figures obtained as part of the Michigan Study are very different. The Michigan Study found that only 19.7 percent of former players between 30 and 49 had ever been divorced.[10] By contrast, 25.6 percent of all American men between 30 and 49 have been divorced.[11]

Of those former players aged 30–49 at the time of the study and who had married before or during their NFL career, 7.6 percent had their marriage end during their career, 13.3 percent had their marriage end less than five years after their career ended, and 6.9 percent had their marriage end five or more years after their career ended.[12]

Figures from a 2014–2015 survey of 763 former players by *Newsday* paint a different picture than those from the Michigan Study. The *Newsday* survey found that 29.8 percent of former players interviewed experienced "marital problems" during their career and 48.2 percent experienced "marital problems" after their career.[13] While "marital problems" are different from divorce, the *Newsday* survey suggests that former players' family lives are not as stable as was suggested in the earlier Michigan Study.

Also, the Michigan Study found that former players between 30 and 49 had a mean of 2.28 children.[14]

Clearly there are many factors that affect the constitution and stability of NFL families. Some players are lucky to have excellent support systems before, during, and after their careers, while others do not. The question is what are the legal and ethical obligations of family members as they concern an NFL player's health?

Before moving on, it is important to know that there are limitations to the *Newsday* and Michigan Study analyses.

The *Newsday* survey is limited as follows: (1) the survey was sent via email and text message by the NFLPA to more than 7,000 former NFL players, thus eliminating former players who were less technologically savvy and also possibly skewing the sample towards those former players closer to the NFLPA; (2) the response rate for the survey was low (approximately 11 percent); and, (3) the study does not discuss the demographics of those that responded, making it difficult to ascertain whether those who responded are a representative sample of all former players.

There are also two potential limitations to the Michigan Study. First, the Michigan Study population only included players who had vested rights under the NFL's Retirement Plan; meaning, the players generally had been on an NFL roster for at least three games in at least three seasons. There is likely a significant but unknown percentage of NFL players who never become vested under the Retirement Plan. Second, responders to the survey were 36.8 percent African American and 61.4 percent white—almost a complete reversal of the NFL's population of current players. While the racial demographics of former players is likely closer to the population of the Michigan

Study, *i.e.*, there were more white players than in the current NFL, the Michigan Study did not provide such data on the former player population and did not adjust or account for the racial demographics of the former player population. In a telephone call with Dr. David Weir, the lead author of the Michigan Study, he explained that: (1) due to limited resources, the population of players to be studied and contacted was limited to the data and contact information available to and provided by the NFL; and, (2) the NFL did not provide racial demographics of former players and thus the study could not adjust for that factor. Weir also believes that the racial demographics of former players is substantially similar to the racial demographics of the Michigan Study's participants. Finally, Weir explained that, during the internal review process with the NFL, the study was leaked to the media, preventing the study from being amended and submitted to a peer-reviewed publication.

(B) Current Legal Obligations[b]

At the outset, it is important to be clear that we are analyzing the obligations of family members to players, rather than the obligations of players to their families. Although players have obligations to their families, that is outside the scope of this Report.

When it comes to legal obligations of family members, there is a significant body of law, family law, that governs these relationships but little of it is relevant to the health of NFL players. The most common understanding of the legal relationship between spouses results from cases of divorce, where the parties have to divide their property and determine alimony and child support obligations in accordance with state law. However, divorce law generally does not elucidate the obligations of spouses to one another while married. Moreover, any such obligations would generally extinguish upon divorce.[c]

There is some case law holding spouses and parents to be fiduciaries and thus subject to fiduciary duties under law.[15] Generally speaking, a fiduciary is "a person who is required to act for the benefit of another person on all matters within the scope of their relationship; one who owes to another the duties of good faith, trust, confidence, and candor; . . . [o]ne who must exercise a high standard of care

in managing another's money or property."[16] Whether a fiduciary relationship exists is a fact-based inquiry into the nature of the relationship.[17] In other words, where an individual trusts and relies on a person to look out for his or her best interests, a fiduciary, and thus a legal, relationship can be formed.

If an NFL player consults with his family about health concerns, *and* a family member is held to be a fiduciary to the player (which may be unlikely), then the family member is legally obligated to provide advice that is in the best interests of the player, regardless of the effect on the family member. For example, if a player explains to his wife-as-fiduciary that he is suffering from post-concussion symptoms and is considering retirement, the wife's advice must be principally concerned with the player's best interests as opposed to how the wife might benefit from the player's continued playing. As a practical matter, these types of conversations and balancing of pros and cons often occur naturally and are the subject of a mutual decision making process. Nevertheless, it is important to understand that family members may have legal obligations to one another. That said, these obligations, even where legally recognized, may not often be enforced.

> Several professional athletes claim to have been led to bankruptcy as a result of letting their parents handle their financial affairs.

In addition, family members might assume fiduciary, contractual or other legal obligations by virtue of taking on roles and responsibilities beyond just being a family member. For example, if a family member undertakes to handle a player's financial or legal affairs, then the family member will likely have assumed a fiduciary role on behalf of the player and could be held to the legal and ethical standards of financial and legal professionals. Indeed, several professional athletes claim to have been led to bankruptcy as a result of letting their parents handle their financial affairs.[18] The legal and ethical obligations of contract advisors are discussed in Chapter 12, and the obligations of financial advisors are discussed in Chapter 13. If and when family members play either of these roles, the content of those chapters would also apply.

---

b   The legal obligations described herein are not an exhaustive list but are those we believe are most relevant to player health.

c   Similarly, family law statutes control the obligations of parents to their children, but only until the child reaches a certain age (typically 18). As all NFL players are legally adults, their parents no longer have any obligations to them that would be governed by family law statutes.

(C) Current Ethical Codes

There are no known ethical codes for family members.

(D) Current Practices

Interviews with players and contract advisors confirmed that family members play a role, but often a secondary one, in player health decisions. Players, of course, have varying relationships with their families, which dictate how involved a family member might be in advising a player or the player's contract advisor on various matters. A family member's involvement might vary depending on the player's point in his career.

When it comes to current players, while they generally discuss their current injuries and health concerns with their partners or other significant family members, they tend to rely most on their contract advisor and the doctors involved (*e.g.,* club and second opinion) to determine the appropriate course of action. Relatedly, it is likely the contract advisor who will handle the logistics of the care.

The below quotations show the differences in player opinion about the involvement of family in player health matters:[d]

- **Current Player 1:** *"[T]hey just kinda offer moral support . . . whatever happened they would have my back . . . . [B]ut it's really up to me – I'll make those decisions for myself."*

- **Current Player 2:** *"[Family members] play a huge role in the mental and emotional health of players."*

- **Current Player 4:** *"I think parents are huge."*

- **Current Player 5:** *"I'm very close to my parents. And they're always actively informed of what my injuries are, they make suggestions. But I would say my family's very, very limited in their involvement in my health and safety."*

- **Current Player 6:** *"As far as career decisions, I think family is a major, major factor . . . . The family can be helpful if somebody has a wife and kids to come home to and they have this structure at home."*

- **Former Player 3:** *"I don't think you can overstate the importance of a solid family unit behind you."*

Players approaching retirement are particularly likely to consult with their family members concerning their health. The players we interviewed discussed sometimes being "torn" between the desires of their family members that they stop playing and their own desires to keep playing.[e] Family members often see a player when he is at his worst, perhaps even unable to move after a game, practice or particular injury. It is in these moments that family members often encourage players to stop playing for the sake of their future health. Nevertheless, encouragement and convincing are often two very different things.

Anna Welker, the wife of wide receiver Wes Welker, provides a positive example. As Wes continued to suffer concussions during his career, Anna educated herself about brain injuries in professional football. Then, at Anna's behest, Wes agreed to get regular MRIs and to see his own neurologist twice a week.[19] Although Anna still had concerns about Wes' continuing to play, she took a proactive step in furthering the health of her husband.

Several players, contract advisors, and financial advisors also affirmed that family members sometimes place excessive pressures, particularly financial, on players. Family members might expect or request gifts, jobs or cash.[20] Former NFL player Phillip Buchanon claimed that his mother demanded $1 million from him when he was drafted in 2002.[21] Current players explained these concerns:

- **Current Player 2:** *"[T]he wrong kind of family member can put a strain on your health. . . . [Y]ou have those family members that are maybe looking for handouts."* *"They think it's an easy meal ticket. I think some women are smart enough to see that and try to take advantage of it."*

- **Current Player 4:** *"There's definitely family members, girlfriends, friends, acquaintances, all those people [that] will ask you for money."*

- **Current Player 6:** *"I know situations where families were a cancer to players . . . Football players have gotten into a lot of trouble because they have problems with their brother who is a troublemaker and they trust in their brother but their brother might have been the worst thing for them."*

- **Current Player 9:** *"It's family members, it's friends, it's those people that it's very hard to say 'no' to."*

- **Former Player 3:** Players might feel pressure from family to continue playing *"because the players might be the breadwinner for, not just for themselves, but maybe for a parent, or taking care of siblings, cousins, uncles, etc."*

---

d   We reiterate that our interviews were intended to be informational but not representative of all players' views and should be read with that limitation in mind.

e   Family members might also want players to keep playing, as was apparently the case when former San Francisco 9ers defensive end Justin Smith retired after the 2014 season. *See* Josh Alper, *Eric Reid: Even Justin Smith's Wife Wants Him To Come Back*, ProFootballTalk (Apr. 9, 2015, 6:33 AM), http://profootballtalk.nbcsports.com/2015/04/09/eric-reid-even-justin-smiths-wife-wants-him-to-come-back/, *archived at* http://perma.cc/9E8F-RRCG.

Additionally, family members might set out to be substantially involved in the player's career, including potentially handling the player's financial matters. These situations can lead to mismanaged finances and broken family relationships. During the 2014 Rookie Symposium, when discussing family members or old friends or girlfriends that do not have the player's best interests in mind, St. Louis Rams running back Zac Stacy bluntly advised rookie players to "cut 'em off."[22] At the same Symposium, former NFL player Donovan Darius discussed the "most consistent concerns of players: How do you deal with females understanding that you're now a target? How do you deal with the entitlement of family members who now see you for what you can give them? Who can I trust to support my interests in the NFL?"[23]

(E) Enforcement of Legal and Ethical Obligations[f]

Litigation between professional athletes and their family members is rare but not without precedent.

---

f   Appendix K is a summary of players' options to enforce legal and ethical obligations against the stakeholders discussed in this Report.

In 2013, Philadelphia Phillies (Major League Baseball) first baseman Ryan Howard was sued by his twin brother, Corey Howard, alleging that Ryan had breached agreements to employ Corey and other family members.[24] Ryan countersued, alleging that Corey and his family members had fraudulently stolen millions of dollars from Ryan under the guise of handling Ryan's financial and legal affairs.[25] Ryan specifically alleged that Corey had abused the relationship of "trust and confidence,"[26] *i.e.,* a fiduciary relationship, between the brothers. The lawsuit was settled on undisclosed terms in October 2014.[27]

In 2012, Dallas Cowboys offensive lineman Tyron Smith was forced to obtain a protective order against his parents and siblings after they allegedly continued to harass him with financial requests.[28]

However, as discussed above, there are minimal legal and ethical obligations between NFL players and their family members in the absence of additional duties like those alleged in the *Howard* case. Thus, while NFL players could conceivably sue family members for breach of contract or breach of fiduciary duty in the appropriate circumstances, such claims are not unique to the relationships between NFL players and their family members.

(F) Recommendations Concerning Family Members

Family members often are and should be one of a player's most trusted allies and confidants in matters concerning their health. In most cases, family members love and care for the players who are their husbands, fathers, sons, or brothers. Nevertheless, just as some players are not prepared for an NFL career, the same is sometimes true for family members. Below are recommendations concerning family members that can help improve the ways in which they support players.

Goal 1: To maximize the supportive role of players' family members in protecting and promoting player health.

Principles Advanced: Respect; Health Primacy; Empowered Autonomy; and, Collaboration and Engagement.

Recommendation 14:1-A: Family members should be cognizant of the gaps in their knowledge concerning the realities of an NFL career, and the NFL and NFLPA should offer programs or materials to help them become better health advocates.

The lives of players and their families are obviously intertwined. A player's career can have meaningful implications for his family members, particularly financially. Nevertheless, despite their best intentions, family members, like most people, might not have an accurate understanding of an NFL player's likely career length and earnings, as well as the physical risks players face in playing the game. Ideally, family members, with the help of the NFL and NFLPA, can understand the tenuous nature of an NFL career and encourage players to think long term. At the same time, family members should be careful about the pressures they might place on players.

Family members often are more in touch with concerns about the player's life than a contract advisor or financial advisor might be. Consequently, family members can help themselves and players by learning about a player's health situations and understanding what might be done to safeguard them, including but not limited to the player's physical, mental, and financial situations.

We do not suggest any formal legal or ethical responsibility for family members to advance player health in these ways, but we do recommend that interested family members be supported with adequate resources. For example, the NFL and NFLPA could provide information and seminars on relevant health issues or support systems and programs for players and families suffering from various conditions.

Goal 2: To separate family members from professional management of players' careers and affairs.

Principles Advanced: Empowered Autonomy; and, Managing Conflicts of Interest.

Recommendation 14:2-A: Players should select and rely on professionals rather than family members for managing their business, financial, and legal affairs.

Player financial and legal matters are complicated issues that should be handled by qualified professionals. Even if a player's family member is qualified, it is often best to preserve relationships by avoiding the conflicts that may arise by mixing family and finances. In Chapter 12: Contract Advisors and Chapter 13: Financial Advisors, we make recommendations for improving those industries to ensure that the professionals player do rely on are well-qualified.

Endnotes

1   *See* Laura A. Siminoff, *Incorporating patient and family preferences into evidence-based medicine,* 13(Suppl. 3) BMC Med. Informatics and Decision Making S6 (2013) ("recognition of the influences family members and other caregivers have within the clinical encounter—by offering opinions and participating in treatment-related decision making—is needed and could lead to more efficient and effective health care."); Carin Reust, *Family involvement in medical decision making,* 28 Fam. Med. 39 (1996) ("patients acknowledge the context of family life in medical decision making, while families actively promote patient autonomy. Consideration of nonmedical burdens related to family roles and relationships takes an equal or higher priority than consideration of medical burdens. Family is, and should be treated as, a significant moral participant in medical decision making.")

2   CBA, Art. 26, § 1(a).

3   *See* Tim Keown, *Financial Requests Overwhelm Smith,* ESPN (Nov. 26, 2014), http://espn.go.com/nfl/story/_/page/hotread141125/dallas-cowboys-tyro, *archived at* http://perma.cc/G8QQ-FUEK; Anna Katherine Clemmons et al., *Money Confidential,* ESPN (Nov. 25, 2014), http://espn.go.com/espn/story/_/id/11931251/nfl-nba-nhl-mlb-stars-divul, *archived at* http://perma.cc/MT5K-CHM9 (survey of 37 professional athletes revealed that, on average, players were asked for a loan from a friend or family member 25.5 times in the last year and that only 27.6 percent of loans are paid back); Robert Pagliarini, *Why Pro Athletes Go Broke,* Chi. Trib., Aug. 6, 2013, http://articles.chicagotribune.com/2013-08-06/lifestyle/sns-201308061630--tms--pagliarictnrp-a20130806-20130806_1_athletes-nfl-player-financial-stability, *archived at* http://perma.cc/M49C-6UST; Pablo S. Torre, *How (and Why) Athletes Go Broke,* Sports Illustrated, Mar. 23, 2009, http://www.si.com/vault/2009/03/23/105789480/how-and-why-athletes-go-broke, *archived at* http://perma.cc/4E3Z-NHL6; Melissa Isaacson, *Paradise Lost, Paradise Found, Big Money Brings Out 'Friends' Young Stars Don't Know They Had,* Chi. Trib., Mar. 5, 2000, *available at* 2000 WLNR 8289967; Mary Judice, *Pro Football Players Make More Money in a Few Years than Most People Do in a Lifetime, But Spend it Like There's No Tomorrow,* New Orleans Times Picayune, Sept. 12, 1999, *available at* 1999 WLNR 1256308.

4   *Id.*

5   David R. Weir, et al., *National Football League Player Care Foundation Study of Retired NFL Players,* Inst. for Social Research at Univ. of Mich. (2009), https://ns.umich.edu/Releases/2009/Sep09/FinalReport.pdf, *archived at* https://perma.cc/6G5Q-LN2M?type=pdf.

6   *Id.*

7   *Id.*

8   *Id.*

9   Torre, *supra* note 3.

10 Weir *supra* note 5.

11 *Id.*

12 *Id.* at 15.

13 *See* Jim Baumbach, *Life After Football,* Newsday, Jan. 22, 2015, http://data.newsday.com/projects/sports/football/life-football/, *archived at* http://perma.cc/77DP-LUUE.

14 Jim Baumbach, *Life After Football,* Newsday, Jan. 22, 2015, http://data.newsday.com/projects/sports/football/life-football, *archived at* http://perma.cc/77DP-LUUE.

15 *See* Swanson v. Morrison, 172 Wash.App. 1040, *2 (Wash. Ct. App. 2013) ("spouses.., owe each other the highest fiduciary duties") (internal quotations omitted); Vickery v. Vickery, 999 S.W.2d 342, 357 (Tex. 1999) ("A husband and wife owe each other special fiduciary duties"); Smith v. Smith, 860 P.2d 634, 643 (Idaho 1993) ("The marital relationship imposes the high duty of care of a fiduciary upon each of the parties"); Unander v. Unander, 506 P.2d 719, 722 n.2 (Or. 1973)

("spouses . . . have a fiduciary duty to each other"); Murphy v. Murphy, 694 A.2d 932, 936 (Me. 1997) (discussing fiduciary duty owed by parent to child); L.C. v. A.D., 971 S.W.2d 512, 517 (Tex. App. 1997) (same); Robinson v. State, Dept. of Health and Rehabilitative Services on Behalf of Robinson, 473 So.2d 228, 230 (Fla. Dist. Ct. App. 1985) (same).

16 "Duty," Black's Law Dictionary (9th ed. 2009).

17 Ritani, LLC v. Aghjayan, 880 F. Supp. 2d 425, 455 (S.D.N.Y. 2012) (applying New York law); Carcano v. JBSS, LLC, 684 S.E.2d 41, 53 (N.C. Ct. App. 2009); L.C. v. R.P., 563 N.W.2d 799, 802 (N.D. 1997); Allen Realty Corp. v. Holbert, 318 S.E.2d 592, 595 (Va. 1984); Murphy v. Country House, Inc., 240 N.W.2d 507, 511 (Minn. 1976).

18 *See* Katie Strang, *Jack Johnson: Little Left Of Earnings,* ESPN (Nov. 21, 2014), http://espn.go.com/nhl/story/_/id/11908361/columbus-blue-jackets-d-jack-johnson-files-bankruptcy-parents-reportedly-blame, *archived at* http://perma.cc/5UEA-CNMK (Columbus Blue Jackets defenseman Jack Johnson forced to file for bankruptcy after entrusting $18 million in career earnings to his parents); Tim Russo, *Bernie Kosar & His Cowardly Dad on ESPN Outside The Lines Story,* Cleveland Leader, Nov. 2, 2014, http://www.clevelandleader.com/node/23339, *archived at* http://perma.cc/7499-HMD5 (former Cleveland Browns quarterback Bernie Kosar forced to file for bankruptcy after entrusting his career earnings to his father).

19 Kevin Van Valkenburg, *Wes Welker Will Not Be Denied,* ESPN The Magazine, Dec. 18, 2014, http://espn.go.com/espn/feature/story/_/id/12046903/is-denver-broncos-wes-welker-putting-future-danger, *archived at* http://perma.cc/V5N6-Q3DW.

20 *See* Michael David Smith, *Trent Richardson says greedy friends and family affected his career,* ProFootballTalk (Aug. 6, 2016, 5:45 AM), http://profootballtalk.nbcsports.com/2016/08/06/trent-richardson-says-greedy-friends-and-family-affected-his-career/, *archived at* https://perma.cc/5FZV-GYC7.

21 Michael David Smith, *Phillip Buchanon's Cautionary Tale: My Mom Demanded $1 Million,* ProFootballTalk (Apr. 11, 2015, 9:50 AM), http://profootballtalk.nbcsports.com/2015/04/11/phillip-buchanons-cautionary-tale-my-mom-demanded-1-million/, *archived at* http://perma.cc/3ASQ-FZXN; *see also* Michael David Smith, *When T-Rich got rich, friends and family had their hands out,* ProFootballTalk (Mar. 26, 2016, 1:09 PM), http://profootballtalk.nbcsports.com/2016/03/26/when-t-rich-got-rich-friends-and-family-had-their-hands-out/, *archived at* https://perma.cc/Z8EX-QZXR.

22 Robert Klemko, *So This is the NFL, Part I,* MMQB (Jul. 8, 2014), http://mmqb.si.com/2014/07/08/nfl-rookie-symposium-part-1/, *archived at* http://perma.cc/2E8R-3S38.

23 Robert Klemko, *So This is the NFL, Part II,* MMQB *(Jul. 9, 2014),* http://mmqb.si.com/2014/07/09/nfl-rookie-symposium-part-2/, *archived at* http://perma.cc/A9ZM-3WDD.

24 *See* Complaint, Howard v. RJH Enterprises, LLC, 13-cv-2518 (E.D.Mo. Dec. 18, 2013), ECF #1.

25 *See* Answer and Counterclaim, Howard v. RJH Enterprises, LLC, 13-cv-2518 (E.D.Mo. Jan. 27, 2014), ECF #8.

26 *Id.* at ¶ 36.

27 Joint Stipulation of Dismissal With Prejudice, Howard v. RJH Enterprises, LLC, 13-cv-2518 (E.D.Mo. Oct. 22, 2014), ECF #40; David Murphy, *The Family Legal Fight Over Ryan Howard's Finances,* Philly (Nov. 19, 2014, 8:43 AM), http://www.philly.com/philly/sports/phillies/The_family_legal_fight_over_Ryan_Howards_finances.html, *archived at* http://perma.cc/H7LD-GNAQ.

28 Tim Keown, *Financial Requests Overwhelm Smith,* ESPN (Nov. 26, 2014), http://espn.go.com/nfl/story/_/page/hotread141125/dallas-cowboys-tyro, *archived at* http://perma.cc/G8QQ-FUEK.

Part 6: **Other Stakeholders**

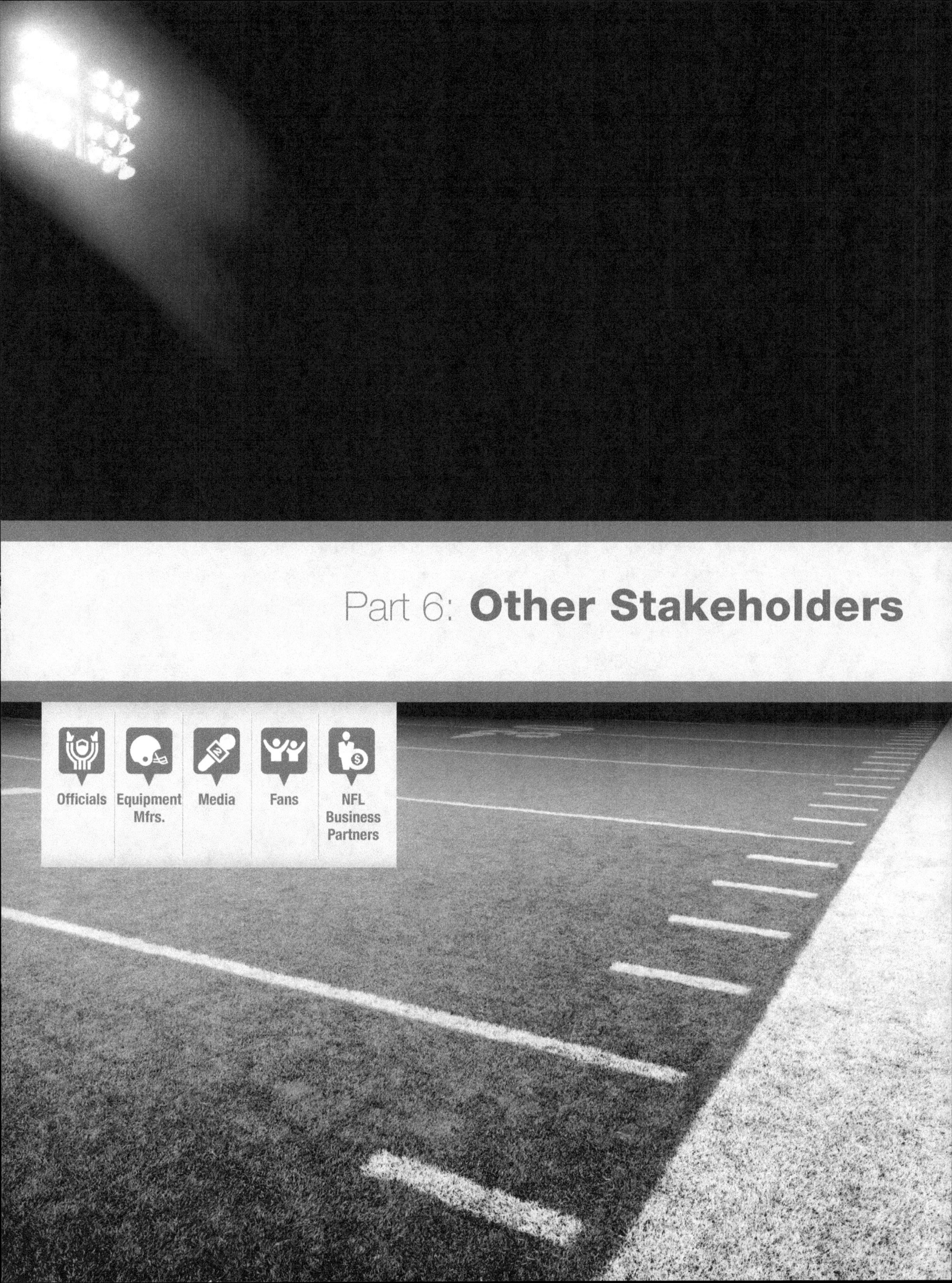

Officials | Equipment Mfrs. | Media | Fans | NFL Business Partners

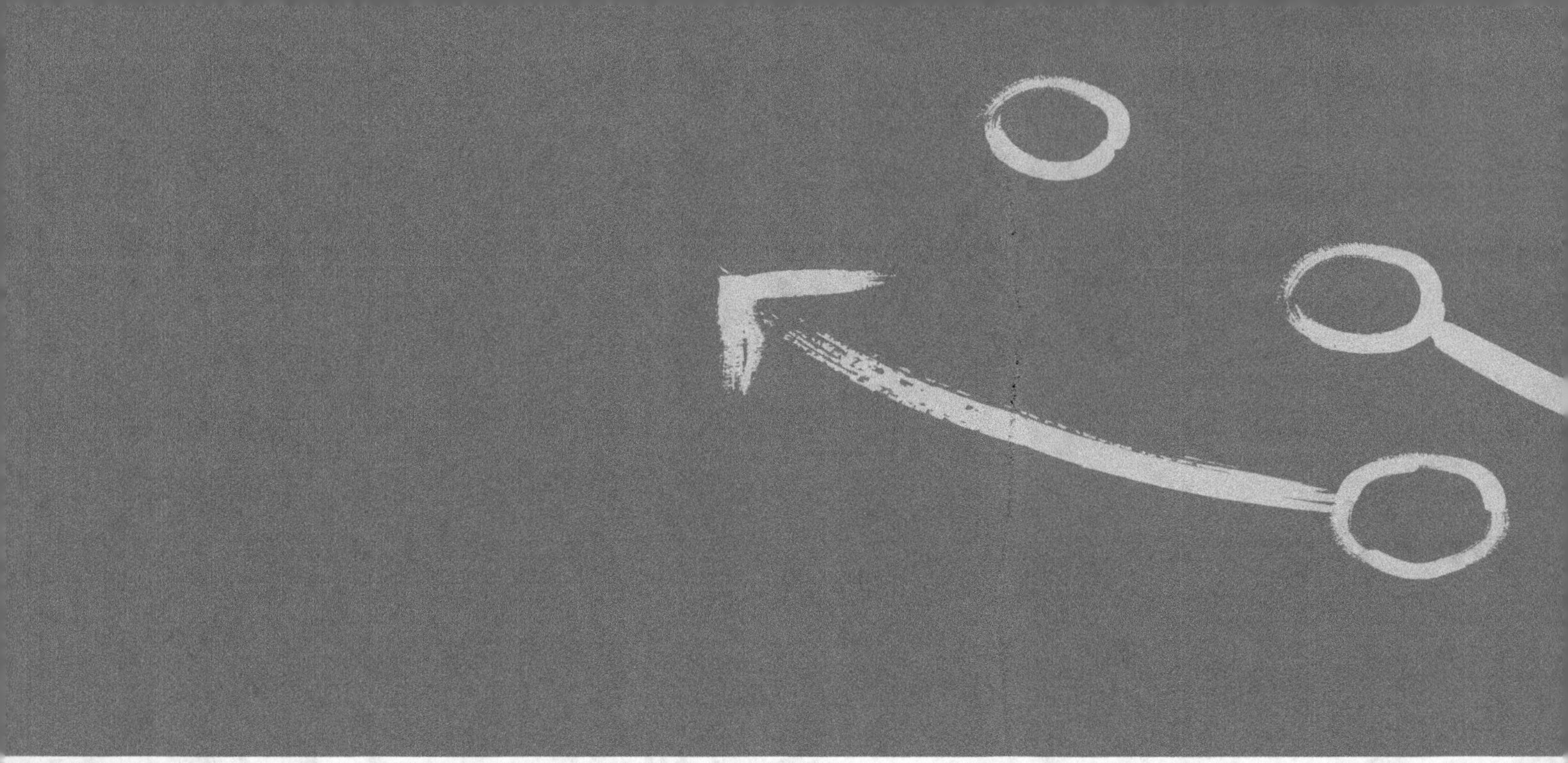

Part 6 discusses several other stakeholders with a variety of roles in player health, including: Officials; Equipment Manufacturers; The Media; Fans; and, NFL Business Partners. Additionally, we remind the reader that while we have tried to make the chapters accessible for standalone reading, certain background or relevant information may be contained in other parts or chapters, specifically Part 1 discussing Players and Part 3 discussing the NFL and the NFLPA. Thus, we encourage the reader to review other parts of this Report as needed for important context.

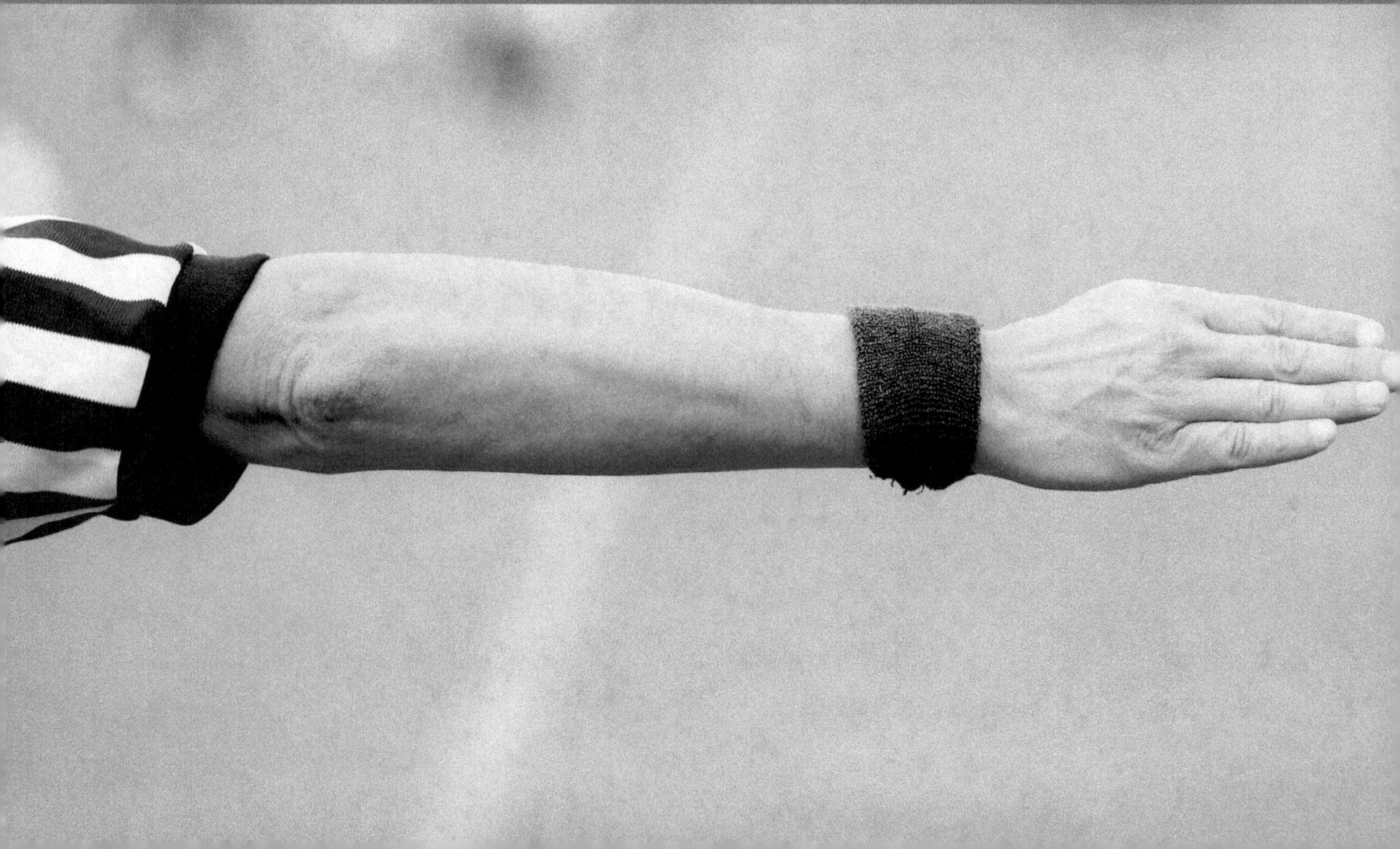

Chapter 15

Officials

Officials, as the individuals responsible for enforcing the Playing Rules, have an important role in protecting player health on the field.

In order to ensure that this chapter was as accurate and valuable as possible, we invited the National Association of Sports Officials (NASO) and the National Football League Referees Association (NFLRA), both described below, to review a draft version of this chapter prior to publication. NASO provided brief comments but also stated that it did "not have any changes [it] feel[s] must be made."[62] The NFLRA declined our invitation.[63]

(A) Background

There are seven officials in an NFL game: Referee; Umpire; Head Linesman; Line Judge; Field Judge; Side Judge; and, Back Judge.[1] Each official is equally responsible for calling penalties during a game.[2] Each official is positioned differently on the field and the Referee is in charge of the officiating crew.

There were 122 officials during the 2015 season, with a mean of 11.5 years' experience in the NFL.[3] Most NFL officials have 10 to 20 years of experience at the high school and college levels before becoming an NFL official.[4] The NFL typically hires its officials from the best college football conferences.[5]

NFL officials are represented by the NFLRA. The NFLRA collectively bargains the terms and conditions of the officials' employment with the NFL. In fall 2012, the NFL locked out the officials after the parties were unable to agree on a new collective bargaining agreement (CBA).[6] The lockout stretched from the preseason through the first quarter of the regular season, during which time replacement officials made numerous questionable calls, drawing the ire of players, coaches, and fans.[7] In early September 2012, NFLPA General Counsel Tom DePaso wrote a letter to the NFL warning that the NFLPA would take "appropriate action" if it was determined that the replacement officials jeopardized the health and safety of the players.[8] The NFLPA may have been concerned that the replacement officials would miss certain penalties, thereby effectively allowing riskier and more dangerous play.

In late September 2012, the parties reached a new CBA running through the 2019 season.[9] The new CBA included a modified retirement structure through which the officials would partially contribute, an increase in pay to $173,000 per year in 2013, rising to $205,000 in 2019, and the option for the NFL to retain full-time officials (officials previously only worked during the preseason and season).[10] The NFL-NFLRA CBA does not address player health issues.[11]

Every NFL official is a member of NASO.[12] The NFLRA automatically enrolls all of its members as NASO members.[13] NASO is a voluntary organization of approximately 22,000 member officials, ranging from the lowest levels of youth sports to the professionals.[14] NASO provides an extensive list of services to its members, including educational programs, legal advocacy, and insurance policies.[15]

NASO, however, does not certify officials.[16] Each sports organization, whether it is a state high school athletic association, the National Collegiate Athletic Association (NCAA), or the NFL, judges the qualifications of its officials during its hiring process.[17]

(B) Current Legal Obligations[a]

Sports officials of all levels of play have generally been held to have the following legal duties: (1) inspect the field of play to ensure it is safe; (2) keep the playing field free of spectators and hazards; (3) ensure the game is played in safe weather conditions; and, (4) enforce equipment rules.[18] These duties might appear limited but courts are historically reluctant to consider review of officials' on-field decisions during the course of play, such as whether an official failed to call a penalty or to apply a rule properly.[19] Additionally, if players or other individuals seek to hold officials liable for a breach of one of the aforementioned duties, they must generally prove that the official acted with "gross negligence," as opposed to simple negligence.[20] The gross negligence requirement has historically applied to volunteer officials[21] and thus it is unclear whether the same standard would apply to professional officials.

Official liability has also been shaped by robust lobbying efforts of the NASO.[22] Sixteen states have passed laws requiring proof of gross negligence by an official before liability can be imposed.[23] The application of these laws is limited to youth sports, amateur sports, or volunteer officials in 13 states.[24] Three states (Tennessee, Mississippi, and Nevada) have laws restricting liability against officials that are not restricted to youth sports, amateur sports, or volunteer officials, and thus would protect NFL officials.[25] However, Tennessee is the only one of these states in which NFL clubs play.

NASO is aware of, and concerned about, the reach of state-level concussion-related legislation, discussed at length in Part 7: Other Interested Parties, Section 3: Governments.[26] NASO is concerned that these laws improperly require lay officials to make medical determinations.[27] NASO is working to educate officials on the skills to recognize and report players with suspected medical conditions, and to always err on the side of caution by requiring players to be removed from play.[28]

---

a   The legal obligations described herein are not an exhaustive list but are those we believe are most relevant to player health.

(C) Current Ethical Codes

NASO also issues a Code of Conduct for Sports Officials, but none of NASO's stated principles concern player health and safety.[29] Moreover, NASO does not itself enforce its Code of Conduct.[30] Instead, it is NASO's intention that its Code of Conduct be adopted and enforced by the athletic associations and sports leagues that have authority over the officials.[31]

The NFLRA does not have a code of ethics.[32]

(D) Current Practices

Many people have argued that the Playing Rules, and thus perhaps also the officials, have become overprotective of players' health and safety. That is, people often think that the Playing Rules, and thus also the officials, too frequently penalize players for certain types of tackles or hits, particularly on quarterbacks.[33] This opinion is held by many members of the media,[34] fans,[35] and players,[36,b] among others.

Officials do play some role in the rulemaking process; they attend NFL Competition Committee meetings and participate in the discussion on proposed rule changes.[37] Moreover, certain rules do permit the official to take into consideration the likelihood of injury in determining whether to call a penalty, including roughing the passer[38] and roughing the holder on a place kick.[39] Nevertheless, the NFL makes the Playing Rules and it is the officials' principal job is to enforce them. On that front, there is generally no criticism that officials are failing to enforce the Playing Rules as enacted by the NFL.

In addition to calling penalties, NFL officials are empowered to call an "Injury Timeout" if he or she "determines a player to be injured."[40] In recent years, the NFL has actively encouraged officials to try and pay particular attention to see if players might be injured and to stop play accordingly.[41] While it might be challenging for officials to determine whether a player is actually injured or faking an injury for competitive reasons, according to NASO, officials are taught to err on the side of caution.[42] However, the Playing Rules also direct that the official "should not try to determine if [a] player is injured."[43] There are likely concerns about officials attempting to make medical determinations. Nevertheless, these two provisions seem to contradict and thus clarification may be warranted.

Despite the officials' ability to prevent play from continuing when a player is injured, during the 2014 season there were several publicized examples of players who continued to play in games after suffering concussions.[44] In the case of San Diego Chargers safety Jahleel Addae, "he looked disoriented and seemed to go into a convulsion while remaining on his feet, but he stayed in the game while fans on social media questioned why he was still playing while displaying such obvious distress."[45] While the Addae incident caused the NFL to advise team medical staffs to be more vigilant about spotting concussions,[46] it also raised concerns about the officials' failure to spot Addae's odd movements and to stop play as a result. Similar concerns were raised when New England Patriots wide receiver Julian Edelman looked "woozy" after suffering a hit in the 2015 Super Bowl.[47] Due partially to these incidents, in 2015 the NFL approved a rule that permits an athletic trainer stationed in the press box to stop play if it appears a player has suffered a head injury.[48]

> In recent years, the NFL has actively encouraged officials to try and pay particular attention to see if players might be injured and to stop play accordingly.

Players that we interviewed seemed to believe that officials are doing an adequate job in enforcing the current rules but are not likely to take any other action concerning player health:[c]

Current Player 5: *"I think that they're doing as good of a job as they can. They're trying to do their best. I think with the targeting rules and the head to head contact, I think they've been overly cautious which, when it comes to protecting players, is probably on the right end. But besides that, I've never seen an official step outside the rule book to protect a player."*

Former Player 2: *"I don't think they play much role other than if they see a guy banged up, they're just going to make sure he seeks medical attention and that's what they're supposed to do. But I don't see them going above and beyond."*

---

b   Current Player 7: "It's . . . taking away from the game that we'll all learned how to play, by being too protective."

c   We reiterate that our interviews were intended to be informational but not representative of all players' views.

(E) Enforcement of Legal and Ethical Obligations[d]

Neither the CBA nor the Constitution and Bylaws address officials' conduct. Thus, it seems that a player would not be bound to arbitrate a claim against an official.[49]

Moreover, litigation against officials seems to be an available remedy for players. It is unclear whether in any such litigations the gross negligence standard that has been applied to volunteer officials would also apply to professional officials officiating professional sports as research has revealed almost no cases where a professional official was sued.

There are only two known litigations concerning NFL officials, neither of which has clearly articulated a standard for judicial review of an official's actions.

In 1972, Baltimore Colts defensive end Charles "Bubba" Smith was injured during a preseason game when he collided with an aluminum yardage marker stuck in the ground on the sideline and which an official had not removed.[50] Smith was forced to sit out the 1972 season and sued the official.[51] After a mistrial resulted in the case being retried, a jury found the official not liable for Smith's injury.[52]

In 1999, Cleveland Browns offensive lineman Orlando Brown was injured when an official threw a penalty flag (weighted with the standard BB pellets) into the air, which struck Brown in the eye.[53] The incident left Brown partially blind in the eye and seemingly unable to continue his football career.[54]

Brown sued the NFL (but not the official) in a New York state court alleging that the NFL had failed to hire and employ competent officials and to properly train and supervise the officials.[55] In addition, Brown sought to hold the NFL vicariously liable for the official's alleged negligence.[56]

The NFL sought to remove Brown's case to federal court and have it dismissed by asserting that his claims were preempted by the Labor Management Relations Act (LMRA) and the terms of the CBA.[57] The United States District Court for the Southern District of New York disagreed, holding that Brown's claims were state law claims which did not require interpretation of the CBA so as to trigger preemption.[58]

The case was remanded to New York state court and reportedly settled for $15 million to $25 million in 2002.[59] Brown nevertheless actually returned to the NFL in 2003 and continued playing through 2005.[60]

---

d   Appendix K is a summary of players' options to enforce legal and ethical obligations against the stakeholders discussed in this Report.

There are only two known litigations concerning NFL officials, neither of which has clearly articulated a standard for judicial review of an official's actions.

(F) Recommendations Concerning Officials

Indications are that officials are generally performing their jobs well concerning player health and safety and thus we have no formal recommendations for them. Officials should be praised for their efforts, particularly considering the high level of scrutiny around these issues. While officials should continue their solid work, they must always be diligent and open to change for additional ways to protect player health. In particular, it has been established that players who suffer brain injuries are at risk of serious aggravation of their conditions if they are injured again shortly after the first injury.[61] While the athletic trainers designated for spotting injuries from the press box can help, officials should exercise their discretion to stop play liberally to ensure, as much as possible, that injured athletes do not remain on the field where they can be exposed to further injury.

Endnotes

1 E-mail from Barry Mano, President, National Association of Sports Officials, to author (Mar. 23, 2016, 2:28 PM) (on file with authors).

2 E-mail from Michael C. Arnold, Arnold, Newbold, Winter & Jackson P.C., to author (Apr. 22, 2016, 10:58 AM), (on file with authors).

3 Official Playing Rules of the National Football League (NFL Playing Rules), Rule 15, Art. 2.

4 Id. at Art. 6–7.

5 NFL Officials, Nat'l Football League, http://operations.nfl.com/the-officials/officiating-development/scouting-the-next-nfl-officials/2015-nfl-officials/ (last visited Sept. 23, 2015), archived at http://perma.cc/K36J-W9LY.

6 Gary Mihoces, Path To Becoming NFL Referee Is Usually Long, USA Today, Sept. 19, 2012, http://usatoday30.usatoday.com/sports/nfl/story/2012/09/19/path-to-becoming-nfl-referee-is-usually-long/57809626/1, archived at http://perma.cc/R6EG-HB7N.

7 Id.; see Josh Katzowitz, NFL releases list of all officials for 2014 season, CBSSPORTS.COM (May 22, 2014, 11:38 AM), http://www.cbssports.com/nfl/eye-on-football/24569855/nfl-releases-list-of-all-officials-for-2014-season, archived at https://perma.cc/A2ZW-F2GY (discussing that the 12 newest officials previously refereed in the Pac-12, SEC, Big 10, Big 12 and ACC).

8 Judy Battista, N.F.L. Reaches Labor Deal With Referees, N.Y. Times, Sept. 26, 2012, http://www.nytimes.com/2012/09/27/sports/football/nfl-and-referees-reach-labor-deal.html?_r=0, archived at https://perma.cc/XTZ8-WWYT?type=pdf.

9 Id.

10 Mike Florio, NFLPA Threatens "Appropriate Action" Over Replacement Officials, ProFootballTalk (Sept. 9, 2012, 7:49 PM), http://profootballtalk.nbcsports.com/2012/09/09/nflpa-threatens-appropriate-action-over-replacement-officials/, archived at http://perma.cc/X887-RPKF.

11 NFL, NFLRA Reach Eight-Year Agreement, NFL (Sept. 27, 2012 12:34 AM), http://www.nfl.com/news/story/0ap1000000066739/article/nfl-nflra-reach-eightyear-agreement, archived at http://perma.cc/4C9Z-CZLR.

12 Id.

13 Interview with Jim Quirk, Executive Director, NFLRA (March 25, 2015).

14 Interview with Barry Mano, President, National Association of Sports Officials (Oct. 29, 2014).

15 Id.

16 Id.

17 Id. For more information on NASO, see its website at http://www.naso.org.

18 Interview with Mano, supra note 14.

19 Id. The Commissioner and the Supervisor of League Game Officials are responsible for selecting officials. See NFL Constitution and Bylaws (2012), § 8.7.

20 Glenn M. Wong, Essentials of Sports Law, § 4.7 (4th ed. 2010) (discussing duties of officials and gathering cases); Eric T. Gilson, Sports Officiating and the Law: A Survey of Risks and Protections, 7 Willamette Sports L.J. 32 (2009) (same).

21 See Alan S. Goldberger, Sports Officiating: A Legal Guide, 206–210 (2007) (stating "[t]he American legal system is traditionally reluctant to become involved in second guessing decisions of referees" and collecting cases); Order, Ind. School Dist. No. I-89 of Okla. County, Okla. v. Okla. Secondary School Activities Ass'n, 2014-cv-2235 (Okla. Cnty. Dec. 11, 2014) (dissolving temporary injunction after high school sued to replay state playoff game based on erroneous application of a rule: "it borders on the unreasonable, and in some respects extends far beyond the purview of the judiciary, to this Court more equipped or better qualified than Defendant to decide the outcome or any portion of a high school football game."); Georgia High School Ass'n v. Waddell, 285 S.E.2d 7 (Ga. 1981) (holding that Courts do not possess the authority to review the decisions of high school football referees).

22 See Marc T. Wolin, Robert D. Lang, Legal Liability for Sports Referees in Today's Litigious World – If You Can't Kill the Ump Then Sue Him, 15 U. Den. Sports & Ent. L.J. 83, 85 (2013); John Cadkin, Sports Official Liability: Can I Sue If the Ref Missed a Call? 2008 Den. U. Sports & Ent. L.J. 51, 52 (2008).

23 Id.

24 See Gilson, supra note 20, at 41 (discussing NASO's lobbying efforts); Cadkin, supra note 22, at 56–57 (same).

25 Sports Officials Legislative Scorecard, Nat'l Ass'n Sports Officials, http://www.naso.org/Resources/Legislation/LegislationStatus/SportsOfficialsLegislativeScorecard.aspx (last visited Aug. 7, 2015), archived at http://perma.cc/JV5L-98PD.

26 See M.G.L.A. 231 § 85V (Massachusetts statute restricting liability against volunteer officials and those working in youth sports); 745 ILCS 80/1 (Illinois statute restricting liability against volunteer officials and those working in youth sports); 42 Pa.C.S.A. § 8332.1 (Pennsylvania statute restricting liability against volunteer officials and those working in youth sports); Gen.Laws 1956, § 9-1-48 (Rhode Island statute restricting liability against officials in youth sports); R.C. § 3707.511 (Ohio statute restricting liability against officials in youth sports); NDCC, 32-03-46 (North Dakota statute restricting liability against volunteer officials); LSA-R.S. 9:2798 (Louisiana statute restricting liability against volunteer officials); N.J.S.A. 2A:62A-6.1 (New Jersey statute restricting liability against youth sports officials); N.J.S.A. 2A:62A-6 (New Jersey statute restricting liability against volunteer officials); 16 Del.C. § 6836 (Delaware statute restricting liability against volunteer officials); Ga. Code Ann.,

§ 51-1-41 (Georgia statute restricting liability against officials for amateur sports); A.C.A. § 16-120-102 (Arkansas statute restricting liability against officials for amateur sports); V.T.C.A., Civil Practice & Remedies Code § 84.004 (Texas statute restricting liability against volunteers of youth sports organizations); MD Code, Courts and Judicial Proceedings, § 5-802 (Maryland statute restricting liability against officials of amateur sports).

27 See T. C. A. § 62-50-202 (Tennessee statute restricting liability against officials "at any level of competition"); Miss. Code Ann. § 95-9-3 (Mississippi statute restricting liability against officials "at any level of competition"); N.R.S. 41.630 (Nevada statute restricting liability against officials "at any level of competition").

28 Interview with Barry Mano, President, National Association of Sports Officials (Oct. 29, 2014).

29 Id.

30 Id.

31 See Code of Conduct for Sports Officials, Nat'l Ass'n Sports Officials, http://www.naso.org/Portals/0/downloads/code_of_conduct.pdf (last visited Aug. 7, 2015), archived at https://perma.cc/35SA-8C6H?type =pdf.

32 Interview with Mano, supra note 14.

33 Id.

34 Interview with Jim Quirk, Executive Director, NFLRA (March 25, 2015).

35 See Kevin Seifert, NFL Nation Says: Too Much QB Protection? ESPN (Nov. 21, 2013), http://espn.go.com/blog/nflnation/post/_/id/102074/nfl -nation-says-too-much-qb-protection, archived at http://perma.cc/J5YP -V78Y.

36 Mark Kiszla, NFL Appears to Prefer Two-Hand Touch, Denver Post, Aug. 8, 2014, available at 2014 WLNR 21946260; Marshall Faulk, Stupid rule endangers running backs' well-being, NFL (March 20, 2013, 11:04 PM) http://www.nfl.com/news/story/0ap1000000152312/article/ crownofhelmet-ban-nfl-rule-draws-criticism-understanding, archived at http://perma.cc/WW22-6HHJ.

37 Mike Florio, On Concussions, Players and Fans Can't Have it Both Ways, ProFootballTalk (May 6, 2012, 10:15 AM), http://profootballtalk.nbcsports .com/2012/05/06/on-concussions-players-and-fans-cant-have-it-both -ways/, archived at http://perma.cc/9KRW-TJGA.

38 Michael David Smith, Vinny Testaverde Thinks the NFL is Overprotective of Quarterbacks, ProFootballTalk (Nov. 20, 2012, 10:45 AM), http://profootballtalk.nbcsports.com/2012/11/20/vinny-testaverde -thinks-the-nfl-is-overprotective-of-quarterbacks/, archived at http://perma.cc/W6NQ-586T; Kevin Seifer, Tim MacMahon, The Associated Press, Critics Blast Kickoff Rule Change, ESPN (Aug. 24, 2011), http://espn.go.com/nfl/story/_/id/6887856/donnie-nickey -formerly-tennessee-titans-latest-rip-new-nfl-kickoff-rule, archived at http://perma.cc/ZVB8-WG36; Gregg Rosenthal, Woodley upset that football is "turning soft", ProFootballTalk (May 25, 2011, 4:32 PM), http://profootballtalk.nbcsports.com/2011/05/25/woodley-upset-that -football-is-turning-soft/, archived at http://perma.cc/2722-L2ZX.

39 NFL Comments and Corrections (June 24, 2016).

40 NFL Playing Rules, § 2, Art. 9.

41 NFL Playing Rules, § 2, Art. 11.

42 NFL Playing Rules, § 5, Art. 2.

43 Interview with Jim Quirk, Executive Director, NFLRA (March 25, 2015).

44 E-mail from Barry Mano, President, National Association of Sports Officials, to author (Mar. 23, 2016, 2:28 PM) (on file with authors).

45 NFL Playing Rules, § 5, Art. 2.

46 Mike Florio, Giants LB Played Nearly Three Quarters with Concussion, ProFootballTalk (Nov. 13, 2014, 8:30 PM), http://profootballtalk .nbcsports.com/2014/11/13/giants-lb-played-nearly-three-quarters -with-concussion/, archived at http://perma.cc/LM4Z-YQJG; Lions' Michael David Smith, Laadrian Waddle Returned to Game After Concussion, ProFootballTalk (Oct. 23, 2014, 10:41 AM), http://profootballtalk .nbcsports.com/2014/10/23/lions-laadrian-waddle-returned-to-game -after-concussion/, archived at http://perma.cc/27UM-X5BJ.

47 Michael David Smith, Chargers Now Admit Jahleel Addae Had a Concussion, ProFootballTalk (Oct. 25, 2014, 6:45 AM) http://profootballtalk .nbcsports.com/2014/10/25/chargers-now-admit-jahleel-addae-had-a -concussion/, archived at http://perma.cc/S96G-CKRW.

48 Mike Florio, Doctors Advise Team Medical Staffs to Be More Vigilant About Concussions, ProFootballTalk (Oct. 30, 2014, 4:42 PM), http://profootballtalk.nbcsports.com/2014/10/30/doctors-advise-team -medical-staffs-to-be-more-vigilant-about-concussions/, archived at http://perma.cc/QFB8-JSX7.

49 Darin Gantt, Injury Timeout Proposal Unanimously Approved by NFL Owners, ProFootballTalk (Mar. 24, 2015, 1:38 PM), http://profootballtalk .nbcsports.com/2015/03/24/injury-timeout-proposal-unanimously -approved-by-nfl-owners/, archived at http://perma.cc/4C5W-ULP9.

50 Id.

51 See 2011 CBA, Art. 43, § 1 (Non-Injury Grievances are the exclusive method for resolving claims concerning "any provision of [the CBA], the NFL Player Contract, the Practice Squad Player Contract, or any applicable provision of the NFL Constitution and Bylaws or NFL Rules pertaining to the terms and conditions of employment of NFL players").

52 Marc T. Wolin, Robert D. Lang, Legal Liability for Sports Referees in Today's Litigious World – If You Can't Kill the Ump Then Sue Him, 15 U. Den. Sports & Ent. L.J. 83, 88 (2013); Byron Rosen, Denver Baseball Flame Brightens, Wash. Post, Feb. 2, 1978, available at 1978 WLNR 229812.

53 Id.

54 Id.

55 Brown v. Nat'l Football League, 219 F. Supp. 2d 372, 376 (S.D.N.Y. 2002).

56 Id.

57 Id. at 376.

58 Id.

59 Id. at 377.

60 Id.

61 Daniel Slotnik, Orlando Brown, Who Sued N.F.L. Over Errant Flag, Dies at 40, N.Y. Times, Sept. 23, 2011, http://www.nytimes.com/2011/09/24/ sports/football/orlando-brown-who-sued-nfl-over-errant-flag-dies-at-40 .html?_r=0, archived at https://perma.cc/32U3-C4SS?type=pdf.

62 Id.

63 Ruben Echemendia et al., Developing guidelines for return to play: consensus and evidence-based approaches. 29 Brain Inj. 185 (2015) ("Risk for recurrent concussion was greater for individuals with prior concussions and appeared greatest in the first 10 days after a sports-related concussion.").

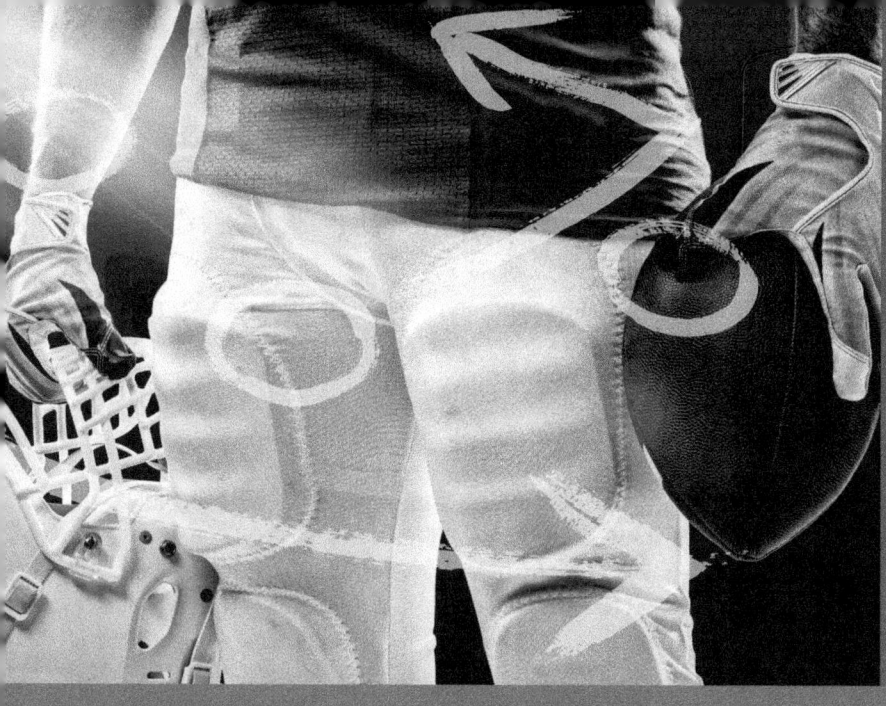

Chapter 16

Equipment Manufacturers

One major strategy for protecting and promoting player health is to offer them the appropriate type and amount of injury-reducing equipment. For this reason, equipment manufacturers play an important role in player health.

In order to ensure that this chapter was as accurate and valuable as possible, we invited two leading equipment manufacturers, Riddell and Schutt, as well as the National Operating Committee on Standards for Athletic Equipment (NOCSAE), described below, to review a draft version of this chapter prior to publication. All three reviewed the chapter and provided comments.

(A) Background

The football equipment market is dominated by Riddell and Schutt, each of which hold at least a 45 percent share of the football equipment market,[1] across all levels of football. Riddell and Schutt offer all pads necessary for the game of football, including but not limited to helmets, faceguards, chin straps, mouth guards, shoulder pads, hip pads, thigh pads, knee pads, and rib pads.[2] Adams, another manufacturer of football equipment, was sold to Schutt's parent company, in 2014.[3] Additionally, Rawlings, also once a manufacturer of football equipment, announced in 2015 that it was leaving the market.[4] Xenith is seemingly one of the lone competitors left to Riddell and Schutt, though it only manufactures helmets and shoulder pads.[5]

The equipment manufacturers have not surprisingly had important interactions with the NFL. In 1988, the NFL and Riddell entered into an agreement without duration whereby Riddell provided free helmets, pads, and jerseys to all NFL clubs in exchange for Riddell receiving the exclusive right to display its logo on NFL helmets.[6] Players were still nonetheless free to wear a helmet from any manufacturer, provided it met NFL standards.[7] Schutt unsuccessfully challenged the NFL-Riddell agreement as a violation of antitrust laws.[8] After litigation was initiated against both the NFL and Riddell concerning concussions (*see* Chapter 7: The NFL and NFLPA), the NFL renegotiated the agreement to conclude with the 2013 season.[9] Following the expiration of NFL's deal with Riddell, the NFL said it would no longer have an official helmet sponsor.[10] Similarly, the NFL does not have an official equipment sponsor. Players are permitted to wear whatever equipment they like, provided it meets NOCSAE standards, as will be discussed below.

For many years, the helmet manufacturers have attempted to develop helmets that reduced the risks of concussions—and market them accordingly—even though it is questionable to what extent helmets can actually reduce the risk of concussions.[11] In comments provided after reviewing a draft of this chapter, Schutt CEO Robert Erb described the challenges of reducing the incidence of concussion as follows:

> [W]hat is happening inside the skull, with the brain suspended in cerebrospinal fluid, is an extraordinarily complex event. There is an infinite array of possible trajectories and circumstances at the point of impact in a game of football, including field conditions, position played, girth and length of neck, medical history, whether one saw the hit coming, temperature, altitude, genetic make-up, area struck, type of turf, helmet implements and accessories, mass, speed, velocity of impact, fit of the helmet, etc., etc.

Indeed, the competition in the equipment manufacturer industry and the concerns about concussions have made the equipment manufacturing industry a challenging landscape. Riddell's development and marketing of the Revolution football helmet is a helpful example.

In 2002, Riddell provided a grant to be used to partially fund a study at the University of Pittsburgh Medical Center (UPMC) of Riddell's recently released Revolution helmet.[12] The study was designed to compare the concussion rates and recovery times for athletes wearing Riddell's Revolution helmet compared to athletes wearing older model helmets manufactured by both Riddell and its competitors.[13] The study was conducted by Micky Collins and Mark R. Lovell, co-owners of ImPACT, the leading concussion diagnostic tool which was used to measure recovery time from concussion during the study.[14]

The study took three years and examined 2,141 high school football players: 1,173 using Revolution helmets and 968 using other helmets.[15] The authors found 5.3 percent of players using Revolution helmets suffered concussions as compared to 7.6 percent of players using other helmets.[16] The authors described the difference as "statistically significant" and said the results "demonstrated a trend toward a lowered incidence of concussion" but that the "limited sample size precludes a more conclusive statement of findings at this time."[17] The study also highlighted that there was a 31 percent decreased relative risk for athletes wearing the Revolution helmet, comparing the 5.3 percent and 7.6 percent concussion rates.[18,a]

Riddell seized on that last statistic and began to advertise that the Revolution helmet reduced the risk of concussion by 31 percent.[19] Although this percentage improvement is technically accurate, the more relevant number in practice (or to players) is likely the absolute reduction in concussion rates, which was only 2.3 percent. Riddell also expanded the claim to all of its helmets even though they had not been a part of the study.[20]

As part of a patent lawsuit brought by Riddell against Schutt, Schutt counterclaimed, alleging Riddell had violated state and federal false advertising laws by claiming that

---

a   When providing comments for this Report, Riddell highlighted the fact that the UPMC study authors extrapolated that, if 1.5 million high school students participate in football each year, the risk reduction found with the Revolution helmet could theoretically mean 18,600–46,500 less concussions per year. Letter from Brian P. Roche, General Counsel, Riddell, Inc., to authors (Apr. 28, 2016) (on file with authors).

Revolution helmets decreased the risk of concussion by 31 percent.[21] The United States District Court for the Western District of Wisconsin ultimately granted Riddell summary judgment,[b] finding that Riddell's claim that "technology" used in its helmets had been "shown to reduce the incidence of concussion" was not "literally false" as required to state a claim.[22]

The 31 percent statistic has also been the subject of other litigation. In at least three cases brought by consumers (none of whom were NFL players), the plaintiffs alleged that Riddell's use of the 31 percent figure was misleading.[23] All three cases are ongoing as of the date of publication.[24] In two court decisions thus far, courts found that the 31 percent statistic could be considered misleading if it was used in advertising helmets that were not involved in the UPMC study.[25]

However, Riddell's claims also caught the attention of the Federal Trade Commission (FTC). The FTC investigated Riddell and concluded that the UPMC study "did not prove that Revolution varsity football helmets reduce concussions or the risk of concussions by 31%."[26] The FTC nevertheless did not sanction Riddell since the company had already discontinued using the 31 percent statistic in marketing.[27] According to Riddell, it ceased using the statistic because it was no longer relevant—the helmets that the Revolution helmet had been compared to in the UPMC study "had largely been phased out of the market."[28]

Notwithstanding the FTC's conclusion about Riddell's characterization of the UPMC study, the Revolution helmet has in other research been shown to reduce the risk of concussions as compared to older model helmets. A 2014 study determined that 2.82 percent of a population of college football players wearing a Revolution helmet suffered a concussion, as compared to 4.47 percent of players using an older Riddell model.[29] The study, like the UPMC study, found this difference to be statistically significant.[30]

Perhaps counterintuitively, there has been an ongoing debate about whether the best way to improve player health is for players to wear *less* equipment. Coaches, commentators and others have long lamented that the helmet and shoulder pads are often used as a weapon by would-be-tacklers, offering the first and hardest blow to ball carriers.[31] Although the NFL has recently increased the penalties for plays on which a player delivers a forcible blow with the top or crown of the helmet,[32] the helmet arguably still provides players with a level of protection that enables them to play the game with a degree of reckless abandon.[33]

A recent rule changes provides a relevant example. In 2013 the NFL reinstated a rule requiring players to wear thigh and knee pads.[34] One might then have expected a reduction in contusions to the hips, thighs and knees that season. However, no such reduction occurred. During the 2013 season, there were 61 reported contusions to these areas.[35] In the four prior seasons, there was a mean of 55.75 contusions to these areas.[36] To be fair, this change was taking place simultaneously with other changes, confounding any strong causal inference, but it does give a reason to resist the assumption that more equipment necessarily equals fewer injuries.

Also of note, the NFL does not mandate the use of mouth guards,[37] despite some but still disputed evidence that mouth guards can help prevent concussions.[38]

Attached as Appendix J is a timeline of equipment-related events and policies in the NFL.

(B) Current Legal Obligations[c]

The principal source of equipment manufacturers' legal obligations is products liability law.[39] Products liability is an area of tort law, which can vary from state to state. The American Law Institute publishes "Restatements of the Law," which are useful summaries of general principles about various areas of law. According to the Restatement of the Law Third, Torts: Products Liability, a manufacturer of consumer products, such as sports equipment, has a duty not to cause personal injury as a result of:

1. selling or distributing products which contain manufacturing defects;[40]

2. selling or distributing products which are defective in design;[41]

3. selling or distributing products without adequate instructions or warnings;[42]

4. misrepresenting a material fact concerning the product;[43]

5. failing "to provide a warning after the time of sale or distribution of a product if a reasonable person in the seller's position would provide such a warning";[44] and

6. failing to recall harmful products.[45]

b Summary judgment is "[a] judgment granted on a claim or defense about which there is no genuine issue of material fact and on which the movant is entitled to prevail as a matter of law." Black's Law Dictionary (9th ed. 2009).

c The legal obligations described herein are not an exhaustive list but are those we believe are most relevant to player health.

While the above list addresses an equipment manufacturers' principal legal obligations concerning player health, it is not an exhaustive list. For example, equipment manufacturers could potentially be subject to liability for common law fraud claims, for violating consumer protection statutes, or for misrepresenting their products.

Although every state legislature has passed a law concerning the treatment of concussions in youth athletes (*see* Part 7: Interested Parties, Section 3: Governments), there are no federal or state laws directly governing athletic equipment standards.[46]

The safety standards for athletic equipment that currently exist are almost exclusively determined by the National Operating Committee on Standards for Athletic Equipment (NOCSAE). NOCSAE is a non-profit organization with the stated purpose of improving athletic equipment and reducing injuries through equipment standards.[47] NOCSAE was formed in 1969 in response to more than 100 high school and college football players killed by skull fractures and acute brain bleeding during the 1960s.[48] NOCSAE's Board of Directors consists of representatives from the American Academy of Pediatrics, American College Health Association, American College of Sports Medicine, American Football Coaches Association, American Medical Society for Sports Medicine, American Orthopaedic Society for Sports Medicine, Athletic Equipment Managers Association, National Athletic Equipment Reconditioners Association, National Athletic Trainers Association, and the Sports & Fitness Industry Association.[49]

> The safety standards for athletic equipment that currently exist are almost exclusively determined by the National Operating Committee on Standards for Athletic Equipment (NOCSAE).

Today, NOCSAE sets general safety standards for equipment in all sports while also providing specific guidance for baseball, softball, football, hockey, lacrosse, polo, and soccer.[50] Equipment manufacturers themselves and not NOSCAE are responsible for testing their equipment and evaluating compliance with the NOSCAE standards.[51] Compliance with NOCSAE standards must then be confirmed by the Safety Equipment Institute, an independent organization that specializes in testing and certifying personal protective equipment.[52] If the equipment complies, the equipment manufacturer may place a NOCSAE trademarked logo on the equipment indicating that it meets NOCSAE standards.[53]

NOCSAE's funding is derived from manufacturers' use of the NOCSAE logo as a symbol of certification.[54] NOCSAE enters into licensing agreements with sports equipment manufacturers whereby the manufacturers are permitted to place the NOCSAE logo on its equipment provided the equipment meets NOCSAE's standards.[55] The licensing agreements also impose ongoing quality control and assurance requirements on the manufacturers.[56] If the equipment does not meet NOCSAE standards, then the manufacturer cannot use the NOCSAE logo, and presumably, NOCSAE does not receive any licensing money from the manufacturer.[d]

Certainly a significant portion of NOCSAE's work has been related to football helmets and concerns about concussions. In reviewing a draft of this chapter, NOCSAE made three points it identified as framing its approach to these matters:

1. There is no concussion specific helmet standard in the world, in ANY activity, sport or otherwise.

2. There is no scientific consensus as to what a concussion performance standard should incorporate as a pass/fail injury threshold.

3. Ethical standards for personal protective equipment must be based on consensus science, must be feasible and effective, and must not create a new risk of injury or increase the risk of injury in other areas.[57]

NOCSAE has two standards relevant to football helmets. First, NOCSAE has a standard that governs helmets in sports generally, known as the ND001 standard.[58] Second, NOCSAE has a standard governing football helmets specifically, known as the ND002 standard.[59] The ND002 standard is subject to any changes made to the broader ND001 standard.[60] While some have suggested that NOCSAE's standards have not meaningfully changed over time,[61] in reviewing this chapter, NOCSAE strongly disagreed.[62]

---

d   According to NOCSAE, since 1996 it has funded more than $8 million of independent research at universities concerning equipment safety. Letter from Mike Oliver, Executive Director/General Counsel, NOCSAE, to authors (Apr. 28, 2016) (on file with authors).

Indeed, a review of the relevant standards demonstrates that the ND001 standard has been substantively revised 16 times since it was first published in 1973, and the ND002 standard has been revised 3 times since it split from the ND001 standard in 1998.[63] Nevertheless, we are not engineers or scientists and thus we cannot opine on the significance of these revisions. Finally, it is important to understand that NOCSAE's standards are performance standards—they measure the helmet's ability to withstand certain physical forces—they do not specify materials or design.[64]

> *Under NOCSAE's standard, the football helmet is placed on a synthetic head model that is filled with glycerin and fitted with various measuring instruments. The head model fitted with the helmet is then dropped sixteen times onto a polymer anvil with two of the drops from a height of sixty inches onto six different locations of the helmet at varying temperatures determined by NOCSAE to simulate different potential game temperatures. After each drop a "Severity Index," which measures the severity of the impact absorbed by the head model at the moment of impact, is determined. Helmets are graded on a pass-fail basis, and the helmets that pass are those meeting an acceptable Severity Index.[65]*

In June 2014, NOCSAE proposed a new standard that would include rotational forces into the analysis for football helmets.[66] The proposed standard was open for comment through June 2015 with NOCSAE scheduled to vote on its adoption in 2016.[67] Again, we lack the scientific expertise to opine on the appropriateness of NOCSAE's standards.[e] Nevertheless, a report by the National Academy of Sciences on youth concussions, citing NOCSAE's research into rotational forces, suggested that NOCSAE's standards are at the forefront of the science in evaluating the efficacy of helmets.[68]

The Consumer Product Safety Commission (CPSC), the federal agency responsible for regulating the safety of thousands of consumer products,[69] does not have any standards for football helmets.[70] Indeed, in 1980 the CPSC denied a petition requesting it set standards for football helmets "to reduce the risks of head, neck, and spinal injuries," citing voluntary standards and purported decreasing injury rates.[71] In 2011, New Mexico Senator Tom Udall proposed the Children's Sports Athletic Equipment Safety Action that would have required the CPSC to develop standards for football helmets, mandate third-party testing of youth football helmets, and instruct the Federal Trade Commission to regulate the manner in which helmet manufacturers advertise the safety specifications of their products.[72] However, the bill was never enacted.[73,f]

(C) Current Ethical Codes

There are no known codes of ethics for sports equipment manufacturers.

(D) Current Practices

Equipment manufacturers have seemingly altered their behavior due to the increased litigation and scrutiny, as discussed above in the background to this chapter. For example, in touting its new SpeedFlex helmet in 2014, Riddell's senior vice president for research and product development was careful not to claim that the helmet could help reduce concussions:

> *We'll let the medical researchers weigh in on the medical data around concussions, because that's kind of a moving target right now because of all the things that are being learned[.] But what we can do is try to reduce the forces of impact to the player's head. I think reducing those forces is unequivocally a good thing.[74,g]*

---

e   In reviewing a draft of this chapter, NOCSAE stated that its standards for football helmets, including third-party certification, exceed those set by the Consumer Product Safety Commission for bicycle helmets and by the Department of Transportation for motorcycle helmets. Letter from Mike Oliver, Executive Director/General Counsel, NOCSAE, to authors (Apr. 28, 2016) (on file with authors). We lack the scientific expertise to evaluate NOCSAE's statement.

f   There is also the possibility (albeit unlikely) that football equipment, helmets in particular, could be regulated by the Food and Drug Administration (FDA). The FDA regulates "medical devices," which includes, among many other things, "an instrument, apparatus, implement, machine, contrivance, implant, in vitro reagent, or other similar or related article, including a component part, or accessory which is . . . intended for use . . . in the cure, mitigation, treatment, or prevention of disease, in man[.]" *What is a Medical Device?*, U.S. Food and Drug Admin., http://www.fda.gov/aboutfda/transparency/basics/ucm211822.htm (last visited Aug. 7, 2015), *archived at* http://perma.cc/VJ9Q-GCUH, *quoting* Federal Food Drug & Cosmetic Act (FDCA) § 201(h), 21 USC 321(h). To the extent that football equipment and helmets are intended to prevent injuries and diseases, they appear to fit within the definition of a medical device. If the FDA chose to regulate football equipment, the manufacturers would be subject to a variety of regulatory requirements, likely including registering the product with the FDA, providing information to the FDA before the product can be sold publicly, and providing accurate and descriptive labeling and literature concerning the product. *Overview of Device Regulation*, U.S. Food and Drug Admin., http://www.fda.gov/MedicalDevices/DeviceRegulationandGuidance/Overview/#labeling (last visited Aug. 7, 2015), *archived at* http://perma.cc/6A6M-SU55. Nevertheless, there is no indication that the FDA is considering regulating football equipment and, as will be discussed below, it appears that football equipment manufacturers are providing the types of warnings that the FDA would likely require.

g   Former Player 2 complained that equipment manufacturers were often misleading about their products: "This helmet is supposed to be safer for your head, but then you go hit somebody and you have a concussion. You're saying 'What the hell is going on?'"

Riddell's website also now contains a wealth of information, articles, and links concerning concussions,[75,h] all of which would militate against claims that Riddell failed to warn consumers about the risks of concussions. Similarly, Schutt's homepage contains a lengthy warning about the risks of concussions that a visitor to the website must check off as having "read and underst[ood]" before visiting any other Schutt webpage.[i]

At the current time, NOCSAE appears to be taking a proactive approach in assessing whether equipment actually meets its standards. In December 2014, NOCSAE announced that the two most popular lacrosse helmets on the market did not meet NOCSAE standards.[76] The helmet manufacturer quickly offered to increase the padding in the helmets at no cost to the consumer, a modification NOCSAE accepted.[77] Had it not made changes to the helmets, the manufacturer would not have been able to continue using the NOCSAE logo as evidence of its compliance with NOCSAE standards.[78]

In addition to NOCSAE, Virginia Tech has also provided valuable information concerning football helmets. Since 2011, The Virginia Tech Department of Biomedical Engineering and Mechanics has been evaluating helmets using a series of biomechanical tests and assigning them a rating from zero stars up to five stars based on the helmet's perceived ability to minimize the risk of concussions.[79] The Virginia Tech ratings have become incredibly important in the industry, as consumers are reluctant to buy anything that has not received five stars from Virginia Tech.[80] According to Virginia Tech, the research "is done as part of Virginia Tech's service mission and is 100% independent of any funding or influence from helmet manufacturers."[81]

(E) Enforcement of Legal and Ethical Obligations[j]

Players' only recourse against equipment manufacturers is a civil lawsuit.

Riddell, along with the NFL, is a defendant in the Concussion Litigation, discussed at length in Chapter 7: The NFL and NFLPA. The plaintiffs' claims against Riddell are summarized by the header to the section of the plaintiffs' Complaint concerning Riddell: "The Riddell Defendants Duty to Protect Against the Long-Term Risk of Concussions."[82] The plaintiffs alleged a variety of intentional and negligent acts on the part of Riddell concerning the design, manufacture, inspection, testing and warnings related to Riddell helmets which allegedly caused plaintiffs to suffer injuries. The plaintiffs further alleged that Riddell has never "acknowledge[d] a link between repeat concussions and later life cognitive problems" and that Riddell has "never warned any Plaintiff or retired player of the long-term health effects of concussions."[83]

In August 2012, Riddell sought to dismiss the plaintiffs' claims arguing, like the NFL, that the claims were preempted by the Labor Management Relations Act (LMRA).[84] Common law claims such as negligence are generally preempted by the LMRA.[85] The LMRA bars or "preempts" state common law claims[k] where the claim is "substantially dependent upon analysis of the terms" of a CBA, i.e., where the claim is "inextricably intertwined with consideration of the terms of the" CBA."[86]

Riddell argued that claims against it are subject to preemption "even though the Riddell Defendants were not parties to the CBAs, because, as the Supreme Court has explained, the doctrine of complete preemption barring state-law claims 'is more aptly expressed not in terms of parties but in terms of the purpose of the lawsuit.'"[87]

---

h   In reviewing this chapter, Riddell indicated that since 1981 its helmets have included a warning that "NO HELMET CAN PREVENT ALL HEAD OR NECK INJURIES A PLAYER MIGHT RECEIVE WHILE PARTICIPATING IN FOOTBALL" and that improper use of the helmet "can result in severe head or neck injuries, paralysis or death." In addition, Riddell indicated that beginning in 2002, its helmets have included warnings that contact in football can result in "CONCUSSION-BRAIN INJURY" and advised players not to "return to a game until all symptoms are gone and you have received MEDICAL CLEARANCE." Letter from Brian P. Roche, General Counsel, Riddell, Inc., to authors (Apr. 28, 2016) (on file with authors).

i   The entire message reads:

WARNING

Scientists have not reached agreement on how the results of impact absorption tests relate to concussions. No conclusions about a reduction of risk or severity of concussive injury should be drawn from impact absorption tests.

NO HELMET SYSTEM CAN PREVENT CONCUSSIONS OR ELIMINATE THE RISK OF SERIOUS HEAD OR NECK INJURIES WHILE PLAYING FOOTBALL.

Keep your head up. Do not butt, ram, spear or strike an opponent with any part of the helmet or faceguard. This is a violation of football rules and may cause you to suffer severe brain or neck injury, including paralysis or death and possible injury to your opponent. Contact in football may result in Concussion/Brain Injury which no helmet can prevent. Symptons (sic) include loss of consciousness or memory, dizziness, headache, nausea or confusion. If you have symptoms, immediately stop and report them to your coach, trainer and parents. Do not return to a game or contact until all symptoms are gone and you receive medial (sic) clearance. Ignoring this warning may lead to another and more serious or fatal brain injury.

NO HELMET SYSTEM CAN PROTECT YOU FROM SERIOUS BRAIN AND/OR NECK INJURIES INCLUDING PARALYSIS OR DEATH. TO AVOID THESE RISKS, DO NOT ENGAGE IN THE SPORT OF FOOTBALL.

See http://www.schuttsports.com/, archived at http://perma.cc/6K6F-PEU9.

j   Appendix K is a summary of players' options to enforce legal and ethical obligations against the stakeholders discussed in this Report.

k   Common law refers to "[t]he body of law derived from judicial decisions, rather than from statutes or constitutions." Black's Law Dictionary (9th ed. 2009). The concept of "preemption" is "[t]he principle (derived from the Supremacy Clause [of the Constitution] that a federal law can supersede or supplant any inconsistent state law or regulation." Id.

The NFL settled the Concussion Litigation in August 2013, approved by the United States District Court for the Eastern District of Pennsylvania in April 2015,[88] and by the United States Court of Appeals for the Third Circuit in April 2016.[89] Riddell was not a party to the settlement and has not reached any settlement of its own. Thus, the Concussion Litigation continues as against Riddell.

Riddell's argument that the LMRA preempts the claims against it seems unlikely to succeed, if for no other reason than it would leave players with no ability to enforce equipment manufacturers' obligations. Players cannot pursue grievances against equipment manufacturers under the CBA because the manufacturers are not parties to the CBA and thus did not agree to arbitrate any such claims.

In addition, as mentioned above, Riddell is currently the subject of several ongoing lawsuits brought by non-NFL player consumers who, like the plaintiffs in the Concussion Litigation, allege a variety of intentional and negligent acts on the part of Riddell concerning the design, manufacture, inspection, testing, warnings, and marketing related to Riddell helmets that allegedly caused plaintiffs to suffer injuries.[90] Schutt is also a defendant in at least one of the lawsuits.[91]

There is, however, one case against Schutt brought by an NFL player that bears mentioning. In 2016, Ryan Mundy, who played in the NFL from 2009 to 2014, sued Schutt alleging that a defect in the helmet caused a laceration on his forehead when he impacted another player.[92] Mundy alleged that the laceration required 17 stitches and left him with permanent scarring.[93] The lawsuit is ongoing as of the date of publication.

Lastly, NOCSAE has minimal enforcement authority against equipment manufacturers. As mentioned above, NOCSAE can only prevent non-conforming equipment from using the NOCSAE logo, substantially precluding the product from being sold. Since all NFL equipment meets NOCSAE standards, there is nothing more that NOCSAE can do in offering players recourse.

(F) Recommendations Concerning Equipment Manufacturers

It appears that equipment manufacturers are generally working to create the safest equipment possible. Equipment manufacturers for a variety of reasons (including both liability and brand image) have generally sought to make equipment safer and the recent increased emphasis on player health and safety can only have accelerated that interest. We thus expect and recommend that equipment manufacturers continue to invest in the research and development of safer equipment. Similarly, at present time it appears equipment manufacturers have been more careful in ensuring they accurately convey the benefits and limitations of their equipment. In this regard, equipment manufacturers should continue to do what they have been doing and there is no need for formal recommendations.

NOCSAE has minimal enforcement authority against equipment manufacturers. As mentioned above, NOCSAE can only prevent non-conforming equipment from using the NOCSAE logo, substantially precluding the product from being sold. Since all NFL equipment meets NOCSAE standards, there is nothing further NOCSAE can offer in terms of player health, other than continued research.

Considering the public interest at hand, football equipment might be an area where additional regulation would be appropriate. Nevertheless, it is unclear who might fill this role of regulating equipment manufacturers. One possibility is for the Government, including the CPSC, to play a greater role in establishing and enforcing equipment standards. For this and other reasons we have included the Government as an Interested Party in Part 7.

Endnotes

1   *See* Lisa Brown, *Rawlings Chases Growth in Football Equipment*, St. Louis Post-Dispatch, Oct. 27, 2013, http://www.stltoday.com/business/local/rawlings-chases-growth-in-football-equipment/article_06babb3c-9483-5115-b42b-8e818693901c.html (last visited Aug. 7, 2015), *archived at* http://perma.cc/MDR4-YFFN (describing each company's market share as exceeding 40%); Lisa Brown, *Rawlings Gaining Ground in the Football Equipment Market*, St. Louis Post-Dispatch, Sept. 18, 2011, http://www.stltoday.com/business/local/rawlings-gaining-ground-in-the-football-equipment-market/article_69329d3b-dd8d-5079-a9a9-9cf8b473b832.html (last visited Aug. 7, 2015), *archived at* http://perma.cc/924L-C74G (describing Riddell and Schutt's combined market share as over 90%).

2   *See Shop*, RIDDELL, http://www.riddell.com/ (last visited Aug. 7, 2015); *Football*, Schutt Sports, http://www.schuttsports.com/aspx/sport/ProductLanding.aspx?sp=3 (last visited Aug. 7, 2015), *archived at* http://perma.cc/HL4K-2EJE.

3   E-mail from Robert Erb, Chief Executive Officer, Kranos Corporation to authors (Mar. 16, 2016) (on file with authors).

4   Lisa Brown, *End of the line for Rawlings' football helmets*, St. Louis Post-Dispatch, June 21, 2015, http://www.stltoday.com/business/local/end-of-the-line-for-rawlings-football-helmets/article_c2a1a349-104c-504e-80d7-ea37c7ddd951.html, *archived at* https://perma.cc/F98N-XUV5.

5   *See Xenith Products*, Xenith, www.xenith.com/products/ (last visited Aug. 7, 2015).

6   *See* Jenny Vrentas, *The First Line of Defense*, MMQB (Oct. 22, 2013), http://mmqb.si.com/2013/10/22/nfl-helmets-head-injury-concussion/, *archived at* http://perma.cc/WL9Q-7PXT (describing Riddell agreement as "indefinite"); *see also* Schutt Athletic Sales Co. v. Riddell, Inc., 727 F.Supp. 1220 (N.D.Ill. 1989) (dismissing Schutt's claim that the NFL-Riddell agreement violated antitrust law).

7   Letter from Brian P. Roche, General Counsel, Riddell, Inc., to authors (Apr. 28, 2016) (on file with authors).

8   *See* Schutt Athletic Sales Co. v. Riddell, Inc., 727 F.Supp. 1220 (N.D.Ill. 1989)

9   Darren Rovell, *NFL, Riddell Ending Helmet Deal*, ESPN, (Oct. 25, 2013, 2:44 PM), http://espn.go.com/nfl/story/_/id/9875758/nfl-end-official-helmet-deal-riddell-2013–14-season, *archived at* http://perma.cc/8LRU-CJHT.

10 Vrentas, *supra* note 6.

11 Steven Rowson et al., *Can Helmet Design Reduce the Risk of Concussion in Football?* 120 J Neurosurgery 919 (2014) ("Although helmet design may never prevent all concussions from occurring in football, evidence illustrates that it can reduce the incidence of this injury."); Don Comrie et al., *Letters to the editor: football helmet design and concussion*, 121 J. Neurosurgery 491 (2014) (criticizing the findings of the Rowson paper); Timothy A. McGuine, et. al., *Protective equipment and player characteristics associated with the incidence of sport-related concussion in high school football players: a multifactorial prospective study*, 42 Am. J. Sports Med. 2470 (2014) ("Incidence of SRC [sport-related concussion] was similar regardless of the helmet brand (manufacturer) worn by high school football players. Players who had sustained an SRC within the previous 12 months were more likely to sustain an SRC than were players without a history of SRC.").

12 Letter from Brian P. Roche, General Counsel, Riddell, Inc., to authors (Apr. 28, 2016) (on file with authors); Micky Collins et al., *Examining Concussion Rates and Return to Play in High School Football Players Wearing Newer Helmet Technology: A Three-Year Prospective Cohort Study*, 58 Neurosurgery 275 (2006).

13 *Id.*; Riddell, Inc. v. Schutt Sports, Inc., 724 F. Supp. 2d 963, 967 (W.D.Wis. 2010).

14 Collins et al., *supra* n. 12.

15 Riddell, Inc. v. Schutt Sports, Inc., 724 F. Supp. 2d 963, 968 (W.D.Wis. 2010).

16 *Id.*

17 *Id.*

18 *Id.* 7.6% less 31% of 7.6% = approximately 5.3%.

19 *Id.*

20 *Id.* at 969.

21 *See id.* at 966.

22 *Id.* at 965.

23 *See In re Riddell Concussion Reduction Litigation*, 121 F. Supp.3d 402 (D.N.J. 2015); *DuRocher v. Riddell, Inc.*, 97 F. Supp.3d 1006 (S.D. Ind. 2015); *Midwestern Midget Football Club Inc. v. Riddell Inc.*, 15-cv-244, 2015 WL 4727438 (S.D. W. Va. Aug. 10, 2015).

24 *See* Thiel v. Riddell, Inc., 13-cv-7585 (D.N.J.); DuRocher v. Nat'l Collegiate Athletic Ass'n, 13-cv-1570 (S.D. Ind.); Midwestern Midget Football Club Inc. v. Riddell, Inc., 15-cv-244 (S.D. W. Va.).

25 *See* Memorandum Opinion and Order, Midwestern Midget Football Club Inc. v. Riddell, Inc., 15-cv-244 (S.D. W. Va. June 17, 2016), ECF No. 78; In re Riddell Concussion Reduction Litigation, 121 F. Supp.3d 402, 416–17 (D.N.J. 2015).

26 Mark Fainaru-Wada & Steve Fainaru, League of Denial: The NFL, Concussions, and the Battle for Truth 316–317 (2013). The FTC's investigation followed an October 19, 2011 hearing before the Senate Commerce entitled "Concussions and the Marketing of Sports Equipment." *Id.*

27 *Id.*

28 Letter from Brian P. Roche, General Counsel, Riddell, Inc., to authors (Apr. 28, 2016) (on file with authors).

29 Steven Rowson et al., *Can Helmet Design Reduce the Risk of Concussion in Football?* 120 J. Neurosurgery 919 (2014).

30 *Id.*

31 *See* Stephen Chapman, *Football Doesn't Have to Resemble Battlefield Footage*, Chi. Trib., Oct. 20, 1988, *available at* 1988 WLNR 1727333; Red Smith, *Headgear as a Weapon*, N.Y. Times, Feb 23, 1981, http://www.nytimes.com/1981/02/23/sports/red-smith-headgear-as-weapon.html, *archived at* http://perma.cc/2LJV-K2RQ.

32 David Barron, *Football: Prevent Defense: From NFL Down, Sport is Legislated to Create a Safer Playing Environment*, Hous. Chron., Aug. 18, 2013, *available at* 2013 WLNR 20617460.

33 To help teach players not to use their heads while making tackles, the University of New Hampshire football team occasionally practices without helmets. *See* Jenny Ventras, *Helmetless Football? It's the New Practice at New Hampshire*, MMQB, (Dec. 4, 2014), http://mmqb.si.com/2014/12/04/helmetless-football-practice-university-of-new-hampshire/, *archived at* http://perma.cc/6CBB-8Y5J.

34 Tom Pelissero, *More Padding Mandatory in NFL, Protection of Knees, Thighs Now Required*, USA Today, July 12, 2013, *available at* 2013 WLNR 16937591.

35 Quintiles, *NFL Injury Data Analysis* (Feb. 19, 2014) (on file with authors).

36 *Id.*

37 Jeffri Chadiha, *10 Steps to Make the Game Safer*, ESPN, (Aug. 30, 2012), http://espn.go.com/nfl/story/_/id/8061129/nfl-10-steps-make-game-safer (last visited Aug. 7, 2015), *archived at* http://perma.cc/E49Q-A6SC.

38 *See* Daniel H. Daneshvar et al., *Helmets and Mouth Guards: The Role of Personal Equipment in Preventing Sport-Related Concussions*, 30 Clinical Sports Med. 145 (2011), http://www.bu.edu/cte/files/2011/07/Daneshvar-et-al.-Helmets-and-Mouth-Guards.-2011.pdf, *archived at* https://perma.cc/Y3DR-UZU5?type=pdf (discussing conflicting evidence as to whether mouthguards help prevent concussions); Paul McCrory, *Do Mouthguards Prevent Concussions?*, 35 Br. J. Sports Med. 81 (2001) (same).

39 "One engaged in the business of selling or otherwise distributing products who sells or distributes a defective product is subject to liability for harm to persons or property caused by the defect." Restatement (Third) of Torts: Products Liability § 1 (1998).

40 A product "contains a manufacturing defect when the product departs from its intended design even though all possible care was exercised in the preparation and marketing of the product." Restatement (Third) of Torts: Products Liability § 2 (1998).

41 A product "is defective in design when the foreseeable risks of harm posed by the product could have been reduced or avoided by the adoption of a reasonable alternative design by the seller or other distributor, or a predecessor in the commercial chain of distribution, and the

omission of the alternative design renders the product not reasonably safe." Restatement (Third) of Torts: Products Liability § 2 (1998). This definition has proven controversial and some states have adopted alternative definitions. *See* Larry S. Stewart, Strict Liability for Defective Product Design: The Quest for a Well-Ordered Regime, 74 Brook. L. Rev. 1039 (2009); Patrick Lavelle, *Crashing Into Proof of a Reasonable Alternative Design: The Fallacy of the Restatement (Third) of Torts: Products Liability*, 38 Duq. L. Rev. 1059 (2000).

42 A product "is defective because of inadequate instructions or warnings . . . when the foreseeable risks of harm posed by the product could have been reduced or avoided by the provision of reasonable instructions or warnings by the seller or other distributor, or a predecessor in the commercial chain of distribution, and the omission of the instructions or warnings renders the product not reasonably safe. Restatement (Third) of Torts: Products Liability § 2 (1998).

43 "One engaged in the business of selling or otherwise distributing products who, in connection with the sale of a product, makes a fraudulent, negligent, or innocent misrepresentation of material fact concerning the product is subject to liability for harm to persons or property caused by the misrepresentation." Restatement (Third) of Torts: Products Liability § 9 (1998).

44 "A reasonable person in the seller's position would provide a warning after the time of sale if: (1) the seller knows or reasonably should know that the product poses a substantial risk of harm to persons or property; and (2) those to whom a warning might be provided can be identified and can reasonably be assumed to be unaware of the risk of harm; and (3) a warning can be effectively communicated to and acted on by those to whom a warning might be provided; and (4) the risk of harm is sufficiently great to justify the burden of providing a warning." Restatement (Third) of Torts: Products Liability § 10 (1998).

45 "One engaged in the business of selling or otherwise distributing products is subject to liability for harm to persons or property caused by the seller's failure to recall a product after the time of sale or distribution if: (a)(1) a governmental directive issued pursuant to a statute or administrative regulation specifically requires the seller or distributor to recall the product; or (2) the seller or distributor, in the absence of a recall requirement under Subsection (a)(1), undertakes to recall the product; and (b) the seller or distributor fails to act as a reasonable person in recalling the product." Restatement (Third) of Torts: Products Liability § 11 (1998).

46 *See* Jason Navia, *Sitting on the Bench: The Failure of Youth Football Helmet Regulation and the Necessity of Government Intervention*, 64 Admin. L. Rev. 265 (2012) (discussing generally youth football helmet regulation and proposed or possible legislation).

47 *About NOSCAE*, Nat'l Operating Comm. Standards for Athletic Equipment, http://nocsae.org/about-nocsae/ (last visited Aug. 7, 2015), *archived at* http://perma.cc/J5DG-43JE.

48 Alan Schwarz, *As Concussions Rise, Scant Oversight for Football Helmet Safety*, N.Y. Times, Oct. 21, 2010, http://www.nytimes.com/2010/10/21/sports/football/21helmets.html?pagewanted=all, *available at* http://perma.cc/2LJV-K2RQ.

49 *NOCSAE Board of Diretors*, Nat'l Operating Comm. Standards for Athletic Equipment, http://nocsae.org/board-of-directors/ (last visited May 2, 2016), *archived at* https://perma.cc/5V87-GJAN.

50 *Standards — General*, Nat'l Operating Comm. Standards for Athletic Equipment, http://nocsae.org/standards/general/ (last visited Aug. 7, 2015), *archived at* http://perma.cc/G9H4-BKNY.

51 *Id.*

52 Letter from Mike Oliver, Executive Director/General Counsel, NOCSAE, to authors (Apr. 28, 2016) (on file with authors); Letter from Brian P. Roche, General Counsel, Riddell, Inc., to authors (Apr. 28, 2016) (on file with authors).

53 *Standards — Statement on Shared Responsibilities*, Nat'l Operating Comm. Standards for Athletic Equipment, http://nocsae.org/nocsae-standard/statement-on-shared-responsibilities/ (last visited Aug. 7, 2015), *archived at* http://perma.cc/G9LB-526U; Letter from Mike Oliver,

Executive Director/General Counsel, NOCSAE, to authors (Apr. 28, 2016) (on file with authors).

54 Letter from Mike Oliver, Executive Director/General Counsel, NOCSAE, to authors (Apr. 28, 2016) (on file with authors).

55 *Id.*

56 *Id.*

57 Letter from Mike Oliver, Executive Director/General Counsel, NOCSAE, to authors (Apr. 28, 2016) (on file with authors).

58 *See* NOCSAE, *Standard Test Method and Equipment Used in Evaluating the Performance Characteristics of Headgear/Equipment* (Modified June 2015), available at http://nocsae.org/standards/general (last visited Apr. 29, 2016).

59 *See* NOCSAE, *Standard Performance Specification for Newly Manufactured Helmets* (Modified June 2015), available at http://nocsae.org/standards/general (last visited Apr. 29, 2016).

60 *See id.* at ¶ 1.2.

61 *See* Alan Schwarz, *As Concussions Rise, Scant Oversight for Football Helmet Safety*, N.Y. Times, Oct. 21, 2010, http://www.nytimes.com/2010/10/21/sports/football/21helmets.html?pagewanted=all, *available at* http://perma.cc/2LJV-K2RQ ("The standard has not changed meaningfully since it was written in 1973"); Jason Navia, *Sitting on the Bench: The Failure of Youth Football Helmet Regulation and the Necessity of Government Intervention*, 64 Admin. L. Rev. 265, 269 (2012) ("NOCSAE's testing standards for football helmets have not changed since 1973").

62 Letter from Mike Oliver, Executive Director/General Counsel, NOCSAE, to authors (Apr. 28, 2016) (on file with authors).

63 *Id.*

64 R. Graham et al., *Sports-Related Concussions in Youth: Improving the Science, Changing the Culture* (2013), available at http://www.nationalacademies.org/hmd/Reports/2013/Sports-Related-Concussions-in-Youth-Improving-the-Science-Changing-the-Culture.aspx (last visited Apr. 29, 2016).

65 *See* Navia *supra* n. 61 at 276–77.

66 Gary Mihoces, *New Helmet Standard To Address Concussion Prevention*, USA Today, June 20, 2014, http://www.usatoday.com/story/sports/nfl/2014/06/20/helmets-safety-concussion-prevention-nocsae/11139183/, *archived at* http://perma.cc/M86U-EDUZ.

67 *Id.*

68 See Graham, supra n. 64 at 250 ("Advances in helmet test standards that incorporate new methods and new injury criteria that evaluate protection in both linear and rotational loading modes are needed before real progress can be made on this issue. NOCSAE, to offer one example, has research under way to develop such test protocols, but the limiting factor may be having sufficiently robust, age-dependent concussion tolerance criteria with which to interpret the results of such tests.")

69 *About CPSC*, U.S. Consumer Product Safety Comm., http://www.cpsc.gov/en/About-CPSC/ (last visited Aug. 7, 2015), *archived at* http://perma.cc/RWB9-RXD8.

70 Brooke de Lench & Lindsey Barton Straus, *Standard-Setting by Non-Governmental Agencies in the Field of Sports Safety Equipment: Promoting the Interests of Consumers or Manufacturers?*, 10 J. Bus. & Tech. L. 47, 47 n.3 (2015).

71 Football Helmets; Denial of Petition, 45 Fed. Reg. 63326 (Sept. 24, 1980).

72 Jason Navia, *Sitting on the Bench: The Failure of Youth Football Helmet Regulation and the Necessity of Government Intervention*, 64 Admin. L. Rev. 265, 270 (2012).

73 *H.R. 1127 (112th): Children's Sports Athletic Equipment Safety Act*, GovTrack.us, https://www.govtrack.us/congress/bills/112/hr1127 (last visited Aug. 7, 2015), *archived at* https://perma.cc/R9SQ-BWUS.

74 The Associated Press, *In Race to Develop Safer Football Helmets, Many Questions Remain*, N.Y. Times, Aug. 23, 2014, http://www.nytimes.com/2014/08/24/sports/football/in-race-to-develop-safer-football-helmets-many-questions-remain.html, *archived at* https://perma.cc/2BYF-VJ5F.

75 *See What is a Concussion?*, Riddell, http://www.riddell.com/education#conclussion-tab (last visited Aug. 7, 2015), *archived at* http://perma.cc/BEX2-6YRP.

76 Mary Pilon, *After 2 Helmets Are Decertified, Lacrosse Faces Safety Concerns*, N.Y. Times, Dec. 5, 2014, http://www.nytimes.com/2014/12/06/sports/safety-organization-deems-popular-helmet-models-unsuitable-for-play.html, *archived at* https://perma.cc/5HDM-FYMK?type=pdf.

77 Mary Pilon, *Maker Agrees to Modify a Lacrosse Helmet That Was Decertified*, N.Y. Times, Dec. 12, 2014, http://www.nytimes.com/2014/12/13/sports/maker-agrees-to-modify-a-lacrosse-helmet-that-was-decertified.html, *archived at* https://perma.cc/S2U3-Y5ZY?type=pdf.

78 Letter from Mike Oliver, Executive Director/General Counsel, NOCSAE, to authors (Apr. 28, 2016) (on file with authors).

79 *See Virginia Tech Helmet Ratings*, Virginia Tech, http://www.beam.vt.edu/helmet/index.php (last visited May 9, 2016), *archived at* https://perma.cc/GJ9H-67UY.

80 Bryan Gruley, *The Truth About the Safety Ratings That Sell Football Helmets*, Bloomberg (Jan. 28, 2015), http://www.bloomberg.com/news/features/2015-01-28/the-controversial-safety-ratings-that-sell-football-helmets, *archived at* https://perma.cc/KM9B-PWXY.

81 *See Virginia Tech Helmet Ratings*, Virginia Tech, http://www.beam.vt.edu/helmet/index.php (last visited May 9, 2016), *archived at* https://perma.cc/GJ9H-67UY.

82 Plaintiffs' Amended Master Administrative Long-Form Complaint at p. 76, In re Nat'l Football League Players' Concussion Injury Litigation, 2:12-md-2323 (E.D.Pa. July 17, 2012), ECF No. 2642.

83 *Id.* at ¶¶ 395–96.

84 *See* Brief in Support of Riddell Defendants' Motion to Dismiss Based on LMRA § 301 Preemption, In re Nat'l Football League Players' Concussion Injury Litigation, 2:12-md-2323 (E.D.Pa. Aug. 30, 2012), ECF No. 3592-1.

85 U.S.C. § 185.

86 Allis-Chambers Corp. v. Lueck, 471 U.S. 202, 213, 220 (1985).

87 *See* Brief in Support of Riddell Defendants' Motion to Dismiss Based on LMRA § 301 Preemption at 2–3, In re Nat'l Football League Players' Concussion Injury Litigation, 2:12-md-2323 (E.D.Pa. Aug. 30, 2012), ECF No. 3592-1, *quoting* Wooddell v. Int'l Bd. of Elec. Workers, 502 U.S. 93, 112 (1991).

88 In re Nat'l Football League Players' Concussion Injury Litigation, 307 F.R.D. 351, 393 (E.D. Pa. 2015).

89 In re Nat'l Football League Players' Concussion Injury Litigation, 821 F.3d 410 (3d Cir. Apr. 18, 2016).

90 *See, e.g.,* Thiel v. Riddell, Inc., 13-cv-7585 (D.N.J.); DuRocher v. Nat'l Collegiate Athletic Ass'n, 13-cv-1570 (S.D. Ind.); Midwestern Midget Football Club Inc. v. Riddell, Inc., 15-cv-244 (S.D. W. Va.).

91 DuRocher v. Nat'l Collegiate Athletic Ass'n, 13-cv-1570 (S.D. Ind.).

92 Complaint at Law, Mundy v. Kranos Corp. d/b/a Schutt Sports, 2016-L-005166 (Ill. Cir. Ct. May 24, 2016).

93 *Id.*

Chapter 17

The Media[a]

Today, the media takes on many forms, including traditional print journalists in newspapers and magazines, television and radio network broadcasters and reporters, and journalists who work for Internet-based news sources, *e.g.,* "blogs." In discussing the media in this chapter, we intend for the term to include all of the aforementioned individuals who report news as a profession, *i.e.,* get paid, as well as their employers.[1,b] The NFL and the media have an important and significant relationship that, as a result, makes the media a stakeholder in player health.

---

a   The portions of this work related to media are the result of collaboration with John Afflect, Knight Chair in Sports Journalism and Society, Penn State University.

b   We recognize that the line between "media" and "social media" is increasingly blurred these days. Nevertheless, we think issues related to social media are properly addressed in Chapter 18: Fans.

In order to ensure that this chapter was as accurate and valuable as possible, we invited the Professional Football Writers Association (PFWA) and the National Sports Media Association (NSMA) to review a draft version of this chapter prior to publication. Both groups declined our invitation.

(A) Background

The NFL currently has television broadcasting agreements with ESPN, NBC, CBS, FOX, NFL Network, and DirecTV. The NFL also has a radio broadcasting agreement with Westwood One and, for at least the 2016 season, a streaming agreement with Twitter.[2] In total, the broadcasting agreements bring in approximately $7 billion in annual revenue to the NFL[3]—58 percent of the NFL's approximate $12 billion in total annual revenue.[4]

The television networks pay the broadcast fees in response to consumer demand. According to The Nielsen Company, during the 2015 season, 46 out of the top 50 rated television programs, including the top 25, were NFL games.[5] In addition, more than 202 million Americans watched an NFL game in 2014—68 percent of the country.[6]

The networks also employ dozens of journalists, broadcasters, and other on-air talent to support their NFL coverage. All of the NFL's television broadcasting partners (except DirecTV) have pre-game shows consisting of various broadcasters, journalists, former players, coaches, and executives. Moreover, ESPN dedicates more than 23 hours of shows each week (not including SportsCenter) exclusively to the NFL during the season, and even created a 90,000 square foot studio exclusively for its NFL coverage.[7]

In addition to the television media, the PFWA consists of hundreds of writers who cover the NFL on a regular basis.[8] These writers consist of traditional journalists as well as those who work for online news organizations.

To assist the media's coverage, the NFL has a robust Media Relations Policy requiring players and coaches to make themselves available to the media and for practices to generally be open to the media.[9] Players diagnosed with concussions are excused from speaking with the media until they have cleared the Concussion Protocol (*see* Appendix A).[10] Players nonetheless do not always cooperate with the Media Relations Policy. In 2014, Seattle Seahawks running back Marshawn Lynch was fined $100,000 for refusing to speak to the media.[11] When he did speak, Lynch repeated the same non-responsive phrases over and over, such as "thanks for asking"[12] or "I'm just here so I won't get fined."[13]

Below, we discuss the media and its historical treatment of player health matters before moving to a discussion of the NFL's Injury Reporting Policy.

1) THE MEDIA AND ITS HISTORICAL TREATMENT OF PLAYER HEALTH

Media have been reporting on injuries since the NFL's inception. At the same time, reporters have also been praising players who played through injuries for just as long. The *Chicago Daily Tribune's* coverage of the NFL champion 1940 Chicago Bears provides some descriptive examples. In the account of a key victory that season, the Bears' 14–7 win over the Green Bay Packers, writer George Strickler declared "the story of the game is written in the second half, when [the Bears' George] Swisher leaped from the bench incased (sic) in tape that protected his recently fractured ribs and brought the breath out of a record-breaking crowd of 45,434[.]"[14] The article went on to praise Packers fullback Clark Hinkle, "who played a good share of the contest with a back injury that would have kept him out of any game except one with the Bears."[15] About a month later, Strickler's preview of the championship matchup between the Bears and the Washington football club devoted a paragraph to Swisher, who had an injured heel but was declared set to play, and to two injured Washington players.[16]

The converse of this praise is that members of the media have also been willing to criticize those players they believe lack toughness,[17] not an uncommon occurrence.

The introduction of television created a powerful new way for fans, through the media, to experience NFL football. For example, in 1960, CBS created a documentary called *The Violent World of Sam Huff*, a New York Giants linebacker. Huff wore a microphone during a game for the documentary, which was narrated by Walter Cronkite.[18]

Perhaps one of the most important events in the media's coverage of the NFL occurred with the creation by Ed Sabol of a small film company that would later become NFL Films, an NFL-controlled corporation. NFL Films created widely acclaimed highlight films using dramatic music, slow motion, and live microphone recordings of players and coaches. In addition, NFL Films excelled at glorifying the violence of the game and toughness of the players.[19] Former NFL Films President Steve Sabol once described NFL Films' work as "movie making perfectly matched to the grace and the beauty and the violence of pro football."[20]

Beginning in 2003,[21] ESPN introduced a segment called "Jacked Up" which also glorified the violence of the game. The segment aired prior to Monday Night Football each week with former player and broadcaster Tom Jackson replaying the weekend's biggest and most ferocious hits while all of the announcers yelled in unison that the player receiving the hit had "got JACKED UP!"[22] The segment was discontinued after the 2008 season[23] after criticism from both the media[24] and fans.[25]

2) THE NFL'S INJURY REPORTING POLICY

A key component of the media's relationship to player health is the NFL's "Personnel (Injury) Report Policy" ("Injury Reporting Policy"). The Injury Reporting Policy requires each club to report information on injured players to both the NFL and the media each game week ("Injury Report").[26] The stated purpose of this reporting is "to provide a full and complete rendering of player availability" to all parties involved, including the opposing team, the media, and the general public. According to the NFL, the policy is of "paramount importance in maintaining the integrity of the NFL,"[27] i.e., preventing gambling on inside information concerning player injuries.[c]

The Injury Report is a list of injured players, each injured player's type or location of injury, and the injured player's status for the upcoming game. Each injury must be described "with a reasonable degree of specificity,"[28] e.g., ankle, ribs, hand or concussion. For a quarterback's arm injury or a kicker's or punter's leg injury, the description must designate left or right. Historically, the player's status for the upcoming game was classified into four categories: Out (definitely will not play); Doubtful (at least 75 percent chance will not play); Questionable (50-50 chance will not play); and, Probable (virtual certainty player will be available for normal duty).[29]

In 2016, the NFL changed the classifications for player injuries by: (1) eliminating the probable designation; (2) changing the definition of "questionable" to "uncertain as to whether the player will play in the game"; (3) changing the definition of "doubtful" to "unlikely the player will participate"; and, (4) only using the "out" designation two days before a game.[30] The Injury Report also indicates whether a player had full, limited, or no participation in practice, whether due to injury or any other cause (e.g., team discipline, family matter, etc.).[31]

Clubs must issue an Injury Report after practice each Wednesday, Thursday, and Friday of game week. If there are any additional injuries after the Friday deadline, the club must report these injuries to the NFL, the club's opponent, the televising network, and the local media on Saturday and Sunday.[32]

The Injury Reporting Policy dictates that all injury reports be "credible, accurate, and specific within the guidelines of this policy." In "unusual situations," clubs are requested to contact the League's Public Relations Office, and when in doubt, clubs should include a player in the Injury Report. Clubs and coaches that violate the policy are subject to disciplinary action. If a player with a game status of "Doubtful" plays, the club must provide a written explanation to the NFL within 48 hours.[33]

Despite the enforcement system and disciplinary action for abuse (typically fines of $5,000 to $25,000[34]), many in the media along with coaches and players have questioned the Injury Report's accuracy and value. A 2007 *USA Today* analysis of two-and-a-half seasons of Injury Reports found a high variance in the number of injuries reported by teams, with 527 reported by the Indianapolis Colts versus just 103 by the Dallas Cowboys; interviews with coaches suggested that the different philosophies of coaches to report even minor injuries versus only major injuries accounted for this variance.[35] In the same article, former Pittsburgh Steelers coach Bill Cowher was quoted as saying that he deliberately changed the location of injuries (e.g., reporting hip instead of knee) to protect his players from having their injuries targeted by opponents.[36] Baltimore Ravens head coach Jim Harbaugh, after being fined for not listing an injured player in 2012, told the media that "[t]here's no credence on the injury report now. . . . It doesn't mean anything. It has no value."[37] In March 2014, two former players on the New England Patriots stated that head coach Bill Belichick filed inaccurate and false injury reports.[38] Many in the media have referred to the Injury Report as a "game" or "joke."[39] Finally, some believed that the 2016 changes to the injury reporting policy allowed for even more gamesmanship.[40] Possibly due to the potential for fines for misreporting injuries on the Injury Report, many clubs have policies prohibiting players from speaking to the media about injuries.[41]

---

c   For more information on gambling and the NFL *see* Chapter 18: Fans.

(B) Current Legal Obligations[d]

Traditionally, the media's main legal obligations toward the individuals it covers are explained in terms of defamation law. Defamation is "[t]he act of harming the reputation of another by making a false statement to a third person."[42] Slander is the spoken form of defamation while libel is the written form.[43] A public figure, which would likely include any NFL player,[44] must prove that the reporter alleged to have committed defamation acted with "actual malice."[45] Actual malice is generally established where the reporter knew the statement was false or acted with reckless disregard of whether the statement was false or not.[46] Thus, media members generally have a legal obligation to work diligently to ensure the accuracy of their reports concerning public figures, including NFL players. Beyond these generalized obligations, there do not appear to be any specific relevant legal obligations that the media has as to NFL players.

(C) Current Ethical Codes

The principal source of media ethical obligations comes from the Society of Professional Journalists (SPJ), a voluntary organization of nearly 10,000 members.[47] The SPJ Code of Ethics includes 35 specific obligations, separated into the following categories: Seek Truth and Report It; Minimize Harm; Act Independently; and, Be Accountable and Transparent.[48] The principles most relevant to NFL players include:

> Ethical journalism treats sources, subjects, colleagues and members of the public as human beings deserving of respect.

> * * *

> Balance the public's need for information against potential harm or discomfort.

> * * *

> Weigh the consequences of publishing or broadcasting personal information.

The PFWA does not have a Code of Ethics but does include as one of its stated purposes "[t]o practice and advance the concepts of professional journalism while using verifiable facts, proper attribution and an objective, appropriate perspective in order to inform and enlighten the public in a credible manner."[49]

(D) Current Practices

Media attention and interest concerning player health and safety has certainly increased in recent years. On the one hand, numerous news articles discussed and cited in this Report brought important attention to player health issues and increased scrutiny of current practices. At the same time, the media's interest in player injury information for reasons unrelated to player health has increased dramatically.

Perhaps the biggest contributing factor to increased media attention to player injuries is fantasy football. As is discussed in more detail in Chapter 18: Fans, tens of millions of NFL fans play fantasy football with billions of dollars at stake. An essential component of fantasy football success is the health of the players on the fan's fantasy football roster. Media companies have responded with a variety of items to assist fans. For example, ESPN has a website called "Injury Central" which tracks injuries to key fantasy players,[50] and CBS Sports partnered with a web application called "Sports Injury Predictor" which is supposed to help fans determine whether a player is likely to get injured.[51] Additionally, every Sunday morning during the season, ESPN broadcasts a two-hour fantasy football show called "Fantasy Football Now." The program includes live updates from reporters on players' health statuses while also debating which players will "benefit" from the injury to another player.[52] Another frequent topic of debate among fantasy football media is whether fans can "trust" a player and his health.[53] Finally, ESPN employs Stephania Bell, "a physical therapist who is a board-certified orthopedic clinical specialist" to provide analysis of player injuries, specifically as they relate to fantasy football.[54]

As is discussed in more detail in Chapter 18: Fans, Section D: Current Practices, some have argued that fantasy football commoditizes and depersonalizes the players.[55] The reason is that media and fan focus is not on the health of players as human beings, but the health of the player as a replaceable unit in a gambling game. For example, when Carolina Panthers quarterback Cam Newton was in a major car crash during the 2014 season, fans quickly took to social media asking what the car crash meant for their fantasy football team.[56]

Another important factor in the media's coverage of players and their health is the increasingly intense 24/7 news cycle. With the rapid demand for and consumption of news, journalists may not have sufficient time to verify the details of a

---

d   The legal obligations described herein are not an exhaustive list but are those we believe are most relevant to player health.

story. If they do, they risk being scooped by competing news outlets. Moreover, news is no longer delivered by a predictable group of traditional news outlets. A large number of websites and Twitter users pass along rumors and other stories about players, many of which make it into the mainstream media as "news." Additionally, several top sports media organizations have websites specifically devoted to "rumors," including ESPN,[57] FOX Sports' Yardbarker,[58] and NBC Sports' ProFootballTalk.[59] National Football Post, another well-read NFL-specific website, includes a column called "The Training Room," written by former San Diego Chargers Club doctor Dr. David Chao.[60] On a weekly basis, Chao speculates on the diagnosis, prognosis, and treatment of player injuries. Of note, Chao resigned as the Chargers Club doctor in 2013 after a series of negative incidents, including a complaint by the NFLPA (*see* Chapter 2: Club Doctors).

An example of the intense interest in player health information occurred during the 2015 offseason when Giants defensive end Jason Pierre-Paul suffered a hand injury that resulted in the amputation of one of his fingers. While Pierre-Paul was in the hospital and the status of his hand still uncertain, ESPN reporter Adam Schefter Tweeted a photo of a hospital surgical record showing that Pierre-Paul's finger was to be amputated.[61] Despite criticism for posting the picture of Pierre-Paul's medical records, ESPN and Schefter defended the Tweet as part of the normal reporting of player injuries.[62] In February 2016, Pierre-Paul sued ESPN and Schefter, alleging they had violated Florida medical confidentiality and privacy laws. In August 2016, the United States District Court for the Southern District of Florida denied ESPN and Schefter's motion to dismiss, finding that Pierre-Paul had properly pled a claim for invasion of privacy.[63] The case is ongoing as of the date of this publication.

Prior to the 2014 season, Green Bay Packers star quarterback Aaron Rodgers lamented the intense interest in player injuries and its effect on players:

> TMI. There's too much information out there[.] There's too much exposure and, at times, undue pressure on players and coaching staffs to play now, win now. Just too much access.[64,e]

Players we interviewed echoed these concerns:[f]

- **Current Player 4:** *"I think at times [the media's coverage of player health issues] could be pretty hurtful .... Their job is to get as much information as possible and you, as a player, don't necessarily want all your business being published in an article."*

- **Current Player 5:** *"I think for the most part the media usually doesn't know what they're talking about. In sports reporting, I think there's a very low bar for accuracy. So I think in general that they don't do a very good job of drawing attention to player safety or reporting the facts."*

- **Former Player 2:** *"I don't know how accurate [the club is] giving proper information to the media ..., so I wouldn't say [the media is] that accurate .... I would say 60 percent confidence that anything the media reports on injuries is true."[g]*

Clubs and the NFL have also placed considerable pressure on the way the media covers the NFL. The NFL and the clubs have websites that employ writers to cover the clubs. Not surprisingly, these writers receive greater access to the clubs, the League, coaches and players than unaffiliated writers, and often write stories favorable to the clubs or League. Additionally, NFL clubs often have public relations staff that monitors or shadows the media during interviews and news conferences. If a journalist writes articles unfavorable to the club, the club might reduce that journalist's access to the club, its coaches, and players.[65] Similarly, when reporter Albert Breer left NFL Network in 2016, he explained that, while with NFL Network, he was prevented or discouraged from reporting on stories problematic for the NFL.[66]

> With the rapid demand for and consumption of news, journalists may not have sufficient time to verify the details of a story. If they do, they risk being scooped by competing news outlets.

---

e   Perhaps as further support for Rodgers' complaint, in July 2014, the satirical news organization *The Onion* ran a story with the following headline: "Report: Majority of Football Fans Better Informed On Health of NFL Players Than Parents." *Report: Majority of Football Fans Better Informed on Health of NFL Players Than Parents*, The Onion (July 29, 2014), http://www.theonion.com/article/report-majority-of-football-fans-better-informed-o-36565, *archived at* http://perma.cc/GJY6-AX2F.

f   We reiterate that our interviews were intended to be informational but not representative of all players' views and should be read with that limitation in mind.
g   Former Player 2 also believed that "the media definitely does" put pressure on players concerning their health.

Despite the increased attention to player health issues, it is still common for journalists to question a player's toughness. For example, when Chicago Bears quarterback Jay Cutler was removed from a 2011 playoff game due to a knee injury, numerous news articles questioned the severity of Cutler's injury and his inability to return to the game.[67] Sometimes the criticism is more implicit. For example, during a 2015 playoff game against the Green Bay Packers, Dallas Cowboys linebacker Rolando McClain left the game after suffering a head injury.[68] McClain had been diagnosed with a concussion earlier in the week after suffering a head injury in the prior week's game against the Detroit Lions.[69] Nevertheless, when McClain was taken out of the Packers game, a Dallas-based ESPN reporter Tweeted: "Rolando McClain to Cowboys locker room. Nobody frustrates training staff more[.]"[70]

Conversely, if the media glorifies players for playing with injuries,[71] it creates pressure on other players to do the same.

The media's portrayal of players can have a powerful influence on the public. In a 2014 article in *Communication & Sport*,[72] researchers reviewed 177 newspaper articles concerning two injury situations: Cutler's, as discussed above, and Washington quarterback Robert Griffin III's efforts to play with a knee injury during a 2013 playoff game against the Seattle Seahawks.[73] Of note, the researchers found that the leading theme from the articles discussing Griffin's injury shifted the blame to the Washington football club (40.67 percent of articles). Meanwhile, 49.24 percent of articles supported Cutler's decision to stop playing while 44.22 percent of articles blamed Cutler in some way, downplayed the severity of his injury or called him

a "sissy" in some way. The authors, citing other studies, reasoned that "[t]he notion that a player who needs to sit out or miss playing time due to an injury is a 'sissy' or less of a 'man' can have extremely unfortunate consequences."[74] Finally, the authors suggested that "[a]s sports journalists take more of an advocacy role and support athletes who make their health a priority, attitudes towards injuries and the players who sustain them may gradually begin to change."[75]

The media's coverage of player health issues has been mixed. Beginning in January 2007, Alan Schwarz of *The New York Times* was one of the leading journalists to report on health problems among former NFL players and problems with the NFL's approach to player health issues, including its Mild Traumatic Brain Injury (MTBI) Committee.[76] Schwarz appropriately received numerous accolades for this work. Mark Fainaru-Wada and Steve Fainaru of ESPN and authors of *League of Denial* similarly exposed problems in the way player health is or has been addressed, and the resulting problems suffered by current and former players. Reporters from all over the country and world have taken the lead from this work and contributed their own stories of problems concerning player health. Without this work, many of the improvements concerning player health that have been made in the last 5 to 10 years may never have happened.[h]

Despite the important work the media has done reporting on player health, there are also concerns. First, the media regularly reports on the perils and drawbacks of football,

---

h   Indeed, Current Player 9 believes the media has done a good job of covering player health "because they've done a good job of bringing awareness."

The media may not always have adequate space or time to convey the implications, and more importantly the limitations, of studies concerning player health.

whether children should be allowed to play,[77] and whether fans should continue to engage with the sport.[78] While these may be legitimate and important aspects to cover, some of this coverage shows a tendency to ignore important benefits to players (including those offered by the NFL and NFLPA) and others, and other positive aspects of the game.[i] In other words, balance in coverage in some instances appears to be lacking.

Another problem relates to accuracy. There have been many important scientific studies concerning the injuries, particularly concussions, suffered by football players. However, the media may not always have adequate space or time to convey the implications, and more importantly the limitations, of these studies.[j,79] The media may not always have adequate space or time to convey the implications, and more importantly the limitations, of studies concerning player health. Similarly, the media has not always accurately reported on player health litigation. For example, on September 12, 2014, the NFL filed an expert report in support of its position that the Concussion Litigation settlement would adequately compensate the plaintiffs.[80] The NFL's experts, using "conservative assumptions," assumed 28 percent of former players would be eligible for benefits under the settlement to demonstrate that the settlement was adequate.[81] The same day, the *New York Times* published a story entitled "Brain Trauma to Affect One in Three Players, N.F.L. Agrees."[82] The *Times'* headline ignored that the number was used by an actuarial firm as a conservative estimate meant to demonstrate the adequacy of the settlement—as opposed to medical data—and misstated 28 percent as "one in three," when it is actually closer to one in four.[k] The scientific and legal nuances are difficult to understand, which makes accurate reporting on them critically important.

(E) Enforcement of Legal and Ethical Obligations

A player's most likely available legal recourse against a member of the media is a civil lawsuit alleging defamation. As discussed above, lawsuits against journalists must overcome the high burden of proving that the journalist acted with actual malice, which should only arise in the rare event a journalist fails to abide by any of the sourcing or fact-checking requirements of the industry. Importantly, statements of opinion cannot be defamatory[83] and truth is an absolute defense to defamation claims.[84] While there are a few instances of sports figures suing journalists or publications for defamation,[85] there are no known cases of an NFL player suing a journalist.

In addition, as demonstrated by the Pierre-Paul case, it is possible more players will look to assert health privacy-related claims against media members.

The PFWA has a "Grievance Committee" that is charged with hearing any complaints about its members but its sanctioning authority as to the media is unclear. Similarly, while the SPJ has an Ethics Committee, it has no mechanism for investigating or enforcing violations of its Code of Ethics.[86] Instead, the SPJ believes the best enforcement of journalism ethics comes from the scrutiny of the public and other journalists.[87]

---

i Former Player 3: "There's thousands, tens of thousands, of former players . . . doing great, physically, mentally, financially, spiritually doing great. So those stories are not told."

j For example, in January 2015, *The New York Times* reported on a study done at the Boston University School of Medicine which, based on tests given to 42 former NFL players, purported to find "that those who began playing tackle football when they were younger than 12 years old had a higher risk of developing memory and thinking problems later in life." Ken Belson, *Study of Retirees Links Youth Football to Brain Problems*, N.Y. Times, Jan. 28, 2015, http://www.nytimes.com/2015/01/29/sports/football/study-points-to-cognitive-dangers-of-tackle-football-before-age-12.html, *archived at* https://perma.cc/G7MC-KGE8?type=pdf. However, the *New York Times* article did not include any responses to the study, including criticism from highly respected neurologist Julian Bailes, which was included in ESPN's coverage of the study. *See* Tom Farrey, *Study Cites Youth Football for Issues*, ESPN (Jan. 29, 2015, 4:04 PM), http://espn.go.com/espn/otl/story/_/id/12243012/ex-nfl-players-played-tackle-football-youth-more-likely-thinking-memory-problems, *archived at* http://perma.cc/V3Y5-EQJH (Bailes told ESPN "that the sample is too small to draw any conclusions from, and that the results of NFL players cannot be compared to that of athletes who never made it to that level.").

k Similarly, in a lengthy article praising the attorney who filed the first concussion-related lawsuit against the NFL, the *New York Times* wrongly asserted that if the NFL had won its motion to dismiss prior to the settlement, the case would have proceeded in "mediation or arbitration." Michael Sokolove, *How One Lawyer's Crusade Could Change Football Forever*, N.Y. Times (Magazine), Nov. 6, 2014, http://www.nytimes.com/2014/11/09/magazine/how-one-lawyers-crusade-could-change-football-forever.html, *archived at* https://perma.cc/4DJ6-XMQV?type=pdf. In reality, dismissal likely would have been the end of the players' claims. *See* Michael McCann, *Retired Players Who Opt Out of NFL Concussion Settlement Taking Big Risk*, Sports Illustrated (Jan. 26, 2015), http://www.si.com/nfl/2015/01/26/nfl-concussion-lawsuit-settlement-retired-players-opt-out, *archived at* http://perma.cc/ZD66-EJ67. *See also* In re Nat'l Hockey League Players' Concussion Injury Litigation, 14-md-2551, 2016 WL 2901736, *22 (D. Minn. May 18, 2016) ("Plaintiffs, as retire[d] [hockey players], would likely be unable to access the arbitration forum and would not have another forum in which to seek relief").

(F) Recommendations Concerning the Media

The media has a powerful and unique voice to shape the way player health issues are perceived and addressed. Below we make recommendations to improve the relationship between the media and the players they cover.

Goal 1: To recognize the media's responsibility in encouraging a culture of health for NFL players.

Principles Advanced: Respect; Health Primacy; Collaboration and Engagement; and, Justice.

Recommendation 17:1-A: The media's reporting on players should take care not to dehumanize them.

The media can both help and hurt players. While many reporters are increasingly taking into consideration players' health, there are still many reporters who are willing to criticize and question the toughness of players who suffer injuries or who do not play with injuries. Such reports impossibly and improperly assume to understand the pain the player may be in or the medical consequences of the player's playing with the injury. Moreover, such reports fail to take into consideration the player's best interests, *e.g.*, the player's short- and long-term health.

Similarly, the fantasy football-related discussions, websites, and applications take on a disturbing tone in some instances. At their worst, they do not acknowledge the players as human beings with medical conditions that could, and in many cases will, affect the quality and length of their lives. Instead, in some instances there is a dehumanization of the player and only a concern for how the player's injury that will affect fantasy football rosters which, relative to player health, is meaningless.[88] While many in the media work hard to avoid dehumanizing players, those media members who participate in and perpetuate such discussions should reconsider the tone and context of their reports and debates. We recognize that this is an aspirational goal and not one that can be readily monitored or enforced, but it is important to acknowledge this behavior as a problem and the role it plays in player health.

Through taking care in its reporting of player injuries and treating players with dignity, the media has the power to draw greater public emphasis to player health and also reduce pressure on players to play while injured.

Recommendation 17:1-B: The media should engage appropriate experts, including doctors, scientists and lawyers, to ensure that its reporting on player health matters is accurate, balanced, and comprehensive.

The media's coverage of player health issues, while excellent at times, also has been occasionally misleading or not entirely accurate. Inaccurate news reports will only undermine the credibility of the serious issues facing NFL players. The medical, scientific and legal issues concerning player health are extremely complicated, which demands that the media take care to avoid making assertions that are not supported or that do not account for the intricacies and nuance of medicine, science, and the law. While we understand the pressures faced by members of the media trying to complete work on tight deadlines, we also emphasize the importance of engaging appropriate experts who can help the media understand these complex issues.

Endnotes

1   *See also* "Media", Oxford Dictionaries, 2015, http://www .oxforddictionaries.com/us/definition/american_english/media (last visited Aug. 7, 2015), *archived at* http://perma.cc/6FGD-CQP7 (defining "media" as "[t]he main means of mass communication (especially television, radio, newspapers, and the Internet) regarded collectively); "Journalist", Oxford Dictionaries, 2015, http://www.oxforddictionaries .com/us/definition/american_english/journalist (last visited Aug. 7, 2015), *archived at* http://perma.cc/37MC-9PZX (defining "journalist" as "[a] person who writes for newspapers or magazines or prepares news to be broadcast"); "Press" Black's Law Dictionary (9th ed. 2009) (defining "press" as "[t]he news media; print and broadcast news organizations collectively").

2   *National Football League and Twitter Announce Streaming Partnership for Thursday Night Football,* NFL (Apr. 5, 2016), https:// nflcommunications.com/Documents/2016%20Releases/NFL%20TWTR %20TNF.pdf, *archived at* https://perma.cc/F5SN-AVRL.

3   Kurt Badenhausen, *The NFL Signs TV Deals Worth $27 Billion,* Forbes (Feb. 14, 2011, 6:13PM), http://www.forbes.com/sites/kurtbadenhausen /2011/12/14/the-nfl-signs-tv-deals-worth-26-billion/, *archived at* https:/ /perma.cc/B64R-2GHV?type=pdf.

4   *See* Daniel Kaplan, *NFL Projecting Revenue Increase of $1B Over 2014,* Sports Bus. Daily (Mar. 9, 2015), http://www.sportsbusinessdaily.com /Journal/Issues/2015/03/09/Leagues-and-Governing-Bodies/NFL -revenue.aspx, *archived at* http://perma.cc/F8B5-233U (discussing NFL's $11.2 billion in revenue for 2014, growing at a rate of approximately $1 billion per year and expected to exceed $12 billion in 2015).

5   *Regular Season Tv Ratings Recap*, Nat'l Football League, https:// nflcommunications.com/PublishingImages/Pages/2015-REGULAR -SEASON-RATINGS-RECAP-/2015%20Regular%20Season%20Ratings %20Recap.pdf (last visited Apr. 7, 2016), *archived at* https://perma.cc/ Q43S-4HBE.

6   B.J. Kissel, *2014 NFL TV Ratings Recap,* Kansas City Chiefs, (Jan. 11, 2015), http://www.kcchiefs.com/news/article-2/2014-NFL-TV-Ratings -Recap/2638f637-5fae-4e89-afd9-8a0da6135588, *archived at* http://perma.cc/7ZME-GGZN.

7   Bill Hofheimer, *ESPN's Coverage of the 2014 NFL Season,* ESPN, (Sept. 3, 2014), http://espnmediazone.com/us/press-releases/2014/09 /espns-coverage-of-the-2014-nfl-season/, *archived at* http://perma.cc/ U5CU-BQ5D.

8   *See* Bob McGinn, *Packers: Scouts Should Determine NFL Awards*, Mil. J. Sentinel, Dec. 18, 2005, *available at* 2005 WLNR 20536517 (discussing "a few hundred PFWA members"); *Young Nabs Honor as NFL's Best,* Buffalo News, Jan. 26, 1995, *available* at 1995 WLNR 1092627 (describing PFWA membership as "400-plus").

9   *NFL Media Access Policy*, Pro Football Writers Am., http://www .profootballwriters.org/nfl-media-access-policy/ (last visited Aug. 7, 2015), *archived at* http://perma.cc/QGS4-HUMW.

10 *Id.*

11 Jeffri Chadiha, *The Misunderstood Marshawn Lynch,* ESPN (Jan. 27, 2015), http://espn.go.com/nfl/playoffs/2014/story/_/id/12232435/the -misunderstood-marshawn-lynch-why-seattle-seahawks-running-back -trust-media, *archived at* http://perma.cc/7CVQ-8XDK.

12 Mike Florio, *Marshawn Has a Very Polite Media Availability,* ProFootball- Talk (Dec. 22, 2014, 9:57 AM), http://profootballtalk.nbcsports.com/2014 /12/22/marshawn-has-a-very-polite-media-availability/, *archived at* http://perma.cc/2QS3-XCP2.

13 Darin Gantt, *Marshawn Lynch Shows Up at Media Day to Avoid Fines*, ProFootballTalk (Jan. 27, 2015, 2:30 PM), http://profootballtalk.nbcsports .com/2015/01/27/marshawn-lynch-shows-up-at-media-day-to-avoid -fines/, *archived at* http://perma.cc/K7GG-TCRX.

14 George Strickler, *45,434 see Bears defeat Packers 14 to 7*, Chi. Trib., Nov. 4, 1940.

15 *Id.*

16 George Strickler, *Bears meet Redskins today for pro football title*, Chi. Trib., Dec. 8, 1940.

17 *See, e.g.,* Dan Pompei, *Gault's Confidence Built on Toughness,* Chi. Sun Times, Nov. 7, 1987, *available at* 1987 WLNR 2135505; Frank Cooney, *Everett's Courage is Being Questioned Around the NFL,* S. F. Examiner, Sept. 12, 1993, *available at* 1993 WLNR 12375; Damon Amendora, *Washington Still Doesn't Know if RGIII is Tough Enough*, CBS Sports Radio (Aug. 21, 2015, 11:40 AM), http://da.radio.cbssports.com/2015/08 /21/da-washington-still-doesnt-know-if-rgiii-is-tough-enough/, *archived at* http://perma.cc/YYM7-ZVCS.

18 *The Violent World of Sam Huff (*CBS October 30, 1960).

19 *See* Bob Raissman, *Concussion Concerns Will Go Over CBS' Head*, N.Y. Daily News, Jan. 25, 2013, *available at* 2013 WLNR 1999106 (discussing role of NFL Films in Concussion Litigation and allegations of glorifying violence); Desmond Ryan, *A Player In The Field Of Film NFL Films Focuses On Gridiron Glory, But Has An Impact Beyond The End Zone*, Phil. Inquirer, May 8, 1995, http://articles.philly.com/1995-05 -08/entertainment/25673540_1_nfl-films-cahiers-critics-and-editors (discussing the style of NFL Films); Bill Lyon, *NFL Films has seen – and filmed – it* all, Seattle Times, Dec. 16, 1990, *available at* 1990 WLNR 887902 (discussing NFL Films' history and, among other things, glorification of violence in the NFL).

20 *NFL Films: Inside the Vault, Vol. 1* (Steve Sabol 2003).

21 Brent Jones, *Billick: Browns fans off base on Modell*, Balt. Sun, Dec. 23, 2003, *available at* 2003 WLNR 2034569 (earliest news article mentioning the "Jacked Up" segment).

22 *See* Aaron Gordon, *When ESPN Cheered Violence*, Salon (Sept. 15, 2013, 10:00 AM), http://www.salon.com/2013/09/15/keep_your_helmet_on _espns_jacked_up_in_retrospect_partner/, *archived at* http://perma.cc /3RDU-4CTP.

23 *See* Chad Finn, *ESPN's Reaction Was Candid And Poignant*, Bos. Globe, Sept. 15, 2014, *available at* 2014 WLNR 25499549 (referencing "Jacked Up" segment ending after the 2008 season).

24 *See* Phil Mushnick, *ESPN Gets 'Jackassed Up!'*, N.Y. Post, Oct. 3, 2004, *available at* 2004 WLNR 19629651.

25 Will Leitch, *ESPN Listens Closely to Its Viewers*, Deadspin (Oct. 4, 2007, 4:10 PM), http://deadspin.com/307063/espn-listens-closely-to-its -viewers, *archived at* http://perma.cc/D3G6-AFA9 (discussing internal ESPN memo citing 200+ complaints about the "Jacked Up" segment during the 2006 season). NFL Columnist Mike Freeman has criticized journalists (including himself) for "glorifying the violence of the sport while not detailing the toll that violence took on the body." Mike Freeman, Two Minute Warning: How Concussions, Crime, and Controversy Could Kill the NFL (and What the League Can Do to Survive) 218 (2015).

26 Both quotes are from the *2008 Personnel (Injury) Report Policy*, Page E32.

27 *Id.*

28 *Id.*

29 *Id. at* E34.

30 Tom Pelissero, *Major change to NFL's injury report will take some getting used to*, USA Today (Aug. 21, 2016, 4:33 PM), http://www.usatoday .com/story/sports/nfl/2016/08/21/injury-report-probable-bill-belichick -patriots/89080582/, *archived at* https://perma.cc/QT4C-MAA6.

31 *Personnel (Injury) Report Policy*, Page E33.

32 *Id.*

33 *Personnel (Injury) Report Policy*.

34 Scott Boeck & Skip Wood, *Analysis: Injury Report Is Game Within The Game*, USA Today, Nov. 22, 2007, *available at* http://usatoday30 .usatoday.com/sports/football/nfl/2007-11-22-injury-report-cover_N .htm, *archived at* http://perma.cc/4MK7-657Q. Midway through the 2012 season, 4 NFL teams had been fined $20,000 each for injury report violations. Mike Florio, *Rams Rack Up an Injury-Reporting Fine, Too*, ProFootballTalk (Nov. 2, 2012, 10:44 PM), http://profootballtalk .nbcsports.com/2012/11/02/rams-rack-up-an-injury-reporting-fine-too/, *archived at* http://perma.cc/W8U5-XTN7. In 2009, the Jets were fined a total $125,000 for former quarterback Brett Favre's injury for the last 5 games of the season ($75,000 for the team and $25,000 each for General Manager Mike Tannenbaum and former Head Coach Eric Mangini), the highest injury-reporting violation fine publicly announced. *See* Greg Bishop, *Jets Still Paying Price for Favre and Mangini*, N.Y. Times, Sept. 16, 2009, http://www.nytimes.com/2009/09/17/sports/football /17favre.html, *archived at* https://perma.cc/M9VT-BF96?type=pdf.

35 Boeck *supra* note 34; *see also* Gregg Rosenthal, *Redskins Play the "Questionable" Game, Again*, ProFootballTalk (Sept. 25, 2010, 10:07 AM), http://profootballtalk.nbcsports.com/2010/09/25/redskins-play -the-questionable-game-again/, *archived at* http://perma.cc/L4PQ-J8LV (players reporting that coaches report the wrong injuries): Michael David Smith, *Spikes, Talib Say Patriots File False Injury Reports*, ProFootball-Talk (Mar. 19, 2014, 7:01 AM), http://profootballtalk.nbcsports.com/2014 /03/19/spikes-talib-say-patriots-file-false-injury-reports/, *archived at* http://perma.cc/A4S9-MQ6Q.

36 *See* Boeck *supra* note 34.

37 Jeff Zrebiec, *John Harbaugh: 'The Injury Report Has No Value'*, Balt. Sun, Nov. 2, 2012, http://www.baltimoresun.com/sports/ravens/ravens -insider/bal-harbaugh-criticizes-nfl-over-injury-report-20121102-story .html, *archived at* http://perma.cc/FS8C-2PHX.

38 Smith *supra* note 35.

39 *See* Rosenthal *supra* note 35; Boeck *supra* note 34. *See also* Carl Prine, *Bloody Sundays*, Pitt. Trib.-Rev., Jan. 9, 2005, http://triblive.com/x/ pittsburghtrib/sports/steelers/s_291033.html#axzz3OdCi5UC7, *archived at* http://perma.cc/GSK3-W254 (finding that "the NFL's 1999 [Injury Reports] data was so suspect, the Trib didn't use it").

40 Mike Florio, *New Injury report creates plenty of questions, concerns*, ProFootballTalk (Aug. 21, 2016, 8:20 PM), http://profootballtalk .nbcsports.com/2016/08/21/new-injury-report-creates-plenty-of -questions-concerns/, *archived at* https://perma.cc/ZMX9-XQT2.

41 *See* Darin Gantt, *Julian Edelman Won't Say Whether He Had Concussion Tests*, ProFootballTalk (Feb. 1, 2015, 11:30 PM), http://profootballtalk .nbcsports.com/2015/02/01/julian-edelman-wont-say-whether-he-had -concussion-tests/, *archived at* http://perma.cc/3WZQ-RU9K (discussing Patriots' policy of prohibiting players from speaking about injuries). In an interview, a current player on a different club also stated that his club prohibited players from speaking to the media about injuries.

42 Black's Law Dictionary (9th ed. 2009).

43 *See id.* (defining "slander" as "[a] defamatory assertion expressed in a transitory form, esp. speech" and "libel" as "[a] defamatory statement expressed in a fixed medium, esp. writing but also a picture, sign, or electronic broadcast").

44 *See* Vilma v. Goodell, 917 F. Supp. 2d 591, 596 (E.D.La. 2013) (describing NFL player Jonathan Vilma as "a public figure" for purposes of defamation claim).

45 N.Y. Times Co. v. Sullivan, 376 U.S. 254, 279–80 (1964).

46 *Id.*

47 *About SPJ*, Soc'y Prof'l Journalists, http://www.spj.org/aboutspj.asp (last visited Aug. 7, 2015), *archived at* http://perma.cc/6TSA-LVN3.

48 *SPJ Code of Ethics*, Soc'y Prof'l Journalists, http://www.spj.org/ ethicscode.asp (last visited Aug. 7, 2015), *archived at* http://perma.cc/ W49E-8MK2.

49 PFWA Constitution and Bylaws (amend. Jan. 30, 2009) (on file with authors).

50 *Injury Central: Tracking Key Injuries*, ESPN (Dec. 26, 2014, 5:41 PM), http://espn.go.com/fantasy/football/story/_/id/11426633/all -latest-fantasy-football-injury-information-injury-central, *archived at* http://perma.cc/WEE8-D764.

51 *Sports Injury Predictor and ASL Extend Partnership*, Advanced Sports Logic (Feb. 20, 2014), http://advancedsportslogic.com/about/asl-in -industry-news/asl-and-sports-injury-predictor-extend-partnership, *archived at* http://perma.cc/EM7E-2938.

52 *See also* Matt Pallister, *Fantasy Football Players Can Benefit From Injuries If They Know Where To Look*, Wash. Times (DC), Aug. 28, 2014, *available at* 2014 WLNR 23671218.

53 Ladd Biro, *Starters and Benchwarmers: Fantasy Football*, S.F. Chron., Nov. 21, 2014, *available at* 2014 WLNR 32864699 ("it's hard to trust Rivers, who apparently is trying to play through a rib injury"); Cecil Lammey, *Fantasy Football Gates' Status Requires a Backup Plan*, Denver Post, Nov. 21, 2010, *available at* 2010 WLNR 23277384 ("Floyd is returning from a hamstring injury, but I can't trust him in the starting lineup this week.").

54 *See Stephania Bell Blog*, ESPN, http://espn.go.com/blog/stephania-bell (last visited Aug. 7, 2015), *archived at* http://perma.cc/59PZ-NC4R.

55 *See* Mónica Guzmán, *Internet Pumps Up Interest in Fantasy Football*, Seattle Times, Nov. 10, 2013, *available at* 2013 WLNR 28440805; Mackenzie Ryan, An Analysis of National Football League Fandom and Its Promotion of Conservative Cultural Ideals about Race, Religion and Gender 9 (Aug. 2012).

56 Josh Hill, *Scumbag NFL Fans Ask Fantasy Football Advice After Cam Newton Car Crash*, FanSided.com (Dec. 9, 2014), http://fansided.com /2014/12/09/fantasy-football-advice-cam-newton-car-crash/, *archived at* http://perma.cc/4RPJ-U9DD.

57 *Rumor Central: ESPN Insiders*, ESPN, http://insider.espn.go.com/blog/ insider/rumors/ (last visited Aug. 7, 2015), *archived at* http://perma.cc/ CJQ2-4P9W.

58 *Yardbarker*, http://www.yardbarker.com/ (last visited Aug. 7, 2015), *archived at* http://perma.cc/YG7W-4KXX.

59 ProFootballTalk, http://profootballtalk.nbcsports.com/category/rumor -mill/ (last visited Aug. 7, 2015), *archived at* http://perma.cc/4F8Z-VFA6.

60 *The Training Room—by Dr. David Chao*, Nat'l Football Post, http://www .nationalfootballpost.com/category/the-training-room/ (last visited Aug. 7, 2015), *archived at* http://perma.cc/GL5E-MYNB.

61 Mike Florio, *Schefter says he "could and should have done more" before posting JPP medical records*, ProFootballTalk (July 12, 2015, 10:39 AM), http://profootballtalk.nbcsports.com/2015/07/12/schefter-says-he-could -and-should-have-done-more-before-posting-jpp-medical-records/, *archived at* http://perma.cc/ZY4D-9ZC5.

62 *Id.*

63 Order on Defendant's Motion to Dismiss After Hearing, Pierre-Paul v. ESPN, Inc., 16-cv-21156 (Aug. 29, 2016, S.D. Fla.), ECF No. 30.

64 Tom Pelissero, *Tony Romo's Injury Shows Pressure QBs Face to Play Hurt*, USA Today, Nov. 3, 2014, http://www.usatoday.com/story/sports/nfl /2014/11/03/tony-romo-quarterback-injuries-aaron-rodgers-alex-smith /18439613/, *archived at* http://perma.cc/QLH9-U4LG.

65 Interview with John Affleck, Knight Chair in Sports Journalism and Society, Penn State University.

66 Mike Florio, *Breer pulls back curtain on working for NFL Network*, Pro-FootballTalk (Apr. 23, 2016, 12:51 PM), http://profootballtalk.nbcsports .com/2016/04/23/breer-pulls-back-curtain-on-working-for-nfl-network/, *archived at* https://perma.cc/KD7Y-BBBA.

67 Nancy Gay, *Cutler Lacks Grit In Loss Against Packers*, FoxSports (Jun. 2, 2014, 1:49 PM), https://web.archive.org/web/20110125180314/http ://msn.foxsports.com/nfl/story/gay-jay-cutler-knee-injury-chicago-bears -nfc-championship-012311, *archived at* https://perma.cc/7MD9-U6C4; *Will Cutler Ever Be Where Rodgers Is?*, Daily Herald (Arlington Heights, IL), Feb. 2, 2011, *available at* 2011 WLNR 2223051; Dave George, *Not Tough Enough?* Palm Beach Post (FL), Jan. 25, 2011, *available at*

2011 WLNR 1562822; Tom Rock, *Cutler's Exit Opens Debate*, Newsday, Jan. 24, 2011, *available at* 2011 WLNR 1423016.

68 Josh Alper, *Cowboys Tie Game, Lose Rolando McClain to Locker Room With Head Injury*, ProFootballTalk (Jan. 11, 2015, 1:36 PM), http://profootballtalk.nbcsports.com/2015/01/11/cowboys-tie-game -lose-rolando-mcclain-to-locker-room-with-head-injury/, *archived at* http://perma.cc/KDS3-GGD8.

69 *Id.*

70 Samer Kalaf, *Concussions Sure Are Frustrating*, Deadspin (Jan. 11, 2015, 2:05PM), http://deadspin.com/concussions-sure-are-frustrating -1678834644, *archived at* http://perma.cc/8HUG-LKM4; *see also* Mike Freeman, Two Minute Warning: How Concussions, Crime, and Controversy Could Kill the NFL (and What the League Can Do to Survive) 219 (2015) (criticizing journalist who "wrote glowingly about the violence of the sport, and condemned players we perceived as soft.")

71 *See* Jeffri Chadiha, *J.J. Watt's nasty bruise evokes memories of great injury moments*, ESPN (May 22, 2015), http://espn.go.com/nfl/story/_/id /12928692/jj-watt-bruise-continues-storied-tradition-athletes-playing -injuries, *archived at* http://perma.cc/W2RU-4VRU (providing examples of "great injury moments" in which athletes played while injured).

72 According to its website, "*Communication and Sport (C&S)* is a cutting-edge, peer-reviewed quarterly journal that publishes research to foster international scholarly understanding of the nexus of communication and sport. *C&S* publishes research and critical analysis from diverse disciplinary and theoretical perspectives to advance understanding of communication phenomena in the varied contexts through which sport touches individuals, society, and culture." *Communication & Sport*, SAGE Publications, https://us.sagepub.com/en-us/nam/communication-sport/ journal202136 (last visited Aug. 7, 2015), *archived at* https://perma.cc/ JA2M-AQ8N?type=pdf.

73 Jimmy Sanderson et al., *A Hero or Sissy? Exploring Media Framing of NFL Quarterbacks Injury Decisions*, Commc'n & Sport, May 28, 2014.

74 *Id.* at 16.

75 *Id.* at 15.

76 *See* Mark Fainaru-Wada & Steve Fainaru, League of Denial: The NFL, Concussions and the Battle for Truth 213, 215, 226, 227, 234, 260, 264, 276, 283–84 (2013).

77 *See, e.g.,* John Guida, *Should Your Child Play Football?* N.Y. Times, Nov. 11, 2014, http://op-talk.blogs.nytimes.com/2014/11/11/should -your-child-play-football/, *archived at* http://perma.cc/5VRC-H4PM; Julie Suratt, *Would You Let This Boy Play Football?* Bos. Mag., Jan. 2015, http://www.bostonmagazine.com/news/article/2015/01/05/let-boy-play -football/, *archived at* http://perma.cc/ND6J-EF9Q; *Opinion Northwest: Would You Let Your Son Play Football?* Seattle Times, Oct. 14, 2013, *available at* 2013 WLNR 25728781; *If You Had A High-School-Age Son, Would You Let Him Play Football?* Ariz. Republic, Sept. 22, 2012, *available at* 2012 WLNR 23906921; Lindsay Schnell, *Oregon Ducks Rundown Column*, Oregonian (Portland, Ore), Oct. 27, 2011, *available at* 2011 WLNR 22155996; *Sports Poll*, San Diego Union-Tribune, Jan. 13, 2013, *available at* 2013 WLNR 1063883.

78 *See, e.g.,* Chuck Klosterman, *Is It Wrong to Watch Football?*, N.Y. Times, Sept. 5, 2014, http://www.nytimes.com/2014/09/07/magazine/is-it -wrong-to-watch-football.html, *archived at* https://perma.cc/STD5 -4GGS?type=pdf; Will Leitch, *Is Football Wrong? Even to a Devoted Fan, It's Getting Harder to Watch the NFL*, N.Y. Magazine, Aug. 10, 2012, http://nymag.com/news/sports/games/nfl-fans-2012-8/, *archived at* http://perma.cc/ZT5D-BBX2; Steve Almond, *Why You Should Stop Watching Football*, Bos. Globe, Aug. 10, 2014, *available at* 2014 WLNR 21887974; Melissa Jeltsen, T*he Moral Case Against Football*, Huffington Post (Sept. 4, 2014, 3:22 PM), http://www.huffingtonpost.com/2014 /09/04/steve-almond-against-football_n_5718939.html, *archived at* http://perma.cc/DK93-ZK6X; Rick Maese & Scott Clement, *Despite Problems, NFL Remains Very Popular*, Wash. Post, Sept. 5, 2012, *available at* 2012 WLNR 18865647.

79 *See* Last Week Tonight With John Oliver: Scientific Studies (HBO) (May 8, 2016), YouTube, https://www.youtube.com/watch?v=0Rnq1NpHdmw.

80 Report of the Segal Group to Special Master Perry Golkin, In re: Nat'l Football League Players' Concussion Injury Litigation, 2:12-md-2323 (Sep. 12, 2014), ECF No. 6168.

81 *Id.* at ¶¶ 18–23.

82 Ken Belson, *Brain Trauma to Affect One in Three Players, N.F.L. Agrees*, N.Y. Times, Sept. 12, 2014, http://www.nytimes.com/2014/09/13/sports /football/actuarial-reports-in-nfl-concussion-deal-are-released.html, *archived at* https://perma.cc/5HFR-N8TV?type=pdf; *see also* Ken Belson, *Dementia Care, Tailored to N.F.L. Retirees*, N.Y. Times, Mar. 22, 2016, http://www.nytimes.com/2016/03/23/sports/dementia-care-tailored-to -nfl-retirees.html, *archived at* https://perma.cc/P3E4-WXRV (also inaccurately describing 28% figure).

83 GreenBelt Co-op Pub. Ass'n v. Bresler, 398 U.S. 6 (1970).

84 Curtis Publishing Co. v. Butts, 388 U.S. 130, 151 (1967).

85 In 2013, St. Louis Cardinals (MLB) slugger Albert Pujols sued former player turned radio announcer Jack Clark for defamation after Clark asserted that Pujols used performance-enhancing drugs. Pujols agreed to drop the lawsuit after Clark retracted his statement and apologized. *See Media Views: The Real Meaning of Jack Clark's Apology*, St. Louis Post-Dispatch, Feb. 21, 2014, *available at* 2014 WLNR 4958206. In 2005, former Alabama football coach Mike Price settled a lawsuit against *Sports Illustrated* in which Price alleged *Sports Illustrated* slandered him about a night of drinking at a strip club. *Price, Time Reach Second Settlement Over Sports Illustrated Article,* Seattle Times, Nov. 15, 2005, http://seattletimes.com/html/sports/2002625534_webprice15.html, *archived at* http://perma.cc/4288-A3LZ.

86 *Frequently Asked Questions*, Soc'y Prof'l Journalists, http://www.spj.org /ethicsfaq.asp (last visited Aug. 7, 2015), *archived at* http://perma.cc/ P36J-633X.

87 *Id.*

88 *See* William C. Rhoden, *Fantasy Sports' Real Crime: Dehumanizing the Athletes*, N.Y. Times, Nov. 25, 2015, http://www.nytimes.com/2015/11 /26/sports/football/fantasy-sports-real-crime-dehumanizing-the-athletes .html?_r=1, *archived at* https://perma.cc/WPG9-GL5A?type=image.

Chapter 18

Fans[a]

Fans are undoubtedly a central component to the NFL's success. Fans engage with NFL football and players in a variety of ways, including by watching on television, attending practices or games in-person, by gambling and playing fantasy sports, and through public events where fans might see or speak with players. These different fan experiences also shape the fan's interests and role in player health.

While in other chapters we provided the stakeholder an opportunity to review a draft of the relevant chapter(s) prior to publication, because there is no well-defined representative for fans, no one reviewed this chapter on behalf of fans prior to publication.

a   The portions of this work related to fans are the result of collaboration with Daniel Wann, Professor, Murray State University.

(A) Background

Below we discuss two components of fandom that have connections to player health: (1) the level at which fans engage with the NFL; and, (2) gambling, an activity that presents particular legal and ethical concerns.

1) FAN ENGAGEMENT

NFL football is the most popular sport in America by a variety of measures.[1] Thirty-five percent of Americans consider professional football (*i.e.*, the NFL) their favorite sport, a number that is increasing yearly.[2] Fifty-five percent of Americans identify themselves as fans of the NFL.[3] According to ESPN, there are more than 85 million "avid" NFL fans—"more than a quarter of the nation."[4] A mean of more than 68,000 people attend every NFL game.[5] NFL games are the most watched television programming: more than 20 million people watch the primetime broadcasts, triple the ratings of the major television networks.[6] The Super Bowl is the most viewed broadcast in television history, with approximately 45-percent of all households (about 53 million) tuning in annually.[7] And, not surprisingly, millions of fans also follow and engage with their favorite NFL clubs via social media.[8]

Indeed, NFL fans have strong psychological connections to their favorite clubs. Being a fan is a central component of their social identity,[9] and fans often have a stronger connection to their favorite club than their religion or alma mater,[10] or their favorite consumer brands such as clothing and food or beverage products.[11]

2) FANS AND GAMBLING[b]

A comprehensive analysis of issues in the NFL, including player health, is not complete without a discussion of gambling,[c] including fantasy sports.[d] The sports gambling industry in the United States is vast and appears to have grown at an exponential rate since the 1970s.[12] The size of the legal college and professional football gambling market is limited to Nevada, Montana, and Delaware by virtue of the Professional and Amateur Sports Protection Act (PASPA), a 1992 federal statute that exempted a small number of states from a federal prohibition on sports gambling.[13]

The legal sports gambling market in Nevada saw, in total, $3.9 billion wagered on sports in 2014, $1.74 billion of which was on football (about 45 percent of the total).[14] In 2014, Nevada sportsbooks won $113.73 million on college and professional football.[15] Delaware recently reported revenue associated with state licensed football pools of $25.4 million.[16] The "Montana Sports Action," a line of games related to fantasy football and racing, sold $179,790 worth of tickets in 2013.[17] Although no monetary amounts are available, the *Houston Chronicle* reported that "the Super Bowl is by far the most wagered on event—legally and illegally—in the country."[18]

Despite the above-referenced figures, illegal gambling still dwarfs legal gambling. In the United States, illegal gambling on professional sports has been estimated at $80-$380 billion annually.[19] If we assume the rate of illegal gambling on football matches Nevada's 45-percent rate of legal gambling on football, one would estimate that there is as much as $170 billion illegally gambled on football each year.[20] While likely off in its specifics, that estimate gives a rough sense of the magnitude of illegal NFL gambling that goes on.

The relationship between gambling and the NFL's popularity is undeniable. As one current club owner recently said in reference to gambling, "our game is made for that."[21] In testimony surrounding the 1999 National Gambling Impact Study (created at Congress' behest), broadcaster Bob Costas stated "there is also no denying that the presence and prevalence of sports gambling benefits those leagues and benefits their television ratings."[22] More recently, NFL commentator Mike Florio opined on the role of fantasy sports and NFL popularity:

> *The unprecedented growth of pro football over the last 20 years has resulted in large part from the ascension of fantasy football. With free agency potentially undermining fan rooting interest in specific teams, the ability to cobble together a team of their own has expanded fan interest far beyond the teams they love and the teams they hate.*[23]

---

b The portions of this work related to gambling are the result of collaboration with Ryan Rodenberg, JD, PhD, Professor, Florida State University.

c For purposes of this report, gambling is defined broadly to include traditional sports gambling (point spreads, money lines, totals, prop bets, in-game wagering, etc.), and fantasy sports (season-long and daily). We acknowledge the ongoing debate about whether fantasy sports constitute gambling but believe it is appropriate to include them in the definition for our purposes. *See, e.g.*, Decision and Order, State of New York v. DraftKings, Inc., Index No. 543054/2015 (N.Y. Sup. Ct. Dec. 11, 2015) (enjoining daily fantasy sports operator from conducting business in New York).

d Although specific forms of fantasy sports have been exempted under the Unlawful Internet Gambling Enforcement Act of 2006 ("UIGEA"), *see* 31 U.S.C. §§ 5361–5367, many suggest that in reality there is no distinction between gambling and fantasy sports, *see, e.g.*, Robert Lipsyte, *Serving Sports Fans Through Journalism*, ESPN (Dec. 3, 2014), http://espn.go.com/blog/ombudsman/tag/_/name/robert-lipsyte, *archived at* http://perma.cc/5G2C-EPTB ("The rise of gambling and fantasy leagues — some would argue often the same thing — will have social consequences that need to be monitored"); Joshua Brustein, *Web Sites Blur Line between Fantasy Sports and Gambling*, N.Y. Times, Mar. 11, 2013, http://www.nytimes.com/2013/03/12/sports/web-sites-blur-line-between-fantasy-sports-and-gambling.html, *archived at* https://perma.cc/C6E5-5J3P?type=pdf.

Gambling and player health have a long history. Following a 1960 incident in which a point spread[24] changed dramatically after publication of a photograph of Pittsburgh Steeler quarterback Bobby Layne's injured arm, the NFL instituted a policy requiring clubs to report player injury status during the week.[25,e] Former NFL security director Jack Danahy explained the purpose of the injury reports during a 1976 deposition:

> We have initiated a program in the [NFL] wherein we require each team to report injuries on Tuesdays, again on Thursdays, and then following Thursday, right up to the time of the game. We publicize these injuries. The purpose of making this information public—and it has been in existence probably as long as I have been in the league . . . is to foreclose the possibility of gamblers attempting to obtain or obtaining confidential information or obtaining information surreptitiously as to the condition of ballplayers. We want it out in the open so that no one can claim an unfair advantage.[26]

For at least the last 50 years, the NFL has been concerned about the possibility of inside information about player injuries making its way into the hands of gamblers, who typically were involved in organized crime. In 1967, NFL assistant to the Commissioner in charge of gambling, William G. Hundley, wrote a letter to a federal probation officer on behalf of organized crime figure Gil Beckley as a result of Beckley's provision of NFL gambling-related information to Hundley.[f] Former NFL commissioner Pete Rozelle admitted in a 1976 deposition that inside information concerning injuries "could be construed as for gambling purposes."[27] Also during a 1976 deposition, NFL security director Jack Danahy stated: "There can be times when maybe there is a key injury and we will have four and five representatives calling in at the same time with point spread changes."[28] In 1977, the NFL admitted that

it "investigates at least one allegedly crooked game a week during a typical season."[29] Additionally, there have been reports of gamblers seeking to obtain information from NFL club doctors.[g]

In the United States, illegal gambling on professional sports has been estimated at $80-$380 billion annually.

(B) Current Legal Obligations[h]

Generally speaking, fans have no legal obligations specific to their status as NFL fans. In other words, fans are generally obligated to treat (and avoid harming) players in the manner as they would any other individual.

Unfortunately, there have been several violent incidents between fans and athletes in a variety of sports over the years. Brawls occurred between Boston Bruins players and New York Rangers fans in 1980 (National Hockey League), and between Indiana Pacers players and Detroit Pistons fans in 2004 (National Basketball Association).[30] Fortunately (relatively speaking), in the NFL, fan and player violence has generally been limited to incidents of players and opposing fans trading snowballs.[31] However, during a 2014 joint practice between the Oakland Raiders and Dallas Cowboys, after players began to fight near fans, a Raiders fan swung a helmet at a Cowboys player, narrowly missing.[32]

While some of these incidents have resulted in criminal charges (typically assault or battery) for the fans and players,[33] there have been no criminal or civil proceedings that would demonstrate that fans have a legal obligation to players unique to the fan-player relationship.

---

e   For more information on the NFL's Injury Reporting Policy, see Chapter 17: The Media.

f   Letter from William G. Hundley to C.L. Williams, Probation Department, Miami, FL, April 20, 1967 ("[Beckley] offered, on a confidential basis, to furnish any information that came into his possession concerning the possibility of endeavors to corrupt professional football players, seek unauthorized information about players [sic] conditions, and supply any other information that might reflect adversely on the integrity of professional football."). A March 2, 1970 *Time Magazine* feature described Beckley as follows: "Handling as much as $250,000 worth of bets daily, Beckley, 58, mastered all the tricks of his arcane trade: (i) wangling information from locker rooms; (ii) computing odds in his head; and (iii) occasionally bribing athletes." *See also* Adam Bernstein, *Lawyer William G. Hundley, 80*, Wash. Post, June 14, 2006, http://www.washingtonpost.com/wp-dyn/content/article/2006/06/13/AR2006061301681.html, *archived at* http://perma.cc/7WZ6-5QHZ (describing Hundley's role at the NFL).

g   *See* Rob Huizenga, M.D., You're Okay, It's Just a Bruise 67–68 (1994) (former Los Angeles Raiders Club doctor explaining ""For the first time in my life I had information that people would pay money for. Big money."")

h   The legal obligations described herein are not an exhaustive list but are those we believe are most relevant to player health.

(C) Current Ethical Codes

The only existing ethical codes for fans are stadium codes of conduct. In 2008, the NFL and its clubs began to implement codes of conducts for fans attending games.[34] The NFL's code requires fans to refrain from:

- Behavior that is unruly, disruptive, or illegal in nature.

- Intoxication or other signs of alcohol impairment that results in irresponsible behavior.

- Foul or abusive language or obscene gestures.

- Interference with the progress of the game (including throwing objects onto the field).

- Failing to follow instructions of stadium personnel.

- Verbal or physical harassment of opposing team fans.

Moreover, in 2012, the NFL began to require that any fan ejected from a stadium be required to take an online course on stadium conduct before being permitted back into an NFL stadium.[35] While these codes of conduct are not specific to the fan-player relationship, if followed, they would seemingly help to minimize the frequency of incidents between fans and players.

(D) Current Practices

1) FAN ENGAGEMENT

Increased attention on football-related injuries has had an effect on fans. A 2014 Bloomberg Politics poll reported that 50 percent of Americans say they will not let their son play football.[36] Major news publications such as the *New York Times* and *Boston Globe* have questioned whether it is ethical to continue to watch football[37] or to let your kids play football.[38] Not surprisingly, between 2010 and 2012, Pop Warner, the country's largest youth football program, saw a 9.5-percent decrease in participation.[39] Although officials at Pop Warner have suggested a number of potential causes for the declining rates (e.g., a poor economy), they admitted that parent concerns about injuries was likely a key contributor to the drop in participation.[40] While other organizations have reported similar declines in participation,[41] the Sports & Fitness Industry Association (SFIA) actually found that participation in tackle football across all leagues and among individuals aged 6 and above increased from 2014 to 2015.[42,i]

Despite all of the scrutiny, fans have generally not been dissuaded from consuming NFL football. Many fans enjoy NFL football (and other physical sports) specifically because of its violent nature.[43] Moreover, in a 2014 *Sports Illustrated* poll, while 26 percent of fans reported being less interested in NFL football as a result of news stories regarding the long-term health risks of playing football, only 8 percent said they actually viewed fewer NFL games than they did two years ago.[44] In contrast, 36 percent of fans said they were watching more NFL games than they previously did.[45] Additionally, after the NFL's mishandling of domestic violence incidents during the 2014 season, only 11 percent of fans said they were less likely to watch as a result.[46]

Nevertheless, in the long term, decreased participation in youth football is likely to result in fewer future NFL fans. Research has frequently found that previous involvement in youth sport is one of the best predictors of interest in sport as a fan.[47] If fewer children participate in football because parents are hesitant to expose them to potential injury, a likely longitudinal consequence will be fewer adults interested in football as a fan years later (or at least less interested than they would have been had they played football).

The same dynamic is evident from older studies. A 1981 study found that fans rated football plays as more entertaining and enjoyable when the plays were violent in nature.[48] In a similar study, published in 1982, fans reported greater enjoyment of watching sport contests when the announcers focused on the hatred and violence between the two teams.[49] It has even been argued by some scholars that some fans are attracted to combative sports such as the NFL specifically for the opportunity to see players be injured.[50] Indeed, it is not uncommon for news articles to compare watching an NFL game to being in attendance at the Roman Colosseum.[51]

A fan's concern for an athlete's injury not surprisingly depends on his or her feelings toward that athlete. Following the 2001 fatal car crash by NASCAR drive Dale Earnhardt, Sr., researchers examined the reactions of NASCAR fans.[52] Those who were not fans of Earnhardt were more likely to trivialize Earnhardt's death and be unsympathetic in their reactions to the crash. Conversely, fans with a strong attachment to Earnhardt were clearly disturbed and psychologically affected by the incident.

---

i   For more discussion on youth football, see Part 7: Other Interested Parties: Youth Leagues.

There are many incidents of fans cheering players' injuries. In one of the more famous examples, in 1999, Philadelphia Eagles fans cheered as Dallas Cowboys star wide receiver Michael Irvin was being placed on a stretcher as a result of head and neck injuries.[53] In a more recent trend, fans have been cheering when their own players (typically poorly performing quarterbacks) are injured, such as Cleveland Browns fans and Derek Anderson in 2008,[54] Kansas City Chiefs fans and Matt Cassel in 2012,[55] and Houston Texans fans and Matt Schaub in 2013.[56]

Fans' occasional disregard for the health of players is not surprising considering past research that has shown that college football fans are more attached to the game of football than they are to the individual players.[57] Some have suggested that as a result of the players' helmets, players become depersonalized,[58] and thus fans do not develop the same sentiment towards players and might not be uncomfortable cheering an injury.

There are, of course, positive relationships between fans and players as well. Research has shown that athletes are viewed positively by fans where the athletes are perceived as "good people off the field,"[59] and exhibit prosocial behavior.[60] Nevertheless, there is no doubt that players often feel pressure from fans to perform.[61]

2) FANS AND GAMBLING

As discussed in the background section of this chapter, the NFL has long been concerned about the commoditization of player health information. These concerns persist today. In a 2011 book discussing the gambling scandal involving former NBA referee Tim Donaghy,[j] professional gambler Jimmy Batista described winning a large amount after receiving a tip from the Philadelphia Eagles' locker room concerning the injury status of star running back Brian Westbrook (who played from 2002 to 2010) right before a game.[62]

Today, the "Personnel (Injury) Report Policy" ("Injury Reporting Policy") makes clear that "it is NFL policy that information on all injured players be supplied by the clubs to the league office."[63] The NFL describes the Injury Reporting Policy as one "of paramount importance in maintaining the integrity of the NFL."[64] The potential abuses of the Injury Reporting Policy, including the possibility that players and coaches target injured players, are discussed in more detail in Chapter 17: The Media.

Perhaps the most visible way in which gambling affects players today is through fantasy sports. An estimated 33.5 million Americans play fantasy sports every year, spending more than $3 billion on fantasy games and related services and products.[65] Moreover, there are many websites where fantasy players, for a fee, can win cash prizes, some exceeding $1 million.[66] These games have been partially exempted under the Unlawful Internet Gambling Enforcement Act of 2006 (UIGEA),[67] a legal status supported by the NFL, MLB, NBA, NHL, and NCAA.[68]

---

j   "Tim Donaghy, a former National Basketball Association (NBA) referee, was caught making picks on games he officiated during the 2006–07 season following an investigation conducted by the Federal Bureau of Investigation. Donaghy bet on dozens of games that he officiated in each of the three prior seasons and had disclosed information regarding player injuries and which referees were assigned to specific games to people betting on NBA games. He was eventually sentenced to a prison term of fifteen months for conspiracy to commit wire fraud and ordered to pay $217,266 USD in restitution by denying his employer the intangible right to his honest services and conspiracy to transmit wagering information." Richard H. McLaren, *Is Sport Losing Its Integrity?* 21 Marq. Sports L. Rev. 551, 566 (2011).

Fans now routinely harass players via social media or in person concerning players' fantasy performance.

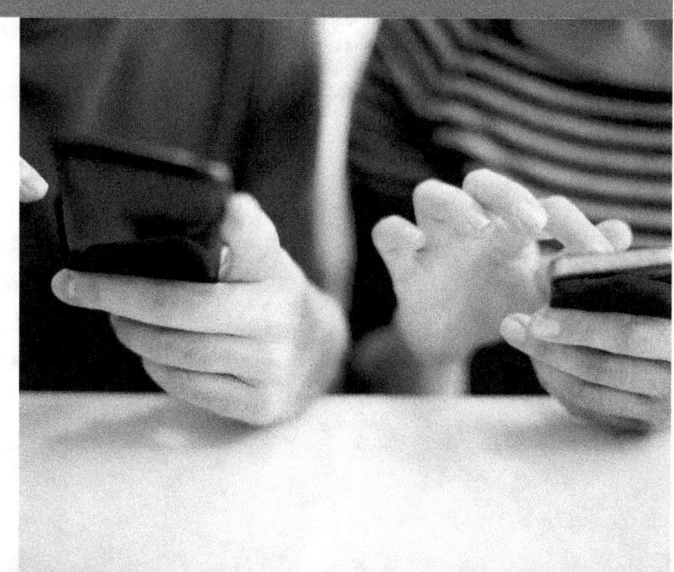

The high stakes of fantasy sports has nevertheless come with a dark side. Fans now routinely harass players via social media or in person concerning players' fantasy performance.[69] Star running backs Jamaal Charles of the Kansas City Chiefs and Arian Foster of the Houston Texans both recalled being pressured by fans to come back from injuries to help the fans' fantasy football performance.[70] Additionally, many of the interactions have come in the form of threats. For example, during the 2013 season, a fan sent the following Tweet to New York Giants running back Brandon Jacobs: "ON LIFE BRANDON IF YOU DON'T RUSH FOR 50 YARDS AND TWO TOUCHDOWNS TONIGHT ITS OVER FOR YOU AND YO FAMILY N---ER."[k] Jacobs reported the incident to NFL security.[71]

Current Player 4 relayed a story in which an injured team-mate had a fan tell the player "to get back in the game" because the fan had the player on his fantasy roster. "[The player] was pretty disgusted that somebody would even suggest something like that."[l] Current Player 6 confirmed "[y]ou feel the pressure and you hear the chatter" and Current Player 7 said players "definitely" feel pressure from fans to play through injuries.[m]

The NFL reportedly has growing concerns about high stakes fantasy sports,[72] but to date has not reversed its position that fantasy sports is not gambling; this is unsurprising since the NFL administers free fantasy leagues (without cash prizes) through its own website,[73] and even recognizes a Fantasy Player of the Year at its annual awards ceremony.[74] Indeed, inside information concerning player injuries is now just as important for fantasy sports as it always has been for more traditional gambling: ESPN offers a subscription service called "Insider Trading," which purportedly includes "a collection of fantasy advice pulled straight from the locker rooms and practice fields of every team."[75]

The relationship between gambling and professional sports has caused some to reconsider its prohibition. In November 2014, NBA Commissioner Adam Silver, accepting that gambling has become widespread, called for the legalization of sports gambling, proposing that it instead be heavily regulated.[76] Indeed, both the NBA and MLB own equity interests in fantasy websites where fans pay entry fees and can win large financial prizes.[77] While the NFL does not have an equity interest in such websites, two NFL club owners do.[78] The NFL, nevertheless, as a collective entity, has been unmoved, stating that Silver's comment "doesn't change our stance that has been articulated for decades: no gambling on N.F.L. games."[79]

(E) Enforcement of Legal and Ethical Obligations

As discussed above, there are no legal obligations unique to the fan-player relationship. To the extent fans assault, batter, threaten or otherwise harm NFL players, NFL players could pursue either criminal charges or a civil lawsuit against the fan.

If fans are acting unruly or in a threatening manner at a game, players can bring that to the attention of security and have the fan ejected.

---

k   In the Tweet to Jacobs, the fan spelled out the entire slur. *See Fantasy Pressure,* ESPN (Dec. 8, 2014, 10:09 AM), http://espn.go.com/video/clip?id=11994138.

l   Other players also expressed concern about the pressures created by fantasy football: Current Player 9: "Yes, definitely [players feel pressure from fans], especially with fantasy football." Former Player 2: "This fantasy football stuff right now has kind of gone crazy."

m   Other players did not believe players felt meaningful pressure from fans. Current Player 2: "I don't think that [fans] play a huge role in putting pressure on guys as they're out on the field. I don't think there's any that have any impact on the guy whether a guy is going to go out there and play hurt or not." Current Player 10: "I don't think the fans or even the media plays that much into it." We reiterate that our interviews were intended to be informational but not representative of all players' views and should be read with that limitation in mind.

(F) Recommendations Concerning Fans

Fans, ultimately, are what drive the success of the NFL. Fans consume the sport in incredible numbers, driving record-breaking television audiences and contracts. Fans, thus, also have incredible power. Without fan interest, the money, power, and prestige disappear. Below we make recommendations that seek to recognize and harness the power of the fans for the betterment of NFL players.

Goal 1: To wield the power of NFL fans to improve the health of NFL players.

Principles Advanced: Respect; Health Primacy; and, Justice.

Recommendation 18:1-A: Fans should recognize their ability to bring about change concerning player health.

As discussed above, fans are tremendously important when it comes to the NFL's success. Fans thus have the leverage to pressure the NFL and other stakeholders into making positive changes for player health. There is precedent for the exercise of such leverage. In 2009, the Sports Fan Coalition was formed by a former White House attorney for the purposes of protecting fans' interests.[80] In its brief history, two items on the Sports Fan Coalition agenda have changed for the better: (1) NCAA college football created a playoff system; and, (2) the Federal Communications Commission eliminated a rule that permitted NFL clubs to "blackout" television broadcasts where the game did not reach a certain attendance level. While the Sports Fan Coalition's importance in these changes is unclear, it seems likely that the Sports Fan Coalition's expression of a collective fan voice had an impact.

Fans could have a similar positive impact on NFL player health, including by putting pressure on the NFL, NFLPA, clubs, and other stakeholders to adopt recommendations like those we have made in this Report.[n]

Recommendation 18:1-B: Fans should recognize that the lives of NFL players are more than entertainment, and that NFL players are human beings who suffer injuries that may adversely affect their health.

While NFL players' profession entails playing a sport largely for the entertainment of fans, an NFL career has real and important short and long-term impacts on players and their families. The fan experience sometimes strips some fans of understanding or sympathy for players—viewing them as mere means rather than human beings. Such a view is incompatible with the principle of Respect we have outlined in this Report. Fortunately, fans have increasingly taken note of the ways in which the game can harm players and through their behavior can help foster a norm of respect. This is a positive trend and hopefully one that will continue.

Recommendation 18:1-C: Fans should not pressure players to play while injured.

n   The long-time NFL columnist Mike Freeman stated, "[i]f there ever comes a time when fans see the players as people and not commodities or gladiators or faceless entities on our fantasy rosters, everything could change." Mike Freeman, Two Minute Warning: How Concussions, Crime, and Controversy Could Kill the NFL (and What the League Can Do to Survive) xx (2015).

Recommendations Concerning Fans – continued

For the reasons discussed above, fans should respect players and their physical and mental conditions. It is obvious that all NFL players often play with varying degrees of injury and pain. No fan—except perhaps former NFL players—can realistically understand the physical limitations of a player's particular injury and whether it can withstand the physical demands of playing in an NFL game. Moreover, fans should respect that the player has legitimate long-term interests in his health at stake. As part of the continuing theme, fans must treat players with dignity and respect, and not as combatants for the fans' amusement.

On a related topic, fans should exercise discretion when communicating with players via social media. While the interaction between players and fans via social media is a great way to build a connection, fans should obviously refrain from crossing the line with racist attacks or other threats. To the extent players are recipients of such communications, they should take them seriously and report them to club and NFL security.

Recommendation 18:1-D: Fans should not advocate, cheer, encourage, or incite player injuries.

It seems obvious that one should not encourage or be happy about the bodily or mental injury of another human being. Nevertheless, fans sometimes express joy when a player, even their own team's player, has been injured. That behavior is incompatible with showing respect for players and treating them as human beings.

Endnotes

1   Regina Corso, *As American As Mom, Apple Pie, and Football?* Harris Poll (Jan. 16, 2014), http://www.harrisinteractive.com/NewsRoom/HarrisPolls/tabid/447/ctl/ReadCustom%20Default/mid/1508/ArticleId/1365/Default.aspx, *archived at* http://perma.cc/9GF9-Y2WP (listing America's favorite sports as, among others, Pro Football (35%), Baseball (14%), College Football (11%), Auto Racing (7%), Men's Pro Basketball (6%), Hockey (4%), Men's College Basketball (3%). 35% is the highest percentage Pro Football has received in the history of the poll, dating back to 1985.).

2   *Id.*

3   Larry Shannon-Missal, *Denver Broncos Are America's Favorite Football Team; Dallas Cowboys Drop to 4th After Six Years at the Top*, Harris Poll (Oct. 14, 2014), http://www.harrisinteractive.com/NewsRoom/HarrisPolls/tabid/447/mid/1508/articleId/1506/ctl/ReadCustom%20Default/Default.aspx, *archived at* http://perma.cc/MB7G-FKX7.

4   Mark Fainaru-Wada & Steve Fainaru, League of Denial: The NFL, Concussions, and the Battle for Truth 5 (2013).

5   *See NFL Attendance – 2015*, ESPN, http://espn.go.com/nfl/attendance (last visited Apr. 7, 2016), *archived at* https://perma-archives.org/warc/3ST3-L4ZB/http://espn.go.com/nfl/attendance.

6   Sara Bibel, *NFL 2013 TV Recap: 205 Million Fans Tuned In; 34 of 35 Most Watched Shows This Fall*, Zap2It (Jan. 8, 2014), http://tvbythenumbers.zap2it.com/2014/01/08/nfl-2013-tv-recap-205-million-fans-tuned-in-34-of-35-most-watched-shows-this-fall/227726/, *archived at* http://perma.cc/NZ7C-WF3C.

7   *Super Bowl XLVIII Draws 111.5 Million Viewers*, Nielsen (Feb. 3, 2014), http://www.nielsen.com/us/en/insights/news/2014/super-bowl-xlviii-draws-111-5-million-viewers-25-3-million-tweets.html, *archived at* http://perma.cc/X38F-ZX59.

8   One.Cool.Customer, *NFL Social Media Rankings: Which Teams Have The Largest Social Media Reach?* SB Nation Blog (Jun 4, 2014, 8:00 PM), http://www.bloggingtheboys.com/2014/6/4/5772834/nfl-social-media-rankings-which-teams-have-the-largest-social-media-reach, *archived at* http://perma.cc/8ZDY-RHDA.

9   *See* K. A. Hunt, T. Bristol, & R. E. Bashaw, *A Conceptual Approach to Classifying Sports Fans*, J Serv. Mktg. 13, 439–452 (1999); D. L. Wann, J. Royalty, & A. Roberts *The Self-Presentation of Sport Fans: Investigating the Importance of Team Identification and Self-Esteem*, J. Sport Behavior 23, 198–206 (2000).

10 S. E. Smith et al., *How Does Sport Team Identification Compare to Identification With Other Social Institutions?* 6 J Contemp. Athletics 69–82 (2011).

11 R. J. Sebastian & D. N. Bristow, *Win or Lose, Take Me Out to the Ballgame! An Empirical Investigation of Loyalty Proneness Among College Students*, 9 Sport Mktg. Quarterly 211, 211–20 (2000).

12 A 1977 New York Times article estimated the illegal sports gambling market in the United States as being worth $50 billion. Steve Cady, *The Need for a Super Security Agency to Police All Major Sports*, N.Y. Times, Feb. 22, 1977, http://query.nytimes.com/gst/abstract.html?res=9C04E0DF143BE63BBC4A51DFB466838C669EDE, *archived at* https://perma.cc/593A-72WT?type=source.

13 PASPA also exempted Oregon from the prohibition on sports gambling. However, in 2005 Oregon voted to abolish the sports wagering lottery at the end of the 2006–2007 NFL season. Carla Hanson, *Oregon Sports Action Laid to Rest*, BlueOregon, Feb. 9, 2007, http://www.blueoregon.com/2007/02/oregon_sports_a/, archived at http://perma.cc/5RYJ-2CBY.

14 David Purdum, *Wagers, Bettor Losses Set Record*, ESPN (Jan. 30, 2015), http://espn.go.com/chalk/story/_/id/12253876/nevada-sports-bettors-wagered-lost-more-ever-2014, *archived at* http://perma.cc/RKR8-WPD7.

15 *Id.*

16 *Delaware State Lottery 2013 Annual Report for the Fiscal Year Ending June 30, 2013*, Del. State Lottery, http://www.delottery.com/pdf/2013_DELott_Annual_Report.pdf (last visited Aug. 7, 2015), *archived at* https://perma.cc/QWD5-CW6B?type=pdf.

17 *Montana Lottery Annual Report 2013,* Mont. Lottery, http://montanalottery.com/forms/annual_report_2013.pdf (last visited Aug. 7, 2015), *archived at* https://perma.cc/5JRT-9GDT?type=pdf.

18 Jerome Solomon, *NFL's Dirty Little Secret: Gambling's Roots Run Deep,* Houston Chron., Jan. 29, 2004, http://www.chron.com/sports/article/NFL -s-dirty-little-secret-Gambling-s-roots-run-1562128.php, *archived at* http://perma.cc/6YEX-JU9R.

19 *See The 1999 National Gambling Impact Study –Chapter 2: Gambling in the United States*, Nat'l Gambling Impact Study Comm'n (June 18, 1999), http://govinfo.library.unt.edu/ngisc/reports/2.pdf, *archived at* https://perma.cc/7VQU-EY39?type=pdf, at Page 2–14. ("Estimates of the scope of illegal sports betting in the United States range anywhere from $80 billion to $380 billion annually, making sports betting the most widespread and popular form of gambling in America.").

20 Unfortunately, the reported numbers make it impossible to bifurcate estimates for professional football and college football.

21 Robert Kraft, Owner, New England Patriots, Deans' Innovation in Sports Challenge Kickoff, Harvard innovation lab (Nov. 21, 2014).

22 Testimony of Bob Costas, N.G.I.S.C Las Vegas Meeting, November 10, 1998.

23 Mike Florio, *Goodell Says Fantasy Football Isn't About Wagering,* ProFootballTalk (January 17, 2014 11:32 AM), http://profootballtalk .nbcsports.com/2014/01/17/goodell-says-fantasy-football-isnt-about -wagering/, *archived at* http://perma.cc/BU2B-YQUB.

24 Generally speaking, the point spread is the number of points by which one team is expected to beat its opponent.

25 Dan Moldea, Interference: How Organized Crime Influences Professional Football, 101–02 (1989). The Steelers were initially pegged as a seven-point favorite over Washington, but the spread closed to one point before kickoff following the publication of a photograph featuring Layne and his injured arm.

26 Deposition of John J. Danahy, NFL v. Governor of Delaware, Oct. 28, 1976, p. 70–71. Danahy's affidavit in the same case elaborates on the motivation: "It is obvious that illegal gambling on NFL games occur and that constant efforts are made by these gamblers to seek information about teams or even influence games." Affidavit of John J. Danahy, NFL v. Governor of Delaware, (August 23, 1976), p. 3.

27 Deposition of Pete Rozelle, NFL v. Governor of Delaware, Oct. 13, 1976, p. 99.

28 Deposition of John J. Danahy, NFL v. Governor of Delaware, Oct. 28, 1976, p. 24. Danahy also revealed: "We have had situations where rumors of injuries have been specifically created by gamblers for the purpose of creating or effecting a gambling coup" (p. 72).

29 Steve Cady, *The Need for a Super Security Agency to Police All Major Sports,* N.Y. Times, Feb. 22, 1977, http://query.nytimes.com/gst/abstract .html?res=9C04E0DF143BE63BBC4A51DFB466838C669EDE, *archived at* https://perma.cc/593A-72WT?type=source.

30 *See* Glenn M. Wong, Essentials of Sports Law, § 16.1.3 (4th ed. 2010) (discussing these and other cases of fan-athlete violence).

31 *See* Rich Cimini, *NFL Hits Ellis with 10G Fine for Snowball,* N.Y. Daily News, Dec. 24, 2008, *available at* 2008 WLNR 24668756 (discussing 2008 incident between Seattle Seahawks fans and New York Jets player Shaun Ellis); Hector Gutierrez, *Snow May Land Fans in Court,* Denver Rocky Mountain News, Nov. 24, 1999, available at 1999 WLNR 811239 (discussing 1999 incident between Denver Broncos fans and Oakland Raiders players); *Snowball Barrage Injures 15,* Denver Rocky Mountain News, Dec. 24, 1995, *available at* 1995 WLNR 657930 (discussing New York Giants fans pelting San Diego Chargers players and coaches with snowballs).

32 Mike Wilkening, *Fan Swings Helmet At Cowboys' Webb During Practice Fight; Webb Swings Back,* ProFootballTalk (Aug. 12, 2014, 10:59 PM), http://profootballtalk.nbcsports.com/2014/08/12/fan-swings-helmet-at -cowboys-webb-during-practice-fight-webb-swings-back/, *archived at* http://perma.cc/RDR2-JFTL.

33 *See* Wong, *supra* note 30.

34 *NFL Teams Implement Fan Code of Conduct,* NFL (Aug. 5, 2008, 04:43 PM, Updated Jul. 26, 2012, 08:20 PM), http://www.nfl.com/news/story /09000d5d809c28f9/article/nfl-teams-implement-fan-code-of-conduct, *archived at* http://perma.cc/X4J4-T3X9.

35 *See* Darren Rovell, *NFL Gets Serious About Fan Conduct,* ESPN (Aug. 17, 2012) http://espn.go.com/nfl/story/_/id/8278886/nfl-require-ejected -fans-take-online-fan-conduct-course, *archived at* http://perma.cc/2N9E -ER4F. The course is available at www.fanconductclass.com/NFL.

36 *Half of Americans Don't Want Their Sons Playing Football, Poll Shows,* Bloomberg (Dec. 10, 2014, 7:00 AM), http://www.bloomberg.com/ politics/articles/2014-12-10/bloomberg-politics-poll-half-of-americans -dont-want-their-sons-playing-football, *archived at* http://perma.cc/ CQ5Q-D7KW.

37 *See* Chuck Klosterman, *Is It Wrong to Watch Football?,* N.Y. Times, Sept. 5, 2014, http://www.nytimes.com/2014/09/07/magazine/is-it -wrong-to-watch-football.html, *archived at* https://perma.cc/STD5-4GGS ?type=pdf; Steve Almond, *Why You Should Stop Watching Football,* Bos. Globe, Aug. 10, 2014, *available at* 2014 WLNR 21887974.

38 John Guida, *Should Your Child Play Football?* N.Y. Times, Nov. 11, 2014, http://op-talk.blogs.nytimes.com/2014/11/11/should-your-child-play -football/, *archived at* http://perma.cc/5VRC-H4PM.

39 Steve Fainaru & Mark Fainaru-Wada, *Youth Football Participation Drops,* ESPN (Nov. 14, 2013), http://espn.go.com/espn/otl/story/_/page/ popwarner/pop-warner-youth-football-participation-drops-nfl-concussion -crisis-seen-causal-factor, *archived at* http://perma.cc/E3GZ-5D65.

40 *Id.*

41 *See* Ryan Wallerson, *Youth Participation Weakens in Basketball, Football, Baseball, Soccer,* Wall St. J., Jan. 31, 2014, http://www.wsj.com/articles /SB10001424052702303519404579350892629229918, *archived at* http://perma.cc/D47A-QTPN (5.4% decrease in youth football participa-tion between 2008 and 2012 according to the Sports and Fitness Industry Association and Physical Activity Council); Emily Attwood, 2013 Editions of NSGA Sports Participation Reports Released, Athletic Bus. (June 2013), http://www.athleticbusiness.com/industry-press -room/2013-editions-of-nsga-sports-participation-reports-released .html, *archived at* http://perma.cc/L5A2-7LZZ (National Sporting Goods Association finding a "nearly 13% decline" in youth football participation between 2011 and 2013).

42 *Date Shows Team Sports Participation Increased in '15, Including Hoops, Football,* Sports Business Daily (Mar. 10, 2016), http://www .sportsbusinessdaily.com/Daily/Issues/2016/03/10/Research-and -Ratings/SFIA.aspx, *archived at* https://perma.cc/PQ86-E29E.

43 *See* Jennings Bryant, *Viewers Enjoyment of Televised Sports Violence,* Media, Sports, and Soc'y, 270–89 (1989); R. Todd Jewell, Afsheen Moati, & Dennis Coates, *A Brief History of Violence and Aggression in Spectator Sports, in* Violence and Aggression in Sporting Contests: Economic, History and Policy 11–26 (2011); Stephanie Lee Sargent, Dolf Zillmann & James B. Weaver III, *The Gender Gap in the Enjoyment of Televised Sports,* 22 J. Sport Soc. Issues 46 (1998); Daniel L. Wann et al., Sport fans: The Psychology and Social Impact of Spectators (2001).

44 Don Banks, *NFL Fan Poll: Should Roger Goodell Keep Job? More State of the Game,* Sports Illustrated, http://www.si.com/nfl-fan-poll-2014 (last visited Aug. 7, 2015), *archived at* http://perma.cc/PM8J-ZTNY.

45 *Id.*

46 Michael David Smith, *Poll Finds NFL Still Has Strong Support Across America,* ProFootballTalk (Sept. 18, 2014, 6:59 PM), http://profootballtalk .nbcsports.com/2014/09/18/poll-finds-nfl-still-has-strong-support -across-america/, *archived at* http://perma.cc/6D3R-PHE4.

47 Daniel L. Wann et al., Sport Fans: The Psychology and Social Impact of Spectators (2001); Matthew D. Shank & Fred M. Beasley, *Fan or Fanatic: Refining a Measure of Sports Involvement,* 21 J. Sport Behavior 435 (1998); Stephen J. Grove et al., *Spectatorship Among a Collegiate Sample: An Exploratory Investigation, in* Michael J. Etzel & John F. Gaski, Applying Marketing Technology to Spectator Sports, 26–40 (1982).

48 Jennings Bryant, Paul W. Comisky & Dolf Zillmann, *The Appeal of Rough-And-Tumble Play in Televised Professional Football,* 29 Commc'n Quarterly 256 (1981).

49 Jennings Bryant et al., *Sports and Spectators: Commentary and Appreciation*, 32 J Commc'n 109 (1982).

50 Dolf Zillmann & Paul B. Paulus *Spectators: Reactions to sports events and effects on athletic performance, in* Robert N. Singer, Milledge Murphey & L. Keith Tennant, Handbook of Res. on Sport Psychol. 600–19 (1993).

51 *See* Michael Powell, *Outrage Over Violence Ends at the Stadium Gates*, N.Y. Times, Sept. 16, 2014, http://www.nytimes.com/2014/09/17/sports/football/reactions-to-adrian-peterson-case-ignore-brutality-on-nfl-fields.html?_r=0, *archived at* https://perma.cc/P82D-CKY6?type=image; Scott Ostler, *How will Martin fit in?*, S.F. Chron., Mar. 13, 2014, *available at* 2014 WLNR 6793584; Matthew Stanmyre, *NFL has tried to make football safer, but violence remains at its core*, Star-Ledger (NJ), Feb. 1, 2014 *available at* 2014 WLNR 2909040; *Cf. Chiefs Players Angry as Fans Cheer Injury*, Pitt. Post-Gazette, Oct. 8, 2012, *available at* 2012 WLNR 21308873 (Kansas City Chiefs offensive lineman and future NFLPA President Eric Winston exclaiming "We are not gladiators and this is not the Roman Colosseum. This is a game" after Chiefs fans cheered the injury of quarterback Matt Cassel).

52 Daniel L., Wann & Paula J. Waddill, *Examining reactions to the Dale Earnhardt crash: The importance of identification with NASCAR drivers*, 30 J. Sport Behav. 94 (2007).

53 Jean-Jacques Taylor, *Crowd Callous About Irvin's Injury: Players Astonished By Fans' Reaction*, Dall. Morning News, Oct. 11, 1999, *available at* 1999 WLNR 7714249.

54 Mary Kay Cabot, *Browns QB Anderson Heard the Jeers After Injury*, Cleveland.com (Nov. 30, 2008, 8:38 PM), http://www.cleveland.com/browns/index.ssf/2008/11/browns_qb_anderson_heard_the_j.html, *archived at* http://perma.cc/FM3C-HST7.

55 Darin Gantt, *Eric Winston Rips Chiefs Fan For Cheering Cassel Injury*, ProFootballTalk (October 7, 2012, 5:48 PM), http://profootballtalk.nbcsports.com/2012/10/07/eric-winston-rips-chiefs-fans-for-cheering-cassel-injury/, *archived at* http://perma.cc/A2KZ-VZVB.

56 Mike Florio, *Texans Players Sound Off on Fans Cheering Matt Schaub Injury*, ProFootballTalk (Oct. 14, 2013, 10:11 AM), http://profootballtalk.nbcsports.com/2013/10/14/texans-players-sound-off-on-fans-cheering-matt-schaub-injury/, *archived at* http://perma.cc/7QS5-ZDWM.

57 Matthew J. Robinson & Galen T. Trail, *Relationships Among Spectator Gender, Motives, Points Of Attachment, And Sport Preference*, 19 J. Sport Mgmt. 58 (2005).

58 *See* Barbara Barker, *Broncos, Seahawks Defenders Bring Sack Dances To Big Stage*, Newsday, Jan. 29, 2014, http://www.newsday.com/sports/football/super-bowl/super-bowl-2014-broncos-seahawks-defenders-bring-sack-dances-to-big-stage-1.6904808, *archived at* http://perma.cc/UZ25-FBGJ; Sally Jenkins, *NFL Violence: It's a Matter Of Choice, Not Just the Rules*, Wash. Post, Dec. 1, 2002, *available at* 2002 WLNR 15895732.

59 Traci A. Giuliano et al., *Gender and the Selection of Public Athletic Role Models*, 30 J. Sport Behav. 161 (2007).

60 Julie A. Stevens, Anna H. Lathrop, & Cheri L. Bradish, *"Who Is Your Hero": Implications for athlete endorsement strategies*, 12 Sport Mktg. Q. 103 (2003).

61 *See* Tom Pelissero, *Tony Romo's Injury Shows Pressure QBs Face To Play Hurt*, USA Today Sports, Nov. 3, 2014, http://www.usatoday.com/story/sports/nfl/2014/11/03/tony-romo-quarterback-injuries-aaron-rodgers-alex-smith/18439613/, *archived at* http://perma.cc/SUW3-9CVX (Green Bay Packers quarterback Aaron Rodgers discussing pressure from fans to play through injuries as a result of publicly released medical information); Joseph White, *Redskins' Sellers: Temptation of steroids was hard to resist*, Virginian-Pilot, May 4, 2010, *available at* 2010 WLNR 9202873 (former Washington Redskins fullback Mike Sellers describing "pressure from fans, family . . . " as reasons players take performance enhancing drugs).

62 Sean Patrick Griffin, Gaming the Game, 68 (2011) ("He was questionable but we got a call out of the locker room before anyone else that he wasn't playing," Battista says. "The Eagles were favored by ten points and the over/under was something like fifty-two. Well, Westbrook being out of the offense was a big deal. The total moved like six points. We bet the dog and buried the under. The under hit and the dog covered.").

63 National Football League, *2008 Personnel (Injury) Report Policy*, Media and Public Relations – General Information, Volume IV, Page E32. The NFL's policy has numerous prongs: (i) "all players with significant or noteworthy injuries must be listed on the report;" (ii) "the intent of the policy is to provide a full and complete rendering of player availability;" (iii) "coaches violating [the] policy are subject to disciplinary action;" and (iv) "injuries must be identified with a reasonable degree of specificity in terms that are meaningful to coaches, other club officials, the media, and the public." The degree of specificity in the reports creates a possible concern about gamblers, coaches, or players targeting injured bodily areas.

64 *Id.*

65 Erik Matuszewski, *Fantasy Sports Luring Wall Street in Its Fastest-Growing Sector*, Bloomberg (Jan. 5, 2014, 10:00 PM), http://www.bloomberg.com/news/2014-01-06/fantasy-sports-luring-wall-street-in-its-fastest-growing-sector.html, *archived at* http://perma.cc/77RF-GAAR.

66 *Id.*

67 *See* 31 U.S.C. §§ 5361–5367. For a detailed academic treatment of the UIEGA carve-out for certain kinds of fantasy sports see Anthony N. Cabot & Louis V. Csoka, *Fantasy Sports: One Form of Mainstream Wagering in the United States*, J. Marshal L. Rev. 40, 1195–219 (2007).

68 *See* Letter from Jeffrey Pash, VP and General Counsel, NFL, Tom Ostertag, Senior VP and General Counsel, MLB, Richard Buchanan, Senior VP and General Counsel, NBA, William Daly, Deputy Commissioner, NHL, and Elsa Kircher Cole, General Counsel, NCAA, to Members of Congress (Feb. 1, 2006) (urging members of Congress to pass the UIEGA).

69 *See Fantasy Pressure*, ESPN (Dec. 8, 2014, 10:09 AM), http://espn.go.com/video/clip?id=11994138.

70 *Id.*

71 *Id.*

72 Mike Florio, *NFL paying attention to influence of high-stakes fantasy football leagues*, ProFootballTalk (July 28, 2014, 3:08 PM), http://profootballtalk.nbcsports.com/2014/07/28/nfl-paying-attention-to-influence-of-high-stakes-fantasy-football-leagues/, *archived at* http://perma.cc/LD2K-KW84.

73 *See Fantasy Football*, NFL, http://www.nfl.com/fantasyfootball (last visited Aug. 7, 2015).

74 *See Fantasy Football Player of the Year Vote*, NFL, http://fantasy.nfl.com/features/playeroftheyearvoteconfirm?votedPlayerId=100025&votingState=pre (last visited Apr. 7, 2016), *archived at* https://perma.cc/6WKF-TN3B.

75 NFL Nation Reports, *Fantasy Advice for Every Team*, ESPN Insider (Sept. 5, 2014), http://insider.espn.go.com/fantasy/football/story/_/id/11467696/insider-trading-fantasy-advice-every-team-week-1-nfl, *archived at* http://perma.cc/KQN7-WS9X ("ESPN Insider has planted 'spies' in every NFL locker room – OK, so they're our 32 NFL Nation team reporters – in order to provide fantasy owners with inside intel to help you win your league.").

76 Adam Silver, *Legalize and Regulate Sports Betting*, N.Y. Times, Nov. 13, 2014, http://www.nytimes.com/2014/11/14/opinion/nba-commissioner-adam-silver-legalize-sports-betting.html, *archived at* https://perma.cc/LUF8-EZM2?type=pdf.

77 Craig Calcaterra, *MLB Owns a Stake in Daily Fantasy Sports*, HardBallTalk.com (Mar. 30, 2015, 11:35 AM), http://hardballtalk.nbcsports.com/2015/03/30/mlb-owns-a-stake-in-daily-fantasy-sports/, *archived at* http://perma.cc/QFH9-R8NT.

78 Mike Florio, *NFL owners may have to dump investments in DFS companies*, ProFootballTalk (Nov. 13, 2015, 7:29 AM), http://profootballtalk.nbcsports.com/2015/11/13/nfl-owners-may-have-to-dump-investments-in-dfs-companies/, *archived at* https://perma.cc/TH7P-W5QJ.

79 Ken Belson, *Will Other Leagues Join N.B.A.? Don't Bet on It*, N.Y. Times, Nov. 14, 2014, http://www.nytimes.com/2014/11/15/sports/not-all-leagues-ready-to-go-all-in-on-legalized-gambling.html, *archived at* https://perma.cc/P8TH-Z3P2?type=pdf.

80 *Who We Are*, SportsFans.org, http://www.sportsfans.org/about/ (last visited Aug. 7, 2015), *archived at* http://perma.cc/QZ7V-GE8Z.

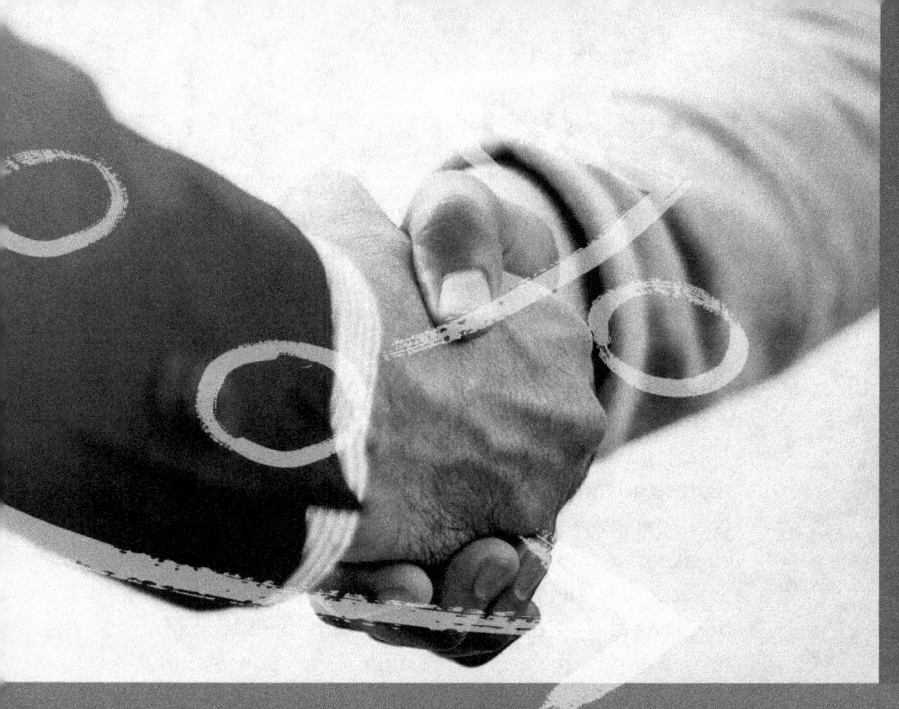

Chapter 19

NFL Business Partners

In the 2015 season, the NFL had approximately 29 official corporate partners,[a] which collectively paid the NFL more than one billion dollars annually.[1] While there are many other companies that might advertise on television during NFL games or around other NFL events, the business partners we are principally focused on here are the ones that have reached an agreement with the NFL to be considered an official partner or sponsor of the NFL. These business partners are an important component in professional football. Such a role includes the potential, and at times the obligation, to also play a role in player health.

---

a   These corporate partners are sponsors of the NFL as opposed to sponsors of particular clubs or players. In addition, none of them are Medical Service Providers, as discussed in Chapter 2: Club Doctors.

In order to ensure that this chapter was as accurate and valuable as possible, we invited nine NFL business partners to review a draft version before publication: Verizon, Anheuser-Busch, Pepsi, and McDonald's did not respond to multiple invitations to review the Report; Gatorade, FedEx, and Nationwide Insurance declined to review the draft; Microsoft reviewed the chapter but did not provide any comments; and, Nike provided a single comment affirming the importance of player health and safety to Nike.[b]

---

b   Nike's full comment: "As a sponsor of the NFL and the sponsor and footwear provider of many individual players, the safety and well-being of players is important to us. Through the years NIKE has worked closely with the both the NFLPA and the NFL in the NFL Foot and Ankle Committee (a subsection of the Player Safety Committee). Additionally, we have always worked directly with athletes, teams and equipment managers on testing, feedback and changes to our products to help athletes perform to their highest ability." E-mail from Nike counsel to author (May 18, 2016, 12:05 PM).

(A) Background

The largest NFL business partners at the time of publication include Verizon ($250 million in sponsorship annually);[2] Anheuser-Busch ($233 million);[3] Nike ($220 million);[4] Pepsi ($100 million);[5] and, Microsoft ($80 million).[6] The relationship with the NFL generally provides the business partners, among other things, advertising during NFL games and through other NFL media, the right to include the NFL logo on their products and in their advertisements, the right to advertise themselves as the "official" brand of the NFL, exclusivity in their brand category, and/or the right to engage in promotional activities at NFL events, such as the Super Bowl. The business partners have clearly determined that the value of their association with the NFL and the related exposure exceeds the millions in sponsorship fees.

Table 19-A:
NFL Sponsors (2015)[7]

Sponsor	Category	Since
Gatorade	Isotonic beverage	1983
Visa USA	Payment systems service	1995
Campbell's Soup	Soup	1998
FedEx	Worldwide package delivery service	2000
Frito-Lay	Salted snack/popcorn/peanuts/dip	2000
Mars Snackfood	Chocolate and non-chocolate confectionery	2002
Pepsi	Soft drinks	2002
Bridgestone	Tire	2009
Procter & Gamble (Gillette, Head & Shoulders, Vicks, Old Spice)	Grooming products, fabric care/air care, household needs	2009
Verizon	Wireless telecommunication service	2010
Barclays	Affinity card/rewards program	2010
Papa John's	Pizza	2010
Castrol	Motor oil	2010
Anheuser-Busch	Beer	2011
USAA	Insurance/military appreciation	2011
Bose	Home theater system	2011
Marriott	Hotel	2011
Xbox (Microsoft)	Video game console, interactive video entertainment console	2011
Nike	Athletic apparel	2012
Quaker	Hot cereal	2012
Procter & Gamble (Tide, Duracell)	Household cleaning, battery power	2012
Lenovo	Computers (desktop, laptop, and computer workstations)	2012
McDonald's	Restaurant	2012
SAP	Cloud software solutions, business and business analytics	2012
Microsoft (Surface, Windows)	Sideline technology (tablet, PC operating system)	2013
Cover Girl	Beauty	2013
Nationwide	Insurance	2014
Extreme Networks	Wi-Fi Analytics Provider	2014
Hyundai	Automobile	2015

(B) Current Legal Obligations[c]

Although NFL players and NFL business partners benefit from one another, there is generally no direct legal relationship between them. While some players might also enter into endorsement agreements with the business partners, these contracts concern marketing matters and would not create any legal obligations for the business partners concerning NFL player health.[8] Similarly, the CBA does not create any obligations on NFL business partners, nor could it, since the CBA is a contract between the clubs and players. Thus, NFL business partners have no legal obligations to NFL players specific to their status as business partners.

(C) Current Ethical Codes

The NFL is supported by a range of business partners whose main focus often has nothing to do with football, but instead centers on reaching the NFL's massive audience for marketing purposes. Reaching consumers is a legitimate and important business goal, but not all advertising venues are fair game. One can imagine a wide variety of unsavory outlets a company would prefer (and ought) to avoid, even if they would be an effective way to reach potential customers. This is because companies are often concerned—either genuinely, or out of fear that negative responses from consumers will affect their bottom line—that they may contribute to some ethically problematic endeavor, thereby becoming complicit in or even exacerbating it. Notably, complicity comes in many forms, ranging from failure to intervene when one has the capacity to provide assistance to offering active support to an ethically problematic activity.

As increasing questions arise about the health of professional football players, NFL business partners (and their customers) may ask themselves, "what is our responsibility?" That is, what level and type of support should they be providing to the NFL, or from a different angle, to the players? At root, these questions are about unclean hands, and whether NFL business partners are profiting on the backs of players who may suffer dire consequences in the long term. While the precise risks and benefits of an NFL career remain subject to debate, the concerns suggest that these are precisely the questions that ethically responsible companies should ask. To avoid complicity, these companies should be concerned with what endeavors they allow their money to support, and in what ways they can and/or should wield their power to affect change.

The concept of corporate social responsibility seeks to address these questions. We find it a useful framework for understanding the ethical obligations NFL business partners might have towards players. The most influential articulation of corporate social responsibility principles is the United Nations Guiding Principles on Business and Human Rights, published in 2011 ("Guiding Principles").[9] Indeed, many NFL business partners have stated their intention to comply with the Guiding Principles.[10]

To be clear, we are not claiming that any of the problems we discuss in this Report or that NFL players face by playing football rise to the level of human rights violations; given the simple fact of consent to play and payment for services, the difficulties players face do not compare to the numerous and ongoing tragedies around the world that human rights law is thought to govern. Nonetheless, the Guiding Principles provide a framework for understanding business enterprises' ethical obligations concerning others. This framework is useful to understanding the relationship between NFL business partners and players, even if we are not discussing human rights violations.

To put the point another way, in asking the question "what ethical obligations should business partners have as to the health of NFL players," it is useful to begin by understanding what recognized ethical obligations they have in the human rights realm, simply as a starting point. The Guiding Principles include several principles that may be relevant to that inquiry:

- Business enterprises should "[s]eek to prevent or mitigate adverse human rights impacts that are directly linked to their operations, products or services by their business relationships, even if they have not contributed to those impacts."[11]

- "[B]usiness enterprises should carry out human rights due diligence" including "assessing actual and potential human rights impacts, integrating and acting upon the findings, tracking responses, and communicating how impacts are addressed."[12]

- Business enterprises should engage in "meaningful consultation with potentially affected groups and other relevant stakeholders."[13]

- Business enterprises should "exercise" leverage "to prevent or mitigate the adverse impact" when possible.[14]

- Business enterprises which lack the leverage to prevent or mitigate the adverse impact should consider "collaborating with other actors."[15]

---

c   The legal obligations described herein are not an exhaustive list but are those we believe are most relevant to player health.

In the corporate context, these responsibilities are considered as defining the ethical business conduct, but the Guiding Principles do not purport to be legally enforceable obligations. Nonetheless, using the Guiding Principles as persuasive authority, we highlight two of the above principles for further discussion.

Importantly, the Guiding Principles do not require that the business enterprises' conduct cause an adverse impact, only that they be "directly linked." NFL business partners' practices almost certainly do not cause player health problems, but for reasons discussed in this chapter, there is a direct link between business partners' practices and player health issues.

Second, the second-to-last bullet point recognizes business enterprises' obligations to exercise leverage where appropriate. Again, for reasons discussed in this chapter, business partners have the ability to wield influence with the NFL. With that influence comes the responsibility to act conscientiously and force others to do the same, including on matters concerning player health.

(D) Current Practices

NFL business partners' approach to NFL player health issues is best highlighted by examining their response to recent NFL controversies. When the NFL faced scrutiny for mishandled domestic violence incidents in the fall of 2014, many of its major sponsors issued generalized statements expressing disappointment in the situation and calling on the NFL to make changes.[16] However, research has not revealed any statements by any NFL corporate sponsor concerning the lawsuits over concussions or painkillers, or any other player health or safety issue.

> Business partners should be concerned with what endeavors they allow their money to support, and in what ways they can and/or should wield their power to affect change.

Much of the relationship between business partners and the NFL occurs behind closed doors. All we can see are the public positions, statements, and actions undertaken by business partners. Taking inspiration from the Guiding Principles (and again emphasizing that there is no claim that we are talking about human rights violations), and evaluating only based on the public record (a limitation, to be sure), it does not appear that NFL business partners have undertaken any of these kinds of efforts to prevent harm to the health of NFL players, or even to influence a culture that recognizes the value and importance of player health. That is, there is no evidence that NFL business partners have: (1) sought to prevent or mitigate player health problems; (2) conducted due diligence concerning player health issues; (3) engaged in meaningful consultation

Research has not revealed any statements by any NFL corporate sponsor concerning the lawsuits over concussions or painkillers, or any other player health or safety issue.

with players concerning player health issues; (4) exercised leverage in an individual capacity to prevent or mitigate player health problems; or, (5) exercised leverage in a collaborative capacity to prevent or mitigate player health problems.[d]

Commentators have opined that one way to push the NFL to make meaningful changes to its policies or course of conduct regarding player health is to threaten financial consequences, *i.e.*, if business partners threatened to stop doing business with the NFL.[17] Thus, there seemingly exists the possibility that NFL business partners have the power to effect change—or to at least begin meaningful conversation about change—concerning player health issues.

Nevertheless, so long as the NFL remains a valuable property with which to be associated, it seems unlikely that individual business partners would risk damaging their relationships with the NFL by either taking adverse positions or putting pressure on the League. At the same time, this may be an era where the economic realities are changing.

Business enterprises that engage in sponsorship like that of the NFL's business partners are principally concerned with deriving economic value from the sponsorship through increased brand awareness and positive association with the sponsored entity, *e.g.*, the NFL. Negative publicity for the NFL or decreased attention to the NFL (*e.g.*, television ratings) lessens the economic value of the business partner's sponsorship. NFL player health issues have created negative attention for the NFL through lawsuits, news articles, and other means. This negative attention has the potential to spread to the NFL's business partners through a "guilt by association" mindset.[e] Thus, this may be the moment where economic and ethical interests align, such that business partners can take on a more prominent role in pressing for protection of player health.

(E) Enforcement of Legal and Ethical Obligations

In the absence of any existing legal or ethical obligations for NFL business partners concerning NFL player health, there can be no enforcement of any such legal or ethical obligations.

---

d   The business partners' conduct must also be viewed in light of Guiding Principle No. 24, which states that "[w]here it is necessary to prioritize actions to address actual and potential adverse human rights impacts, business enterprises should first seek to prevent and mitigate those that are most severe or where delayed response would make them irremediable." Thus, some business partners might believe there are issues of a human rights nature that deserve greater attention and immediacy than their involvement in NFL player health matters.

e   Such concerns are not hypothetical. In 2014, five sponsors (Sony, Emirates Airlines, Castrol, Continental and Johnson & Johnson) pulled their sponsorship of FIFA's World Cup due to extensive allegations of corruption within the international soccer organization. *See* Peter Sharkey, *Cup Joy's a World Apart From FIFA 'Toxic Brand'*, Birmingham Post (UK), Jan. 29, 2015, *available at* 2015 WLNR 2794660.

(F) Recommendations Concerning NFL Business Partners

NFL business partners, due to the power of their purses, have a unique ability to influence the NFL to make positive changes concerning player health. Below we make recommendations that can improve business partners' approaches to player health issues, to the benefit of both players and the business partners. In making these recommendations, we also stress that while we recommend and encourage business partners to act independently when necessary, that if business partners collaborated and worked collectively on these issues they would be more likely to achieve positive changes quickly and effectively.

Goal 1: To encourage NFL business partners to work towards advancing a culture of health for NFL players.

Principles Advanced: Respect; Health Primacy; Collaboration and Engagement; and, Justice.

Recommendation 19:1-A: NFL business partners should not remain silent on NFL player health-related policies.

During the 2014 season, the NFL's business partners condemned the NFL's failures to handle and address domestic violence issues. Several of the business partners' statements reflected on the NFL's place in our society and emphasized the need for ethical conduct and leadership.[18] However, none of the business partners have ever made any statements concerning the risks players face in playing professional football and the tolls of such a career. Moreover, the business partners never made any statement concerning the allegations in the Concussion Litigation (*see* Chapter 7: The NFL and NFLPA) that for many years the NFL misrepresented the risks of playing professional football to players. Why this asymmetry? It is quite possible that business partners' comments on the domestic violence issue were in response to greater public pressure, and the more diffuse public pressure on player health has not yet reached the same crescendo.

Nevertheless, for the same reasons business partners commented on the NFL's domestic violence issues, they should also make their voices heard on player health-related issues. Business partners, like everyone in the professional football universe, need to understand and accept their responsibilities and role concerning player health.

A recent useful example is the energy bar company Clif Bar. Clif Bar sponsors adventure sports athletes, including mountain climbers. After determining that some of these athletes were taking risks that were excessive (such as not using safety ropes or BASE jumping), Clif Bar pulled their sponsorships of some of these athletes and issued a statement clarifying the types of risks Clif Bar felt comfortable supporting. Of particular relevance, Clif Bar indicated that it "no longer [felt] good about benefitting from the amount of risk certain athletes [we]re taking[.]"[19]

Recommendation 19:1-B: NFL business partners should consider applying pressure on the NFL to improve player health.

The NFL is a business and, like any business, does not want to suffer a drop in revenue. Individually, the business partners might not represent a significant portion of the NFL's revenue, but collectively the business partners' sponsorship fees comprise more than 10 percent of the NFL's revenue. Thus, collectively, the business partners have leverage, *i.e.*, the ability to force the NFL to make change at the threat of losing hundreds of millions of dollars. The business partners, consistent with the spirit of the Guiding Principles and other social responsibility initiatives and aspirations they have, should use their power of the purse to help the players from whom they derive considerable financial value.[f]

To be fair, business partners might reasonably be concerned that any exercise of such leverage will only result in the NFL replacing them with a competitor. However, the NFL has reasons to maintain continuity with its business partners. Sponsor turnover is bad for brand loyalty and identification for both the sponsor and the NFL, thus decreasing the value of the replacement partner's sponsorship. For example, Pepsi is currently the official soft drink of the NFL. If Pepsi were to be replaced by Coca-Cola, many fans might still believe Pepsi is the official soft drink or be confused as to which brand is the official soft drink, decreasing the value of Coca-Cola's sponsorship and the amount it would be willing to pay to the NFL.[20]

The recommendations made in this Report and other outlets that have discussed changes to player health provide guidance on the types of issues for which business partners should exercise leverage.

Recommendation 19:1-C: NFL business partners should consider supporting organizations conducting due diligence into player health issues.

The Guiding Principles, generally speaking, instruct business enterprises to conduct due diligence into how their actions and business relationships affect others. If business partners are going to make fully informed decisions about their relationships with the NFL, it would be advisable that they consider research and data on NFL players and the issues they face. While the business partners themselves likely lack the capabilities or expertise to conduct research into player health issues, they have the resources to support organizations conducting such research.

Recommendation 19:1-D: NFL business partners should engage players concerning player health issues.

As discussed above, NFL business partners receive tremendous economic value from their association with, and from the work of, NFL players. In such situations, the Guiding Principles direct that the business enterprise should engage the stakeholders involved to understand the impact of the business enterprise's conduct on the health of the stakeholder. Such conversations have the possibility to improve relations between the stakeholder and business enterprise, the business enterprise's own business operations, and the health of the stakeholder. In this context, NFL business partners could hold conversations with current or former players to better understand them and the issues that matter to them. Additionally, through these conversations, the business partners could learn how they might adopt more consistent messaging concerning professional football, apply pressure on the NFL where appropriate, and what types of causes or organizations concerning football the business partners should support. Such conversations would establish a better dynamic between players and business partners and enhance the business partners' reputation for social responsibility.

---

f   FIFA again provides a useful example. In 2015, major sponsors Coca-Cola, Visa, and McDonald's demanded FIFA take actions to address allegations of corruption and criminal activity and requested a meeting to voice their concerns. Brian Homewood, *FIFA to meet sponsors after reproaches from Coke, Visa, McDonald's*, Reuters, (Jul. 24, 2015, 8:48 AM), http://www.reuters.com/article/2015/07/24/us-soccer-fifa-sponsors-idUSKCN0PY1IC20150724, *archived at* http://perma.cc/VF4G-JHJ4.

Endnotes

1 *Spons-o-Meter: NFL Lines Up 26 Partners To Start '13 Season*, Sports Bus. Daily (Sept. 13, 2013), http://www.sportsbusinessdaily.com/Daily/Issues/2013/09/06/NFL-Season-Preview/Sponsometer.aspx, *archived at* http://perma.cc/U4S2-TLUJ. For several years, Sports Business Daily published an annual list of the NFL's official sponsors. However, for unknown reasons, Sports Business Daily did not publish any such list in 2014 or 2015.

2 Matthew Futterman and Spencer Ante, *Verizon Pads NFL Deal*, Wall St. J., Jun. 4, 2013, http://online.wsj.com/news/articles/SB10001424127887324563004578525060861520512, *archived at* http://perma.cc/53SG-7U4H.

3 Michael David Smith, *Bud Light sponsorship will pay the NFL $1.4 billion over six years*, ProFootballTalk (Nov. 4, 2015, 10:28 AM), http://profootballtalk.nbcsports.com/2015/11/04/bud-light-sponsorship-will-pay-the-nfl-1-4-billion-over-six-years/, *archived at* http://perma.cc/6YVT-FKJY.

4 Kristi Dosh, *Steep Price Paid by Nike Likely to Pay Off*, ESPN (Apr. 3, 2012), http://espn.go.com/blog/playbook/dollars/post/_/id/554/steep-price-paid-by-nike-likely-to-pay-off, *archived at* http://perma.cc/2MRR-UBHJ.

5 Matthew Futterman, *NFL Back On Field, And Deals Pile Up*, Wall St. J., Sept. 6, 2011, http://online.wsj.com/news/articles/SB10001424053111904900904576552773485086198, *archived at* http://perma.cc/6QXS-GP4K. Gatorade, Frito-Lay, and Quaker are all brands owned by PepsiCo and are included in Pepsi's deal with the NFL, which runs through the 2022 season.

6 *NFL Sponsorship Revenue Totals $1.07 Billion In 2013 Season*, IEG Sponsorship Report, Jan. 27, 2014, http://www.sponsorship.com/IEGSR/2014/01/27/NFL-Sponsorship-Revenue-Totals-$1-07-Billion-In-20.aspx, *archived at* http://perma.cc/SD88-HK2L.

7 *See Spons-o-Meter: NFL Lines Up 26 Partners To Start '13 Season*, Sports Bus. Daily (Sept. 13, 2013), http://www.sportsbusinessdaily.com/Daily/Issues/2013/09/06/NFL-Season-Preview/Sponsometer.aspx, *archived at* http://perma.cc/U4S2-TLUJ (providing the bulk of the list's data); *New Deal Establishes Nike As League's Official Uniform Provider*, NFL (Oct. 12, 2010, 1:25 PM), http://www.nfl.com/news/story/09000d5d81b4559b/article/new-deal-establishes-nike-as-leagues-official-uniform-provider, *archived at* http://perma.cc/R7PZ-393X (discussing sponsorship agreement between Nike and NFL); *Nationwide Insurance Teams Up With The National Football League As An Official Sponsor*, Nationwide Ins. (Aug. 4, 2014), http://www.nationwide.com/about-us/080414-nfl-announcement.jsp, *archived at* http://perma.cc/K74G-4WZV (discussing sponsorship agreement between Nationwide and NFL); *Extreme Networks Named Official Wi-Fi Analytics Provider of National Football League*, Extreme Networks (Jan. 15, 2014), http://investor.extremenetworks.com/releasedetail.cfm?releaseid=819515, *archived at* http://perma.cc/9LFY-ZSBD (discussing sponsorship agreement between Extreme Networks and NFL).

8 Additionally, players routinely enter into sponsorship agreements with competitors of the NFL's business partners. *See* Cindy Boren, *Colin Kaepernick Sticks with Beats by Dre—With a Little Tape Over the Logo*, Wash. Post, Oct. 14, 2014, *available at* 2014 WLNR 28601543.

9 United Nations Office of the High Commission, *Guiding Principles on Business and Human Rights*, A/HRC/17/31 (Jun. 16, 2011) *available at* http://www.ohchr.org/Documents/Publications/GuidingPrinciplesBusinessHR_EN.pdf?v=1392752313000/_/jcr:system/jcr:versionstorage/12/52/13/125213a0-e4bc-4a15-bb96-9930bb8fb6a1/1.3/jcr:frozennode, *archived at* https://perma.cc/U36F-S7YR?type=pdf [hereinafter, "Guiding Principles"].

10 The NFL business partners that have stated their intention to comply with the Guiding Principles include, but are not limited to: Pepsi, *see*

PepsiCo Code of Conduct, PepsiCo, http://www.pepsico.com/Purpose/Talent-Sustainability/Human-Rights, *archived at* http://perma.cc/5YN4-WRPW?type=live (last visited Aug. 7, 2015); *see Report of the Sustainability and Corporate Responsibility Committee of the Board of Directors of McDonald's Corporation*, McDonalds Corp., Jan. 9, 2014, http://www.aboutmcdonalds.com/content/dam/AboutMcDonalds/Investors/Investor%202014/Human%20Rights.pdf, *archived at* https://perma.cc/QN4Y-XMBR?type=pdf (last visited Aug. 7, 2015); *Corporate Citizenship*, Microsoft, http://www.microsoft.com/about/corporatecitizenship/en-us/working-responsibly/principled-business-practices/human-rights/, *archived at* http://perma.cc/EVJ3-H2KK (last visited Aug. 7, 2015); and P&G Corporate Newsroom *A Renewed Commitment to Respect Human Rights*, Procter & Gamble, (Apr. 21, 2014, 2:33 PM) http://news.pg.com/blog/social-responsibility/renewed-commitment-respect-human-rights, *archived at* http://perma.cc/MN33-JNEF.

11 Guiding Principles, *supra* note 9 at 14.

12 *Id.* at 17.

13 *Id.* at 19.

14 *Id.* at 22.

15 *Id.*

16 Laurie Kulikowski, *Will These 10 NFL Sponsors Quit Funding Football Over Domestic Violence?*, Street (Sept. 24, 2014, 2:04 PM), http://www.thestreet.com/story/12885981/1/10-nfl-sponsors-upset-over-the-handling-of-domestic-abuse-scandals.html, *archived at* http://perma.cc/5P8L-9KFN (discussing statements by ten NFL sponsors expressing disappointment, including Anheuser-Busch, General Motors, Verizon, USAA, McDonald's, Pepsi, Bose, FedEx, Marriott and Campbell Soup).

17 *See* Michael David Smith, *Anheuser-Busch Disappointed, Concerned, Dissatisfied With NFL*, ProFootballTalk (Sept. 16, 2014, 3:47 PM), http://profootballtalk.nbcsports.com/2014/09/16/anheuser-busch-disappointed-concerned-dissatisfied-with-nfl/, *archived at* http://perma.cc/4G5C-6FFN; Juliet Macur, *Time for N.F.L. Sponsors to Demand Change*, N.Y. Times, Feb. 14, 2014, http://www.nytimes.com/2014/02/15/sports/football/time-for-nfl-sponsors-to-demand-change.html, *archived at* https://perma.cc/PC9J-5PMF?type=pdf.

18 *See* Kulikowski, *supra* note 16 (Anheuser-Busch stating that the players' actions "so clearly go against our own company culture and moral code."; USAA stating: "USAA's founding values of service, loyalty, honesty and integrity will always govern how we ultimately move forward, and we've made this clear to the NFL."; PepsiCo CEO Indra Nooyi stating: "Given PepsiCo's long-standing partnership with the NFL, I know Roger Goodell. We have worked together for many years. I know him to be a man of integrity, and I am confident that he will do the right thing for the league in light of the serious issues it is facing.").

19 *See* The Clif Bar Team, *A Letter to the Climbing Community*, Clif Bar, http://www.clifbar.com/text/a-letter-to-the-climbing-community (last visited Aug. 14, 2015), *archived at* http://perma.cc/VA9L-QSKN; John Branch, *A Sponsor Steps Away From the Edge*, N.Y. Times, Nov. 14, 2014, http://www.nytimes.com/2014/11/16/sports/clif-bar-drops-sponsorship-of-5-climbers-citing-risks-they-take.html, *archived at* https://perma.cc/7TFM-UK3V?type=pdf.

20 SportsBusiness Journal, in conjunction with Turnkey Sports & Entertainment, conducts an annual poll measuring fans' ability to correctly identify a league's official sponsor is various categories as opposed to a competing brand. *See* David Broughton, *Awareness up across the board for sponsors*, Sports Bus. Daily (June 16, 2014), http://www.sportsbusinessdaily.com/Journal/Issues/2014/06/16/Research-and-Ratings/NHL-Sponsor-Loyalty.aspx, *archived at* http://perma.cc/6VKS-DWX8.

Part 7: **Other Interested Parties**

NCAA | Youth Leagues | Govern- ment | Workers' Comp. Attys | Health- related Companies

As described in the Introduction to this Report, the stake-holders analyzed were: those that as individuals, groups, and organizations *directly impact* player health, for example, as employers or caregivers; those who *reap substantial financial benefits* from players' work; and/or those who have some *capacity to influence* player health. Additionally, as described in depth in the Introduction and throughout this Report, we are generally focused on current players.

Nevertheless, there are a variety of parties that do not fit well into the criteria outlined above but have some role in NFL player health. In particular, some have more direct roles in the health of future or former players. And while the roles of these parties are not as integral as the stake-holders already discussed, they still merit identification and discussion. These other parties that have at least some role in NFL player health are: (a) the National Collegiate Athletic Association (NCAA); (b) youth leagues; (c) governments; (d) workers' compensation attorneys; and, (e) health-related companies. Additionally, these parties should consider the recommendations in this Report and how they might be applied to their environment. For example, the NCAA should strongly consider our recommendations concerning improvements to the structure of player healthcare.

1) THE NCAA

The NCAA is a non-profit unincorporated association headquartered in Indianapolis through which the nation's colleges and universities govern their athletic programs. The NCAA consists of more than 1,200 member institutions, all of which participate in the creation of NCAA rules and voluntarily submit to its authority.[1] The NCAA's member institutions hire a President to oversee its affairs, currently Mark Emmert, formerly the President of the University of Washington.

The NCAA is divided into three Divisions (I, II, and III) depending on the size, resources, and number of sports teams of the schools, with Division I being the largest and Division III being the smallest. When it comes to football, Division I is further divided between the Football Bowl Subdivision (FBS) and the Football Championship Subdivision (FCS). FBS schools are the largest schools with the greatest financial and physical resources. In 2015, there were 125 schools playing in the FBS and 127 schools playing in the FCS.[2]

Due to the NFL's requirement that a player be at least three years removed from his high school graduation before he is eligible for the NFL Draft,[3] almost all NFL players played college football at an NCAA Division I member institution.[a] A handful of players come from Division II or III schools, international schools, or played for a college that is a member of the National Association of Intercollegiate Athletics, the NCAA's significantly smaller alternative.

Because the NCAA governs college football, it, its member institutions, and employees of member institutions have important legal and ethical obligations to current football student-athletes. In many respects, those obligations might track the obligations of the NFL, NFL clubs, and NFL club employees discussed herein.[b] However, those responsibilities largely if not entirely disappear once a player leaves an NCAA member institution. Thus, the NCAA generally has no current legal or ethical obligations toward current NFL players.

Nevertheless, the NCAA is an important and powerful component of the football ecosystem. The NCAA's member institutions, for better or worse, serve as the training ground for many NFL players, coaches, doctors, athletic trainers, and others working in the NFL. It is at these member institutions where policies and practices are learned and become part of the football culture.

It is perhaps thus not surprising that the NCAA, like the NFL, has faced litigation concerning concussions. In 2013, multiple lawsuits brought by student-athletes alleging that the NCAA had failed to institute appropriate safeguards concerning concussions were consolidated in the United States District Court for the Northern District of Illinois.[4] In October 2014, the parties reached a proposed settlement that included: (a) $70 million in a medical monitoring fund whereby former student-athletes could obtain medical evaluations concerning possible medical problems related to concussions; (b) $5 million for concussion-related research; and, (c) revised concussion protocols by the NCAA.[5] The court rejected the initial settlement on several procedural grounds, including that the class was not sufficiently represented by former student-athletes and those that played non-contact sports.[6] In April 2015, the parties submitted a revised proposed settlement agreement resolving the procedural issues but which did not change the financial

---

a   FBS team rosters are limited to 105 student-athletes. NCAA Division I Manual § 17.10.2.1.2. FCS rosters are limited to 95 student-athletes. NCAA Division I Manual § 17.10.2.1.3. Thus, each year there are approximately 25,000 student-athletes playing Division I college football. According to the NCAA, only 1.6 percent of all Division I football student-athletes will ever play professionally. Jake New, *A Long Shot*, Inside Higher Ed, Jan. 27, 2015, https://www.insidehighered.com/news/2015/01/27/college-athletes-greatly-overestimate-their-chances-playing-professionally, *archived at* https://perma.cc/MR9S-DZ7A.

b   A key distinction is that generally student-athletes are not considered employees of the institution. *See* Steven L. Wilborn, *College Athletes as Employees: An Overflowing Quiver*, 69 U. Miami L. Rev. 65 (2014).

components of the settlement.[7] In January 2016, the Court approved the settlement.[8,c]

The principal document governing intercollegiate athletics and setting forth relevant policies is the NCAA's Division I Manual, a complex set of thousands of rules. The Manual covers topics such as, but not limited to, ethical conduct, conduct and employment of athletics personnel, amateurism and athletics eligibility, recruiting, financial aid, scholarships, playing and practice seasons, championships, and enforcement.

The Division I Manual includes several provisions related to the health of student-athletes. In Section 2.2, entitled "The Principle of Student-Athlete Well-Being," the Division I Manual declares that "[i]ntercollegiate athletics programs shall be conducted in a manner designed to protect and enhance the physical and educational well-being of student-athletes."[9] Section 2.2 goes on to list and describe several principles relevant to student-athlete health, including: overall educational experience; cultural diversity and gender equity; health and safety; student-athlete/coach relationship; fairness, openness and honesty; and, student-athlete involvement. Moreover, in 2010, the Division I Manual was amended to require each member institution to create a concussion management plan for its student-athletes.[10]

The NCAA has recently made additional important progress on player health issues. In January 2014, the NCAA hosted a Safety in College Football Summit.[11] The stated purpose of "the summit was to bring together a multi-faceted group of experts who share a common interest in improving the culture of safety in intercollegiate sports in general, and football in particular."[12] The summit working group consisted of 65 people, including doctors, athletic trainers, NCAA officials and consultants, school athletic department officials, athletic conference officials, military officials, attorneys, and others.[13] The summit resulted in "consensus guidelines for three paramount safety issues in intercollegiate athletics: (1) Independent medical care in the collegiate setting; (2) Concussion diagnosis and management; and (3) Football practice contact." These guidelines substantially supplement the Division I Manual and are an important step forward for the health of college football players.

In addition, the NCAA has a Committee on Competitive Safeguards and Medical Aspects of Sports, which monitors student-athlete health and safety issues, and promulgates a Sports Medicine Handbook, which establishes requirements and guidelines regarding student-athlete health and safety issues.[14]

While the NCAA does not have direct dealings with current NFL players, many NFL players' health issues may stem (at least in part) from their collegiate careers and earlier. The NCAA's policies and practices influence and guide those playing or working in college football who might later play or work in the NFL. Additionally, the NCAA is a powerful organization and has the authority to influence positive policy and culture changes around player health. And similarly, the NCAA is likely to be influenced and affected by changes made at the NFL level. For these reasons, the NCAA is an interested and important party concerning the health of football players, particularly future players, and should strongly consider the recommendations made in this Report. At the same time, because of their overlapping interests, it is advisable for the NFL, the NCAA and youth leagues (discussed next) to discuss and create a bottom-up approach to solving many of the health and safety issues that impact football players at all levels.

2) YOUTH LEAGUES

Youth football leagues present important opportunities for children to learn and play the game of football. Even though the number of children who play youth football and who ultimately play in the NFL is infinitesimal,[d] youth football is still almost always the first step in a future NFL player's career.

There are approximately 2.8 million children between the ages of 6 and 14 who play football each year.[15] According to numerous media reports, this number has declined over the last decade,[16] though the Sports & Fitness Industry Association (SFIA) found that participation in tackle football among individuals aged 6 and above increased from 2014 to 2015.[17] Moreover, according to SFIA, 40 percent of adolescent boys play football, tied with basketball as the sport most likely to be played by young boys.[18]

These children play in hundreds of different leagues, the largest being Pop Warner.[19] Pop Warner has a participation level of approximately 225,000 annually, and, reportedly, 60 to 70 percent of current NFL players began playing football in a Pop Warner league.[20] Most youth football

---

c   The settlement did not preclude additional lawsuits against individual schools (as opposed to schools collectively in the form of the NCAA). As a result, new lawsuits were brought against individual schools. See Ben Strauss, *Six Concussion Suits Are Filed Against Colleges and N.C.A.A.*, N.Y. Times, May 17, 2016, http://www.nytimes.com/2016/05/18/sports/ncaafootball/six-head-injury-suits-filed-in-new-front-against-colleges-and-ncaa.html?_r=0, *archived at* https://perma.cc/5JY5-VEZT.

d   According to the NCAA, of 1,093,234 high school football players in 2013–2014, only 6.5 percent of those players will play college football. *Research — Football*, NCAA (Feb. 25, 2015), http://www.ncaa.org/about/resources/research/football, *archived at* http://perma.cc/73HT-TTLW. And, of those that play college football, only 1.6 percent will play in the NFL. By multiplying the figures together, it appears that only about 1 in every 1,000 high school football players will reach the NFL.

leagues, including Pop Warner, are members of USA Football, a non-profit organization based in Indianapolis that acts as the sport's national governing body for youth football.[21] USA Football is supported by or affiliated with the NFL, NCAA, National Federation of State High School Associations (NFHS), the American Football Coaches Association, and the five most powerful conferences in college football (ACC, Big 12, Big Ten, Pac-12 and SEC).[22] Additionally, NFL Commissioner Roger Goodell sits on USA Football's Board of Directors.[23]

While Pop Warner leagues govern children between the ages of 5 and 14, NFHS generally creates the rules for high school football. NFHS is an organization consisting of each of the 50 states' high school athletic associations,[24] and makes rules of play that are generally adopted by each of its members.[25] For example, NFHS' rules for football require all equipment meet the standards set forth by the National Operating Committee on Standards for Athletic Enforcement (NOCSAE),[26] as discussed in Chapter 16: Equipment Manufacturers.

Like the NFL, both Pop Warner and NFHS have many rules concerning player safety, some of which were added in recent years. For example, in 2010, Pop Warner instituted rules that required a player who may have a concussion to receive clearance from a doctor before he can return to play.[27] Then, in 2012, Pop Warner prohibited certain drills that cause helmet-to-helmet collisions and limited the amount of contact during practice to one-third of the practice time.[28] Similarly, in 2010, NFHS instituted rules requiring clearance by a doctor before a player suspected of having suffered a concussion can return to play.[29] Then, in 2016, Pop Warner banned kickoffs, believed to be the most dangerous play in the game.[30] Additionally, all youth leagues must comply with the Lystedt Laws, which are discussed below in the Government section.

Youth sports leagues can be held liable for the negligent actions of its employees when those employees are engaged in work on behalf of the league.[31] However, youth sports leagues are sometimes protected by statutes that provide immunity to non-profit or volunteer organizations[32] as well as the assumption of risk doctrine.[33] Similarly, while some state courts have found "that state high school athletic associations owe a duty of care to their participating athletes and that duty of care includes the responsibility to establish and enforce rules to protect the health and safety of participating athletes,"[34] high school athletic associations, which are often largely intertwined with the state government, may be protected, at least in part, by sovereign immunity laws.[35]

The possibility of litigation and heightened scrutiny concerning player health has caused concerns for youth leagues. Pop Warner has faced multiple lawsuits from former players alleging they had suffered serious injuries as a result of playing Pop Warner football,[36] settling some for undisclosed sums.[37] Moreover, dwindling participation and cautious exclusion of potentially injured athletes has forced schools to forfeit games or give up the sport.[38] Finally, increased liability exposure has increased leagues' insurance premiums,[39] potentially threatening the financial viability of the leagues.[40]

Despite decreasing participation, millions of children still play football. Consequently, youth football leagues remain important to both the game of football and those who play it.[e] The youth leagues teach players how to play the game and how to play it safely and thus also promote lifelong interest in the game. For these reasons, many of the issues and recommendations discussed in this Report are relevant to youth leagues. And again, as recommended above, because of their overlapping interests, it is advisable for the NFL, the NCAA, and youth leagues to work together in addressing these issues.

3) GOVERNMENTS

The federal government has occasionally involved itself in professional sports. In 1961, Congress passed the Sports Broadcasting Act (at the NFL's prompting), which, among other things, immunizes the NFL, NBA, NHL, and MLB from the antitrust laws when the leagues want to collectively sell their television rights;[41] in 1992, Congress passed the Professional and Amateur Sports Protection Act (again, at the NFL's prompting), a federal statute that generally forbids state-sponsored sports gambling;[42] and, in the mid-2000s, Congress held a series of hearings concerning performance-enhancing drugs in sports.[43] Of most relevance, in 2007 Congress held hearings concerning retirement and disability benefits for former NFL players,[44] in 2009 held a hearing concerning concussions in the NFL,[45] and in 2016 held a hearing concerning concussions generally.[46]

While Congress has never passed legislation specifically concerned with NFL player health, the possibility exists. Moreover, although governments' interest in sports is sporadic, the power that governments wield makes them a potentially powerful change agent. For example, shortly after the 2009 hearing, the NFL overhauled the Mild

---

e   "The mission of Pop Warner . . . is to enable young people to benefit from participation in team sports and activities in a safe and structured environment." *The Pop Warner Mission*, Pop Warner Little Scholars, http://www.popwarner.com/About_Us/mission.htm (last visited Aug. 7, 2015), *archived at* http://perma.cc/3UMX-YGGF.

Traumatic Brain Injury (MTBI) Committee[f] by removing its controversial leaders, renaming it the Head, Neck and Spine Committee, and appointing respected, independent neurosurgeons to lead the Committee and the NFL's research into concussions.[47]

State governments have taken more action concerning football player health, focusing on youth football. Since youth football players have no sophisticated union to represent their interests, government actions to protect their health have been particularly important. The most important of these initiatives are known as "Lystedt Laws," after Zackery Lystedt, who, as a 13-year old in October 2006, suffered brain hemorrhaging after he returned to a youth football game 15 minutes after having suffered a concussion.[48] Lystedt's experience left him in a coma for nine months, on a feeding tube for two years, and with severe physical disabilities.[49]

In 2009, as a result of Lystedt's experience, Washington, Lystedt's home state, passed a law in his name that: (1) requires youth athletes suspected of having sustained a concussion or head injury in a practice or game to be removed from competition at that time; and, (2) prevents the youth athlete from returning to play "until the athlete is evaluated by a licensed health care provider trained in the evaluation and management of concussion and receives written clearance to return to play from that health care provider."[50] Soon, other states began passing similar legislation.

In 2010, NFL Commissioner Roger Goodell sent a letter to the Governors of 44 states that had not yet passed a version of the Lystedt Law, urging them to do so.[51,g] In 2014, with the passage of the Mississippi Youth Concussion Act, all 50 states and the District of Columbia had passed a version of the Lystedt Law.[52]

Nearly all states' Lystedt Laws also require concussion-related information to be provided to youth athletes.[53] Nevertheless, there is substantial variation in the laws concerning the content of the information and whether the athletes must acknowledge receipt of the information.[54] The content can vary concerning the nature of a concussion, the risks of a concussion, the risk of continued play after a suspected concussion, actions to be taken in response to a concussion, return to play guidelines, and the short- and long-term consequences of concussions.[55] Thirty-five states require that both the athlete and his or her parents acknowledge receipt of the information while an

additional eight states require only that the parent acknowledge receipt.[56]

The application of the Lystedt Laws in the event of non-compliance is unclear. None of the state statutes provide for criminal or civil penalties.[57] In the only case to date concerning Washington's law, the court seemingly used the law as a guideline for determining whether the defendants were negligent. After briefly discussing the law's requirements, the court found that "[t]he Administrators and Coaches responsible for the football program . . . were not negligent in administering the eligibility requirements or monitoring the safety and health of the players on the team."[58]

Governments are appropriately aware of situations posing threats to the health of the public, including practices in particular industries. While any problems concerning NFL player health are generally best left to the collective bargaining process, it might be appropriate for the government to involve itself if the situation is particularly concerning. More importantly, governments can play a more robust role in changing the culture around football safety by protecting youth football players, some of whom are future NFL players.

4) WORKERS' COMPENSATION ATTORNEYS

As discussed in Chapter 8: NFL Clubs, NFL clubs' obligations to pay for workers' compensation benefits to players has been a contentious issue. Although the benefits a player might receive are quite small compared to the amounts he earned while playing, the player will have medical care stemming from a football-related injury covered for life. Workers' compensation attorneys are a crucial part of players receiving benefits to which they are entitled.

To assist NFL players with workers' compensation claims, the NFLPA makes available to players and their contract advisors a document describing the benefits claim process, benefits amount, and statutes of limitations. Additionally, the NFLPA has recommended workers' compensation attorneys in each city in which an NFL club plays (collectively, the "Panel"). The Panel consists of approximately 60 attorneys. Because players play in many states, they are often eligible for workers' compensation benefits in many states. The advantage of the Panel is coordination and communication (with the NFLPA' assistance) that permits a player to determine which state will provide the player with the best benefits. Finally, contract advisors are prohibited from referring a player to a workers' compensation attorney who is not a member of the Panel.[59]

---

f   For more on the MTBI Committee, see Chapter 7: The NFL and NFLPA.
g   Dr. Richard Ellenbogen, Lystedt's treating physician and the co-chairman of the NFL Head, Neck and Spine Committee was also involved in the efforts to have the laws passed.

The Panel provides NFL players with easy access to attorneys experienced in workers' compensation and sensitive to the specific issues that might arise concerning NFL players. In addition, the Panel attorneys are generally the first to know of changes in the workers' compensation laws, whether by judicial decision or legislative action, and can alert the NFLPA accordingly.

Workers' compensation attorneys are also in a relatively unique position to judge a player's post-career health. Workers' compensation claims generally must be filed within 1 to 3 years from the date of injury. Professional football players are most likely to file claims for career-ending or threatening injuries when the likelihood of future compensation becomes less certain. Workers' compensation attorneys are thus likely working with players whose careers are about to end or have recently ended. Moreover, as part of the workers' compensation claim, the attorney will undoubtedly become familiar with the player's medical history and issues and the likely effect of those issues on the player's quality of life moving forward.

Many of the issues discussed in this Report potentially contribute and are relevant to workers' compensation claims. Consequently, workers' compensation attorneys' are well-versed in many of these issues. For these reasons, we believe it would help players and their health if workers' compensation attorneys reviewed this Report and considered the ways in which they can help improve player health.

5) HEALTH-RELATED COMPANIES

Many technology companies are creating biological and other health-related products principally geared towards a sports application. Some of these companies are working on biological technologies while others are working on genetic ones. Additional detail on these technologies and tests, and their legal and ethical implications as they relate to NFL players, are discussed at length in our forthcoming law review article, *Evaluating NFL Player Health and Performance: Legal and Ethical Issues*.[60]

Several companies are putting cutting-edge technology into devices that can generate a variety of biological data. For example, there are technologies that can be used to track player movement (Catapult Sports, Zebra Technologies), or measure the force exerted by players (Catapult Sports, PUSH, EliteForm), a player's readiness for practice or competition (Omegawave, BioForce HRV), a player's heart rate (Polar, Proteus Digital Health, BioForce HRV), the quality of a player's sleep (Fatigue Science), a player's body temperature (Proteus Digital Health, HQInc.), a player's hydration level (Atago), and head impacts (X2 Biosystems,

Riddell). Many of these products are already being utilized by NFL clubs.

As these technologies get smaller and smaller, and thus easier to incorporate into equipment, the trend will be toward more robust data generation and collection over time. In all of these situations, the companies are responding to market demands, including for technologies that can help athletes (professional and amateur) improve their performance and also those that can help athletes be healthier and safer. Recognizing that these demands are principal concerns of the NFL and many other powerful sports leagues provides strong economic incentives for the continued creation and expansion of biotechnologies.

Turning to products focused on genetics, a 2011 study in the *Journal of Personalized Medicine* found 13 companies providing sports-specific DNA tests or analyses to American consumers.[61] The tests were given names such as "Sports DNA Test," "Sports X Factor Standard Panel," "Athletic Gene Test," "Sports Gene Test," and "Athletics Profile Test" and ranged in price from $99 to about $1,000.[62] However, in August 2013, the Food and Drug Administration (FDA) ordered one of the leading companies offering sports-specific DNA tests, 23andMe, to stop advertising its genetic tests without authorization from the FDA.[63] At that time, the FDA had not developed any rules for direct-to-consumer (DTC) genetic testing. Thus, the FDA was concerned about whether the test was clinically validated and how consumers might interpret genetic test results provided to them.[64] Shortly thereafter, 23andMe and its American competitors ceased offering the DTC genetic tests.[65]

The reliability of these genetic tests is suspect. A 2013 article summed up the state of research: "A favorable genetic profile, when combined with an optimal training environment, is important for elite athletic performance; however, few genes are consistently associated with elite athletic performance, and none are linked strongly enough to warrant their use in predicting athletic success."[66] This opinion is not uniformly held, and indeed a 2013 *Journal of Sports Medicine* article took an even dimmer view of the current science, arguing that: "Current genetic testing has zero predictive power on talent identification and should not be used by athletes, coaches or parents."[67]

Nevertheless, interest in genetic testing in sports remains extremely high. Researchers and companies have claimed there are more than 200 genes associated with physical performance and that at least 20 of them might be tied to elite athletic performance.[68] In February 2015, 23andMe received FDA approval to begin marketing a genetic test designed to determine whether prospective parents carry mutations that could cause a rare disorder known as Bloom syndrome in their children.[69] Thus, it seems likely that 23andMe and other American companies will seek or already are seeking FDA approval for sports-specific genetic tests.

Many of the issues discussed in this Report are decades old—ingrained in the culture and nature of the NFL. The health-related technology companies are an interesting component of the future of the NFL. Nevertheless, these technologies have the potential to be bad for players—by contributing to many of the problems discussed in this Report—or good for players—by using their technologies in ways that are principally designed to protect and promote player health. Health-related technologies can both contribute to many of the problems discussed in this Report and be used in ways that are principally designed to protect and promote player health. Health-related technology companies should review the issues discussed in this Report and carefully consider what their role in player health will be moving forward.

> Health-related technologies can both contribute to many of the problems discussed in this Report and be used in ways that are principally designed to protect and promote player health.

Endnotes

1 *See Who We Are*, Nat'l Collegiate Athletic Ass'n, http://www.ncaa.org/about/who-we-are (last visited Aug. 7, 2015), *archived at* http://perma.cc/2S7M-GL89; *Membership*, Nat'l Collegiate Athletic Ass'n, http://www.ncaa.org/about/who-we-are/membership (last visited Aug. 7, 2015), *archived at* http://perma.cc/5J5P-RQ2V (describing membership as more than 1,200 schools).

2 *See NCAA Members by Division*, http://web1.ncaa.org/onlineDir/exec2/divisionListing (last visited Aug. 7, 2015), *archived at* https://perma.cc/EJP3-S2V4?type=pdf.

3 *See* 2011 CBA, Art. 6 § 2(b).

4 *See* In re: Nat'l Collegiate Athletic Ass'n Student-Athlete Concussion Injury Litigation, 13-cv-9116, 2014 WL 7237208, *1-3 (N.D. Ill. Dec. 17, 2014) (discussing procedural history of case).

5 *See id.* at *3-4 (discussing terms of proposed settlement).

6 *See* In re: Nat'l Collegiate Athletic Ass'n Student-Athlete Concussion Injury Litigation, *supra* note 4, *6-10.

7 *See* Ben Strauss, *Former Player Opposes Settlement in N.C.A.A. Concussion Suit*, N.Y. Times, June 9, 2015, http://www.nytimes.com/2015/06/10/sports/football/former-player-opposes-settlement-in-ncaa-concussion-suit.html, *archived at* https://perma.cc/WE4D-7JJR?type=source.

8 *In re: Nat'l Collegiate Ath. Ass'n Student-Athlete Concussion Injury Litigation,* 13-cv-9116, 2016 WL 305380 (N.D. Ill. Jan. 26, 2016).

9 NCAA Division I Manual at § 2.2.

10 *See id.*

11 *Health and Safety—Appendix,* Nat'l Collegiate Athletic Ass'n, http://www.ncaa.org/health-and-safety/appendix (last visited Apr. 30, 2015), *archived at* http://perma.cc/9XSN-6RZ6.

12 *Id.*

13 *Id.*

14 *Committee on Competitive Safeguards and Medical Aspects of Sports,* NCAA, http://www.ncaa.org/governance/committees/committee-competitive-safeguards-and-medical-aspects-sports (last visited Dec. 11, 2015), *archived at* https://perma.cc/785B-5WDV?type=source .

15 Steve Fainaru & Mark Fainaru-Wada, *Youth Football Participation Drops*, ESPN (Nov. 14, 2013), http://espn.go.com/espn/otl/story/_/page/popwarner/pop-warner-youth-football-participation-drops-nfl-concussion-crisis-seen-causal-factor, *archived at* http://perma.cc/FHB7-ZU5C.

16 *See id.* (discussing Pop Warner's reported 6.7-percent decline in participation from 2010 to 2011 and 4.0-percent decline from 2011 to 2012); Neil Paine, *Fewer Kids Are Playing Football, But Mark Cuban Might Be Wrong About Why*, FiveThirtyEight (Mar. 25, 2014, 4:37 PM), http://fivethirtyeight.com/datalab/fewer-kids-are-playing-football-but-mark-cuban-might-be-wrong-about-why/, *archived at* http://perma.cc/22EQ-XB8X (discussing a Wall Street Journal study that found a 5.4% decline in youth football between 2008 and 2014); Bob Cook, *Why Is Football Participation Declining? The Answer Isn't Concussions*, Forbes, Nov. 26, 2013, http://www.forbes.com/sites/bobcook/2013/11/26/why-is-football-participation-declining-the-answer-isnt-concussions/, *archived at* https://perma.cc/Y9C9-X579?type=image (discussing a National Sporting Goods Association report finding a 13% decline from 2011 to 2012).

17 *Date Shows Team Sports Participation Increased in '15, Including Hoops, Football*, Sports Business Daily (Mar. 10, 2016), http://www.sportsbusinessdaily.com/Daily/Issues/2016/03/10/Research-and-Ratings/SFIA.aspx, *archived at* https://perma.cc/PQ86-E29E.

18 Bruce Kelley & Carl Carchia, *Hey, Data Data—Swing!* ESPN (Jul. 16, 2013), http://espn.go.com/espn/story/_/id/9469252/hidden-demographics-youth-sports-espn-magazine, *archived at* http://perma.cc/TQ4P-TUQG.

19 Fainaru & Fainaru-Wada, *supra* note 15.

20 *See id.*

21 *USA Football,* USA Football, http://usafootball.com/about-us (last visited Aug. 7, 2015), *archived at* http://perma.cc/V48Q-37P6.

22 *Id.*

23 *Directory,* USA Football, http://usafootball.com/contact_us (last visited Aug. 7, 2015), *archived at* http://perma.cc/R4W8-K3D7.

24 *About Us,* Nat'l Fed'n State High Sch. Ass'ns, http://www.nfhs.org/who-we-are/aboutus (last visited Apr. 30, 2015), *archived at* http://perma.cc/2FWC-LURF.

25 *Id.*

26 *See Football Rules Book,* Nat'l Fed'n State High Sch. Ass'ns (2012), http://goodofficials.files.wordpress.com/2012/08/2012-football-rules2.pdf, *archived at* https://perma.cc/93Y8-A4LQ?type=pdf (containing multiple provisions requiring equipment meet NOCSAE standards).

27 Bill Brink, *Pop Warner Football Issues Strict Rules on Concussions*, Pittsburgh Post-Gazette, Nov. 19, 2010, *available at* 2010 WLNR 23068024.

28 *Limited Contact in Practice Rule*, Pop Warner Little Scholars, http://www.popwarner.com/safety/practice_contact.htm (last visited Aug. 7, 2015), *archived at* http://perma.cc/8XUX-PW7A.

29 *−11 NFHS Rule Book Changes on Concussion*, Nat'l Fed'n State High Sch. Ass'ns, http://www.fhsaa.org/sites/default/files/orig_uploads/health/pdf/concussion.pdf (last visited Aug. 7, 2015), *archived at* https://perma.cc/LRZ8-3SEL?type=pdf.

30 Ken Belson, *Pop Warner Bans Kickoffs in Hopes of Protecting Its Youngest Players*, N.Y. Times, May 12, 2016, http://www.nytimes.com/2016/05/13/sports/football/pop-warner-bans-kickoffs-concussions-nfl.html, *archived at* https://perma.cc/U52D-GBRK.

31 Marie-France Wilson, *Young Athletes at Risk: Preventing and Managing Consequences of Sports Concussion in Youth Athletes and the Related Legal Issues*, 21 Marq. Sports L. Rev. 241, 260–68 (2010) (discussing liability of youth sports leagues).

32 Thomas A. Baker, Daniel P. Connaughton, & James J. Zhang *An Examination of Immunity Statutes Regarding the Liability of Recreational Youth Sport Organizations for the Pedophilic Actions of Coaches, Administrators, and Officials*, 5 J. Int'l Council for Health, Physical Educ., Recreation, Sport & Dance 54 (2010).

33 Wilson, *supra* note 31 at 260–68.

34 *Id.* at 263.

35 *See* Isler v. New Mexico Activities Ass'n, 893 F. Supp. 2d. 1145 (D.N.M. 2012) (state high school athletic association entitled to immunity); University Interscholastic League v. Southwest Officials Ass'n, Inc., 319 S.W.3d 952 (Tex. App. 2010) (same); Yanero v. Davis, 65 S.W.3d 510 (Ky. 2001) (same); Coughlon v. Iowa High School Athletic Ass'n, 150 N.W.2d 660 (Iowa 1967) (same). *But see* Wissel v. Ohio High School Athletic Association, 605 N.E.2d 458 (Ohio Ct. App. 1992) (state high school athletic association not entitled to sovereign immunity).

36 *See* Complaint, Pyka v. Pop Warner Little Scholars, Inc., 15-cv-57 (Feb. 5, 2015), ECF No. 1; Ken Belson, *Family Sues Pop Warner Over Suicide of Player Who Had Brain Disease,* N.Y. Times, Feb. 5, 2015, http://www.nytimes.com/2015/02/06/sports/family-of-player-with-cte-who-killed-himself-sues-pop-warner.html, *archived at* https://perma.cc/YF26-F4ER; Trial Order, Dixon v. Pop Warner Little Scholars, Inc., No. BC526842, 2015 WL 9583749 (Sup. Ct. Dec. 22, 2015) (tentative ruling denying Pop Warner's motion for summary judgment in case brought by former player).

37 *See* Michael Martinez, *Pop Warner settles concussion suit filed by former player who committed suicide*, CNN (Mar. 9, 2016, 3:54 PM), http://www.cnn.com/2016/03/09/us/pop-warner-concussion-lawsuit-settlement-player-suicide/, *archived at* https://perma.cc/9GBA-VAKK;

Stipulaton of Dismissal With Prejudice, Pyka v. Pop Warner Little Scholars, Inc., 15-cv-57 (Mar. 10, 2016), ECF No. 54.

38 John Branch & Billy Witz, *Injury Lists Grow Longer, and High School Seasons Are Cut Short*, Oct. 29, 2014, http://www.nytimes.com/2014/10/30/sports/football/football-injuries-lead-to-steady-stream-of-high-school-forfeitures.html, *archived at* https://perma.cc/82JC-NU7R?type=pdf.

39 Ken Belson, *Concussion Liability Costs May Rise, and Not Just for N.F.L.*, N.Y. Times, Dec. 10, 2012, http://www.nytimes.com/2012/12/11/sports/football/insurance-liability-in-nfl-concussion-suits-may-have-costly-consequences.html, *archived at* https://perma.cc/739V-3QGN?type=pdf.

40 *See* Kevin Brandwein, *Goals and Obstacles in Legislating Concussion Management in Youth Sports*, 10 Willamette Sports L.J. 28, 38 (2013) (collecting and discussing news articles arguing that increased insurance premiums threaten football leagues).

41 U.S.C. §§1291-1295 (1961).

42 U.S.C. § 3702. *See also* Chil Woo, *All Bets Are Off: Revisiting the Professional and Amateur Sports Protection Act (PASPA)*, 31 Cardozo Arts & Ent. L.J. 569 (2013) (discussing, among other things, PASPA's history and the NFL's involvement).

43 NFL Commissioner Paul Tagliabue and NFLPA Executive Director Gene Upshaw were forced to appear in front of the House Government Reform Committee in April 2005. Jarrett Bell, *NFL Touts Tweaks to Drug Policy*, USA Today, Apr. 28, 2005, *available at* 2005 WLNR 6652843, and the House Energy and Commerce Committee in May 2005, concerning performance-enhancing drugs; Leonard Shapiro, *Leagues Draw Praise, Rebuke; Congress Says NFL Is 'Excellent' on Drug Policy, but NBA Is 'Weak'*, Wash. Post, May 20, 2005, *available at* 2005 WLNR 27746472.

44 *See* Paul Daugherty, *NFL No Match For Aging Ex-Players*, Cincinnati Enquirer, June 28, 2007, *available at* 2007 WLNR 27417382 (describing June 26, 2007 hearing before the House Judiciary Committee); Greg Johnson, *NFL Admits to Flaws in Pension System*, L.A. Times, Sept. 19, 2007, *available at* 2007 WLNR 18319286 (describing September 19, 2007 hearing before the Senate Commerce Committee).

45 *See* Wayne Coffey, *Goodell, NFL Grilled Over Concussions*, N.Y. Daily News, Oct. 29, 2009, *available at* 2009 WLNR 21575530 (describing October 29, 2009 hearing before the House Judiciary Committee).

46 Broad Review of Concussions: Initial Roundtable Before the House Committee on Energy, Commerce, Oversight and Investigations, 114th Congress (2016).

47 *See* Mark Fainaru & Steve Fainaru, League of Denial: The NFL, Concussions, and the Battle for Truth 279–88 (2013).

48 Chantal Anderson, *State Lawmakers Approve Concussion Bills for Young Athletes*, Seattle Times, Mar. 11, 2009, *available at* 2009 WLNR 4637806.

49 Sheila Mickool, *The Story Behind the Zackery Lystedt Law*, Seattle Mag., Fall/Winter 2012, http://www.seattlemag.com/article/story-behind-zackery-lystedt-law, *archived at* http://perma.cc/3KLL-KWYY.

50 Wash. Rev. Code § 28A.600.190.

51 *NFL's Goodell Urges States to Adopt Concussion Law*, Ottawa Citizen (Canada), May 24, 2010, *available at* 2010 WLNR 26175330.

52 Nat'l Football League, 2014 Player Health & Safety Report 11 (2014), http://www.nflevolution.com/healthandsafetyreport/, *archived at* http://perma.cc/TPR2-5DE9.

53 Christine M. Baugh et al., *Requiring Athletes to Acknowledge Receipt of Concussion-Related Information and Responsibility to Report Symptoms: A Study of the Prevalence, Variation, and Possible Improvements*, 42 J. L., Med., & Ethics 297, 299 (2014) (explaining that Colorado, Connecticut, Mississippi, and New Hampshire are the only states that do not require the dissemination of such information).

54 *Id.*

55 *Id.*

56 *Id.*

57 Phoebe Anne Amberg, *Protecting Kids' Melons: Potential Liability and Enforcement Issues with Youth Concussion Laws*, 23 Marq. Sports L. Rev. 171, 183 (2012).

58 Ingram v. U.S., 12-cv-5892, 2014 WL 934363 (W.D.Wash. Mar. 10, 2014).

59 NFLPA Regulations, § 3(B)(28).

60 Jessica L. Roberts, et al., *Evaluating NFL Player Health and Performance: Legal and Ethical Issues*, U. Penn. L. Rev. (forthcoming 2017).

61 Jennifer K. Wagner & Charmaine D. Royal, *Field of Genes: An Investigation of Sports-Related Genetic Testing*, 12 J Pers. Med. 119 (2012) (the companies identified were: 23andMe, Inc.; Advanced Health Care Inc.; American International Biotechnology Services; Asper Bio Tech; Athleticode, Inc.; Atlas Sports Genetics, LLC; Cosmetics DNA; CyGene Direct; DNA4U; Family Tree DNA; Genetic Technologies Limited; My Gene; and, Warrior Roots).

62 *Id.*

63 George J. Annas & Sherman Elias, *23andMe and the FDA*, 370 N. Engl. J. Med. 985 (2014).

64 *Id.*

65 *Id.* It was determined that 23andMe's American competitors ceased offering DTC genetic tests by attempting to visit their websites. Specifically, Warrior Gene, Athleticode, Inc. and Cygene Direct no longer offer their sports-specific genetic tests.

66 Lisa M. Guth & Stephen M. Roth, *Genetic Influence on Athletic Performance*, 25 Curr. Opin. Pediatr. 653 (2013).

67 Yannis Pitsiladis et al., *Genomics of Elite Sporting Performance: What Little We Know and Necessary Advances*, 47 Br. J. Sports Med. 550 (2013).

68 *Id.*

69 Andrew Pollack, *F.D.A. Reverses Course on 23andMe DNA Test in Move to Ease Restrictions*, N.Y. Times, Feb. 19, 2015, http://www.nytimes.com/2015/02/20/business/fda-eases-access-to-dna-tests-of-rare-disorders.html?_r=0, *archived at* https://perma.cc/9ER6-UQTW?type=pdf.

Conclusion

We began this Report by explaining the pressing need for research into the overall health of NFL players; the need to address player health from all angles, both clinical and structural; and, the challenges presented in conducting such research and analysis. The issues and parties involved are numerous, complex, and interconnected. To address these issues—and ultimately, to protect and improve the health of NFL players—requires a diligent and comprehensive approach to create well-informed and meaningful recommendations for change. This has been precisely the focus of this Report.

We examined the wide variety of stakeholders in NFL player health and addressed the pertinent legal and ethical issues. Beginning with interviews of various stakeholders, we also took care to subject the Report to review by expert peer reviewers, our own Law & Ethics Advisory Panel, and the stakeholders themselves. Only by undertaking such a thorough approach is it possible to abide by our commitment to make realistic ethical and policy recommendations that can advance player health.

Nevertheless, our recommendations are only as useful as their implementation. For this reason, we make the following final recommendations.

Final Recommendation 1: The NFL, NFLPA and other stakeholders should actively engage with and publicly respond to this Report.[a]

We recognize that analyzing and implementing (or not) the recommendations contained in this Report will be complicated and challenging. Nevertheless, it is important that the stakeholders (particularly the NFL and NFLPA) take proactive steps to fulfill their respective and shared responsibilities for player health. We think a useful first step in that process is to review and publicly respond to this Report in such a way that demonstrates the steps they will take to fulfill their obligations as described herein.

As discussed in the Section: Ensuring Independence and Disclosure of Conflicts, we invited both the NFLPA and NFL to write a response to this Report, which we offered to publish on The Football Players Health Study website alongside the Report. The NFL took us up on this offer while the NFLPA did not.[b] While the NFL may disagree with us on certain issues, we nonetheless appreciate the time it took in reviewing our Report and providing a response. We remain hopeful that the NFL will engage with this Report and other stakeholders to implement our recommendations for improving player health. Similarly, although the NFLPA declined to write a response, we remain hopeful that the NFLPA will engage with this Report and other stakeholders to implement our recommendations for improving player health.

---

a   We recognize that certain stakeholders might not have a clearly defined representative to respond to this Report, such as second opinion doctors, family members, and fans. Nevertheless, we urge individuals within these stakeholder groups to engage with the Report and welcome their responses.

b   In declining the opportunity to write a response, the NFLPA stated as follows: "[O]ur primary objective in funding Harvard is to advance independent research on the many complex issues facing our members. Harvard's publications further that objective without formal comment by the PA."

Final Recommendation 2: The stakeholders identified in this Report, media, academics, and others should actively advocate, encourage, and monitor the promotion of player health.

Following this Report, we do not intend to be a passive voice in the process of improving player health. It is our hope to be able to periodically review the progress of the stakeholders in improving player health, and provide additional reports. However, in addition to any progress reports from the authors of this Report or The Football Players Health Study at Harvard University, we urge and trust that others, in particular the stakeholders themselves, will heed the messages in this Report and hold other stakeholders accountable.

The stakeholders' efforts to protect and promote player health would almost certainly be aided by communication and collaboration. Thus, when possible, the stakeholders should engage with one another to consider the issues discussed in this Report and consider actions to be taken.

Final Recommendation 3: As recommended throughout the Report, various stakeholders (e.g., club doctors, athletic trainers, coaches, contract advisors, and financial advisors) should adopt, improve and enforce Codes of Ethics.

Many of the stakeholders discussed in this Report have some form of an existing Code of Ethics that potentially regulates their interactions with players, including club doctors, athletic trainers, second opinion doctors, neutral doctors, personal doctors, coaches, equipment managers, contract advisors, financial advisors, and the media. These Codes of Ethics seem to have varying degrees of strength and record of enforcement, and thus have varying degrees of usefulness to players. There are important changes that need to be made to some of these Codes of Ethics. We have recommended that both the NFL Physicians Society (Recommendation 2:1-B) and NFL Coaches Association (9:1-A) adopt Codes of Ethics responsive to the unique circumstances of their employment in the NFL. We have also recommended that the Professional Football Athletic Trainers Society substantially amend its Code of Ethics to better reflect athletic trainers' obligations to players (3:1-B). In addition, we have recommended that substantial changes be made to the NFLPA's regulations governing contract advisors (12:2-A, 12:2-D, 12:2-E) and the NFLPA's regulations governing financial advisors (13:1-B). These changes are important steps these stakeholders can take in protecting and promoting player health.

In addition, enforcement is essential. Violations of a professional code of ethics should include meaningful punishments, ranging from warnings and censures to fines and suspensions. In order to be effective, the enforcement and disciplinary schemes for some of these stakeholders might need to be included in the CBA.

* * *

NFL football has a storied history and holds an important place in this country. The men who play it deserve to be protected and have their health needs met and it is our fervent hope that the health needs of these men will be met. We hope this Report succeeds in furthering that cause.

Appendices

APPENDIX A \ Concussion Protocol

**NFL Head, Neck and Spine Committee's Protocols Regarding
Diagnosis and Management of Concussion**

Introduction

Concussion is an important injury for the professional football player, and the diagnosis, prevention, and management of concussion is important to the National Football League, its players and member Clubs, and the National Football League Players Association. The NFL's Head, Neck and Spine Committee has developed a comprehensive set of protocols with regard to the diagnosis and management of concussions in NFL players.

The diagnosis and management of concussion is complicated by the difficulty in identifying the injury as well as the complex and individual nature of managing this injury. Ongoing education of players, NFL team physicians and athletic trainers regarding concussion is important, recognizing the evolving advances in concussion assessment and management. The objective of these protocols is to provide medical staffs responsible for the health care of NFL players with a process for diagnosing and managing concussion.

Concussion Defined: For purposes of these protocols, the term *concussion* is defined as (reference McCrory et al BJSM '13): A complex pathophysiological process affecting the brain induced by biomechanical forces. Several common features that incorporate clinical, pathologic and biomechanical injury constructs that may be utilized in defining the nature of a concussive head injury include:

1. Concussion may be caused either by a direct blow to the head, face, neck or elsewhere on the body with an "impulsive" force transmitted to the head.

2. Concussion typically results in the rapid onset of transient impairment of neurologic function that resolves spontaneously. However, in some cases, symptoms and signs may evolve over a number of minutes to hours.

3. Concussion may result in neuropathological changes, but the acute clinical symptoms largely reflect a functional disturbance rather than a structural injury and, as such, no abnormality is seen on standard structural neuroimaging studies.

4. Concussion results in a graded set of clinical symptoms that may or may not involve loss of consciousness. Resolution of the clinical and cognitive symptoms typically follows a sequential course; however, it is important to note that, in some percentage of cases, post-concussive symptoms may be prolonged.

2

Potential Concussion Signs (Observable)

- Any loss of consciousness;
- Slow to get up following a hit to the head ("hit to the head" may include secondary contact with the playing surface);
- Motor coordination/balance problems (stumbles, trips/falls, slow/labored movement);
- Blank or vacant look;
- Disorientation (e.g., unsure of where he is on the field or location of bench);
- Clutching of head after contact;
- Visible facial injury in combination with any of the above.

Potential Concussion Symptoms (Player reported, following direct or indirect contact)

- Headache;
- Dizziness;
- Balance or coordination difficulties;
- Nausea;
- Amnesia for the circumstances surrounding the injury (i.e., retrograde/anterograde amnesia);
- Cognitive slowness;
- Light/sound sensitivity;
- Disorientation;
- Visual disturbance;
- Tinnitus.

NFL Sideline Concussion Assessment:

The NFL Sideline Concussion Assessment is the standardized acute evaluation that has been developed by the NFL's Head Neck and Spine Committee to be used by team's medical staffs to evaluate potential concussions during practices and on game day. This evaluation is based on the Standardized Concussion Assessment Tool (SCAT2) published by the Concussion in Sport Group (McCrory '09), modified for use in the NFL in 2011, and consistent with the SCAT3 published in 2013 by the same international Concussion in Sport Group (McCrory '13) (Attachment A). The NFL Sideline Concussion Assessment can be used to aide in the diagnosis of concussion even if there is a delayed onset of symptoms. The NFL Sideline Concussion Assessment is also designed for serial testing, which allows it to be used across multiple occasions to track player recovery. Clubs shall maintain all NFL Sideline Concussion Assessment exams and a copy of the same shall be given to both the player and the team medical staff.

Being able to compare the results from the Sideline Concussion Assessment to the baseline information obtained in the preseason improves the value of this instrument. In all circumstances, the Team Physician or other physician designated by the Team Physician (e.g. neurosurgeon or Neurotrauma Consultant) shall assess the player in person. The Team Physician shall be responsible for determining whether the player is diagnosed as having a concussion

APPENDIX B \ Summary Of Health-Related Changes To The Collective Bargaining Agreements

Note: The below summaries represent our efforts to identify and describe those changes to the collective bargaining agreements (CBAs) that we believe affected player health as defined in this Report, but the summaries are not necessarily exhaustive.

CBA NUMBER: ONE

Date of Execution: November 20, 1968

Effective Begin Date: July 15, 1968

Effective End Date: February 1, 1970

Changes to Player Health Provisions:

1. Creation of "Bert Bell NFL Player Retirement Plan and Trust Agreement" ("Retirement Plan").

2. Creation of Group Medical Insurance policy.

3. Creation of Injury Grievance mechanism.

4. Creation of provision requiring clubs to provide worker's compensation benefits.

5. Creation of Injury Protection benefit.

CBA NUMBER: TWO

Date of Execution: March 29, 1971

Effective Begin Date: February 1, 1970

Effective End Date: January 31, 1974

Changes to Player Health Provisions:

1. Injury Grievances: Added impartial arbitration process; clarified filing and hearing process.

2. Creation of Disability Benefits plan.

3. Creation of Life Insurance policy.

4. Creation of Dental Benefits program for players and their families.

5. Off-Season Workouts: Parties "agree that no veteran player shall be required to perform any activities relating to professional football during the off-season except on a voluntary basis."

CBA NUMBER: THREE

Date of Execution: March 1, 1977

Effective Begin Date: February 1, 1974

Effective End Date: July 15, 1982

Changes to Player Health Provisions:

1. Retirement/Pension Plan: Vesting requirement reduced from five to four Credited Seasons for players who achieve fourth Credited Season in 1974 or later.

2. Group Medical Insurance: Major medical coverage increased to $250,000. Eighty percent of the first $3,000 and 100 percent of the excess eligible medical expenses will be reimbursed.

3. Disability Benefits: Benefits increased to $1,000/month for football injuries and $500/month for non-football injuries + $50/month for each dependent child.

4. Life Insurance: Coverage increased to $30,000 for rookies and an additional $5,000 per year for each Credited Season up to $50,000.

5. Dental Benefits: Coverage increased to $1,000 per year and orthodontics coverage added.

6. Off Season Workouts: Each club can hold one mandatory off-season training camp for veteran players which cannot exceed three days in length and will not include contact work. Teams with new coaches can hold two off-season camps and there is no limit on off-season camps for rookies. Players injured during off-season camps are protected "in the same manner as if injured during the club's pre-season training camp."

7. Pre-Season Training Camps: No player required to report to training camp more than 15 days before first preseason game or July 15, whichever is later.

8. Joint Committee on Player Safety and Welfare established "for the purpose of discussing the player safety and welfare aspects of playing equipment, playing surfaces, stadium facilities, playing rules, player-coach relationships, drug abuse prevention programs and any other relevant subjects." Committee has no power to bind either NFL or NFLPA on any issue.

9. Days Off: Players are entitled to at least four off days a month, though players can be required to receive medical treatment and quarterbacks can be required to attend meetings.

10. PUP List: Any player placed on the Physically Unable to Perform List will be paid at the rate of his full contract salary while on the List.

CBA NUMBER: FOUR

Date of Execution: December 11, 1982

Effective Begin Date: July 16, 1982

Effective End Date: August 31, 1987

Changes to Player Health Provisions:

1. Group Medical Insurance: Major medical coverage increased to $1 million.

2. Workers' Compensation: Addition of arbitration mechanism if amount of benefits is disputed.

3. Injury Protection: Maximum benefit increased to $65,000.

4. Disability Benefits: Benefits increased to $4,000/month for football injuries and $750/month for non-football injuries.

5. Life Insurance: Coverage increased to $50,000 for rookies and an additional $10,000 per year for each Credited Season up to $100,000.

6. Dental Benefits: Coverage increased to $2,000 per year.

7. Season Length: NFL must give 90 days' notice before increasing season to 16 games and must negotiate with NFLPA with regard to additional compensation, subject to arbitration if no agreement reached. Regular season cannot be extended beyond 18 games.

8. Severance Pay: Any player with at least two Credited Seasons who leaves the NFL is entitled to severance payment ranging from $5,000 to $140,000 depending on length of service.

9. Club Doctors: "Each club will have a board certified orthopedic surgeon as one of its club physicians. The cost of medical services rendered by club physicians will be the responsibility of the respective clubs. If a club physician advises a coach or other club representative of a player's physical condition which could adversely affect the player's performance or health, the physician will also advise the player."

10. Club Athletic Trainers: All full-time athletic trainers must be certified by the National Athletic Trainers Association.

11. Second Medical Opinion: Players entitled to second medical opinion paid for by club provided player first consults with club doctor and club doctor is provided with report from second opinion doctor.

12. Players' Right to a Surgeon of His Choice: Player entitled to choose his own surgeon at the club's cost provided player first consults with club doctor.

13. Pre-Season Physical: Each player will undergo a standardized minimum pre-season physical examination conducted by the club doctor.

14. Chemical Dependency: Clubs to pay for education and treatment related to chemical dependence.

15. Drug Testing: "The club physician may, upon reasonable cause, direct a player to [a treatment facility] for testing for chemical abuse or dependency problems. There will not be any spot checking for chemical abuse or dependency by the club or club physician."

16. Access to Medical Records: Player entitled to review his medical records twice per season. Players' doctor may obtain copies for use in rendering a medical opinion, but such copies cannot be released to the player or any other person.

CBA NUMBER: FIVE

Date of Execution: May 6, 1993

Effective Begin Date: March 29, 1993

Effective End Date: March 1, 2000

Changes to Player Health Provisions:

1. Retirement Plan: Future contributions to be made by NFL clubs as necessary to fund the Plan pursuant to certain actuarial assumptions and methods. Vesting requirement reduced to three Credited Seasons for players with at least one Credited Season during 1993. Early Retirement Option eliminated for players beginning career in 1993 or later. Amendment of Plan to include benefits for players who played prior to 1959.

2. Group Medical Insurance: Lifetime benefits increased up to a maximum of $1 million.

3. Injury Grievances: Addition of "presumption of fitness" if player passes preseason physical.

4. Worker's Compensation: Addition of joint study on workers' compensation laws and moratorium on lobbying on workers' compensation laws.

5. Injury Protection: Maximum benefits increased to $150,000–200,000 depending on year.

6. Disability Benefits: Benefits divided into five categories: (1) Active Football: $4,000/month; (2) Active Nonfootball: $4,000/month; (3) Football Degenerative: $4,000/month; (4) Inactive Nonfootball: $1,500/month; and, (5) Dependent Child: $100/month. Also, included retroactive increases for payments due under prior CBAs.

7. Life Insurance: Coverage increased to $100,000 for rookies and an additional $20,000 per year for each Credited Season up to $200,000.

8. Off-Season Workouts: Creation of minicamps instead. Clubs can conduct offseason workout programs for no more than sixteen weeks with four workouts per week. No more than 14 team practices. Contact work prohibited.

9. PUP List: Player's contract tolled if in last year and unable to perform after sixth regular season game.

10. Severance Pay: Players with at least two Credited Seasons to receive $5,000 for each Credited Season between 1989 and 1992 and $10,000 for each Credited Season between 1993 and 1999.

11. Club Doctors: If a player's "condition could be significantly aggravated by continued performance, the physician will advise the player of such fact in writing before the player is again allowed to perform on-field activity."

12. Pre-Season Physical: Substantially the same, plus inclusion of permission to "conduct random testing for steroids" with limits to be negotiated between Commissioner and NFLPA.

13. Access to Medical Records: Addition of player's permission to obtain records during the off-season upon request.

14. Creation of Steroid Testing: Clubs permitted to "conduct random testing for steroids" with limits to be negotiated between Commissioner and NFLPA.

15. Creation of Second Career Savings Plan: Each NFL club to contribute a total of $215,000 to plan per year. Participants in plan can receive various payout structures after age 45 if no longer employed by NFL club.

16. Creation of Supplemental Disability Insurance: Creation of a Voluntary Employees' Beneficiary Association (VEBA).[a] Increases benefit amounts due under the Retirement Plan.

17. Creation of Benefit Arbitrator to arbitrate any disputes concerning player benefits.

CBA NUMBER: SIX

Date of Execution: June 6, 1996

Effective Begin Date: March 29, 1993

Effective End Date: March 1, 2003

Changes to Player Health Provisions:

1. Injury Protection: Maximum benefits increased to $225,000 for 2000–2002.

2. Life Insurance: Coverage increased to $150,000 for rookies and an additional $30,000 per year for each Credited Season up to $300,000.

3. Off-Season Workouts: Healthy, veteran players prohibited from participating in club activities within 10 days prior to training camp; coaches can be fined if club does not comply with rules.

CBA NUMBER: SEVEN

Date of Execution: February 25, 1998

Effective Begin Date: March 29, 1993

Effective End Date: March 1, 2005

Changes to Player Health Provisions:

1. Retirement Plan: Increase in benefits for Credited Seasons prior to 1997; retroactive decrease in vesting requirement from five to four years for players prior to 1975.

2. Group Medical Insurance: Lifetime benefits increased up to a maximum of $2 million.

3. Worker's Compensation: Lobbying moratorium to end June 1, 1999.

4. Injury Protection: Maximum benefits increased to $250,000 for 2003–2004; players allowed to argue they should not have passed post-season physical.

5. Disability Benefits: Change in definitions: "A disability will be deemed 'permanent' if it has persisted or is expected to persist for at least 12 months from the date of its occurrence and if the Player is not an Active Player." Players can obtain disability benefits for psychological disorders caused by NFL activities.

6. Creation of Player Annuity Program: Establishment of program with NFL contribution $33 million in 1998 up to $73 million in 2001; player annuity amounts dependent on experience (four Credited Seasons minimum).

CBA NUMBER: EIGHT

Date of Execution: January 8, 2002

Effective Begin Date: March 29, 1993

Effective End Date: March 1, 2008

Changes to Player Health Provisions:

1. Group Medical Insurance: Lifetime benefits increased up to a maximum of $2.5 million.

2. Worker's Compensation: No moratorium on lobbying.

3. Injury Protection: Maximum benefits increased to $275,000 for 2006–2007.

4. Disability Benefits: Disability definition changed to that of the American Medical Association's "Guides to the Evaluation of Permanent Impairment."

5. Off-Season Workouts: Off-season workout programs reduced from 16 to 14 weeks; players cannot be at facility for more than four hours per day and not on the field for more than 90 minutes per day; NFLPA given authority to commence investigations; potential discipline against violators increased up to a 4th round draft pick for repeat offenders.

6. Joint Committee on Safety and Welfare: NFLPA has right to commence an investigation before the Joint Committee if it believes "that the medical care of a team is not adequately taking care of player safety." Neutral doctor will investigate and issue a report concerning the complaint.

7. Supplemental Disability Benefits: Payments to be made automatically to qualifying players unless they have waived the right to receive such benefits.

8. Creation of Tuition Assistance Plan: Establishment of plan whereby clubs will reimburse players for tuition up to $15,000/year.

---

a   A VEBA is a tax-free account created for the purpose of providing benefits to employees, such as insurance benefits, severance pay, sick leave, vacation benefits, etc.

CBA NUMBER: NINE

Date of Execution: March 8, 2006

Effective Begin Date: March 8, 2006

Effective End Date: March 1, 2013

Changes to Player Health Provisions:

1. Worker's Compensation: Clarifies method for calculating a club's right to offset a player's salary with any workers' compensation award.

2. Injury Protection: Maximum benefits increased to $350,000 for 2012.

3. Life Insurance: Coverage increased to $300,000 for rookies and an additional $100,000 per year for each Credited Season up to $800,000.

4. Severance Pay: Payments increased to $12,500 for each season between 2000 and 2008 and $15,000 for each season between 2009 and 2011.

5. Player Annuity Program: Clubs to contribute $65,000 per player with at least four Credited Seasons.

6. Tuition Assistance Plan: Program extended to players retired within last three years.

7. Creation of Health Reimbursement Account: NFL clubs to contribute based on actuarial assumptions and methods. Account credits up to $300,000 depending on number of Credited Seasons.

8. Creation of 88 Benefit: Establishment of plan to provide players with dementia up to $88,000 per year, paid for by NFL.

CBA NUMBER: TEN

Date of Execution: August 4, 2011

Effective Begin Date: August 4, 2011

Effective End Date: March 1, 2021

Changes to Player Health Provisions:

1. Retirement Plan: Benefit amounts increased for past seasons.

2. Group Medical Plan: Elimination of maximum coverage.

3. Injury Grievances: Establishment of Grievance Settlement Committee.

4. Worker's Compensation: Joint committee established to address workers' compensation in California.

5. Injury Protection: Maximum benefits increased to $1 million in 2011–2012 up to $1.2 million in 2019–2020. Players can now get "Extended Injury Protection" in second season after injury for $500,000 in 2012–2014 up to $575,000 in 2019–2020.

6. Disability Benefits: New plan created, providing for benefits up to $30,000 per year. "A disability will be deemed 'permanent' if it has persisted or is expected to persist for at least twelve months from the date of its occurrence." Categories of disability include: Active Football; Active Nonfootball; Inactive A; and, Inactive B.

7. Life Insurance: Coverage increased to $600,000 for rookies and an additional $200,000 per year for each Credited Season up to $1.6 million.

8. Off-Season Workouts: Offseason program reduced to nine weeks in three phases of varying intensity; establishment of uniform workout agreement.

9. Pre-Season Training Camps: Limitations imposed on two-a-day practices. Maximum of three hours of padded practice. All practices to be filmed.

10. Days Off: Generally, one off-day every seven days in preseason and four per month during regular and postseason.

11. Season Length: NFL can increase the number of regular season games only with NFLPA approval which may be withheld at the NFLPA's sole discretion.

12. Severance Pay: $17,500 for each season between 2012 and 2013 up to $22,500 for each season between 2017 and 2020.

13. Club Physicians: Clubs required to have orthopedic surgeon and internal, family medicine or emergency medicine physician. Club doctors must have Certificate of Added Qualification in Sports Medicine. Club required to have the following consultants: neurological; cardiovascular; nutrition; and, a neuropsychologist. New provision declaring that "each Club physician's primary duty in providing player medical care shall not be to the Club but instead to the player-patient."

14. Pre-Season Physical: Each player will undergo a standardized minimum pre-season physical examination conducted by the club physician. Clubs prohibited from conducting their own tests for PEDs or drugs or alcohol.

15. Access to Medical Records: Prohibition against showing records to any other person removed. NFL to develop and implement online, electronic medical record system.

16. Minicamps: Greater restrictions on types of activities, pursuant to off-season workout rules. Clubs can hold voluntary veteran minicamp. All minicamps must be videotaped.

17. Supplemental Disability Plan: Incorporated into new NFL Player Disability.

18. Player Annuity Program: Club contributions increase to $95,000 in 2018–2020.

19. Tuition Assistance Plan: Reimbursement amount increased to $20,000 in 2015–2020. Program available to players retired within the last four years if they have five Credited Seasons.

20. Health Reimbursement Account: Account credits cannot exceed $350,000.

21. 88 Benefit: Benefits increased to $100,000 per year, $130,000 beginning in 2016.

22. Regular Season and Post-Season Practices: Clubs limited to fourteen padded practices during the season and one per week in the postseason. On-field activities limited to three hours. Four days off during bye weeks. All practices to be filmed.

23. Role of NFLPA Medical Director: NFLPA Medical Director to be a voting member on all NFL healthy and safety committees and will have same access to data as NFL Medical Advisor.

24. Home Game Neutral Physician: "All home teams shall retain at least one [Rapid Sequence Intubation] RSI physician who is board certified in emergency medicine, anesthesia, pulmonary medicine, or thoracic surgery, and who has documented competence in RSI intubations in the past twelve months. This physician shall be the neutral physician dedicated to game-day medical intervention for on-field or locker room catastrophic emergencies."

25. Creation of Accountability and Care Committee: Committee established "which will provide advice and guidance regarding the provision of preventive, medical, surgical and rehabilitative care for players by all clubs." Committee has several identified tasks, including conducting a confidential survey every two years to solicit players' input regarding adequacy of medical care.

26. Creation of Legacy Benefit: Establishment of benefit for players who played prior to 1993. NFL to contribute $620 million.

27. Long Term Care Insurance Plan: Continues plan already in existence — players are able to obtain a long-term care insurance policy providing maximum benefits of $150/day for four years.

28. Creation of Former Player Life Improvement Plan: Plan formerly known as NFL Player Care Plan. Plan permits qualifying retired players not otherwise covered by health insurance to receive up to $250,000 in medical costs for "joint replacements, prescription drugs, assisted living, Medicare supplemental insurance, spinal treatment, and neurological treatment."

29. Neuro-Cognitive Disability Benefit: Permits qualifying retired players to receive no less than $3,000 per month for a maximum of 180 months. The medical standards for qualifying for this benefit were to be agreed upon by a Special Committee created by the parties made up of three healthcare professionals with expertise in neuro-cognitive disorders.

30. Support for Former Players: $22 million annually allocated to healthcare, benefits, funds and programs for former players as determined by the NFLPA.

31. Medical Research: $11 million annually allocated for medical research.

APPENDIX C \ Summary of Collectively Bargained Health-Related Programs and Benefits

Preliminary Note: The descriptions below are of various collectively bargained health-related programs and benefits. These programs are mentioned in the collective bargaining agreement (CBA) but the actual plan and benefit documents are separate from the CBA. The descriptions below are merely summaries as the actual plan and benefit documents are substantially longer and contain much greater detail and nuance. These descriptions should be not be taken as a complete statement of the benefits, rights, and obligations under the various plans.

Additionally, as a preliminary matter, player eligibility for many of the collectively bargained benefits discussed below depends on the number of "Credited Seasons" a player has earned. Generally, a player earns a Credited Season when he is entitled to be paid for at least three regular season games.[1]

RETIREMENT PLAN

First Created: 1968

Last Amended: 2011

2011 CBA Provision: Art. 53

Administrator: The Retirement Board, which consists of three members selected by the NFL Management Council (NFLMC)[a] and three members selected by the NFLPA. The current NFLMC members are: Dick Cass, President, Baltimore Ravens; Katie Blackburn, Executive Vice President, Cincinnati Bengals; and, Ted Phillips, President, Chicago Bears. The National Football League Players Association (NFLPA) members are former players Jeff Van Note, Robert Smith, and Sam McCullum. NFL Commissioner Roger Goodell is a nonvoting member and Chairman.

The members of the Retirement Board also serve as the members of the Disability Board, Savings Board, 88 Board, Annuity Board, and HRA Board, the plans of which are discussed in further detail below.

Description: Provides eligible players with retirement benefits, and offers survivor benefits for players' wives and family.

Eligibility: Generally, only "Vested Players" are eligible for retirement benefits. A Vested Player is a player who fits one of the following criteria: (1) has three or more Credited Seasons, including at least one Credited Season after 1992; (2) has four or more Credited Seasons, including at least one Credited Season after 1973; or, (3) has five or more Credited Seasons. In addition, regardless of the number of Credited Seasons a player has, if the player qualifies for permanent and total disability benefits under the Disability & Neurocognitive Disability Benefit Plan (discussed below) while an active player, the player can receive benefits under the Retirement Plan.

When Eligible: Vested Players can receive monthly retirement benefits for life beginning at age 55. Players with a Credited Season before 1993 can receive reduced monthly benefits as early as age 45. A player can elect to receive retirement benefits until his death or defer some of the benefits to his family upon death.

Payor: Contributions are made into a trust fund by NFL clubs each year according to certain actuarial assumptions.

Payment Type: Monthly.

Enrollment Type: Player must file for retirement benefits upon reaching age 55, but will automatically begin receiving the benefits at age 65 if nothing is filed.

---

a   NFL Management Council is the official name of the organization that collectively bargains on behalf of the NFL clubs.

Benefit Amount:

Table C-A:

Retirement Benefits (If taken after age 55)

Credited Season	Monthly Benefit Credit per Credited Season
Before 1982	$250
1982 through 1992	$255
1993 through 1994	$265
1995 through 1996	$315
1997	$365
1998 through 2011	$470
2012 through 2014	$560
2015 through 2017	$660
2018 through 2020	$760

In addition, the Retirement Plan includes $620 million in Legacy Benefits created as part of the 2011 CBA for players that played before 1993. The Legacy Benefits listed below are in addition to the Retirement Benefits listed above.

Table C-B:

Legacy Benefits

Credited Season	Monthly Benefit Credit per Credited Season
Before 1975	$124
1975 through 1992	$108

Additional Notes: According to the NFL, as of 2015, 3,641 former players receive an average monthly retirement benefit of $1,656,[2] for a total of approximately $72,353,952 annually. In addition, about 90 percent of those former players also received Legacy Benefit payments, with an average monthly payment of $723.85,[3] for a total of approximately $28,464,677 in Legacy Benefit payments. Thus, in 2015, the NFL Retirement Plan paid a little more than $100 million to former NFL players.

The Retirement Plan—which until 2011 also covered disability benefits—has historically been viewed negatively by former players. The filing process has been considered complex and lengthy,[4] resulting in many former players suing the Retirement Plan concerning their benefits.[5] During a 2007 hearing before the United States Senate Committee on Commerce, Science, and Transportation, it was revealed that only 317 former players were receiving disability benefits, out of the thousands that were eligible.[6]

Of additional concern, in recent years the NFLPA has been warning players that the Retirement Plan is underfunded.[7] Currently, the Plan only takes in enough money to cover about 54.5 percent of what it pays out,[8] jeopardizing its ability to pay retirement benefits in the future.

DISABILITY & NEUROCOGNITIVE BENEFIT PLAN

First Created: Disability benefits were first offered in 1970 and were historically available as part of the Retirement Plan. The Neurocognitive Disability Benefit was created as part of the 2011 CBA. The 2011 CBA also agreed to combine the disability components of the Retirement Plan, the Supplemental Disability Plan and the Neurocognitive Disability Benefit into this plan.

Last Amended: 2014

2011 CBA Provisions: Arts. 61, 65

Administrator: The Disability Board, which consists of the same members as the Retirement Board.

Description: Provides eligible players with disability benefits, including benefits based on neurocognitive disability.

Eligibility: A player is eligible for "Total and Permanent Disability Benefits" if the Initial Claims Committee[b] or Disability Board determines "(1) that he has become totally disabled to the extent that he is substantially prevented from or substantially unable to engage in any occupation or employment for remuneration or profit . . . , and (2) that such condition is permanent."

Each player is awarded benefits pursuant to one of four categories: (1) Active Football: the player is an active player and the disability "results from League football activities";[c] (2) Active Nonfootball: the player is an active player but the disability does not result from League football activities; (3) Inactive A: the player is a former player who filed for disability benefits within 15 years of his last Credited Season; or (4) Inactive B: the player is a former player who filed for disability benefits more than 15 years of his last Credited Season. Inactive A and Inactive B disability benefits are not dependent on the disability resulting from League football activities.

---

b   The Initial Claims Committee consists of three members: one appointed by the NFL, one appointed by the NFLPA, and a medical professional jointly chosen by the parties.
c   League football activities include any NFL "pre-season, regular-season, or post-season game, or any combination thereof, our out of League football activity supervised by a[] [Club], including all required or directed activities."

A player is eligible for "Line-of-Duty Disability Benefits" if the Initial Claims Committee or Retirement Board determines that the player "incurred a substantial disablement . . . arising out of [NFL] football activities." Line-of-Duty Disability Benefits address those injuries or disabilities that are not considered permanent.

A player is eligible for Neurocognitive Disability Benefits if: (1) the player is vested under the Retirement Plan; (2) the player is under age 55; (3) the player had at least one Credited Season after 1994; (4) the player does not receive Retirement Benefits; (5) the player does not receive Total and Permanent Disability Benefits; (6) the player executes a release releasing the NFL and clubs from any liability for head or brain injuries;[d] and, (7) the player is determined to have mild or moderate neurocognitive impairment.

A player has "mild neurocognitive impairment if he has problems with one or more domains of cognitive functioning which reflect acquired brain dysfunction but are not severe enough to cause marked interference in day-to-day activities."

A player has "moderate neurocognitive impairment if he has problems with one or more domains of cognitive functioning which reflect acquired brain dysfunction resulting in marked interference with everyday life activities, but not severe enough to prevent the Player from working."

A player must submit to a medical examination by a doctor of the Disability Board's choosing to determine if the player has neurocognitive impairment.

When Eligible: A player can receive Total and Permanent Disability Benefits as soon as the disability is established, retroactive to the time of application. Total and Permanent Disability Benefits continue so long as the player remains disabled and submits to medical examinations.

A player can receive Line-of-Duty Disability Benefits as soon as the disability is established, retroactive to the time of application, for a maximum of 90 months.

A player can receive Neurocognitive Disability Benefits as soon as the disability is established, retroactive to the time of application, for a maximum of 180 months. Also, the Neurocognitive Disability Benefits terminate

upon the player's 55th birthday regardless of when the benefits began.

Generally, a player cannot receive both retirement and disability benefits at the same time.

Payor: Contributions are made into a trust fund by NFL clubs each year.

Payment Type: Monthly.

Enrollment Type: Player must file for disability benefits.

Benefit Amount:

Table C-C:
Total and Permanent Disability Benefits

Type of Disability	Monthly Benefit
Active Football	$22,084
Active Nonfootball	$13,750
Inactive A	$11,250
Inactive B	$5,000

- **Line-of-Duty Disability Benefits:** $3,000/month.

- **Mild Neurocognitive Disability Benefits:** $2,250/month.

- **Moderate Neurocognitive Disability Benefits:** $4,000/month.

Additional Notes: As of July 31, 2015, 1,881 players are receiving disability benefits for an average of $5,178.33 a month,[9] for a total of approximately $116,885,264.

According to a 2010 analysis of the NFLPA's disability claims database, disability benefit applications had never exceeded 200 applications in a year until 2008 and 2009, when there were more than 400 claims in both years.[10] As of 2010, NFL disability benefit claims were approved approximately 38 percent of the time.[11] Importantly, the benefits criteria changed after the 2011 CBA, so current data would not be comparable. Moreover, according to the same analysis, of the players who filed for disability benefits, the mean age at which they retired from the NFL was 30.2 years.[12] Additionally, the mean age at which the player filed for disability benefits was 38.1 years.[13]

Finally, through the year 2009, there had been a total of 2,670 disability benefit claims, with 2,423 (90.7 percent) for orthopedic conditions, 52 (1.9 percent) for neurological conditions, 18 (0.7 percent) for psychological conditions, 18 (0.7 percent) for cardiovascular conditions, and 159 for other unspecified conditions (6.0 percent).[14]

---

d   The requirement of this release might prevent many otherwise qualified players from receiving Neurocognitive Disability Benefits to which they would otherwise be entitled. When asked, the NFL stated it was unable to provide the number of former players currently receiving neurocognitive disability benefits "without the consent of the NFL Players Association." The NFLPA declined to provide this consent or the number of former players who have filed for or are receiving these benefits, citing "player privacy and confidentiality concerns." We are not sure if we agree with these concerns. This information is de-identified aggregate data that is unlikely to reveal the personal medical information of any player.

SEVERANCE PAY

First Created: 1982

Last Amended: 2011

2011 CBA Provision: Art. 60

Administrator: NFLMC

Description: Player is eligible to receive severance pay for each Credited Season.

Eligibility: A player with at least two Credited Seasons, at least one of which was in 1993 or after.

When Eligible: 12 months after your last contract expired or was terminated. Payments generally begin within the quarter after claim accepted.

Payor: The club with whom the player last earned a Credited Season.

Payment Type: Single lump sum.

Enrollment Type: Player must file a claim with NFLMC.

Benefit Amount:

Table C-D:
Severance Pay Benefits[e]

Seasons	Amount for Each Credited Season
1989–92	$5,000
1993–99	$10,000
2000–08	$12,500
2009	$15,000
2010	0
2011	$15,000
2012–13	$17,500
2014–16	$20,000
2017–20	$22,500

PLAYER INSURANCE PLAN

First Created: 1968

Last Amended: 2011

2011 CBA Provision: Art. 59

Administrator: Aon Hewitt; Cigna

Description: Provides players and their family with life insurance, accidental death and dismemberment insurance, medical coverage, dental coverage, and wellness benefits. The wellness benefits include access to clinicians for mental health, alcoholism, and substance abuse, child and parenting support services, elder care support services, pet care services, legal services, and identity theft services.

Eligibility: Any player in the NFL, including practice squad players. Players who are vested under the Retirement Plan continue to receive coverage for five years after their career ends. Players who are not vested are only covered through the end of the plan year.

After their career has ended, players have the option of continuing coverage pursuant to the Consolidated Omnibus Budget Reconciliation Act (COBRA)[f] for a period of 18, 29 or 36 months. Players are required to pay the full cost of coverage plus 2 percent for administrative costs.

When Eligible: Generally, players are eligible on the first day of training camp.

Payor: Generally speaking, the clubs pay for the costs of the insurance programs, which, under the terms of the CBA, reduces the amount of money that can be paid to players in salary.

The club pays the entire cost of life insurance and accidental death and dismemberment insurance.

The players are responsible for copayments and deductibles of varying amounts depending on the types of medical and dental treatment being provided.

Payment Type: Insurance coverage and reimbursement as appropriate.

Enrollment Type: Player must complete enrollment paperwork.

---

e   Pursuant to the terms of the 2006 CBA, the NFL was not required to fund several benefit plans, including the Severance Pay Plan in 2010 if the 2010 season was not played with a Salary Cap — a situation which would only exist if the NFL and NFLPA were unable to agree to an extension of the CBA, which is what actually transpired. See 2006 CBA, Art. L; Art. LVI.

f   COBRA, 29 U.S.C. §§ 1161–69, requires continuation coverage to be offered to covered employees, their spouses, former spouses, and dependent children when group health coverage would otherwise be lost due to certain specific events, including, as would be relevant in the NFL, "the termination (other than by reason of such employee's gross misconduct), or reduction of hours, of the covered employee's employment." 29 U.S.C. § 1163(2).

Benefit Amount:

Table C-E:

Life Insurance Benefits

Number of Credited Seasons	Benefit Amount
6 or more	$1,600,000
5	$1,400,000
4	$1,200,000
3	$1,000,000
2	$800,000
1 or 0	$600,000

- **Accidental Death and Dismemberment Insurance:** Up to $50,000 depending on the injured body part.

- **Medical Coverage:** So long as the player is a member of the insurance plan, there is no limit to the amount of benefits the player can obtain.

- **Dental Coverage:** Limited to $2,000 per person per year.

SECOND CAREER SAVINGS PLAN

First Created: 1993

Last Amended: 2011

2011 CBA Provision: Art. 54

Administrator: The Savings Board, which consists of the same members as the Retirement Board.

Description: A 401(k) plan that helps players save for retirement in a tax-favored manner.

Eligibility: All NFL players, regardless of the number of Credited Seasons.

When Eligible: Players can receive their benefits after the player is 45 provided the player is not employed by a club, or after the player is 59½.

Payor: Players and their clubs.

Payment Type: The player can receive the benefits in a variety of forms: (1) a single lump sum payment; (2) installments over ten years; (3) an annuity for the player's life; and, (4) an annuity for the player's life and surviving spouse's life.

Enrollment Type: Players are automatically enrolled in the plan, with 10 percent of their pre-tax salary going towards the plan. Players can change the amount of their contributions or opt out of the plan at any time.

Benefit Amount: Players can contribute up to the maximum permitted by the IRS ($18,000 in 2016). The player's club is required to contribute a minimum of: $1,000 if the player has exactly one Credited Season; $7,200 if the player has exactly two Credited Seasons; and, $3,600 if the player has three or more Credited Seasons.

In addition, the club will contribute $2 for every $1 contributed by a player during a year in which the player earned a Credited Season, provided the player has at least one Credited Season, up to a maximum of $26,000 between 2015–18, and $28,000 between 2019–20.

Notes: According to the NFLPA, 99 percent of NFL players are enrolled in the Second Career Savings Plan.[15]

TUITION ASSISTANCE PLAN

First Created: 2002

Last Amended: 2011

2011 CBA Provision: Art. 56

Administrator: NFLMC

Description: Players receive reimbursement for tuition, fees, and books from attending an eligible education institution.

Eligibility: All current NFL players with at least one Credited Season. Former players with at least five Credited Seasons are also eligible provided that the costs are incurred within four years of the player's last season.

When Eligible: Players must have received a "C" or better in the course and submit their claim for reimbursement within six months of when the final grade is issued.

Payor: The player's club pays the benefits. NFLMC pays administrative costs and expenses.

Payment Type: Lump-sum payment within 75 days after player's application is received.

Enrollment Type: Player must complete application and include copies of all receipts.

Benefit Amount: The maximum reimbursement is $20,000 per year. A former player with at least five Credited Seasons is eligible for up to $60,000 in reimbursements.

Note: For context, according to the College Board, the average tuition at a public four-year university for an in-state student is $9,410; the average tuition at a public four-year university for an out-of-state student is $23,893; and, the average tuition at a private four-year university is $32,405.[16]

THE 88 PLAN

First Created: 2006

Last Amended: 2012

2011 CBA Provision: Art. 58

Administrator: The 88 Board, which consists of the same members as the Retirement Board.

Description: Provides former players suffering from dementia, amyotrophic lateral sclerosis (ALS) or Parkinson's disease with benefits. The 88 Plan is named for John Mackey, a Hall of Fame tight end for the Baltimore Colts and San Diego Chargers from 1963 to 1972, who wore number 88 during his career. Mackey suffered from dementia later in life and died in 2011 at the age of 69.

Eligibility: Vested Players under the Retirement Plan and players who have received Total and Permanent Disability Benefits under the Disability & Neurocognitive Benefit Plan who have been diagnosed with dementia, ALS, or Parkinson's disease. The 88 Committee, consisting of an NFLMC designee and an NFLPA designee, determine whether the player qualifies for the benefit.

When Eligible: A player is eligible upon diagnosis.

Payor: Contributions are made into a trust fund by NFL clubs each year.

Payment Type: The 88 Plan will reimburse or pay the following costs for medical care that are related to a player's dementia, ALS, or Parkinson's disease: institutional care; home custodial care provided by an unrelated third party; physician services; durable medical equipment; and, prescription medication.

The player must file claims for reimbursement within 12 months of the later of the date medical care was rendered or the date the bill for covered expenses was received.

Enrollment Type: Player must apply for the benefits.

Benefit Amount: A maximum of $130,000 per year.

Notes: As of 2014, 214 former players were receiving funds from The 88 Plan.[17]

FORMER PLAYER LIFE IMPROVEMENT PLAN

First Created: 2007

Last Amended: 2011

2011 CBA Provision: Art. 64

Administrator: Aon Hewitt

Description: Plan permits qualifying former players (and in some cases their dependents) not otherwise covered by health insurance to receive reimbursement for medical costs for "joint replacements, prescription drugs, assisted living, Medicare supplemental insurance, spinal treatment, and neurological treatment."

Eligibility: Former NFL players who are vested under the Retirement Plan. However, there are many benefits under this plan, some of which have additional eligibility requirements, so not every player is eligible for every benefit.

When Eligible: Generally, upon the end of the player's career.

Payor: Contributions to the plan are made by the clubs on a per-capita basis to a trust in amounts sufficient to pay estimated benefits and expenses.

Payment Type: Reimbursement and grants to assist eligible players in need.

Enrollment Type: Player must file.

Benefit Amount:

- **Joint Replacement Benefits:** A maximum of $5,250, or $10,500 in the case of a bilateral procedure.

- **Discount Prescription Drug Benefits:** Unspecified discounts for prescription drugs.

- **Life Insurance Benefits:** Term life insurance in an amount equal to $20,000, plus $2,000 for each Credited Season in excess of the number of Credited Seasons the player was required to have to vest under the Retirement Plan, up to a maximum of $50,000.

- **Assisted Living Benefits:** Special discounts and preferred access at Brookdale Senior Living and Silverado Senior Living facilities.

- **Medicare Benefit:** A range of Medicare Supplemental Insurance plans to former players are available.

- **Spine Treatment Benefit:** Access to top tier medical centers that have particular expertise in treating spinal conditions. However, the plan generally does not cover the costs of any treatment or provide for any discounts.

- **Neurological Benefit:** Access to top tier medical centers that have particular expertise in treating neurological conditions. However, the plan generally does not cover the costs of any treatment or provide for any discounts.

- **Wellness Benefit:** Includes access to clinicians for mental health, alcoholism, and substance abuse, child and parenting support services, elder care support services, pet care services, legal services, and identity theft services.

PLAYER ANNUITY PLAN

First Created: 1998

Last Amended: 2011

2011 CBA Provision: Art. 55

Administrator: The Annuity Board, which consists of the same members as the Retirement Board.

Description: Provides deferred compensation to players. The Annuity Plan invests the players' collective deferred compensation. The Annuity Plan is divided between a Qualified Account and a Nonqualified Account. The Qualified Account includes the maximum amount of compensation that can be deferred on a pre-tax basis pursuant to IRS rules. The maximum amount that could be deferred on a pre-tax basis in 2016 was $53,000.[18] The amount contributed to the Annuity Plan above this amount is the Nonqualified Account portion and must be taxed before being invested as part of the Annuity Plan.

Eligibility: A current or former player with at least one Credited Season. A player does not vest in his Qualified Account until he has earned at least three Credited Seasons. In contrast, a player is always vested in his Nonqualified Account.

When Eligible: A player can elect to receive a distribution at any time after he is done playing, provided the player is at least 45, or is at least 35 and five years have elapsed since the player last earned a Credited Season. Distributions must begin no later than the first day of the month after the player turns 65.

Payor: Paid from player's own deferred compensation.

Table C-F:
Annuity Plan Benefits

Credited Seasons	Total Amount Allocated to Annuity Plan for That Season
1	$0
2	$5,000
3	$5,000
4	$70,000
5 or more	$80,000

The reason for the large increase in allocation from the third to fourth Credited Season is likely due to the vesting requirements. As stated earlier, a player is not vested in his Qualified Account—which represents the bulk of the Annuity Plan contribution—until after his third Credited Season. If he does not vest in the Qualified Account, it is forfeited. Thus, by minimizing the amounts allocated before players vest in the Annuity Plan, the Annuity Plan minimizes the amount of deferred compensation that might be forfeited.

Payment Type: Players may elect different distributions forms for each of their accounts and different dates for payments to begin. Payment forms include: (1) annual installments until the player reaches 45; (2) an annuity for life; (3) a reduced annuity for your life, with a survivor annuity beginning after the player's death; (4) a lump sum, if the former player is at least 45 when the lump sum is to be paid; and, (5) a partial lump sum, if the player is at least 45 when the partial lump sum is paid, with the remainder paid in one of the other payment forms.

Enrollment Type: Automatic.

Benefit Amount: The benefit the player receives depends on: the value of the player's account; the player's age; the player's marital status; and, the type of payment plan selected by the player.

HEALTH REIMBURSEMENT ACCOUNT PLAN

First Created: 2006

Last Amended: 2011

2011 CBA Provision: Art. 63

Administrator: The HRA Board, which consists of the same members as the Retirement Board.

Description: Helps to pay out-of-pocket healthcare expenses after players are no longer employed by an NFL Club and after the period of extended medical coverage under the Player Insurance Plan that is paid by the NFL has ended.

Eligibility: (1) Players with at least eight Credited Seasons and whose last Credited Season was in 2004 or 2005; or (2) Players with at least three Credited Seasons and whose last Credited Season was in 2006 or later.

When Eligible: Player is eligible to withdraw amounts from Health Account for medical expenses incurred provided he files for reimbursement within 24 months of receiving the medical bill to be reimbursed.

Payor: Clubs contribute the amounts to the Health Account. Players do not contribute their own money to their Health Account.

Payment Type: Lump sum.

Enrollment Type: Automatic.

Benefit Amount:

Table C-G:
Health Reimbursement Account Benefits[g]

Credited Seasons	Health Account Contribution per Credited Season
2009 and prior	$25,000
2010	$0
2011 through 2015	$25,000
2016 through 2020	$30,000

LONG TERM CARE INSURANCE PLAN

First Created: 2011

Last Amended: 2011

2011 CBA Provision: Art. 62

Administrator: NFL

Description: Provides medical insurance to cover the costs of long-term care.

Eligibility: Vested players under the Retirement Plan who are between the ages of 50 and 76, who have been certified by a licensed healthcare provider as requiring critical supervision, or requiring the presence of another person within arm's reach due to inability to perform a required number of defined activities of daily living.

When Eligible: Player is eligible for the insurance as soon as he meets the eligibility requirements.

Payor: It is uncertain what the NFL and players' obligations are with respect to the Long Term Care Insurance Plan, as we were unable to obtain Plan documents.

Payment Type: Uncertain.

Enrollment Type: Player must enroll.

Benefit Amount: $150 a day for a maximum of four years.

---

g   Pursuant to the terms of the 2006 CBA, the NFL was not required to fund several benefit plans, including the Health Reimbursement Account in 2010 if the 2010 season was not played with a Salary Cap — a situation which would only exist if the NFL and NFLPA were unable to agree to an extension of the CBA, which is what actually transpired. See 2006 CBA, Art. L; Art. LVI.

Endnotes

1   *See* Bert Bell/Pete Rozelle NFL Player Retirement Plan (Apr. 1, 2012) § 1.11 (defining "Credited Season"); 2011 CBA, Art. 26, § 2 (same).

2   Aaron Gordon, *Battle for Benefits, Part 3: "Don't Make Proud Men Beg"*, Vice Sports (Sept. 18, 2015), https://sports.vice.com/en_us/article/battle -for-benefits-part-3-dont-make-proud-men-beg, *archived at* https:// perma.cc/YP4J-8AGY.

3   *Id.*

4   *See* Mark Fainaru & Steve Fainaru, League of Denial: The NFL, Concussions, and the Battle for Truth 86–87 (2013).

5   Pursuant to the Employee Retirement Income Security Act ("ERISA"), individuals claiming entitlement to benefits under a retirement plan are entitled to bring a civil action to enforce or clarify their rights under the plan. 29 U.S.C. § 1132(a). Former players routinely sue the Retirement Plan alleging they were wrongfully denied benefits, with mixed success. *See, e.g.,* Atkins v. Bert Bell/Pete Rozelle NFL Player Retirement Plan, 694 F.3d 557 (5th Cir. 2012) (plan administrator's determination that player was not entitled to additional benefits was not an abuse of discretion); Giles v. Bert Bell/Pete Rozelle NFL Player Retirement Plan, 925 F. Supp. 2d 700 (D.Md. 2012) (Retirement Board's classification of participant's disability as "Inactive" rather than "Football Degenerative" was not reasonable decision supported by substantial evidence in the record); Moore v. Bert Bell/Pete Rozelle NFL Player Retirement Plan, 282 Fed.Appx. 599 (9th Cir. 2008) (Retirement Board's decision to terminate player's benefits was not based on reasonable interpretation of plan's terms); Johnson v. Bert Bell/Pete Rozelle NFL Player Retirement Plan, 468 F.3d 1082 (8th Cir. 2006) (plan administrator did not abuse its discretion in setting date of disability as time of disability determination by physician to whom plan had referred former player); Boyd v. Bert Bell/ Pete Rozelle NFL Players Retirement Plan, 410 F.3d 1173 (9th Cir. 2005) (administrator did not abuse its discretion in rejecting retiree's claim, given ambiguity as to cause of neurologic disability at issue); Courson v. Bert Bell NFL Player Retirement Plan, 75 F. Supp. 2d 424 (W.D.Pa. 1999) *aff'd* 214 F.3d 136 (3d Cir. 2000) (plan administrator's determination that former player was not disabled was not arbitrary or capricious); Brumm v. Bert Bell NFL Retirement Plan, 995 F.2d 1433 (8th Cir. 1993) (trustees' interpretation of ERISA plan to allow higher level of disability benefits only in cases involving single, identifiable football injury, and excluding cases of disability resulting from football career's overall impact on body was unreasonable in light of plan's goals).

6   *Oversight of the National Football League (NFL) Retirement System: Hearing Before the Comm. On Commerce, Sci. & Transp.*, 110th Cong. 1177 (2007), *available at* http://www.gpo.gov/fdsys/pkg/CHRG -110shrg76327/html/CHRG-110shrg76327.htm, *archived at* https:// perma.cc/RK38-GBYQ?type=pdf.

7   Aaron Gordon, *Battle for Benefits, Part 3: "Don't Make Proud Men Beg"*, Vice Sports (Sept. 18, 2015), https://sports.vice.com/en_us/article/battle -for-benefits-part-3-dont-make-proud-men-beg, *archived at* https:// perma.cc/YP4J-8AGY.

8   *Id.*

9   Aaron Gordon, *Battle for Benefits, Part 1: "Why Do I Have to Fight You Now?"*, Vice Sports (Sept. 16, 2015), https://sports.vice.com/en_us /article/battle-for-benefits-part-1-why-do-i-have-to-fight-you-now, *archived at* https://perma.cc/FK7X-G3BN.

10 Edgeworth Economics, *DRAFT Dangers of the Game: Injuries in the NFL —Analysis for the NFLPA* (Sept. 6, 2010), http://esq.h-cdn.co/assets /cm/15/07/54dae83730ce3_-_Dangers-of-the-Game-Draft-Esquire.pdf, *archived at* https://perma.cc/X976-GYPU?type=pdf.

11 *Id.*

12 *Id.*

13 *Id.*

14 *Id.*

15 *Quotes from NFLPA Press Conference*, NFLPA (Feb. 4, 2016), https ://www.nflpa.com/news/all-news/quotes-from-nflpa-sb50-press -conference, *archived at* https://perma.cc/2GZH-FQ37.

16 *See Average Published Undergraduate Charges by Sector, 2015–16*, CollegeBoard, http://trends.collegeboard.org/college-pricing/figures-tables/ average-published-undergraduate-charges-sector-2015-16 (last visited Mar. 17, 2016), *archived at* https://perma.cc/HNW6-FBKG.

17 Ken Belson, *Dementia Care, Tailored to N.F.L. Retirees*, N.Y. Times, Mar. 22, 2016, http://www.nytimes.com/2016/03/23/sports/dementia -care-tailored-to-nfl-retirees.html, *archived at* https://perma.cc/P3E4 -WXRV.

18 *See IRS Announces 2016 Pension Plan Limitations; 401(k) Contribution Limit Remains Unchanged at $18,000 for 2016*, Internal Revenue Service, Oct. 21, 2015, https://www.irs.gov/uac/Newsroom/IRS -Announces-2016-Pension-Plan-Limitations%3B-401(k)-Contribution -Limit-Remains-Unchanged-at-$18,000-for-2016, *archived at* https:// perma.cc/G28S-9K6R.

APPENDIX D \ Summary Of Programs Offered by NFL's Player Engagement Department[a]

To Whom Available	Program	Program Description (According to NFL)
High School Student-Athletes	NFL PREP 100	Program includes: Classroom sessions on player health and safety; On-field instructions highlighting technical drills and techniques; Insight on the academic and athletic experiences of a professional athlete from current and former NFL players; Leadership Development training by the National Guard; and, classroom sessions led by NCAA representatives to explain the most up-to-date information regarding eligibility, recruiting, and compliance information for parents and student-athletes.
High School Student-Athletes	NFL Prep Sports Career Expo	The NFL Prep Sports Career Expo, produced in conjunction with Why Not Sports, Inc., enlists professionals from all aspects of the sports industry to inform, educate, and enlighten student-athletes on career opportunities within the professional sports arena. Students are educated about the academic requirements needed to successfully transition from high school to college and are enlightened about a broad spectrum of career opportunities within the sports industry outside of being a professional athlete.
Rising Senior High School Student-Athletes	Prep Leadership Program	Program includes: Basics of Leadership — assessments, styles, motivating others; Professional Development — life skills, social media; Career Development — preparing for the future (resume, mock-interview, public speaking, networking); Financial Education — introduction to financial terms, tools, and the role of financial advisors; and, Basics of Management.
High School Student-Athletes in Baltimore	1st & Goal Program	The 1st & Goal program focuses on supporting student athletes with meeting and exceeding academic standards including improving grades, attendance, and graduation rates. The program supports the social-emotional growth of each athlete through a curriculum that focuses on financial literacy, character development, conflict resolution, mentoring, communications and health, safety and wellness. NFL Player Engagement has partnered with the Family League of Baltimore and selected The Academies at Frederick Douglass High School as the target athletic program. The Family League of Baltimore is a non-profit organization that convenes, coordinates, and funds programs to strengthen the lives of children and families in the Baltimore area with the hope of improving the lives of the city's youth from birth to their entry into adulthood.

a   These programs can be found at the NFL's Player Engagement Department website at https://www.nflplayerengagement.com.

To Whom Available	Program	Program Description (According to NFL)
NCAA Student-Athletes	NFL-NCAA Life Skills Roundtable	The NFL-NCAA Life Skills Roundtable for Student-Athletes is designed to provide student-athletes with a forum to discuss the resources and support that they need in order to meet their personal and professional goals. Through intimate discussions with a diverse representation of student-athletes (sport, gender, ethnicity), the NFL and the NCAA will gain a better understanding of the personal and professional development needs and goals of student-athletes. The student-athletes will also afford the opportunity to participate in professional development seminars as well as assessments to increase self-awareness.
Rookie NFL players	Rookie Transition Program	The NFL Rookie Transition Program is an orientation for all drafted and undrafted rookies based on the four principles of NFL History, Total Wellness, Experience and Professionalism. The symposium includes presentations, videos, and workshops focused on these principles as well as other topics, including player health and safety, decision making, mental health, substance abuse and domestic violence prevention, non-discrimination, and maintaining positive relationships. Rookies are provided with resources and best practices to assist them with their shared responsibility in successfully identifying off-the-field challenges and transitioning from college to the professional level. *The Rookie Transition Program is the only program listed here that is mandatory.*
Current players	Continuing Education	The Continuing Education Program (CEP) assists current and former NFL players to complete their undergraduate degree, pursue graduate studies and utilize other educational opportunities to prepare for life after football. The CEP partners with colleges and universities across the country to design detailed plans to assist players in reaching their educational goals. By working closely with academic advisors, these individualized educational plans may include opportunities to pursue coursework in a player's franchise city, at his original institution or through distance learning via Internet-based coursework. Players who have already completed their undergraduate degree may opt to participate in graduate school or professional certification programs aimed at enhancing their skills and abilities. The CEP can assist players to identify appropriate, accredited schools, provide guidance on admission requirements including graduate exams (GRE, GMAT, LSAT, etc.) and assist players in the preparation of their graduate application.
Current players	Financial Education	The National Football League Financial Education Program (FEP) provides players with valuable knowledge to manage their personal finances and improve financial decision-making. The objective of the program is to ensure the long-term financial stability of players throughout the League. The program offers players resources and a realistic perspective on the current economic environment. The non-credit seminars teach players about cash management, insurance, tax planning, estate planning, investments, retirement planning and other related topics.

Appendix D: Summary Of Programs Offered By NFL's Player Engagement Department (continued)

To Whom Available	Program	Program Description (According to NFL)
Current and former NFL players	Broadcast Boot Camp	A hands-on program that offers current and former NFL players the opportunity to explore multiple on-air job functions in the television/media business. The program includes sessions on tape study, editing, show preparation, radio production, control room operation, studio preparation, production meetings, field reporting and game preparation. Each player has the opportunity to tape segments in a studio environment as a game analyst and as a field reporter. Players are also able to experience what life is like in the broadcast booth and in other media positions.
Current and former NFL players	NFL Business Management and Entrepreneurial Program	The NFL Business Management and Entrepreneurial Program is a joint effort between the NFL, the NFLPA and premiere graduate business schools. These custom programs seek to improve players' ability to evaluate business opportunities through interactive workshops, stimulating discussions and practical knowledge. This program is ideal for NFL players interested in owning, operating or building their own businesses. Topics covered include: personal investments, non-profit and social awareness foundations, business plan review and assessment, property management, operations and cash-flow management, recruiting, hiring, and human resource management. Players are provided the opportunity to look at realistic business scenarios and dissect opportunities they may be considering. The Wharton School, University of Pennsylvania, Harvard Business School, Kellogg School of Management, Northwestern University, University of Notre Dame, and, the Stanford Graduate School of Business are all participating schools in the program.
Current and former NFL players	Business of Music Boot Camp	The NFL Business of Music Boot Camp is an intensive immersion program for current and former NFL players who are interested in understanding the essential components and make up of today's music industry. Utilizing the world-renowned faculty of NYU's Clive Davis Institute of Recorded Music, top industry professionals, and internationally recognized artists, participants experience the creative process first-hand via classroom sessions and round table discussions. Over the course of four days, participants will engage in discussions and interactive workshops covering all contemporary aspects of the music industry including production, artist development, digital music, publishing, artist management, marketing, and touring. Participants will gain a better understanding of the steps they should take to pursue a successful career in the music industry and will learn how to turn their creative ideas into concrete business plans.
Current and former NFL players	Hospitality & Culinary Management Workshop	Hosted at New York City's award winning Institute for Culinary Education, the Hospitality & Culinary Management Workshop introduces participants to the fundamental skills required for success in the hospitality and culinary industries. Whether you're considering owning or managing a small inn, a large hotel chain, a local café, or a five-star restaurant, learning from some of the best in the business will help you avoid the pitfalls of the industry and get a head start on your future career.

To Whom Available	Program	Program Description (According to NFL)
Current and former NFL players	NFL-NCAA Coaches Academy	The program provides 30 current and former NFL players with tools and networking opportunities for potential careers as football coaches. Many of the participants currently have high school or college coaching positions. The NCAA also invites football coaches who have less than eight years of college coaching experience to take part. This is an excellent opportunity for players who are looking to continue their careers on the football sidelines to learn leadership, management and administrative skills from football coaches at all levels.
		Sessions include instruction from NFL, college and high school coaches, business leaders and athletic administrators. Topics include how to build a personal and professional brand; managing budgets; successful networking; media messaging; coaching contracts; building relationships in college; effective leadership; understanding the academic landscape; and, the interview process. Participants also experience mock interview sessions.
Current and former NFL players	Pro Hollywood Boot Camp	The NFL Pro Hollywood Boot Camp is an intensive filmmaking workshop for players aspiring to careers in the motion picture industry. Through classroom learning and practical application, current and former NFL players receive a crash course in the art of moviemaking and are introduced to various disciplines and careers in the film business.
Current and former NFL players	Consumer Products Boot Camp	The NFL Consumer Products department is the architect of the NFL's brand as it relates to Retail products, On-Field product, Club Practice Gear and Promotional items. This division works with NFL licensing partners and retailers to identify key product trends and new business opportunities.
		This custom program is tailored to those who are interested in learning more about the consumer products design, licensing, and manufacturing industries. Under the guidance of faculty from the University of Maryland Robert H. Smith School of Business and official NFL Licensees, participants will receive an overview of the consumer products field with a focus on business planning, product marketing, and industry trends and practices. A tour of a licensee campus and an exclusive visit to the NFL's Consumer Products Summit will enhance the lessons learned in classroom sessions and provide a great backdrop for the extensive mentoring and networking opportunities available.
		The four days will culminate in a Group Pitch Project in which participants will compete in groups to develop, create, and deliver a product pitch to a panel comprised of League executives and industry experts.

Appendix D: Summary Of Programs Offered By NFL's Player Engagement Department (continued)

To Whom Available	Program	Program Description (According to NFL)
Current and former NFL players, along with spouses	Franchising Boot Camp	The NFL Franchising Boot Camp, open to current and former players and their significant others, focuses on the franchising industry and how to take advantage of the resources and business practices franchisors provide to their franchisees. The program will cover the types of businesses that rely on franchising, where to get information about them, how to devise a franchise business plan, what annual and daily operational costs to expect, how to put together a winning team and whether or not franchising is right for each player and spouse.
Former NFL players	Legends Community	The NFL Legends Community is designed to connect former players with each other, their former teams and the NFL. Twenty Legends will lead the outreach and assist the NFL in administering the NFL Legends Community.
Former NFL players and spouses	Transition Assistance Program	The NFL Transition Assistance Program (TAP) marks the evolution of the NFL Career Transition Program (CTP), which hosted over 250 former NFL players from 2010–2013. TAP has been created in a partnership with former players and Georgia Tech faculty experts. The purpose of TAP is to provide transitioning players and their significant others peer to peer support through relationships with trained NFL Transition Coaches (former players) who will emphasize a holistic approach to Total Wellness. Transition is a continuous process unique to each individual's situation. At TAP, all attendees will chart their specific course through conversations with others who have experienced the physical, psychological, and social aspects of transition. The curriculum also features sessions pertaining to fitness, nutrition, career development, financial success, and much more. Upon completion of the program, attendees will leave with their Transition Playbook resource guide, which includes customized tools for success, Player Engagement resources, and NFL Player Benefits information.
Minorities interested in coaching	Bill Walsh NFL Minority Coaching Fellowship	The Bill Walsh NFL Minority Coaching Fellowship is an annual program administered by the NFL Management Council and NFL Player Engagement. The program's objective is to use NFL clubs' training camps, offseason workout program and minicamps to give talented minority coaches opportunities to: observe; participate; gain experience; and, ultimately gain a full-time NFL coaching position. Designed as a vocational tool to increase the number of full-time NFL minority coaches, all 32 NFL clubs participate in the program on an annual basis. Participants are hired for the duration of training camp, including all pre-season games, and clubs are encouraged to hire a minimum of four participants.

To Whom Available	Program	Program Description (According to NFL)
Potential head coaches	NFL-NCAA Champion Forum	The NFL-NCAA Champion Forum is an educational forum where individuals who have been identified as a potential head coaches by administrators in the membership will simulate the intercollegiate interview process from researching the position to their first staff meeting after becoming a head coach. By achieving the following objectives, the forum is providing tailored education to future head coaches at the intercollegiate level.
Potential college football coaches	NFL-NCAA Future Football Coaches Academy	The NFL-NCAA Future Football Coaches Academy is an educational forum where individuals who have recently completed their collegiate eligibility, and have a desire to enter the college football coaching profession, will learn about and explore football coaching careers with a primary focus on intercollegiate athletics. By achieving the following objectives, the academy is educating participants on the various aspects of securing, managing and excelling as a coach at the intercollegiate level.
Head football coaches, athlete development professionals, clinicians, and directors of football operations from the NCAA and NFL	NFL-NCAA Summit	The summit allows each group participating individual sessions focused on becoming a more informed and educated administrator and coach. A clinician led session provides attendees with valuable skill enhancement and professional development education focused on protecting the mental and physical well-being of athletes. In addition, participants spend time together to discuss key cross collaboration opportunities that will allow them to serve student-athletes, professional athletes and executives in a more informed and efficient fashion.
Aspiring journalists and communications professionals	Sports Journalism & Radio Boot Camp	Hosted at Bowling Green State University, the Sports Journalism & Radio Boot Camp will provide aspiring journalist and communications professionals the opportunity to hear the latest from industry leaders; find out what social media options are available, including creating your own blog; and, learn what it would take to become a sports communications professional at the pro or college level.

APPENDIX E \ Summary of Programs Offered by the NFLPA[1]

To Whom Available	Program	Program Description (According to NFLPA)
Current players	Externship Program	Matches current players with companies for a 3-week internship during the offseason. In 2015, the NFLPA matched 25 players with 9 organizations, including an ESPN radio station, Comcast SportsNet, Under Armour, and two college athletic departments.
Current players	Business Classes	The NFLPA has partnered with Indiana University's Kelley School of Business to give players the opportunity to participate in a variety of webinars, business certificate courses, professional courses, and for-credit courses toward an M.B.A. The Trust, below, runs a similar program in collaboration with Babson College.
Current players	Coaching Internship	The NFLPA partnered with the American Football Coaches Association (AFCA) to place former players as coaching interns at Division II, Division III, and National Association of Intercollegiate Athletics (NAIA) institutions for an entire football season.
Former players with at least 2 Credited Seasons	The Trust	A "set of resources, programs and services designed to provide former players with the support, skills and tools to help ensure success off the field and in life after football." The Trust has partnered with a variety of organizations and institutions to assist former players in the areas of physical health, career transitioning, and financial health. For example, in the area of physical health, the University of North Carolina, the Tulane University Institute of Sport Medicine, the Cleveland Clinic, and Massachusetts General Hospital will all provide former players with a full body physical examination, including but not limited to musculoskeletal, neurological, and cardiovascular analyses. According to the NFLPA, more than 1,500 former players have availed themselves of The Trust's resources since it was launched in 2013.
Former players	Gene Upshaw Player Assistance Trust Fund	"The Gene Upshaw Players Assistance Trust assists former players who are facing financial hardship due to unforeseen crisis, unaffordable medical situations and players who wish to go back to school to finish their undergraduate degrees."

Endnote

1. For more on these programs, see NFLPA Externship Program Enters Second Year, NFLPA (Feb. 23, 2015), https://nflpa.com/news/all-news/nflpa-externship-program-enters-second-year, archived at https://perma.cc/G2HJ-TCRU; A Winning Team: Kelley School of Business and the NFLPA, Kelley Sch. Business, https://nflpawebqa.blob.core.windows.net/media/Default/PDFs/Player%20Development/NFLPA-Kelley_%20Program.pdf (last visited Aug. 7, 2015), archived at https://perma.cc/8WPH-A8GD?type=pdf; Career, Trust, http://playerstrust.com/your-trust/career (last visited Aug. 7, 2015), archived at http://perma.cc/QZJ5-9URR; Active Players – Grow Experience, NFLPA, https://nflpa.com/active-players/playerdevelopment/experience (last visited Aug. 7, 2015), archived at https://perma.cc/5JPR-RR9E (However, we note that it is unclear why Division I institutions are not included. Additionally, it would seem very possible that players could obtain such positions without the internship program); Emily Kaplan, The Games Go On, And So Does Life, MMQB (Dec. 26, 2013), http://mmqb.si.com/2013/12/26/nfl-nflpa-the-trust-player-retirement-benefits/, archived at http://perma.cc/Z2LH-V8PM (discussing creation of the Trust); Frequently Asked Questions, Trust, http://playerstrust.com/frequently-asked-questions (last visited Aug. 7, 2015), archived at http://perma.cc/7NLC-HDTB (describing The Trust and its purpose); Brain and Body, Trust, http://playerstrust.com/your-trust/brain-and-body (last visited Aug. 7, 2015), archived at http://perma.cc/4HN3-HSHL; Gene Upshaw Player Assistance Trust Fund, https://www.yourpaf.com/gupat/#.VuhhvnOrLIU (last visited Mar. 15, 2016), archived at https://perma.cc/S9T8-RYHF.

APPENDIX F \ Article 39 of the 2011 Collective Bargaining Agreement—Players' Rights to Medical Care and Treatment

Note: Below is the current text of Article 39 of the 2011 Collective Bargaining Agreement, entitled "Players' Rights to Medical Care and Treatment." In Appendix G, we provide a revised, Model Article 39 based on the recommendations made in this Report.

ARTICLE 39
PLAYERS' RIGHTS TO MEDICAL CARE AND TREATMENT

Section 1. **Club Physician:**

    (a)   **Medical Credentials.** Each Club will have a board-certified orthopedic surgeon as one of its Club physicians, and all other physicians retained by a club to treat players shall be board-certified in their field of medical expertise. Each Club will also have at least one board-certified internist, family medicine, or emergency medicine physician (non-operative sports medicine specialist). Any Club medical physician (internist, family medicine or emergency medicine) hired after the effective date of this Agreement must also have a Certification of Added Qualification (CAQ) in Sports Medicine; any head team physician (orthopedic or medical) hired after the effective date of this Agreement must have a CAQ in Sports Medicine; and any current team physician promoted to head team physician after the effective date of this Agreement has until February 2013 to obtain a CAQ in Sports Medicine or relinquish the position.

    (b)   **Team Consultants.** All Clubs shall have the consultants with the following certifications:

        (i)   Neurological (head trauma): Board certification in neurosurgery, neurology, sports medicine, emergency medicine, or psychiatry, with extensive experience in mild and moderate brain trauma;

        (ii)   Cardiovascular: Board certified in cardiovascular disease;

        (iii)   Nutrition (athletes): licensed;

        (iv)   Neuropsychologist: Ph.D and certified/licensed.

    (c)   **Doctor/Patient Relationship.** The cost of medical services rendered by Club physicians will be the responsibility of the respective Clubs, but each Club physician's primary duty in providing player medical care shall be not to the Club but instead to the player-patient. This duty shall include traditional physician/patient confidentiality requirements. In addition, all Club physicians and medical personnel shall comply with all federal, state, and local requirements, including all ethical rules and standards established by any applicable government and/or other authority that regulates or governs the medical profession in the Club's city. All Club physicians are required to disclose to a player any and all information about the player's physical condition that the physician may from time to time provide to a coach or other Club representative, whether or not such information affects the player's performance or health. If a Club physician advises a coach or other Club representative of a player's serious injury or career threatening physical condition which significantly affects the player's performance or health, the physician will also advise the player in writing. The player, after being advised of such serious injury or career-threatening physical condition, may request a copy of the Club physician's record from the examination in which such physical condition was diagnosed and/or a written explanation from the Club physician of the physical condition.

    (d)   **NFLPA Medical Director.** The NFL recognizes that the NFLPA Medical Director has a critical role in advising the NFLPA on health and safety issues. Accordingly, the NFL agrees that the NFLPA Medical Director shall be a voting member of all NFL health and safety committees, including but not limited to the NFL Injury & Safety Panel and its subcommittees and shall have access to all of the same data,

Article 39: Players' Rights to Medical Care and Treatment (continued)

records and other information provided to the NFL Medical Advisor and/or any other members of such committees.

(e) **Home Game Medical Coverage-Neutral Physician:** All home teams shall retain at least one RSI physician who is board certified in emergency medicine, anesthesia, pulmonary medicine, or thoracic surgery, and who has documented competence in RSI intubations in the past twelve months. This physician shall be the neutral physician dedicated to game-day medical intervention for on-field or locker room catastrophic emergencies.

Section 2. **Club Athletic Trainers:** All athletic trainers employed or retained by Clubs to provide services to players, including any part time athletic trainers, must be certified by the National Athletic Trainers Association and must have a degree from an accredited four-year college or university. Each Club must have at least two full-time athletic trainers. All part-time athletic trainers must work under the direct supervision of a certified athletic trainer. In addition, each Club shall be required to have at least one full time physical therapist who is certified as a specialist in physical therapy to assist players in the care and rehabilitation of their injuries.

Section 3. **Accountability and Care Committee:**

(a) The parties agree to establish an Accountability and Care Committee, which will provide advice and guidance regarding the provision of preventive, medical, surgical, and rehabilitative care for players by all clubs during the term of this Agreement. The Committee shall consist of the NFL Commissioner and the NFLPA Executive Director (or their designees). In addition, the Commissioner and Executive Director shall each appoint three additional members of the Committee, who shall be knowledgeable and experienced in fields relevant to health care for professional athletes.

(b) The Committee shall meet in person or by conference call at least three times per year, or at such other times as the Commissioner and Executive Director may determine.

(c) The Committee shall: (i) encourage and support programs to ensure outstanding professional training for team medical staffs, including by recommending credentialing standards and continuing education programs for Team medical personnel; sponsoring educational programs from time to time; advising on the content of scientific and other meetings sponsored by the NFL Physicians Society, the Professional Football Athletic Trainers Association, and other relevant professional institutions; and supporting other professional development programs; (ii) develop a standardized preseason and postseason physical examination and educational protocol to inform players of the primary risks associated with playing professional football and the role of the player and the team medical staff in preventing and treating illness and injury in professional athletes; (iii) conduct research into prevention and treatment of illness and injury commonly experienced by professional athletes, including patient care outcomes from different treatment methods; (iv) conduct a confidential player survey at least once every two years to solicit the players' input and opinion regarding the adequacy of medical care provided by their respective medical and training staffs and commission independent analyses of the results of such surveys; (v) assist in the development and maintenance of injury sur-

Article 39: Players' Rights to Medical Care and Treatment (continued)

veillance and medical records systems; and (vi) undertake such other duties as the Commissioner and Executive Director may assign to the Committee.

(d)   If any player submits a complaint to the Committee regarding Club medical care, the complaint shall be referred to the League and the player's Club, which together shall determine an appropriate response or corrective action if found to be reasonable. The Committee shall be informed of any response or corrective action. Nothing in this Article, or any other Article in this Agreement, shall be deemed to impose or create any duty or obligation upon either the League or NFLPA regarding diagnosis, medical care and/or treatment of any player.

(e)   Each Club shall use its best efforts to ensure that its players are provided with medical care consistent with professional standards for the industry.

Section 4. **Player's Right to a Second Medical Opinion:** A player will have the opportunity to obtain a second medical opinion. As a condition of the Club's responsibility for the costs of medical services rendered by the physician furnishing the second opinion, such physician must be board-certified in his field of medical expertise; in addition, (a) the player must consult with the Club physician in advance concerning the other physician; and (b) the Club physician must be furnished promptly with a report concerning the diagnosis, examination and course of treatment recommended by the other physician. A player shall have the right to follow the reasonable medical advice given to him by his second opinion physician with respect to diagnosis of injury, surgical and treatment decisions, and rehabilitation and treatment protocol, but only after consulting with the club physician and giving due consideration to his recommendations.

Section 5. **Player's Right to a Surgeon of His Choice:** A player will have the right to choose the surgeon who will perform surgery provided that: (a) the player will consult unless impossible (e.g., emergency surgery) with the Club physician as to his recommendation regarding the need for, the timing of and who should perform the surgery; (b) the player will give due consideration to the Club physician's recommendations; and (c) the surgeon selected by the player shall be board-certified in his field of medical expertise. Any such surgery will be at Club expense; provided, however, that the Club, the Club physician, trainers and any other representative of the Club will not be responsible for or incur any liability (other than the cost of the surgery) for or relating to the adequacy or competency of such surgery or other related medical services rendered in connection with such surgery.

Section 6. **Standard Minimum Preseason Physical:** Each player will undergo the standardized minimum preseason physical examination and tests outlined in Appendix K, which will be conducted by the Club physician(s) as scheduled by the Club. No Club may conduct its own individual testing for anabolic steroids and related substances or drugs of abuse or alcohol.

Section 7. **Substance Abuse:**
(a)   **General Policy.** The parties agree that substance abuse and the use of anabolic steroids are unacceptable within the NFL, and that it is the responsibility of the

Article 39: Players' Rights to Medical Care and Treatment (continued)

parties to deter and detect substance abuse and steroid use and to offer programs of intervention, rehabilitation, and support to players who have substance abuse problems.

(b) **Policies.** The parties confirm that the Program on Anabolic Steroids and Related Substances will include both annual blood testing and random blood testing for human growth hormone, with discipline for positive tests at the same level as for steroids. Over the next several weeks, the parties will discuss and develop the specific arrangements relating to the safe and secure collection of samples, transportation and testing of samples, the scope of review of the medical science, and the arbitrator review policy, with the goal of beginning testing by the first week of the 2011 regular season. Pending agreement by both parties regarding the implementation of this program of blood testing, and such other policy amendments as the parties may agree upon, the Policy and Program on Substances of Abuse and the Policy on Anabolic Steroids and Related Substances, will remain in full force and effect as each existed during the 2010 season.

APPENDIX G \ Model Article 39 of the Collective Bargaining Agreement — Players' Medical Care and Treatment

Preliminary Note: Below is a model collective bargaining agreement (CBA) provision setting forth our proposed recommendation for the structure of NFL player healthcare, discussed at length in Chapter 2: Club Doctors. This CBA provision would replace the existing Article 39, which governs "Players' Medical Care and Treatment." In particular, the model CBA provision is focused on the creation of a Medical Committee to select, review, and terminate the doctors that care for players. We leave the processes for such selection, review, and termination to medical experts and the proposed Medical Committee. Nevertheless, it seems at a minimum that the Players' Medical Staff should be reviewed each year.

This model CBA provision does not address certain related issues. First, it does not address medical sponsorships, discussed in detail in Chapter 2: Club Doctors, Section (A)(i). While medical sponsorship is an important issue, it is not an issue that has been collectively bargained, *i.e.*, has not been included in Article 39 or prior CBA provisions governing player medical care. Consequently, we do not address the issue in our model Article 39. Second, our proposal may be complicated to implement. The logistics of implementation, including any phasing in process, are determinations best left to the NFL and NFLPA and thus are not addressed here. Third, the model CBA provision does not include a dispute resolution mechanism. There are a variety of dispute resolution mechanisms in the 2011 CBA, and which one is best for resolving issues under our model CBA provision is not our principal focus and thus not addressed here.

ARTICLE 39: Players' Medical Care and Treatment

SECTION 1: MEDICAL COMMITTEE

(a) **Responsibilities.** The Medical Committee shall be responsible for selecting, reviewing, and terminating (as necessary) the Players' Medical Staff, as described in Section 2. The process for selecting, reviewing, and terminating members of the Players' Medical Staff is at the Medical Committee's discretion.

(b) **Composition.** The NFL and NFLPA shall each select three medical professionals to serve on the Medical Committee. The NFL and NFLPA must each select two doctors (either M.D. or D.O.) and one athletic trainer (certified by the Board of Certification for the Athletic Trainer). The six members collectively chosen by the NFL

and NFLPA shall then jointly select a seventh medical professional to serve as Chairperson of the Medical Committee. The NFL and NFLPA retain the right to select and replace their three members of the Medical Committee according to their discretion, provided neither the NFL or NFLPA shall take any action that interferes or potentially interferes with a member of the Medical Committee performing his or her obligations as described in this Article with the utmost professionalism and independence. The Chairperson may only be replaced or removed by a majority vote of the other members of the Medical Committee.

(c) **Funding.** The NFL and NFLPA shall be jointly responsible for providing the Medical Committee with funding sufficient to permit the Medical Committee to carry out its obligations as described in this Article, including but not limited to hiring other professionals the Medical Committee determines to be necessary. Nothing in this Article shall be deemed to impose or create any duty or obligation upon the NFL, NFLPA or Medical Committee regarding diagnosis, medical care and/or treatment of any player.

SECTION 2: PLAYERS' MEDICAL STAFF

(a) **Players' Doctors.** For each Club, the Medical Committee shall select two appropriately qualified "Players' Doctors" who shall be responsible for providing medical care to the Club's players in accordance with all applicable laws and ethical standards, except as otherwise provided for in this Article. The Medical Committee shall designate one of the two Players' Doctors as the Head Players' Doctor, who shall be responsible for directing and supervising the work of the other members of the Players' Medical Staff, as defined in this Section. The Players' Doctors must have a Certificate of Added Qualification in Sports Medicine at the time of their selection.

(b) **Players' Specialists.** In addition to the Players' Doctors, for each Club, the Medical Committee shall also select a doctor board-certified in each of the following specialties or sub-specialties to be available for the treatment of players as determined to be necessary by the Head Players' Doctor ("Players' Specialists"):

i. Orthopaedic surgery;

ii. Internal medicine;

iii. Emergency medicine;

iv. Family medicine;

v. Cardiovascular disease or interventional cardiology; and,

vi. Neurological surgery.

If one of the Players' Doctors is certified in one or more of the above-listed specialties or sub-specialties, the Medical Committee need not select an additional Players' Specialist with the same specialty or sub-specialty. The Specialists shall be responsible for providing medical care to the Club's players in accordance with all applicable laws and ethical standards, except as otherwise provided for in this Article. The Players' Specialists will at all times provide medical care and advice that is in the player's best interests, taking into account the player's own goals and interests, without regard to any interest of the Club.

(c) **Players' Athletic Trainers.** For each Club, the Medical Committee shall select four athletic trainers who shall be responsible for providing medical care to the Club's players in accordance with all applicable laws and ethical standards, except as otherwise provided for in this Article. The Medical Committee shall designate one of the four Players' Athletic Trainers as the Head Players' Athletic Trainer, who shall be responsible for directing and supervising the work of the other Players' Athletic Trainers. The Head Players' Doctor shall supervise and direct the work of all Players' Athletic Trainers. The Players' Athletic Trainers must be certified by the Board of Certification for the Athletic Trainer at the time of their selection.

(d) **EMRs.** The Players' Athletic Trainers shall be responsible for entering all diagnosis and treatment notations into the electronic medical record ("EMR") system, including the notations of any examinations performed on a player during a game and any consultation with, or treatment provided by, Second Opinion Doctors as described in Section 5 below.

(e) **Players' Other Medical Professionals.** In addition to the Players' Doctors, Players' Specialists, and Players' Athletic Trainers, for each Club, the Medical Committee shall also select one of each of the following medical professionals to be available for the treatment of players as reasonably determined to be necessary by the Head Players' Doctor:

    i. Physical therapist;

    ii. Massage therapist;

    iii. Nutritionist;

    iv. Psychiatrist; and,

    v. Neuropsychologist.

(f) **Access to Club Facilities and Events.** The Players' Doctors, Players' Specialists, Players' Athletic Trainers, and Players' Other Medical Professionals (collectively, "Players' Medical Staff"), shall have access to Club facilities and events (including but not limited to locker rooms, practices, and games) as needed to perform their duties as described in this Article. The Club shall be responsible for providing all equipment and supplies as reasonably determined by the Head Players' Doctor to be necessary for the Players' Medical Staff to perform their duties as described in this Article.

(g) **Compensation Arrangement.** The Club is responsible for compensating the Players' Medical Staff, in amounts to be determined by the Medical Committee. All members of the Players' Medical

Staff shall enter into written contracts detailing the terms of the arrangement between the Players' Medical Staff member and the Club. The contract between the Players' Medical Staff member and the Club must be approved by the Medical Committee prior to execution and shall explicitly reference this Article as controlling and superseding any provision of the contract in the event of a conflict. The Club has no authority to select, control, or terminate any member of the Players' Medical Staff. It is the intention of the NFL and NFLPA that each member of the Players' Medical Staff be considered and treated as an independent contractor under all applicable laws and regulations.

(h) **Avoidance of Conflicts.** The Players' Medical Staff will at all times provide medical care and advice that is in the player's best interests, taking into account the player's own goals and interests, without regard to any interest of the Club. No member of the Players' Medical Staff shall have any obligation to the Club, except for the Player Health Report, discussed below in Section 4.

SECTION 3: CLUB MEDICAL STAFF

(a) **Retention and Duties.** Each Club is free to retain any qualified medical professional to provide services to the Club ("Club Medical Staff"). The Club Medical Staff shall not provide medical care to any player, except in emergency situations. The Club Medical Staff shall have no communication with players or the Players' Medical Staff, except as otherwise described in this Article.

(b) **Physical Examinations.** Within the limitations set forth below, the Club shall be permitted to conduct physical examinations of players via Club Medical Staff. During any such physical examinations, the player will make full and complete disclosure of any physical or mental condition known to him which might impair his performance under his contract and will respond fully and in good faith when questioned by the Club Medical Staff about his condition.

(c) A player under contract to a Club shall, upon the Club's request, submit to a complete physical examination by the Club Medical Staff at the following times:

    i. Once within seven days following the Club's last game of the season.

    ii. After seven days following the Club's last game of the season, once before two days prior to the commencement of preseason training camp, provided the player is otherwise with the Club, e.g., during offseason workouts or minicamps.

    iii. Once within two days prior and two days after commencement of the Club's preseason training camp.

    iv. After two days following commencement of the Club's preseason training camp and before the last game of the season, upon the Club's reasonable request.

(d) In addition to a physical examination, the Club may also request that the player submit to drills or other football-related activities for the purpose of assessing the player's fitness-to-play, unless the Head Players' Doctor states in writing that such drills or football-related activities create an unreasonable risk of worsening the player's condition or delaying his recovery from such condition.

(e) A player not currently under contract may be required to submit to any physical examination, drills or other football-related activities requested by a Club as part of the negotiation of a prospective contract between the player and Club, provided such physical examinations, drills or other football-related activities otherwise comply with all applicable laws and regulations.

(f) **Access to Medical Records.** The Club Medical Staff shall have full access to the EMRs of each player on its roster, subject to applicable law.

(g) **Compliance with the Law.** All examinations (physical or otherwise) and possession or use of medical records by Club Medical Staff must comply with all applicable laws.

SECTION 4: PLAYER HEALTH REPORT

(a) **Content.** The Players' Medical Staff, under the direction of the Head Players' Doctor and Head Players' Athletic Trainer, are responsible for providing the Club with a regular status report of all players currently receiving medical treatment for a diagnosed condition ("Player Health Report"). The Player Health Report shall briefly describe: (1) the player's condition; (2) the player's permissible level of participation in practice and other Club activities; (3) the player's current status for the next game; (4) any limitations on the player's potential participation in the next game; and, (5) an estimation of when the player will be able to return to full participation in practice and games.[a] The Players' Medical Staff shall complete the Player Health Report in a good faith effort to permit the Club to be properly prepared for its next game.

(b) **Provision of Player Health Report.** The Player Health Report will be provided to an individual designated by the Club at the following times:

i. At least one hour before practice on the day of the practice;

ii. Within two hours of the conclusion of practice on the day of the practice;

iii. Between 28 and 20 hours prior to kickoff of a game;

iv. Between 3 and 2 hours prior to kickoff of a game;

v. Within 2 hours after the conclusion of a game (provided there are games or the possibility of games remaining in the season);

vi. By the end of the day following a game (provided there are games or the possibility of games remaining in the season); and,

vii. On days where there is no practice or game, by the end of the day if and only if a player has received medical care or testing that day.

To the extent that any of the above-required dates on which the Player Health Report must be provided overlap, the Player Health Report need only be provided once within the relevant time frame. The Club representative receiving the Player Health Report is permitted to share the Player Health Report with all coaches, front office personnel and Club Medical Staff as are reasonably necessary to help the Club prepare for the next game.

(c) **Clearance to Practice.** The Head Players' Doctor's determinations, as detailed in the Player Health Report, concerning whether a player can practice or participate in football-related activities, including with any relevant limitations, are controlling, subject to Section 5 below. A Club shall not permit a player to practice or participate in football-related activities beyond the limitations set forth in the Player Health Report. If a player suffers an injury or other condition during the course of a practice, the Head Players' Doctor and Head Athletic Trainer will make best efforts to advise a designated Club representative of a player's status for the remainder of the practice as soon as is practicable.

(d) **Clearance to Play.** As part of the Player Health Report provided between 3 and 2 hours prior to kickoff of a game, the Head Players' Doctor will declare: (i) whether the player can or cannot play; and, (ii) if the player can play, any relevant limitations on the player's playing. The Head Players' Doctor's determinations, as detailed in the Player Health Report, concerning whether a player can play, or whether the player can play with limitations, are controlling as to the player's status to play, subject to Section 5 below. A Club shall not permit a player to play beyond the limitations set forth in the Player Health Report. If a player suffers an injury or other condition during the course of a game, the Head Players' Doctor and Head Athletic Trainer will make best efforts to advise a designated Club representative of a player's status for the remainder of the game as soon as is practicable.

(e) **Communication with Club Medical Staff.** The Club Medical Staff may seek reasonable clarification or explanation of the information contained in the Player Health Report via direct communication with only the Head Players' Doctor. The Head Players' Doctor shall make reasonable efforts to respond in good faith to all reasonable inquiries from the Club Medical Staff concerning the Player Health Report. At no time other than provided for in this Section shall the Players' Medical Staff communicate with any employee, representative, consultant or agent of the Club concerning the medical care or condition of a player.

(f) **Compliance with the Law.** The creation, possession and use of the Player Health Report must comply with all applicable laws.

---

a   We recommend that the NFL and NFLPA jointly agree on the form of the Player Health Report, which should be completed electronically and automatically incorporated into the players' EMRs. Additionally, the Player Health Report should mirror the terminology historically used by the NFL's Injury Reporting Policy concerning a player's status: Out (definitely will not play); Doubtful (at least 75 percent chance will not play); Questionable (50-50 chance will not play); and, Probable (virtual certainty player will be available for normal duty).

SECTION 5: PLAYERS' RIGHT TO A SECOND MEDICAL OPINION

(a) **Second Opinion Doctors List.** The Medical Committee shall create a list of doctors with whom players are permitted to consult for the purposes of providing a medical opinion other than that of the Players' Medical Staff ("Second Opinion Doctors"). In creating the Second Opinion Doctors List, the Medical Committee shall seek to identify well-qualified doctors in all relevant specialties for which a player might seek a second medical opinion. A player can request that a doctor be added to the Second Opinion Doctors List by submitting such a request to the Medical Committee Chairperson prior to the consultation or treatment. The NFL, NFLPA or a Club can request a doctor be added to or removed from the Second Opinion Doctors List by submitting such a request to the Medical Committee detailing the reason for the request. The Medical Committee shall act promptly with regard to all requests. Where a player has requested a doctor be added to the Second Opinion Doctors List, a doctor need not be added to the Second Opinion Doctors List in advance of such consultation or treatment to be considered a Second Opinion Doctor; so long as the doctor is at some point added to the Second Opinion Doctors List per the player's request. The existence of the Second Opinion Doctor List shall in no way limit players to their own choice of personal doctor. Players need only consult with a Second Opinion Doctor for purposes of Payment, discussed in Section (b) below, and Clearance to Practice or Play, discussed in Section (c) below.

(b) **Payment.** The Club is responsible for the payment of any consultation with, or treatment provided by, a Second Opinion Doctor provided the following conditions are met:

   i. The player has first consulted in good faith with the Head Players' Doctor;

   ii. At the time of the consultation or treatment, the Second Opinion Doctor is on the Second Opinion Doctor List, or the player has requested the doctor the doctor be added to the Second Opinion Doctors List in accordance with Section 5(a) above and the doctor is added pursuant to the player's request; and,

   iii. All relevant records from the consultation or treatment are either incorporated into the player's EMR or provided to the Club within two business days of their receipt by the player or the player's NFLPA-certified Contract Advisor.

(c) **Clearance to Practice or Play.** If at any time on the Player's Health Report, the Head Players' Doctor has limited a player's clearance to practice or has determined that a player is "Out," "Doubtful," or "Questionable" for the next game, the player has the right to seek clearance to practice or play from a Second Opinion Doctor. If the Second Opinion Doctor states in writing that the player can practice or play in a manner more extensive than that determined by the Head Players' Doctor, the player, at his sole discretion, has the right to practice or play up to the limits imposed by the Second Opinion Doctor, if any. If the Second Opinion Doctor states in writing that the player can practice or play in a manner less extensive than that determined by the Head Players' Doctor, the player, at his sole discretion, has the right to practice or play up to the limits imposed by the Head Players' Doctor.

SECTION 6: TREATMENT DETERMINATIONS

(a) **Surgery.** A player has the right to choose the surgeon who will perform any surgery on him. A player is not obligated to undergo any surgery, regardless of the recommendations of the Players' Medical Staff, a Second Opinion Doctor, the Club Medical Staff, or any other party.

(b) **Payment.** The Club is responsible for the payment of any surgery provided:

   i. The surgery is performed by: (x) a member of the Players' Medical Staff; (y) a surgeon who, at the time of the surgery, is on the Second Opinion Doctor List, or the player has requested the doctor be added to the Second Opinion Doctors List in accordance with Section 5(a) above and the doctor is added pursuant to the player's request and, the player has first consulted in good faith with the Head Players' Health Doctor; or, (z) any other medical professional in an emergency situation.

   ii. All relevant records from the surgery are either incorporated into the player's EMR or provided to the Club within two business days of their receipt by the player or the player's NFLPA-certified Contract Advisor.

SECTION 7: HOME GAME EMERGENCY MEDICAL COVERAGE

(a) For each game, the Medical Committee shall select one doctor who is board-certified in emergency medicine, anesthesiology, pulmonary disease, or thoracic and cardiac surgery, and who has documented competence in rapid sequence intubations in the past twelve months. This doctor shall be responsible for game-day medical intervention for catastrophic emergencies.

APPENDIX H \ Medical Malpractice Cases Against Club Doctors[a]

1. Butkus v. Chicago Bears, Fox

In 1976, former Chicago Bears linebacker and Hall of Famer Dick Butkus settled a lawsuit against the Bears and their doctor Theodore Fox for $600,000 after Butkus alleged that Fox negligently and repeatedly injected Butkus' knee with painkillers and refused to cooperate with Butkus' efforts to obtain a second opinion following a 1971 surgery.[1]

2. Siani v. Oakland Raiders, Rosenfeld

In 1980, former Oakland Raiders wide receiver Mike Siani settled a lawsuit against the Raiders and Raiders doctor Robert Rosenfeld for $120,000.[2] Siani alleged that Rosenfeld repeatedly injected Siani's foot with painkillers to numb Siani's broken toes which eventually caused the removal of the bones from his toes.[3]

3. Hendy v. San Diego Chargers, Losse[4]

In 1988, former San Diego Chargers defensive back John Hendy sued the Chargers and club doctor Gary Losse alleging that: (1) the Chargers were negligent in their hiring and retention of Losse; (2) Losse intentionally and negligently withheld medical information from Hendy concerning the extent of Hendy's knee injury; and, (3) Losse misrepresented to Hendy that he was fit to play.[5] The United States Court of Appeals for the Ninth Circuit held that the Chargers' hiring obligations and Losse's duty to disclose were not controlled by the CBA and thus not preempted.[6] The Ninth Circuit thus remanded the case to state court for consideration of the state tort law claims.[7]

The case eventually reached the Supreme Court of California.[8] Rephrased as a "medical malpractice" claim, the Supreme Court of California held that Hendy's claims were barred by California's workers' compensation statutes.[9] In so doing, the Supreme Court of California relied on Hendy's allegation that Losse was an employee of the Chargers and that Hendy had not alleged any facts which would have permitted him to amend his complaint to allege that Losse was instead an independent contractor.[10]

Hendy's claims against the Chargers were found to be preempted by the Labor Management Relations Act and dismissed.[11]

4. Krueger v. San Francisco 49ers, Taylor, Millburn

In 1988, former San Francisco 49ers offensive lineman Charlie Krueger settled a lawsuit against the 49ers and the 49ers' doctors Lloyd Taylor and Lloyd Millburn for approximately $1.5 million.[12] Krueger alleged that Taylor injected Krueger's knee with painkilling injections dozens of times a season between a 1963 knee surgery and the end of Krueger's career in 1973 without informing him of the true condition of his knee.[13]

5. Easley v. Seattle Seahawks, Scranton, Whitesel, Whitehall Laboratories

In 1989, former Seattle Seahawks safety Kenny Easley sued the Seahawks, the Seahawks doctor Pierce Scranton, athletic trainer James Whitesel and Whitehall Laboratories, a maker of Advil.[14] Easley alleged that his use of Advil, as prescribed by the club doctors, caused him kidney damage which the doctors failed to treat or disclose and ultimately necessitated a transplant.[15] Easley settled the case for an undisclosed sum in 1991.[16]

6. Daniels v. Seattle Seahawks, Auld

In 1992, then-Seattle Seahawk David Daniels was treated by the Seahawks' orthopedist, Dr. Merrit Auld, for an apparent groin strain. Daniels was unable to play due to the pain and it was later determined he had a fractured rectus femoris. Daniels alleged he was never able to fully recover from his injury, contributing to the end of his career. Daniels sued Auld for medical malpractice. A Washington state court held that because Auld, like Daniels, was an employee of the Seahawks, Daniels' lawsuit was barred by Washington's workers' compensation laws.[17]

The result of Daniels' claims against the Seahawks is unclear.

---

a   The cases listed here were found through searching legal and news databases or otherwise discovered during our research. This list should not be considered an exhaustive list of medical malpractice cases by NFL players against club doctors. For example, the list does not include non-published case dispositions which were not reported in the news. Additionally, we know of one case pending as of the date of publication brought by former Miami Dolphins wide receiver O.J. McDuffie. See McDuffie v. Mills, Docket No. 2002-014638-CA-01 (Fla. Cir. Ct.).

7. Novak v. Lucie

In 1999, former Jacksonville Jaguars offensive lineman Jeff Novak sued the Jaguars' doctor Stephen Lucie alleging Lucie improperly operated on him in the locker room, a non-sterile environment, resulting in a hematoma and infection in his leg.[18] Lucie settled the case for $2.2 million.[19]

8. Hoge v. Munsell

In 2000, former Chicago Bears running back Merrill Hoge won a $1.55 million jury award in a lawsuit against former Bears' doctor John Munsell.[20] Hoge alleged that Munsell failed to properly treat Hoge's concussions and negligently cleared Hoge to play, resulting in further injury and Hoge's forced retirement.[21]

9. Stringer v. Minnesota Vikings, et al.

In 2001, Minnesota Vikings Pro Bowl offensive tackle Korey Stringer died of complications from heat stroke after collapsing during training camp.[22] Stringer's family later sued the Vikings, Vikings coaches and affiliated doctors, the NFL and Riddell. Stringer's family reached undisclosed settlements with one of the three doctors involved, David Knowles,[23] after a Minnesota trial court determined that Dr. Knowles was an independent contractor.[24] The claims against the two other Vikings doctors (Sheldon Burns and David Fischer) were dismissed on the ground that they were employees of the Vikings and the claims were thus barred by workers' compensation laws.[25]

In 2003, a Minnesota trial court granted summary judgment[b] in favor of the Vikings and its coaches.[26] The *Stringer* case is discussed in greater detail in Chapter 3: Athletic Trainers, Chapter 7: The NFL and NFLPA, and Chapter 9: Coaches.

10. Wilson v. Prusmack

In 2008, former Denver Broncos linebacker Al Wilson sued the Broncos' Club doctor, Chad Prusmack, alleging that Prusmack failed to treat properly a neck injury, requiring Wilson's retirement.[27] Wilson commenced the action approximately one month after an arbitrator ruled his grievance against the Broncos concerning the same issue was time-barred.[28] In 2011, a jury found that Prusmack was not negligent.[29]

11. Jurevicius v. Cleveland Browns, Figler, Miniaci[30]

In 2009, Cleveland Browns wide receiver Joe Jurevicius sued the Browns and Browns' doctors (Richard Figler and Anthony Miniaci) in Ohio state court, alleging causes of action for negligence, negligent misrepresentation, fraud, constructive fraud, breach of fiduciary duty, common law intentional tort and statutory intentional tort against the Browns. Jurevicius generally alleged that the Browns and their doctors failed to take proper precautions to prevent staph infections and lied to players about what steps the club had taken to prevent infections.[31] The Browns and the doctors attempted to remove the case to federal court, arguing that Jurevicius' claims were barred by the CBA.[32] In a March 31, 2010 decision, the United States District Court for the Northern District of Ohio determined that Jurevicius' negligence, negligent misrepresentation, fraud, common law intentional tort and statutory intentional tort claims were not preempted while the constructive fraud and breach of fiduciary duty claims were. Concerning the doctors, the Court found that the CBA did not address the alleged obligations of club doctors to warn players about the conditions at a medical facility and thus the claims were not preempted.[33] The lawsuit settled a few months after the Court's decision.[34]

12. Jones v. Gill, Zarins

In 2009, former New England Patriots defensive back Tebucky Jones sued Patriots doctors Tom Gill and Bertram Zarins alleging they failed to tell him that he had suffered a tear in his knee ligament during a 2006 game.[35] Jones claimed that the doctors' failure to inform him of his condition delayed proper treatment and caused further problems which ultimately caused the end of his career.[36] A jury awarded Jones $3.75 million but the verdict was overturned by a Massachusetts judge for reasons which are unclear.[37]

13. Rolle v. Brigham

In 2014, former Baltimore Ravens cornerback Samari Rolle was awarded $650,000 in a medical malpractice lawsuit against then-Carolina Panthers Club doctor Craig Brigham and his OrthoCarolina healthcare practice.[38] In September 2008, Rolle was referred to Brigham by the Ravens' doctors for spinal surgery, an area of Brigham's expertise.[39] Rolle alleged that Brigham cleared Rolle to return to play too soon.[40] Rolle required a second surgery by Andrew Dossett, the Dallas Cowboys' Spine Consultant, which, although performed properly, forced Rolle to retire.[41] Dossett, a member of the NFL Physicians Society, testified against Brigham, also a member of the NFL Physicians Society, at trial.[42]

---

b   Summary judgment is "[a] judgment granted on a claim or defense about which there is no genuine issue of material fact and on which the movant is entitled to prevail as a matter of law." Black's Law Dictionary (9th ed. 2009).

Endnotes

1   Fred Mitchell, *Butkus Recalls Battles with Docs*, Chic. Trib., Nov. 1, 2007, *available at* 2007 WLNR 21518086; Dick Butkus & Pat Smith, Butkus — Flesh and Blood, 227–30, 257,279–95 (1997) (describing Fox's treatment of Butkus' knee conditions and lawsuit).

2   Angelo Cataldi & Glen Macnow, *Shots for the Pain Led to Permanent Damage*, Phil. Inquirer, Jun. 21, 1989, http://articles.philly.com/1989-06 -21/sports/26105705_1_injections-cortisone-robert-rosenfeld, *archived at* http://perma.cc/LFL5-2N72.

3   *Id.*

4   F.2d 1470 (9th Cir. 1991).

5   *Id.*

6   *Id.*

7   *Id.*

8   P.2d 1, 54 Cal.3d 723 (Cal. 1991).

9   *Id.*

10 *Id.* at 743.

11 *See Hendy v. Losse*, 274 Cal.Rptr. 31, 33 (Cal. App. 1990).

12 Jennifer Lynn Woodlief, *The Trouble with Charlie: Fraudulent Conceal- ment of Medical Information in Professional Football*, 9 SPG Ent. & Sports L. 3, 3 (1991). *See also* Krueger v. San Francisco Forty Niners, 234 Cal.Rptr. 579 (Cal.App. 1987) (ordering judgment in favor of Krueger and remanding for further proceedings).

13 *Id.*

14 Tom Farrey, *Easley Settles with Doctors, Drug Maker,* Seattle Times, Sept. 18, 1991, *available at* 1991 WLNR 984467; Glenn Nelson, *Courting Danger Krueger's Advice to Easley: Put Up Fight,* Seattle Times, May 31, 1989, *available at* 1989 WLNR 654489.

15 *Id.*

16 Tom Farrey, *Easley Settles with Doctors, Drug Maker,* Seattle Times, Sept. 18, 1991, *available at* 1991 WLNR 984467.

17 *See* Daniels v. Seattle Seahawks, 92 Wash.App. 576 (Wash. Ct. App. 1998).

18 Tom Farrey, *At What Price a Player's Pain?* ESPN (updated Nov. 4, 2002, 10:44 AM), http://espn.go.com/gen/s/2002/0912/1431095.html, *archived at* http://perma.cc/TRN5-GQE6.

19 Jason Cole, Lawsuits Are Bad Medicine for Pro Sports Doctors, Wash. Post, Apr. 27, 2003, available at 2003 WLNR 19263311.

20 Mark Fainaru-Wada & Steve Fainaru, League of Denial: The NFL, Concussions, and the Battle for Truth 121 (2013).

21 *See id.* at 41–46 (discussing treatment provided by Munsell to Hoge).

22 Stringer v. Minnesota Vikings Football Club, LLC, 705 N.W.2d 746, 748 (Minn. 2005).

23 *See* Stringer v. Minnesota Vikings Football Club, LLC, No. 02-415, 2003 WL 25766738 (Minn.Dist.Ct. Dec. 8, 2003) (mentioning settlement with W. David Knowles, MD and Mankato Clinic, Ltd.).

24 Pam Louwagie & Kevin Seifert, *Stringer Claims Against Vikings Dismissed*, Newspaper — Twin Cities (Minneapolis), Apr. 26, 2003, *available at* 2003 WLNR 14250471.

25 *See* Memorandum and Order, Stringer v. Minn. Vikings Football Club, No. 02-415, 20–23 (Minn. Dist. Ct. Apr. 25, 2003).

26 *See* Memorandum and Order, Stringer v. Minnesota Vikings Football Club, LLC, No. 02-415 (Minn. Dist. Ct. Apr. 25, 2003); Stringer v. Min- nesota Vikings Football Club, LLC, No. 02-415, 2003 WL 25766738 (Minn. Dist. Ct. Dec. 8, 2003) (discussing Court's prior order). Follow- ing Stringer's death, the NFL now issues an annual memorandum to NFL Clubs warning them about the risks of players overheating during training camp. *See, e.g.,* Memorandum from NFL Injury and Safety Panel (Elliott Hershman, M.D., Chairman), to General Managers, Head Coaches, Team Physicians, and Team Athletic Trainers re: 2014 Training Camps — Adverse Weather Conditions (July 11, 2014) (on file with author).

27 Felisa Cardona, *Jury finds doctor not negligent in advice to former Bronco Al Wilson*, Denver Post, June 17, 2011, http://www.denverpost .com/ci_18296823, *archived at* http://perma.cc/T4QV-7SBD; Wilson v. Prusmack, Case # 2008CV-010376 (Col.Dist.Ct. 2008).

28 (Townley, Arb. Oct. 29, 2008), available as Exhibit 16 to the Declaration of Dennis L. Curran in Support of Defendant National Football League's Motion to Dismiss Second Amended Complaint (Section 301 Preemp- tion), Dent v. Nat'l Football League, 14-cv-2324 (N.D. Cal. Sep. 24, 2014), ECF No. 73.

29 Cardona *supra* note 27.

30 Jurevicius v. Cleveland Browns Football Co. LLC, 09-cv-1803, 2010 WL 8461220 (N.D.Ohio Mar. 31, 2010).

31 *Id.*

32 *Id.*

33 *Id.*

34 *Jurevicius Settles Lawsuit with the Browns*, ESPN (June 15, 2010, 6:37 PM), http://sports.espn.go.com/nfl/news/story?id=5289486, *archived at* http://perma.cc/JJH7-CR37.

35 Jessica Farge, *Jones Claims Pats Docs Cut Short Career,* Bos. Herald, Aug. 9, 2009, *available* at 2009 WLNR 15475294.

36 *Id.*

37 Bob Hohler, *Lawsuit Won't Change Jones's Loyalties*, Bos. Globe, Feb. 2, 2012, *available* at 2012 WLNR 2249010.

38 Erin Bacon, *Former NFL Player Wins Lawsuit Against Orthocaro- lina for $650,000*, Charlotte Observer, Sept. 5, 2014, http://www .charlotteobserver.com/2014/09/05/5152485/former-nfl-player-wins -lawsuit.html#.VFfaBWe9b2o, *archived at* http://perma.cc/98V7-4ENF. Additional information concerning Rolle's case was gathered from a November 3, 2014 interview with Gary Fox of Stewart Tilghman Fox Bianchi & Cain, P.A. in Miami, Florida. Fox represented Rolle in the lawsuit. The case did not include any motions to dismiss or for summary judgment. Thus, there were no court orders on the substantive legal issues discussed in this Report.

39 *Id.*

40 *Id.*

41 Interview with Fox, *supra* note 38.

42 *Id.*

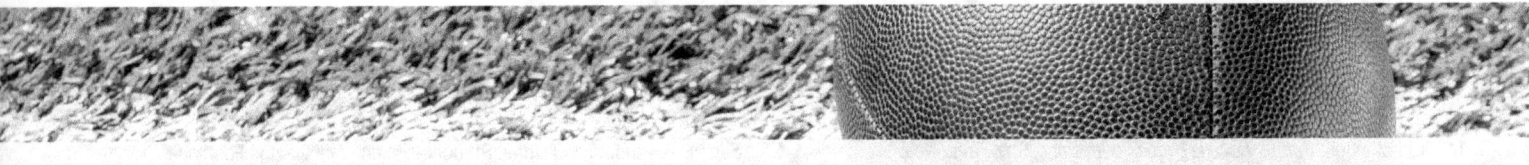

APPENDIX I \ History of Health-Related NFL Playing Rules Changes[a]

For an explanation of how rule changes take place, see Chapter 7: The NFL and NFLPA, Section A(ii): Rule Changes.

1955:

- The ball is dead immediately if the runner touches the ground with any part of his body except his hands or feet while in the grasp of an opponent.

1956:

- The ball is dead immediately if a runner touches the ground with any part of his body except his hands or feet after being contacted by a defensive player.

- Grasping the face mask of any opponent except a runner is illegal use of hands. Penalty: Five yards.

1962:

- Grasping the face mask of an opponent is illegal. Penalty: 15 yards.

1966:

- All goal posts must be offset from the goal line.

1971:

- A team will not be charged a timeout for an injured player unless the injury occurs in the last two minutes of either half.

1973:

- A defensive player who jumps or stands on a teammate or who is picked up by a teammate cannot attempt to block an opponent's kick. Penalty: 15 yards.

1974:

- Eligible receivers who take a position more than two yards from the offensive tackle, whether on or behind the line, may not be blocked below the waist at or behind the line of scrimmage.

- No receiver can be blocked below the waist after moving beyond the line of scrimmage.

- An offensive player who is aligned in a position more than two yards laterally outside of the offensive tackle may not contact an opponent below the waist if the blocker is moving toward the position of the ball either at the snap or after it is made, and contact occurs within an area three yards on either side of the line of scrimmage. This is known as a crackback block. Penalty: 15 yards.

1976:

- A defender cannot place a hand or hands on a teammate to gain additional height in an attempt to block a kick.

- A defender is not permitted to run or dive into a ball carrier who has fallen to the ground untouched.

1977:

- It is illegal for a defensive lineman to strike an opponent above the shoulders (head slap) during his initial charge. (Previously, it was legal only during the first step.)

- The crackback prohibition is extended to running backs who move outside the tight end and back inside to deliver a block below the waist.

1979:

- Mandatory equipment is specified for all players to wear during a game.

- Players on the receiving team are prohibited from blocking opponents below the waist during kickoffs, punts, and field goal attempts.

- The crackback zone is extended from three yards to five yards on either side of the line of scrimmage.

- Officials will declare the ball dead as soon as the quarterback is clearly in the grasp and control of any tackler.

- A player may be penalized for unsportsmanlike conduct for non-contact acts such as throwing a punch or a forearm, or kicking at an opponent.

- It is unnecessary roughness if a tackler uses his helmet to butt, spear, or ram an opponent, or if any player uses the crown or top of the helmet unnecessarily.

- A player in the backfield is prohibited from chopping an outside rusher on a pass play.

1980:

- A Chop block (below the waist) is also prohibited by a tight end against an outside rusher. The prohibition applies to pass plays and any plays in which the player receiving the snap initially shows pass.

---

a   For rule changes through the year 2012, we relied on an NFL website that lists "NFL rule changes focused on protecting player health and safety[.]" *See Evolution of the Rules: From Hashmarks to Crackback Blocks*, NFL Evolution (Aug. 2, 2013, 01:23 AM), http://www.nfl.com/news/story/0ap1000000224872/article/evolution-of-the-rules-from-hashmarks-to-crackback-blocks, *archived at* http://perma.cc/WZ8Q-GM43 (discussing rule changes from 1920–2012). For rule changes after 2012, we relied on news articles as indicated.

1981:

- Chop blocks (at or below the knee) are prohibited by interior linemen on passing plays or plays in which a lineman shows an attempt to pass block. If an offensive player who fires out at the snap blocks an opponent at or below the knee, the defender cannot be double-teamed by a teammate of the offensive player.

1982:

- It is illegal for any player to use the crown or top of his helmet against a passer, a receiver in the act of catching a pass, or a runner who is in the grasp of a tackler.

1983:

- All mandatory player equipment must be designed and made by a professional manufacturer and cannot be altered, except by direction of the club doctor.

- A player who uses a helmet he is not wearing as a weapon shall be ejected.

- The chop block rule applies to blocks at "thigh or lower."

1985:

- During the last two minutes of a half, the play ends when a quarterback kneels or simulates kneeling on the ground.

- The ball is dead when any runner slides to the ground feet first, thereby declaring himself down.

1986:

- Blocking below the waist on punts is prohibited during the entire down.

- The "lure" technique is prohibited. When an offensive tackle shows pass set, a teammate lined up outside him cannot chop a defender who is lined up over the tackle, even if the tackle and defender are not engaged (a "lure").

1987:

- An offensive lineman may not clip a defender who, at the snap, is aligned on the line of scrimmage opposite another offensive lineman who is more than one position away, when the defender is responding to the flow of the ball away from the blocker. Example: A tackle cannot clip the nose tackle on a sweep to the opposite side.

- It is illegal for the kicking team to block below the waist after a free kick or punt has been made. (Low blocks by the receiving team became illegal in 1979).

- Both teams are prohibited from blocking below the waist after a change of possession.

1989:

- A defender (approaching from any direction) who has an unrestricted path to the quarterback is prohibited from flagrantly hitting him in the area of the knee(s).

1990:

- A player who butts, spears, or rams an opponent may be disqualified if the action is flagrant or vicious.

1991:

- Officials will whistle the play dead whenever a defensive lineman clearly penetrates beyond the neutral zone before the ball is snapped and continues unabated toward the quarterback.

1992:

- For the first time the chop block is illegal on some running players: It is illegal on a running play for an offensive player who is lined up in the backfield at the snap to deliberately block a defensive player in the thigh or lower (chop) if the defensive player is engaged by an offensive player who was on the line of scrimmage at the snap. This action is prohibited whether on or behind the line of scrimmage in an area that extends laterally to the position originally occupied by the tight end on either side.

- When a defensive player runs forward and leaps in an attempt to block an extra point or field goal, it is a foul only if the leaping player lands on other players.

1994:

- Defensive players are prohibited from blocking low during a punt, field goal, or extra point attempt (kick), except those defensive players at the snap that are lined up on or inside the normal tight end position. Previously, all players on the defensive team could block low during the field goal or extra point attempt.

1995:

- Protection for defenseless players is clarified and expanded. Since 1982, a defensive player was prohibited from using the crown or top of his helmet against a passer, a receiver in the act of catching a pass, or a runner who is in the grasp of a tackler. The clarification provided that:

  – Defenseless players included a kickoff or punt returner attempting to field a kick in the air, and a player on the ground at the end of a play.

  – Defensive players are prohibited from lowering their heads to make forcible contact with the facemask, or with the "hairline" or forehead part of the helmet, against an opponent, instead of only with the top/crown.

  – Defensive players are prohibited from forcibly hitting the defenseless player's head, neck, or face with the helmet or facemask.

  – Defensive players are prohibited from launching into a defenseless player in a way that causes the defensive player's helmet or facemask to forcibly strike the defenseless player's head, neck, or face, even if the initial contact of the defender's helmet or facemask is lower than the defenseless player's neck.

- When tackling a passer during or just after throwing a pass, a defensive player is prohibited from unnecessarily and violently throwing him down and landing on top of him with all or most of the defender's weight.

1996:

- On running plays, a chop block is prohibited by an offensive player who is aligned more than one position away from the engaged defender when the block occurs away from the flow of the play.

- A defender cannot be chopped even after he has disengaged from an offensive opponent, if he is still confronting the offensive player.

- Prohibition of the "lure" technique is applicable all along the offensive line, instead of only to a player outside a tackle.

- Blocking from behind, at, or below the knees in the clipping zone is prohibited.

2002:

- The Chop block technique is illegal on all kicking plays.

- It is illegal to hit a quarterback helmet-to-helmet any time after a change of possession.

2005:

- It is illegal to grab the inside collar of the shoulder pads to tackle a runner ("horse-collar tackle").

- Unnecessarily running, diving into, or throwing the body against a player who should not have reasonably anticipated such contact by an opponent is unnecessary roughness. Previously, the rule only protected a player who is out of the play.

- A kicker/punter must not be unnecessarily contacted by the receiving team through the end of the play or until he assumes a distinctly defensive position. An opponent may not unnecessarily initiate helmet-to-helmet contact to the kicker/punter during the kick or during the return.

- An offensive player who is aligned in the tackle box at the snap and moves to a position outside the box is prohibited from initiating contact on the side or below the waist of an opponent if the blocker is moving toward his own end line and approaches the opponent from behind or from the side ("Peel Back Block"). The near shoulder of the blocker must be in front of his opponent's body.

2006:

- Low hits on the quarterback are prohibited when a rushing defender has an opportunity to avoid such contact.

- Blocks in the back above the waist by the kicking team while the ball is in flight during a scrimmage kick are illegal.

- The definition of a "horse-collar tackle" is expanded to include grabbing the inside collar of the jersey.

- During a field-goal attempt or a try, a defensive player who is within one yard of the line of scrimmage at the snap must have his helmet outside the snapper's shoulder pad.

2007:

- A block below the waist against an eligible receiver while the quarterback is in the pocket is a 15-yard penalty instead of a 5-yard penalty (an illegal cut block).

2009:

- Teams are not permitted to intentionally form a wedge of more than two players on a kickoff return in an attempt to block for the runner. Penalty: 15 yards.

- The "bunch" formation on kickoffs is eliminated. The kickoff team must have at least three players outside each hash mark, one of whom must be outside the yard-line number.

- It is an illegal "blindside" block if the blocker is moving toward his own endline and approaches the opponent from behind or from the side, and the initial force of the contact by the blocker's helmet, forearm, or shoulder is to the head or neck area of an opponent. Penalty: 15-yards.

- It is an illegal hit on a defenseless receiver if the initial force of the contact by the defender's helmet, forearm, or shoulder is to the head or neck area of the receiver. Penalty: 15 yards.

- Clarified rule regarding low hits on passers:

  – A defender cannot initiate a roll or lunge and forcibly hit the passer in the knee area or below, even if he is being contacted by another player.

  – It is not a foul if the defender swipes, wraps, or grabs a passer in the knee area or below in an attempt to tackle him.

2010:

- During a field-goal attempt, punt, or try-kick, a defensive team player, who is within one yard of line of scrimmage at snap, must have his entire body outside the snapper's shoulder pads.

- A player who has just completed a catch is protected from blows to the head or neck by an opponent who launches.

- All "defenseless players" are protected from blows to the head delivered by an opponent's helmet, forearm, or shoulder.

- Kickers and punters during the kick and return, and quarterbacks after a change of possession, are protected from blows to the head delivered by an opponent's helmet, forearm, or shoulder, instead of just helmet-to-helmet contact.

- The ball is declared dead at the spot if a runner's helmet comes completely off.

2011:

- The restraining line for the kicking team is moved from the 30- to the 35-yard line in an effort to increase touchbacks.

- All kicking team players other than the kicker must be lined up no more than five yards behind their restraining line, eliminating the 15–20 yard running "head start" that had become customary for many players.

- The list of "defenseless players" is expanded to include a kicker/punter during the kick or during the return, a quarterback at any time after a change of possession, and a player who receives a "blindside" block when the blocker is moving toward his own endline and approaches the opponent from behind or from the side. Previously, these players were protected against blows to the head, but not against blows delivered by an opponent with the top/crown or forehead/"hairline" parts of the helmet against other parts of the body.

- A receiver who has completed a catch is a "defenseless player" until he has had time to protect himself or has clearly become a runner. A receiver/runner is no longer defenseless if he is able to avoid or ward off the impending contact of an opponent. Previously, the receiver who had completed a catch was protected against an opponent who launched and delivered a blow to the receiver's head.

2012:

- The list of "defenseless players" is expanded to include defensive players on crackback blocks, making it illegal to hit them in the head or neck area.

- Players are required to wear protective knee and thigh pads beginning with the 2013 season.

2013:[1]

- Ball-carriers who grab and twist, turn or pull on an opponent's face mask, or grab the face mask and use it to control an opponent will be penalized 15 yards.

- "Peel back" blocks are illegal inside the tackle box. Previously they were only illegal outside the tackle box.

- Ball-carriers and tacklers cannot lead with the crown of their helmets when both players are outside of the tackle box.

- Long-snappers, while in the act of snapping the ball, are considered defenseless players.

2014:[2]

- Blockers cannot hit an opponent in the side of the legs. Rule previously only prohibited blockers from hitting an opponent in the back of the legs.

2015:[3]

- Defensive players prohibited from pushing teammates at the line of scrimmage when the offense is in punt formation.

- Offensive players prohibited from engaging in peel back blocks.

- Wide receivers are given defenseless player protection when a pass is intercepted.

- Running backs prohibited from chop blocking a defensive player engaged above the waist by another offensive player outside the tackle box.

- Allows the athletic trainer in the press box designated for spotting injuries to stop the game if a player appears to have suffered a concussion.

2016:[4]

- Prohibited all forms of the chop block.

- On a one-year trial basis, any player who is penalized twice in one game for certain types of unsportsmanlike conduct fouls is ejected.

- On a one-year trial basis, any touchback resulting from a kickoff will give the receiving team the ball at the 25-yard line (as opposed to the 20-yard line under the prior rule).

- Expanded the horse collar tackle rule to also prohibit grabbing the jersey at the name plate or above and pulling a runner to the ground.

Endnotes

1 Brian McIntyre, *2013 NFL Rule Changes Include Elimination of 'Tuck Rule', Peel-Back Blocks*, Yahoo! Sports (Aug. 6, 2013 3:03 PM), http://sports.yahoo.com/blogs/shutdown-corner/2013-nfl-rule-changes -elimination-tuck-rule-peel-190327171.html, *archived at* http://perma .cc/8RL7-C3S9.

2 Michael David Smith, *Five Rules Changes Get NFL Owners' Approval at League Meeting,* ProFootballTalk (Mar. 26, 2014, 10:11 AM), http://profootballtalk.nbcsports.com/2014/03/26/five-rules-changes -pass-as-nfl-owners-vote-at-league-meeting/, *archived at* http://perma .cc/CV3R-TWXN.

3 Michael David Smith, *NFL Passes Five Player Safety Rules*, ProFootball-Talk (Mar. 24, 2015, 3:06 PM), http://profootballtalk.nbcsports.com/2015 /03/24/nfl-passes-five-player-safety-rules/, *archived at* http://perma.cc /WT9Z-3CU8.

4 Lorenzo Reyes, *NFL approves automatic ejection rule and touchbacks moved to 25-yard line for 2016*, USA Today, Mar. 23, 2016, http://www .usatoday.com/story/sports/nfl/2016/03/23/rule-changes-automatic -ejections-touchback-25-yard-line/82158540/, *archived at* https:// perma.cc/SAN7-KC3C.

APPENDIX J \ Timeline of Equipment-Related Events and Policies[a]

Note: Below we discuss the evolution and advances made in football equipment. Nevertheless, we generally do not know when, if at all, the newer equipment models were first used in the NFL.

1869:
- Rutgers University and Princeton University played the first game of what would become American football.[1]

1905:
- After 45 players died between 1890 and 1905, President Teddy Roosevelt summoned a meeting of college football coaches to broker changes in the rules that would make the game safer.[2] Among the changes were the introduction of the forward pass and the stoppage of play when the ball carrier was down.[3]

1920:
- The American Professional Football Conference begins play, changing its name to the National Football League in 1922.[4]

1920s:
- Players used a hardened leather helmet and shoulder pads made of felt wool and leather.[5]

1929:
- John T. Riddell, a high school football coach in Indiana, creates the equipment company bearing his name after inventing the removable football cleat.[6]
- Introduction of fibershell helmets, which would be used into the 1950s.[7]

1930s:
- Introduction of molded leather helmets, foam pads and facemasks.[8]

1940:
- Introduction of hardened leather shoulder pads, used into the 1960s.[9]
- Introduction of the plastic helmet.[10] The plastic was brittle and would tend to break upon impact.[11]
- Introduction of the leather chin strap to help hold the helmet in place.[12]

1943:
- Helmets become mandatory in the NFL.[13]

1950s:
- Introduction of fibershell shoulder pads, used into the 1960s, and a plastic helmet with pads on the interior.[14]

1963:
- Riddell[15] introduces first helmet that uses air inflation for fitting the helmet snug to the head. [16]

1969:
- National Operating Committee on Standards for Athletic Equipment (NOCSAE) is formed as a non-profit organization with the purpose of improving athletic equipment and reducing injuries through equipment standards.[17] NOCSAE was formed in response to more than 100 high school and college football players killed by skull fractures and acute brain bleeding.[18]

1973:
- NOSCAE introduces its first helmet testing standards. Today, "under NOCSAE's standard, the football helmet is placed on a synthetic head model that is filled with glycerin and fitted with various measuring instruments. The head model fitted with the helmet is then dropped sixteen times onto a polymer anvil with two of the drops from a height of sixty inches onto six different locations of the helmet at varying temperatures determined by NOCSAE to simulate different potential game temperatures. After each drop a "Severity Index," which measures the severity of the impact absorbed by the head model at the moment of impact, is determined. Helmets are graded on a pass-fail basis, and the helmets that pass are those meeting an acceptable Severity Index."[19] For more information on NOCSAE, see Chapter 16: Equipment Manufacturers.

1970s:
- Introduction of plastic shoulder pads; facemasks expand beyond the single bar.[20]

---

a   To create this timeline, we relied on a timeline included on an NFL website, *see NFL Evolution—Health & Safety,* NFL Evolution, http://www.nflevolution.com/nfl-timeline/index. html (last visited Aug. 7, 2015), *archived at* http://perma.cc/PVP6-PA6C, a timeline included on Riddell's website, *See History,* Riddell, http://www.riddell.com/history (last visited Aug. 7, 2015), *archived at* http://perma.cc/A9DF-MF5V, and a variety of other news sources. It should not be considered an exhaustive list. More information and context is available in Chapter 16: Equipment Manufacturers.

1979:

- NFL mandates the use of thigh and knee pads. The rule is revoked in 1994, but reinstated in 2013.[21]

1982:

- Riddell introduces helmet with a combination of foam and liquid-filled cells used for padding.[22]

1983:

- All mandatory player equipment must be designed and made by a professional manufacturer and cannot be altered, except by the direction of the club doctor.[23]

1988:

- NFL and Riddell entered into agreement without duration whereby Riddell provides free helmets, pads and jerseys to all NFL clubs in exchange for Riddell receiving the exclusive right to display its logo on Riddell helmets used by NFL players. Competing helmet manufacturers could not display its logo on its helmets used by NFL players. Schutt Athletic, a Riddell competitor, lost its antitrust challenge to the agreement.[24]

1992:

- Riddell introduces the Variable Size Range (VSR) series, designed with additional inflation points for a more customized fit.[25] As a result of its agreement with the NFL, VSR helmets would come to be used by more than 60 percent of NFL players.[26]

1994:

- NFL removes rule requiring players to wear thigh and knee pads. Rule reinstated in 2013.[27]

2001:

- Minnesota Vikings Pro Bowl offensive tackle Korey Stringer died of complications from heat stroke after collapsing during training camp.[28] Stringer's family later sued the Vikings, Vikings coaches and affiliated doctors, the NFL, and Riddell. Stringer's family reached undisclosed settlements with one of the doctors involved,[29] the NFL[30] and Riddell.[31]

2002:

- Riddell introduces the Riddell Revolution helmet, designed with the intent of reducing concussion risk.[32]

- Riddell also funds research project led by two University of Pittsburgh Medical Center professors and a Riddell employee designed to compare the concussion rates and recovery times for athletes wearing Riddell's Revolution helmet compared to athletes wearing older model helmets manufactured by both Riddell and its competitors.[33] After tracking 2,141 Pennsylvania high school football players, the authors found 5.3 percent of players using Revolution helmets suffered concussions as compared to 7.6 percent of players using other helmets.[34] The authors described the difference as "statistically significant" and said the results "demonstrated a trend toward a lowered incidence of concussion" but that the

"limited sample size precludes a more conclusive statement of findings at this time."[35] The study also highlighted that there was a 31-percent decreased relative risk for athletes wearing the Revolution helmet, comparing the 5.3-percent and 7.6-percent concussion rates.[36] Riddell seized on that last statistic and began to advertise that the Revolution helmet reduced the risk of concussion by 31 percent.[37] Riddell's competitor, Schutt Sports, later lost a lawsuit alleging Riddell's advertisements were false and based on an unreliable study.[38] The study has nonetheless been controversial, as discussed in Chapter 16: Equipment Manufacturers.

2008:

- Introduction of shoulder pads which allow cold air to be pumped through them while on the sidelines.[39]

2010:

- NFL clubs test new girdles with built-in padding at the hip, thigh and tailbone during training camp and preseason with hope of encouraging more players to wear leg pads.[40]

2011:

- Chicago Bears become the first NFL club to adopt Riddell RipKord shoulder pads. According to Riddell, "[b]y pulling a single cord, shoulder pads outfitted with RipKord can be quickly and easily removed by two trained professionals without elevating a player," providing "more efficient and immediate access to an athlete's chest and airway in the event of a suspected head, spine or chest injury."[41]

- NFL begins relationship with the United States military aimed at preventing and treating head injuries.[42]

- NFL players begin to put Kevlar in their helmets, generating controversy.[43]

- Riddell introduces 360 Helmet, designed to disperse the energy of frontal impacts as a result of examining over 1.4 million impacts collected through Riddell's impact-tracking technology.[44]

- The first lawsuits against the NFL and Riddell concerning concussions are filed. Hundreds followed.[45]

2012:

- All cases concerning concussions are consolidated in the United States District Court for the Eastern District of Pennsylvania *In re National Football League Players' Concussion Injury Litigation,* 12-md-23-23 (E.D.Pa.). Claims generally allege that NFL knew of risk of concussions and intentionally and fraudulently concealed those risks from NFL players, and that Riddell made defective helmets while failing to inform players of the risks of using their helmets.[46]

2013:

- NFL sends memo to clubs reminding them that players must have the opportunity to see and try "a wide range of helmets from leading manufacturers," at no cost to the player. NFL locker rooms include large posters with 18 helmets from six different brands including their ratings according to Virginia Tech's "STAR" evaluation system.[47]

- NFL institutes policy whereby teams playing games in "throwback" uniforms must still use their current, regular helmets.[48]

- NFL reinstates rule requiring players to wear thigh and knee pads. The NFL estimated that, prior to reinstating the rule, 70 percent of players were not wearing thigh and knee pads.[49] Nevertheless, even with the existence of the rule, players have a long-standing practice of modifying and minimizing the required pads in favor of speed and mobility.[50]

- NFL's indefinite agreement with Riddell expired as a result of NFL negotiations. NFL states that there will no longer be an official helmet of the NFL.[51]

- NFL announces a $40 million research and development program with General Electric and Under Armour to improve concussion diagnosis and treatment, including $10 million incentive programs aimed at discovering new and improved technology.[52]

2014:

- NFL and Riddell enter into five-year agreement by which Riddell would be the exclusive licensee for collectible helmets.[53]

- Riddell introduces SpeedFlex helmet, which includes a five-sided indentation on the crown of the helmet.[54] The helmets are adopted by several major college football programs.

2015:

- United States District Court for the Eastern District of Pennsylvania approves settlement between NFL and plaintiffs *In re National Football League Players' Concussion Injury Litigation,* providing for compensation to qualifying former NFL players depending on the severity of their medical conditions. The settlement does not limit the total amount the NFL might eventually have to pay to satisfy its obligations under the settlement.[55] The lawsuit was not settled with Riddell.

2016:

- United States Court of Appeals for the Third Circuit affirms the District Court's approval of the settlement between NFL and plaintiffs *In re National Football League Players' Concussion Injury Litigation.* Claims against Riddell remain in litigation.

Endnotes

1. *Chronology of Professional Football*, 2013 NFL Record & Fact Book, 353, 353–54 (2013), http://static.nfl.com/static/content/public/image/history/pdfs/History/2013/353-372-Chronology.pdf, *archived at* https://perma.cc/TT7V-PK84?type=pdf.

2. Katie Zezima, *How Teddy Roosevelt Helped Save Football*, Wash. Post, May 29, 2014, http://www.washingtonpost.com/blogs/the-fix/wp/2014/05/29/teddy-roosevelt-helped-save-football-with-a-white-house-meeting-in-1905/, *archived at* http://perma.cc/8EMV-4RJF.

3. *Id.*

4. *Chronology of Professional Football*, *supra* note 1 at 353–54

5. *NFL Evolution — Health & Safety*, NFL Evolution, http://www.nflevolution.com/nfl-timeline/index.html (last visited Aug. 7, 2015), *archived at* http://perma.cc/PVP6-PA6C ("NFL Evolution").

6. *History*, Riddell, http://www.riddell.com/history (last visited Aug. 7, 2015), *archived at* http://perma.cc/A9DF-MF5V ("Riddell History").

7. NFL Evolution.

8. NFL Evolution.

9. NFL Evolution.

10. NFL Evolution.

11. Riddell History.

12. Riddell History.

13. NFL Evolution.

14. NFL Evolution.

15. Mentions of Riddell mean all the various entities which generally operate under the name "Riddell."

16. Riddell History.

17. *About NOSCAE,* Nat'l Operating Comm. on Standards for Athletic Equipment, http://nocsae.org/about-nocsae/ (last visited Aug. 7, 2015), *archived at* http://perma.cc/6AD8-UJ96.

18. Alan Schwarz, *As Concussions Rise, Scant Oversight for Football Helmet Safety*, N.Y. Times, Oct. 21, 2010, http://www.nytimes.com/2010/10/21/sports/football/21helmets.html?pagewanted=all, *available at* http://perma.cc/2LJV-K2RQ.

19. Jason Navia, *Sitting on the Bench: The Failure of Youth Football Helmet Regulation and the Necessity of Government Intervention*, 64 Admin. L. Rev. 265, 276–77 (2012).

20. NFL Evolution.

21. Tom Pelissero, *More Padding Mandatory in NFL, Protection of Knees, Thighs Now Required*, USA Today, July 12, 2013, *available at* 2013 WLNR 16937591.

22. Riddell History.

23. NFL Evolution.

24. *See* Schutt Athletic Sales Co. v. Riddell, Inc., 727 F.Supp. 1220 (N.D.Ill. 1989); *see also* Jenny Vrentas, *The First Line of Defense*, MMQB (Oct. 22, 2013), http://mmqb.si.com/2013/10/22/nfl-helmets-head-injury-concussion/print/, *archived at* http://perma.cc/WL9Q-7PXT (describing Riddell agreement as "indefinite").

25. Riddell History.

26. *Id.*

27. Pelissero, *supra* note 21.

28. Stringer v. Minnesota Vikings Football Club, LLC, 705 N.W.2d 746, 748 (Minn. 2005).

29. *See* Stringer v. Minnesota Vikings Football Club, LLC, No. 02-415, 2003 WL 25766738 (Minn.Dist.Ct. Dec. 8, 2003) (mentioning settlement with W. David Knowles, MD and Mankato Clinic, Ltd.).

30. *Stringer's Widow Settles Lawsuit With N.F.L.,* N.Y. Times, Jan. 27, 2009, http://www.nytimes.com/2009/01/27/sports/football/27stringerbox.html?ref=topics, *archived at* http://perma.cc/L39K-9BB2.

31   *Jackson Ends His Holdout, Saying He Always Wanted to Remain an Eagle*, N.Y. Times, Aug. 9, 2011, http://www.nytimes.com/2011/08/09/sports/football/eagles-desean-jackson-ends-holdout-after-11-days.html, *archived at* http://perma.cc/L39K-9BB2.

32   Riddell History.

33   *See* Riddell, Inc. v. Schutt Sports, Inc., 724 F. Supp. 2d 963, 967 (W.D.Wis. 2010) (describing background of the study).

34   *Id.*

35   *Id.*

36   *Id.* 7.6% less 31% of 7.6% = approximately 5.3%.

37   *Id.*

38   *See id.*

39   Janet Cromley, *Air-Conditioned Pads Make Football Cooler*, Star-Ledger (Newark, NJ), Aug. 5, 2008, *available at* 2008 WLNR 14600368.

40   Judy Battista, *N.F.L. Gives Lower-Body Padding a Tryout*, N.Y. Times, Aug. 6, 2010, http://www.nytimes.com/2010/08/06/sports/football/06pads.html, *archived at* http://perma.cc/R3EQ-46LP.

41   *Chicago Bears to be First NFL Team to Adopt New Riddell RipKord Shoulder Pad Technology*, PR Newswire (Aug. 1, 2011), http://www.prnewswire.com/news-releases/chicago-bears-to-be-first-nfl-team-to-adopt-new-riddell-ripkord-shoulder-pad-technology-126508183.html, *archived at* http://perma.cc/DGH8-Y9HM.

42   Bill Bradly, *Department of Defense, Veterans Affairs Focus on Brain Injuries*, NFL (Aug. 22, 2013, 10:41 PM), http://www.nfl.com/news/story/0ap1000000232809/article/department-of-defense-veterans-affairs-focus-on-brain-injuries, *archived at* http://perma.cc/6DMF-KCQB.

43   Sean Conboy, *The Helmet Con: How to Make a Buck Off the Concussion Crisis*, Deadspin (Aug. 21, 2013), http://deadspin.com/the-helmet-con-how-to-make-a-buck-off-the-concussion-c-1173019556, *archived at* http://perma.cc/J9JV-XBVD.

44   Riddell History.

45   *See Court Documents*, NFL Concussion Litigation.com, http://nflconcussionlitigation.com/?page_id=18 (last visited Aug. 7, 2015), *archived at* http://perma.cc/FYW5-NN7A.

46   *See* Plaintiffs' Amended Master Administrative Long-Form Complaint, In re National Football League Players' Concussion Injury Litigation, 2:12-md-2323 (E.D.Pa. July 17, 2012), ECF No. 2642.

47   Jenny Vrentas, *The First Line of Defense*, MMQB (Oct. 22, 2013), http://mmqb.si.com/2013/10/22/nfl-helmets-head-injury-concussion/print/, *archived at* http://perma.cc/WL9Q-7PXT.

48   Paul Lukas, *Uni Watch: Impact of Helmet Policy*, ESPN (Sept. 19, 2013), http://espn.go.com/espn/print?id=9694560&type=Columnist&imagesPri, *archived at* http://perma.cc/6D33-32UL.

49   Tom Pelissero, *More Padding Mandatory in NFL, Protection of Knees, Thighs Now Required*, USA Today, July 12, 2013, *available at* 2013 WLNR 16937591.

50   See Jere Longman, *Slim is In*, N.Y. Times, Jan. 31, 2014, http://www.nytimes.com/2014/01/31/sports/football/shoulder-pads-slim-down-in-faster-sleeker-nfl.html, *archived at* https://perma.cc/K9VJ-U8NS; *When it Comes to Pads, Fewer the Better*, Indianapolis Star, Aug. 22, 2010, *available at* 2010 WLNR 16781303; Stefan Fatsis, *Padded Stats: Protective Gear in Today's NFL is Becoming an Endangered Species as Players Gladly Sacrifice Equipment for Speed and Mobility*, Nat'l Post (Canada), Dec. 24, 2004, *available at* 2004 WLNR 14897899; Steve Aschburner, *Tricks of the Trade: Protective Paraphernalia Puts Players at Peace*, Star Trib. (Minneapolis, St. Paul), Oct.9, 1988, *available at* 1988 WLNR 1648115.

51   Vrentas, *supra* note 47.

52   Gary Mihoces, *NFL Offering Millions for Helmet Innovations*, USA Today, Sept. 4, 2013, http://www.usatoday.com/story/sports/nfl/2013/09/04/helmets-concussions-roger-goodell/2768237/, *archived at* http://perma.cc/37F6-MHDT.

53   *Riddell Enters New Agreement with NFL into 2019*, J. Engineering, Apr. 9, 2014, *available at* 2014 WLNR 8998904.

54   *In Race to Develop Safer Football Helmets, Many Questions Remain*, N.Y. Times, Aug. 23, 2014, http://www.nytimes.com/2014/08/24/sports/football/in-race-to-develop-safer-football-helmets-many-questions-remain.html?mabReward=RI%3A7, *archived at* https://perma.cc/W8MD-774C?type=pdf.

55   Michael David Smith, *NFL, Concussion Plaintiffs Announce Revised Settlement*, ProFootballTalk (June 25, 2014,12:05 PM), http://profootballtalk.nbcsports.com/2014/06/25/nfl-concussion-plaintiffs-announce-revised-settlement/, *archived at* http://perma.cc/LL9Q-D6NK.

APPENDIX K \ Players' Options to Enforce Stakeholders' Legal and Ethical Obligations[a]

Stakeholder Against Whom Relief is Sought	Enforcement Mechanism	Strengths	Weaknesses
Players	Civil lawsuit	• Potential for jury award	• Length of time • Cost • Conduct must have been intentional, reckless, or willful and wanton • Potentially preempted by CBA • Almost definitely barred by workers' compensation statutes if injured by player's own teammate
Athletic Trainers	Accountability and Care Committee — Art. 39	• Inexpensive • Informal • Private	• Claim is referred to NFL and club • Committee has no binding authority • No neutral adjudicatory process
	Non-Injury Grievance — Art. 43	• Less costly and faster than court action • Private • Money damages explicitly available • Can allege ethical violations	• CBA likely cannot be enforced in an action against athletic trainers • Almost definitely barred by workers' compensation statutes • 50-day statute of limitations strictly enforced • No jury • Less public scrutiny than court action
	Joint Committee on Player Safety and Welfare — Art. 50	• Inexpensive • Informal • Private • Review by neutral doctors	• Claim is referred to NFL and club • Committee has no binding authority • No neutral adjudicatory process

a   The chart here includes players' options to enforce a stakeholder's legal and ethical obligations, except for The Media, Fans, and NFL Business Partners. Enforcement against those stakeholders is too unlikely and tangential to be included among these enforcement options.

APPENDIX K: Players' Options To Enforce Stakeholders' Legal And Ethical Obligations (continued)

Stakeholder Against Whom Relief is Sought	Enforcement Mechanism	Strengths	Weaknesses
Athletic Trainers (continued)	Civil lawsuit	• Potential for jury award • Public scrutiny	• Length of time • Cost • Very likely barred by workers' compensation statutes • Potentially preempted by CBA
	File complaint with Professional Football Athletic Trainers Society (PFATS).	• Inexpensive • Informal • Private	• Unlikely to result in tangible benefit to player
	File complaint with National Athletic Trainers Association (NATA).	• Inexpensive • Informal • Private	• Unlikely to result in tangible benefit to player
	File complaint with Board of Certification for the Athletic Trainer.	• Inexpensive • Informal • Private	• Unlikely to result in tangible benefit to player
Club Doctors	Accountability and Care Committee — Art. 39	• Inexpensive • Informal • Private	• Claim is referred to NFL and club • Committee has no binding authority • No neutral adjudicatory process
	Non-Injury Grievance — Art. 43	• Less costly and faster than court action • Private • Money damages explicitly available • Can allege ethical violations	• CBA likely cannot be enforced in an action against club doctors • Might be barred by workers' compensation statutes • 50-day statute of limitations strictly enforced • No jury • Less public scrutiny than court action
	Joint Committee on Player Safety and Welfare — Art. 50	• Inexpensive • Informal • Private • Review by neutral doctors	• Unclear whether Committee has any authority to compensate player

Stakeholder Against Whom Relief is Sought	Enforcement Mechanism	Strengths	Weaknesses
Club Doctors (continued)	Civil lawsuit	• Potential for jury award • Public scrutiny	• Length of time • Cost • Potentially preempted by CBA • Possibly barred from workers' compensation statutes (depending on relationships between club and doctor)
	File complaint with the doctor's state licensing board	• Potential for jury award • Public scrutiny	• Unlikely to result in tangible benefit to player
Second Opinion Doctors	Civil lawsuit	• Potential for jury award • Public scrutiny	• Length of time • Cost
	File complaint with the doctor's state licensing board	• Inexpensive • Informal • Private	• Unlikely to result in tangible benefit to player
Neutral Doctors	Non-Injury Grievance — Art. 43	• Less costly and faster than court action • Private • Money damages explicitly available • Can allege ethical violations	• 50-day statute of limitations strictly enforced • No jury • Less public scrutiny than court action
	Civil lawsuit	• Potential for jury award • Public scrutiny	• Length of time • Cost • Potentially preempted by CBA
	File complaint with the doctor's state licensing board.	• Inexpensive • Informal • Private	• Unlikely to result in tangible benefit to player
Personal Doctors	Civil lawsuit	• Potential for jury award • Public scrutiny	• Length of time • Cost
	File complaint with the doctor's state licensing board	• Inexpensive • Informal • Private	• Unlikely to result in tangible benefit to player

APPENDIX K: Players' Options To Enforce Stakeholders' Legal And Ethical Obligations (continued)

Stakeholder Against Whom Relief is Sought	Enforcement Mechanism	Strengths	Weaknesses
The NFL	Non-Injury Grievance — Art. 43	• Less costly and faster than court action • Private • Money damages explicitly available	• 50 day statute of limitations strictly enforced • No jury • Less public scrutiny than court action
	Civil lawsuit	• Potential for jury award • Public scrutiny	• Length of time • Cost • Claims often preempted by CBA
The NFLPA	Civil lawsuit	• Potential for jury award • Public scrutiny	• Length of time • Cost • Potentially preempted by CBA and National Labor Relations Act (NLRA)
	Arbitration pursuant to NFLPA Constitution	• Less costly and faster than court action • Private	• Mechanism has never been used • Unclear if damages available to injured player
NFL Clubs	Accountability and Care Committee — Art. 39	• Inexpensive • Informal • Private	• Claim is referred to NFL and club • Committee has no binding authority • No neutral adjudicatory process
	Non-Injury Grievance — Art. 43	• Less costly and faster than court action • Private • Money damages explicitly available • Can allege ethical violations	• 50 day statute of limitations strictly enforced • No jury • Less public scrutiny than court action
	Joint Committee on Player Safety and Welfare — Art. 50	• Inexpensive • Informal • Private • Review by neutral doctors	• Unclear whether Committee has any authority to compensate player
	Civil lawsuit	• Potential for jury award • Public scrutiny	• Length of time • Cost • Claims likely preempted by CBA

Stakeholder Against Whom Relief is Sought	Enforcement Mechanism	Strengths	Weaknesses
Coaches	Non-Injury Grievance — Art. 43	• Less costly and faster than court action • Private • Money damages explicitly available	• CBA likely cannot be enforced in an action against coaches • Almost definitely barred by workers' compensation statutes • 50-day statute of limitations strictly enforced • No jury • Less public scrutiny than court action
	Civil lawsuit	• Potential for jury award • Public scrutiny	• Length of time • Cost • Almost definitely barred by workers' compensation statutes • Potentially preempted by CBA
	File complaint with the American Football Coaches Association (AFCA)	• Inexpensive • Fast • Private	• AFCA cannot order recompense to the injured player • AFCA generally not involved in NFL coach matters
Club Employees	Non-Injury Grievance — Art. 43	• Less costly and faster than court action • Private • Money damages explicitly available	• CBA likely cannot be enforced in an action against club employees • Almost definitely barred by workers' compensation statutes • 50-day statute of limitations strictly enforced • No jury • Less public scrutiny than court action
	Civil lawsuit	• Potential for jury award • Public scrutiny	• Length of time • Cost • Very likely barred by workers' compensation statutes • Potentially preempted by CBA

APPENDIX K: Players' Options To Enforce Stakeholders' Legal And Ethical Obligations (continued)

Stakeholder Against Whom Relief is Sought	Enforcement Mechanism	Strengths	Weaknesses
Equipment Managers	Non-Injury Grievance — Art. 43	• Less costly and faster than court action • Private • Money damages explicitly available • Can allege ethical violations	• CBA likely cannot be enforced in an action against equipment managers • Almost definitely barred by workers' compensation statutes • 50-day statute of limitations strictly enforced • No jury • Less public scrutiny than court action
	Civil lawsuit	• Potential for jury award • Public scrutiny	• Length of time • Cost • Almost definitely barred by workers' compensation statutes • Potentially preempted by CBA
	File complaint with Athletic Equipment Managers Association (AEMA)	• Inexpensive • Informal • Private	• Unlikely to result in tangible benefit to player • Not all Equipment Managers are members of the AEMA
Contract Advisors	Grievance pursuant to Contract Advisor Regulations	• Less costly and faster than court action • Private	• No jury • Less public scrutiny than court action
	Civil lawsuit	• Potential for jury award • Public scrutiny	• Length of time • Cost • Almost definitely barred by Contract Advisor Regulations
	File complaint with Committee on Agent Regulation and Discipline (CARD)	• Inexpensive • Informal • Private	• Unlikely to result in tangible benefit to player
	File complaint with the contract advisor's state bar (if contract advisor is attorney)	• Inexpensive • Informal • Private	• Unlikely to result in tangible benefit to player

Stakeholder Against Whom Relief is Sought	Enforcement Mechanism	Strengths	Weaknesses
Financial Advisors	File grievance with Financial Industry Regulation Authority (FINRA)	• Less costly and faster than court action • Private	• No jury • Less public scrutiny than court action
	File complaint with NFLPA	• Inexpensive • Informal • Private	• Unlikely to result in tangible benefit to player
	Civil lawsuit	• Potential for jury award • Public scrutiny	• Length of time • Cost • Likely barred by arbitration clause in financial advisor agreement
	File complaint with the financial advisor's relevant professional societies	• Inexpensive • Informal • Private	• Unlikely to result in tangible benefit to player
Family Members	Civil lawsuit	• Potential for jury award • Public scrutiny	• Length of time • Cost • Public airing of family matters
Officials	Civil lawsuit	• Potential for jury award • Public scrutiny	• Length of time • Cost • Potentially preempted by CBA
Equipment manufacturers	Civil lawsuit	• Potential for jury award • Public scrutiny	• Length of time • Cost • Potentially preempted by CBA

APPENDIX L \ Authorization for Use and Disclosure of Records and Information

Note: Below is a form executed by players permitting their medical records to be used by and disclosed among the NFL, NFL clubs, and related parties. This form was collectively bargained between the NFL and NFLPA.

INSERT CLUB NAME AND/OR LOGO

AUTHORIZATION FOR USE AND DISCLOSURE OF RECORDS AND INFORMATION

Name: _____   D.O.B.: _____

Address: _____

1. Persons/Entities Authorized to Release and Disclose Information:

I hereby authorize and give my permission to the following persons and/or entities to release and disclose my medical records and/or protected health information ("PHI") (as defined under the Health Insurance Portability and Accountability Act, as amended ("HIPAA") and the regulations thereunder) in the manner described in this Authorization:

> *[INSERT CLUB NAME]*, ("Club"), the National Football League and each of its member Clubs, as now existing or at any time in the future, the National Football League Drug Advisers, National Invitational Camp, Inc., National Football Scouting, Inc., the advisors to the National Football League's Policy and Program on Substances of Abuse, the advisors to the National Football League's Policy on Anabolic Steroids and Related Substances, and respective representatives, agents, and/or employees, owners, officers, servants, staff members, and contractors, any NFL Club medical staff members, team physicians, athletic training staff members, as well as any outside or third-party physicians, physician groups, hospitals, clinics, laboratories, consulting physicians, specialists, and/or healthcare professionals engaged by the NFL or NFL Clubs, and any present and future electronic medical record vendors used by the NFL or NFL Clubs, including, but not limited to, eClinicalWorks, Inc., Infinitt, Inc., and/or Surescripts.

2. Personal Health Information to Be Used and Disclosed:

I hereby authorize the following medical records and/or PHI to be used and disclosed as described in this Authorization to the Authorized Parties:

> My entire health or medical record and/or PHI relating to any injury, sickness, disease, mental health condition, physical condition, medical history, medical or clinical status, diagnosis, treatment or prognosis from any source, including without limitation all written and/or electronic information or data, clinical notes, progress notes, discharge summaries, lab results, pathology reports, operative reports, consultations, physicals, physicians' records, athletic trainers' records, diagnoses, findings, treatments, history and prognoses, test results, laboratory reports, x-rays, MRI, and/or imaging results, outpatient notes, physical therapy records, occupational therapy records, prescriptions, and any and all other information pertaining to my past or present medical condition, diagnosis, treatment, history, and prognosis. This Authorization expressly <u>includes</u> all records and PHI relating to any mental health treatment, therapy, and/or counseling, but expressly excludes psychotherapy notes.

> For purposes of use and disclosure to the National Football League this disclosure shall be subject to the limitations set forth in Section 4(f) below.

3. Persons/Entities Authorized to Receive and Use:

I hereby authorize the following persons and/or entities to receive and use my medical records and/or PHI only for the purposes that are permitted under this Authorization. These persons and entities will be referred to as the "Authorized Parties":

[*INSERT CLUB NAME*], the National Football League and each of its member Clubs, as now existing or at any time in the future, the National Football League Drug Advisers, National Invitational Camp, Inc., National Football Scouting, Inc., the advisors to the National Football League's Policy and Program on Substances of Abuse, the advisors to the National Football League's Policy on Anabolic Steroids and Related Substances, and respective representatives, agents, and/or employees, owners, officers, servants, staff members, and contractors, any NFL Club medical staff members, team physicians, athletic training staff members, as well as any outside or third-party physicians, physician groups, hospitals, clinics, laboratories, consulting physicians, specialists, and/or healthcare professionals engaged by the NFL or NFL Clubs, and any present and future electronic medical record vendors used by the NFL or NFL Clubs, including, but not limited to, eClinicalWorks, Inc., Infinitt, Inc., and/or Surescripts.

4. Purpose of the Disclosure:

For purposes relating only to my actual or potential employment in the National Football League including the provision of healthcare, evaluation, consultation, treatment, therapy, and related services, which purposes are limited to reviewing, discussing, transmitting, disclosing, sharing, and/or using my medical records and PHI: (a) between and among any of the Authorized Parties; (b) with any of my healthcare providers and/or mental health providers; (c) for employment-related injury reports; (d) for the activities of the National Football League Drug Advisors, the advisors to the National Football League's Policy and Program on Substances of Abuse, and/or the advisors to the National Football League's Policy on Anabolic Steroids and Related Substances, specifically limited to due diligence and audit activities, investigations of possible violations of the Policies or eligibility for a "therapeutic-use" exception under either Policy; (e) for ophthalmic examinations, consultations or treatment; and/or (f) with respect to disclosure to the National Football League, this authorization shall not be used by the NFL or its member Clubs to obtain documents, evidence, or material for purposes of litigation, grievances, or any dispute with the National Football League or its member clubs, except as contemplated by the August 4, 2011 Collective Bargaining Agreement (CBA), and as is necessary for the NFL and its member Clubs to fulfill their obligations under the CBA.

5. Expiration Event: This Authorization will expire two years from the date on which I was last employed by any NFL Club.

6. Photocopy: A photostatic copy of this Authorization shall be considered as effective and valid as the original.

7. Signature: By my signature below, I acknowledge that I have read this Authorization, understand my rights as described herein, understand that I am allowing medical and mental healthcare providers to disclose my PHI, and have had any questions answered to my satisfaction. I also acknowledge and understand that: this Authorization has been collectively bargained for by the National Football League and the National Football League Players Association.

Signature:_____   Date: _____

NOTICE: You are entitled to a copy of this Authorization after you sign it. You have the right to revoke this Authorization any time by presenting a written request to the Club's Head Athletic Trainer or his designee, except to the extent that any Authorized Party has relied upon it. Revocation will not apply: 1) to information that has already been released in connection with this Authorization, 2) during a contestability period under applicable law, or 3) if the Authorization was obtained as a condition of obtaining insurance coverage. We may not condition treatment, payment, enrollment or eligibility for benefits on your execution of this authorization, except for the purpose of creating protected health information for disclosure to a third party on provision of Authorization. Information disclosed pursuant to this Authorization may be re-disclosed by the recipient(s) and no longer protected by federal or state privacy laws or regulations. Information disclosed pursuant to this Authorization may include records created by a healthcare provider or mental healthcare provider other than the disclosing party, unless access to such PHI has been restricted as permitted under HIPAA or such provider has expressly prohibited such re-disclosure.

2

APPENDIX M \ Authorization for Release and Disclosure of Medical & Mental Health Records

Note: Below is a form executed by players permitting their medical providers to release their medical records to the NFL, NFL clubs, and related parties. This form was collectively bargained between the NFL and NFLPA.

INSERT CLUB NAME AND/OR LOGO
**AUTHORIZATION FOR RELEASE & DISCLOSURE
OF MEDICAL & MENTAL HEALTH RECORDS**

Player Name: _____   Date of Birth: _____

Club Name: _____

1.   Persons/Entities Authorized to Release and Disclose Information. I hereby authorize, empower, request, and direct all healthcare providers, physicians, hospitals, mental health providers, counselors, therapists, clinics, schools, universities, colleges, student health services, dispensaries, sanatoriums, any other agencies, NFL Clubs, professional football teams, athletic trainers, all other amateur or professional teams or organizations, facilities, and/or entities that may possess my medical records and/or my protected health information ("PHI") (as defined under the Health Insurance Portability and Accountability Act, as amended ("HIPAA") and the regulations thereunder): (1) to release, disclose, and to make these records and/or PHI freely available to the persons and entities identified on this Authorization as the Authorized Parties; and (2) to discuss the contents of these records and PHI with the Authorized Parties and their representatives. I hereby release and discharge all persons and institutions from any and all claims by reason of their releasing such records and information.

2.   Persons/Entities Authorized to Receive and Use the Information. I hereby authorize, empower, and give permission to the following persons and/or entities and their representatives to receive, inspect, copy, obtain copies, examine, and/or use of any and all medical records and PHI described in this Authorization. These persons and entities will be referred to as the "Authorized Parties":

> *[INSERT CLUB NAME]*, hereinafter "Club", the National Football League and each of its member Clubs, as now existing or at any time in the future, the National Football League Drug Advisers, National Invitational Camp, Inc., National Football Scouting, Inc., the advisors to the National Football League's Policy and Program on Substances of Abuse, the advisors to the National Football League's Policy on Anabolic Steroids and Related Substances, respective representatives, agents, and/or employees, owners, officers, servants, staff members, and contractors, any NFL Club medical staff members, team physicians, athletic training staff members, as well as any outside or third-party physicians, physician groups, hospitals, clinics, laboratories, consulting physicians, specialists, and/or healthcare professionals engaged by the NFL or NFL Clubs, and any present and future electronic medical record vendors used by the NFL or NFL Clubs, including, but not limited to, eClinicalWorks, Inc., Infinitt, Inc., and/or Surescripts.

786673.1

3.   Description of the Information to be Released and Disclosed. I hereby authorize, empower, direct, and give permission for the following medical records and/or PHI to be released and disclosed to the Authorized Parties:

My entire health or medical record and/or PHI relating to any injury, sickness, disease, mental health condition, physical condition, medical history, medical or clinical status, diagnosis, treatment or prognosis from any source, including without limitation all written and/or electronic information or data, clinical notes, progress notes, discharge summaries, lab results, pathology reports, operative reports, consultations, physicals, physicians' records, athletic trainers' records, diagnoses, findings, treatments, history and prognoses, test results, laboratory reports, x-rays, MRI, and/or imaging results, outpatient notes, physical therapy records, occupational therapy records, prescriptions, and any and all other information pertaining to my past or present medical condition, diagnosis, treatment, history, and prognosis. This Authorization applies to any and all medical records and/or PHI, including medical records and/or PHI which the Persons/Entities Authorized to Release and Disclose Information may have received from another provider, unless access to such PHI has been restricted as permitted under HIPAA or that provider has expressly prohibited re-disclosure.

This Authorization expressly includes all records and PHI relating to any mental health treatment, therapy, and/or counseling, but expressly excludes psychotherapy notes.

4.   Purpose of the Disclosure. For purposes relating only to my actual or potential employment in the National Football League including the provision of healthcare, evaluation, consultation, treatment, therapy, and related services, which purposes are limited to reviewing, discussing, transmitting, disclosing, sharing, and/or using my medical records and PHI: (a) between and among any of the Authorized Parties; (b) with any of my healthcare providers and/or mental health providers; (c) for employment-related injury reports; (d) for the activities of the National Football League Drug Advisors, the advisors to the National Football League's Policy and Program on Substances of Abuse, and/or the advisors to the National Football League's Policy on Anabolic Steroids and Related Substances, specifically limited to due diligence and audit activities, investigations of possible violations of the Policies or eligibility for a "therapeutic-use" exception under either Policy; (e) for ophthalmic examinations, consultations or treatment; and/or (f) with respect to disclosure to the National Football League, this authorization shall not be used by the NFL or its member Clubs to obtain documents, evidence, or material for purposes of litigation, grievances, or any dispute with the National Football League or its member

786673.1

clubs, except as contemplated by the August 4, 2011 Collective Bargaining Agreement (CBA), and as is necessary for the NFL and its member Clubs to fulfill their obligations under the CBA.

5.   Expiration Event. This Authorization will expire two years from the date on which my employment with any NFL Club ceases.

6.   Photocopy. A photostatic copy of this Authorization shall be considered as effective and valid as the original.

7.   Signature. By my signature below, I acknowledge that I have read this Authorization, understand my rights as described herein, understand that I am allowing medical and mental healthcare providers to disclose my PHI, and have had any questions answered to my satisfaction. I expressly and voluntarily authorize the release, disclosure, and use of my medical records and/or PHI as described in this Authorization. I also acknowledge and understand that: this Authorization has been collectively bargained for by the National Football League and the National Football League Players Associations.

_____   _____
Signature   Date

If a personal representative signs this Authorization on behalf of the Player, complete the following:

Personal Representative's Name: _____

Relationship to Individual: _____

NOTICE: You are entitled to a copy of this Authorization after you sign it. You have the right to revoke this Authorization any time by presenting a written request to the Club's Head Athletic Trainer or his designee, except to the extent that any Authorized Party has relied upon it. Revocation will not apply: 1) to information that has already been released in connection with this Authorization, 2) during a contestability period under applicable law, or 3) if the Authorization was obtained as a condition of obtaining insurance coverage. We may not condition treatment, payment, enrollment or eligibility for benefits on your execution of this authorization, except for the purpose of creating protected health information for disclosure to a third party on provision of Authorization.   Information disclosed pursuant to this Authorization may be re-disclosed by the recipient(s) and no longer protected by federal or state privacy laws or regulations.   Information disclosed pursuant to this Authorization may include records created by a healthcare provider or mental healthcare provider other than the disclosing party, unless access to such PHI has been restricted as permitted under HIPAA or such provider has expressly prohibited such re-disclosure.

786673.1

APPENDIX N \ Reviewers of This Report

After this Report was reviewed by The Football Players Health Study team at Harvard, we subjected it to review by numerous advisors, experts, readers, and stakeholders before publication. We identify these reviewers below.

Importantly, while the below reviewers had the opportunity to comment, and their comments in many instances did inform the content of this Report, we retained control over its final content. Thus, review alone should not necessarily be considered an individual endorsement by that reviewer of the final Report in its entirety.

LAW & ETHICS ADVISORY PANEL (LEAP)

The LEAP is a multidisciplinary group of individuals who advise the Law & Ethics Initiative of The Football Players Health Study. We hold semi-annual meetings or conference calls with members of the LEAP to update them on our projects and receive their feedback. In addition, we communicate with individual members of the LEAP from time to time if they have expertise relevant to a particular issue we are facing or working through. The LEAP members are not paid for their assistance.

Specific to the LEAP's role in reviewing this Report, we consulted with LEAP members early in the drafting process, and members were given the opportunity to comment on the Report's organization, selection of stakeholders, and relevant ethics principles. They also had the opportunity to review a complete draft of the Report and provide detailed feedback. We listened to this feedback, and where appropriate, made changes.

APPENDIX N-A:
LEAP Members

LEAP Member	Relevant Titles and Affiliations	Relevant Expertise
Nita Farahany, J.D., M.A., Ph.D.	Professor, Duke University and Duke University School of Law; Member, Presidential Commission for the Study of Bioethical Issues.	Farahany is an expert in bioethics and the law.
Joseph J. Fins, M.D., M.A.C.P.	Professor, Attending Physician and Chief of Division of Medical Ethics, Weill Cornell Medical College.	Fins is an expert in medicine, public health, and bioethics.
Ashley Foxworth, J.D., M.A.	Attorney; Student, Harvard Graduate School of Education.	Foxworth is an attorney and her husband, Domonique, played in the NFL from 2005–11 and was President of the NFLPA from 2012–14.
Walter Jones	Former NFL Player.	Jones is a former offensive lineman and a member of the Pro Football Hall of Fame. Jones played with the Seattle Seahawks from 1997–2009.

APPENDIX N-A: LEAP Members (continued)

LEAP Member	Relevant Titles and Affiliations	Relevant Expertise
Isaiah Kacyvenski, M.B.A.	Former NFL Player; Head of Sport & Fitness, MC10 Inc.	Kacyvenski played in the NFL from 2000–07. After earning his M.B.A. at Harvard Business School, Kacyvenski joined the health technology company MC10.
Bernard Lo, M.D.	President, Greenwall Foundation; Professor of Medicine Emeritus and Director of the Program in Medical Ethics Emeritus, University of California, San Francisco.	Lo is an expert in medicine and bioethics.
Chris Ogbonnaya, B.A., B.S.	Former NFL Player (current player at the time of joining LEAP).	Ogbonnaya played in the NFL from 2009–14.
Dick Vermeil, M.A.	Former NFL Coach.	Vermeil coached in the NFL for 29 years, including 15 as a head coach. Vermeil won Super Bowl XXXIV as the coach of the St. Louis Rams in 1999.

PEER REVIEWERS:

Following LEAP review, we provided each of the below reviewers a draft copy of the Report and asked them, within 30 days, to provide written comments focusing on the following items:

a) Does the Report contain any legal or factual errors or omissions?

b) Is the Report fair in its tone and analysis?

c) Is the Report understandable? Do you have any suggestions for improving the Report's accessibility?

d) Is the Report missing anything that would help contribute to player health?

e) Are the Report's recommendations meaningful and realistic?

f) Are there additional recommendations you would make, or recommendations that should be excluded?

g) Do you have any other comments or feedback concerning the Report?

We reviewed the reviewers' comments and made the changes we believed were necessary and appropriate. The reviewers were paid $5,000 each for their work.

Gabriel Feldman, Associate Professor of Law and Director, Sport Law Program, Tulane University Law School, additionally served as a "lead" peer reviewer. Professor Feldman provided his own comments on the Report and also reviewed the comments of the other reviewers as well as any changes we made in response to those comments to ensure we had properly considered and addressed the comments of the reviewers. In light of his increased responsibilities, Professor Feldman was paid $10,000 for his work. Professor Feldman's review of our work is further described in Appendix O.

APPENDIX N-B:
Peer Reviewers

Reviewer	Relevant Titles and Affiliations	Relevant Expertise
Andrew Brandt, J.D.	Director, Moorad Center for Sports Law, Villanova University; Contributor on NFL legal and business affairs, ESPN and Sports Illustrated.	Brandt is an expert in sports law and business, including particular expertise in the law and business of the NFL. Prior to his current positions, Brandt was an NFLPA-certified Contract Advisor, the General Manager of an NFL World League Club, and Vice President of the Green Bay Packers from 1999–2008.
Gabriel Feldman, M.A., J.D.	Associate Professor of Law and Director, Sport Law Program, Tulane University School of Law; Associate Provost for NCAA Compliance, Tulane University; Board Member, Sports Lawyers Association.	Feldman is an expert in sports law, including particular expertise in the application of antitrust law to the sports industry.
Michelle Mello, M.Phil., Ph.D., J.D.	Professor, Stanford Law School and Stanford University School of Medicine.	Mello is an expert in health law, including particular expertise in medical liability, patient safety and medical ethics.
Matt Mitten, J.D.	Professor of Law and Director, National Sports Law Institute, Marquette University Law School; Arbitrator, Court of Arbitration for Sport; Board Member and Current President, Sports Lawyers Association.	Mitten is an expert in sports law, including particular expertise in the application of tort law and health law in the sports setting.
William Sage, M.D., J.D.	Professor, University of Texas School of Law; Member, National Academy of Medicine; Fellow, The Hastings Center.	Sage, a licensed attorney and doctor, is an expert in health law and bioethics.
Paul Wolpe, M.A., M.Phil., Ph.D.	Professor of Bioethics, Director, Center for Ethics, Emory University; Senior Bioethicist, National Aeronautics and Space Administration; Fellow, The Hastings Center.	Wolpe is an expert in bioethics.
Cindy Chang, M.D.	Sports Medicine Specialist, University of California, San Francisco, Benioff Children's Hospitals and Sports Medicine Center for Young Athletes; Team doctor, University of California, Berkeley; Former President, American Medical Society for Sports Medicine.	Chang is a sports medicine expert and practitioner, having served as a physician for University of California, Berkeley athletic teams, Ohio State University athletic teams and the United States Olympic teams.

ADDITIONAL READERS:

We provided each of the below readers a draft copy of the Report (or parts thereof) and asked them to provide written comments on those chapters or areas relevant to their expertise. We reviewed the readers' comments and made the changes we believed were necessary and appropriate but did not provide Professor Feldman with the comments from the readers. Each of them has a perceived or potential conflict of commitment that differentiates them from the peer reviewers discussed above. Consequently, Carfagna, Goldberg, and Robertson were not paid for their comments. Gusmano, Maschke, and Solomon were not paid directly for their comments, but The Hastings Center does receive compensation from The Football Players Health Study at Harvard University pursuant to an agreement between The Hastings Center and Harvard University under which The Hastings Center is a collaborator on certain Football Players Health Study research projects. Through that agreement, The Hastings Center also arranged the review by Dr. Hoberman.

APPENDIX N-C:
Additional Readers

Reader	Relevant Titles and Affiliations	Relevant Expertise
Peter Carfagna, J.D.	Lecturer, Harvard Law School; Chairman, Lake County Captains; Board Member; Concussion Legacy Foundation.	Carfagna is an expert in sports law.
John Goldberg, M.A., M.Phil., J.D.	Professor, Harvard Law School.	Goldberg is an expert in tort law.
Michael Gusmano, M.A., Ph.D.	Research Scholar, The Hastings Center; Lecturer, Yale University.	Gusmano is an expert in health policy.
John Hoberman, Ph.D.	Professor, University of Texas.	Hoberman is an expert in the culture and history of sports and medicine.
Karen Maschke, M.A., Ph.D.	Research Scholar, The Hastings Center.	Maschke is an expert in bioethics and health policy.
Christopher Robertson	Associate Professor, University of Arizona College of Law; Affiliate, Edmond J. Safra Center for Ethics, Harvard University; Affiliate, Petrie-Flom Center for Health Law Policy, Biotechnology, and Bioethics, Harvard Law School.	Robertson is an expert in health law and bioethics.
Mildred Solomon, Ed.D.	President and Chief Executive Officer, The Hastings Center.	Solomon is an expert in bioethics, health policy, and social science research.

STAKEHOLDER REVIEWERS:

After the peer review process, we offered most of the stakeholders covered in this Report the opportunity to review the chapter or chapters concerning them. For example, players only reviewed Chapter 1: Players, but the NFL Physicians Society (NFLPS) reviewed Chapter 2: Club Doctors, Chapter 3: Athletic Trainers, Chapter 4: Second Opinion Doctors, Chapter 5: Neutral Doctors, and Chapter 6: Personal Doctors. To protect the confidentiality of the Report prior to publication, only the NFL and NFLPA were offered the opportunity to review the *entire* Report before publication.

Other than the NFL and NFLPA, all of the stakeholders are a group of individual persons or entities. We could not realistically provide each individual person or entity within these groups the opportunity to respond to the Report. Thus, where possible, we provided an organization that represents these individual persons or entities an opportunity to do so. Additionally, in certain cases, we offered certain individuals or entities within the group the opportunity to review the Report.

Below is a list of individuals and entities we invited to review the Report on behalf of each stakeholder. Some of the stakeholders do not have a well-defined representative to review the Report. Thus, there was no review on behalf of these stakeholders, as is explained in further detail in Table N-D. Table N-D also identifies those individuals or entities that accepted our invitation to review the Report. None of the stakeholders were compensated in any way for their review.

In providing each of the stakeholders the opportunity to review the Report, we requested written comments within 30 days. We reviewed the stakeholders' comments and made the changes we believed were necessary and appropriate.

APPENDIX N-D:
Stakeholder Reviewers

Stakeholder	Invited Reviewer(s)	Reviewer(s)
Chapter 1: Players	All 13 players confidentially interviewed as part of this Report.	Seven of the 13 players that we confidentially interviewed as part of this Report agreed to review the Report; three provided comments.
Chapter 2: Club Doctors	We invited the NFL to arrange review by Club doctors of the NFL's choosing and through the NFLPS.	The NFLPS reviewed relevant parts of the Report and provided its own set of comments via the NFL. The NFLPS also provided a commentary in a Special Report of The Hastings Center Report discussing our recommendations concerning club doctors.
Chapter 3: Athletic Trainers	(1) National Athletic Trainers Association (NATA); and, (2) we invited the NFL to arrange review by athletic trainers of the NFL's choosing and through the Professional Football Athletic Trainers Society (PFATS).	NATA reviewed relevant parts of the Report and provided comments. PFATS reviewed relevant parts of the Report and provided their own set of comments via the NFL.
Chapter 4: Second Opinion Doctors	We did not seek a second opinion doctor reviewer because there is no readily available list of such doctors as described in this Report.	No one reviewed the Report on behalf of second opinion doctors.
Chapter 5: Neutral Doctors	We did not seek a neutral doctor reviewer because there is no readily available list of such doctors as described in this Report.	No one reviewed the Report on behalf of neutral doctors.

APPENDIX N-D: Stakeholder Reviewers (continued)

Stakeholder	Invited Reviewer(s)	Reviewer(s)
Chapter 6: Personal Doctors	We did not seek a personal doctor reviewer because there is no readily available list of such doctors as described in this Report.	No one reviewed the Report on behalf of personal doctors.
Chapter 7: NFL	We invited the NFL to arrange review by a maximum of 15 NFL employees or persons working with the NFL, *e.g.,* outside counsel.	The NFL reviewed the entire Report and provided comments.
Chapter 7: NFLPA	We invited the NFLPA to arrange review by NFLPA employees as it deemed appropriate. The NFLPA's review was broader than the NFL's due to the contract between Harvard and the NFLPA, including relevant confidentiality provisions.	The NFLPA reviewed the entire Report and provided comments.
Chapter 8: NFL Clubs	We invited the NFL to arrange review by club officials of the NFL's choosing.	The NFL reviewed the Report and provided comments.
Chapter 9: Coaches	(1) NFL Coaches Association; (2) American Football Coaches Association; and, (3) we invited the NFL to arrange review by coaches of the NFL's choosing.	The NFL, the American Football Coaches Association, and the NFL Coaches Association reviewed relevant parts of the Report and provided comments.
Chapter 10: Club Employees	We invited the NFL to arrange review by club employees of the NFL's choosing.	The NFL reviewed the Report and provided comments.
Chapter 11: Equipment Managers	(1) American Equipment Managers Association; and, (2) we invited the NFL to arrange review by equipment managers of the NFL's choosing.	The NFL and the American Equipment Managers Association reviewed relevant parts of the Report and provided comments.
Chapter 12: Contract Advisors	All 6 contract advisors confidentially interviewed as part of this Report.	Five of the six contract advisors that we confidentially interviewed as part of this Report agreed to review relevant parts; three provided comments.
Chapter 13: Financial Advisors	All 3 financial advisors confidentially interviewed as part of this Report.	Two of the three financial advisors confidentially interviewed as part of this Report agreed to review its relevant parts; Mark Doman, one of the financial advisors interviewed, was the only one who provided comments and asked to be identified.
Chapter 14: Family Members	The Off the Field Players' Wives Association (OTFPWA).	The President of the OTFPWA, Ericka Lassiter, who is also a Family Advisor to The Football Players Health Study at Harvard University, arranged for three wives of former NFL players to review relevant parts of the Report; two provided comments.

Stakeholder	Invited Reviewer(s)	Reviewer(s)
Chapter 15: Officials	(1) NFL Referees Association; and, (2) National Association of Sports Officials.	The National Association of Sports Officials reviewed relevant parts of the Report and provided comments. The NFL Referees Association declined our invitation to review the Report.
Chapter 16: Equipment Manufacturers	(1) National Operating Committee on Standards for Athletic Equipment (NOCSAE); (2) Riddell; and, (3) Schutt.	NOCSAE, Riddell and Schutt all reviewed relevant parts of the Report and provided comments.
Chapter 17: The Media	(1) Pro Football Writers Association; and, (2) National Sports Media Association.	The Pro Football Writers Association and the National Sports Media Association both declined to review the Report.
Chapter 18: Fans	We did not seek a fans reviewer because: (1) NFL fans are too heterogeneous of a group to allow review by only a small sample; and, (2) most (if not all) of the other reviewers of this Report are also fans.	No one reviewed the Report on behalf of fans.
Chapter 19: NFL Business Partners	(1) Verizon; (2) Nike; (3) Anheuser-Busch; (4) Pepsi; (5) Microsoft; (6) Gatorade; (7) McDonald's; (8) Nationwide Insurance; and, (9) FedEx.	Verizon, Anheuser-Busch, Pepsi, and McDonald's did not respond to multiple invitations to review the Report. Gatorade, FedEx, and Nationwide Insurance declined to review the Report. Nike and Microsoft reviewed relevant parts of the Report and provided comments.

APPENDIX O \ Certification From Gabriel Feldman

Tulane University

TULANE LAW SCHOOL

Gabe Feldman
Paul and Abram B Barron Associate Professor of Law
Director, Tulane Sports Law Program
Associate Provost for NCAA Compliance,
Tulane University

To Whom It May Concern:

The authors of this Report have demonstrated a strong commitment to ensuring their integrity and independence as academic researchers. To help ensure the quality of their work, the authors of this Report sought peer reviews from well-respected experts in the relevant fields addressed by the Report, and asked me to serve as "lead reviewer" to certify the adequacy and integrity of the peer review process. In that role, I have reviewed the comments from the reviewers, the changes the authors made to the Report in light of those comments, and the authors' explanations for changes not made. I have also provided my own comments on the Report and have reviewed the authors' response to those comments. Based on this review, I certify that the peer reviewers possess the appropriate expertise to review this Report, the authors adequately, fully, and fairly considered the comments received and the Report reflects appropriate changes where warranted.

It is my understanding that the stakeholders discussed in this report also submitted comments to the authors. My certification only applies to the comments made by the peer reviewers. Review and response to the comments made the respective stakeholders was part of a separate process.

Sincerely,

/Gabe Feldman

John Giffen Weinmann Hall, 6329 Freret St., New Orleans, LA 70118-6231 *tel* 1.504.865.5948 *fax* 1.504.862.8855
gfeldman@tulane.edu   www.law.tulane.edu

APPENDIX P \ Glossary of Terms and Relevant Persons and Institutions

88 Plan: Provides benefits for former players suffering from dementia, amyotrophic lateral sclerosis (ALS), or Parkinson's disease. For additional details, *see* Appendix C: Summary of Collectively Bargained Health-Related Programs and Benefits.

ACC: *See* Accountability and Care Committee.

Accountability and Care Committee (ACC): A CBA-mandated committee consisting of the NFL Commissioner (or his designee), the NFLPA Executive Director (or his designee), and six additional members "experienced in fields relevant to health care for professional athletes," three appointed by the Commissioner and three by the NFLPA Executive Director. The ACC is to "provide advice and guidance regarding the provision of preventive, medical, surgical, and rehabilitative care for players by all clubs."[1]

Accrued Season: A player receives an Accrued Season "for each season during which he was on, or should have been on, full pay status for a total of six or more regular season games."[2] Accrued Seasons are used for calculating a player's right to be a Restricted Free Agent and Unrestricted Free Agent, as differentiated from a Credited Season.

AEMA: *See* Athletic Equipment Managers Association.

AFCA: *See* American Football Coaches Association.

AFL: *See* American Football League.

Agent: *See* Contract advisor.

All Revenue (AR): "[T]he aggregate revenues received or to be received on an accrual basis, for or with respect to a League Year during the term of [the CBA], by the NFL and all NFL Clubs (and their designees), from all sources, whether known or unknown, derived from, relating to or arising out of the performance of players in NFL football games," with a few specific exceptions.[3] The term was introduced as part of the 2011 CBA. From 1993 to 2006, All Revenue was known as Defined Gross Revenue ("DGR"), and from 2006 to 2011, was known as Total Revenue ("TR").

AMA: *See* American Medical Association.

American Football Coaches Association (AFCA): A voluntary organization of more than 11,000 high school, college or professional football coaches, but principally focused on college coaches.

American Football League (AFL): A major professional American football league that operated from 1960 until 1969, when it merged with the NFL.

American Medical Association (AMA): a voluntary professional association for physicians with the leading code for ethical medical practice.

Appeals Panel: A three-member arbitration panel designated to hear appeals of System Arbitrations. The Appeals Panel currently consists of Georgetown Law professor James Oldham, former judge on the United States District Court for the Northern District of California Fern Smith, and former judge on the United States District Court for the Southern District of New York Richard Holwell.

AR: *See* All Revenue.

Athletic Equipment Managers Association (AEMA): A voluntary organization which provides certification to equipment managers working in sports across the country.

Benefits Arbitrator: An arbitrator appointed to hear player complaints concerning the benefits available under the CBA.

Board of Certification for the Athletic Trainer (BOC): The nation's only accredited certification program for entry-level athletic trainers, setting the standards and codes of conduct for the practice of athletic training.

BOC: *See* Board of Certification for the Athletic Trainer.

Brady v. NFL, 11-cv-639 (D. Minn.): A class action antitrust lawsuit brought by NFL players in 2011 against the NFL challenging the NFL's policies on compensation, free agency and the NFL Draft. The settlement of the case resulted in the 2011 CBA. New England Patriots quarterback Tom Brady was the lead plaintiff in the case. *See also White v. NFL.*

Canadian Football League (CFL): A professional football league in Canada that largely follows the same playing rules of the NFL. The CFL has nine teams and it is common for players to leave the CFL for the NFL.

CARD: *See* Committee on Agent Regulation and Discipline.

Casson, Ira: Neurologist and member of the MTBI Committee from 1994–2009.

CBA: *See* Collective Bargaining Agreement.

CFL: *See* Canadian Football League.

Chronic Traumatic Encephalopathy (CTE): A "progressive neurodegenerative disease."[4] Retrospective case reports have found CTE pathology in the brains of former athletes—including former professional football players—who manifested mood disorders, headaches, cognitive difficulties, suicidal ideation, difficulties with speech, and aggressive behavior.[5] The vast majority of cases in these studies were associated with repetitive head trauma.[6] However, a mechanistic connection between head trauma and CTE remains elusive.[7] Similarly, whether CTE is distinct from other neurodegenerative diseases[8] or whether repetitive head traumas are necessary and sufficient to cause CTE has not been definitively established.[9]

Club: One of 32 separate professional football franchises which collectively, via the NFL's Constitution and Bylaws, make up the NFL.

Collective Bargaining Agreement (CBA): "A contract between an employer and a labor union regulating employment conditions, wages, benefits, and grievances."[10] The NFL and NFLPA have executed ten CBAs, the first in 1968 and the most recent in 2011.

Commissioner: The Chief Executive Officer of the NFL, as elected by NFL club owners pursuant to the NFL Constitution and Bylaws. The current NFL Commissioner is Roger Goodell.

Committee on Agent Regulation and Discipline (CARD): A committee made up of three to five players responsible for investigating and taking disciplinary action against contract advisors pursuant to the NFLPA Regulations Governing Contract Advisors.

Concussion: As defined in the Concussion Protocol, a complex pathophysiological process affecting the brain induced by biomechanical forces.

Concussion Protocol: Officially titled the NFL Head, Neck and Spine Committee's Protocols Regarding Diagnosis and Management of Concussion (Appendix A), the Concussion Protocol is the procedures required to be followed by NFL club medical staff in diagnosing and managing players suspected of suffering a concussion.

Constitution and Bylaws of the NFL: The governing and operating agreement among the 32 member NFL clubs that dictates and controls many aspects of the NFL's operations.

Contract advisor: An individual certified by the NFLPA to act as a player's representative in contract negotiations with NFL clubs. More commonly known as an "agent." Contract advisors are governed by the NFLPA Regulations Governing Contract Advisors.

Contract Advisor Regulations: *See* NFLPA Regulations Governing Contract Advisors.

Covington & Burling LLP: Washington, D.C. law firm that has served as the NFL's chief outside counsel since the early 1960s. *See also* Tagliabue, Paul and Pash, Jeffrey.

Credited Season: A player receives a Credited Season "for each season during which he was on, or should have been on, full pay status for a total of three or more regular season games."[11] Credited Seasons are used for calculating a player's right to financial benefits under the CBA, as differentiated from an Accrued Season.

CTE: *See* Chronic Traumatic Encephalopathy.

Defined Gross Revenue (DGR): *See* All Revenue.

DePaso, Tom: NFLPA General Counsel since 2012. DePaso played in the NFL for one year in 1978.

Disability & Neurocognitive Benefit Plan: Provides eligible players with disability benefits, including benefits based on neurocognitive disability. For additional details, *see* Appendix C: Summary of Collectively Bargained Health-Related Programs and Benefits.

Dissolution: The legal process of removing a labor organization as the representative of a group of employees for purposes of collective bargaining with one or more employers. The NFLPA has dissolved itself twice: from December 1989 to March 1993, and from March 2011 to July 2011. Dissolution permits the employees to bring antitrust claims which are otherwise unavailable while represented by a union. Dissolution is sometimes referred to as "disclaimer" or "decertification" but each of these terms has specific legal significance under federal labor and antitrust laws. The distinction is complex and not relevant to this Report and thus, for our purposes here, "dissolution" captures both terms.

DGR: *See* All Revenue.

Extended Injury Protection: An Injury Protection benefit that permits a player to earn 50 percent of his salary up to $500,000 for the **second** season after suffering an injury that prevented the player from continuing to play. *See also* Injury Protection.

Féderation Internationale de Médicine du Sport (FIMS): The world's leading sports medicine organization, comprised of national sports medicine associations across five continents which seeks to maximize athlete health and performance.

FIMS: *See* Féderation Internationale de Médicine du Sport.

Financial advisor: A financial professional providing services to NFL players in the areas of tax planning, investment advice and services, budgeting, financial planning, insurance, estate planning, and/or retirement planning.

Financial Advisor Regulations: *See* NFLPA Regulations and Code of Conduct Governing Registered Player Financial Advisors.

Former Player Life Improvement Plan: A medical plan that permits qualifying former players (and in some cases their dependents) not otherwise covered by health insurance to receive reimbursement for medical costs for "joint replacements, prescription drugs, assisted living, Medicare supplemental insurance, spinal treatment, and neurological treatment." For additional details, *see* Appendix C: Summary of Collectively Bargained Health-Related Programs and Benefits.

Free Agency: A system by which players are able to sign contracts with new clubs after a certain number of seasons played (*see* Accrued Season), provided their prior contract is expired. *See also* Unrestricted Free Agent and Restricted Free Agent.

Garvey, Ed: Former labor attorney with the Minneapolis law firm Lindquist & Vennum, PLLP, and the NFLPA's first Executive Director, a post he held from 1971–1983.

General Manager: The individual generally responsible for the overall control and direction of an NFL club, including player personnel decisions.

Goodell, Roger: Commissioner of the NFL since 2006, and NFL employee since 1981. Son of former New York Senator Charles Goodell and 1981 graduate of Washington & Jefferson College.

Head, Neck and Spine Committee: Formerly known as the MTBI Committee, an NFL Committee of doctors and scientists that exists for the purpose of studying head, neck and spine injuries in the NFL. The current co-chairmen of the Head, Neck and Spine Committee are Drs. Richard Ellenbogen and Hunt Batjer.

Health (for purposes of this Report): A state of overall wellbeing in fundamental aspects of a person's life, including physical, mental, emotional, social, familial, and financial components.

Health Reimbursement Account: Helps to pay out-of-pocket healthcare expenses after players are no longer employed by an NFL club and after the period of extended medical coverage under the NFL Player Insurance Plan that is paid by the NFL has ended. For additional details, *see* Appendix C: Summary of Collectively Bargained Health-Related Programs and Benefits.

Injured Reserve (IR): A roster designation for players who are injured and are unable to return that season, with the exception of one player per season per club who can be placed on the IR but designated to be able to return. Players on IR do not count towards the club's 53-man Active/Inactive List.

Injury Grievance: "[A] claim or complaint that, at the time a player's NFL Player Contract or Practice Squad Player Contract was terminated by a Club, the player was physically unable to perform the services required of him by that contract because of an injury incurred in the performance of his services under that contract."[12] If successful, the club must pay the player his salary for the duration of his injury, but only for the season of injury. An Injury Grievance is a much narrower claim than a Non-Injury Grievance—Non-Injury Grievances can include a wide variety of claims related to player health.

Injury Protection: A benefit available to NFL players where the player has met the following criteria: (a) "[t]he player must have been physically unable, because of a severe football injury in an NFL game or practice, to participate in all or part of his Club's last game of the season, as certified by the Club physician following a physical examination after the last game; or the player must have undergone Club-authorized surgery in the off-season following the season of injury; and (b) [t]he player must have undergone whatever reasonable and customary rehabilitation treatment his Club required of him during the off-season following the season of injury; and (c) [t]he player must have failed the preseason physical examination given by the Club physician for the season following the season of injury because of such injury and as a result his Club must have terminated his contract for the season following the season of injury." In 2015, an NFL player can receive Injury Protection in "an amount equal to 50 percent of his Paragraph 5 Salary for the season following the season of injury, up to a maximum payment of" $1,100,000. A player is only entitled to Injury Protection once in his career.[13] *See also* Extended Injury Protection.

Injury Report: A list of injured players, each injured player's type or location of injury, and the injured player's status for the upcoming game. Each injury must be described "with a reasonable degree of specificity," *e.g.*, ankle, ribs, hand or concussion. For a quarterback's arm injury or a kicker's or punter's leg injury, the description must designate left or right. The player's status for the upcoming game is classified into three categories: Out (will not play) (designation not used until 2 days prior to the game); Doubtful (unlikely the player will participate); and, Questionable (uncertain as to whether the player will play in the game). The Injury Report also indicates whether a player had full, limited or no participation in practice, whether due to injury or any other cause (*e.g.*, team discipline, family matter, etc.). The Injury Report is issued after practice each Wednesday, Thursday and Friday. *See also* Injury Reporting Policy.

Injury Reporting Policy: An NFL policy that requires each club to report information on injured players to both the NFL and the media each game week. The stated purpose of this reporting is "to provide a full and complete rendering of player availability" to all parties involved, including the opposing team, the media, and the general public. *See also* Injury Report.

***In re National Football League Players' Concussion Injury Litigation*, 12-md-2323 (E.D.Pa.) ("Concussion Litigation"):** A lawsuit consisting of several hundred consolidated lawsuits whereby approximately 5,500 former NFL players alleged that the NFL had negligently and fraudulently concealed the risk of brain injury associated with playing football. The case was settled in 2013, approved by the United States District Court for the Eastern District of Pennsylvania in 2015, and affirmed by the United States Court of Appeals for the Third Circuit in 2016.

IR: *See* Injured Reserve.

Joint Committee on Player Safety and Welfare ("Joint Committee"): A CBA-mandated committee consisting of three club representatives and three NFLPA representatives that discusses "player safety and welfare aspects of playing equipment, playing surfaces, stadium facilities, playing rules, player-coach relationships, and any other relevant subjects."[14] The Joint Committee is merely advisory and has no binding decision-making authority.

Kessler, Jeffrey: Partner with the law firm of Winston Strawn LLP and the NFLPA's chief outside counsel. Kessler has represented the NFLPA and NFL players since the early 1980s, having previously practiced at Weil, Gotshal & Manges LLP and Dewey & LeBoeuf.

Labor Management Relations Act (LMRA): A federal statute (also known as the Taft-Hartley Act), which, in conjunction with the National Labor Relations Act, governs relationships between labor organizations and employers. The LMRA is most often relevant in the NFL due to the fact that it often "preempts" or bars common law claims against the NFL and/or NFLPA. *See also* Preemption.

League Policies for Players: An annual document provided by the NFL to players describing various policies, including for discipline, uniforms, media, community relations, personal conduct, workplace conduct, guns and weapons, commercial substances and endorsements, gambling, ticket scalping, bounties, and HIV/AIDS.

League Year: The fiscal and operational year for the NFL and NFLPA, generally beginning and ending in March.[15]

Legacy Benefit: As part of the 2011 CBA, the NFL contributed $620 million in benefits to players who played prior to 1993 through credits as part of the Retirement Plan. Players who played before 1975 received a $124/month credit and those who played between 1975 and 1992 received a $108/month credit. For additional details, *see* Appendix C: Summary of Collectively Bargained Health-Related Programs and Benefits.

LMRA: *See* Labor Management Relations Act.

Long Term Care Insurance Plan: Provides medical insurance to cover the costs of long-term care for NFL players (but not their family members). For additional details, *see* Appendix C: Summary of Collectively Bargained Health-Related Programs and Benefits.

Lystedt Law: A form of concussion-related legislation, initially passed in Washington state, generally requiring that youth athletes suspected of sustaining a concussion or head injury be removed from practice or the game and not return to play until approved by a healthcare provider. The law is named after Zackery Lystedt who, at the age of 13 in 2006, suffered brain hemorrhaging after he returned to a youth football game fifteen minutes after having suffered a concussion. All 50 states have some form of the Lystedt Law.

Mackey-White Committee: A Committee created by the NFLPA in 2009 consisting of current players, former players, doctors, and others for the purpose of "assist[ing] the NFLPA in its development of policies concerning workplace safety and the health of NFLPA members."[16]

Major League Baseball (MLB): The world's premier professional baseball organization, consisting of 30 member clubs and headquartered in New York City. With the NFL, NBA and NHL, sometimes known as part of the "Big Four."

Mayer, Thom: Medical Director of the NFLPA since 2001 and CEO of the physician group Best Practices.

Mild Traumatic Brain Injury (MTBI) Committee: A committee created by the NFL in 1994 for the purpose of studying concussions and other head injuries to NFL players. The committee initially consisted of several club doctors, two club athletic trainers, a consulting engineer, a club equipment manager, neurologist Ira Casson (who had studied boxers), and Hank Feuer, an Indianapolis neurosurgeon who worked with the Colts. New York Jets Club doctor Elliot Pellman, a rheumatologist, was designated as Chairman of the Committee by Commissioner Paul Tagliabue. The MTBI Committee was renamed the Head, Neck and Spine Committee in 2010.

MLB: *See* Major League Baseball.

MTBI Committee: *See* Mild Traumatic Brain Injury Committee.

Nabel, Elizabeth: The NFL's Chief Health and Medical Advisor, President of Brigham and Women's Hospital in Boston and a professor of medicine at Harvard Medical School.

NASO: *See* National Association of Sports Officials.

NATA: *See* National Athletic Trainers Association.

National Association of Sports Officials (NASO): A voluntary organization of approximately 20,000 member officials, ranging from the lowest levels of youth sports to the professionals. NASO provides an extensive list of services to its members, including educational programs, legal advocacy and insurance policies. Every NFL official is a member of NASO.

National Athletic Trainers Association (NATA): A voluntary professional membership association for certified athletic trainers across all levels of competition. NATA's stated mission "is to enhance the quality of health care provided by certified athletic trainers and to advance the athletic training profession."

National Basketball Association (NBA): The world's premier professional basketball organization, consisting of 30 member clubs and headquartered in New York City. With the NFL, MLB and NHL, sometimes known as part of the "Big Four."

National Collegiate Athletic Association (NCAA): A non-profit unincorporated association headquartered in Indianapolis through which the nation's colleges and universities govern their athletic programs. The NCAA consists of more than 1,200 member institutions, all of which participate in the creation of NCAA rules and voluntarily submit to its authority.

National Hockey League (NHL): The world's premier professional ice hockey organization, consisting of 30 member clubs and headquartered in New York City. With MLB, the NFL and NBA, sometimes known as part of the "Big Four."

National Football League (NFL): An unincorporated association of 32 member clubs operating as the world's premier professional football league. The NFL has its headquarters in New York City and is led by Commissioner Roger Goodell. With MLB, the NBA and NHL, sometimes known as the "Big Four."

National Football League Players Association (NFLPA): A Virginia nonprofit, tax-exempt corporation and labor organization which, pursuant to the National Labor Relations Act, is "the exclusive representative[] of all the employees in [the bargaining] unit for the purposes of collective bargaining in respect to rates of pay, wages, hours of employment, or other conditions of employment." The NFLPA has its headquarters in Washington, D.C., and is led by Executive Director DeMaurice Smith.

National Labor Relations Act (NLRA): A federal labor law statute that governs labor relations between employees and employers in the private sector and obligates both sides to negotiate in good faith concerning the wages, hours, and other terms and conditions of employment.

National Labor Relations Board (NLRB): An independent agency of the United States government responsible for administering and enforcing the provisions of the NLRA, including investigating and remedying unfair labor practices.

National Operating Committee on Standards for Athletic Equipment (NOCSAE): A nonprofit organization with the purpose of improving athletic equipment and reducing injuries through equipment standards. Safety standards for athletic equipment are almost exclusively determined by NOCSAE.

NBA: *See* National Basketball Association.

NCAA: *See* National Collegiate Athletic Association.

Neuro-Cognitive Disability Benefit: A medical benefit that permits qualifying retired players to receive no less than $3,000 per month for a maximum of 180 months as part of the Disability Plan. For additional details, *see* Appendix C: Summary of Collectively Bargained Health-Related Programs and Benefits.

NFL: *See* National Football League.

NFLCA: *See* NFL Coaches Association.

NFL Combine: An annual event held each February in Indianapolis in which approximately 300 of the best college football players undergo medical examinations, intelligence tests, interviews, and multiple football and other athletic drills and tests. NFL club executives, coaches, scouts, doctors and athletic trainers attend the Combine to evaluate the players for the upcoming NFL Draft (usually in April). The NFL Combine is organized by National Football Scouting, Inc., a Delaware corporation that is not owned or controlled by the NFL.

NFL Coaches Association (NFLCA): "[A] voluntary non-union association that represents the over six hundred coaches and assistant coaches currently employed by the thirty-two individual National Football League Clubs, as well as many retired coaches formerly employed by the NFL teams." David Cornwell is the NFLCA's Executive Director in a part-time capacity.

NFL Draft: An annual event held each April/May whereby NFL clubs select former college football student-athletes to join their roster. The Draft consists of seven rounds. Clubs are permitted to trade draft picks and players eligible for the Draft but who are not drafted are become Unrestricted Free Agents and are free to sign with any club.

NFL Injury Surveillance System (NFLISS): The standardized system, created in 1980, used by the NFL and NFL clubs to track and analyze NFL injuries and to provide data for medical research. Injury information is entered by club athletic trainers. Since 2011, the NFLISS is managed by the international biopharmaceutical services firm Quintiles.

NFLISS: *See* NFL Injury Surveillance System.

NFLPA: *See* National Football League Players Association.

NFLPA Constitution: The governing and operating document of the NFLPA, as voted on by its Board of Player Representatives.

NFLPA Regulations Governing Contract Advisors (Contract Advisor Regulations): The NFLPA's rules of certification and conduct for contract advisors, *i.e.,* "agents." First instituted in or about 1983, last amended in 2012.

NFLPA Regulations and Code of Conduct Governing Registered Player Financial Advisors (Financial Advisor Regulations): The NFLPA's rules of registration and conduct for Financial Advisors. First instituted in 2002, last amended in 2012.

NFL Physicians Society (NFLPS): A voluntary professional membership association for club doctors. NFLPS' mission is "to provide excellence in the medical and surgical care of the athletes in the National Football League and to provide direction and support for the athletic trainers in charge of the care for these athletes."

NFLPS: *See* NFL Physicians Society.

NFLRA: *See* NFL Referees Association.

NFL Referees Association (NFLRA): The labor organization that represents NFL officials in CBA negotiations and related proceedings with the NFL.

NHL: *See* National Hockey League.

NLRA: *See* National Labor Relations Act.

NLRB: *See* National Labor Relations Board.

NOCSAE: *See* National Operating Committee on Standards for Athletic Equipment.

Non-Injury Grievance: "Any dispute . . . arising after the execution of [the CBA] and involving the interpretation of, application of, or compliance with, any provision of [the CBA], the NFL Player Contract, the Practice Squad Player Contract, or any applicable provision of the NFL Constitution and Bylaws or NFL Rules pertaining to the terms and conditions of employment of NFL players."[17] A Non-Injury Grievance is a much broader claim than an Injury Grievance and would include player complaints about their healthcare.

Paragraph 5 Salary: A player's base compensation as outlined in Paragraph 5 of the Standard Player Contract. Paragraph 5 Salary is generally not guaranteed.

Pash, Jeffrey: Executive Vice President and General Counsel of the NFL. Pash was formerly an attorney with Covington & Burling LLP and joined the NFL in 1997.

PASPA: *See* Professional and Amateur Sports Protection Act.

Pellman, Elliot: Former New York Jets Club doctor, current NFL Medical Director and Chairman of the MTBI Committee from 1994 to 2009.

PES Policy: *See* Policy on Performance-Enhancing Substances.

PFATS: *See* Professional Football Athletic Trainers Society.

PFWA: *See* Pro Football Writers of America.

Physically Unable to Perform (PUP) List: A roster designation for players that have failed the preseason physical and are unable to participate in training camp but are expected to be able to play later in the season. A player on the PUP List cannot practice or play until after the sixth game of the regular season and does not count towards the club's 53-man Active/Inactive List during that time.

Player Annuity Program: A plan that provides deferred compensation to players. For additional details, *see* Appendix C: Summary of Collectively Bargained Health-Related Programs and Benefits.

Player Benefit Costs: The total amounts the NFL and its clubs spend on NFL player benefits, programs and medical care.

Player Cost Amount: The players' share of All Revenue ("AR"), which is equal to: (1) 55 percent of League Media, which consists of all NFL broadcasting revenues; (2) 45 percent of NFL Ventures/Postseason revenue, which includes all revenues arising from the operation of postseason NFL games and all revenues arising from NFL-affiliated entities, including NFL Ventures, NFL Network, NFL Properties, NFL Enterprises, NFL Productions, and NFL Digital; and, (3) 40 percent of Local Revenues, which includes those revenues not included in League Media or NFL Ventures/Postseason, and specifically includes revenues from the sale of preseason television broadcasts.

Player Insurance Plan: An insurance plan that provides players and their family with life insurance, accidental death and dismemberment insurance, medical coverage, dental coverage, and wellness benefits. The wellness benefits include access to clinicians for mental health, alcoholism, and substance abuse, child and parenting support services, elder care support services, pet care services, legal services, and identity theft services. For additional details, *see* Appendix C: Summary of Collectively Bargained Health-Related Programs and Benefits.

Players, Inc.: A Virginia for-profit entity formed by the NFLPA responsible for group licensing of NFL player rights.

Playing Rules: Rules governing the playing of professional football on the field. The NFL amends the Playing Rules from time to time, pursuant to the applicable voting procedures of the NFL Constitution and Bylaws.

Policy and Program on Substances of Abuse (Substance Abuse Policy): A collectively bargained document prohibiting players from using common street drugs, such as cocaine, marijuana, amphetamines, opiates, opioids, PCP, and MDMA (ecstasy). The Substance Abuse Policy includes treatment and disciplinary provisions.

Policy on Performance-Enhancing Substances (PES Policy): A collectively bargained document prohibiting players from using performance enhancing drugs. The PES Policy includes disciplinary but not treatment provisions.

Preemption: "The principle . . . that a federal law can supersede or supplant any inconsistent state law or regulation."[18] In the NFL context, the Labor Management Relations Act will preempt, *i.e.,* bar, common law (*i.e.,* non-statutory) claims where the claim is "substantially dependent upon analysis of the terms" of a CBA, *i.e.,* where the claim is "inextricably intertwined with consideration of the terms of the" CBA.[19] The preemption doctrine corresponds with the law's general preference that complaints between employees and employers be resolved through the collectively bargained grievance and arbitration mechanisms, where applicable.

Professional and Amateur Sports Protection Act (PASPA): A federal statute that outlaws sports betting nationwide, exempting certain states which had previously allowed sports betting activities, including Delaware, Montana, Nevada, and Oregon.

Professional Football Athletic Trainers Society (PFATS): A voluntary professional membership association for club athletic trainers.

Pro Football Writers of America (PFWA): A voluntary organization of journalists and writers that cover the NFL and its 32 clubs on a daily basis.

Restricted Free Agent: A "player with three Accrued Seasons, but less than four Accrued Seasons [who] . . . at the expiration of his last Player Contract . . . shall be completely free to negotiate and sign a Player Contract with any Club, and any Club shall be completely free to negotiate and sign a Player Contract with any such player, subject to" certain restrictions set forth in the CBA, including rights of first refusal and draft pick compensation.[20] *See also* Unrestricted Free Agent.

Retirement Plan: A retirement plan that provides eligible players with retirement benefits, and offers survivor benefits for players' wives and family. For additional details, *see* Appendix C: Summary of Collectively Bargained Health-Related Programs and Benefits.

Riddell: One of the leading manufacturers for football equipment across all levels of football. Riddell offers all pads necessary for the game of football, including but not limited to helmets, faceguards, chin straps, mouth guards, shoulder pads, hip pads, thigh pads, knee pads and rib pads. Riddell is headquartered in Rosemost, Illinois and between 1988 and 2013 was the official helmet sponsor of the NFL.

Rozelle, Pete: NFL Commissioner from 1960 to 1989, widely credited with making the NFL one of the most successful sports leagues in the world.

Salary Cap: "[T]he absolute maximum amount of Salary that each Club may pay or be obligated to pay or provide to player . . . at any time during a particular League Year." The Salary Cap is determined by subtracting Player Benefit Costs from the Player Cost Amount and dividing by the number of clubs in the NFL.

Schutt: One of the leading manufacturers for football equipment across all levels of football. Schutt offers all pads necessary for the game of football, including but not limited to helmets, faceguards, chin straps, mouth guards, shoulder pads, hip pads, thigh pads, knee pads and rib pads. Schutt is headquartered in Litchfield, Illinois.

Second Career Savings Plan: A 401(k) plan that helps NFL players save for retirement in a tax-favored manner. All NFL players are eligible for the Plan, regardless of the number of Credited Seasons. For additional details, *see* Appendix C: Summary of Collectively Bargained Health-Related Programs and Benefits.

Severance Pay: A benefit a player is eligible to receive as severance for each Credited Season. For additional details, *see* Appendix C: Summary of Collectively Bargained Health-Related Programs and Benefits.

Smith, DeMaurice: Executive Director of the NFLPA since 2009. Former Assistant United States Attorney for the District of Columbia and Partner with the law firms of Latham & Watkins and Patton Boggs LLP.

Society of Professional Journalists (SPJ): A voluntary organization of nearly 10,000 journalists that promotes and protects the interests of journalism and journalists.

SPJ: *See* Society of Professional Journalists.

SRA: *See* Standard Representation Agreement.

Standard Representation Agreement (SRA): The standard contract between contract advisors and players as provided for in the NFLPA Regulations Governing Contract Advisors, subject to minimal variation as agreed upon by the parties.

Substance Abuse Policy: *See* Policy and Program on Substances of Abuse.

System Arbitration: A legal process for the resolution of disputes between the NFL and the NFLPA and/or a player concerning a subset of CBA provisions that are central to the NFL's operations and which invoke antitrust and labor law concerns, including but not limited to the NFL player contract, NFL Draft, rookie compensation, free agency, and the Salary Cap. System Arbitrations are presided over by the System Arbitrator and subject to appeal before the Appeals Panel.

System Arbitrator: The arbitrator designated to hear System Arbitrations. The current System Arbitrator is University of Pennsylvania Law School Professor Stephen B. Burbank.

Tagliabue, Paul: NFL Commissioner from 1989 to 2006. Prior to becoming Commissioner, Tagliabue was the NFL's chief outside counsel with the Washington, D.C. law firm of Covington & Burling LLP, the firm to which he returned after retiring as Commissioner.

Termination Pay: A player benefit whereby a player who has at least four years of credited service under the Retirement Plan is eligible to receive the unpaid balance of his Paragraph 5 Salary for a season after having had his contract terminated during that season, provided he was on the club's Active/Inactive List for at least one game that season. A player is entitled to Termination Pay only once during his career.

Toradol: The brand name for ketorolac tromethamine, a non-steroidal anti-inflammatory drug used for short-term relief of acute pain.

Total Revenue: *See* All Revenue.

TR: *See* All Revenue.

Tuition Assistance Plan: A benefit that permits players to receive reimbursement for tuition, fees and books from attending an eligible education institution. For additional details, *see* Appendix C: Summary of Collectively Bargained Health-Related Programs and Benefits.

Unrestricted Free Agent: A "player with four or more Accrued Seasons [who] . . . at the expiration of his Player Contract . . . shall be completely free to negotiate and sign a Player Contract with any Club, and any Club shall be completely free to negotiate and sign a Player Contract with such player without penalty or restriction[.]"[21] *See also* Free Agency and Restricted Free Agent.

Upshaw, Eugene: Hall of Fame offensive lineman with the Oakland Raiders from 1967 to 1981 and Executive Director of the NFLPA from 1983 to 2008.

***White v. NFL,* 92-cv-906 (D. Minn.):** A class action antitrust lawsuit brought by NFL players in 1992 against the NFL challenging the NFL's policies on compensation, free agency and the NFL Draft. The settlement of the case formed the basis of the 1993 CBA and every CBA since. Hall of Fame defensive end Reggie White was the lead plaintiff in the case. *See also Brady v. NFL.*

Workers' Compensation: A state-based system which provides workers injured during the course of their employment with wages and medical benefits and which, as a tradeoff, generally bars employees from suing their employers and co-employees for negligence.

Endnotes

1   CBA, Art. 39, § 3.

2   CBA, Art. 8, § 1(a).

3   CBA, Art. 12, § 1.

4   *See* Michelle Saulle M & Brian D. Greenwald, *Chronic Traumatic Encephalopathy: A Review,* 2012 Rehabil. Res. Pract. 1 (2012) (defining CTE as "a progressive neurodegenerative disease that is a long-term consequence of single or repetitive closed head injuries for which there is no treatment and no definitive pre-mortem diagnosis."); Bennet Omalu et al., *Emerging Histophormorphic Phenotypes of Chronic Traumatic Encephalopathy in American Athletes,* 69 Neurosurgery 173 (2011) (defining CTE as "a progressive neurodegenerative syndrome caused by single, episodic or repetitive blunt force impacts to the head and transfer of acceleration–deceleration forces to the brain."); Ann McKee et al., *Chronic Traumatic Encephalopathy in Athletes: Progressive Tauopathy After Repetitive Head Injury,* 68 J. Neuropathology & Experimental Neurology 709 (2009) (describing CTE as "shar[ing] many features of other neurodegenerative disorders").

5   *See* Joseph C. Maroon et al. *Chronic Traumatic Encephalopathy in Contact Sports: A Systematic Review of All Reported Pathological Cases,* PLOS ONE (2015) (summarizing CTE case studies to date); Ann C. McKee et al., *The spectrum of disease in chronic traumatic encephalopathy,* 136 Brain 43 (2013); Bennet I. Omalu, *Chronic Traumatic Encephalopathy, Suicides and Parasuicides in Professional American Athletes,* 31 Am. J. Forensic Med. Pathol. 130 (2010); *What is CTE?* BU CTE Center, http://www.bu.edu/cte/about/what-is-cte/ (last visited Mar. 31, 2016), *archived at* https://perma.cc/W86H-886C (CTE is associated with "athletes (and others) with a history of repetitive brain trauma," and "is associated with memory loss, confusion, impaired judgment, impulse control problems, aggression, depression, and, eventually, progressive dementia.")

6   *See* Maroon, *supra* note 5.

7   *See id.;* Paul McCrory et al., *Consensus statement on concussion in sport: the 4th Int'l Conference on Concussion in Sport held in Zurich, November 2012,* 47 Br. J. Sports Med. 250, 254, 257 (2013).

8   *See* Maroon, *supra* note 5.

9   *See* McCrory, *supra* note 7, at 257.

10 Black's Law Dictionary (9th ed. 2009).

11 CBA, Art. 26, § 2.

12 CBA, Art. 44, § 1.

13 CBA, Art. 45, § 1.

14 CBA, Art. 50, § 1.

15 CBA, Art. 1.

16 NFLPA Mackey-White Committee Charter, ¶ 2.

17 CBA, Art. 43, § 1.

18 Black's Law Dictionary (9th ed. 2009).

19 Allis-Chambers Corp. v. Lueck, 471 U.S. 202, 213, 220 (1985).

20 CBA, Art. 9, § 2.

21 CBA, Art. 9, § 1(a).

Index